Frommer's®

Canada

15th Edition

by Leslie Brokaw, Hilary Davidson, Paul Karr, Bill McRae & Donald Olson

WILEY

Wiley Publishing, Inc.

Published by:

Wiley Publishing, Inc.

111 River St.
Hoboken, NJ 07030-5774

ISBN 978-0-470-25706-7
Editor: mcd editorial. with William Travis
Production Editor: Eric T. Schroeder
Cartographer: Elizabeth Puhl
Photo Editor: Richard Fox
Production by Wiley Indianapolis Composition Services

Front cover photo: Banff National Park: Moraine Lake, early spring
Back cover photo: Prince Royal Island: Bear fishing in fast flowing river

For information on our other products and services or to obtain technical support, please contact our Customer Care Department within the U.S. at 800/762-2974, outside the U.S. at 317/572-3993 or fax 317/572-4002.

Wiley also publishes its books in a variety of electronic formats. Some content that appears in print may not be available in electronic formats.

Manufactured in the United States of America

5 4 3 2 1

Contents

4   New Brunswick   114

by Paul Karr

5   Prince Edward Island   149

by Paul Karr

6   Newfoundland & Labrador   172

by Paul Karr

13 Manitoba & Saskatchewan   486

by Bill McRae

14 Alberta & the Rockies   537

by Bill McRae

15 Vancouver   630

by Donald Olson

16 Victoria & British Columbia 689

by Bill McRae & Donald Olson

17 The Yukon, Northwest Territories & Nunavut 780

by Bill McRae

Appendix: Canada in Depth 821

by Bill McRae

Index 831

List of Maps

About the Authors

Leslie Brokaw is frequent traveler to Montréal and Québec City from her home base in Boston. She teaches at Emerson College, writes a film column for *The Boston Globe,* and covers travel, business, and entertainment for a wide variety of other publications and websites. Brokaw spent her early career at *Inc.* magazine as a writer and Web editor.

Toronto native **Hilary Davidson** now calls New York City home, thanks to her persuasive Manhattan-born husband, Daniel. She is a contributing editor at *Chatelaine* magazine and has written for *American Archaeology, Discover, Executive Travel, Fitness, Glow, House & Home,* and *Martha Stewart Weddings.* She is also the author of *Frommer's Toronto* and *Frommer's New York City Day by Day.* She can be reached at hcdavidson@gmail.com.

Paul Karr has written, co-authored, or edited more than 25 guidebooks, including *Vancouver & Victoria For Dummies; Frommer's Nova Scotia, New Brunswick & Prince Edward Island; Frommer's New England; Frommer's Vermont, New Hampshire & Maine;* and *Frommer's Maine Coast.* He also has contributed to *Frommer's Irreverent Guides* to Rome and Vancouver. In addition, he has written articles for *Sierra* and *Sports Illustrated,* among other publications. He divides his time among New England, both coasts of Canada, Europe, and Japan.

Bill McRae was born and raised in rural eastern Montana, though he spent the better years of his youth attending university in Great Britain, France, and Canada. He has previously written about Montana, Utah, and Oregon for Moon Publications and about the Pacific Northwest and Seattle for Lonely Planet. Other publications he has written for include *National Geographic,* Microsoft Expedia, and *1,000 Places to See in the U.S.A. and Canada Before You Die* for Workman Press. Bill also is co-author of *Frommer's British Columbia & the Canadian Rockies.* He makes his home in Portland, Oregon.

Donald Olson is a novelist, playwright, and travel writer. He has published several novels, most recently *The Confessions of Aubrey Beardsley* and, under the pen name of Swan Adamson, *My Three Husbands* and *Confessions of a Pregnant Princess.* His plays have been staged in the U.S. and Europe. Donald Olson's travel stories have appeared in *The New York Times, Travel & Leisure, Sunset, National Geographic* books, and many other publications. He is the author of *England For Dummies* (winner of the 2002 Lowell Thomas Travel Writing Award for Best Guidebook), *London For Dummies, Germany For Dummies, Frommer's London from $95 a Day, Frommer's Portable London from $95 a Day,* and *Frommer's Irreverent Guide to London.*

An Invitation to the Reader

In researching this book, we discovered many wonderful places—hotels, restaurants, shops, and more. We're sure you'll find others. Please tell us about them, so we can share the information with your fellow travelers in upcoming editions. If you were disappointed with a recommendation, we'd love to know that, too. Please write to:

Frommer's Canada, 15th Edition
Wiley Publishing, Inc. • 111 River St. • Hoboken, NJ 07030-5774

An Additional Note

Please be advised that travel information is subject to change at any time—and this is especially true of prices. We therefore suggest that you write or call ahead for confirmation when making your travel plans. The authors, editors, and publisher cannot be held responsible for the experiences of readers while traveling. Your safety is important to us, however, so we encourage you to stay alert and be aware of your surroundings. Keep a close eye on cameras, purses, and wallets, all favorite targets of thieves and pickpockets.

Other Great Guides for Your Trip:

Frommer's Nova Scotia, New Brunswick & Prince Edward Island

Frommer's Montréal & Québec City

Frommer's Toronto

Frommer's British Columbia & the Canadian Rockies

Frommer's Vancouver & Victoria

Frommer's Alaska Cruises & Ports of Call

Frommer's Ottawa with Kids

Frommer's Toronto with Kids

Frommer's Vancouver with Kids

Frommer's Star Ratings, Icons & Abbreviations

Every hotel, restaurant, and attraction listing in this guide has been ranked for quality, value, service, amenities, and special features using a **star-rating system.** In country, state, and regional guides, we also rate towns and regions to help you narrow down your choices and budget your time accordingly. Hotels and restaurants are rated on a scale of zero (recommended) to three stars (exceptional). Attractions, shopping, nightlife, towns, and regions are rated according to the following scale: zero stars (recommended), one star (highly recommended), two stars (very highly recommended), and three stars (must-see).

In addition to the star-rating system, we also use **seven feature icons** that point you to the great deals, in-the-know advice, and unique experiences that separate travelers from tourists. Throughout the book, look for:

Finds	Special finds—those places only insiders know about
Fun Fact	Fun facts—details that make travelers more informed and their trips more fun
Kids	Best bets for kids and advice for the whole family
Moments	Special moments—those experiences that memories are made of
Overrated	Places or experiences not worth your time or money
Tips	Insider tips—great ways to save time and money
Value	Great values—where to get the best deals

The following **abbreviations** are used for credit cards:

AE	American Express	DISC	Discover	V	Visa
DC	Diners Club	MC	MasterCard		

Frommers.com

Now that you have this guidebook to help you plan a great trip, visit our website at **www. frommers.com** for additional travel information on more than 3,600 destinations. We update features regularly to give you instant access to the most current trip-planning information available. At Frommers.com, you'll find scoops on the best airfares, lodging rates, and car rental bargains. You can even book your travel online through our reliable travel booking partners. Other popular features include:

- Online updates of our most popular guidebooks
- Vacation sweepstakes and contest giveaways
- Newsletters highlighting the hottest travel trends
- Online travel message boards with featured travel discussions

What's New in Canada

The Canadian tourism industry is dealing with something of a triple whammy these days: In addition to new U.S. passport requirements, the strength of the loonie has sent Canadian tourists out of the country and kept foreign visitors from spending as freely as they have in the past. Plus, the federal Visitor Rebate Program that allowed nonresident guests to recoup taxes they paid on purchases and lodging was eliminated in 2007. The following offers additional hints of new developments awaiting travelers to Canada.

NOVA SCOTIA There's a new lobster festival, **Lobsterpalooza** (© **902/270-3330;** www.lobsterpalooza.ca), in the province: a month-long bash of lobster suppers, cultural events, and tours spread across various parts of 'Scotia (many are concentrated on Cape Breton Island). Check with the festival office about the 2008 schedule, when events will take place from late May to the end of June.

The Manse in Mahone Bay, one of Atlantic Canada's finest and friendliest inns, has closed. On Cape Breton Island, the Duffus House Inn in Baddeck has also closed.

NEW BRUNSWICK It's getting easier to reach this province. Where you once had to fly into Saint John first, **Continental** (© **800/523-FARE;** www.continental. com) now flies directly from Newark, New Jersey's Liberty International Airport to Moncton.

PRINCE EDWARD ISLAND The island will go gaga for the **100th anniversary** of the June 1908 publication of Lucy Maud Montgomery's novel *Anne of Green Gables,* with a full program of events including a children's literary festival, readings, plays, and the release of a new prequel novel written by a local children's author. Check the provincial tourism office's special Anne page at **www. gentleisland.com/anne** for more details and an event schedule.

Delta (© **800/221-1212;** www.delta. com) has begun offering a new direct summer flight from Boston's Logan International Airport to Charlottetown.

MONTREAL In summer 2007, the Québec province officially inaugurated the new *Route verte* (Green Route), a 4,000km (2,485-mile) bike network that stretches from one end of the province to the other and links up all regions and cities. Accredited accommodations along the way provide safe bike storage, basic tools, information about where to make repairs nearby, and high-carb meals.

Where to Stay There's an inexpensive new entry in downtown: The decor of **Hôtel Le Dauphin,** 1025 rue de Bleury (© **888/784-3888**), may be just a step up from dorm-room functional, but each of its 72 rooms is equipped with a computer terminal and free Internet access.

The plush **Hôtel Nelligan,** 106 rue St-Paul ouest (© **877/788-2040**) in

Vieux-Montréal, expanded in 2007 from 63 to 105 rooms. The **Ritz-Carlton Montréal,** 1228 rue Sherbrooke ouest (© **800/363-0366**), is planning a C$100-million renovation to begin sometime in 2008 that will last for 15 months.

Where to Dine In downtown, the very good Spanish resto **Pintxo** has added a new outpost at 2 rue Sherbrooke est at the corner of bd. St-Laurent. On Ile Ste-Hélène, **Nuances** (© **514/392-2708**), the restaurant atop the city's casino, got a dazzling face-lift in 2007 and now looks as contemporary as the food on its plates. And at press time, Québec City restaurant hotshot Daniel Vézina was said to be preparing **Laurie Raphaël Montréal,** to open in the restaurant space within the Hôtel Le Germain; and the founders of the well-liked **Joe Beef** had just opened an Italian eatery, **Liverpool House,** at 2501 rue Notre-Dame ouest (© **514/313-6049**), just a few doors away.

QUEBEC CITY Québec has spent the last few years gearing up for its 400th anniversary party in 2008. Although celebrations are scheduled year-round, most events take place from June to September 2008. The biggest days will be July 3 to 6, with ceremonies, concerts, and huge outdoor parties. The waterfront has been spruced up, museums will show anniversary-related exhibits, and the Cirque du Soleil and other artists will be performing. **Espace 400ᵉ,** a new pavilion on the waterfront where the Centre d'Interprétation du Vieux-Port used to be, will be homebase. More details are at **www.myquebec2008.com**.

Where to Stay In Québec City's burgeoning arts and gastronomic community St-Roch, the new **Auberge Le Vincent,** 295 rue St-Vallier est (© **418/523-5000**), has sophisticated rooms and luxe features.

Where to Dine The physical overhaul of **Laurie Raphaël,** 117 rue Dalhousie (© **418/692-4555**), keeps it atop the local food pyramid: It's now endlessly eclectic *and* sophisticated.

OTTAWA & EASTERN ONTARIO The **Diefenbunker** (© **613/839-0007;** www.diefenbunker.ca), a former H-bomb bunker in the countryside outside Ottawa converted into a fascinatingly chilling museum, added two spectacular new permanent exhibitions in 2006: One very graphically archives the terrible physical toll (on structures *and* people) of nuclear weapons; the other is an exhibition about peacekeeping and peacekeepers around the world. Tours of the Diefenbunker are offered daily and the two new exhibits can be seen at the conclusion of the tour.

The **Great Canadian Theatre Company** (© **613/236-5196;** www.gctc.ca) has moved into a brand-new theater facility known as the **Irving Greenberg Theatre Centre.** It holds three performance spaces and is located at 1233 Wellington St. W. (at Holland Ave.).

But it's not all good news: The **Storyland family park** outside Ottawa closed its doors in September 2007 after 42 years of amusements, and the venerable **Café Henry Burger** in Gatineau—one of the very longest-standing restaurants in the Ottawa area in recent memory—has also been shuttered.

TORONTO The transformation of the **Royal Ontario Museum (ROM)** is almost complete: 10 new Daniel Libeskind–designed galleries are already open, and the World Culture and Natural World galleries will be unveiled in 2008. The Frank Gehry–designed renovation at the **Art Gallery of Ontario (AGO)** will continue in 2008, with most of the building closed to the public while work is ongoing. There are also updates and expansions going on at the **Ontario Science Centre,** but that child-pleasing museum will stay open while the work is being done.

Toronto was already blessed with plenty of parkland, but in 2007 a particularly interesting new green space opened: **Ireland Park,** on the waterfront. It's a memorial to the 38,000 Irish who arrived in the city in 1847; the "Arrival" figures by Rowan Gillespie are the counterpoint to his "Departure" figures on Dublin's Liffey quayside.

Where to Stay The newest place to stay is actually Toronto's oldest continuously operating hotel. **The Gladstone,** 1214 Queen St. W. (© **416/531-4635;** www. gladstonehotel.com), opened in 1889, but for the past several decades it had languished. However, with the march of gentrification moving steadily west along Queen Street, it was time for a top-to-toe reno by a new owner. The results employ the work of local artists in the unique rooms, and there's plenty going on to recommend the place. However, the West Queen West neighborhood won't appeal to all visitors—it's cleaned up from what it used to be, but it's still rough around the edges.

Where to Dine Sampling all of Toronto's best new restaurants will have you running all over town. There's **Thuet,** 609 King St. W. (© **416/603-2777**), an opulent bistro and bakery; **Perigee** in the Distillery District (55 Mill St.; © **416/364-1397**), a dining room that is set up almost like a theater, only instead of a stage, there's an open kitchen; **Cava,** 1560 Yonge St. (© **416/979-9918**), an uptown tapas bar from Chris McDonald, one of Toronto's greatest chefs; and **Asia Republik,** 372 Bloor St. W. (© **416/921-6787**), which has the best lunch deal in the city.

SOUTHWESTERN ONTARIO If you're a cyclist, you'll appreciate Via Rail's new **Toronto-Niagara Bike Train,** which is available in the summer months; you can take the train to Niagara Falls and store your bike in a cargo car till you get

there. While you're in the area, you might want to check out the increasingly popular **Fort George Ghost Tours,** which explore one of Ontario's best-known "haunted" places.

NORTHERN ONTARIO The Muskoka region has been a magnet for visitors since the 19th century, but only recently has its natural charms been rivaled by man-made ones. Several of the region's top-rated golf courses—including **Taboo** and the Mark O'Meara Course at **Grandview**—have joined forces to create the **Muskoka Golf Trail** (© **800/465-3034** or 905/755-0999; www.golfmuskoka.com). Luxurious spas at the **Deerhurst Resort** and Taboo attract both sexes (visit www.spasontario. com for offerings). On the restaurant front, **3 Guys and a Stove** (© **705/789-1815**) and **Elements Restaurant, Culinary Theatre & Lounge** (© **705/687-2233**) are in top form.

MANITOBA & SASKATCHEWAN The former Gull Harbour Resort in Hecla/Grindstone Provincial Park, an island in massive Lake Winnipeg, reopens in 2008 as the **Hecla Oasis Resort** (© **800/267-6700;** www.heclaoasis.com) after a C$15-million remodel and the addition of a family water park, full-service day spa with mineral pool, and a health and wellness center.

Since the Royal Canadian Mounted Police (RCMP) arrived on the Saskatchewan prairies in the 1870s, Regina's RCMP Training Academy has served as the primary training facility for the Mounties. In 2007, the **RCMP Heritage Centre,** (© **306/780-5838;** www. rcmpheritagecentre.com), opened on the academy grounds. The striking new building, designed by famed Canadian architect Arthur Erickson, presents the story of the RCMP from the days of frontier justice to its current role as the Canadian national police force.

The South Saskatchewan Riverfront in the heart of Saskatoon is about to gain another landmark civic structure. **Persephone Theatre** (www.persephonetheatre. org), the city's top acting troupe, is building a two-theater performance center that will also offer workshop space and house a year-round farmer's market.

ALBERTA & THE ROCKIES The **Kensington Riverside Inn** (ⓒ 877/313-3733; www.kensingtonriversideinn.com), a small boutique lodging across the Bow River from downtown Calgary, has expanded its small dining area into a 25-seat dining room with two seatings each evening. The manager characterizes the planned menu as "French Laundry meets the Canadian heartland," referring to the Napa Valley restaurant known for its many small courses of exquisite, locally sourced food.

The **Art Gallery of Alberta** (ⓒ 780/422-6223; www.artgalleryalberta.com), whose long-time home in Winston Churchill Square is undergoing complete restructuring, has a new temporary home. Until the new building is complete (scheduled for 2009), the AGA is mounting shows and displaying works from its permanent collection at Enterprise Square, 10230 Jasper Ave. (formerly the Hudson Bay Building).

Near the Alberta Legislature Building and a few blocks from downtown, the **Matrix Hotel** (ⓒ 866/465-8150; www. matrixedmonton.com) is taking over a 1964 structure built as Edmonton's first luxury high-rise hotel. The slightly severe Moderne facade is the perfect foil for the Matrix Hotel's 185 urban-chic rooms and suites; we haven't reviewed it yet, but the manager promises cool decor and warm hospitality.

VANCOUVER Prices are sure to rise for the 2010 Olympics, but for now, fabulous restaurants and accommodations in Vancouver are still priced lower than those in Toronto, Montréal, or any major U.S. city. This is true even with the weakening value of the U.S. dollar.

Getting Around Parts of Vancouver are torn up for the construction of **Canada Line,** a new light-rail hookup from Vancouver International Airport. When it begins operation in 2009, visitors will be able to board the train at the airport and arrive downtown or in Yaletown in 22 minutes.

Frontier Airlines has introduced a new daily nonstop service between its Denver hub and Vancouver, the first U.S. low-cost carrier to serve Vancouver.

Where to Stay Situated in Vancouver's downtown close to the Granville Street entertainment district, the **Moda Hotel,** 900 Seymour St. (ⓒ 604/683-4251), offers lots of style and excellent value. The hotel, located in a 1908 heritage building, recently opened its doors after receiving a significant makeover. Rooms feature a sleekly minimal European look.

Where to Dine After 18 years, Chef Hidekazu Tojo relocated **Tojo's Restaurant** (ⓒ 604/872-8050) to a stunning new space at 1133 W. Broadway. Designed by sculptor and architect Colin Kwok, the 604-sq.-m (6,500-sq.-ft.) vaulted restaurant is a blend of Zen spatial dynamics, crisp modern forms, and an underlying Japanese sensibility. The restaurant features an open-kitchen concept set behind the sushi bar.

An inexpensive and very welcome addition to Gastown's dining scene, **Salt,** in Blood Alley (ⓒ 604/633-1912), is Vancouver's only charcuterie and serves cured meats and artisan cheeses.

What to See & Do Gale-force winds in December 2006 wreaked havoc on **Stanley Park,** toppling thousands of trees. Expect some hiking trails to be closed well into 2008.

2010 Winter Olympics Update Construction of **The Richmond Oval,** where 12 speed skating events will be held, began in November 2006. The facility will house a 400m track and seating for 8,000 spectators. Post-games, the Oval will become a multipurpose sports, recreation, and wellness facility.

Construction is also underway on **Hillcrest/Nat Bailey Stadium Park.** Located about 15 minutes from downtown Vancouver, the facility will host the men's and women's curling competitions for the games, as well as the wheelchair curling tournament for the Paralympic Games. Post-games, Hillcrest/Nat Bailey Stadium Park will become a multipurpose community recreation center that will include an ice hockey rink, gymnasium, library, and a new aquatic center with a 50m (164-ft.) lap and leisure pool. The multipurpose center has been designed using leading environmental and business practices.

It's also been announced that the freestyle skiing site at West Vancouver's Cypress Mountain in **Cypress Provincial Park** is now competition-ready. The mountain, just 30 minutes from downtown, will serve as the venue for snowboarding, freestyle skiing, and the new ski cross events. In winter 2008, Cypress will open nine new runs for high-level intermediate/expert skiers and snowboarders, a 40% increase in the mountain's skiable terrain.

VICTORIA & BRITISH COLUMBIA

A ferry accident in March 2006 sank the *Queen of the North,* the BC Ferries (© **888/223-3779** or 250/386-3431; www.bcferries.com) vessel that previously sailed through the Inside Passage between Port Hardy and Prince Rupert. As of press time, schedule and vessel changes are possible along this route until a replacement ferry is put in operation. Service will continue on all the runs, but dates and times may be different from published schedules.

Getting Around   Delta Airlines (www. delta.com) now offers a direct flight to Victoria from Salt Lake City.

The mile-long, three-lane Highway 97 bridge that connects Westbank to Kelowna across Okanagan Lake long ago ceased to handle the traffic load in this fast-growing resort and wine-growing mecca. A new five-lane bridge is scheduled for completion in 2008, which may ease congestion in this otherwise beautifully scenic area. But of course, build it and they will come: Within the decade, the new bridge's designers expect the span to carry nearly 70,000 vehicles a day (30% more than today).

Where to Stay As the name suggests, the **Grand Okanagan Lakefront Resort** (© **800/465-4651;** www.grandokanagan. com), is the grandest place to stay in Kelowna. However, with the opening of the **Royal Private Residence Club,** a new building of opulent and spacious suites adjacent to the existing resort, the Grand Okanagan takes luxury to a new height. With rich but comfortable decor, fully equipped designer kitchens, multiple bathrooms and TVs, and views over the marina, these accommodations are perfect for a special occasion. You'll also want to watch the sunset from the top floor's heated infinity pool.

The small agricultural town of Oliver has been the hub of Okanagan Valley fruit production since the 1930s, and more recently it's become the locus of the valley's burgeoning wine industry. However, the town of Oliver itself has offered little for the traveling wine connoisseur. That's about to change: The **Oliver Wine Village** (www.oliverwinevillage.com), a mixed-use development that includes a condo hotel, fine-dining restaurant, and spa is slated to open in 2008. The grounds will also include the Okanagan Wine Interpretive Centre, which will educate wine lovers on the wine-making process, and the Okanagan Culinary Arts Centre, where food lovers can enjoy cooking lessons and food classes, and, of course, learn more about pairing wines with food.

Whistler With the Winter Olympics' skiing and sliding events coming to Whistler in 2010, the news in this world-renowned ski resort is always of building and rebuilding. The **continuing road construction on the Sea to Sky Highway (Hwy. 99)** between Horseshoe Bay and Whistler will probably have the most impact on pre-Olympics visitors. Expect delays of between 45 and 60 minutes. Note also that the entire route may be closed for most of the night (between midnight and 6am), due to blasting.

Check the links under "Driving to Whistler" at www.tourismwhistler.com for the latest updates on construction schedules and closures.

One of the largest construction projects in Whistler history opens in winter 2008. Intrawest, the corporation behind Whistler Blackcomb Resort, is building a record-defying gondola that will link together the peaks of Whistler (elev. 2,182m/7,160 ft.) and Blackcomb (elev. 2,284m/7,494 ft.) mountains. The **Peak to Peak Gondola** will have the longest free-span lift in the world, at 3.024km (1¾ miles) and a total length of 4.4km (2¾ miles). The Peak to Peak Gondola will also be the highest detachable lift in the world, at 415m (1,362 ft.) above the valley floor. The gondola will be open in winter to skiers and in summer to sightseers seeking an adrenaline rush.

The Best of Canada

Planning a trip to such a vast and diverse country can present you with a bewildering array of choices. We've scoured all of Canada in search of the best places and experiences, and in this chapter we share our very personal and opinionated choices. We hope they'll give you some ideas and get you started.

1 The Best Travel Experiences

- **Exploring the Cabot Trail** (Nova Scotia): This wildly scenic driving loop around Cape Breton Highlands National Park delivers a surplus of dramatic coastal scenery. Take a few days to explore the area. You can hike blustery headlands, scope for whales on a tour boat, and dabble around a cove or two in a sea kayak. See chapter 3.

- **Hiking Gros Morne National Park** (Newfoundland): When the earth's land masses broke apart and shifted 500 million years ago, a piece of the mantle, the very shell of the planet, was thrust upward to form awesome tableland mountains of rock here. Spend a week or more trekking coastal trails, venturing to scenic waterfalls, and strolling alongside landlocked fjords. See "Gros Morne National Park: One of Canada's Treasures" in chapter 6.

- **Watching the World Go by at a Québec City Cafe** (Québec): Perched just overlooking the pedestrian-only rue du Petit-Champlain, the terrace of **Le Marie-Clarisse** restaurant offers a catbird seat to the world. A more pleasant hour cannot be passed anywhere in Québec City than here on a summer afternoon, over a platter of shrimp or pâtés. (In winter, cocoon by the stone fireplace inside: The rooms are formed of rafters, brick, and 300-year-old walls, and evoke the feel of a small country inn.) See p. 286.

- **Checking Out Toronto Theater, Dance, and Music** (Ontario): Sure, Toronto likes its blockbuster shows, which are usually housed at the Royal Alexandra or the Princess of Wales theaters. However, the offerings from the CanStage, Soulpepper, Opera Atelier, Tafelmusik, and the Lorraine Kimsa Theatre for Young People are innovative and consistently excellent, too. And seeing the Canadian Opera Company or the National Ballet of Canada onstage at their new home—the Four Seasons Centre for the Performing Arts—is breathtaking. See "Toronto After Dark" in chapter 10.

- **Seeing the Polar Bears in Churchill** (Manitoba): In October or November, travel by train or plane to Churchill and the shores of Hudson Bay to view hundreds of magnificent polar bears, which migrate to the bay's icy shores and even lope into Churchill itself. In the evening, you can glimpse the famous aurora borealis (northern lights). Either take **VIA**

Rail's *Hudson Bay* train (© **888/VIA-RAIL** in Canada, or 800/561-3949 in the U.S.), a 2-night/1-day trip from Winnipeg, or fly in on **Calm Air** (© **800/839-2256**). See "On to the Far North & Churchill, the World's Polar Bear Capital" in chapter 13.

- **Horseback Riding in the Rockies** (Alberta): Rent a cabin on a rural guest ranch and get back in the saddle again. Spend a day fishing, then return to the lodge for a country dance or barbecue. Ride a horse to a backcountry chalet in the rugged mountain wilderness. Forget the crowded park highways and commercialized resort towns and just relax. **Brewster's Kananaskis Guest Ranch**

(© **800/691-5085** or 403/673-3737) in Kananaskis Village, near Banff, offers a variety of guided horseback trips, including food, lodging, and the horse you ride in on. See p. 575.

- **Sailing the Great Bear Rain Forest** (British Columbia): About halfway up B.C.'s west coast is an isolated region of mountains, fjords, bays, rivers, and inlets. It's one of the last places where grizzly bears are still found in large numbers, plus salmon, killer whales, otters, and porpoises. **Maple Leaf Adventures** (© **888/599-5323** or 250/386-7245) runs a number of trips on a 28m (92-ft.) schooner to this magic part of the world. See p. 694.

2 The Best Family Vacations

- **Fundy National Park and Vicinity** (New Brunswick): You'll find swimming, hiking, and kayaking at this extraordinary national park—and plenty of attractions and programs for kids, too. Don't overlook biking in the hills east of the park or rappelling and rock climbing at Cape Enrage, either. See "Fundy National Park: Exploring the Wild Coast" in chapter 4.

- **Prince Edward Island's Beaches:** The red-sand beaches here might turn white swim trunks a bit pinkish, but it's hard to beat a day or two splashing around these tepid waters while admiring pastoral island landscapes. The island possesses several children's amusements nearby, as well. See chapter 5.

- **Mont-Tremblant Ski Resort** (Montréal): The pearl of the Laurentians is Mont-Tremblant, just an hour and a half from Montréal and the highest peak in eastern Canada at 968m (3,176 ft.). It's a mecca in the winter

for skiers and snowboarders from all over and is repeatedly voted the top resort in eastern North America by *Ski* magazine. Development has been particularly heavy in the resort town; the area gains back some of its charm in the summer with thinned-out traffic. See "North into the Laurentian Mountains" in chapter 7.

- **Ottawa** (Ontario): In this family-friendly city, you and your kids can watch soldiers strut their stuff and red-coated Mounties polish their equestrian and musical skills. Canoeing or skating on the canal is lots of fun, and Ottawa boasts a host of lively museums to explore—such as the Canada Aviation Museum, the Canadian Museum of Civilization, and the Canada Science and Technology Museum. See chapter 9.

- **The Muskoka Lakes** (Ontario): This region is filled with resorts that welcome families. Kids can swim, canoe, bike, fish, and more. Because most resorts offer children's programs, parents can enjoy a rest as well. And once you tell the small fries that Santa's Village is open year-round in the town of Bracebridge, you won't be able to keep them away. See "The Muskoka Lakes: A Land of Resorts" in chapter 12.

- **Whistler/Blackcomb Ski Resorts** (British Columbia): Whistler and Blackcomb's twin ski resorts offer lots of family-oriented activities. You'll find everything from downhill and cross-country skiing, snowboarding, snowshoeing, and snowmobiling lessons in winter to horseback riding, mountain biking, in-line skating, swimming, kayaking, and rafting summer trips designed for families with school-age children. See "Whistler: One of North America's Premier Ski Resorts" in chapter 16.

- **Travel the Klondike Gold Rush Route** (The Yukon): Follow the Klondike Gold Rush, traveling from Skagway, Alaska, up and over White Pass, to the Yukon's capital, Whitehorse. Canoe through the once-daunting Miles Canyon on the mighty Yukon River. Drive to Dawson City, and visit the gold fields, walk the boardwalks of the old town center, and listen to recitations of Robert Service poetry. Pan for gold and attend an old-fashioned musical revue at the opera house. Inexpensive public campgrounds abound in the Yukon, making this one of the more affordable family vacations in western Canada. See chapter 17.

3 The Best Nature & Wildlife Viewing

- **Whales at Digby Neck** (Nova Scotia): For a chance to see fin, minke, or humpback whales, choose from a plethora of whale-watching outfitters located along this narrow peninsula of remote fishing villages. Right, sperm, blue, and pilot whales, along with the infrequent orcas, have also been seen over the years. Getting to the tip of the peninsula is half the fun—it requires two ferries. See "From Digby to Yarmouth: A Taste of the Other Nova Scotia" in chapter 3.

- **Birds and Caribou on the Avalon Peninsula** (Newfoundland): In one busy day you can see a herd of caribou, the largest puffin colony in North America, and an extraordinary gannet colony visible from mainland cliffs. See "The Southern Avalon Peninsula" in chapter 6.

- **Whales at Baie Ste-Catherine** (Québec): About a 2-hour drive north of Québec City in the upper Charlevoix region, hundreds of resident minke and beluga whales are joined by blue, fin, and humpback whales in the summers. Mid-June to early October is the best time to see them. They can be spotted from land, but whale-watching cruises offer closer looks. The website www.whales-online.net provides up-to-date info on activity in the region. See "Upper Charlevoix: St-Siméon, Baie Ste-Catherine, & Tadoussac" in chapter 8.

- **Pelicans in Prince Albert National Park** (Saskatchewan): On Lavallee Lake roosts the second-largest pelican colony in North America. Bison, moose, elk, caribou, black bear, and red fox also roam free in this 400,000-hectare (1 million-acre) wilderness. See "Prince Albert National Park: A Jewel of the National Park System" in chapter 13.

- **Orcas off Vancouver Island** (British Columbia): The waters surrounding Vancouver Island teem with orcas (killer whales), as well as harbor seals, sea lions, bald eagles, and harbor and Dahl's porpoises. In Victoria, **Seafun Safaris Whale Watching** (© **877/360-1233** or 250/360-1200; www.seafun.com), is one of many companies offering whale-watching tours in Zodiacs and covered boats. See chapter 16.

4 The Best Views

- **Cape Enrage** (New Brunswick): Just east of Fundy National Park, you'll find a surprisingly harsh coastal terrain of high rocky cliffs pounded by the sea. Route 915 offers a wonderful detour off the beaten path. See "Fundy National Park: Exploring the Wild Coast" in chapter 4.

- **Signal Hill** (Newfoundland): Signal Hill marks the entrance to St. John's harbor. Besides the history that was made here, it's uncommonly scenic, with views of a coast that hasn't changed in 500 years. The North Head Trail is one of Newfoundland's most dramatic—and it's entirely within city limits. See p. 194.

- **Bonavista Peninsula** (Newfoundland): The peninsula's northernmost tip offers a superb vantage point for spotting icebergs, even into midsummer. You'll also see puffins, whales, and one of the most scenic lighthouses in eastern Canada. See "The Bonavista Peninsula: Into Newfoundland's Past" in chapter 6.

- **Terrasse Dufferin in Québec City** (Québec): Every narrow street, leafy plaza, sidewalk cafe, horse-drawn *caléche,* and church spire in Québec City breathes recollections of the provincial cities of the mother country of France. Atop the bluff overlooking the St. Lawrence River, this handsome boardwalk promenade, with its green-and-white–topped gazebos, looks much as it did 100 years ago, when ladies with parasols and gentlemen with top hats strolled it on sunny afternoons, with the turrets of the Château Frontenac as a backdrop. At night, the river below is the color of liquid mercury, and music from the *boîtes* in Lower Town echoes faintly. See chapter 8.

- **Niagara Falls** (Ontario): This is still a wonder of nature despite its commercial exploitation. You can experience the falls from the cockpit of a helicopter or from the decks of the *Maid of the Mist,* which takes you into the roaring maelstrom. The least intimidating view is from the Skylon Tower. See "Niagara-on-the-Lake & Niagara Falls" in chapter 11.

- **Agawa Canyon** (Ontario): To see the northern Ontario wilderness that inspired the Group of Seven, take the Agawa Canyon Train Tour on a 184km (114-mile) trip from the Soo to Hearst through the Agawa Canyon, where you can spend a few hours exploring scenic waterfalls and vistas. The train snakes through a vista of deep ravines and lakes, hugging the hillsides and crossing gorges on skeletal trestle bridges. See "Some Northern Ontario Highlights: Driving along Highways 11 & 17" in chapter 12.

- **Moraine Lake in Banff National Park** (Alberta): Ten snow-clad peaks towering up to 3,000m (9,843 ft.) rear up dramatically behind this gem-blue tiny lake. Rent a canoe and paddle to the mountains' base. See "Banff National Park: Canada's Top Tourist Draw" in chapter 14.

- **Vancouver** (British Columbia): With the most beautiful setting of any city in Canada or indeed the world, there are numerous places to take in the view of mountains, city, and ocean: on the oft-snow-clad peaks of **Grouse Mountain** (© **604/984-0661**), accessible via a quick tram ride; or from the window of your harborside hotel room in the **Pan Pacific Hotel Vancouver** (© **604/662-8111**). But the best way remains the cheapest: Round about sunset wander to English Bay Beach near the corner of Denman and Davie streets, grab an ice cream or a coffee or nothing at all, and watch as the sun shimmers red, and then descends behind Vancouver Island, lighting the Coast Mountains, Vancouver, and English Bay in a warm red glow. See chapter 15.

5 The Most Dramatic Drives

- **Cape Breton's Cabot Trail** (Nova Scotia): This 300km (186-mile) loop through the uplands of Cape Breton Highlands National Park is a world-class excursion. You'll see Acadian fishing ports, pristine valleys, and some of the most picturesque coastline anywhere. See chapter 3.

- **Viking Trail** (Newfoundland): Travelers looking to leave the crowds behind needn't look any farther. This beautiful drive to Newfoundland's northern tip is wild and solitary, with views of curious geology and a wind-raked coast. And you'll end up at one of the world's great historic sites— L'Anse aux Meadows. See "The Great Northern Peninsula: Way Off the Beaten Path" in chapter 6.

- **Icefields Parkway** (Hwy. 93 through Banff and Jasper national parks, Alberta): This is one of the world's grandest mountain drives. Cruising along it is like a trip back to the ice ages. The parkway climbs past glacier-notched peaks to the Columbia Icefields, a sprawling cap of snow, ice, and glacier at the very crest of the Rockies. See "Banff National Park: Canada's Top Tourist Draw" in chapter 14.

- **Highway 99** (British Columbia): The Sea to Sky Highway from Vancouver to Lillooet takes you from a dramatic seacoast past glaciers, pine forests, and a waterfall that cascades from a mountaintop and through Whistler's majestic glacial mountains. The next leg of the 4-hour drive winds up a series of switchbacks to the thickly forested Cayoosh Creek valley and on to the craggy mountains surrounding the Fraser River gold-rush town of Lillooet. See chapter 16.

- **Dempster Highway** (from Dawson City to Inuvik, Northwest Territories): Canada's most northerly highway, the Dempster is a year-round gravel road across the top of the world. From Dawson City, the road winds over the Continental Divide three times, crosses the Arctic Circle, and fords the Peel and Mackenzie rivers by ferry before reaching Inuvik, a Native community on the mighty Mackenzie River delta. See chapter 17.

6 The Best Walks & Rambles

- **Halifax's Waterfront** (Nova Scotia): Take your time strolling along Halifax's working waterfront. You can visit museums, board a historic ship or two, enjoy a snack, and take an inexpensive ferry ride across the harbor and back. Come evening, there's fiddle and guitar playing at the pubs.

See "Halifax: More Than a Natural Harbor" in chapter 3.

- **Cape Breton Highlands National Park** (Nova Scotia): You'll find bog and woodland walks aplenty at Cape Breton, but the best trails follow rugged cliffs along the open ocean. The Skyline Trail is among the most dramatic pathways in the province. See "Cape Breton Highlands National Park" in chapter 3.

- **Green Gardens Trail** (Gros Morne, Newfoundland): This demanding hike at Gros Morne National Park takes you on a 16km (9.4-mile) loop, much of which follows coastal meadows atop fractured cliffs. It's demanding but worth every step. See "Gros Morne National Park: One of Canada's Treasures" in chapter 6.

- **Vieux-Montréal** (Montréal): The architectural heritage of the historic Vieux-Montréal, or "Old Montréal," district and the Vieux-Port (Old Port) waterfront promenade adjacent has been substantially preserved. Several small but intriguing museums are housed in historic buildings, and restored 18th- and 19th-century structures have been adapted for use as shops, galleries, boutique hotels, cafes, studios, bars, and apartments. In the evening, many of the finer buildings are illuminated. Today, especially in summer, activity centers around Place Jacques-Cartier, where street performers, strolling locals and tourists congregate. See chapter 7.

- **Toronto's Art & Design District** (Ontario): The stretch of Queen Street that runs west of Bathurst Avenue has been recently reinvented as the Art & Design District. This isn't just a marketing ploy—the title is well deserved. The area is home to the Museum of Contemporary Canadian Art and to private art collections such as the Stephen Bulger Gallery; it's also the neighborhood to see some of the best local design talent, with block after block of unique boutiques, small but edgy galleries, and plenty of cafes. See chapter 10.

- **Lake Superior Provincial Park** (Ontario): Follow any trail in this park to a rewarding vista. The 16km (10-mile) Peat Mountain Trail leads to a panoramic view close to 150m (about 500 ft.) above the surrounding lakes and forests. The moderate Orphan Lake Trail offers views over the Orphan Lake and Lake Superior, plus a pebble beach and Baldhead River falls. The 26km (16-mile) Toawab Trail takes you through the Agawa Valley to the 25m (82-ft.) Agawa Falls. See "Some Northern Ontario Highlights: Driving along Highways 11 & 17" in chapter 12.

- **Johnston Canyon** (Banff National Park, Alberta): Just 24km (15 miles) west of Banff, Johnston Creek cuts a deep, very narrow canyon through limestone cliffs. The trail winds through tunnels, passes waterfalls, edges by shaded rock faces, and crosses the chasm on footbridges before reaching a series of iridescent pools, formed by springs that bubble up through highly colored rock. See "Banff National Park: Canada's Top Tourist Draw" in chapter 14.

- **Plain of Six Glaciers Trail** (Lake Louise, Alberta): From Chateau Lake Louise, a lakeside trail rambles along the edge of emerald-green Lake Louise, and then climbs to the base of Victoria Glacier. At a rustic teahouse, you can order a cup of tea and a scone—each made over a wood-burning stove—and gaze up at the rumpled face of the glacier. See "Banff National Park: Canada's Top Tourist Draw" in chapter 14.

- **Stanley Park** (Vancouver, British Columbia) is something of a miracle—a huge, lush park (one of the largest city parks in the world) right on the edge of a densely populated urban neighborhood. Stroll the famous seawall that skirts the entire park, visit a striking collection of First Nation totem poles, or simply wander among the giant trees and magnificent plantings. See p. 665.

- **Long Beach** (Vancouver Island, British Columbia): Part of Pacific Rim National Park, Long Beach is more than 16km (10 miles) long and hundreds of meters wide and is flanked by awe-inspiring rain forests of cedar, fir, and Sitka spruce. Beyond the roaring surf you'll see soaring eagles, basking sea lions, and occasionally even migrating gray whales. See chapter 16.

7 The Best Biking Routes

- **Nova Scotia's South Shore:** Not in a hurry to get anywhere? Peddling peninsulas and coasting along placid inlets is a great tonic for the weary soul. You'll pass through graceful villages such as Shelburne, Lunenburg, and Chester and rediscover a quiet way of life en route. See "The South Shore: Quintessential Nova Scotia" in chapter 3.

- **Prince Edward Island:** This island province sometimes seems like it was created specifically *for* bike touring. The villages here are reasonably spaced apart, hills are virtually nonexistent, the coastal roads are picturesque in the extreme, and a new island-wide bike path offers detours through marshes and quiet woodlands. See chapter 5.

- **Montréal's Lachine Canal** (Montréal): Montréal boasts an expanding network of more than 350km (217 miles) of cycling paths and year-round bike lanes on city streets. The Lachine Canal was inaugurated in 1824 so ships could bypass the Lachine Rapids on the way to the Great Lakes, and the canal now has a nearly flat 11km (6.8-mile) bicycle path on either side of it that travels peacefully alongside locks and over small bridges. You can rent bikes in the Old Port. See "Outdoor Activities & Spectator Sports" in chapter 7.

- **Québec province's *Route verte* (Green Route):** In summer 2007, the province officially inaugurated the *Route verte,* a 4,000km (2,485-mile) bike-path network that stretches from one end of Québec to the other and links up all regions and cities. The idea is modeled on the Rails-to-Trails program in the U.S. and cycling routes in Denmark and Great Britain. Inns along the route are especially focused on serving bikers, with covered and locked storage for overnight stays and carb-heavy meals. See p. 275.

- **Niagara Region** (Ontario): The flatlands here make for terrific biking terrain. A bike path runs along the Niagara Parkway, which follows the Niagara River. You'll bike past fruit farms, vineyards, and gardens with picnicking spots. See "Niagara-on-the-Lake & Niagara Falls" in chapter 11.

- **Highways 1 and 93 through Banff and Jasper National Parks** (Alberta): Also called the Icefields Parkway, this well-maintained wide highway winds through some of the world's most dramatic mountain scenery. Take the Bow Valley Parkway, between Banff and Lake Louise, and Parkway 93A between Athabasca Falls and Jasper for slightly quieter peddling. Best of all, there are seven hostels (either rustic or fancy) at some of the most beautiful sights along the route, so you don't have to weigh yourself down with camping gear. See chapter 14.

- **Stanley Park Seawall** (Vancouver, British Columbia): Vancouver's Seawall surrounds the Stanley Park shoreline on the Burrard Inlet and English Bay. Built just above the high-tide mark, it offers nonstop breathtaking views, no hills, and no cars. See chapter 15.

8 The Best Culinary Experiences

- **Fresh Lobster** (Nova Scotia & New Brunswick): Wherever you see wooden lobster traps piled on a wharf, you'll know a fresh lobster meal isn't far away. The most productive lobster fisheries are around Shediac, New Brunswick, and all along Nova Scotia's Atlantic coast. Sunny days are ideal for cracking open a crustacean while sitting at a wharfside picnic table, preferably with a locally brewed beer close at hand. See chapters 3 and 4.

- **Newfoundland Berries:** The unforgiving rocky and boggy soil of this blustery island resists most crops, but it also produces some of the most delicious berries in Canada. Look for roadside stands or pick your own blueberries, strawberries, partridgeberries, or bakeapples. Many restaurants add these berries to desserts (cheesecake, custard) when they're in season, too. See chapter 6.

- **Pigging Out in Montréal** (Montréal): See what its cultish fans have been raving about. **Au Pied de Cochon** (🕿 **514/281-1114**) looks like just another storefront restaurant, but it's packed to the walls 6 nights a week because of its slabs of meat, especially pork. "The Big Happy Pig's Chop," weighing in at more than a pound, is emblematic. Foie gras comes in nearly a dozen combinations, including stuffed into a ham hock, with *poutine,* and in a goofy creation called Duck in a Can which does, indeed, come sealed in a can with a can opener. See p. 234.

- **Indulging in a Tasting Menu Dinner in Québec City** (Québec): Higher-end establishments in both Montréal and Québec City are increasingly offering menus that let you sample the chef's wildest concoctions, and "surprise menus" are equally popular—you don't know what you're getting until it's right in front of you. The imaginative menu at **Laurie Raphaël** (🕿 **418/692-4555**) has included silky-smooth foie gras on a teeny ice-cream paddle with a drizzle of port reduction, Alaskan snow crab with a bright-pink pomegranate terrine, and an egg yolk "illusion" of thickened orange juice encapsulated in a skin of pectin served in a puddle of maple syrup. Dazzling! See p. 285.

- **Indulging in Toronto's Gastonomic Scene** (Ontario): Toronto is blessed with a host of stellar chefs, such as Mark McEwan (**North 44,** 🕿 416/487-4897), Susur Lee (**Susur,** 🕿 416/603-2205), Chris McDonald (**Cava,** 🕿 416/979-9918), Marc Thuet (**Thuet,** 🕿 416/603-2777), and Jamie Kennedy (**Jamie Kennedy Wine Bar,** 🕿 416/362-1957). This is your chance to find out why they're household names. See "Where to Dine" in chapter 10.

- **Tasting the World in Toronto** (Ontario): The United Nations has called Toronto the world's most multicultural city, so it's no surprise that the restaurant scene reflects that diversity. Whether you try the excellent sushi at **Hiro Sushi** (🕿 416/304-0550), modern Indian cooking at **Xacutti** (🕿 416/323-3957), classic French cuisine at **Bistro 990** (🕿 416/921-9990), or imaginatively updated Greek at **Pan on the Danforth**

(© 416/466-8158), your taste buds will thank you. See "Where to Dine" in chapter 10.

- **Dining along the Wine Route** (Ontario): The Niagara Region enjoys its own unique microclimate, a fact that explains why this is one of the lushest, most bountiful parts of Canada. Sampling the local wines is a great way to spend an afternoon, particularly if you add lunch and dinner to your itinerary at a vineyard restaurant such as **On the Twenty** (© 905/562-7313) or **Vineland Estates** (© 888/846-3526 or 905/562-7088). See "Niagara-on-the-Lake & Niagara Falls" in chapter 11.

- **Cutting Edge in Winnipeg** (Manitoba): After Makoto Ono took first place honors as Canada's top chef in 2007, his small and quirky **Gluttons Bistro** (© 204/475-5714) suddenly became a must-dine destination for gourmands from across the country. Putting an Asian spin on traditional Canadian foods, Ono delivers seriously delicious and inventive food that's the perfect summation of Winnipeg's multicultural yet emphatically midcontinent spirit. See p. 505.

- **Going Organic in Calgary** (Alberta): You'll walk through a quiet tree-filled park on an island in the Bow River to reach the bustling **River Café** (© 403/261-7670). An immense wood-fired oven and grill produces soft, chewy flat breads and smoky grilled meats and vegetables, all organically grown and freshly harvested. On warm summer evenings, picnickers loll in the grassy shade, nibbling this and that from the cafe's picniclike menu. See p. 554.

- **Dining at a Hotel in Lake Louise** (Alberta): At its cozy dining room in an old log lodge, the **Post Hotel** (© 800/661-1586 or 403/522-3989) serves up the kind of sophisticated yet robust cuisine that perfectly fits the backdrop of glaciered peaks, deep forest, and glassy streams. Both the wine list and the cooking are French and hearty, with the chef focusing on the best of local ingredients—lamb, salmon, and Alberta beef. After spending time out on the trail, a meal here will top off a quintessential day in the Rockies. See p. 597.

- **Serving Up Exquisite Canadian Cuisine in Edmonton** (Alberta): The **Hardware Grill** (© 780/423-0969) is a stylish restaurant in a historic storefront with one of western Canada's finest dining rooms. The chef captures the best of local produce and meats without being slave to the indigenous foods movement, instead taking a Pan-Canadian view of fine dining. Fresh B.C. oysters and salmon, Alberta steaks, Québec foie gras, and Maritime lobsters are artfully prepared, and it's especially exciting to make a meal of the menu's ample selection of small plates—savoring these exquisite culinary explosions is the gastronomic equivalent of foreplay. See p. 624.

- **Enjoying Dim Sum in Vancouver's Chinatown** (British Columbia): With its burgeoning Chinese population, Vancouver's Chinatown has more than half a dozen dim-sum parlors where you can try steamed or baked barbecued-pork buns, dumplings filled with fresh prawns and vegetables, or steamed rice-flour crepes filled with spicy beef. One favorite is **Sun Sui Wah** (© 604/872-8822). See p. 663.

- **Eating Local in Lotus Land** (British Columbia): Self-sufficiency is the new watchword on the west coast, with top chefs sourcing all their ingredients locally. On Vancouver Island, the **Sooke Harbour House** (© 800/889-9688 or 250/642-3421) offers lamb from nearby Salt

Spring Island, seasoned with herbs from the chef's own garden. See p. 721. In Vancouver, the **Raincity Grill** (© **604/685-7337**) makes a specialty of fresh-caught seafood and local game, while the vast selection of B.C. wines by the glass makes dinner an extended road trip through the west coast wine country, with no need for a designated driver. See p. 660.

9 The Best Festivals & Special Events

- **International Busker Festival** (Halifax, Nova Scotia): In early August, the 10-day International Busker Festival brings together talented street performers from around the world, performing in their natural habitat. Best of all, it's free. See p. 87.

- **Newfoundland and Labrador Folk Festival** (St. John's, Newfoundland): How did such a remote island develop such a deep talent pool? That's one of the questions you'll ponder while tapping your feet at this 3-day festival, which is laden with local talent. It's cheap, folksy, and fun. See p. 194.

- **Montréal Jazz Festival** (Montréal): The city has a long tradition in jazz, and this enormously successful July festival has been celebrating America's art form since 1979. Spread out over 11 days, close to 150 indoor shows are scheduled. Wynton Marsalis, Harry Connick, Jr., and even Bob Dylan have been featured in recent years, with smaller shows that highlight everything from Dixieland to the most experimental. See p. 259.

- **Carnaval de Québec** (Québec): Never mind that temperatures in Québec can plummet in February to –40°F (–40°C). Canadians happily pack the family up to come out and play for the 17 days of the city's winter festival. There's a monumental ice palace, dog-sled racing, ice sculptures competitions, outdoor hottubing, zip-line rides over crowds, and dancing at night at outdoor concerts. See p. 296.

- **Toronto International Film Festival** (Ontario): Second only to Cannes, this film festival draws Hollywood's leading luminaries to town for 10 days in early September; more than 250 films are on show. See p. 406.

- **Stratford Festival** (Ontario): This world-famous festival of superb repertory theater, launched by Tyrone Guthrie in 1953, has featured major players such as the late Sir Alec Guinness, Christopher Plummer, Dame Maggie Smith, and the late Sir Peter Ustinov. Productions, which run from May to October or early November on four stages, range from classic to contemporary. You can also participate in informal discussions with company members. See "Stratford & the Stratford Festival" in chapter 11.

- **Festival du Voyageur** (Winnipeg): There's no better antidote to February cabin fever than a midwinter festival, and this is western Canada's largest. The festival celebrates the French-Canadian trappers and explorers called voyageurs who traveled the waterways of Canada in canoes. Held in St. Boniface (Winnipeg's French Quarter), the festival brings together traditional French-Canadian food, music and high spirits. See p. 494.

- **Calgary Stampede** (Alberta): In all North America, there's nothing quite like the Calgary Stampede. Of course it's the world's largest rodeo, but it's also a series of concerts, an art show, an open-air casino, a carnival, a street dance—you name it, it's undoubtedly going on somewhere. In early July, all of Calgary is converted into a party and everyone's invited. See "Calgary: Home of the Annual Stampede" in chapter 14.

- **Celebration of Light** (Vancouver, British Columbia): This 4-night fireworks extravaganza in late July and early August (www.celebration-of-light.com) takes place over English Bay. Three of the world's leading manufacturers are invited to represent their countries in competition against one another, setting their best displays to music. On the fourth night, all three companies launch their finales. Up to 500,000 people show up each night. The best seats are at the "Bard on the Beach" Shakespeare festival across False Creek. See chapter 15.

10 The Best Luxury Hotels & Resorts

- **Keltic Lodge** (Cape Breton Island, Nova Scotia; © **800/565-0444** or 902/285-2880): It's got grand natural drama in the sea-pounded cliffs that surround it, plus a generous measure of high culture. (Jackets on men at dinner, please!) The adjacent golf course is stupendous, and some of the national park's best hikes are close at hand. See p. 107.

- **Kingsbrae Arms Relais & Châteaux** (St. Andrews, New Brunswick; © **506/529-1897**): This deluxe inn manages the trick of being opulent and comfortable at the same time. The shingled manse is lavishly appointed, beautifully landscaped, and well situated for exploring charming St. Andrews. See p. 123.

- **Dalvay-by-the-Sea** (Grand Tracadie, Prince Edward Island; © **902/672-2048**): This intimate resort (it has fewer than 35 rooms and cottages total) is on a quiet stretch of beach. The Tudor mansion was built by a business partner of John D. Rockefeller, and the woodwork alone is enough to keep you entertained during your stay. Bring your bike. See p. 159.

- **Hôtel Le St-James** (Montréal; © **866/841-3111** or 514/841-3111): Old Montréal's surge of designer hotels spans the spectrum from superminimalist to gentlemen's club. The opulent Le St-James sits squarely at the gentlemen's club end of the range. A richly paneled entry leads to a grand hall with carved urns, bronze chandeliers, and balconies with gilded metal balustrades, and the 60 units are furnished with entrancing antiques and impeccable reproductions. A stone-walled, candle-lit spa offers massage and full-body water therapy. See p. 225.

- **Fairmont Le Château Frontenac** (Québec; © **800/441-1414** or 418/692-3861): The turreted hotel opened in 1893 and has hosted Queen Elizabeth and Prince Philip; during World War II, Winston Churchill and Franklin D. Roosevelt had the entire place to themselves for a conference. Luxurious rooms are outfitted with regal decor and elegant château furnishings. Bathrooms have marble touches and every mattress was replaced in 2006 and 2007. Fairmont Gold floors, with a separate concierge and a lounge with an honor bar, offer expansive views of the St. Lawrence River and the old city below. See p. 277.

- **Park Hyatt Toronto** (© **800/233-1234** or 416/925-1234): Talk about having it all—the Park Hyatt boasts a beautifully renovated Art Deco building, a creative dining room (Annona), a serene spa, top-notch service, and one of the best views in the city from the rooftop terrace lounge (where they mix a mighty martini, too). This is a place to relax and let yourself be pampered. See p. 385.

- **Langdon Hall** (Cambridge, Ontario; © **800/268-1898** or 519/740-2100): This quintessential English country house, built in 1902 for the grand-daughter of John Jacob Astor, is now a small hotel where you can enjoy 81 hectares (200 acres) of lawns, gardens, and woodlands. The guest rooms feature the finest amenities, fabrics, and furnishings. Facilities include a full spa, a pool, a tennis court, a croquet lawn, and an exercise room. The airy dining room overlooking the lily pond offers fine Continental cuisine. See p. 452.

- **Delta Bessborough** (Saskatoon, Saskatchewan; © **800/268-1133** or 306/244-5521): Canada is famous for its historic, turn-of-the-20th-century luxury hotels built by the railways, but none is more unexpected than this massive French château in the midst of the Saskatchewan prairies. Beautifully restored, the Bessborough is more than a relic—it's a celebration of the past. Expect exemplary service, comfortable rooms, and the giddy feeling that you're on the Loire, not the South Saskatchewan River. See p. 530.

- **The Fairmont Chateau Lake Louise** (Banff National Park, Alberta; © **800/441-1414** or 403/522-3511): First of all, there's the view: Across a tiny gem-green lake rise massive cliffs shrouded in glacial ice. And then there's the hotel: Part hunting lodge, part European palace, the Chateau is its own community, with sumptuous boutiques, sports-rental facilities, seven dining areas, two bars, magnificent lobby areas, and beautifully furnished guest rooms. See p. 595.

- **Fairmont Hotel Macdonald** (Edmonton, Alberta; © **800/441-1414** or 780/424-5181): When the Canadian Pacific bought and refurbished this landmark hotel in the 1980s, all the charming period details were preserved, while all the inner workings were modernized and brought up to snuff. The result is a regally elegant but friendly small hotel, a real class act. See p. 620.

- **Westin Bayshore Resort & Marina** (Vancouver, British Columbia; © **800/937-8461** or 604/682-3377): Vancouver's only resort hotel with its own marina, the Westin Bayshore looks out across the Burrard Inlet to the mountains and west to the vast expanse of Stanley Park. The finishes throughout are top quality, the beds divine, the pool is one of the largest in North America, and the size of the hotel (which includes a spa and conference center) makes it like a small, luxurious city. See p. 452.

- **The Wickaninnish Inn** (Tofino, British Columbia; © **800/333-4604** in North America, or 250/725-3100): No matter which room you book in this beautiful new lodge, you'll wake to a magnificent view of the untamed Pacific. The inn is on a rocky promontory, surrounded by an old-growth spruce and cedar rainforest and the sprawling sands of Long Beach. In summer, try golfing, fishing, or whale-watching. In winter, shelter by the fire in the Pointe restaurant and watch the wild Pacific storms roll in. See p. 745.

- **Brentwood Bay Lodge & Spa** (Victoria, British Columbia; © **888/544-2079** or 250/544-2079): Every detail has been carefully considered and beautifully rendered in this contemporary timber-and-glass lodge located on a pristine inlet about 20 minutes north of downtown Victoria. With its contemporary rooms, fabulous spa, fine-dining room, and host of amenities, guests experience the luxurious best of the Pacific Northwest. See p. 721.

- **Four Seasons Resort Whistler** (Whistler, British Columbia; © **888/935-2460** or 604/935-3400): This grand—even monumental—hotel is the classiest place to stay in Whistler,

which is saying something. This is a hotel with many moods, from the Wagnerian scale of the stone-lined lobby to the precise gentility of the guest rooms to the faint and welcome silliness of the tiled and back-lit stone fixtures of the restaurant. This is a great hotel that's not afraid to make big statements. See p. 766.

11 The Best Bed & Breakfasts

- **Shipwright Inn** (Charlottetown, Prince Edward Island; © **888/306-9966** or 902/368-1905): This in-town, nine-room B&B is within easy walking distance of all of the city's attractions yet has a settled and pastoral feel. It's informed by a Victorian sensibility without being over the top about it. See p. 163.
- **At Wit's Inn** (St. John's, Newfoundland; © **877/739-7420** or 709/739-7420): This centrally located B&B is bright, cheerful, and whimsical. Opened in 1999 by a restaurateur from Toronto, the inn preserves the best historical elements of its century-old home while graciously updating things for modern tastes. See p. 198.
- **Beild House** (Collingwood, Ontario; © **888/322-3453** or 705/444-1522): On Fridays, you can sit down to a splendid five-course dinner before retiring to the bed that belonged to the duke and duchess of Windsor. A sumptuous breakfast will follow the next morning. This handsome 1909 house contains 11 rooms, 7 with private bathroom. See p. 459.

- **Thea's House** (Banff, Alberta; © **403/762-2499**): Thea's House manages to combine rustic charm and modern elegance, right in the heart of Banff. This refined log-and-stone lodging is a short walk from the busy throngs along Banff Avenue, but it feels miles away in terms of restful comfort. Expect antiques, pine furniture, luxurious amenities, and a friendly but discreet welcome. See p. 587.
- **The Haterleigh Heritage Inn** (Victoria, British Columbia; © **866/234-2244** or 250/384-9995): This exceptional B&B captures the essence of Victoria's romance with a combination of antique furniture, original stained-glass windows, and attentive personal service. The spacious rooms boast high ceilings, large windows, sitting areas, and enormous bathrooms, some with hand-painted tiles and Jacuzzi tubs. Everything is immaculate, and the suites make for wonderful romantic weekends. See p. 716.

12 The Best Camping & Wilderness Lodges

- **Green Park Provincial Park** (Tyne Valley, Prince Edward Island; © **902/831-7912**): Can't afford your own well-maintained estate? This provincial campground makes a decent

substitute. Set on a quiet inlet, the 88-hectare (217-acre) park is built around an extravagant gingerbread mansion that's still open to the public. See

"Prince County: PEI in the Rough" in chapter 5.

- **Gros Morne National Park** (Newfoundland): Backpackers will find wild, spectacular campsites in coastal meadows along the remarkable Green Gardens Trail; car campers should head for Trout River Pond, at the foot of one of Gros Morne's dramatic landlocked fjords. See "Gros Morne National Park: One of Canada's Treasures" in chapter 6.

- **Arowhon Pines** (Algonquin Park, Ontario; © **866/633-5661,** or 705/633-5661 in summer, 416/483-4393 in winter): Located 8km (5 miles) off the highway down a dirt road, this is one of the most entrancing places anywhere. You can enjoy peace, seclusion, and natural beauty, plus comfortable accommodations and good fresh food. There are no TVs or phones—just the call of the loons, the gentle lapping of the water, the croaking of the frogs, and the splash of canoe paddles cutting the surface of the lake. See p. 473.

- **Tunnel Mountain** (Banff, Alberta; © **403/762-1500**): If you find Banff too expensive and too crowded, these campgrounds—three within 5km (3 miles) of town—are a great antidote. Most sites have full hookups, with showers and real toilets. And you'll pay just one-tenth of what hotel dwellers are paying for equally good access to the Rockies. See "Banff National Park: Canada's Top Tourist Draw" in chapter 14.

- **Clayoquot Sound** (British Columbia): The best place to camp in B.C. is on a wild beach on the shores of this vast forested fjord, with only the eagles for company by day and an endless supply of burnable driftwood at night. Much of the coastline is Crown or public land, so there are limitless places to camp (and it's free). The only trick is you need a kayak to take you there. Along the way you'll see thousand-year-old trees and glaciers and whales and bald eagles. See chapter 16.

2

Planning Your Trip to Canada

Canada is a vast country—in fact, it is the world's second-largest nation. This chapter can save you money, time, and headaches as you plan your visit.

1 The Regions in Brief

Bounded by the Atlantic, Pacific, and Arctic oceans, Canada is a land of extraordinary natural beauty, with dramatic land and seascapes, and vibrant cosmopolitan cities. The country is divided into 10 provinces and 3 territories:

- **Nova Scotia:** The heart of Canada's maritime provinces, Nova Scotia has brooding landscapes, wild seacoasts, and historic fishing villages. Its name means New Scotland, after all. Centered on a beautiful natural harbor, Halifax is one of Canada's most charming small cities, with lots of 18th-century stone architecture. See chapter 3.
- **New Brunswick:** Wedged between the Gulf of St. Lawrence and the Bay of Fundy, New Brunswick is truly maritime. At Fundy National Park, you can view some of the world's most powerful tides along a wilderness coastline. Grand Manan and Campobello Islands are famed for wildlife and birding opportunities. The warm and sandy beaches along the Gulf of St. Lawrence are popular summer holiday destinations. See chapter 4.
- **Prince Edward Island:** Canada's smallest province is a green and bucolic island in the Gulf of St.

Lawrence that's seemingly far from the stress and hurry of one's regular life. The capital city of Charlottetown is a lovely brick-built city clustered around a quiet bay, but the real attraction here is the quiet countryside covered with forests and farms (a setting that served as the inspiration for *Anne of Green Gables*) and the beaches along the island's north coast. See chapter 5.

- **Newfoundland and Labrador:** So remote that they occupy their own time zone, Newfoundland and Labrador form Canada's wild east. Rocky and windswept, they have a long history that includes the Vikings and other seafaring adventurers. Today, craggy fishing villages and the austere tablelands and fjords of Gros Morne National Park attract travelers who value isolation and dramatic landscapes. See chapter 6.
- **Québec:** Canada's French-speaking homeland, Québec boasts two fascinating cities. Montréal, in many ways, the cultural center of Canada, has a rich history, excellent food, vibrant arts scene, and an indomitable sense of style. Québec City is at once a modern capital and one of the most historic cities in North America. Dating from

Canada

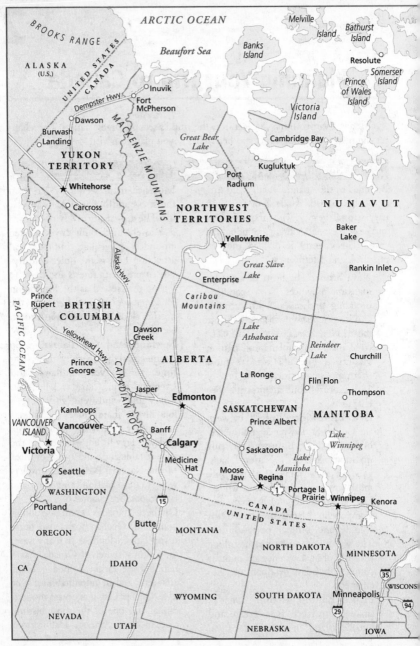

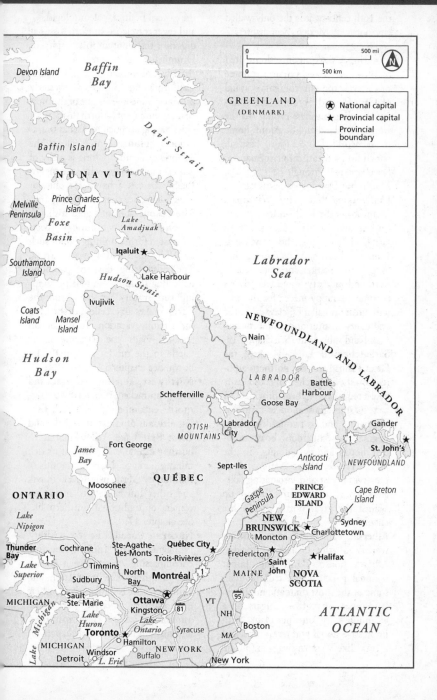

0 ———— 500 mi
0 ———— 500 km

★ National capital
★ Provincial capital
— Provincial boundary

Devon Island

Baffin Bay

GREENLAND
(DENMARK)

Davis Strait

Baffin Island

N U N A V U T

Prince Charles Island

Melville Peninsula

Foxe Basin

Lake Amadjuak

Iqaluit ★

Southampton Island

Hudson Strait

Lake Harbour

Coats Island

Mansel Island

Ivujivik

Labrador Sea

Nain

Hudson Bay

NEWFOUNDLAND AND LABRADOR

LABRADOR

Battle Harbour

Schefferville

Goose Bay

James Bay

Fort George

OTISH MOUNTAINS

Labrador City

Gander

St. John's ★

NEWFOUNDLAND

ONTARIO

Moosonee

QUÉBEC

Sept-Iles

Anticosti Island

Cape Breton Island

Gaspé Peninsula

PRINCE EDWARD ISLAND

Sydney

NEW BRUNSWICK ★

Charlottetown

Lake Nipigon

Thunder Bay

Cochrane

Ste-Agathe-des-Monts

Québec City ★

Moncton

Fredericton ★

Lake Superior

Timmins

Trois-Rivières

Saint John

★ Halifax

Sudbury

North Bay

Montréal

MAINE

NOVA SCOTIA

MICHIGAN

Sault Ste. Marie

Lake Huron

Ottawa ★

Kingston

81

VT

95

ATLANTIC OCEAN

Lake Michigan

Toronto

Lake Ontario

Syracuse

NH

Boston

MICHIGAN

Windsor

Hamilton

NEW YORK

MA

Detroit

L. Erie

Buffalo

New York

the 16th century, it is the only walled city north of Mexico. See chapters 7 and 8.

- **Ontario:** A vast province dominated by the Great Lakes, Ontario is home to Ottawa, the governmental capital of Canada, and Toronto, the country's bustling business capital. To the west is farmland and Stratford, home to the world-class Stratford Festival, famed for its theatrical performances. See chapters 9 through 12.

- **Manitoba:** Dominated by its capital, hardworking but artsy Winnipeg, Manitoba is the land bridge between eastern and western Canada. Half farmland, half lake, the province is Canada's heartland. Winnipeg has long been a center for trade, transport, and industry; more recently it's become a scrappy mecca for the arts, with great art galleries, classical music and dance institutions, and a rousing rock-band subculture. See chapter 13.

- **Saskatchewan:** Located where the Great Plains meet the northern arboreal forests, Saskatchewan is too easily neglected as the flyover province. In fact, its immigrant pioneer history is fascinating and its two leading cities, Regina and Saskatoon, boast excellent hotels and restaurants. To the north, Prince Albert National Park preserves a vast and fascinating lakeland where the prairies bump up against the great north woods. See chapter 13.

- **Alberta:** Famed for the stunning scenery of the Canadian Rockies, Alberta boasts Banff and Jasper national parks, which truly contain some of the most dramatic mountain landscapes on earth. Calgary is a gleaming City on the Plain, with impressive hotels and restaurants and a Texas-like Western swagger. Out on the eastern prairies, paleontologists—and eager travelers—unearth fossils at digs near the dinosaur fossil capital of Drumheller. See chapter 14.

- **British Columbia:** B.C. is Canada's California. In this most westerly province, Vancouver is one of the most cosmopolitan of North American cities, facing as much to Asia as to traditional cultural centers along the Atlantic seaboard. Victoria is a city of genteel English ways, while the rugged Pacific coast is a haven for outdoor adventurers. See chapters 15 and 16.

- **The Yukon:** Born of a gold rush, the Yukon preserves its historic prospecting past at former mining camps such as Whitehorse and Dawson Creek. The ripsnorting days of gambling halls, dog sledding, and claim jumping isn't history yet here, and the Yukon makes an excellent destination for a family vacation. To the north, seasonal roads lead past the Arctic Circle to the tundra land of the far north. See chapter 17.

- **Northwest Territories:** Vast and largely untracked, the Northwest Territories encompass the outback fishing nirvanas of Great Slave Lake and Great Bear Lake. Yellowknife is its bustling capital, still proud of its rich mining heritage. Near the mouth of the mighty Mackenzie River, Inuvik and other Inuvialuit settlements are centers of traditional northern life. See chapter 17.

- **Nunavut:** Canada's newest territory, Nunavut is the Inuit homeland, encompassing Arctic Ocean islands and coastline. The population and cultural center is Baffin Island, where extraordinary Native art and astounding ice-age landscapes draw adventurous travelers. See chapter 17.

2 Visitor Information & Maps

In addition to the provincial tourism websites listed below, take a look at the official tourism and travel site for Canada at **www.travelcanada.ca.** Each of the provinces and territories can provide excellent road maps for free or a small fee.

- **Nova Scotia Dept. of Tourism, Culture, and Heritage,** P.O. Box 456, 1800 Argyle St., Halifax, NS B3J 2R5 (© **800/565-0000** or 902/425-5781; http://novascotia.com).
- **New Brunswick Department of Tourism and Parks,** P.O. Box 12345, Campbellton, NB E3N 3T6 (© **800/561-0123;** www.tourism newbrunswick.ca).
- **Tourism Prince Edward Island,** P.O. Box 2000, Charlottetown, PEI C1A 7N8 (© **800/463-4734;** www.gentleisland.com).
- **Newfoundland and Labrador Dept. of Tourism, Culture and Recreation,** P.O. Box 8700, St. John's, NL A1B 4J6 (© **800/563-6353** or 709/729-2831; www.new foundlandandlabradortourism.com).
- **Tourisme Québec,** P.O. Box 979, Montréal, PQ H3C 2W3 (© **877/266-5687** or 514/873-2015; www.bonjourquebec.com).
- **Ontario Tourism,** Hearst Block, 10th Floor, 900 Bay St., Toronto, ON M7A 2E1 (© **800/668-2746;** www.ontariotravel.net).
- **Travel Manitoba,** (mailing) 7th Floor, 155 Carlton St., Winnipeg, MB R3C 3H8; (visitors center) Explore Manitoba Center, 21 Forks Market Rd., Winnipeg, MB R3C 4T7 (© **800/665-0040;** www.travel manitoba.com).
- **Tourism Saskatchewan,** 1922 Park St., Regina, SK S4P 3V7 (© **877/237-2273** or 306/787-9600; www.sasktourism.com).

- **Travel Alberta,** Box 2500, Edmonton, AB T5J 2Z4 (© **800/252-3782** or 780/427-4321; www.travelalberta.com).
- **Tourism British Columbia,** 200 Burrard St., Plaza Level, Vancouver, BC V6C 3L6 (© **800/HELLO-BC** or 604/683-2000; www.hellobc.com).
- **Tourism Yukon,** P.O. Box 2703, Whitehorse, YT Y1A 2C6 (© **800-661-0494;** www.travelyukon.com).
- **NWT Arctic Tourism,** P.O. Box 610, Yellowknife, NWT X1A 2N5 (© **800/661-0788** or 867/873-7200; www.explorenwt.com).
- **Nunavut Tourism,** P.O. Box 1450, Iqaluit, NU X0A 0H0 (© **866/686-2888** or 867/979-6551; www.nunavuttourism.com).

For general information about Canada's national parks, contact **Parks Canada National Office,** 25 Eddy St., Hull, PQ K1A 0M5 (© **888/773-8888;** www.pc.gc.ca).

CITY SITES Internet city guides are a good way to navigate without getting lost in the virtual countryside. Here are some to check out for Canada's top cities:

- Montréal: **www.tourism-montreal.org** (Bonjour à la Montréal), **http://english.montrealplus.ca** (Montréal Plus), or **www.montreal.worldweb.com** (Montréal Worldweb)
- Québec: **www.quebecregion.com** (Québec City and Area Tourism and Convention Bureau), **www.quebecplus.ca** (Québec Plus), or **www.quebec.worldweb.com** (Québec Worldweb)
- Ottawa: **www.ottawakiosk.com** (Ottawa Kiosk) or **www.ottawaplus.ca** (Ottawa Plus)
- Toronto: **www.toronto.com** (Toronto.com), **www.torontotourism.com**

(Tourism Toronto), **www.toronto. worldweb.com** (Toronto Worldweb), or **www.gaytoronto.com** (Gay Toronto)

- Winnipeg **www.destinationwinnipeg. ca** (Destination Winnipeg)
- Calgary: **www.tourismcalgary.com** (Tourism Calgary), **www.discover calgary.com** (Calgary Worldweb), or **www.calgaryplus.ca** (Calgary Plus)
- Edmonton: **www.edmonton.ca** (City of Edmonton), **www.discover edmonton.com** (Edmonton Worldweb), **www.edmontonplus.ca** (Edmonton Plus), or **www.edmonton. com** (Edmonton Tourism)
- Vancouver: **www.tourism-vancouver. org** (Tourism Vancouver), **www. vancouverplus.ca** (Vancouver Plus), or **www.whistler.com** (Whistler Resort Guide)
- Victoria: **www.city.victoria.bc.ca** (City of Victoria), or **www.victoria bc.com** (Victoria BC)

3 Entry Requirements

PASSPORTS

For information on how to get a passport, go to "Passports" in the "Fast Facts" section of this chapter—the websites listed provide downloadable passport applications as well as the current fees for processing passport applications. For an up-to-date, country-by-country listing of passport requirements around the world, go to the "Foreign Entry Requirement" webpage of the U.S. State Department site at http://travel.state.gov.

The U.S. **Intelligence Reform and Terrorism Prevention Act of 2004** requires that travelers to and from Canada (and other neighboring countries) have a passport or other secure, accepted document to enter or reenter the United States. The goal of the initiative is to strengthen U.S. border security while facilitating entry for U.S. citizens and legitimate foreign visitors by providing standardized documentation that enables the Department of Homeland Security to quickly and reliably identify a traveler.

The implementation of these new travel document requirements has been anything but clear and methodical, with the deadline for full compliance with the new border security laws pushed out further and further into the future.

At press time, here are the document requirements for travelers between the U.S. and Canada, as taken from the U.S. Department of State website at http:// travel.state.gov/travel/cbpmc/cbpmc_22 23.html (be sure to consult this website for the latest information if you are planning to cross the border using any other documents besides a valid passport):

All persons traveling by air between the United States and Canada are required to present a passport or other valid travel document to enter or reenter the United States. A birth certificate and photo ID is **not** acceptable for air travel.

For persons traveling by land or sea between the U.S. and Canada, the situation remains a bit murkier. By January 31, 2008, U.S. and Canadian citizens will need to present a Western Hemisphere Travel Initiative (WHTI) compliant travel document. These include passports, passport cards (high-tech identity cards which are still under development), trusted traveler cards such as NEXUS, FAST, or SENTRI; a valid Merchant Mariner Document (MMD) when traveling in conjunction with official maritime business; or a valid U.S. military identification card when traveling on official orders. For the time being, U.S. citizens (*not* Canadians) can still cross the border using a government-issued photo ID, such as a driver's license, plus proof of citizenship, such as a birth certificate (use an original, as photocopies can be refused).

However, WHTI does demand the eventual requirement for passports or other secure, accepted travel documents (*not* a driver's license and birth certificate) at land and sea border crossings, perhaps as early as summer 2008. Clearly, to avoid any potential hassles, it is easiest for U.S. citizens to simply procure a passport and use it as documentation when crossing into and returning from Canada.

Permanent U.S. residents who aren't U.S. citizens must be prepared to present their Alien Registration Cards (green cards). If you plan to drive into Canada, be sure to bring your car's registration papers and proof of insurance.

An important point: Any person under 18 traveling alone requires a letter from a parent or guardian granting him or her permission to travel to Canada. The letter must state the traveler's name and the duration of the trip. It's essential that teenagers carry proof of identity, usually a passport, though see the above website for alternatives; otherwise, their letter is useless at the border.

Although it is rare, immigration officials may prevent the entry of visitors who appear to pose a health risk, those they doubt will be able to support themselves and their dependents in Canada, or those whose willingness and means to return to their home country is in doubt. Also, immigration officials can prevent the entry of foreign nationals who have a criminal record. This includes any convictions for driving while intoxicated; anyone with a felony conviction will find it very challenging to enter Canada.

BRINGING CHILDREN INTO CANADA

If you are traveling with children under age 18, you should carry identification for each child. Passports are best, though birth certificates are still accepted, though this may change. Divorced parents who share custody of their children should carry copies of the legal custody documents. Adults who are not parents or guardians should have written permission from the parents or guardians to supervise the children. When traveling with a group of vehicles, parents or guardians should travel in the same vehicle as the children when arriving at the border. Customs officers are looking for missing children and may ask questions about the children who are traveling with you.

VISAS

Citizens of the U.S., most European countries, most former British colonies, and certain other countries (Israel, Korea, and Japan, for instance) do not need visas but must carry passports to enter Canada. Entry visas are required for citizens of more than 130 countries. Entry visas must be applied for and received from the Canadian embassy in your home country. For more information on entry requirements to Canada, see the Citizenship and Immigration Canada website visitors' services page at **www.cic.gc.ca/english/visit/index.asp**.

CUSTOMS

For information on what you can bring into and take out of Canada, go to **"Customs"** in the **"Fast Facts"** section of this chapter.

4 When to Go

When to go to Canada depends a lot on what you plan to do when you get there. Although much of Canada lies above the 49th parallel, and therefore has long and often intense winter weather, this isn't particularly a negative if you are going to Canada to ski. Although some tourist facilities in small centers are closed in winter, most remain open (after all,

Canadians live in Canada year-round and require a full network of services).

Summer, from late June to August, brings the finest weather and not surprisingly the largest influx of travelers. Prices are highest, accommodations are frequently booked up, and crowds fill the wilderness. In many ways, the fall months, particularly September and October, are the most pleasant time to travel, as the weather is frequently very pleasant, the crowds have dispersed, and prices begin to fall. If you are looking for value, spring is the best time to visit Canada. However, it's not a good time to plan a trip centering on outdoor activities as it is also the "mud season" when all that snow melts.

THE WEATHER

In southern and central Canada, the weather is the same as that in the northern United States. As you head north, the climate becomes arctic, meaning long and extremely cold winters, brief and surprisingly warm summers (with lots of insects), and magical springs.

As a general rule, **spring** runs mid-March to mid-May, **summer** mid-May to mid-September, **fall** mid-September to mid-November, and **winter** mid-November to mid-March. Pick the season best suited to your tastes and temperament, and remember that your car should be winterized through March and that snow sometimes falls as late as April (in 1995, a foot of snow blanketed Prince Edward Island in May). September and October bring autumn foliage and great opportunities for photographers.

Evenings tend to be cool everywhere, particularly on or near water. In late spring and early summer, you'll need a supply of insect repellent if you're planning bush travel or camping.

With the huge size of some provinces and territories, you naturally get considerable climate variations inside their borders. Québec, for instance, sprawls all the way from the temperate south to the Arctic, and the weather varies accordingly. For up-to-date weather conditions and forecasts for any Canadian destination, check out Environment Canada's weather center online at **www.weatheroffice.gc.ca**.

Daily Mean Temperature & Total Precipitation for Vancouver, BC

	Jan	Feb	Mar	Apr	May	June	July	Aug	Sept	Oct	Nov	Dec
Temp (°F)	38	41	45	40	46	62	66	67	61	42	48	39
Temp (°C)	3	5	7	4	8	17	19	19	16	6	9	4
Precipitation (in.)	5.9	4.9	4.3	3.0	2.4	1.8	1.4	1.5	2.5	4.5	6.7	7.0

Daily Mean Temperature & Total Precipitation for Calgary, AB

	Jan	Feb	Mar	Apr	May	June	July	Aug	Sept	Oct	Nov	Dec
Temp (°F)	26	31	38	51	62	69	74	73	63	55	37	28
Temp (°C)	–4	0	3	11	16	21	23	23	17	13	3	–2
Precipitation (in.)	.5	.4	.6	1	2.1	3	2.8	1.9	1.9	.6	.5	.5

Daily Mean Temperature & Total Precipitation for Winnipeg, MB

	Jan	Feb	Mar	Apr	May	June	July	Aug	Sept	Oct	Nov	Dec
Temp (°F)	8	15	29	50	66	74	79	77	66	52	31	14
Temp (°C)	–13	–10	–2	10	19	23	26	25	19	11	–1	–10
Precipitation (in.)	.8	.6	.9	1.4	2.4	3.3	2.8	3	2	1.2	.8	.7

Daily Mean Temperature & Total Precipitation for Toronto, ON

	Jan	Feb	Mar	Apr	May	June	July	Aug	Sept	Oct	Nov	Dec
Temp (°F)	28	29	39	53	65	75	80	78	70	57	45	33
Temp (°C)	–3	–2	4	12	18	24	27	26	21	14	7	1
Precipitation (in.)	1.8	1.8	2.2	2.5	2.6	2.7	3	3.3	2.9	2.5	2.8	2.6

Daily Mean Temperature & Total Precipitation for Montreal, QC

	Jan	Feb	Mar	Apr	May	June	July	Aug	Sept	Oct	Nov	Dec
Temp (°F)	22	24	36	51	65	74	79	76	68	55	41	27
Temp (°C)	–6	–4	2	11	19	23	26	25	20	13	5	–3
Precipitation (in.)	2.5	2.2	2.7	2.9	2.7	3.2	3.4	3.9	3.4	3	3.7	3.4

Daily Mean Temperature & Total Precipitation for Halifax, NS

	Jan	Feb	Mar	Apr	May	June	July	Aug	Sept	Oct	Nov	Dec
Temp (°F)	29	29	37	46	59	68	74	73	66	55	45	34
Temp (°C)	–2	–2	3	8	15	20	23	23	19	13	7	1
Precipitation (in.)	5.8	4.7	4.8	4.9	4.4	3.9	3.8	4.3	3.7	5.1	6.1	6.6

CANADA CALENDAR OF EVENTS

Canadians love a festival, and not even the chill of winter will keep them from celebrating. The Canadian festival calendar is jammed with events celebrating ethnic cultures, food and wine, historical events and characters, the arts, rodeos, music and theater—even salmon, lobsters, and whales. Following is a seasonal list of festival highlights from across Canada; see individual chapters for more festival options.

For an exhaustive list of events beyond those listed here, check http://events. frommers.com, where you'll find a searchable, up-to-the-minute roster of what's happening in cities all over the world.

Winter

- **Winter Carnival** (www.carnaval.qc. ca) is a celebration of all things winter in Québec City. February.
- **Festival du Voyageur** (© 204/237-7692; www.festivalvoyageur.mb.ca) is Winnipeg's celebration of the 18th-century French voyageurs who

explored Canada by canoe, with music, wine, and winter fun. February.
- **Yukon Quest** (www.yukonquest.org) brings hundreds of sled dogs and mushers to Whitehorse, Yukon, for one of the world's top dog-sledding events. February.

Spring

- **Pacific Rim Whale Festival** (© 250/726-4641; www.pacificrimwhale festival.org), celebrates the yearly return of up to 20,000 gray whales to the waters off Tofino and Ucluelet, Vancouver Island, B.C. March.
- **Canadian Tulip Festival** (© 888/465-1867; http:/tulipfestival.ca), features thousands of tulips in bloom, plus art fairs and concerts, in Ottawa, Canada's capital. May.

Summer

- **Stratford Festival** (© 800/567-1600; www.stratfordfestival.ca) presents over a dozen theatrical productions, a mix of Shakespeare and contemporary works, in a delightful Ontario country town. May through October.

- **Montreal International Fireworks Competition** (© 514/397-2000; www.internationaldesfeuxloto-quebec.com) is North America's largest fireworks competition, with fireworks makers from around the world competing for the Gold Jupiter award, the pinnacle of pyrotechnics. June through August.
- **Calgary Stampede** (© 800/661-1767; www.calgarystampede.com), is the world's largest and richest rodeo, and Calgary's opportunity to celebrate its cowboy past. July.
- **Vancouver Folk Festival** (© 604/602-9798; www.thefestival.bc.ca) is one of North America's top folk music events, bringing Summer of Love musical stylings to a gorgeous bayside park. July.
- **RCMP Training Academy Sunset Retreat Ceremony** (© 306/780-5838; www.rcmp-grc.gc.ca/depot) is a stirring drill practice and flag ceremony with dress-uniformed Mounties plus pipe-and-bugle bands at Regina's century-old RCMP training facility. July through August.
- **Banff Summer Arts Festival** (© 800/413-8368; www.banffcentre.ca) is a celebration of classical and jazz music in the heart of the Canadian Rockies. July through August.
- **International Busker Festival** (© 902/429-3910; www.buskers.ca) brings street musicians and performers from around the world to Halifax's bustling waterfront. August.
- **Newfoundland and Labrador Folk Festival** (© 709/576-8508; www.sjfac.nf.net) is a major folk music festival held at the center of St. Johns, Newfoundland. August.

Fall

- **Toronto International Film Festival** (© 416/968-FILM; www.tiffg.ca) is a glittering celebration of stars and cinema, and the world's second-largest film festival. September.
- **Celtic Colours** (© 877/285-2321; www.celtic-colours.com) is the largest Celtic music and arts festival outside of Britain, held on Cape Breton Island, Nova Scotia. October.
- **Okanagan Wine Festival** (© 250/861-6654; www.owfs.com) celebrates B.C.'s Okanagan Valley's fall harvest with wine tastings, winery open houses, and dining events. October.

5 Getting There

BY PLANE

Vancouver (YVR), Toronto (YYZ), and Montréal (YUL) serve as the dominant hubs for international flights, and are served by most international carriers including British Air, Air France, Qantas, Singapore Airlines, Lufthansa, SAS, and many U.S. airlines. Smaller airports such as Calgary and Winnipeg also have some international flights, particularly in summer.

Air Canada (© 888/247-2262; www.aircanada.com) is by far the largest carrier in Canada; in 1999, it subsumed Canadian Airlines, giving it and its subsidiary companies dominance over internal and external Canadian air travel.

FLYING FOR LESS: TIPS FOR GETTING THE BEST AIRFARE

Nearly all airlines flying into Canada are served by the Internet travel sites such as Travelocity and Expedia, and strategies for getting the best fares are discussed below.

- Passengers who can book their ticket either **long in advance or at the last minute,** or who **fly midweek** or **at less trafficked hours** may pay a fraction of the full fare.

- Search **the Internet** for cheap fares. The most popular online travel agencies are **Travelocity** (www.travelocity.com and www.travelocity.co.uk); **Expedia** (www.expedia.com, www.expedia.co.uk, and www.expedia.ca); and **Orbitz** (www.orbitz.com). In the U.K., go to **Travelsupermarket** (℃ **0845/345-5708;** www.travelsupermarket.com), a flight search engine that offers flight comparisons for the budget airlines whose seats often end up in bucket-shop sales. Other websites for booking airline tickets online include **Cheapflights. com, SmarterTravel.com, Priceline.com,** and **Opodo** (www.opodo.co.uk). Metasearch sites (which find and then direct you to airline and hotel websites for booking) include **Sidestep.com** and **Kayak.com**—the latter includes fares for budget carriers like JetBlue and Spirit as well as the major airlines. **Lastminute.com** is a great source for last-minute flights and getaways. In addition, most **airlines** offer online-only fares that even their phone agents know nothing about.
- **Consolidators,** also known as bucket shops, are wholesale brokers in the airline-ticket game. Consolidators buy deeply discounted tickets from airlines and sell them to online ticket agencies, travel agents, tour operators, corporations, and, to a lesser degree, the general public. They can be great sources for cheap international tickets. On the down side, bucket-shop tickets are often rigged with restrictions, such as stiff cancellation penalties (as high as 50% to 75% of the ticket price). And keep in mind that most of what you see advertised is of limited availability. Several reliable consolidators are worldwide and available online. **STA Travel** (www.statravel.com) is the world's leading consolidator for students, but its fares are competitive for travelers of all ages. **Flights.com** (℃ **800/TRAV-800;** www.flights.com) has excellent fares worldwide.
- Join **frequent-flier clubs.** Frequent-flier membership doesn't cost a cent, but it does entitle you to free tickets or upgrades when you amass the airline's required number of frequent-flier points. But keep in mind that award seats are limited, seats on popular routes are hard to snag, and more and more major airlines are cutting their expiration periods for mileage points. To play the frequent-flier game to your best advantage, consult the community bulletin boards on **FlyerTalk** (www.flyertalk.com) or go to Randy Petersen's **Inside Flyer** (www.insideflyer.com). Petersen and friends review all the programs in detail and post regular updates on changes in policies and trends.

BY CAR

Because Canada has the longest open border on earth, it makes sense that many U.S.-based travelers will consider taking their own car to Canada as a road-trip destination. There are scores of border crossings between Canada and the U.S. (the U.S. freeway system enters at 13 different locations). However, not all border crossings keep the same hours, and many are closed at night. Before you set off to cross the border at a remote location, ascertain if it will be open when you arrive there.

In addition to having the proper ID to cross into Canada, drivers may also be asked to provide proof of car insurance and show the car registration. If you're driving a rental car, you may be asked to show the rental agreement. It's always a good idea to clean your car of perishable foodstuff before crossing the border; fruit, vegetables, and meat products may be confiscated and may lead to a full search of the car. Remember that firearms are allowed across the border only in special circumstances; handguns are almost completely outlawed.

RENTAL CARS   Canada has scores of rental-car companies, including **Hertz** (ⓒ 800/654-3001 in the U.S., or 800/263-0600 in Canada; www.hertz.com), **Avis** (ⓒ 800/331-1212 in the U.S and Canada; www.avis.com), **Dollar** (ⓒ 800/800-4000; www.dollar.com), **Thrifty** (ⓒ 800/THRIFTY; www.thrifty.com), **Budget** (ⓒ 800/527-0700 in the U.S., or 800/268-8900 in Canada; www.budget.com), **Enterprise** (ⓒ 800/261-7331; www.enterprise.com), and **National Car Rental** (ⓒ 800/CAR-RENT; www.nationalcar.com). Nevertheless, rental vehicles tend to get tight during the tourist season, from around mid-May through August. It's a good idea to reserve a car as soon as you decide on your vacation.

Several rental-car agencies offer roadside assistance programs in Canada. In case of an accident, a breakdown, a dead battery, a flat tire, a dry gas tank, getting stuck, or locking yourself out of your car, call your agency's 24-hour number. For **Hertz** call ⓒ 800/654-5060, for **Avis** call ⓒ 800/354-2847, for **Dollar** call ⓒ 800/235-9393, for **Budget** call ⓒ 800/334-2847, for **National** call ⓒ 800/367-6767 or 800/227-7368, and for **Enterprise** call 800/307-6666.

None of the above rental agencies enforce a mandatory upper-age cutoff for renting cars to seniors, but individual franchisers can impose their own age limits. The minimum age for renting cars in Canada is usually 21, though rates are high. Standard rates for drivers kick in at 25 years of age.

For booking rental cars online, the best deals are usually found at rental-car company websites, although all the major online travel agencies also offer rental-car reservations services. Priceline and Hotwire work well for rental cars, too; the only "mystery" is which major rental company you get, and for most travelers the difference between Hertz, Avis, and Budget is negligible.

Members of the **American Automobile Association (AAA)** should remember to take their membership cards since the **Canadian Automobile Association (CAA)** (ⓒ **800/222-4357;** www.caa.ca) extends privileges to them in Canada.

BY TRAIN

Amtrak (ⓒ **800/USA-RAIL;** www.amtrak.com) can get you into Canada at a few border points, where you can connect up with Canada's **VIA Rail** (ⓒ **888/VIARAIL;** www.viarail.ca) system. On the East Coast, Amtrak's *Adirondack* starts at New York City's Pennsylvania Station and travels daily via Albany and upstate New York to Montréal. The *Maple Leaf* links New York City and Toronto via Albany, Rochester, Buffalo, and Niagara Falls, departing daily from Penn Station. On the West Coast, the *Cascades* runs from Eugene, Oregon, to Vancouver, British Columbia, with stops in Portland and Seattle. Amtrak-operated buses may also connect segments of these routes.

Amtrak and VIA Rail both offer a North American Railpass, which gives you 30 days of unlimited economy-class travel in the U.S. and Canada. Remember that the Railpass doesn't include meals; you can buy meals on the train or carry your own food.

BY BUS

Greyhound (ⓒ **800/661-8747** in Canada, www.greyhound.ca; in the U.S. ⓒ 800/231-2222, www.greyhound.com) operates the major intercity bus system in Canada, with frequent cross-border links to cities in the U.S. northern tier (many more than what's offered by Amtrak). In general, Greyhound offers cross-border service along routes where the U.S. freeway system enters Canada.

BY FERRY

Ocean ferries operate from Maine to Nova Scotia and New Brunswick, and from Seattle, Anacortes, and Port Angeles, Washington, to Victoria, British Columbia. For details, see the relevant chapters.

6 Money & Costs

Prices for goods and services are comparable between Canada and the U.S.—particularly now that the Canadian dollar is at par with its U.S. counterpart. On a day-to-day basis, traveling in Canada will cost about the same as traveling in the U.S., as long as restraint is used when making hotel and dining selections. European travelers using euros and the British pound will find that Canadian prices for comparable goods and services are generally lower than those in their home countries.

CURRENCY

Canadian currency is counted in dollars and cents, just like the currency system in the U.S. However, in addition to pennies, nickels, dimes, and quarters, there are one- and two-dollar coins (there are no dollar or two-dollar bills). Dollar coins are bronze-plated coins and bear the picture of a loon—hence their nickname "loonies." There's also a two-toned $2 coin sometimes referred to as a "toonie." Paper currency begins with $5 bills.

Exchanging currency is pretty straightforward, particularly if you are changing U.S. dollars into Canadian. Most banks on both sides of the border will exchange U.S. and Canadian currency even if they don't normally advertise as foreign exchange services. However, the easiest way to procure Canadian currency is simply to withdraw money from an ATM (see below).

Often, Canadian businesses will accept U.S. dollars in payment, making the currency value exchange, if any, at the till.

It's always advisable to bring money in a variety of forms on a vacation: a mix of cash, credit cards, and traveler's checks. You should also exchange enough petty cash to cover airport incidentals, tipping, and transportation to your hotel before you leave home, or withdraw money upon arrival at an airport ATM.

THE CANADIAN DOLLAR & THE U.S. DOLLAR The prices cited in this guide are given first in Canadian dollars (C$), then in U.S. dollars (US$) and British pounds (£); amounts over $10 are rounded to the nearest dollar or pound, and amounts under $10 are rounded to the nearest nickel. Note that the Canadian dollar is now equal (or greater) in value than the American dollar. As we go to press, US$1 is worth about C$1, and the British pound is worth about US$2 or C$2; these were the equivalencies used to figure the approximate prices in this guide.

ATMs

The easiest and best way to get cash away from home is from an ATM (automated teller machine), sometimes referred to as a "cash machine" or a "cashpoint." ATMs also offer the best exchange rates. Avoid exchanging money at commercial exchange bureaus and hotels, which often have the highest transaction fees.

The **Cirrus** (© 800/424-7787; www.mastercard.com) and **PLUS** (© 800/843-7587; www.visa.com) networks span the globe. Go to your bank card's website to find ATM locations at your destination. Be sure you know your daily withdrawal limit before you depart. *Note:* Many banks impose a fee every time you use a card at another bank's ATM, and that fee can be higher for international transactions (up to $5 or more) than for domestic ones (where they're rarely more than $2). In addition, the bank from which you withdraw cash may charge its own fee. For international withdrawal fees, ask your bank.

Note: Banks that are members of the **Global ATM Alliance** charge no transaction fees for cash withdrawals at other Alliance member ATMs; these include Bank of America, Scotiabank (Canada, Caribbean & Mexico), Barclays (U.K. and parts of Africa), Deutsche Bank (Germany, Poland, Spain, and Italy), and BNP Paribus (France).

CREDIT CARDS

Credit cards are another safe way to carry money. They also provide a convenient record of all your expenses, and they generally offer relatively good exchange rates. You can withdraw cash advances from your credit cards at banks or ATMs but high fees make credit card cash advances a pricey way to get cash. Keep in mind that you'll pay interest from the moment of your withdrawal, even if you pay your monthly bills on time. Also, note that many banks now assess a 1% to 3% "transaction fee" on **all** charges you incur abroad (whether you're using the local currency or your native currency).

Canadian businesses honor the same credit cards as in the U.S and the U.K. Visa and MasterCard are the most common, though American Express is also normally accepted in hotels and restaurants catering to tourists. Discover and Diner's Club cards are somewhat less frequently accepted.

For tips and telephone numbers to call if your wallet is stolen or lost, go to "Lost & Found" in the "Fast Facts" section of this chapter.

TRAVELER'S CHECKS

You can buy traveler's checks at most banks. They are offered in denominations of $20, $50, $100, $500, and sometimes $1,000. Generally, you'll pay a service charge ranging from 1% to 4%.

The most popular traveler's checks are offered by **American Express** (© 800/807-6233 or © 800/221-7282 for card holders—this number accepts collect calls, offers service in several foreign languages, and exempts Amex gold and platinum cardholders from the 1% fee.); **Visa** (© 800/732-1322)—AAA members can obtain Visa checks for a $9.95 fee (for checks up to $1,500) at most AAA offices or by calling © 866/339-3378; and **MasterCard** (© 800/223-9920).

Be sure to keep a record of the traveler's checks serial numbers separate from your checks in the event that they are stolen or lost. You'll get a refund faster if you know the numbers.

American Express, Thomas Cook, Visa, and **MasterCard** offer **foreign currency traveler's checks,** useful if you're traveling to one country or to the euro zone; they're accepted at locations where dollar checks may not be.

Another option is the new prepaid traveler's check cards, reloadable cards that work much like debit cards but aren't linked to your checking account. The **American Express Travelers Cheque Card,** for example, requires a minimum deposit, sets a maximum balance, and has a one-time issuance fee of US$15. You can withdraw money from an ATM (for a fee of US$2.50 per transaction, not including bank fees), and the funds can be purchased in dollars, euros, or pounds. If you lose the card, your available funds will be refunded within 24 hours.

All the above companies also offer travelers checks denominated in Canadian dollars. If you are planning to use travelers checks frequently while in Canada, there are advantages to buying them in Canadian dollars, as there is usually no fee to reimburse them, and they can be used like cash in most retail situations.

7 Travel Insurance

The cost of travel insurance varies widely, depending on the destination, the cost and length of your trip, your age and health, and the type of trip you're taking, but expect to pay between 5% and 8% of the vacation itself. You can get estimates from various providers through **InsureMyTrip. com**. Enter your trip cost and dates, your age, and other information, for prices from more than a dozen companies.

U.K. citizens and their families who make more than one trip abroad per year may find an annual travel insurance policy works out cheaper. Check **www.money supermarket.com**, which compares prices across a wide range of providers for single- and multitrip policies.

Most big travel agents offer their own insurance and will probably try to sell you their package when you book a holiday. Think before you sign. **Britain's Consumers' Association** recommends that you insist on seeing the policy and reading the fine print before buying travel insurance. **The Association of British Insurers** (© 020/7600-3333; www.abi. org.uk) gives advice by phone and publishes *Holiday Insurance,* a free guide to policy provisions and prices. You might also shop around for better deals: Try **Columbus Direct** (© 0870/033- 9988; www.columbusdirect.net).

TRIP-CANCELLATION INSURANCE

Trip-cancellation insurance will help retrieve your money if you have to back out of a trip or depart early, or if your travel supplier goes bankrupt. Trip cancellation traditionally covers such events as sickness, natural disasters, and State Department advisories. The latest news in trip-cancellation insurance is the availability of **expanded hurricane coverage** and the **"any-reason"** cancellation coverage—which costs more but covers cancellations made for any reason. You won't

get back 100% of your prepaid trip cost, but you'll be refunded a substantial portion. **TravelSafe** (© **888/885-7233;** www.travelsafe.com) offers both types of coverage. Expedia.com also offers any-reason cancellation coverage for its air-hotel packages.

For details, contact one of the following recommended insurers: **Access America** (© 866/807-3982; www.access america.com); **Travel Guard International** (© 800/826-4919; www.travel guard.com); **Travel Insured International** (© 800/243-3174; www.travel insured.com); and **Travelex Insurance Services** (© 888/457-4602; www. travelex-insurance.com).

MEDICAL INSURANCE

For travel overseas, most U.S. health plans (including Medicare and Medicaid) do not provide coverage, and the ones that do often require you to pay for services upfront and reimburse you only after you return home.

As a safety net, you may want to buy travel medical insurance, particularly if you're traveling to a remote or high-risk area where emergency evacuation might be necessary. If you require additional medical insurance, try **MEDEX Assistance** (© **410/453-6300;** www.medex assist.com) or **Travel Assistance International** (© 800/821-2828; www.travel assistance.com; for general information on services, call the company's **Worldwide Assistance Services, Inc.,** at © 800/ 777-8710).

LOST-LUGGAGE INSURANCE

On international flights (including U.S. portions of international trips), baggage coverage is limited to approximately $9.07 per pound, up to approximately $635 per checked bag. If you plan to check items more valuable than what's covered by the standard liability, see if your homeowner's policy covers your valuables, get baggage insurance as part of your comprehensive travel-insurance package, or buy Travel Guard's "BagTrak" product.

If your luggage is lost, immediately file a lost-luggage claim at the airport, detailing the luggage contents. Most airlines require that you report delayed, damaged, or lost baggage within 4 hours of arrival. The airlines are required to deliver luggage, once found, directly to your house or destination free of charge.

8 Health

STAYING HEALTHY

In general, Canada poses no particular health threats to travelers. Nonetheless, you may want to check the CDC's (Centers for Disease Control) travel advisory site at wwwn.cdc.gov/travel for any last-minute alerts.

If you suffer from a chronic illness, consult your doctor before your departure. For conditions such as epilepsy, diabetes, or heart problems, wear a **MedicAlert identification tag** (© **800/825-3785;** www.medicalert.org), which will immediately alert doctors to your condition and give them access to your records through MedicAlert's 24-hour hot line.

Pack **prescription medications** in your carry-on luggage, and carry prescription medications in their original containers, with pharmacy labels—otherwise they won't make it through airport security. Also bring along copies of your prescriptions in case you lose your pills or run out. Don't forget an extra pair of contact lenses or prescription glasses. Carry the generic name of prescription medicines, in case a local pharmacist is unfamiliar with the brand name.

GENERAL AVAILABILITY OF HEALTH CARE

Canada's health-care system is similar to that in the U.S. except that its health insurance for Canadian citizens is managed nationally by the federal government. Hospitals, clinics, and pharmacies are as common as in the U.S. and western Europe. Contact the **International Association for Medical Assistance to** **Travelers** (IAMAT) (© **716/754-4883** or, in Canada, 416/652-0137; www.iamat.org) for tips on travel and health concerns in Canada. **Travel Health Online** (www.tripprep.com), sponsored by a consortium of travel medicine practitioners, may also offer helpful advice on traveling abroad. You can find listings of reliable medical clinics overseas at the **International Society of Travel Medicine** (www.istm.org).

WHAT TO DO IF YOU GET SICK AWAY FROM HOME

Canadian hospitals have emergency rooms open 24 hours for emergency care. In addition, most cities also have walk-in clinics where nonemergency treatment is available. Look in the local Yellow Pages under "Clinics, Medical" for walk-in clinics; these clinics usually take charge cards though they may be able to bill your private insurance directly. You can also inquire at your hotel, as some hotels have relationships with private practitioners to treat the emergency needs of guests.

Pharmacies are common, and most large cities have at least one 24-hour operation. You'll have no trouble having prescriptions filled; in fact, you may note that prescription drugs are substantially cheaper in Canada than in the U.S. Also, certain drugs are available over the counter in Canada that are available only by prescription in the U.S.

In most cases, your existing health plan will provide the coverage you need, though you may need to pay upfront and request reimbursement later. But double-check; you may want to buy **travel medical insurance** instead. Bring your insurance ID card with you when you travel.

Medicare and Medicaid do not provide coverage for medical costs outside the U.S. Before leaving home, find out what medical services your health insurance covers. To protect yourself, consider buying medical travel insurance (see "Medical Insurance," under "Travel Insurance," above).

Very few health insurance plans pay for medical evacuation back to the U.S. (which can cost $10,000 and up). A number of companies offer medical evacuation services anywhere in the world. If you're ever hospitalized more than 150 miles from home, **MedjetAssist** (© 800/ 527-7478; www.medjetassistance.com) will pick you up and fly you to the hospital of your choice virtually anywhere in the world in a medically equipped and staffed aircraft 24 hours a day, 7 days a week. Annual memberships are $225 individual, $350 family; you can also purchase short-term memberships.

9 Safety

STAYING SAFE

Canada is one of the least violent countries on earth—at least off the hockey ice. Using common sense, most travelers should experience few if any threatening situations during a trip to Canada. In fact, most Canadians are unfailingly polite and helpful.

The weather and wildlife are probably a greater threat to the average traveler than violence from other human beings. If driving in winter, be sure to carry traction devices such as tire chains in your vehicle, plus plenty of warm clothes and a sleeping bag.

Wildlife is really only dangerous if you put yourself into their habitat: being in the wrong place, wrong time can be dangerous. Elk can often seem tame, particularly those that live near human civilization. However, during calving season, mother elk can mistake your doting attention as an imminent attack on her newborn, Hiking trails are often closed to hikers during calving season, so be sure to obey all trail postings.

Moose are more dangerous, as they are truly massive and when surprised are apt to charge first and ask questions later. Give a moose plenty of room, and resist the temptation to feed them snacks. Chances are they will come looking for more.

Bears are the most dangerous wilderness denizens to humans. Canada is home to grizzly bears, one of the largest carnivores in North America, and to black bears, a smaller, less fearsome cousin (unless you're traveling along the polar ice floes, you're extremely unlikely to see a polar bear). Grizzly bears tend to keep their distance from humans, preferring mountain meadows to human garbage dumps. However, black bears can coexist much more readily with humans, and in some ways pose a more persistent threat. Never come between a bear and its cub, or its food source. Never hike alone in the backwoods, and if camping keep food items away from tents.

DEALING WITH DISCRIMINATION

Canada has one of the most open and cosmopolitan cultures in the world and an extremely ethnically diverse population. Gay and lesbian rights are enshrined as part of the federal bill of rights. It's unlikely that travelers will encounter discrimination while visiting Canada. It's possible to get into heated conversations regarding U.S. foreign policy, but little discrimination will result from this kind of dispute over political issues.

10 Specialized Travel Resources

TRAVELERS WITH DISABILITIES

Most disabilities shouldn't stop anyone from traveling. There are more options and resources for disabled travelers than ever before.

A clearinghouse of official Canadian federal government information on disability issues, including those related to travel and transportation, is available from **Persons with Disabilities Online** at www.pwd-online.ca. The **Canadian Paraplegic Association** (© 613/723-1033; www.canparaplegic.org) can offer advice for mobility-challenged travelers as well as address issues for those with spinal-cord injuries or with other physical disabilities. From the national website, you can click to find provincial organizations.

Organizations that offer a vast range of resources and assistance to disabled travelers include **MossRehab** (© 800/CALL-MOSS; www.mossresourcenet.org); the **American Foundation for the Blind (AFB)** (© 800/232-5463; www.afb.org); and **SATH (Society for Accessible Travel & Hospitality)** (© 212/447-7284; www.sath.org). **AirAmbulanceCard.com** is now partnered with SATH and allows you to preselect top-notch hospitals in case of an emergency.

Access-Able Travel Source (© 303/232-2979; www.access-able.com) offers a comprehensive database on travel agents from around the world with experience in accessible travel; destination-specific access information; and links to such resources as service animals, equipment rentals, and access guides.

Many travel agencies offer customized tours and itineraries for travelers with disabilities. Among them are **Flying Wheels Travel** (© 507/451-5005; www.flyingwheelstravel.com) and **Accessible Journeys** (© 800/846-4537 or 610/521-0339; www.disabilitytravel.com).

Flying with Disability (www.flying-with-disability.org) is a comprehensive

information source on airplane travel. **Avis Rent a Car** (© 888/879-4273; www.avis.com) has an "Avis Access" program that offers services for customers with special travel needs. These include specially outfitted vehicles with swivel seats, spinner knobs, and hand controls; mobility scooter rentals; and accessible bus service. Be sure to reserve well in advance.

Also check out the quarterly magazine *Emerging Horizons* (www.emerginghorizons.com), available by subscription ($16.95 per year U.S.; $21.95 outside U.S).

The "Accessible Travel" link at **Mobility-Advisor.com** (www.mobility-advisor.com) offers a variety of travel resources to disabled persons.

British travelers should contact **Holiday Care** (© 0845-124-9971 in U.K. only; www.holidaycare.org.uk) to access a wide range of travel information and resources for disabled and elderly people.

GAY & LESBIAN TRAVELERS

Canada is one of the most gay-tolerant travel destinations in the world. Witness the fact that gay marriage is legal in Canada and that the entire nation has nondiscrimination protection for gays and lesbians. While not every rural village is ready for the circuit party set, most gay travelers will encounter little adversity.

A good clearinghouse for information on gay Canada is the website **www.gaycanada.com**, which features news and links to gay-owned or -friendly accommodations and business across Canada. Another guide for gay-based travel information for destinations worldwide is www.gay.com.

The **International Gay and Lesbian Travel Association (IGLTA)** (© 800/448-8550 or 954/776-2626; www.iglta.org) is the trade association for the gay and lesbian travel industry, and offers an online directory of gay- and lesbian-friendly travel businesses and tour operators.

Many agencies offer tours and travel itineraries specifically for gay and lesbian travelers. San Francisco–based **Now, Voyager** (© **800/255-6951;** www.now voyager.com) offers worldwide trips and cruises, and **Olivia** (© **800/631-6277;** www.olivia.com) offers lesbian cruises and resort vacations.

Gay.com Travel (© **800/929-2268** or 415/644-8044; www.gay.com/travel or www.outandabout.com), is an excellent online successor to the popular *Out & About* print magazine. It provides regularly updated information about gay-owned, gay-oriented, and gay-friendly lodging, dining, sightseeing, nightlife, and shopping establishments in every important destination worldwide. British travelers should click on the "Travel" link at **www.uk.gay.com** for advice and gay-friendly trip ideas.

The Canadian website **GayTraveler** (www.gaytraveler.ca) offers ideas and advice for gay travel all over the world.

The following travel guides are available at many bookstores, or you can order them from any online bookseller: *Spartacus International Gay Guide,* 35th edition (Bruno Gmünder Verlag; www.spartacus world.com/gayguide) and *Odysseus: The International Gay Travel Planner,* 17th edition (www.odyusa.com); and the *Damron* guides (www.damron.com), with separate, annual books for gay men and lesbians.

SENIOR TRAVEL

Mention the fact that you're a senior while traveling in Canada, and frequently you can receive discounted admission prices to cultural and tourist attractions. In most Canadian cities, people over the age of 65 qualify for reduced admission to theaters, museums, and other attractions, as well as discounted fares on public transportation. It is less common to receive discounts on lodging, though it does happen so it is worth asking when you make your lodging reservations.

Members of **AARP,** 601 E St. NW, Washington, DC 20049 (© **888/687-2277;** www.aarp.org), get discounts on hotels, airfares, and car rentals. AARP offers members a wide range of benefits, including *AARP: The Magazine* and a monthly newsletter. Anyone over 50 can join.

Many reliable agencies and organizations target the 50-plus market. **Elderhostel** (© **800/454-5768;** www.elder hostel.org) arranges worldwide study programs for those aged 55 and over. **ElderTreks** (© **800/741-7956** or 416/558-5000 outside North America; www. eldertreks.com) offers small-group tours to off-the-beaten-path or adventure-travel locations, restricted to travelers 50 and older.

Recommended publications offering travel resources and discounts for seniors include: the quarterly magazine *Travel 50 & Beyond* (www.travel50andbeyond. com) and the bestselling paperback *Unbelievably Good Deals and Great Adventures That You Absolutely Can't Get Unless You're Over 50 2005–2006,* 16th edition (McGraw-Hill), by Joann Rattner Heilman.

FAMILY TRAVEL

Canada makes an especially great family-vacation destination because of its fantastic national park system and abundance of recreational activities. Destinations such as the Canadian Rockies are especially attractive, as outfitters make it easy to arrange guided hiking, biking, white-water rafting, and horseback riding excursions simply by talking to your hotel's concierge. Destinations on both the Atlantic and Pacific coast provide opportunities to learn to sea kayak or to journey out onto the seas to view marine wildlife, while the prairie provinces feature guest ranches and Old West activities.

To locate accommodations, restaurants, and attractions that are particularly kid-friendly, refer to the "Kids" icon throughout this guide.

Recommended family travel websites include **Family Travel Forum** (www.familytravelforum.com), a comprehensive site that offers customized trip planning; **Family Travel Network** (www.familytravelnetwork.com), an online magazine providing travel tips; and **TravelWithYourKids.com** (www.travelwithyourkids.com), a comprehensive site written by parents for parents offering sound advice for long-distance and international travel with children.

STUDENT TRAVEL

The **International Student Travel Confederation (ISTC)** (www.istc.org) was formed in 1949 to make travel around the world more affordable for students. Check out its website for comprehensive travel services information and details on how to get an **International Student Identity Card (ISIC)**, which qualifies students for substantial savings on rail passes, plane tickets, entrance fees, and more. It also provides students with basic health and life insurance and a 24-hour help line. The card is valid for a maximum of 18 months. You can apply for the card online or in person at **STA Travel** (© 800/781-4040 in North America; www.statravel.com), the biggest student travel agency in the world; check out the website to locate STA Travel offices worldwide. If you're no longer a student but are still under 26, you can get an **International Youth Travel Card (IYTC)**, which entitles you to some discounts. **Travel CUTS** (© 800/592-2887; www.travelcuts.com) offers similar services for both Canadians and U.S. residents. Irish students may prefer to turn to **USIT** (© 01/602-1904; www.usit.ie), an Ireland-based specialist in student, youth, and independent travel.

SINGLE TRAVELERS

On package vacations, single travelers are often hit with a "single supplement" to the base price. To avoid it, you can agree to room with other single travelers or find a compatible roommate before you go, from one of the many roommate-locator agencies.

Travel Buddies Singles Travel Club (© 800/998-9099; www.travelbuddiesworldwide.com), based in Canada, runs small, intimate, single-friendly group trips and will match you with a roommate free of charge. **TravelChums** (© 212/787-2621; www.travelchums.com) is an Internet-only travel-companion matching service with elements of an online personals-type site, hosted by the respected New York–based Shaw Guides travel service.

Many reputable tour companies offer singles-only trips. **Singles Travel International** (© 877/765-6874; www.singlestravelintl.com) offers singles-only escorted tours to places like London, Alaska, Fiji, and the Greek Islands. **Backroads** (© 800/462-2848; www.backroads.com) offers "Singles + Solos" active-travel trips to destinations worldwide.

For more information, check out Eleanor Berman's classic *Traveling Solo: Advice and Ideas for More Than 250 Great Vacations,* 5th edition (Globe Pequot), updated in 2005.

TRAVELING WITH PETS

Dogs, cats, and most pets can enter Canada with their owners, though you must have proof of rabies vaccinations within the last 36 months for pets over 3 months old.

Finding hotels that allow pets is easy with www.petswelcome.com, www.pettravel.com, and www.travelpets.com. Several hotel chains make a point of welcoming pets, including Motel 6, Fairmont, and Westin.

11 Sustainable Tourism/Eco-Tourism

Each time you take a flight or drive a car, CO_2 is released into the atmosphere. You can help neutralize this danger to our planet through "carbon offsetting"—paying someone to reduce your CO_2 emissions by the same amount you've added. Carbon offsets can be purchased in the U.S. from companies such as **Carbonfund.org** (www.carbonfund.org) and **TerraPass** (www.terrapass.org), and from **Climate Care** (www.climatecare.org) in the U.K.

Although one could argue that any vacation that includes an airplane flight can't be truly "green," you can go on holiday and still contribute positively to the environment. You can offset carbon emissions from your flight in other ways. Choose forward-looking companies that embrace responsible development practices, helping preserve destinations for the future by working alongside local people. An increasing number of sustainable tourism initiatives can help you plan a family trip and leave as small a "footprint" as possible on the places you visit.

Responsible Travel (www.responsibletravel.com) contains a great source of sustainable travel ideas run by a spokesperson for responsible tourism in the travel industry. **Sustainable Travel International** (www.sustainabletravelinternational.org) promotes responsible tourism practices and issues an annual "Green Gear & Gift Guide."

You can find eco-friendly travel tips, statistics, and touring companies and associations—listed by destination under "Travel Choice"—at the TIES website, www.ecotourism.org. Also check out **Conservation International** (www.conservation.org)—which, with *National Geographic Traveler*, annually presents **World Legacy Awards** (www.wlaward.org) to those travel tour operators, businesses, organizations, and places that have made a significant contribution to sustainable tourism. **Ecotravel.com** is part online magazine and part eco-directory that lets you search for touring

Frommers.com: The Complete Travel Resource

It should go without saying, but we highly recommend **Frommers.com,** voted Best Travel Site by *PC Magazine.* We think you'll find our expert advice and tips; independent reviews of hotels, restaurants, attractions, and preferred shopping and nightlife venues; vacation giveaways; and an online booking tool indispensable before, during, and after your travels. We publish the complete contents of over 128 travel guides in our **Destinations** section covering nearly 3,800 places worldwide to help you plan your trip. Each weekday, we publish original articles reporting on **Deals and News** via our free **Frommers.com Newsletter** to help you save time and money and travel smarter. We're betting you'll find our new **Events** listings (http://events.frommers.com) an invaluable resource; it's an up-to-the-minute roster of what's happening in cities everywhere—including concerts, festivals, lectures and more. We've also added weekly **podcasts, interactive maps,** and hundreds of new images across the site. Check out our **Travel Talk** area featuring **Message Boards** where you can join in conversations with thousands of fellow Frommer's travelers and post your trip report once you return.

companies in several categories (water-based, land-based, spiritually oriented, and so on).

In the U.K., **Tourism Concern** (www.tourismconcern.org.uk) works to reduce social and environmental problems connected to tourism and find ways of improving tourism so that local benefits are increased.

The **Association of British Travel Agents (ABTA)** (www.abta.com) acts as a focal point for the U.K. travel industry and is one of the leading groups spearheading responsible tourism.

The **Association of Independent Tour Operators (AITO)** (www.aito.co.uk) is a group of interesting specialist operators leading the field in making holidays sustainable.

12 Staying Connected

TELEPHONES

The Canadian phone system is exactly the same as the system in the United States. Canadian phone numbers have 10 digits: The first three numbers are the area code, which corresponds to a province or division thereof, plus a seven-digit local number. To call a number within the same locality, usually all you have to dial is the seven-digit local number. If you're making a long-distance call (out of the area or province), you need to precede the local number with 1 plus the area code.

Pay phones are easy to find, particularly in hotels and at public transportation hubs. You can use coins to operate the phone (dial the number, then insert coins as directed by the automated voice), or credit cards. It's far cheaper to use pre-paid phone cards, which are widely available in pharmacies and post offices. Phone cards are available in various denominations and can be used to make either domestic or international calls. Or you can order virtual phone cards over the Internet on websites such as **www.pingo.com** and **www.zaptel.com**; these phone card services are activated immediately and can be "recharged" through the company website.

To make international calls: Dial the international access code 011, followed by the country code (44 for the U.K., 353 for Ireland, 61 for Australia, and 64 for New Zealand), then dial the city code (without the initial 0 for U.K. and Ireland numbers) and then the number.

For directory assistance: Dial 411 if you're looking for a number inside Canada or the U.S. Fees for these directory assistance calls range from C$1.25 to C$3.50 (US$1.25–US$3.50/65p–£1.75). For international directory assistance, dial 00 and ask for the international directory assistance operator. These calls cost C$8.95 (US$8.95/£4.50) each. It is free to use Web-based phone directories, such as www.whitepages.com or www.anywho.com, to research phone numbers.

For operator assistance: If you need operator assistance in making a call, dial 0.

Toll-free numbers: Numbers beginning with 800, 888, 877, and 866 within Canada are toll-free.

CELLPHONES

Most U.S. travelers with cellphones will find that their phones will probably work just fine in Canada. Call your service provider to make certain, but nearly all U.S. providers have reciprocal relationships with national Canadian networks. Calls on a U.S. phone using a Canadian network can be expensive, however, usually more than the standard roaming charges incurred within the U.S.

For cellphone users from Asia, Australia and Europe, the situation is a bit more complicated. The three letters that define much of the world's wireless capabilities are **GSM** (Global System for Mobile

Online Traveler's Toolbox

Veteran travelers usually carry some essential items to make their trips easier. Following is a selection of handy online tools to bookmark and use.

- **Airplane Food** (www.airlinemeals.net)
- **Airplane Seating** (www.seatguru.com and www.airlinequality.com)
- **Foreign Languages for Travelers** (www.travlang.com)
- **Maps** (www.mapquest.com)
- **Subway Navigator** (www.subwaynavigator.com)
- **Time and Date** (www.timeanddate.com)
- **Travel Warnings** (http://travel.state.gov, www.fco.gov.uk/travel, www.voyage.gc.ca, or www.smartraveller.gov.au)
- **Universal Currency Converter** (www.xe.com/ucc)
- **Visa ATM Locator** (www.visa.com), **MasterCard ATM Locator** (www.mastercard.com)
- **Weather** (www.intellicast.com and www.weather.ca)

Communications), a big, seamless network that makes for easy cross-border cellphone use throughout Europe and dozens of other countries worldwide. In Canada and the U.S., GSM networks are much less common. In the U.S., T-Mobile, AT&T Wireless, and Cingular offer some GSM services; in Canada, Microcell and Rogers use some GSM networks.

GSM phones function with a removable plastic SIM card, encoded with your phone number and account information. If your cellphone is on a GSM system and you have a world-capable multiband phone such as many Sony Ericsson, Motorola, or Samsung models, you can make and receive calls across civilized areas around much of the globe. Just call your wireless operator and ask for "international roaming" to be activated on your account. Unfortunately, per-minute charges can be high.

For some, **renting** a phone when visiting Canada may be a good idea. A quick search of the Web reveals many cellphone rental companies that provide service in Canada, including **Cellular Abroad**

(© **800/287-5072** or www.cellularabroad.com) and **Planet Omni** (© **877/327-5076**; www.planetomni.com). Cellphone rental charges range between C$30 to C$35 (US$30–US$35/£15–£18) a week, but fees can quickly mount as you'll also need to buy a SIM card and pay dearly (up to C60¢ a minute) for both incoming and outgoing calls. To rent a phone, you'll need to contact the rental company in advance of your departure and await the arrival of your phone.

Buying a phone once you arrive in Canada can be more economically attractive. Two of Canada's largest carriers, **Rogers** (www.shoprogers.com) and **Telus Mobility** (www.telusmobility.com) offer pay-as-you-go plans, which don't require users to sign up for lengthy contract plans. Once you arrive at your destination, stop by a local cellphone shop (both Rogers and Telus Mobility have stores everywhere in urban centers; the websites give locations) and ask for the cheapest pay-as-you-go package. You'll need to purchase a phone, but if you resist splurging on a high-end model, these can cost as little as C$50 (US$50/£25). Pay-as-you-go plans start at C$1 per day, or C25¢ per minute, depending on the plan. Incoming calls are free. The downside is that you'll end up with a non-GSM phone, but you'll be prepared for your next trip to Canada or the States.

VOICE-OVER INERNET PROTOCOL (VOIP)

If you have Web access while traveling, you might consider a broadband-based telephone service (in technical terms, **Voice over Internet Protocol,** or **VoIP**) such as Skype (www.skype.com) or Vonage (www.vonage.com), which allows you to make free international calls if you use their services from your laptop or in a cybercafe. The people you're calling must also use the service for it to work; check the sites for details.

INTERNET/E-MAIL
WITHOUT YOUR OWN COMPUTER

To find cybercafes in your destination check **www.cybercaptive.com** and **www.cybercafe.com**.

Most major airports have **Internet kiosks** that provide basic Web access for a per-minute fee that's usually higher than cybercafe prices. Check out copy shops like **Kinko's** (FedEx Kinko's), which offers computer stations with fully loaded software (as well as Wi-Fi). Most hotels also offer a desktop computer with Internet access for the use of guests.

WITH YOUR OWN COMPUTER

More and more hotels, resorts, airports, cafes, and retailers are going **Wi-Fi** (wireless fidelity), becoming "hot spots" that offer free high-speed Wi-Fi access or charge a small fee for usage. Most laptops sold today have built-in wireless capability. To find public Wi-Fi hot spots at your destination, go to **www.jiwire.com**; its Wi-Fi Hotspot Finder holds the world's largest directory of public wireless hot spots.

For dial-up access, most business-class hotels throughout the world offer dataports for laptop modems, and a few thousand hotels in Europe now offer free high-speed Internet access.

Wherever you go, bring a **connection kit** of the right power and phone adapters, a spare phone cord, and a spare Ethernet network cable—or find out whether your hotel supplies them to guests. (Both phone and electrical cables in Canada are exactly the same as the U.S.)

13 Packages for the Independent Traveler

Package tours are simply a way to buy the airfare, accommodations, and other elements of your trip (such as car rentals, airport transfers, and sometimes even activities) at the same time and often at discounted prices.

One good source of package deals is the airlines themselves, including **Air Canada,** which offers an array of package deals specially tailored to trim the costs of your vacation. Collectively, these packages come under the title "Air Canada Vacations." This term covers a whole series of travel bargains ranging from city packages to fly/drive tours, escorted tours, motorhome travel, and ski holidays. For details, pick up the brochure from an Air Canada office, or follow the links at www.aircanadavacations.com.

Other airlines offer Canadian package holidays, including **American Airlines Vacations** (© 800/321-2121; www.aavacations.com), **Delta Vacations** (© 800/221-6666; http://deltares.deltavacations.com), **Continental Airlines Vacations** (© 800/301-3800; www.covacations.com), and **United Vacations** (© 888/854-3899; www.unitedvacations.com).

Several big online travel agencies—Expedia, Travelocity, Orbitz, and Lastminute.com—also do a brisk business in packages. Travel packages are also listed in

> **Tips   Ask Before You Go**
>
> Before you invest in a package deal or an escorted tour:
>
> - Always ask about the **cancellation policy.** Can you get your money back? Is there a deposit required?
> - Ask about the **accommodations choices and prices** for each. Then look up the hotels' reviews in a Frommer's guide and check their rates online for your specific dates of travel. Also find out what types of rooms are offered.
> - Request a complete **schedule.** (Escorted tours only)
> - Ask about the **size** and demographics of the group. (Escorted tours only)
> - Discuss what is included in the **price** (transportation, meals, tips, airport transfers, etc.). (Escorted tours only)
> - Finally, look for **hidden expenses.** Ask whether airport departure fees and taxes, for example, are included in the total cost—they rarely are.

the travel section of your local Sunday newspaper. Or check ads in national travel magazines such as *Budget Travel Magazine, Travel + Leisure, National Geographic Traveler,* and *Condé Nast Traveler.*

14 Escorted General-Interest Tours

Escorted tours are structured group tours, with a group leader. The price usually includes everything from airfare to hotels, meals, tours, admission costs, and local transportation.

Collette Tours, 62 Middle St., Pawtucket, RI 02860 (© **800/340-5158;** www.collettevacations.com), offers a wide variety of escorted trips by bus and train, including several in the Atlantic provinces, the Pacific Northwest, and the Rockies. A 10-day tour of Newfoundland includes the seldom-visited northern peninsula and the Viking site at L'Anse aux Meadows, as well as a visit to Labrador. Shorter trips explore the Toronto/Niagara area, and some combine Atlantic Canada with New England or Western Canada with Alaska. An escorted train tour goes from Vancouver to Banff aboard the *Rocky Mountaineer* (see below). Order any of Collette's tour brochures by phone or on their website.

Brewster Transportation and Tours, P.O. Box 1140, Banff, AB T0L 0C0 (© **877/791-5500;** www.brewster.ca) offers a wide variety of tours throughout Canada, both escorted and independent. Their offerings include motorcoach and train excursions, ski and other winter vacations, city and resort combination packages, chartered day tours by bus, and independent driving tours. Highlights include a visit to the Columbia Icefields in Jasper National Park, Alberta, and one to Yellowknife, Northwest Territories, to view the aurora borealis. Many packages in the Rockies include stays at guest ranches.

Travel by train lets you see the Rockies as you never would in a bus or behind the wheel of a car. The **Rocky Mountaineer Vacations,** 1150 Station St., 1st Floor, Vancouver, BC V6A 2X7 (© **877/460-3200;** www.rockymountaineer.com), bills its *Rocky Mountaineer* as "The Most Spectacular Train Trip in the World." During daylight hours between mid-April and mid-October, this sleek blue-and-white train winds past foaming waterfalls, ancient glaciers, towering snowcapped peaks, and roaring mountain streams. The *Rocky Mountaineer* gives you the options of traveling east from Vancouver; traveling west from Jasper, Calgary, or Banff; or taking round-trips. A new rail service offers travel to/from Vancouver and Jasper via Whistler and Prince George. There's also a tour offering a VIA Rail connection from Toronto, or packages that include links to the Inside Passage from Prince Rupert to Victoria. Tours range from 2 to 12 days, with stays in both the mountains and cities.

John Steel Railtours (© **800/988-5778** or fax 604/886-2100; www.john steel.com) offers both escorted and independent tour packages, many through the Rockies and the west and a few in other regions, which combine train and other forms of travel. VIA Rail and BC Rail operate the train portions of John Steel tours. Packages run from 5 to 12 days, at all times of year, depending on the route, and combine stays in major cities and national parks.

Despite the fact that escorted tours require big deposits and predetermine hotels, restaurants, and itineraries, many people derive security and peace of mind from the structure they offer. Escorted tours—whether they're navigated by bus, motorcoach, train, or boat—let travelers sit back and enjoy the trip without having to drive or worry about details. They take you to the maximum number of sights in the minimum amount of time with the least amount of hassle. They're particularly convenient for people with limited mobility and they can be a great way to make new friends.

On the downside, you'll have little opportunity for serendipitous interactions with locals. The tours can be jampacked with activities, leaving little room for individual sightseeing, whim, or adventure—plus they often focus on the heavily touristed sites, so you miss out on many a lesser known gem.

15 The Outdoor Adventure Planner

OUTFITTERS & ADVENTURE-TRAVEL OPERATORS

Most outfitters offer trips in specific geographic areas only, though some larger outfitters package trips across the country. In the chapters that follow, we'll recommend lots of local operators and tell you about the outings they run. We've found a few, though, that operate in more than one region of Canada.

The Great Canadian Adventure Company, 6714 101 Ave., Edmonton, AB T6A 0H7 (© **888/285-1676** or 780/414-1676; fax 780/424-9034; www.adventures.ca), offers over 40 different types of guided activities and expeditions—including all of the standards plus such options as Native (First Nations and Inuit) cultural tours, helicopter- or snowcat-transported backcountry snowboarding, and a submersible excursion—in

every province and just about every nook of the country.

Nahanni River Adventures, P.O. Box 312033, Whitehorse, YT Y1A 5P7 (© **800/297-6927** or 867/668-3180; fax 867/668-3056; www.nahanni.com), offers white-water and naturalist float trips in rivers across western and northern Canada, with the Nahanni River a specialty.

Canusa Cycle Tours, Box 35104, Sarcee RPO, Calgary, AB T3E 7C7 (© **800/938-7986;** fax 403/254-8361; www.canusacycletours.com), offers guided cycle tours along some of western Canada's most scenic highways.

Ecosummer Expeditions, P.O. Box 177, Clearwater, BC V0E 1N0 (© **800/465-8884** or 250/674-0102; fax 250/674-2197; www.ecosummer.com), offers a wide variety of sea kayaking, white-water rafting, dog sledding, photography, and other expeditions in British Columbia, the Yukon, the Northwest Territories, and Nunavut. Ecosummer also offers trips to Greenland, as well as destinations in South and Central America.

Black Feather Wilderness Adventure Company, 250 McNaughts Rd., R.R. 3, Parry Sound, ON P2A 2W9 (*©* **888/849-7668** or 705/746-1372; fax 705/746-7048; www.blackfeather.com), leads kayaking, canoeing, and hiking trips in British Columbia, the Northwest Territories, Nunavut, Ontario, and Labrador.

SHOULD YOU USE AN OUTFITTER OR PLAN YOUR OWN TRIP?

A basic consideration for most people who embark on an adventure vacation is time versus money. If you have time on your hands and have basic skills in dealing with sports and the outdoors, then planning your own trip can be fun. On the other hand, making one phone call and writing one check makes a lot more sense if you don't have a lot of time and lack the background to safely get you where you want to go.

TRANSPORTATION & EQUIPMENT

In general, the more remote the destination, the more you should consider an outfitter. In many parts of Canada, simply getting to the area where your trip begins requires a great deal of planning. Frequently, outfitters will have their own airplanes or boats or work in conjunction with someone who does. These transportation costs are usually included in the price of an excursion and are usually cheaper than the same flight or boat trip on a chartered basis.

The same rule applies to equipment rental. Getting your raft or canoe to an out-of-the-way lake can be an adventure in itself. But hire an outfitter and they'll take care of the hassle.

Another option is to use an outfitter to "package" your trip. Some outfitters offer their services to organize air charters and

provide equipment for a fee but leave you to mastermind the trip.

SAFETY   Much of Canada is remote and given to weather extremes. What might be considered a casual camping trip or boating excursion in more populated or temperate areas can become life-threatening in the Canadian backcountry—which often starts right at the edge of town. Almost all outfitters are certified as first-aid providers, and most carry two-way radios in case there's a need to call for help. Local outfitters also know the particular hazards of the areas where they lead trips. In some areas, such as the Arctic, where hazards range from freakish weather to ice-floe movements and polar bears, outfitters are nearly mandatory.

OTHER PEOPLE   Most outfitters will lead groups on excursions only after signing up a minimum number of participants. This is usually a financial consideration for the outfitter, but for participants this can be both good and bad news. Traveling with the right people can add to the trip's enjoyment, but the wrong companions can lead to exasperation and disappointment. If you're sensitive to other peoples' idiosyncrasies, ask the potential outfitter specific questions regarding who else is going on the trip.

SELECTING AN OUTFITTER

An outfitter will be responsible for your safety and your enjoyment of the trip, so make certain you choose one wisely. All outfitters should be licensed or accredited by the province and should be happy to provide you with proof. This means they're bonded, carry the necessary insurance, and have the money and organizational wherewithal to register with the province. This rules out fly-by-night operations and college students who've decided to set up business for the summer. If you're just starting to plan an excursion, ask the provincial tourist authority for its complete list of licensed outfitters.

Tips **A Warning**

All outfitters should be licensed by their province, and local tourist offices can provide listings of outfitters licensed to operate in the areas you intend to visit.

Often, a number of outfitters offer similar trips. When you've narrowed down your choice, call and talk to those outfitters. Ask questions and try to get a sense of who these people are; you'll be spending a lot of time with them, so make sure you feel comfortable. If you have special interests, such as bird- or wildlife-watching, be sure to mention them. A good outfitter will also take your interests into account when planning a trip.

If there's a wide disparity in prices between outfitters for the same trip, find out what makes the difference. Some companies economize on food. If you don't mind having cold cuts for each meal of your weeklong canoe expedition, then perhaps the least expensive outfitter is okay. However, if you prefer a cooked meal, alcoholic beverages, or a choice of entrees, then be prepared to pay more. On a long trip, it may be worth it to you.

Ask how many years an outfitter has been in business and how long your particular escort has guided this trip. While a start-up outfitting service can be perfectly fine, you should know what level of experience you're buying. If you have questions, especially for longer or more dangerous trips, ask for referrals.

WHAT TO PACK

Be sure that it's clearly established between you and your outfitter what you're responsible for bringing along. If you need to bring a sleeping bag, find out what weight of bag is suggested for the conditions you'll encounter. If you have any special dietary requirements, find out whether you can be accommodated or need to pack and prepare accordingly.

While it's fun and relatively easy to amass the equipment for a backcountry expedition, none of it will do you any good if you don't know how to use it. Even though compasses aren't particularly accurate in the North, bring one along and know how to use it (or maybe consider using a GPS device). Detailed maps are always a good idea. If you're trekking without guidance, make sure you have the skills appropriate to your type of expedition, plan your packing well (with contingencies for changes in weather), and bring along a good first-aid kit.

For all summer trips in Canada, make sure to bring along insect repellent, as mosquitoes are particularly numerous and hungry in the North. If you know you're heading into bad mosquito country, consider buying specialized hats with mosquito netting attached. Sunglasses are a must, even above the Arctic Circle. The farther north you go in summer, the longer the sun stays up; the low angle of the sun can be particularly annoying. In winter, the glare off snow can cause sun blindness. For the same reasons, sunscreen is a surprising necessity.

Summer weather is changeable in Canada. If you're planning outdoor activities, be sure to bring along wet-weather gear, even in high summer. The more exposure you'll have to the elements, the more you should consider bringing high-end Gore-Tex and artificial-fleece outerwear. The proper gear can make the difference between a miserable time and a great adventure.

If you're traveling in Canada in winter, you'll want to have the best winter coat, gloves, and boots you can afford. A coat with a hood is especially important, as arctic winds can blow for days at a time.

16 Getting Around Canada

BY CAR

Once in Canada, drivers will find that roads are generally in good condition. There are two major highway routes that cross Canada east to west. Highway 1— the Trans-Canada Highway—which is largely four-lane, travels from Victoria on the Pacific to St. John's in Newfoundland a total of 8,000km (5,000 miles)—with some ferries along the way. The Yellowhead Highway (Hwy. 16) links Winnipeg to Prince Rupert in B.C. along a more northerly route.

GASOLINE   As in the United States, the trend in Canada is toward self-service stations, and in some areas you may have difficulty finding the full-service kind. Though Canada (specifically Alberta) is a major oil producer, gasoline isn't particularly cheap. Gas sells by the liter and pumps for anywhere from about C90¢ to C$1.15 (US90¢–US$1.15/45p–58p) per liter, or about C$3.90 to C$4.40 (US$3.90–US$4.40/£1.95–£2.20) per U.S. gallon. (Note that the term "gallon" in Canada usually refers to the imperial gallon, which amounts to about 1.2 U.S. gal.) Gasoline prices will vary from region to region.

DRIVING RULES   Canadian driving rules are similar to regulations in the United States. Wearing seat belts is compulsory (and enforced) in all provinces, for all passengers. Children under 5 must be in child restraints. Motorcyclists must wear helmets. Throughout the country, pedestrians have the right of way and crosswalks are sacrosanct. The speed limit on the autoroutes (limited-access highways) is usually 110kmph (70 mph). In all provinces but Québec, right turns on red are permitted after a full stop, unless another rule is posted. Drivers must carry proof of insurance in Canada at all times.

SAMPLE DRIVING DISTANCES BETWEEN MAJOR CITIES   Here are some sample driving distances between major Canadian cities. The distances are calculated based on a particular route, possibly the fastest, but not necessarily the shortest: Montréal to Vancouver, 4,910km (3,051 miles); Vancouver to Halifax, 6,295km (3,912 miles); Toronto to Victoria, 4,700km (2,920 miles); Winnipeg to St. John's, 5,100km (3,169 miles); Calgary to Montréal, 3,710km (2,305 miles); St. John's to Vancouver, 7,625km (4,738 miles); Ottawa to Victoria, 4,810km (2,989 miles). To get driving directions online, check MapQuest (www.mapquest.ca) or Yahoo! Canada Maps (http://ca.maps.yahoo.com) and select driving directions.

BY PLANE

Canada is undergoing a renaissance in regional air travel. If you're fans of Southwest, JetBlue, or Ryanair, you're in for a treat. It's actually cheaper now to fly between Canadian cities than take the bus or train, as deregulation has resulted in a number of excellent new airlines that offer no-frills but perfectly comfortable air travel. These airlines rely on the Internet to create savings in booking flights and other information gathering, so you'll want Internet access to learn about these flights. **WestJet** (© **888/937-8538;** www.westjet.com) offers the largest service area, with flights spanning the country from Victoria to St. John's.

BY TRAIN

Most of Canada's passenger rail traffic is carried by the government-owned **VIA Rail** (© **888/VIARAIL** in Canada, 888/842-7245 in the U.S., www.viarail.ca). You can traverse the continent very comfortably in sleeping cars, parlor coaches, bedrooms, and roomettes. Virtually all of Canada's major cities (save Calgary and Regina) are connected by rail, though service is less frequent than it used to be.

Some luxury trains, such as *The Canadian,* boast dome cars with panoramic picture windows, hot showers, and dining cars. Reduced regular fares are available for students, seniors, and children traveling with adults.

The problem with traveling on VIA Rail, particularly in western Canada, is that the train only runs 3 days a week. If you want to link your visit between destinations in Alberta and Saskatchewan with a train journey, you may be out of luck unless your schedule is very flexible. Also, if sightseeing and not just transport is part of your vacation agenda, then you may also find that your train journey takes place overnight. Because of the way the train is scheduled in many parts of rural Canada, there's just one schedule per train, so the leg between Winnipeg and Edmonton, for instance, will always be overnight, no matter which train you take.

You can buy a **Canrailpass,** C$837 (US$837/£419) in high season and C$523 (US$523/£262) in low season, giving you 12 days of unlimited economy-class travel in one 30-day period throughout the VIA Rail national network. Seniors 60 and over, students, and youths 17 or under receive a 10% discount on all fares. Class upgrades are available for a fee each time you ride. A similar but less expensive package is available for 10 days of unlimited travel on the Québec-Windsor corridor, serving Toronto, Niagara Falls, Ottawa, Montréal, and Québec City.

BY BUS

While many Americans may not relish the option of traveling by bus while in Canada, in fact Greyhound Canada (© **800/661-8747;** www.greyhound.ca) offers far superior service and coverage than does Greyhound in the U.S. Not only are the buses newer and cleaner, and the bus stations better kept up than in the U.S., Greyhound is often the only option for land transport in many parts of Canada due to the relatively minimal coverage by VIA Rail.

17 Tips on Accommodations

Travelers to Canada are lucky: The quality of hotels and lodging in Canada is very high. In fact, along with the Swiss, Canadians seem to have a natural gift for the hospitality industry.

A national accommodations rating system is in place in Canada. Called **Canada Select,** it rates lodgings between one and five stars based on the evaluation of an independent adjudicator. The system is more prominent in some provinces than in others; it is also completely voluntary, so the absence of stars doesn't necessarily mean that the property is substandard. In fact, the Canada Select program is most popular and meaningful for smaller inns and B&Bs, where an independent evaluation is often reassuring.

Generally speaking, most travelers would be comfortable staying in accommodations with at least three stars. These accommodations may not be fancy, but they will be clean and pleasant. Four-star accommodations are usually top-notch. It's worthwhile noting that the gradations between four and five stars have to do with features that may not directly affect the comfort or pleasure of your stay—types of curtains, types of door locks, and so on. In other words, you may not even recognize the supposed superiority of a five-star property over one with four stars.

Every Canadian city will have a selection of upscale luxury or business hotels. The preeminent Canadian chain of luxury hotels is **Fairmont Hotels and Resorts** (© **800/257-7544;** www.fairmont.com), which is the company that now controls many of the historic and utterly fabulous hotels built by the Canadian railroads around the turn of the 20th century. These include a number of hotels that are practically symbols of Canada, such as the Empress in Victoria, the Château Lake Louise, the Banff Springs, and the Château Frontenac in Québec City. These Fairmont hotels have been lovingly restored, but you'll have to decide if their astonishingly steep rates are worth it to you—certainly, a stay at one of these vintage beauties will be a highlight of any stay in Canada (some Fairmont hotels are modern, though of equally high quality).

Many business hotel chains familiar from the U.S. and Europe are also found in Canada, including Hilton, Radisson, Hyatt, Ramada, and Westin. An excellent Canadian-based chain of upscale business hotels is **Delta Hotels** (✆ 888/890-3222; www.deltahotels.com). Delta hotels (not related to the airline) are very high quality and are frequently among the top hotels in major Canadian business destinations. A smaller chain of business hotels in western Canada is **Coast Hotels and Resorts** (✆ 800/716-6199; www.coasthotels.com), which also keeps very high standards. As in other parts of North America, the **Best Western** chain (✆ 800/780-7234; www.bestwestern.com) is well represented in Canada and offers a guarantee of good, midlevel quality.

Canada is also known for its small inns and bed-and-breakfasts. There are many more high-quality B&B inns available than this guide could possibly cover. However, the text usually offers the phone number and website information to contact local B&B organizations. A good Canada-wide clearinghouse for B&Bs is the website **www.bbcanada.com**.

Another Canadian specialty is its backcountry lodges and country inns. These are sometimes located in remote regions, at the end of a long and bumpy road. However, the lodges found in this guide are rustic in spirit only, and offer high-quality lodging and dining in beautiful and remote areas.

18 Tips on Dining

Dining habits in Canada are quite similar to those in the U.S. Evening meals are generally eaten between 6 and 8pm. A tip of 15% to 20% is usually expected for good service. The quality of food in Canada is generally quite high; you'll have no problem finding excellent dining options across the country.

Canada is a country of recent immigrants. You can ask locals for recommendations to the best neighborhood Chinese, Lebanese, Pakistani, Jamaican, or other ethnic restaurant. As these restaurants tend to come and go pretty quickly, they may not appear in this guide. However, almost every Canadian city and town has an offering of ethnic restaurants that will provide inexpensive and delicious dining.

Traditional Canadian cooking is often excellent. In Maritime Canada, this will include wondrous all-you-can-eat lobster buffets in out-of-the-way diners and church basements, while in Québec it will include rotisserie chicken, smoked beef, and the heart-stopping but delicious fast food called *poutine* (fried potatoes with cheese and gravy). Out west, local beef steaks are on every menu, and along the Pacific coast, fresh salmon is almost always available in restaurants, right off the boat and absolutely fresh.

However, Canada is also home to a more modern cooking ethic that focuses on organic, locally grown meats and produce and fresh fish and seafood; unusual meats such as bison and game meats such as venison, elk, moose, and caribou are also common on upscale menus. New Canadian cuisine is frequently excellent. It is intensely dedicated to local products, but it also draws on the combined strength of pioneer cooking, including the traditional cooking of French and British settlers, as well as the subtle cuisines of more recent immigrant communities, particularly from Asia.

If you haven't heard of—much less tried—Canadian wines, you're in for a treat. The Niagara area of Ontario is famed for its dessert ice wines, while the Okanagan Valley in central British Columbia is home to a burgeoning wine industry featuring excellent vintages made from traditional French varietals. Most Canadian towns and cities also have a number of brewpubs that feature locally brewed beer and ales as well as flavorful casual dining.

FAST FACTS: Canada

AAA Members of the **American Automobile Association (AAA)** are covered by the **Canadian Automobile Association (CAA)** while traveling in Canada. Bring your membership card and proof of insurance. The 24-hour hot line for emergency service is ℂ 800/222-4357. Most mobile phones can call ℂ *CAA (*222) to reach emergency road service. See www.caaquebec.com for more. The AAA card also provides discounts at many hotels and restaurants.

American Express See the city chapters that follow for the locations of individual American Express offices. To report lost or stolen traveler's checks, call ℂ 800/ 221-7282.

ATM Networks See "Money & Costs," p. 33.

Business Hours Standard business hours in Canada are similar to those in the U.S., usually 10am to 6pm. It is common for stores to be closed on Sundays, particularly outside of the larger cities and major tourist areas.

Customs **What You Can Bring Into Canada**
Customs regulations are very generous in most respects but get pretty complicated when it comes to firearms, plants, meats, and pets. You can bring in free of duty up to 50 cigars, 200 cigarettes, and 200 grams (about a half-pound) of tobacco, providing you're over 18. Those of age (18 or 19, depending on the province) are also allowed about 1.15 liters (40 oz.) of liquor, 1.5 liters (50 oz.) of wine, or 24 355-milliliter (12-oz.) containers of beer or ale. Dogs, cats, and most pets can enter Canada with their owners, though you must have proof of rabies vaccinations within the last 36 months for pets over 3 months old.

Canada has complex requirements, restrictions, and limits that apply to importing meat, eggs, dairy products, fresh fruits and vegetables, and other food from around the world. You can avoid problems by not bringing such goods into Canada.

As for firearms, visitors can bring rifles for the purposes of hunting into Canada during hunting season. Handguns and automatic rifles are generally not allowed. Fishing tackle poses no problems, but the bearer must possess a nonresident license for the province or territory where he or she plans to use it. For more details concerning Customs regulations, contact the **Canada Border Service Agency** (ℂ 800/461-9999 within Canada, or 204/983-3500; www.cbsa-asfc.gc.ca).

What You Can Take Home from Canada

U.S. Citizens: Returning **U.S. citizens** who have been away for at least 48 hours are allowed to bring back, once every 30 days, US$800 worth of merchandise duty-free. You'll be charged a flat rate of 3% duty on the next US$1,000 worth of purchases. Be sure to have your receipts handy. With some exceptions, you cannot bring fresh fruits and vegetables into the United States. Travelers 18 and older are allowed to bring back 1 liter of alcohol, 100 cigars, or 200 cigarettes duty-free. For specifics on what you can bring back and the corresponding fees, download the invaluable free pamphlet *Know Before You Go* online at **www.cbp.gov**. (Click on "Travel," and then click on "Know Before You Go"). Or contact the **U.S. Customs & Border Protection (CBP),** 1300 Pennsylvania Ave., NW, Washington, DC 20229 (✆ **877/287-8667)** and request the pamphlet.

U.K. citizens returning from Canada have a customs allowance of 200 cigarettes or 50 cigars or 250 grams of smoking tobacco; 2 liters of still table wine; 1 liter of spirits or strong liqueurs (over 22% volume); 2 liters of fortified wine, sparkling wine, or other liqueurs; 60cc (ml) perfume; 250cc (ml) of toilet water; and £145 worth of all other goods, including gifts and souvenirs. People under 17 cannot have the tobacco or alcohol allowance. For more information, contact **HM Revenue and Customs** at ✆ **0845/010-9000** (from outside the U.K., 020/8929-0152), or consult their website at www.hmce.gov.uk.

Australian Citizens: The duty-free allowance in Australia is A$900 or, for those under 18, A$450. Citizens can bring in 250 cigarettes or 250 grams of loose tobacco, and 2.25 liters of alcohol (for travelers 18 and older). If you're returning with valuables you already own, such as foreign-made cameras, you should file form B263. A helpful brochure available from Australian consulates or Customs offices is "Know Before You Go." For more information, call the **Australian Customs Service** at ✆ **1300/363-263,** or log on to www.customs.gov.au.

New Zealand Citizens: The duty-free allowance for New Zealand is NZ$700. Citizens over 17 can bring in 200 cigarettes, 50 cigars, or 250 grams of tobacco (or a mixture of all three if their combined weight doesn't exceed 250g), plus 4.5 liters of wine and beer, or 1.125 liters of liquor. New Zealand currency does not carry import or export restrictions. Fill out a certificate of export, listing the valuables you are taking out of the country; that way, you can bring them back without paying duty. Most questions are answered in a free pamphlet available at New Zealand consulates and Customs offices: New Zealand Customs Guide for Travellers, Notice no. 4. For more information, contact **New Zealand Customs,** The Customhouse, 17–21 Whitmore St., Box 2218, Wellington (✆ **0800/428-786** or 04/473-6099; www.customs.govt.nz).

Drugstores Drugstores and pharmacies are found throughout Canada. As in the U.S., there are a number of national chain pharmacies, including Shoppers Drug Mart and Rexall. In addition, many grocery stores in Canada also have in-store pharmacies. Many prescription-only drugs in the United States are available over the counter in Canada, and pharmacists are more likely to offer casual medical advice than their counterparts in the States. If you're not feeling well, a trip to see a pharmacist may save you a trip to the doctor.

Electricity Canada uses the same electrical plug configuration and current as the United States: 110 to 115 volts, 60 cycles.

Embassies & Consulates All embassies are in Ottawa, the national capital; the **U.S. embassy** is at 490 Sussex Dr., Ottawa, ON K1N 1G8 (✆ **613/688-5335**; http://canada.usembassy.gov/). The mailing address for the embassy's consular services is P.O. Box 866, Station B, Ottawa, ON K1P 5T1. For the other embassies in Ottawa, see "Fast Facts: Ottawa," in chapter 9.

U.S. consulates are in the following locations: **Nova Scotia, Newfoundland, New Brunswick, and Prince Edward Island**—Suite 904, Purdy's Wharf Tower II, 1969 Upper Water St., Halifax, NS B3J 3R7 (✆ **902/429-2480**); **Québec**—2 place Terrasse-Dufferin (behind Château Frontenac), P.O. Box 939, Québec City, PQ G1R 4T9 (✆ **418/692-2095**), and 1155 St. Alexander St., P.O. Box 65, Postal Station Desjardins, Montréal, PQ H5B 1G1 (✆ **514/398-9695**); **Ontario**—360 University Ave., Toronto, ON M5G 1S4 (✆ **416/595-1700** or 416/201-4100 for emergency after-hours calls); **Alberta, Saskatchewan, Manitoba,** and the **Northwest Territories**—615 Macleod Trail S.E., 10th Floor, Calgary, AB T2G 4T8 (✆ **403/266-8962**); **British Columbia** and the **Yukon**—Mezzanine, 1095 W. Pender St., Vancouver, BC V6E 2M6 (✆ **604/685-4311**). Visit the American Citizen Information Services website (www.amcits.com) for further U.S. consular services information.

There's a **British consulate general** at 777 Bay St., Suite 2800, Toronto, ON M5G 2G2 (✆ **416/593-1290**; for more information see www.britainincanada.org), and an **Australian consulate general** at Suite 1100, South Tower,175 Bloor St. E., Suite 316, Toronto, ON M4W 3R8 (✆ **416/323-1155**; for more information see www.ahc-ottawa.org).

Emergencies Dial ✆ **911** for emergency.

Holidays National holidays are celebrated throughout the country; all government facilities and banks are closed, but some department stores and a scattering of smaller shops stay open. If the holiday falls on a weekend, the following Monday is observed.

Language Canada has two official languages, English and French. French is the dominant language in Québec; however, most Québecers can also speak passable English, particularly if they work in the tourist industry. However, it's a good idea to dust off your high-school French if you're traveling to Québec destinations outside of Montréal or Québec City. Not only is it a courtesy to address people in their native tongue, you'll be treated with greater respect if you don't start barking English orders to waiters and hotel staff.

Liquor Laws Laws regarding beer, wine, and liquor vary from province to province. In some provinces, all beer, wine, and spirits are sold only in government liquor stores, which keep very restricted hours and are usually closed on Sundays. Only Alberta and Québec have liquor laws that resemble those in the United States. In those provinces and Manitoba, the minimum drinking age is 18; in all others, it's 19.

Lost & Found Be sure to tell all of your credit card companies the minute you discover your wallet has been lost or stolen and file a report at the nearest police precinct. Your credit card company or insurer may require a police report number or record of the loss. Most credit card companies have an emergency toll-free number to call if your card is lost or stolen; they may be able to wire you a cash advance immediately or deliver an emergency credit card in a day or two. Visa's U.S. emergency number is © 800/847-2911 or 410/581-9994. American Express cardholders and traveler's check holders should call © 800/221-7282. MasterCard holders should call © 800/307-7309 or 636/722-7111. For other credit cards, call the toll-free number directory at © 800/555-1212.

If you need emergency cash over the weekend when all banks and American Express offices are closed, you can have money wired to you via **Western Union** (© 800/325-6000; www.westernunion.com).

Mail Standard mail in Canada is carried by **Canada Post** (© 800/267-1177 in Canada, or 416/979-8822 in the U.S.; www.canadapost.ca). At press time, it costs C52¢ (US52¢/26p) to send a first-class letter or postcard within Canada and C93¢ (US93¢/47p) to send a first-class letter or postcard from Canada to the United States. First-class airmail service to other countries is C$1.55 (US$1.55/78p) for the first 20 grams. Rates go up frequently. If you put a return address on your letter, make sure it's Canadian; otherwise, leave it without. Delivery time can be unaccountably slow between Canada and the States, and all U.S. letter mail travels by air: Expect a letter from Calgary to take a week to reach Seattle.

Measurements Canada uses the metric system, though many Canadians still use miles to measure distance and are familiar with other U.S. forms of measurement. See the chart on the inside front cover of this book for details on converting metric measurements to nonmetric equivalents.

Newspapers & Magazines In addition to local newspapers, the *Globe and Mail* and the *National Post,* both based out of Toronto, are distributed nationally. *Macleans* is a Canadian weekly newsmagazine along the lines of *Newsweek* or *Time.*

Passports Allow plenty of time before your trip to apply for a passport; processing normally takes 3 weeks but can take much longer during busy periods (especially spring). And keep in mind that if you need a passport in a hurry, you'll pay a higher processing fee.

For Residents of Australia: You can pick up an application from your local post office or any branch of Passports Australia, but you must schedule an interview at the passport office to present your application materials. Call the **Australian Passport Information Service** at © 131-232, or visit the government website at www.passports.gov.au.

For Residents of Ireland: You can apply for a 10-year passport at the **Passport Office,** Setanta Centre, Molesworth Street, Dublin 2 (© 01/671-1633; www.irlgov.ie/iveagh). Those under age 18 and over 65 must apply for a 3-year passport. You can also apply at 1A South Mall, Cork (© 021/272-525), or at most main post offices.

For Residents of New Zealand: You can pick up a passport application at any New Zealand Passports Office or download it from their website. Contact the **Passports Office** at © 0800/225-050 in New Zealand or 04/474-8100, or log on to www.passports.govt.nz.

For Residents of the United Kingdom: To pick up an application for a standard 10-year passport (5-year passport for children under 16), visit your nearest passport office, major post office, or travel agency or contact the **United Kingdom Passport Service** at ✆ **0870/521-0410** or search its website at www.ukpa.gov.uk.

For Residents of the United States: Whether you're applying in person or by mail, you can download passport applications from the U.S. State Department website at **http://travel.state.gov**. To find your regional passport office, either check the U.S. State Department website or call the **National Passport Information Center** toll-free number (✆ **877/487-2778**) for automated information.

Police In emergencies, dial ✆ **911.**

Safety See section 9, "Safety."

Smoking Smoking indoors is much more restricted in Canada than in much of the U.S. or Europe. Ten of the country's 13 provinces and territories have now passed smoking bans prohibiting cigarettes in the workplace and public buildings, bars and restaurants. In some jurisdictions, there are even regulations on how closely one can smoke to public entrances to buildings.

Taxes Throughout Canada, you will be charged a federal **goods and services tax (GST),** a 5% tax on virtually all goods and services (the tax was reduced from 6% in January 2008). In all provinces except Alberta, there is an additional provincial sales tax added to purchases and financial transactions, and all provinces and some municipalities levy a hotel room tax. Some provinces (the Maritimes) instead levy a 15% **harmonized sales tax (HST),** which combines their provincial sales taxes with the GST. Some hotels and shops include the GST or HST in their prices; others add it on separately. When included, the tax accounts for the odd hotel rates, such as C$66.05 per day, that you may find on your final bill.

As of April 2007, **the Canadian government no longer offers GST or HST rebates** of hotel bills or the cost of goods you've purchased in Canada.

Time Zone Six time zones are observed in Canada. In winter, when it's 7:30pm Newfoundland standard time, it's 6pm Atlantic Standard Time (Labrador, Prince Edward Island, New Brunswick, and Nova Scotia); 5pm Eastern Standard Time (Québec and most of Ontario); 4pm Central Standard Time (western Ontario, Manitoba, and most of Saskatchewan); 3pm Mountain Standard Time (northwestern Saskatchewan, Alberta, eastern British Columbia, and the Northwest Territories); and 2pm Pacific Standard Time (the Yukon and most of British Columbia).

Each year, on the second Sunday in March, daylight saving time comes into effect in most of Canada, and clocks are advanced by 1 hour. On the first Sunday in November, Canada reverts to standard time. During these summer months, all of Saskatchewan observes the same time zone as Alberta.

Tipping The rules for tipping in Canada parallel those in the United States. For good service in a restaurant, tip 15% to 20%. Tip hairdressers or taxi drivers 10%. Bellhops get C$1 (US$1/50p) per bag for luggage taken to your room; for valets who fetch your car, a C$2 (US$2/£1) tip should suffice.

Useful Phone Numbers U.S. Dept. of State Travel Advisory: ☎ 202/647-5225 (staffed 24 hrs.)

U.S. Passport Agency: ☎ 202/647-0518

U.S. Centers for Disease Control International Traveler's Hotline: ☎ 404/332-4559

Water The water in Canada is legendary for its purity. You can drink water directly from the tap anywhere in the country. Bottled water is also widely available.

3

Nova Scotia

by Paul Karr

Nova Scotia is difficult to characterize. It generally feels more cultured and British than wild, a better place to buy a wool sweater and shoot a round of golf than to actually get your feet wet. That is, until you stumble upon the blustery, boggy uplands and crags of Cape Breton Highlands National Park (which seems like a proper home for druids and trolls), then hear the wild strains of some local Celtic band's fiddling emanating from a tiny pub.

It's a province full of rolling hills and cultivated farms, especially near the Northumberland Straits on the northern shore . . . but then you find the vibrant, edgy, and lively arts and entertainment scene that is Halifax, a city possessing more intriguing street life than many cities three times its size.

There's a tremendous variety of landscapes and low-key attractions here, and the scene changes kaleidoscopically as you travel Nova Scotia's winding roads: from dense forests to bucolic farmlands, from ragged coast to melancholy bogs, and from historic villages to tall ships lazing about impressively at port to dynamic little downtowns serving up everything from fish and chips and a pint to the occasional gourmet eatery. Even in its most populated sections, it's possible to find a sense of remoteness, of being surrounded by big space and a profound history.

1 Exploring the Province

Visitors to Nova Scotia should spend a little time poring over a map (and this travel guide) before leaving home. Your biggest challenge is narrowing down your options before you set off; numerous loops and circuits are possible here, and the available permutations multiply once you factor in the various ferry links to the United States, New Brunswick, Prince Edward Island, and Newfoundland. Figuring out where to go—and then how to get there—is the hardest work you'll need to do in a place that is relatively easy to travel in.

ESSENTIALS

VISITOR INFORMATION Every traveler to Nova Scotia should have a copy of the massive (400+ page) official tourism guide, which is the province's best effort to put travel-guide writers like me out of business. It's comprehensive, colorful, well organized, and free, listing all hotels, campgrounds, and attractions within the province, with brief descriptions and current prices. (Restaurants are given only limited coverage, however; investigate those on your own, using this book and your own nose for eats.)

The tome, called the *Nova Scotia Doers' & Dreamers' Guide,* is available starting each March by phone (© **800/565-0000** or 902/425-5781), fax (902/424-2668), mail

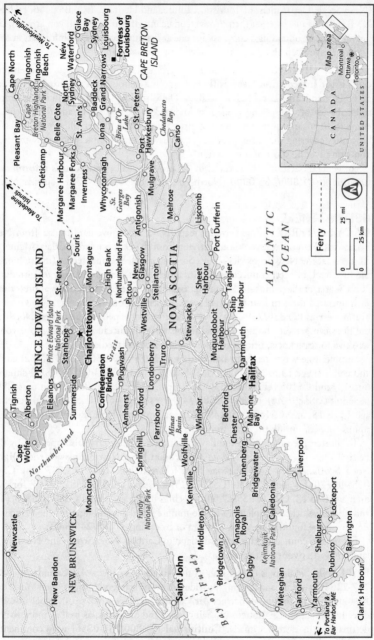

(Nova Scotia Department of Tourism, Culture, and Heritage, P.O. Box 456, Halifax, NS B3J 2R5), and Internet (http://novascotia.com). If you wait until you arrive in the province before obtaining a copy, ask for one at the numerous visitor information centers, where you can also request the excellent free road map.

TOURIST OFFICES   The provincial government administers about a dozen official **Visitor Information Centres** (known as VICs) throughout the province, as well as in Portland and Bar Harbor, Maine. These mostly seasonal centers are amply stocked with brochures and tended by knowledgeable staffers. In addition, virtually every town of any note has a local tourist information center filled with racks of brochures covering the entire province, staffed with local people who know the area. You won't ever be short of information.

For general questions about travel in the province, call **Nova Scotia's information hot line** at ✆ **800/565-0000** (North America) or 902/425-5781 (outside North America).

GETTING THERE
BY CAR & FERRY   Most travelers reach Nova Scotia overland by car from New Brunswick. Plan on at least 4 hours driving from the U.S. border at Calais, Maine, to Amherst (at the New Brunswick–Nova Scotia border). Seasonal ferries (figure June to the first week of Oct) connect both Portland and Bar Harbor, Maine, to Yarmouth, Nova Scotia, at the peninsula's southwest end, though neither runs daily; at press time, each operated three to four times per week, depending on the season.

Bay Ferries (✆ **888/249-7245;** www.catferry.com) operates the ferries. Note that the rides can get very bumpy depending on wave and ocean conditions, so if you're sensitive to seasickness, bring and take motion-sickness medicine.

Summer one-way rates from Bar Harbor in 2007 were C$63 (US$63/£32) adults and children age 13 to 18, C$58 (US$58/£29) seniors, C$43 (US$43/£22) children 6 to 13, and C$105 (US$105/£53) and up per vehicle. From Portland, it cost C$89 per adult (US$89/£45), C$85 (US$85/£43) per senior, C$59 (US$59/£30) per child age 13 to 18, and C$149 (US$149/£75) and up per vehicle. Reservations for both routes are *vital* during the peak summer season.

To shorten the slog around the Bay of Fundy, a 3-hour ferry (also operated by Bay Ferries) known as the *Princess of Acadia* links **Saint John, New Brunswick** with **Digby, Nova Scotia.** Peak season one-way fares (charged June–Oct) in 2007 were C$40 (US$40/£20) for adults, C$30 (US$30/£15) for seniors, C$25 (US$25/£13) for children age 6 to 13, C$5 (US$5/£2.50) per child under age 6, and C$80 (US$80/£40) and up per vehicle. Complete up-to-the-minute schedules and fares for the *Princess of Acadia* can be found at www.nfl-bay.com or by calling ✆ **888/249-SAIL.**

Ferries also connect Prince Edward Island to Caribou, Nova Scotia, and Newfoundland to North Sydney, Nova Scotia.

BY PLANE   Halifax is the air hub of the Atlantic Provinces. **Air Canada** (✆ **888/ 247-2262;** www.aircanada.com) provides daily direct service from New York and Boston, using its commuter partner **Air Canada Jazz** (www.flyjazz.ca), which also flies directly to Sydney, Charlottetown, Saint John, and St. John's, as well as more remote destinations in eastern Canada. **Continental** (✆ **800/231-0856;** www.continental. com) flies direct from Newark to Halifax several times daily in summer; American Airlines' **American Eagle** (✆ **800/433-7300;** www.aa.com) service has added a daily flight between New York's LaGuardia Airport and Halifax. If you're coming from anywhere other than New York, you will probably need to connect in Montréal or Toronto, which can turn into a half-day excursion or more.

BY TRAIN   VIA Rail (℃ **888/842-7245;** www.viarail.com) offers train service 6 days a week between Halifax and Montréal; the entire trip takes between 18 and 21 hours, depending on direction, with a basic summertime fare of about C$240 (US$240/£120) each way, not counting sleeping accommodations. The sleeping berths and private cabins are available at extra cost—the cheapest bed, in a double-bunked cabin, is about twice the cost of the no-bed fare—and VIA also recently added a higher class of service on its overnight run from mid-June through mid-October. The train runs daily each direction year-round except Tuesdays; check the VIA Rail website for updates on routes, schedules, and online booking.

THE GREAT OUTDOORS

Nova Scotia's official travel guide (the aforementioned *Doers' & Dreamers' Guide*) has a very helpful "Outdoors" section in the back that lists camping outfitters, bike shops, whale-watching tour operators, and the like. A free brochure that lists adventure outfitters is published by the **Nova Scotia Adventure Tourism Association,** 1099 Marginal Rd., Ste. 201, Halifax, NS B3H 4P7 (℃ **800/948-4267** or 902/423-4480). Write or call for a copy.

BIKING   The low hills of Nova Scotia and the gentle, largely empty roads make for wonderful cycling. Cape Breton is the most challenging of destinations; the south coast and Bay of Fundy regions yield wonderful ocean views while making fewer demands on cyclists. A number of bike outfitters can aid in your trip planning. **Freewheeling Adventures** (℃ **800/672-0775** or 902/857-3600; www.freewheeling.ca) offers guided bike tours throughout Nova Scotia (as well as Prince Edward Island and Newfoundland). Walter Sienko's guide, *Nova Scotia & the Maritimes by Bike: 21 Tours Geared for Discovery,* is helpful in planning a bike excursion. For an Internet introduction to cycling in Nova Scotia and beyond, visit the website of **Atlantic Canada Cycling** (www.atl-canadacycling.com).

BIRD-WATCHING   More than 400 species of birds have been spotted in Nova Scotia, ranging from odd and exotic birds blown off course in storms to majestic **bald eagles,** of which some 250 nesting pairs reside in Nova Scotia, mostly on Cape Breton Island. Many whale-watching tours also offer specialized sea bird–spotting tours, including trips to **puffin colonies.**

CAMPING   With backcountry options rather limited, Nova Scotia's forte is drive-in camping. The 20 or so provincial parks with campgrounds are uniformly clean, friendly, well managed, and reasonably priced, and offer some 1,500 campsites among them. For a brochure and map listing all provincial campsites, write to **Nova Scotia Department of Natural Resources, Parks and Recreation Division,** R.R. #1, Belmont, NS B0M 1C0; or call ℃ **902/662-3030.** As usual, the province's *Doers' and Dreamers' Guide* contains the fullest campground listings available.

Also check with the Campground Owners Association of Nova Scotia (COANS): Its website at www.campingnovascotia.com lists a number of privately held campgrounds. The free and helpful *Campers Guide,* available at visitor information centers, lists this information as well.

CANOEING   Nova Scotia offers an abundance of accessible canoeing on inland lakes and ponds. The premier destination is **Kejimkujik National Park** in the southern interior, which has plenty of backcountry sites accessible by canoe. A number of other fine canoe trails allow paddlers and portagers to venture off for hours or days. General information is available from **Canoe Kayak Nova Scotia,** 5516 Spring Garden Rd., 4th floor, Halifax, NS B3J 1G6 (② **902/425-5454,** ext. 316).

FISHING   Saltwater-fishing tours are easily arranged on charter boats berthed at many of the province's harbors. Inquire locally at the visitor information centers, or consult the "Boat Tours & Charters" section of the *Doers & Dreamers Guide.* No fishing license is required to fish *most* saltwater species for those on charters. For questions, current fishing regulations, or lists of licensed fishing guides, contact the Nova Scotia **Department of Fisheries and Aquaculture** in Halifax at ② **902/424-4560,** or go to their website at www.gov.ns.ca/fish.

Salmon licenses must be obtained from a provincial office, campground, or licensed outfitter; other freshwater species popular with anglers are brown trout, shad, smallmouth bass, rainbow trout, and speckled trout.

GOLF   Nova Scotia lays claim to more than 50 golf courses. Among the most memorable: **Highland Links** (② **800/441-1118** or 902/285-2600) in Ingonish, which features a dramatic oceanside setting; and **Bell Bay Golf Club** (② **800/565-3077** or 902/295-1333) near Baddeck, which is also wonderfully scenic, and was voted "Best New Canadian Golf Course" by *Golf Digest* in 1998.

New courses are always being constructed, or rumored to be. For one-stop shoppers, tourism office–run **Golf Nova Scotia** (② **800/565-0000,** ext. 007; www.golf novascotia.com) represents about two dozen well-regarded properties around the province, and can arrange customized golfing packages at its member courses. A handy directory of Nova Scotia's golf courses (with phone numbers) is published as a separate brochure and in the "Outdoors" section of the *Doers' & Dreamers' Guide,* as well.

HIKING & WALKING   Serious hikers make tracks for Cape Breton Highlands National Park, which is home to the most dramatic terrain in the province. But other options abound—trails are found throughout Nova Scotia, although in many cases they're a matter of local knowledge. (Ask at the visitor information centers.) Published hiking guides are widely available at local bookstores. Especially helpful are the back pocket–size guides published by **Nimbus Publishing;** call for a catalog (② **800/646-2879** or 902/454-7404; www.nimbus.ns.ca).

WHALE-WATCHING   If you're on the coast, it's likely you're not far from a whale-watching operation. Around two dozen whale-watching outfits offer trips in search of finback, humpback, pilot, and minke whales, among others. The richest waters for whale-watching are found on the Fundy Coast, where the endangered right whale is often seen feeding in summer. Digby Neck (a thin strand extending southwest from the town of Digby) has the highest concentration of whale-watching excursions, but you'll find them in many other coves and harbors. Just ask the staff at visitor information centers to direct you to the whales.

2 Wolfville: Introduction to the Annapolis Valley ⋆

90km (56 miles) NW of Halifax, 234km (145 miles) NE of Yarmouth

The trim and tidy Victorian village of Wolfville (pop. 3,500) has a distinctly New England feel to it, in both its handsome architecture and its layout—a small commercial downtown just 6 blocks long is surrounded by shady neighborhoods of elegant homes. And it's not hard to trace that sensibility to its source. The area was largely populated in the wake of the American Revolution by transplanted New Englanders, who forced off the Acadian settlers who had earlier done so much to tame the wilds.

The town has emerged in recent years as a popular destination for weekending Halifax residents, who come to relax at the many fine inns, wander the leafy streets, and explore the countryside. Also a consistent draw is the **Atlantic Theatre Festival** (© 800/ 337-6661 or 902/542-4242), which has attracted plaudits in the few years it has been presenting shows. Performances are staged throughout the summer season in a comfortable 500-seat theater. Check upcoming performances on their website (www.atf.ns.ca).

EXPLORING WOLFVILLE

Strolling the village is the activity of choice. The towering elms and maples that shade the extravagant Victorian architecture provide the dappled light and rustling sounds for an ideal walk. A good place to start is the **Wolfville Tourist Bureau** at Willow Park (© 902/542-7000) on the north edge of the downtown.

Several **trails** through rugged landscapes and intriguing geological formations are on **Cape Split,** the hook of land that extends far into the Bay of Fundy north of Wolfville.

At **Blomidon Provincial Park** (© 902/582-7319), 24km (15 miles) north of Route 101 (Exit 11), some 14km (8.7 miles) of trail at the park take walkers through forest and along the coast. Among the most dramatic trails is the 6km (3.7-mile) **Jodrey Trail**, which follows towering cliffs that offer broad views over the Minas Basin. It's open mid-May through early October.

One of the more intriguing sights in town occurs each summer day at dusk, in an unprepossessing park surrounded by a parking lot a block off Main Street. At **Robie Swift Park,** a lone chimney (dating from a long-gone dairy plant) rises straight up like a stumpy finger pointed at the heavens. Around sunset, between 25 and 100 chimney swifts flit about and then descend into the chimney for the night.

Grand-Pré National Historic Site Long before roving New Englanders arrived in this region, hardworking Acadians had vastly altered the local landscape. They did this in large part by constructing a series of dikes outfitted with ingenious log valves, which allowed farmers to convert the saltwater marshes to productive farmland. At Grand-Pré, a short drive east of Wolfville and just off Route 1, you can learn about these dikes along with the tragic history of the Acadians, who populated the Minas Basin between 1680 and their expulsion in 1755.

More a memorial park than a living history exhibit, Grand-Pré (which means "great meadow") has superbly tended grounds that are excellent for idling, a picnic lunch, or simple contemplation. Among the handful of buildings on the grounds is a graceful stone church, built in 1922 on the presumed site of the original church. Evangeline Bellefontaine, the revered (albeit fictional) heroine of Longfellow's epic poem, was said to have been born here; look for the statue of this tragic heroine in the garden. It was created in 1920 by Canadian sculptor Philippe Hérbert, and the image has been reproduced widely since.

2241 Grand-Pré Rd. (P.O. Box 150), Grand-Pré B0P 1M0. © 902/542-3631. www.grand-pre.com. Admission C$7.15 (US$7.15/£3.60) adults, C$5.90 (US$5.90/£2.95) seniors, C$3.45 (US$3.45/£1.75) children 6–16, C$18 (US$18/£9) families. Daily mid-May to mid-Oct 9am–6pm. Closed mid-Oct to mid-May.

WHERE TO STAY
Gingerbread House Inn The ornate, brightly painted Gingerbread House Inn was originally the carriage house for the building now housing Victoria's Historic Inn

(see below). A former owner went wood shop wild, adding all manner of swirly accouterments and giving the place a convincingly authentic air. Some have since been updated and modernized with the times; most guest rooms here are now a modern interpretation of the gingerbread style and are quite comfortable, though the two units in the back are darkest and smallest of the lot. Each has its own private exterior entrance, adding to the privacy, and each has its own feel: The airy Gaspereau Suite features luxe touches like a modernistic propane fireplace, interior loft, big-screen television, and huge eight-person hot tub; the Country and Sunrise suites are more gingerbready. Even some of the simpler rooms sport hot tubs. Breakfasts tend toward the elaborate and are served by candlelight.

8 Robie Tufts Dr. (P.O. Box 819), Wolfville, NS B0P 1X0. © 888/542-1458 or 902/542-1458. Fax 902/542-4718. www.gingerbreadhouse.ca. 9 units. May–Oct C$115–C$129 (US$115–US$129/£58–£65) double, C$165–C$199 (US$165–US$199/£83–£100) suite; Nov–Apr C$85–C$119 (US$85–US$119/£43–£60) double, C$130–C$189 (US$130–US$189/£65–£95) suite. Rates include full breakfast. Ask about golf packages. AE, MC, V. No children permitted in suites. **Amenities:** Dining room. *In room:* A/C, TV, DVD, Jacuzzi (some), no phone.

Tattingstone Inn 🐀🐀 "We sell romance and relaxation," says innkeeper Betsey Harwood. And that pretty well sums it up. This handsome Italianate-Georgian mansion, named after one of Harwood's forebears' ancestral town in England, dates from 1874 and overlooks the village's main drag. The inn is furnished with a mix of reproductions and antiques, and traditional and modern art blend well. The attitude isn't as over-the-top Victorian as one might guess by looking at the manse, but instead decorated with a deft touch mixing informal country antiques with regal Empire pieces. The rooms in the Carriage House are a bit smaller than those in the main house, but they are still pleasant and showcase fine examples of modern Canadian art. Inquire about the blue-and-cream Toad Hall room in the carriage house, for instance: There's a living room downstairs with electric fireplace and an exposed-beam ceiling, while upstairs sports a queen bed and two-person Jacuzzi. The spacious semiformal dining room is rather refined, and diners sup amid white tablecloths and stern Doric columns. The heated outdoor pool is a bonus, as is the enclosed sun porch, which captures the lambent, early-evening light to good effect.

620 Main St. (P.O. Box 98), Wolfville, NS B0P 1X0. © 800/565-7696 or 902/542-7696. www.tattingstone.ns.ca. 10 units. July–Oct C$148–C$178 (US$148–US$178/£74–£89) double; Nov–June C$88–C$165 (US$88–US$165/£44–£83) double. AE, MC, V. **Amenities:** Restaurant; outdoor pool; tennis court; steam room. *In room:* A/C, TV/VCR, hair dryer, iron/ironing board, Jacuzzi (some), fireplace (some), no phone.

Victoria's Historic Inn 🐀🐀 Victoria's Historic Inn was constructed by apple mogul William Chase in 1893 and is architecturally elaborate. This sturdy Queen Anne–style building features bold pediments and massed pavilions, which have been adorned with balusters and ornate Stick Style trim. Inside, the effect seems a bit as if you'd wandered into one of those stereoscopic views of a Victorian parlor. Whereas the nearby Tattingstone Inn resists theme decor, Victoria's Historic Inn embraces it (there's a Cranberry Room, a Sunflower Room, a Nautical Room, and so on). There's dense mahogany and cherry woodwork throughout, along with exceptionally intricate ceilings. The deluxe two-room Chase Suite features a large sitting room with a gas fireplace, double Jacuzzi, queen bed, and an oak mantle. The less expensive third-floor rooms are smaller and somewhat less historic in flavor. Several of the inn's suites have fireplaces and Jacuzzis.

600 Main St., Wolfville, NS B4P 1E8. © 800/556-5744 or 902/542-5744. Fax 902/542-7794. www.victoriashistoric inn.com. 15 units. High season C$118–C$245 (US$118–US$245/£59–£123) double; Nov–Mar C$99–C$175 (US$99–US$175/£50–£88) double. Rates include full breakfast. AE, MC, V. **Amenities:** Laundry service. *In room:* A/C, TV/VCR, Jacuzzi (some).

WHERE TO DINE

Acton's Grill and Café ★ (© **902/542-7525**) at 406 Main St. is the best fancy restaurant in town, perfect for lamb, steak, veal, chicken, and local seafood with a French twist; it's open daily for lunch and dinner, year-round. For lower-brow fare, get your java and coffeehouse-culture fix at **The Coffee Merchant & Library Pub,** 472 Main St. (© **902/542-4315**), possibly the hippest place in town. Musicians sometimes show up to gig here, too.

Many of the inns in Wolfville also open their dining rooms at night and serve fancy food to the public, though at prices to match.

Al's Homestyle Café ⟨*Value*⟩ DELI   Randy and Linda Davidson now operate this place in the nearby hamlet of Canning (about 16km/10 miles northwest of Wolfville, on Rte. 358), but Al Waddell's popular recipes for sausages live on—choose from Polish, German, hot Italian, and honey garlic. Buy some links to cook later, or order up a quick road meal. You won't find a better cheap lunch: A sausage on a bun with a cup of soup will run you less than C$5 (US$5/£2.50).

9819 Main St., Canning. © **902/582-7270**. Most selections C$2–C$4 (US$2–US$4/£1–£2). V. Mon–Sat 8am–6pm; Sun 11am–5pm.

3 Annapolis Royal: Nova Scotia's Most Historic Town ★★

197km (122 miles) W of Halifax, 128km (80 miles) NE of Yarmouth

Annapolis Royal is arguably Nova Scotia's most historic town—it even bills itself, with justification, as "Canada's birthplace." The nation's first permanent settlement was established at Port Royal, just across the river from the present-day Annapolis Royal, in 1605 by a group of doughty settlers that included Samuel de Champlain. (Champlain called the beautiful Annapolis Basin "one of the finest harbours that I have seen on all these coasts.") The strategic importance of this well-protected harbor was proven in the tumultuous later years, when a series of forts was constructed on the low hills overlooking the water.

Annapolis Royal today is truly a treat to visit. Because the region was largely overlooked by later economic growth (trade and fishing moved to the Atlantic side of the peninsula), it requires little in the way of imagination to see Annapolis Royal as it once was. (The current population is just 700.) The original settlement was rebuilt on the presumed site. Fort Anne overlooks the upper reaches of the basin, much as it did when abandoned in 1854. And the village itself maintains much of its original historic charm, with narrow streets and historic buildings fronting the now-placid waterfront.

ESSENTIALS

GETTING THERE   Annapolis is located at Exit 22 of Route 101. It is 200km (124 miles) from Halifax, and 129km (80 miles) from Yarmouth.

VISITOR INFORMATION   The **Annapolis District Tourist Bureau** (© **902/ 532-5454**) is 1km (½ mile) north of the town center (follow Prince Albert Rd. and look for the Annapolis Royal Tidal Generating Station). It's open daily in summer 8am to 8pm, and 10am to 6pm in spring and fall.

EXPLORING THE TOWN

Start at the tourist bureau, which is located at the **Annapolis Royal Tidal Power Project** (© **902/532-5454**), where the extreme fall in the tides has been harnessed since

---

Moments **Sunset at Fort Anne**

A good strategy for visiting the fort is to come during the day to tour the museum and get a feel for the lay of the land. Then return for the evening sunset, long after the bus tours have departed, to walk the **Perimeter Trail** ✪ with its river and valley vistas.

1984 to produce electricity for the area in a generating station. Before leaving the center, be sure to request a copy of the free "Footprints with Footnotes" walking-tour brochure. Take a moment to note that as you walk down lower St. George Street, you're walking down the oldest street in Canada.

Children and adults alike adore the **Upper Clements Parks** ✪ (© **888/248-4567** or 902/532-7557; www.upperclementsparks.com) on Route 1, about 5 minutes south of Annapolis Royal. This is a wonderfully old-fashioned amusement park (you arrive after driving through an old orchard). It's full of low-key amusements and attractions that will especially delight younger kids. It's open daily in season from 11am to 7pm.

Fort Anne National Historic Site ✪   What you'll likely remember most from a visit here are the impressive grassy earthworks that cover some 14 hectares (35 acres) of high ground overlooking the confluence of the Annapolis River and Allains Creek. The French built the first fort here around 1643. Since then, dozens of buildings and fortifications have occupied this site. You can visit the 1708 gunpowder magazine (the oldest building of any Canadian National Historic Site), then peruse the museum located in the 1797 British field officer's quarters. The model of the site as it appeared in 1710 is particularly intriguing. If you find all the history a bit tedious, ask a guide for a croquet set and practice your technique on the lush rolling lawns.

Entrance on St. George St. © 902/532-2397. Admission C$3.95 (US$3.95/£2) adults, C$3.50 (US$3.50/£1.75) seniors, C$1.95 (US$1.95/£1) children, C$9.90 (US$9.90/£4.95) families. May 15–Oct 15 9am–6pm; off season by appointment only (grounds open year-round).

Historic Gardens ✪   You don't need to be a flower nut to enjoy an hour or two at these exceptional gardens. The 4-hectare (10-acre) grounds are uncommonly beautiful, with a mix of formal and informal gardens dating from varied epochs. Set on a gentle hill, the plantings overlook a beautiful salt marsh (now diked and farmed), and they include a geometric Victorian garden, a knot garden, a rock garden, and a colorful perennial border garden. Rose fanciers should allow plenty of time—some 2,000 rose bushes track the history of rose cultivation from the earliest days through the Victorian era to the present day. A garden cafe offers an enticing spot for lunch.

441 St. George St. © 902/532-7018. www.historicgardens.com. Admission C$8.50 (US$8.50/£4.25) adults, C$7.50 (US$7.50/£3.75) seniors and students, C$23 (US$23/£11) families. July–Aug daily 8am–dusk, spring and fall daily 9am–5pm. Closed Nov–Apr.

Port-Royal National Historic Site ✪   Canada's first permanent settlement, Port-Royal was located on an attractive point with sweeping views of the Annapolis Basin. After spending the dreadful winter of 1604 on an island in the St. Croix River (along the current Maine–New Brunswick border), the survivors moved to this better-protected location. Settlers lived here for 8 years in a high style that approached decadent given the harsh surroundings. Many of the handsome, compact, French-style farmhouse buildings were designed by Samuel de Champlain to re-create the comfort they might have enjoyed at home. Although the original settlement was abandoned and eventually destroyed, this 1939 re-creation is convincing in all the details. You'll find a handful of costumed interpreters engaged in traditional handicrafts like woodworking, and they're happy to fill you in on life in the colony during those difficult early years, an "age of innocence" when the French first forged an alliance with local Natives. Allow 1 or 2 hours to wander and explore.

10km (6 miles) south of Rte. 1, Granville Ferry (turn left shortly after passing the tidal generating station). ℂ 902/ 532-2898. Admission C$3.95 (US$3.95/£2) adults, C$3.50 (US$3.50/£1.75) seniors, C$1.95 (US$1.95/£1) children, C$9.90 (US$9.90/£4.95) families. May 15–Oct 15 daily 9am–6pm. Closed Oct 16–May 14.

WHERE TO STAY

Garrison House Inn ★   The historic Garrison House sits across from Fort Anne in the town center and has bedded and fed guests since it first opened to accommodate officers at Fort Anne (which sits right across the road) in 1854. The rooms are nicely appointed with antiques, some worn, some pristine. There's no air-conditioning but fans are provided; the top floor can still get a bit stuffy on warm days. Room no. 2 is appealing, with wide pine floors, braided rug, and wing-back chairs, though it faces the street and at times can be a bit noisy. Room no. 7 is tucked in the back of the house, away from the hubbub of St. George Street, and it has two skylights and a big demilune window to let in the wonderfully dappled light. In addition to the restaurant (see below), there's a screened-in veranda with food (fish and lobster, mostly) and drink service. Note that there are no phones, which could be a blessing.

350 St. George St., Annapolis Royal, NS B0S 1A0. ℂ 866/532-5750 or 902/532-5750. Fax 902/532-5501. www. garrisonhouse.ca. 7 units. May–Nov C$69–C$149 (US$69–US$149/£35–£75) double; call in advance for weekends rest of year. AE, MC, V. Street parking. **Amenities:** Restaurant; bar. *In room:* AC, TV/DVD, no phone , Jacuzzi (1 unit).

King George Inn ★ *Kids*   The handsome King George Inn was built as a sea captain's mansion in 1868, and served a stint as a rectory before becoming an inn. It's befittingly busy and cluttered for its era; guest rooms are furnished entirely with antiques, most of the country Victorian ilk. Think commodes, bowls and pitchers, rocking chairs, Oriental rugs, and Tara-worthy lamps. (Those who prefer clean lines might find a surplus of decor and frippery here.) Most rooms have queen-size beds— ask if you want a king or twins—and the two family suites have separate bedrooms and a bathroom that's shared between them. The best in the house might be room no. 7, the Duchess of Kent suite, with its Jacuzzi and small private deck off the back of the house overlooking the garden. A second Jacuzzi room was added in 2001, in the Queen Victoria suite, which also has a king bed, bay window, and gigantic headboard (if you're into that). The inn also features a pump organ and a 19th-century grand piano, and helpfully provides bikes for guests.

548 Upper St. George St., Annapolis Royal, NS B0S 1A0. ℂ 888/799-5464 or 902/532-5286. Fax 902/532-0144. www.kinggeorgeinn.com. 8 units. C$80–C$160 (US$80–US$160/£40–£80) double. MC, V. Closed Jan–Apr. **Amenities:** Bikes. *In room:* A/C, coffeemaker, hair dryer, no phone.

Queen Anne Inn ★   This Second Empire mansion, built in 1865, looks like the city hall of a small city. You won't miss it driving into town. Like the Hillsdale House across the street, the Queen Anne (built for the sister of the Hillsdale's owner) has benefited from a preservation-minded owner, who restored the Victorian detailing to its former luster. There's a zebra-striped dining-room floor (alternating planks of oak and maple) and a grand central staircase. The guest rooms are quite elegant and furnished appropriately to the Victorian era, although have been updated to include Jacuzzis.

With their towering elms, the parklike grounds are shady and inviting. Breakfast is a three-course affair.

494 St. George St., Annapolis Royal, NS B0S 1A0. © **877/536-0403** or 902/532-7850. Fax 902/532-2078. www.queen anneinn.ns.ca. 12 units. May–June C$99–C$169 (US$99–US$169/£50–£85) double; July–Oct C$119–C$209 (US$119–US$209/£60–£105) double. Rates include full breakfast. MC, V. Closed Nov–Apr. *In room:* TV, no phone.

WHERE TO DINE

For a more relaxed bite than the choice described below, swing by **Ye Olde Town Pub** (© **902/532-2244**) at 9 Church St. Housed in an 1884 brick building that was once a bank (hence the bars on the windows), it's said to be the smallest pub in Nova Scotia—not only now, but in the history of the province. It's open daily from 11am to 11pm most days. There's beer, an all-day-open kitchen, and a kids' menu.

Garrison House ✿✿ ECLECTIC The Garrison House is the most intimate and attractive of the village's restaurants. The three cozy dining rooms in this historic home each have a different feel, some with colonial colors, some contemporary, most with black Windsor chairs and modern piscine art. (My favorite room is the one with the green floors and the humpback whale.) The menu is also tricky to categorize, with yummy starters such as house-cured salmon with flatbread, Acadian seafood chowder, mussels steeped in wine, and a Thai shrimp soup, and entrees ranging from jambalaya, shrimp and chicken in a Vietnamese curry over basmati rice, or salmon with a bourbon-maple glaze to Digby scallops or a simple pasta with seafood or garden vegetables. There are Jamaican influences in the cooking, as well.

350 St. George St. (inside the Garrison House Inn). © **902/532-5750.** Reservations recommended in summer. Main courses C$14–C$27 (US$14–US$27/£7–£14). AE, MC, V. May–Oct daily 5:30–8:30pm; open by arrangement in off season.

4 Kejimkujik National Park ✿

About 45km (28 miles) southeast of Annapolis Royal is a popular national park that's a world apart from coastal Nova Scotia. Kejimkujik National Park, founded in 1968, is located in the heart of southcentral Nova Scotia, and it is to lakes and bogs what the south coast is to fishing villages and fog. Bear and moose are the full-time residents here; park visitors are the transients. The park, which was largely scooped and shaped during the last glacial epoch, is about 20% water, which makes it especially popular with canoeists. A few trails also weave through the park, but hiking is limited; the longest hike in the park can be done in 2 hours. Bird-watchers are also drawn to the park in search of the 205 species that have been seen both here and at the seaside adjunct of the park, a 22-sq.-km (8.5-sq.-mile) coastal holding west of Liverpool. Among the more commonly seen species are pileated woodpeckers and loons, and at night you can listen for the raspy call of the barred owl.

ESSENTIALS

GETTING THERE Kejimkujik National Park is approximately midway on Kejimkujik Scenic Drive (Rte. 8), which extends 115km (71 miles) between Annapolis Royal and Liverpool. The village of Maitland Bridge (pop. 130) is near the park's entrance. Plan on about 2 hours' drive from Halifax.

VISITOR INFORMATION The park's **visitor center** (© **902/682-2772**) is open daily and features slide programs and exhibits about the park's natural history.

FEES The park opens daily at 8am year-round, though the visitor center cuts its hours substantially, closing at 4pm instead of 8pm, between Labour Day and mid-June. Fees are C$5.45 (US$5.45/£2.75) for adults, C$4.70 (US$4.70/£2.35) for seniors, C$2.70 (US$2.70/£1.35) ages 6 to 16, and C$14 (US$14/£7) for families. Seasonal passes can cut the cost of a longer stay; they cost C$27 (US$27/£14) adults, C$24 (US$24/£12) seniors, C$14 (US$14/£7) children ages 6 to 16, and C$68 (US$68/£34) for families.

EXPLORING THE PARK

The park's 381 sq. km (147 sq. miles) of forest, lake, and bog are peaceful and remote. Part of what makes the terrain so appealing is the lack of access by car. One short, forked park road from Route 8 gets you partway into the park. Then you need to continue by foot or canoe. A stop at the visitor center is worthwhile, both for the exhibits on the region's natural history and for a preliminary walk on one of the three short trails. The Beech Grove loop (2km/1.3 miles) takes you around a glacial hill called a drumlin. The park has a taped walking tour available for use; ask at the information center.

Canoeing is the optimal means of traversing the park. Bring your own, or rent a canoe at **Jake's Landing** (3km/2 miles along the park access road) for C$7.50 (US$7.50/£3.75) per hour or C$28 (US$28/£14) per day. Similar rates apply to rentals of bikes, paddleboats, kayaks, and rowboats. Canoeists can cobble together wilderness excursions from one lake to the other, some involving slight portaging. Multiday trips are easily arranged to backcountry campsites and are the best way to get to know the park. Canoe route maps are provided at the visitor center. Rangers also lead short, guided canoe trips for novices.

The park also has 15 **walking trails,** ranging from short easy strolls to, well, longer easy strolls. (There's no elevation gain to speak of.) The 6km (4-mile) **Hemlocks and Hardwoods Trail** loops through stately groves of 300-year-old hemlocks; the 3km (1.8-mile) **Merrymakedge Beach Trail** skirts a lakeshore to end at a beach. A free map that describes the trails is available at the visitor center.

CAMPING

Backcountry camping is the park's chief draw. The canoe-in and hike-in sites are assigned individually, which means you needn't worry about noisy neighbors playing loud music on their car stereo. Backcountry rangers keep the sites in top shape, and each is stocked with firewood for the night (the wood is included in the campsite fee). Most sites can handle a maximum of six campers. Naturally, there's high demand for the best sites; you're better off here midweek, when fewer weekenders are down from Halifax. You can also reserve backcountry sites (C$23/US$23/£12 per site) up to 60 days in advance for an additional fee; call the **visitor center** (© 902/682-2772).

The park's drive-in campground at **Jeremy's Bay** ⊛ offers about 360 sites, a few quite close to the water's edge. Campground rates are C$18 to C$25 (US$18–US$25/£9–£13) per night. Starting early every April reservations at the drive-in campground may be made for an additional fee by calling © **877/RESERVE** or online at the website www.pccamping.ca.

---

5 From Digby to Yarmouth: A Taste of the Other Nova Scotia

Two towns serving as gateways to Nova Scotia bracket this 113km (70-mile) stretch of coast. Whereas the South Shore—the stretch between Yarmouth and Halifax—serves to confirm popular conceptions of Nova Scotia (small fishing villages, shingled homes), the Digby-to-Yarmouth route seems determined to confound them. Look for Acadian enclaves, fishing villages with more corrugated steel than weathered shingle, miles of sandy beaches, and spruce-topped basalt cliffs that seem transplanted from Labrador.

DIGBY & DIGBY NECK

The unassuming port town of **Digby** is located on the water at Digby Gap—where the Annapolis River finally forces an egress through the North Mountain coastal range. Set at the south end of the broad watery expanse of the Annapolis Basin, Digby is home to the world's largest inshore scallop fleet, which drags the ocean bottom for tasty and succulent Digby scallops. The town is an active community where life centers around fishing boats, neighborhoods of wood-frame houses, and no-frills seafood restaurants. It also serves as Nova Scotia's gateway for those arriving from Saint John, New Brunswick, via ferry. The ferry terminal is on Route 303 west of Digby.

Digby Neck is a long, bony finger of high ridges, spongy bogs, dense forest, and expansive ocean views. The last two knuckles of this narrow peninsula are islands, both of which are connected via 10-minute ferries across straits swept with currents as strong as 9 knots. Although neither the neck nor the islands have much in the way of services for tourists, it's worth the drive if you're a connoisseur of end-of-the-world remoteness. The town of **Sandy Cove** on the mainland is picture perfect, with its three prominent church steeples rising from the forest. **Tiverton** on Long Island and Westport on **Brier Island** are unadorned fishing villages, and bird-watching on the island is excellent.

ESSENTIALS

GETTING THERE Digby is Nova Scotia's gateway for those arriving from Saint John via ferry. The ferry terminal is on Route 303 west of Digby. If you're arriving by ferry and want to visit the town, watch for signs directing you downtown from the bypass. From other parts of Nova Scotia, Digby is accessible via Exit 26 off Route 101.

Route 217 runs 72km (45 miles) south from Digby to Brier Island. Two **ferries** fill in when you run out of mainland. Ferries leave East Ferry (about a 45-min. drive from Digby) on the mainland for Long Island every hour on the half-hour; they depart from Long Island for Brier Island on the hour. Then you take another ferry from Long Island to Brier Island. Fares are C$4 (US$4/£2) per car round-trip on each ferry; fares are collected on the outbound leg only.

VISITOR INFORMATION The province maintains a **visitor information center** (© 902/245-2201) in Digby on Route 303 (on your right shortly after you disembark from the Saint John ferry). It's open April through November. There's also the municipal Visitor Information Centre located on the harbor at 110 Montague Row. It's open daily 8:30am to 8:30pm May through mid-October, and daily 9am to 5pm during spring and fall.

A seasonal **information booth** (© 902/839-2853) is located at the local historical museum in Tiverton on Long Island. It's supposedly open from 9am to 7:30pm in July and August, though hours are sometimes more erratic than that.

EXPLORING DIGBY NECK

Brier Island offers an ideal destination for mountain bikers. Maps are available free at island stores and lodges. If you park your car on the Long Island side and take your bike over on the ferry, you'll save money; there's no charge for bikes or pedestrians. Bike rentals are available at **Backstreet Bicycles** in Digby (© 902/245-1989).

Whale-Watching at Digby Neck ⊛

In the Bay of Fundy, ocean currents mingle and the vigorous tides cause upwelling, which brings a rich assortment of plankton to the surface. That makes it an all-you-can-eat buffet for **whales,** which feed on these minuscule bits of plant and animal. The number of fishermen offering whale-watching tours has boomed.

Right, sperm, blue, and pilot whales, along with the seldom-seen orcas, have all been spotted over the years. Plan on spending around C$35 to C$45 (US$35–US$45/£18–£23) per adult for a 3- to 4-hour cruise, less for children. **Mariner Cruises** (ⓒ **800/239-2189** or 902/839-2346) in Westport on Brier Island sails aboard the 14m (45-ft.) *Chad and Sisters Two,* which is equipped with a heated cabin. Both whale- and bird-watching tours are offered. **Pirate's Cove Whale & Seabird Cruises** (ⓒ **888/480-0004** or 902/839-2242), located in Tiverton, has been leading offshore cruises since 1990; several tours are offered daily aboard the 13m (42-ft.) vessels *Fundy Cruiser* and *Fundy Voyager.* **Petite Passage Whale Watch** (ⓒ **902/834-2226**) sails out of East Ferry aboard the 14m (45-ft.), 45-passenger *Passage Provider 04* and has a partially covered deck. It runs two to three cruises daily from June to October.

For a saltier adventure, **Ocean Explorations** (ⓒ **877/654-2341** or 902/839-2417) offers tours on rigid-hulled inflatable Zodiacs. The largest boat holds up to a dozen passengers and moves with tremendous speed and dampness through the fast currents and frequent chop around the islands and the open bay; guests are provided with survival suits for warmth and safety. The 2- to 3-hour trips cost C$55 (US$55/£28) per adult, less for children, seniors, students, and group members.

On Long Island, two short but rewarding woodland hikes take you to open vistas of St. Mary's Bay and the Bay of Fundy. The trail head for the half-mile hike to **Balancing Rock** is 4km (2½ miles) south of the Tiverton ferry on Route 217; look for the well-marked parking area on the left. A series of boardwalks leads you over the surging ocean to get a dead-on view of the tall column of basalt balancing improbably atop another column. For another short hike, return to the parking lot and drive 5km (3 miles) south to the picnic area on the right. From the parking lot atop the hill, a hike of 1km (.5 mile) descends gradually through a forest of moss, ferns, and roots to the remote Fundy shore.

Farther along, **Brier Island** is laced with **hiking trails** ⊛, offering fantastic opportunities for seaside exploration. A good place to start is the Grand Passage Lighthouse (turn right after disembarking the ferry).

WHERE TO STAY & DINE

Brier Island Lodge ⊛ *Finds*   Built to jump-start local eco-tourism, the Brier Island Lodge has a rustic-modern motif, with log-cabin construction and soaring glass windows overlooking the Grand Passage 40m (131 ft.) below. The rooms on two floors all have great views, the usual motel amenities, and some unexpected touches (double

Jacuzzis in the pricier rooms). A well-regarded dining room serves up traditional favorites, and local fishermen congregate in an airy lounge in the evening to play cards and watch the satellite TV. There's a small but good selection of field guides near the upholstered chairs in the corner of the lounge; hiking trails connect directly from the lodge to the Fundy shore.

Westport, Brier Island. (℃) **800/662-8355** or 902/839-2300. Fax 902/839-2006. www.brierisland.com. 40 units. C$60–C$139 (US$60–US$139/£30–£70) double. MC, V. **Amenities:** Bike rental; game room. *In room:* A/C, TV, Jacuzzi (4 rooms).

Digby Pines Golf Resort and Spa ☆☆
Digby Pines is actually located in the town of Digby, and is situated on 120 hectares (300 acres) with marvelous views of the Annapolis Basin. The resort is redolent of an earlier era when old money headed to fashionable resorts for an entire summer. Built in 1929 in a Norman château style, the inn today is owned and operated by the province of Nova Scotia, and it should silence those who believe that government can't do anything right. The imposing building of stucco and stone is surrounded by the eponymous pines, which rustle softly in the wind. Throughout, the emphasis is more on comfort than historical verisimilitude, although the gracious lobby features old-world touches like Corinthian capitals, floral couches, and parquet floors. The guest rooms vary slightly as to size and views (ask for a waterview room; there's no extra charge), and all now have ceiling fans or air-conditioning. The cottages have one to three bedrooms and most feature fireplaces and air-conditioning. An Aveda spa offers a full menu of treatments and services, and an 18-hole Stanley Thompson–designed golf course threads its way through pines and over a babbling brook.

Shore Rd., P.O. Box 70, Digby, NS B0V 1A0. (℃) **800/667-4637** or 902/245-2511. Fax 902/245-6133. www.digby pines.ca. 84 units, 30 cottages. From C$160–C$325 (US$160–US$325/£80–£163) double. AE, DC, DISC, MC, V. Closed mid-Oct to mid-May. **Amenities:** Restaurant; bar; heated outdoor pool; golf course; 2 tennis courts; health club; spa; sauna; bike rentals; children's center; concierge; tour desk; courtesy car; babysitting; dry cleaning; laundry service. *In room:* A/C (cottages only), TV, dataport, coffeemaker.

YARMOUTH

The constant lament of Yarmouth restaurateurs and shopkeepers is this: The summer tourists who steadily stream off the incoming ferries rarely linger long enough to appreciate the city before they mash the accelerator and speed off to higher-marquee venues along the coast. There might be a reason for that. Yarmouth is a pleasant burg that offers some noteworthy historic architecture dating from the golden age of seafaring. But the town's not terribly unique, and thus not high on the list of places to spend a few days. It has more the flavor of a handy pit stop than a destination, though recent redevelopment efforts have spruced up the waterfront a bit and added evening entertainment during the summer months, a very welcome sign.

ESSENTIALS
GETTING THERE   Yarmouth is at the convergence of two of the province's principal highways, Route 101 and Route 103. It's approximately 300km (180 miles) from Halifax. Yarmouth is the gateway for ferries connecting to Bar Harbor, Maine.

VISITOR INFORMATION   The **Yarmouth Visitor Centre** ((℃) **902/742-6639** or 902/742-5033) is at 228 Main St., just up the hill from the ferry in a modern, shingled building you simply can't miss. Both provincial and municipal tourist offices are located here, open mid-May through late October daily from about 8am to 7pm.

EXPLORING THE TOWN

The tourist bureau and the local historical society publish a very informative walking tour brochure covering downtown Yarmouth. It's well worth requesting at the **Yarmouth Visitor Centre** (see above). The guide offers general tips on what to look for in local architectural styles (how do you tell the difference between Georgian and Classic Revival?), as well as brief histories of significant buildings. The whole tour is 4km (2½ miles) long.

The most scenic side trip—and an ideal excursion by bike or car—is to **Cape Forchu** and the **Yarmouth Light** ⨀. Head west on Main Street (Rte. 1) for 2km (1¼ miles) from the visitor center, then turn left at the horse statue. The road winds picturesquely out to the cape, past seawalls and working lobster wharves, meadows, and old homes. When the road finally ends, you'll be at the red-and-white-striped concrete lighthouse that marks the harbor's entrance. Leave enough time to ramble around the dramatic rock-and-grass bluffs—part of Leif Eriksson Picnic Park—that surround the lighthouse; don't miss the short trail out to the point below the light, either.

Firefighters' Museum of Nova Scotia (Kids)

This two-story museum will appeal mostly to confirmed fire buffs, historians, and impressionable young children. The museum is home to a varied collection of early firefighting equipment, with hand-drawn pumpers the centerpiece of the collection: Kids love the 1933-vintage Chev Bickle Pumper (yes, that's its real name), where they can don helmets and take the wheel. Also showcased here are uniforms, badges, helmets, and pennants. Look for the photos of notable Nova Scotian fires (i.e., "Hot Shots").

451 Main St. © 902/742-5525. Admission C$3 (US$3/£1.50) adults, C$2.50 (US$2.50/£1.25) seniors, C$1.50 (US$1.50/75p) children, C$6 (US$6/£3) families. July–Aug Mon–Sat 9am–9pm, Sun 10am–5pm; June and Sept Mon–Sat 9am–5pm; Oct–May Mon–Fri 9am–4pm, Sat 1–4pm.

WHERE TO STAY

Yarmouth is also home to a number of chain motels, mostly on Main Street.

Harbour's Edge B&B ⨀ (Finds)

Now this is truth in advertising: This exceptionally attractive early Victorian home (1864) sits on a quiet hectare (2 acres) and 76m (250 ft.) of harbor frontage, changing the scenery twice per day with the tides. This was the very first parcel of land in Yarmouth to be owned by a Caucasian, but before that local Native Canadians had camped and fished here. Today you can lounge on the lawn watching herons, hawks, and kingfishers below. It's hard to believe you're just a few minutes from the international ferry terminal. The inn opened in 1997 after 3 years of intensive restoration, and the rooms are lightly furnished, which nicely highlights the architectural integrity of the design. All four rooms sport high ceilings and handsome spruce floors. The attractive Audrey Kenney Room is biggest, but the Clara Caie has better views of the harbor, even if the private bathroom and its claw-foot tub are down the hall. The Georgie Allen has a private hallway and clear harbor view, as well. You'll feel safe here, too: One of the innkeepers is a Royal Mountie (in other words, a Canadian cop).

12 Vancouver St., Yarmouth, NS B5A 2N8. © 902/742-2387. www.harboursedge.ns.ca. 4 units. C$125–C$140 (US$125–US$140/£63–£70) double. Rates include full breakfast. MC, V. Head toward Cape Forchu; watch for the inn shortly after turning at the horse statue. *In room:* Iron/ironing board, no phone.

Lakelawn Motel

The clean, well-kept Lakelawn Motel offers basic motel rooms done up in freshened bluish colors, newer carpeting, and so forth very close to the ferry landing. It's been a downtown Yarmouth mainstay since the 1950s, when the centerpiece Victorian house (where the office is located) was moved back from the road to make room for the motel wings. Looking for something a bit cozier? The house also has four B&B-style guest rooms upstairs, each furnished simply with antiques. Breakfast, however, costs extra.

641 Main St., Yarmouth, NS B5A 1K2. ℂ 877/664-0664 or 902/742-3588. www.lakelawnmotel.com. 34 units. C$59–C$99 (US$59–US$99/£30–£50) double. Meals available. AE, DC, DISC, MC, V. Closed Nov–Apr. *In room:* TV, no phone (some units).

WHERE TO DINE

Quick-N-Tasty *(Kids)* SEAFOOD   The name about says it all. This country-cooking joint a mile or two from the incoming ferries from Maine has long been a hit with locals. The restaurant is adorned with the sort of paneling that was au courant in the 1970s, and meals are likewise old-fashioned and generous. The emphasis here is on seafood; you can order fish either fried or broiled, but go for the hot open-faced lobster club sandwich—it's gaining international foodie acclaim. The seafood casserole and the blueberry desserts are also notable.

Rte. 1, Dayton (from downtown Yarmouth, follow Rte. 3 east to Rte. 3). ℂ 902/742-6606. Sandwiches C$3–C$12 (US$3–US$12/£1.50–£6); main courses C$7–C$18 (US$7–US$18/£3.50–£9). AE, DC, MC, V. Daily 11am–8pm (winter until 7:30pm). Closed mid-Dec to Feb. Original location just east of Yarmouth on the north side of Rte. 1; 2nd location across from ferry terminal.

Rudder's Seafood Restaurant & Brewpub *(★)* BREWPUB   Yarmouth's first (and Nova Scotia's fourth) brewpub opened in 1997 on the newly spiffed-up waterfront. It occupies an old warehouse dating from the mid-1800s, and you can see the wear and tear of the decades on the battered floor and the stout beams and rafters. The place has been nicely spruced up, and the menu features creative pub fare, with additions including Acadian and Cajun specialties such as rappie pie, and jambalaya, as well as lobster suppers and planked salmon. The steaks are quite good, as is the beer, especially the best bitter. In summer, there's outdoor seating on a deck with a view of the harbor across the parking lot.

96 Water St. ℂ 902/742-7311. Sandwiches C$4–C$11 (US$4–US$11/£2–£5.50); entrees C$10–C$24 (US$10–US$24/£5–£12). AE, DC, MC, V. Mid-Apr to mid-Oct daily 11am–11pm (shorter hours spring and fall). Closed mid-Oct to mid-Apr.

6 The South Shore: Quintessential Nova Scotia *(★★★)*

The Atlantic coast between Yarmouth and Halifax is that quaint, maritime Nova Scotia you see on laminated place mats and calendars. It's all lighthouses and weathered, shingled buildings perched at the rocky edge of the sea, as if tenuously trespassing on the ocean's good graces. But as rustic and beautiful as this area is, you might find it a bit stultifying to visit every quaint village along the entire coastline—involving about 340km (211 miles) of twisting road along the water's edge. If your heart is set on exploring this fabled landscape, be sure to leave enough time to poke in all the nooks and crannies along this stretch of the coast—towns such as Lunenburg, Mahone Bay, and Peggy's Cove are well worth the time.

SHELBURNE

Shelburne is a historic town with an unimpeachable pedigree. Settled in 1783 by United Empire Loyalists fleeing New England after the unfortunate outcome of the late war, the town swelled with newcomers and by 1784 was believed to have a population of 10,000—larger than Montréal, Halifax, or Québec. With the decline of

> **Tips A Fog Alert**
>
> In addition to the scenic considerations, it's sensible to allow more time on the South Shore for a practical reason—fog. When the cool waters of the arctic currents mix with warm summer air over land, the results are predictable and soupy. The fog certainly adds atmosphere. It also can slow driving to a crawl.

boat building and fishing in this century, the town edged into that dim economic twilight familiar to other seaside villages (it now has a population of about 3,000), and the waterfront began to deteriorate, despite valiant preservation efforts.

And then Hollywood came calling. In 1992, the film *Mary Silliman's War* was filmed here. Two years later, director Roland Joffe arrived to film the spectacularly miscast *Scarlet Letter,* starring Demi Moore, Gary Oldman, and Robert Duvall. When the crew departed, it left behind three buildings and an impressive shingled steeple you can see from all over town. Among the "new old" buildings is the waterfront cooperage across from the Cooper's Inn. Today, barrel makers painstakingly make and sell traditional handcrafted wooden barrels in what amounts to a souvenir of a notable Hollywood flop.

ESSENTIALS

GETTING THERE   Shelburne is 216km (134 miles) southwest of Halifax on Route 3. It's a short hop from Route 103 via either Exit 25 (southbound) or Exit 26 (northbound).

VISITOR INFORMATION   The **Shelburne Tourist Bureau** (© **902/875-4547**) is located in a tidy waterfront building at the corner of King and Dock streets. It's open daily mid-May through October; hours are 9am to 8pm during peak season, 10am to 6pm off season.

EXPLORING SHELBURNE

The central historic district runs along the waterfront, where you can see legitimately old buildings, Hollywood fakes (see above), and spectacular views of the harbor from small, grassy parks. A block inland from the water is Shelburne's more commercial stretch, where you can find services that include banks, shops, and a wonderful bakery (see "Where to Dine," below).

Shelburne Historic Complex ⭐ *Kids*   The historic complex is an association of four local museums located within steps of one another. The most engaging is the **Dory Shop Museum,** right on the waterfront. On the first floor you can admire examples of the simple, elegant boats (said to be invented in Shelburne) and view videos about the late Sidney Mahaney, a master builder who worked in this shop from the time he was 17 until he was 96. Then head upstairs, where all the banging is going on. While you're there, ask about the difference between a Shelburne dory and a Lunenburg dory.

The **Shelburne County Museum** features a potpourri of locally significant artifacts from the town's Loyalist past. Most intriguing is the 1740 fire pumper; it was made in London and imported here in 1783. Behind the museum is the austerely handsome **Ross-Thomson House,** built in 1784 through 1785. The first floor contains a general store as it might have looked in 1784, with bolts of cloth and cast-iron teakettles.

Upstairs is a militia room with displays of antique and reproduction weaponry. The fourth museum, the **Muir-Cox Shipyard** and its Interpretive Centre, was added most recently and features, as you might guess, maritime displays of barks, sailboats, yachts, and more.

Dock St. (P.O. Box 39), Shelburne, NS B0T 1W0. (✆ **902/875-3141**. Admission to all 4 museums C$8 (US$8/£4) adults, free for children under 16; individual museums C$3 (US$3/£1.50) adults, free for children under 16. June to mid-Oct daily 9:30am–5:30pm. Closed mid-Oct to May (Dory Shop closes end of Sept).

WHERE TO STAY

Just across the harbor from Shelburne is **The Islands Provincial Park** (✆ **902/875-4304**), which offers 64 campsites on 193 hectares (477 acres) from mid-May to early September. Some are right on the water and have great views of the historic village across the way. There are no hookups for RVs. The sites cost C$19 (US$19/£9.50) apiece.

The Cooper's Inn ★★ *Finds*   Located facing the harbor in the Dock Street historic area, the impeccably historic Cooper's Inn was originally built by Loyalist merchant George Gracie in 1785. Subsequent additions and updates have been historically sympathetic. The downstairs sitting and dining rooms set the mood nicely, with worn wood floors, muted wall colors (mustard and khaki green), and classical music in the background. The rooms in the main building mostly feature painted wood floors (they're carpeted in the cooper-shop annex), and they are decorated in a comfortably historic-country style. The third-floor suite features wonderful detailing, two sleeping alcoves, and harbor views. It's worth stretching your budget for. The George Gracie Room has a four-poster bed and water view; the small Roderick Morrison Room has a wonderful claw-foot tub perfect for a late-evening soak; and the Harbour Suite features a harbor-view tub and massage chair. The two small, elegant **dining rooms** ★★ here serve the best meals in town.

36 Dock St., Shelburne, NS B0T 1W0. (✆ **800/688-2011** or 902/875-4656. Fax 902/875-4656. www.thecoopersinn. com. 7 units. C$100–C$185 (US$100–US$185/£50–£93) double. Rates include full breakfast. MC, V. **Amenities:** 2 dining rooms. *In room:* TV/VCR, kitchenette (1 unit), coffeemaker (most units), hair dryer.

WHERE TO DINE

For a full dinner out, see the Cooper's Inn, above.

Mr. Fish ★ *Value* SEAFOOD   You can't miss this little fried-fish stand on the side of busy Route 3, near a shopping center; what the place lacks in location, it more than makes up for in character and good simple seafood. The matronly line cooks fry up messes of haddock, scallops, and shrimp, perfectly jacketed in light crusts. As if that weren't good enough, they then dole out great fries and crunchy coleslaw on the side—plus a smile. You eat outside on the picnic tables (but watch out for bees); if it's raining, you'll have to eat in your car.

104 King St. (Rte. 3, north of town center). (✆ **902/875-3474**. Meals C$2.60–C$13 (US$2.60–US$13/£1.30–£6.50). V. Mon–Sat 10am–7pm (Fri and holidays until 9pm); Sun noon–7pm.

Shelburne Café ★ *Value* BAKERY/CAFE   When a family of German chefs set about to open the Shelburne Pastry shop in 1995, the idea was to sell fancy pastries. But everyone who stopped by during the restoration of the Water Street building asked whether they would be selling bread. So they added bread. And today their loaves are among the best you'll taste in the province—especially the delectable Nova Scotian oatmeal brown bread. Though the place is under new ownership, it still offers great pastries (try the pinwheels) as well as satisfying sandwiches and filling meals from an expanding menu that might include seafood entrees such as almond-crusted salmon or poached haddock with a dill-wine sauce, lobster crepes and sandwiches, and seafood pastas. Everything is made from scratch, and everything (except the marked-down day-old goods) is just-baked fresh. Soft-serve ice cream and macaroons are two more new additions. You'll get good value for your loonies here.

171 Water St. © 902/875-1164. Sandwiches C$3.50–C$4.25 (US$3.50–US$4.25/£1.75–£2.15); main courses C$8–C$17 (US$8–US$17/£4–£8.50). V. Mon–Fri 8am–7pm.

LUNENBURG ✸✸

Lunenburg is one of Nova Scotia's most historic and appealing villages, a fact recognized in 1995 when UNESCO declared the old downtown a World Heritage Site. The town was first settled in 1753, primarily by German, Swiss, and French colonists. It was laid out on the "model town" plan then in vogue (Savannah, Georgia, and Philadelphia, Pennsylvania, were also set out along these lines), which meant seven north-south streets intersected by nine east-west streets. Such a plan worked quite well in the coastal plains. Lunenburg, however, is located on a harbor flanked by steep hills, and implementers of the model town plan saw no reason to bend around these. As a result, some of the streets can be exhausting to walk.

About 70% of the downtown buildings date from the 18th and 19th centuries, and many of these are possessed of a distinctive style and are painted in bright colors. Looming over all is the architecturally unique Lunenburg Academy, with its exaggerated mansard roof, pointy towers, and extravagant use of ornamental brackets. It sets the tone for the town the way the Citadel does for Halifax. The first two floors are still used as a public school (the top floor was deemed a fire hazard some years ago), and the building is open to the public only on special occasions.

ESSENTIALS

GETTING THERE Lunenburg is 100km (62 miles) southwest of Halifax on Route 3.

VISITOR INFORMATION The **Lunenburg Tourist Bureau** (© 902/634-8100 or 902/634-3656) is located at the top of Blockhouse Hill Road. It's open from May to October daily 9am to 8pm. It's not in an obvious location, but the brown "?" signs posted around town—or helpful locals—will point you there. The staff here is especially good at helping you find a place to spend the night if you've arrived without reservations. You can also find local information online at www.lunenburgns.com.

EXPLORING LUNENBURG

Leave plenty of time to explore Lunenburg by foot. An excellent walking tour brochure is available at the tourist office on Blockhouse Hill Road, though supplies are getting limited. If that's gone, contact the **Lunenburg Board of Trade** (© 902/634-3170) for the excellent local and regional map they have created.

St. John's Anglican Church ✸✸ at the corner of Duke and Cumberland streets had been one of the most impressive architectural sights in all of eastern Canada. All this changed on Halloween night in 2001, however: A fire nearly razed the place, gutting its precious interior and much of the ornate exterior as well. In June 2005, it reopened after a painstaking 3-year restoration project and can be viewed once more.

Guided 1½-hour **walking tours** (© 902/634-3848) that include lore about local architecture and legends are hosted daily by Eric Croft, a knowledgeable Lunenburg

The Dauntless *Bluenose*

Take an old Canadian dime—one minted before 2001, that is—out of your pocket and have a close look. That graceful schooner on one side? That's the *Bluenose,* Canada's most recognized and most storied ship.

The *Bluenose* was built in Lunenburg in 1921 as a fishing schooner. But it wasn't just any schooner. It was an exceptionally fast schooner. U.S. and Canadian fishing fleets had raced informally for years. Starting in 1920 the *Halifax Herald* sponsored the International Fisherman's Trophy, which was captured that first year by Americans sailing out of Massachusetts. Peeved, the Nova Scotians set about taking it back. And did they ever. The *Bluenose* retained the trophy for 18 years running, despite the best efforts of Americans to recapture it. The race was shelved as World War II loomed; in the years after the war, fishing schooners were displaced by long-haul, steel-hulled fishing ships, and the schooners sailed into the footnotes of history. The *Bluenose* was sold in 1942 to labor as a freighter in the West Indies. Four years later it foundered and sank off Haiti.

What made the *Bluenose* so unbeatable? A number of theories exist. Some said it was because of last-minute hull design changes. Some said it was frost "setting" the timbers as the ship was being built. Still others claim it was blessed with an unusually talented captain and crew.

The replica *Bluenose II* was built in 1963 from the same plans as the original, in the same shipyard, and even by some of the same workers. It's been owned by the province since 1971, and it sails throughout Canada and beyond as Nova Scotia's seafaring ambassador. The *Bluenose*'s location varies from year to year, and it schedules visits to ports in Canada and the United States. In midsummer, it typically alternates between Lunenburg or Halifax, during which time visitors can sign up for 2-hour harbor sailings (C$35/US$35/£18 adults, C$20/US$20/£10 children age 3–12). To hear about the ship's schedule, call the *Bluenose II* **Preservation Trust** (© **866/579-4909**).

native who's in possession of a sizable store of good stories. Tours depart at 10am, 2pm, and 9pm (by candlelight) from Bluenose Drive, across from the parking lot for the Atlantic Fisheries Museum; the cost is about C$15 (US$15/£7.50) adults, C$10 (US$10/£5) children.

Several boat tours operate from the waterfront, most tied up near the Fisheries Museum. **Lunenburg Whale Watching Tours** (© **902/527-7175**) sails in pursuit of several species of whales, along with seals and seabirds on 3-hour excursions. There are four departures daily from May to October, with reservations recommended. **Star Charters** (© **877/247-7075** or 902/634-3535; www.novascotiasailing.com) takes visitors on a mellow 45-minute tour of Lunenburg's inner harbor (no swells!) in a converted fishing boat. The same folks also offer 1½-hour sailing trips on the *Eastern Star,* a 14m (48-ft.) wooden ketch, from June to October.

Fisheries Museum of the Atlantic ★ (Kids) The sprawling Fisheries Museum is professionally designed and curated, and it manages to take a topic that some might consider a little, well, dull and make it fun and exciting. It's also been upgraded and expanded recently. You'll find aquarium exhibits on the first floor, including a touch tank for kids. (Look also for the massive 15-lb. lobster, estimated to be 25–30 years old.) Detailed dioramas depict the whys and hows of fishing from dories, colonial schooners, and other historic vessels. You'll also learn a whole bunch about the *Bluenose*, a replica of which ties up in Lunenburg when it's not touring elsewhere (see "The Dauntless *Bluenose*" box, above). Outside, you can tour two other ships—a trawler and a salt-bank schooner—and visit a working boat shop. Allow at least 2 hours to probe all the corners of this engaging waterfront museum.

On the waterfront. © 866/579-4909 or 902/634-4794. http://museum.gov.ns.ca/fma. Mid-May to mid-Oct admission C$9 (US$9/£4.50) adults, C$7 (US$7/£3.50) seniors, C$3 (US$3/£1.50) children 6–17, C$22 (US$22/£11) families; rest of the year, C$4 (US$4/£2) per person (free for children). May–Oct daily 9:30am–5:30pm (July–Aug Tues–Sat till 7pm); Nov–Apr Mon–Fri 9:30am–4pm.

WHERE TO STAY

Boscawen Inn ⓐ   This imposing 1888 mansion occupies a prime hillside site in a cute neighborhood just a block from the heart of town; it was built in 1888 by local Senator H. A. N. Kaulbach, an influential figure in local history, as a wedding gift for his daughter. Today it is considered one of Lunenburg's finest examples of Queen Anne Revival style of architecture. The interior decor is Victorian, although not aggressively so, and it's almost worth staying here just to get access to the main-floor deck and its views of the harbor. Most of the simply furnished rooms are in the main building, which had a newer wing added in 1945. (Two of the spacious suites are located in the 1905 MacLachlan House, just below the main house and across Lincoln St., with its little octagonal tower.) Note that guests housed on the third floor will need to navigate some steep steps. The inn's restaurant serves reliable, sometimes imaginative dinners nightly in season from 5:30 to 9pm.

150 Cumberland St., Lunenburg, NS B0J 2C0. © 800/354-5009 or 902/634-3325. Fax 902/634-9293. www.boscawen.ca. 17 units. C$95–C$195 (US$95–US$195/£48–£100) double. Rates include continental breakfast. AE, DISC, MC, V. **Amenities:** 2 restaurants; bar; laundry service. *In room:* TV, hair dryer, iron/ironing board, Jacuzzi (1 unit), no phone (except by request).

Kaulbach House Historic Inn ⓐⓐ   One of the few local inns to have upscaled with the times, the right-in-town Kaulbach House is decorated appropriately for its elaborate architecture: in high Victorian style, but rendered somewhat less oppressive with un-Victorian color schemes. The house also reflects the era's prevailing class structure, since the nicest room (the tower room) is on top. It features two sitting areas and a great view. (The least intriguing rooms are the former servants' quarters on street level.) Recent renovations by the new owners have spruced up the building a good bit: New windows, mattresses, comforters, and hot-water heating had been installed in 2000, to which they have added great shower heads, fresh flowers, fluffy robes, and DVD players. The hearty three-course, included breakfast is worth coming for alone. And this is a good choice in another regard: This is one of the few small Lunenburg inns in which all the guest rooms have their own private bathrooms.

75 Pelham St., Lunenburg, NS B0J 2C0. © 800/568-8818 or 902/634-8818. Fax 902/640-3036. www.kaulbachhouse.com. 6 units. C$109–C$169 (US$109–US$169/£55–£85) double. Rates include full breakfast. MC, V. Closed Nov–May. **Amenities:** Laundry service. *In room:* A/C, TV, hair dryer, no phone.

Lennox Inn Bed & Breakfast   In 1991, this strikingly handsome but simple house in a quiet residential area of Lunenburg was condemned and slated for demolition.

Robert Cram didn't want to see it go, so he bought it and spent several years restoring it to its original 1791 appearance, filling it with antiques and period reproduction furniture. It's more rustic than opulent (translation: the wood-floored rooms are pretty spare), but this fine inn should still be high on the list for anyone fond of authentically historic houses. In fact, it claims, quite plausibly, to be the oldest unchanged inn in Canada. Three of the four spacious second-floor rooms have the original plaster, and all four have the original fireplaces (nonworking). A country breakfast is served in the former tavern; be sure to note the ingenious old bar.

69 Fox St. (P.O. Box 254), Lunenburg, NS B0J 2C0. ⓒ **888/379-7605**, 902/634-4043, or 902/521-0214. www.lennox inn.com. 4 units, 2 with private bathroom. C$95–C$120 (US$95–US$120/£48–£60) double. Rates include full breakfast. MC, V. Open year-round; by reservation only mid-Oct to Apr. *In room:* No phone.

Lunenburg Arms 𝄞𝄞   In a town where nearly all the lodgings consist of converted old seamen's homes, this hotel—opened in June 2002 and also converted from a gutted former tavern and boardinghouse—stands out as a modern alternative, one in which nearly everything you see is new. It's the only accommodation in town where rooms are wheelchair accessible, there's an elevator, pets are welcomed with open paws, and each unit is wired up for high-speed Internet access at no extra charge. Rooms are furnished in pleasant carpeting and queen and king beds that wouldn't look out of place in a New York boutique hotel, yet there are also thoughtfully homey touches such as wood-laminate floors and a stuffed teddy bear (or two) placed in each room. The smallish bathrooms feature pedestal sinks and all-new fixtures. No two rooms here are laid out exactly alike, so examine a few if possible to get the configuration you want—some rooms have Jacuzzis, some feature the town's best harbor views, and there are two bi-level loft suites with beds up small sets of stairs. The hotel added a spa featuring Aveda products in 2006; its facilities include a soaker tub, a hot tub, and aromatherapy-delivering steam showers.

94 Pelham St., Lunenburg, NS B0J 2C0. ⓒ **800/679-4950** or 902/640-4040. Fax 902/640-4041. www.lunenburg arms.com. 26 units. Peak season C$129–C$299 (US$129–US$299/£65–£150) double. AE, MC, V. **Amenities:** Dining room; spa; conference room. *In room:* A/C, TV, dataport, coffeemaker, hair dryer.

WHERE TO DINE

Historic Grounds Coffee House 𝄞 *Value* CAFE   More than just great coffee drinks, this youthful place in decidedly unhip Lunenburg serves up hearty breakfasts, good chowders, sandwiches, salads, and fish cakes throughout most of the day, and always with a smile (they've been doing it since the mid-1990s, so this isn't one of those flash-in-the-pan, designer java huts). Wash it down with real Italian espresso, something called a frappé (which is not an American-style frappé, but rather more like a frozen espresso), smoothies, or sodas. Ice cream and interesting dessert items are also available. Go for a table on the tiny balcony if you can snag one—they've got the best dining view in town, at a fraction of the cost of what you'd pay for a meal anywhere else. Good choices at lunch include the Caesar salad wrap, the turkey club, and even a lobster sandwich.

100 Montague St. ⓒ **902/634-9995**. Lunch items C$3.95–C$8.95 (US$3.95–C$8.95/£2–£4.50). AE, DISC, MC, V. June to mid-Sept Mon–Fri 7:30am–10pm, Sat–Sun 8am–10pm; mid-Sept to May daily 7:30am–6pm.

The Knot 𝄞 *Value* PUB FARE   Good beers on tap and a convivial English atmosphere make this pub a great place to take a break from more upscale eateries in town. Located smack in the center of a tiny commercial district, it serves surprisingly good pub fare—think juicy burgers, fried fish, local sausage, and a warming mussel soup—plus a selection of bitters and ales, some of them brewed locally in Halifax. The crowd is an agreeable mixture of fishermen, local families, and tourists, and bar staff are all too happy to help you decide what's good that day.

4 Dufferin St. Ⓒ **902/634-3334.** Meals C$6–C$10 (US$6–US$10/£3–£5). AE, MC, V. Daily 10am–midnight; kitchen closes 9pm in summer, 8:30pm in winter.

Old Fish Factory Restaurant ⭐ SEAFOOD The Old Fish Factory Restaurant is—no surprise—located in a huge old fish-processing plant, which it shares with the Fisheries Museum. This large and popular restaurant can swallow whole bus tours at once; come early and angle for a window seat or a spot on the patio. Also no surprise: The specialty is seafood, which tends to involve medleys of varied fish. At lunch you might order a fish sandwich or a salmon filet. At dinner, lobster is served four different ways, along with bouillabaisse, snow crab, local haddock and scallops, and a curried mango seafood pasta. There's steak, lamb, and chicken for more terrestrial tastes.

68 Bluenose Dr. (at the Fisheries Museum). Ⓒ **800/533-9336** or 902/634-3333. www.oldfishfactory.com. Reservations recommended (ask for a window seat). Lunch C$8–C$19 (US$8–US$19/£4–£9.50); dinner C$14–C$35 (US$14–US$35/£7–£18). AE, DC, DISC, MC, V. Daily 11am–9pm. Closed late Oct to early May.

MAHONE BAY ⭐⭐

Mahone Bay, first settled in 1754 by European Protestants, is picture-perfect Nova Scotia. It's tidy and trim with an eclectic Main Street that snakes along the bay and is lined with inviting shops. This is a town that's remarkably well cared for by its 1,100 residents, a growing number of whom live here and commute to work in Halifax. Architecture buffs will find a range of styles to keep them ogling.

ESSENTIALS
GETTING THERE Mahone Bay lies 10km (6 miles) east of Lunenburg on Route 3.

VISITOR INFORMATION A **visitor information center** (Ⓒ **888/624-6151** or 902/624-6151; www.mahonebay.com) is located at 165 Edgewater St., near the three church steeples. It's open daily in summer 9am to 7:30pm, until 5:30pm in shoulder seasons.

EXPLORING THE TOWN
The free **Mahone Bay Settlers Museum,** 578 Main St. (Ⓒ **902/624-6263**), provides historic context for your explorations from June to early September; it's open Tuesday through Saturday 10am to 5pm, and Sunday 1 to 5pm. A good selection of historic decorative arts is on display. Before leaving, be sure to request a copy of "Three Walking Tours of Mahone Bay," a handy brochure that outlines easy historic walks around the compact downtown.

Thanks to the looping waterside routes nearby, this is a popular destination for bikers. And the deep, protected harbor offers superb sea kayaking. If you'd like to give kayaking a go, contact **East Coast Outfitters** (Ⓒ **877/852-2567** or 902/852-2567), based in the Peggy's Cove area near Halifax. They offer half-day introductory classes and a 5-day coastal tour of the area. Among the more popular adventures is the daylong introductory tour, in which paddlers explore the complex shoreline and learn about kayaking in the process. The price is about C$115 (US$115/£58) per person, C$35 (US$35/£18) extra for a lobster lunch. Rentals are also available, starting at about C$45 (US$45/£23) per half-day for a single kayak.

WHERE TO STAY

You'll find a clutch of bed-and-breakfast choices in and around Mahone Bay; consult the local website (www.mahonebay.com) for a fairly complete listing. **Ocean Trail Retreat** (© **888/624-8824** or 902/624-8824; fax 902/624-8899) on Route 3 at Mader's Cove is a relatively new property with 15 airy motel-style rooms and 3 two-bedroom chalets. It's very popular with families, largely because of the heated outdoor swimming pool. This might be the area's best choice if you're bringing children. Rooms go for C$99 to C$119 (US$99–US$119/£50–£60) per night, and a few ocean-view chalets renting for C$1,200 (US$1,200/£600) per week, or C$175 (US$175/£88) per night during the off-peak months.

Then, right in the center of town, **Mahone Bay Bed & Breakfast** at 558 Main St. (© **866/239-6252** or 902/624-6388) is a more Victorian option with four rooms at rates from C$75 to C$125 (US$75–US$125/£38–£63) per night. The restored, bright-yellow 1860s-era house was built by one of the town's many former shipbuilders. There's also **Fisherman's Daughter** (97 Edgewater St.; © **902/624-0483**), with its maritime theme and four rooms costing C$100 to C$125 (US$100–US$125/£50–£63) per night.

WHERE TO DINE

The seasonally open **Gazebo Cafe** ⚓ at 567 Main St. (© **902/624-6484**) is one of my favorite places in the area—an affable and affordable waterside cafe dishing up filling, healthy sandwiches and thick bowls of seafood chowder. They also do juices, smoothies, and top-flight coffee. Fresh desserts are delivered several times weekly. This place is rapidly becoming the arts headquarters of the town, too; check the bulletin board for news of local art shows and musical performances, some of which take place right at the cafe.

Innlet Café ⚓⚓ SEAFOOD/GRILL   Former owners Jack and Katherine Sorensen served up great meals here for 2 decades, and new ownership is holding true to the menu they created, which brought back legions of customers. Everything is good, especially the seafood. The menu is all over the place (oven-braised lamb shank to scallop stir-fry), but the smart money hones in on the unadorned seafood. Notable are the "smoked and garlicked mackerel" and the mixed seafood grill. The best seats are on the stone patio, which has a view of the harbor and the famous three-steepled townscape of Mahone Bay. If you end up inside, nothing lost. The clean lines and lack of clutter make it an inviting spot, and the atmosphere is informal and relaxed.

249 Edgewater St. © **902/624-6363**. Reservations recommended for dinner. Main courses C$12–C$21 (US$12–US$21/£6–£11). MC, V. Daily 11:30am–9pm.

CHESTER ⚓⚓

Chester has the feel of an old-money summer colony, perhaps somewhere along the New England coast in the 1920s. It was first settled in 1759 by immigrants from New England and Great Britain, and today it has a population of 1,250. The village is noted for its regal homes and quiet streets, along with the picturesque islands offshore. The atmosphere here is uncrowded, untrammeled, lazy, and slow—the way life used to be in summer resorts throughout the world. Change may be on the horizon: Actors and authors have discovered the place and are snapping up waterfront homes in town and on the islands as private retreats, giving a bit of an edge to the lazy feel of the spot.

ESSENTIALS

GETTING THERE   Chester is located on Route 3 and is a short drive off Route 103, 21km (13 miles) east of Mahone Bay.

VISITOR INFORMATION   The **Chester Visitor Information Centre** (© 902/ 275-4616; www.chesterns.com) is in the old train station on Route 3 on the south side of town. It's open daily from 9am to 7pm in July and August, from 10am to 5pm in spring and fall.

EXPLORING THE TOWN

Like so many other towns in Nova Scotia, Chester is best seen out of your car. But unlike other towns, where the center of gravity seems to be in the commercial district, here the focus is on the graceful, shady residential areas that radiate out from the Lilliputian village.

In your rambles, plan to head down Queen Street to the waterfront, and then veer around on South Street, admiring the views out toward the mouth of the harbor. Continue on South Street past the yacht club, past the statue of the veteran (in a kilt), past the sundial in the small square. Then you'll come to a beautiful view of Back Harbour. At the foot of the small park is a curious municipal saltwater pool, filled at high tide. On warmer days, you'll find what appears to be half the town out splashing and shrieking in the bracing water.

Some creative shops are beginning to find a receptive audience in and around Chester, and there's good browsing for new goods and antiques both downtown and in the outlying areas. One such shop is **Fiasco,** 54 Queen St. (© **902/275-2173**), which has an appealing selection of funky and fun home accessories and clothing. Another good stop is the **Village Emporium** at 11 Pleasant St. (© **902/275-4773**), an eclectic clustering of folk-arty purveying anything from lavender soaps to simple pottery to knit purses; it's in the same building as the Kiwi Café (see below).

In the evening, the intimate **Chester Playhouse,** 22 Pleasant St. (© **800/363- 7529** or 902/275-3933; www.chesterplayhouse.ns.ca), hosts plays, concerts, and other high-quality performances throughout the summer season. Tickets are usually around C$20 (US$20/£10) adults. Call for a schedule or reservations.

WHERE TO STAY

Graves Island Provincial Park ★★ (© **902/275-4425**) is 3km (1¾ miles) north of the village on Route 3 in East River. The 50-hectare (125-acre) estatelike park is one of the province's more elegant campgrounds, as befits moneyed Chester. The park has 73 sites, many dotting a high grassy bluff with outstanding views out to the spruce-clad islands of Mahone Bay, available mid-May through early October. No hookups are available; the camping fee is C$19 (US$19/£9.50) per night.

Mecklenburgh Inn *(Value)*   This wonderfully funky and appealing inn, built around 1890, is located on a low hill in one of Chester's residential neighborhoods. The building is dominated by broad porches on the first and second floors, which invariably are populated with guests sitting and rocking and watching the town wander by (which it does—the post office is just next door). Innkeeper Suzi Fraser has been running the place with casual bonhomie since the late 1980s, and she's a great breakfast cook to boot. Rooms are modern Victorian and generally quite bright. What's the catch? The four rooms share two hallway bathrooms, but guests often end up feeling like family, so it's usually not much of a bother.

78 Queen St., Chester, NS B0J 1J0. (C) **902/275-4638.** www.mecklenburghinn.ca. 4 units, 1 with private bathroom. C$85–C$135 (US$85–US$135/£43–£68) double. Rates include full breakfast. AE, V. Closed Jan–Apr. *In room:* Hair dryer, no phone.

WHERE TO DINE

In addition to the two eateries listed below, there's also **The Rope Loft,** at 36 Water St. ((C) **902/275-3430**) serving dependable pastas, pizza, fried clams, Digby scallops, lobster, and other seafood by the water—ask for a deck chair, if you can get one. The restaurant also serves brunch on both weekend days, from 11am to 2 pm.

The Kiwi Café (*Finds* CAFE A little enclave of New Zealand culture on the nautical coast of Nova Scotia? Yes, indeed. The former Luigi's bookshop/cafe right in the heart of downtown Chester was sold in 2004 and reinvented as the Kiwi, a thank-goodness-it's-still-fun place in what can be an occasionally starchy town. Proprietor Lynda Flynn—yes, she's really from New Zealand, and received training in the culinary arts in Auckland—serves up breakfast eggs and bagels (try the lobster scramble), plus an assortment of sandwiches, wraps, panini, fresh soups, Nova Scotian fish cakes with mango salsa, and gourmet salads for lunch. Wash it down with wine, Nova Scotia beer, or good, Halifax-roasted coffee served in an inventive set of coffee drinks. On the go? No problem: Grab a "dinner-in-a-box" (Flynn also runs a catering business) or some New Zealand honey from the little provisions shop on premises.

19 Pleasant St. (C) **902/275-1492.** www.kiwicafechester.com. Main courses C$4.50–C$8.50 (US$4.50–US$8.50/£2.25–£4.25). V. Daily 8:30am–4pm.

La Vista CONTINENTAL/SEAFOOD This dining room, located inside the Oak Island Resort spa and convention center just north of Chester down a side peninsula, offers a serviceable upscale alternative to traveling diners in the Chester area. Meals begin with such starters as a Lunenburg seafood chowder flavored with dill, a French onion soup with Gruyère, a smoked-salmon Napoleon, Thai crab cakes, or local mussels in white wine, and main courses such as sesame-crusted salmon over basmati rice, cedar-planked salmon with maple butter, pan-roasted halibut with pepper and lemon grass, roasted tenderloin with a Stilton crust, a Madras seafood curry, and shrimp-and-lobster pasta.

36 Treasure Dr. (inside the Oak Island Resort), Western Shore. (C) **902/627-2600.** Main courses C$18–C$21 (US$18–US$21/£9–£11). MC, V. Daily 7am–2pm and 5–9pm. Take Hwy 103 to exit 9, continue 2km (1½ miles) to Rte. 3, turn onto Rte. 3, continue 5km (3 miles) to resort.

7 Halifax: More Than a Natural Harbor

322km (200 miles) NE of Yarmouth

Halifax's unusually pleasing harborside setting, now home to a city of some 115,000 (about three times as many in the greater metro area), first attracted Europeans in 1749, when Col. Edward Cornwallis established a military outpost here. (The site was named after George Montagu Dunk, second earl of Halifax. Residents tend to agree that it was a great stroke of luck that the city avoided the name Dunk, Nova Scotia.) The city plodded along as a colonial backwater for the better part of a century; one historian wrote that it was generally regarded as "a rather degenerate little seaport town."

But its natural advantages—including that well-protected harbor and its location near major fishing grounds and shipping lanes—eventually allowed it to emerge as a major port and military base. In recent years, the city has grown aggressively (it

Halifax

ACCOMMODATIONS ■
Cambridge Suites **15**
Delta Halifax **6**
Halifax Heritage House
   Hostel **24**
Halifax Waverley Inn **23**
The Halliburton **22**
The Lord Nelson Hotel
   and Suites **16**

DINING ◆
Bish World Cuisine **21**
Cheapside Café **13**
daMaurizio **20**
Henry House **26**
Il Mercato **17**
Ryan Duffy's Steak
   and Seafood **18**
Satisfaction Feast **2**
Sweet Basil Bistro **8**

ATTRACTIONS ●
Art Gallery of Nova Scotia **13**
Barrington Place **7**
Fairview Lawn Cemetery **1**
Halifax Citadel National
   Historic Site **4**
Historic Properties **9**
Maritime Museum
   of the Atlantic **14**

Nova Scotia Museum
   of Natural History **3**
Old Burying Ground **19**
Old City Hall **10**
Old Town Clock **5**
Pier 21 **27**
Point Pleasant Park **25**
Province House **12**
St. Paul's Anglican Church **11**

annexed adjacent suburbs in 1969) and carved out a niche as the vital commercial and financial hub of the Maritimes. The city is also home to a number of colleges and universities, which gives it a youthful, edgy air. Skateboards and bicycles often seem to be the vehicles of choice. In addition to the many attractions, downtown Halifax is home to a number of fine restaurants and hotels.

ESSENTIALS

GETTING THERE BY PLANE   Halifax International Airport (www.hiaa.com) is 34km (21 miles) north of downtown Halifax in Elmsdale; take Route 102 to Exit 6. Nova Scotia's notorious fogs make it advisable to call before heading out to the airport to reconfirm flight times. Airlines serving Halifax include Air Canada and its commuter airline Jazz, WestJet, American Eagle, and Canjet. (See "Getting There" in section 1, earlier in this chapter, for phone numbers.) The **Airporter** (© **902/873-2091**) offers frequent shuttles from the airport to major downtown hotels daily from 6:30am to 11:15pm. The rate is C$18 (US$18/£9) one-way.

GETTING THERE BY CAR   Coming from New Brunswick and the west, the most direct route is via Route 102 from Truro; allow about 2 to 2½ hours from the provincial border at Amherst.

GETTING THERE BY RAIL   VIA Rail (© **888/842-7245**) offers train service 6 days a week between Halifax and Montréal. The entire trip takes between 18 and 21 hours, depending on direction. Stops include Moncton and Campbellton (with bus connections to Québec). Halifax's train station, at Barrington and Cornwallis streets, is within walking distance of downtown attractions.

VISITOR INFORMATION   Halifax's two main visitor centers are conveniently located downtown, and both open year-round. The info booth in **Scotia Square** (© **902/490-5963**) and the VIC by the waterfront at Sackville Landing (© **902/424-4248**) each open daily from 8:30am to 9pm in summer (until 5pm in winter). They're staffed with friendly folks who will point you in the right direction or help you make room reservations in a pinch. A third year-round VIC is located in the domestic arrivals area of the main terminal of the **airport** (© **902/873-1223**), open 9am to 9pm daily. From mid-May to mid-October, still another VIC opens downtown at 1598 Argyle St. (at the corner of Sackville). Also during the summer, travel counselors also cruise the waterfront and boardwalk on Segway scooters. For online information about Halifax, visit the website **www.halifaxinfo.com**.

GETTING AROUND   Parking in Halifax can be problematic. Long-term metered spaces are in high demand downtown, and many of the parking lots and garages fill up fast. If you're headed downtown for a brief visit, you can usually find a 2-hour meter. But if you're looking to spend a day, I'd suggest venturing out early to ensure a spot at a parking lot. The city's most extensive parking (fee charged) is available near Sackville Landing. Or try along Lower Water Street, south of the Maritime Museum of the Atlantic, where you can park all day for around C$6 (US$6/£3).

Metro Transit operates buses throughout the city. Route and timetable information is available at the information centers or by phone (© **902/490-4000**). Bus fare is C$2 (US$2/£1) adults, C$1.25 (US$1.25/65p) seniors and children.

Daily throughout the summer (early July through late Oct), a bright green bus named **FRED** (© **902/490-4000**) cruises a loop through the downtown, passing each stop about every 30 minutes from 10:30am until 5:30pm. It's free. Stops include the

Maritime Museum, Water Street, the Grand Parade, the Citadel, and Barrington Place. Request a schedule and map at the visitor center.

SPECIAL EVENTS & FESTIVALS   The annual **Royal Nova Scotia International Tattoo** (© 902/420-1114; www.nstattoo.ca) features military and marching bands totaling some 2,000 plus military and civilian performers. This rousing event takes place over the course of a week in early July and is held indoors at the Halifax Metro Center. Tickets are C$18 to C$50 (US$18–US$50/£9–£25).

The annual **Atlantic Jazz Festival** (© 800/567-5277 or 902/492-2225; www.jazz east.com) has performances ranging from global and avant-garde to local and tradi-tional music each July. Venues include area nightclubs and outdoor stages, and prices vary considerably; consult the website for the latest details and specifics of perform-ance and price.

In early August, expect to see a profusion of street performers ranging from fire-eaters to comic jugglers. They descend on Halifax each summer for the 10-day **Halifax Inter-national Busker Festival** (© 866/773-0655 or 902/429-3910; www.buskers.ca). Per-formances take place along the waterfront walkway all day long and are often quite remarkable. The festival is free, though donations are requested.

The **Atlantic Film Festival** (© 902/422-3456; www.atlanticfilm.com) offers screenings of more than 150 films in mid-September. The focus is largely on Cana-dian filmmaking, with an emphasis on independent productions and shorts. Some films are free, while those with a charge cost about C$5 to C$15 (US$5–US$15/£2.50–£7.50) each.

EXPLORING HALIFAX

Halifax is fairly compact and easily reconnoitered on foot or by mass transportation. The major landmark is the **Citadel**—the stone fortress that looms over downtown from its grassy perch. From the ramparts, you can look into the windows of the tenth floor of downtown skyscrapers. The Citadel is only 9 blocks from the waterfront—albeit 9 sometimes steep blocks—and you can easily see both the downtown and the waterfront areas in 1 day.

A lively neighborhood worth seeking out runs along **Spring Garden Road,** between the Public Gardens and the library (at Grafton St.). You'll find intriguing boutiques, bars, and restaurants along these 6 blocks, set amid a mildly bohemian street scene. If you have strong legs and a stout constitution, you can start on the waterfront, stroll up and over the Citadel to descend to the Public Gardens, and then return via Spring Garden to downtown, perhaps enjoying a meal or two along the way.

THE WATERFRONT ✷

Halifax's rehabilitated waterfront is at its most inviting and vibrant between Sackville Landing (at the foot of Sackville St.) and the Sheraton Casino, near Purdy Wharf. (You could keep walking, but north of here the waterfront lapses into an agglomera-tion of charmless modern towers with sidewalk-level vents that assail passersby with unusual odors.) On sunny summer afternoons, the waterfront is bustling with tourists enjoying the harbor, business folks playing hooky while sneaking an ice-cream cone, and baggy-panted skateboarders striving to stay out of trouble. Plan on about 2 to 3 hours to tour and gawk from end to end.

The city's most extensive parking (fee charged) is available near Sackville Landing, and that's a good place to start a walking tour. Make your first stop the waterfront's crown jewel, the **Maritime Museum of the Atlantic** (see below).

In addition to the other attractions listed below, the waterfront walkway is studded with small diversions, intriguing shops, take-out food emporia, and minor monuments. Think of it as an alfresco scavenger hunt.

Among the treasures, look for **Summit Place,** commemorating the historic gathering of world leaders in 1995, when Halifax hosted the G-7 Economic Summit. There's North America's oldest operating **Naval Clock,** which was built in 1767 and chimed at the Halifax Naval Dockyard from 1772 to 1993. You can visit the **Ferry Terminal,** which is hectic during rush hour with commuters coming and going to Dartmouth across the harbor. (It's also a cheap way to enjoy a sweeping city and harbor view.) The passenger-only ferry runs at least every half-hour, and the fare is C$2 (US$2/£1) per adult each way, cheaper for seniors and children age 5 to 15.

The waterfront's shopping core is located in and around the 3-block **Historic Properties,** near the Sheraton. These stout buildings of wood and stone are Canada's oldest surviving warehouses and were once the center of the city's booming shipping industry. Today, the historic architecture is stern enough to provide ballast for the somewhat precious boutiques and restaurants they now house. Especially appealing is the granite-and-ironstone **Privateers' Warehouse,** which dates from 1813.

If you're feeling that a pub crawl might be in order, the Historic Properties area is also a good place to wander around after working hours in the early evening. There's a contagious energy that spills out of the handful of public houses, and you'll find a bustling camaraderie and live music.

Maritime Museum of the Atlantic ★★ (Kids)   All visitors to Nova Scotia owe themselves a stop at this standout museum on a prime waterfront location. The exhibits are involving and well executed, and you'll be astounded at how fast 2 hours can fly by. Visitors are greeted by a 3m (10-ft.) lighthouse lens from 1906, and then proceed through a parade of shipbuilding and seagoing eras. Visit the deckhouse of a coastal steamer (ca. 1940), or learn the colorful history of Samuel Cunard, a Nova Scotia native (born 1787) who founded the Cunard Steam Ship Co. to carry the royal mail and along the way established an ocean dynasty. Another highlight is the exhibit on the tragic Halifax Explosion of 1917, when two warships collided in Halifax harbor not far from the museum, detonating tons of TNT. More than 1,700 people died, and windows were shattered 100km (60 miles) away. But perhaps the most poignant exhibit is the lone deck chair from the *Titanic*—150 victims of the *Titanic* disaster are buried in Halifax, where rescue efforts were centered. Also memorable are the "Age of Steam" exhibit, Queen Victoria's barge, and the interesting new "Shipwreck Treasures of Nova Scotia" section with its stories and artifacts from more than a dozen local shipwrecks.

1675 Lower Water St. © 902/424-7490. www.maritime.museum.gov.ns.ca. Admission May–Oct C$8.50 (US$8.50/ £4.25) adults, C$7.50 (US$7.50/£3.75) seniors, C$4.50 (US$4.50/£2.25) children 6–17, C$22 (US$22/£11) family. Lower-price admission Nov–Apr. May–Oct daily 9:30am–5:30pm (to 8pm Tues); Nov–Apr closed Mon and shorter hours Sun 1–5pm.

C.S.S. *Acadia*   This unusually handsome 1913 vessel is part of the Maritime Museum ("our largest artifact"), but it can be viewed independently for a small fee. The *Acadia* was used by the Canadian government to chart the ocean floor for 56 years, until its retirement in 1969. Much of the ship is open for self-guided tours, including the captain's quarters, upper decks, wheelhouse, and oak-paneled chart room. If you want to see more of the ship, ask about the guided half-hour tours (four times daily), which offer access to the engine room and more. You probably wouldn't need more than a half-hour here.

On the water, in front of the Maritime Museum, 1675 Lower Water St. ℂ **902/424-7490.** Free admission with Maritime Museum ticket, which costs C$8.50 (US$8.50/£4.25) adults, C$7.50 (US$7.50/£3.75) seniors, C$4.50 (US$4.50/£2.25) children 6–17, C$22 (US$22/£11) family. Mon–Sat 9:30am–5:30pm; Sun 1–5:30pm. Closed mid-Oct to May 1.

HMCS *Sackville*   This blue-and-white corvette (a speedy warship smaller than a destroyer) is tied up along a wood-planked wharf behind a small visitor center. There's a short multimedia presentation to provide some background. The ship is outfitted as it was in 1944, and it is now maintained as a memorial to the Canadians who served in World War II. Plan to spend about a half-hour here.

Sackville Landing (summer), HMC dockyard (winter). ℂ **902/429-2132.** Admission C$3 (US$3/£1.50) adults, C$2 (US$2/£1) seniors and students. June–Oct daily 10am–5pm; off-season hours vary.

Pier 21 ⭐ *(Kids*   Between 1928 and 1971 more than one million immigrants arrived in Canada by disembarking at Pier 21, Canada's version of New York's Ellis Island. In 1999, the pier was restored and reopened, filled with engaging interpretive exhibits, which aid visitors in vividly imagining the confusion and anxiety of the immigration experience. The pier is divided roughly into three sections, which recapture the boarding of the ship amid the cacophony of many languages, the crossing of the Atlantic (a 26-min. multimedia show recaptures the voyage in a shiplike theater), and the dispersal of the recent arrivals throughout Canada via passenger train. For those seeking more in-depth information (one in five Canadians today can trace a link back to Pier 21), there's a reference library and computer resources. Plan to spend at least an hour here.

1055 Marginal Rd. (on the waterfront behind the Westin Hotel). ℂ **902/425-7770.** www.pier21.ca. C$8.50 (US$8.50/£4.25) adults, C$7.50 (US$7.50/£3.75) seniors, C$5 (US$5/£2.50) children 6–16, C$21 (US$21/£11) family. May–Nov daily 9:30am–5:30pm; Dec–March Tues–Sat 10am–5pm; Apr Mon–Sat 10am–5pm.

THE CITADEL & DOWNTOWN

Downtown Halifax cascades 9 blocks down a slope between the imposing stone Citadel and the waterfront. There's no fast-and-ready tour route; don't hesitate to follow your own desultory course, alternately ducking down quiet streets and striding along busy arteries. A good spot to regain your bearings periodically is the **Grand Parade,** where military recruits once practiced their drills. It's a lovely urban landscape—a broad terrace carved into the hill, presided over on either end by St. Paul's (see below) and Halifax's **City Hall.**

Art Gallery of Nova Scotia   Located in a pair of sandstone buildings between the waterfront and the Grand Parade, the Art Gallery is arguably the premier gallery in the Maritimes, with a focus on local and regional art. You'll also find a selection of other works by Canadian, British, and European artists, with a well-chosen selection of folk and Inuit art. In 1998, the gallery expanded to include the Provincial Building next door, where the entire house (it's tiny) of Nova Scotian folk artist Maud Lewis has been reassembled and is on display. The museum can be comfortably perused in 60 to 90 minutes; consider a lunch break in the attractive Cheapside Café (p. 96).

1723 Hollis St. (at Cheapside). ℂ **902/424-5280.** Admission C$12 (US$12/£6) adults, C$10 (US$10/£5) seniors, C$5 (US$5/£2.50) students, C$3 (US$3/£1.50) children age 6–17, C$25 (US$25/£13) families. Daily 10am–5pm (Thurs till 9pm).

Halifax Citadel National Historic Site ⭐⭐   Even if the stalwart stone fort weren't here, it would be worth the uphill trek for the astounding views alone. The panoramic sweep across downtown and the harbor finishes up with vistas out toward the broad Atlantic beyond. At any rate, an ascent makes it obvious why this spot was chosen for the harbor's most formidable defenses: There's simply no sneaking up on the place.

Four forts have occupied the summit since Col. Edward Cornwallis was posted to the colony in 1749. The Citadel has been restored to look much as it did in 1856, when the fourth fort was built out of concern over bellicose Americans. The fort has never been attacked.

The site is impressive to say the least: Sturdy granite walls topped by grassy embankments form a rough star; in the sprawling gravel and cobblestone courtyard you'll find convincingly costumed interpreters in kilts and bearskin hats marching in unison, playing bagpipes, and firing the noon cannon. The former barracks and other chambers are home to exhibits about life at the fort. If you still have questions, stop a soldier, bagpiper, or washerwoman and ask.

The Citadel is the perfect place to launch an exploration of Halifax: It provides a good geographic context for the city and anchors it historically as well. This National Historic Site is the most heavily visited in Canada, and it's not hard to see why. You won't need more than 45 minutes or an hour here, though.

Citadel Hill. ⓒ 902/426-5080. Admission June to mid-Sept C$11 (US$11/£5.50) adults, C$9.15 (US$9.15/£4.60) seniors, C$5.45 (US$5.45/£2.75) youths (6–16), C$27 (US$27/£14) family; spring and fall C$7.15 (US$7.15/£3.60) adults, C$5.90 (US$5.90/£2.95) seniors, C$3.45 (US$3.45/£1.75) youths 6–16, C$18 (US$18/£9) family; free in winter. July–Aug daily 9am–6pm; May–June and Sept–Oct daily 9am–5pm. Visitor center closed, grounds open Nov–Apr; no guides in fall or winter.

Nova Scotia Museum of Natural History   Situated on the far side of the Citadel from downtown, this modern, midsize museum offers a good introduction to the flora and fauna of Nova Scotia. Galleries include geology, botany, mammals, and birds, plus exhibits of archaeology and Mi'kmaq culture. Especially noteworthy are the extensive collection of lifelike ceramic fungus and the colony of honeybees that freely come and go from their indoor acrylic hive through a tube connected to the outdoors. Allow about 1 hour.

1747 Summer St. ⓒ 902/424-7353. Admission June to mid-Oct C$5.50 (US$5.50/£2.75) adults, C$5 (US$5/£2.50) seniors, C$3.50 (US$3.50/£1.75) children 6–17, C$11–C$16 (US$11–US$16/£5.50–£8) families, free admission Wed nights; mid-Oct to May admission C$3.50 (US$3.50/£1.75) adults, C$3 (US$3/£1.50) seniors, C$2.50 (US$2.50/£1.25) children 6–17, C$7.50–C$10 (US$7.50–US$10/£3.75–£5) families. June to mid-Oct Mon–Sat 9:30am–5:30pm (Wed until 8pm), Sun 1–5:30pm; mid-Oct to May Tues–Sat 9:30am–5pm (Wed until 8pm), Sun 1–5pm.

Province House   Canada's oldest seat of government, Province House has been home to the Nova Scotian legislature since 1819. This exceptional Georgian building is a superb example of the rigorously symmetrical Palladian style. And like a jewel box, its dour stone exterior hides gems of ornamental detailing and artwork inside; note especially the fine plasterwork, rare for a Canadian building of this era. A well-written free booklet is available when you enter and provides helpful background about the building's history and architecture. If the legislature is in session, you can obtain a visitor's pass and sit up in the gallery and watch the business of the province take place.

Within the building also roost a number of fine stories. My favorite: the headless falcons in several rooms. It's said they were decapitated by an agitated legislator with a free-swinging cane who mistook them for eagles during a period of feverish anti-American sentiment in the 1840s. History buffs should allow an hour for this visit.

1776 Hollis St. (near Prince St.). ⓒ 902/424-4661. Free admission. July–Aug Mon–Fri 9am–5pm, Sat–Sun and holidays 10am–4pm; Sept–June Mon–Fri 9am–4pm.

St. Paul's Anglican Church ⍟   Forming one end of the Grand Parade, St. Paul's was the first Anglican cathedral established outside of England and is Canada's oldest Protestant place of worship. Part of the building, which dates from 1750, was fabricated in Boston and erected in Halifax with the help of a royal endowment from King George II. A classic white Georgian building, St. Paul's has fine stained-glass windows. A piece of flying debris from the explosion of 1917 (see Maritime Museum of the Atlantic, above) is lodged in the wall over the doors to the nave. Just a quick drop in is enough to get a sense of the place; take one of the summer-only guided tours if you want to see more.

1749 Argyle St. (on the Grand Parade near Barrington St.). ℭ **902/429-2240**. Mon–Fri 9am–4:30pm; Sun services 8, 9:15, and 11am. Free guided tours June–Aug Mon–Sat.

GARDENS & OPEN SPACE

Fairview Lawn Cemetery ⍟   When the *Titanic* went down April 15, 1912, nearly 2,000 people died. Ship captains from Halifax were recruited to help retrieve the corpses (you can learn about this grim mission at the Maritime Museum, described above). Some 121 victims, mostly ship crew members, were buried at this quiet cemetery located a short drive north of downtown Halifax. Some of the simple graves have names; others just numbers. Interpretive signs highlight some of the stories that survived the tragedy. A brochure with driving directions to this and two other *Titanic* cemeteries may be found at the Maritime Museum and visitor information centers. It's definitely worth an hour or more for *Titanic* fans; others might just spend a few minutes here. Without a car, skip it.

Chisholm Ave., off Connaught Ave., about 4km (2½ miles). Northwest of the Citadel. ℭ **902/490-4883**. Daylight hours year-round.

Point Pleasant Park ⍟   Point Pleasant is one of Canada's finer urban parks, and there's no better place for a walk along the water on a balmy day. This 74-hectare (183-acre) park occupies a wooded peninsular point, and it served for years as one of the linchpins in the city's military defense. You'll find the ruins of early forts and a nicely preserved Martello tower. Halifax has a 999-year lease from Great Britain for the park, for which it pays 1 shilling—about US10¢—per year. You'll also find a lovely gravel carriage road around the point, a small swimming beach, miles of walking trails, and groves of graceful fir trees. The park is located about 2km (1¼ miles) south of the Public Gardens. No bikes are allowed on weekends or holidays.

Point Pleasant Dr. (south end of Halifax). Free admission. Daylight hours. Head south on S. Park St. near Public Gardens and continue on Young.

Public Gardens ⍟⍟ *Kids*   The Public Gardens literally took seed in 1753, when it was founded as a private garden. It was acquired by the Nova Scotia Horticultural Society in 1836, and it assumed its present look in 1875, during the peak of the Victorian era. As such, the garden is one of the nation's Victorian masterpieces, more rare and evocative than any mansard-roofed mansion. You'll find wonderful examples of many 19th-century trends in outdoor landscaping, from the "natural" winding walks and ornate fountains to the duck ponds and fussy Victorian bandstand. (Stop by at 2pm Sun in summer for a free concert.) There are lots of leafy trees, lush lawns, cranky ducks who have long since lost their fear of humans, and tiny ponds. The overseers have been commendably stingy with memorial statues and plaques. You'll usually find dowagers and kids feeding pigeons, and smartly uniformed guards slowly walking the grounds.

Spring Garden and S. Park St. Free admission. Spring to late fall 8am–dusk.

Tips A Side Trip to Peggy's Cove ⍟⍟

About 42km (26 miles) southwest of Halifax is the picturesque fishing village of **Peggy's Cove** ⍟⍟ (pop. 120). The village offers a postcard-perfect tableau: an octagonal lighthouse (surely one of the most photographed in the world), tiny fishing shacks, and graceful fishing boats bobbing in the postage stamp–size harbor. The bonsailike perfection hasn't gone unnoticed by the big tour operators, however, so it's a rare summer day when you're not sharing the experience with a few hundred of your close, personal bus-tour friends. The village is home to a handful of B&Bs, and a gallery, but scenic values draw the day-trippers with cameras and lots of film. While there, make sure to check out the touching **Swissair Flight 111 Memorial** ⍟ among the rocks just before the turnoff to the cove; this site memorializes the passengers of that flight, which crashed into the Atlantic just off the coast here in 1998.

Want to stay awhile? One good lodging choice in the area is **Peggy's Cove B&B** (© **888/634-8973** or 902/634-4543), a restored three-bedroom fisherman's home close to the lighthouse with rooms at C$95–$C165 (US$95–US$165/£48–£83) per night. If it's full, **Code's Oceanside Inn** (© **888/823-2765**), about 3km (2 miles) away in West Dover, has two rooms and a suite for C$105 to C$195 (US$105–US$195/£53–£98) per night

WHERE TO STAY
EXPENSIVE

Cambridge Suites ⍟ (Kids)   The attractive, modern Cambridge Suites is nicely located near the foot of the Citadel and is well positioned for exploring Halifax. It's perfect for families—40 of the units are two-room suites featuring kitchenettes with microwaves, two phones, coffeemakers, and hair dryers. Expect comfortable, inoffensive decor, and above-average service; everything in the place was freshened up in 2001. Dofsky's Grill on the first floor is open for all three meals, which are palatable if not exciting. Look for pasta, blackened haddock, burgers, and jerked chicken.

1583 Brunswick St., Halifax, NS B3J 3P5. © **888/417-8483** or 902/420-0555. Fax 902/420-9379. www.cambridge suiteshalifax.com. 200 units. C$119–C$299 (US$119–US$299/£60–£150) suite. Children under 18 stay free in parent's room. AE, DC, MC, V. Valet or self-parking C$14 (US$14/£7). **Amenities:** Restaurant; health club; Jacuzzi; sauna; concierge; room service; babysitting; coin-op laundry; dry cleaning. *In room:* A/C, TV, dataport, kitchenette (some units), minibar, fridge (some units), coffeemaker, hair dryer, iron.

Delta Halifax ⍟   The Delta Halifax is a slick and modern (built in 1972) downtown hotel that offers premium service. It's located just a block off the waterfront, to which it's connected via skyway, but navigating it involves an annoying labyrinth of parking garages and charmless concrete structures. The lobby is streetside; guests take elevators up above a six-floor parking garage to reach their rooms. The hotel is frequented largely by business travelers during the week. Ask for a room in the so-called "resort wing" near the pool, which feels a bit further away from the chatter of downtown and the press of business. A number of rooms have balconies and many have harbor views; ask when you book. Rooms are in two classes—either 28 or 46 sq. m (300 or 500 sq. ft.)—and all are furnished simply and unexceptionably with standard-issue hotel furniture. The Crown Bistrot restaurant (run by the same chef who runs the nearby, affiliated Delta Barrington's cafe) offers good Continental, Asian, and Maritime-inflected cuisine. Sam Slick's Lounge features a surprisingly varied bar menu.

1990 Barrington St., Halifax, NS B3J 1P2. © **877/814-7706** or 902/425-6700. Fax 902/425-6214. www.deltahalifax. com. 296 units. C$134–C$284 (US$134–US$284/£67–£142) double. AE, MC, V. Valet parking C$22 (US$22/£11), self-parking C$19 (US$19/£9.50). **Amenities:** Restaurant; bar; indoor pool; health club; Jacuzzi; sauna; concierge; car-rental desk; shopping arcade; limited room service; babysitting; laundry service; dry cleaning. *In room:* A/C, TV, dataport, minibar, coffeemaker, hair dryer, iron.

The Halliburton ℛ
The Halliburton is a well-appointed, well-run, and elegant country inn located in the heart of downtown. Named after former resident Sir Brenton Halliburton (Nova Scotia's first chief justice), the inn is spread among three town house–style buildings, which are connected via gardens and sun decks in the rear but not internally. The main building was constructed in 1809 and was converted to an inn in 1995, when it was modernized without any loss of its native charm. All guest rooms are subtly furnished with fine antiques, but few are so rare that you'd fret about damaging them. The rooms are rich and masculine in tone, and light on frilly stuff. Among the best: room no. 113, relatively small but with a lovely working fireplace and unique skylighted bathroom. Room nos. 102 and 109 are both suites with wet bars and fireplaces; there's also a studio apartment. Halliburton is popular with business travelers, yet it's also a romantic spot for couples to hide out in. The intimate first-floor dining room **Stories** ℛ serves nightly; it's dusky and wonderful, with a menu that's small yet inventive. The seafood has always been reliable, but there's also a new emphasis on other tastes such as game and duck.

5184 Morris St., Halifax, NS B3J 1B3. © **888/512-3344** or 902/420-0658. Fax 902/423-2324. www.halliburton.ns.ca. 29 units. C$145–C$350 (US$145–US$350/£73–£175) double. All rates include continental breakfast and parking (limited). AE, MC, V. **Amenities:** Restaurant; room service; babysitting; dry cleaning. *In room:* A/C, TV, coffeemaker, hair dryer.

The Lord Nelson Hotel and Suites ℛ
The Lord Nelson was built in 1928, and was for years the city's preeminent hostelry. It gradually sank in esteem and eventually ended up as a flophouse. In 1998, it was purchased and received a long-overdue top-to-bottom renovation. It certainly has location going for it: It's right across from the lovely Public Gardens and abuts lively Spring Garden Road. Rooms are furnished with Georgian reproductions. The business-class Flagship Rooms feature desks, ergonomic office chairs, robes, free local calls, and morning newspapers. The hotel charges a premium for a room that faces the street or the gardens, but it's worth it; others face into a rather bleak courtyard filled with service equipment. The Victory Arms is a cozy and convincing English-style pub located off the handsome coffered lobby. There's British pub fare like bangers and mash and fish and chips, but also more inventive cuisine such as Singapore noodles, naan pizzas, and Cajun-spiced cod sandwiches.

1515 S. Park St., Halifax, NS B3J 2L2. © **800/565-2020** or 902/423-6331. Fax 902/491-6148. www.lordnelsonhotel. com. 260 units. C$139–C$259 (US$139–US$259/£70–£130) double. Valet parking C$20 (US$20/£10), self-parking C$15 (US$15/£7.50). AE, DC, DISC, MC, V. Pets allowed with C$100 (US$100/£50) deposit. **Amenities:** Restaurant; bar; health club; sauna; concierge; limited room service; babysitting; laundry; dry cleaning. *In room:* A/C, TV, coffeemaker, hair dryer, iron.

MODERATE
Halifax Waverley Inn ℛ
The Waverley is adorned in high Victorian style, as befits its 1866 provenance. Flamboyant playwright Oscar Wilde was a guest in 1882, and

one suspects he had a hand in the decorating scheme. There's walnut trim, red uphol-stered furniture, and portraits of sourpuss Victorians at every turn. The headboards in the guest rooms are especially elaborate—some look like props from Gothic horror movies. Room no. 130 has a unique Chinese wedding bed and a Jacuzzi (about 10 rooms have private Jacuzzis).

1266 Barrington St., Halifax, NS B3J 1Y5. ℂ 800/565-9346 or 902/423-9346. Fax 902/425-0167. www.waverleyinn. com. 34 units. June–Oct C$99–C$279 (US$99–US$279/£50–£140) double. Rates include continental breakfast, snacks, afternoon tea, and parking. DC, MC, V. *In room:* A/C, TV, hair dryer (some units), Jacuzzi (some units), no phone (some units).

INEXPENSIVE

The 75-bed **Halifax Heritage House Hostel** (ℂ 902/422-3863) is located at 1253 Barrington St., within walking distance of downtown attractions. You'll usually share rooms with other travelers (several private and family rooms are available); there are lockers in each room, shared bathrooms, and a shared, fully equipped kitchen. Rates are C$20 (US$20/£10) and up per person in dormitories, C$50 (C$50/£25) for a double bed in a private room.

A short way from downtown but convenient to bus lines are university dorm rooms open to travelers during the summer, when school isn't in session (that is, mid-May through mid-August). **Dalhousie University** (ℂ 888/271-9222 or 902/494-8840) rents out a range of one-, two-, and three-bedroom units—furnished with plain sin-gle beds each—to the public. Note that a 2-night minimum stay is required for some of these units.

WHERE TO DINE
EXPENSIVE

Bish World Cuisine ★★★ *Finds* FUSION   Maurizio strikes again! The culinary wiz-ard behind the deservedly popular daMaurizio (see below) in the Brewery Market has daringly opened a second high-tone eatery—practically across the street from the other one—and, against the odds in a tough economic moment, it's already supplant-ing his original fine dining establishment as the "in" place to paint this town red. Tucked into a harborside location at the back of the upscale Bishop's Landing devel-opment (hence the name—I think), this place combines Asian and Continental influ-ences to fine effect, much like a hot young chef in Manhattan might do.

Exhibit A: appetizers and first courses of mussels in garlic and wine, pulled-pork quesadillas, a tomato-chèvre tart, foie gras with blueberries and cassis, tempura scal-lops with ponzu sauce, a lobster-corn chowder, and the like. Exhibit B: main courses such as seared Angus medallions and cremini mushrooms, lamb served with mint or curry, Kobe beef burgers, roasted duck with wild cherries and port sauce, sesame-crusted tuna, or a peanutty chicken and shrimp pad Thai. There's also local lobster, of course, here split and garlic-broiled. Finish your meal off with house-made ice creams or sorbets, crème caramel, a rhubarb-ginger crisp, a peanut brittle sundae (yum!), or perhaps a lemon tart. The water views, professional service, and fine bar and wine list only enhance the experience of having temporarily traded in New Scotland for New York. Dress smartly, expect Halifax's finest to be out in force on the weekends, and reserve early in anticipation of that fact.

1475 Lower Water St. (in Bishop's Landing, entrance at end of Bishop St.). ℂ 902/425-7993. Reservations highly recommended. Main courses C$20–C$27 (US$20–US$27/£10–£14). AE, DC, MC, V. Mon–Sat 5:30–10pm.

daMaurizio ☆☆☆ ITALIAN   DaMaurizio does everything right. Located in a cleverly adapted former brewery, the vast space has been divided into a complex of hives with columns and exposed brick that add to the atmosphere and heighten the anticipation of the meal. The decor shuns decorative doodads for clean lines and simple class. Much the same might be said of the menu. You could start with an appetizer such as squid quick-fried with olive oil, tomato, and chiles; pick through a romaine salad with grapefruit and candied walnuts; go for risotto or minestrone; or just order simple ravioli with sausage. The main courses tax even the most decisive of diners: On a given night, they might include pastas featuring such accoutrements as lobster, leeks, white wine, cream, and fresh ginger; pan-seared scallops with chile-and-port sauce; or a whole lobster, gratinéed with sweet peppers, onions, brandy, and cream, among many other inspired choices. Desserts run beyond tiramisu and gelati to cake, panna cotta, a fruit, nut, and cheese plate, and tartufo: a molded almond gelato, filled with chocolate and topped with crumbled amaretti and sided with crème anglaise and a chocolate ganache. The kitchen doesn't try to dazzle with outlandish creativity but rather relies instead on the best ingredients and a close eye on perfect preparation.

1496 Lower Water St. (in the Brewery). ✆ **902/423-0859.** Reservations highly recommended. Main courses C$28–C$33 (US$28–US$33/£14–£17); pasta dishes C$11–C$16 (US$11–US$16/£5.50–£8). AE, DC, MC, V. Mon–Sat 5–10pm.

MODERATE

Ryan Duffy's ☆ STEAKHOUSE   Located on the upper level of a small shopping mall on Spring Garden, Ryan Duffy's may at first strike diners as a knockoff of a middlebrow chain, like T.G.I. Friday's. It's not—it's a couple of notches above. The house specialty is steak, for which the place is justly famous. The beef comes from corn-fed Hereford, black Angus, and Shorthorn, and it is nicely tender. (When the waiter delivered me an oversize steak knife, he said, "You don't really need this, but it's all part of the show.") Steaks are grilled over a natural wood charcoal and can be prepared with garlic, cilantro butter, or other extras upon request. The more expensive cuts, such as the strip loin, are trimmed right at the table. If you move away from steak on the menu, expect less consistency; the shrimp cocktail is disappointing, but the Caesar salad is wonderful. Americans who are disappointed that they can't order rare steak much anymore owing to liability concerns will like it here—you can even order it "blue-rare."

5640 Spring Garden Rd. ✆ **902/421-1116.** Reservations recommended. Main courses C$9–C$15 (US$9–US$15/£4.50–£7.50) lunch, C$19–C$38 (US$19–US$38/£9.50–£19) dinner. AE, DC, MC, V. Mon–Fri 11:30am–2pm and 5–10pm; Sat–Sun 5–10pm.

Sweet Basil Bistro ☆☆ *(Finds)* UPMARKET PASTA   Of the waterfront's many highbrow and lowbrow spots, Sweet Basil might be my very favorite. It has the casual feel of a local trattoria, but the elegant menu transcends the limited regional offerings you might expect. The chef somehow manages to meld Thai influences, pasta, cream sauces, and local seafood cooked in fusion style without going overboard, resulting in truly interesting creations: a bouillabaisse of lobster, scallops, mussels, shrimp, and haddock, for example; pork tenderloin with a crabapple butter; pistachio-crusted chicken breast with chevre, pears, and basil cream; a Guinness-brined rack of lamb; and a partridgeberry-stuffed duck breast with a white truffle demiglace. Desserts such as a warmed apple cake, caramelized banana split over a coconut macaroon, or a Grand Marnier–flavored chocolate pâté make very fitting finishes. A recent addition to this winner is the weekend brunch, from 10am to 3pm Saturdays and Sundays: Look for crepes, breakfast burritos, egg dishes, fish cakes, and a hearty filled brioche French toast—all for just C$10 (US$10/£5) per person.

1866 Upper Water St. ✆ 902/425-2133. Reservations recommended. Main courses C$8–C$16 (US$8–US$16/£4–£8) lunch, C$14–C$24 (US$14–US$24/£7–£12) dinner. AE, DC, MC, V. Daily 11:30am–10pm.

INEXPENSIVE

Cheapside Café (*Value* (*Kids* CAFE   Yes, it's cheap, but the name actually comes from an open market that once occupied this street, named after a similar market in London. The cheerful and lively Cheapside Café is tucked inside the Provincial Building, one of two structures housing the Art Gallery of Nova Scotia. The interior is almost like a little museum with its fun artwork on the walls and table settings. The daily card of soups and sandwiches might feature choices like chicken breast with avocado-and-mango chutney, roast beef with fried onions, or smoked salmon served with an egg pancake and asparagus. Other daily fare might include jerked pork, pasta primavera, fish cakes, Thai chicken salads with peanut sauce, quiche, poached salmon, and cold open-faced shrimp sandwiches. Desserts are delicious—especially notable is the Cheapside Café Torte, with its hazelnut crunch.

1723 Hollis St. (inside the Art Gallery of Nova Scotia). ✆ 902/425-4494. Sandwiches and entrees C$10–C$13 (US$10–US$13/£5–£6.50). MC, V. Tues–Sat 10am–5pm; Sun noon–5pm.

Henry House (*R* BREWPUB   Eastern Canada's pioneer brewpub—this was the first—is housed in an austere building far down Barrington Street. The starkly handsome 1834 stone building has a medium-fancy dining room upstairs with red tablecloths and captains' chairs. (The pub downstairs is more boisterous and informal.) You can order off the same menu at either spot, and it's what you'd expect at a brewpub, only better tasting: Entrees include beer-battered fish, steak sandwiches, an excellent smoked-salmon club sandwich, burgers, beef-and-beer stew, salads, and meatloaf. The beer here is fresh and good; they also do Sunday brunches.

1222 Barrington St. ✆ 902/423-5660. Main courses C$7–C$14 (US$7–US$14/£3.50–£7). AE, DC, MC, V. Mon–Sat 11:30am–12:30pm; Sun noon–11pm.

Il Mercato (*R* ITALIAN   Light-colored Tuscan sponged walls and big rustic terracotta tiles on the floor set an appropriate mood at this popular spot amid the clamor of Spring Garden. Come early or late or expect to wait a bit (no reservations accepted), but it's worth making the effort. You'll find a great selection of meals at prices that approach bargain level. Start by selecting antipasti from the deli counter in the front (you point; the waitstaff will bring them to your table). The focaccias are superb and come with a pleasing salad, while the ravioli with roast chicken and wild mushrooms is sublime. There are plenty of pastas and thin-crust pizzas on the menu to satisfy your fix, while non-Italian entrees include grilled rack of lamb with Dijon, a seafood medley cooked up with peppers, and a strip steak topped with Gorgonzola.

5650 Spring Garden Rd. ✆ 902/422-2866. Reservations not accepted. Main courses C$12–C$20 (US$12–US$20/£6–£10). AE, DC, MC, V. Mon–Sat 11am–11pm.

Satisfaction Feast VEGETARIAN   Located along the newly cool stretch of Grafton Street, Satisfaction Feast, Halifax's original vegetarian restaurant (it opened in 1981), has been voted one of the top 10 veggie restaurants in Canada by the *Globe and Mail.* It's funky and fun, with a certain spare grace inside and a canopy and sidewalk tables for summer lounging. Entrees include lasagna, bean burritos, pesto pasta, veggie burgers, and a macrobiotic rice casserole. There's also "neatloaf" and tofu-and-rice-based "peace burgers" for those who like their food with cute names. The vegan fruit crisp is the dessert to hold out for. They also do takeout; consider a hummus-and-pita picnic atop nearby Citadel Hill.

3559 Robie St. ✆ **902/422-3540**. http://satisfaction-feast.com. Main courses C$5–C$12 (US$5–US$12/£2.50–£6). AE, DC, MC, V. Daily 11:30am–9:30pm (winter till 8:30pm).

HALIFAX BY NIGHT

THE PERFORMING ARTS   **Shakespeare by the Sea** (✆ 902/422-0295) stages a whole line of Bardic and non-Bardic productions July through August at several alfresco venues around the city. Most are held at Point Pleasant Park, where the ruins of old forts and buildings are used as the stage settings for delightful performances, with the audience sprawled on the grass, many enjoying picnic dinners with their *Taming of the Shrew* or *All's Well That Ends Well*. Shows are technically free, though the players ask a suggested donation of C$10 (US$10/£5) per person. The occasional, more elaborate productions (past shows have included *King Lear* at the Citadel and *Titus Andronicus* at the park's Martello Tower) at other locations have limited seating, with ticket prices that might range up to C$30 (US$30/£15).

The **Neptune Theatre,** 1593 Argyle St. (✆ **902/429-7070**), benefited from a C$13.5-million renovation and now also includes an intimate 200-seat studio theater. Top-notch dramatic productions are offered throughout the year. (The main season runs Sept–May, with a summer season filling in the gap with eclectic performances.) Main-stage tickets range generally from around C$15 to C$45 (US$15–US$45/£7.50–£23).

CLUB & BAR SCENE

The young and restless tend to congregate in pubs, in nightclubs, and at street corners along two axes that converge at the public library: Grafton Street and Spring Garden Road. If you're thirsty, wander the neighborhoods around here, and you're likely to find a spot that could serve as a temporary home for the evening. One of the coolest places to hang out is **Economy Shoe Shop** (✆ 902/423-7463) at 1663 Argyle St. In the evening (and late afternoons on Sat), you'll also find lively Maritime music and good beer at the **Lower Deck Pub** (✆ 902/425-1501), one of the restaurants in the Historic Properties complex on the waterfront. There's music nightly, and often on Saturday afternoons. Among the clubs offering local rock, ska, and the like are the **Marquee Club,** 2041 Gottingen St. (✆ 902/423-2072), and **The Attic,** 1741 Grafton St. (✆ 902/423-0909). **Maxwell's Plum** at 1600 Grafton St. (✆ 902/423-5090) is a free-for-all English pub where peanut shells litter the floor and there are dozens of selections of import and Canadian draft and bottled beers.

8 The Eastern Shore: Rugged Coastline from Halifax to Cape Breton Island

Heading from Halifax toward Cape Breton Island (or vice versa), you need to choose between two basic routes. If you're burning to get to your destination, take the main roads of Route 102 connecting to Route 104, the Trans-Canada Highway (the one with the maple leaf). If you're in no particular hurry and are most content venturing down narrow lanes, destination unknown, by all means allow a couple of days to wind along the Eastern Shore, mostly along Route 7. (Note that official tourism materials refer to this stretch as the Marine Drive instead of the Eastern Shore, for whatever reason.)

Along the way you'll be rewarded with glimpses of a rugged coastline that's wilder and more remote than the coast south of Halifax. Communities here tend to be farther apart, less genteel, and stocked with far fewer services—or tourists. With its rugged terrain and remote locales, this region is a good bet for those drawn to the outdoors and seeking coastal solitude.

ESSENTIALS

GETTING THERE   Route 107 and Route 7 run along or near the coast from Dartmouth to Stillwater (near Sherbrooke). A patchwork of other routes—including 211, 316, 16, and 344—continues onward along the coast to the causeway to Cape Breton. (It's all pretty obvious on a map.) An excursion along the entire coastal route—from Dartmouth to Cape Breton Island with a detour to Canso—is 407km (253 miles).

VISITOR INFORMATION   Several tourist information centers are staffed along the route. You'll find the best-stocked and most-helpful centers in **Sheet Harbour,** next to the waterfall (© **902/885-2595;** daily in summer 10am–7pm); in **Sherbrooke Village**, at the museum (© **902/522-2400;** daily in summer 9:30am–5:30pm), and in **Canso** at 1297 Union St. (© **902/366-2170;** daily in summer 9am–6pm).

EXPLORING THE EASTERN SHORE

This section assumes travel northeastward from Halifax toward Cape Breton. If you're traveling the opposite direction, hold this book upside down (just kidding).

Between Halifax and Sheet Harbour the route plays hide-and-seek with the coast, touching the water periodically before veering inland. The most scenic areas are around wild and open **Ship Harbour,** as well as **Spry Harbour,** noted for its attractive older homes and islands looming offshore.

Between Ship and Spry harbours is the town of Tangier, home to **Coastal Adventures** (© **877/404-2774** or 902/772-2774), which specializes in kayak tours. It's run by Scott Cunningham, who literally wrote the book on Nova Scotia kayaking (he's the author of the definitive guide to paddling this coast). This well-run operation is situated on a beautiful island-dotted part of the coast, but it specializes in multiday trips throughout Atlantic Canada. You're best off writing (P.O. Box 77, Tangier, NS B0J 3H0) or calling for a brochure well in advance of your trip.

There's also a terrific little fish-smoking business just outside Tangier, **Willie Krauch & Sons Smokehouse** (© **800/758-4412** or 902/772-2188). Krauch (pronounced "craw") and family sell wood-smoked Atlantic salmon, mackerel, and eel in an unpretentious little store; they'll also give you a tour of the premises, if you like, where you can check out the old-style smoking process in action. Take some to go for a picnic. It's open until 6pm daily.

Adjacent to the well-marked Liscombe Lodge (see below), and just over the main bridge, is the **Liscomb River Trail** system. Trails follow the river both north and south of Route 7. The main hiking trail follows the river upstream for 5km (3 miles), crosses it on a suspension bridge, and then returns on the other side. The Mayflower Point Trail follows the river southward toward the coast, then loops back inland.

Continuing on Route 211 beyond historic Sherbrooke Village (see description below), you'll drive through a wonderful landscape of lakes, ocean inlets, and upland bogs and soon come to the scenic **Country Harbour Ferry** (© **902/389-2200**). The 12-car cable ferry crosses each direction every half-hour when open; it's a picturesque crossing of a broad river encased by rounded and wooded bluffs. The fare is C$5

(US$5/£2.50) per car, which includes driver and passengers. If the ferry isn't running, you'll have to turn right around and head back, so it's wise to check at the Canso or Sherbrooke visitor centers before detouring this way.

Farther along (you'll be on Rte. 316 after the ferry), you'll come to **Tor Bay Provincial Park.** It's 4km (2½ miles) off the main road, but well worth the detour on a sunny day. The park features three sandy crescent beaches backed by grassy dunes and small ponds that are slowly being taken over by bog and spruce forest. The short boardwalk loop is especially picturesque.

Way out on the eastern tip of Nova Scotia's mainland is the end-of-the-world town of Canso (pop. 1,200). It's a rough-edged fishing and oil-shipping town, often windswept and foggy. (If you're coming to Canso in summer, watch out for the annual folk music festival created to honor Nova Scotia's own Stan Rogers.) The chief attraction here is **Grassy Island Fort National Historic Site** (*©* 902/295-2069), part of the newly created Canso Islands National Historic Site.

First stop by the small interpretive center on the waterfront (daily 10am–6pm June through mid-Sept) and ask about the boat schedule. A park-run boat takes you out to Grassy Island, which once housed a bustling community of fishermen and traders from New England—the interpretive center features artifacts recovered from the island. A trail also links several historic sites within the island, which feels a bit melancholy whether it's foggy or not. Boat fares are by donation; I always give them a few dollars per person.

Sherbrooke Village *★★* *(Kids)* About half of the town of Sherbrooke comprises Sherbrooke Village, a historic section surrounded by low fences, water, and fields. (It's managed as part of the Nova Scotia Museum.) You'll have to pay admission to wander around, but the price is well worth it. This is the largest restored village in Nova Scotia, and it's unique in several respects. For one, almost all of the buildings are on their original sites (only two have been moved). Also, many homes are still occupied by local residents, and private homes are interspersed with the buildings open to visitors. About two dozen buildings have been restored and opened to the public, from a convincing general store to an operating blacksmith shop and post office. Look also for the former temperance hall, courthouse, printery, boat-building shop, drugstore, and schoolhouse. These are all staffed by genial costumed interpreters, who can tell you about what life was like in the 1860s around here. Be sure to ask about the source of the town's early prosperity; you might be surprised. Plan to spend up to a half-day here, depending on your (and your kids') interest level.

Rte. 7, Sherbrooke. *©* 902/522-2400. Admission C$9 (US$9/£4.50) adults, C$6.50 (US$6.50/£3.65) seniors, C$3.75 (US$3.75/£1.90) children, C$25 (US$25/£13) families. June to mid-Oct daily 9:30am–5pm.

WHERE TO STAY & DINE

Other than a handful of motels and B&Bs, few accommodations are available on the Eastern Shore.

Liscombe Lodge *★★* *(Kids)* This modern complex, owned and operated by the province, consists of a central lodge and a series of smaller cottages and outbuildings. It's situated in a remote part of the coast, adjacent to hiking trails and a popular boating area at the mouth of the Liscomb River. The lodge bills itself as "the nature lover's resort," and indeed it offers good access to both forest and water. But it's not exactly rustic, with well-tended lawns, bland modern architecture, shuffleboard, a marina, and even an oversize outdoor chessboard. In addition, plenty of kid-friendly offerings (table tennis, horseshoe pitches, and so forth) make this a good choice for vacationing families. The rooms are modern and motel-like; the cottages and chalets have multiple bedrooms and are good for families. The dining room is open to the public and serves resort fare.

Rte. 7, Liscomb Mills, NS B0J 2A0. (C) **800/665-6343** or 902/779-2307. Fax 902/779-2700. www.signatureresorts. com. 68 units. C$140–C$350 (US$140–US$350/£70–£175) double. Inquire about packages. AE, DISC, MC, V. Closed mid-Oct to mid-May. Pets allowed in chalets. **Amenities:** Restaurant; indoor pool; tennis court; fitness center; free bikes; coin-op washers and dryers; shuffleboard. *In room:* TV w/VCR (some units), fridge (some units), hair dryer, iron, no phone.

SeaWind Landing Country Inn ★★   What to do when your boat-building business plummets because the fisheries business is on the downturn? How about opening an inn instead? That's what Lorraine and Jim Colvin decided to do, and their 8-hectare (20-acre) oceanfront compound is the delightful result. Some of the guest rooms here are located in the 130-year-old main house, which has been tastefully modernized and updated. The rest are in a more recent outbuilding—anything that's been lost in historic charm is more than recovered by the brightness, great ocean views, and double Jacuzzis these units possess. The Colvins are especially knowledgeable about local art (much of the work on display here was produced in the area), and they have compiled a literate and helpful guide to the region for guests to use while exploring. The property also has three private sand beaches, and coastal boat tours and picnic lunches can easily be arranged for an extra charge. The inn also serves **dinner** ★ nightly, to inn guests only, featuring local products prepared in country-French style washed down with wines from the inn's own wine cellar.

1 Wharf Rd., Charlos Cove, NS B0H 1T0. (C) **800/563-4667** or 902/525-2108. Fax 902/525-2108. www.seawind landing.com. 10 units. C$95–C$169 (US$95–US$169/£48–£85) double. AE, MC, V. Closed mid-Oct to mid-May. **Amenities:** Dining room; laundry service. *In room:* Hair dryer, Jacuzzi (most units), no phone.

9 Cape Breton Island ★★★

Isolated and craggy Cape Breton Island—Nova Scotia's northernmost landmass— should be high on the list of don't-miss destinations for travelers, especially those with an adventurous bent. The island's chief draw is **Cape Breton Highlands National Park,** far north on the island's western lobe. But there's also the historic fort at **Louisbourg** and scenic **Bras d'Or Lake,** the inland saltwater lake that nearly cleaves the island in two. Above all, there are the picturesque drives. It's hard to find a road that's not a scenic route in Cape Breton. By turns the vistas are wild and dramatic, then settled and pastoral.

When traveling on the island, be alert to the cultural richness. Just as southern Nova Scotia was largely settled by English Loyalists fleeing the United States after they lost the War of Independence, Cape Breton was principally settled by Highland Scots whose families came out on the wrong side of rebellions against the Crown. You can still see that heritage in the accents of elders in some of the more remote villages, and in the great popularity of Scottish-style folk music.

You'll often hear references to the **Cabot Trail** ★★★ when on the island. This is the official designation for the 300km (186-mile) roadway around the northwest part of the island, which encompasses the national park. It's named after John Cabot, who many believe first set foot on North American soil near Cape North. (However, many disagree, especially in Newfoundland.)

Cape Breton Island

Note: Jump ahead to section 10 for information on adventures in Cape Breton Highlands National Park.

ESSENTIALS

GETTING THERE   Cape Breton is connected to the mainland via the Canso Causeway, a 24m-wide (79-ft.), 65m-deep (213-ft.), 1,290m-long (4,232-ft.) stone causeway built in 1955 with 10 million tons of rock. (You can see a half mountain, the other half of which was sacrificed for the cause, as you approach the island on the Trans-Canada Hwy.) The causeway is 262km (163 miles) from the New Brunswick border at Amherst, 272km (169 miles) from Halifax.

VISITOR INFORMATION   Nine tourist information centers dot the island. The best stocked (and a much recommended first stop) is the bustling **Port Hastings Info**

Centre ((C) **902/625-4201**), located on your right just after crossing the Canso Causeway. It's open daily from 8am to 8:30pm most of the year, although closed January through late April.

SPECIAL EVENTS   Celtic Colours ✸✸✸ ((C) **877/285-2321** or 902/562-6700; www.celtic-colours.com) is a big annual music shindig timed to approximate the peak of the lovely highland foliage. It usually begins around the second week of October and lasts a full foot-stompin', pennywhistlin', fiddle-playin' week. The musical performances are the obvious highlight, though they can cost as much as C$60 (US$60/£30) per person for a real headline act. More typical *ceilidh* (pronounced *kay*-lee) nights of music and storytelling cost more like C$20 (US$20/£10), and the more popular local performers sell out months in advance; call well ahead if you've got your heart set on some particular act or another. Otherwise, just buy a ticket to anything. You almost can't go wrong.

MABOU & VICINITY ✸✸

The little village of Mabou (pop. 600) sits on a deep, protected inlet along the island's picturesque western shore. This former coal-mining town has made itself over as a lobster-fishing town, though you don't come here for crustaceans; instead, scenery and culture beckon. Attractive drives and bike rides are easy to find in the area; almost any road you choose will yield opportunities to break out the camera or just lean against your vehicle and enjoy the panorama. The town itself consists of a short main street, a clump of homes, a gas station, a few eateries and services, and (if you can find it) a scenic little beach.

But there's a hidden bonus to the area, giving it an importance all of proportion to its size: Local residents are strongly oriented toward **music,** even more so than is usual on already-musical Cape Breton Isle. The local kids, nearly all of Scots descent, grow up playing instruments, singing, and dancing; amazingly, this tiny town has produced not only several international hit Celtic music acts, but also the current premier of Nova Scotia (Rodney MacDonald), a former step dancer and fiddler elected to the post in February 2006 at the age of just 34. Evening entertainment here revolves around fiddle playing, square dancing, or the traditional gathering of musicians and storytellers known as a **ceilidh** ✸✸✸. These events take place in pubs, civic buildings, outdoors, people's homes . . . anywhere. To find out where things are going on, your best bets are to stop by the village grocery stores and pubs.

In a handsome valley between Mabou and Inverness is the distinctive post-and-beam **Glenora Distillery** ✸ ((C) **800/839-0491** or 902/258-2662). This modern distillery—said to be North America's only single-malt whisky producer—began producing spirits from a pure local stream in 1990, and began selling it in 2000; they'll tell you that the Cape Breton water is what makes all the difference, and is the reason the owner chose to put the factory here—seemingly in the middle of nowhere. Production runs take place in the fall, but tours of the facility are offered throughout the year. Tours cost C$7 (US$7/£3.50) and last about a half-hour (daily 9am–5pm), culminating in free samples; the tours conveniently end near the gift shop.

WHERE TO STAY

Glenora Inn & Distillery Resort ✸✸   So, when was the last time you spent the night at a distillery? This distiller of single-malt whiskey added nine modern rooms in a building next to the pub, which in turn is located next to the actual distillery. The contemporary yet rustic architecture has a pleasant feel to it, but the real attraction is easy access to the pub and restaurant on the premises, which often features live performers from the area. The distillery has the feel of being in a remote vale in the Scottish highlands. Honeymooners will appreciate the half-dozen modern chalets, located on the hills overlooking the distillery: each has a Jacuzzi, satellite TV, and a wonderful view of the mist-covered valley below. (Do be prepared for a bone-rattling ride up the hill on a gravel road.) These chalets are available in one-, two-, or three-bedroom configurations.

Rte. 19, Glenville, NS B0E 1X0. © **800/839-0491** or 902/258-2662. Fax 902/258-3572. www.glenoradistillery.com. 15 units. C$120–C$150 (US$120–US$150/£60–£75) double; C$175–C$240 (US$175–US$240/£88–£120) chalet. AE, MC, V. Closed mid-Oct to mid-May. **Amenities:** Restaurant; bar. *In room:* TV, Jacuzzi (some units).

Mabou River Inn 🌦 *Finds*   Located not far from the river and adjacent to the Mother of Sorrows Pioneer Shrine, this former boarding school has been converted twice, first into a winning youth hostel and then into this homey little inn just off the main road. Hosts Donna and David Cameron keep things running smoothly and dispense great advice; nature lovers will appreciate the opportunity to hike, kayak, fish, and mountain bike on the scenic Ceilidh Trail using the inn's rental equipment, while night owls can stroll a few minutes across the bridge and into town to check out the local traditional music offerings that fill Mabou in summer. Note that while all nine of the main inn rooms come with their own private bathrooms, you have to put on your slippers and walk to get to seven of them. The kitchen and dining room for guests are useful; there are also three two-bedroom apartment suites good for families, since they come with TVs, VCRs, kitchens, and phones. At night the staff cooks up some good pizzas and serves beer and wine with them.

19 SW Ridge Rd. (P.O. Box 255), Mabou, NS B0E 1X0. © **888/627-9744** or 902/945-2356. Fax 902/945-2605. www. mabouriverinn.com. 12 units. C$75–C$99 (US$75–US$99/£38–£50) double; C$125–C$155 (US$125–US$155/ £63–£78) suite. AE, MC, V. **Amenities:** Restaurant; bike and sea kayak rentals; game room. *In room:* TV/VCR (some units), kitchenette (some units), no phone (some units).

WHERE TO DINE

The Red Shoe Pub 🌶 *Finds* PUB FARE   You won't find a more local pub than The Shoe, which was formerly operated by the famous Rankin family of musicians. The menu here features basic pub fare such as soups, salads, ribs, and wings; there are a few beers on tap, plus all the obvious bottles. The real highlight, though, is the frequent musical performances in the pub—the next area Celtic music star might be playing for peanuts on the night you swing by. Be aware that the place is small and, when crowded, can get a bit claustrophobic; it helps to know a local, though the influx of summer tourists coming for music and beer keeps the mix interesting. With the modern times has come another change: This is now a completely nonsmoking venue (even the patio), which was definitely not the case for many years here. A small kids' menu and a line of surprisingly upscale desserts like sticky toffee pudding, gingerbread, lemon pavlova with lemon curd, and berry cobbler have also been added.

Main St. (Hwy. 19), Mabou. © **902/945-2996.** Meals C$5–C$12 (US$5–US$12/£2.25–£6). MC, V. Mon–Wed 11:30am–midnight; Thurs–Sat 11:30am–2am; Sun noon–midnight.

MARGAREE VALLEY 🌶

West of Baddeck and south of Chéticamp, the Margaree Valley region consists of the area from the village of Margaree Valley near the headwaters of the Margaree River, down the river to Margaree Harbor on Cape Breton's west coast. Some seven small communities are clustered in along the valley floor, and it's a world apart from the rugged drama of the surf-battered coast; instead, it's vaguely reminiscent of, say, the rolling farm country of upstate New York. The Cabot Trail gently rises and falls on the shoulders of gently rounded hills flanking the valley, offering views of the farmed floodplains and glimpses of the shining river. In autumn, the foliage here is often among eastern Canada's best.

The **Margaree River** has been accorded celebrity status in fishing circles—it's widely regarded as one of the most productive Atlantic salmon rivers in North America, and salmon have continued to return to spawn here in recent years, which is unfortunately not the case in many other waterways of Atlantic Canada. The river has been closed to all types of fishing except fly-fishing since the 1880s, and in 1991 it was designated a Canadian Heritage River.

Learn about the river's heritage at the **Margaree Salmon Museum** ⭐ (© 902/248-2848) in North East Margaree. The handsome building features a brief video about the life cycle of the salmon, and exhibits include fisherman photos by the score as well as antique rods (including one impressive 5m/18-footer), examples of poaching equipment, and hundreds of hand-tied salmon flies. Museum docents can help you find a guide to try your hand on the water; late spring and early fall are the best times to get a catch. The museum is open June to mid-October daily from 9am to 5pm. Admission is C$1 (US$1/50p) adult, C25¢ (US25¢/15p) child. The whole area is best explored by slow and aimless driving, or by bike or canoe if you've brought one along with you.

WHERE TO STAY & DINE

Normaway Inn ⭐ Down a drive lined with Scotch pines, the Normaway is a throwback. The property was built in 1928 and has been run by the same family since the 1940s; while it might have once been the sort of place you would run into gentlemen anglers dressed in tweed, it's neither a fishing resort nor a truly luxury getaway today. Instead, it appeals to families and honeymooners interested in fresh air, the sounds of crickets, the strain of pipes, and nothing more. Nine of the rooms on the 200-hectare (494-acre) property are situated in the main lodge; the first-floor rooms, which are larger and have corner windows for better ventilation, are probably best here. The cottages are spread around the property but an easy walk to the main lodge, with hardwood floors and a spare interior decor. The oldest of these cottages were built in the 1940s and are a bit smaller and rougher around the edges; eight newer cottages have Jacuzzis, all but two have woodstoves, and some have two bedrooms.

The dining room, decorated in a simple country farmhouse style, is known for its salmon and lamb, which is raised specially for the inn about 16km (10 miles) away. (No, those sheep wandering the property are not destined for your dinner plate.) The Normaway's strong suit is its laid-back evening entertainment, with events ranging from films to live performances—Acadian music, storytelling, local fiddling, and the like. A weekly square dance, held in the inn's barn, attracts hundreds of locals and tourists alike; there's a small fee to attend.

P.O. Box 121, Margaree Valley, NS B0E 2C0. © 800/565-9463 or 902/248-2987. Fax 902/248-2600. www.normaway. com. 26 units. C$79–C$249 (US$79–US$249/£40–£125) double and cottage. Late-afternoon same-day booking discounts. Breakfast about C$11 (US$11/£5.50) extra. DC, MC, V. Closed late Oct to May. Pets allowed in cottages only. **Amenities:** Dining room; tennis court; free bikes. *In room:* No phone.

CHETICAMP

The Acadian town of Chéticamp is the western gateway to Cape Breton Highlands National Park, and the center for French-speaking culture on Cape Breton. The change is rather obvious as you drive northward from Margaree Harbour—the family names suddenly go from MacDonald to Doucet, and the whole culture and cuisine turn on their head all at once.

The town itself is an assortment of restaurants, boutiques, and tourist establishments spread along Main Street, which closely hugs the harbor. A winding boardwalk follows the harbor's edge through much of town, and offers a good spot to stretch your legs and get your bearings. (Chéticamp Island sits just across the water; the tall coastal hills of the national park are visible just up the coast.) This is an adequate stop for provisioning, topping off the gas tank, and finding shelter.

Chéticamp is noted worldwide for its hooked rugs, a craft perfected by early Acadian settlers. Those curious about the craft should allow time for a stop at Les Trois Pignons, which houses the **Elizabeth LeFort Gallery and Museum.** It is located on Main Street in the north end of town (© **902/224-2642;** www.lestroispignons.com) and displays some of the 300 fine tapestries, many created by Elizabeth LeFort, who was Canada's premier rug-hooking artist for many decades until she passed away in 2005. It's open daily from 8am to 7pm in July and August; 9am to 5pm spring and fall; and 8:30am to 4:30pm in winter. Admission is C$4.50 (US$4.50/£2.25) adult, C$4 (US$4/£2) seniors, C$3.50 (US$3.50/£1.75) students, C$15 (US$15/£7.50) family, free for ages 12 and under.

In the 1930s artisans formed the **Co-operative Artisanale de Chéticamp,** located at 5067 Main St. (© **902/224-2170**). A selection of hooked rugs—from the size of a drink coaster on up—are sold here, along with other trinkets and souvenirs. There's often a weaver or other craftsperson at work in the shop. A small museum downstairs (admission is free) chronicles the life and times of the early Acadian settlers and their descendants. It's closed from mid-October to May.

WHERE TO STAY
A handful of motels service the thousands of travelers who pass through each summer. **Laurie's Motor Inn,** Main Street (© **800/959-4253** or 902/224-2400), has more than 50 motel rooms in three buildings well situated right in town, with rates of C$99 to C$149 (US$99–US$149/£50–£75) double. The inn also manages some nicer suites and apartments around town; inquire if you're interested in something larger, coming with a family, staying awhile, or need cooking facilities.

Parkview Motel   The basic yet comfortable Parkview's best claim is its location—within walking distance of the national park's visitor center, and away from the hubbub of Chéticamp's downtown. Don't expect anything fancy and you won't be disappointed; at least it has cable television and recently upgraded bathrooms. There's a dining room and lounge in a separate building across the street, where the six newest rooms are located. These units offer additional amenities to the traveler such as coffeemakers, refrigerators, and microwave ovens unavailable in the main building.

Cabot Trail, Chéticamp, NS B0E 1H0. © **902/224-3232.** Fax 902/224-2596. www.parkviewresort.com. 17 units. C$75–C$109 (US$75–US$109/£38–£55) double. AE, MC, V. Closed mid-Oct to early May. **Amenities:** Dining room; bar; bike rentals. *In room:* A/C (some units), TV, coffeemaker (some units), fridge (TV).

Pilot Whale Chalets ⚑   These spare, modern cottages (constructed in 1997) each have two bedrooms and full housekeeping facilities, including microwaves. They may have a bit of an antiseptic, condo air, but they are nevertheless well equipped with TVs and VCRs, gas barbecues for firing up steaks, coffeemakers, decks, and wood stoves; some even have Jacuzzis and fireplaces, as well. The best feature, though, is the grand view northward toward the coastal mountains. (Cottages 1, 2, 4, and 5 have the best vistas.) The lodge added apartments to the walk-out basements beneath two of the cottages in 1999, which impinges slightly on the privacy of those both upstairs and down, and also added a three-bedroom cottage very recently.

Rte. 19, Chéticamp, NS B0E 1H0. (℃) **902/224-1040**. Fax 902/224-1540. www.pilotwhales.com. 13 units. C$95–C$199 (US$95–US$199/£48–£100) double. AE, MC, V. *In room:* TV/VCR, kitchenette (some units), coffeemaker, Jacuzzi (some units), no phone.

WHERE TO DINE

La Boulangerie Aucoin (℃) **902/224-3220**) has been a staple of Chéticamp life since 1959. Located just off the Cabot Trail between the town and the national park (look for signs), the bakery is constantly restocking its shelves with fresh-baked goods; ask what's warm when you order at the counter. Among the options: croissants, scones, loaves of fresh bread, and berry pies. This is a recommended stop to fuel up on snack foods before setting off into the park.

For an informal and quick lunch in town, there's **L&M Chéticamp Seafoods, Ltd.** (℃) **902/224-1688**) on Main Street. It's a take-out spot with a few picnic tables inside and outside. It's best known for its fish and chips, but also offers hamburgers and chicken fingers. If you're camping in the park, this is also the spot for fresh fish for the grill. It's open from 8am to 8pm daily May through mid-September.

Restaurant Acadien ACADIAN This restaurant is attached to a crafts shop on the south side of town (the Co-operative Artisanale; see above) and has the uncluttered feel of a cafeteria. Servers here wear costumes inspired by traditional Acadian dress, and the menu draws on local Acadian traditions, as well. Look for *fricot* (a kind of chicken-potato soup), stewed potatoes, and the meat pies for which this region is renowned. Also on the menu: blood pudding, for the brave, and butterscotch pie.

15067 Main St. (℃) **902/224-3207**. Reservations recommended. Breakfast C$3.50–C$5 (US$3.50–US$5/ £1.75–£2.50); lunch and dinner C$3.50–C$17 (US$3.50–US$17/£1.75–£8.50). AE, MC, V. Daily 7am–9pm. Closed Nov to mid-May.

INGONISH ⚘

The Ingonish area includes a gaggle of similarly named towns (Ingonish Centre, Ingonish Ferry, South Ingonish Harbor), which have a population of probably 1,300 or so in total. Like Chéticamp on the peninsula's east side, Ingonish serves as a gateway to the national park and is home to a park visitor information center and a handful of motels and restaurants. Oddly, there's really no critical mass of services here—instead, they're spread along a lengthy stretch of the Cabot Trail, so there's never any real sense of having arrived in town. You pass a liquor store, some shops, a bank, a post office, and a handful of cottages. And that's it: Suddenly you're there, in the park. Highlights in the area include a sandy beach (near Keltic Lodge) good for some chilly splashing around, and a number of shorter hiking trails. (See "Cape Breton Highlands National Park," later in this chapter.)

For golfers, windswept **Highlands Links course** ⚘⚘⚘ (℃) **800/441-1118** or 902/ 285-2600; www.highlandslinksgolf.com), adjacent to the Keltic Lodge (see below) is considered one of the best in Nova Scotia, if not all of Atlantic Canada. Rounds cost about C$88 (US$88/£44) per golfer, less if you tee off in the late afternoon, in spring and fall, or if you're a teenager or child.

South of Ingonish the **Cabot Trail** ⚘⚘⚘ climbs and descends the hairy 300m-high (984-ft.) promontory of Cape Smokey, which explodes into panoramic views from the top. At the highest point, there's a provincial park where you can cool your engine and admire the views. An 11km (7-mile) hiking trail leads to the tip of the cape along the high bluffs, studded with unforgettable viewpoints along the way.

WHERE TO STAY & DINE

A number of serviceable cottage courts and motels are located in this area. (If booking by phone, be sure to find out which Ingonish you're staying in; the town names around here all sound the same, leading to possible confusion.) In addition to the choices below, **Glenghorm Beach Resort** in Ingonish (© **800/565-5660** or 902/285-2049) has about 75 units on a spacious 8-hectare (20-acre) property that fronts a sandy beach. Some rooms feature painted cinder-block walls, and the decorating is a bit dated, with avocado or gold hues that recall a bygone era. Options include motel rooms and efficiencies, along with cottages and some elaborate suites. Prices are C$80 to C$129 (US$80–US$129/£40–£65) for the motel rooms, C$120 to C$189 (US$120–US$189/£60–£95) for the cottages, and C$195–C$399 (US$195–US$399/£98–£200) for the suites.

Keltic Lodge Resort and Spa ⊛   The Keltic Lodge is reached after a series of dramatic flourishes: You pass through a grove of white birches, cross an isthmus atop cliffs, then arrive at a vaguely Tudor-looking resort. The views are extraordinary. Owned and operated by the province, this resort is comfortable without being slick, worn without being threadbare. Some rooms are painted in a soothing mint green that was popular in the 1940s; most are furnished rather plainly with run-of-the-mill motel furniture. (You might expect more for the price.) The cottages are set amid birches and have three bedrooms each, but you share some space with other travelers; if you rent just one bedroom, you will share a common living room with two other sets of guests. Some units are located in the more modern Inn at Keltic building a few hundred meters away, which has better views though a more sterile character. (One reader wrote to lament the inadequate soundproofing in this annex, recommending an upstairs room here to avoid hearing heavy footfalls.)

The food in the main **Purple Thistle dining room** ⊛⊛ (6–9pm nightly) is among the best on the island; the excellent fixed-price dinner menu—which is included in your room rates—offers selections such as prime rib, lemon-pepper salmon filet, and the like. A less formal option is the newer Atlantic Restaurant, with its high post-and-beam ceiling, views, and lighter fare.

Middle Head Peninsula, Ingonish Beach, NS B0C 1L0. © **800/565-0444** or 902/285-2880. Fax 902/285-2859. www.signatureresorts.com. 72 standard units, 10 cottage units. C$175–C$442 (US$175–US$442/£88–£221) double and cottage. Rates include breakfast and dinner. Packages available. AE, DC, DISC, MC, V. Closed late Oct to late May. **Amenities:** 2 restaurants; outdoor pool; golf course; spa; game room; laundry service. *In room:* A/C (2 units), TV (most units), fridge (some units), hair dryer, iron, no phone.

BADDECK

Although Baddeck (pronounced *Bah*-deck) is at a distance from the national park, it's often considered the de facto "capital" of the Cabot Trail. The town offers the widest selection of hotels and accommodations along the whole loop, an assortment of restaurants, and a handful of useful services like grocery stores and laundromats. Baddeck is also famed as the summer home of inventor Alexander Graham Bell, memorialized at a national historic site here. It's a compact and easy town to reconnoiter by foot, scenically located on the shores of Bras d'Or Lake, and within striking distance of the Fortress at Louisbourg. That makes it the most practical base for those with limited vacation time who are planning to drive the Cabot Trail in 1 day (figure on 6–8 hr.).

The useful **Baddeck Welcome Center** (✆ **902/295-1911**) is located just south of the village at the intersection of Route 105 and Route 205. It's open daily in season (June to mid-Oct) from 9am to 7pm.

EXPLORING THE TOWN

Baddeck is much like a modern New England village, skinny and centered around a single commercial boulevard (Chebucto St.) just off the lake. Ask for a free walking tour brochure at the welcome center. A complete tour of the village's architectural highlights won't take much more than 15 or 20 minutes.

Government Wharf (head down Jones St. from the Yellow Cello restaurant) is home to boat tours, which offer the best way to experience **Bras d'Or Lake.** For fishing buffs, Captain Donald Tutty's outfit **Fan-A-Sea** (✆ **902/295-1900**) runs charter fishing trips from Baddeck mid-May through mid-October, and with some luck you may land cod, haddock, or trout. Bait and rods are supplied; the rate is about C$40 (US$40/£20) per person, and a minimum of two people is required per tour. Cheaper harbor tours are also offered.

Also in Baddeck, **Loch Bhreagh Boat Tours** (✆ **902/295-2016**) offers thrice-daily sightseeing tours on a 42-foot cruiser motorboat that pass Alexander Graham Bell's palatial former estate and other attractions at this end of the lake from May through October. Moonlight tours are available by arrangement, if you've got a group together.

About 180m (591 ft.) offshore from the downtown wharf is Kidston Island, owned by the town. It has a wonderful sand beach with lifeguards and an old lighthouse to explore. The Lion's Club offers frequent pontoon boat shuttles across St. Patrick's Channel; the crossing is free, but donations are encouraged.

Alexander Graham Bell National Historic Site 🌟🌟 *(Kids)*   Each summer for much of his life, the inventor Alexander Graham Bell—of Scottish descent, but his family emigrated to Canada while he was young—fled the oppressive heat and humidity of Washington, D.C., for this hillside retreat perched above Bras d'Or Lake at the northern end of Baddeck. The mansion, still owned and occupied by the Bell family, is visible across the harbor from various spots around town. But to learn more about the inventor's career and restless mind, you should visit the modern exhibit center. You'll find extensive exhibits about Bell's invention of the telephone at age 29, as well as considerable information about his less lauded contraptions: ingenious kites, hydrofoils, and airplanes, among others. (Bell also invented the metal detector.) Science buffs will love it, and it's surprising to learn Bell actually died in this home and is buried on this mountaintop. There's an extensive "discovery" section, as well, where kids are encouraged to apply their intuition and creativity in solving problems. All in all, it's a very well-thought-out attraction—and attractive, besides.

Chebucto St., Baddeck. ✆ **902/295-2069.** Admission C$7.15 (US$7.15/£3.60) adults, C$5.90 (US$5.90/£2.95) seniors, C$3.45 (US$3.45/£1.75) youth age 6–16, C$18 (US$18/£9) family. June daily 9am–6pm; July to mid-Oct daily 8:30am–6pm; May and mid- to late Oct daily 9am–5pm; Nov–Apr by appointment only.

WHERE TO STAY & DINE

If the places below are booked, try **Auberge Gisele's,** 387 Shore Rd. (✆ **800/304-0466** or 902/295-2849), a modern 75-room hotel that's open May to late October and popular with bus tours; regular rooms cost C$135 to C$175 (US$135–US$175/£68–£88), the suites C$40 to C$100 (US$40–US$100/£20–£50) more. Or try the **Cabot Trail Motel,** Route 105, 1.6km (1 mile) west of Baddeck (✆ **902/295-2580**), with 38 motel units and four chalets overlooking the lake, as well as a heated outdoor pool and private saltwater beach. Doubles run around C$95 to C$115 (US$95–US$115/£48–£58), the cabins a bit more.

Green Highlander Lodge   The Green Highlander is located atop the Yellow Cello, a popular in-town eatery. The three rooms are nicely decorated in a sort of gentleman's fishing camp motif. Rooms are named after Atlantic salmon flies: Blue Charm, for instance, has a private sitting room and blue-quilted twin beds. All three have private decks with views looking out toward Kidston Island, with Lady Amherst perhaps having the best. Ask about the moonlight paddle trips, kayak rentals, and the private beach located a mile away.

525 Chebucto St., Baddeck, NS B0E 1B0. ✆ 902/295-2303 or 902/295-2240. Fax 902/295-1592. www.green highlanderlodge.com. 3 units. C$90–C$120 (US$90–US$120/£45–£60) double. Rates include full breakfast. AE, MC, V. Closed Nov to mid-May. **Amenities:** Kayak rentals, laundry. *In room:* TV, hair dryer, no phone.

Inverary Resort 🐕 *Kids*   This sprawling resort, located on 5 lakeside hectares (12 acres) within walking distance of town, is a good choice for families with active kids. The slew of activities runs the gamut from fishing and paddleboats to nightly bonfires on the beach. Sports fans will love the volleyball, tennis, and shuffleboard courts. Guest rooms and facilities are spread all over the well-maintained grounds, mostly in buildings painted dark-chocolate brown with white trim and green roofs. The rooms vary in size and style, but most are comfortable, even the snug motel-style units in the cottages; several two-bedroom units are offered, and a few units have kitchens. The resort has two dining rooms: a cafe overlooking the resort's small marina serves informal fare such as various pastas; the more formal dining room in the main lodge serves classier food, in a sun-porch setting.

Shore Rd. (P.O. Box 190), Baddeck, NS B0E 1B0. ✆ 800/565-5660 or 902/295-3500. Fax 902/295-3527. www.cape bretonresorts.com. 138 units. C$119–C$189 (US$119–US$189/£60–£95) double; C$159–C$390 (US$159–US$390/£80–£195) suite. AE, DC, MC, V. Closed Dec–May. **Amenities:** 2 restaurants; pub; indoor pool; 3 tennis courts; spa; Jacuzzi; sauna; watersports equipment; bike; playground; room service. *In room:* A/C, TV (VCR in some units), kitchenette (some units).

Telegraph House   The rooms in this 1861 hotel right on Baddeck's bustling main street are divided between the original inn and motel units on a rise behind the main building. This is where Alexander Graham Bell stayed when he first visited Baddeck, and the units are still rooming-house small. Four rooms on the top floor share two bathrooms between them, an arrangement that works fine for families but might give others a bit of pause. Guests can linger on a front or side porch (there are several sitting nooks) and watch commerce happen on the main drag. The larger, if unexciting, motel rooms in back (especially room nos. 22–32) are actually better unless you want to watch the town's coming and goings; some have small sitting decks outside their front doors, with glimpses of the lake. The dining room serves traditional meals at lunch and dinner. Expect shepherd's pie, meatloaf, turkey, fish cakes, and big desserts.

Chebucto St. (P.O. Box 8), Baddeck, NS B0E 1B0. ✆ 902/295-1100. Fax 902/295-1136. www.baddeck.com/telegraph. 41 units. C$70–C$119 (US$70–US$119/£35–£60) double; C$150–C$195 (US$150–US$195/£75–£98) cabin. AE, MC, V. **Amenities:** Restaurant. *In room:* A/C (1 unit), TV, no phone.

LOUISBOURG 🐕🐕

In the early-18th-century **Louisbourg on Cape,** Breton's remote and windswept easternmost coast, was home to an ambitious French fortress and settlement. Despite its brief prosperity and durable construction of rock, it virtually disappeared after the British finally forced the French out (for the second time) in 1760. Through the miracle of archaeology and historic reconstruction, much of the imposing settlement has been re-created, and today Louisbourg is among Canada's most ambitious national historic parks. It's an attraction everyone coming to Cape Breton Island should make an effort to visit. The site, 36km (22 miles) east of Sydney, isn't on the way to any-place else, and it's an inconvenient detour from Cape Breton Highlands National Park. But if you're interested in Louisbourg, commit yourself to going. A few hours spent wandering the wondrous rebuilt town, then walking amid ruins and out along the coastal trail, might be one of the highlights of your trip to Atlantic Canada.

EXPLORING THE VILLAGE

The hamlet of Louisbourg—which you'll pass through en route to the historic park—is low-key, still looking for ways to rebound from the cessation of the local railway, the decline in local boatbuilding, and the decline of local fisheries. Louisbourg is now striv-ing to gear its economy more toward tourism, and it's making progress on this front.

A short **boardwalk** with interpretive signs fronts the town's tiny waterfront. (You'll get a glimpse of the national historic site across the water.) Nearby is a faux-Elizabethan theater, the **Louisbourg Playhouse** (© **902/733-2996;** www.louisbourgplayhouse. com), at 11 Aberdeen St. Various performances and concerts are staged here throughout the summer.

Fortress of Louisbourg National Historic Site 🇫🇫 🇰ids   The historic and pic-turesque French village of Louisbourg has had three lives. The first was early in the 18th century, when the French first colonized this area aggressively in a bid to stake their claim in the New World. They built an imposing fortress of stone. It was impos-ing but not impregnable, as the British would prove when they captured the fort in 1745. The fortress had a second, short-lived heyday when it was returned to the French following negotiations in Europe. War soon broke out again, however, and the British recaptured it in 1758; this time they blew it up for good measure. The final resurrection came during the 1960s, when the Canadian government decided to rebuild one-fourth of the stone-walled town—creating a whole settlement from some grass hummocks and a few scattered documents about what once had been.

The park was built to re-create life as it might have looked in 1744, when this was still an important French military capital and seaport; visitors today arrive at the site after walking through an interpretive center and boarding a bus for the short ride to the site. (Keeping cars at a distance does much to enhance the historic flavor.) You come through an impressive gatehouse—perhaps being challenged by a costumed guard on the look-out for English spies—then begin wandering narrow lanes and poking around faux-his-toric buildings, some of which contain informative exhibits, others of which are restored and furnished with convincingly worn reproductions; chickens, geese, and barnyard ani-mals peck and cluck, while vendors hawk freshly baked bread out of wood-fired ovens. It really does feel like old Europe. Ask for a free tour, and don't hesitate to question the costumed guides, who are knowledgeable and friendly. Allow at least 4 hours here.

Louisbourg, NS. © **902/733-2280** or 902/733-3546. www.louisbourg.ca. June–Sept admission C$16 (US$16/£8) adults, C$14 (US$14/£7) seniors, C$8.15 (US$8.15/£4.10) children, C$41 (US$41/£21) family; May and Oct admission discounted 60%. July–Aug daily 9am–5:30pm; mid-May to June and Sept to mid-Oct daily 9:30am–5pm. Costumed interpreters limited in off season. Closed late Oct to mid-May.

WHERE TO STAY & DINE

Cranberry Cove Inn 🇰   You can't miss this attractive, in-town inn en route to the fortress—it's the three-story Victorian farmhouse painted cranberry red, with

cranberry-tinged meals to match. Inside, it's decorated in a light Victorian motif. Upstairs rooms are carpeted and furnished on themes—Anne's Hideaway is the smallest, but has a nice old tub and butterfly collection; Isle Royale is done up in Cape Breton tartan. The quirky Field and Stream room has a twig headboard, mounted deer head, and a pheasant. Breakfast includes cranapple sauce and "cran-bran" muffins; dinner is served nightly from 5 to 8:30pm in a handsome first-floor dining room of polished wood floors and cherrywood tables and chairs. Entrees could range from charbroiled Atlantic salmon to (you guessed it) cranberry-marinated breast of chicken. Note that, due to the three-story open staircase, this inn isn't suitable for toddlers.

12 Wolfe St., Louisbourg, NS B1C 2J2. $\textcircled{C}$ **800/929-0222** or 902/733-2171. www.louisbourg.com/cranberrycove. 7 units. C$105–C$160 (US$105–US$160/£53–£80) double. Rates include breakfast. MC, V. Closed Nov–Apr. **Amenities:** Dining room. *In room:* TV (some units), hair dryer, no phone (some units).

Louisbourg Harbour Inn $\mathcal{R}\mathcal{R}$ This golden-yellow, century-old clapboard home is conveniently located in the village, a block off the main street and overlooking fishing wharves, the blue waters of the harbor, and, across the way, the Fortress of Louisbourg. The inn's lovely pine floors have been nicely restored, and all guest rooms are tidy and attractive, some fussier than others, but all are comfortable. The best rooms are on the third floor, requiring a bit of a trek: Room no. 6 is bright and cheerful, with a Jacuzzi tub; Room no. 7, one of my favorites, is spacious and also boasts an in-room Jacuzzi, plus a handsome wooden bed and a pair of rockers from which to monitor the happenings at the fish pier. Room nos. 1 and 3 also have private balconies, and yet again Jacuzzis. A three-course dinner is sometimes available by advance reservations to guests in the first-floor dining room. All in all, an excellent choice.

9 Lower Warren St., Louisbourg, NS B1C 1G6. $\textcircled{C}$ **888/888-8466** or 902/733-3222. www.louisbourg.com/louisbourg harbourinn. 8 units. C$100–C$180 (US$100–US$180/£50–£90) double. Rates include breakfast. MC, V. Closed mid-Oct to mid-June. *In room:* Fridge (some units), coffeemaker, Jacuzzi (some units), no phone.

10 Cape Breton Highlands National Park $\mathcal{R}\mathcal{R}\mathcal{R}$

Cape Breton Highlands National Park is one of the two crown-jewel national parks in Atlantic Canada (Gros Morne in Newfoundland is the other). Covering some 950 sq. km (367 sq. miles) and stretching across a rugged peninsula from the Atlantic to the Gulf of St. Lawrence, the park is famous for its starkly beautiful terrain. It also features one of the most dramatic coastal drives east of Big Sur, California. One of the great pleasures of the park is that it holds something for everyone, from tourists who prefer to sightsee from the comfort of their car, to those who prefer backcountry hiking in the company of bear and moose.

The mountains of Cape Breton are probably unlike those you're familiar with elsewhere. The heart of the park is fundamentally a huge plateau. In the vast interior, you'll find a flat and melancholy landscape of wind-stunted evergreens, bogs, and barrens. This is called the taiga, a name that refers to the zone between tundra and the northernmost forest. In this largely untracked area (which is also Nova Scotia's largest remaining wilderness), you might find 150-year-old trees that are only knee-high.

But it's the park's edges that capture the attention. On the western side of the peninsula, the tableland has eroded into the sea, creating a dramatic landscape of ravines and ragged, rust-colored cliffs pounded by the ocean. The Cabot Trail, a paved road built in 1939, winds dramatically along the flanks of the mountains, offering extraordinary vistas at every turn. On the park's other coastal flank—the eastern, Atlantic side—the terrain is less dramatic, with a coastal plain interposed between mountains and sea. But the lush green hills still offer a backdrop that's exceptionally picturesque.

Note that this section focuses only on the park proper, which offers no lodging or services other than camping. You will find limited lodging and restaurants in the handful of villages that ring the park. See "Cape Breton Island," earlier in this chapter.

ESSENTIALS

GETTING THERE   Access to the park is via the Cabot Trail, one of several tourist routes well marked by provincial authorities. The entire loop is 300km (186 miles). The distance from the park entrance at Chéticamp to the park entrance at Ingonish is 105km (65 miles). Although the loop can be done in either direction, I would encourage visitors to drive it in a clockwise direction solely because the visitor center in Chéticamp offers a far more detailed introduction to the park.

VISITOR INFORMATION   Visitor information centers are located at both Chéticamp and Ingonish and are open daily summers from 8am to 8pm. The Chéticamp center has more extensive information about the park, including a 10-minute slide presentation, natural history exhibits, a large-scale relief map, and a very good bookstore specializing in natural and cultural history. The park's main phone number is © **902/224-2306.**

FEES   Entrance permits are required from mid-May to mid-October and can be purchased either at information centers or at tollhouses at the two main park entrances. Permits are required for any activity along the route, even stopping to admire the view. Daily fees are C$6.90 (US$6.90/£3.45) adults, C$5.90 (US$5.90/£2.95) seniors, C$3.45 (US$3.45/£1.75) children age 6 to 16, and C$17 (US$17/£8.50) family.

CAMPING

The park has five drive-in campgrounds. The largest are at **Chéticamp** (on the west side) and **Broad Cove** (on the east), both of which have the commendable policy of never turning campers away. Even if all regular sites are full, they'll find a place for you to pitch a tent or park an RV. All the national park campgrounds are well run and well maintained. Chéticamp and Broad Cove offer three-way hookups for RVs. Rates run from around C$18 to C$35 (US$18–US$35/£9–£18) per night, depending on the level of services you require and the campground you've selected. Remember that you're also required to buy a day-use permit when camping at Cape Breton, and that you can only make advance reservations at Chéticamp, where half the sites are set aside for advance bookings, using the website www.pccamping.ca. At all the other campgrounds, it's first come, first served.

Cape Breton also has some backcountry campsites at **Fishing Cove** that are especially attractive, set on a pristine cove; just remember to plan for an 8km (5-mile) hike in from the Cabot Trail and your car. Once there, however, you can watch for pilot whales at sunset from the cliffs. The current fee is C$9.90 (US$9.90/£4.95) per person per night; make arrangements at one of the visitor information centers.

HIKING

The park offers no less than 27 distinct hiking tracks departing from the Cabot Trail. Many excursions are quite short and have the feel of a casual stroll rather than a vigorous tromp, but those determined to be challenged will find suitable destinations. All trails are listed, with brief descriptions, on the reverse side of the map you'll receive when you pay your park entry fee at the gates.

Tips **A Scenic Drive**

Cape Breton Highlands National Park offers basically one drive, and with few lapses it's scenic along the entire route. The most breathtaking stretch is the 43km (27-mile) **route from Chéticamp to Pleasant Bay** ✸✸✸ along the western coast. Double the time you figure you'll need to drive this itinerary, because you'll want to spend lots of time at the pullouts gawking at the views, perusing the signs, and snapping digital photos. (If it's foggy, though, save yourself the entrance fee and gas money. Without the views, there's little reason to travel and you'd be well advised to wait until the fog lifts.) You can also hike in the foggy forest or across the upland bogs, or explore some of the nearby villages in an atmospheric mist.

You'll want to be very confident in your car's brakes before setting out on the Cabot Trail. The road rises and falls with considerable drama, and when cresting some ridges you might feel mildly afflicted with vertigo. Especially stressful on the brakes (when traveling the Cabot Trail clockwise) are the descents to Pleasant Bay, into the Aspy Valley, and off Cape Smokey.

The **Skyline Trail** ✸✸✸ offers oodles of altitude and views, but no climbing. You ascend the tableland from Chéticamp by car, then follow a 7km (4.3-mile) hiking loop out along dramatic bluffs and through wind-stunted spruces and firs. A spur trail descends to a high, exposed point overlooking the surf; it's capped with blueberry bushes. Moose are often spotted along this trail. The downside: It's a very popular trek, and thus often crowded.

Farther along the Cabot Trail, the .8km (.5-mile) **Bog Trail** ✸ offers a glimpse of the tableland's unique bogs from a dry boardwalk. **Lone Shieling** ✸ is an easy .8km (.5-mile) loop through a verdant hardwood forest in a lush valley that includes 350-year-old sugar maples. A re-creation of a hut of a Scottish crofter (shepherd) is a feature along this trail.

If you're looking to leave the crowds behind, the **Glasgow Lake Lookoff** ✸ is a relatively gentle 8km (5-mile) round-trip hike that takes you through barrens and scrub forest to a rocky bald overlooking a series of pristine highland lakes with distant views of the ocean. The trail is alternately swampy and rocky, so rugged footwear is advised.

On the eastern shore, try the superb 4km (2.5-mile) **hike to Middle Head** ✸✸, beyond the Keltic Lodge resort. This dramatic, rocky peninsula thrusts well out into the Atlantic. The trail is wide and relatively flat, you'll cross open meadows with wonderful views north and south. The tip is grassy and open, and it offers a fine spot to scan for whales or watch the waves crash in following a storm. Allow about 2 hours for a relaxed excursion out and back.

4

New Brunswick

by Paul Karr

Sometimes New Brunswick seems like it could be the Rodney Dangerfield of Atlantic Canada—it just gets no respect. It's probably better known within Canada for its pulp mills, industrial forests, cargo ports, and oil refineries (the huge Irving Oil conglomerate is based here) than for its many quaint villages and charming byways. And that's a shame.

Travelers, as well, tend to view New Brunswick as a place to be driven through as quickly as possible en route from Québec or Maine to the rest of Atlantic Canada—and the building of a fast toll road through the western section of the province hasn't helped mitigate that impression at all.

But rest assured: New Brunswick *does* in fact have pockets of wilderness and scenic beauty the equal of those anywhere in eastern Canada. The province's appeal just tends to be a bit more hidden than that of other locales. With a little homework, you can discover surprisingly warm ocean waters lapping up on sand beaches that hold their own to anything Prince Edward Island's got to offer; rocky, surf-pounded headlands; huge tides that will stun you with their drop; and a salty, pubby maritime city (Saint John) that makes a nice run at Halifax as a place with enough culture to shake a stick at.

1 Exploring the Province

If you're drawn to rugged beauty, you should plan to focus on the Fundy Coast with its stupendous drop of tides, rocky cliffs, and boreal landscape. This part of the coast actually feels a lot more remote and northerly than the more densely settled (and tamer-looking) northeastern coast. Those interested in Acadian history or sandy beaches should veer toward the Gulf of St. Lawrence and its fishing heritage and laid-back feel. And those who want to sip a pint to the strains of traditional music and shop at a great farmer's market could do a lot worse than a swing through Saint John and its lovely associated fishing towns. Those simply interested in hurrying through the province to get to Prince Edward Island or Nova Scotia? Take at least a day en route and detour down through Fundy National Park and visit Cape Enrage and Hopewell Rocks.

ESSENTIALS

VISITOR INFORMATION New Brunswick publishes several free annual directories and guides that are helpful in planning a trip to the province, including **"Experience New Brunswick,"** with listings of attractions, accommodations, campgrounds, and multiday and daylong adventure packages, as well as an official "New Brunswick Travel

New Brunswick & the Gaspé Peninsula

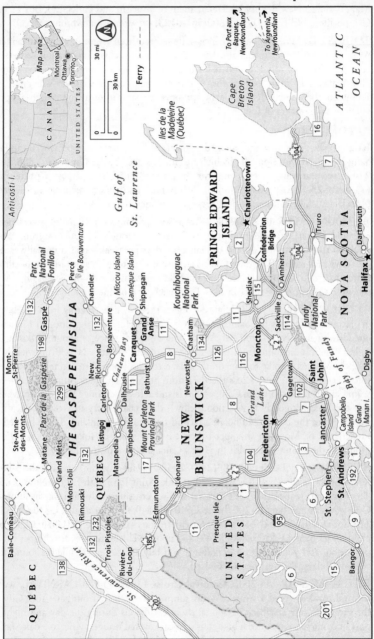

Map." Contact **New Brunswick Department of Tourism and Parks,** P.O. Box 12345, Campbellton, NB E3N 3T6 (© **800/561-0123;** www.tourismnewbrunswick.ca).

TOURIST OFFICES   The province staffs seven official visitor information centers; most cities and larger towns also have their own municipal information centers. A complete listing of phone numbers for these centers can be found in the "Experience New Brunswick" guide, or look for "?" direction signs on the highway when driving. Phone numbers and addresses for the appropriate visitor information centers are provided in each section of this chapter.

GETTING THERE

BY PLANE   The province's main airports are at Fredericton (the provincial capital), Saint John, and Moncton, all of which are chiefly served by **Air Canada** (© **888/247-2262;** www.aircanada.com) and the major car-rental companies. **Continental** (© **800/523-FARE;** www.continental.com) now also flies nonstop from Newark, New Jersey's Liberty International Airport to Moncton.

BY TRAIN   **VIA Rail** (© **888/842-7245;** www.viarail.com), Canada's government-operated national train service, offers train service through the province from Montréal (on the way from Montréal to Halifax) 6 days per week—operating daily except Tuesdays year-round. The train follows a northerly route, with stops in Campbellton, Miramichi, and Moncton. Check out the rail line's website for more details on routes, schedules and stopping times in New Brunswick, and online booking.

BY CAR   The Trans-Canada Highway bisects the province, entering from Québec at St. Jacques. It follows the Saint John River Valley before veering through Moncton and exiting into Nova Scotia at Aulac. The entire distance is about 530km (329 miles). The fastest route from New England to southwestern New Brunswick is to take the Maine turnpike to Bangor, then head east on Route 9 to connect to Route 1 into Calais, which is just across the river from St. Stephen, New Brunswick. A more scenic variation is to drive to Campobello Island across the bridge from Lubec, Maine (see the Passamaquoddy Bay section, below), then take a ferry to Deer Island, drive the length of the island, and board a second ferry to the mainland. Those headed to Fredericton or Moncton will speed their trip somewhat by following U.S. I-95 to Houlton, then connecting with the Trans-Canada after crossing the border.

BY FERRY   **Bay Ferries** (© **888/249-7245;** www.nfl-bay.com) operates the 3-hour ferry known as the *Princess of Acadia* that links Saint John with Digby, Nova Scotia. The ferry sails year-round, with as many as three crossings daily each way in summer. One-way summer fares in 2007 were C$40 (US$40/£20) for adults, C$30 (US$30/£15) for seniors, C$25 (US$25/£13) for children ages 6 to 13, C$5 (US$5/£2.50) per child under 6, and C$80 (US$80/£40) and up per vehicle; all fares are cheaper in the off season, and you also get a discount if you buy a ticket to complete a round-trip within 30 days. Reservations are advised.

BY CRUISE SHIP   In 2007, **Carnival Cruise Lines** (© **888/CARNIVAL;** www.carnival.com) unveiled a series of 4-day summertime cruises from New York City to the Bay of Fundy and back. Optional shore excursions during the day and night at port in Saint John included a bike tour of local covered bridges; visits to a dairy farm; kayak trips around the bay; and a visit to the Moosehead Brewery.

I don't speak sign language.

A hotel can close for all kinds of reasons.
Our Guarantee ensures that if your hotel's undergoing construction, we'll let you know in advance. In fact, we cover your entire travel experience. See www.travelocity.com/guarantee for details.

THE GREAT OUTDOORS

The province has put together a well-conceived campaign to encourage visitors of all budgets to explore its outdoor attractions and activities. The provincial travel guide outlines dozens of multiday and day adventures ranging from a C$10 (US$10/£5) guided hike at Fundy National Park to C$276 (US$276/£138) biking packages that include inn accommodations and gourmet dinners. For more information on the program, call the tourism department at © 800/561-0123.

BACKPACKING Among the best destinations for a backcountry tromp are **Mount Carleton Provincial Park** and **Fundy National Park,** both of which maintain backcountry campsites for visitors. These two landscapes are quite different to hike through, however; see the appropriate sections later in this chapter for more information on each park, then make your choice.

BICYCLING The islands and peninsulas of **Passamaquoddy Bay** lend themselves nicely to cruising in the slow lane—especially Campobello, which also has good dirt roads for mountain biking. **Grand Manan** holds appeal for cyclists, although the main road (Rte. 776) has rather narrow shoulders and some fast local cars. Some of the best coastal biking is around **Fundy National Park**—especially the back roads to Cape Enrage, and the **Fundy Trail Parkway,** an 11km (6.8-mile) multiuse trail that hugs the coast west of the national park. Along the Acadian Coast, **Kouchibouguac National Park** has limited but unusually nice biking trails through mixed terrain (rentals available).

A handy guide is *Biking to Blissville,* by Kent Thompson. It covers 35 rides in the Maritimes, and costs about C$15 (US$15/£7.50). Look in local bookshops, online bookstores, or directly with the publisher: Goose Lane Editions, 500 Beaverbrook Ct., Suite 500, Fredericton, NB E3B 5X4 (© **888/926-8377;** www.gooselane.com).

BIRD-WATCHING **Grand Manan** is probably the province's most noted destination for birders, located right on the Atlantic flyway. (John James Audubon lodged here when studying bird life more than 150 years ago.) Over the course of a typical year, as many as 275 species can be observed on the island, with September usually the best month for sightings. Boat tours from Grand Manan can take you to Machias Seal Island, with its colonies of puffins, arctic terns, and razorbills. It's fun to swap information with other birders: on the ferry, look for excitable folks with binoculars and floppy hats dashing from port to starboard and back. (If they're *not* the birders, oh well, you might have just made new friends from Brisbane or Iowa.)

On **Campobello Island,** the mixed terrain also attracts a good mix of birds, including sharp-shinned hawk, common eider, and black guillemot. Ask for a checklist and map at the visitor center. Shorebird enthusiasts flock to **Shepody Bay National Wildlife Area,** which maintains preserves in the mud flats between Alma (near Fundy National Park) and Hopewell Cape. Also offering excellent birding is the marsh that surrounds **Sackville,** near the Nova Scotia border.

CANOEING New Brunswick has 3,500km (2,175 miles) of inland waterways, plus lakes and protected bays. Canoeists can find everything from glass-smooth waters to daunting rapids. In Kouchibouguac National Park, for example, there is a rental and tour concession based at **Ryans Recreational Equipment Rental Centre** (© **506/ 876-8918**) from mid-May to mid-September (open weekends only May and Sept, daily June–Aug). More experienced canoeists looking for a longer expedition should head to the **St. Croix River** on the U.S. border, where you can embark on a multiday paddle trip and get lost in the woods, spiritually if not in fact.

FISHING The **Miramichi River** has long attracted anglers both famous and obscure. In some considered opinions, this ranks among the best salmon rivers in the world. There are strict laws regarding river fishing of the salmon: the fish must be caught using flies, and nonresidents must hire a licensed guide when fishing for them. For other freshwater species, including bass, as well as open-ocean saltwater angling, the provincial restrictions are less onerous. Get up to date on the rules and regulations by requesting two brochures: "Sport Fishing Summary" and "Atlantic Salmon Angling." These are available from the **Fisheries Section** of the Department of Natural Resources, reached by phone at © **506/453-2440** or by snail mail at P.O. Box 6000, Fredericton, NB E3B 5H1. The website can be found at the memorable address www.gnb.ca/0254.

GOLF In St. Andrews, the **Algonquin hotel**'s newly expanded and redesigned golf course is a beauty—easily among eastern Canada's top 10. It features 9 newer inland holes (the front 9) and 9 older seaside holes that become increasingly spectacular as you approach the point of land separating New Brunswick from Maine. Service and upkeep are impeccable here, and there's both a snack bar on premises and a roving club car with sandwiches and drinks. Greens fees are C$79 to C$99 (US$79–US$99/£40–£50) for 18 holes (carts extra; discount at twilight time). Lessons are offered, and there's a short-game practice area in addition to a driving range; call © **888/460-8999** or 506/529-8165 for tee times. In Fredericton, **Kingswood** (© **800/423-5969** or 506/443-3333; www.golfnb.com/kingswood1.html) was recognized by *Golf Digest* as the best new Canadian golf course in 2003. It features 27 holes, a par-3 course, and a double-ended driving range. A round of 18 holes cost C$50 to C$65 (US$50–US$65/£25–£33) in 2007.

HIKING The province's highest point is in the center of the woodlands region, at **Mount Carleton Provincial Park.** Several demanding hikes in the park yield glorious views. There's also superb hiking at **Fundy National Park,** with a mix of coastal and woodland hikes on well-marked trails. The multiuse 11km (6.8-mile) **Fundy Trail Parkway** has terrific views of the coast and is wheelchair accessible. **Grand Manan** is a good destination for independent-minded hikers who enjoy the challenge of finding the trail as much as the hike itself. An excellent resource is *A Hiking Guide to New Brunswick,* published by Goose Lane Editions. It's C$15 (US$15/£7.50) and available in bookstores around the province, or directly from the publisher, Goose Lane Editions, at 500 Beaverbrook Ct., Suite 500, Fredericton, NB E3B 5X4 (© **888/ 926-8377;** www.gooselane.com).

SEA KAYAKING The huge tides that make kayaking so fascinating along the **Bay of Fundy** also make it exceptionally dangerous—even the strongest kayakers are no match for a fierce ebb tide if they're in the wrong place. Fortunately, the number of skilled sea-kayaking guides has really boomed in recent years.

Among the most extraordinary places to explore is **Hopewell Rocks.** The rocks stand like amazing Brancusi statues on the ocean floor at low tide, then offer sea caves and narrow channels to explore at high tide. **Baymount Outdoor Adventures** (© **877/601-2660** or 506/734-2660), run by the Faulkners in Hillsborough, offers 90-minute sea kayak tours of Hopewell Rocks for C$55 (US$55/£28) adults, C$45 (US$45/£23) children. Other good kayak outfitters along the Fundy Coast include

FreshAir Adventure (© 800/545-0020 or 506/887-2249) in Alma and **Seascape Kayak Tours** (© 866/747-1884 or 506/747-1884) on Deer Island, both charging basically the same rates as Baymount.

WHALE-WATCHING   The **Bay of Fundy** is rich with plankton, and therefore rich with whales. Some 15 types of whales can be spotted in the bay, including finback, minke, humpback, the infrequent orca, and the endangered right whale. Whale-watching expeditions sail throughout the summer from Campobello Island, Deer Island, Grand Manan, St. Andrews, and St. George. Any visitor information center can point you in the right direction; the province's travel guide also lists many of the tours, which typically cost around C$40 to C$50 (US$40–US$50/£20–£25) for 2 to 4 hours of whale-watching.

2 Around Passamaquoddy Bay: Campobello Island & More

The Passamaquoddy Bay region is often the first point of entry for those arriving over-land from the United States. The deeply indented bay is wracked with massive tides that produce currents powerful enough to stymie even doughty fishing boats. It's a place of lasting fogs, spruce-clad islands, bald eagles, and widely scattered develop-ment. It's also home to a grand old summer colony and a peninsula that boasts two five-star inns and a rambling turn-of-the-20th-century resort.

CAMPOBELLO ISLAND 🐦

Campobello is a compact island (about 16km/10 miles long and 5km/3 miles wide) at the mouth of Passamaquoddy Bay. It's connected by a graceful modern bridge to Lubec, Maine, and is thus easier to get to from the United States than from Canada. (To get here from the Canadian mainland without driving through the United States requires two ferries, one of which operates only during the summer.) This is a great quick trip into Canada for a quick taste of New Brunswick when you're already in Downeast Maine. Campobello has been home to both humble fishermen and wealthy families over the years, and both have coexisted nicely. (Locals approved when sum-mer folks built golf courses earlier this century, for example, since it gave them a place to graze their sheep.) Today, the island is a mix of elegant summer homes and hum-ble local dwellings.

ESSENTIALS

GETTING THERE   Campobello Island is accessible year-round from the United States. From Route 1 in Whiting, Maine, take Route 189 to Lubec, where a bridge links Lubec with Campobello. In the summer, there's another option. From the Cana-dian mainland, take the free ferry to Deer Island, drive the length of the island, and then board the small seasonal ferry to Campobello. The ferry is operated by **East Coast Ferries** (© 506/747-2159) and runs from late June to September. The fare is C$14 (US$14/£7) for car and driver, C$3 (US$3/£1.50) for each additional passenger.

VISITOR INFORMATION   The **Campobello Welcome Center,** 44 Route 774, Welshpool, NB E5E 1A3 (© 506/752-7043), is on the right side just after you cross the bridge from Lubec. It's open mid-May to early September daily from 9am to 7pm, and from 10am to 6pm until mid-October.

EXPLORING THE ISLAND

Roosevelt Campobello International Park 🐦🐦   Like a number of other afflu-ent Americans, the family of Franklin Delano Roosevelt made an annual trek to the prosperous summer colony at Campobello Island. The island lured folks from the sultry cities with a promise of cool air and a salubrious effect on the circulatory system. The future U.S. president came to this island every summer between 1883, the year after he was born, and 1921, when he was stricken with polio. Franklin and his siblings spent those summers exploring the coves and sailing around the bay, and he always recalled his time here fondly. (It was his "beloved island," he said, coining a phrase that gets no rest in local brochures.)

Be sure to save some time to explore farther afield in the 1,120 hectares (2,768-acre) park, which offers scenic coastline and 14km (8.7 miles) of walking trails. While the park's Visitor Centre closes on Canada's Thanksgiving Day in late October, these extensive grounds and parklands remain open to the public year-round. Maps and walk suggestions are available at the visitor center. The park, should you find your way here, is easily worth a half-day.

459 Rte. 774, Welshpool. ⓒ 506/752-2922. www.fdr.net. Free admission. Daily 10am–6pm; last tour at 5:45pm. Visitor center closed mid-Oct to mid-May; grounds open year-round.

WHERE TO STAY & DINE

There is camping at **Herring Cove Provincial Park** (ⓒ **506/752-7010**) for C$22 to C$24 (US$22–US$24/£11–£12), with discounts for seniors.

Lupine Lodge ✦ (Value) (Kids)   In 1915, cousins of the Roosevelts built this handsome compound of log buildings not far from the Roosevelt cottage. A busy road runs between the lodge and the water, but the buildings are located on a slight rise and have the feel of being removed from the traffic. Guest rooms are in two long lodges adjacent to the main building and restaurant. The rooms with bay views cost a bit more but are worth it—they're slightly larger and better furnished in a log-rustic style. All guests have queen-bedded rooms (some rooms add another double bed or fireplace) and access to a deck that overlooks the bay. You won't find phones, TVs, luxury bathrooms, or wireless Internet, but you will find a pleasing vibe—they welcome even small children, and will pack a lunch for your explorations, though they cannot accept pets.

The lodge's attractive **dining room** ✦ is a great place for a meal, exuding rustic summer ease with log walls, a double stone fireplace, bay views of the fishing fleets, and mounted moose and swordfish. Three meals are served daily (go for blueberry pancakes at breakfast), and dinners have been recently upscaled: Entrees now include such choices as maple-glazed salmon and a turkey dinner, in addition to longtime favorites like rib-eye steak, seafood, and lobster chowder.

610 Rte. 774, Welshpool, Campobello Island, NB E5E 1A5. ⓒ 888/912-8880 or 506/752-2555. www.lupinelodge. com. 11 units. C$99–C$150 (US$99–US$150/£50–£75) double. MC, V. Closed Nov–Apr. **Amenities:** Restaurant. *In room:* No phone.

Owen House, A Country Inn & Gallery   This three-story clapboard captain's house dates from 1835 and sits on 4 tree-filled hectares (10 acres) at the edge of the bay. The first-floor common rooms are nicely decorated in a busy Victorian manner with Persian and braided carpets and mahogany furniture; view the water from the nautical-feeling, airy sun room and its big windows. The guest rooms are a mixed lot, furnished with an eclectic mélange of antique and modern furniture; some are bright and airy and filled with salty air (room no. 1 is the largest, with waterfront views on two sides); others, like room no. 5, are tucked under stairs and a bit dark, though the Owens are renovating the house. Third-floor rooms share a single bathroom but also have excellent views. A filling hot breakfast served family-style is included in the room rates, and ask to see the owner's in-house watercolor gallery if you're an art buff.

11 Welshpool St., Welshpool, Campobello, NB E5E 1G3. © **506/752-2977.** www.owenhouse.ca. 9 units, 2 with shared bathroom. C$107–C$210 (US$107–US$210/£54–£105) double. Rates include full breakfast. MC, V. Closed Nov–Apr. No children under 6 in Aug. *In room:* No phone.

ST. ANDREWS ★★

The lovely village of St. Andrews—or St. Andrews By-the-Sea, as the chamber of commerce persists in calling it—traces its roots back to the days of the Loyalists. After the American Revolution, New Englanders who supported the British in the struggle were made to feel unwelcome. They decamped first to lovely little Castine, Maine, which they presumed was safely on British soil. But it wasn't; the St. Croix River was later determined to be the border between Canada and the United States. Forced to uproot once again, the Loyalists dismantled their new homes, loaded the pieces aboard ships, and rebuilt them on the welcoming peninsula of St. Andrews, which is not so far away by water. Some of these remarkably resilient saltbox houses still stand in town today.

Beautifully sited at the tip of a long, wedge-shaped peninsula, the community later emerged as a fashionable summer resort in the late–19th century, when many of Canada's affluent and well-connected built homes and gathered annually here for social activities. Around this time, the Tudor-style Algonquin Hotel (now known as The Fairmont Algonquin) was built on a low rise overlooking the town in 1889, and quickly became the town's social hub and defining landmark.

ESSENTIALS

GETTING THERE   St. Andrews is located at the apex of Route 127, which dips southward from Route 1 between St. Stephen and St. George. It's an easy drive north from St. Stephen or south from Saint John (more scenic coming from Saint John), and the turnoff is well marked from either direction. In case you don't have wheels, **Acadien Bus Lines** (© **800/567-5151** or 506/529-3101; www.smtbus.com) runs one daily bus trip between St. Andrews and Saint John; the one-way fare in 2007 was C$22 (US$22/£11) adult one-way, C$37 (US$37/£19) round-trip. Even better, the bus line offers discounts of 15% to 40% for children, students, and seniors.

VISITOR INFORMATION   St. Andrews' seasonal **Welcome Centre** (© **506/529-3556**), is located at 46 Reed Ave., on your left as you enter the village. It's in a handsome 1914 home overarched by broad-crowned trees. It's open daily from 8am to 8pm in July and August, from 9am to 5pm in May, June, and from September until it closes in early October. The rest of the year, contact the **Chamber of Commerce** in the same building (© **800/563-7397** or 506/529-3555) by writing P.O. Box 89, St. Andrews, NB E0G 2X0.

EXPLORING ST. ANDREWS

The chamber of commerce produces two brochures, the "Town Map and Directory" and the "St. Andrews by-the-Sea Historic Guide," both of which are free and can be found at the two visitor information centers. Also look for "A Guide to Historic St. Andrews," produced by the St. Andrews Civic Trust. With these in hand you'll be able to launch an informed exploration. To make it even easier, many of the private dwellings in St. Andrews feature plaques with information on their origins. Look in particular for the saltbox-style homes, some of which are thought to be the original Loyalist structures that traveled here by barge.

The village's compact and handsome downtown flanks Water Street, a lengthy commercial street that parallels the bay. You'll find low, understated commercial architecture, much of it from the turn-of-the-20th century, that encompasses a gamut of styles. Allow an hour or so for browsing at boutiques and art galleries. There's also a mix of restaurants and inns.

Two blocks inland on King Street, you'll get a dose of local history at the **Ross Memorial Museum,** 188 Montague St. (© **506/529-5124**). The historic home was built in 1824; in 1945 the home was left to the town by Rev. Henry Phipps Ross and Sarah Juliette Ross, complete with their eclectic and intriguing collection of period furniture, carpets, and paintings. The museum is open June to early October, Monday through Saturday from 10am to 4:30pm. Admission is by donation.

Kingsbrae Garden *Kids*   This 11-hectare (27-acre) public garden opened in 1998, using the former grounds of a long-gone estate. The designers incorporated the existing high hedges and trees, and have ambitiously planted open space around the mature plants. The entire project is very promising, and as the plantings take root and mature it's certain to become a noted stop for garden lovers. The grounds include almost 2,000 varieties of trees (including old-growth forest), shrubs, and plants. Among the notable features: a day lily collection, an extensive rose garden, a small maze, a fully functional Dutch windmill that circulates water through the two duck ponds, and a children's garden with an elaborate Victorian-mansion playhouse.

220 King St. © 866/566-8687 or 506/529-3335. Admission C$9 (US$9/£4.50) adults, C$7.60 (US$7.60/£3.80) students and seniors, C$24 (US$24/£12) family, free for children under 6. Daily 9am–6pm. Closed early Oct to mid-May.

Ministers Island Historic Site/Covenhoven *Kids*   This rugged, 200-plus-hectare (500-acre) island is linked to the mainland by a sandbar at low tide, and the 2-hour tours are scheduled around the tides. (Call for upcoming times.) You'll meet your tour guide on the mainland side, then drive your car out convoy-style across the ocean floor to the magical island estate created in 1890 by Sir William Van Horne, of the Canadian Pacific Railway, and the person behind the extension of the rail line to St. Andrews. He then built a sandstone mansion (Covenhoven) with some 50 rooms (including 17 bedrooms), a circular bathhouse, and one of Canada's largest and most impressive barns. The estate also features heated greenhouses, which produced grapes and mushrooms, along with peaches that weighed up to 2 pounds each. You'll learn all this, and more, on the tours.

Rte. 127 (northeast of St. Andrews), Chamcook. © 506/529-5081. Admission C$8 (US$8/£4) adults, C$7 (US$7/£3.50) seniors and students, C$25 (US$25/£13) family, free for children 6 and under. Closed mid-Oct to mid-May.

WHERE TO STAY
Those traveling on a budget instead of seeking the luxury digs below might head for the **Picket Fence Motel,** 102 Reed Ave. (© **506/529-8985**). This trim and tidy property is near the handsome, newly expanded Algonquin golf course (see "Golf," earlier in this chapter) and within walking distance of St. Andrews' village center. Rooms cost C$69 to C$85 (US$69–US$85/£35–£43) double.

Or, for something slightly more upscale yet unlikely to break your bank, contact the **Europa** *Kids* restaurant (see below); the owners rent out a series of rooms, suites, and an apartment collectively rated at 3½ stars by Canada's government hotel-rating agency for C$69 to C$149 double (US$69–US$149/£35–£75). The suites and apartment have kitchenettes.

The Fairmont Algonquin 🏵🏵   The Algonquin's distinguished pedigree dates from 1889, when it opened its doors to wealthy vacationers seeking respite from city heat. The original structure was destroyed by fire in 1914, but the surviving annexes were rebuilt in Tudor style; in 1993 an architecturally sympathetic addition was built across the road, linked by a gatehouse-inspired bridge. The red-tile-roofed resort commands one's attention through its sheer size and aristocratic bearing (not to mention through its kilt-wearing, bagpipe-playing staff). The inn is several long blocks from the water's edge, perching on the brow of a hill, and affords panoramic bay views from the second-floor roof garden and many guest rooms. The rooms have been refreshed, and are comfortable and tasteful. In addition to the outstanding seaside golf course (see "Golf," earlier), there's a spa at the hotel featuring a full card of treatments ranging from facials and nail services to body wraps and massage. The resort's main **dining room** 🏵🏵, open May through October, is one of the more enjoyable spots in town.

184 Adolphus St., St. Andrews, NB E5B 1T7. ℂ 800/441-1414 or 506/529-8823. Fax 506/529-7162. www.fairmont.com. 234 units. C$99–C$459 (US$99–US$459/£50–£230) double; C$299–C$1,169 (US$299–US$1,169/£150–£585) suite. Rates include continental breakfast. AE, DC, MC, V. Valet parking. Small cats and dogs C$25 (US$25/£13) per night. **Amenities:** 2 restaurants; 2 bars; outdoor heated pool; golf course; 2 tennis courts; health club; spa; Jacuzzi; sauna; bike rentals; children's programs; game room; concierge; salon; massage; babysitting; laundry service; dry cleaning. *In room:* TV, dataport, minibar, coffeemaker, hair dryer, iron.

Kingsbrae Arms Relais & Châteaux 🏵🏵🏵   Kingsbrae Arms, part of the Relais & Châteaux network, is a five-star inn informed by an upscale European feel. Located at the top of King Street, the inn occupies an 1897 manor house, where the furnishings all seem to have a story to tell. The home, built by prosperous jade merchants in 1897, occupies .4 hectares (1 acre), all of which has been well employed. Guests will feel pampered, with amenities including 325-thread-count sheets, plush robes, and a complete guest-services suite stocked with complimentary snacks and refreshments. Some rooms have Jacuzzis; all have gas fireplaces. Guests can also enjoy a five-course meal around a stately table in the dining room during peak season. (This dining room is not open to the public.) One meal is offered nightly, and the *nouveau* Canadian-style cuisine is ever-changing and good. Note that rates are in American dollars, rather than Canadian.

219 King St., St. Andrews, NB E5B 1Y1. ℂ 506/529-1897. Fax 506/529-1197. www.kingsbrae.com. 8 units. US$585–US$985 (C$585–C$985/£293–£493) double. 2-night minimum; 3-night minimum July–Aug weekends. 5% room service charge additional. AE, MC, V. Closed Nov–Apr. Pets allowed with advance permission. **Amenities:** Babysitting; laundry service; dry cleaning. *In room:* A/C, TV, coffeemaker, hair dryer, iron/ironing board, Jacuzzi (some units).

WHERE TO DINE

Europa 🏵🏵 *(Finds)* CONTINENTAL   In an intriguing yellow building that once housed a movie theater and dance hall, Bavarian husband-and-wife transplants Markus and Simone Ritter whip up great French-, Swiss-, and German-accented Continental cuisine for a 35-seat room. Starters include smoked salmon with rösti and capers; a house specialty of seared scallops in Mornay sauce, baked with cheese; French onion soup; and escargots. Main courses run to several versions of schnitzel (grilled pork or veal steak), each with distinct fillings, toppings, and sauces; beef stroganoff; duck a l'Orange; rack of lamb; haddock in lemon butter or champagne sauce; steak in Bearnaise sauce; and tiger shrimp in mango-curry sauce. All are prepared with skill and restraint. Finish with chocolate mousse, homemade almond parfait, or one of about a dozen homemade ice creams or sorbets. The wine list is also surprisingly strong given that this is such a small, out-of-the-way town. All in all, consider this restaurant a gem—a must-visit spot if you're in the area.

48 King St. ⓒ **506/529-3818.** Reservations recommended. Main courses C$18–C$27 (US$18–US$27/£9–£14). MC, V. Mid-May to Sept daily 5–9pm; Oct Tues–Sat 5–9pm; Nov to mid-Feb Thurs–Sat 5–9pm. Closed mid-Feb to mid-May.

The Gables SEAFOOD/PUB FARE   This informal eatery is located in a trim home with prominent gables fronting Water Street, though you enter down a narrow alley where sky and water views suddenly break through a soaring window from a spacious outside deck. Inside is a bright and lively local spot with a casual maritime decor and fare; outside there's a plastic porch furniture informality. Breakfast is served during peak season only, with homemade baked goods and rosemary potatoes. Lunch and dinner options include burgers, steaks, and seafood items such as breaded haddock, daily catches, and a lobster clubhouse—a chopped lobster salad with cheese, cucumber, lettuce, and tomato. There's a kids' menu as well, while margaritas and sangria are available by the pitcher for the adults in the party. The view tends to pull rank on the menu, but if you like simple fare, both will satisfy.

143 Water St. ⓒ **506/529-3440.** Main courses C$3.95–C$6.95 (US$3.95–US$6.95/£2–£3.50) breakfast, C$7.50–C$25 (US$7.50–US$25/£3.75–£13) lunch and dinner. MC, V. July–Aug daily 8am–11pm; Sept–June daily 11am–9pm.

3 Grand Manan Island ⓧ

Geologically rugged, profoundly peaceable, and indisputably remote, this handsome island of 2,800 year-round residents is a 90-minute ferry ride from the port of Blacks Harbour, which is just southeast of St. George. Despite being located incredibly close to Maine (and the U.S.), Grand Manan is a much-prized destination for adventurous travelers—sometimes a highlight of their vacation. Yet the island also remains a mystifying puzzle for others who fail to be smitten by its rough-edged charm. Either this is your kind of place, or it isn't; perhaps there's no in between. The only way to find out is to visit.

Grand Manan is a special favorite both among serious **birders** and serious enthusiasts of Pulitzer Prize–winning novelist Willa Cather, who found her way from Nebraska and New York to a summer cottage here. Hiking the island's famous trails, don't be surprised to come across knots of very quiet people peering intently through binoculars. These are the birders, not the Cather fans. Nearly 300 different species of birds either nest here or stop by the island during their long migrations, and it's a good place to add mightily to your "life list," if you're into such a pursuit; with birds ranging from bald eagles to puffins (though you'll need to sign up for a boat tour to catch a glimpse at the latter) here, you're sure to see something with wings you've never seen before except in books.

Cather kept a cottage here and wrote some of her books while staying on the island. Her die-hard fans are as easy to spot as the birders, say locals, and something of a wild breed; during one Cather conference some years ago, several dozen got up, wrapped themselves in sheets, and danced around a bonfire during the summer solstice—I'm not sure what that was all about, but there you have it.

ESSENTIALS

GETTING THERE   Grand Manan is connected to Blacks Harbour on the mainland via frequent ferry service in summer. **Coastal Transport ferries** (ⓒ **506/642-0520;** www.coastaltransport.ca), each capable of hauling 60 cars, depart from the mainland and the island every 2 hours between 7:30am and 5:30pm during July and August; a ferry makes three to four daily trips the rest of the year. The round-trip fare was C$11 (US$11/£5.50) per passenger (C$5.20/US$5.20/£2.60 ages 5–12) and

C$31 (US$31/£16) per car in 2007. Boarding the ferry on the mainland is free; you purchase tickets when you leave the island.

Reserve your return trip at least a day ahead to avoid getting stranded on the island, and get in line early to secure a spot. A good strategy for departing from Blacks Harbour is to bring a picnic lunch, arrive an hour or two early, put your car in line, and head to the grassy waterfront park adjacent to the wharf. It's an attractive spot; there's even an island to explore at low tide.

VISITOR INFORMATION   The island's **Visitor Information Centre,** Route 776, Grand Manan, NB E5G 4E9 (© **888/525-1655** or 506/662-3442), is open Monday through Friday in summer (8am–5pm except Sun, when it's open 9am–1pm) in the town of Grand Harbour. It's closed mid-September to early June; if so, ask at island stores or inns for a free island map published by the **Grand Manan Tourism Association** (www.grandmanannb.com), which has a listing of key island phone numbers.

EXPLORING THE ISLAND

Start your explorations before you arrive. As you come abreast of the island aboard the ferry, head to the starboard side. You'll soon see **Seven Day's Work** in the rocky cliffs of Whale's Cove, where seven layers of hardened lava and sill (intrusive igneous rock) have come together in a sort of geological Dagwood sandwich.

You can begin to open the puzzle box that is local geology at the **Grand Manan Museum** (© **506/662-3424**) in Grand Harbour, one of three villages on the island's eastern shore. The museum's geology exhibit, located in the basement, offers pointers about what to look for as you roam the island. Birders will enjoy the Allan Moses collection upstairs, which features 230 stuffed and mounted birds in glass cases. The museum also has an impressive lighthouse lens from the Gannet Rock Lighthouse, and a collection of stuff that's washed ashore from the frequent shipwrecks. The museum is open from June to September Monday through Friday 10am to 4pm; it's also open Sundays from 1 to 5pm in July and August. Admission is C$4 (US$4/£2) adults, C$2 (US$2/£1) seniors and students, and free for children under 12.

Numerous hiking trails lace the island, and they offer a popular diversion throughout the summer. Trails can be found just about everywhere, but most are a matter of local knowledge. Don't hesitate to ask at your inn or the Visitor Information Centre, or to ask anyone you might meet on the street. *A Hiking Guide to New Brunswick* (Goose Lane Editions; © **506/450-4251**) lists 12 hikes with maps; this handy book is often sold on the ferry. The most accessible clusters of trails are at the island's northern and southern tips. Head north up Whistle Road to Whistle Beach, and you'll find both the **Northwestern Coastal Trail** ⚐ and the **Seven Day's Work Trail** ⚐, both of which track along the rocky shoreline. Near the low lighthouse and towering radio antennae at Southwest Head (follow Rte. 776 to the end), trails radiate out along cliffs topped with scrappy forest; the views are remarkable when the fog's not in.

WHALE-WATCHING & BOAT TOURS

A fine way to experience island ecology is to mosey offshore. Several outfitters offer complete nature tours, providing a nice sampling of the world above and beneath the sea. On an excursion you might see minke, finback, or humpback whales, along with exotic birds including puffins and phalaropes. **Sea Watch Tours** (© **506/662-8552**), run by Peter and Kenda Wilcox, operates a series of 5-hour excursions from mid-June to early August, with whale sightings guaranteed or your money back, aboard a 13m

(43-ft.) vessel with canopy. The rate is C$59 (US$59/£30) for adults and C$39 (US$39/£20) per child.

WHERE TO STAY

Anchorage Provincial Park ✸ (ℭ **506/662-7022**) has about 100 campsites scattered about forest and field, available late May to mid-September. There's a small beach and a hiking trail on the property, and it's well situated for exploring the southern part of the island. It's very popular midsummer; call before you board the ferry to ask about campsite availability. Sites are C$22 to C$35 (US$22–US$35/£11–£18), some with hookups for RVs and some better suited for a simple tent.

Inn at Whale Cove Cottages ✸✸   The Inn at Whale Cove is a delightful, family-run compound set in a grassy meadow overlooking a quiet and picturesque cove. The original building is a cozy farmhouse that dates to 1816. It's been restored rustically with a nice selection of simple country antiques. The three guest rooms in the main house are comfortable (Sally's Attic has a small deck and a large view); the living room has a couple years' worth of good reading and a welcoming fireplace. Five cottages are scattered about the property, and they vary in size from one to four bedrooms; some only rent by the week, others daily. One of the older units was author Willa Cather's famous cottage, while the newer John's Flat and Cove View cottages are the most modern, with such amenities as extra bedrooms and dining rooms, decks, televisions, a laundry, and in one case a Jacuzzi. Views are lovely. The 4-hectare (10-acre) grounds, especially the path down to the quiet coveside beach, are wonderful to explore. Innkeeper Laura Buckley received her culinary training in Toronto, and her **dining room** ✸ demonstrates a deft touch with local ingredients.

Whistle Rd. (P.O. Box 233), North Head, Grand Manan, NB E0G 2M0. ℭ **506/662-3181**. 3 rooms, 5 cottages (some only rented by week). C$105–C$150 (US$105–US$150/£53–£75) double; C$800–C$900 (US$800–US$900/£400–£450) weekly cottage. Rates include full breakfast. MC, V. All but 1 unit closed Nov to Apr. Pets accepted for C$5 (US$5/£2.50) per day. **Amenities:** Dining room. *In room:* TV (2 units), kitchenette (3 units), Jacuzzi (1 unit).

Shorecrest Lodge ✸ *Value* *Kids*   This century-old inn is a place to put your feet up and unwind. Located just a few hundred yards from the ferry, the inn is nicely decorated with a mix of modern furniture and eclectic country antiques. Most of the guest rooms have private bathrooms, a rarity for Grand Manan. The best might be Room no. 8 with its burgundy leather chairs and a great harbor view. Kids like the TV room in back, which also stocks games and a library that's long on local natural history. The country-style dining room has a fireplace and hardwood floors, and a menu of local fresh seafood, pizza, chicken, and beef tenderloin.

100 Rte. 776, North Head, Grand Manan, NB E5G 1A1. ℭ **506/662-3216**. www.shorecrestlodge.com. 10 units, 8 with private bathroom. C$65–C$119 (US$65–US$119/£33–£60) double. Rates include continental breakfast. MC, V. Closed Nov–May. **Amenities:** Restaurant; fitness room. *In room:* No phone.

WHERE TO DINE

Options for dining out aren't exactly extravagant on Grand Manan. The inns listed above offer good meals, and you'll encounter a few more family restaurants and grocers along the road, as well. If you're here on Saturday morning, check out the weekly **farmer's market** in North Head.

In the mood for a dare? Try walking into **North Head Bakery** ✸✸ (ℭ **506/662-8862**) at 199 Rte. 776 and walking out without buying anything. It cannot be done. This superb bakery (Tues–Sat 6am–6pm) has used traditional baking methods and whole grains since it opened in 1990. Breads made daily include a crusty, seven-grain

Saint John Valley bread and a delightful egg-and-butter bread. Nor should the choco-late-chip cookies be overlooked. The bakery is on Route 776 on the left when you're heading south from the ferry.

4 Saint John: New Brunswick's Largest City ⟨★

152km (94 miles) SW of Moncton, 112km (70 miles) SE of Fredericton

Centered on a good-size commercial harbor, Saint John is New Brunswick's largest city and the center of much of the province's industry. Spread out over a low hill with good rocky views, the downtown boasts wonderfully elaborate Victorian flourishes on its rows of commercial buildings. (Be sure to look high along the cornices to appreci-ate the intricate brickwork.) And a handful of impressive mansions lord over the side streets, their interiors a forest of intricate wood carving—appropriately so, as timber barons built most of them.

There's an industrial grittiness to Saint John that some find unappealing and oth-ers find charming. It all depends on your outlook. Just don't expect a tidy garden city with lots of neat homes; this isn't that sort of place. Instead, Saint John offers a surfeit of brick architecture in various states of repair. From throughout the downtown you'll get glimpses of its past and present industry: large shipping terminals, oil storage facil-ities, and paper mills of the sort that were so popular with Ashcan artists.

Don't let this put you off, though; think about taking a detour from the main coastal highway downtown. It does take some effort—the traffic engineers have been very mischievous here, leading you around rather than into the city. When you finally arrive, though, you'll discover an intriguing place to stroll around for an afternoon while awaiting the ferry to Digby, to grab a delicious bite to eat and a pint of ale, and possibly break up your driving and cute-village-hopping with an urban overnight. The streets here often bustle with everyone from skateboarders to out-for-the-weekenders to dowagers shopping at the public market.

ESSENTIALS

GETTING THERE BY PLANE   Saint John's **airport** (© 506/696-0200; www. saintjohnairport.com), coded YSJ, has regular flights to and from Montréal, Toronto, and Halifax; contact **Air Canada Jazz** (© 888/247-2262; www.aircanada.com) for more information about the vast majority of them. **WestJet** (© 800/538-5696; www.westjet.com) also runs occasional service from Toronto. There are auto rental kiosks in the terminal, and a taxi ride into the city costs about C$30 (US$30/£15).

GETTING THERE BY FERRY   Year-round ferry service connects Saint John to Digby, Nova Scotia. See "Exploring the Province" at the beginning of this chapter for information.

GETTING THERE BY CAR   Saint John is located on Route 1. It's 106km (66 miles) from the U.S. border at St. Stephens, and 427km (265 miles) from Halifax, Nova Scotia.

VISITOR INFORMATION   Saint John (www.tourismsaintjohn.com) is fully stocked with *three* (count 'em) **visitor information centers.** Arriving from the west, look for a contemporary triangular building just off the Route 1 West off-ramp, open mid-May to early October, where you'll find a trove of information and brochures (© 506/658-2940). A smaller seasonal **information center,** reached by exits 119A

> **Fun Fact Spell It Out**
>
> Saint John is *always* spelled out, just as I have done in this sentence. It's never abbreviated as "St. John." That's to keep mail destined for St. John's in Newfoundland from ending up here by mistake, and vice versa.

and 119B, is located inside the observation building overlooking Reversing Falls on Route 100 (© **506/658-2937**). It's also open mid-May to early October.

If you've already made your way downtown, or need info outside of the peak seasons, look for the city's **City Centre Tourist Information Centre** (© **886/GO-FUNDY** or 506/658-2855) inside Market Square, a downtown shopping mall just off the waterfront reached via Exit 22. Find the info center by entering the square at street level at the corner of St. Patrick and Water streets. During peak season (mid-June to mid-Sept) the center is open daily from 9am to 7pm. The rest of the year it's open daily 9am to 5:30pm.

EXPLORING SAINT JOHN

If the weather's cooperative, start by wandering around near the **waterfront.** Tourism Saint John has published three walking tour brochures that offer plenty of history and architectural trivia. Saint John is noted for the odd and interesting gargoyles and sculpted heads that adorn the brick and stone 19th-century buildings downtown. If you have time for only one tour, I'd opt for **"Prince William's Walk,"** an hour-long, self-guided tour of the impressive commercial buildings. Obtain the tour brochures at the **Market Square information center.**

If the weather's disagreeable (and it might be), just head indoors. Over the past two decades, Saint John has been busy linking its downtown malls and shops with an elaborate network of underground and overhead pedestrian walkways, dubbed **"The Inside Connection."** It's not only for shopping—two major hotels, the provincial museum, the city library, the city market, the sports arena, and the aquatic center are all part of this network.

Loyalist House   A mandatory destination for serious antique buffs, this stately Georgian home was built in 1817 for the Merritt family, who were wealthy Loyalists from Rye, New York. Inside is an extraordinary collection of furniture dating from before 1833, most pieces of which were original to the house and have never left. Especially notable are the extensive holdings of Duncan Phyfe Sheraton furniture and a rare piano-organ combination. Other unusual detailing includes the doors steamed and bent to fit into the curved sweep of the stairway, and the carvings on the wooden chair rails. Tours last 30 to 45 minutes, depending on the number of questions you ask. Note that this house is open only 2 months of the year, though it does sometimes open in the fall when cruise ships are at port in the harbor. Failing to catch one of those in town, you might get together a small interested group or big family and give these folks a call, asking them nicely to open the house.

120 Union St. © 506/652-3590. C$3 (US$3/£1.50) adults, C$1 (US$1/50p) children, C$7 (US$7/£3.50) families. July–Aug daily 10am–5pm; June Mon–Fri 10am–5pm; Sept to Apr by appointment only.

New Brunswick Museum ★ (Kids   The New Brunswick Museum is an excellent stop for anyone in the least bit curious about the province's natural or cultural history. The collections are displayed on three open floors, and they offer a nice mix of traditional

Saint John

ACCOMMODATIONS ■

Earle of Leinster B&B **6**

Hilton Saint John **2**

Homeport Historic
Bed & Breakfast **1**

DINING ◆

Beatty and the Beastro **5**

Billy's Seafood Co. **3**

Taco Pica **4**

artifacts and quirky objects. (Among the more memorable items is a frightful looking "permanent wave" machine from a 1930s beauty parlor.) The exhaustive exhibits include the complete interior of Sullivan's Bar (where longshoremen used to slake their thirst a few blocks away), a massive section of a ship frame, a wonderful geological exhibit, and even a sporty white Bricklin from a failed New Brunswick automobile manufacturing venture in the mid-1970s. "The Wind, Wood and Sail" exhibit describes 19th-century shipbuilding in the province. Allow at least 2 hours to enjoy these eclectic and uncommonly well-displayed exhibits.

1 Market Sq. ✆ **506/643-2300**. Admission C$6 (US$6/£3) adults, C$4.75 (US$4.75/£2.40) seniors, C$3.25 (US$3.25/£1.65) students and children 4–18, C$13 (US$13/£6.50) families. June–Oct Mon–Fri 9am–5pm (Thurs until 9pm), Sat 10am–5pm, Sun noon–5pm; closed Mon Nov–May.

Old City Market ★★   Hungry travelers venture here at their peril! This spacious, bustling, and bright marketplace is crammed with vendors hawking meat, fresh seafood, cheeses, flowers, baked goods, and bountiful fresh produce. You can even sample dulse, a snack of dried seaweed from the Bay of Fundy. (One traveler has compared the experience to licking a wharf.) The market was built in 1876, and it has been a center of commerce for the city ever since. Note the construction of the roof: Local lore says it resembles an inverted ship because it was made by boat builders who didn't know how to build anything else. And watch for the small, enduring traces of tradition: The handsome iron gates at either end have been in place since 1880, and the loud bell is rung daily by the deputy market clerk, who signals the opening and closing of the market. A number of vendors offer meals to go, and there's a bright seating area in an enclosed terrace on the market's south side. It's worth an hour or two (including a stop to eat, of course).

47 Charlotte St. © 506/658-2820. Mon–Thurs 7:30am–6pm; Fri 7:30am–7pm; Sat 7:30am–5pm. Closed holidays.

WHERE TO STAY

Budget travelers should head to Manawagonish Road for lower-priced motels. Unlike many other motel strips, which tend to be notably unlovely, Manawagonish Road is reasonably attractive. It winds along a high ridge of residential homes west of town, with views out to the Bay of Fundy. It's about a 10-minute drive into downtown. Rates at most Manawagonish motels are approximately C$50 to C$60 (US$50–US$60/£25–£30) peak season. The **Econo Lodge,** 1441 Manawagonish Rd. (© **800/55ECONO** or 506/635-8700), is somewhat more expensive but a bit more comfortable, and the rooms have sweeping views.

In-town camping is available summers at **Rockwood Park** (© **506/652-4050**). Some 80 sites are spread across a rocky hill; many overlook downtown, the highway, and a rail yard (expect nighttime noise). RVs requesting full hookups are directed to an area resembling a parking lot, but it's quite serviceable. Other sites vary widely in privacy and scenic attributes. Rates range from about C$18 (US$18/£9) for a tent site to around C$24 (US$24/£12) for hookups. Follow signs to the park from either Exit 122 or Exit 125 off Route 1.

Earle of Leinster "Inn Style" Bed & Breakfast *Value*   For more than a decade, Lauree and Stephen Savoie have operated the Earle of Leinster, a handsome Victorian row house in a working-class neighborhood a 5-minute walk from King's Square. It's a welcoming and casual place, nothing fancy, with a kitchen for guests to make themselves at home, and a pool table and TV in the basement. The Fitzgerald and Lord Edward rooms in the main house are the most historic, with high ceilings and regal furniture. Most of the remaining rooms are in the carriage house and are a bit more motel-like, although the second-floor loft is quite spacious. (Some rooms can be musty after a rainy spell.) The bathrooms are private, but they're also small. Added bonus: There's a free self-serve washer and dryer, plus VCRs in all rooms and a small library of films to select from. Recently the owner has expanded some of the smaller rooms, making them into minisuites with small kitchenette facilities.

96 Leinster St., Saint John, NB E2L 1J3. © 506/652-3275. http://earleofleinster.tripod.com. 7 units. C$65–C$96 (US$65–US$96/£33–£48) double. Rates include full breakfast. AE, DC, MC, V. Pets allowed. **Amenities:** Laundry service. *In room:* TV/VCR, fridge, hair dryer, no phone.

Hilton Saint John ★   This 12-story waterfront hotel was built in 1984 and has the amenities one would expect from an upscale chain hotel. Rooms on the top two Plaza

Floors were repainted, redecorated, and upgraded to include perks such as electronic safes, cordless phones, bigger desks, and terry-cloth robes. This property boasts the best location in Saint John, overlooking the harbor yet just steps from the rest of downtown by street or indoor walkway. Windows in all guest rooms open, a nice touch when the breeze is coming from the sea. The Hilton is connected to the convention center and attracts major events; ask whether anything's scheduled before you book if you don't want to be overwhelmed by conventioneers.

The hotel's lounge offers light meals from 11:30am to midnight daily. For more refined fare, head for the main dining room, which serves three meals daily in an understated and classical harborside setting. Entrees include creatively prepared steaks, pheasant, and salmon.

1 Market Sq., Saint John, NB E2L 4Z6. © 800/561-8282 in Canada, 800/445-8667 in the U.S., or 506/693-8484. Fax 509/657-6610. www.hiltonsaintjohn.com. 197 units. C$119–C$219 (US$119–US$219/£60–£110) double. AE, DC, DISC, MC, V. Self-parking C$15 (US$15/£7.50) per day. Pets allowed. **Amenities:** 2 restaurants; bar; indoor pool; fitness room; Jacuzzi; sauna; game room; concierge; car-rental desk; business center; salon; 24-hr. room service; babysitting; laundry service. *In room:* A/C, TV, dataport, minibar, coffeemaker, hair dryer, iron, safe.

Homeport Historic Bed & Breakfast 🎁🎁 *Kids*   This architecturally impressive Italianate home built by a prominent shipbuilding family sits high atop a rocky ridge on the north side of Route 1, overlooking downtown and the harbor. Built around 1858 (that's before Canada was even Canada yet), this is one of southern New Brunswick's best options for an overnight if you're a fan of old houses and furnishings. Rooms are fitted out eclectically with materials gleaned from local auctions and shops; all units have individually controlled heat, a rarity in such an inn. Look for such touches as sleigh beds, (nonworking) marble fireplaces, and such. The Veranda Room is one favored room; it's spacious, has fine harbor views, and gets superb afternoon sun. The walls are decorated with steel engravings commemorating the laying of the first trans-Atlantic cable, floors are wide-board hand-cut pine, and there's antique furniture that was made by a local woodworker. The Harbour Master Suite has a four-posted bed and a small separate sitting room that's ideal for those traveling with a child or two. "Come-hungry" breakfasts are served family-style around a long antique table in the formal dining room.

80 Douglas Ave. (take Exit 121 or 123 to Main St.), Saint John, NB E2K 1E4. © 888/678-7678 or 506/672-7255. Fax 506/672-7250. www.homeport.nb.ca. 10 units. C$110–C$175 (US$110–US$175/£55–£88) double. Rates include full breakfast. AE, MC, V. Free parking. *In room:* A/C, TV, dataport, fridge (1 unit), kitchenette (1 unit).

WHERE TO DINE

For lunch, don't overlook the Old City Market, mentioned above. With a little snooping you can turn up tasty light meals and fresh juices in the market, then enjoy your finds in the alley atrium.

Beatty and the Beastro *Finds* 🎁 BISTRO/CONTINENTAL   Ignore the jokey name. This large-windowed establishment is the most handsome eatery in Saint John, with its attractive interior fronting King's Square and a mild European-moderne look. Service is cordial and efficient, and the meals are among the best in the city. Lunch includes soups, salads, omelets, curry wraps, and elaborate gourmet sandwiches (but the simple grilled fish sandwich isn't bad, either). At dinner the restaurant is noted for its lamb, the preparation of which varies nightly according to the chef's desire; the house curry dish is also recommended, as is chicken parmigiana, a schnitzel served with spaetzle, steaks, fish, and a pepper-chicken dish of the restaurant's creation. When dessert time rolls around, be aware that both the butterscotch pie and the lemon chess pie have large local followings.

60 Charlotte St. (on King's Sq.). ⓒ 506/652-3888. Reservations recommended weekends and when shows are slated at the Imperial Theatre. Main courses C$7–C$10 (US$7–US$10/£3.50–£5) lunch, C$20–C$22 (US$20–US$22/ £10–£11) dinner. AE, DC, MC, V. Mon–Fri 11:30am–3pm and 5–9pm; Sat 5–10pm.

Billy's Seafood Co. ⓖ SEAFOOD   Billy Grant's restaurant off King's Square boasts a congenial staff, exceptionally fresh seafood (they sell to City Market customers by day), and slightly better prices than the more tourist-oriented waterfront seafood restaurants. The chef at this classy-yet-casual eatery knows how to prepare fish without overcooking. Specialties include cedar-planked salmon, and Billy's bouillabaisse is also quite good. Lunch entrees are surprisingly versatile, too, including Thai curried mussels and seafood crepes. Offerings of beef, veal, and pasta fill out the menu for those not in the mood for fish.

49–51 Charlotte St. (at City Market). ⓒ 506/672-3474. Reservations suggested. Light meals C$5.95–C$11 (US$5.95– US$11/£3–£5.50); dinner entrees C$16–C$29 (US$16–US$29/£8–£15). AE, DC, MC, V. Mon–Thurs 11am–10pm; Fri–Sat 11am–11pm; Sun 4–10pm.

Taco Pica LATIN AMERICAN   This cooperative is owned and run by a group of Guatemalans and their friends. It's bright, festive, and just a short stroll off King Street. The restaurant has developed a devoted local following since it opened in 1994, featuring a menu that's a notch above the usual staid Canadian adaptations of Mexican and Latin American fare. Among the most reliable dishes are *pepian* (a spicy beef stew with chayote), garlic shrimp, and the shrimp taco with potatoes, peppers, and cheese. Vegetarian offerings are available as well. There's a good selection of fresh juices here, and the restaurant possesses a liquor license—which means you can quaff any of a variety of fruit margaritas to put out the fire.

96 Germain St. ⓒ 506/633-8492. Reservations recommended on weekends. Main courses C$7.95–C$17 (US$7.95– US$17/£4–£8.50). AE, MC, V. Mon–Sat 10am–10pm.

5 Fredericton

174km (108 miles) W of Moncton, 112km (70 miles) NW of Saint John

New Brunswick's provincial capital is a compact, historic city of brick and concrete that unfolds lazily along the banks of the wide Saint John River. The handsome buildings, broad streets, and wide sidewalks make the place feel more like a big, tidy village than a small city. Keep an eye out for two icons that mark Fredericton: the stately elm trees that have stubbornly resisted Dutch elm disease and still shade the occasional park and byway, and the Union Jack, which you'll occasionally see fluttering from various buildings attesting to long-standing historic ties with the Loyalists who shaped the city.

For travelers, the city can be seen as divided into three zones: the malls and motels atop the hills and near the Trans-Canada Highway; the impressive, Georgian-style University of New Brunswick on the hillside just south of town; and the downtown itself, with its casual blend of modern and historic buildings. Most visitors focus on downtown. The main artery—where you'll find the bulk of the attractions and restaurants— is Queen Street, which parallels the river just inland. An ill-considered four-lane roadway separates much of downtown from the river, but you can reach water's edge via The Green pathway or by crossing a pedestrian bridge at the foot of Carleton Street.

ESSENTIALS

GETTING THERE BY PLANE   The **Fredericton Airport** (ⓒ **506/444-6100;** www.frederictonairport.ca), coded YFC, is located 10 minutes southeast of downtown

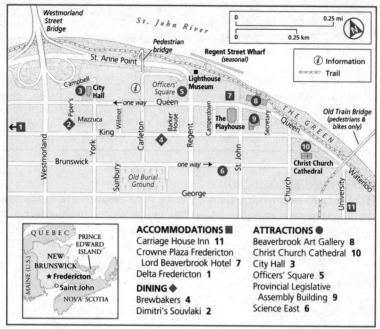

ACCOMMODATIONS ■
Carriage House Inn **11**
Crowne Plaza Fredericton
  Lord Beaverbrook Hotel **7**
Delta Fredericton **1**

DINING ◆
Brewbakers **4**
Dimitri's Souvlaki **2**

ATTRACTIONS ●
Beaverbrook Art Gallery **8**
Christ Church Cathedral **10**
City Hall **3**
Officers' Square **5**
Provincial Legislative
  Assembly Building **9**
Science East **6**

on Route 102 and is served by cab and rental car companies. For flight information, contact **Air Canada Jazz** (© 888/247-2262; www.aircanada.com). There's also a new direct **Delta Connection** (© 800/221-1212; www.delta.com) shuttle service from Boston.

GETTING THERE BY CAR   A major relocation and widening of the Trans-Canada Highway near Fredericton has relieved traffic congestion somewhat. Look for signs directing you to downtown; from the west, follow Woodstock Road, which tracks along the river to downtown. From Saint John, look for Route 7 to Regent Street, and then turn right down the hill.

VISITOR INFORMATION   Always careful to cater to visitors, Fredericton maintains no less than three center-city visitor information centers: the original in **City Hall** at 397 Queen St. (© 506/460-2041; daily 8am–5pm and to 8pm in the summer), and a second, newer one at **11 Carleton St.**, which also has racks of information year-round; it's the central tourism office, so it's only open normal business hours, i.e., weekdays from 8:15am to 4:30pm. Call © 888/888-4768 or 506/460-2041 to reach either. Then there's a third information center at **Kings Landing** (© 506/460-2191), just west of town in River Valley, open from mid-May to early October as well. No matter which one you find first, ask for a visitor parking pass, which allows visitors from outside the province to park free at city lots and meters in town for up to 3 days without penalty. You can also request travel information in advance by visiting the city's website at www.tourismfredericton.ca.

Tips **Fredericton: The Land of Wi and Fi?**

Surprisingly, Fredericton has been named one of the most "wired" cities in all of North America; it's easy to find a hot spot with your laptop anywhere in the city, thanks to the 2003 installation of city-wide Wi-Fi. Known as Fred-e-Zone, the project now offers hundreds of access points—not only downtown, but at the Greater Fredericton Airport, in shopping malls, and even in parks and sports arenas (think: hockey) throughout the city. You can even rent a portable PC from the **Lighthouse Adventure Centre** (© **506/460-2939**) for just C$3 (US$3/£1.50) per half-hour. Thumbs up, guys. Now get me my laptop.

EXPLORING FREDERICTON

The free **"Fredericton Visitor Guide,"** available at the information centers and many hotels around town, contains a well-written and informative **walking tour** of the downtown. It's worth tracking down before launching an exploration of the city.

City Hall, at 397 Queen St., is an elaborate Victorian building with a prominent brick tower and 2.4m (8-ft.) clock dial. The second-floor City Council Chamber occupies what was the opera house until the 1940s. Small, folksy tapestries adorn the **visitor's gallery** and tell the town's history. Learn about these and the rest of the building during the free building tours, which are offered twice daily from mid-May to mid-October (both in English and French). In the off season, call © **506/460-2120** to schedule a tour.

Officers' Square, on Queen Street between Carleton and Regent, is now a handsome city park. In 1785, the park was the center of military activity and used for drills, first as part of the British garrison, and later (until 1914) by the Canadian Army. Today, the only soldiers are local actors who put on a show for the tourists. Look also for music and dramatic events staged at the square in the warmer months. The handsome colonnaded stone building facing the parade grounds is the former officer's quarters, now the York-Sunbury Historical Society Museum.

Two blocks upriver of Officers' Square are the Soldiers' Barracks, housed in a similarly grand stone building. Check your watch against the sundial high on the end of the barracks, a replica of the original timepiece. A small exhibit shows the life of the enlisted man of the 18th century. Along the ground floor, local craftspeople sell their wares from small shops carved out of former barracks.

One entertaining and enlightening way to learn about the city's history is to sign up for a walking tour with the **Calithumpians Theatre Company** ⚑. Costumed guides offer free tours daily in July and August, pointing out highlights with anecdotes and dramatic tales. Recommended is the nighttime "Haunted Hike" tour, done by lantern light, which runs 5 nights each week. This evening tour is about 2 hours and costs C$13 (US$13/£6.50) for adults, C$8 (US$8/£4) for children; call © **506/457-1975** for more information.

Fredericton recently expanded its trail system for walkers and bikers. The centerpiece of the system is **The Green** ⚑, a 5km (3-mile) pathway that follows the river from the Sheraton hotel to near the Princess Margaret Bridge. It's a lovely walk, and you'll pass the **Old Government House,** downtown, and the open parklands near Waterloo Row.

Beaverbrook Art Gallery ⊛ *Value*   This surprisingly good museum overlooks the waterfront and is home to an impressive collection of British paintings, including works by Reynolds, Gainsborough, Constable, and Turner. Antiques buffs gravitate to the rooms with period furnishings and early decorative arts. Most visitors find themselves drawn to Salvador Dalí's massive *Santiago El Grande,* and studies for an ill-fated portrait of Winston Churchill. A new curator has brought in more controversial modern art exhibits of late; one focused on nudity, featuring various artistic perceptions of the unclothed human form, for example. But other shows have touched on more conventional ground, such as 19th-century French realism and a show on the cities of Canada drawn from the Seagram Collection. Stop by to find out what's currently on display.

703 Queen St. © 506/458-2028. www.beaverbrookartgallery.org. Admission C$5 (US$5/£2.50) adults, C$4 (US$4/£2) seniors, C$2 (US$2/£1) students, C$10 (US$10/£5) family; Thurs evenings pay what you wish. Daily 9am–5:30pm (Thurs until 9pm).

Provincial Legislative Assembly Building ⊛   The assembly building, constructed starting in 1880, boasts an exterior designed in that bulbous, extravagant Second Empire style. But that's just the prelude. Inside, it's even more dressed up and fancy. Entering takes a bit of courage if the doors are closed; they're heavy and intimidating, with slits of beveled glass for peering out. (They're reminiscent of the gates of Oz.) Inside, it's creaky and wooden and comfortable, in contrast to the cold, unyielding stone of many seats of power. In the small rotunda, look for the razor-sharp prints from John James Audubon's elephant folio, on display in a special case.

The assembly chamber nearly takes the breath away, especially when viewed from the heights of the visitor gallery on the upper floors. (You ascend via a graceful wood spiral stairway housed in its own rotunda.) The chamber is ornate and draperied in that fussy Victorian way, which is quite a feat given the vast scale of the room. Note all the regal trappings, including the portrait of the young Queen Elizabeth. This place just feels like a setting for high drama, whether or not it actually delivers when the chamber is in session. Half-hour long tours are available; plan to spend at least an hour here.

706 Queen St. (across from the Beaverbrook Art Gallery). © 506/453-2527. Free admission. June to mid-Aug daily 9am–7pm (last tour at 6:30pm); off season Mon–Fri 9am–4pm.

Science East ⊛ *Value* *Kids*   Children enjoy a visit to this newish (1999) science center for two reasons. First, it's located in the old county jail, a sturdy stone structure built in the 1840s. (It was still being used as a jail as late as 1996.) And then there are the great exhibits—more than 100 interactive displays indoor and out, including a huge kaleidoscope, a periscope for people-watching, a solar-powered water fountain, and a minitornado. It's an ideal destination for a family on a chilly or rainy day, and there's plenty to do in the outdoors portion on nice days too—a garden of native New Brunswick plants is in the works, for example. If you have kids, this place is easily worth up to 2 hours of your time.

668 Brunswick St. © 506/457-2340. www.scienceeast.nb.ca. Admission C$5 (US$5/£2.50) adults, C$3 (US$3/£1.50) students and seniors, C$14 (US$14/£7) families. June–Aug Mon–Sat 10am–5pm, Sun 1–4pm; rest of year Mon–Fri noon–5pm, Sat 10am–5pm, Sun 1–4pm.

AN ATTRACTION OUTSIDE OF TOWN
Kings Landing Historical Settlement ⊛   Kings Landing, on the bank of the St. John River, is 34km (21 miles) and about 150 years from Fredericton. The authentic re-creation brings to life New Brunswick from 1790 to 1910, with 10 historic houses

and nine other buildings relocated here and saved from destruction by the flooding during the Mactaquac hydro project. The aroma of freshly baked bread mixes with the smell of horses and livestock, and the sound of the blacksmith's hammer alternates with that of the church bell. More than 160 costumed "early settlers" chat about their lives. You could easily spend a day exploring the 120 hectares (297 acres), but if you haven't that much time, focus on the Hagerman House (with furniture by Victorian cabinetmaker John Warren Moore), the Ingraham House with its fine New Brunswick furniture and formal English garden, the Morehouse House (where you'll see a clock Benedict Arnold left behind), and the Victorian Perley House.

Exit 253 off the Trans-Canada Hwy. (Rte. 2 west). (506/363-4999. www.kingslanding.nb.ca. Admission C$15 (US$15/£7.50) adults, C$13 (US$13/£6.50) seniors, C$12 (US$12/£6) students over 16, C$10 (US$10/£5) children 6–16, C$36 (US$36/£18) families. June to early Oct daily 10am–5pm. Closed mid-Oct to May.

WHERE TO STAY

In addition to the listings below, a handful of motels and chain hotels are located in the bustling mall zone on the hill above town, mostly along Regent and Prospect streets.

Carriage House Inn   Fredericton's premier bed-and-breakfast is located a short stroll from the riverfront pathway in a quiet residential neighborhood. A former mayor built the imposing three-story Victorian manse in 1875. Inside, it's a bit somber in that Victorian way, with dark-wood trim and deep colors, and feels solid enough to resist glaciers. Rooms are eclectically furnished and comfortable without being overly opulent. High-speed wireless Internet is available throughout the inn, and delicious, elaborate breakfasts included with your rate are served in a sunny ballroom in the rear of the house. It's furnished with art and antiques.

230 University Ave., Fredericton, NB E3B 4H7. (800/267-6068 or 506/452-9924. Fax 506/452-2770. www.carriage house-inn.net. 10 units. C$95–C$125 (US$95–US$125/£48–£63) double. Rates include full breakfast. AE, MC, V. Small, well-trained pets allowed. **Amenities:** Restaurant. In room: A/C, TV, hair dryer.

Crowne Plaza Fredericton Lord Beaverbrook Hotel ★ (Kids)   This hulking 1947 waterfront hotel is severe and boxy in an early Deco kind of way, a look that may at first suggest that it houses the Ministry of Dourness. But inside, the mood lightens considerably, with composite stone floors, Georgian pilasters, and chandeliers. The downstairs indoor pool and recreation area are positively whimsical, a sort of Tiki-room grotto that kids adore. The guest rooms are nicely appointed with traditional reproduction furniture in dark wood—and they've been seriously freshened up since the Crowne Plaza folks acquired the property. Standard rooms can be somewhat dim, and most of the windows don't open (ask for a room with opening windows when you book). However, the suites are spacious, and many have excellent river views. This is the best accommodation for those who want the convenience of a downtown location and who enjoy the solid architectural touches of an old-fashioned hotel. Those looking for a modern polish may be more content at the Delta.

659 Queen St., Fredericton, NB E3B 5A6. (866/444-1946 or 506/455-3371. Fax 506/455-1441. www.cpfredericton. com. 168 units. C$139–C$199 (US$139–US$199/£70–£100) double. AE, DC, MC, V. **Amenities:** 3 restaurants; pub; indoor pool; Jacuzzi; sauna; business center; babysitting; laundry service; dry cleaning. In room: A/C, TV, dataport, cof-feemaker, hair dryer, iron.

Delta Fredericton ★★   This modern resort hotel, built in 1992, occupies a prime location along the river about 10 minutes' walk from downtown via the riverfront pathway. Much of summer life revolves around the outdoor pool (with its own poolside bar) on the deck overlooking the river, and on Sundays the lobby is surrendered to an over-the-top brunch buffet. Although decidedly up-to-date, the interior is done with classical styling and is comfortable and well appointed. The hotel lounge is an active and popular spot on many nights, especially weekends. Across the lobby is Bruno's Seafood & Chop-house, which offers a good alternative to the restaurants downtown. The chef wisely focuses on whatever's fresh at the city farmer's market; thus, look for seasonal and regional specialties, including fiddleheads in early summer and local vegetables and fruits in season. Bruno's also cooks good steaks.

225 Woodstock Rd., Fredericton, NB E3B 2H8. © 888/462-8800 or 506/457-7000. Fax 506/457-7000. www.delta fredericton.com. 222 units. C$99–C$229 (US$99–US$229/£50–£115) double, royal suites up to C$800 (US$800/£400). AE, DC, MC, V. Free parking. Pets accepted. **Amenities:** Restaurant; 2 bars; heated indoor and outdoor pools; fitness room; Jacuzzi; sauna; salon; room service; babysitting. *In room:* A/C, TV, minibar, coffeemaker, hair dryer, iron/ironing board.

WHERE TO DINE

Brewbakers 𝒶 ITALIAN/SANDWICH   Brewbakers is a convivial pub, cafe, and restaurant, located on three levels in a cleverly adapted downtown building. It's a bustling and informal spot, creatively cluttered with artifacts and artworks, and does boomtown business during lunch hours and early evenings. The cafe section is quieter, as is the mezzanine dining room above the cafe, while the third floor bustles with its open kitchen. Pastas used to be the main attraction here, served up with the usual array of sauces, but recent years have brought a few more upscaled versions (a maple-curry-chicken-cream pasta is just one). Also good here are the personal pizzas, the roasted chicken, the grilled strip loin, and the herb-crusted tenderloin. Lunch features sandwiches that are getting fancier all the time, with choices like smoked salmon, a Morrocan salsa-topped sirloin burger, and a sandwich of oven-roasted peppers and garlicky mayo.

546 King St. © 506/459-0067. Reservations recommended. Main courses C$9–C$14 (US$9–US$14/£4.50–£7) lunch, C$12–C$24 (US$12–US$24/£6–£12) dinner. AE, DC, MC, V. Mon–Wed 11:30am–10pm; Thurs–Fri 11:30am–midnight; Sat 4pm–midnight; Sun 4–10pm.

Dimitri's Souvlaki *Value* GREEK   Dimitri's is hard to find, and easy to walk past even after you've found it. But the generic, chain-restaurant interior belies better-than-average cooking that will appeal to budget-conscious diners. You'll get a big plate of food here without dropping a lot of money. Greek specialties include moussaka (with and without meat), souvlakia, and dolmades, and all are quite good. (Avoid the mystery-meat donairs, though.) Deluxe dinner plates are served with delicious potatoes—hearty wedges that are cooked crispy on the outside and remain hot and soft on the inside. The meats are sometimes on the tough side, but most budget-happy diners will find this place to be a good value.

349 King St. (in Piper's Lane area). © 506/452-8882. Main courses C$8.25–C$18 (US$8.25–US$18/£4.15–£9). AE, DC, MC, V. Mon–Wed 11am–11pm; Thurs–Sat 11am–11:30pm.

6 Fundy National Park: Exploring the Wild Coast 𝒶/𝒶

The Fundy Coast between Saint John and Alma is for the most part wild, remote, and unpopulated. It's plumbed by few roads other than the Fundy Drive, making it difficult to explore unless you have a boat. The best access to the wild coast is through Fundy National Park, a gem of a destination that's hugely popular with travelers with an outdoor bent. Families often settle in here for a week or so, filling their days with activities in and around the park that include hiking, sea kayaking, biking, and splashing around a seaside pool. Nearby are lovely drives and an innovative adventure center at **Cape Enrage.** If a muffling fog moves in to smother the coast, head inland for a hike to a waterfall or through lush forest. If it's a day of brilliant sunshine, venture along the rocky shores by foot or boat.

ESSENTIALS

GETTING THERE Route 114 runs through the center of Fundy National Park. If you're coming from the west, follow the prominent national park signs just east of Sussex. If you're coming from Prince Edward Island or Nova Scotia, head southward on Route 114 from Moncton.

VISITOR INFORMATION The park's main **Visitor Centre** (𝒞 506/887-6000) is located just inside the Alma (eastern) entrance to the park. The stone building is open daily during peak season from 8am to 10pm (only to 4:30pm in the spring and fall). You can watch a video presentation, peruse a handful of exhibits on wildlife and tides, and shop at the nicely stocked nature bookstore. The smaller **Wolfe Lake Information Centre** (𝒞 506/432-6026) is at the park's western entrance and is open daily, mid-June to mid-August only, from 10am to 6pm. The small town of **Alma** also maintains an information center at 8584 Main St. (𝒞 506/887-6127).

FEES Park entry fees are charged from mid-May to mid-October. The fee is C$6.90 (US$6.90/£3.45) adults, C$5.90 (US$5.90/£2.95) seniors, C$3.45 (US$3.45/£2.75) children ages 6 to 16, and C$17 (US$17/£8.50) families. Seasonal passes and spring season discount rates are also available.

EXPLORING THE PARK

Most national park activities are centered around the Alma (eastern) side of the park, where the park entrance has a cultivated and manicured air, as if part of a landed estate. Here you'll find stone walls, well-tended lawns, and attractive landscaping, along with a golf course, amphitheater, lawn bowling, and tennis. Also in this area is a **heated saltwater pool,** set near the bay with a sweeping ocean view. There's a lifeguard on duty, and it's a popular destination for families. The pool is open late June through August. The cost is C$3 (US$3/£1.50) adults, C$2.50 (US$2.50/£1.25) seniors, C$1.50 (US$1.50/75p) children, and C$7.50 (US$7.50/£3.75) families.

Sea kayaking tours are a way to get a good, close look at the ocean landscape and the tides. **FreshAir Adventure** (𝒞 800/545-0020 or 506/887-2249) in Alma offers tours that range from 2 hours to several days. The half-day tours explore marsh and coastline (C$45–C$57/US$45–US$57/£23–£29 including lunch); the full-day adventure includes a hot meal and 6 hours of exploring the wild shores (C$85–C$105/US$85–US$105/£43–£53).

The park maintains 105km (65 miles) of trails for hikers and walkers. These range from a 20-minute loop to a 4-hour trek, and they pass through varied terrain. The trails are arranged such that several can be linked into a 48km (30-mile) backpacker's loop, dubbed the **Fundy Circuit,** which typically requires 3 nights in the backcountry. Pre-registration is required for the overnight trek, so ask at the Visitor Centre. Among the most accessible hikes is the **Caribou Plain Trail** 𝔾, a 3km (2-mile) loop that provides a wonderful introduction to the local terrain. **Third Vault Falls Trail** 𝔾𝔾 is a 7.5km (4.7-mile) in-and-back hike that takes you to the park's highest waterfall, about 14m (46 ft.) high.

Seeking Adventure on Cape Enrage

Cape Enrage is a blustery and bold cape that juts impertinently out into Chignecto Bay. It's also home to a wonderful adventure center that could be a model for similar centers worldwide.

Cape Enrage Adventures ⚘ traces its roots to 1993, when a group of Harrison Trimble High School students in Moncton decided to do something about the decay of the cape's historic lighthouse, which had been abandoned in 1988. They put together a plan to restore the light and keeper's quarters and establish an adventure center. It worked. Today, with the help of experts in kayaking, rock climbing, rappelling, and other rugged sports, a couple dozen high-school students staff and run this program throughout the summer months. The program closes in late August, when the student-managers head back to school.

Part of what makes the program so notable is its flexibility. Day adventures are scheduled throughout the summer, from which you can pick and choose, as if from a menu. These include **rappelling workshops, rock-climbing lessons, kayak trips,** and **canoeing excursions.** Prices are about C$50 (US$50/£25) per person for a 2-hour rock-climbing or rappelling workshop, about C$60 (US$60/£30) for a half-day kayak trip. Parents should note that this is an ideal spot to drop off restless teens while you indulge in scenic drives or a trip to Hopewell Rocks.

As if running the center didn't keep the students busy enough, they also operate a restaurant (open to the public), called the **Keepers' Lunchroom.** Light but tasty meals include a notable fish chowder made with fresh haddock from a recipe provided by a local fisherman's wife, served with hot biscuits. A few other selections are offered—like grilled cheese and cheesecake—but the smart money gets the chowder. Finish with blueberry-and-whipped-cream-topped biscuits.

For more information about the program, which runs May through September, contact **Cape Enrage Adventures** (✆ 888/280-7273 or 506/887-2273; www.capenrage.com).

All the park's trails are covered in the pullout trail guide you'll find in "Salt & Fir," the booklet you'll receive when you pay your entry fee.

CAMPING   The national park maintains four drive-in campgrounds and about 15 backcountry sites. The two main campgrounds are near the Alma entrance. **Headquarters Campground** ⚘ is within walking distance of Alma, the saltwater pool, and numerous other attractions. Since it overlooks the bay, this campground tends to be cool and subject to fogs. **Chignecto North Campground** ⚘ is higher on the hillside, sunnier, and warmer. You can hike down to Alma on an attractive hiking trail in 1 to 2 hours. Both campgrounds have hookups for RVs, flush toilets, and showers, and sites can be reserved in advance (✆ 877/737-3783; www.pccamping.ca); sites cost C$15 to C$33 (US$15–US$33/£7.50–£17) per night, depending on services offered.

The **Point Wolfe** and **Wolfe Lake** campgrounds lack RV hookups and are slightly more primitive, but they are the preferred destinations for campers seeking a quieter camping experience. Rates at Point Wolfe, where showers and flush toilets are available, are about C$25 (US$25/£13); Wolfe Lake lacks showers and has only pit toilets, thus a night there costs only about C$15 (US$15/£7.50).

Backcountry sites are scattered throughout the park, with only one located directly on the coast (at the confluence of the coast and Goose River). Ask at the visitor centers for more information or to reserve a site (mandatory). Backcountry camping fees are about C$10 (US$10/£5) per person per night.

A SIDE TRIP TO HOPEWELL ROCKS

There's no better place to witness the extraordinary power of the Fundy tides than at **Hopewell Rocks** ⭐ (© 877/734-3429; www.thehopewellrocks.ca), located about 40km (25 miles) northeast of Fundy National Park on Route 114. Think of it as a natural sculpture garden. At low tide (the best time to visit), eroded columns as high as 15m (49 ft.) tower above the ocean floor. They're sometimes called the "flowerpots," on account of the trees and plants that still flourish on their narrowing summits.

You park at the visitor center and restaurant and wander down to the shore. (There's also a shuttle service that runs from the interpretive center to the rocks for a small fee.) Signboards fill you in on the natural history. If you're here at the bottom half of the tide, you can descend the steel staircase to the sea floor and admire these wondrous free-standing rock sculptures, chiseled by waves and tides.

The site can be crowded, but that's understandable. If your schedule allows it, come early in the day when the sun is fresh over Nova Scotia across the bay, the dew is still on the ground, and most travelers are still sacked out in bed. The park charges an entry fee of C$8 (US$8/£4) adults, C$6.75 (US$6.75/£3.40) seniors, C$5.75 (US$5.75/£2.90) children ages 5 to 18, and C$20 (US$20/£10) families. It's open mid-May to mid-June daily 9am to 5pm, then 8am to 8pm from mid-June until mid-August (mid-Aug to late Aug only to 6pm), and from 9am to 5pm through the end of September.

If you arrive at the top half of the tide, consider a sea kayak tour around the islands and caves. **Baymount Outdoor Adventures** (© 877/601-2660 or 506/734-2660) runs 90-minute tours daily for C$55 (US$55/£28) adults, C$45 (US$45/£23) youths. Caving tours at nearby caverns are also offered; inquire for details.

WHERE TO STAY

Broadleaf Guest Ranch ⭐ *Kids*   The two-bedroom cottages at this homey, family-operated ranch are a great choice for families or couples traveling together, particularly those with an interest in horses: The ranch offers trail rides of varying duration, cattle checks, and some basic spa packages. Think of it as a dude ranch without the rattlesnakes. The cottages feature full kitchens, a small sitting area with gas stove, TV and VCR, and lovely, sweeping views of the ranch's 600 hectares (1,483 acres) and the bay. Bedrooms are furnished with bunk beds (a single over a double) plus a single bed. You won't mistake these lodgings for a luxury experience, but staying here is like sinking into a favored armchair at the end of the day: comforting and satisfying. The same could be said of the home-cooking Broadleaf dishes up in its large, cafeteria-style dining area. There are also three simple bed-and-breakfast rooms in the main house (known as Broadleaf "Too") and a campground, as well.

5526 Rte. 114, Hopewell Hill, Fundy, Albert County, NB E4H 3N5. ℂ 800/226-5405 or 506/882-2349. Fax 506/882-2075. www.broadleafranch.com. 7 units. Main inn rooms C$60–C$75 (US$60–US$75/£30–£38) double; chalets and apts C$150–C$200 (US$150–US$200/£75–£100). Ask about packages. MC, V. **Amenities:** Restaurant; spa; watersports equipment; bike rentals; business center; room service; laundry service. *In room:* TV/VCR (some units), kitchenette (some units), no phone.

Fundy Highlands Inn and Chalet ★ (Kids) This recently renovated property was brought to my attention by several Frommer's readers, who wrote me to give it high recommendations. Indeed, its 24 cottages and 20 motel rooms—managed by New Brunswick natives Doug and Donna Stewart—are each furnished with color televisions, beach towels, and kitchenette units. Some of the cottages even have built-in bunk beds, making those a good choice for travelers with young children. It's also notable for its expansive grounds, 18 acres in all of grassy knolls, rose beds, and the like, and the good views of the bay and coastline from many of the rooms and cottages.

8714 Hwy. 114, Fundy National Park, NB E4H 4V3. ℂ 888/883-8639 or 506/887-2930. Fax 506/887-2453. www.fundyhighlandchalets.com. 44 units (24 cabins, 20 rooms). Cottages C$74–$C105 (US$74–US$105/£37–£53); motel rooms C$65–C$85 (US$65–US$85/£33–£43). MC, V. *In room:* TV, kitchenette.

Parkland Village Inn (Value) (Kids) The Parkland opened the same day as the park in 1948. It's an old-fashioned seaside hotel in the village of Alma, with five two-room suites that have been modernized and thinly furnished in a sort of budget-motel modern style. Some rooms have been set up as two-bedroom units, others with a sitting room and bedroom. All have fine views of the bay. It's not deluxe by any means, but it's handy to the park and offers good value for families. The inn also manages a small cottage about 10km (6 miles) away, renting for C$125 (US$125/£63) per night with a 3-night minimum stay required. The downstairs dining room, the Tides, has 110 seats and specializes in (of course) seafood, prepared with little fuss or flair. It's open for breakfast as well, in July and August only.

8601 Main St. (Rte. 114), Alma, NB E4H 1N6. ℂ 866/668-4337 or 506/887-2313. Fax 506/887-2315. www.parklandvillageinn.com. 5 units. C$75–C$135 (US$75–US$135/£38–£68) double. Discounts in off season. MC, V. Closed Dec–Apr. **Amenities:** Restaurant. *In room:* TV, Jacuzzi (some units), no phone.

WHERE TO DINE

Seawinds Dining Room PUB FARE/CANADIAN Seawinds overlooks the park's golf course, and it serves as a de facto clubhouse for hungry duffers—and tourists in the area. The handsome and open dining room has hardwood floors, a flagstone fireplace, and wrought-iron chandeliers. The menu offers enough variations to please most anyone. Lunch selections include a variety of hamburgers, fish and chips, and bacon and cheese dogs; dinner is somewhat more refined, with main courses like grilled trout, roast beef, and fried clams.

47 Fundy Park Chalet Rd. (near park headquarters), Fundy National Park, NB E4H 4Y8. ℂ 506/887-2808. Reservations recommended. Sandwiches C$3–C$7 (US$3–US$7/£1.50–£3.50); main courses C$9–C$16 (US$9–US$16/£4.50–£8). AE, MC, V. Summer daily 8am–9:30pm. Closed Oct–May.

7 Moncton: A Rival to Saint John

152km (94 miles) NE of Saint John, 174km (108 miles) E of Fredericton

Moncton makes the plausible claim that it's at the crossroads of the Maritimes, and it hasn't been bashful about using its geographic advantage to promote itself as a business hub. As such, much of the hotel and restaurant trade caters to people in suits, at least on weekdays. But walk along Main Street in the evening or on weekends, and you're likely to spot spiked hair, grunge flannel, skateboards, and other youthful fashion statements from current and lapsed eras. There is some life here.

For families, Moncton offers a decent stopover if you're traveling with kids. Magnetic Hill and Crystal Palace both offer entertaining (albeit somewhat pricey) ways to fill an afternoon.

ESSENTIALS

GETTING THERE BY PLANE   The airport is about 10 minutes from downtown on Route 132 (head northeast on Main St. from Moncton and keep driving). **Air Canada** (© 888/247-2262; www.aircanada.com) has traditionally served the city, but the upstart carrier **WestJet** (© 888/937-8538; www.westjet.com) now also connects Moncton with Halifax, Toronto, St. John's, and Calgary, which can then be connected onward to Florida, Los Angeles, and Las Vegas without switching airlines.

GETTING THERE BY RAIL   VIA Rail's (© 888/842-7245; www.viarail.com) train from Montréal to Halifax stops in Moncton 6 days a week. The rail station is downtown on Main Street, next to Highfield Square.

GETTING THERE BY CAR   Moncton is at the crossroads of several major routes through New Brunswick, including Route 2 (the Trans-Canada Hwy.) and Route 15. The airport is about 10 minutes from downtown on Route 132 (head northeast on Main St. from Moncton and keep driving).

VISITOR INFORMATION   Moncton has three staffed visitor information centers, all open seasonally. One is located at the **Moncton airport** (© 506/877-7782), open from late May to Labour Day. The second is near **Magnetic Hill,** in a McDonald's restaurant off Exit 450 of the Trans-Canada Highway (© 506/855-8622); it's also open from late May until Labour Day. Then there's a downtown visitor information center located centrally in **Bore Park,** just off Main Street at 10 Bendview Court (© 506/853-3540), open daily from late May until early October.

The rest of the year, you can find an unstaffed kiosk of tourist information in the lobby of the modern **City Hall** at 655 Main St. The city's tourism website is located at www.gomoncton.com.

EXPLORING MONCTON

Moncton's downtown can be easily reconnoitered on foot—once you find parking, which can be vexing. (Look for the paid lots a block or so north and south of Main St.) **Downtown Moncton Inc.** publishes a nicely designed "Historic Walking Tour" brochure that touches on some of the most significant buildings; ask for it at one of the visitor centers.

The most active stretch of Main Street is the few blocks between City Hall and the train underpass. Here you'll find cafes, newsstands, hotels, and restaurants, along with a handful of intriguing shops. Note the sometimes-jarring mix of architectural styles, the earlier examples of which testify to Moncton's historic prosperity as a commercial center.

Crystal Palace *(Kids)*   The indoor amusement park at Crystal Palace will make an otherwise endless rainy day go by quickly. The spacious enclosed park includes a four-screen cinema, shooting arcades, numerous games (ranging from old-fashioned Skee-Ball to cutting-edge video games), a medium-size roller coaster, a carousel, a swing ride, laser tag, bumper cars, miniairplane and miniature semitruck rides, minigolf, batting cages, and a virtual-reality ride. From late June to early September, outdoor activities include go-karts and bumper boats. The park will particularly appeal to kids under the age of 12, although teens will likely find a video game to occupy them. To really wear the kids down, you can stay virtually inside the park by booking a room at the adjoining Ramada Plaza Crystal Palace Hotel (see below).

At Champlain Place Shopping Centre (Trans-Canada Hwy. Exit 504-A W), 499 Paul St., Dieppe. ℰ 877/856-4386 or 506/859-4386. www.crystalpalace.ca. Free admission. Rides are 1–4 tickets each (book of 25 for C$20/US$20/£10). Unlimited ride bracelets C$20 (US$20/£10) adults, C$17 (US$17/£8.50) children, C$62 (US$62/£31) families. July–Aug daily 10am–10pm; Sept–June Mon–Thurs noon–8pm, Fri noon–9pm, Sat 10am–9pm, Sun 10am–8pm.

WHERE TO STAY

In addition to the listings below, familiar chain hotels have set up shop near the complex of services that have sprouted around Magnetic Hill (from the Trans-Canada Hwy., take Exit 450 to reach these hotels).

Delta Beauséjour ⛄ The downtown Delta Beauséjour, constructed in 1972, is boxy, bland, and concrete, and the entrance courtyard is sterile and off-putting in a Cold War Berlin sort of way. But inside, the decor is inviting in a spare, International Modern manner. The property is well maintained, with rooms and public areas recently renovated. The third-floor indoor pool offers year-round swimming. (There's also a pleasant outdoor deck overlooking the distant marshes of the Petitcodiac River.) The hotel is a favorite among business travelers, but in summer and on weekends, leisure travelers largely have it to themselves. In addition to the elegant Windjammer (see below), the hotel has a basic cafe/snack bar; a piano bar and lounge; and a rustic, informal restaurant called L'Auberge that serves three meals a day.

750 Main St., Moncton, NB E1C 1E6. ℰ 888/351-7666 or 506/854-4344. Fax 506/858-0957. www.deltahotels.com. 310 units. C$129–C$199 (US$129–US$199/£65–£100) double. Rates include continental breakfast. AE, DC, MC, V. **Amenities:** 3 restaurants; bar; indoor heated pool; fitness center; business center; shopping arcade; salon; 24-hr. room service; babysitting; laundry service; dry cleaning. *In room:* A/C, TV, fax (some units), dataport, minibar, coffeemaker, iron/ironing board.

Ramada Plaza Crystal Palace Hotel *(Overrated)*   This modern, three-story chain hotel (built in 1990) adjoins the Crystal Palace amusement park and is a short walk from the region's largest mall. As such, it's surrounded by acres of asphalt and has little in the way of native charm. Most rooms are modern but unexceptional—not counting the 12 fantasy suites that go over the top with themes like "Deserted Island" (sleep in a thatched hut) or "Rock 'n' Roll" (sleep in a 1959 replica pink Cadillac bed). Some rooms face the indoor pool, others, the vast parking lot. For entertainment nearby, there's the amusement park, obviously. Also within the amusement complex is the hotel's restaurant, McGinnis Landing, which offers basic pub fare. Prices are high for what you get for main dinner courses; but specials are always available, and the restaurant caters well to younger appetites.

499 Paul St., Dieppe, NB E1A 6S5. ℰ 800/528-1234 or 506/858-8584. Fax 506/858-5486. 115 units. www.crystalpalacehotel.com. C$90–C$275 (US$90–US$275/£45–£138) double. Ask about packages, some of which include amusement-park passes. AE, DC, DISC, MC, V. **Amenities:** Restaurant; bar; indoor pool; Jacuzzi; sauna; limited room service; babysitting; dry cleaning. *In room:* A/C, TV, minibar, coffeemaker.

WHERE TO DINE

Boomerang's Classic Grill ⛄ *Kids* STEAK   Though it has changed its name to reduce confusion, Boomerang's is still likely to remind diners of the Aussie-themed Outback Steakhouse chain, right down to the oversized knives here. Though there is now a second location in the town of Dartmouth, this is *not* a chain; service is rather more personal, and the Aussie-whimsical decor is done with a lighter hand. It's a handsome spot with three dining rooms, all quite dim with slatted dividers, drawn shades, and ceiling fans, which create the impression that it's blazingly hot outside (a real trick in February in New Brunswick). The menu features lobster and all the usual stuff from the barbie, including grilled chicken breasts and ribs. But the steak selection is the reason you come, ranging from an 8-ounce bacon-wrapped tenderloin to a 14-ounce porterhouse; you can even get them "blue-rare" if you want. Side it with an Aussie baked potato if you like. Boomerang's burgers are also excellent, and the plethora of lunch offerings and "cut lunch" specials is nothing short of amazing—every kid and parent can find something good to eat here.

130 Westmoreland St. ℭ 506/857-8325. Call-ahead seating in lieu of reservations. Lunch C$9–C$15 (US$9–US$15/ £4.50–£7.50); dinner C$17–C$28 (US$17–US$28/£8.50–£14). AE, DC, DISC, MC, V. Sun–Wed 4–10pm; Thurs–Sat 4–11:30pm.

The Windjammer ✦✦ SEAFOOD/CONTINENTAL   Tucked off the lobby of Moncton's best hotel is The Windjammer, probably its best restaurant; this dining room is considered in some circles to be one of Canada's top hotel eateries. With its heavy wood and nautical theme, it resembles the private officer's mess of an exclusive ship. Yet this isn't a fish and chips joint: The menu is ambitious, and the dining room has garnered an excellent reputation for its dishes, including an appetizer of oysters, a cold seafood "martini," and a bison ragout; entrees such as squid-ink linguine with fiddleheads, a ginger-garlic filet salmon, the pan-roasted black cod, an herbed arctic char, and simple lobster are similarly winning. Despite the seafaring decor, the chef serves up plenty of treats for carnivores, including roasted New Brunswick rack of lamb, a chateaubriand of bison, and a tenderloin flambé prepared tableside and then garnished with a peppercorn sauce.

750 Main St. (in the Delta Beauséjour). ℭ 506/877-7137. Reservations recommended. Main courses C$22–C$42 (US$22–US$42/£11–£21). AE, DC, MC, V. Mon–Sat 5:30–10pm.

8 Kouchibouguac National Park ✦

Much is made of the fact that this sprawling park has all sorts of ecosystems worth studying, from sandy barrier islands to ancient peat bogs. But that's a little bit like saying Disney World has nice lakes—that perception entirely misses the point. In fact, this artfully designed national park is a wonderful destination for relaxing biking, hiking, and beach-going. If you can, plan to spend a couple of days here doing a whole lot of nothing. The varied ecosystems (which, incidentally, are spectacular) are just an added attraction. Kouchibouguac is, above all, a place for bikers and families.

ESSENTIALS
GETTING THERE   Kouchibouguac National Park is between Moncton and Miramichi. The exit for the park off Route 11 is well marked.

VISITOR INFORMATION   The park is open from mid-May to mid-October. The **Visitors Centre** (ℭ 506/876-2443) is just off Route 134, a short drive past the park entrance. It's open from 8am to 8pm during peak season, with shorter hours in the off season. There's a slide show to introduce you to the park's attractions, and a small collection of field guides to peruse.

> *Tips* **A Weather Warning**
>
> Be aware that this is a fair-weather destination—if it's blustery and rainy, there's little to do except take damp and melancholy strolls on the beach. So it's best to save a visit here for more cooperative days.

FEES A daily pass is C$6.90 (US$6.90/£3.45) adults, C$5.90 (US$5.90/£2.95) seniors, C$3.45 (US$3.45/£1.75) children 6 to 16, and C$17 (US$17/£8.50) families. (From Apr–June and Oct–Nov, rates are discounted about 40%.)

EXPLORING THE PARK

Hiking and biking trails here are as short and undemanding as they are appealing. The one hiking trail that requires slightly more fortitude is the **Kouchibouguac River Trail,** which runs for some 13km (8 miles) along the banks of the river. The **Bog Trail** ✦ is just 2km (1.2 miles) each way, but it opens the door to a wonderfully alien world. The boardwalk crosses to the thickest, middle part of the bog. Where the boardwalk stops, you can feel the bouncy surface of the bog—you're actually standing on a mat of thick vegetation that's floating atop water.

  Callanders Beach and **Cedar Trail** ✦ are both located at the end of a short dirt road. They're a good alternative for those who'd prefer to avoid the larger crowds at Kellys Beach.

BEACHES

The park features some 15km (9 miles) of sandy beaches, mostly along barrier islands of sandy dunes, delicate grasses and flowers, and nesting plovers and sandpipers. **Kellys** ✦ is the principal beach, and it's one of the best-designed and best-executed recreation areas in eastern Canada. At the forest's edge, a short walk from the main parking area, you'll find showers, changing rooms, a snack bar, and some interpretive exhibits. From here, you walk some 540m (1,800 ft.) across a winding boardwalk that's plenty fascinating on its own. It crosses a salt marsh, lagoons, and some of the best-preserved dunes in the province.

  The long, sandy beach features water that's comfortably warm, with the waves that are usually quite mellow—they lap rather than roar, unless a storm's offshore. Lifeguards oversee a roped-off section of about 90m (300 ft.); elsewhere, you're on your own. For very young children who still equate waves with certain death, there's supervised swimming on a sandy stretch of the quiet lagoon.

  Ryans (© **506/876-8918**)—a cluster of buildings between the campground and Kellys Beach—is the place for renting bikes, kayaks, paddleboats, and canoes seasonally. Bikes rent for around C$5 (US$5/£2.50) per hour. Most of the watersports equipment (including canoes and pedal boats) rent for around C$7 (US$7/£3.50) per hour, with double kayaks at C$12 (US$12/£6) per hour. Canoes may be rented for longer excursions; it's around C$30 (US$30/£15) daily, or C$45 (US$45/£23) for 2 days. Ryans is located on the lagoon, so you can explore up toward the dunes or upstream on the winding river.

WHERE TO STAY & DINE

South Kouchibouguac ✦, the main campground, is centrally located and very nicely laid out with 311 sites, most rather large and private. Sites are about C$21 to C$30

(US$21–US$30/£11–£15) per night, depending on time of year and the level of comfort you require. Reservations are accepted for about half of the campsites; call © **506/ 876-2443** starting in late April. The remaining sites are doled out first come, first served.

Other camping options within the park: Across the river on Kouchibouguac Lagoon is the more remote, semiprimitive **Côte-à-Fabien.** It lacks showers and some sites require a short walk, but it's more appealing for tenters. The cost is about C$15 (US$15/£7.50) per night. The park also maintains three backcountry sites. **Sipu** is on the Kouchibouguac River and is accessible by canoe or foot; **Petit Large** by foot or bike; **Pointe-à-Maxime** by canoe only. Backcountry sites cost C$9.90 (US$9.90/ £4.95) per night.

Habitant Motel and Restaurant (★ (Value)   At about 15km (9 miles) from the park entrance, the Habitant is the best choice for overnighting if you're exploring Kouchibouguac by day. It's a modern, mansard-roofed, Tudor-style complex—well, let's just say "architecturally mystifying"—with a restaurant and small campground on the premises. The rooms are decorated in a contemporary motel style and are very clean. The motel features a distinctive indoor pool, along with a fitness center and sauna. The restaurant next door serves three meals a day and is reasonably priced.

9600 Main St. (Rte. 134), Richibucto, NB E4W 4E6. © **888/442-7222** or 506/523-4421. Fax 506/523-9155. www. habitant.nb.ca. 29 units. C$65–C$140 (US$65–US$140/£33–£70) double. AE, DC, MC, V. Small, well-trained pets allowed. **Amenities:** Restaurant; indoor pool; sauna. *In room:* A/C, TV.

9 The Acadian Peninsula

The Acadian Peninsula is that bulge on the northeast corner of New Brunswick, forming one of the arms of the Baie des Chaleurs (Québec's Gaspé Peninsula forms the other). It's a land of tidy if generally nondescript houses, miles of shoreline (much of it beaches), modern concrete harbors filled with commercial fishing boats, and residents proud of their Acadian heritage. You'll see everywhere the stella maris flag—the French tricolor with a single gold star in the field of blue.

On a map it looks like much of the coastline would be wild and remote here. But it's not. Although a number of picturesque farmhouses dot the route and you'll occasionally come upon brilliant meadows of hawkweed and lupine, this part of the coast is more defined by manufactured housing that's been erected on squarish lots between the sea and fast two-lane highways than anything else. Other than the superb Acadian Village historical museum near Caraquet, there are few organized attractions in this region. It's more a place to unwind while walking on a beach, or sitting along harbors while watching fishing boats come and go.

ESSENTIALS

GETTING THERE   Route 11 is the main highway serving the Acadian Peninsula.

VISITOR INFORMATION   Each of the areas mentioned below maintains a visitor information center. **Caraquet Tourism Information** is at 35 du Carrefour Ave. (© **506/726-2676**), a seasonal (late May to mid-Sept) office, and offers convenient access to other activities in the harbor (see below) and there's plenty of parking. **Shippagan** dispenses information from a wooden lighthouse near the Marine Centre at 200 Hotel de Ville Ave. (© **506/336-3993**).

CARAQUET ✿

The historic beach town of Caraquet—widely regarded as the spiritual capital of Acadian New Brunswick—just keeps on going and going . . . geographically speaking, anyway. It's spread thinly along a commercial boulevard parallel to the beach. Caraquet once claimed the honorific "longest village in the world" when it ran to some 21km (13 miles) long. As a result of its length, Caraquet lacks a well-defined downtown or any sort of urban center of gravity; there's one stoplight, and that's where Boulevard St-Pierre Est changes to Boulevard St-Pierre Ouest. (Most establishments mentioned below are somewhere along this boulevard.)

A good place to start a tour is the **Carrefour de la Mer** (51 Blvd. St-Pierre Est), a modern complex overlooking the man-made harbor. It has a spare, Scandinavian feel to it, and you'll find the tourist information office (see above), a seafood restaurant, a snack bar, a children's playground, and two short strolls that lead to picnic tables on jetties with fine harbor views.

Village Historique Acadien ✿   New Brunswick sometimes seems awash in Acadian museums and historic villages. If you're interested in visiting just one such site, this is the place to hold out for. Some 45 buildings—most of which were dismantled and transported here from other villages on the peninsula—depict life as it was lived in an Acadian settlement between the years 1770 and 1890. The historic buildings are set throughout 183 hectares (452 acres) of woodland, marsh, and field. You'll learn all about the exodus and settlement of the Acadians from costumed guides, who are also adept at skills ranging from letterpress printing to blacksmithing. Plan on spending at least 2 to 3 hours exploring the village.

In June 2002, the village opened a major addition, which focuses on a more recent era. Some 26 buildings (all but one are replicas) are devoted to continuing the saga, showing Acadian life from 1890 to 1939, with a special focus on industry. The attractive yellow Chateau Albert Hotel, which mostly houses students enrolled in multiday workshops in traditional Acadian arts and crafts, was part of this new construction project; the simple rooms lack phones and televisions, but there is a dining room, convivial bar area and a thrown-back-in-time vibe (which is intentional). Rooms run from about C$70 to C$125 (US$70–US$125/£35–£63) double.

Rte. 11 (10km/6 miles west of Caraquet). ✆ 506/726-2600. www.villagehistoriqueacadien.com. Admission C$15 (US$15/£7.50) adults, C$13 (US$13/£6.50) seniors, C$10 (US$10/£5) children, C$30 (US$30/£15) family. June to mid-Sept daily 10am–6pm, mid-Sept to mid-Oct 10am–5pm. Closed mid-Oct to May.

WHERE TO STAY & DINE

Auberge de la Baie   The Auberge de la Baie is your basic year-round motel that has dressed itself up with a modern lobby and dining room. The rooms are cheerless but adequate (some have cinder-block walls, some have bay views). Particularly inviting is the broad lawn that descends from the property toward the water; stake your claim to a lawn chair and dive into a book. There's a small beach for swimming, as well. The oaky and spare restaurant is open daily for all three meals, specializing in seafood dinners.

139 Blvd. St-Pierre Ouest, Caraquet, NB E1W 1B7. ✆ 506/727-3485. 54 units. C$79–C$139 (US$79–US$139/ £40–£70) double. AE, MC, V. **Amenities:** Dining room; bar. *In room:* A/C, no phone.

Hôtel Paulin ✿✿   This attractive Victorian hotel, built in 1891 as the first hotel in Caraquet, has been operated by the Paulin family for the past three generations and has recently gone a bit more upscale with added units—and rising prices to match. It's a three-story red clapboard building with a green-shingled mansard roof, located just off the main boulevard and overlooking the bay. (Some of the charm has been compromised by buildings nearby, however.) The lobby immediately puts one in mind of summer relaxation, with royal blue wainscoting, canary yellow walls, and stuffed furniture upholstered in white with blue piping. Expect rooms, including four suites, to be comfortably but sparely furnished with antiques; only one suite has an ocean view. The hotel's first floor houses a handsome, well-regarded **restaurant** ⓧ.

143 Blvd. St-Pierre Ouest, Caraquet, NB E1W 1B6. ⓒ **866/727-9981** or 506/727-9981. Fax 506/727-4808. www.hotel paulin.com. 12 units. Mid-June to mid-Sept C$199–C$315 (US$199–US$315/£100–£158) double; mid-Sept to mid-June C$179–C$235 (US$179–US$235/£90–£118) double. MC, V. **Amenities:** Restaurant, massage. *In room:* A/C, TV, hair dryer, iron, no phone.

GRANDE-ANSE

Grande-Anse is a wide-spot-in-the-road village of low, modern homes near bluffs overlooking the bay. The town is lorded over by the stone Saint Jude church. The best view of the village, and a good spot for a picnic, is along the bluffs just below the church. (Look for the sign indicating QUAI 45m/148 ft. west of the church.) Here you'll find a small man-made harbor with a fleet of fishing boats, a tiny sand beach, and some grassy bluffs where you can park overlooking the bay.

If you'd prefer picnic tables, head a few miles westward to **Pokeshaw Park** (ⓒ **506/ 732-5423**), open mid-June through August. Just offshore is a large kettle-shaped island ringed with ragged cliffs that rise from the waves, long ago separated from the cliffs on which you're now standing. An active cormorant rookery thrives among the skeletons of trees, lending the place a bit of a haunted and melancholy air. There's a small picnic shelter for use in inclement weather. The park is open daily from 9am to 9pm; a small admission fee is charged.

For the full-blown ocean swimming experience, head to **Plage Grande-Anse,** located 2km (1¼ miles) east of town. This handsome beach has a snack bar near the parking area and is open from 10am to 9pm daily. There's a small entrance fee.

5

Prince Edward Island

by Paul Karr

Prince Edward Island (PEI) may not be the world's leading manufacturer of relaxation, but it's certainly a major distribution center. Visitors soon realize there's something about the richly colored landscape of azure seas and henna-tinged cliffs capped with purple and green farm fields that triggers some obscure relaxation hormone, resulting in a pleasant ennui. It's sometimes difficult to believe that PEI and boggy, blustery Newfoundland share the same planet, never mind the same gulf.

The northern coast is lined with red-sand beaches, washed by the warm waters of the Gulf of St. Lawrence. Swimming here isn't quite like taking a tepid dip in North Carolina, but it's warmer than in Maine or New Hampshire. Away from these beaches you'll find low, rolling hills blanketed in trees and crops, especially potatoes, for which the island is justly famous. Small farms make up the island's backbone—one-quarter of the island is dedicated to agriculture, with that land cultivated by more than 2,300 individual farms.

The island is compact and its roads are usually well marked. It's difficult to become disoriented—but you should try. Whether you're on bicycle or traveling by car, it can be quite pleasurable indeed to get lost on PEI's back roads.

1 Exploring the Island

ESSENTIALS

VISITOR INFORMATION   Tourism PEI publishes a comprehensive free guide to island attractions and lodgings that's well worth picking up. The **Visitors Guide** is available at all information centers on the island, or in advance by calling ℭ **800/463-4734** or 902/368-4444. You can also request it by mail (P.O. Box 2000, Charlottetown, PEI C1A 7N8), e-mail (gentleisland@pei.gov.pe.ca), or fax (**902/368-4438**). The official PEI website is located at www.gentleisland.com.

TOURIST OFFICES   PEI's splashy main information center is in **Gateway Village** (ℭ **902/437-8570**), just as you arrive on the island via the Confederation Bridge. It's a good spot for gathering brochures and asking last-minute questions. There's also a well-laid-out interpretive center featuring nicely designed exhibits about island history and culture. Other information centers are scattered around the island.

GETTING THERE

BY PLANE   The island's main airport, Charlottetown Airport (airport code YYG; www.flypei.com), is a few miles north of the city. The daily **Air Canada Jazz** (ℭ **888/247-2262**; www.flyjazz.com) commuter flights from Halifax take just a half-hour, and Jazz also flies to Toronto and Montréal. In 2007, **Delta** (ℭ **800/221-1212**;

www.delta.com) announced a new direct summertime service from Boston, joining **Northwest** (© 800/447-4747; www.nwa.com), which has flown to the island from Detroit daily in summer for several years.

A taxi ride into the city from the airport costs C$11 (US$11/£5.50) for the first passenger, C$3 (US$3/£1.50) for additional passengers. There are also limousine firms and four car-rental outfits represented in the terminal.

BY CAR   If you're coming from the west by car, you'll arrive via the **Confederation Bridge,** open 24 hours a day. It takes about 10 to 12 minutes to cross. Unless you're high up in a van, a truck, or an RV, however, the views are mostly obstructed by the concrete Jersey barriers that form the guardrails along the sides.

The bridge toll in 2007 was C$41 (US$41/£21) round-trip for cars, more for vehicles with more than two axles. No fare is paid when you travel to the island; the entire toll is collected when you leave. Credit cards are accepted. Call © 888/437-6565 for more information.

BY FERRY   For those arriving from Cape Breton Island or other points east, **Northumberland Ferries Limited** (© 888/249-7245; www.nfl-bay.com) provides seasonal service between Caribou, Nova Scotia (just north of Pictou), and Woods Island, PEI. Ferries with a 250-car capacity run from May to mid-December. During peak season (June to mid-Oct), ferries depart each port approximately every 90 minutes throughout the day, with the last ferry departing at 7:30pm or 9pm, depending on which direction you are traveling. The crossing takes about 75 minutes.

No reservations are accepted, except for buses; it's best to arrive at least an hour before departure to boost your odds of securing a berth on the next boat. Early-morning ferries tend to be less crowded. Fares are C$12 to C$14 (US$12–US$14/£6–£7) per person and C$59 (US$59/£30) for a regular-sized car (more for campers and RVs). Major credit cards are honored.

THE GREAT OUTDOORS

BICYCLING   The main off-road bike trail is the **Confederation Trail** ℱ. The pathway is covered mostly in rolled stone dust, which makes for good travel with a mountain bike or hybrid. Services are slowly developing along the route, with bike rentals and inns cropping up. An excellent place to base yourself for exploring the trail is the **Trailside Café** in Mount Stewart, where several spurs of the trail converge. **MacQueen's Island Tours & Bike Shop** (© 800/969-2822 or 902/368-2453; www.macqueens.com), located at 430 Queen St. in Charlottetown, organizes a range of bicycle tour packages with all-inclusive prices covering bike rentals, accommodations, route cards, maps, luggage transfers, and emergency road repair service. For just rentals, check out **Smooth Cycle** (© 800/310-6550 or 902/566-5530) at 330 University Ave. in Charlottetown.

FISHING   For a taste of deep-sea fishing, head to the north coast, where you'll find plenty of outfitters happy to take you out on the big swells. The greatest concentrations of services are at North Rustico and Covehead Bay; see "Queens County: The Land of Anne," below. Rates are quite reasonable, generally about C$20 (US$20/£10) for 3 hours or so.

GOLF   PEI's reputation for golf has soared in the last few years. One of the best-regarded courses is the **Links at Crowbush Cove** ℱℱ (© 800/235-8909 or 902/368-5761); another perennial favorite is the **Brudenell River Golf Course** (© 800/235-8909 or 902/652-8965) near Montague along the eastern shore. Golf PEI

Prince Edward Island

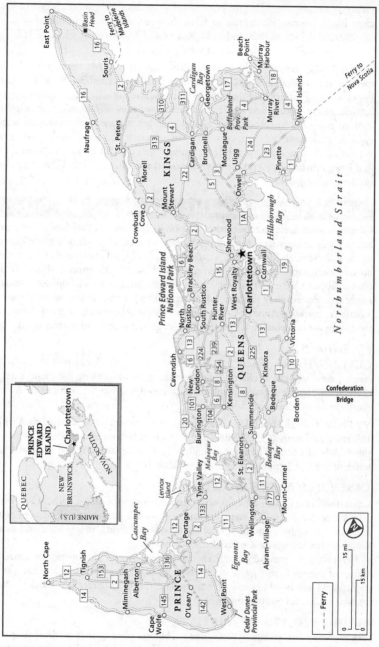

publishes a booklet outlining the essentials of about 20 island courses. Request a copy from island information centers or from the provincial tourist information office (© 902/368-4653), or write to 565 N. River Rd., Charlottetown, PEI C1E 1J7. The information is also available online at www.golfpei.com.

SWIMMING   Among PEI's chief attractions are its red-sand beaches. You'll find them all around the island, tucked in among dunes and crumbling cliffs. Thanks to the moderating influence of the Gulf of St. Lawrence, the water temperature is more humane here than elsewhere in Atlantic Canada, and it usually doesn't result in unbridled shrieking among bathers. The most popular beaches are at Prince Edward Island National Park along the north coast, but you can easily find other beaches with great swimming. Among my favorites: Cedar Dunes Provincial Park on the southwest coast, Red Point Provincial Park on the northeast coast, and Panmure Island Provincial Park on the southeast coast.

2 Queens County: The Land of Anne

Queens County occupies the center of the province, is home to the island's largest city, and hosts the greatest concentration of traveler services. The county is neatly cleaved by the Hillsborough River, which is spanned by a bridge at Charlottetown. Cavendish on the north shore is the most tourist-oriented part of the entire province; if the phrase "Ripley's Believe It or Not Museum" lacks positive associations for you, you might consider avoiding this area, which has built a vigorous tourist industry around a fictional character, Anne of Green Gables. On the other hand, much of the rest of the county—not including Charlottetown—is quite pastoral and untrammeled.

ESSENTIALS

GETTING THERE   Route 2 is the fastest way to travel east-west through the county, although it lacks charm. Route 6 is the main route along the county's north coast; following the highway involves a number of turns at intersections, so keep a sharp eye on the directional signs.

VISITOR INFORMATION   The snazzy, well-stocked little **Cavendish Visitor Information Centre** (© 902/963-7830) is open daily from 8am to 9pm mid-May to the middle of October (only until 4:30pm in shoulder seasons) and is located just north of the intersection of Route 13 and Route 6.

CAVENDISH: ANNE'S HOMETOWN

Cavendish is the home of the fictional character Anne of Green Gables. If you mentally screen out the tourist traps constructed over the past couple of decades, you'll find the area to be a bucolic mix of woodlands and fields, rolling hills, and sandy dunes—a fine setting for a series of pastoral novels.

However, the tremendous and enduring popularity of the novels has attracted droves of curious tourists, who in turn have attracted droves of entrepreneurs who've constructed new buildings and attractions. The bucolic character of the area has thus become somewhat compromised.

SEEING EVERYTHING ANNE

Green Gables Heritage Site *Overrated*   The best place to start an Anne tour is at Green Gables itself. The house is operated by Parks Canada, which also operates a helpful visitor center on the site. You can watch a short video presentation about Montgomery, view a handful of exhibits, and then head out to explore the farm and

> *Fun Fact* **The Birth of Anne Shirley**
>
> Visitors to Prince Edward Island owe it to themselves to think about picking up a copy of *Anne of Green Gables* at some point. Not that you won't enjoy your stay here without doing so, but if you don't read it, you might feel a bit out of touch and unable to understand the inside references that seem to seep into many aspects of PEI culture.
>
> Some background: In 1908 island native Lucy Maud Montgomery published *Anne of Green Gables,* her first book—and it was an instant smash. The book is a fictional account of one Anne Shirley, a precocious and bright 11-year-old who's mistakenly sent from Nova Scotia to the farm of the taciturn and dour Matthew and Marilla Cuthbert. (The plot device driving the conflict? The Cuthberts had requested an orphan *boy* to help them with their farm chores.)
>
> Anne's vivid imagination and outsized vocabulary get her into a series of ever-more-hilarious pickles, from which she generally emerges beloved by everyone who encounters her. It's a bright, bittersweet story, and it went on to huge popular success, spawning a number of sequels.

trails. The farmhouse dates from the mid–19th century and belonged to cousins of Montgomery's grandfather. It was the inspiration for the Cuthbert farm, and it has been furnished according to descriptions in the books.

2 Palmers Lane (just off Rte. 6), Cavendish (just west of intersection with Rte. 13). ✆ **902/963-7874**. Admission C$7.15 (US$7.15/£3.60) adults, C$5.90 (US$5.90/£2.95) seniors, C$3.45 (US$3.45/£1.75) children, C$18 (US$18/£9) families. Discounted rates spring and fall. May–Oct daily 9am–5pm; Nov–Dec and Apr Sun–Thurs 10am–4pm; Jan–Mar Sun–Thurs noon–4pm.

Cavendish Cemetery   This historic cemetery was founded in 1835, but it's best known now as the final resting spot for author Lucy Maud Montgomery. It's not hard to find her gravesite: Follow the pavement blocks from the arched entryway, which is across from the Anne Shirley Motel.

Intersection of Rte. 13 and Rte. 6, Cavendish. Free. Daily dawn to dusk.

Avonlea *(Kids)*   This development of faux historic buildings was opened in 1999 with the idea of creating the sort of a village center you might find in reading the Anne novels. It's located on a large lot amid amusement parks and motels, and the new buildings have been constructed with an eye to historical accuracy. Several Anne-related buildings and artifacts are located on the site, including the schoolhouse in which Montgomery taught (moved here from Belmont), and a Presbyterian church (moved from Long River), which Montgomery occasionally attended. There's also a variety show, hayrides, staff in period dress, restaurant, several stores (including an art gallery and music shop), and a spot for ice cream and candy. It's a bit overpriced, however.

Rte. 6, Cavendish. ✆ **902/963-3050**. www.avonlea.ca. Day pass admission C$19 (US$19/£9.50) adults, C$17 (US$17/£8.50) seniors, C$15 (US$15/£7.50) children 6–16, C$64 (US$64/£32) family. Musical variety show, small extra charge. June daily 10am–5pm; July–Aug daily 10am–6pm; Sept daily 10am–4pm. Closed Oct–May.

Lucy Maud Montgomery Birthplace   Very near the Anne of Green Gables Museum is the Lucy Maud Montgomery Birthplace, where the author was born in 1874. The house is decorated in the Victorian style of the era, and it includes Montgomery mementos like her wedding dress and scrapbook. It's worth 45 minutes, but only for die-hard Anne fans.

Intersection of Rte. 6 and Rte. 20, New London. (℅ **902/886-2099** or 902/836-5502. Admission C$3 (US$3/£1.50) adults, C50¢ (US50¢/25p) children 6–12. Mid-May to mid-Oct daily 9am–5pm. Closed mid-Oct to mid-May.

Anne of Green Gables Museum at Silver Bush   About 20km (12 miles) west of Cavendish near the intersection of Route 6 and Route 20 is the Anne of Green Gables Museum at Silver Bush. It's located in the home of Montgomery's aunt and uncle; the author was married here in 1911. The building still holds some of Montgomery's furniture, linens, photos, and other personal effects. For the best view of the "Lake of Shining Waters," take the wagon ride. It's hardly essential, but a half-hour visit might be in order if you're ticking off Anne destinations.

Rte. 20, Park Corner. (℅ **800/665-2663** or 902/886-2884 (weekends only). Admission C$3 (US$3/£1.50) adults, C$1 (US$1/50p) children age 6 to 16. Mid-Oct to May daily 11am–4pm; June and Sept 10am–4pm; July–Aug daily 9am–5pm.

WHERE TO STAY
Cavendish Beach Cottages   Location, location, location. This compound of 13 cottages is located on a grassy rise within the national park, just past the gatehouse into the park. The pine-paneled cottages are available in one-, two-, or three-bedroom configurations, and all feature ocean views, kitchenettes with microwaves, and outdoor propane barbecue grills. Some of the better-equipped cottages have dishwashers, making them great for families, and all are a 2-minute walk from the beach. There's also easy access to Gulf Shore Drive, where you'll find some of the island's premier biking trails.

Gulf Shore Dr., Cavendish (mailing address: 166 York Lane, Charlottetown, PEI C1A 7W5). (℅ **902/963-2025.** Fax 902/963-2025. www.cavendishbeachcottages.com. 13 units. C$115–C$209 (US$115–US$209/£58–£105) double. MC, V. Closed Oct to mid-May. **Amenities:** Laundry. *In room:* A/C, TV, kitchenette, no phone.

Green Gables Bungalow Court   Located next to the Green Gables house, this pleasant cluster of one- and two-bedroom cottages began as a government make-work project promoting tourism in the 1940s. As a result, they're quite sturdily built, and nicely arrayed among lawn and pines. All have kitchens with refrigerators and coffeemakers, and many have outdoor gas grills for an evening barbecue. The linoleum floors and spartan furnishings take on a certain retro charm after a few hours of settling in. Some cabins were trimmed with cheap sheet paneling, while others have the original pine paneling; ask for one with the latter. The beach is about 1km (½ mile) away, and there's a small heated outdoor pool on the premises.

Rte. 6 (Hunter River R.R. 2), Cavendish, PEI C0A 1N0. (℅ **800/965-3334** or 902/963-2722. www.greengablesbungalow court.com. 40 cottages. Up to 4 people C$65–C$135 (US$65–US$135/£33–£68) nightly; C$655–C$899 (US$655–US$899/£328–£450) weekly. AE, MC, V. Closed Oct–June. **Amenities:** Outdoor heated pool. *In room:* TV, kitchenette, fridge, no phone.

WHERE TO DINE
Cavendish itself offers limited opportunities for creative dining, although it's stocked with restaurants offering hamburgers, fried clams, and the like. For better dining, head for New Glasgow and these two places.

Café on the Clyde ★★ (Value) (Kids) ECLECTIC   This cafe is part of the noted Prince Edward Island Preserve Co, itself a worthwhile stop for the delicious homemade preserves. Light meals are served in the bright and modern dining room just off the preserve showroom. In this popular and often crowded spot, you can order from a menu that has expanded to include appealing breakfasts, lunches, and dinners. A smoked fish platter or the lobster chowder are just the ticket on a drizzly afternoon, and they've also got pastas, crepes, foccaccia and BLT sandwiches, island fish cakes, lobster rolls, and even a cheesy potato pie with maple cream. There's beer and wine, a kids' menu, and pies, cakes, and cheesecakes, making this a legitimate dining destination in a rural area where there is not much else to eat besides the Olde Mill (see below). Just be prepared for the tour bus crowd: Buses get their own parking lot here, close to the door.

Intersection of Rte. 224 and Rte. 258 (6.5km/4 miles south of Rte. 6 on Rte. 13), New Glasgow. ② 902/964-4301. Main courses C$6–C$13 (US$6–US$13/£3–£6.50) breakfast and lunch, C$11–C$18 (US$11–US$18/£5.50–£9) dinner. AE, DC, MC, V. July–Aug daily 9am–9pm; June and Sept limited hours. Closed Oct–May.

Olde Glasgow Mill Restaurant ★ REGIONAL/CANADIAN   This casual restaurant, formerly a 19th-century feed mill in twee little New Glasgow, is nicely shielded from the tourist throngs at Cavendish. The place overlooks a small pond and features an eclectic assortment of regional food. Appetizers include seafood chowder, along with salads and PEI mussels. Lunch entrees are uncomplicated, but dinner is more serious. Besides Atlantic salmon and scallops, you'll find rack of lamb swabbed in Dijon mustard and rosemary-herb crust served with a rosemary-peppercorn sauce, cheese-and-spinach-stuffed chicken breast in puff pastry, peppery strip loin, and the like. There's a leisurely brunch on the weekends.

Rte. 13, New Glasgow. ② 902/964-3313. Reservations recommended. Lunch C$9–C$12 (US$9–US$12/£4.50–£6); dinner C$14–C$29 (US$14–US$29/£7–£15). AE, MC, V. June–Oct Mon–Sat noon–10pm, Sun 10am–10pm; shorter hours in winter.

NORTH & SOUTH RUSTICO TO BRACKLEY BEACH

A few miles east of Cavendish are the Rusticos, of which there are five: North Rustico, South Rustico, Rusticoville, Rustico Harbour, and Anglo Rustico. The region was settled by Acadians in 1790, and many residents are descendants of those original settlers. North and South Rustico are both attractive villages that have fewer tourist traps and are more amenable to exploring by foot or bike than Cavendish. Although out of the hubbub, they still provide easy access to the national park and Anne-land, with beaches virtually at your doorstep.

North Rustico clusters around a scenic harbor with views out toward Rustico Bay. Plan to park and walk around, perusing the deep-sea fishing opportunities (see below) and peeking in the shops. The village curves around Rustico Bay to end at North Rustico Harbour, a sand spit with fishing wharves, summer cottages, and a couple of informal restaurants. A wood-decked promenade follows the water's edge from the town to the harbor, and is a worthy destination for a quiet afternoon ramble or a picnic.

In **South Rustico** ★★, turn off Route 6 onto Rte. 243 and ascend the low hill overlooking the bay. Here you'll find a handsome cluster of buildings that were home to some of the more prosperous Acadian settlers. Among the structures is the sandstone **Farmers' Bank of Rustico Museum** ★ (② 902/963-3168), beside the church. It helped inspire the credit union movement in Canada and North America. Renovations of the building have been ongoing for several years, and it's looking much better these days; the bank is open for tours June through September Monday through Saturday 9:30am to 5pm and Sundays 1 to 5pm. It's free.

Finds   A PEI Tradition: The Lobster Supper

The north shore of Prince Edward Island is home to famous lobster suppers, which are a good bet if you have a craving for one of the succulent local crustaceans. These suppers first took root years ago as informal gatherings held in local church basements, in which parishioners would bring covered hot dishes to share and the church would provide a lobster. Everyone would contribute some money, and the church netted a few dollars from the fun get-together. Outsiders (and travel writers like me) began discovering these good deals and showing up; the fame of the dinners spread; and today several establishments offer the bountiful lobster dinners, which have become almost a cottage industry. Figure on C$25 to C$50 (US$25–US$50/£13–£25) per person, depending on the size lobster you want and the options available.

   St. Ann's Church Lobster Suppers (② 902/621-0635) remains a charitable organization, as it was in 1963 when it claims it created the first lobster supper on PEI. Located in a modern church hall in the small town of St. Ann, just off Route 224 between routes 6 and 13, St. Ann's has a full liquor license and the home-cooked food is served at your table (no buffet lines). Lobster dinners are served mid-June to late September Monday through Saturday from 4 to 8:30pm. (As befits a church, it's closed Sun.) Credit cards are accepted.

   Fisherman's Wharf Lobster Suppers (② 877/289-1010 or 902/963-2669) in North Rustico boasts an 18m (60-ft.) salad bar to go with its lobster; it's open daily from noon to 9pm, mid-May to mid-October (shorter hours in May and June). It offers a children's menu. And near the PEI Preserve Company in New Glasgow is the barnlike **New Glasgow Lobster Suppers** (② 902/964-2870). Meals here include unlimited mussels and chowder, thus it's a bit more pricey; it's on Route 258 (just off Rte. 13) and is open June to mid-October daily from 4 to 8:30pm. This eatery also offers roast beef suppers and its own kids' menu.

Next door to the bank are two more structures worth investigating. **Doucet House** ✪, a sturdy log building of Acadian construction dating from 1772, was the home of one Jean Doucet who arrived in these parts by boat. (The house was moved from its waterside location in 1999, and completely restored—which it badly needed.) Period furnishings have been added to bring back that two-plus-centuries-ago flavor.

   Then the handsome **St. Augustine's Parish Church** (dating from 1838, with a cemetery beyond) should be visited if possible. If the church's door is open, head in for a look at this graceful structure.

   Brackley Beach is the gateway to the eastern section of the national park, and has the fewest services of all. It's a quiet area with no village center to speak of; it will be best appreciated by those who prefer their beach vacations unadulterated.

WHERE TO STAY & DINE
Barachois Inn ✪✪ *(Finds)*   The proudly Victorian Barachois (say "Bar-a-*schwa*") Inn was built in 1870, and it is a soothing retreat for road-weary travelers. Located amid

a cluster of historic buildings on a gentle rise overlooking Rustico Bay—see "North & South Rustico to Brackley Beach," above—it's a winner. Factor in some time to just stroll around the neighborhood and enjoy both the village and the inn's tidy garden. It's topped with a lovely mansard roof adorned with pedimented dormers, and it boasts a fine garden and historic furnishings throughout. Innkeepers Judy and Gary MacDonald bought the place as derelict property in 1982, and have done an outstanding job bringing it back from the brink, adding modern art along the way to soften the staid Victorian architecture.

2193 Church Rd., Rustico (mailing address: Hunter River R.R. 3, PEI C0A 1N0). ℭ **902/963-2194.** Fax 902/963-2906. www.barachoisinn.com. 8 units, 1 with private bathroom in hallway. June–Sept C$160–C$275 (US$160–US$275/ £80–£138) double; Oct–May rates lower. Rates include full breakfast. Ask about packages. AE, MC, V. **Amenities:** Sauna; laundry service. *In room:* A/C, VCR, kitchenette, hair dryer, iron, no phone.

Shaw's Hotel ⟨★⟩   Shaw's is a delightfully old-fashioned compound located down a tree-lined dirt road along a marsh-edged inlet. It's been in the same family since 1860, and even with modern touches such as a sun deck, a bar, and a dining room addition that accommodates 40 more people, the place still has the feel of a farm-stay vacation in the 19th century. It remains mostly the kind of place where the aging carpets in the hallways add to the charm rather than detract from it. The hotel's centerpiece is a Victorian farmhouse with a lipstick-red mansard roof. Fifteen guest rooms are located upstairs; they are "boarding-house style," which is to say, small. The cottages vary in size and vintage. None are lavish, but most have the essentials (some with kitchenettes, some just with cube refrigerators) and some are downright comfy (double Jacuzzis have been installed in some of them).

Rte. 15, Brackley Beach, PEI C1E 1Z3. ℭ **902/672-2022.** Fax 902/672-3000. www.shawshotel.ca. 41 units. Inn rooms July–Aug C$145–C$240 (US$145–US$240/£73–£120) double; rest of the year C$75–C$135 (US$75– US$135/£38–£68); cottages C$190–C$710 (US$190–US$710£95–£355). Meal plans available. AE, MC, V. Closed Nov to late May. Pets allowed in cottages only. **Amenities:** 2 restaurants; canoe, kayak, and bike rental; secretarial services; babysitting; laundry. *In room:* TV (some units), kitchenette, no phone.

3 Prince Edward Island National Park ⟨★⟩⟨★⟩

Prince Edward Island National Park encompasses a 40km (25-mile) swath of red-sand beaches, wind-sculpted dunes topped with marran grass, vast salt marshes, and placid inlets. The park is located along the island's sandy northcentral coast, which is broached in several spots by broad inlets that connect to harbors. As a result, you can't drive along the entire park's length in one shot. The coastal road is disrupted by inlets, requiring backtracking to drive the entire length. And, actually, there's little point in trying to tour the whole length. It's a better use of your time to pick one spot, then settle in and enjoy your surroundings.

The national park also oversees the Green Gables house and grounds; see "Cavendish: Anne's Hometown," earlier in this chapter.

ESSENTIALS

GETTING THERE   From Charlottetown, Route 15 offers the most direct route to the eastern segments of the park. To head to the Cavendish area, take Route 2 to Hunter River, then head north on Route 13.

VISITOR INFORMATION   The **Cavendish Visitor Information Centre** (ℭ **902/ 963-7830**), near the intersection of routes 6 and 13, furnishes information on the park's destinations and activities; it's open daily from 9am to 10pm in the peak summer season (it closes earlier during the shoulder seasons). Inside the park, the modern **Greenwich Interpretation Centre** (*C* 902/961-2514) is open daily from 9am to 5pm mid-May through early October. For other questions or during the off season, the park administration (located in Charlottetown) can be reached at *C* **902/672-6350.**

FEES The park is open year-round. Between mid-June and mid-October, however, visitors to the national park must stop at one of the tollhouses and pay entry fees. Daily rates are C$6.90 (US$6.90/£3.45) adults, C$5.90 (US$5.90/£2.95) seniors, C$3.45 (US$3.45/£1.75) children 6 to 16, and C$17 (US$17/£8.50) per family; all rates are lower in June. Ask about multiday passes if you plan to visit for more than 3 days.

EXPLORING THE PARK

Hiking is limited here, compared to Atlantic Canada's other national parks, but you can still find a handful of pleasant strolls. Of course, there's also the beach, which is perfect for long leisurely walks. The park maintains eight trails adding up to a total of 20km (12 miles). Among the most appealing is the **Homestead Trail** *⚘*, which departs from the Cavendish campground. The trail offers a 5.2km (3.2-mile) loop and an 8km (5-mile) loop. The trail skirts wheat fields, woodlands, and estuaries, with frequent views of the distinctively lumpy dunes at the west end of the park.

Biking along the shoreline roads in the park is sublime. The traffic is light, and it's easy to make frequent stops to explore beaches, woodlands, or the marshy edges of inlets. The two **shoreline roads** *⚘⚘* within the national park—between Dalvay and Rustico Island, and from Cavendish to North Rustico Harbour—are especially beautiful on a clear evening as sunset edges into twilight. Snack bars are located at Brackley Beach and Covehead Bay.

Your can rent bikes easily in **Charlottetown.** Try **Smooth Cycle** (*C* **800/310-6550** or 902/566-5530) in its new location at 330 University Ave. Rentals including a helmet, water bottle, and a lock cost C$25 (US$25/£13) per day. Note that the shop is closed Sundays.

You can often find rentals closer to the beach, as well. In Brackley Beach, a good option is **Northshore Rentals** (*C* **902/672-2022**), located at Shaw's Hotel; their rentals cost C$7 (US$7/£3.50) per hour and C$20 (US$20/£10) per day.

BEACHES

PEI National Park is nearly synonymous with its beaches. The park is home to two kinds of sandy strands: popular and sometimes crowded beaches with changing rooms, lifeguards, snack bars, and other amenities; and all the other beaches. Where you go depends on your temperament. If it's not a day at the beach without the aroma of other people's coconut tanning oil, head to **Brackley Beach** or **Cavendish Beach.** The latter is within walking distance of the Green Gables house and many other amusements (see "Cavendish: Anne's Hometown," earlier in this chapter) and makes a good destination for families.

If you'd just as soon be left alone with the waves, sun, and sand, you'll need to head a bit farther afield, or just keep walking far down the beaches away from parking-area access points until you have left the crowds behind. I won't reveal the best spots here for fear of crowding. But suffice it to say that they're out there.

WHERE TO STAY & DINE

Prince Edward Island National Park maintains three excellent campgrounds, which open for the short season in early June. Reservations are not accepted, so plan to arrive early in the day for the best selection of sites. Campground fees start at about C$25 (US$25/£13) per night, with serviced sites costing up to C$33 (US$33/£17). For more information, contact the **Cavendish Visitors Centre** (✆ 902/963-7830).

The most popular (and first to fill) is **Cavendish,** located just off Route 6 west of Green Gables. It has more than 300 sites spread among piney forest and open, sandy bluffs; the sites at the edge of the dunes overlooking the beach are the most popular. The sites aren't especially private or scenic. A limited number of two-way hookups are available for RVs, and the campground has free showers, kitchen shelters, and evening programs. Note that this campground closes for the season in late August.

The **Stanhope** ✶ campground lies just across the park road from lovely Stanhope Beach, which is on the eastern segment of the park (enter through Brackley Beach). The road isn't heavily traveled, so you don't feel much removed from the water's edge. Most sites are forested, and you're afforded more privacy here than at Cavendish. Two-way hookups, free showers, and kitchen shelters are offered. It's also open later, until early October.

Also see listings for "Cavendish: Anne's Hometown," earlier in this chapter, and "North & South Rustico to Brackley Beach," above.

Dalvay-by-the-Sea ✶✶   This imposing Tudor mansion was built in 1895 by Alexander MacDonald, a partner of John D. Rockefeller. The place is unusually large for a private home, yet rather intimate for a luxury inn. There are glimpses of the ocean across the road from the upper floors, even as the landscaping largely focuses on a beautiful freshwater pond out front. Inside, you'll be taken aback by the extraordinary cedar woodwork in the main entryway, and by the grand stone fireplace. The guest rooms are elegantly appointed and wonderfully solid and quiet, though they have intentionally been kept free of any phones or televisions; this is true rusticating. As a result, in the evening you'll hear mostly the roar of the sea, since the inn overlooks one of the park's best beaches. Rates are steep, though that partly disguises the fact that breakfast and dinner are included in all rates, whether you want it or not. (So eat up.) The eight newer and lovely three-bedroom pine cottages are in big demand thanks to their size, open design, and amenities like wet bars and propane stoves. The hotel also serves afternoon tea each day from 2 to 4pm. Next morning? Hike off all those extra calories at one of the many walking trails nearby.

Off Rte. 6, Grand Tracadie (mailing address P.O. Box 8, Little York, PEI C0A 1P0). ✆ 902/672-2048. Fax (summer only) 902/672-2741. www.dalvaybythesea.com. 34 units. June to late Sept C$270–C$390 (US$270–US$390/£135–£195) double; cottages C$450–C$490 (US$450–US$490/£225–£245) double. Extra charges for children and infants. All rates include breakfast and dinner. Ask about packages. National park entrance fees also charged. 2-night minimum in summer. AE, DC, MC, V. Closed late Sept to May. **Amenities:** Tennis court; bike rentals; croquet; lawn bowling; horseshoes; canoeing. *In room:* Minibar (cottage only), fridge (cottage only), coffeemaker (cottage only), no phone.

4 Charlottetown ✶

56km (35 miles) E of Borden-Carleton, 61km (38 miles) NW of Wood Islands

It's not hard to figure out why early settlers put the province's political and cultural capital where they did: It's on a point of land between two rivers and within a large protected harbor. For ship captains plying the seas, this quiet harbor with ample anchorage and wharf space must have been a welcome sight. Of course, travelers rarely arrive by water these days (unless a cruise ship is in port), but the city's harborside location translates into a lovely setting for one of Atlantic Canada's most graceful and relaxed cities.

Named after Queen Charlotte, consort of King George III, Charlottetown is home to some 40,000 people—nearly one of every three islanders. Within Canada, the city is famous for hosting the 1864 conference that 3 years later led to the creation of the independent Dominion of Canada. For this reason, you're never far from the word *confederation*, which graces buildings, malls, and bridges. (In a historic twist, PEI itself actually declined to join the new confederation until 1873.)

Today, the downtown has a brisk and busy feel to it, with a pleasing mix of modern and Victorian commercial buildings, as well as government and cultural centers. The capital also has by far the island's best selection of inns and hotels, and a fine assortment of restaurants that ensure you can dine out every night for a week and still be pleasantly surprised. As for scheduling time for exploring the city itself—save that for a rainy day or those early-morning or late-afternoon moments.

ESSENTIALS

GETTING THERE   Coming by car from the mainland, both Route 1 (the Trans-Canada Hwy.) and Route 2 pass through or near Charlottetown. For information on arriving by air, see "Exploring the Island" at the beginning of this chapter. If you're coming from Montréal by train, debark at Moncton and take an **Acadien bus** (© 800/567-5151; two to three times daily) to Charlottetown; the cost is C$30 (US$30/£15) adults for the 3-hour trip. Or, if you have flown into Halifax, **PEI Express Shuttle** (© 877/877-1771; www.peishuttle.com) offers transportation by van between Charlottetown and Halifax for C$55 (US$55/£28) one-way for adults, C$50 (US$50/£25) students and seniors, C$45 (US$45/£23) children under age 5.

VISITOR INFORMATION   The city's main **Visitor Information Centre** (© 902/368-7795) is a modern structure known as **Founders Hall** at 6 Prince St. (the end of the street, at the entrance to Confederation Landing Park). Look for brown "?" signs to direct you to this brick building with helpful staffers, an interactive computer kiosk, cafe, free Internet, and an ample supply of brochures. There's also a vacancy board to let you know where rooms are currently available. The center is open daily in July and August from 8am to 10pm, Monday through Friday only in the off season from 8am to 5pm. Charlottetown's **City Hall** also maintains an info kiosk, though it is less comprehensive.

EXPLORING CHARLOTTETOWN

Charlottetown is a compact city that's easy to reconnoiter once you park your car. Three main areas merit exploration: the waterfront, the downtown area near Province House and the Confederation Court Mall, and the parks and residential areas over near Victoria Park.

You're best off first heading to the main **Visitor Information Centre** (see above), by the waterfront, and then starting your tour from there. At the visitor center, be sure to ask for a map and one of the free walking tour brochures. The **waterfront** has been spruced up in recent years with the addition of **Peake's Wharf,** a collection of touristy boutiques and restaurants that attracts hordes in summer (it's open mid-May to mid-Oct). To see the city from the water, sign up with **Peake's Wharf Boat Cruises** (© 902/566-4458), which offers three tours daily for about C$16 to C$22 (US$16–US$22/£8–£11).

Next to the wharf is **Confederation Landing Park** ⽊, an open, modern park with a boardwalk along the water's edge, lush lawns, and benches nicely situated for indolence.

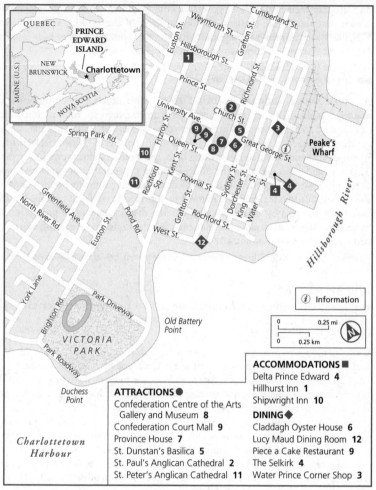

From Peake's Wharf, you can stroll up **Great George Street** ★★★. This is surely one of the most handsome streets in all of Canada, with leafy trees, perfectly scaled Georgian row houses, and stately churches.

Confederation Centre of the Arts Gallery and Museum   Part of the Confederation Centre of the Arts (which includes three theaters), this is the largest art gallery in Atlantic Canada. The center is housed in a bland and boxy modern complex of glass and rough sandstone; about the best that can be said of it is that it doesn't detract too much from the stylishly classical Province House next door. (Canadian writer Will Ferguson has referred to the building as "one of the greatest unprosecuted crimes of urban planning in Canadian history.") Inside, however, the gallery is spacious and nicely arranged on two levels, and it features displays from the permanent collection as well as imaginatively curated changing exhibits. Shows might range from an exhibit on Canadian legal history to Uruguayan paintings to knit works or photographs of islands, but mostly the museum focuses on hanging the work of up-and-coming Canadians such as prize-winning Inuit artist Annie Pootoogook (who hails from the Northwest Territories). Spend an hour here if you enjoy art.

145 Richmond St. ℰ 902/628-6142. www.confederationcentre.com. Free admission. Late May to early Oct daily 9am–5pm; off season Wed–Sat 11am–5pm, Sun 1–5pm.

Province House National Historic Site ✸ This neoclassical downtown land-mark was built in 1847 in an area set aside by town fathers for colonial administration and church buildings. When it served as a colonial legislature, the massive building rose up from vacant lots of dust and mud; today, as the provincial legislature, it's ringed by handsome trees, an inviting lawn, and a bustling downtown just beyond. This stern and imposing sandstone edifice occupies a special spot in Canadian history as the place where the details of the Confederation were hammered out in 1864. In the early 1980s, the building was restored to appear as it would have looked in that year. Start your tour by viewing a well-made film that documents the process of confederation. Afterward, wander the halls and view the Legislative Assembly, where legislators have been meeting since 1847.

2 Palmer's Lane. ℰ 902/566-7626. Free admission (donations requested). July–Sept daily 8:30am–5pm; Oct–June Mon–Fri 8:30am–5pm.

WHERE TO STAY

For those traveling on a tight budget, there are also a number of moderately priced motels situated along the main access roads running into town (coming from the Confederation Bridge) and beside the airport.

Delta Prince Edward ✸✸ *Kids* A modern, boxy, 10-story hotel overlooking the harbor, the Prince Edward Hotel is part of the Canadian Pacific chain and has all the amenities expected by business travelers and upscale tourists, including free exercise bikes delivered to your room and cordless phones (in about half the rooms). The better guest rooms are furnished with reproduction Georgian-style furniture; others have those oak and beige-laminate furnishings that are virtually invisible. Higher rooms have better views; there's a premium for water views, but the city views are actually nicer and you can usually still glimpse the water. Kids will love the children's wading pool indoors, while adults hang out in the adjacent heated lane pool and hot tub, or work the Nordic tracks in the fitness center. The in-hotel **Selkirk** restaurant (p. 164) might be the city's best, with upscale service and presentation to complement a fine menu. There's also a pubby lounge. Summers only, a more informal restaurant serves tasty lunches on a patio near the harbor. Raining? No problem: Try out the hotel's golf simulator.

18 Queen St., Charlottetown, PEI C1A 8B9. ℰ 888/890-3222 or 902/566-2222. Fax 902/566-2282. www.delta princeedward.com. 211 units. Peak season C$169–C$390 (US$169–US$390/£85–£195) double, C$225–C$905 (US$225–US$905/£113–£453) suite; call for off-season rates. AE, DC, DISC, MC, V. Valet parking C$18 (US$18/£9); self-parking C$14 (US$14/£7) per day. Pets allowed. **Amenities:** 2 restaurants; indoor pool; fitness room; Jacuzzi; sauna; concierge; business center; shopping arcade; salon; room service; babysitting; laundry; dry cleaning; golf simulator. *In room:* A/C, TV, minibar, coffeemaker, hair dryer, iron/ironing board.

Hillhurst Inn ✸ Another fine mansion built in 1897 in another fine neighborhood (3 blocks northeast of Province House), Hillhurst features a raft of nice touches, not the least of which is the extraordinarily detailed woodworking carved by some of the city's shipbuilders. When built, locals called it "the crystal palace" because of its profusion of windows. The rooms are varied in size and style and have been upgraded over time; two even have Jacuzzis. As is often the case, third-floor rooms require a bit of a hike, and are smaller and cozier than rooms on the second floor. Only drawback? Many of the bathrooms are small (often shoehorned into closets). Also, the furnishings are a bit less historic and creative than those at the comparatively priced Shipwright (see below).

181 Fitzroy St., Charlottetown, PEI C1A 1S3. (C) **877/994-8004** or 902/894-8004. Fax 902/892-7679. www.hillhurst. com. 9 units. Mid-June to mid-Sept C$135–C$235 (US$135–US$235/£68–£118) double; spring and fall C$99–C$165 (US$99–US$165/£50–£83) double. Closed Dec–Apr. Rates include full breakfast. AE, DISC, MC, V. Free parking. **Amenities:** Business center. *In room:* A/C, TV, dataport, hair dryer, Jacuzzi (2 units).

Shipwright Inn ★★★ This understated Victorian home was built by a shipbuilder, and expertly renovated and refurbished. It's decorated with period furniture and with a deft touch—no over-the-top Victoriana here—and equipped with modern amenities. All rooms have lovely wood floors (some with original ship-planking floors), and three are in a recent addition, which was built with a number of nice touches. Among the best rooms are those with extra somethings: the Officer's Wardroom, a suite with an Asian feel, living-room fireplace, and skylight-view bathtub; the airy Crow's Nest luxury apartment, with its plush king bed, claw-foot Jacuzzi (yes, really), and lovely unvarnished wood furniture; and even the simpler Purser's Stateroom, which shares a lovely deck with another room. The business center, with its computer and fax machine, is a nice bonus; afternoon tea service is a good introduction to the island; and innkeepers Judy and Trevor Pye and their staff are unfailingly helpful. This inn is located right in the city, yet it has a settled, pastoral farmhouse feel to it nonetheless— a perfect combination.

51 Fitzroy St., Charlottetown, PEI C1A 1R4. (C) **888/306-9966** or 902/368-1905. Fax 902/628-1905. www.shipwright inn.com. 9 units. May–Oct C$149–C$289 (US$149–US$289/£75–£145) double, Nov–Apr C$99–C$199 (US$99– US$199/£50–£100). Rates include full breakfast. AE, DC, MC, V. Free parking. **Amenities:** Dining room; business center. *In room:* A/C, TV, kitchenette (some units), minibar, fridge (most units), hair dryer, iron, Jacuzzi (some units).

WHERE TO DINE

Claddagh Oyster House ★ SEAFOOD Despite the Irish name and the Olde Dublin Pub located downstairs, the Claddagh Room isn't the place for corned beef. Instead, as the rest of its name indicates, it's a place for seafood—starting with oysters, which have become a focus of the recently retooled menu. The seafood chowder is very tasty, or go for seared scallops over sweet potato pancakes, mussels of the day, or oysters Rockfeller. For the main meal, you might choose from the raw oyster bar or go for a boiled lobster, lemony shrimp, sesame seed-encrusted salmon, citrus-shallot haddock, and the like; there are also strip loin steaks, maple pork chops, and other landlubber entrees. There's no harbor view, as there is at other seafood places in town, but the preparation and service here are a notch above. Live Irish entertainment is often featured downstairs in the pub during the summer months.

131 Sydney St. (C) **902/892-9661.** Reservations recommended. Main courses C$18–C$29 (US$18–US$29/£9–£15); oysters C$1.60–C$1.90 (US$1.60–US$1.90/80p–85p) each. AE, DISC, MC, V. Mon–Fri 11:30am–2pm; Sun–Thurs 5–10pm; Fri–Sat 5–10:30pm.

Lucy Maud Dining Room ★★ REGIONAL The Lucy Maud Dining Room is located on the respected Culinary Institute of Canada's Charlottetown campus. The building itself is a bit institutional and charmless, and the 80-seat dining room has much the feel of a hotel restaurant. But plenty of nice touches offset the lack of personality. Among them: custom china and a beautiful view of the bay and Victoria Park from oversize windows. Best of all, diners get to sample some of the best of island cuisine, prepared and served by institute students eager to please. The lunch and dinner menus change each semester, but typical dinner entrees might include duck breast with a sour-cherry sauce or venison loin with a blueberry-peppercorn sauce (the kitchen is noted for its venison). There's always salmon on the menu here, and often a curry-flavored seafood chowder with fresh tarragon. A short wine list is also available.

4 Sydney St. ⓒ **902/894-6868**. Reservations recommended June–Sept for lunch and dinner. Main courses C$8–C$13 (US$8–US$13/£4–£6.50) lunch, C$15–C$28 (US$15–US$28/£7.50–£14) dinner. AE, MC, V. Tues–Fri 11:30am–1:30pm; Tues–Sat 6–8pm. Closed holiday weekends.

Piece a Cake Restaurant 🐵🐵 ECLECTIC   This modern, handsome restaurant occupies the second floor of a building that's part of the Confederation Court Mall. With hardwood floors, high ceilings, rich custard-colored walls, and window frames suspended whimsically from the ceiling, there's a welcoming, airy grace to it. It's the kind of place where friends who don't see each other often get together and relax over a lively meal. The menu is wonderfully far-ranging, and it's hard to imagine someone not finding something appealing—lunches might range from a teriyaki salmon wrap to Thai scallop salad to Tuscan grilled chicken sandwiches. Dinners are similarly eclectic and include a range of adventurous pastas, such as Penne on Fire (with charred onions, grilled zucchini, toasted pecans, and a tangerine relish.) Other dinner options have included a medley of Thai seafood; blackened salmon; and a pecan-encrusted pork loin. Also ask about the gourmet brown-bag lunches, about C$10 to C$14 (US$10–US$14/£5–£7) including dessert and beverage, with choices that could run to a lobster salad croissant or a jerk chicken pasta salad.

119 Grafton St. (upstairs in the Confederation Court Mall). ⓒ **902/894-4585**. Reservations recommended. Main courses C$6–C$12 (US$6–US$12/£3–£6) lunch, C$9–C$18 (US$9–US$18/£4.50–£9) dinner. AE, DC, MC, V. Mon–Sat 11am–10pm.

The Selkirk 🐵🐵🐵 NEW CANADIAN   Charlottetown's most stylish restaurant is smack in the middle of the lobby of the high-end Delta Prince Edward Hotel. Yet it has a more informal character than many upscale hotel restaurants, with an eclectic mix of chairs and a piano player providing the live soundtrack. The menu is also more ambitious and creative than you'll find elsewhere in the city. Start with a local seafood chowder or some island-smoked salmon. Main courses from chef Mark Gregory could include a bouillabaisse, spicy smoked beef ribs, a pan-roasted pork loin chop, a potato-crusted filet of salmon with a spinach-onion confit stuffing and a ruby grapefruit *gastrique*, or a PEI lobster feed of a sea salt–boiled crustacean, chowder, mussels, potato, and veggies. Ask about the seasonal prix-fixe three-course dinners (C$35/US$35/£18 in 2007). The lobby location gets noisy at times, especially when conferees are in town, so ask for a table under the mezzanine, nearer the piano.

In the Delta Prince Edward, 18 Queen St. ⓒ **902/566-2222**. Reservations recommended. Main courses C$11–C$25 (US$11–US$25/£5.50–£13) at dinner. AE, DC, DISC, MC, V. Daily 5:30–9pm; Mon–Fri 7am–1:30pm; Sat 7–11am; Sun 7am–2pm.

Water Prince Corner Shop 🐵🐵 *Finds* SEAFOOD   This place is a real find, tucked into an attractive corner building at Water and Prince streets (thus the name) that looks at first glance like a simple newsstand or convenience store. Inside, though, you'll find one of the city's most convivial seafood joints, serving lobster dinners, superb seafood chowder, cooked mussels, and even lobster rolls to an appreciative mixture of tourists and locals. There's a liquor license if you want to tip a few (and you might). If the weather's good, try to get a seat on the street near sundown: You can see the waterfront from some tables. Even if it's not, don't miss the exceptionally rare blue lobster kept here on display (alive)—it was caught off the west coast of PEI in 2002.

141 Water St. ✆ 902/368-3212. Reservations recommended. Lunch C$4.95–C$11 (US$4.95–US$11/£2.50–£5.50); dinner C$6.95–C$25 (US$6.95–US$25/£3.50–£13). AE, DISC, DC, MC, V. May–June and Sept–Oct daily 9am–8pm; July–Aug daily 9am–10pm.

5 Kings County: An Escape from Anne's Land

After a visit to Charlottetown and the island's central towns, Kings County comes as a bit of a surprise. It's far more tranquil and uncluttered than Queens County (Anne's reach is much diminished here), and the landscapes feature woodlots alternating with corn, grain, and potato fields. Although much is made of the county's two great commercial centers on the coast—Souris and Montague—it's good to keep in mind that each of these has a population of around 1,500. In some parts of North America, that wouldn't even rate a dot on the map.

ESSENTIALS

GETTING THERE   Several main roads—including highways 1, 2, 3, and 4—connect eastern PEI with Charlottetown and western points. The ferry to Nova Scotia sails from Woods Island on the south coast. See "Exploring the Island," earlier in this chapter, for more information about the ferry.

VISITOR INFORMATION   There's a provincial **Visitor Information Centre** (✆ 902/687-7030) at 95 Main St. in Souris, open daily from mid-June to mid-October. There's another VIC in St. Peter's Bay (✆ 902/961-3540), on Route 2 at the intersection of routes 313 and 16; this center, bordering the lovely Confederation Trail, opens daily June through October.

MONTAGUE

Montague may be the Kings County region's main commercial hub, but it's a hub in low gear: compact and attractive, with a handsome business district on a pair of flanking hills sloping down to a bridge across the Montague River. (In fact, a century and a half ago, the town was called Montague Bridge.) Shipbuilding was the economic mainstay in the 19th century; today, it's dairy and tobacco.

EXPLORING THE OUTDOORS

Cruise Manada (✆ 800/986-3444 or 902/838-3444; www.cruisemanada.com) offers seal- and bird-watching tours daily during peak season aboard restored fishing boats; the cost is C$22 (US$22/£11) adults, C$20 (US$20/£10) seniors and students, C$12 (US$12/£6) children age 5 to 13. Trips depart from the marina on the Montague River, just below the visitor center in the old railway depot, three times daily in July and August, once daily from mid-May to June and in September. Reservations are advised. Allow at least 2 hours. Cruise Manada also does "floating ceilidhs" (Celtic folk dances) for about C$36 (US$36/£18) per adult.

Southeast of Montague (en route to Murray River) is the **Buffaloland Provincial Park** (✆ 902/652-8950), where you'll spot a small herd of buffalo. These magnificent animals were a gift to PEI from the province of Alberta, and they now number about two dozen. Walk down the 90m (295-ft.) fenced-in corridor into the paddock and ascend the wooden platform for the best view of the shaggy beasts. Often they're hunkered down at the far end of the meadow, but they sometimes wander nearer. The park is right off Route 4; watch for signs. It's open daily year-round, and—like so many of PEI's parks—free to enter.

Brudenell River Provincial Park is one of the province's better-bred parks, and a great spot to work up an athletic glow on a sunny afternoon. On its 600 riverfront hectares (1,482 acres) you'll find two well-regarded golf courses, a golf academy, a full-blown resort (see below), tennis, lawn bowling, a wildflower garden, a playground, a campground, and nature trails. Kids' programs—including Frisbee golf, shoreline scavenger hunts, and crafts workshops—are scheduled daily in summer. You can also rent canoes, kayaks, and jet skis from private operators located within the park. The park is open daily mid-May to early October from 9am to 9pm, and admission is free. Head north of Montague on Route 4, then east on Route 3 to the park signs.

WHERE TO STAY

Rodd Brudenell River Resort 🏃🏃 *Kids*   The attractive Brudenell River Resort was built in 1991, and its open, vaguely Frank Lloyd Wright–esque design reflects its recent vintage. This is an especially popular destination for golfers—it's set among two golf courses that have been garnering raves and hosted international tournaments and exhibitions. Guests choose from three types of rooms. The hotel proper has nearly 100 well-appointed guest rooms, most with a balcony or terrace. The expensive cottages each have two bedrooms, cathedral ceilings, fireplaces, and large-screen TVs; then, there are a set of more basic cabins—the best choice for those traveling on a budget, though these aren't as fresh and the units are clustered together oddly like pavilions in a long-gone world exposition.

In addition to the two excellent golf courses (one with a golf academy offering lessons), the resort maintains indoor and outdoor pools, as well as a newer **spa** 🏃 which opens from mid-May to mid-October only. The dining room on the first level of this property overlooks one of the golf courses; it's huge, but the high-backed chairs carve out a sense of intimacy. The kitchen serves dinners of what might be described as creative country-club cuisine, with entrees including charbroiled steak, sole in puff pastry, and pasta primavera.

Rte. 3 (P.O. Box 67), Cardigan, PEI C0A 1G0. (℄) **800/565-7633** or 902/652-2332. Fax 902/652-2886. www.rodd-hotels.ca. 165 units. Hotel C$131–C$353 (US$131–US$353/£116–£177) double; C$87–C$178 (US$87–US$178/£44–£89) cabin; C$167–C$536 (US$167–US$536/£84–£268) cottage. AE, DC, MC, V. Closed mid-Oct to mid-May. Pets allowed with C$10 (US$10/£5) fee per pet per night. **Amenities:** 2 restaurants; 2 bars; indoor and outdoor pools; golf course (with academy); 2 tennis courts; fitness center; spa; Jacuzzi; sauna; canoe/kayak/bike rental; children's center; babysitting; dry cleaning. *In room:* A/C, TV, dataport, kitchenette (some units), minibar (some units), fridge (some units), coffeemaker, hair dryer, iron.

WHERE TO DINE

Windows on the Water Café 🏃 SEAFOOD   If you haven't yet dined on PEI mussels, this is the place to let loose. The blue mussels are steamed in a root *mirepoix* (soup base), with sesame, ginger, and garlic—a great idea. Main courses might include sole stuffed with crab and scallop and topped with hollandaise, or a filet mignon served with sweet peppers, red onion, and mushrooms in a peppercorn sauce. Lunches are lighter, with choices that could include a grilled chicken and mandarin salad or house-made fish cakes. The appealing, open dining room features press-back chairs and a lively buzz, but if the weather's agreeable, angle for a seat under the canopy on the deck and enjoy the great view of the Montague River.

106 Sackville St. (corner of Main St.), Montague. © 902/838-2080. Reservations recommended. Main courses C$7.50–C$9.95 (US$7.50–US$9.95/£3.75–£5) lunch, C$15–C$21 (US$15–US$21/£7.50–£11) dinner. AE, DC, MC, V. June–Oct daily 11:30am–9:30pm. Closed Nov–May.

SOURIS & NORTHEAST PEI

Some 42km (26 miles) northeast of Montague is the town of Souris, an active fishing town attractively set on a gentle hill overlooking the harbor. Souris (pronounced Soo-*ree*) is French for "mouse"—so named because early settlers here were beset by voracious field mice that destroyed their crops. The town is the launching base for an excursion to the Magdalen Islands, and it also makes a good base for exploring northeastern PEI, which is considered by some Charlottetown types to be the island's version of either Mayberry, RFD or the Outback—in other words, a place that's remote and sparsely populated. You'll find it to be somewhat less agricultural and more forested (especially away from the coast) than the rest of the island, too.

EXPLORING THE AREA

Several good beaches can be found ringing this wedge-shaped peninsula that points like an accusing finger toward Nova Scotia's Cape Breton Island. **Red Point Provincial Park** (© 902/357-3075) is 13km (8 miles) northeast of Souris. Open from June until mid-September, it offers a handsome beach and supervised swimming, along with a campground that's popular with families; sites cost about C$19 to C$25 (US$19–US$25/£9.50–£13). Another inviting and often empty **beach** ⊛ is a short distance northeast at Basin Head, which features a "singing sands" beach that allegedly sings (actually, it's more like squeaks) when you walk on it. The dunes here are especially appealing.

At the island's far eastern tip is the aptly named **East Point Lighthouse** ⊛ (© 902/357-2718). You can simply enjoy the dramatic setting or take a tour of the building (mid-June to Aug only). Ask for your East Point ribbon while you're here. If you make it to the North Cape Lighthouse on the western shore, you'll receive a Traveller's Award documenting that you've traveled PEI tip-to-tip. Admission to the octagonal lighthouse tower is C$3 (US$3/£1.50) adults, C$2 (US$2/£1) seniors and students, C$1 (US$1/50p) children, and C$8 (US$8/£4) families. There are daily tours in season; from September to mid-June, you'll need to call to try to schedule one. There's now a craft shop on-site, as well, purveying jewelry, soap, sand paintings, local books and music, and other island goods.

WHERE TO STAY & DINE

Inn at Bay Fortune ⊛⊛ This exceptionally attractive, shingled compound on 18 hectares (45 acres) was built by playwright Elmer Harris in 1910 as a summer home, and it quickly became the nucleus for a colony of artists, actors, and writers. Innkeeper David Wilmer pulled out the stops in renovating, bringing it back from the brink of decay. In 1998 he added a wing with six new rooms (several with Jacuzzis), including the wonderful North Tower Room no. 4, with a high ceiling and balcony overlooking the lodge and bay beyond. The best room, though, remains South Tower Room no. 4, which requires a hike up a narrow staircase—but feels like another world once you reach the perchlike destination. Newer rooms are bigger than older ones, yet all are cozy with mixes of antiques and custom-made furniture. About half of the units have wood-burning fireplaces. This is also home to one of PEI's best **restaurants** ⊛; the chef's always-shifting menu rarely fails to produce a great prix-fixe meal.

Rte. 310 (off Rte. 2), Bay Fortune, PEI C0A 2B0. ℂ 902/687-3745 or off season 860/296-1348. Fax 902/687-3540. www.innatbayfortune.com. 18 units. C$150–C$335 (US$150–US$335/£75–£168) double. Rates include full breakfast. DC, MC, V. Closed mid-Oct to mid-May. **Amenities:** Restaurant.

Inn at Spry Point 𝓡𝓡 *(Finds)*   This inn was founded in the 1970s on a remote point of land as a United Nations–funded self-sufficient community affiliated with the New Alchemy Institute—think windmills, solar power, greenhouses, trout ponds, and some serious hippy-dippy talk. But oil prices dropped, interest in conservation waned, and the experiment faded. Enter David Wilmer, owner of Inn at Bay Fortune (see above). He bought the 32-hectare (79-acre) property and has undertaken the monumental task of bringing it up to date. All 15 rooms have canopied king-size beds and are tastefully appointed with comfortable sitting areas. Most have their own private balconies, and four have a garden terrace. Outside, the location is top-rate—2,440m (8,000 ft.) of undeveloped shorefront that invite exploration—and you can walk along trails that traverse red-clay cliffs with views of the Northumberland Strait. Later, dine in the outstanding contemporary **dining room** 𝓡𝓡 featuring locally grown organic vegetables and island seafood; prix-fixe meals cost about C$45 (US$45/£22) per person, and you can also order a la carte.

Spry Pt. Rd. (off Rte. 310), Little Pond, PEI C0A 2B0. ℂ 902/583-2400. Fax 902/583-2176. www.innatsprypoint.com. 15 units. C$185–C$335 (US$185–US$335/£93–£168) double. Rates include full breakfast. DC, MC, V. Closed Oct to mid-June. **Amenities:** Restaurant. *In room:* A/C.

The Matthew House Inn 𝓡   Kimberly and Franco Olivieri came to PEI on vacation from Italy in 1995. They fell in love with the island's grand old homes, and before their holiday had ended they found themselves owners of this fine B&B. ("My husband is very impulsive by nature," says Kimberly.) Located atop a pleasant lawn overlooking the harbor and ferry to the Magdalen Islands, this stately Victorian dates from 1885 and maintains many of the original flourishes inside and out. Eastlake-style furnishings and William Morris touches give the place an architectural richness without seeming too grandmotherly about it; for big families, a two-bedroom cottage adjacent to the inn rents by the week and is equipped with a kitchen and laundry. This place will be appreciated by those passionate about historic architecture.

15 Breakwater St. (P.O. Box 151), Souris, PEI C0A 2B0. ℂ 902/687-3461. Fax 902/687-3461. www.matthewhouse inn.com. 8 units. C$105–C$175 (US$105–US$175/£53–£88) double. Rates include full breakfast. AE, MC, V. Closed early Sept to mid-June. Children over 10 welcome. **Amenities:** Dining room; laundry service; fax service. *In room:* TV/VCR, hair dryer.

6 Prince County: PEI in the Rough

Prince County encompasses the western end of PEI and offers a varied mix of lush agricultural land, rugged coastline, and unpopulated sandy beaches. With a few exceptions, this region is a bit more ragged around the edges in a working-farm, working-waterfront kind of way. It lacks the pristine-village charm or polish of Kings County or much of Queens County. Within this unrefined landscape, however, you'll find pockets of considerable charm such as the village of Victoria on the south coast at the county line, and in Tyne Valley near the north coast, which is reminiscent of a Cotswold hamlet.

ESSENTIALS

GETTING THERE   Route 2 is the main highway connecting Prince County with the rest of the island. Smaller feeder roads typically lead you to or from Route 2. The

Confederation Bridge from the mainland connects to Prince County at Borden Point, southeast of Summerside.

VISITOR INFORMATION   The best source of travel information for the county is **Gateway Village** (*©* **902/437-8570**) at the end of the Confederation Bridge. It's open daily year-round.

VICTORIA 🌟🌟

The town of **Victoria**—located a short detour off Route 1 between the Confederation Bridge and Charlottetown—is a tiny and unusually scenic village that has attracted a number of artists, boutique owners, and craftspeople. The village is perfect for strolling—parking is near the wharf and off the streets, keeping the narrow lanes free for foot traffic. Wander the short, shady lanes while admiring the architecture, much of which is in elemental farmhouse style, clad in clapboard or shingle and constructed with sharply creased gables. (Some elaborate Victorians break the mold.) What makes the place so singular is that the village, which was first settled in 1767, has utterly escaped the creeping sprawl that has plagued so many otherwise attractive places. The entire village consists of 4 square blocks, which are surrounded by potato fields and the Northumberland Strait.

EXPLORING VICTORIA

The **Victoria Seaport Museum** (no phone) is located inside the shingled, square **lighthouse** near the town parking lot. (You can't miss it.) You'll find a rustic local history museum with the usual assortment of artifacts from the past century or so. In summer, it's open most afternoons; admission is by donation.

In the middle of town is the well-regarded **Victoria Playhouse** (*©* **902/658-2025**). Built in 1913 as a community hall, the building has a unique raked stage (it drops 18cm/7 in. over 6.5m/21 ft.) to create the illusion of space, four beautiful stained-glass lamps, and a proscenium arch (also unusual for a community hall). Plays staged here from late June through September attract folks out from Charlottetown for the night. It's hard to say what is more enjoyable: the high quality of the acting or the wonderful big-night-out air of a professional play in a small town where nothing else is going on. There's also a Monday-night concert series, with performers offering up everything from traditional folk to Latin jazz. Most tickets are C$24 (US$24/£12) adults, C$22 (US$22/£11) seniors, and C$18 (US$18/£9) students, though a few performance are priced higher; matinees cost about C$18 (US$18/£9).

WHERE TO STAY

Orient Hotel 🌟   The Orient has been a Victoria mainstay for years—a 1926 guide notes that the inn had 20 rooms at C$2.50 per night (of course, back then a trip to the bathroom required a walk to the carriage house). It has been modernized in recent years (all rooms now have private bathrooms), but it retains much of its antique charm. The century-old building with its yellow shingles and maroon trim is at the edge of the village overlooking potato fields lurid with purple blooms in late summer. Rooms are painted in warm pastel tones and furnished eclectically with flea-market antiques; most have good water views. Some of the updating diminished the charm a bit, but the place has a friendly low-key demeanor, much like the village itself; the enthusiastic owners have also added a combination television/games room set up for cribbage and crokinole (an old-fashioned Maritime game), and ceilidhs (Celtic folk dances) have been known to pop up, too. Mrs. Proffit's Tea Shop, on the first floor, serves lunch and afternoon tea.

34 Main St. (P.O. Box 55, Victoria, PEI C0A 2G0). ℂ 800/565-6743 or 902/658-2503. 8 units. C$80–C$150 (US$80–US$150/£40–£75) double. Rates include full breakfast. Dinner and theater packages available. MC, V. Closed mid-Oct to mid-May. Not suitable for children under 12. **Amenities:** Tearoom. *In room:* TV.

WHERE TO DINE
Landmark Café CAFE   Located across from the Victoria Playhouse, the Landmark Café occupies a small, cozy storefront teeming with shelves filled with crockery, pots, jars, and more, some of which is for sale. But the effect is more funky than Ye Olde Quainte, and the limited menu is inviting. Daily offerings might include steamed mussels, vine leaves with feta cheese, salads, lasagna, a meat pie, or a salmon steamed in tarragon.

12 Main St. ℂ 902/658-2286. Reservations recommended. Sandwiches around C$5.50 (US$5.50/£2.75); main courses C$11–C$16 (US$11–US$16/£5.50–£8). MC, V. Daily 11am–9:30pm. Closed mid-Sept to late June.

TYNE VALLEY ℟
The village of Tyne Valley is just off Malpeque Bay and is one of the most attractive and pastoral areas in all of western PEI. There's little to do here, but much to admire. Verdant barley and potato fields surround a village of gingerbread-like homes, and azure inlets encroach on the view from afar; these are the arms of the bay, world-famous for its succulent Malpeque oysters. A former 19th-century shipbuilding center, the village now attracts artisans and others in search of a quiet lifestyle within sight of gorgeous scenery. A handful of good restaurants, inns, and shops here cater to visitors.

EXPLORING TYNE VALLEY
Just north of the village on Route 12 is lovely **Green Park Provincial Park** ℟ (ℂ 902/831-7912), open from mid-June through early September. Once the site of an active shipyard, the 88-hectare (217-acre) park is now a lush riverside destination with emerald lawns and leafy trees, and it has the feel of a turn-of-the-20th-century estate, which, in fact, it was. In the heart of the park is the extravagant gingerbread mansion (1865) once owned by James Yeo, a merchant, shipbuilder, and landowner who in his time was the island's wealthiest and most powerful man.

The historic Yeo House and the **Green Park Shipbuilding Museum** (ℂ 902/831-7947), open June through September, are now the park's centerpieces. Managed by the Prince Edward Island Museum and Heritage Foundation, exhibits in two buildings provide a good view of the prosperous life of a shipbuilder and the golden age of PEI shipbuilding. The museum and house are open daily from mid-June through summer, 9am to 5:30pm, closing for the season around Labour Day. Admission is C$5 (US$5/£2.50) plus tax adults; C$3.50 (US$3.50/£1.75) students; C$12 (US$12/£6) families; and free for children under 12.

When leaving the area, consider taking the highly scenic drive along the bay on Route 12 from Tyne Valley to MacDougall.

WHERE TO STAY
Green Park Provincial Park ℟℟ (ℂ 902/831-7912) may be the most gracious and lovely park on the island, and offers camping on 58 grassy sites overlooking an arm of Malpeque Bay. Cost is about C$19 to C$25 (US$19–US$25/£9.50–£13) per night.

Caernarvon Cottages, B&B, and Gardens *(Kids)* The sense of quiet and the views over Malpeque Bay across the road are the lure at this attractive, well-maintained cottage complex on 2 hectares (5 acres) a few minutes' drive from Tyne Valley. The four modern (ca. 1990) pine cottages are furnished simply but comfortably. Each has two bedrooms and a sleeping loft, outdoor gas barbecue, cathedral ceiling, and porch with a bay view. This is a good choice if you're looking to get away, but it's also popular with families—there's a playground out back, so it may not be the best option for a romantic escape, even with the pretty 10m-high (33-ft.) gazebo on the lawn just steps from the bay. (The gazebo is encircled by three large flower beds filled with peonies, lilies, and hardy roses.) Three simply furnished rooms are available in the main house; a full breakfast is included in those rates.

4697 Hwy. 12, Bayside, PEI (mailing address: Richmond RR1, C0B 1Y0). (C) **800/514-9170** or 902/854-3418. www. cottagelink.com/cottlink/pei/pe10018.html. 7 units. Main inn C$120 (US$120/£60) double; cottages C$110 (US$110/ £55) double; C$770 (US$770/£385) weekly for two. Inn rates include full breakfast. V. Cottages closed mid-Sept to mid-June. Pets in cottages only. *In room:* TV/VCR (some units), kitchenette (some units), hair dryer, iron, no phone.

Doctor's Inn *(R) (Value)* A stay at the Doctor's Inn is a bit like visiting relatives you didn't know you had. Upstairs in this handsome in-town farmhouse are just two guest rooms, which share a bathroom. (Note that you could rent both for less than the cost of a room at many other PEI inns.) There's an upstairs sitting area, and extensive organic gardens out back to peruse. It's a pleasant retreat, and innkeepers Jean and Paul Offer do a fine job of making guests feel relaxed and at home. (There's also a cottage available for rent.) The Offers also serve up one of Atlantic Canada's most memorable dining experiences in its **dining room** *(R)(R)* by prior arrangement for up to six diners.

Rte. 167, Tyne Valley, PEI C0B 2C0. (C) **902/831-3057.** www.peisland.com/doctorsinn. 2 units. C$60 (US$60/£30) double; cottage C$360–C$450 (US$360–US$450/£180–£225) weekly. All rates include breakfast. MC, V. Well-mannered pets allowed. **Amenities:** Dining room. *In room:* No phone.

WHERE TO DINE

Also see the "Doctor's Inn," above, for fine dining.

The Shipwright's Café REGIONAL This locally popular restaurant is elegant yet informal, and you'd be comfortable here in either neat jeans or predinner sport clothes. Expect good service, a modest but useful wine list, and salads with organic greens from the Offers just down the street (see Doctor's Inn, above). Justly popular dishes include local oysters broiled with spinach and cheese; island-raised lamb; Atlantic salmon; and a seafood chowder rich with plenty of those famous plump PEI mussels.

11869 Rte. 6 (at junction of Rte. 33), Margate, PEI C0B 1M0. (C) **902/836-3403.** Reservations recommended in summer. Lunch C$9.95–C$17 (US$9.95–US$17/£5–£8.50); dinner C$15–C$20 (US$15–US$20/£7.50–£10), more for lobster. MC, V. June–Sept daily 11:30am–8:30pm. Closed Oct–May.

6

Newfoundland & Labrador

by Paul Karr

Newfoundland and Labrador might be the eastern seaboard's last best place. (These two distinct geographic areas are administered as one province, thus the phrase "Newfoundland and Labrador" sometimes refers to a single province of Canada, sometimes to the two physically separate places.) Wild, windswept, and isolated, the province often reveals a powerful paradox. Although the landscape is as rocky and raw as expected—at times it looks as though the glaciers had only receded a year or two ago, instead of a hundred thousand—residents here display a warmth that puts visitors to shame even as it makes them feel right at home.

Tourists only recently started arriving here in numbers, and longtime residents more often than not love to chat up the place, offering advice and listening to outsiders' impressions. Even the sort of traveler who's usually reluctant to engage a stranger is likely to drop that hesitation after an encounter or two here.

An excursion to The Rock—as the island of Newfoundland is often called in Canada—can indeed be a magical experience on many levels, not only for this extraordinary northern landscape and its curious northern light as well its gracious inhabitants, but also for the rich history that catches many first-time visitors off guard. This is where European civilization made landfall in the New World twice: first by Vikings, then later by fishermen and settlers in the wake of John Cabot's arrival in 1497. You'll therefore find traces of North America's original history at almost every turn here. History isn't buried here; it's right on the surface. And Mother Nature is never far away, either.

1 Exploring Newfoundland & Labrador

This is a big place, and the amount of time to travel anywhere on the island goes up accordingly. A couple of weeks is enough for a bare-bones tour of the island, though you'll still be frustrated by all that gets left out. You're better off selecting a few regions and focusing on those.

ESSENTIALS

VISITOR INFORMATION Visitor information centers aren't as numerous or well organized in Newfoundland as they are in Nova Scotia or Prince Edward Island, areas where almost every small community has a place to stock up on truckloads of pretty color brochures (and ask lots of annoying questions). In Newfoundland, you're better off stocking up on maps and information either in St. John's or just after you disembark from the ferries, where excellent centers are maintained.

The Newfoundland and Labrador Travel Guide, published by the province's department of tourism, is hefty and helpful, with listings of all attractions and accommodations.

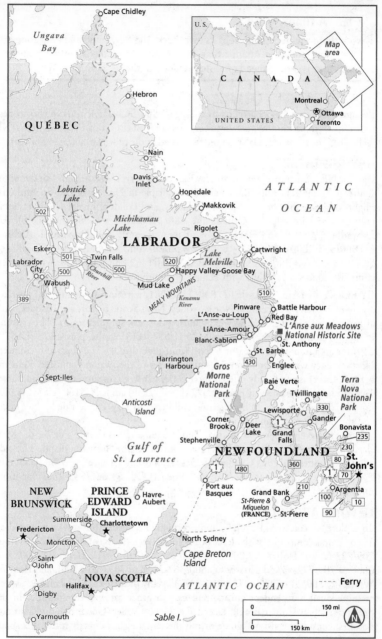

Cape Chidley

Ungava
Bay

U.S.

Map
area

C A N A D A

Montreal
Ottawa
Toronto

UNITED STATES

Hebron

QUÉBEC

Nain

Davis
Inlet

Lobstick
Lake

Hopedale

502

Michikamau
Lake

Makkovik

ATLANTIC

OCEAN

Rigolet

Esker

501

LABRADOR

Lake
Melville

Cartwright

Twin Falls

520

Labrador
City

500

Churchill
River

500

Happy Valley-Goose Bay

Wabush

389

Mud Lake

MEALY MOUNTAINS

Kenamu
River

510

Pinware

Battle Harbour

L'Anse-au-Loup

Red Bay

L'Anse-Amour

L'Anse aux Meadows
National Historic Site

Blanc-Sablon

St. Anthony

Harrington
Harbour

St. Barbe

430

Englee

Sept-Iles

Gros
Morne
National
Park

Baie Verte

Terra
Nova
National
Park

Anticosti
Island

Twillingate

Lewisporte

330

Corner
Brook

Deer
Lake

Gander

Bonavista

235

Gulf of
St. Lawrence

Stephenville

Grand
Falls

230

NEWFOUNDLAND

1

80

St.
John's

1

NEW
BRUNSWICK

PRINCE
EDWARD
ISLAND

Havre-
Aubert

480

360

70

Port aux
Basques

210

Argentia

Summerside

Charlottetown

Grand Bank

St-Pierre &
Miquelon
(FRANCE)

100

St-Pierre

10

90

Fredericton

Moncton

Saint
John

North Sydney

Cape Breton
Island

NOVA SCOTIA

Digby

Halifax

ATLANTIC OCEAN

Yarmouth

Sable I.

--- Ferry

0   150 mi

0   150 km

N

> **Tips** **A Timely Note**
>
> Note that Newfoundland keeps its own clock. The Newfoundland time zone is
> a half-hour ahead of Atlantic time (which the rest of the Atlantic provinces
> keep), and 1½ hours ahead of Eastern Standard (that is, New York) Time.

Request a free copy before arriving by calling © **800/563-6353.** You can also request
it by e-mail (tourisminfo@mail.gov.nf.ca) or snail mail (P.O. Box 8700, St. John's, NL
A1B 4J6). The guide is available on the ferries and at the province's information centers.

GETTING THERE

BY PLANE   Air transportation to Newfoundland is typically through Gander or St.
John's, although scheduled flights are also available to Deer Lake and St. Anthony.
Flights originate in Montréal, Toronto, Halifax, and London, England. Airlines serv-
ing the island include **Air Canada** (© **888/247-2262;** www.aircanada.com), **Air
Labrador** (© **800/563-3042;** www.airlabrador.com), and **Provincial Airlines**
(© **800/563-2800** or 709/576-1666; www.provair.com). Flight time from Toronto to
St. John's is about 3 hours. Calgary-based **WestJet** (© **888/937-8538;** www.westjet.
com) also connects St. John's with Halifax and Toronto.

BY FERRY   Marine Atlantic (© **800/341-7981;** www.marine-atlantic.ca) operates
a year-round ferry service from North Sydney, Nova Scotia to Port aux Basques, with
as many as four sailings each way daily during the peak summer season. The crossing
is about 5 hours; one-way fares are C$25 (US$25/£13) adults, plus C$78 (US$78/
£39) for an automobile. A seasonal ferry (mid-June through late Sept) also connects
North Sydney with Argentia on the southwest tip of the Avalon Peninsula. Remember that this crossing is only offered three times per week, in summer only, and takes
14 to 15 hours. The one-way fare is C$77 (US$77/£39) adults, C$160 (US$160/£80)
for regular-size vehicles. On both ferries, children 5 to 12 years old ride for half price,
and the ride's free for children under 5.

If you're traveling between the two land masses, a much shorter ride on the M/V
Apollo connects Blanc-Sablon, Labrador, with St. Barbe, Newfoundland. The ride
takes 20 minutes and costs C$23 (US$23/£12) one-way for autos, C$7.50 (US$7.50/
£3.75) adults and C$6 (US$6/£3) for students. Call © **866/535-2567** for more
information.

GETTING AROUND

To explore the countryside, you'll almost certainly need a car (bus service is sporadic).
Major rental companies with fleets in St. John's include **Avis** (© 800/879-2847 or
709/722-6620), **Dollar** (© 800/800-4000 or 709/726-1791), **Hertz** (© 800/263-
0600 or 709/722-4333), **Thrifty** (© 800/367-2277 or 709/722-6000), and **Rent-A-
Wreck** (© 800/239-7990 or 709/753-2277). Many of these car-rental chains, as well
as some small independent outfits, rent cars in other gateway communities in the
province such as Corner Brook, Deer Lake, Happy Valley–Goose Bay, and Port aux
Basques; consult the visitors' guide or call the rental chains directly for details about
some of these other locations.

Sock away some extra cash for gasoline when traveling the island: The price of fuel
on Newfoundland tends to be a bit higher than in other Atlantic provinces.

THE GREAT OUTDOORS

BIKING   Bike touring in Newfoundland is not for the out-of-shape. It's not that the hills here are necessarily brutal (though many are). It's the *weather* that can be downright demoralizing. Expect more than a handful of blustery days, complete with horizontal rains that seem to swirl around from every direction and can bring forward pedaling progress to a standstill.

Freewheeling Adventures, P.O. Box 100, Norris Point, NL A0K 3V0 (© **800/ 672-0775** or 902/857-3612; www.freewheeling.ca), runs van-supported trips based in hotels and B&Bs. Its Viking Tour of the northern coast of Newfoundland is a week of pure pleasure; it costs C$2,000 to C$2,400 (US$2,000–US$2,400/£1,000–£1,200), depending on whether you use their guides or do your own itinerary yourself. Lodging is included in both plans, but the full monty includes all your meals, equipment rental, van transfers, a bonus fjord boat trip, and a whale/iceberg-watching boat trip in the package. Freewheeling offers a similar 8-day tour of the Avalon Peninsula (very near St. John's), as well.

Aspenwood Tours, P.O. Box 622, Springdale, NL A0J 1T0 (© **709/673-4255**), arranges mountain biking trips in and around the central sections of Newfoundland.

BIRD-WATCHING   If you're from a temperate climate, bird-watching doesn't get much more interesting or exotic than in Newfoundland and Labrador: It's one of the most intensive areas on the continent (and the world) for certain birds. Seabirds typically attract the most attention, and eastern Newfoundland and the Avalon Peninsula are especially rich in bird life. Just south of St. John's—it's offshore from Route 10, near Deer Lake—is **Witless Bay Ecological Reserve** (© **709/635 4520**), a cluster of several islands hosting the largest colony of breeding puffins and kittiwakes in the western Atlantic. On the southern Avalon Peninsula, **Cape St. Mary's** features a remarkable sea stack just yards from easily accessible cliffs that's home to a cacophonous colony of northern gannets.

CAMPING   In addition to the two national parks, Newfoundland maintains a number of provincial parks open for car camping. (About a dozen of these were "privatized" in 1997 and are now run as commercial enterprises, although many still appear on maps as provincial parks.) These are all listed in the provincial travel guide, where you'll also find information about most of the province's private campgrounds.

CANOEING   A glance at a map shows that rivers and lakes abound in Newfoundland and Labrador. Canoe trips can range from placid puttering around a pond near St. John's to world-class descents of Labrador rivers hundreds of miles long. The

---

Tips Sailing by Night

You may find it more convenient to take an **overnight ferry** from North Sydney to Port aux Basques; the ferry sails most nights of the week, departing around midnight and arriving early in the morning. Of course, you'll need to pay extra for your bunk bed or private cabin—but you'll also wake up refreshed for the long driving ahead. In 2007, dormitory-style bunks cost C$16 (US$16/£8) per person and private cabins (which sleep four passengers) cost C$99 (US$99/£50). Check with Marine Atlantic ferries for the latest details and fares of the sleeper service.

It's All in a Name . . .

The official name of this province is "Newfoundland and Labrador." But if I kept writing that out, this book would be twice as long (and heavy). So I'm going to abbreviate it to just "Newfoundland" for most purposes in this chapter. Labradoreans, bear with us. We know you're there.

Department of Tourism produces a free brochure outlining several canoe trips; call 🕿 **800/563-6353.** A popular guide to provincial canoeing is sold in bookstores around the province.

FISHING   Newfoundland and Labrador are legendary among serious anglers, especially those stalking the cagey Atlantic salmon, which can weigh up to 18kg (40 lbs.). Other prized species include landlocked salmon, lake trout, brook trout, and northern pike. More than 100 fishing-guide services on the island and mainland can provide everything from simple advice to complete packages that include bush-plane transportation, lodging, and personal guides. One fishing license is needed for Atlantic salmon, one for other fish, so be sure to read the current *Newfoundland & Labrador Hunting and Fishing Guide* closely for current regulations. It's available at most visitor centers, or by calling 🕿 **800/563-6353.** To request it by mail, write the provincial tourism office at P.O. Box 8700, St. John's, NL A1B 4J6.

HIKING & WALKING   Newfoundland has an abundance of trails, but you'll have to work a bit harder to find them here than in the provinces to the south. The most obvious hiking trails tend to be centered around national parks and historic sites, where they are often fairly short—good for a half-day's hike, rarely more. But Newfoundland has hundreds of trails, many along the coast leading to abandoned communities. Some places are finally realizing the recreational potential for these trails, and are now publishing maps and brochures directing you to them. The Bonavista Peninsula and the Eastport Peninsula, both on Newfoundland's east coast, are two areas that are attracting attention for world-class trails that were all but overlooked until recently.

The best-maintained trails are at **Gros Morne National Park** ⭐⭐⭐, which has around 100km (60 miles) of trails. In addition to these, there's also off-track hiking on the dramatic Long Range for backpackers equipped to set out for a couple of days. Ask at the park visitor center for more information.

SEA KAYAKING   With all its protected bays and inlets, Newfoundland is ideal for exploring by sea kayak. But there's a catch: the super-frigid water. You'll need to be well prepared in the event you end up in the drink. Experts traveling with their own gear can pick and choose their destinations; the area northeast of **Terra Nova National Park,** with its archipelago centering around St. Brendan's Island, is one great choice. Novices should stick to guided tours. The aforementioned **Aspenwood** (🕿 **709/673-4255**) in Springdale does half- and full-day guided paddles and rentals, in addition to its mountain-biking options; **Eastern Edge Kayak Adventures** (🕿 **(866/ 782-5925** or 709/773-2201) offers tours and clinics of 1 day and up, mostly on the Avalon Peninsula. **Coastal Safari** (🕿 **877/888-3020** or 709/579-3977; www.coastal safari.com), based in St. John's, is a similar outfitter offering extended paddling tours from May through the end of August.

2 Western Newfoundland: Your Introduction to The Rock

For most travelers arriving by ferry, this region is their first introduction to The Rock. It's like starting a symphony without a prelude, jumping right to the crescendo: There's instant drama in the brawny, verdant Long Range Mountains that run parallel to the Trans-Canada Highway en route to Corner Brook. Then come the towering seaside cliffs of the Port au Port Peninsula, and intriguing coastal villages just waiting for your exploration. This is a polar-opposite travel experience to, say, flying into Charlottetown and lazing along the back roads of Prince Edward Island.

ESSENTIALS

GETTING THERE BY FERRY   Port aux Basques is commonly reached via ferry from Nova Scotia. See "Exploring Newfoundland & Labrador," earlier, for ferry information. The Trans-Canada Highway (Rte. 1) links the major communities of southwestern Canada. Port aux Basques is 874km (543 miles) from St. John's via the Trans-Canada Highway.

GETTING THERE BY PLANE   Western Newfoundland is served by two airports, **Deer Lake,** 50km (30 miles) east of Corner Brook, and **Stephenville,** 80km (50 miles) south of Corner Brook. Both offer service to St. John's, and Goose Bay, Labrador. There are car-rental agencies at both airports and there is a shuttle available from Deer Lake to Corner Brook.

VISITOR INFORMATION   In Port aux Basques, the **Provincial Interpretation and Information Centre** (✆ 709/695-2262) is located on the Trans-Canada Highway about 3km (2 miles) from the ferry terminal. You can't miss it: It's the modern, ecclesiastical-looking building on the right. Inside are displays to orient you regarding the island's regions, and racks aflutter with great forests of brochures. It's open from mid-May to the middle of October daily from 6am to 11pm.

PORT AUX BASQUES

Port aux Basques is a major gateway for travelers arriving in Newfoundland, with ferries connecting the town to Nova Scotia year-round. It's a good way station for those arriving late on a ferry or departing early in the morning; otherwise, it can comfortably be viewed in a couple of hours while either coming or going, or even skipped over altogether en route to much greater scenic treasures.

The **Gulf Museum,** 118 Main St. (✆ **709/695-7604**), across from the Town Hall, has a quirky assortment of artifacts related to local history. The museum's centerpiece is a Portuguese astrolabe dating from 1628, which was recovered from local waters in 1981. Also intriguing is a display about the *Caribou,* a ferry torpedoed by a German U-boat in 1942; 137 people died in the tragedy. The museum is open daily in summer from 9am to 7pm; admission is C$3.50 (US$3.50/£1.75) adults, C$1 (US$1/50p) children, C$5 (US$5/£2.50) family.

On the way out of town you'll pass the **Port aux Basques Railway Heritage Centre,** Route 1 (✆ **709/695-2646**), dedicated to the memory of the *Newfie Bullet,* a much-maligned but now much-reminisced-about passenger train that ran between Port aux Basques and St. John's from 1898 to 1969. (The highway across the island opened in 1966, dooming the train.) The train required 27 hours to make the trip (going a respectable average speed of 48kmph/30 mph), and during a tour of several restored rail cars you'll learn how the train made the run through deep snows of winter, how the passengers slept at night (very cozily, it turns out), and what life aboard the mail car and caboose was like. Tours given by railway-costumed staff last 15 minutes and cost C$2 (US$2/£1) for adults, C$5 (US$5/£2.50) per family, free for students. It's a good quick stop for rail enthusiasts or those with kids. The museum is open from mid-June through mid-September daily 9 am to 9 pm.

Departing from the edge of Railway Heritage Centre is the **T'Railway** ⊛, a coast-to-coast, nearly 900km (560-mile) pathway being converted from the old train line. It's used by pedestrians, bikers, and ATVers, and in this stretch it runs through marsh and along the ocean to Cheeseman Park and beyond. It's a good spot to get your mountain bike limbered up for further adventures.

WHERE TO STAY

About a half-dozen hotels and B&Bs offer no-frills shelter to travelers at Port aux Basques. The two largest are **Hotel Port aux Basques,** Route 1 (🕐 **877/695-2171** or 709/695-2171), and **St. Christopher's Hotel,** Caribou Road (🕐 **800/563-4779** or 709/695-3500). Both might be described as "budget modern," with clean, basic rooms in architecturally undistinguished buildings. I'd give St. Christopher's the edge since it's located on a high bluff with views of the town and the harbor. Both have around 50 rooms and charge from around C$75 to C$150 (US$75–US$150/ £38–£75) for a double.

WHERE TO DINE

Dining opportunities are limited. Both hotels mentioned above have dining rooms, serving basic, filling meals. A short walk from the ferry terminal on the boardwalk is the **Harbour Restaurant,** at easy-to-remember 1 Main St. (🕐 **709/695-3238**). It's a family-style restaurant that serves budget-friendly meals with entrees around C$5 to C$14 (US$5–US$14/£2.50–£7), most C$10 (US$10/£5) or less. Expect fried fish, fried chicken, fish cakes, sandwiches, and the like. Most tables have good views of the harbor.

CORNER BROOK

Corner Brook is Newfoundland's second-largest city. Like St. John's, it's also dramatically sited—in this case, on the banks of the glimmering Humber River, which winds down through verdant mountains from beyond Deer Lake, then turns the corner to flow into Humber Arm. The hills on the south shore of the Humber are nearly as tall as those in **Gros Morne National Park,** making a great backdrop for the town, which has gradually expanded up the shoulders of the hills.

This is a young city with a long history. The area was first explored and charted in 1767 by Capt. James Cook, who spent 23 days mapping the islands at the mouth of the bay. But it wasn't until early in the 20th century that the city started to take its present shape. Copper mines and the railroad brought in workers; in the early 1920s the paper mill, which still dominates downtown, was constructed. By 1945 it was the largest paper mill in the world.

The city has grown beyond its stature as a mill town, and has a more vibrant feel than other spots anchored by heavy industry. This is no doubt aided in large part by the energy from two institutions of higher learning: **Sir Wilfred Grenfell College of Memorial University of Newfoundland,** and the **College of the North Atlantic.** You'll also find well-developed services and suppliers, including grocery stores, banks, hotels, and restaurants. This is your last chance to stock up and indulge if you're headed to Gros Morne—from here on out, you'll be dependent on small grocery stores and mom-and-pop restaurants.

The **Corner Brook Museum and Archive,** 2 West St. (📞 **709/634-2518**), is housed in a solid 1920s-era building that once was home to customs offices, the court, and the post and telegraph offices. A visit here offers a quick way to learn just how young the city really is (grainy black-and-white photos show empty hills surrounding the paper mill as late as the 1920s), and how civilized it has become since its establishment. An assortment of locally significant artifacts (a prominent doctor's desk, ship models) rounds out the collection. The museum is open daily from 9am to 7pm, mid-June through August; the rest of the year, by appointment only. Admission is C$5 (US$5/£2.50) adults, C$3 (US$3/£1.50) students, and children under age 12 enter for free.

WHERE TO STAY

Corner Brook is home to several convenient chain motels. Among others, you'll find the **Mamateek Inn,** 64 Maple Valley Rd. (📞 **800/563-8600** or 709/639-8901), near the tourist information booth, and the **Greenwood Inn & Suites,** 47 West St. (📞 **800/399-5381** or 709/634-5381), which is within walking distance of the city's best restaurant (see below); it recently changed hands and upgraded itself. Double rooms go for C$90 up to C$120 (US$90–US$120/£45–£60) at the Mamateek, and up to C$195 (US$195/£98) at the Greenwood. Camping is offered on the north banks of the Humber at **Kinsmen Prince Edward Park** *(★★* (© **709/637-1580**), with 80 sites spread along a bluff. Both fully serviced (C$20/US$20/£10) and unserviced sites (C$15/US$15/£7.50) are available. The campground is open from June to mid-September.

Glynmill Inn *(★ Value*   This Tudor inn is set in a quiet, parklike setting—an easy stroll to the services and shops of West Street. Built in 1924 and extensively renovated in 1994, the four-story hotel's appealing detailing will charm you. (The place was designated a Registered Heritage Structure in 2001.) Rooms are tastefully decorated with colonial reproductions; the popular Tudor Suite has a private Jacuzzi. You'll get far more character here than at the chain motels in town, for about the same price. The inn's two eating rooms, the Carriage Room and the Wine Cellar, are quite popular among local diners; the setting can feel a bit institutional (they do a rousing business with conventions and banquets), but the food is nevertheless pretty good. There's also a commodious pub and a little art gallery on the inn premises.

1 Cobb Lane (near West St.), Corner Brook, NL A2H 6E6. © **800/563-4400** or 709/634-5181. Fax 709/634-5106. www.glynmillinn.ca. 81 units. C$79–C$155 (US$79–US$155/£40–£78) double. AE, DC, MC, V. **Amenities:** 2 dining rooms; bar; fitness center; business center; laundry service. *In room:* A/C, TV, fridge (some units), coffeemaker, hair dryer, iron/ironing board.

WHERE TO DINE
Thirteen West *(★★* GLOBAL   Western Newfoundland's best restaurant can easily hold its own with the top restaurants in St. John's, both in terms of quality of food and with its casual but professional service. Tucked along shady West Street in an unobtrusive building (there's a patio fronting the street for that rare balmy night), the kitchen does an outstanding job preparing top-notch meals and the staff knows how to make good service seem easy. At lunchtime look for offerings like grilled strip loin spiced Montréal style, salmon salad, or a warm seafood salad of mussels, shrimp, scallops, and bacon. In the evening, you might find a menu of such items as grilled salmon with a dill pesto, roasted rack of lamb, barbecued chicken with Cajun shrimp and black-pepper sauce, or a seafood platter. Don't leave without sampling at least one of the delightful desserts, which have usually included such standards as crème caramel and profiteroles along with more inventive selections such as sautéed bananas with a rum-pecan-caramel sauce and vanilla ice cream.

13 West St. © **709/634-1300**. Reservations recommended. Main courses C$6–C$13 (US$6–US$13/£3–£6.50) lunch, C$16–C$28 (US$16–US$28/£8–£14) dinner. AE, DC, MC, V. Mon–Fri 11:30am–2:30pm and 5:30–9:30pm (Fri until 10:30pm); Sat 5:30–10:30pm; Sun 5:30–9:30pm (summer until 10:30pm).

3 Gros Morne National Park: One of Canada's Treasures *(★(★(★*

Gros Morne National Park is one of Canada's greatest natural treasures, and few who visit here fail to come away with a sense of awe. In fact, it's officially designated as one of the *world's* greatest natural treasures: In 1987, the park was declared a UNESCO World Heritage Site, largely due to the importance of a section of the park known as the **Tablelands.** This geological quirk formed eons ago, when a portion of the earth's mantle broke loose during continental drifting and was forced to the surface, creating an eerie, rust-colored tableau. (See "Journey to the Center of the Earth," below, for more information.)

The park is divided into two sections, north and south, riven by the multiarmed Bonne Bay (locally pronounced like "Bombay"). Alas, a ferry connecting the two areas has not operated for years, so exploring both sections by car requires some backtracking. The park's visitor center and most tourist services are found in the village of **Rocky Harbour** in the north section—but you'd be shortchanging yourself to miss a detour through the dramatic **southern section,** a place that looks to have had a rough birth, geologically speaking.

To do Gros Morne justice, plan on spending at least 3 days here. (A week would not be too much if you're an ardent hiker.) Excellent hikes and awe-inspiring boat rides can take you right into the heart of the park's wildest places. If you'd prefer to let someone else do the planning for you, contact **Gros Morne Adventures** (© 800/685-4624 or 709/458-2722; www.grosmorneadventures.com), which organizes guided sea kayaking and hiking excursions throughout the park.

ESSENTIALS

GETTING THERE   From the Trans-Canada Highway in Deer Lake, turn west on Route 430 (the Viking Trail). This runs through the northern section of the park; it's 71km (44 miles) in all from Deer Lake to Rocky Harbour. To reach the southern section, turn left (south) on Route 431 in Wiltondale; from the turn, it's 27km (17 miles) to Woody Point.

VISITOR INFORMATION   The park's main **visitor information center** (© 709/458-2417) is just south of Rocky Harbour on Route 430. It's open daily from 9am to 9pm in summer, from 9am to 5pm most days in spring and fall (but weekdays only in early May and Oct), and closed from November to April. The center features exhibits on park geology and wildlife; there's also a short film about the park that's picturesque but not terribly informative. Interactive media kiosks are exceptionally well done; you can view video clips depicting highlights of all hiking trails and other attractions simply by touching a video screen. The center is also the place to stock up on field guides, as well as to request backcountry camping permits.

Across the bay just outside of Woody Point on Route 431 en route to Trout River is the new **Discovery Centre.** This building is an enlightening stop, with interactive exhibits, a fossil room, and a multimedia theater to help make sense of the Gros Morne landscape. It's open mid-May through early October; more information is available at the visitor center.

FEES   All visitors must obtain a permit for any activity within the park. From mid-May through early October, the daily entrance fees are C$8.90 (US$8.90/£4.45) adults, C$7.65 (US$7.65/£3.80) seniors, C$4.45 (US$4.45/£2.20) children 6 to 18, and C$18 (US$18/£9) family; in the off season, fees are somewhat lower. Annual passes are available for about C$45 (US$45/£23) per adult or C$89 (US$89/£45) per family, a great deal if you'll be entering the park on at least 3 different days.

GROS MORNE'S SOUTHERN SECTION

The road through the southern section of Gros Morne dead-ends at Trout River, and accordingly it seems to discourage convenience-minded visitors who prefer loops and through-routes. That's too bad, because the south contains some of the park's most dramatic terrain. Granted, you can glimpse the rust-colored Tablelands from north of Bonne Bay near Rocky Harbour and call it a day, thereby saving the 48km (30-mile) detour. But without actually walking through that desolate landscape, you miss much of its impact. The southern section also contains several lost-in-time fishing villages that predate the park's creation in 1973, and a new Discovery Centre (see above) with exhibits documenting the park's natural history.

The region's scenic centerpiece is **Trout River Pond,** a landlocked fjord some 15km (9 miles) long. You can hike along the north shore to get a great view of the Narrows, where cliffs nearly pinch the pond in two. For a more relaxed view, sign up for a boat tour, which surrounds you with breathtaking panoramic views. From late May to mid-October, the **Trout River Pond Boat Tour** ⚓ (© **866/751-7500** or 709/451-7500) is an excursion on the pond aboard a 40-passenger boat. The 2½-hour trips are offered three times daily in summer, once daily in the shoulder seasons; cost is C$35 (US$35/ £18) per adult, C$18 (US$18/£9) children ages 7 to 17, and C$75 (US$75/£38) families. Tickets are sold at a gift shop between the village of Trout River and the pond; watch for signs.

For a superb panorama encompassing ocean and mountains, watch for the **Lookout Trail** ⚓ just outside of Woody Point en route to Trout River. This steep trail is about 5km (3 miles) round-trip. The **Tablelands Trail** departs from barren Trout River gulch and follows an old gravel road up to Winterhouse Brook Canyon. You can bushwhack along the rocky river a bit farther upstream, or turn back. It's about 2km (1.2 miles) each way, depending on how adventurous you feel. This is a good trail to get a feel for the unique ecology of the Tablelands. Look for the signboards that explain the geology at the trail head, and at the roadside pull-off on your left before reaching the trail head.

Experienced hikers looking for a challenge should seek out the **Green Gardens Trail** ⚓⚓⚓. There are two trail heads to this loop; I recommend the second one (closer to Trout River). You begin by trekking through a rolling, infertile landscape, and then the plunge begins as you descend down, down, and down wooden steps and a steep trail toward the sea. The landscape grows lusher by the moment, until you're walking through extraordinary coastal meadows on crumbling bluffs high above the churning surf.

The trail then follows the shore northward for about 4 or 5km (2.5–3 miles) more, and this next stretch might be one of the most picturesque coastal trails in the world. In July, the irises and a whole symphony of wildflowers bloom wildly. The entire loop is about 16km (9.4 miles), and is rugged and very hilly; allow about 5 or 6 hours for the hike. An abbreviated version involves walking clockwise on the loop to the shore's edge, then retracing one's steps back uphill. That's about 9km (5.5 miles) in total.

WHERE TO STAY

The two **drive-in campsites** in the southern section—**Trout River Pond** and **Lomond**—both offer showers and nearby hiking trails. Of the two, Trout River Pond is more dramatic, located on a plateau overlooking the pond; a short stroll brings you to the pond's edge with wonderful views up the fjord. Lomond is near the site of an old lumber town and is popular with anglers. Camping is about C$18 to C$25 (US$18–US$25/£9–£13) per site. Three exceptional **backcountry campsites** are located along the Green Garden Trail; registration at the park visitor center is required, and the fee is about C$10 (US$10/£5) per night.

Victorian Manor B&B This 1920s home is one of the most impressive in the village, though that doesn't mean it's extravagant. It's more solid than flamboyant, set in a residential neighborhood near the town center and a few minutes' walk to the harbor. The attractive guesthouse has its own whirlpool. If that's booked, ask for one of the efficiencies, which cost about the same as the inn rooms but afford much greater convenience, especially considering the slim dining choices around town.

Journey to the Center of the Earth

If you see folks wandering around the **Tablelands** 𝒜𝒜 looking all twitchy and excited, they're probably amateur geologists. The Tablelands are one of the world's great geological celebrities, and a popular destination among pilgrims who come to worship at the altar of classic rock—not rock and roll. *Rocks.*

To the uninitiated, the Tablelands area—south of Woody Point and the south arm of Bonne Bay—seem rather bleak and barren. These muscular hills rise up, rounded and rust-colored, devoid of trees or even the slightest green haze of vegetation. Up close, you discover just how barren they are—little plant life seems to have established a toehold here yet.

There's a reason for that. Some 570 million years ago, this rock was part of the earth's mantle—the part of the earth lying just underneath its crust. Riding on continental plates, two landmasses collided forcefully, and this piece of mantle was driven up and over the crust, rather than being forced under (as is usually the case). Years of erosion followed, and what's left is a rare X-ray of the earth's oldest bones. But this rare, ancient rock is so rich in magnesium that few plants can stand to live here, giving the landscape a barrenness that seems more appropriate for a desert landscape than for the rainy mountains of Newfoundland.

Main Rd. (P.O. Box 165), Woody Point, NL A0K 1P0. ⓒ 866/453-2485 or 709/453-2485. www.grosmorne.com/ victorianmanor. 7 units. C$60–C$95 (US$60–US$95/£30–£50) double. Rates include continental breakfast. AE, MC, V. **Amenities:** Jacuzzi; coin-op washers and dryers. *In room:* TV, kitchenette, fridge, coffeemaker, no phone.

WHERE TO DINE

Seaside Restaurant 𝒜 SEAFOOD   The Seaside has been a Trout River institution for years; it's a notch above the tired fare you often find in tiny coastal villages, though service can be slow if the place fills up. The restaurant is nicely polished without being swank, and it features magnificent harbor views. The pan-fried cod is superb, as are a number of other seafood dishes. (Sandwiches and burgers are at hand for those who don't care for seafood.) Desserts are quite good; inquire about whether the partridge-berry parfait is on the menu.

Main St., Trout River. ⓒ 709/451-3461. Main courses C$10–C$19 (US$10–US$19/£5–£9.50). MC, V. Daily noon–8pm. Closed mid-Oct to June.

GROS MORNE'S NORTHERN SECTION

Gros Morne's northern section flanks Route 430 for some 72km (45 miles) between Wiltondale and St. Paul's. The road winds through the abrupt, forested hills south of Rocky Harbour; beyond these, the road levels out, following a broad coastal plain covered mostly with bog and tuckamore. East of the plain rises the extraordinarily dramatic monoliths of the Long Range. This section contains the park's visitor center as well as the park's one must-see attraction: **Western Brook Pond.**

The hardscrabble fishing village of Rocky Harbour is your best bet for tourist services, including motels, B&Bs, laundromats, and such. *One caveat:* This area lacks a good, big grocery store or supply depot of the sort you would expect to be located near a big national park of such international significance. What you'll find instead are a few modest grocers.

If you have time for only one activity in Gros Morne—and heaven forbid that's the case—make it the **BonTours boat trip** (© **888/458-2016** or 709/458-2016; www.bontours.ca) up **Western Brook Pond** ✹✹. The trip begins with a 20-minute drive north of Rocky Harbour. Park at the Western Brook Pond trail head, then set off on an easy 2-mile, 45-minute hike across the northern coastal plain, with interpretive signs explaining the wildlife and bog ecology you'll see along the way. (Keep an eye out for moose.) Always ahead, the mighty monoliths of the Long Range rise high above, inviting and mystical, more like a 19th-century scene from the Rockies than the Atlantic seaboard.

You'll soon arrive at pond's edge, where there's a small collection of outbuildings near a wharf. This is where the tour boats dock up. Once aboard one of the vessels (there are two), you'll set off into the maw of the mountains, winding between the sheer rock faces that define this landlocked fjord. The spiel on the boat is recorded, but even that unfortunate bit of cheese fails to detract from the grandeur of the scene. You'll learn about the glacial geology and the remarkable quality of the water, which is considered among the purest in the world. Bring lots of film and a wide-angle lens. The trip lasts about 2½ hours and costs C$39 (US$39/£20) adults, C$15 (US$15/ £7.50) students 12 to 16 (must be accompanied by an adult), C$12 (US$12/£6) children under 11, and C$79 (US$79/£40) per family—they only take cash, no credit cards. Buy tickets for the tour at the dock, or at the Ocean View Motel in Rocky Harbour. Also note that you must acquire a **park admissions pass** before arrival to take this tour.

Even if you're not planning on signing up for the Western Brook Pond boat tour, you owe yourself a walk up to the pond's wharf and possibly beyond. The 45-minute one-way trek from the parking lot north of Sally's Cove follows a well-trod trail and boardwalk through boglands and boreal forest. When you arrive at the wharf, the **view** ✹✹ to the mouth of the fjord will take your breath away. A well-executed outdoor exhibit explains how glaciers shaped the dramatic landscape right in front of you.

Two spur trails continue on either side of the pond for a short distance. The **Snug Harbour Trail** ✹✹, which follows the northern shore to a primitive campsite (registration required), is especially appealing. After crossing a seasonal bridge at the pond outlet, you'll pass through scrubby woods before emerging on a long and wonderful sand and pebble beach; this is a great destination for a relaxed afternoon picnic and requisite nap. The hike all the way to Snug Harbour is about 8km (5 miles) one-way.

WHERE TO STAY & DINE

The main campground is **Berry Hill,** which is just north of Rocky Harbour. There are nearly 150 drive-in sites, plus a handful of walk-in sites on the shores of the pond itself. It's just 10 minutes' drive from the visitor center, where evening activities and presentations are held. **Shallow Bay** ✹ has 50 campsites and is near the park's northern border and an appealing 4km (2½-mile) sand beach. Both of these campgrounds have showers and flush toilets; sites at each cost C$18 to C$25 (US$18–US$25/£9–£13) per night, depending on the time of year. **Green Point** ✹✹ is an intimate, popular campground with just 18 sites; it's a "primitive" campsite, meaning there are only pit toilets (no flush toilets) and showers. These campgrounds fill up fast; it's best to arrive as soon after the 2pm checkout time as possible to secure a site. Reservations are very helpful for all three sites during summer; call © **800/563-6353.**

Tips Visiting More than One Park? We'll Take a (Viking) Pass

If you're going to be visiting Gros Morne National Park, and then also folding one or another of the province's natural and historic treasures into your trip before or after going there—L'Anse aux Meadows, Red Bay, Port au Choix, or the Grenfell Historic Properties—pick up a **Viking Trail Pass** (valid for 7 days from the date of issue) at any of the park offices listed. This pass gives you unlimited admission to all of them for one flat fee. It costs C$40 (US$40/£20) per adult, C$34 (US$34/£17) seniors, C$19 (US$19/£11) children, and C$81 (US$81/£41) for a family of four.

The largest motel in town is the **Ocean View Motel** (© 800/563-9887 or 709/458-2730), located on the harbor. It has 52 rather basic rooms (some with small balconies and bay views). The motel is popular with bus tours, and often fills up early in the day. Rooms are C$115 to C$155 (US$115–US$155/£58–£78) double in season.

Gros Morne Cabins   The best thing about the Gros Morne Cabins? Pulling up and seeing long lines of freshly laundered sheets billowing in the sea breeze, like a Christo installation. Two dozen trim, tidy log cabins are clustered along a grassy rise overlooking Rocky Harbour, and all have outstanding views toward the Lobster Cove Head Lighthouse. Inside they're new and clean (even sporting good televisions and wireless Internet access), more antiseptic and modern than time-worn. Each is equipped with a kitchenette, while gas barbecues are scattered about the property. The complex also includes a store and a laundromat, and there's a pizza place across the street for relaxed sunset dining at your own picnic table.

Main St. (P.O. Box 151), Rocky Harbour, NL A0K 4N0. © 888/603-2020 or 709/458-2020. Fax 709/458-2882. 25 units. C$99–C$179 (US$99–US$179/£50–£90) double. AE, DC, MC, V. Pets allowed. **Amenities:** Laundry service. *In room:* TV, kitchenette, Jacuzzi (1 unit).

Sugar Hill Inn *&*   This appealing green-shingled inn opened in 1991 on the road between Rocky Harbour and Norris Point. The six rooms are quite comfortable, though some guests might find them a bit condolike or sterile. Nice touches abound, like hardwood floors in all units, plenty of natural wood trim, well-selected furnishings, phones and televisions throughout, and a shared sauna and hot tub in a cedar-lined common room. The upstairs sitting room is spacious and bright, with a fireplace and modern furnishings; it's a good spot to swap local adventure ideas with other guests. The inn's dining room serves breakfast and dinner daily, and there's now a cottage for rent (with queen bed and a Jacuzzi), as well. Surprisingly, this inn is open all year-round—a bonus if you're visiting off season.

115–129 Sexton Rd. (P.O. Box 100), Norris Point, NL A0K 3V0. © 888/299-2147 or 709/458-2147. Fax 709/458-2166. www.sugarhillinn.nf.ca. 7 units. C$89–C$175 (US$89–US$175/£45–£88). Rates include continental breakfast. AE, MC, V. **Amenities:** Restaurant; bar; Jacuzzi; sauna; laundry service. *In room:* A/C, TV, fridge, Jacuzzi (some units).

Wildflowers Country Inn   This 1930s home near the village center was modernized and updated before its opening as a B&B in 1997, giving it a casual country look inside. Rooms here are tastefully appointed if a bit small, though two newer rooms have private bathrooms and are a bit larger. The neighborhood isn't especially scenic (there's an auto repair shop across the way, for instance), but the house is peaceful, the innkeepers exceptionally friendly, and this is a great choice for those seeking reason-ably priced lodging with a comfortable, homey feel.

Main St. N (P.O. Box 291), Rocky Harbour, NL A0K 4N0. © **888/811-7378** or 709/458-3000. Fax 709/458-3080. www.wildflowerscountryinn.com. 6 units. C$89–C$129 (US$89–US$129/£45–£65) double. Rates include full break-fast. Mid-Oct to May, call about availability. MC, V. **Amenities:** Restaurant; bar; laundry service. *In room:* TV, no phone.

4 The Great Northern Peninsula: Way Off the Beaten Path

On a map, the Great Northern Peninsula looks like a stout cudgel threatening the shores of Labrador. If Newfoundland can even be said to have a beaten track, rest assured that this peninsula is well, well off it. It's not nearly as mountainous or starkly dramatic as Gros Morne, but the road here unspools for miles through tuckamore and evergreen forest, along coastline and the base of geologically striking hills. There are few services and even fewer organized diversions. But it has early history in spades, a handful of fishing villages clustering along its rocky coast, and some of the most unspoiled terrain you'll find in North America. The road here is in good condition, the chief hazard being the occasional stray moose or caribou—or, in spring, the infre-quent polar bear wandering through, hungry after a long trip south on ice floes.

ESSENTIALS
GETTING THERE BY CAR   Route 430, also called the Viking Trail, runs from Deer Lake (at the Trans-Canada Hwy.) to St. Anthony, a 419km (260-mile) jaunt.

GETTING THERE BY PLANE   Tiny **St. Anthony Airport** (airport code YAY; © **709/454-3192**), where rental cars are available, serves the area. The airport is on Route 430 approximately 30km (18 miles) west of St. Anthony. Two Newfoundland airlines service the airstrip with flights: **Air Labrador** (© **800/563-3042** or 709/758-0002; www.airlabrador.com) and **Provincial Airlines** (© **800/563-2800** or 709/576-1666; www.provair.com).

VISITOR INFORMATION   For information about the Great Northern Peninsula and the Viking Trail, contact the **Viking Trail Tourism Association,** P.O. Box 251, St. Anthony, NL A0K 4T0 (© **877/778-4546** or 709/454-8888; www.vikingtrail.org).

PORT AU CHOIX
A visit to Port au Choix (pronounced "Port a shwaw") means a short, 13km (8-mile) detour off the Viking Trail, out to a knobby peninsula that's home to a sizable fishing fleet. The windswept landscape overlooking the sea here is low, predominantly flat, and lush with wind-blown grasses. Simple homes speckle the landscape; most are of recent vintage.

Port au Choix National Historic Site ★★ *Kids*   Back in 1967 a local businessman began digging the foundation for a new movie theater in Port au Choix. Seems inno-cent enough. Suddenly, he came upon some bones. A lot of bones. In fact, what he stumbled upon turned out to be a remarkable burying ground for what are now called the Maritime Archaic Indians. These early Natives relied chiefly on the sea, and among the artifacts recovered here are slate spears and antler harpoon tips, which fea-tured an ingenious toggle that extended into the fish as sort of a delayed-action mech-anism after being thrust into flesh. You'll learn about this fascinating historic episode at the modern visitor center. Staff here can also direct you to nearby sites including the original burial ground, now surrounded by village homes. (Don't miss Philip's

---

Tips **The Viking Trail**

This beautiful drive to Newfoundland's northern tip is wild and solitary, with views of curious geology and a wind-raked coast. You'll pass Gros Morne National Park and Port au Choix, and you'll end up at one of the world's great historic sites—L'Anse aux Meadows.

Garden.) You can also visit a nearby **lighthouse,** scenically located on a blustery point thrusting into the Gulf of St. Lawrence. Plan to spend about 90 minutes exploring the area.

Point Riche Rd., Port au Choix. © **709/861-3522.** Admission C$7.15 (US$7.15/£3.60) adults, C$5.90 (US$5.90/£2.95) seniors, C$3.45 (US$3.45/£1.75) children 6–16, C$18 (US$18/£9) families. Visitor center June to early Oct daily 9am–6pm.

L'Anse aux Meadows *✮✮✮ Value*   Newfoundland's northernmost tip is not only exceptionally remote and dramatic, it is also one of the most historically significant archaeological sites in the world. A Viking encampment dating from A.D. 1000 was discovered here in 1960, and has been thoroughly documented by archaeologists in the decades since. An especially well-conceived and managed National Historic Site probes this earliest chapter in European expansion, and an afternoon spent here piques one's imagination. This ancient Norse encampment included three large halls, along with a forge where nails were made from locally mined pig iron. As many as 100 Vikings lived here for a time, including some women; the Vikings abandoned the settlement after a few years to return to Greenland and Denmark, thus ending the first experiment in the colonization of North America by Europeans. It's telling that no graves have ever been discovered here.

Start your visit by viewing the recovered artifacts in the visitor center and watching the half-hour video about the site's discovery. Then sign up for one of the free guided tours of the site. The guides here offer considerably more information than the simple markers around the grounds do.

Rte. 436, L'Anse aux Meadows. © **709/623-2608.** Admission C$10 (US$10/£5) adults, C$8.90 (US$8.90/£4.45) seniors, C$5.20 (US$5.20/£2.60) children 6–16, C$26 (US$26/£13) families. June to early Oct daily 9am–8pm; rest of the year, call ahead for status.

WHERE TO STAY & DINE

Lightkeeper's Seafood Restaurant *✮* SEAFOOD   Located at scenic Fishing Point Park, this cafe with the amazing view is housed in a simple but handsome white building with fire-engine-red trim overlooking the ocean. Inside, it's sparsely decorated and flooded with natural light. You can't beat the panoramic scenery, and the proprietors have helpfully placed binoculars on the windowsills for you to scope out the whales and icebergs while waiting for your meal. The daily specials are fresh and tasty. Perennial favorites include butter-fried cod, cod tongues, steaks, burgers, ribs, and seafood chowder; the truly famished can order the Commissioner's Feast, which includes samples of "all the seafood in the house" plus lobster or crab.

Fishing Point Park. © **877/454-4900** or 709/454-4900. Reservations not accepted. Main courses C$8–C$22 (US$8–US$22/£4–£11). AE, MC, V. Daily 11:30am–9pm. Closed Nov–May.

Tickle Inn at Cape Onion *✮ Finds*   If you're seeking that end-of-the-world flavor, you'll be more than a little content here. Set on a remote cove at the end of a road near

Newfoundland's northernmost point (you can see Labrador across the straits), the Tickle Inn occupies a solid fisherman's home built around 1890 by the great-grandfather of the current innkeeper, David Adams. (He's a retired school counselor from St. John's.) After lapsing into decrepitude, the home was expertly restored in 1990, and has recaptured the charm of a Victorian outport home. Its rooms are small but comfortable; all of them share three communal bathrooms.

Before dinner, guests often gather in the parlor and enjoy snacks and complimentary cocktails; afterward, there's often music or other entertainment. **Dining room** ✯ meals are served family-style each evening. (Your only other option is to drive a considerable distance to the nearest restaurant.) The food is excellent, featuring local cuisine—Cape Onion soup with a touch of port, or paella with local seafood, for instance. Time your visit for berry season and you can expect them to pop up in the flan or other desserts. One of the highlights of a stay here is the small but superb network of hiking trails maintained by the Adams family; they ascend open bluffs to amazingly beautiful views of the Labrador Straits. The inn is about a 40-minute drive from L'Anse aux Meadows.

R.R. 1 (Box 62), Cape Onion, NL A0K 4J0. ℂ 866/814-8567 or 709/452-4321. Fax 709/452-2030. www.tickleinn.net. 4 units, none with private bathroom. C$55–C$70 (US$55–US$70/£28–£35) double. Rates include deluxe continental breakfast. MC, V. Closed Oct–May. **Amenities:** Dining room. *In room:* No phone.

5 Terra Nova National Park

Terra Nova National Park is an exceedingly pleasant spot with lots of boreal forest and coastal landscape, along with a surplus of low, rolling hills. Within its boundaries, forest and shoreline are preserved for wildlife and recreation and make for excellent exploration. But the terra, however nova it is, isn't likely to take your breath away (with one possible exception: the cliffs and hills at the mouth of Newman Sound). More than likely, a visit here will simply leave you soothed and relaxed. Activities and facilities at Terra Nova have mostly been designed with families in mind.

If your goal is to put some distance between yourself and the noisy masses, head for the backcountry section of the park. A number of campsites are accessible by foot, canoe, or ferry only; once there, you'll be able to scout for bald eagles and shooting stars in complete silence.

ESSENTIALS

GETTING THERE   Terra Nova is located on the Trans-Canada Highway. It's about 232km (144 miles) from St. John's, and 609km (378 miles) from Port aux Basques.

VISITOR INFORMATION   The **Visitor Interpretation Centre** (ℂ 709/533-2801) at the Saltons Day-Use Area, about 5km (3 miles) north of the Newman Sound Campground, is open daily June to mid-October from 9am to 7pm (limited hours after Labour Day, closed Oct to early Jan). There's a kiosk at the campground, as well, open 8am to midnight in high season, shorter hours out of season.

FEES   A park entry fee is required of all visitors, even those just overnighting at a park campground. Fees are C$5.45 (US$5.45/£2.75) per day adults, C$4.70 (US$4.70/£2.35) seniors, C$2.70 (US$2.70/£1.35) children 6 to 16, C$14 (US$14/£7) family. Annual passes are available for about C$27 (US$27/£14) per adult or C$68 (US$68/£34) per family.

EXPLORING THE PARK

A trip to the park should begin with a visit to the spiffy, modern **Visitor Information Centre** (see above). It's located on a scenic part of the sound, encased in verdant hills, and from here the sound looks suspiciously like a lake. Oceangoing sailboats tied up at the wharf will suggest otherwise, however. The center has a handful of exhibits focusing on local marine life, and many are geared toward kids. There's a touch tank where you can scoop up starfish and other aquatic denizens, and informative displays on life underwater. Especially nifty is an underwater video monitor that allows you to check out the action under the adjacent wharf with a joystick and zoom controls. There's also a **Wet Lab,** where you can conduct experiments under the guidance of a park naturalist. The center is free with your paid park admission. You'll also find a snack bar and gift shop here.

The park has 77km (48 miles) of maintained **hiking trails.** Many of these are fairly easy treks of an hour or so through undemanding woodlands. The booklet you'll receive when you pay your entrance fee offers descriptions of the various trails. Among the more popular is the 4.5km (2.8-mile) **Coastal Trail** 𝒜𝒜, which runs between Newman Sound Campground and the information center. You get great views of the sound, and en route you pass the wonderfully named **Pissing Mare Falls.**

The park also lends itself quite nicely to **sea kayaking.** If you've brought your own boat, ask for route suggestions at the information center. (Overnight trips to Minchin and South Broad coves are good options, as are day trips to Swale Island.)

For a more passive view from the water, consider a tour with **Ocean Watch Tours** (© **709/533-6024**), which sails in a converted fishing boat four times daily from the wharf at the visitor center. You're all but certain to spot bald eagles and, with some luck, whales and icebergs. The tours typically cost around C$35 (US$35/£18) for a 2-hour tour and around C$45 (US$45/£23) for a 3-hour tour, half price for children. Reservations are recommended during peak season, when the tours take place three times daily.

WHERE TO STAY & DINE

Campgrounds are the only option within the park itself; the main campground is at **Newman Sound.** It has 355 campsites (mostly of the gravel-pad variety) set in and around spruce forest and sheep laurel clearings. Amenities include free showers, limited electrical hookups, grocery store and snack bar, evening programs, laundromat, and hiking trails. Be aware that the campground can be quite noisy and bustling in peak season. Fees are C$18 to C$28 (US$18–US$28/£9–£14), depending on the level of services and time of year.

At the north end of the park, the town of Eastport is 16km (10 miles) from the Trans-Canada Highway on Route 310, and offers several places to stay overnight. From May to the end of October, try **The Doctor's Inn Bed & Breakfast,** 5 Burden's Rd., Eastport, NL A0G 1Z0 (© **877/677-3539** or 709/677-3539), with six rooms priced at C$70 to C$95 (US$70–US$95/£35–£48). Right on a sandy beach are the **Seaview Cottages,** 325 Beach Rd., Eastport, NL A0G 1Z0 (© **709/677-2271**), open May through September, with 23 basic cottages, a small indoor heated pool, minigolf, a barbecue area, and other family-friendly amenities. Rates are C$60 to C$75 (US$60–US$75/£30–£38).

Terra Nova Golf Resort 𝒜 (Kids)   This modern three-story resort is a short drive off Route 1, about 2km (1¼ miles) south of the park's southern entrance; it sits on 220

acres of oceanfront property. Even better, it's adjacent to both the 6,546-yard, par 71 **Twin River Golf Course** 🏌️🏌️—one of Atlantic Canada's most scenic, best-regarded links even if it's sometimes overlooked in favor of Nova Scotian courses—and the 9-hole Eagle Creek Golf Course. This hotel isn't lavish at all; it features bland, cookie-cutter rooms. On the other hand, it's clean, comfortable, and well located for a golfing holiday or exploring the park. It's a popular spot with families, since kids can roam the grounds, splash around the pool, and congregate at the downstairs video games. Note that about two-thirds of the rooms consist of two double beds; the rest are king-bedded, queen-bedded, have pullout sofas, or (in a few cases) are suites with full kitchens. The resort's dining room is open daily for breakfast and dinner.

Rte. 1, Port Blandford, NL A0C 2G0. © **709/543-2525**. Fax 709/543-2201. www.terranovagolf.com. 89 units. C$101–C$157 (US$101–US$157/£51–£79) double. AE, DC, DISC, MC, V. **Amenities:** 2 restaurants; bar; outdoor pool; 2 tennis courts; Jacuzzi; sauna; game room. *In room:* A/C, TV, kitchenette (some units).

6 The Bonavista Peninsula: Into Newfoundland's Past 🏛

The Bonavista Peninsula juts northeast into the sea from just south of Terra Nova National Park. It's a worthy side trip for travelers fascinated by the island's past. You'll find a historic village, a wonderfully curated historic site, and one of the province's most intriguing lighthouses. It's also a good spot to see whales, puffins, and icebergs.

Along the south shore of the peninsula is **Trinity**, an impeccably maintained old village. (It's the only village in Newfoundland where the historic society has say over what can and cannot be built.) Some longtime visitors grouse that it's becoming overly popular and a bit dandified with B&Bs and traffic restrictions. That may be, but there's still a palpable sense of tradition in this profoundly historic spot. Anyway, it's the place for miles to find good shelter and a decent meal.

From Trinity it's about 40km (25 miles) out to the tip of the peninsula. Somewhere along the route, which isn't always picturesque, you'll wonder whether it's worth it. But keep going; it will be worth it. Plan to spend at least a couple of hours exploring the dramatic, ocean-carved point and the fine fishing village of **Bonavista** with its three excellent historic properties.

ESSENTIALS

GETTING THERE Depending on the direction you're coming from, the Bonavista Peninsula can be reached from the Trans-Canada Highway via Route 233, Route 230, or Route 230A. Route 230 runs all the way to the tip of the cape; Route 235 forms a partial loop back and offers some splendid water views along the way. The round-trip from Clarenville to the tip is approximately 232km (144 miles).

VISITOR INFORMATION Consult the **Discovery Trail Tourism Association** (© **866/420-3255** or 709/466-3845; www.thediscoverytrail.org) at 54 Manitoba Dr. in Clarenville. Take Rte. 230A off the Trans-Canada Highway, about 40km (25 miles) south of Terra Nova National Park and 75km (47 miles) from Trinity.

TRINITY 🏛

The tiny coastal hamlet of Trinity, with a year-round population of just 200, once had more residents than St. John's. For more than 3 centuries, from its first visit by Portuguese fishermen in the 1500s until well into the 19th century, Trinity benefited from a long and steady tenure as a hub for traders, primarily from England, who supplied the booming fishing economy of Trinity Bay and eastern Newfoundland. Technological advances (including the railroad) doomed Trinity's merchant class, and the

town lapsed into an extended economic slumber. But even today, you can see lingering traces of the town's former affluence, from the attractive flourishes in much of the
architecture to the rows of white picket fences all around the village.

Start your voyage into the past at the **Trinity Interpretation Centre** (© 709/
464-2042) at the Tibbs House, open 10am to 5:30pm daily from mid-May through
late September. (It's a bit tricky to find.) Here you can purchase tickets, pick up a
walking-tour map, and get oriented with a handful of history exhibits. Entry costs
C$3 (US$3/£1.50) per adult. This ticket also admits you to the Lester-Garland property and the Hiscock House (see below), which keep the same seasons and hours as
the interpretation center.

A minute's walk away is the brick **Lester-Garland Premises** (© 709/464-2042),
often the first stop on travelers' Trinity itineraries. Here you can learn about the
traders and their times. This handsome Georgian-style building is a convincing replica
(built in 1997) of one of the earlier structures, built in 1819. The original was occupied until 1847, when it was abandoned and began to deteriorate. It was torn down
(much to the horror of local historians) in the 1960s, but parts of the building hardware, including some doors and windows, were salvaged and warehoused until the
rebuilding.

Next door is the Ryan Building, where a succession of the town's most prominent
merchants kept shop. The grassy lots between these buildings and the water were once
filled with warehouses, none of which survived. The **Rising Tide Theatre** (© 888/464-
3377 or 709/464-3232) was architecturally styled after one of the warehouses (a good
imagination is helpful in envisioning the others). The 255-seat theater is a good stop
if you enjoy the arts. A short walk away, just past the parish house, is the **Hiscock
House** (© 709/464-2042), a handsome home restored to appear as it might have
been in 1910, and helpful guides fill in the details. Again, the combination Trinity
ticket gets you in here for C$3 (US$3/£1.50) per adult; children under 13 enter for
free.

An entertaining way to learn about the village's history is during the summertime
Trinity Pageant. Local actors lead a peripatetic audience through the streets, acting
out episodes from Trinity's past. For dates and tickets, contact the innovative **Rising
Tide Theatre** (see above).

WHERE TO STAY

Campbell House Bed & Breakfast Inn ★ *Finds*   This handsome 1840 home and
two nearby cottages are set amid lovely gardens on a twisting lane overlooking Fisher
Cove. Two rooms are on the second floor of the main house, and these have a nice historic flair, even to the point that they'll require some stooping under beams if you're
over 5 feet, 10 inches tall. Two rooms are located in a lovely and simple pine-paneled
house just beyond the gardens, and they feature an adjacent waterfront deck and a full
kitchen on the first floor; the Twine Loft (home to a restaurant) also overlooks the
water. An affiliated property, the **Artisan Inn,** offers three similar simple rooms at
C$115 to C$135 (US$115–US$135/£58–£68) double occupancy. Innkeeper Tineke
Gow and her family are great sources of information on local adventures and maintain a wine cellar on the premises. Reserve well in advance for July and August, when
the inn rarely has a free room.

High St., Trinity, Trinity Bay, NL A0C 2S0. © 877/464-7700 or 709/464-3377. www.trinityvacations.com. 3 units plus
3 units in Artisan Inn. C$109–C$230 (US$109–US$230/£55–£115). Rates include full breakfast. AE, DC, MC, V. Closed
Nov–May. **Amenities:** Laundry. *In room:* TV, dataport, kitchenette, hair dryer, iron, no phone.

Village Inn This handsome old inn, located on what passes for a busy street in Trinity (busy with pedestrians, that is), has a pleasantly lived-in feel with its eclectic-but-leaning-toward-Victorian furniture, a front porch for relaxing, and a small dining room that feels as if it hasn't changed a whit in 75 years. The folksy sitting room, with its fireplace, piano, and collections of books and board games, is a popular chill-out spot. Innkeepers Christine and Peter Beamish do a fine job of making guests feel at home here; they also run Ocean Contact, a whale-watch operation that uses an 8m (26-ft.) rigid-hull inflatable. Ask about tour availability when you book.

Taverner's Path (P.O. Box 10), Trinity, Trinity Bay, NL A0C 2S0. ⓒ 709/464-3269. Fax 709/464-3700. www.ocean contact.com. 6 units. From C$100 (US$100/£50) double. Packages available. MC, V. Closed except by arrangement Nov–Apr. Small, well-behaved pets allowed. **Amenities:** 2 dining rooms; pub. *In room:* No phone.

WHERE TO DINE

Eriksen Premises 𝒻 TRADITIONAL   Despite some inelegant touches, this is Trinity's best restaurant and it offers good value. The restaurant shares the first floor of a B&B with a gift shop, and has a homey feel with oak floors, beadboard ceiling, and Victorian accents. (There's also dining on an outside deck, which is especially inviting at lunchtime.) Meals are mostly traditional: cod tongue, broiled halibut, scallops, liver and onion, chicken, and the like. The service and food are a notch above the expected, though. Desserts, like the cheesecake with fresh berry toppings, are especially good.

West St. ⓒ 877/464-3698 or 709/464-3698. Reservations recommended during peak season. Main courses C$5–C$7 (US$5–US$7/£2.50–£3.50) lunch, C$10–C$19 (US$10–US$19/£5–£9.50) dinner. MC, V. Daily 8am–9:30pm. Closed Nov–May.

Village Inn 𝒻 *Finds* TRADITIONAL/VEGETARIAN   The pleasantly old-fashioned dining room at the Village Inn (see "Where to Stay," above) has been known to serve good vegetarian meals, which is an extremely rare species in the Newfoundland kitchen. The options might include a lentil shepherd's pie or a rice-nut casserole. Of course, those looking for comfort food are also well served, with options like chowder, meatloaf, fried cod, liver and onions, a ham plate, or a seafood platter. This is country cooking at its best, everything made from scratch, soups to dessert.

Taverner's Path. ⓒ 709/464-3269. Main courses C$8–C$20 (US$8–US$20/£4–£10); lunch items less. MC, V. Daily 8am–9pm.

BONAVISTA 𝒻

Bonavista is a 45-minute drive from Trinity, and is a strongly recommended day trip for those spending a night or two in the area. The bay here is noted for its icebergs.

The **Ryan Premises National Historic Site** 𝒻 (ⓒ 709/468-1600) opened in 1997, with Queen Elizabeth herself presiding over the ceremonies. Located in downtown Bonavista, the newish site is a very photogenic grouping of white clapboard buildings at the harbor's edge. For more than a century, this was the town's most prominent salt-fish complex, where fishermen sold their catch and bought all the sundry goods needed to keep an outport functioning. The spiffy complex today features an art gallery, local museum, gift shop, hand-crafted furniture store, and an exhibit on the role of the codfish in Newfoundland's history. An hour or two here will go a long way toward helping you make sense of the rest of your visit to this singular island. The property is open daily mid-May through late October from 10am to 6pm. Admission is C$3.95 (US$3.95/£2) adults, C$3.45 (US$3.45/£1.75) seniors, C$1.95 (US$1.95/£1) youths, and C$9.90 (US$9.90/£4.95) family.

On the far side of the harbor, and across from a field of magnificent irises, is the beautiful **Mockbeggar Plantation** ((C) **709/468-7300**). With a few telltale exceptions (note the wonderful 1940s-era carpet in the formal dining room), it shows a strong Victorian influence. The house is managed as a Provincial Historic Site, and admission is C$3 (US$3/£1.50) adults, free for children 12 and under; this ticket also gets you admission to the Cape Bonavista Lighthouse (see below). The house is open to the public mid-May through late September daily from 10am to 5:30pm.

A replica of the ***Matthew*** ((C) **877/468-1497** or 709/468-1493), the ship John Cabot sailed when he first landed in Newfoundland in 1497, floats in Bonavista's harbor. This compact ship is an exacting replica, based on plans of the original ship. (Don't confuse this ship with the other *Matthew* replica, which crossed the Atlantic and sailed around Newfoundland in 1997.) An interpretive center and occasional performances staged wharfside provide context for your tour aboard the ship, which is designed as a floating museum. The ship is open from June to mid-October daily from 10am to 6pm (to 8pm in summer). Admission is C$6.50 (US$6.50/£3.25) adults, C$6 (US$6/£3) seniors, C$2.25 (US$2.25/£1.15) children ages 6 to 16, C$16 (US$16/£8) per family; plan to spend an hour touring the ship.

The extraordinary **Cape Bonavista Lighthouse Provincial Historic Site** (*(C)* 709/468-7444) is located 6km (3¾ miles) north of town on a rugged point. Built in 1843, the lighthouse is fundamentally a stone tower around which a red-and-white wood-frame house has been constructed. You can clamber up narrow stairs to the light and inspect the ingenious clockwork mechanism that kept six lanterns revolving all night, every night between 1895 and 1962. The lighthouse is open daily from mid-May to late September from 10:30am to 5:30pm; admission is C$3 (US$3/£1.50) per adult, free for children 12 and under. (This ticket also includes admission to the Mockbeggar Plantation; see above.)

7 St. John's: Bright Lights, Big City

905km (562 miles) W of Port aux Basques

St. John's (always abbreviated, never spelled out) is a world apart from the rest of Newfoundland. The island's small fishing villages and long empty roads through spruce and bog are imbued with loneliness, quietude, and wildness. St. John's, on the other hand, is surprisingly vibrant, cultured, and bustling. Coming into this city after traveling the hinterlands is like stepping from Kansas into Oz—the picture suddenly seems to burst with color and life.

This attractive port city of more than 100,000 residents crowds the steep hills around a deep harbor. Like Halifax, Nova Scotia, and Saint John, New Brunswick, St. John's also serves as a magnet for youth culture throughout the entire province, and the clubs and restaurants tend to have a more cosmopolitan feel and sharper edge than you might expect from such a provincial, conservative island. The presence of Memorial University—the province's premiere institution of higher learning, less than 2 miles west of the harbor—gives the city yet another shot in the cultural arm.

ESSENTIALS

GETTING THERE BY PLANE   St. John's International Airport ((C) **709/758-8500**; www.stjohnsairport.com) receives flights from Halifax, Montréal, Ottawa, Toronto, and even internationally. The airport is 6.5km (4 miles) from downtown;

taxis from the airport to downtown hotels cost C$15 to C$20 (US$15–US$20/ £7.50–£10).

GETTING THERE BY CAR   St. John's is located 127km (79 miles) from the ferry at Argentia, 874km (543 miles) from Port aux Basques.

VISITOR INFORMATION   The city's main **tourist information office** (© 709/ **576-8106**) is located at 348 New Water St., and open year-round: 9am to 5pm in summer, weekdays from 9am to 4:30pm in the off season. The city's tourism website is at www.stjohns.ca.

GETTING AROUND   Metrobus serves much of the city. Fares are C$2 (US$2/£1) for a single trip. Route information is available at the visitor information center or by calling © **709/722-9400.**

SPECIAL EVENTS   The annual **Newfoundland and Labrador Folk Festival** ✹✹ (© **800/576-8508** or 709/576-8508; www.nlfolk.com) is a 3-day shindig usually held during the first weekend in August; performers from all over the province gather to play at Bannerman Park downtown. (Bring a lawn chair.) It costs C$12 (US$12/ £6) per adult (less for seniors and children) for an afternoon pass or evening pass allowing you access to the entire slate of performers, or C$50 (US$50/£25) for an all-weekend pass.

EXPLORING ST. JOHN'S

The city produces a free, informative and comprehensive pocket-size brochure detailing walking and driving tours of the metro area; it's an outstanding resource for planning and executing your visit to the city. Ask for it at the tourist information office (see above).

DOWNTOWN

Provincial Museum of Newfoundland and Labrador ✹✹ (Kids)   This downtown museum found a new home in 2005, moving to a complex known as The Rooms (the Provincial Art Gallery and Provincial Archives are also located here). It offers a good introduction to the natural and cultural history of the island, through exhibits that both kids and adults can understand and enjoy. The second level features a lesson on canoe building from an Innu Native, while the third level focuses on the process of change as glaciers retreated and Native peoples settled the province; you'll learn about flora and fauna, finding out for example that the moose is *not* native to Newfoundland. (Who knew?) The fourth level suggests how 19th-century life was lived by the province's British settlers, with a recreated fort and stories about Newfoundland's fisheries and a history of the constabulary (in other words, the fuzz). While here, watch for delicate carvings of bear heads and exhibits highlighting the awesome power of the polar bear; special exhibitions include a Canadian heritage quilt project. Allow about an hour for a leisurely tour.

9 Bonaventure Ave. © **709/757-8020.** www.therooms.ca/museum. C$5 (US$5/£2.50) adult, C$4 (US$4/£2) senior, C$3 (US$3/£1.50) children 6–16, C$15 (US$15/£7.50) family. Additional charge for special exhibits; free Wed 6–9pm. June to mid-Oct Mon–Sat 10am–5pm (Wed–Thurs to 9pm), Sun noon–5pm; mid-Oct to May Tues–Sat 10am–5pm (Wed–Thurs to 9pm), Sun noon–5pm.

Signal Hill ✹✹ (Value)   You'll come for the history, but stay for the views. Signal Hill is St. John's most visible and visit-worthy attraction. This rugged, barren hill is the city's preeminent landmark, rising up above the entrance to the harbor and topped

St. John's

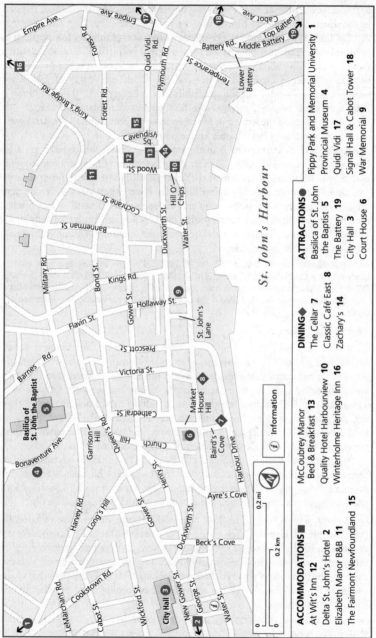

ACCOMMODATIONS ■
At Wit's Inn **12**
Delta St. John's Hotel **2**
Elizabeth Manor B&B **11**
The Fairmont Newfoundland **15**

McCoubrey Manor
Bed & Breakfast **13**
Quality Hotel Harbourview **10**
Winterholme Heritage Inn **16**

DINING ◆
The Cellar **7**
Classic Café East **8**
Zachary's **14**

ATTRACTIONS ●
Basilica of St. John
the Baptist **5**
The Battery **19**
City Hall **3**
Court House **6**

Pippy Park and Memorial University **1**
Provincial Museum **4**
Quidi Vidi **17**
Signal Hall & Cabot Tower **18**
War Memorial **9**

ⓘ Information

0.2 mi
0.2 km

St. John's Harbour

with a craggy "castle" complete with flag fluttering overhead—the "signal" referred to in the name. The layers of history here are rich and complex: Flags have flown atop this hill since 1704, and over the centuries a succession of military fortifications have occupied these strategic slopes, as did three different hospitals. The castlelike structure (which is officially called Cabot Tower) dates from 1897, when it was built in honor of Queen Victoria's Diamond Jubilee and the 400th anniversary of John Cabot's arrival in the new world. The hill secured its spot in history in 1901, when Nobel laureate Guglielmo Marconi received the first wireless transatlantic broadcast—three short dots indicating the letter *S* in Morse code, sent from Cornwall, England—on an antenna raised 120m (394 ft.) on a kite in powerful winds.

A good place to start a tour is in the interpretive center, where you'll get a good briefing about the hill's history. (Military drills and cannon firings still sometimes take place in the field next to the center; check here if you're interested.) From the center, you can follow serpentine trails up the hill to the tower, where you'll be rewarded with breathtaking **views** ✦ of the Narrows and the open ocean beyond—Cape Spear can even be seen in the distance to the south, and look for icebergs in the early summer and whales anytime. Interpretive placards, scattered about the summit, feature engaging photos from various epochs.

Atop Signal Hill at the entrance to St. John's harbor. ✆ **709/772-5367.** Free admission to grounds; admission to interpretive center C$3.95 (US$3.95/£2) adults, C$3.45 (US$3.45/£1.75) seniors, C$1.95 (US$1.95/£1) children 6–16, C$9.90 (US$9.90/£4.95) families. Grounds open year-round; Interpretation Center mid-May to mid-Oct daily 10am–6pm, rest of the year Mon–Fri 8:30am–4:30pm; Cabot Tower Apr to mid-Jan daily 9am–5pm, closed mid-Jan to March.

FARTHER AFIELD
Quidi Vidi ✦   Pronounced "kitty vitty," this tiny harbor village sets new standards for the term *quaint.* The village is tucked in a narrow, rocky defile behind Signal Hill, where a narrow ocean inlet provides access to the sea. It's photogenic in the extreme and a wonderful spot to investigate by foot or bike (it's rather more difficult by car). The village consists mostly of compact homes, including the oldest home in St. John's, with very few shops. Visit here while you can; in recent years, following rancorous local debate, development plans were approved for the addition of modern housing in the area. (There's a microbrewery already, if you're into that.)

To get to Quidi Vidi, follow Signal Hill Road to Quidi Vidi Road; turn right onto Forest Road. From here you can easily connect to Quidi Vidi Lake, where St. John's Regatta is held the first Wednesday in August, as it has been since 1826. Look for the trail leading to the lake from near the entrance to Quidi Vidi, or ask locally.

Fluvarium ✦ *Finds* *Kids*   This low, octagonal structure at the edge of Long Pond (near Memorial University, a few miles west of downtown) actually descends three stories into the earth. The second level features exhibits on river ecology, including life in the riffles (that's where trout spawn) and in shallow pools, which are rich with nutrients. On the lowest level you'll find yourself looking up into a deep pool that's located alongside the building. Watch for brown trout swimming lazily by. Plan to spend about 45 minutes here.

Pippy Park, off Allandale Rd. ✆ **709/754-3474.** www.fluvarium.ca. Admission C$5.50 (US$5.50/£2.75) adults, C$4.50 (US$4.50/£2.25) seniors and students, C$3.50 (US$3.50/£1.75) children under 14. Hours variable but weekdays usually daily 9am–5pm in summer, closed or shorter hours weekends in off season. Guided tours on the half-hour in summer; feeding time 4pm.

Memorial University Botanical Garden ⊛   An abundant selection of northern plants makes this garden well worth seeking out (it's tucked over a wooded ridge on the city's western edge, behind Pippy Park). The main plots are arranged in gracious "theme gardens," including a cottage garden, a rock garden, and a peat garden. Among the most interesting is the Newfoundland Heritage Garden, with examples of 70 types of perennials traditionally found in island gardens. The floral displays aren't as ostentatious or exuberant as you'll find in other public gardens in Atlantic Canada (the gardens of Halifax and Annapolis Royal come to mind), but they will be of great interest to amateur horticulturists curious about boreal plants. Behind the gardens are winding hiking trails leading down to marshy Oxen Pond. Allow an hour for this visit.

306 Mt. Scio Rd. ⓒ 709/737-8590. www.mun.ca/botgarden. Summer admission C$5 (US$5/£2.50) adults, C$3 (US$3/£1.50) seniors, C$1.15 (US$1.15/60p) children 6–18, C$10 (US$10/£5) family. Spring and fall rates discounted. May–Sept daily 10am–5pm; Oct daily 10am–4pm. Take Thorburn Rd. past Avalon Mall; turn right on Mt. Scio Rd.

OUTDOOR PURSUITS

Pippy Park ⊛ (ⓒ 709/737-3655) is on the city's hilly western side adjacent to the university and contains 1,340 hectares (3,311 acres) of developed recreation land and quiet trails. You should definitely visit if you're coming with kids. This popular park is home to the city campground and Fluvarium (see above), as well as miniature golf and regulation-sized golf courses, picnic sites, playgrounds, hiking trails, and more.

One highly recommendable hike (but only if you are *not* afraid of heights) is the **North Head Trail** ⊛⊛, which runs from Signal Hill to an improbable cluster of small buildings between the rock face and the water called **The Battery.** Don't tackle this unless you are reasonably fit; it's no easy stroll.

Here's how to get there: On foot, follow Duckworth Street between the Hotel Newfoundland and **Devon House,** then bear right onto Battery Road. Stay on the main branch (a few smaller branches may confuse you) as the pathway narrows, rises, and falls while skirting a rock face. First you reach the so-called **Outer Battery.** The former fishermen's homes here are literally inches from the road—and not much farther from the water—and most have drop-dead views of the Narrows and the city skyline. There's a whimsical, storybook character to this place, and this real estate is now much sought-after by city residents.

At the end of the Battery you'll cross someone's front porch (it's okay), and it's here that the North Head Trail begins in earnest. It runs along the **Narrows,** past old gun emplacements, up and down heroic sets of steps, and along some narrow ledges (chains are bolted to the rocks as handrails for a little extra security in one place). The trail ascends an open headland before looping back and starting a final ascent up Signal Hill. After some time exploring and soaking up the view, you can save time on the return by walking a paved road back downhill to Duckworth Street where you began.

WHERE TO STAY
EXPENSIVE
Delta St. John's Hotel ⊛⊛ (Kids)   The sleek and modern Delta St. John's is located downtown near City Hall and caters largely to businesspeople. It must be doing something right: It has nearly doubled in room count in recent years. The Delta lacks the views and ineffable sense of class that you'll find at the Fairmont (see below), but has nice touches like ship models in the lobby and a handsome pool table as the centerpiece of the lounge. It's also well situated for prowling the city, and features a number of amenities that choosy travelers will appreciate, such as hair dryers and coffeemakers in

all of the rooms. Management runs a number of children's programs and offers babysitting services as well. The hotel's chummy Mickey Quinn's restaurant, off the lobby, offers breakfast, lunch, and dinner daily.

120 New Gower St., St. John's, NL A1C 6K4. © 888/890-3222 or 709/739-6404. Fax 709/570-1622. www.deltahotels. com. 403 units. C$99–C$650 (US$99–US$650/£50–£325) double. AE, DC, DISC, MC, V. Valet parking C$18 (US$18/ £9); self-parking C$8 (US$8/£4) per day. Pets allowed with advance permission. **Amenities:** Restaurant; indoor pool; health club; Jacuzzi; sauna; children's program; concierge; limited room service; babysitting; laundry service; dry cleaning. *In room:* A/C, TV, minibar, fridge (some units), coffeemaker, hair dryer, iron.

The Fairmont Newfoundland 🏨🏨 The Newfoundland was built in 1982 in a starkly modern style, yet it boasts a refined sensibility and attention to detail that's vaguely reminiscent of a lost era. The designers and architects have been subtle about their best surprises; the lobby has one of the best views of the Narrows in town, but you have to hunt around to find it. It's a wonderful effect, and one that's used nicely throughout. (This helps compensate for the somewhat generic, conference-hotel feel of much of the decor.) The rooms themselves are standard-size and unremarkable, though all have coffeemakers and bathrobes. About half have harbor views. The hotel's lobby is home to three dining establishments.

115 Cavendish Sq. (P.O. Box 5637), St. John's, NL A1C 5W8. © 800/441-1414 or 709/726-4980. Fax 709/576-0554. www.fairmont.com. 301 units. C$219–C$349 (US$219–US$349/£110–£175) double. AE, DC, DISC, MC, V. Valet parking C$17 (US$17/£8.50) per day; self-parking free. Pets C$20 (US$20/£10) extra per night. **Amenities:** 3 restaurants; indoor pool; health club; Jacuzzi; sauna; concierge; business center; salon; 24-hr. room service; babysitting; laundry service; dry cleaning. *In room:* A/C, TV, minibar.

Winterholme Heritage Inn 🏨🏨 This stout, handsome Victorian mansion was built in 1905 and is as architecturally distinctive a place as you'll find in Newfoundland, with prominent turrets, bow-front windows, bold pediments, elaborate molded plaster ceilings, and woodwork extravagant enough to stop you in your tracks. Room 1 is oval-shaped (the original master bedroom to the home) and occupies one of the turrets; it has a Jacuzzi, as well as a king bed. Room no. 7 is another of the most lavish; this former billiards room features a fireplace and a two-person Jacuzzi, along with a plasterwork ceiling and a supple leather wing chair. Attic-level rooms here are less extraordinary, but still appealing with their odd angles and nice touches. The mansion is located about a 10-minute walk from downtown. Limited spa services are available at the inn by appointment.

79 Rennies Mill Rd., St. John's, NL A1C 3R1. © 800/599-7829 or 709/739-7979. Fax 709/753-9411. www.winterholme. com. 11 units. C$129–C$249 (US$129–US$249/£65–£125) double. Rates include full breakfast. AE, DC, MC, V. Free parking. *In room:* TV/DVD, coffeemaker, hair dryer, iron.

MODERATE

At Wit's Inn 🏨🏨 *Finds* Forgive the innkeepers their pun. This lovely century-old home was wonderfully restored and opened as an inn in 1999 by a former Toronto restaurateur. Decorated with a sure eye for bold color and simple style, this is a welcoming urban oasis just around the corner from the Fairmont. The four rooms are not terribly spacious, but neither are they uncomfortably small, and each is nicely furnished with down duvets and VCRs. (The largest room is on the top floor, requiring a bit of a hike.) The beautifully refinished floors and elaborately carved banister here are notable, as are many of the old fixtures (such as the servant's intercom) that have been left intact. A full breakfast is served in the first-floor dining room, wine and cheese are offered in the late afternoon, and there's a butler's pantry for snacking in between times. At Wit's Inn offers luxury touches at a relatively affordable price.

3 Gower St., St. John's, NL A1C 1M9. ⓒ 877/739-7420 or 709/739-7420. www.atwitsinn.ca. 4 units. C$109–C$139 (US$109–US$139/£55–£70) double. Rates include breakfast. AE, MC, V. Free parking. In room: TV/VCR.

Elizabeth Manor B&B ⓐ (Value)   Lodging history note: This is said to have been the first modern B&B proper in St. John's. The Elizabeth—long known as the Prescott, until a recent ownership change—is composed of an unusually attractive grouping of wood-frame town houses. They were substantially renovated and upgraded in 2004, adding more Jacuzzis, as well as sleigh and four-poster beds. Some rooms have carpeting; others have hardwood floors. All are furnished with eclectic antiques; the lower-priced rooms are among the city's better bargains. Guests are welcome to relax on the shared balcony that runs along the back of the building. The same owners also manage a group of suites known as the Randall-Shea suites; inquire about those if you've brought a family.

21 Military Rd. (P.O. Box 204), St. John's, NL A1C 2C3. ⓒ 888/263-3786 or 709/753-7733. Fax 709/738-7434. www.elizabethmanor.nl.ca. 6 units. Peak season C$80–C$199 (US$80–US$199/£40–£100) double; off season C$60–C$169 (US$60–US$169/£30–£85) double. Rates include full breakfast. AE, DC, MC, V. Free parking. Pets allowed. In room: TV, fridge, Jacuzzi (some).

McCoubrey Manor Bed & Breakfast ⓐⓐ (Kids)   McCoubrey Manor offers a convenient downtown location with Victorian charm, and yet also a nicely casual atmosphere. These adjoining 1904 town houses are decorated in what might be called a "contemporary Victorian" style, and its six rooms are quite inviting. Upstairs rooms have private double Jacuzzis; Room no. 1 is brightest and faces the street, while Room no. 2 has a sunken Jacuzzi, oak-mantled fireplace, and trim of British Columbian fir. Just around the corner, the property manages a few other spacious apartments with full kitchens—what they lack in elegance, they make up for in space. Families take note. Evening tea get-togethers and breakfasts in the main inn only add to its charm.

6–8 Ordnance St., St. John's, NL A1C 3K7. ⓒ 888/753-7577 or 709/722-7577. Fax 709/579-7577. www.mccoubrey.com. 6 units plus 4 off-site apts. Peak season C$139–C$199 (US$139–US$199/£70–£100) double; off season C$89–C$179 (US$89–US$179/£45–£90) double. Rates include full breakfast. AE, DC, MC, V. Free parking. Amenities: Laundry. In room: A/C (some units), TV/VCR, kitchenette (some units), fridge (some units), no phone (most units).

Quality Hotel Harbourview   Courteous service and a great downtown location with free parking are among the merits of this modern chain hotel. The rooms are standard-size, but comfortable and clean; they're set apart mainly by their views—ask for one overlooking the Narrows. You can easily walk downtown to restaurants and attractions in a few minutes; the Battery and Signal Hill are a pleasant hike in the other direction. The better-than-average restaurant on-site serves three meals daily.

2 Hill O'Chips, St. John's, NL A1C 6B1. ⓒ 800/228-5151 or 709/754-7788. Fax 709/754-5209. 160 units. C$99–C$159 (US$99–US$159/£50–£80) double. Off-season discounts available. AE, DC, DISC, MC, V. Free parking. Amenities: Restaurant. In room: A/C, TV, coffeemaker, hair dryer, iron.

WHERE TO DINE

Budget travelers should wander up the city's hillside to the intersection of LaMarchant and Freshwater streets. Within a 2-block radius, you'll find numerous options for cheap eats at both eat-in and take-out establishments.

EXPENSIVE

The Cellar 𝄐𝄐 ECLECTIC   The classy interior is a surprise here—the restaurant looks nondescript from the outside. Inside, however, it's as intimate and warm (though never as stuffy) as a fine gentleman's club. The kitchen has been turning out fine meals for a while now, developing a local following for its creativity and consistency. Look for standbys like gravlax, homemade bread, and pastas. Fish is prepared especially well; cuts are often paired with innovative flavors such as ginger or pear. Lunches are even a better bargain: past menus have featured such tasty and offbeat offerings as baked brie in phyllo (with a red-currant chutney) and scallop crepes.

189 Water St. ℂ 709/579-8900. Reservations recommended. Main courses C$9–C$21 (US$9–US$21/£4.50–£11) lunch, C$10–C$34 (US$10–US$34/£5–£17) dinner. AE, DC, DISC, MC, V. Mon–Fri 11:30am–2:30pm and 5:30–9:30pm (Fri until 10:30pm); Sat 5:30–10:30pm; Sun 5:30–9:30pm.

MODERATE

Classic Café East CANADIAN   This come-as-you-are eatery is appropriately named: It's your classic St. John's spot, and everyone in town seems to drop by here at some point. Breakfast is served until 4pm daily, but don't expect toast and tea; the macho entrees (sirloin with eggs, toast, home fries, and baked beans is one) appeal to everyone from burly longshoremen to hungover musicians. Lunch and dinner portions, running to usual diner fare and seafood, are equally generous and surprisingly good.

73 Duckworth St. ℂ 709/726-4444. Main courses C$6–C$8 (US$6–US$8/£3–£4) breakfast and lunch, C$8–C$17 (US$8–US$17/£4–£8.50) dinner. DC, MC, V. Daily 24 hr.

Zachary's TRADITIONAL   This informal spot with wood-slat booths offers a slew of Newfoundland favorites, such as fish cakes, fried bologna (really), and Acadian-style *toutons* (dough fried in pork fat)—and that's just for breakfast. Dinners emphasize seafood; entrees might include grilled salmon, seafood fettuccine, pan-fried cod, and lobster most of the year, and you'll also find plenty of steaks and chicken. Desserts here are homemade; especially tempting are the cheesecake, carrot cake, and date squares. You'll find more inventive spots for dinner, but you probably can't do better for reliable quality when on a budget. Breakfasts, served all day, are outstanding.

71 Duckworth St. ℂ 709/579-8050. Reservations recommended. Main courses C$3.30–C$7.50 (US$3.30–US$7.50/£1.65–£3.75) breakfast, C$6–C$9 (US$6–US$9/£3–£4.50) lunch, C$11–C$20 (US$11–US$20/£5.50–£10) dinner. AE, MC, V. Daily 7am–11pm.

ST. JOHN'S AFTER DARK

The nightlife in St. John's is extraordinarily vibrant, and you will be doing yourself an injustice if you don't spend at least one evening on a pub crawl.

Your first stop for local music and cordial imbibing should be **George Street** 𝄐, which runs for several blocks near New Gower and Water streets, close to City Hall. Every St. John's resident confidently asserts that George Street is home to more bars per square foot than anywhere else on the planet; being unable to track down a global authority that tracks and verifies pubs per square foot, I cannot verify this mighty large boast. But the street is packed with energetic pubs and lounges—some fueled by beer, others by testosterone, still others (these are my favorite) by lively Celtic fiddling. At places with live music, cover charges are universally cheap, and rarely top C$5 (US$5/£2.50).

For blues and traditional music, there's the lively **Fat Cat Blues Bar,** 5 George St. (ℂ 709/739-5554), with acts scheduled almost every single night. (It's closed Mon, however.) For a more upscale spot with lower decibel levels, try **Christian's Bar,** 23

George St. (© **709/753-9100**), which also serves specialty coffees. **Trapper John's,** 2 George St. (© **709/579-9630**), is known for its outstanding provincial folk music.

The Ship Inn, at 265 Duckworth St. (© **709/753-3870**), is a St. John's mainstay featuring a variety of local musical acts that complement rather than overwhelm the place's cozy atmosphere.

8 The Southern Avalon Peninsula

The Avalon Peninsula—or just The Avalon, as it's commonly called—is home to some of Newfoundland's most memorable and dramatic scenery, including high coastal cliffs and endless bogs. More good news: It's also relatively compact and manageable, and is closed enough to the big city that it can be viewed either on longish day trips from St. John's or in a couple of days of poking around. It's a good destination for anyone who's short on time yet wants to get a taste of the islander's particular brand of wildness. The area is especially notable for its bird colonies, as well as its herd of wild caribou. The bad news? It's physically thrust out into the north Atlantic, a place where cold and warm currents collide—resulting in legendary fogs and blustery, moist weather. Bring a rain suit and come prepared for bone-numbing dampness and occasional slow driving through pea-soup conditions.

ESSENTIALS

GETTING THERE   Several well-marked and well-maintained highways follow the coast of the southern Avalon Peninsula, though few roads cross the damp and spongy interior. A map is essential.

VISITOR INFORMATION   Your best bet is to stop in the **St. John's tourist information office** (see earlier in this chapter) or at the well-marked tourist bureau just up the hill from the Argentia ferry before you begin your travels. Witless Bay has a **tourist information booth** (© 709/334-2609) stocked with a handful of brochures. It's open irregularly.

WITLESS BAY ECOLOGICAL RESERVE

The Witless Bay area, about 34km (21 miles) south of St. John's, makes an easy day trip from the city, or can serve as a launching point for an exploration of the Avalon Peninsula. The main attraction here is the **Witless Bay Ecological Reserve** ⭐ (© 709/635-4520), comprising four islands a short boat ride offshore. Literally millions of seabirds nest and fish here, and it's a spectacle even if you're not a bird-watcher.

On the islands you'll find the largest puffin colony in the western Atlantic Ocean, with some 60,000 puffins burrowing into the grassy slopes above the cliffs, and awkwardly launching themselves from the high rocks. The tour boats are able to edge right along the shores, about 6 or 7.5m (20–25 ft.) away, allowing puffin-watching on even foggy days. Also on the islands is North America's second-largest murre colony.

While the islands are publicly owned and managed, access is via privately operated tour boat, several of which you'll find headquartered along Route 10 in Bay Bulls and Bauline East. It's worth shopping around since prices can vary considerably.

Bay Bulls is the closest town to St. John's, and is home to three of the more popular tours: **Mullowney's** (© 877/783-3467 or 709/334-3666), operating late May through late September; **O'Brien's** (© 877/639-4253 or 709/753-4850), operating mid-April through mid-October; and **Gatherall's** (© 800/419-4253 or 709/334-2887).

Two-and-a-half-hour tours from here range generally between C$32 and C$45 (US$32–US$45/£16–£23) per adult, though you'll want to check ahead for the latest rates.

FERRYLAND 🍴

Historic Ferryland is among the most picturesque of the Avalon villages, set at the foot of rocky hills on a harbor protected by a series of abrupt islands at its mouth.

Ferryland was among the first permanent settlements in Newfoundland. In 1621, the Colony of Avalon was established here by Sir George Calvert, first baron of Baltimore (he was also behind the settlement of Baltimore, Maryland). Calvert sunk the equivalent of C$4 million into the colony, which featured luxe touches like cobblestone roads, slate roofs, and fine ceramics and glassware from Europe. So up to date was the colony that privies featured drains leading to the shore just below the high-tide mark, making these the first flush toilets in North America (or so the locals insist). Later the Dutch, and then the French, sacked the colony during ongoing squabbles over territory, and eventually it was abandoned.

Recent excavations have revealed much about life here nearly 4 centuries ago. Visit the **Colony of Avalon Interpretation Centre** 🍴 (© 877/326-5669 or 709/432-3200) with its numerous glass-topped drawers filled with engrossing artifacts, and then ask for a tour of the six archaeological sites currently being excavated (the tour is included in the cost of admission). Other interpretive exhibits include a reproduction of a 17th-century kitchen, and three gardens of the sort you might have overseen had you lived 400 years ago. After your tour, take a walk to the lighthouse at the point (about 1 hr. round-trip), where you can scan for whales and icebergs. Ask for directions at the museum.

The site is open daily mid-May through early October, usually from 9am to 7pm (10am–5pm May–June); admission is C$6 (US$6/£3) adults, C$5 (US$5/£2.50) seniors, C$4 (US$4/£2) students, C$3 (US$3/£1.50) children age 5 to 14, and C$15 (US$15/£7.50) families.

WHERE TO STAY & DINE

The Downs Inn   Overlooking the harbor, this building served as a convent between 1914 and 1986, when it was converted to an inn. The rather simple furnishings might reflect its heritage as an institution, rather than a historic building. (Much of the religious statuary was left in place.) Ask for one of the two front rooms, where you can watch for whales from your windows. The front parlor has been converted to a tea-room, where you can order a pot of tea and a light snack such as carrot cake or a rhubarb tart.

Irish Loop Dr. (P.O. Box 69), Ferryland, NL A0A 2H0. © 877/432-2808 or 709/432-2808. Fax 709/432-2659. acostello@nf.sympatico.ca. 4 units. C$55–C$75 (US$55–US$75/£28–£38) double. Rates include full breakfast. MC, V. Closed mid-Nov to mid-May. Small pets allowed. **Amenities:** Laundry service. *In room:* No phone.

AVALON WILDERNESS RESERVE

Where there's bog, there are **caribou** 🍴. Or at least that's true in the southern part of the Avalon, which is home to the island's largest caribou herd, numbering some 13,000 of these magnificent animals. You'll see signs warning you to watch for them along the roadway. The caribou roam freely throughout a 1,700-sq.-km (656-sq.-mile) reserve, so it's largely a matter of happenstance to find them. Your best bet is to scan the high upland barrens along Route 10 between Trepassey and Peter's River—an area that's actually just outside the reserve.

On Route 90 between St. Catherines and Hollyrood is the **Salmonier Nature Park** ꜛꜛ (ⓒ **709/229-7189**), where you're certain to see caribou—along with other wildlife—if you can't find the herd on the reserve described above. This intriguing and well-designed park is fundamentally a 2.5km-long (1.5-mile) nature trail, almost entirely on boardwalk, which tracks through boglands and forest and along streams and ponds. Along the route are more than a dozen unobtrusive pens, in which orphaned or injured wildlife can be observed. (It's the only such facility in the province.) Among the animals represented: arctic fox, snowy owl, moose, bald eagle, mink, otter, beaver, and lynx. It's located 11km (6¾ miles) south of the Trans-Canada Highway; and admission is free. The gates open in summer daily from 10am to 6pm, then to 4pm from Labour Day until (the Canadian) Thanksgiving Day, when the park closes for winter. It remains closed from early October to the end of May.

CAPE ST. MARY'S

Cape St. Mary's Ecological Reserve ranks high on my list of favorite places on Newfoundland. Granted, it's off the beaten track—some 97km (60 miles) from the Trans-Canada Highway—but it's worth every mile.

Cape St. Mary's Ecological Reserve ꜛꜛ   This natural reserve is home to some 5,500 pairs of northern gannets: big, noisy, beautiful, graceful white birds with cappuccino-colored heads and black wingtips. While they can be seen wintering off the coast of Florida and elsewhere to the south, they're seldom seen in such cacophonous numbers as they are here. Most are nesting literally right on top of one another on a compact, 100m (328-ft.) sea stack. At any given moment hundreds are flying above, around and below you, too, which is all the more impressive given their huge, nearly 2m (6½-ft.) wingspan.

You needn't take a boat ride to see the colony. Start your visit at the visitor center, which offers a quick and intriguing introduction to the indigenous bird life. Then walk 15 minutes along a grassy cliff-top pathway—through harebell, iris, and dandelion—until you arrive at a dizzying cliff just a couple of dozen yards from the sea stack (it's close enough to be impressive even in a dense fog). You'll be looking straight down onto the birds. Also nesting on and around the island are some 10,000 pairs of murre, 10,000 kittiwakes, and 100 razorbills. Guided tours are offered for a fee, and are worthwhile; so is the summer performance series of evening concerts, if it's on. Note that admission to the reserve was free in 2007, though this could change in the future.

14km (9 miles) off Rte. 100 (5km/3 miles east of St. Bride's). ⓒ **709/277-1666**. Free admission. 1½-hr. guided tours C$7 (US$7/£3.50). Daily 9am–7pm. Grounds open year-round; interpretive center May–Oct.

WHERE TO STAY & DINE

Atlantica Inn and Restaurant   The Atlantica won't win points for charm—it's a basic, aluminum-sided box among some of the newer houses in the village. But it offers great value at the price, and the three rooms are well enough maintained and comfortable, if a bit small. The attached restaurant is by and large the only game in town, offering inexpensive meals daily.

Rte. 100, St. Bride's, NL A0B 2Z0. ⓒ **888/999-2860** or 709/337-2860. Fax 709/337-2860. 3 units. C$45–C$55 (US$45–US$55/£23–£28) double. MC, V. **Amenities:** Restaurant. *In room:* No phone.

Bird Island Resort ꜛ (Value) (Kids)   This modern, unaffected motel (a resort it is emphatically *not*) is located behind the town food market, where you'll stop in to ask for a room. It's the best choice in town, especially for families, and offers unexpected amenities such as a laundry room open to guests, tiny fitness room, and minigolf course (rooms come with clubs and balls). Rooms themselves vary in size; three-quarters of them are cottages. The double efficiency cottage units feature separate sitting rooms, and some have good newish kitchenettes, which come in handy given the dearth of restaurants in town. Families with kids will especially appreciate those. Room nos. 1 through 5 all have these kitchenettes, in fact, and all face the ocean—which means terrific views, assuming the fog hasn't moved in yet. The motel units here are basic, but as clean and updated as those at a Hampton This or a Comfort That.

Rte. 100, St. Bride's, NL A0B 2Z0. (© 888/337-2450 or 709/337-2450. Fax 709/337-2903. www.birdislandresort.com. 20 units. C$69–C$99 (US$69–US$99/£35–£50) double. AE, MC, V. *In room:* TV, kitchenette (some units), coffeemaker.

9 The Labrador Coast: Wilderness Adventure & More

Yes, Labrador may be highly remote and poorly understood. Despite that, however, it has long played an outsized role in the history of Atlantic Canada. For centuries, its many-toothed coastline was famed for robust fisheries, and itinerant fleets plied these waters both harvesting a bounty of Atlantic seafood. The empty landscape here has served much the same function that the American West frontier has played in the course of American history—it has become a land of opportunity, seemingly bottomless with natural resources (once fish and furs, but now primarily raw ore), as well as a place where tough outdoorspeople historically test their mettle against a harsh environment, stalking big game, big salmon, big views, and big quiet.

Only about 30,000 people live in all of Labrador: about 13,000 in western Labrador, about 8,000 in Happy Valley–Goose Bay, and the remainder spread thinly along and around the many-tongued coast. Approximately four-fifths of those born here remain here for life; strong ties bind family and neighbors, although these close-knit communities typically welcome visitors warmly. Many visitors come here for the sportfishing of brook trout, Atlantic salmon, arctic char, lake trout, white fish, and northern pike. Others come for wilderness adventure, hiking, and camping beneath the undulating northern lights. Still others are simply curious to see such a remote part of the world.

THE LABRADOR STRAITS

The Labrador Straits are the easiest part of Labrador to explore from Newfoundland. The southeast corner of Labrador is served by ferries shuttling between St. Barbe, Newfoundland, and Blanc Sablon, Québec (which is almost right on the Québec-Labrador border). From Blanc Sablon, you then travel on the (only) road, which runs 77km (48 miles) northward, dead-ending at the hamlet of Red Bay; plans call for extending this road in the future, but that could take another decade.

Ferries are timed such that you can cross over in the morning, drive to Red Bay, and still be back for the later ferry to Newfoundland. Such a hasty trip isn't recommended, however. It's better to spend a night, when you'll have a chance to meet the people, who offer the most compelling reason to visit.

The **MV** *Apollo* (© 866/535-2567) ferry runs from mid-April until ice season, usually sometime in mid-January. The crossing takes about 1 hour and 30 minutes, and reservations are encouraged in summer because some seats are first come, first served. The one-way fares in 2007 were C$23 (US$23/£12) for a car and driver, C$7.50 (US$7.50/£3.75) per additional passenger; there are discounts for seniors and youths. Remember that you pay a nonrefundable C$10 (US$10/£5) deposit if you do reserve in advance; miss the boat, and you don't get it back.

The terrain along the Labrador Straits is rugged, the colors muted except for a vibrant stretch of green along the Pinware River. The few small houses are clustered close together; during winter, it's nice to have neighbors so nearby. Homes here are often brightened up with "yard art"—replicas of windmills, wells, churches, and the like.

In summer, icebergs float by the coast while whales breach and spout offshore. The landscape is covered with cotton grass, clover, partridgeberries, bakeapples, fireweed, buttercups, and bog laurel. Fogs roll in frequently; they will either stay awhile, or roll right back out again. Capelin come and go as well—these tiny migrating fish crash-land onshore by the thousands during a week in late June or early July, when local residents rush to the beach, scoop up the fish, and carry them proudly home where they become the unfortunate stars of quick and easy suppers.

In past years, there has been a "Gateway to the Labrador Straits" visitor information center set up in the small, restored St. Andrews Church in **L'Anse-au-Clair,** the first town you will pass through after the ferry landing; check to see if it's open as you're passing through. The local tourism association has developed several footpaths and trails in the area. Don't forget to ask about the mysterious "fairy holes," either. (I'm not giving the secret away here.)

If you come in mid-August, plan to attend the annual **Bakeapple Folk Festival,** celebrating the local berry that stars in desserts both here and in Newfoundland.

EXPLORING THE LABRADOR STRAITS

Drive the "slow road" that connects the villages of the Labrador Straits. Traveling southwest to northeast, here's some of what you'll find along the way.

In L'Anse-au-Clair, **Moores Handicrafts,** 8 Country Rd., just off Route 510 (© **709/ 931-2186**), sells handmade summer and winter coats, traditional cassocks, moccasins, knitted items, handmade jewelry, and other crafts, as well as homemade jams. They also do traditional embroidery on Labrador cassocks and coats, and if you stop on the way north and choose your design, they'll finish it by the time you return to the ferry—even the same day. Prices are quite reasonable. The shop, run by the Moores family, is open daily in season from 9am to as late as 10pm.

The **Point Amour Lighthouse** ★★ (© 709/927-5825), at the western entrance to the Strait of Belle Isle, is the tallest lighthouse in the Atlantic provinces and the second tallest in all of Canada. The walls of this slightly tapered, circular tower (built in 1858) are 2m (6½-ft.) thick at the base; the dioptric lens up top was imported from Europe for the princely sum of C$10,000—a lot at the time. This light kept watch for submarines during World War II, and is still in use; in fact, it was maintained by a resident lightkeeper right up until 1995. Remember to climb the 122 steps to reach good views from the top. The lighthouse is open to the public daily from mid-May to September 10am to 5:30pm, with an admission fee of C$3 (US$3/£1.50) adults, free for children 12 and under. This is about a 3km (2-mile) detour off the main road.

After you pass the fishing settlements of **L'Anse-au-Loup** ("Wolf's Cove") and West St. Modeste, the road follows the scenic Pinware River, where the trees start becoming noticeably taller. Along this stretch of road, you'll also see glacial erratics— big odd boulders deposited by the melting ice cap. **Pinware River Provincial Park** ★ (© 709/927-5516), open June through mid-September, is about 42km (26 miles) from L'Anse au Clair and offers a picnic area, hiking trails, and 15 simple campsites with neither flush toilets nor showers for C$10 (US$10/£5) per night. There's a C$5 (US$5/£2.50) fee per car to enter the park. The 81km-long (50-mile) Pinware River, which passes through the park, is known for its trout and salmon fishing; ask the rangers about the provincial rules and license requirements if you're interested.

The highway ends in **Red Bay.** Here, the interesting **Red Bay National Historic Site** 𝒜𝒜 (𝒞 **709/920-2051** or 709/920-2142) showcases artifacts from the late 1500s, when Basque whalers came here in numbers to hunt right and bowhead whales. Beginning in 1977, excavations began turning up whaling implements, pottery, glassware, and even partially preserved seamen's clothing. If you're really gung-ho about this sort of thing, you can arrange tours of sites on **Saddle Island** 𝒜, the home of Basque whaling stations in the 16th century. Or you can simply scope out the island from afar: the observation deck on the third floor of the visitor center has a good view of it. Admission to the historic site complex is C$7.15 (US$7.15/£3.60) adults, C$5.90 (US$5.90/£2.95) seniors, C$3.45 (US$3.45/£1.75) ages 6 to 16, C$18 (US$18/£9) family. The site is open daily from 9am to 6pm early June through early October, closed the rest of the year.

WHERE TO STAY & DINE

Beachside Hospitality B&B 𝒜 A stay here offers an excellent opportunity to meet a local family and learn firsthand about life in this region of Labrador. Three bedrooms each have separate entrances, though two must share use of a bathroom. There's a whirlpool bath in the house, and guests have access to a communal phone and television room. Home-style meals are available by arrangement, or you can cook your own in a kitchen or outdoors on the grill; the friendly owners also sell homemade breads, jams, and jellies, and sometimes arrange Newfoundland jigs or other events.

9 Lodge Rd., L'Anse-au-Clair, Labrador, A0K 3K0. 𝒞 **709/931-2338.** Fax 709/931-2275. 3 units, 1 with private bathroom. C$45 (US$45/£23) double. Rates include continental breakfast. MC, V. **Amenities:** Jacuzzi. *In room:* Kitchenette, no phone.

Grenfell Louie A. Hall Bed & Breakfast *Value* History buffs love the Grenfell Hall—it was built in 1946 by the International Grenfell Association as a nursing station, and there's plenty of reading material about the coast's early days. The rooms here are furnished with basic, contemporary-country furniture, and all share bathrooms; there's also a common room with TV, VCR, and fireplace. A sixth unit, a private cottage, sports four double beds. The innkeepers can arrange to transport you to and from the ferry, if needed. (If you're just curious about the place and want to visit it, museum-style, you're invited to stop in for a small donation.) Evening meals are available by advance arrangement, and usually feature seafood such as cod or salmon along with homemade bread, preserves, and dessert. A full breakfast costs extra.

3 Willow Ave. (P.O. Box 137), Forteau, Labrador, A0K 2P0. 𝒞 **877/931-2916** or 709/931-2916. Fax 709/931-2916. 6 units (5 with shared bathroom). Inn rooms C$50–C$65 (US$50–US$65/£25–£33) double; cottage C$75–C$100 (US$75–US$100/£38–£50). MC, V. Rates include continental breakfast. MC, V. Closed Nov–Apr. *In room:* Iron, no phone.

Lighthouse Cove B&B Hosts Cecil and Rita Davis have lived in this simple home, overlooking rocks, water, and beach, for more than 4 decades, so they can tell you much about the region—and, since they live here, it's one of the rare inns in the province that stays open year-round. A light breakfast is included in your room rate; full breakfast and seafood supper can be requested, with a charge for the dinners. From the house you can walk a footpath right to the Point Amour Lighthouse, a great bonus.

3 Main St. (P.O. Box 225), L'Anse-Amour, Labrador, A0K 3J0. 𝒞 **709/927-5690.** Fax 709/927-5690. 3 units share 2½ bathrooms. C$40 (US$40/£20) double. Rates include continental breakfast. MC, V. *In room:* No phone.

Northern Light Inn ⭐ *Kids*   The largest and most modern hotel in the region, and the one closest to the ferry, the Northern Light has long offered comfortable, well-maintained rooms, a good gift shop, friendly staff, and a big dining room. All the inn's rooms possess modern, business-hotel amenities such as air-conditioning, hair dryers, voicemail, and even (in some cases) Jacuzzis. In addition to the pasta and seafood doled out in the dining room, there are fried-chicken and pizza chain outlets on-site as well, making this perhaps a good choice for those with restless kids.

58 Main St. (P.O. Box 92), L'Anse au Clair, Labrador, A0K 3K0. © 800/563-3188 from Atlantic Canada or 709/931-2332. Fax 709/931-2708. www.northernlightinn.com. 59 units. C$89–C$159 (US$89–US$159/£45–£80) double. AE, DC, MC, V. **Amenities:** Restaurant; business center; laundry service. *In room:* A/C, TV, hair dryer, Jacuzzi (some units).

7

Montréal

by Leslie Brokaw

Montréal and Québec City, just 3 hours apart by car, have a stronger foreign flavor than other cities in Canada. Here you can best see the duality of the country's French and British roots. One Canada, English and Calvinist in origin, is said to be staid, smug, and work-obsessed. The other, French and Catholic but highly secular, is thought of as more creative, lighthearted, and inclined to see pleasure as the end purpose of labor. Or so go the stereotypes.

The blending occurs in particularly intense fashion in Québec province's largest city, Montréal. The first language of the majority of residents is French (Francophones); most of the remaining population speaks English primarily (Anglophones). A growing number of residents have another primary tongue, and many younger residents blend both French and English phrases into their conversation, making up a unique regional patois.

Travelers will likely find Montréal an urban near-paradise. The subway system, called the Métro, is modern and swift. Streets are safe. Montréal's best restaurants are the equals of their south-of-the-border compatriots in every way.

Just 10 years ago, something of a bleak mood prevailed throughout the region. It was driven by a lingering recession and the possibility that the province would fling itself into independence from the rest of Canada. Lately, though, something else has been going on. Provincial elections in early 2007 dealt a crushing defeat to the separatist Parti Québécois. The Canadian dollar, as every traveler will discover, has strengthened against its U.S. and European counterparts.

In Montréal, a building boom has filled vacant lots all over downtown, and the city has become modern in every regard, with skyscrapers in unexpected shapes and uncorporate colors. The historic Vieux-Montréal, or "Old Montréal" district, and the Vieux-Port (Old Port) waterfront promenade have been beautifully preserved. And a large residential neighborhood, the Plateau Mont-Royal, is filled with boutiques, cafes, artist lofts, and miles of restaurants. The city above ground is mirrored by another below: The underground city is a labyrinth of shops, restaurants, and offices where an entire winter can be avoided in coatless comfort.

Montréal is terrific for walking and has miles of bike paths on its urban streets and out of the city into green spaces. And not many cities have a mountain at their core. True, reality insists that Montréal doesn't either, because what it calls a "mountain" most other people would call a "large hill." Still, Montréal is named for Mont-Royal—the "Royal Mountain"—and the park that surrounds it is a soothing urban pleasure. Stroll through it or, for a more romantic trip, take a horse-drawn calèche to the top for a sunset view of the city and St. Lawrence River.

1 Essentials
GETTING THERE
BY PLANE   The **Aéroport International Pierre-Elliot-Trudeau de Montréal** (© 800/465-1213 or 514/394-7377; www.admtl.com; airport code YUL), known less cumbersomely as Montréal-Trudeau Airport, is 23km (14 miles) southwest of downtown. A C$716-million expansion was completed in 2006, although work is still underway to build a new area that will encompass a U.S. Customs area and preboarding screening checkpoint. Wi-Fi is available throughout the airport. **Aéroport Mirabel,** 55km (34 miles) northwest of the city, is an all-cargo facility.

Montréal-Trudeau is served by the shuttle bus **L'Aérobus** (© 514/631-1856; www.laerobus.qc.ca), which travels between the airport and four downtown stops, including The Fairmont The Queen Elizabeth (Fairmont Le Reine Elizabeth) hotel at 900 bd. René-Lévesque ouest. One-way fares are C$14 (US$14/£7) for adults, C$13 (US$13/£6.50) for seniors, and C$11 (US$11/£5.50) for children. Free minibuses take passengers to 39 major hotels from its last stop at Station Centrale Berri (also known as the Station Centrale d'Autobus, the city's main bus terminal). Buses from Montréal-Trudeau run approximately every 20 to 30 minutes between 7am and 2am daily. The ride to the Fairmont stop is about 25 minutes if traffic isn't tangled.

A taxi trip to downtown Montréal is a flat fare of C$35 (US$35/£18) plus tip.

BY TRAIN   Montréal has one intercity rail terminus, **Gare Centrale (Central Station)**, 895 rue de la Gauchetière ouest (© 514/989-2626), below The Fairmont The Queen Elizabeth hotel. The station is connected to the Métro subway system (Bonaventure Station).

BY BUS   The central bus station, called **Station Centrale d'Autobus** (© 514/842-2281), is at 505 bd. de Maisonneuve est. It has a bar, a cafeteria, and an information booth. Beneath the terminal is the Berri-UQAM Métro station, the junction of several important Métro lines and a good starting point for trips to most quarters of the city. (UQAM—pronounced "*Oo*-kahm"—stands for Université de Québec à Montréal.) Alternatively, taxis usually line up outside the terminal building.

BY CAR   Driving north from the U.S., the entire ride is on expressways. From New York City, all but the last 40 or so miles of the 603km (375-mile) trip are within New York State on Interstate 87. At the border, I-87 links up with Canada's Autoroute 15, which goes straight to Montréal.

From Boston, I-93 north goes up through New Hampshire (and the beautiful Franconia Notch in the White Mountains) and merges into I-91 north to cross the tip of Vermont. At the border, I-91 becomes Autoroute 55. Signs lead to Autoroute 10 west to Montréal. From Boston to Montréal is about 518km (322 miles).

VISITOR INFORMATION
The main information center for visitors in downtown Montréal is the large **Info-touriste Centre,** at 1255 rue Peel (© 877/266-5687 or 514/873-2015; Métro: Peel). It's open daily and the bilingual staff can provide suggestions for accommodations, dining, car rentals, and attractions.

In Vieux-Montréal (Old Montréal) there's a small **Tourist Information Office** at 174 rue Notre-Dame est, at the corner of Place Jacques-Cartier (Métro: Champ-de-Mars). It's open daily in warmer months, Wednesday through Sunday in winter, and has brochures, maps, and a helpful staff.

Tips **Montréal: Where the Sun Rises in the South**

For the duration of your visit to Montréal, you'll need to accept local directional conventions, strange as they may seem. The city borders the St. Lawrence River, and as far as locals are concerned, that's south, looking toward the United States. Never mind that the river, in fact, runs almost north and south at that point. For this reason, it has been observed that Montréal is the only city in the world where the sun rises in the south. Don't fight it: Face the river. That's south. Turn around. That's north. *Tout est clair?*

To ease the confusion, the directions given throughout the Montréal chapters conform to this local directional tradition. However, the maps in this book also have the true compass on them.

The city of Montréal maintains a terrific website at **www.tourisme-montreal.org**, and the Québec province an equally good one at **www.bonjourquebec.com**.

CITY LAYOUT

MAIN ARTERIES & STREETS   In **downtown Montréal,** the principal streets running east-west include boulevard René-Lévesque, rue Ste-Catherine (*rue* is the French word for "street"), boulevard de Maisonneuve, and rue Sherbrooke. The north-south arteries in downtown and **Vieux-Montréal** include rue Crescent, rue McGill, rue St-Denis, and, most importantly, boulevard St-Laurent, which serves as the line of demarcation between east and west Montréal. Most of the areas in this book lie to the west of boulevard St-Laurent.

(In earlier days, Montréal was split geographically along ethnic lines: Anglophones lived predominantly west of boulevard St-Laurent, and Francophones were concentrated to the east. That's reflected in the names of streets: Peel and Atwater on the English-speaking side, and St-Laurent and Beaudry on the French side.)

Other major streets in Vieux-Montréal are rue St-Jacques, rue Notre-Dame, rue St-Paul, and rue de la Commune, which hugs the waterfront promenade bordering the St. Lawrence River (Flueve Saint-Laurent, in French). In **Plateau Mont-Royal,** northeast of the downtown area, major streets are avenue du Mont-Royal and avenue Laurier.

In addition to the maps in this book, neighborhood street plans are available online at www.tourisme-montreal.org and from the information centers listed above.

FINDING AN ADDRESS   Boulevard St-Laurent is the dividing point between the east and west sides (*est* and *ouest*) of Montréal. There's no equivalent division for north and south (*nord* and *sud*)—the numbers start at the river and climb from there, just as the topography does. The odd numbers are on the east and the even numbers on the west.

For the streets that run east to west, the numbers start at boulevard St-Laurent and then go *in both directions.* That means that an address at 500 *est* is actually very far from 501 *ouest*, as opposed to directly across the street. Make sure you know your east from your west, and confirm the cross street for all addresses.

Greater Montréal

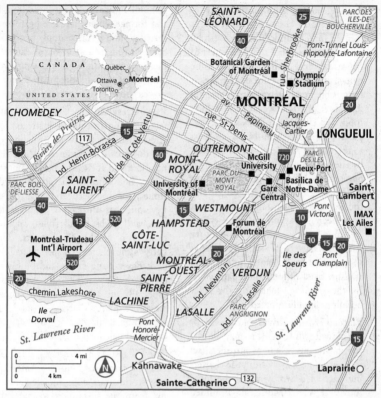

Map labels:
SAINT-LÉONARD · 25 · PARC DES ILES-DE-BOUCHERVILLE · 40 · Pont-Tunnel Louis-Hippolyte-Lafontaine · Botanical Garden of Montréal · rue Sherbrooke · Olympic Stadium · CANADA · Québec · Ottawa · Montréal · Toronto · UNITED STATES · av. Papineau · MONTRÉAL · 20 · CHOMEDEY · Rivière des Prairies · rue St-Denis · Pont Jacques-Cartier · LONGUEUIL · 117 · 13 · bd. Henri-Bourassa · 15 · bd. de la Côte-Vertu · 40 · OUTREMONT · MONT-ROYAL · McGill University · 720 · PARC DES ILES · Vieux-Port · PARC DU MONT-ROYAL · Basilica de Notre-Dame · PARC BOIS-DE-LIESSE · SAINT-LAURENT · University of Montréal · Gare Central · Saint-Lambert · 40 · 15 · WESTMOUNT · Pont Victoria · IMAX Les Ailes · 13 · 520 · HAMPSTEAD · Forum de Montréal · 10 · Montréal-Trudeau Int'l Airport · CÔTE-SAINT-LUC · Ile des Soeurs · 10 · 15 · 20 · Pont Champlain · 520 · MONTRÉAL-OUEST · 20 · 20 · SAINT-PIERRE · VERDUN · bd. Newman · LaSalle · St. Lawrence River · 15 · chemin Lakeshore · LACHINE · PARC ANGRIGNON · bd. LaSalle · Ile Dorval · LASALLE · bd. · St. Lawrence River · Pont Honoré-Mercier · 0 4 mi · 0 4 km · N · Kahnawake · Laprairie · Sainte-Catherine · 132

THE NEIGHBORHOODS IN BRIEF

Centre Ville/Downtown This area contains the most striking elements of the dramatic Montréal skyline and includes most of the city's large luxury and first-class hotels, principal museums, corporate headquarters, main railroad station, and department stores. The district is loosely bounded by rue Sherbrooke to the north, boulevard René-Lévesque to the south, boulevard St-Laurent to the east, and rue Drummond to the west.

Within this neighborhood is the area known as "The Golden Square Mile," an Anglophone district once characterized by dozens of mansions erected by the wealthy Scottish and English merchants and industrialists who dominated the city's politics and social life well into the 20th century. Many of those stately homes were torn down when skyscrapers began to rise here after World War II, but some have been preserved. At the northern edge of the downtown area is the urban campus of prestigious McGill University, which retains its Anglophone identity.

Vieux-Montréal The city was born here in 1642, down by the river at Pointe-à-Callière. Today, especially in summer, activity centers around Place Jacques-Cartier, where cafe tables line narrow terraces and street performers, strolling locals, and tourists congregate. The area is larger than it might seem at first, bounded on the north by rue St-Antoine, once the Wall Street of Montréal and still home to some banks, and on the south by the Vieux-Port (Old Port), a waterfront promenade that provides welcome breathing room for cyclists, in-line skaters, and picnickers. Vieux-Montréal is bordered to the east by rue Berri and to the west by rue McGill.

Several small but intriguing museums are housed in historic buildings, and the architectural heritage of the district has been substantially preserved. Restored 18th- and 19th-century structures have been adapted for use as shops, galleries, boutique hotels, cafes, studios, bars, offices, and apartments. In the evening, many of the finer buildings are illuminated.

Plateau Mont-Royal Northeast of the downtown area, this may be the part of the city where Montréalers feel most at home—away from the chattering pace of downtown and the more touristed Vieux-Montréal. Bounded roughly by boulevard St-Joseph to the north, rue Sherbrooke to the south, avenue Papineau to the east, and rue St-Urbain to the west, the Plateau has a vibrancy and ethnicity that fluctuates with each new surge in immigration.

Rue St-Denis (see below) runs the length of the district and is to Montréal what boulevard St-Germain is to Paris, while boulevard St-Laurent, running parallel, has a more polyglot flavor. Without its gumbo of languages and cultures, St-Laurent (known to all as "The Main"), could be another urban eyesore. But ground-floor windows here are filled with glistening golden chickens, collages of shoes and pastries, curtains of sausages, and far-fetched garments of designers on the forward edge of Montréal's active

fashion industry. Many warehouses and former tenements have been converted to house this panoply of shops, bars, and high- and low-cost eateries, their often-garish signs drawing eyes away from the still-dilapidated upper stories above.

Rue Crescent One of Montréal's major dining and nightlife streets, rue Crescent lies in the western shadow of the downtown skyscrapers. While the northern end at rue Sherbrooke houses luxury boutiques in Victorian brownstones, the southern end near René-Lévesque has dozens of restaurants, bars, and clubs of all styles, spilling over onto neighboring streets. The party atmosphere that pervades after dark never quite fades, and builds to crescendos as weekends approach, especially in warm weather. That's when the quarter's largely 20- and 30-something denizens flock to sidewalk cafes and balcony terraces.

The Village The city's gay and lesbian enclave, one of North America's largest, runs east along rue Ste-Catherine from rue St-Hubert to rue Papineau and onto side streets. A compact but vibrant district, it's filled with dance clubs, clothing stores, antiques shops, and cafes. A rainbow, symbolic of the gay community, marks the Beaudry Métro station in the heart of the neighborhood. Two major annual festivals are Divers/Cité in July and Black & Blue in October.

St-Denis Rue St-Denis, running from downtown near rue Ste-Catherine est and continuing north into the Plateau Mont-Royal district, is the thumping central artery of Francophone Montréal, thick with cafes, bistros, offbeat shops, and lively nightspots.

At the southern end of St-Denis, near the concrete campus of the Université du Québec à Montréal (UQAM), the avenue is student oriented, with inexpensive bars and the visual messiness that characterizes student/bohemian quarters. Farther north, above Sherbrooke, a raffish quality persists along the facing rows of three- and four-story Victorian row houses, but the average age of residents and visitors nudges past 30. Prices are higher, and some of the city's better restaurants are located here. This is a district for taking the pulse of Francophone life over bowls of cafe au lait at any of the numerous terraces that line the avenue.

Mile End Adjoining Plateau Mont-Royal at its upper west corner, this blossoming neighborhood is contained by rue St-Laurent on the east, avenue Du Parc on the west, and boulevard St-Joseph on the south. Although it is outside the usual tourist orbit, there has been a surge of worthwhile restaurants here in recent years.

Ile Ste-Hélène & Ile Notre-Dame These two islands, visible from Vieux-Montréal, are accessible by subway, bicycle, ferry, and car. They're connected by two bridges and now comprise the recently designated Parc Jean-Drapeau. St. Helen's Island was altered extensively to become the site of Expo '67, Montréal's very successful World's Fair in 1967. Construction crews doubled its surface area with landfill then created beside it an island that hadn't existed before, Ile Notre-Dame. When Expo closed, the city government preserved the site and a few of the exhibition buildings. Today Ile Ste-Hélène is home to Montréal's popular casino and an amusement park, La Ronde. In June, the Grand Prix of Canada is held on the racing track on Ile Notre-Dame. The islands are both nearly car-free.

The Underground City During Montréal's long (long) winters, life slows on the streets of downtown as people escape into *la ville souterraine*, a parallel subterranean universe. In this controlled climate it's always spring, and it's possible to arrive at the railroad station, check into a hotel, go out for dinner, and see a movie without ever donning an overcoat or putting on snow boots.

This underground "city" evolved when major building developments in the downtown put their below-street-level areas to profitable use, leasing space for shops and other enterprises. Over time, in fits and starts and with no master plan in place, these spaces became connected with Métro stations and then with each other. There are now more than 1,700 shops, hundreds of restaurants and food courts, and 40 cinemas and theaters underground.

The maze covers a vast area without the convenience of a logical street grid, and it can be confusing. There are plenty of signs, but it's wise to make careful note of landmarks at key corners along your route if you want to return to the same starting point. Expect to get lost anyway, and consider it part of the fun.

2 Getting Around

The city of Montréal has 1.6 million residents, and the greater metropolitan area has 3.6 million. Still, getting oriented is remarkably easy. The Métro (subway) system is fast and easy to navigate. Walking, of course, is the best way to enjoy and appreciate this vigorous, multidimensional city, neighborhood by neighborhood.

BY METRO OR BUS

For speed and economy, nothing beats Montréal's Métro system for getting around. The stations are marked on the street by blue-and-white signs that show a circle enclosing a down-pointing arrow. Although starting to show its age (the system has run at a deficit in recent years), and recently afflicted with waves of graffiti, the Métro's relatively clean trains whisk passengers through an expanding network of tunnels. In 2007, the orange line (no. 2 on our map) was extended three stops further into the north. The new end station is Montmorency, the train "direction" you'll see on platforms.

Fares are by the ride, not by distance. **Single rides** cost C$2.75 (US$2.75/£1.35), a **strip of six tickets** is C$12 (US$12/£6), and a **weekly pass,** good for unlimited rides, is C$19 (US$19/£9.50). Reduced fares are available to children and, with special Métro ID cards, seniors and students. **Tourist passes** are good for short visits: unlimited rides for 1 day for C$9 (US$9/£4.50) or 3 days for C$17 (US$17/£8.50). Buy tickets at the booth in any station or from a convenience store.

To enter the system, slip your ticket into the slot in the turnstile or show your pass to the attendant in the booth. If you plan to transfer to a bus, take a transfer ticket *(correspondence)* from the machine just inside the turnstile; every Métro station has one, and it allows you a free transfer to a bus wherever you exit the subway. Remember to take the transfer ticket at the station where you *first* enter the system.

The Métro runs from about 5:30am to 12:30am. If you plan to be out late, check the website at www.stm.info or call ⓒ **514/786-4636** for the exact times of the last train on each line.

The Métro is not immune to transit strikes; an action in May 2007, for instance, led to reduced hours of operation for several days. And *one caveat:* Convenient as the Métro is, there can be substantial distances when making a transfer between lines. Accessibility is sometimes difficult for people with mobility problems.

Buses cost the same as Métro trains, and Métro tickets are good on buses, too. Exact change is required to pay bus fares in cash. Although they go throughout the city (and give riders the decided advantage of traveling above ground), buses don't run as frequently or as swiftly as the Métro. If you start a trip on the bus and want to transfer to the Métro, ask the bus driver for a transfer ticket.

BY TAXI

There are plenty of taxis run by several companies. Cabs come in a variety of colors and styles, so their principal distinguishing feature is the plastic sign on the roof. At night, the sign is illuminated when the cab is available. The initial charge is C$3.15 (US$3.15/£1.55) at the flag drop, and then C$1.45 (US$1.45/70p) per kilometer (⅗ mile), and C55¢ (US55¢/25p) per minute of waiting. A short ride downtown usually costs about C$8 (US$8/£4). Tip about 15%. Members of hotel and restaurant staffs can call cabs, many of which are dispatched by radio. Cabs line up outside most large hotels or can be hailed on the street.

Montréal taxi drivers range in temperament from sullen cranks to the unstoppably loquacious. Some know their city well, others have sketchy knowledge and poor language skills, so it's a good idea to have your destination written down—with cross street—to show your driver.

For cyclists, several taxi companies participate in the "Taxi+Vélo" (*vélo* means bicycle) program. Call one of them, specify that you have a bike to transport, and a cab with a specially designed rack arrives. Up to three bikes can be carried for an extra fee

Montréal Métro

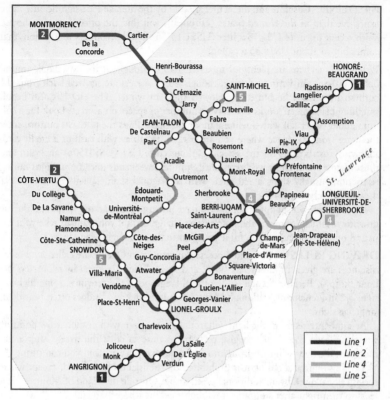

of C\$3 (US\$3/£1.50) each. The companies are listed at www.velo.qc.ca (search for "taxi"), or call ℂ **514/521-8356.**

BY CAR

Although Montréal is an easy city to navigate by car, visitors arriving by plane or train will probably want to rely on public transportation and cabs. A rental car can come in handy, though, for trips outside of town or if you plan to drive to Québec City.

RENTALS Terms, cars, and prices for rentals are similar to those in the United States, and all the larger U.S. companies operate in Canada. Basic rates are about the same from company to company, although a little comparison shopping can unearth modest savings.

All of the companies listed here have counters at Montréal-Trudeau Airport; the local numbers at the terminal are listed here. Major car-rental companies include **Avis** (ℂ **800/437-0358** or 514/636-1902), **Budget** (ℂ **800/268-8900** or 514/636-0052), **Hertz** (ℂ **800/263-0600** or 514/636-9530), **National** (ℂ **800/387-4747** or 514/636-9030), and **Thrifty** (ℂ **800/367-2277** or 514/631-5567).

If you'll be doing much driving in Montréal, pick up the pocket-sized atlas by JDM Géo. It's published by MapArt (**www.mapart.com**) and available at gas stations.

GASOLINE   Gasoline and diesel fuel are sold by the liter, and are significantly more expensive than in the United States (Europeans will find the prices less of a shock). With recent prices of C$1.15 a liter (US$1.15/55p), and 3.78 liters to 1 gallon, that comes out to about US$4.35 a gallon.

PARKING   There are plenty of metered spaces throughout the city. Look around before walking off without paying, though: some meters are set well back from the curb so they won't be buried by plowed snow in winter. The city has also begun installing black metal kiosks that serve a number of spaces on a street. Look for a column about 6 feet tall with a white P in a blue circle. Press the ENGLISH button, enter the letter from the space where you are parked, then pay with cash or a credit card, following instructions on the screen. Parking costs C$1 (US$1/50p) an hour, and most meters are in effect weekdays until 9pm and weekends until 6pm. Signs noting restrictions usually show a red circle with a diagonal slash. LIVRAISON SEULEMENT means "delivery only."

Most downtown shopping complexes have underground parking lots, as do the big downtown hotels. Some of the hotels don't charge extra if you want to take your car in and out during the day, useful if you plan to do some sightseeing by car.

DRIVING RULES   The limited-access expressways in Québec are called *autoroutes,* distances are given in kilometers (km), and speed limits are given in kilometers per hour (kmph). Because French is the official language of the province, some highway signs are in French only, although Montréal's autoroutes and bridges often bear dual-language signs.

At some intersections, the light will initially turn green with just an arrow pointing straight ahead. This is just to give pedestrians time to cross the street. After a few moments the light will turn from arrow to regular green light and you can turn.

Turning right at a red light is prohibited on the island of Montréal, except where specifically allowed by an additional green arrow. Outside the island of Montréal, it is legal to turn right after stopping at red lights except where marked.

Seat-belt use is required by law while driving or riding in a car in Québec province.

FAST FACTS: Montréal

AAA   Members of the **American Automobile Association (AAA)** are covered by the **Canadian Automobile Association (CAA)** while traveling in Canada. Bring your membership card and proof of insurance. The 24-hour hot line for emergency service is 🕿 **514/861-1313** in Montréal and 🕿 **800/222-4357** in the rest of Québec province and Canada. Most mobile phones can call 🕿 ***CAA** (*222) to reach emergency road service. See www.caaquebec.com for more. The AAA card also provides discounts at many hotels and restaurants.

American Express   In Montréal, 10 travel agencies are licensed to provide American Express Travel Services. One centrally located agency is **Excellent Travel** at 383 rue St. Jacques (🕿 **514/345-1121**), on the northern edge of Vieux-Montréal. For other agencies and general information, call 🕿 **800/668-2639**. For lost or stolen cards, call 🕿 **800/869-3016**.

Currency Exchange   There are currency-exchange offices (sometimes called *bureaux de change*) near most locations where they're likely to be needed: at the airports, in the train station, near **Infotouriste Centre**, at 1255 rue Peel on Dorchester Square.

Doctors & Dentists The front desks at hotels can contact a doctor quickly. For less serious illness, you can see a doctor at a community health center called a CLSC. These are smaller clinics, and there is one in every neighborhood. Medical treatment in Canada isn't free for foreigners, and hospitals make you pay your bills at the time of service. Check if your insurance policy covers you while traveling in Canada, especially for hospitalization abroad. For dental emergencies, call ⓒ **514/721-6006** or visit www.carrefourdentaire.com. In a medical emergency, dial ⓒ **911.**

Drugstores A pharmacy is called a *pharmacie*, a drugstore is a *droguerie*. A large chain in Montréal is Pharmaprix. Its branch at 5122 Cote-Des-Neiges (ⓒ **514/738-8464;** www.pharmaprix.ca), just 2 blocks from the Basilique Notre Dame, is open 24 hours a day, 7 days a week.

Embassies & Consulates All embassies are in Ottawa, the national capital. The U.S. has a consulate office in Montréal at 1155 rue St-Alexandre (ⓒ **514/398-9695**). The United Kingdom has a consulate general in Montréal at 1000 rue de la Gauchetière ouest, Ste. 4200 (ⓒ **514/866-5863**).

Emergencies Dial ⓒ **911** for the police, firefighters, or an ambulance.

Hospitals In Montréal, hospitals with emergency rooms include **Hôpital Général de Montréal**, 1650 rue Cedar (ⓒ **514/934-8090**), and **Hôpital Royal Victoria**, 687 av. des Pins ouest (ⓒ **514/934-1934**), both of which are associated with McGill University. **Hôpital de Montréal pour Enfants**, 2300 rue Tupper (ⓒ **514/412-4400**), and **Centre Hospitalier Universitaire Sainte-Justine**, 3175 Chemin de la Côte-Sainte-Catherine (ⓒ **514/345-4931**), are children's hospitals.

Internet Access Cybercafes seem to be fading in Montréal, as more restaurants and hotels offer Wi-Fi hotspots. Many hotels provide computers for use by guests; some offer Internet access via in-room televisions. Ask your hotel about your options.

Liquor & Wine Hard liquor and spirits in Québec province are sold through official government stores operated by the Québec Société des Alcools (look for maroon signs with the acronym SAQ). Wine and beer can be bought in grocery stores and convenience stores, called *dépanneurs*. The legal drinking age in the province is 18.

Newspapers & Magazines Montréal's primary English-language newspaper is the **Montréal Gazette** (www.montrealgazette.com). The leading French-language newspaper is *Le Soleil*. For information about current arts happenings, pick up the Friday or Saturday edition of the *Gazette*. Most large newsstands and those in the larger hotels carry the *Wall Street Journal, The New York Times,* and the *International Herald Tribune*. Major newsstands include the multibranch **Maison de la Presse Internationale**, with one location at 1166 rue Ste-Catherine ouest (at rue Stanley).

Pets Some Montréal hotels now accept pets, and some even offer walking services and little beds for dogs. Most hotels charge an extra fee of C$25 (US$25/£13) or more and have strict restrictions.

Police Dial ⓒ **911** for the police. There are three types of officers in Québec: **municipal police** in Montréal, Québec City, and other towns; **Sûreté de Québec officers,** comparable to state police or the highway patrol in the United States; and **RCMP (Royal Canadian Mounted Police),** who are similar to the FBI and handle cases involving infraction of federal laws.

Taxes Most goods and services in Canada are taxed 5% by the federal government (the GST, or goods and services tax). On top of that, the province of Québec has an additional 7.5% tax (the TVQ). A 3% accommodation tax is also in effect in Montréal. The tax rebate that nonresident visitors used to be able to apply for was eliminated in April 2007.

Telephones The Canadian telephone system, operated by Bell Canada, closely resembles the U.S. model. All operators (dial ⓒ **00** from Canada to get one) speak English as well as French, and respond in the appropriate language as soon as callers speak to them. Pay phones in Québec province cost C25¢ (US25¢/15p) for a 3-minute local call. Directory information (dial ⓒ **411**) is free. Remember that local and long-distance calls usually cost more from hotels—sometimes a lot more, so check. When making a local call within Québec province, you must dial the area code before the seven-digit number. The area code for Montréal Island is **514,** and surrounding areas use **450.**

Time Montréal and the Laurentian mountain area north are in the eastern time zone. Daylight saving time is observed as in the U.S., moving clocks ahead an hour in the spring and back an hour in the fall.

3 Where to Stay

Montréal hoteliers go the extra mile to make guests feel welcome, at least in part because there are proportionally more hotel rooms here than in other North American cities of similar size, with still more constructed every year. Hotels prices have held stable and, in some cases, gone down in the last few years. While it's not quite a buyer's market, there's opportunity to negotiate rates, particularly in the off season.

Accommodations options range from soaring glass skyscrapers to grand boulevard hotels to converted row houses. Stylish inns and boutique luxury hotels appear in ever-increasing numbers, especially in Vieux-Montréal. Visitors can almost always count on discounts and package deals, especially on weekends, when the hotels' business clients have packed their bags and gone home.

The tourist authorities in Québec province have a six-level rating system (zero to five stars) for all establishments offering six or more rooms to travelers. An ocher-and-brown shield bearing the assigned rating is found near the entrance to most hotels and inns. The Québec system is based on quantitative measures such as the range of services and amenities. However, the stars in the reviews below are of the zero- to three-star Frommer's system.

Nearly all hotel staff members are reassuringly bilingual. The busiest times are July and August, especially during the frequent summer festivals, during holiday periods (Canadian or American), and during winter carnival. At those times, reserve well in advance. Most other times, expect to find plenty of available rooms.

The listings below are categorized first by neighborhood, then by price. All rooms have private bathrooms unless otherwise noted. Many hotels have stopped providing coffeemakers in their rooms, so check if this feature is important to you. Many hotels are also in the process of adding Wi-Fi to parts or all of their facilities; ask about availability when booking. Most hotels in Montréal are entirely nonsmoking; those that aren't have a limited number of smoking rooms available, so check with the hotel before booking.

DOWNTOWN
VERY EXPENSIVE

The Fairmont The Queen Elizabeth (Le Reine Elizabeth) 🐾🐾 Montréal's largest hotel—it has over a thousand rooms—has lent its august presence to the city since 1958. Its 21 floors sit atop VIA Rail's Gare Centrale, the main train station, with the Métro and popular shopping areas such as Place Ville-Marie and Place Bonaventure accessible through underground arcades. This desirable location makes "the Queenie" a frequent choice for heads of state and touring celebrities, even though other hotels in town offer more luxurious pampering. The Fairmont Gold 18th and 19th floors, which anyone can stay on for a price, have a private concierge lounge serving complimentary breakfasts and cocktail-hour canapés. Less exalted rooms on floors 4 through 17 are entirely satisfactory, furnished traditionally and featuring easy chairs, ottomans, and bright reading lamps. A full on-site spa was renovated in 2006.

900 bd. René-Lévesque ouest (at rue Mansfield), Montréal, PQ H3B 4A5. © 800/441-1414 or 514/861-3511. Fax 514/954-2296. www.fairmont.com. 1,039 units. C$229–C$599 (US$229–US$599/£115–£300) double. Children 18 and under stay free in parent's room. Packages available. AE, DC, MC, V. Valet parking C$24 (US$24/£12). Métro: Bonaventure. Pets accepted. **Amenities:** 3 restaurants; 2 bars; heated indoor pool; exceptional health club and spa w/Jacuzzi, steam room, and instructors; concierge; business center; shopping arcade; 24-hr. room service; babysitting; laundry service; same-day dry cleaning; executive floors. *In room:* A/C, TV, high-speed Internet; minibar, coffeemaker, hair dryer, iron.

Hôtel Le Germain 🐾🐾🐾 This undertaking by the owner of equally desirable boutique hotels in Québec City and Toronto brought a shot of panache to the downtown lodging scene. Le Germain features a magical mix of Asian minimalism combined with all the Western comforts that international executives might anticipate—and a few they might not. Signature touches include big wicker chairs with fat cushions and beds with goose-down duvets. Self-serve breakfasts feature perfect croissants, excellent cafe au lait fabricated by a magical machine, and newspapers in French and English, all set out near the lobby fireplace. A little too sophisticated for families, this gem of a hotel is ideal for any other travelers.

2050 rue Mansfield (at av. du President-Kennedy), Montréal, PQ H3A 1Y9. © 877/333-2050 or 514/849-2050. Fax 514/849-1437. www.hotelgermain.com. 101 units. C$210–C$500 (US$210–US$500/£105–£250) double. Packages available. Rates include breakfast. AE, DC, MC, V. Valet parking C$23 (US$23/£12). Métro: Peel. Pets accepted. **Amenities:** Restaurant; bar; exercise room; concierge; business center, limited room service; in-room massage; babysitting; dry cleaning. *In room:* A/C, TV, CD player, free Wi-Fi, minibar, hair dryer, iron, safe.

Sofitel 🐾🐾 This representative of the French chain transformed a bland 1970s office tower into a coveted destination for visiting celebrities and the power elite. It wows from the moment of arrival, from the light-filled stone-and-wood lobby to the universally warm welcome of the staff. The 100 standard rooms (called "Superior") make full use of current technology and offer 3m (10-ft.) walls decorated with photos of Montréal by local photographers. Although sitting chairs with right-angled backs

Downtown Montréal

Parc du Mont-Royal

Royal-Victoria Hospital

Shriner's Hospital

Redpath Crescent

avenue Cedar

Montréal General Hospital

avenue des Pins

chemin de la Côte-des-Neiges

av. Docteur - Penfield

McGill University

Parc Rutherford

rue Simpson
rue Redpath
rue du Musée
rue de la Montagne
rue Drummond
rue Stanley
rue Peel
rue McTavish
rue University
rue Aylmer

McGill University

Pollack Concert Hall

rue Sherbrooke

rue Sherbrooke

QUARTIER DU MUSÉE

rue du Fort
rue St-Marc
rue Lincoln
rue Mathieu

GUY-CONCORDIA

SHAUGHNESSY VILLAGE

bd. de Maisonneuve

PEEL

rue Metcalfe
rue Mansfield
McGill College
rue University

av. du Président - Kennedy

McGILL

Concordia University

rue Ste - Catherine

DOWNTOWN

Square Phillips

ACCOMMODATIONS ■

Auberge Bonaparte **42**
Auberge Les Passants du Sans Soucy **46**
Auberge du Vieux-Port **47**
Fairmont The Queen Elizabeth (Le Reine Elizabeth) **19**
Château Versailles **2**
Hostellerie Pierre du Calvet **55**
Hôtel XIXe Siècle **32**
Hôtel du Fort **1**
Hôtel Gault **30**
Hôtel Nelligan **67**
Hôtel Inter-Continental Montréal **35**
Hôtel Le Dauphin **34**
Hôtel Le Germain **11**
Hôtel Le Saint-Sulpice **66**
Hôtel Le St-James **37**
Hôtel Omni Mont-Royal **10**
Hôtel St-Paul **29**
Le Centre Sheraton **18**
Le Place d'Armes Hôtel & Suites **36**
Le Square Phillips Hôtel & Suites **25**
Loews Hôtel Vogue **15**
L'Hôtel de la Montagne **14**
Ritz-Carlton Montréal **7**
Sofitel **7**
W Montréal **31**

rue Mackay
rue Bishop
rue Crescent
rue de la Montagne
rue Drummond
rue Stanley
rue Peel

Square Dorchester

bd. René - Lévesque

LUCIEN-L'ALLIER

Place du Canada

Centre Bell

Gare Windsor

rue de la Cathédrale

rue Belmont

Gare Centrale

rue de la Gauchetière

BONAVENTURE

Place Bonaventure

SQUARE-VICTORIA

rue St-Antoine

rue St - Jacques

rue Notre-Dame

rue St-Maurice

rue St-Henri

rue St-Paul

rue de Longueuil

Hallé

rue William

rue Nazareth

rue Duke

rue Ottawa

av. rue

rue des Soeurs-Grises

rue Prince

rue King

rue Wellington

DINING ◆

Au Pied du Cochon **62**
Aux Vivres **59**
Boustan **6**
Brunoise **63**
BU **59**
Café Méliès **57**
Chez l'Epicier **53**
Chez Queux **50**
Chez Schwartz **59**
Cluny ArtBar **28**
Europea **13**
Ferreira Café **16**
Gandhi **44**
Joe Beef **17**
Julien **24**
L'Express **61**
La Montée de Lait **61**
Le Blanc **56**
Le Bourlingueur **45**

Le Club Chasse et Peche **52**
Le Garde Manger **41**
Le Taj **8**
Leméac **59**
Maestro S.V.P. **58**
Marché de la Villete **38**
Moishes **59**
Nuances **27**
Pintxo **60**
Toqué! **33**
Wilensky Light Lunch **59**

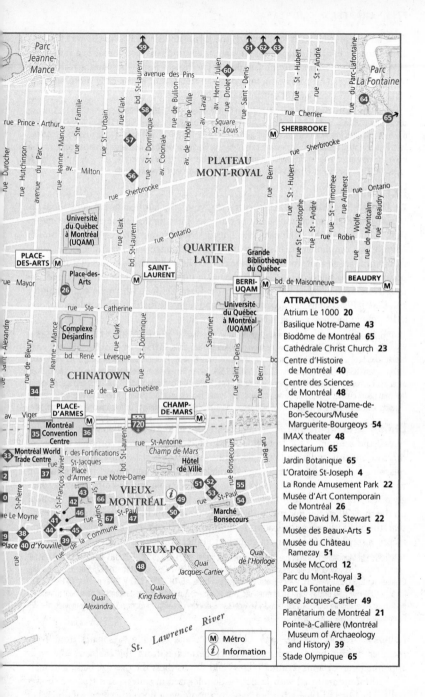

ATTRACTIONS ●

Atrium Le 1000 **20**
Basilique Notre-Dame **43**
Biodôme de Montréal **65**
Cathédrale Christ Church **23**
Centre d'Histoire
de Montréal **40**
Centre des Sciences
de Montréal **48**
Chapelle Notre-Dame-de-
Bon-Secours/Musée
Marguerite-Bourgeoys **54**
IMAX theater **48**
Insectarium **65**
Jardin Botanique **65**
L'Oratoire St-Joseph **4**
La Ronde Amusement Park **22**
Musée d'Art Contemporain
de Montréal **26**
Musée David M. Stewart **22**
Musée des Beaux-Arts **5**
Musée du Château
Ramezay **51**
Musée McCord **12**
Parc du Mont-Royal **3**
Parc La Fontaine **64**
Place Jacques-Cartier **49**
Planétarium de Montréal **21**
Pointe-à-Callière (Montréal
Museum of Archaeology
and History) **39**
Stade Olympique **65**

are a bit too overdesigned for comfort, the thrust-desks attached to the wall are easy to use from either side. Bathrooms have an Asian touch (bamboo spear in a vase, dimmer lights). Some floors are nonsmoking. The hotel's Renoir restaurant features an outdoor terrace. The exercise room is open 24 hours, and in the early morning, towels and chilled water are put out in the lobby for joggers.

1155 rue Sherbrooke ouest (at Peel), Montréal, PQ H3A 2N3. © **514/285-9000.** Fax 514/289-1155. www. sofitel.com. 258 units. C$195–C$405 (US$195–US$405/£98–£203) double; suites from C$295 (US$295/£148). Children under 12 stay free in parent's room. Packages available. AE, DC, MC, V. Valet parking C$26 (US$26/£13). Métro: Peel. Pets accepted. **Amenities:** Restaurant; bar; 24-hr. exercise room w/sauna; concierge; business center; Wi-Fi in lobby and restaurant; 24-hr. room service; in-room massage; babysitting; laundry service; same-day dry cleaning. *In room:* A/C, TV w/pay movies, CD player, high-speed Internet, minibar, hair dryer, iron, safe.

EXPENSIVE

Le Centre Sheraton ✦   This representative of the familiar brand goes about its business with efficiency and surety of purpose. That figures, since earnest people in suits make up much of the clientele. They gravitate toward the Club rooms, which offer guests complimentary breakfast and a private lounge with expansive views. Standard rooms are clean if worn around the edges. The health club/spa includes an indoor pool, a sauna, a fully equipped fitness center, a massage studio, and a landscaped terrace. Near to the central Dorchester Square, Gare Centrale (the main train station), and the high-stepping rue Crescent dining and nightlife district, the hotel has as good a downtown location as might be asked.

1201 bd. René-Lévesque ouest (between rue Drummond and rue Stanley), Montréal, PQ H3B 2L7. © **800/325-3535** or 514/878-2000. Fax 514/878-3958. www.sheraton.com/lecentre. 825 units. C$179–C$599 (US$179–US$599/£90–£300) double (club floor additional). Children under 17 stay free in parent's room. Packages available. AE, DC, DISC, MC, V. Valet parking C$26 (US$26/£13); self-parking C$19 (US$19/£9.50). Métro: Bonaventure. Entrance is on rue Drummond. Dogs accepted, but must be caged when owner is out. **Amenities:** Restaurant; bar; indoor pool; health club and spa; concierge (for Club floor); business center; shopping arcade; salon; limited room service; babysitting; laundry service; same-day dry cleaning; executive floors. *In room:* A/C, TV, high-speed Internet, video games, minibar, coffeemaker, hair dryer, iron, safe.

L'Hôtel de la Montagne ✦   There's a little bit of Vegas here: Two white lion sculptures stand sentinel at the front door, and the crowded lobby incorporates a pair of carved elephants and a nude female figure with stained-glass butterfly wings atop a splashing fountain. A cabaret lounge off the lobby has a piano player and jazz duos on weekends and leads into Thursday's, a popular singles bar and restaurant with a spangly disco and a terrace onto lively rue Crescent. Lunches are available beside the pool on the roof, 20 stories up, and in the evening there's dancing under the stars. After all that, the relatively serene bedrooms seem downright bland. But given all these inducements, a stay here is a bargain in contrast to other downtown options.

1430 rue de la Montagne (north of rue Ste-Catherine), Montréal, PQ H3G 1Z5. © **800/361-6262** or 514/288-5656. Fax 514/288-9658. www.hoteldelamontagne.com. 135 units. C$160–C$225 (US$160–US$225/£80–£113) double. Children up to 11 stay free in parent's room. Packages available. AE, DC, DISC, MC, V. Valet parking C$15, or C$30 for SUV (US$15/£7.50 or US$30/£15). Métro: Peel. Pets accepted. **Amenities:** 2 restaurants; 4 bars; heated outdoor pool; concierge; limited room service; laundry service; same-day dry cleaning. *In room:* A/C, TV w/pay movies, free Wi-Fi, minibar, coffeemaker, hair dryer.

Loews Hôtel Vogue ✦✦ *Kids*   Confidence and capability resonates from every member of this hotel's staff, and luxury permeates from the lobby to the well-appointed guest rooms. Feather pillows and duvets dress the oversize beds, and marble bathrooms are fitted with Jacuzzis—double-sized in suites—and separate shower stalls. The hotel's L'Opéra Bar is a two-story room with floor-to-ceiling windows. For families, Loews goes beyond lending libraries of games and has special children's menus, Gameboys, and supervised recreational programs. A springtime Sugar Season package includes a private trip to a traditional sugar shack and advice from the hotel's executive chef, who doubles as a "syrup sommelier." An early-morning joggers' station offers bottled water, towels, and maps to trails on nearby Mont Royal.

1425 rue de la Montagne (near rue Ste-Catherine), Montréal, PQ H3G 1Z3. (©) 866-LOEWSWB (563-9792) or 514/285-5555. Fax 514/849-8903. www.loewshotels.com. 142 units. C$179–C$399 (US$179–US$399/£90–£200) double. Children under 18 stay free in parent's room. Packages available. AE, DC, DISC, MC, V. Valet parking C$30 (US$30/£15). Métro: Peel. Pets accepted. **Amenities:** Restaurant; bar; 24-hr. exercise room; children's programs; concierge; business center; 24-hr. room service; babysitting; laundry service; same-day dry cleaning. In room: A/C, TV w/pay movies, CD player, high-speed Internet, minibar, hair dryer, iron.

Ritz-Carlton Montréal ✹✹   In 1912, the Ritz-Carlton opened its doors to the carriage trade, and that clientele has remained faithful—even as their Pierce-Arrows gave way to Rolls-Royces and Mercedes. The **Café de Paris** is favored for its high tea and weekday power breakfasts, and the **Le Jardin du Ritz** is an oasis next to the hotel's famous duck pond and its ducklings. However, the Ritz announced plans in late 2007 for a major C$100-million renovation that will transform its 229 rooms into 130 rooms and suites, 35 condo-residencies, and 15 condo-suites. Work is expected to take 15 months starting sometime in 2008, and hotel staff were unclear at the time of this writing if the hotel would be closed for any of that period. Call for current information.

1228 rue Sherbrooke ouest (at rue Drummond), Montréal, PQ H3G 1H6. (©) 800/363-0366 or 514/842-4212. Fax 514/842-3383. www.ritzmontreal.com. 229 units. C$180–C$239 (US$180–US$239/£90–£119) double; from C$248 (US$248/£124) suite. Packages available. AE, DC, MC, V. Valet parking C$30 (US$30/£15). Métro: Peel. Pets accepted. **Amenities:** 2 restaurants; bar; 24-hr. exercise room; access to off-site pool and gym; concierge; 24-hr. business center; 24-hr. room service; in-room massage; babysitting; laundry service; same-day dry cleaning. In room: A/C, TV w/pay movies, high-speed Internet, minibar, hair dryer, iron, safe.

MODERATE

Château Versailles ✹   This long-popular facility is one of the city's snappy boutique hotels. It began as a European-style pension in 1958, expanding into adjacent pre–World War I town houses. The spacious rooms have enjoyed the full decorator treatment, with navy-and-gold decor, fine modern furnishings with faint Deco tinges, and some Second Empire touches. Some rooms have fireplaces. A buffet breakfast is served in the main living room, where you can sit at a small table or in an easy chair at the fireplace. Only one deficiency remains: the lack of an elevator to deal with the three floors. Because the hotel is the official lodging of the nearby **Musée des Beaux-Arts** (p. 240) and near the popular rue Sherbrooke shopping area, reserve well in advance.

1659 rue Sherbrooke ouest (at rue St-Mathieu), Montréal, PQ H3A 1E3. (©) 888/933-8111 or 514/933-3611. Fax 514/933-8401. www.versailleshotels.com. 65 units. C$155–C$300 (US$155–US$300/£78–£150) double; suites from C$380 (US$380/£190). Rates include breakfast. Packages available. AE, DC, DISC, MC, V. Valet parking C$23 (US$23/£12). Métro: Guy-Concordia. Pets accepted. **Amenities:** 24-hr. exercise room w/sauna; business center; limited room service; babysitting; laundry service; same-day dry cleaning. In room: A/C, TV w/pay movies, CD player, high-speed Internet, Wi-Fi, minibar, coffeemaker, hair dryer, iron, safe.

Hôtel du Fort ⓚⁱᵈˢ   While hardly grand, this reliable hotel takes as its primary duty providing lodging to longer-term business travelers. That includes providing a fitness room (newly renovated) sufficient for a thorough morning workout, basic kitchenettes with fridges and microwave ovens in all rooms (the concierge can get groceries delivered), and an underground parking garage. Since all rooms are good-size and many have sofas with hide-a-beds, those same attributes are useful for small families. A buffet breakfast is served in the hotel's Louis XV Club Lounge and other meals can be taken at the Café Suprême in the adjoining Complexe du Fort mall, which also provides room service.

1390 rue du Fort (at rue Ste-Catherine), Montréal, PQ H3H 2R7. © **800/565-6333** or 514/938-8333. Fax 514/938-2078. www.hoteldufort.com. 124 units. C$135–C$175 (US$135–US$175/£68–£88) double; suites from C$165 (US$165/£83). Children under 12 stay free in parent's room. AE, DC, MC, V. Métro: Guy-Concordia. **Amenities:** Exercise room; concierge; business center; limited room service; babysitting; laundry service; same-day dry cleaning. *In room:* A/C, TV w/pay movies and Nintendo, Internet, coffeemaker, hair dryer, iron, safe.

Hôtel Omni Mont-Royal ⚡ *Kids*   This Omni outpost's health club, spa, and outdoor pool complex offers everything from Lifecyles to yoga classes to massages; nonguests can use it for C$25 (US$25/£13) adults and C$7 (US$7/£3.50) children. Many rooms are large, with fresh-looking furnishings, and are offered in escalating categories of relative luxury. The hotel provides information for parents traveling with children at a special website, www.omnikidsrule.com, and special kids' meals and games.

1050 rue Sherbrooke ouest (at rue Peel), Montréal, PQ H3A 2R6. © **800/843-6664** or 514/284-1110. Fax 514/845-3025. www.omnihotels.com. 299 units. C$129–C$299 (US$129–US$299/£64–£150) double. Children under 17 stay free in parent's room. Packages available. AE, DC, DISC, MC, V. Valet parking C$23 (US$23/£12); self-parking C$15 (US$15/£7.50). Métro: Peel. Pets accepted. **Amenities:** 2 restaurants; year-round heated outdoor pool; impressive 24-hr. health club and spa; games for children; concierge; 24-hr. business center; shopping arcade; salon; 24-hr. room service; babysitting; laundry service; same-day dry cleaning. *In room:* A/C, TV w/pay movies, CD player, free Wi-Fi, minibar, coffeemaker, hair dryer, iron, safe.

Le Square Phillips Hôtel & Suites *Kids*   Originally designed as a warehouse by the noted Québec architect Ernest Cormier, the building was converted to its present use in 2003. The vaguely cathedral-like spaces were largely retained, making for capacious studio bedrooms and suites fully equipped for long stays and vacationing families. Full kitchens in every unit come with all essential appliances—toasters, fridges, stoves, dishwashers, crockery, and pots and pans. There's an indoor pool on the roof adjoining an exercise room with exercise machines. A laundry room is available for guest use. The location is ideal, at the edge of the downtown shopping district and an easy walk to Vieux-Montréal and the rue Crescent nightlife district. On our last visit, the mattress was very, very firm.

1193 Square Phillips (south of rue Ste-Catherine), Montréal, PQ H3B 3C9. © **866/393-1193** or 514/393-1193. Fax 514/393-1192. www.squarephillips.com. 160 units. C$132–C$277 (US$132–US$277/£66–£138) double; discounts for stays of 7 or more days. Rates include breakfast. AE, DC, DISC, MC, V. Métro: McGill. Pets accepted. **Amenities:** Heated indoor rooftop pool; exercise room; concierge; business center; babysitting; coin-op laundry facilities; dry cleaning. *In room:* A/C, TV w/pay movies, free high-speed Internet, coffeemaker, hair dryer, iron.

INEXPENSIVE

Hôtel Le Dauphin *Value*   This downtown location of the small Dauphin hotel chain opened in February 2007. Its nine floors are decorated in bland tans and putty, and room furnishings are just a step up from dorm-room functional. However, the bathrooms are sleek with black counters and glass-walled shower stalls, and—get this—every room is equipped with a computer terminal and free Internet access. Rooms also have large unstocked refrigerators. A key is required to access the elevator, for an added bit of safety. All in all, a great new option for travelers on a budget.

1025 rue de Bleury (near av. Viger), Montréal, PQ H2Z 1M7. © **888/784-3888** or 514/788-3888. Fax 514/788-3889. www.hoteldauphin.ca. 72 units. C$109–C$140 (US$109–US$140/£55–£70) double. Rates include breakfast. AE, MC, V. Métro: Place d'Armes. **Amenities:** Access to gym; coin-op washers and dryers. *In room:* A/C, TV/DVD, computer w/free high-speed Internet, fridge, coffeemaker, hair dryer, iron, safe.

VIEUX-MONTREAL (OLD MONTREAL)
VERY EXPENSIVE

Hôtel Le St-James ✦✦✦   A triumph of the union of design and preservation. Montréal's surge of new designer hotels spans the spectrum from superminimalist to gentlemen's club. Le St-James sits squarely at the gentlemen's club end of the range. It began life as a merchant's bank in 1870, and the opulence of that station of privilege has been both retained and upgraded. The richly paneled entry hall leads to a grand hall with carved urns, bronze chandeliers, and balconies with gilded metal balustrades. Rooms are furnished with entrancing antiques and impeccable reproductions. All have video screens that control lights, room temperature, and even the do-not-disturb sign. The stone-walled, candle-lit **Le Spa,** with both a regular massage table and full-body water therapy, has to be seen to be believed. Breakfast, lunch, afternoon tea, and dinner are served right in the entry Banker's Hall, often accompanied by harp music.

355 rue St-Jacques ouest, Montréal, PQ H2Y 1N9. ✆ **866/841-3111** or 514/841-3111. Fax 514/841-1232. www. hotellestjames.com. 60 units. C$350–C$400 (US$350–US$400/£175–£200) double; C$475 (US$475/£238) and way up suite. AE, DC, MC, V. Valet parking C$30 (US$30/£15). Métro: Square Victoria. Pets accepted. **Amenities:** Restaurant; bar; exercise room; high-end spa; concierge; 24-hr. room service; babysitting; laundry service; same-day dry cleaning; laptop for loan. *In room:* A/C, TV w/pay movies, CD player, high-speed Internet, minibar, hair dryer, iron, safe.

Hôtel Le Saint-Sulpice ✦✦ *(Kids)*   Another of the high-style boutique hotels that has washed across Vieux-Montréal, Le Saint-Sulpice impresses with an all-suites configuration and courtly service. Suites come with myriad conveniences and gadgets, including a cordless phone, mini-kitchens with microwave ovens, stoves, and fridges. Children's services include gaming consoles in every room, board games, kid-friendly TV programming, a children's menu, and daycare service.

414 rue St-Sulpice (next to the Basilique Notre-Dame), Montréal, PQ H2Y 2V5. ✆ **877/785-7423** or 514/288-1000. Fax 514/288-0077. www.lesaintsulpice.com. 108 units. C$189–C$569 (US$189–C$569/£95–£285) suite. Children under 13 stay free in parent's room. AE, DC, DISC, MC, V. Valet parking C$25, or C$32 for SUV (US$25/£13 or US$32/£16). Métro: Place d'Armes. Pets accepted. **Amenities:** Restaurant; bar; compact health club and spa; concierge; business center; 24-hr. room service; babysitting; laundry service; same-day dry cleaning. *In room:* A/C, TV w/pay movies, high-speed Internet, minibar, coffeemaker, hair dryer, iron, safe.

W Montréal ✦✦✦   The high standards set in recent years by several of the city's boutique hotels were exceeded as soon as this exemplar of the growing W chain opened in late 2004 on the edge of where downtown meets Vieux-Montréal. If it weren't for the reception and concierge desks at each end, the lobby would suggest an exclusive dance club, what with the ice-blue and fire-engine-red glow of the wall panels and the 4m (12-ft.) waterfall. Bedrooms follow through, with pillowtop mattresses, goose-down comforters, and 350-count Egyptian cotton sheets. That flat-screen TVs, DVD players, and high-speed Internet access are standard even in the basic (called "Cozy") rooms is only to be expected. The hotel restaurant, Otto, attracts a sleek crowd favoring black and Armani, while the intimate W Café/Bartini features specialty martinis and the Wunderbar lounge is a dance club with DJs.

901 rue Square-Victoria, Montréal, PQ H2Z 1R1. ✆ **888/627-7081** or 514/395-3100. Fax 514/395-3150. www.whotels. com/montreal. 152 units. From C$255 (US$255/£127) double. Packages available. AE, DC, DISC, MC, V. Valet parking C$35 (US$35/£18). Métro: Square Victoria. Pets accepted. **Amenities:** Restaurant; 3 bars; exercise room and spa; concierge; business center; 24-hr. room service; in-room massage; babysitting; laundry service; same-day dry cleaning. *In room:* A/C, TV/DVD, high-speed Internet, minibar, hair dryer, iron, safe.

EXPENSIVE

Auberge du Vieux-Port ✿✿   This romantic luxury inn, housed in an 1882 building facing the waterfront, features polished hardwood floors, exposed brick and stone walls, massive beams, and the original windows in the hideaway bedrooms. There's an inviting cellar restaurant and a wine bar on the main floor, while both snacks and full dinners are served on the rooftop terrace, which has unobstructed views of the Vieux-Port—a particular treat during those summer nights when there are fireworks on the river. A complimentary glass of wine is served each afternoon in a sophisticated lounge off the lobby. The Auberge also runs the **Lofts du Vieux-Port** (www.loftsduvieuxport. com), suitelike rentals that have kitchenettes for longer stays.

97 rue de la Commune est (near rue St-Gabriel), Montréal, PQ H2Y 1J1. ✆ 888/660-7678 or 514/876-0081. Fax 514/876-8923. www.aubergeduvieuxport.com. 27 units. C$180–C$295 (US$180–US$295/£90–£148) double. Rates include afternoon wine and cheese, and full breakfast. AE, DC, DISC, MC, V. Valet parking C$21 (US$21/£11). Métro: Champs-de-Mars. Pets accepted in certain loft rooms. **Amenities:** Restaurant; concierge; limited room service; in-room massage; babysitting; laundry service; dry cleaning; laptop and mobile phone rentals. In room: A/C, TV, CD player, free Wi-Fi, minibar, coffeemaker (upon request), hair dryer, iron, safe.

Hostellerie Pierre du Calvet ✿   Step from cobblestone streets into an opulent 18th-century home with broad dark-wood floors, beamed ceilings, velvet curtains, gold-leafed writing desks, and four-poster beds made of teak mahogany. This wildly atmospheric inn transports guests to an elegant Breton manor in France, with public rooms furnished with original antiques, not reproductions, and a voluptuous dining room, **Les Filles du Roy,** suggesting a 19th-century hunting lodge. Some bedrooms have fireplaces and room no. 6 even has a stone-walled shower stall. New flat-screen TVs are as discordant as Victoria Beckham at Versailles but can be removed upon request. Door locks are rickety and best imagined as period pieces. An outdoor courtyard with a small fountain serves lunch and dinner; it's a wonderful little hideaway.

405 rue Bonsecours (at rue St-Paul), Montréal, PQ H27 3C3. ✆ 866/544-1725 or 514/282-1725. Fax 514/282-0456. www.pierreducalvet.ca. 9 units. C$265–C$295 (US$265–US$295/£132–£147). Rates include full breakfast. AE, MC, V. Métro: Champ-de-Mars. **Amenities:** Restaurant; laundry service; dry cleaning. In room: A/C, TV, free Wi-Fi, hair dryer, iron (on request).

Hôtel Gault ✿   This designer hotel explores the far reaches of minimalism, and guest responses vary from dismay to delight. Design aficionados will love its raw, monumental, concrete walls and brushed-steel work surfaces. Its structural austerity is tempered by lollipop-colored reproductions of Modern furniture from the 1950s to keep it more playful than chilly. The large bedrooms on the hotel's five floors are all loft-style to create a home-away-from-home feeling (they start at 29 sq. m/310 sq. ft. and go up), and use curtains instead of walls to define spaces. Bedding comes from the high-end Italian company FLOU, and hypoallergenic pillows are available. The first-floor Existential rooms feature the highest ceilings. The lobby with massive arched windows doubles as a bar/cafe/breakfast area.

449 rue Ste-Hélène, Montréal, PQ H2Y 2K9. ✆ 866/904-1616 or 514/904-1616. Fax 514/904-1717. www.hotel gault.com. 29 units. C$200–C$299 (US$200–US$299/£100–£150) double. Rates include breakfast. AE, MC, V. Métro: Square Victoria. Pets accepted. **Amenities:** Bar; gym access; concierge; 24-hr. room service; laundry service; same-day dry cleaning; newspapers in lobby. In room: A/C, TV/DVD, CD player, free high-speed Internet, minibar, safe.

Hôtel Inter-Continental Montréal ✿✿✿   Only a few minutes' walk from the Basilique Notre-Dame and the restaurants and nightspots of Vieux-Montréal, this striking luxury hotel has two arms: the tower houses the sleek reception area and guest rooms, while the restored 1888 Nordheimer building contains a bar-bistro; take a look at the early-19th-century vaults below. Guest rooms are quiet, well lit, and decorated with photographs and lithographs by local artists. The turret suites are fun, with their round bedrooms and wraparound windows, and Club rooms have access to an exclusive lounge serving complimentary continental breakfast and afternoon hors d'oeuvres, beer, and wine.

360 rue St-Antoine ouest (near rue de Bleury), Montréal, PQ H2Y 3X4. © 514/987-9900. Fax 514/987-9904. www. montreal.intercontinental.com. 357 units. C$159–C$309 (US$159–US$309/£79–£154) double. Packages available. AE, DC, DISC, MC, V. Valet parking C$26 (US$26/£13) with in-out privileges or C$19 (US$19/£9.50) without. Métro: Square Victoria. **Amenities:** 2 restaurants; bar; small enclosed rooftop lap pool; health club w/sauna and steam rooms; concierge; substantial 24-hr. business center; 24-hr. room service; massage; laundry service; same-day dry cleaning; executive floors. *In room:* A/C, TV w/pay movies and video games, Internet, minibar, coffeemaker, hair dryer, iron, safe.

Hôtel Nelligan ✿✿✿ Occupying adjoining 1850 buildings, the Nelligan had a major expansion in 2007, going from 63 to 105 units. Over half the units are now suites. Bedrooms are dark-wooded masculine retreats with puffy goose-down duvets and heaps of pillows. The building has beautiful spaces, from the sun-splashed atrium on the ground floor to the rooftop terrace, where drinks and light meals are served in good weather. Rooms on the fifth floor are steps away from both the terrace and the exercise room. The Nelligan is named for the 19th-century Québecois poet Emile Nelligan, whose lines are excerpted on the walls. The one distraction: Because the hotel is built around the center atrium, noise from the bar can filter up to the rooms. Still, claiming an enveloping lobby chair facing the open front to the street, with a book and a cold drink at hand, is one definition of utter contentment.

106 rue St-Paul ouest (at rue St-Sulpice), Montréal, PQ H2Y 1Z3. © 877/788-2040 or 514/788-2040. Fax 514/788-2041. www.hotelnelligan.com. 105 units. C$235–C$260 (US$235–US$260/£118–£130) double; suites from C$335 (US$335/£168). Rates include afternoon wine and cheese, and breakfast. Packages available. AE, DC, DISC, MC, V. Valet parking C$24 (US$24/£12). Métro: Place d'Armes. **Amenities:** 2 restaurants; bar; exercise room; concierge; computer for guest use; limited room service; in-room massage; babysitting; laundry service; same-day dry cleaning. *In room:* A/C, TV, CD player, free high-speed Internet, Wi-Fi, minibar, hair dryer, iron, safe.

Hôtel St-Paul ✿✿ Another in the ranks of worthwhile old buildings converted to contemporary hotels: The exterior is a product of the Beaux Arts school, but minimalism prevails inside, with simple lines and muted tones (many of the guests are equally trim and understated). A floor-to-ceiling alabaster fireplace anchors one end of the astere lobby. Elevators and hallways are hushed and bordering on pitch black, but open into bright rooms with walls and furnishings in shades of cream. Marble sinks are square, as are the clear plastic cubes covering the toiletries. Mobile phones and laptops are available upon request. Many rooms face the less touristed far western edge of Vieux-Montréal, with its mixture of stone and brick buildings in midconversion to modern condos and office space.

355 rue McGill (at rue St-Paul), Montréal, PQ H2Y 2E8. © 866/380-2202 or 514/380-2222. Fax 514/380-2200. www.hotelstpaul.com. 120 units. C$189–C$279 (US$189–US$279/£95–£140) double; suites from C$339 (US$339/ £170). Rates include breakfast. Children under 12 stay free in parent's room. Packages available. AE, DC, MC, V. Valet parking C$19 (US$19/£9.50). Pets accepted. Métro: Square Victoria. **Amenities:** Restaurant; bar; 24-hr. exercise room; concierge; 24-hr. business center; free Wi-Fi in public areas; limited room service; in-room massage and yoga; babysitting; laundry service; same-day dry cleaning. *In room:* A/C, TV w/pay movies, CD player, fax, free high-speed Internet, minibar, coffeemaker, hair dryer, iron, safe.

Le Place d'Armes Hôtel & Suites ✿✿ This highly desirable property is housed in three cunningly converted adjoining buildings dating from the late–19th and early–20th centuries. The elaborate architectural details of that era are in abundant evidence inside, with high ceilings and richly carved capitals and moldings. Many bedrooms have original brick walls and all are decorated in simple, contemporary fashion: slate floors in the bathrooms, deluxe bedding with down comforters, spotlight lighting. Many bathrooms feature rain showers. A complimentary afternoon wine-and-cheese party is held in the ground-floor lounge, which becomes a popular gathering place in the evenings, and there's a rooftop sun deck. A free morning shuttle takes guests to several downtown business locations. The elaborate **Rainspa** incorporates a hammam—a traditional Middle Eastern steam bath—in addition to offering massages, microdermabrasions, and body wraps.

55 rue St-Jacques ouest, Montréal, PQ H2Y 3X2. 🕾 **888/450-1887** or 514/842-1887. Fax 514/842-6469. www.hotel placedarmes.com. 135 units. From C$225 (US$225/£112) double; C$325 (US$325/£162) and up suite. Rates include afternoon wine and cheese, and breakfast. Packages available. AE, DC, DISC, MC, V. Valet parking C$24 (US$24/£12). Métro: Place d'Armes. **Amenities:** Restaurant; bar; exercise room; large spa; concierge; secretarial services; 24-hr. room service; babysitting; same-day laundry service; same-day dry cleaning. *In room:* A/C, TV, CD player, Wi-Fi, high-speed Internet, minibar, hair dryer, safe.

MODERATE

Auberge Bonaparte 🏵   The restaurant of the same name on the ground floor—romantic and faded in a Left Bank of Paris sort of way—has long been a Vieux-Montréal favorite. It was accorded massive renovations in 1999, and while the owners were at it they transformed the overhead floors into this fashionable urban inn. The auberge continues the restaurant's romantic style: Even the smallest rooms are spacious and feature a variety of combinations of furniture (such as double beds) that are useful for families. Of the eight units on each floor, four have whirlpool tubs with separate showers. All guests can spend time on the rooftop terrace, which overlooks the Basilique Notre-Dame. The auberge's one suite offers superb views of the basilica's cloistered gardens.

447 rue St-François-Xavier (north of rue St-Paul), Montréal, PQ H2Y 2T1. 🕾 **514/844-1448.** Fax 514/844-0272. www.bonaparte.com. 31 units. C$145–C$215 (US$145–US$215/£73–£108) double; C$305–C$355 (US$305–US$355/ £152–£178) suite. Rates include full breakfast. AE, DC, MC, V. Parking C$15 (US$15/£7.50) per calendar day. Métro: Place d'Armes. **Amenities:** Restaurant; access to nearby health club; concierge; limited room service; in-room massage; babysitting; laundry service; same-day dry cleaning. *In room:* A/C, TV/VCR, Wi-Fi, hair dryer, iron.

Hôtel XIXe Siècle   This tidy little hotel is worth seeking out for its central location and quiet demeanor. The building began life in 1870 as a bank in the Second Empire style, and the interior reflects these stately origins, with a lobby that looks like a Victorian library. Rooms are spacious, with 4.5m (15-ft.) ceilings, and even the nonsuite rooms have good-size areas for sitting and working at a desk. A handful of rooms have whirlpool tubs. Rooms facing the nondescript inner courtyard might not be scenic but are nearly silent and a treat for light sleepers. Three vaults remain from the building's original use as a bank, with one converted to a small bedroom. Despite its faintly aristocratic air, the hotel gives nods to green living, with energy-saving light bulbs and newspaper recycling buckets in each room.

262 rue St-Jacques ouest (at rue St-Jean), Montréal, PQ H2Y 1N1. 🕾 **877/553-0019** or 514/985-0019. Fax 514/985-0059. www.hotelxixsiecle.com. 59 units. C$145–C$260 (US$145–US$260/£73–£130) double. AE, DC, MC, V. Valet parking C$20 (US$20/£10). Métro: Place d'Armes. **Amenities:** Bar; concierge; laundry service; same-day dry cleaning. *In room:* A/C, TV, Wi-Fi, hair dryer, iron.

INEXPENSIVE

Auberge Les Passants du Sans Soucy ★ *Value*   This cheery bed-and-breakfast in the heart of Vieux-Montréal is a former 1723 fur warehouse gracefully converted into an inn. The marble-floored front entry doubles as a gallery space, setting an immediately relaxed and urbane tone. Rooms feature mortared stone walls, beamed ceilings, wrought-iron or brass beds, buffed wood floors, and lace curtains (photos of all nine are posted online). They also have jet tubs, flat-screen TVs, and electric fireplaces. A breakfast nook with a skylight has communal tables on either side of a fireplace brought over from Bordeaux, and substantial morning meals include chocolate croissants and made-to-order omelets.

171 rue St-Paul ouest (at rue St-François-Xavier), Montréal, PQ H2Y 1Z5. © **514/842-2634.** Fax 514/842-2912. www.lesanssoucy.com. 9 units. C$115–C$185 (US$115–US$185/£58–£93) double; C$145–C$215 (US$145–US$215/£73–£108) suite. Rates include full breakfast. AE, MC, V. Self-parking C$13 (US$13/£6.50). Métro: Place d'Armes. *In room:* A/C, TV, free Wi-Fi, hair dryer, iron.

4 Where to Dine

A generation ago, most restaurants in Montréal served only French cuisine. A few *temples de cuisine* delivered haute standards of gastronomy, while accomplished bistros served up humbler ingredients in less grand settings and folksy places featured the hearty fare that long employed the ingredients available in New France—caribou, maple syrup, root vegetables. Everything else was considered "ethnic." Québec province was French, and that was that.

Over the last 10 years, this attitude changed dramatically. A recession in the 1990s put many restaurateurs out of business and forced others to reexamine their operations. Immigration continued to increase, and along with it, the cooking styles of the city's chefs. Montréalers now routinely indulge in once-exotic edibles found in the storefront eateries all around them—Portuguese, Indian, Moroccan, Thai, Turkish, Mexican.

Intermingling of styles, ingredients, and techniques were inevitable, and Montréal, long one of the world's elite gastronomic centers, is now as cosmopolitan in its offerings as any city on the continent. In some eyes, it has taken Canada's leadership role in gastronomy.

Deciding where to dine among the many tempting choices can be bewildering. The establishments recommended here include some of the most popular and honored restaurants in town, but getting to any of them involves passing many other worthy possibilities, because good restaurants—called "restos" in the colloquial—often cluster together in certain neighborhoods or along particular streets, such as Laurier, St-Denis, or St-Laurent. Nearly all of them post menus outside for a little salivation-inducing reading and comparison shopping.

One thing to always look for is table d'hôte (fixed-price) meals. Entire two- to four-course meals, often with a beverage, can be had for little more than the price of an a la carte main course alone. Even the best restaurants offer them, making it easy to sample excellent venues without breaking the bank. Many higher-end establishments also offering tasting menus, and "surprise menus" are equally popular—you don't know what you're getting until it's there in front of you. Remember that an *entrée* is an appetizer, not the main course, which is *le plat principal.*

Websites featuring reviews and observations about the local dining scene include www.montrealfood.com and http://endlessbanquet.blogspot.com. The delightful reviews of food critic Lesley Chesterman of the *Montréal Gazette* are online at www.montrealgazette.com.

It's a good idea to make a reservation if you wish to dine at one of the city's top restaurants. Dress codes are all but nonexistent, but Montréalers are a fashionable lot and manage to look smart even in casual clothes. Smoking in bars and restaurants was banned by law in 2006.

CENTRE VILLE/DOWNTOWN
EXPENSIVE

Europea ☆☆ FRENCH CONTEMPORARY   When viewed from the outside, Europea looks like any of the city's multitude of low-brow cellar eateries. Even once inside, the low ceiling, bare wood floors, and brick walls are more simple that stunning. But then comes the food. The *amuse* (pre-appetizer) is in a three-segment dish with different tasty nibbles in each; it's followed by an unannounced "teaser," a demitasse of lobster bisque with a shot of truffle oil. Gaps in the procession are short, leading to the main event, maybe the roasted Alaska crab legs and warm lobster salad, or the beef fillet. For the full treatment, order the nine-course *menu degustation* for C$76 (US$76/£38). Europea doesn't court the family trade, and the average age of diners tends toward the far side of 40. Service is watchful and efficient.

1227 rue de la Montagne (at rue Ste-Catherine). ⓒ **514/398-9229.** www.europea.ca. Reservations strongly recommended. Main courses C$26–C$40 (US$26–US$40/£13–£20); table d'hôte dinner C$46 (US$46/£23), lunch C$26 (US$26/£13). AE, DC, MC, V. Mon–Fri noon–2pm; daily 6–10pm. Métro: Peel.

Ferreira Café ☆ SEAFOOD   *Cataplana* is the name of both a venerated Portuguese recipe and the hinged copper clamshell-style pot in which it is cooked. Ingredients vary depending on the cook, but at this extremely popular downtown spot, that means a fragrant stew of mussels, clams, potatoes, *chouriço* sausage, and chunks of cod and salmon. Mostly middle-aged and dressed in business wear, customers fill every seat at lunchtime but go home at night, which is when to visit if you prefer a bit of tranquillity with your grilled squid or pan-seared salted cod. Many dishes are priced according to the daily market, so they can be higher than outlined below.

1446 rue Peel (near bd. de Maisonnueve). ⓒ **514/848-0988.** www.ferreiracafe.com. Reservations recommended. Main courses C$28–C$45 (US$28–US$45/£14–£23). AE, MC, V. Mon–Fri 11:30am–3pm and 5:30–11pm; Sat 5:30–11:30pm. Métro: Peel.

Julien FRENCH CONTEMPORARY   A quiet downtown block in the financial district has been home to this relaxed Parisian-style bistro for years, hosting businesspeople at lunch and for cocktails after work and mostly tourists from nearby hotels in the evening. Much of the year diners have the option of tables in the heated terrace/garden. The chef isn't interested in being edgy, although he has been known to start out with a trendy *amuse* of marinated salt cod in a porcelain Chinese spoon. Sautéed duck breast is served with armillaire mushrooms and potato purée, and grilled red tuna with parsnip purée. There's a gluten-free vegetarian pasta option. The cheese selection is good, as is the tiramisu. Solid food without the pyrotechnics.

1191 av. Union (at bd. René-Lévesque). ⓒ **514/871-1581.** www.restaurantjulien.com. Reservations recommended. Main courses C$21–C$35 (US$21–US$35/£11–£18); table d'hôte dinner from C$22 (US$22/£11), lunch from C$18 (US$18/£9). AE, DC, MC, V. Mon–Fri 11:30am–2:30pm; Mon–Sat 5:30–10pm. Métro: McGill.

MODERATE
Le Taj *Value* INDIAN   This remains one of the tastiest bargains downtown. The price of the lunch buffet has barely changed since Le Taj opened in 1985, and the five-course

dinner costs C$28 (US$28/£14). The kitchen specializes in the mughlai cuisine of the subcontinent, and dishes are perfumed with turmeric, saffron, ginger, cumin, mango powder, and *garam masala*. For a real treat, order the marinated boneless lamb chops roasted in the tandoor; they arrive at the table sizzling and nested on braised vegetables. Vegetarians have ample choices, the chickpea-based *channa masala* among the most complex. Main courses are huge, arriving in a boggling array of bowls, saucers, cups, and dishes, all accompanied by *naan* (the pillowy flat bread) and basmati rice. Evenings are quiet, and lunchtimes are busy but not hectic.

2077 rue Stanley (near rue Sherbrooke). ✆ 514/845-9015. www.restaurantletaj.com. Main courses C$7.95–C$25 (US$7.95–US$25/£3.95–£13); lunch buffet C$12 (US$12/£6); table d'hôte dinner C$28 (US$28/£14). AE, DC, MC, V. Mon–Fri 11:30am–2:30pm and 5–10:30pm; Sat 5–11pm; Sun noon–2:30 and 5–10:30pm. Métro: Peel.

INEXPENSIVE

Boustan *Finds* LEBANESE   In the middle of the hubbub among the bars and clubs on rue Crescent, this completely nondescript Lebanese pizza-parlor-style eatery gets lines out the door at 2pm (office workers) and again at 2am (late-night partiers), all for its famed falafel, shish taouk, or shawarma sandwiches. Yes, that's former Prime Minister Pierre Trudeau in the photo at the cash register; he was a regular.

2020 rue Crescent (at bd. de Maisonneuve). ✆ 514/843-3576. www.boustan.ca. Most items under C$10 (US$10/£5). AE, MC, V. Daily 11am–4am. Métro: Peel.

VIEUX-MONTREAL
VERY EXPENSIVE

Toqué! *✫✫✫* FRENCH CONTEMPORARY   Toqué! is a gem that single-hand-edly raised the gastronomic expectations of the entire city. A meal here is obligatory for anyone who admires superb food, dazzlingly presented. "Post-nouvelle" might be an apt description for the creations of Normand Laprise, for while presentations are eye-opening, the portions are quite sufficient and the singular combinations of ingredients are intensely flavorful. Asian and related fusion influences are more evident these days, but the chef is still grounded in principles of the French contemporary kitchen. A short menu and top-of-the-bin ingredients, some of them rarely seen in combination—for example, cauliflower soup with foie gras shavings and milk foam—ensure that options are never set in stone. If you choose one of the tasting menus—and on weekends, up to 80% of the crowd does—you can opt for a wine pairing with glasses selected to complement each preparation.

900 Place Jean-Paul-Riopelle (near rue St-Antoine). ✆ 514/499-2084. www.restaurant-toque.com. Reservations required. Main courses C$32–C$45 (US$32–US$45/£16–£23); degustation dinner C$92 (US$92/£46) or C$104 (US$104/£52). AE, DC, MC, V. Tues–Sat 5:30–10:30pm. Métro: Square Victoria.

EXPENSIVE

Chez l'Epicier *✫* FUSION   This crisp little eatery opposite the Marché Bonsecours does double duty: It's both a high-end restaurant and a gourmet delicatessen with an abundance of tempting prepared foods, so remember it when you are planning a pic-nic. Over time, the kitchen has shifted to fashionable, extravagant preparations. While lunches are certainly well done, the dinner hour has seen creative flourishes equaled only in a few other local establishments. Asian ingredients and techniques are part of the mix, as are witty surprises: Witness a humble turnip appetizer that the waiter injected with tomato confit . . . using a syringe!

331 rue St-Paul est (at rue St-Claude). ✆ 514/878-2232. www.chezlepicier.com. Main courses C$26–C$34 (US$26–US$34/£13–£17), 6-course menu degustation C$80 (US$80/£40). AE, DC, MC, V. Mon–Fri 11:30am–2pm; daily 5:30–10pm. Métro: Champ-de-Mars.

Chez Queux ✿ FRENCH TRADITIONAL   No fancy foams or nasturtiums on these plates. Chez Queux is a throwback to a time when the only cuisine was French, and that meant chateaubriand for two, showy tableside preparations, and flaming desserts. In the baronial setting of a mansion built for a mayor of the city in 1862, deep paneling contrasts with fringed lampshades over the tables, a baby grand, and a two-sided gas fireplace that casts shadows over all. The waiters even wear tuxedos. The food is decidedly retro but the execution is superb: Shellfish bisque, Dover sole meunière, sweetbreads with morels, and even crêpes suzette are better than those of a certain age will recall and will be a revelation to those too young to remember rotary phones. A summer dining terrace adds views of the Vieux-Port to the experience.

158 rue St-Paul est (near Place Jacques Cartier). ✆ 514/866-5194. www.chezqueux.com. Reservations recommended. Main courses C$28–C$41 (US$28–US$41/£14–£21); table d'hôte C$25–C$40 (US$25–US$40/£13–£20). AE, DC, DISC, MC, V. Tues–Fri 11:30am–2:30pm; Tues–Thurs 5–10pm; Fri–Sat 5–10.30pm. Métro: Place-d'Armes.

Le Club Chasse et Peche ✿ FUSION   The name "Hunting and Fishing Club" doesn't suggest fine dining, but this restaurant received enthusiastic reviews after its 2005 opening and works hard to keep earning them. The short menu seems simple enough until the waiter comes, kneels beside the table, and describes them in considerable detail. Happily, the food is witty in combination. The recent version of what it calls the "new school surf and turf" is a combination of crisp sweetbread, *boulangères* (potatoes), mushrooms, and bacon. At lunch, two courses run from C$20 to C$26 (US$20–US$26/£10–£13). The restaurant's website is a quirky blog of reviews, YouTube films, and random stuff the staff likes.

423 rue St-Claude (between rue St-Paul and rue Notre Dame). ✆ 514/861-1112. www.leclubchasseetpeche.com. Reservations recommended. Main courses C$27–C$35 (US$27–US$35/£14–£18). AE, DC, MC, V. Tues–Fri 11:30am–2pm; Tues–Sat 6–10:30pm. Métro: Champ-de-Mars.

Le Garde Manger SEAFOOD   Nothing delicate about this newcomer. From the baseball-capped servers to the dark roadhouse decor, this buzzing resto is a smackdown to its gentrified Vieux-Montréal neighbors. On the plus side, the food is pretty good and generously portioned. The menu changes nightly, but we liked the Chilean sea bass and beef cheeks with bok choy, although the General Tao's lobster was terrifically hot and heavy. You'll need a lead stomach to survive a whole portion of a fried Mars bar, the signature dessert, unless roaring rock music helps you digest.

408 rue St-François-Xavier (north of rue St-Paul). ✆ 514/678-5044. Reservations recommended. Main courses C$22–C$35 (US$22–US$35/£11–£18). AE, MC. Tues–Sun 6–11pm; bar open until 3am. Métro: Place d'Armes.

MODERATE

Gandhi ✿ *Value* INDIAN   Classy but still inexpensive enough that both student and retiree budgets can afford it, Gandhi is so busy that the owners expanded into the adjacent building in 2007, doubling their seating space. Rooms are bright, service is polite but brisk, and the cooking is mostly to order and arrives fresh from the pot, pan, or oven. Flavors are delicate and subtle, but ask that they be ramped up to spicier levels and the kitchen will oblige. (Request "Madras hot" for medium heat.) Tandoori duck and lamb and chicken tikka are popular, and there are many vegetarian dishes.

230 rue St-Paul ouest (near rue St-François-Xavier). ✆ 514/845-5866. www.restaurantgandhi.com. Reservations recommended. Main courses C$14–C$19 (US$14–US$19/£7–£9.50); table d'hôte dinner C$20–C$22 (US$20–US$22/£10–£11). AE, MC, V. Mon–Fri noon–2pm; daily 5–10:30pm. Métro: Place d'Armes.

INEXPENSIVE

Cluny ArtBar *Finds* BREAKFAST/LIGHT FARE   The loft and factory district west of avenue McGill, at the edge of Vieux-Montréal, is showing signs of rebirth. Artists and high-tech businesses are moving in, although the streets are still very quiet. Among the pioneers is the Darling Foundry, an avant-garde exhibition space that provides room for Cluny, which serves breakfasts and coffee and, at lunch, antipasti and sandwiches such as tuna melts and smoked salmon panini. Although it's called an Art-Bar, its main hours are during the daylight, when the sun streams through mammoth industrial windows; it's open past 5 pm only on Thursdays.

257 rue Prince (near rue William). (C) 514/866-1213. www.cluny.info. Most items under C$10 (US$10/£5). MC, V. Daily 8am–5pm (Thurs until 10pm). Métro: Square Victoria.

Le Bourlingueur *Value* FRENCH BISTRO   This restaurant charges almost unbelievably low prices for several four-course meals daily. The blackboard menu changes depending on what's available at the market that day. Roast pork with apple sauce, glazed duck leg, and *choucroute garnie* (sauerkraut with meat) are likely to show up, but the specialty of the house is seafood—watch for the shrimp in Pernod sauce. Well short of chic, but the decor hardly matters at these prices and relative quality. The crowd has a wide range of ages and occupations.

363 rue St-François-Xavier (at rue St-Paul). (C) 514/845-3646. Reservations recommended on weekends. Main courses and table d'hôte lunch and dinner C$10–C$17 (US$10–US$17/£5/£8.50). MC, V. Daily 11:30am–9pm. Métro: Place d'Armes.

Marché de la Villette *Finds Value* FRENCH TRADITIONAL   Charming in its simplicity, and if you close your eyes you could convince yourself you're tucked into a shop in a quiet French village. While it started life as an atmospheric *boucherie* and charcuterie specializing in cheeses, meats, and breaks, the shop now serves breakfast, snacks, and table d'hôte lunches costing as little as C$9.95 (US$9.95/£4.95). The changing tables d'hôte are sturdily satisfying, but the several available platters of merguez and Toulouse sausages, various cheeses, and smoked meats are as beguiling. Quiches, foie gras, sandwiches, and savory and sweet crêpes are other possibilities. Wine is available.

324 rue St-Paul ouest (at rue St-Pierre). (C) 514/807-8084. Reservations not accepted. Most items under C$13 (US$13/£6.50). Mon–Sat 9am–6pm; Sun 9am–5pm. Métro: Square Victoria.

PLATEAU MONT-ROYAL & OUTER DISTRICTS
VERY EXPENSIVE

Brunoise *Finds* FUSION   The kitchen half of this two-man partnership takes full advantage of ingredients. His mussel-and-potato *bourride* (similar to bouillabaisse), for instance, gives off a stronger aroma of saffron than those from cooks who simply use it as coloring. Mains include influences as broad as Asian and Mediterranean and as focused as Catalan. With simpler preparations you can expect sublime satisfaction. *One caveat:* Prices here rank among the highest in town, and only prix-fixe menus are now offered. The owners expanded in early 2007 with **La Brasserie Brunoise** next to the Bell Centre at 1012 rue de la Montagne, where most mains are under C$20 (US$20/£10).

3807 rue St-Andre (at rue Roy). (C) 514/523-3885. www.brunoise.ca. Reservations recommended. Prix-fixe and tasting menus C$48–C$70 (US$48–US$70/£24–£35). MC, V. Tues–Sat 5:30–10:30pm. Métro: Sherbrooke.

Moishes ✪ STEAKHOUSE   Those who care to spend serious money for a slab of charred beef should take their credit ratings here. The oldest steak-and-seafood house in town is also arguably its finest, and less afflicted with tourists than the popular Gibby's in Vieux-Montréal. It now gets the trim new breed of up-and-coming executives as well as those of the older generation who didn't know about triglycerides until it was too late. The former are more likely to go for the chicken teriyaki or arctic char while the latter stick with the steak. The wine list is substantial, and the restaurant offers wine-tasting evenings.

3961 bd. St-Laurent (north of rue Prince Arthur). ✆ 514/845-3509. www.moishessteakhouse.com. Reservations recommended. Main courses C$27–C$52 (US$27–US$52/£14–£26). AE, DC, MC, V. Mon–Fri 11:30am–2:30pm and 5:30–11pm; Sat–Sun 5–11pm. Métro: Sherbrooke.

Nuances ✪✪ FRENCH CONTEMPORARY   Haute cuisine in a gambling casino, as unlikely as that seems. Ensconced atop four floors of blinking lights and the crash of cascading jackpots, this dazzling entry into Montréal's gastronomic sweepstakes got a face-lift in early 2007 that made the decor as contemporary and elegant as the food. A dramatic crystal chandelier may evoke the ghost of Liberace, but gone is the dark presidential decor and in are creamy walls, white linen, and pale-green leather banquettes. Every member of the staff is a sommelier and qualified to advise on appropriate wines. Recent triumphs have included loin of caribou (killed by arrow by an Inuit, we were told) with parsley gnocchi and caramelized squash, and Chilean sea bass with wine-butter emulsion. Dress code is business attire, but women will feel equally comfortable in business dress or a little red dress. A room with real star power.

1 av. du Casino (in the Casino de Montréal, Ile Ste-Hélène). ✆ 514/392-2708. www.casino-de-montreal.com. Reservations strongly recommended. Main courses C$43–C$46 (US$43–US$46/£21–£23); 3 table d'hôte options C$65–C$110 (US$65–US$110/£32–£55). AE, DC, MC, V. Sun–Thurs 5:30–11pm; Fri–Sat 5:30–11:30pm. Métro: Parc Jean-Drapeau.

EXPENSIVE

Au Pied de Cochon ✪✪ QUEBECOIS   Though it looks like another of the amiable but mediocre storefront restos that line most streets in the neighborhood, this Plateau restaurant is packed to the walls 6 nights a week and has become something of a cult (famed American chef Anthony Bourdain loves the place). As the name—"The Pig's Foot"—suggests, this is all about slabs of meat, especially pork. The Big Happy Pig's Chop, weighing in at more than a pound, is emblematic. Chef Martin Picard gets clever with one pervasive product: foie gras. It comes in nearly a dozen combinations, including stuffed into a ham hock, with *poutine,* and in a goofy creation called Duck in a Can which does, indeed, come to the table in a can with a can opener. When you feel like another bite will send you into a cholesterol-induced coma, sugar pie is the only fitting finish.

536 rue Duluth est (near rue St-Hubert). ✆ 514/281-1114. www.restaurantaupieddecochon.ca. Reservations strongly recommended. Main courses C$13–C$45 (US$13–US$45/£6.50–£23). MC, V. Tues–Sun 5pm–midnight. Métro: Sherbrooke.

Joe Beef ✪ SEAFOOD/ STEAKHOUSE   Owner David McMillan used to ride the fast track with interests in some of the most glamorous resto-clubs in town, and he opened this little beef-and-fish house in a neighborhood where the warehouses haven't all turned into high-end lofts yet. Ensconced in a narrow storefront that keeps diners elbow to elbow, the restaurant has a menu and wine list written on the big blackboard occupying one wall. Customary starters are oysters and the *salade Joe Beef,* a tangy tangle of haricots vert, boiled potatoes, pickled beets, jicama straws, slices of duck breast, leaves of Parmesan, and a poached egg. Mains can include trout and suckling pig, and the strip sirloin must be 14 ounces and 2 inches thick. In fall 2007, McMillian and partners opened an Italian eatery, **Liverpool House,** just down the block at no. 2501, with plans to add a gourmet grocery story in the same strip.

2491 rue Notre-Dame ouest (near av. Atwater). ✆ 514/935-6504. Reservations strongly recommended. Main courses C$24–C$36 (US$24–US$36/£12–£18). AE, MC, V. Tues–Sat 6–10pm. Métro: Lionel-Groulx.

La Montée de Lait ✦ *finds* FRENCH BISTRO   This compact bistro began life as a celebrator of dairy products (the "cheese and milk" of its name). The staff quickly opened up their menu, and now the cramped corner space is filled nightly with neighborhood regulars, post-grads, and monied gourmands from upscale *quartiers.* Starters include red deer tartare (Québécois don't need euphemisms for their food) and main dishes such as scallops in a cream sauce touched with egg, buttery tuna over pencil asparagus and mushrooms, and crispy rectangles of pork belly with molasses and Brussels sprouts. The cheese selection is impeccable. Lunch is the best deal, for a fixed price of C$20 (US$20/£10).

371 rue Villeneuve est (corner of rue Drolet). ✆ 514/289-9921. Reservations strongly recommended. Table d'hôte dinner C$40 (US$40/£20) for 4 courses, C$60 (US$60/£30) for 7 courses. MC, V. Tues–Sun 6–10pm; Wed–Fri noon–2pm. Métro: Mont-Royal.

Le Blanc ✦ FUSION   Once a jinxed location that had seen three other restaurants crash in no time, this latest manifestation has lasted almost a decade, and 24m (80-ft.) stretch limos regularly pull up to the door. Le Blanc shifted its formula in early 2007 to more of a club and lounge atmosphere, but office workers still take advantage of the inexpensive fixed-price lunches before moving aside for a 20- and 30-something crowd in the evening. The pleasingly Art Deco space has a few romantically secluded booths to one side and the front opens to the street in good weather.

3435 bd. St-Laurent (north of rue Sherbrooke). ✆ 514/288-9909. www.restaurantleblanc.com. Main courses C$26–C$45 (US$26–US$45/£13–£23). AE, DC, MC, V. Mon–Fri 11am–3pm and 5:30pm–midnight (until 1am Thurs–Fri), Sat–Sun 5:30pm–midnight; bar until 3am daily. Métro: Sherbrooke.

Maestro S.V.P. SEAFOOD   Smaller and more relaxed than many restaurants packed in the 2 blocks of The Main north of Sherbrooke, the highlight of this bistro is its oysters. A typical night features 14 varieties from the Atlantic (New Brunswick, PEI, Nova Scotia) and Pacific (British Columbia, Japan), and Maestro claims it has the biggest selection 12 months a year of any city venue. Main-course options include grilled shrimp with a fennel-and-spinach purée and Madagascar scallops, and the Maestro Platter, an extravagant medley of clams, mussels, calamari, a half lobster, *and* king crab. There's a tapas menu weekdays until 5pm and Tuesday and Wednesday nights with 30 items under C$10 (US$10/£5).

3615 bd. St-Laurent (at rue Prince Arthur). ✆ 514/842-6447. www.maestrosvp.com. Reservations recommended. Main courses C$16–C$56 (US$16–US$56/£8–£28). AE, DC, MC, V. Mon–Fri 11am–11pm; Sat–Sun 5–11pm. Métro: Sherbrooke.

MODERATE

BU ITALIAN   Not just another award-winning designer bar, BU strikes an exquisite balance between wine and food. The eats in question are antipasti, with The Assiette BU, for instance, a satisfying assortment of meats, cheese, and grilled vegetables. Some guests come just for BU's silky rendition of *vitello tonnato*—veal and crème of tuna.

There are three hot dishes offered nightly, but the purpose of all the food is to complement, not do battle with, the wines. The long card of 500 selections eschews the same old bottlings, and about 25 wines are available by the glass. The crowd gets younger as the night rolls on.

5245 bd. St-Laurent (at av. Fairmount). ℭ 514/276-0249. www.bu-mtl.com. Reservations recommended. Antipasti C$9–C$20 (US$9–US$20/£4.50–£10). AE, DISC, MC, V. Daily 5pm–1am. Métro: Laurier.

Café Méliès FRENCH CONTEMPORARY   In a section of The Main that is almost bristling with hipness, hurrah for the well-appointed but lower-key Café Méliès, whose decor is best described as "space-age submarine" (there are portholes throughout). Located inside the Ex-centris film center, this cafe-lounge has grown into a neighborhood favorite. It can be utilized for a quick dinner before a movie, but people drop in for light or bountiful breakfasts on the weekend, a snack such as risotto with four mushrooms and truffle oil, or simply an espresso or a glass of wine. Single folks will feel comfortable here. Steel, chrome, and glass define the generous space, updating the traditional bistro concept.

3540 bd. St-Laurent (near av. des Pins). ℭ 514/847-9218. www.cafemelies.com. Main courses C$19–C$32 (US$19–US$32/£9.50–£16). AE, MC, V. Daily noon–10pm (till 11pm Fri–Sat); Sat–Sun brunch 8:30am–3pm. Métro: Sherbrooke.

Leméac ℛ FRENCH BISTRO   This sprightly member of the Laurier scene has a long tin-topped bar along one side, well-spaced tables, and, far from least, a cheerful waitstaff. While the bistro dishes sound conventional on the page, they are put together in freshly conceived ways: a curried mussel soup was capped by a nicely browned pillow of puff pastry, and the salmon *pot-au-feu* was a perfectly cooked filet laid over a healthful selection of small potatoes, carrots, tender Brussels sprouts, and their broth. Food is different but not startlingly so, and served in an atmosphere that invites lingering. Weekend brunch is popular, as is the C$22 (US$22/£11) appetizer-plus-main menu that kicks in at 10pm. There's a terrace in warm weather.

1045 av. Laurier ouest (corner of av. Durocher). ℭ 514/270-0999. www.restaurantlemeac.com. Reservations recommended on weekends. Main courses C$18–C$36 (US$18–US$36/£9–£18); table d'hôte lunch C$18–C$23 (US$18–US$23/£9–£12); late-night menu C$22 (US$22/£11). AE, DC, MC, V. Mon–Fri 11:45am–midnight; Sat–Sun 10:30am–midnight. Métro: Laurier.

L'Express ℛ FRENCH BISTRO   No obvious sign announces the presence of this restaurant, only its name discreetly spelled out in white tiles in the sidewalk. There's no need to call attention to itself, since *tout* Montréal knows exactly where this most classic of Parisian-style bistros is. While there are no table d'hôte menus, the food is fairly priced for such an eternally busy place and costs the same at midnight as it does at noon. Opt for one of the lighter main courses, such as the *ravioli maison,* round pasta pockets filled with a flavorful mixture of beef, pork, and veal. Or simply stop by for a bowl of *soupe de poissons* or a simple croque monsieur. This is honest, unpretentious food, thoroughly satisfying. Although reservations are usually necessary, single diners can often find a seat at the zinc-topped bar, where meals are also served.

3927 rue St-Denis (just north of rue Roy). ℭ 514/845-5333. Reservations recommended. Main courses C$13–C$21 (US$13–US$21/£6.50–£11). AE, DC, MC, V. Mon–Fri 8am–3am; Sat–Sun 10am–3am. Métro: Sherbrooke.

Pintxo ℛℛ 𝘝𝘢𝘭𝘶𝘦 SPANISH   Pronounced "Peent-choo," the Basque word for "tapas," this tucked-away resto draws from the Spanish Basque tradition, going in for exquisitely composed dishes at fair prices in pleasant surroundings. Each pintxo is true tapa size, only three or four bites, so order recklessly. Some of our favorites: the braised beef cheek, the seared fois gras on a bed of lentils, and the white asparagus with Serrano ham and fried onion cut so fine it looked like tinsel. The best budget resto in town, it has opened a second, smaller space at 2 rue Sherbrooke est at the corner of boulevard St-Laurent, open weekdays for lunch and Tuesday through Saturday for dinner.

256 rue Roy est (2 blocks west of St-Denis). (C) **514/844-0222.** Individual pintxo from C$3 (US$3/£1.50); main courses C$18–C$21 (US$18–US$21/£9–£11). MC, V. Wed–Fri noon–2pm; Mon–Sat 6–11pm. Métro: Sherbrooke.

INEXPENSIVE

Aux Vivres VEGAN   In business since 1997, this bright restaurant with white Formica tables, raw blonde walls, and pink Chinese lanterns has been extra busy since moving in 2006 to its current location. A large menu includes bowls of chili with gua-camole and bok choi with grilled tofu and peanut sauce, as well as salads, sandwiches, desserts, and a daily chef special. All foods are vegan and the kitchen uses local organic vegetables, tofu, and tempeh. In addition to inside tables, there is a juice bar off to one side and a back terrace.

4631 bd. St-Laurent (at av. du Mont-Royal). (C) **514/842-3479.** Most items under C$11 (US$11/£5.50). No credit cards. Tues–Sun 11am–11pm. Métro: Mont-Royal.

Chez Schwartz Charcuterie Hébraïque de Montréal ⭐ DELI   French-first lan-guage laws turned this old-line delicatessen into a linguistic mouthful, but it's still known simply as Schwartz's to its ardent fans. Many are convinced it's the only place to indulge in the guilty treat of *viande fume*—smoked meat, which is a kind of brisket. Housed in a long, narrow storefront, with a lunch counter and simple tables and chairs crammed impossibly close to each other, this is as unassuming a culinary land-mark as you'll find. Sandwiches or plates are described either as small (meaning large) or large (meaning humongous), heaped with meat and piles of rye bread. Most peo-ple also order sides of fries and mammoth garlicky pickles.

3895 bd. St-Laurent (just north of rue Roy). (C) **514/842-4813.** www.schwartzsdeli.com. Sandwiches C$4.25–C$4.95 (US$4.25–US$4.95/£2.20–£2.45), with most other items under C$14 (US$14/£7). No credit cards. Sun–Thurs 8am–12:30am; Fri 8am–1:30am; Sat 8am–2:30am. Métro: Sherbrooke.

Wilensky Light Lunch LIGHT FARE   Wilensky's has been a Montréal tradition since 1932 and has its share of regular pilgrims nostalgic for its grilled-meat sand-wiches, low prices, curt service, and utter lack of decor. The ambience is Early Jewish Immigrant, and there are nine counter stools, no tables. The house special is grilled salami and bologna with mustard, thrown on a bun and squashed on a grill. You can wash it down with an egg cream or cherry Coke jerked from the rank of syrups—this place has drinks typical of the old-time soda fountain that it is.

34 rue Fairmount ouest (1 block west of bd. St-Laurent). (C) **514/271-0247.** Most items under C$4 (US$4/£2). No credit cards. Mon–Fri 9am–4pm. Métro: Laurier.

PICNIC FARE

If you're planning a picnic, bike ride, or simply an evening in, supplies are available in Vieux-Montréal at several shops along rue St-Paul. On the west end of the street is **Olive & Gourmando** ((C) **514/350-1083**) at 351 rue St-Paul ouest, a local favorite that sells near-perfect baguettes, cheeses and sausages from a cold case, and sandwiches. Just across the street, the **Marché de la Villette** ((C) **514/807-8084**), at 324 rue St-Paul ouest (p. 233) has similar fare. On the east end of rue St-Paul, a block and a half from the main plaza Place Jacques-Cartier, is **Chez l'Epicier** ((C) **514/878-2232**), at 331 rue

> **Fun Fact**   *Poutine,* **Smoked Meat & the World's Best Bagels**
>
> While you're in Montréal, be sure to indulge in at least a couple Québec standards. Although you'll find them dolled up on some menus, these are generally thought of as basic comfort foods:
>
> - *Poutine,* french fries doused with gravy and cheese curds
> - **Smoked meat,** a maddeningly tasty sandwich component that hovers in the neighborhood of pastrami and corned beef
> - *Queues de Castor,* literally "beaver tail," a deep-fried pastry the size of a man's footprint served with chocolate or cinnamon
> - *Tarte au sucre,* maple sugar pie
> - **Bagel,** the doughnut-shaped roll that in Montréal is smaller, chewier, and— it must be said—more deliciously sublime than its New York brethren

St-Paul est (p. 231). It's an ambitious restaurant with a gourmet delicatessen of take-out goodies.

Better still, use this as an excuse to make a short excursion by bicycle or Métro (the Lionel-Groulx stop) to **Marché Atwater,** the public farmer's market at 138 av. Atwater, which is open 7 days a week. The long interior shed is bordered by stalls of gleaming produce and flowers, the two-story center section given to wine purveyors, butchers, food counters, bakeries, and cheese stores. The **Boulangerie Première Moisson** (© 514/932-0328) fills the space with the tantalizing aromas of baskets of breads and cases of pastries—oh, the pastries!—and has a seating area for nibbling on toasted baguettes or sipping a bowl of cafe au lait. Two of the best cheese purveyors are the **Fromagerie du Deuxième** (© 514/932-5532), whose knowledgeable attendants know every detail of production of the scores of North American and European cheeses on offer, and the **Fromagerie du Marché Atwater** (© 514/932-4653), which has over 500 different cheeses, some 50 of them from Québec, and also sells pâtés and charcuterie. Marché Atwater is right on the revamped Lachine Canal, where you can stroll and find a picnic table.

5 Seeing the Sights

Montréal offers a feast of choices, able to satisfy the desires of both physically active and culturally curious visitors. Walk up the city's small mountain, Mont-Royal, in the middle of the city; cycle for miles beside 19th-century warehouses and locks on the Lachine Canal; take in artworks and ephemera at museums and historic buildings; party until dawn on rue Crescent and The Main; or soak up the concrete and spiritual results of some 400 years of conquest and immigration: It's all here for the taking.

Once you've decided what you want to do, getting from hotel to museum to attraction is easy. Montréal has an efficient Métro system, a logical street grid, wide boulevards, and a vehicle-free underground city that all aid in the swift, largely uncomplicated movement of people from place to place.

If you're planning to hit up several museums, consider the **Montréal Museums Pass** (see "Sightseeing Savings," p. 241). You might also want to note which museums have cafes so that you can plan a meal there. Most museums, although not all, are closed Mondays.

For families with children, few cities assure kids of as good a time as this one. There are riverboat rides, the fascinating Biodôme—which replicates four distinct ecosystems—the creepy crawlies of the Insectarium, a sprawling amusement park, the Vieux-Port Centre des Sciences de Montréal, and magical performances by the city's hometown Cirque du Soleil circus company. Recommended attractions are flagged with a *Kids* symbol, and an "Especially for Kids" section is on p. 246.

DOWNTOWN & MONT-ROYAL

Cathédrale Christ Church   This Anglican cathedral, in the heart of downtown, stands in glorious Gothic contrast to the city's commercial skyscrapers. It's sometimes called the "floating cathedral" because of how it was elevated during the construction of adjacent underground malls. The original steeple was too heavy for the structure and replaced by a lighter aluminum version in 1940. The choirs of the cathedral offer music each Sunday at 10am and at Choral Evensong at 4pm, and are broadcast over the Internet. The church also hosts concerts throughout the year.

635 rue Ste-Catherine (at rue University). © 514/843-6577, ext. 371 (recorded information about services and concerts). www.montreal.anglican.org/cathedral. Free admission; donations accepted. Daily 10am–6pm; services Sun 8am, 10am, and 4pm. Métro: McGill.

L'Oratoire St-Joseph 🎆   This huge Catholic church—consecrated as a basilica in 2004 and dominating the north slope of Mont-Royal—is seen by some as inspiring, by others as forbidding. At 236m (774 ft.), it is the highest point in Montréal. It came into being through the efforts of Brother André, a lay brother in the Holy Cross order who enjoyed a reputation as a healer. By the time he had built a small wooden chapel in 1904 on the mountain, he was said to have performed hundreds of cures. His powers attracted supplicants from great distances, and he performed his work until his death in 1937. In 1982, he was beatified by the pope—a status one step below sainthood—and his dream of building a shrine to honor St. Joseph, patron saint of Canada, became a completed reality in 1967. The church is largely Italian Renaissance in style, its giant copper dome recalling the shape of the Duomo in Florence, but of greater size and less grace. Inside is a sanctuary and museum where a central exhibit is **the heart of Brother André.** His original wooden chapel, with its tiny bedroom, is on the grounds and open to the public. There is a modest 14-room hostel called the Jean XXIII Pavilion on the grounds, too, with rooms that start at C$45 (US$45/£23).

3800 chemin Queen Mary (on the north slope of Mont-Royal). © 514/733-8211. www.saint-joseph.org. Free admission, but donations are requested. Crypt and votive chapel daily 6am–10:30pm; basilica and exhibition on Brother André daily 7am–9pm. The 56-bell carillon plays Thurs–Fri noon–3pm, Sat–Sun noon–2:30pm. Métro: Côtes-des-Neiges. Bus: 166.

Musée d'Art Contemporain de Montréal 🎆   Montréal's Museum of Contemporary Art is the only museum in Canada devoted exclusively to contemporary art, "contemporary" defined here as since 1939. Much of the permanent collection of some 7,000 works is composed of the work of Québécois artists such as Jean-Paul Riopelle and Betty Goodwin, but it also includes work by international artists Richard Serra, Bruce Nauman, Sam Taylor-Wood, and Nan Goldin. No single style prevails, so expect to see installations, video displays, and examples of Pop Art and Abstract Expressionism. That the works often arouse strong opinions signifies a museum that is doing something right. On Friday Nocturnes on the first Friday of the month, the museum is open until 9 p.m. with live music, bar service, and tours of the exhibition galleries. Its restaurant has a summer dining terrace.

185 rue Ste-Catherine ouest. © 514/847-6226. www.macm.org. Admission C$8 (US$8/£4) adults, C$6 (US$6/£3) seniors, C$4 (US$4/£2) students, free for children under 12, free to all Wed 6–9pm. Tues–Sun 11am–6pm (until 9pm Wed). Métro: Place des Arts.

Musée des Beaux-Arts 🏛🏛🏛   Montréal's Museum of Fine Arts is the city's most prominent museum, opened in 1912 in Canada's first building designed specifically for the visual arts. The original neoclassical pavilion is on the north side of Sherbrooke. A striking new annex was built in 1991 directly across the street and tripled exhibition space, adding sub-street-level floors and underground galleries that connect to the old building. Art on display is nearly always dramatically mounted, carefully lit, and diligently explained in both French and English.

Our recommendation is to enter the annex on the south side of rue Sherbrooke, take the elevator to the top, and work your way down. The permanent collection totals more than 33,000 works and is largely devoted to international contemporary art and Canadian art created after 1960, and to European painting, sculpture, and decorative art from the Middle Ages to the 19th century. On the upper floors are many of the gems of the collection: paintings by Hogarth, Brueghel, El Greco, and portraitist George Romney; and works—representative, if not world-class—by more recent artists including Renoir, Monet, Picasso, Cézanne, and Rodin. French-Canadian landscape watercolorist Marc-Aurèle Fortin (1888–1970) is well represented; a separate museum that had been devoted just to him donated its entire collection to Beaux-Arts in 2007.

Temporary exhibitions can be dazzling. A show a few years back brought the treasures of Catherine the Great, including her spectacular Coronation Coach, from the Hermitage Museum of Saint Petersburg. An exhibition of art from Cuba is scheduled for 2008. The museum's street-level store on the south side of rue Sherbrooke has an impressive selection of quality books, games, and folk art. A good cafe is adjacent.

1379–1380 rue Sherbrooke ouest (at rue Crescent). © 514/285-2000. www.mmfa.qc.ca. Free admission to the permanent collection (donations happily accepted). Admission to temporary exhibitions: C$15 (US$15/£7.50) adults, C$7.50 (US$7.50/£3.75) seniors and students, free for children 12 and under, C$30 (US$30/£15) family (1 adult and 3 children 16 and under, or 2 adults and 2 children 16 and under); half price Wed 5–9pm. AE, MC, V. Tues 11am–5pm; Wed–Fri 11am–9pm; Sat–Sun 10am–5pm. Métro: Guy-Corcordia. Bus: 24.

Musée McCord   Associated with McGill University, the McCord Museum of Canadian history showcases the eclectic—and not infrequently eccentric—collections of scores of benefactors from the 19th century through today. More than 16,600 costumes, 65,000 paintings, and 1,250,000 historical photographs documenting the history of Canada are rotated in and out of storage and onto display. In general, expect to view furniture, clothing, china, silver, paintings, photographs, and folk art that reveal rural and urban life as it was lived by English-speaking immigrants of the past 3 centuries. A First Nations room displays portions of the museum's extensive collection of objects from Canada's Native population, including meticulous beadwork, baby carriers, and fishing implements. Exhibits are intelligently mounted, with texts in English and French. There's a popular cafe near the front entrance, and a shop that sells Native and Canadian arts and crafts, pottery, and more.

690 rue Sherbrooke ouest (at rue Victoria). © 514/398-7100. www.mccord-museum.qc.ca. Admission C$12 (US$12/£6) adults, C$9 (US$9/£4.50) seniors, C$6 (US$6/£3) students, C$4 (US$4/£2) ages 6–12, free for children 5 and under; free admission on the first Sat of the month 10am–noon. Tues–Fri 10am–6pm; Sat–Sun 10am–5pm. In summer and on holiday weekends it's also open Mon 10am–5pm. Métro: McGill. Bus: 24.

Tips   Sightseeing Savings

- **Buy the Montréal Museums Pass.** Good for 3 consecutive days, the pass gives entry to 32 museums and attractions, including most mentioned in this chapter. Cost is C$45 (US$45/£23) for a pass that includes unlimited access to public transportation and C$35 (US$35/£18) for just the museums. There are no separate rates for seniors or children. It's available at all participating museums, many hotels, and the tourist offices at 174 rue Notre-Dame (in Vieux- Montréal) and 1255 rue Peel (downtown). To find out more, call ℭ 877/266-5687 or visit www.montrealmuseums.org.
- **Flash your AAA card.** Members of the American Automobile Association get the same discounts as members of its Canadian sister, the CAA. That includes reduced rates at many museums as well as hotels and restaurants.
- **Time your trip to coincide with Montréal Museums Day.** On the last Sunday in May, over two dozen museums are free during a citywide open house. There are complimentary shuttle buses to get around.

VIEUX-MONTREAL (OLD MONTREAL)

The central plaza of Vieux-Montréal is **Place Jacques-Cartier,** and it's the focus of much activity in the warm months. The plaza has two repaved streets bracketing a center promenade that slopes down from rue Notre-Dame to the Old Port, with venerable stone buildings from the 1700s along both sides. Horse-drawn carriages that gather at the plaza's base, outdoor cafes, street performers, and flower sellers recall a Montréal of a century ago. Its official website is **www.vieux.montreal.qc.ca**.

The Vieux-Port area—Montréal's Old Port, at the edge of Vieux-Montréal—was transformed in 1992 from a dreary commercial wharf area into a 2km-long (1¼-mile), 53-hectare (131-acre) promenade and public park with bicycle paths, exhibition halls, and a variety of family activities, including the **Centre des Sciences de Montréal** (see below). The area is most active from mid-May to October, when harbor cruises set out from here and bicycles, in-line skates, and family-friendly **quadricycle** carts are available for rent. The **Cirque du Soleil** raises its tents here for 2 months every spring, and warm months also bring 45-minute guided tours in the open-sided **La Balade tram** and information booths staffed by bilingual attendants. In the winter, things are quieter, but an outside ice-skating rink brings people out. There's an information booth at the Centre des Sciences. The Vieux-Port stretches along the waterfront parallel to rue de la Commune from rue McGill to rue Berri.

Basilique Notre-Dame ✦✦✦   Breathtaking in the richness of its interior furnishings and big enough to hold 4,000 worshipers, this magnificent structure was designed in 1824 by James O'Donnell, an Irish-American Protestant architect from New York. So profoundly was O'Donnell moved by the experience that he converted to Catholicism after the basilica was completed; the impact is understandable. Of the hundreds of churches on the island of Montréal, Notre-Dame's interior is the most stunning, with a wealth of exquisite detail, most of it carved from rare woods that have been delicately gilded and painted.

The main altar was carved from linden wood. Behind it is the **Chapelle Sacré-Coeur** (Sacred Heart Chapel), much of it destroyed by an arsonist in 1978 but rebuilt and rededicated in 1982. The altar has 32 bronze panels representing birth, life, and death, cast by Charles Daudelin of Montréal. A 10-bell carillon resides in the east tower, while the west tower contains a single massive bell nicknamed **"Le Gros Bourdon"** which weighs more than 12 tons and has a low, resonant rumble that vibrates right up through your feet. Twenty-minute guided tours in English are offered throughout the day, beginning at 9am. Depending on his availability, the church's organist Pierre Grandmaison gives 90-minute tours of the organ on occasional Wednesday, Thursday, and Friday mornings.

110 rue Notre-Dame ouest (on Place d'Armes). (℃ 514/842-2925. www.basiliquenddm.org. Basilica C$4 (US$4/£2) adults, C$2 (US$2/£1) ages 7–17. Basilica daily 8am–5pm; tours daily 9am–4pm. Métro: Place d'Armes.

Centre des Sciences de Montréal 𝐾𝑖𝑑𝑠   Running the length of a central pier in Vieux-Port (Old Port), this ambitious complex focuses on science and technology with interactive displays and a cinema as well as a popular **IMAX theater** (p. 246). Designed to make energy conservation, 21st-century communications, and life sciences vivid, it uses computers and electronic visual displays. Admission fees vary according to whatever combination of exhibits and movie showings you want. Pre-order tickets for special exhibits to avoid long lines. There's an indoor cafe and, in summer, an outdoor bistro.

Vieux-Port, Quai King Edward. (℃ 514/496-4724. www.montrealsciencecentre.com. Admission from C$10 (US$10/£5) adults, C$9 (US$9/£4.50) seniors and ages 13–17, C$7 (US$7/£3.50) ages 4–12, free for children under 4. MC, V. Weekdays from 8:30am; weekends from 9am; closing times vary. Métro: Place d'Armes or Champ-de-Mars.

Centre d'Histoire de Montréal   Built in 1903 as Montréal's Central Fire Station, this red-brick-and-sandstone building is now the Montréal History Center, which traces the development of the city from its first residents, the Amerindians, to the European settlers who arrived in 1642, to the present day. Imaginative exhibits, videos, and slide shows trace the development of the railroad, Métro, and related infrastructure. A recent exhibit recreated the trial of a woman accused of setting the massive fire that destroyed much of Vieux-Montréal in April of 1734. Allow about an hour for a visit.

335 Place d'Youville (at rue St-Pierre). (℃ 514/872-3207. www.ville.montreal.qc.ca/chm. Admission C$4.50 (US$4.50/£2.25) adults; C$3 (US$3/£1.50) seniors and children 6–17; free for children under 6. May–Aug Tues–Sun 10am–5pm; Sept–Apr Wed–Sun 10am–5pm. Métro: Square Victoria.

Chapelle Notre-Dame-de-Bon-Secours/Musée Marguerite-Bourgeoys   This is called the Sailors' Church because of the special attachment that fishermen and other mariners have to it; their devotion is manifest in the several ship models hanging from the ceiling inside. The attached museum, housed in a restored 18th-century crypt, focuses on the life and work of an energetic teacher named Marguerite Bourgeoys who came from France in 1653 to undertake the education of the children of Montréal. Later, she and several other teachers founded the Congregation of Notre-Dame, Canada's first nuns' order. The pioneering Bourgeoys was canonized in 1982 as the Canadian Church's first woman saint and in 2005, for the chapel's 350th birthday, her remains were brought to the church and interned in the left-side altar. Another part of the museum displays artifacts from the archaeological site under the chapel, including ruins and materials from the earliest days of the colony and an Amerindian fire pit dated to 400 B.C.

400 rue St-Paul est (at the foot of rue Bonsecours). ℂ 514/282-8670. www.marguerite-bourgeoys.com. Free admission to chapel. Museum C$6 (US$6/£3) adults, C$4 (US$4/£2) seniors and students, C$3 (US$3/£1.50) children ages 6–12, free for children under 6; archaeological site and museum C$8 (US$8/£4). May–Oct Tues–Sun 10am–5pm; Nov to mid-Jan and Mar–Apr Tues–Sun 11am–3:30pm. Closed mid-Jan to Feb. Métro: Champ-de-Mars.

Musée du Château Ramezay ☆ *Kids*   Claude de Ramezay, the 11th governor of the colony, built his residence at this site in 1705. The château became home to the city's royal French governors for almost 4 decades, until Ramezay's heirs sold it to a trading company in 1745. Fifteen years later it was taken over by British conquerors, and in 1775 an army of American revolutionaries invaded and held Montréal, using the château as their headquarters. For 6 weeks in 1776, Benjamin Franklin spent his days here, trying to persuade the Québécois to rise with the American colonists against British rule (he failed). After the American interlude, the house was used as a courthouse, a government office building, and headquarters for Laval University, before being converted into a museum in 1895.

Sculpted gardens ringed by a low stone wall evoke 18th-century Parisian estates and are a soothing respite from the busyness of Place Jacques-Cartier, a few steps away. In summer a cafe overlooks the gardens, which host workshops on soap making, paper marbling, and more. Between October and May, the château has a family event on the last Sunday of each month making bread using its 18th-century hearth.

280 rue Notre-Dame est. ℂ 514/861-3708. www.chateauramezay.qc.ca. Admission C$8 (US$8/£4) adults, C$6 (US$6/£3) seniors, C$5 (US$5/£2.50) students, C$4 (US$4/£2) ages 5–17, free for children 4 and under, C$17 (US$17/£8.50) families. MC, V. June to late Nov daily 10am–6pm; late Nov to May Tues–Sun 10am–4:30pm. Métro: Champ-de-Mars.

Pointe-à-Callière (Montréal Museum of Archaeology and History) ☆☆☆ *Kids* A first visit to Montréal might best begin here. Built on the very site where the original colony was established in 1642 (Pointe-à-Callière), the modern Museum of Archaeology and History engages visitors in rare, beguiling ways. The triangular new building echoes the Royal Insurance building (1861) that stood here for many years. Go first to the 16-minute multimedia show in an auditorium that actually stands above exposed ruins of the earlier city. The show is accompanied by music and a playful bilingual narration that keeps the history slick and painless if a little chamber-of-commerce upbeat (children under 12 will likely find it a snooze, however).

Pointe-à-Callière was the spot where the St-Pierre River merged with the St. Lawrence. Evidence of the area's many inhabitants—from Amerindians to French trappers to Scottish merchants—was unearthed during archaeological digs that took more than a decade. Artifacts are on view in display cases set among the ancient building foundations and burial grounds below street level. Wind your way on the self-guided tour through the subterranean complex until you find yourself in the former Custom House, where there are more exhibits and a well-stocked gift shop. Allow at least an hour for a visit. The exhibit is wheelchair accessible. The main building contains **L'Arrivage cafe** and has a fine view of Vieux-Montréal and the Vieux-Port.

350 Place Royale (at rue de la Commune). ℂ 514/872-9150. www.pacmuseum.qc.ca. Admission C$13 (US$13/£6.50) adults, C$8.50 (US$8.50/£4.25) seniors, C$7 (US$7/£3.50) students, C$5 (US$5/£2.50) children 6–12, free under 6. Family rates available. AE, MC, V. July–Aug Mon–Fri 10am–6pm, Sat–Sun 11am–6pm; Sept–June Tues–Fri 10am–5pm, Sat–Sun 11am–5pm. Métro: Place d'Armes.

ILE STE-HELENE/PARC JEAN-DRAPEAU

The small Ile Ste-Hélène and adjacent Ile Notre-Dame sit in the St. Lawrence River near Montréal Vieux-Port waterfront. Connected by two bridges, they now comprise the recently designated **Parc Jean-Drapeau,** almost entirely car-free and accessible by Métro, bicycle, or foot.

Musée David M. Stewart ✦ *(Kids)* If you're in downtown Montréal and hear what sounds like a gun salute, check your watch: If it's just before noon, the sound is coming from here. After the War of 1812, the British prepared for a possible future American invasion by building a moated fortress, which now houses the David M. Stewart Museum. Completed in 1824, it was never involved in armed conflict. Today the low stone barracks and blockhouses contain the museum and staff in period costume performing firing drills, tending camp fires, attempting to recruit visitors into the King's army, and generally doing all they can to bring this piece of history alive. The museum displays maps and scientific instruments that helped Europeans explore the New World, military and naval artifacts, and related paraphernalia from the time of Jacques Cartier (1535) through 1763, the end of the colonial period. From late June through late August the fort really comes to life, with daily reenactments of military parades and retreats by La Compagnie franche de la Marine and The Olde 78th Fraser Highlanders. If you absolutely must be photographed in stocks, they are provided on the parade grounds.

Vieux-Fort, Ile Ste-Hélène. ✆ 514/861-6701. www.stewart-museum.org. Admission C$10 (US$10/£5) adults, C$7 (US$7/£3.50) seniors and students, free for children under 7. Summer daily 10am–6pm; fall to late spring Wed–Mon 10am–5pm. Métro: Parc Jean-Drapeau, then a 15-min. walk. By car: Take the Jacques-Cartier Bridge to the Parc Jean-Drapeau exit, then follow the signs.

OLYMPIC PARK

A 20-minute drive east on rue Sherbrooke or easy Métro ride from downtown is an area known as **Olympic Park,** which has four attractions: the Stade Olympique (Olympic Stadium), Biodôme de Montréal, Jardin Botanique (Botanical Garden), and Insectarium de Montréal. The first three are described below, and the Insectarium on p. 246. All four are walking distance from each other, and there's a free shuttle in summer. You could easily spend a day here, and kids will especially love the Biodôme and Insectarium. **Combination ticket packages** are available, and the Biodôme, Jardin, and Insectarium are all included in the **Montréal Museums Pass** (see "Sightseeing Savings," p. 241). Underground parking at the Olympic Stadium is C$12 (US$12/ £6) a day, with additional parking at the Jardin Botanique and Insectarium.

Biodôme de Montréal ✦✦✦ *(Kids)* Perhaps the most engaging attraction in the city for children of any age, the Biodôme houses replications of four ecosystems: a tropical rainforest, a Laurentian forest, the St. Lawrence marine system, and a polar environment. Visitors walk through each and hear the animals, smell the flora, and, except in the polar region (which is behind glass), feel the changes in temperature. The rainforest area is the most engrossing (the subsequent rooms increasingly less so), so take your time here. It's a kind of "Where's Waldo" challenge to find all the critters, from the huge groundhog called a capybara to the golden lion tamarin monkeys that swing on branches only an arm's length away. Only the bats, fish, and polar penguins and puffins are behind glass. A giant tank in the St. Lawrence region has Atlantic sturgeon nearly 1.5m (5 ft.) long, while the open-air space features hundreds of shore birds whose shrieks can transport you to the beach. The facility also has a game room for kids called Naturalia, a shop, a bistro, and a cafeteria.

4777 av. Pierre-de-Coubertin (next to Stade Olympique). ✆ 514/868-3000. www.biodome.qc.ca. Admission C$16 (US$16/£8) adults, C$12 (US$12/£6) seniors and students, C$8 (US$8/£4) children 5–17, C$2.50 (US$2.50/£1.25) children 2–4. Binocular rentals available. AE, MC, V. Daily 9am–5pm (until 6pm late June to Aug). Closed most Mon Sep–Dec. Métro: Viau.

Jardin Botanique ✦✦✦   Spread across 75 hectares (185 acres), Montréal's Botanical Garden is a fragrant oasis 12 months a year. Ten large conservatory greenhouses each have a theme: orchids, begonias and African violets, ferns, flora from the rainforest. Outdoors, things really kick in in spring: lilacs in May, lilies in June, and roses from mid-June. The **Chinese Garden,** a joint project of Montréal and Shanghai, evokes the 14th- to 17th-century era of the Ming Dynasty and was built according to Chinese landscape principles of yin and yang. It incorporates pavilions, inner courtyards, ponds, and myriad plants indigenous to China. The serene **Japanese Garden** fills 6 hectares (15 acres) and includes a cultural pavilion with an art gallery, a tearoom where ancient tea ceremonies are performed, a stunning bonsai collection, and a Zen garden. A small train runs through the gardens from mid-May through October and is worth the small fee charged to ride it. The grounds are also home to the **Insectarium** (p. 246), displaying some of the world's most beautiful and sinister insects. Birders should bring along binoculars to spot some of the more than 190 species that have been spotted here. An extensive website provides details on everything.

4101 rue Sherbrooke est (opposite Olympic Stadium). ✆ 514/872-1400. www.ville.montreal.qc.ca/jardin. Admission includes access to the Insectarium. May 15–Oct C$16 (US$16/£8) adults, C$12 (US$12/£6) seniors and students, C$8 (US$8/£4) children 5–17, C$2.50 (US$2.50/£1.25) children 2–4. Rates drop about 15% rest of the year. MC, V. Daily 9am–5pm (until 6pm in summer, until 9pm mid-Sept to Nov). Closed Mon Nov to mid-May. No bicycles or dogs. Métro: Pie-IX, then walk up the hill; or take free shuttle bus from Olympic Park (Métro: Viau).

Stade Olympique *Overrated*   Centerpiece of the 1976 Olympic Games and looking like a giant stapler, Montréal's controversial Olympic Stadium provides moderate interest for tourists. Thirty-minute guided tours that describe the 1976 Olympic Games and current center are available daily for a fee. The main event is the 175m (574-ft.) **inclined tower,** which leans at a 45-degree angle and does duty as an observation deck, with a funicular that whisks passengers to the top in 95 seconds. On a clear day, the deck bestows an expansive view over Montréal and into the neighboring Laurentian mountains, but at C$14 (US$14/£7) the price is as steep as the tower.

The complex also includes a stadium that seats up to 56,000 for rock concerts and the like, and was home to the Montréal Expos baseball team before it relocated to Washington, D.C., in 2005. A **Sports Centre** houses five swimming pools open for public swims and classes, including a pool that's 15m deep (49 ft.) for scuba diving.

4141 av. Pierre-de-Coubertin ✆ 514/252-4141. www.rio.gouv.qc.ca. Tower admission C$14 (US$14/£7) adults, C$11 (US$11/£5.50) seniors and students, C$7 (US$7/£3.50) ages 5–17. Packages available that include guided tour. Public swims scheduled daily, with low admission rates. Tower daily 9am–7pm in summer; until 5pm in winter; closed mid-Jan to mid-Feb. Métro: Viau

PARKS & GARDENS

Also see **Jardin Botanique,** above.

Parc du Mont-Royal   Montréal is named for this 232m (761-ft.) hill that rises at its heart—the "Royal Mountain." Walkers, joggers, cyclists, dog owners, and skaters all use this largest of the city's green spaces, which was designed by the American landscape architect Frederick Law Olmsted, who created New York City's Central Park. In summer, **Lac des Castors** (Beaver Lake) is surrounded by sunbathers and picnickers (no swimming allowed, however). In winter, cross-country skiers follow miles of paths and snowshoers tramp along trails laid out for their use. The refurbished **Chalet du Mont-Royal** near the crest of the hill is a popular destination, providing a sweeping view of the city from its terrace and an opportunity for a snack. Up the hill behind the chalet is the spot where, tradition says, Paul de Chomedey, sieur de Maisonneuve

(1612–1676), erected a wooden cross after the colony survived a flood threat in 1643. The present incarnation of the steel **Croix du Mont-Royal** was installed in 1924 and is lit at night. It usually glows white, although it was lit red in the 1980s during a march against AIDS and purple in 2005 to announce the death of Pope John Paul II. On its far slope are two **cemeteries,** one that used to be Anglophone and Protestant, the other Francophone and Catholic—reminders of the linguistic and cultural division that persists in the city.

C 514/843-8240 for the Maison Smith information center in the park's center. www.lemontroyal.qc.ca. Métro: Mont-Royal. Bus: 11; get off at Lac des Castors (Beaver Lake).

Parc La Fontaine   The European-style park in Plateau Mont-Royal is one of the city's oldest and most popular. Illustrating the traditional dual identities of the city's populace, half the park is landscaped in the formal French manner, the other in the more casual English style. The central lake is used for pedal boating in summer and ice skating in winter. Snowshoe and cross-country trails wind past trees in winter, as do bike paths in the warmer months, and there are tennis courts on the premises. An open amphitheater, the **Théâtre de Verdure,** features free outdoor theater, movies, and tango dancing in summer. The northern end is more pleasant than the southern end (along rue Sherbrooke).

Southern end: rue Sherbrooke; northern end: rue Rachel; western side: av. Parc LaFontaine; eastern side: av. Papineau. *C* 514/872-2644, or *C* 514/872-3626 for tennis court reservations. Free; fee for use of tennis courts. Park daily 24 hr. Métro: Sherbrooke.

ESPECIALLY FOR KIDS

In addition to the other attractions flagged in this chapter as especially appealing to children, here are some spots that cater primarily to the under-18 crowd.

Atrium Le 1000 *Kids*   This indoor ice-skating rink in the heart of downtown Montréal is open year-round. Skate rentals are available on-site, and restaurants ring the rink. There is a Tiny Tot hour for children 12 and under and their parents from 10:30 to 11:30am weekends in summer and Sunday mornings in winter. Saturdays feature DJ Nites after 7pm for ages 13 years and older.

Downtown, 1000 rue de la Gauchetière ouest. *C* 514/395-0555. www.le1000.com. Admission C$5.75 (US$5.75/£2.85) adults, C$3.75 (US$3.75/£1.85) children 12 and under. Skate rental C$5 (US$5/£2.50). MC, V. Daily from 11:30am (10:30am some weekend days for children); closed Mon in summer. Métro: Bonaventure.

IMAX Theater *Kids*   The images and special effects are larger than life, always visually dazzling and often vertiginous, thrown on a five-story screen in the renovated theater of the **Centre des Sciences de Montréal** (p. 242). Recent movies have focused on mountain climbing in the Alps, sea monsters, and a haunted castle. Running time is usually under an hour and about a quarter of the screenings are in English. Tickets can be ordered online.

Vieux-Port, Quai King Edward. *C* 877/496-4724 or 514/496-4724. www.montrealsciencecentre.com. Admission from C$10 (US$10/£5) adults, C$9 (US$9/£4.50) seniors and ages 13–17, C$7 (US$7/£3.50) ages 4–12, free for children under 4. MC, V. Shows from 10am–10pm. Métro: Place d'Armes or Champ-de-Mars.

Insectarium de Montréal *Kids*   Live exhibits featuring scorpions, tarantulas, hissing cockroaches, assassin bugs, praying mantises, and other "misunderstood creatures, which are so often wrongly feared and despised," as the Insectarium puts it, are displayed in this two-level structure near the rue Sherbrooke gate of the **Jardin Botanique** (p. 245). Needless to say, kids are delighted by the creepy critters. More

> **Fun Fact** **Cirque du Soleil: Montréal's Hometown Circus**
>
> Cirque du Soleil began in Baie-Saint-Paul, a river town an hour north of Québec City. The artists included stilt walkers, fire breathers, and musicians, raising a small ruckus with one pure intention: to entertain. The troupe formally founded as Cirque du Soleil ("circus of the sun") in 1984.
>
> With no animals, this circus has grown into a spectacle like no other. Using human-sized gyroscopes, trampoline beds, trapezes suspended from massive chandeliers, and more, Cirque creates worlds that are sensual and otherworldly. Over 900 acrobats, contortionists, jugglers, clowns, dancers, and singers are part of the Cirque operation, touring the world in companies simultaneously. There are resident shows in Las Vegas and Orlando, Florida.
>
> The company's offices are in Montréal in the northern Saint-Michel district, just beyond the Mile End neighborhood. The Cirque has a small campus of buildings in the industrial zone: all new artists live in residences on-site and train in acrobatic rehearsal rooms, a dance studio, and a space large enough to erect a circus tent. Some 1,600 people work at the Montréal facility, including 300 in costumes alone. The Cirque celebrates its 25th year in 2009.
>
> Performances have taken place in Montréal from April to June in recent years, in the Cirque's signature yellow-and-blue tents temporarily erected on the Quays (piers) of Vieux-Port. Tickets start at C$60 (US$60/£30) for adults. Details are available at © 800/361-4595 and www.cirquedusoleil.com.

than 3,000 mounted butterflies, beetles, maggots, tarantulas, and giraffe weevils also are featured, and during the summer, the Butterfly House is full of beautiful live specimens fluttering among the nectar-bearing plants. In September, visitors can watch monarch butterflies being tagged and released for their annual migration to Mexico.

4581 rue Sherbrooke est. © **514/872-1400.** www.ville.montreal.qc.ca/insectarium. Admission includes access to the Botanical Garden next door. May 15–Oct C$16 (US$16/£8) adults, C$12 (US$12/£6) seniors and students, C$8 (US$8/£4) children 5–17, C$2.50 (US$2.50/£1.25) children 2–4. Rates drop about 15% rest of the year. See p. 244 for info about combination tickets with the Stade Olympique and Biodôme de Montréal. MC, V. Daily 9am–5pm Nov 1–May 14; daily 9am–6pm May 15–Sept 6; daily 9am–9pm Sept 7–Oct 31. Métro: Pie-IX or Viau.

La Ronde Amusement Park (Kids)   Montréal's amusement park, opened in 1967 as part of the Expo '67 (World's Fair), was run for its first 34 years by the city. The American-owned Six Flags theme park empire bought it in 2001 and added new rides. Like hot sauces, they're categorized by "thrill rating": moderate, mild, or max. Over a dozen rides are in the "max thrill" category, including Le Vampire, a suspended coaster where riders experience five head-over-heels loops at over 80kmph (50 mph). There are also Ferris wheels, carnival booths, and plenty of places to eat and drink. An antique carousel, Le Galopant, was added in 2007; it was built by Belgian artisans in 1885 and part of the Belgian Pavilion at the 1964 New York World's Fair. The Minirail, an original from La Ronde's 1967 opening, is an elevated train that circles the park. Young children have ample selection including the Tchou Tchou Train and *Bob* l'éponge 3D, a 10-minute SpongeBob SquarePants simulated ride. A section called **Le Pays de Rib-ambelle** houses family-friendly rides and daily concerts.

Parc Jean-Drapeau Ile Ste-Hélène. (C) 514/397-2000. www.laronde.com. Admission C$37 (US$37/£19) for patrons 137cm (54 inches) or taller, C$25 (US$25/£13) for patrons shorter than 137cm (54 inches), free for children under 3. Parking C$13 (US$13/£6.50). Daily 10:30am–10:30pm June–Aug; weekends only noon–7pm in spring and fall; closed winter. Métro: Papineau then bus no. 169, or Parc Jean-Drapeau then bus no. 167.

Planétarium de Montréal *Kids*   A window on the night sky with mythical monsters and magical heroes, Montréal's planetarium is right downtown in the heart of the city. Shows in the 20m (66-ft.) dome dazzle and inform at the same time, with up to five different shows screened daily. A Christmas show, "Season of Light," can be seen November through early January. Shows in English alternate with those in French.

1000 rue St-Jacques ouest (at Peel). (C) 514/872-4530. www.planetarium.montreal.qc.ca. Admission C$8 (US$8/£4) adults, C$6 (US$6/£3) seniors and students, C$4 (US$4/£2) children 5–17. MC, V. Hours vary according to show schedule; call for details. Métro: Bonaventure (exit toward rue de la Cathédrale).

6 Special Events & Festivals

In January, **La Fête des Neiges (Snow Festival)** ((C) **514/872-6120;** www.fetedes neiges.com) is Montréal's winter carnival with outdoor events such as dogsled runs, a mock survival camp, street hockey, ice skating, and tobogganing. The less athletically inclined can cheer from the sidelines and then inspect the snow and ice sculptures. It all takes place on Ile Ste-Hélène.

In late May, the **Montréal Bike Fest** (www.velo.qc.ca) attracts tens of thousands of enthusiasts in a variety of cycling competitions over 8 days, including a nocturnal bike ride (Un Tour la Nuit) and the grueling Tour de l'Ile, a 50km (31-mile) race around the rim of the island that draws 30,000 cyclists, shuts down roads and attracts over 100,000 spectators.

On nearly a dozen Wednesdays and Saturdays from June to August, **L'International des Feux Loto-Québec (International Fireworks Competition)** ((C) **514/ 397-2000;** www.internationaldesfeuxloto-quebec.com) pits the pyrotechnics of different countries against each other. Tickets are sold to watch from the open-air theater in La Ronde amusement park on Ile Ste-Hélène, although the fireworks can be enjoyed for free from almost anywhere overlooking the river (tickets do include entrance to the amusement park).

In July, the **Festival International de Jazz de Montréal** *GG* is one of the monster events on the city's calendar. Montréal has a long tradition in jazz, and this enormously successful festival has been celebrating America's art form since 1979. See p. 259.

In October, the **Black & Blue Festival** ((C) **514/875-7026;** www.bbcm.org) is one of the biggest gay festivals on the planet. And when we say big, we mean *big:* The main event for the 2007 fest was held at Olympic Stadium.

7 Outdoor Activities & Spectator Sports

Even if you come to Montréal without your outdoor gear, it's easy to get outside and join the fun.

OUTDOOR ACTIVITIES
BICYCLING & IN-LINE SKATING

Both bicycling and rollerblading are hugely popular in Montréal, and the city helps people indulge that passion: It boasts an expanding network of more than 350km

(217 miles) of cycling paths and year-round bike lanes, and in warm months, car lanes in heavily biked areas are blocked off with concrete barriers and turned into two-way lanes for people-powered vehicles.

If you're serious about biking, get in touch with the nonprofit organization **Vélo Québec** (© 800/567-8356 or 514/521-8356 in Montréal; www.velo.qc.ca). Vélo (which means bicycle) was behind the development of a 4,000km (2,485-mile) bike network called **Route verte** (Green Route) that stretches from one end of the Québec province to the other. The route was officially inaugurated in the summer of 2007. The Vélo website has the most up-to-date information on the state of the paths, the **Montréal Bike Fest** (see "Special Events," above), road races, new bike lanes, and more. (*Tip:* Several taxi companies have bike racks and charge just C$3 (US$3/£1.50) extra for each bike. They're listed at the Vélo Québec website—search for "taxi"—or call the Vélo office.)

If you're looking to rent a bike or pair of skates for an afternoon, the shop **CaRoule/ Montréal on Wheels** (© 514/866-0633; www.caroulemontreal.com) at 27 rue de la Commune est, the waterfront road bordering the Vieux-Port, offers rentals from April to October (by appointment in Mar and Nov). Bikes cost C$9 (US$9/£4.50) an hour and C$30 (US$30/£15) a day on the weekend, rollerblades a little less. Helmets are included and a deposit is required. The staff will set you up with a map (download-able from their website) and can point you toward the peaceful **Lachine Canal,** a nearly flat 11km (6.8-mile) *piste cyclable* (bicycle path) that travels alongside locks and over small bridges. The canal starts just a few blocks away. (The path is open year-round and maintained by Parks Canada from mid-Apr to Oct.) Other options for short rides from Vieux-Port are Ile Notre-Dame, where the Grand Prix auto racing track is a biker's dream less than 20 minutes away, or simply along the 2.5km (1½-mile) promenade that runs along the piers.

BOATING & KAYAKING

It's easy to rent kayaks, pedal boats, and small eco-friendly electric boats on the **Lachine Canal,** just to the west of Vieux-Port. The company **H2O Adventures** (© 514/842-1306; www.h2oadventures.com) won a 2007 Grand Prix du tourisme Québécois award for being a stand-out operation and has rentals starting at C$10 (US$10/£5) an hour. It also offers 2-hour introductory kayak lessons for C$35 (US$35/£18) on weekdays (C$4/US$4/£2 more on weekends). It's open daily. Find it at the **Marché Atwater** farmer's market, where you can pick up lunch from the inside *boulangerie* and *fromagerie,* adjacent to the canal (Métro: Lionel-Groulx).

BOAT TOURS

Le Bateau-Mouche (© 800/361-9952 or 514/849-9952; www.bateau-mouche.com) and **Croisières AML Cruises** (© 800/563-4643 or 514/842-3871; www.croisieresaml. com) both offer trips ranging from 60-minute tours that pass under bridges and provide sweeping views of the city to 4-hour dinner cruises. Prices start at about C$21 (US$21/ £11) for adults.

Croisière historique sur le canal de Lachine (© 866/846-0448 or 514/846-0428) is a leisurely Parks Canada trip up the Lachine Canal, which was inaugurated in 1824 so ships could bypass the Lachine Rapids on the way to the Great Lakes. The canal now has bike paths on either side of it and warehouses that are being converted into high-end condominiums.

Les Sautes-Moutons (© 514/284-9607; www.jetboatingmontreal.com) and **Les Descentes sur le St-Laurent** (© 514/767-2230; www.raftingmontreal.com) both offer hydrojet rides down the Lachine Rapids with trips that start at C$48 (US$48/ £24) for adults and up.

CROSS-COUNTRY SKIING

Parc Mont-Royal has an extensive cross-country course, as do many of the other city parks. Skiers have to supply their own equipment. Just an hour north from the city in the Laurentides (see section 10, later in this chapter), there are numerous options for skiing and rentals.

HIKING

The most popular hike is to head to the top of **Parc Mont-Royal.** They call it a mountain, but it's really more of a large hill. There are a web of options for trekking through it, from the broad and handsome pedestrian-only **chemin Olmsted** (a bridle path named for Frederick Law Olmsted, the park's landscape architect) to smaller paths and a steep set of stairs. The park is well marked and small enough that you can wander without fear of getting too lost.

ICE SKATING

In the winter, outdoor rinks are set up in Vieux-Port, Lac des Castors (Beaver Lake), and other spots around the city; check tourist offices for your best options. One of the most agreeable venues is the **Atrium Le 1000** (p. 246) in downtown. For one thing, it's indoors and warm, and for another, it's surrounded by cafes. And yes, it's even open in the summer.

JOGGING

There are many possibilities for running. In addition to the areas described above for biking and hiking, consider heading to either of the city's most prominent parks: **Parc La Fontaine** in the Plateau Mont-Royal neighborhood (p. 246), or **Parc Maisonneuve** in the east side of the city, adjacent to the **Jardin Botanique** (p. 245). Both are formally landscaped and well used for recreation and relaxation.

SWIMMING

The downtown **Hôtel Omni Mont-Royal** (p. 224) features a terrific health club, spa, and outdoor pool complex, with exercise machines, yoga classes, massages, steam rooms and saunas, and a year-round outdoor pool accessible from the inside on cold days. Nonguests can use it for C$25 (US$25/£13) adults and C$7 (US$7/£3.50) children, and it's open weekdays 6am to 9pm and weekends 7am to 8pm. The hotel is at 1050 rue Sherbrooke ouest, at rue Peel (© **514/284-1110**).

SPECTATOR SPORTS

Montréalers are as devoted to ice hockey as other Canadians are, with plenty of enthusiasm left over for U.S.-style football, soccer, and the other distinctive national sport, curling. (They liked baseball too, but not enough: In 2005, the Montréal Expos, plagued by poor attendance, left for Washington, D.C., where the team became the Nationals.) The biggest single event on the Montréal sports calendar is its version of the Indy 500: the Grand Prix car race that roars into town for 3 days each summer.

FOOTBALL

You might not expect U.S.-style professional football in Canada, but the **Montréal Alouettes** (French for "larks") claim, dubiously, that "Montréal is synonymous with football." No matter; the team does enjoy considerable success, frequently appearing in the Grey Cup, the Canadian Football League's version of the U.S. Super Bowl. The Als play at McGill University's Percival-Molson Memorial Stadium on a schedule that runs from June into November. Tickets start at C$22 (US$22/£11); details are at ✆ **514/871-2255** and www.montrealalouettes.com.

GRAND PRIX

For 3 days in early June, Montréal's entire focus is on the Grand Prix, the FIA's only stop in Canada. Over 110,000 people pour each day onto the island of Ile Notre-Dame, where a permanent track is installed (the rest of the year the circuit is used by cyclists and walkers) and watch race cars make 70 laps at up to 318kmph (198 mph). In the rest of the city, particularly rue Crescent in downtown, Formula 1 cars get put on display, streets shut down, and revelers party deep into the night. Hotel prices typically double and most require 3-night stays. Three-day Grand Prix tickets cost C$90–C$495 (US$90–US$495/£45–£247). Details and tickets sales are at ✆ **514/350-0000** and www.grandprix.ca.

HARNESS RACING

Popularly known as Blue Bonnets Racetrack, the **Hippodrome de Montréal** (✆ **514/739-2741;** www.hdem.com) celebrated its 100th birthday in 2007. It's the host facility for international harness-racing events, including the Coupe des Elevers (Breeders Cup). Parimutuel betting and free admission makes for a satisfying evening or Sunday-afternoon outing. The Hippodrome is located in the northwest of the city at 7440 bd. Décarie (corner of rue Jean-Talon; Métro: Namur, then take a shuttle bus).

HOCKEY

Fans were beside themselves with frustration over the cancellation of the 2004–05 NHL hockey season, but the contract problems were resolved in 2005 and all was well in the world again. The beloved **Montréal Canadiens** play right downtown at the Centre Bell arena. The team has won over 20 Stanley Cup championships since 1918, but hasn't enjoyed much success in recent years. The season runs from October into April, with playoffs continuing into June. Tickets from C$22–C$192 (US$22–US$192/£11–£96). Check www.canadiens.com for schedule and ticketing or call ✆ **514/790-1245.**

8 Shopping

Shopping ranks right up there with dining out as a prime activity among native Montréalers. Most are of French ancestry and seem to believe that impeccable taste bubbles through the Gallic gene pool. The city has produced a thriving fashion industry, from couture to ready-to-wear, with a history that reaches back to the earliest trade in furs and leather. *But note:* The Visitor Rebate Program, which used to allow nonresident visitors to apply for a rebate on tax they paid on most items purchased in Québec, was eliminated in 2007.

Best buys include **Canadian Inuit sculptures** and quilts, drawings, and carvings by Amerindian and other folk artists. The province's daring **clothing designers** produce some appealing fashions at prices that are often reasonable. And while demand has diminished, superbly constructed **furs and leather goods** are high-ticket items.

Ice cider *(cidre de glace)* and **ice wines** made in Québec province from apples and grapes left out after the first frost are inexpensive products to bring home. They are sold in duty-free shops at the border in addition to the provincial **Société des Alcools du Québec (SAQ)** stories throughout the region.

For fashion, art, and luxury items, head to **rue Sherbrooke** in downtown. Also downtown, **rue Ste-Catherine** is home to the city's top department stores and myriad satellite shops. Nearby, **rue Peel** is known for its men's fashions.

In Vieux-Montréal, the western end of **rue St-Paul** has a growing number of art galleries, clothing boutiques, and jewelry shops.

In Plateau Mont-Royal, the funkier **boulevard St-Laurent** sells everything from budget practicalities to off-the-wall handmade fashions. Look along **avenue Laurier** between boulevard St-Laurent and avenue de l'Epée for French boutiques, home furniture and accessories shops, and young Québécois designers. **Rue St-Denis** north of Sherbrooke has strings of shops filled with fun items.

The **underground city** (p. 213) is a warren of passageways connecting more than 1,700 shops in 10 shopping malls that have levels both above and below street level. Typical is the **Complexe Desjardins** (© **514/845-4636**), a downtown mall that has waterfalls and fountains, trees and hanging vines, lanes of shops going off in every direction, and elevators whisking people up to one of the four tall office towers. The main thing to remember is that when you enter a street-level shopping emporium, it's likely that you'll be able to head to a lower level and connect to the maze of tunnels and shopping hallways that will lead you to another set of stores.

ANTIQUES

Antiques can be found along rue Sherbrooke near the Musée des Beaux-Arts and on the little side streets near the museum. More antiques and collectibles, in more than 50 tempting shops one after another, can be found along the lengthening "Antiques Alley" of rue Notre-Dame, especially concentrated between rue Guy and avenue Atwater.

Antiques Puces-Libres   Three fascinatingly cluttered floors are packed with pine and oak furniture, lamps, clocks, vases, and more, most of it 19th- and early-20th-century French-Canadian Art Nouveau. 4240 rue St-Denis (near rue Rachel), Plateau Mont-Royal. © **514/842-5931.**

ARTS & CRAFTS

In warmer months, stroll Vieux-Montréal: Artists display and sell their unremarkable but nevertheless competent works along short **rue St-Amable,** just off Place Jacques-Cartier. Some of the best stores in Montréal are found in city museums. Tops among them are shops in **Pointe-à-Callière** (the Montréal Museum of Archaeology and History), in Vieux-Montréal; shops in the **Musée des Beaux-Arts** and the **Musée McCord,** both on rue Sherbrooke in downtown; and the shop at the **Musée d'Art Contemporain** in the Place-des-Arts, on rue Ste-Catherine ouest, also downtown.

Guilde Canadienne des Métier d'Art Québec   A small but choice collection of craft items is displayed in a meticulously arranged gallery setting. Among the objects are blown glass, paintings on silk, pewter, tapestries, and ceramics. The store is particularly strong in avant-garde jewelry and Inukjuak sculpture. A small carving might be had for C$100 to C$300 (US$100–US$300/£50–£150), while the larger, more important pieces go for hundreds, even thousands, more. 1460 rue Sherbrooke ouest (near rue Mackay), downtown. © **514/849-6091.**

L'Empreinte   This is a *coopérative artisane* (craftspersons' collective). The ceramics, textiles, and glassware often occupy that vaguely defined territory between art and craft. Quality is uneven but usually tips toward the high end. 272 rue St-Paul est (next to the Marché Bonsecours), Vieux-Montréal. © **514/861-4427.**

BATH & BODY

Fruits & Passion   Like The Body Shop, Lush, and other shops full of good smells and a natural aesthetic, this Québec-based chain trades in its own variation of funky soaps, creams, and more (avocado body butter, eco-spa vegetable soap with shavings of panama wood, and so forth). The chain has made only limited inroads to the U.S. and Europe so far. 4159A rue Saint-Denis (near rue Rachel), Plateau Mont-Royal. ⓒ 514/282-9406.

Spa Dr. Hauschka   A chi-chi spa for high-end pampering and getting "in touch with your inner beauty," as the materials put it. On-site treatments include facials, lavender baths, mud baths, and more, but you can also buy the Dr. Hauschka products and indulge at home. 1444 rue Sherbrooke ouest (at rue Redpath), downtown. ⓒ 514/286-1444.

DEPARTMENT STORES

Montréal's major downtown shopping emporia stretch along rue Ste-Catherine from rue Guy eastward to Carré Phillips at Aylmer (department store Holt Renfrew is north on rue Sherbrooke ouest, parallel). An excursion along the 12-block stretch of Ste-Catherine can keep a diligent shopper busy for days. Also look for these stores' branches in the underground city.

Henry Birks et Fils ⟨★⟩   Across from Christ Church Cathedral at the corner of rue Ste-Catherine stands Henry Birks et Fils, a highly regarded jeweler since 1879. This beautiful old store, with its dark-wood display cases, stone pillars, and marble floors, is a living part of Montréal's Victorian heritage. Products also include pens and desk accessories, watches, leather goods, and china. 1240 Phillips Sq. (at rue Ste-Catherine), downtown. ⓒ 514/397-2511.

Holt Renfrew ⟨★⟩   HR began as a furrier in 1837 and is now a showcase for the best in international style, displayed in miniboutiques and focusing on fashion for men and women. Brands include Giorgio Armani, Prada, Gucci, and Chanel, and are displayed with a tastefulness bordering on solemnity. 1300 rue Sherbrooke ouest (at rue de la Montagne), downtown. ⓒ 514/842-5111.

La Baie ⟨★⟩   No retailer has an older or more celebrated name than that of the Hudson's Bay Company, a name shortened in recent years to "The Bay," then transformed into "La Baie" by the language laws that decreed French the lingua franca. The main store focuses on clothing but also offers crystal, china, Inuit carvings, and its famous Hudson's Bay blankets. The company was incorporated in Canada in 1670 and bought by an American investor in 2006, an event that caused understandable consternation among some Canadians. 585 rue Ste-Catherine ouest (near rue Aylmer), downtown. ⓒ 514/281-4422. www.hbc.com.

Maison Simons   This branch was the first foray out of its home area for Québec City's long-established family-owned department store. Most Montréalers had never heard of it, but that changed fast given the fairly priced fashions that fill the refurbished floors of a building that once housed the venerable Simpson's department store. 977 rue Ste-Catherine ouest (at rue Mansfield), downtown. ⓒ 514/282-1840.

Ogilvy ⟨★★⟩   The most vibrant of a classy breed of department store that appears to be fading from the scene. Established in 1866, Ogilvy has been at this location since 1912. A bagpiper still announces the noon hour and special events, and glowing chandeliers and wide aisles enhance the shopping experience. Ogilvy has always had a reputation for quality merchandise and now contains more than 50 boutiques, including Louis Vuitton, Anne Klein, Burberry, and Jones New York. It's also known for its eagerly awaited

Christmas windows. The basement-level Café Romy has quality sandwiches, salads, and desserts. 1307 rue Ste-Catherine ouest (at rue de la Montagne), downtown. ☎ 514/842-7711.

EDIBLES

The food markets described in "Picnic Fare" (p. 237) carry abundant assortments of cheeses, wines, and packaged food products that can serve as gifts or delicious reminders of your visit when you get home.

Canadian Maple Delights *Kids*   Everything maple-y is presented here by a consortium of Québec producers of pastries, gelati, gift baskets, truffles, and, of course, every grade of syrup. A cute cafe serves gelato and sweets. 84 rue St-Paul est (near Place Jacques-Cartier), Vieux-Montréal. ☎ 514/765-3456.

Les Chocolats de Chloé *Finds*   If you approach chocolate the way others approach wine or cheese—that is, pining for the best of the best—then this teeny shop will bring great delight. Chocolates are made on-site, and tastes can be had for as little as C$2.50 (US$2.50/£1.25). Especially adorable: a hollow chocolate fish filled with three little chocolate fishes, for C$9 (US$9/£4.50). 375 rue Roy est (at St-Denis), Plateau Mont-Royal. ☎ 514/849-5550.

FASHION FOR MEN

Eccetera & Co.   Favoring ready-to-wear from such higher-end manufacturers as Hugo Boss and Canali, this store lays out its stock in a soothing setting with personalized service. As it says on the door: GOOD CLOTHES OPEN ALL DOORS. 2021 rue Peel (near bd. de Maisonneuve), downtown. ☎ 514/845-9181.

Harry Rosen *★*   For over 50 years, this well-known retailer of designer suits and accessories has been making men look good in Armani, Versace, and the "Harry Rosen Made in Italy" line. Les Cours Mont-Royal, 1455 rue Peel (at bd. de Maisonneuve), downtown. ☎ 514/284-3315. www.harryrosen.com.

Kamkyl   High style with an Asian influence for "young moderns," presented in 186 sq. m (2,000 sq. ft.) nearly empty save for two black sofas, a coffee machine, and suspended steel racks displaying suits, jackets, and slacks. The owners of this spare boutique are also the clothing's designers. 439 rue St-Pierre, Vieux-Montréal. ☎ 514/281-8221.

FASHION FOR WOMEN

Collection Méli Mélo *Finds*   This shop used to focus a mix of exotica and furniture from Morocco to Thailand down into sub-Saharan Africa. There's still some of that, but a shift in 2007 brought a new concentration on women's clothes by Montréal's chic designers. The collection includes Helmer, Anastasia Lomonova, and Eugenia Design. 205 St-Paul ouest (at rue St-François-Xavier), Vieux-Montréal. ☎ 514/285-5585.

Kaliyana *★*   Vaguely Japanese, certainly minimalist, these free-flowing garments are largely asymmetrical separates. Made by a Canadian designer, they come in muted tones of solid colors, with simple complementary necklaces. 4107 rue St-Denis (near rue Rachel), Plateau Mont-Royal. ☎ 514/844-0633.

Kyoze   The eye-catching creations of Québécois and other Canadian designers, including jewelry and accessories, are featured here. Items are moderate to expensive. 380 St-Antoine ouest (near rue de Bleury), downtown. ☎ 514/847-7572.

Mango   This is the first downtown outlet of a Spanish-owned international chain. Much of its merchandise is upmarket jeans and tees, but the dressier separates intrigue with quiet tones and jazzy cuts—very Euro. 1000 rue Ste-Catherine ouest (at rue Metcalfe), downtown. © 514/397-2323.

FASHION FOR MEN & WOMEN

Montréal's long history as a center for the fur trade buttresses the many wholesale and retail furriers, which have outlets downtown and in Plateau Mont-Royal. Nowhere are fur shops more concentrated than on the "fur row" of **rue Mayor,** downtown between rue de Bleury and rue City Councillors.

Club Monaco   Awareness of this expanding Canadian-owned international chain is growing, as is appreciation of its minimalist, largely monochromatic garments for men and women, along with silver jewelry, eyewear, and cosmetics. Think Prada but affordable, with a helpful young staff. In Les Cours Mont-Royal shopping complex, 1455 rue Peel (north of rue Ste-Catherine), downtown. © 514/499-0959.

Le Château   The merchandizing philosophy here is to move it in then move it out fast. Inveterate shoppers drop by regularly to see what's arrived each week. What they find are affordable shirts, pants, dresses, and suits. 1310 rue Ste-Catherine ouest (near rue de la Montagne), downtown. © 514/866-2481.

HOUSEWARES

Arthur Quentin ⊛   Doling out household products of quiet taste and discernment for over 25 years, this St-Denis stalwart is divided into departments specializing in tableware, kitchen gadgets, and home decor. That means lamps and Limoges china, terrines and tea towels, mandolins and mezzalunas. 3960 rue St-Denis (south of av. Duluth), Plateau Mont-Royal. © 514/843-7513.

Senteurs de Provence   The sunny south of France is evoked in pottery that's hand-painted in the creamy-bright colors of Provence, complemented by cunning collections of bath soaps and gels, printed linens, and lightly perfumed lotions and creams. Several locations. 363 rue St-Paul est (near Marché Bonsecours), Vieux-Montréal. ((© 514/395-8686).

9 Montréal After Dark

Montréal's reputation for effervescent nightlife reaches back to the Roaring Twenties—specifically to the United States' 13-year experiment with Prohibition from 1920 to 1933. Americans streamed across the border for temporary relief from alcohol deprivation (while Canadian distillers and brewers made fortunes—few of them with meticulous regard for legalistic niceties). Montréal already enjoyed a sophisticated and slightly naughty reputation as the Paris of North America, which added to the allure.

Nearly a century later, clubbing and barhopping remain popular activities, with nightspots keeping much later hours in Montréal than in archrival Toronto, which still heeds Calvinist notions of propriety and early bedtimes.

The city boasts its own outstanding symphony, dozens of French- and English-language theater companies, and the incomparable performance company Cirque du Soleil (p. 247). It's also on the concert circuit that includes Chicago, Boston, and New York, so internationally known entertainers, music groups, and dance companies pass through frequently. A decidedly French enthusiasm for film, as well as the city's ever-increasing reputation as a movie-production center, ensures support for cinemas showcasing experimental, offbeat, and foreign films.

A discount ticket office for Montréal cultural events opened in 2007. Called **Vitrine culturelle de Montréal** ("cultural window of Montréal"; © 514/285-4545;

Tips   **Resources: Checking What's on in Montréal Nightlife**

For details on performances or special events on when you're in town, pick up a copy of the free *Montréal Scope* (www.montrealscope.com), a weekly ads-and-events booklet usually available in hotel receptions, or the free weekly papers *Mirror* (www.montrealmirror.com) and *Hour* (www.hour.ca), both in English. Listings of largely mainstream cultural and entertainment events are posted at **www.canada.com** and **www.montrealplus.ca**.

---

www.vitrineculturelle.com), it's located at 145 rue Sainte-Catherine ouest in Place des Arts. It includes full-price tickets as well as last-minute deals.

THE PERFORMING ARTS
CIRCUS
Also see **Cirque du Soleil** (p. 247).

Pavillon de la TOHO *Value*   Next door to the Cirque du Soleil's training complex and company offices, TOHO is a performance facility devoted to the circus arts. Acrobats and performers from the National Circus School, Québec's Productions à Trois Têtes, and the Imperial Acrobats of China have all put on shows here in the in-the-round hall done up like an old-fashioned circus tent. TOHO is also a green building, built with recycled pieces of an amusement park bumper-car ride and heated by biogas from the adjacent landfill. Worth a special trip only if you're a circus nut or environmental architecture fan—guided tours of the small space are available with advance reservations—but certainly check if there's a show playing and build a visit around that. The venue is located in the lower-income Saint-Michel district well north of downtown, but accessible by Métro and bus. Open daily from 9am to 5pm. 2345 rue Jarry est (corner of rue d'Iberville, where Jarry crosses Autoroute 40). © 888/376-TOHU. www.tohu.ca. Free to view the facility and exhibits. Performance tickets from C$23 (US$23/£12) adults, C$14 (US$14/£7) children 12 and younger. Métro: Jarry or Iberville and bus. 8km (5 miles) from downtown, north on rue St-Denis to where it meets Autoroute 40.

CLASSICAL MUSIC & OPERA
L'Opéra de Montréal ✮✮✮   Founded in 1980, this outstanding opera company mounts six productions a year, with artists from Québec and abroad participating in such shows as *La Traviata, Don Giovanni, Aida,* and *Otello.* Performances are held from September to June in theaters at Place des Arts and occasionally at other venues. Place des Arts, Salle Wilfrid-Pelletier hall, 260 bd. de Maisonneuve ouest, downtown. © 514/985-2258. www.operademontreal.com. Tickets from C$44 (US$44/£22). Métro: Place des Arts.

L'Orchestre Symphonique de Montréal (OSM) ✮✮   Kent Nagano was brought on as conductor in 2005 and has focused the repertoire on programs featuring works by Franck and Bruckner in addition to Ravel, Mozart, and Bach. All is not staid: The orchestra has also partnered with local rockers Les Respectables for Pops events. It performs at Place des Arts and the Notre-Dame Basilica. Place des Arts, Salle Wilfrid-Pelletier hall, 260 bd. de Maisonneuve ouest, downtown. © 514/842-9951 for tickets. www.osm.ca. Tickets from C$25 (US$25/£13). Métro: Place des Arts.

Orchestre Métropolitain du Grand Montréal   This orchestra's 2008 schedule includes symphonies by Bruckner, Mahler, and Haydn, and a celebration of Glenn

Gould. In the summer, it puts on free outdoor concerts at the Théâtre de Verdure in Parc La Fontaine. Place des Arts, Maisonneuve Theatre, 260 bd. de Maisonneuve ouest, downtown. ℭ 514/ 842-2112. www.orchestremetropolitain.com. Tickets from C$21 (US$21/£11). Métro: Place des Arts.

CONCERT HALLS & AUDITORIUMS

Centre Bell   Seating up to 21,500, Centre Bell is the home of the Montréal Canadiens hockey team and host to international rock and pop stars on the order of Justin Timberlake, the White Stripes, The Police reunion, and Beyoncé, as well as such dissimilar attractions as Disney on Ice and Meat Loaf (not together, alas). 1260 rue de la Gauchetière ouest, downtown. ℭ 514/ 989-2841. www.centrebell.ca. Métro: Bonaventure.

Metropolis   Starting life as a skating rink in 1884, the Metropolis is now a prime showplace for traveling rock groups, hosting Joss Stone and Queens of the Stone Age in recent years. While it is primarily a concert venue that can hold up to 2,300 customers, it is also home to a small attached lounge, Le Savoy. 59 Ste-Catherine est, downtown. ℭ 514/844-3500. www.spectrumdemontreal.ca/metropolis. Métro: St-Laurent or Berri-UQAM.

Place des Arts 🏵🏵   Since 1992, Place des Arts has been the city's central entertainment complex, mounting performances of musical concerts, opera, dance, and theater in five halls: **Salle Wilfrid-Pelletier** (2,982 seats), where the Orchestre Symphonique de Montréal often performs; the **Théâtre Maisonneuve** (1,458 seats), where the Orchestre Métropolitain de Montréal and Les Grands Ballets Canadiens perform; the **Théâtre Jean-Duceppe** (755 seats); the **Cinquième Salle** (417 seats); and the small **Studio-Théâtre Stella Artois** (138 seats). Portions of the city's many arts festivals are staged in the halls and outdoor plaza here, as are traveling productions of Broadway shows. 260 bd. de Maisonneuve ouest (ticket office), downtown. ℭ 514/842-2112 for information and tickets. www.pda.qc.ca. Métro: Place des Arts.

Pollack Concert Hall   In a landmark building dating from 1899 and fronted by a statue of Queen Victoria, this McGill University venue is in nearly constant use, especially during the school year with concerts and recitals by university students and professionals from the music faculty. On the McGill University campus, 555 rue Sherbrooke ouest, downtown. ℭ 514/398-4547. www.music.mcgill.ca. Performances are usually free. Métro: McGill.

Théâtre de Verdure *(Value)*   Tango nights are popular at this open-air theater nestled in a popular park in Plateau Mont-Royal. Everything is free: music, dance concerts and theater, often with well-known artists and performers. Many in the audience pack picnics. Performances are held from June to August; check the tourist office for days and times. Parc La Fontaine. Métro: Sherbrooke.

DANCE

Frequent appearances by notable dancers and troupes from other parts of Canada and the world—among them Paul Taylor, the Feld Ballet, and Le Ballet National du Canada—augment the accomplished resident companies.

Les Grands Ballets Canadiens 🏵🏵   This prestigious touring company, performing both a classical and a modern repertoire, has developed a following far beyond national borders in its 50 years (it was founded in 1957). In the process, it has brought prominence to many gifted Canadian choreographers and composers. The troupe's annual production of *The Nutcracker* is always a big event. Performances are held October through May. Place des Arts, 175 Ste-Catherine ouest (main entrance), downtown. ℭ 514/842-2112. www.grandsballets.qc.ca. Tickets from C$25 (US$25/£13) and way up. Métro: Place des Arts.

THEATER

Centaur Theatre   The city's principal English-language theater is housed in a former stock-exchange building (1903). A mix of classics, foreign adaptations, and works by Canadian playwrights such as Michel Tremblay are staged here. 453 rue St-François-Xavier (near rue Notre-Dame), Vieux- Montréal. ℭ 514/288-3161. www.centaurtheatre.com. Tickets from C$31 (US$31/£16). Métro: Place d'Armes.

Saidye Bronfman Centre for the Arts   Montréal's Yiddish theater, founded in 1937, the center is a branch of the YM-YWHA Montréal Jewish Community Centres and host to dance and music recitals, occasional lectures, and plays in both Yiddish and English. Recent productions have included Noël Coward's *Fallen Angels* and the Dora Wasserman Yiddish Theatre's production of *Those Were the Days*. The center is a considerable distance from downtown and the taxi fare is substantial, but it is on the subway line. 5170 Côte-Ste-Catherine (near bd. Décarie), Plateau Mont-Royal. ℭ 514/739-2310. www.saidyebronfman.org. Tickets from C$34 (US$34/£17). Métro: Côte-Ste-Catherine. Bus: 29 ouest.

COMEDY & MUSIC CLUBS
COMEDY

The once red-hot market for comedy clubs across North America may have cooled, but it lives on in Montréal, mostly because the city is the home to the highly regarded **Juste pour Rire (Just for Laughs) Festival** (ℭ 888/244-3155; www.hahaha.com) held every summer. Those who have so far avoided the comedy-club experience should know that profanity, bathroom humor, and ethnic slurs are common fodder for performers. To avoid becoming objects of the comedians' barbs, it's wise to sit well back from the stage. Check before buying tickets if the show is in French or English.

Comedyworks   There's a full card of comedy at this long-running club situated on a jumping block of rue Bishop south of rue Ste-Catherine. Shows here are in English, and Monday is open-mic night, Tuesday and Wednesday improv, and Thursday through Saturday international headliners. No food is served, just drinks. Reservations are recommended, especially on Friday, when it may be necessary to arrive early to secure a seat. Shows are nightly at 9pm with additional 11:15pm shows on Fridays and Saturdays. 1238 rue Bishop (at rue Ste-Catherine), downtown. ℭ 514/398-9661. www.comedyworks montreal.com. Cover C$3–C$12 (US$3–US$12/£1.50–£6). Métro: Guy-Concordia.

DANCE CLUBS

As elsewhere, Montréal's dance clubs change in popularity in the blink of an eye and new ones sprout like toadstools after a heavy rain, withering just as quickly. For the latest, quiz concierges or waiters—whoever looks as if they might follow the scene—and visit **www.martiniboys.com**, an insouciant site that is, it says, "a study of all things cool." Also see the clubs listed in "The Village" (p. 262).

Club Balattou   An infectious, sensual tropical beat issues from this club-with-a-difference on The Main, a hot, happy variation from the prevailing grunge and murk that seeps out of mainstream music clubs. Things get going about 10pm every night but Monday. 4372 bd. St-Laurent (at rue Marie-Anne), Plateau Mont-Royal. ℭ 514/845-5447. Métro: Mont-Royal.

Newtown   Huge fanfare trumpeted the 2001 opening of this tri-level club in the white-hot center of rue Crescent nightlife. One of the owners is Formula 1 race car driver and local hero Jacques Villeneuve, whose last name can be translated as "New Town." Adjoining town houses were scooped out to make one big trendy nightspot at a reported cost of C$6 million at the time, with a disco in the basement, big barroom on the main floor, restaurant one floor up, and rooftop terrace in summer. Reservations are usually required for the restaurant, but admission to the bar and dance floor shouldn't be a problem. The bar and restaurant are open daily, and the disco is open Friday and Saturday. 1476 rue Crescent (at de Maisonneuve), downtown. ℂ 514/284-6555. www. newtown.ca. Métro: Peel.

Time Supper Club   Though food is served, it isn't the prime attraction, Time gives its fabulous crowd a chance to get up from the tables and work off the calories to rock, house, and hip-hop that thumps on till closing at 3am. The waitstaff is startlingly attractive—okay, downright sexy. Dress well, look good, and approach the door with confidence. It's located in a dreary industrial neighborhood south of the downtown core, so you may wish to arrive by car or taxi. 997 rue St-Jacques ouest (near rue Peel), downtown. ℂ 514/392-9292. Métro: Bonaventure.

FOLK, ROCK & POP

Montréal has a strong showing of innovative alternative rock, with homegrown outfits that include Arcade Fire, Wolf Parade, and Godspeed You! Black Emperor. (The band Of Montreal, however, is from Georgia.) Scores of bars, cafes, theaters, clubs, and even churches present live music on at least an occasional basis.

Club Soda   This long-established club, in a seedy part of lower St. Laurent, remains one of the prime destinations for performers just below the megastar level, including U.S. rockers Dinosaur Jr. and Québec's own Xavier Caféine. It also hosts several of the city's comedy festivals and acts for the annual jazz festival. 1225 bd. St-Laurent (at rue Ste-Catherine), downtown. ℂ 514/286-1010. www.clubsoda.ca. Tickets from C$15 (US$15/£7.50). Métro: St-Laurent.

Hurley's Irish Pub   The Irish have always been one of the largest immigrant groups in Montréal, and their musical tradition thrives here. In front is a street-level terrace, and Celtic instrumentalists perform every night of the week, usually starting around 9:30pm. 1225 rue Crescent (at rue Ste-Catherine), downtown. ℂ 514/861-4111. www.hurleysirishpub. com. Métro: Guy-Concordia.

Les Deux Pierrots ℛ   Perhaps the best known of Montréal's *boîtes-à-chansons* (song clubs). The main section is an intimate French-style cabaret, with a couple of attached rooms, La Boîte à Spectacles and Le Resto-Bar Le Pierrot. The singers interact animatedly with the crowd, often bilingually, from 8pm until 3 in the morning. 104 rue St-Paul est (west of place Jacques-Cartier), Vieux-Montréal. ℂ 514/861-1270. www.lespierrots.com. Cover from C$5 (US$5/£2.50). Métro: Place d'Armes.

JAZZ & BLUES

Montréal's major **Festival International de Jazz** ℛℛ is held every summer and caters to the public's interest in this original American art form. During the 11 days, close to 150 indoor shows are scheduled, with countless outdoor, ad-hoc performances as well. Wynton Marsalis, Harry Connick, Jr., Keith Jarrett, and even Bob Dylan have been featured in recent years, although it costs serious money to hear stars of such magnitude and tickets sell out months in advance. Fortunately, hundreds of other concerts are free. "Jazz" is broadly interpreted to include everything from Dixieland to reggae, world beat, and the unclassifiable experimental. For information on the festival, call ℂ 888/515-0515 or visit www.montrealjazzfest.com.

Casa del Popolo   This scruffy storefront might seem an unlikely place to launch an increasingly visible summer music festival, but that it has. While jazz and blues dominate the regular schedule, there's plenty of room for percussion specialists, bagpipe, calypso, and reggae. A sister performance space, **La Sala Rossa,** across the street at 4848 bd. St-Laurent, brings in bigger acts. Food is available—strictly vegetarian—and draft beer by the pint is the beverage preferred by the leftie bohemian clientele. Don't overdress. 4873 bd. St-Laurent (near bd. St-Joseph), Plateau Mont-Royal. ℂ 514/284-3804. www. casadelpopolo.com. Cover C$6–C$15 (US$6–US$15/£3–£7.50). Métro: Laurier.

Maison de Jazz ★ Right downtown, this New Orleans–style jazz venue has been on the scene for decades. Lovers of barbecued ribs and jazz, most of them well past the bloom of youth, start early in filling the room, which is decorated in mock Art Nouveau style with tiered levels. Live music starts around 7:30pm and continues until closing time. The ribs are okay and the jazz is of the swinging mainstream variety, with occasional digressions into more esoteric forms. 2060 rue Aylmer (south of rue Sherbrooke), downtown. ℂ 514/842-8656. www.houseofjazz.ca. Cover C$5 (US$5/£2.50). Métro: McGill.

Modavie In the winter, set aside Friday or Saturday night for dinner with jazz at this popular Vieux-Montréal bistro-bar-lounge; in the summer, come in any night at 7pm. Single-malt scotches and cigars are at the ready. Music is usually mainstream jazz, by duos or trios. It's a friendly place, and the food is good, too. 1 rue St-Paul ouest (corner of rue St-Laurent), Vieux-Montréal. ℂ 514/287-9582. Métro: Place d'Armes.

Upstairs Jazz Bar & Grill Name aside, this small room is *down* a few steps from the street. Big names are infrequent, but the jazz groups appearing every night are more than competent. Performances usually begin at 9pm. Decor is largely vintage record album covers and fish tanks. Pretty good food ranges from bar snacks to more substantial meals. Most patrons are edging toward their middle years or are already there. 1254 rue Mackay (near rue Ste-Catherine), downtown. ℂ 514/931-6808. www.upstairsjazz. com. Cover usually about C$10 (US$10/£5). Métro: Guy-Concordia.

BARS & CAFES

An abundance of restaurants, bars, and cafes line the streets near the downtown commercial district, from rue Stanley to rue Guy between rue Ste-Catherine and boulevard de Maisonneuve. **Rue Crescent,** in particular, hums with activity from late afternoon until far into the evening, especially after 10pm on summer weekend nights, when the street swarms with people careening from bar to restaurant to club.

In the Plateau Mont-Royal neighborhood, **boulevard St-Laurent,** or The Main, as it's known, is another nightlife strip, abounding in bars and clubs, most with a distinctive European—particularly French—personality, as opposed to the Anglo flavor of the rue Crescent area.

In Vieux-Montréal, **rue St-Paul** west of place Jacques-Cartier falls somewhere in the middle on the Anglophone-Francophone spectrum.

In all cases, bars tend to open around 11:30am and stay open late. Many of them have *heures joyeuses* (happy hours) from as early as 3pm to as late as 9pm, but usually for a shorter period within those hours. At those times, two-for-one drinks are the rule. Otherwise, given the high taxes on alcoholic beverages, the beverage of choice is most often beer. Look for a sign reading BIERES EN FUT—beer on draft. Last call for orders is 3am, but patrons are often allowed to dawdle over those drinks until 4am.

DOWNTOWN/RUE CRESCENT

Le Cabaret In L'Hôtel de la Montagne and within sight of the trademark lobby fountain with its nude bronze sprite sporting stained-glass wings, this appealing piano bar draws a crowd of youngish to middle-aged professionals after 5:30pm. In summer, there's a terrace bar on the roof by the pool for sunbathing, swimming, meals, drinks,

and dancing; it's open to nonguests, too. 1430 rue de la Montagne (north of rue Ste-Catherine).
© 514/288-5656. Métro: Guy-Concordia.

Le Tour de Ville Memorable and breathtaking. We're talking about the view, that is, from Montréal's only revolving restaurant and bar (the bar part doesn't revolve, but you still get a great view). The best time to go is when the sun is setting and the city lights are beginning to blink on. Open daily from 5:30pm, and on Sunday mornings for brunch. In the Delta Centre-Ville Hôtel, 777 rue University. © 514/879-4777 for reservations. Métro: Square Victoria.

Ritz Bar A mature, prosperous crowd seeks out the quiet Ritz Bar in the Ritz-Carlton, adjacent to the semilegendary Café de Paris restaurant. Anyone can take advantage of the tranquil room and the professionalism of its staff, but because the atmosphere is rather formal, most men will be more at ease with a jacket. The bar is just off the hotel lobby, to the right. In the Ritz-Carlton Hôtel, 1228 rue Sherbrooke ouest (at rue Drummond). © 514/842-4212. Métro: Peel.

Sir Winston Churchill Pub ⟨ The three levels of bars and cafes incorporated here have been operating for over 40 years and are rue Crescent landmarks. The New Orleans–style sidewalk and first-floor terraces (open in summer and enclosed in winter) make perfect vantage points for checking out the pedestrian traffic. The burgers and such have to look up to see mediocrity, but the mixed crowd of questing young professionals don't seem to mind. Open daily 11:30am to 3am. 1459 rue Crescent (near rue Ste-Catherine). © 514/288-3814. Métro: Guy-Concordia.

W Hotel With its Le Plateau Lounge, W Bartini, and Wunderbar open daily until 3 a.m., W attracts some of the best-looking partiers in town. In the W Hotel, 901 Victoria Sq. (at rue McGill). © 516/395-3100. Métro: Square Victoria.

VIEUX-MONTRÉAL

Aszú This classy wine bar features a selection of 450 labels—all private import. Better still, on any night, between 60 and 70 are available by the glass. A menu of oysters, tartar trio, seasonal mushrooms and the like provides accompaniment to the main event. With room for about 30 people at the bar, 40 at inside tables, and 75 on a cute side terrace, this is a cozy find. 212 rue Notre Dame ouest (at rue St-François-Xavier). © 514/845-5436. Métro: Place d'Armes.

Le Jardin Nelson Near the foot of **Place Jacques Cartier**, the main plaza in Vieux-Montréal, a passage leads into a tree-shaded garden court in back of a stone building dating from 1812. A pleasant hour or two can be spent listening to jazz every noontime and evening, and afternoons from Thursday through Sunday. Food takes second place, but the kitchen does well with its pizzas and crêpes. When the weather's nice, it's open until 2am. Closed November through mid-April. 407 place Jacques-Cartier (at rue St-Paul). © 514/861-5731. Métro: Place d'Armes or Champ de Mars.

Suite 701 When the Hôtel Place d'Armes converted its old lobby and wine bar to a spiffy lounge, yuppies young and not-so got the word fast. They crowd in nightly, but especially Thursdays. Upscale bar food includes mac-'n'-cheese with chipotle peppers and beef short rib *poutine*. Happy hour is 5 to 8pm. Corner rue St-Jacques and côte de la Place d'Armes. © 514/904 1201. Métro: Place d'Armes.

PLATEAU MONT-ROYAL & MILE END

Laïka Amidst the plethora of St-Laurent watering stops, this bright little *boîte* stands out for its open front in summer and the fresh flowers on the bar and some of the tables. Tasty sandwiches and tapas are served, and the Sunday brunch is popular. DJs spin house, funk, and whatnot to 3am for the mostly 18- to 35-year-old crowd. 4040 bd. St-Laurent (near rue Duluth). ⓒ 514/842-8088. Métro: Sherbrooke.

Whisky Café   Those who enjoy scotch, particularly single-malts like Laphraoig and Glenfiddich, will find over 150 different labels to sample here. (Because the Québec government applies stiff taxes for the privilege, many of the patrons—suits to grad students—seem to stick to beer.) The decor is sophisticated, with exposed beams and vents, handmade tiled tables, and large wood-enclosed columns. Another decorative triumph: The men's urinal has a waterfall acting as the *pissoir*. Attached is a separate cigar lounge, with leather armchairs and Cubans on sale until 3am. 5800 bd. St-Laurent (at rue Bernard). ⓒ 514/278-2646. Métro: Laurier.

THE VILLAGE

The city's lively **Quartier Gai (Gay Village),** or simply The Village, comprises a stretch of rue Ste-Catherine from rue St-Hubert to rue Papineau. One of the largest gay and lesbian communities in North America, it is action central for both natives and visitors. That's true on any night, really, but especially during such annual events as the weeklong celebration of sexual diversity known as **Divers/Cité** in late July and early August (www.diverscite.org) and the **Black & Blue Festival** (www.bbcm.org), probably the world's largest circuit party with a week of entertainment and club dancing held for a week in October. In 2006, Montréal added another pink feather to its cap by hosting the **1st World Outgames,** attracting more than 16,000 athletes.

If you're looking for a more low-key time without all the muscle, disco, and traces of seediness that surround the edges of the neighborhood, you'll find the city overall to be tolerant and nonplussed by same-sex couples. The official **Tourisme Montréal** website at **www.tourisme-montreal.org** offers a "Montréal Gay to Z" minisite that includes listings of gay-friendly accommodations, links, and more. **The Village Tourism Information Centre** at 576 rue Ste-Catherine est, Suite 200 (ⓒ 888/595-8110 or 514/522-1885) is open daily in the summer and weekdays the rest of the year. In addition, the **Québec Gay Chamber of Commerce** has a website at **www.ccgq.ca**.

Chez Mado   The glint of the sequins can be blinding! Inspired by 1920s cabaret theater, this determinedly trendy place has both performances and dancing. Every night of the week has a different theme, from Monday's karaoke and Wednesday's variety events to Friday and Saturday's festive drag shows. Happy hour is from 4 to 9pm. Look for the massive pink-haired drag queen on the retro marquee. 1115 rue Ste-Catherine est (near rue Amherst). ⓒ 514/525-7566. Métro: Beaudry.

Club Unity Montréal   The former dance club Unity II was one of the biggest and most popular discos in town before it was severely damaged in an April 2006 fire. It reopened as Club Unity Montréal a few months later and once again draws well-dressed, friendly, mixed crowds Fridays and Saturdays to its three-rooms, with top-of-the-line lighting and sound systems, and large outdoor roof terrace. 1171 Ste-Catherine est. ⓒ 514/523-2777. www.clubunitymontreal.com. Métro: Beaudry.

Gotha Salon Bar Lounge   For a quieter venue in The Village, this cozy lounge for both men and women has a fireplace, live piano on Sunday night, and a relaxed vibe. It's at street level below the Aubergell Bed & Breakfast on rue Amherst, a road with antique shops chock-a-block with vintage and collectible goodies from the 1930s to 1980s. 1641 rue Amherst. ⓒ 514/526-1270. Métro: Beaudry.

Sky Club & Pub ☆   A complex that includes a pub which serves dinner Monday through Saturday and brunch on weekends, the Nirvana male strip club, and a spacious dance floor, Sky is thought by many to be the city's hottest spot for the young and fabulous. It continues to thrive after expensive recent renovations, and the spiffy decor and pounding (usually house) music in the disco contribute to the popularity. There are also drag performances in the cabaret room and a roof terrace. 1474 rue Ste-Catherine est (near rue Amherst). ℂ 514/529-6969. www.complexesky.com. Métro: Beaudry.

CASINO

The **Casino de Montréal** (ℂ **800/665-2274** or 514/392-2746; www.casino-de-montreal.com), Québec's first, is housed in recycled space: the complex reuses what were the French and Québec Pavilions on Ile Notre-Dame during Expo '67 (the World's Fair that Montréal hosted). Asymmetrical and groovy, the buildings provide a dramatic setting for games of chance.

Four floors contain more than 115 game tables, including roulette, craps, blackjack, baccarat, and varieties of poker, and there are more than 3,200 slot machines. Its four restaurants get good reviews, especially the elegant **Nuances** (p. 234). The casino is open 24 hours a day, 7 days a week. No alcoholic beverages are served in the gambling areas, and patrons must be 18 and dressed neatly (the full dress code is posted online). There are live shows in the Cabaret, a 500-seat performance hall. Overnight packages are available. Drive or take the Métro to the Parc Jean-Drapeau stop and then walk or take the casino shuttle bus (no. 167). From May to October, there's also a free shuttle bus *(navette)* that leaves on the hour from the Bonjour Québec tourist center at 1001 rue du Square-Dorchester. Call ℂ **514/392-2746** for information on the shuttle and its other downtown stops.

10 North into the Laurentian Mountains

You don't have to travel far from Montréal to get to ski mountains, parks, or bike trails; just 30 minutes north, for instance, gets you to the base of the resort region of the Laurentian mountain range. You won't find spiked peaks or high ragged ridges—the rolling hills and rounded mountains of the Laurentian Shield are among the oldest in the world, worn down by wind and water over eons. They average between 300m and 520m (984 ft. and 1,706 ft.) in height. Nearer to Montréal, the terrain resembles a rumpled quilt, its folds and hollows cupping a multitude of lakes large and small. Farther north the summits are higher and craggier.

The pearl of the Laurentians (also called the Laurentides) is Mont-Tremblant, the highest peak in eastern Canada at 968m (3,176 ft.) and a mecca in the winter for skiers and snowboarders from all over North America. Development has been particularly heavy in the resort town, a kind of Aspen-meets-Disneyland development that is just 1½ hours from Montréal. The resort village has the prefabricated look of a theme park, but at least planners used the Québécois architectural style of pitched or mansard roofs in bright colors, not ersatz Tyrolean or Bavarian Alpine flourishes (for a sweeping view, take the free gondola from the bottom of the village to the top; it zips over the walkways, candy-colored hotels, shops, and outdoor swimming pools).

The **Mont-Tremblant Ski Resort** (www.tremblant.ca) draws the biggest downhill crowds in the Laurentians, and is repeatedly voted the top resort in eastern North America by *Ski Magazine*. It has snowmaking capability to cover 253 hectares (625 acres). Of the 94 total downhill runs and trails, half are expert terrain, about a third are intermediate, and the rest beginner. There is plenty of cross-country action on maintained trails and another 112km (70 miles) of ungroomed trails in the adjacent national park. The region has dozens of other ski centers, too, with scores of trails at every level of difficulty.

The area loses none of its charm in the summer, and in fact gains some of it back with thinned-out traffic. That's when ski resorts become attractive green mountain rental properties close to biking, fishing, golf at the renowned **Le Diable** and **Le Géant** courses, tennis, boating, swimming, and hiking. Bird-watchers of both intense and casual bent can be fully occupied; loon lovers, in particular, should know that the lakes of Québec province's mountains are home to an estimated 16,000 of the native waterfowl that gives its name to the dollar coin.

Other warm-weather activities include the downhill **dry-land luge run** right in the resort village. The engineless sleds are gravity propelled, reaching speeds of up to 48kmph (30 mph) if you choose. Rides cost C$10 (US$10/£5). The resort has other games and diversions to keep families occupied for days. Also in the village, the **Tremblant Film Festival** takes place for 5 days in June.

One unusual activity is the opportunity to participate in a real cattle round-up. The adventure lasts 5 hours and takes place at the **Ranch Mont-Tremblant,** 40 minutes from the mountain. Cost is C$120 (US$120/£60). Call ℭ **819/681-4848.**

The busiest times are in February and March for skiing, July and August for summer vacation, and during the Christmas to New Year holiday period. Other times of the year, reservations are easier to get and prices of virtually everything are lower. May and September are often characterized by warm days, cool nights, and just enough people that the streets don't seem deserted.

A few words of clarification about the abundant use of the name Tremblant: There is Mont-Tremblant, the mountain. At the base of its slope is Tremblant, the growing resort village that is sometimes called Mont-Tremblant Station or the pedestrian village. Just adjacent is Lac (Lake) Tremblant. And there is the small former village of Mont-Tremblant, known today as the old village, about 5km (3 miles) northwest of the resort. Clear as mud?

Because the people of the region rely heavily on tourism for their livelihoods, knowledge of at least rudimentary English is widespread, even outside such obvious places as hotels and restaurants.

GETTING THERE

BY CAR   The fast and scenic Autoroute des Laurentides, also known as Autoroute 15, goes straight from Montréal to the Laurentian mountains. About 103km (64 miles) north of Montréal, the autoroute ends and Route 117 becomes the major artery for the region. Mont-Tremblant is 130km (81 miles) north of Montréal.

BY BUS   **Groupe Galland** buses depart Montréal's **Terminus Voyageur,** 505 bd. de Maisonneuve est, stopping in the larger Laurentian towns including Mont-Tremblant; call ℭ **514/333-9555** or check www.galland-bus.com for schedules. The ride to Mont-Tremblant takes just under 3 hours. Some of the major resorts provide their own bus service from Montréal at an additional charge, so ask when booking.

BY PLANE   The newly renovated **Mont-Tremblant International Airport** (airport code YTM; ℭ **877/425-7919;** www.mtia.ca), 24 miles north of Mont-Tremblant, began receiving direct flights from Newark Liberty International Airport (EWR) via Continental Airlines in late 2007. The service is scheduled to be seasonal for the ski-season months only. **Aéroport International Pierre-Elliot-Trudeau de Montréal** (airport code YUL; ℂ **800/465-1213** and 514/394-7377; www.admtl.com) is about 60 minutes south of Mont-Tremblant.

WHERE TO STAY

There are abundant options for housing in the area. Reservations for lodgings in the resort itself can be made through a central number (ℂ **888/738-1777** or 514/876-7273) or the website www.tremblant.ca. In addition to hotel rooms, there are options to rent fully equipped condos and single-family residences. Bed-and-breakfast lodgings are listed at www.bbtremblant.com. For camping options within **Parc national du Mont-Tremblant,** visit www.parcsquebec.com.

Auberge La Porte Rouge *Value* This unusual motel, run by a third-generation owner, is located in the old village of Mont-Tremblant. Wake to a view of Lake Mercier through the picture window (every unit has one), or gaze at the lake from your little balcony. Some rooms have both fireplaces and whirlpool baths. Later in the day, take lunch on the terrace facing the lake or wind down in the cocktail lounge. Deluxe rooms accommodate 2 to 3 people, while the cottages have room for 10 people. Rowboats, canoes, and pedal boats are available, and the motel is directly on the regional bike and cross-country ski path called Le P'tit Train du Nord. Rates include dinner and breakfast for two.

1874 Chemin du Village, Mont-Tremblant, PQ J8E 1K4. ℂ 800/665-3505 or 819/425-3505. Fax 819/425-6700. www.aubergelaporterouge.com. 26 units. C$138–C$234 (US$138–US$234/£69–£117) double. Rates include dinner and breakfast. Packages available. MC, V. **Amenities:** Restaurant; heated outdoor pool; watersports equipment; bike rental. *In room:* A/C, TV, free Wi-Fi, coffeemaker, iron (on request).

Ermitage du Lac *Kids* You'll find this recent entry in the pedestrian village's lodging-go-round slightly to the right and behind the 19th-century church located at the main entrance. It's just the place for families on long vacations, with all of its units large studios or one- to three-bedroom suites, and its locale directly next to Parc Plage, the beach on Lac Tremblant. Fireplaces and balconies are standard, as are kitchens fully equipped with oven ranges, microwaves, unstocked fridges, and necessary cookware and crockery (only some have dishwashers, though). There is a secure underground parking garage, which is free.

150 Chemin du Curé-Deslauriers, Mont-Tremblant, PQ J8E 1C9. ℂ 800/461-8711 or 819/681-2222. Fax 819/681-2223. www.tremblant.ca. 67 units. From C$155 (US$155/£78) double. Rates include breakfast. AE, MC, V. **Amenities:** 4 restaurants; outdoor pool and hot tub in summer; exercise room; concierge; business center; laundry facilities; dry cleaning. *In room:* A/C, TV w/pay movies, Wi-Fi, free high-speed Internet, kitchen, coffeemaker, hair dryer, iron.

The Fairmont Mont Tremblant This 1996 luxury lodging stands on a crest above the village, as befits its stature among the Tremblant hostelries. Although young compared with the Fairmont chain's Château Frontenac in Québec City and Le Reine Elizabeth in Montréal, it hews closely to the high standards of its siblings across Canada. Inside the plain exterior, the enlarged lobby area has a north-woods look, with a wood-burning fireplace and antiques and folk art prominent in public areas. Guests use the outdoor pool right through the winter, and they can ski out and ski in to the hotel, which is close to the bottom of the chairlift. Even visitors staying elsewhere in the resort troop past the tantalizing buffet lines of in-house restaurant **Windigo** for nightly dinner. The concierge can arrange bike, blade, and ATV rentals, as well as golf, tennis, fishing, tubing, and horseback rides.

> ### *Tips* Biker's Paradise: The New 4,000km Route Verte
>
> Québec is bike crazy. In the summer 2007, the Québec province officially inaugurated the new **Route verte** (Green Route), a 4,000km (2,485-mile) bike network that stretches from one end of the province to the other and links up all regions and cities. The idea is modeled on the Rails-to-Trails program in the U.S. and cycling routes in Denmark, Great Britain, and along the Danube and Rhine rivers. It was initiated by the nonprofit biking organization **Vélo Québec** (www.velo.qc.ca) with support from the Québec Ministry of Transportation.
>
> Included in the network is the long-popular **P'tit Train du Nord bike trail** that goes north into the Laurentians to Mont-Tremblant and beyond. It's built on a former railway track and passes through the pretty villages of Ste-Adèle, Val David, and Ste-Agathe-des-Monts. Cyclists can get food and bike repairs at renovated railway stations along the way and hop on for just a day trip or a longer tour. Access fees are C$5 (US$5/£2.50) a day for adults, C$3 (US$3/£1.50) ages 6 to 17, and free for children under 6. Season passes are available.
>
> The Route verte website at www.routeverte.com has maps of all the paths and links to bed-and-breakfasts, campsites, and hotels that are especially focused on serving bikers. Accredited accommodations have a BIENVENUE CYCLISTES! **sticker** and provide a covered and locked place for overnight bicycle storage.
>
> The free *Official Tourist Guide to The Laurentians* put out by regional tourist office (www.laurentides.com) has a 32-page section on biking. The company **Transport du parc linéaire** (✆ 888/686-1323 or 450/569-5596; www.transportduparclineaire.com) provides baggage transport from inn to inn.

3045 Chemin de la Chapelle, Mont-Tremblant, PQ J8E 1B1. ✆ **800/441-1414** or 819/681-7000. Fax 819/681-7099. www.fairmont.com. 314 units. From C$199 (US$199/£100) double. Packages available. AE, DC, DISC, MC, V. Pets accepted. **Amenities:** Restaurant; cafe; bar; indoor lap pool and heated outdoor pools; health club; spa; concierge; business center; shopping arcade; limited room service; babysitting; laundry service; same-day dry cleaning. *In room:* A/C, TV w/in-house movies and video games, high-speed Internet, minibar, coffeemaker, hair dryer, iron, safe.

Homewood Suites by Hilton   Taking up the interiors of several buildings meant to look like separate candy-colored row houses, the most desirable rooms are those that overlook the Place St-Bernard, the central gathering space of the pedestrian village: many of the resort's restaurants and shops form the perimeter of the plaza. All accommodations are crisply furnished suites, with fireplaces and equipped kitchens. Ski lockers are available to guests, who have ready access to the slopes. An on-site laundromat is provided.

3035 Chemin de la Chapelle, Mont-Tremblant, PQ J8E 1E1. ✆ **888/288-2988** or 819/681-0808. Fax 819/681-0331. www.homewoodsuitestremblant.com. 103 units. C$159–C$595 (US$159–US$595/£80–£298) suite. Rates include breakfast and afternoon snack (Mon–Thurs). AE, DC, DISC, MC, V. **Amenities:** Restaurant; access to health club; babysitting; coin-op laundry facilities; same-day dry cleaning. *In room:* A/C, TV, Internet, kitchen, fridge, coffeemaker, hair dryer, iron.

Hôtel Mont-Tremblant *Value*   This modest hotel down the block from the Auberge La Porte Rouge (see above) is in the old village of Mont-Tremblant. It's popular both with skiers who want to avoid the resort village's higher prices (there's a shuttle bus stop to the mountain across the street) and, in summer, with cyclists who like the location directly on Le P'tit Train du Nord cycling path (see "Biker's Paradise: The New 4,000km Route Verte," p. 266). Rooms all have private bathrooms, most have twin or double beds, and a few have sitting areas. The 1902 inn also houses the popular restaurant **Le Bernardin,** which has a covered front terrace. All meals are served, with dinner main courses from C$15 to C$35 (US$15–US$35/£7.50–£18). Room prices include dinner and breakfast for two.

1900 Chemin du Village, Mont-Tremblant, PQ J8E 1K4. © **888/887-1111** or 819/425-3232. Fax 819/425-9755. www.hotelmonttremblant.com. 25 units. C$140–C$190 (US$140–US$190/£70–£95) double. Rates include dinner and breakfast. MC, V. **Amenities:** Restaurant; bar; beach nearby; bike storage. *In room:* A/C, TV, hair dryer.

Quintessence 🏵🏵🏵   Go in assuming that virtually every service you might find in a much larger deluxe hotel will be available to you . . . then concentrate on the extras. Check-in is in your room—make that "suite"—so you don't have to stand around at a reception desk. Discover the hugely comfortable bed with the 4-inch-thick feather mattress cover. Note that the bathroom floor is heated, that the jets in the tub are controlled by a remote, and that the shower is of the drenching rainforest variety. Maybe order a massage in your room, in front of the wood-burning fireplace. Take in the view of the lake, and if it's warm, book a picnic and a ride on the hotel's gorgeous 1910 mahogany powerboat. Float in the outdoor infinity pool, followed by a steam and a sauna. Anticipate a lavish dinner with a goblet of wine from the 18m-long (59-ft.) wine cellar. There is a separate honeymoon cottage, although no sacrifice is made by booking one of the less expensive units.

3004 Chemin de la Chapelle, Mont-Tremblant, PQ J8E 1E1. © **866/425-3400** or 819/425-3400. Fax 819/425-3480. www.hotelquintessence.com. 30 units. From C$299 (US$299/£150) suite and way up. Packages available. AE, DC, MC, V. **Amenities:** Restaurant; bar; heated outdoor pool and hot tubs; health club; spa; concierge; business center; 24-hr. room service; massage; babysitting; laundry service; same-day dry cleaning. *In room:* A/C, TV w/pay movies, CD player, Wi-Fi, high-speed Internet, minibar, hair dryer, iron, safe.

WHERE TO DINE

Although most Laurentian inns and resorts have their own dining facilities and often require that guests use them (especially in winter), there are some good independent dining options.

Aux Truffes 🏵 FRENCH CONTEMPORARY   The management and kitchen of this restaurant right within the resort village are more ambitious than just about any on the mountain, evidenced by a wine cellar that sails through Canadian, Californian, Argentinean, Spanish, and many admirable French bottlings, up to a Château Latour '86 for C$900 (US$900/£450). Put yourself in the hands of the knowledgeable wine steward and go from there. Meals proceed from a heartier-than-usual *amuse-bouche* to imaginative mains such as caribou chop marinated in black currant and cocoa, or roasted duck breast *magret* stuffed with foie gras and a black truffle sauce. Close with selections from the *plateau* of raw-milk Québec cheeses.

688 rue de Saint-Jovite (in the resort village). © 819/681-4544. www.auxtruffes.com. Main courses C$29–C$46 (US$29–US$46/£15–£23). AE, MC, V. Daily 6–10pm.

Le Cheval de Jade FRENCH   Chef Oliver Tali is what is known in the culinary world as a *maître canardier,* or master chef in the preparation of duck. In fact there is only one *maître canardier* in all of Canada recognized by France's *l'ordre des canardiers,* and he's it. Normally that would mean that at this modest-looking roadside restaurant with a dozen tables and country decor about 20 minutes from the mountain, the only choice is the house specialty, *Caneton des Laurentides à la Rouennaise* (regional duckling). But the bouillabaisse and salmon tartar are also standouts. If you are interested in the duck, you have to call in advance and make a special reservation.

688 rue de Saint-Jovite (in the St-Jovite sector). (℃ **819/425-5233.** www.chevaldejade.com. Reservations recommended. Main courses C$29–C$34 (US$29–US$34/£15–£17); table d'hôte from C$29 (US$29/£15); 7-course gastronomic menu C$173 (US$173/£87) for 2. AE, MC, V. Tues–Sat 5:30–10pm.

Patrick Bermand ⭐ MEDITERRANEAN   If you cherish seafood, appetizers here are especially satisfying and have included garlicky, buttery escargot served in individual ceramic pots and cool chunks of tuna rolled in black sesame seeds accompanied by cold sesame noodles. Main courses are good, too, and large—a lot of leftovers walk out the door. Housed in a roadside log cabin–style building, the restaurant is in the quiet former village of Mont-Tremblant, a short drive from the raucous pedestrian village.

2176 Chemin du Village (Rte. 327 in the old village). (℃ **819/425-6333.** www.patrickbermand.com. Main courses C$26–C$43 (US$26–US$43/£13–£22). AE, MC, V. Daily 5–10pm; sometimes closed Mon in slow months.

8

Québec City & the Gaspé Peninsula

by Leslie Brokaw

Few municipalities are as breathtaking as Québec City. Situated along the majestic St. Lawrence River, much of the oldest part of the city—Vieux-Québec—sits atop Cap Diamant, a rock bluff that once provided military defense. Fortress walls still encase the upper portion of the old city, and the soaring Château Frontenac, a hotel with castlelike turrets, dominates the landscape. Hauntingly evocative of a coastal town in the motherland of France, the tableau is as romantic as any in Europe.

Québec City is the soul of New France and holds that history dear. It was the first significant settlement in Canada, founded in 1608, by Samuel de Champlain. The city has spruced up for its 400th anniversary celebrations in 2008, adding more access to the waterfront and a new pavilion called Espace 400ᵉ that will be the central location for celebrations throughout the year (after 2008, it will become a Parks Canada centre).

The city is almost entirely French in feeling, spirit, and language, and 95% of the population is Francophone, or French-speaking. But many people know some English, especially those who work in hotels, restaurants, and shops. Although it is often more difficult in Québec City than

in Montréal to get by without French, the average Québécois goes out of his or her way to communicate—in halting English, sign language, simplified French, or a combination of all three. Most of the Québécois are uncommonly gracious, even with the city being the capital of the politically prickly Québec province.

A stroll through Québec is comparable to walking in similar *quartiers* in northern European cities. Stone houses huddle close together; carriage wheels creak behind muscular horses; sunlight filters through leafy canopies; drinkers and diners lounge in sidewalk cafes; and laughter echoes down cobblestone streets.

Ile d'Orléans, an agricultural and resort island within sight of Vieux-Québec, is less than a half-hour by car and an easy day trip. Consider, too, a visit a few hours up the northern coast of the St. Lawrence past the shrine of **Ste-Anne-de-Beaupré,** the waterfalls near **Mont Ste-Anne,** and on to pastoral **Charlevoix** and the Saguenay River, where whales come to play. Two days away, the province ends at the eastern most tip of Canada on the **Gaspé Peninsula,** where you'll find **Rocher Percé**—Percé Rock, in English—a monumental butte that rises from the sea.

1 Essentials

GETTING THERE

BY PLANE   Jean-Lesage International Airport (airport code: YQB; ℭ **418/640-2700;** www.aeroportdequebec.com) is small, despite the grand name. A taxi to downtown Québec City is a fixed-rate C$30 (US$30/£15). There are no buses between the airport and the city.

BY TRAIN   The handsome train station in Québec City, **Gare du Palais,** 450 rue de la Gare-du-Palais, was designed by Bruce Price, who is also responsible for the Château Frontenac. The Lower Town location isn't central, though, so plan on a strenuous hike or a C$6 to C$9 (US$6–US$9/£3–£4.50) cab ride to the Upper Town or other areas of the Lower Town.

BY BUS   The bus terminal, at 320 rue Abraham-Martin (ℭ **418/525-3000**), is just next to the train station. As from the train station, it is an uphill climb or quick cab ride to the Upper Town or other parts of the Lower Town.

BY CAR   Driving north from the U.S., the entire ride is on expressways. Québec City is 867km (539 miles) from New York City and 644km (400 miles) from Boston, and about 3 hours northeast from Montréal. From New York, follow the directions to Montréal in chapter 7 and then pick up Autoroute 20 to Québec. From Boston, follow the directions to Montréal, but at Autoroute 10 go east instead of west to stay on Autoroute 55. Pick up Autoroute 20 to Québec.

Coming into Québec City, follow signs for the bridge Pont Pierre-Laporte. Shortly after crossing the bridge, turn right onto boulevard Wilfrid-Laurier (Rte. 175). It changes names first to boulevard Laurier and then to Grande-Allée, the grand boulevard that leads directly into the central Parliament Hill area and the old city.

Another appealing option when you're approaching from the south is to follow Route 132 to the town of Lévis. A car-ferry there, **Traverse Québec-Lévis** (ℭ **418/644-3704**), provides a 10-minute ride across the river and a dramatic introduction to the city. Although the schedule varies substantially according to time of day, week, and season, the ferry leaves at least once an hour from 6am to 2am. One-way costs C$5.95 (US$5.95/£2.95) for the car and driver, and C$2.65 (US$2.65/£1.30) for each additional adult. It's cash only; if you arrive without Canadian dollars, there's an ATM in the small transport terminal next door.

VISITOR INFORMATION

The Greater Québec Area Tourism and Convention Bureau operates an information center in the Discovery Pavilion at 835 av. Wilfrid-Laurier (ℭ **877/783-1608** or 418/641-6290; www.quebecregion.com), near La Citadelle, just outside the walls of the old city. It has racks of brochures and attendants who can answer questions and make hotel reservations and is open daily 8:30am to 7:30pm from June 24 to Labour Day; daily 8:30am to 6:30pm Labour Day to mid-October; and the rest of the year 9am to 5pm Monday through Saturday, 10am to 4pm Sunday.

The Québec Government's tourism department operates a **Centre Infotouriste de Québec** on Place d'Armes, across from the Château Frontenac, at 12 rue Ste-Anne (ℭ **877/266-5687;** www.bonjourquebec.com). It's open from 8:30am to 7:30pm daily from June 21 to early September, and from 9am to 5pm the rest of the year. The office has brochures, information about cruise and bus tour operators, a 24-hour ATM *(guichet automatique),* a currency-exchange office, and a free lodging reservation service. Also in front of the Château is the independent **Kiosque Frontenac** (© **418/ 692-5483**), which sells tickets for tours (walking, bus, boat) and does currency exchange. It's open daily from 9am until 8pm or 9pm in summer.

From early June to Labour Day, student staff of the tourist office pilot motorscooters through the tourist districts of the Upper and Lower towns, making themselves available for questions. (They are also in force on foot during the Winter Carnival season.) In French, they're called the *service mobile,* and their blue mopeds bear flags with a large "?". Just hail them as they approach; they're bilingual.

CITY LAYOUT

MAIN AVENUES & STREETS Within the walls of Old Québec's **Haute-Ville (Upper Town),** the principal streets are rues St-Louis (which becomes the Grande-Allée outside the city walls), Ste-Anne, and St-Jean, and the pedestrian-only Terrasse Dufferin, which overlooks the river in front of the Château Frontenac. In Old Québec's **Basse-Ville (Lower Town),** major streets are St-Pierre, Dalhousie, St-Paul, and, parallel to St-Paul, St-André. There are good maps of the Upper and Lower towns and the metropolitan area available at any tourist office.

FINDING AN ADDRESS If it were larger, the historic old district, with its winding and plunging streets, might be confusing to negotiate. However, it's very compact, so most visitors have little difficulty finding their way around. Most streets are only a few blocks long, making it fairly easy to find a specific address.

THE NEIGHBORHOODS IN BRIEF

Vieux-Québec: Haute-Ville Old Québec's Upper Town, surrounded by thick ramparts, occupies the crest of Cap Diamant and overlooks the *Fleuve Saint-Laurent* (St. Lawrence River). It includes many of the sites for which the city is famous, including the Château Frontenac, Place d'Armes, Basilica of Notre-Dame, and Québec Seminary and Museum. At a still higher elevation, to the south of the Château and along the river, is the Citadelle, a partially star-shaped fortress begun by the French in the 18th century and augmented often by the English well into the 19th century. With most buildings at least 100 years old and made of granite in similar styles, Haute-Ville is visually harmonious, with few jarring modern intrusions. Terrasse Dufferin is a pedestrian promenade with magnificent views of the river and its water traffic, which includes ferries, cruise ships, and freighters putting in at the harbor below.

Vieux-Québec: Basse-Ville and Vieux-Port Old Québec's Lower Town includes the old port district and highlights including the Place Royale, perhaps the most attractive of the city's many squares; the impressive Museum of Civilization; newly spruced up riverside paths; and the restored Quartier du Petit-Champlain, including rue du Petit-Champlain, a pedestrian-only lane that is touristy but not unpleasantly so, with many agreeable cafes and shops. Most visitors travel between Lower and Upper towns by the cliffside elevator *(funiculaire)* at the north end of rue du Petit-Champlain, or by the adjacent stairway.

Parliament Hill Once you pass through the walls at the St-Louis Gate, you're still in Haute-Ville (Upper Town), but no longer in the old city. Rue St-Louis becomes Grande-Allée, a wide boulevard that passes the stately Parliament building on the right and runs parallel to the broad expanse of

Québec City

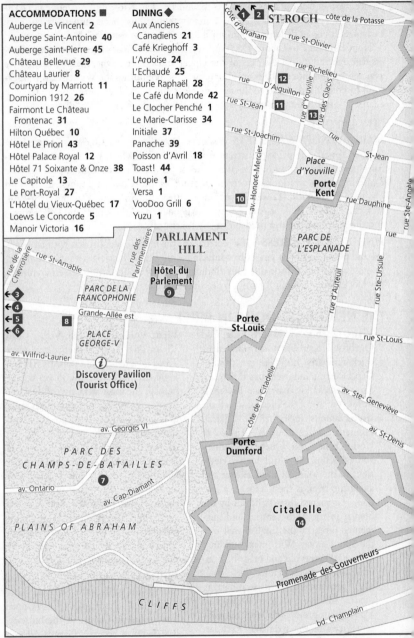

ACCOMMODATIONS ■

Auberge Le Vincent **2**
Auberge Saint-Antoine **40**
Auberge Saint-Pierre **45**
Château Bellevue **29**
Château Laurier **8**
Courtyard by Marriott **11**
Dominion 1912 **26**
Fairmont Le Château
 Frontenac **31**
Hilton Québec **10**
Hôtel Le Priori **43**
Hôtel Palace Royal **12**
Hôtel 71 Soixante & Onze **38**
Le Capitole **13**
Le Port-Royal **27**
L'Hôtel du Vieux-Québec **17**
Loews Le Concorde **5**
Manoir Victoria **16**

DINING ◆

Aux Anciens
 Canadiens **21**
Café Krieghoff **3**
L'Ardoise **24**
L'Echaudé **25**
Laurie Raphaël **28**
Le Café du Monde **42**
Le Clocher Penché **1**
Le Marie-Clarisse **34**
Initiale **37**
Panache **39**
Poisson d'Avril **18**
Toast! **44**
Utopie **1**
Versa **1**
VooDoo Grill **6**
Yuzu **1**

ST-ROCH

côte de la Potasse

côte d'Abraham

rue St-Olivier

rue Richelieu

rue D'Aiguillon

rue d'Youville

rue des Glacis

rue

rue St-Jean

St-Jean

rue St-Joachim

Place
d'Youville

Porte
Kent

rue Dauphine

rue Ste-Angèle

av. Honoré-Mercier

PARC DE
L'ESPLANADE

rue

PARLIAMENT
HILL

Hôtel du
Parlement

rue des
Parlementaires

rue de la
Chevrotière

rue St-Amable

PARC DE LA
FRANCOPHONIE

Grande-Allée est

PLACE
GEORGE-V

rue d'Auteuil

rue Ste-Ursule

Porte
St-Louis

rue St-Louis

av. Wilfrid-Laurier

Discovery Pavilion
(Tourist Office)

côte de la Citadelle

av. Ste- Geneviève

av. Georges VI

Porte
Dumford

av. St-Denis

PARC DES
CHAMPS-DE-BATAILLES

av. Ontario

av. Cap-Diamant

Citadelle

PLAINS OF ABRAHAM

Promenade des Gouverneurs

CLIFFS

bd. Champlain

ATTRACTIONS ●

Basilique Notre-Dame **22**
Chapelle/Musée des
Ursulines **20**
Château Frontenac **32**
Espace 400e **19**
Hôtel du Parlement **9**
La Citadelle **14**

Maison Chevalier **35**
Musée de l'Amérique Française **23**
Musée de la Civilisation **41**
Musée des Beaux-Arts du Québec **4**
Musée du Fort **33**
Parc de l'Artillerie **15**
Parc des Champs-de-Bataille **7**
Place-Royale **36**

the Plains of Abraham, where the lively Carnaval de Québec is held each winter. Two blocks after the Parliament, the Grande-Allée becomes lined with terraced restaurants and cafes. The city's large modern hotels are in this area, and the Musée des Beaux-Arts is a pleasant 20-minute walk up the Allée.

St-Roch Northwest of Parliament Hill and enough of a distance from Vieux-Québec to warrant a cab ride, this neighborhood in transition has some of the trendiest restaurants in the city.

Money has been given to artists to renovate the interior and exterior of their industrial buildings, and there's been an influx of new technology and media companies. Much of St-Roch remains nondescript and a little grubby. But the blocks gravitating from central rue St-Joseph and small rue du Parvis are increasingly home to top-notch restaurants and cute boutiques; Hugo Boss moved in with a massive store at the intersection. (*Note:* On older maps, rue du Parvis was called rue de l'Eglise.)

2 Getting Around

Once you're within or near the walls of the Haute-Ville, virtually no place of interest, hotel, or restaurant is beyond walking distance. In bad weather, or when you're traversing between opposite ends of Lower and Upper towns, a taxi might be necessary. In general, walking is the best way to explore the city.

BY BUS

Local buses run often and cost C$2.50 (US$2.50/£1.25) in exact change. One-day passes cost C$5.95 (US$5.95/£2.95), and discounts are available for seniors and students with proper ID. Bus stops have easy-to-follow signs that state the bus numbers and direction of travel for each route. Flag down the bus as it approaches so the driver knows to stop. The Québec City museum card includes 2 days of unlimited public transport in addition to free entrance to 24 museums for 3 days.

Bus routes are listed online at **www.rtcquebec.ca**. Buses in the most touristed areas include no. 7, which travels up and down rue St-Jean, and no. 10 and no. 11, which shuttle along Grande-Allée/rue St-Louis.

BY FUNICULAR

To get between the Upper Town and Lower Town, there are streets, staircases, and a cliffside elevator, which has long operated along an inclined 64m (210-ft.) track. It was closed for a couple of years after a fatal accident in 1996. Repaired now, the **upper station** is near the front of the Château Frontenac and Place d'Armes, while the **lower station** is at the northern end of rue du Petit-Champlain, inside the Maison Louis-Jolliet. The funicular offers excellent aerial views of the historic Lower Town on the short trip, and runs daily from 7:30am until 11pm all year, and to midnight in high season. Wheelchairs are accommodated. The one-way fare is C$1.75 (US$1.75/85p).

BY TAXI

Taxis are abundant and often parked in front of the big hotels and in some of the larger squares of the Upper Town. In theory, they can be hailed, but they are best obtained by locating one of their stands, such as at the Place d'Armes or in front of the Hôtel-de-Ville (City Hall). Restaurant managers and hotel bell captains will also summon them if you ask. The starting rate is C$3.15 (US$3.15/£1.55), and each kilometer costs C$1.45 (US$1.45/70p). Tip 10% to 15%. A taxi from the train station to one of the big hotels is about C$6 to C$9 (US$6–US$9/£3–£4.50) plus tip. To call a cab, try **Taxi Coop** (© 418/525-5191) or **Taxi Québec** (© 418/525-8123).

BY CAR

The phone numbers listed here are for car-rental companies' general information and their desks at the airport terminal: **Avis** (© 800/437-0358 or 418/872-2861); **Budget** (© 800/268-8900 or 418/872-9885); **Hertz** (© 800/263-0600 or 418/871-1571).

The basic map from the rental agency should suffice for Québec City, which is compact if a little tricky to navigate. There are few roads between Upper Town and Lower Town and many streets are one-way.

On-street parking is difficult in the cramped quarters of Old Québec. When you find a rare space on the street, be sure to check the signs for the hours when parking is permissible. Meters cost C50¢ (US50¢/25p) per 15 minutes. Some meters go up to 5 hours. Metered spots generally have to be paid for Monday through Saturday 9am to 9pm, and Sunday 10am to 9pm. But double-check: Spots along the Parc des Champs-de-Bataille (Battlefields Park), for instance, are in effect 24 hours.

Parking lots are clearly marked on the foldout city map available at tourist offices. They include, in Upper Town, the lot next to the Hôtel-de-Ville (City Hall), and, in Lower Town, the lot across the street from the Musée de la Civilisation, on rue Dalhousie. Many smaller hotels have special arrangements with local garages, with discounts for guests of 25% off the usual C$12 (US$12/£6) or more per day. Check with your hotel first before parking in any lot or garage.

BY BICYCLE

Given the city's hilly topography, tight quarters, and cobblestones, cycling isn't a particularly attractive option right in town. But outside is another story. Like Montréal, Québec has a good network of cycling paths called the *Route verte* (Green Route). There are local paths as well as access to long-distance paths. **Promo-Vélo** (www.promo-velo.org) has information in French.

Cyclo Services at the Marché du Vieux-Port at 160 rue du Quai St-André (© 418/692-4052; www.cycloservices.net), rents bicycles for C$12 (US$12/£6) an hour or C$20 (US$20/£10) for 4 hours. It also rents electric bikes and tandems.

FAST FACTS: Québec City

AAA Members of the **American Automobile Association (AAA)** are covered by the **Canadian Automobile Association (CAA)** while traveling in Canada. Bring your membership card and proof of insurance. The 24-hour hot line for emergency service is © 418/624-4000 in Québec City and © 800/222-4357 in the rest of the province and Canada. Most mobile phones can call © *CAA (*222) to reach emergency road service. Visit **www.caaquebec.com** for more. The AAA card also provides discounts at a wide variety of hotels and restaurants in Québec province.

American Express There is no American Express office in the city, but for lost traveler's checks or credit cards, call © 800/869-3016.

Currency Exchange Main branch banks and *caisses populaires* (credit union offices) will exchange most foreign currencies. In Québec City, **Caisse Populaire** at 19 rue des Jardins (© **418/522-6806**) is open daily in the summer and Monday through Friday the rest of the year. Tourism offices can often exchange money or point you to a place that will.

Doctors & Dentists The front desks at hotels can contact a doctor quickly. For less serious illness, you can see a doctor at a community health centre called a CLSC. These are smaller clinics, and there is one in every neighborhood. Medical treatment in Canada isn't free for foreigners, and hospitals make you pay your bills at the time of service. Check if your insurance policy covers you while traveling in Canada, especially for hospitalization abroad. For dental emergencies, call © **514/721-6006** or visit www.carrefourdentaire.com. In a medical emergency, dial © **911.**

Drugstores A pharmacy is called a *pharmacie,* a drugstore is a *droguerie.* **Caron & Bernier,** in Upper Town, 38 Côte du Palais (at rue Charlevoix; © **418/692-4252**), is open 8:15am to 8pm Monday through Friday, and 9am to 3pm on Saturday. **Pharmacie Brunet,** in the suburbs in Les Galeries Charlesbourg, 4250 av. Première, in Charlesbourg (© **418/623-1571**), is open 8:30am to 10:30pm 7 days a week.

Emergencies Dial © **911** for the police, firefighters, or an ambulance. Québec Poison Control Centre is at © **800/463-5060.**

Internet With the rise in Wi-Fi hot spots, there are fewer cybercafes today in Québec than a few years ago. One place still doing good business is **Centre Internet,** 52 Cote du Palais (© **418/692-3359**), in the Upper Town of Old Québec—it's 1 block off of rue St-Jean.

Liquor & Wine Hard liquor and spirits in Québec province are sold through official government stores operated by the Québec Société des Alcools (look for maroon signs with the acronym SAQ). Wine and beer can be bought in grocery stores and convenience stores, called *dépanneurs.* The legal drinking age in the province is 18.

Newspapers & Magazines The leading French-language newspaper is *Le Soleil.* Most large newsstands and those in the larger hotels carry the *Wall Street Journal, New York Times,* and *International Herald Tribune.* Major newsstands include the multibranch **Maison de la Presse Internationale** at 1050 rue St-Jean inside the walls of Vieux-Québec.

Pets Some Québec City hotels now accept pets, and some even offer walking services and little beds for dogs. Most hotels charge an extra fee of C$25 (US$25/£13) or more and have strict restrictions.

Police Dial © **911** for the police. There are three types of officers in Québec: **municipal police** in Québec City, Montréal, and other towns; **Sûreté de Québec officers,** comparable to state police or the highway patrol in the United States; and **RCMP (Royal Canadian Mounted Police),** who are similar to the FBI and handle cases involving infraction of federal laws.

Taxes Most goods and services in Canada are taxed 5% by the federal government (the GST, or goods and services tax). On top of that, the province of Québec has an additional 7.5% tax (the TVQ). The tax rebate that nonresident visitors used to be able to apply for was eliminated in April 2007.

Telephones The Canadian telephone system, operated by Bell Canada, closely resembles the U.S. model. All operators (dial © **00** from Canada to get one) speak English as well as French, and respond in the appropriate language as soon as callers speak to them. Pay phones in Québec province cost C25¢ (US25¢/15p) for a 3-minute local call. Directory information (dial © **411**) is free. Remember that local and long-distance calls usually cost more from hotels— sometimes a lot more, so check. When making a local call within Québec province, you must dial the area code before the seven-digit number. The area code for Québec City, north into Charlevoix, and all the way to Gaspé, is **418**.

3 Where to Stay

A clutch of new boutique hotels and small inns in the Lower Town has greatly enhanced the lodging stock. Some of the top ones are listed here. If you prefer the conveniences of large chain hotels, check just outside the ancient walls in Parliament Hill. High-rise hotels there are within walking distance or a quick bus or taxi ride away from the attractions in the old city.

Staying in one of the small hotels within or below the walls of Vieux-Québec can be one of your trip's most memorable experiences. From rooms with private bathrooms, minibars, cable TVs, and wireless Internet connections to walk-up budget accommodations with linoleum floors and toilets down the hall, Québec City has a wide enough variety of lodgings to suit most tastes and wallets. Unless otherwise noted, all rooms in the lodgings listed below have private bathrooms—*en suite,* as they say in Canada. Be aware that standards of amenities and prices fluctuate wildly from one small hotel to another, and even from one room to another within a single establishment. It is wise to examine any room offered before booking it.

Prices drop significantly from November to May, except for such events as the winter Carnaval de Québec in February and the Christmas holiday. As a rule, the prices in the listings below are rack rates for a double-occupancy room. That means that you'll rarely, if ever, have to pay that much. Many hotels offer special deals through their websites or AAA discounts.

There are the dozens of bed-and-breakfasts in and around Vieux-Québec. With rates mostly in the C$70 to C$120 (US$70–US$120/£35–£60) range, they don't represent substantial savings over the small hotels, but they do give you the opportunity to get to know some of the city dwellers.

A very useful *Official Accommodation Guide,* put out by Québec City Tourism and revised annually, is available at the tourist offices. It lists every member of the Greater Québec Area Tourism and Convention Bureau, from B&Bs to five-star hotels, providing details about number of rooms, prices, and facilities.

Many hotels in Québec are now completely nonsmoking. If you are a smoker, check before booking.

VIEUX-QUEBEC: HAUTE-VILLE (UPPER TOWN)
VERY EXPENSIVE
The Fairmont Le Château Frontenac ★★★ *Kids*   Québec's magical "castle" opened in 1893 and has been wowing visitors ever since. It was built in phases, following the landline, so the wide halls take crooked paths. Bathrooms have marble

touches, every mattress was replaced in 2006 and 2007, and some 400 rooms were renovated in the same period. Anyone can stay on the more princely (and pricey) Fairmont Gold floors, which have a separate lounge with an honor bar in the afternoons and breakfast in the mornings. Room prices depend on size, location, and when the room was renovated. River views garner top dollar, but lower-priced rooms overlooking the inner courtyard can be eminently appealing: The gables are quite romantic, and children might imagine Harry Potter swooping past the turrets in a Quidditch match. The **Véranda Saint-Laurent** is a casual piano bar with dancing on the weekends. An archeological excavation of parts of the Terrace Dufferin just outside will continue through 2008, so ask for a room not directly on top of the work.

1 rue des Carrières (at Place d'Armes), Québec City, PQ G1R 4P5. ℂ 800/441-1414 or 418/692-3861. Fax 418/692-1751. www.fairmont.com/frontenac. 618 units. May–Oct from C$249 (US$249/£125) double; Nov–Apr from C$199 (US$199/£100) double; suites from C$499 (US$499/£250) and way up. Children under 18 stay free in parent's room. Children 5 and under eat free, 6-12 get 50% off meals. AE, DC, DISC, MC, V. Valet parking C$31 (US$31/£16). Pets accepted. **Amenities:** 3 restaurants; bar; indoor pool and kiddie pool w/outdoor terrace; expansive health club; spa; whirlpool; concierge; business center; Wi-Fi in lobby and bar; shopping arcade; salon; limited room service; in-room massage; babysitting; same-day dry cleaning; executive floors. *In room:* A/C, TV w/pay movies and some Web access, high-speed Internet, minibar, coffeemaker, hair dryer, iron.

EXPENSIVE
L'Hôtel du Vieux-Québec *(Kids* This century-old brick hotel has been renovated with care. Some guest rooms are equipped with sofas and two double beds, and six have kitchenettes. With these homey layouts, the hotel is popular with families, skiers, and the groups of visiting high school students who descend upon the city in late spring. Six rooms were renovated in 2007. There are many moderately priced nightspots and restaurants nearby, including **Les Frères de la Côte** on the ground floor. In the summer, the hotel offers complimentary walking tours of the area.

1190 rue St-Jean (at rue de l'Hôtel Dieu), Québec City, PQ G1R 1S6. ℂ 800/361-7787 or 418/692-1850. Fax 418/692-5637. www.hvq.com. 44 units. July to mid-Oct C$184–C$300 (US$184–US$300/£92–£150) double; late Oct to June C$94–C$154 (US$94–US$154/£47–£77) double. Packages available. AE, MC, V. *In room:* A/C, TV, hair dryer, iron.

Manoir Victoria *(★* With its lobby of stained glass and maroon curtains, this hotel has an air of a grand old-timer. It sprawls all the way from the main entrance on Côte de Palais to adjacent St-Jean, zigzagging around a couple of stores. The proximity to the rue St-Jean restaurant and bar scene is a plus for many, and the indoor pool, rare in this city, is an added extra. A spa, added in 2004, offers body wraps in mud or algae or chocolate (!), along with Swedish massages and exfoliations with sea salt. There's a long staircase to get to the lobby, but elevators make the trip to most of the rooms.

44 Côte du Palais (rue St-Jean), Québec City, PQ G1R 4H8. ℂ 800/463-6283 or 418/692-1030. Fax 418/692-3822. www.manoir-victoria.com. 156 units. May–Oct C$159–C$219 (US$159–US$219/£79–£109) double; Nov–Apr C$109–C$169 (US$109–US$169/£54–£84) double. Packages available. AE, DC, DISC, MC, V. Valet parking C$18 (US$18/£9). **Amenities:** 2 restaurants; 1 bar; heated indoor pool; exercise room; expansive spa; concierge; Internet lounge; limited room service; babysitting; same-day laundry service; same-day dry cleaning. *In room:* A/C, TV w/pay movies, free Wi-Fi, free high-speed Internet, minibar, coffeemaker, hair dryer, iron.

MODERATE
Château Bellevue Occupying several row houses at the top of the Jardin des Gouverneurs, this mini-hotel has a helpful staff as well as some of the creature comforts of larger facilities. Although the rooms are small and unspectacular, they are quiet for the most part, have private bathrooms, and offer one or two double beds or a queen. A few higher-priced units overlook the park. If this place is full, there are some dozen other small lodgings within a block in any direction.

16 rue de la Porte (at av. Ste-Geneviève), Québec City, PQ G1R 4M9. ℰ 800/463-2617 or 418/692-2573. Fax 418/ 692-4876. www.oldquebec.com. 58 units. May–Oct 15 C$109–C$239 (US$109–US$239/£54–£119) double; Oct 16– Apr C$94–C$174 (US$94–US$174/£47–£87) double. Children under 18 stay free in parent's room. Packages available. AE, DC, DISC, MC, V. Valet service. **Amenities:** Concierge; small business center. *In room:* A/C, TV w/pay movies, free Wi-Fi, hair dryer, iron (on request).

VIEUX-QUEBEC: BASSE-VILLE (LOWER TOWN)/VIEUX-PORT
VERY EXPENSIVE
Auberge Saint-Antoine 🐸🐸🐸   This uncommonly attractive property began life as an 1830 maritime warehouse. It kept the soaring ceilings, dark beams, and stone floors, and is now one of the city's landmark luxury boutique hotels. Ancient walls remain in view, and artifacts unearthed in the development are on display throughout the hotel— in public areas, at the door to each room, and at bedside, lit with an underwater-like blue glow. Bedrooms are modern and sleek with details that include luxury linens, plush robes, Bose sound systems, heated bathroom floors, and bathing nooks with rain-shower nozzles directly overhead. Many have balconies or terraces, six have fireplaces, and a few suites have kitchenettes. A striking lounge serves breakfast, lunch, snacks, and drinks, while a fine high-end restaurant, **Panache** (p. 285), is in the original warehouse lobby.

8 rue St-Antoine (next to the Musée de la Civilisation), Québec City, PQ G1K 4C9. ℰ 888/692-2211 or 418/692-2211. www.saint-antoine.com. 94 units. C$159–C$379 (US$159–US$379/£79–£189) double; C$299–C$549 (US$299–US$549/£150–£275) suite. Children under 12 stay free in parent's room. AE, DC, MC, V. Valet garage parking C$23 (US$23/£12). **Amenities:** Restaurant; bar; concierge; business center; Wi-Fi in public areas; limited room service; in-room massage; babysitting; same-day laundry service/dry cleaning weekdays. *In room:* A/C, TV, free high-speed Internet, coffeemaker, hair dryer, iron, safe.

Dominion 1912 🐸🐸🐸   Old Québec meets new in one of the most romantic boutique hotels in the city. The owners stripped the 1912 building down to the studs and pipes and started over, keeping the angular lines and adding soft touches. Québec-made beds have mattresses that are deep, soft, and enveloping, heaped with pillows and feather duvets. Custom-made bedside tables swing into place or out of the way, and even the least expensive rooms are large. About a third of the rooms have only showers, while the rest include tubs. Room no. 206 is a dandy, with a shower that shares a glass wall with the bedroom and views of the city's centuries-old former-industrial buildings. A hearty continental breakfast is set out along with morning newspapers near the fireplace in the handsome lobby. There's a basement fitness room.

126 rue St-Pierre (at rue St-Paul), Québec City, PQ G1K 4A8. ℰ 888/833-5253 or 418/692-2224. Fax 418/692-4403. www.hoteldominion.com. 60 units. May–Oct C$205–C$375 (US$205–US$375/£103–£188) double; Nov–Apr C$169–C$239 (US$169–US$239/£85–£120) double. Rates include breakfast. AE, DC, MC, V. Valet parking C$16 (US$16/£8). Pets accepted. **Amenities:** Espresso bar; exercise room; concierge; computer w/Internet in lobby for guests; limited room service; babysitting; laundry service; same-day dry cleaning. *In room:* A/C, TV, CD player, free Wi-Fi, high-speed Internet, minibar, coffeemaker, hair dryer, iron, safe.

Hôtel 71 Soixante & Onze 🐸🐸   Owned by the same people as the adjacent **Auberge Saint-Pierre** (below), the two properties share a bar, but where the *auberge* is faux-country in style, Hôtel 71 is superslick and ultra-contemporary. Room no. 620 is typical with 5m (15-ft.) creme-colored walls and curtains that extend nearly floor to ceiling, warmed up with deep-red velveteen chairs and cloth panels that serve as closet doors. Bathrooms are in the open style common to the boutique hotels of the area, with sea-foam-green glass separating the shower from the sink area and shower nozzles of the big-disk variety (all rooms have showers, and four have bathtubs as well). Rooms are on floors four to seven and many feature bird's-eye views of the tops of the 19th-century buildings of Old Québec, the St. Lawrence River, or the ramparts of the fortress wall.

71 rue St-Pierre (near rue St-Antoine), Québec City, PQ G1K 4A4. ℂ **888/692-1171** or 418/692-1171. Fax 418/692-0669. www.hotel71.ca. 40 units. C$165–C$295 (US$165–US$295/£83–£148). Rates include a complimentary cocktail and breakfast. Packages available. AE, MC, V. Valet parking C$18 (US$18/£9). **Amenities:** Restaurant; bar; exercise room w/river view; concierge; 24-hr. business center w/river view; room service; massage; babysitting; laundry service; dry cleaning. *In room:* A/C, TV/DVD, CD player, free Wi-Fi, free high-speed Internet, coffeemaker (on request), hair dryer, iron (on request), safe.

EXPENSIVE

Auberge Saint-Pierre (★   One of the city's country-cozy *auberge* options. Most rooms are surprisingly spacious, and the even more commodious suites are a luxury on a longer visit, especially since they have modest kitchen facilities. The made-to-order furnishings suggest traditional Québec styles, although in some rooms the furniture is a bit crowded. Most units have original brick or stone walls. With all rooms on the fourth to seventh floors, some have a river view. Most (35 of 41) have whirlpool tubs but only a few have showers. All rooms got new paint in early 2007. The full breakfasts, included in the price, are cooked to order by the chef in an open kitchen.

79 rue St-Pierre (behind the Musée de la Civilisation), Québec City, PQ G1K 4A3. ℂ **888/268-1017** or 418/694-7981. Fax 418/694-0406. www.auberge.qc.ca. 41 units. May–Aug C$119–C$275 (US$119–US$275/£60–£138) double; Sept–Apr C$99–C$239 (US$99–US$239/£49–£119) double. Rates include full breakfast. AE, DC, DISC, MC, V. Valet parking C$16 (US$16/£8). **Amenities:** Bar; concierge; in-room massage; babysitting; laundry service; dry cleaning. *In room:* A/C, TV, free Wi-Fi, coffeemaker, hair dryer, iron.

MODERATE

Hôtel Le Priori   A playful Art Deco interior livens up the somber facade of a 1726 house; you'll find conical stainless-steel sinks in the bedrooms and, in 4 units, clawfoot tubs beside duvet-covered queen-size beds. Table lamps enliven the formerly dim lighting. Suites have sitting rooms with wood-burning fireplaces, kitchens, and Jacuzzis, and several, including no. 10, are quite masculine, with brown walls in the bedroom, an animal skin rug, and fur throws. Several suites are up stairs with no elevator. Rooms face either the small street out front or a leafy inner courtyard. The inventive restaurant **Toast!** is off the lobby and moves into the courtyard in summer.

15 rue Sault-au-Matelot (at rue St-Antoine), Québec City, PQ G1K 3Y7. ℂ **800/351-3992** or 418/692-3992. Fax 418/692-0883. www.hotellepriori.com. 26 units. Summer C$169–C$229 (US$169–US$299/£85–£150) double; winter C$129–C$189 (US$129–US$189/£65–£95); suites from C$229 (US$229/£115). Rates include breakfast. Packages available. AE, MC, V. Self-parking C$15 (US$15/£7.50) per day. **Amenities:** Restaurant; bar; concierge; limited room service; in-room massage; babysitting; dry cleaning. *In room:* A/C, TV/DVD, CD player, free Wi-Fi, coffeemaker, hair dryer, iron.

Le Port-Royal (*Kids*   Open since 2005, this bright corner near the water is giving serious competition to the best hotels of Basse-Ville. Its 18th-century structure was hollowed out to make 40 suites, the smallest of which is 37 sq. m (398 sq. ft.). They all have well-equipped kitchenettes with microwave ovens and range tops. Four to six people can be accommodated in each unit, making this an excellent choice for families as well as long-stay businesspeople. From May to October the hotel operates at near total capacity, so book early. A fitness center and roof garden are planned for 2009. **Le 48,** a restaurant under separate management with an entrance from the lobby, provides room service.

1144 rue St-Pierre (rue St-Andre), Québec City, PQ G1K 4A8. ℂ **418/692-2777.** Fax 418/692-2778. www.hotelport royalsuites.com. 40 units. Nov–Apr C$159–C$259 (US$159–US$259/£80–£130) suite; May–Oct C$189–C$349 (US$189–US$349/£95–£175) suite. AE, MC, V. Parking C$15 (US$15/£7.50). Pets accepted. **Amenities:** Restaurant;

Québec's Ice Hotel: The Coldest Reception in Town

For C$15 (US$15/£7.50) you can visit, but for C$199 per person (US$199/£99) you can say you slept there. Québec's Ice Hotel (© 877/505-0423; www.ice-hotel-canada.com) is built each winter at the Station Touristique Duchesnay, a woodsy resort a half-hour outside Québec City. Crafted from 500 tons of ice, everything is clear or white, from the ice chandelier in the 5.5m (18-ft.) vaulted main hall, to the thick square ice shot glasses in which vodka is served, to the pillars and arches and furniture. That includes the frozen slabs they call beds—deer skins and sleeping bags provide insulation. Overnight guests get their rooms after visitors leave at 8pm and clear out before the next day's arrivals at 10am. Some rooms are themed and vaguely grand; others bring the words "monastic" or even "cell block" to mind. Bear in mind that except for in the hot tub, temperatures everywhere hover between 23° and 28°F (–5° to –2°C). Refrigerators are used not to keep sodas cold but to *keep them from freezing.*

In 2007, the hotel had 36 rooms and suites, a wedding chapel, and a disco where guests could shake the chill from their booties. Open each January, the Hôtel de Glace takes guests until April or the first thaw, whichever comes first.

Locals have a bemused reaction to all the fuss. As a waitress down the road told one guest: "I would have charged you half as much and let you sleep in a snowbank behind the pub."

bar; limited room service; laundry service; same-day dry cleaning. *In room:* A/C, TV/DVD, CD player, free Wi-Fi, coffeemaker, hair dryer, iron.

Parliament Hill/On or Near the Grande-Allee
EXPENSIVE

Courtyard by Marriott ☞ Sidestepping the conventional template of the parent chain by renovating a handsome building from the 1930s, the Marriott makes a substantial contribution to the ongoing enhancement of Place d'Youville, the central plaza of Upper Town. Rooms got a luxe upgrade in 2006 in bedding, with five pillows per bed and sheet covers on the duvets. All rooms have either a sofa bed or an oversize chair that pulls out into a single bed. There are washing machines for guest use next to a small exercise room. The lobby impresses with a balustraded second floor above a fireplace flanked by leather sofas, and a first-floor bar leads to a full-service restaurant.

850 Place d'Youville (near rue St-Jean), Québec City, PQ G1R 3P6. © 800/321-2211 or 418/694-4004. Fax 418/694-4007. www.marriott-quebec.com. 111 units. C$199–C$299 (US$199–US$299/£100–£150) double; Packages available. AE, DC, DISC, MC, V. Valet parking C$20 (US$20/£10); self-park C$17 (US$17/£8.50). **Amenities:** Restaurant; bar; exercise room w/Jacuzzi; concierge; business center; free Wi-Fi in lobby; limited room service; babysitting; self-service laundry; dry cleaning. *In room:* A/C, TV w/pay movies, free high-speed Internet, fridge, coffeemaker, hair dryer, iron.

Hilton Québec ☞☞ This Hilton is entirely true to the breed, the clear choice for executives and those leisure travelers who want their gadgets. The location—across the street from the city walls and near the Parliament—is excellent. Guest rooms are tastefully appointed in light blues and mustard golds, although it helps if you like mirrors because in some units they make up entire walls in the bathroom and hallway. Ask for an upper-floor room on the side facing the St. Lawrence River and Old Québec, and see the sun rise over the Citadelle. The busy boulevard René-Lévesque provides a steady hum of cars but is not overly distracting. The hotel is connected to the Place Québec shopping complex.

1100 bd. René-Lévesque est, Québec City, PQ G1K 7K7. ⓒ 800/HILTONS (445-8667) or 418/647-2411. Fax 418/647-6488. www.hiltonquebec.com. 571 units. Summer from C$169 (US$169/£84) double and way up; winter C$109–C$225 (US$109–US$225/£54–£112) double. Children stay free in parent's room. Packages available. AE, DC, DISC, MC, V. Valet parking C$21 (US$21/£11). Pets accepted. **Amenities:** Restaurant; bar; heated outdoor pool (year-round); well-equipped health club w/sauna and massage; concierge; car-rental desk; business center; limited room service; babysitting; laundry service; same-day dry cleaning; executive floors. *In room:* A/C, TV w/pay movies, high-speed Internet, minibar, coffeemaker, hair dryer.

Le Capitole 🅐   Located in the heart of Place d'Youville, Le Capitole is as gleefully eccentric as the business hotels it competes with are conventional. Rooms are all curves and obtuse angles, borrowing from Art Deco, and feature stars on the carpets and painted clouds on the ceiling. Beds have down duvets, and some rooms feature a bathtub in the corner. Mostly this works to its advantage, although some of the angles and funky furniture are tests to practicality. The hotel's owner runs the adjacent music and theater venue (also called Le Capitole; p. 282) and Ristorante Il Teatro.

972 rue St-Jean (1 block outside the old city walls; entrance is next to the theater marquee), Québec City, PQ G1R 1R5. ⓒ 800/363-4040 or 418/694-4040. www.lecapitole.com. 40 units. May 27–Oct 13 C$199–C$219 (US$199–US$219/£100–£110) double; rest of the year C$135–C$175 (US$135–US$175/£68–£88); suites from C$175 (US$175/£88). Packages available. AE, DC, DISC, MC, V. Valet parking C$19 (US$19/£9.50). **Amenities:** Restaurant; bar; concierge; limited room service; in-room massage; laundry service; dry cleaning. *In room:* A/C, TV/VCR, CD player, CD and video library, free Wi-Fi, free high-speed Internet, minibar, coffeemaker, hair dryer.

Loews Le Concorde 🅐   From outside, the skyscraper that houses this hotel is something of a visual insult to the skyline, rising from a neighborhood of late-Victorian town houses. But its height means spectacular views of the river and the old city, even from the lower floors. Standard rooms have marble bathrooms, plush robes, and three phone lines. Of all the hotels listed here, this is the farthest from Vieux-Québec: about a 10-minute walk to the walls and then another 10 minutes to the center of the Haute-Ville. **L'Astral,** a revolving rooftop restaurant with a bar and live piano music on weekends, has better food than usually can be expected of such sky-high venues.

1225 cours du Général de Montcalm (at Grande-Allée), Québec City, PQ G1R 4W6. ⓒ 800/463-5256 or 418/647-2222. Fax 418/647-4710. www.loewshotels.com. 406 units. May–Oct C$199–C$299 (US$199–US$299/£100–£150) double; Nov–Apr C$139–C$239 (US$139–US$239/£70–£120) double. Two children under 18 stay free in parent's room. Packages available. AE, DC, DISC, MC, V. Valet parking C$23 (US$23/£12); self-parking C$21 (US$21/£11). Pets accepted. **Amenities:** Restaurant; 2 bars; heated outdoor pool (in season); well-equipped health club w/sauna; concierge; business center; limited room service; babysitting; laundry service; same-day dry cleaning. *In room:* A/C, TV w/pay movies, high-speed Internet, minibar, coffeemaker, hair dryer, iron, safe.

MODERATE

Château Laurier 🅐🅐   Right on the action-filled Grande-Allée, this property has perked up considerably in recent years. A saltwater pool and Finnish sauna opened in 2007, and the health center and restaurant were both renovated in 2007 as well. There are now nine categories of rooms and suites, thanks to nearly continual expansion in recent years. Some have working fireplaces, whirlpools, and king beds; all enjoy the comforts and doodads of a first-class hotel. The new rooms are clearly more desirable than those in the plainer and more cramped original wing, with good-size desks and leather sitting chairs with reading lamps. Many rooms on the higher floors have views of the Citadelle and St. Lawrence River. The hotel is 2 blocks west of the fortress wall and St-Louis Gate.

1220 Place Georges V ouest (at Grande-Allée), Québec City, PQ G1R 5B8. ℂ 800/463-4453 or 418/522-8108. Fax 418/524-8768. www.oldquebec.com. 291 units. May–Oct 28 C$114–C$309 (US$114–US$309/£57–£155) double; Oct 29–Apr C$94–C$269 (US$94–US$269/£47–£135) double; suites from C$159 (US$159/£80). Children under 18 stay free in parent's room. Packages available. AE, DC, MC, V. Parking C$19 (US$19/£9.50). **Amenities:** Restaurant; indoor saltwater pool; sauna; concierge; business center; limited room service; babysitting; laundry service; dry cleaning. *In room:* A/C, TV w/pay movies, CD player, free Wi-Fi, high-speed Internet, coffeemaker, hair dryer, iron, safe.

Hôtel Palace Royal 🏵🏵   The newest and most luxurious addition to a small, family-owned Québec hotel group, this property elevates the standards of the business hotels outside the city walls. Lots of bronze statuary and marble are lavished on the lobby areas, while inner-atrium room balconies overlook a kidney-shaped indoor pool at the heart of a sort-of-tropical garden. Two-thirds of the units are suites, with fridges, microwave ovens, and, in four rooms, whirlpool baths big enough for two.

775 av. Honoré-Mercier (at Place d'Youville), Québec City, PQ G1R 6A5. ℂ 800/567-5276 or 418/694-2000. Fax 418/380-2553. www.jaro.qc.ca. 234 units. From C$134 (US$134/£67) double; from C$154 (US$154/£77) suite. Packages available. AE, DC, DISC, MC, V. Valet parking C$19 (US$19/£9.50). **Amenities:** Restaurant; bar; indoor pool; whirlpool; exercise room; sauna; concierge; business center; limited room service; babysitting; same-day dry cleaning on weekdays; tanning beds. *In room:* A/C, TV, high-speed Internet, coffeemaker, hair dryer, iron.

INEXPENSIVE

Relais Charles-Alexander (Value)   On the ground floor of this attractive brick-faced small hotel is an art gallery, which also serves as the breakfast room. This stylish use of space extends to the bedrooms as well, which are decorated with eclectic antique and wicker pieces and reproductions. Rooms in front are larger, and most have showers (three have tubs). They are quiet, for the most part, given that the inn is just outside the orbit of the sometimes-raucous Grande-Allée terrace bars. The fortress walls and St-Louis Gate are less than 15 minutes away by foot, and the pleasant shopping avenue Cartier is just around the corner.

91 Grande-Allée est (2 blocks east of av. Cartier), Québec City, PQ G1R 2H5. ℂ 418/523-1220. Fax 418/523-9556. www.quebecweb.com/rca. 23 units. June–Oct and Carnaval C$124–C$134 (US$124–US$134/£62–£67) double; Nov–May C$89–C$99 (US$89–US$99/£44–£50) double. Rates include breakfast. MC, V. Parking C$7 (US$7/£3.50). **Amenities:** Breakfast room; dry cleaning. *In room:* A/C, TV, hair dryer.

ST-ROCH
MODERATE

Auberge Le Vincent 🏵 (Value)   The emerging "Le Nouvo St-Roch" neighborhood has restaurants worth going out of your way for, and joining the neighborhood of technology companies, skateboard punks, and well-heeled hipsters is the Van Gogh–inspired Le Vincent, which opened its 10 rooms in August 2006. Housed in a renovated 100-year-old building, the sophisticated accommodations are a good value for all the luxe features: goose duvets, 400-count sheets, custom-made dark-cherry-wood furniture, and generous lighting options. Breakfasts are made to order in a brick-walled seating area off the lobby, whose floor is painted in Van Gogh–style sun-bursts and roiling blue curves. Bike storage and repair is available. Rooms are up either one or two flights of stairs. The hotel is a short walk from rue St-Jean, with its boutiques and restaurants, and Place D'Youville.

295 rue St-Vallier est (corner of rue Dorchester), Québec City, PQ G1K 3P5. ℂ 418/523-5000. Fax 418/523-5999. www.aubergelevincent.com. 10 units. C$119–C$149 (US$119–US$149/£60–£75) double; C$150–C$179 (US$150–US$179/£75–£90) suite. Rates include breakfast. Packages available. AE, MC, V. Valet parking C$15

(US$15/£7.50). **Amenities:** Concierge; in-room massage; laundry service; dry cleaning; bike storage. *In room:* A/C, TV/DVD, CD player, free Wi-Fi, free high-speed Internet, coffeemaker, hair dryer, iron (on request).

4 Where to Dine

Not long ago, it was fair to say that this gloriously scenic city had no *temples de cuisine* comparable to those of Montréal or Manhattan. That has changed. There are now restaurants comparable in every way to the most honored establishments of any North American city. What's more, surprising numbers of creative and ambitious young chefs and restaurateurs are bidding to achieve similar status. It is now easy to eat well in the capital—*quite* well, in an increasing number of cases.

By sticking to any of the many competent French bistros and jazzy fusion eateries, you will likely be more than content. Even the blatantly touristy restaurants along rue St-Louis in Upper Town and around the Place d'Armes, many of them with hawkers outside and showy tableside presentations inside, can produce decent meals. They're entirely satisfactory for breakfast or simple lunches, particularly useful if you're staying in a guesthouse or hotel that serves no meals.

The best dining deals are the table d'hôte—fixed-price—meals. Nearly all full-service restaurants offer them. As a rule, they include at least soup or salad, a main course, and a dessert. Some places add in an extra appetizer and/or a beverage. The total price is approximately what you'd pay for the main course alone.

Game is popular, including caribou, wapiti (North American deer), and quail. Many menus feature emu and lamb raised just north of the city in Charlevoix. Mussels and salmon are also standard.

At the better places and even some that might seem inexplicably popular, reservations are essential during the holidays and festivals that pepper the social calendar. Other times, it's usually only necessary to book ahead for weekend evenings. Dress codes are rarely stipulated, but "dressy casual" works almost everywhere.

Remember that for the Québécois, *dîner* (dinner) is lunch, and *souper* (supper) is the evening meal. The word "dinner" is used below in the common American sense. Also note that an *entrée* in Québec is an appetizer, while a *plat principal* is a main course.

Smoking in restaurants, bars, and most other public places in the Québec province has been banned since 2006.

VIEUX-QUEBEC: HAUTE-VILLE (UPPER TOWN)
EXPENSIVE
Aux Anciens Canadiens ✪ QUEBECOIS   This venerable restaurant is in what is probably the oldest (1677) house in the city; note the small windows whose original glass came over from France packed in barrels of molasses. It's smack in the middle of the tourist swarms and inundated during peak months, but the food at this famous establishment is, surprisingly, both fairly priced—at least at lunch—and well prepared. It's one of the best places in La Belle Province to sample cooking that has its roots in the earliest years of New France. Caribou figures into many of the ancient Québécois recipes, as does maple syrup (with the duckling, goat-cheese salad, and luscious sugar pie). Servings are large enough to ward off hunger for a week. Servers are in costume, and there are carved wooden bas-reliefs of regional scenes.

34 rue St-Louis (at rue des Jardins). ✆ **418/692-1627.** www.auxancienscanadiens.qc.ca. Reservations recommended. Main courses C$26–C$50 (US$26–US$50/£13–£25); table d'hôte dinner C$39–C$62 (US$39–US$62/£20–£31), lunch C$15 (US$15/£7.50). AE, DC, MC, V. Daily noon–10pm.

VIEUX-QUEBEC: BASSE-VILLE (LOWER TOWN)/VIEUX-PORT

VERY EXPENSIVE

Initiale ✮✮✮ FRENCH CONTEMPORARY   Initiale is not only one of the capital's elite restaurants, it is one of the best of the entire province. The palatial setting of tall windows, columns, and a deeply recessed ceiling sets a gracious tone, and the welcome is both cordial and correct. Prix-fixe menus of three to six courses are the way to go. As an example, one dinner started with a buckwheat crepe folded around an artichoke, a round of crabmeat with a creamy purée of onions, and a flash-fried leaf of baby spinach that added a delicate crackle, all arrayed on the plate as on an artist's palette. It continued with grilled tuna supported by sweet garlic, lemon marmalade, and a swirl of pasta with marguerite leaves. Québec cheeses are an impressive topper. This is a place to celebrate important events. Men should wear jackets; women can pull out the stops.

54 rue St-Pierre (corner of Côte de la Montagne). ✆ 418/694-1818. Reservations recommended on weekends. Main courses C$38–C$45 (US$38–US$45/£19–£22); table d'hôte dinner C$64 or C$94 (US$64 or US$94/£32 or £47). AE, DC, MC, V. Tues–Fri 11:30am–2pm; Tues–Sat 6–9pm.

Laurie Raphaël ✮✮✮ FUSION   The owners of this smashingly creative restaurant tinker relentlessly with their handiwork. Against an eclectically sophisticated decor (tempered by dashes of eye-popping red and electric pink), the platings are prettier than ever. Silky-smooth foie gras arrives on a teeny ice-cream paddle, drizzled with a port and maple-syrup reduction. Alaskan snow crab is accompanied by a bright pink pomegranate terrine. Rabbit is served two ways: as a braised leg atop a traditional cassoulet, and trimmed like a rack of lamb. An egg yolk "illusion" of thickened orange juice encapsulated in a skin of pectin is served in a puddle of maple syrup in an Asian soup spoon. And so on. Service falls within the friendly/correct range, and the pace of the meal is spot on. Recent renovations added a fancy public kitchen where chef/owner Daniel Vézina gives cooking classes.

117 rue Dalhousie (at rue St-André). ✆ 418/692-4555. www.restaurantinitiale.com. Reservations recommended. Main courses C$38–C$49 (US$38–US$49/£19–£25); gourmet dinner menu C$94 (US$94/£47); 3-course chef's inspiration C$60 (US$60/£30); table d'hôte lunch C$23 (US$23/£12). AE, DC, DISC, MC, V. Tues–Fri 11:30am–2pm; Tues–Sat 5:30–10pm.

Panache ✮✮ FRENCH CONTEMPORARY   The restaurant of the superb **Auberge Saint-Antoine** (p. 279) started life in 2004 with a big advantage: It is housed in a former 19th-century warehouse delineated by massive wood beams and rough stone walls. A center fireplace, velvet couches, and generous space between tables enhance the inherent romantic aura, and some tables are tucked into second-floor eves. Aiming to serve up *cuisine Québécoise revisitée*—French Canadian cuisine with a twist—the frequently changing menu is heavy on locally sourced game, duck, fish, and vegetables. Appetizers have included emu tartare folded with capers and a lightly flavored vinaigrette, and "Mushrooms from my friend, Michel" served with duck confit, foie gras, and celery ravioli. The Angus beef prepared two ways—grilled rump steak and rib tips—coupled with turnip and shitake gnocchi, is a knockout.

10 rue St-Antoine (in Auberge Saint-Antoine). ✆ 418/692-1022. www.saint-antoine.com. Reservations recommended at dinner. Main courses C$37–C$45 (US$37–US$45/£19–£22); tasting menu C$149 (US$149/£74). AE, DC, MC, V. Breakfast Mon–Sat 6:30–10:30am; lunch Mon–Fri noon–2pm; brunch Sun 11am–2pm; dinner daily 6–10pm.

EXPENSIVE

L'Echaudé ✮ FRENCH BISTRO   The most polished of several restaurants adorning this Vieux-Port corner, this bistro is like a good cashmere sweater, able to be dressed up or down with ease. Tables are covered with butcher paper and there are stools at a stainless-steel bar. Two walls of mirrors reflect the bright amber light, and the businessman's lunch is written on the mirror, Parisian style. Grilled meats and fishes and the seafood stews are very satisfying and an excellent value. Among the classics are steak frites, lobster bisque, duck confit, and salmon tartare. Less expected is the lobster and scallops cannelloni in a white-wine sauce, and the wild-deer medaglioni pasta with cranberry sauce. The owner keeps an important cellar with 150 varieties of wine, about a dozen available by the glass. In the summer, the small street in front of the patio is closed off to car traffic.

73 rue Sault-au-Matelot (near rue St-Paul). (℄ 418/692-1299. www.echaude.com. Reservations recommended on weekends. Main courses C$18–C$38 (US$18–US$38/£9–£19); table d'hôte dinner cost of the main plus C$15 (US$15/£7.50). AE, DC, MC, V. Mon–Fri and Sun 11:30am–2:30pm; daily 5:30–10pm.

Le Marie-Clarisse ✿ FRENCH BISTRO/SEAFOOD   At the bottom of Breakneck Stairs and perched just overlooking the pedestrian-only rue du Petit-Champlain, Le Marie-Clarisse sits where the streets are awash with day-packers and shutterbugs. It serves terrific seafood and the menu changes often, so look closely at the long list of specials posted on chalkboards. A more pleasant hour cannot be passed anywhere in Québec City than here, out on the terrace on a summer afternoon over a platter of shrimp or pâtés. In winter, cocoon by the stone fireplace inside, indulging in the dense bouillabaisse—a stew of mussels, scallops, tuna, tilapia, and shrimp, with a boat of saffron mayo. Try a Québec wine to wash it down. The inside rooms are formed of rafters, brick, and 300-year-old stone walls, and evoke the feel of a small country inn.

12 rue du Petit-Champlain (at the Funiculaire). (℄ 418/692-0857. www.marieclarisse.qc.ca. Main courses C$30–C$33 (US$30–US$33/£15–£17); table d'hôte dinner from C$38 (US$38/£19). AE, MC, V. Mon–Sat 11:30am–10pm; terrace daily Apr–Oct.

Poisson d'Avril SEAFOOD   Nautical trappings include model ships, marine prints, and mounted sailfish, and they make the intent clear: The menu is packed with seafood, including some combinations of costly crustaceans responsible for the stiffer prices noted below. The crowded Provençal bouillabaisse has calamari, scallops, shrimp, mussels, and rouille, while a special platter called *L'assiette du commodore* is laden with snow crabs, half a lobster, and the fish of the day. Mixed grill and pastas are also available. In good weather, there's a covered dining terrace. With the restaurant located almost directly next to Espace 400ᵉ, the new exhibition pavilion, this will be a crowded location, so make reservations for weekend meals.

115 quai Saint-André (in Vieux-Port, near Espace 400ᵉ). (℄ 418/692-1010. www.poissondavril.net. Reservations recommended. Main courses C$13–C$67 (US$13–US$67/£6.50–£33); table d'hôte the price of the main plus C$13 (US$13/£6.50). AE, DC, MC, V. Daily 5–10pm.

Toast! ✿ FUSION   This zesty restaurant has its base in the French idiom but takes off in many directions. You'll see it in a pecan-crusted rack of rabbit with a cold purée of potato, cream, and horseradish, perked with a basil foam and Parmesan. Or fennel soup followed by chopped tuna, spiced with ginger and lemon zest, shaped into a burger and then grilled—but on just one side. Every dish is like that: audacious, sprightly, and attentive to joined tastes and textures. The interior room has a crimson glow from a wall of fire-engine-red tiles, retro-modern lights, and red Plexiglas paneling in the windows. Try for the outdoor dining terrace out back, if it's warm enough: with wrought-iron furniture and big leafy trees overhead, it's an oasis.

17 rue Sault-au-Matelot (at rue St-Antoine). (℄ 418/692-1334. www.restauranttoast.com. Reservations recommended on weekends. Main courses C$27–C$45 (US$27–US$45/£14–£23). AE, DC, MC, V. Mon–Fri 11:30am–2pm; Sun 10:30am–2pm; daily 6–10:30pm (until 11pm Thurs–Sun).

MODERATE

L'Ardoise FRENCH BISTRO   This is one of several appealing bistros that wrap around the intersection of rues St-Paul and Sault-au-Matelot. A new owner took over in the fall of 2006 but kept the orange-and-cobalt decor. Mussels are staples at Québec restaurants, prepared in the Belgian manner with bowls of fries on the side. L'Ardoise's mussels and fries *(moules et frites)* have 11 sauce options, from Dijon mustard to curry, for C$16 (US$16/£8), with seconds for C$7 (US$7/£3.50). On a recent chilly day, a bowl of penne pasta with salmon, broccoli pesto, and aged cheddar hit the spot just right. There's a brunch menu from 10:30am to 3pm on weekends. With jaunty Piaf-style vocals on the stereo, this is a good place to sip a double espresso and leaf through a book.

71 rue St-Paul (near rue du Sault-au-Matelot). ✆ 418/694-0213. www.lardoiseresto.com. Reservations recommended at dinner. Main courses C$15–C$36 (US$15–US$36/£7.50–£18); table d'hôte the price of the main plus C$15 (US$15/£7.50). AE, DC, MC, V. Mon–Fri 11:30am–3pm; Sat–Sun 10:30am–3pm; daily 5:30–10pm (closing earlier in winter).

Le Café du Monde 🐝 *Value* FRENCH/INTERNATIONAL   A long-time and entirely convivial eating venue, the Café du Monde moved in 2002 to its current location adjoining Le Terminal de Croisières—the cruise terminal. It's a larger, Parisian-style space, seating 135 inside and another 75 on a terrace overlooking the St. Lawrence River and Ile d'Orléans. The staff is as amiable as ever, the food a touch more creative but still within bistro conventions. The short menu continues to feature classic French preparations of pâtés, duck confit, onion soup, smoked salmon tartare, and four versions of mussels with frites. A recent brunch plate—scrambled eggs with salmon, dill, potatoes, fruit, and a croissant, for C$9 (US$9/£4.50)—was served fast and with a smile, even on a busy holiday weekend.

84 rue Dalhousie (next to the cruise terminal). ✆ 418/692-4455. www.lecafedumonde.com. Reservations recommended. Main courses C$12–C$27 (US$12–US$27/£6–£14); table d'hôte C$12–C$16 (US$12–US$16/£6–£8). AE, DC, MC, V. Mon–Fri 11:30am–11pm; Sat–Sun and holidays 9:30am–11pm.

PARLIAMENT HILL/ON OR NEAR THE GRANDE-ALLEE

EXPENSIVE

VooDoo Grill 🐝 FUSION   Of all the unlikely places to expect a decent meal, this one takes the laurels. Wait staff is clad in all-black, African carvings adorn the walls, thumping music sets the pace, and conga drummers circulate nightly, beating out insistent rhythms—a tremendous distraction. It's all loud, young, and casual. The menu is divided into three categories: "Air," "Water," and "Land," with features such as a filet mignon from Québec's Charlevoix region grilled with mushrooms and asparagus and a plate featuring shrimps, scallops, and Chinese ravioli stuffed with seafood. There's an attached cigar lounge, the Société Cigare, with 200 offerings.

575 Grande-Allée est (corner of rue de la Chevrotière). ✆ 418/647-2000. www.voodoogrill.com. Reservations recommended. Main courses C$17–C$48 (US$17–US$48/£8.50–£24). AE, DC, MC, V. Mon–Fri 11am–2am; Sat–Sun 5pm–2am.

INEXPENSIVE

Café Krieghoff LIGHT FARE   Walk down Grande-Allée about 10 minutes from the Parliament, and turn right on avenue Cartier. This 5-block strip is the heart of the Montcalm residential neighborhood, with bakeries, boutiques, restaurants, and bars. In the middle of it all is this cheerful cafe, which features an outdoor terrace a few steps up from the sidewalk. On weekend mornings it's packed with artsy locals of all ages, whose tables get piled high with bowls of cafe au lait and huge plates of egg dishes, sweet pasteries, or classics like steak frites. Service is efficient and good-natured. There's also a modest *auberge* upstairs with seven rooms.

1091 av. Cartier (north of Grande-Allée). ℂ 418-522-3711. www.cafekrieghoff.qc.ca. Most items under C$10 (US$10/£5). MC, V. Sun–Thurs 7am–11pm; Fri–Sat 7am–midnight.

ST-ROCH
EXPENSIVE

Utopie ⊛ *(Finds)* FUSION   Utopie has proven so far to have the essential ingredients for its considerable success: the clientele has a stylish sheen, the interior is almost painfully chic (stands of birch trunks march down the middle of the high-ceilinged space), the location is sufficiently out of the way to require that customers are those in the know, and the food isn't same-old. Sautéed *lotte* (monkfish) was joined with translucent baby bok choy and wild asparagus no thicker than bean sprouts one night, with garlic cream another. Duck confit with braised endive and onion compote is a menu staple. The all-out meal is the six-course degustation menu with a wine pairing for C$105 (US$105/£52).

226½ rue St-Joseph est (near rue Caron). ℂ 418/523-7878. www.restaurant-utopie.com. Reservations recommended on weekends. Main courses C$22–C$27 (US$22–US$27/£11–£14); table d'hôte dinner C$29–C$65 (US$29–US$65/£15–£33). AE, MC, V. Tues–Fri noon–2pm; Tues–Sun 6–9pm.

MODERATE

Le Clocher Penché ⊛ *(Finds)* FRENCH BISTRO   Open since 2000 and owned by two self-styled "artisan chefs," the evolution of this unpretentious neighborhood bistro parallels the polishing up this neighborhood has seen during the same period. With its caramel-toned woods, tall ceilings, and walls serving as gallery space for local artists, Le Clocher Penché has a casual European sophistication. The short menu changes regularly and can include duck confit and wild boar. The rich blood sausage *(boudin noir)* was served on a delicate pastry bed with caramelized onions and yellow beets, and the tamer but just-right risotto had mushrooms and big chunks of asparagus. The menu touts that much of the food is sourced locally. The wine list features 187 choices, with 96% private importation and 73% organic or "biodynamic," and about 10 wines are sold by the glass. Service is amiable and without flourishes.

203 rue St-Joseph est (at rue Caron). ℂ 418/640-0597. Reservations recommended. Main courses C$16–C$23 (US$16–US$23/£8–£12); weekend brunch C$14 (US$14/£7). AE, DC, MC, V. Mon–Fri 11:30am–3pm; Sat–Sun 9am–3pm; daily 5–10pm.

Versa FUSION   This is a destination to remember when with a group in a partying mood. Translucent panels behind the back bar pulse with a rainbow of colors, highlighting the pride of the barkeeps, their inventive roster of cocktails—one begins with muddled grapes and fresh ginger before 2 ounces of icy vodka are poured on top. Dinners might feature mussels four ways, soufflé of black crab, leg of lamb with maple syrup, or, for the less hungry or demanding, a "Diablo dog" or tartare burger. A communal table illuminated by pin lights and a disco ball is just the arena for friendly extroverts. The windows along the front open in good weather, and the after-dinner action floats between here and the Boudoir Lounge across the street, a hot nightspot.

432 rue du Parvis (at rue St-Françoise). ℂ 418/523-9995. www.versarestaurant.com. Main courses C$12–C$32 (US$12–US$32/£6–£16); table d'hôte dinner C$21–C$35 (US$21–US$35/£11–£18), lunch C$9–C$18 (US$9–US$18/£4.50–£9). MC, V. Mon–Fri 11am–midnight; Sat–Sun 5pm–midnight.

Yuzu ⊛ SUSHI/JAPANESE   At the epicenter of the renovated section of St-Roch, Québec's low-key retail district that's getting a new youthful pop, Yuzu's sushi and Japanese preparations are its focus. Authenticity isn't sought, not with foie gras on the card (and as expensive as you expect). Individual sushi run C$4–C$15

(US$4–US$15/£2–£7.50), and there are tasting menus of C$65 (US$65/£32) for five courses and C$85 (US$85/£42) for seven.

438 rue du Parvis (at bd. Charest). ℂ 418/521-7253. www.yuzu.ca. Reservations recommended. Main courses C$12–C$22 (US$12–US$22/£6–£11). AE, DC, MC, V. Mon–Fri 11:30am–2:30pm; Sun–Wed 5–10pm; Thurs–Sat 5pm–midnight.

5 Seeing the Sights

Almost all of a visit to Québec City can be spent on foot in the old Lower Town—which hugs the river below the bluff—and in the old Upper Town—atop the Cap Diamant (Cape Diamond).

Wandering at random through Vieux-Québec is a singular pleasure, comparable to exploring a provincial capital in Europe. You can happen upon an ancient convent, blocks of gabled houses with steeply pitched roofs, a battery of 18th-century cannons in a leafy park, or a bistro with a blazing fireplace on a wintry day.

Special events are planned in 2008 for the city's 400th anniversary (see "2008: Québec Throws Itself a Party," p. 291). The colonial city was first built right down by the St. Lawrence: It was here that the earliest French merchants, traders, and boatmen earned their livelihoods, and Basse-Ville (Lower Town) became primarily a district of wharves and warehouses. That trend has been reversed, with new *auberges* (inns) and many attractive bistros, shops, and museums bringing new life to the area. The district maintains the architectural feel of its origins, with narrow cobbled streets.

Unfriendly fire from the British and Amerindians in the 1700s moved residents to safer houses atop the cliffs that form the rim of the Cap. Haute-Ville (Upper Town) turned out to not be immune to cannon fire (as the British General James Wolfe was to prove in 1759 when he took the city from the French). Nevertheless, the division into Upper and Lower towns persisted for obvious topographical reasons. The Upper Town remains enclosed by fortification walls, making Québec the only walled city north of Mexico.

Everything is so compact that it is hardly necessary to plan precise sightseeing itineraries. Start at the Terrasse Dufferin and go off on a whim, perhaps down the funicular or adjacent Breakneck Stairs (Escalier Casse-Cou) to the Quartier du Petit-Champlain and Place Royale, or along the river to the Citadel and the Plains of Abraham, where Generals James Wolfe and Louis-Joseph, Marquis de Montcalm, fought to their mutual deaths in the 20-minute battle between England and France that changed the destiny of the continent.

While the Upper Town is hilly, with sloping streets, only people with physical limitations are likely to experience difficulty. If rain or ice discourages exploration on foot, tour buses and horse-drawn calèches are options.

VIEUX-QUEBEC: BASSE-VILLE (LOWER TOWN)/VIEUX-PORT

Espace 400ᵉ   Occupying what used to be the Centre d'Interprétation du Vieux-Port on the waterfront, this newly renovated and expanded pavilion is the central location for Québec's 400th anniversary celebrations in 2008. It will host exhibits, performances, conferences, and shows throughout the year, and after 2008 will be a Parks Canada discovery center.

100 quai St-Andre (at rue Rioux). www.myquebec2008.com.

Maison Chevalier   Built in 1752 for ship owner Jean-Baptiste Chevalier, the house incorporated buildings dating from 1675 and 1695. It was run as an inn throughout the

19th century, and after the Québec government restored the house it became a museum in 1965. The interior has exposed wood beams, wide-board floors, and stone fireplaces. A permanent exhibit, "A Sense of the Past," shows how people lived in the 18th and 19th centuries. While exhibit texts are in French, guidebooks in English are available at the front desk. The house also serves as an air-conditioned refuge on hot days.

50 rue du Marché-Champlain (near rue Notre-Dame). www.mcq.org. Free admission. Late June to Labour Day daily 9:30am–5pm; Sept to mid-Oct and Dec 19–Jan 1 Tues–Sun 10am–5pm; the rest of the year Sat–Sun 10am–5pm.

Musée de la Civilisation ★★★ Kids

Try to set aside at least 2 hours for a visit to this special museum, one of the most engrossing in all of Canada. Opened in 1988, the Museum of Civilization is an innovative presence on the waterfront of historic Basse-Ville. The precise mission of the museum has never been entirely clear. Recent temporary exhibits, for example, have included the science and fiction of dragons, 110 years of Québec cinema, and the opportunity to solve a faux murder. But never mind. Through highly imaginative display techniques, hands-on devices, holograms, and even an ant farm, the curators have ensured that visitors will be so enthralled by the experience that they won't pause to question its intent.

A dramatic atrium-lobby sets the tone with a representation of the St. Lawrence River with an ancient ship beached on the shore. If time is short, definitely use it to take in "People of Québec . . . Then and Now," a permanent exhibit that is a sprawling examination of Québec history, moving from the province's roots as a fur-trading colony to the present to provide visitors with a rich sense of Québec's daily life over the generations. Another permanent exhibition called "Encounter with the First Nations" examines the products and visions of the Native Canadian tribes that inhabit Québec. Exhibit texts are in French and English, and there's a cafe on the ground floor.

85 rue Dalhousie (at rue St-Antoine). ✆ 418/643-2158. www.mcq.org. Admission C$10 (US$10/£5) adults, C$9 (US$9/£4.50) 65 and over, C$7 (US$7/£3.50) students over 16, C$4 (US$4/£2) children 12–16, free for children under 12; free to all Tues Nov 1–May 31 and Sat 10am–noon Jan–Feb. Late June to Labour Day daily 9:30am–6:30pm; day after Labour Day to late June Tues–Sun 10am–5pm.

Place-Royale ★★★ Kids

This small but picturesque plaza is considered by Québecois to be the literal and spiritual heart of Basse-Ville—in grander terms, the birthplace of French America. In the 17th and 18th centuries, "Royal Square" was the town marketplace and the center of business and industry. Today, folk dances and other festive gatherings are often held near the **bust of Louis XIV** in the center.

The **Eglise Notre-Dame-des-Victoires** dominates the plaza. The oldest stone church in Québec, it was built in 1688 after a massive fire destroyed 55 homes in 1682, and then was restored in 1763 and 1969. Its paintings, altar, and large model boat suspended from the church ceiling were votive offerings brought by early settlers to ensure safe voyages. The church is open daily to visitors May through October. Sunday masses are held at 10:30am and noon.

All the buildings on the square have been restored, although some of the walls are original. The **Centre d'Interprétation de Place-Royale** offers a 20-minute multimedia show and other exhibitions detailing the city's 400-year history. Guided tours of the area are available from the interpretation center in both English and French. Walk past the center with it on your left and to the end of the block, and turn around to view a *trompe l'oeil* mural depicting citizens of the early city.

Admission to the Place-Royale and Eglise Notre-Dame-des-Victoires is free. Centre d'Interprétation de Place-Royale, 27 rue Notre-Dame. ✆ 418/646-3167. C$5 (US$5/£2.50) adults, C$4.50 (US$4.50/£2.25) seniors, C$2 (US$2/£1) ages 12–16, free for children under 12. June 24–Sept 6 daily 9:30am–5pm; Sept 7–June 23 Tues–Sun 10am–5pm.

> ## (*Tips*) 2008: Québec Throws Itself a Party
>
> In 1608, Samuel de Champlain founded a settlement at Kebec, at the foot of Cape Diamond. That settlement became the city of Québec. The city has been sprucing itself up for blow-out celebrations for 2008, to commemorate its 400th anniversary. For the most up-to-date information about events and tickets, go to www.myquebec2008.com. Among the happenings:
>
> - **The opening of Espace 400ᵉ**, a new pavilion on the waterfront where the Centre d'Interprétation du Vieux-Port used to be. It will host special 400th anniversary exhibits, performances, conferences, gardens, and shows from June through September. After 2008, it will become a Parks Canada discovery center.
> - **Four days of "exceptional events" (July 3–6),** including an official ceremony, mass at the Basilique Notre-Dame, tie-in concerts with the Québec City Summer Festival, an "urban opera," and an aerial photograph of the Plains of Abraham that everyone is invited to be a part of.
> - **Nightly projections of video onto the silos** across the water from Espace 400ᵉ—what organizers says will be one of the largest projections of its kind.
> - **Special exhibits at museums** and tourist venues across the city, including "Québec, a City and Its Artists" and an exhibit of works from the Louvre, both at the Musée des Beaux-Arts du Québec.
> - A **closing event** by Cirque du Soleil on October 19.

VIEUX-QUEBEC: HAUTE-VILLE (UPPER TOWN)

Basilique Notre-Dame ⨍   Notre-Dame Basilica, representing the oldest Christian parish north of Mexico, has weathered a tumultuous history of bombardment, reconstruction, and restoration. Parts of the existing basilica date from the original 1647 structure, including the bell tower and portions of the walls, but most of today's exterior is from the reconstruction completed in 1771. The interior is a re-creation undertaken after a fire in 1922 and flamboyantly neo-baroque, with shadows wavering by the fluttering light of votive candles. Paintings and ecclesiastical treasures still remain from the time of the French regime, including a chancel lamp given by Louis XIV. Over 900 people are buried in the **crypt,** including four governors of New France (Frontenac, Vaudreuil, Callières, and Jonquière). The basilica is connected to the group of old buildings that make up Québec Seminary. There is an **organ concert** the first Sunday of every month at 3:30pm.

16 rue Buade (at Côte de la Fabrique). 🕐 **418/692-2533.** Cathedral fee C$2 (US$2/£1) adults, free for ages 16 and younger. Crypt fee C$2 (US$2/£1) adults, C$1 (US$1/50p) ages 16 and younger. Guided tour fee same as crypt fee. Organ concert suggested donation C$5 (US$5/£2.50). Free admission for those who come for prayers and services. Mon–Sat 7:30am–6pm in summer (closing at 4pm the rest of the year); Sun 8:30am–6pm. Guided tours May–Oct daily.

Chapelle/Musée des Ursulines   This chapel is notable for the sculptures in its pulpit and two richly decorated altarpieces, created by Pierre-Noël Levasseur between 1726 and 1736. The tomb of the founder of the Ursulines teaching order, Marie de l'Incarnation, is to the right of the entry. She arrived in Québec City in 1639 at the age of 40 and was beatified by Pope John Paul II in 1980. The Ursuline convent was built originally as a girls' school in 1642 and is the oldest in North America.

The museum tells the story of the nuns, who were also pioneers and artists. Included are vestments woven with gold thread and a cape made of the drapes from the bedroom of Anne of Austria, which was given to Marie de l'Incarnation when she left for New France in 1639. There are also musical instruments and Amerindian crafts, including the *flèche*, or arrow sash, which is still worn during the winter carnival. Some of the docents are nuns of the still-active order.

12 rue Donnacona (des Jardins). (℃ 418/694-0694. www.patrimoine-religieux.com. Free admission to chapel. Museum C$6 (US$6/£3) adults, C$5 (US$5/£2.50) seniors, C$4 (US$4/£2) students 17 and over, C$3 (US$3/£1.50) ages 12–16, free for children under 12. Museum May–Sept Tues–Sat 10am–noon and 1–5pm, Sun 1–5pm; Oct–Apr Tues–Sun 1–5pm. Chapel May–Oct Tues–Sat 10–11:30am and 1:30–4:40pm.

Château Frontenac ⋆ Opened in 1893 to house railroad passengers and encourage tourism, this monster version of a Loire Valley palace is Québec City's emblem— its Eiffel Tower. The hotel can be seen from almost every quarter, commanding its majestic position atop Cap Diamant, the rock bluff adjacent to the St. Lawrence River that once provided military defense. Visitors can take a 50-minute guided tour of the interior; reservations are recommended.

1 rue des Carrières, at Place d'Armes. (℃ 418/691-2166. Tours C$8.50 (US$8.50/£4.25) adults, C$7.75 (US$7.75/ £3.85) for seniors, C$6 (US$6/£3) children ages 6–16. May 1–Oct 15 daily 10am–6pm; Oct 16–Apr 30 Sat–Sun 1–5pm (departures on the hour).

La Citadelle ⋆⋆ The duke of Wellington had this partially star-shaped fortress built at the south end of the city walls in anticipation of renewed American attacks after the War of 1812. Some remnants of earlier French military structures were incorporated into The Citadelle, including a 1750 magazine. Dug into the Plains of Abraham high above Cap Diamant ("Cape Diamond"), the fort has a low profile that keeps it all but invisible until walkers are actually upon it. The facility has never actually exchanged fire with an invader but continues its vigil for the state: Since 1920 it has been home to Québec's Royal 22ᵉ Régiment, the only fully Francophone unit in Canada's armed forces. That makes it the largest fortified group of buildings still occupied by troops in North America.

The public may visit The Citadelle and its 25 buildings by guided tour only. Another option is to attend the ceremonies of the **changing of the guard** (daily at 10am in summer) or **beating the retreat** (Fri at 7pm in summer). Walk or drive up the Côte de la Citadelle from the St-Louis Gate; there are many parking spaces inside the walls.

Côte de la Citadelle (enter off rue St-Louis). (℃ 418/694-2815. www.lacitadelle.qc.ca. Admission C$10 (US$10/£5) adults, C$9 (US$9/£4.50) seniors and students over 17, C$5.50 (US$5.50/£2.75) age 17 and younger. Apr daily 10am–4pm; May–June daily 9am–5pm; July to Labour Day daily 9am–6pm; Sept (after Labour Day) daily 9am–4pm; Oct daily 10am–3pm; Nov–Mar 1 bilingual tour a day at 1:30pm. Changing of the guard (30 min.) June 24 to Labour Day daily at 10am; beating the retreat (20 min.) July to early Sept 7pm Fri, and 7pm Sat–Sun at the Esplanade Park. May be canceled in the event of rain.

Musée de l'Amérique Française Located at the Québec Seminary, which dates from 1663, the Museum of French America focuses on the evolution of French culture in North America. Its extensive collections include paintings by European and Canadian artists, engravings from the early French regime, rare books, early scientific instruments, and even mounted animals and an Egyptian mummy. The mix makes for a mostly engrossing visit, although parts of the museum can be rather dry. The beautiful François-Ranvoyze section has extensive *trompe l'oeil* ornamentation and served

> **Value Québec City Museum Card**
>
> Good for 3 consecutive days, the **Québec City Museum Card** (© **418/641-6172;** www.museocapitale.qc.ca/cartema.htm) gives entry to 24 museums and attractions, including many mentioned here. Cost is C$40 (US$40/£20). There are no separate rates for seniors or children. The pass includes two 1-day bus passes and is available at all participating attractions and at the Québec City Tourism Information Bureau in the Discovery Pavilion.

as a chapel for the seminary priests and students. Concerts are often held in the chapel, which was visited by Pope John Paul II in 1984.

2 Côte de la Fabrique (next to Basilique Notre-Dame). © 418/692-2843. www.mcq.org. Admission C$6 (US$6/£3) adults, C$5 (US$5/£2.50) seniors, C$3.50 (US$3.50/£1.75) students 17 and older, C$2 (US$2/£1) children 12–16, free for children under 12, free to all Tues Nov–May. Late June to Labour Day daily 9:30am–5pm; Sept to mid-June Tues–Sun 10am–5pm. Guided tours (call for reservations) of exhibitions and buildings 10am and 3:30pm in summer; call for times the rest of the year.

Musée du Fort   A long-running but still effective multimedia show combines film, light, stirring music, and a 36-sq.-m (400-sq.-ft.) scale model of the city and environs to tell the story of the several battles that flared here in the 18th century. At less than 25 minutes, it is a sufficiently engrossing presentation during which only the very young are likely to grow restless. Check in advance when shows in English are scheduled.

10 rue Ste-Anne, Place d'Armes. © 418/692-2175. www.museedufort.com. Admission C$7.50 (US$7.50/£3.75) adults, C$6 (US$6/£3) seniors, C$5 (US$5/£2.50) students. Apr 1–Oct 31 daily 10am–5pm; Nov 1–Mar 31 Thurs–Sun 11am–4pm; Dec 26 to first Sun in Jan daily 11am–4pm. Open to groups with reservations in winter months.

Parc de l'Artillerie   Fortifications erected by the French in the 17th and 18th centuries enclose Artillery Park. In addition to protecting the garrison, the defensive works contained an ammunition factory that was functional until 1964. On view are the old officers' mess and quarters, an iron foundry, and a scale model of the city created in 1806. Costumed docents give tours. In July and August, there are twice-daily musket demonstrations; hours vary. (It may be a blow to romantics and history buffs to learn that the nearby St-Jean Gate in the city wall was built in 1940, the fourth in a series that began with the original 1693 entrance, which was replaced in 1747, and then replaced again in 1867.)

2 rue d'Auteuil (near Porte St-Jean). © 418/648-4205. www.pc.gc.ca/artillerie. Admission C$3.95 (US$3.95/£2) adults, C$3.45 (US$3.45/£1.70) seniors, C$1.95 (US$1.95/95p) ages 6–16, free for children under 6. Additional fees for audio guide, special activities, and tea ceremony. Apr 1–Oct 7 daily 10am–5pm; by reservation only the rest of the year.

PARLIAMENT HILL/ON OR NEAR THE GRANDE-ALLEE

Hôtel du Parlement   Since 1968, what the Québécois call their "National Assembly" has occupied this imposing Second Empire château constructed in 1886. Twenty-two bronze statues of some of the most prominent figures in Québec's tumultuous history gaze out from the facade. Highlights are the Assembly Chamber and the Legislative Council Chamber, where parliamentary committees meet. Throughout the building, representations of the fleur-de-lis and the initials VR (for Victoria Regina) remind visitors of Québec's dual heritage. The building can be toured unaccompanied, but there are free 30-minute guided tours in English, French, Spanish, and Italian. Call for tour times and languages. The Beaux Arts–style restaurant **Le Parlementaire**

(© 418/643-6640) is open to the public. Featuring Québec products and cuisine, it serves breakfast and lunch Monday through Friday most of the year.

Entrance at corner of Grande-Allée est and av. Honoré-Mercier. © 418/643-7239. www.assnat.qc.ca. Free admission. Guided tours in summer Mon–Fri 9am–4:30pm; Sat–Sun and holidays 10am–4:30pm; in winter Mon–Fri 9am–4:30pm.

Musée des Beaux-Arts du Québec 🏛🏛 (Kids)   Toward the southern end of the Parc des Champs-de-Bataille (Battlefields Park), just off the Grande-Allée, the Musée du Québec (as it's known in shorthand) is the city's major art museum. It occupies two buildings, one a former prison, linked together by a soaring glass-roofed Grand Hall housing the reception area, a stylish cafe, and a shop.

The original 1933 Gérard-Morisset Pavilion has much of the permanent collection—the largest aggregation of Québécois art in North America, filling eight galleries with works from the beginning of the colony to the present. The museum tilts to the modern in addition to the indigenous, with a permanent exhibition of works by famed Québec Abstract-Expressionist-Surrealist Jean-Paul Riopelle. In 2005, the museum acquired an important Inuit art collection assembled over many years by Raymond Brousseau. Much of the work has been produced in the last 20 years, and about 300 works from the 2,635-piece collection are on display, including a small whimsical statue called *Woman Pulling Out Grey Hairs.*

The second building is the 1867 Charles-Baillairgé Pavilion, a former prison. Make sure to keep climbing until you get to the tower room: It's a small widow's walk, accessible only by spiral staircase, and the highest point in the museum. In addition to housing the massive wooden sculpture of a body in motion by Irish artist David Moore, it offers terrific views of the city in every direction. A craft projects room occupies children, and an accomplished cafe-restaurant serves table d'hôte lunch Monday through Friday, brunch on the weekend, and dinner on Wednesdays.

Parc des Champs-de-Bataille, near where av. Wolfe-Montcalm meets Grande Allée © 418/643-2150. www. mnba.qc.ca. Free admission to permanent collection. Admission for special exhibitions C$12 (US$12/£6) adults, C$10 (US$10/£5) seniors, C$5 (US$5/£2.50) students over 16, C$3 (US$3/£1.50) ages 12–16, free for children under 12. June 1 to Labour Day daily 10am–6pm (until 9pm Wed); day after Labour Day to May 31 Tues–Sun 10am–5pm (until 9pm Wed). Bus: 11.

Parc des Champs-de-Bataille 🏛🏛 (Kids)   Covering 108 hectares (267 acres) of grassy hills and sunken gardens, Québec's Battlefields Park is Canada's first national urban park. It stretches over the Plains of Abraham, where Britain's General James Wolfe and France's Louis-Joseph, Marquis de Montcalm, engaged in their short but crucial battle in 1759, resulting in the British defeat of the French troops (and the death of both military leaders). Today it is a favorite place for all Québécois when they want some sunshine or a bit of exercise.

From the spring through the fall, visit the **Jardin Jeanne d'Arc (Joan of Arc Garden)**, just off avenue Wilifrid-Laurier near the Loews le Concorde Hôtel. This spectacular garden combines French classical style with British-style flower beds, and close to 6,000 trees representing more than 80 species blanket the fields. Prominent among these are sugar maple, Norway maple, and American ash. Within the park are also two Martello towers, cylindrical stone defensive structures built between 1808 and 1812, when Québec feared an invasion from the United States.

The national anthem "Ô Canada" was first performed here, and free concerts are given during the summer at a bandstand, the Kiosque Edwin-Bélanger. Theatrical events are also presented during the summer.

The **Discovery Pavilion of the Plains of Abraham,** at 835 av. Wilfrid-Laurier (© **418/648-4071**), is at the eastern end of the park near The Citadelle and has a gift shop, bathrooms, and, in winter, cross-country ski rentals. The tourism bureau has an office here. A multimedia exhibit is presented in English, French, Spanish, and Japanese.

Park is open at all times. www.ccbn-nbc.gc.ca. Discovery Pavilion, 835 av. Wilfrid-Laurier. © 418/648-4071. Odyssey show C$10 (US$10/£5) adults, C$8 (US$8/£4) seniors and ages 13–17, free for 12 and under. Daily 8:30am–5pm.

ESPECIALLY FOR KIDS

Children who like Arthurian tales of fortresses and castles or the adventures of Harry Potter often delight in simply walking around this storybook city. Start at **Terrasse Dufferin** in the Upper Town, which has those coin-operated telescopes that kids find so engaging. In decent weather, there are always street entertainers, ranging from Peruvian musical groups to men who play wine glasses. Archeological digs under the northern end of the Terrasse will still be underway into 2008, although they may include some new viewing stations put in for the city's 400th anniversary celebrations.

A few steps away at Place d'Armes are **horse-drawn carriages,** and not far in the same direction is the **Musée du Fort** (p. 293). Also at Place d'Armes is the top of **Breakneck Stairs.** Halfway down, across the road, are giant **cannons** ranged along the battlements on rue des Ramparts. The gun carriages are impervious to the assaults of small humans, so kids can scramble over them at will. At the bottom of the Breakneck Stairs, on the left, is a **glass-blowing workshop,** the Verrerie la Mailloche. It's less impervious but still kid-friendly: in the downstairs room, craftsmen give intriguing and informative glass-blowing demonstrations.

Also in the Lower Town, the terrific **Musée de la Civilisation** (p. 290) can occupy children for hours. The **ferry** across the St. Lawrence to Lévis, which leaves not far from the museum, makes for an inexpensive faux-cruise. The crossing, over and back, takes less than an hour.

If military sites are appealing, **La Citadelle** has tours of the grounds and buildings, although the distances covered and the narration are apt to give kids the fidgets. You might be better off taking them to the colorful changing of the guard and beating retreat ceremonies (p. 292). To run off some excess energy, head for **Parc des Champs-de-Bataille (Battlefields Park),** also called the **Plains of Abraham,** directly next to the Citadelle. Acres of grassy lawn give children room to roam and provide the perfect spot for a family picnic (p. 294).

On Wednesdays and Saturdays from late July to mid-August, the city hosts a grand fireworks competition, **Les Grands Feux Loto-Québec.** It takes place at the scenic Montmorency Falls 15 minutes north of city center, with international pyrotechnical teams presenting their own program each evening. Tickets get you admission to the base of the falls. Call © **888/523-3473** for details; tickets can be purchased online at www.quebecfireworks.com.

When in doubt, though, head to the water. The **Village Vacances Valcartier** (© **418/844-1239;** www.valcartier.com) at 1860 bd. Valcartier in St-Gabriel-de-Valcartier, is about a half-hour drive northwest of downtown. In summer, it has 35 slides, a huge wave pool, two "theme rivers," and diving shows. In winter, those same facilities are put to use for snow rafting on inner tubes, sliding down ice slides, and skating. The **Canyon Ste-Anne** (© **418/827-4057;** www.canyonste-anne.qc.ca) about 45 minutes northeast, offers thrilling bridge walks over a rushing waterfall, particularly spectacular in spring when the snow begins to melt (p. 310).

Cruises are offered by **Croisières AML** (© **800/563-4643** or 418/692-1159 in season; www.croisieresaml.com) and **Croisères Dufour** (© **800/463-5250** or 418/692-0222; www.groupedufour.com). Basic cruises last about 1½ hours, with several daily departures in high season. Prices run about C$28 (US$28/£14) for adults, half that for younger children. Board at quai (pier) Chouinard, 10 rue Dalhousie.

6 Special Events & Festivals

The big event on the city calendar is the **Carnaval de Québec** *ππ*, held for 17 days in February. Never mind that temperatures in Québec can plummet to –40°F (–40°C) (fun fact: that's the point where Fahrenheit equals Celsius). Canadians are extraordinarily good-natured about eyeball-freezing cold. They happily pack the family up to come out and play when the symbolic snowman called Bonhomme (Good Fellow) shuffles around town to preside over the merriment. Revelers eddy around a monumental ice palace and ice sculptures that fill snowy fields, cheer a dog-sledding race on the narrow streets of old town, play a human-size version of the table game of Foosball, fly over crowds on a zip line, and dance in the evenings at outdoor concerts.

The party is family-friendly, even given the wide availability of plastic trumpets filled with a nasty concoction called "Caribou," the principal ingredients of which are cheap liquor and sweet red wine. Try not to miss the canoe race that has teams rowing, dragging and stumbling across the treacherous ice floes of the St. Lawrence, an homage to how the city used to break up the ice in order to keep a path open to the town across the river. A C$10 (US$10/£5) pass provides access to most activities. Hotel reservations must be made far in advance. Call © **866/422-7628** or visit www.carnaval.qc.ca.

Honoring Saint John the Baptist, the patron saint of French Canadians, **Jean-Baptiste Day** on June 24 is marked by more festivities and far more enthusiasm throughout Québec province than Canada Day on July 1. It's Québec's own "national" holiday (*fête nationale*) and is celebrated with fireworks, music in parks, and parades.

The **Festival d'Eté (Summer Festival)** *ππ* is what organizers say is the largest cultural event in the French-speaking world. It's held for about 2 weeks each July. Highlights include the free jazz and folk combos who perform in an open-air theater next to City Hall. Since 2007, some of the action has shifted into the St-Roch neighborhood. For details, call © **888/992-5200,** or check www.infofestival.com.

7 Outdoor Activities & Spectator Sports
OUTDOOR ACTIVITIES

The waters and hills around Québec City provide countless opportunities for outdoor recreation, from summer swimming, rafting, and fishing, to winter skiing, snowmobiling, and sleigh rides. There are three centers in particular to keep in mind, all within easy drives from the capital. The provincial **Parc de la Jacques-Cartier** (© **418/848-3169** in summer; 418/528-8787 in winter; www.sepaq.com/pq/jac/en) is off Route 175 north; **Station Touristique Duchesnay** (© **877/511-5885** or 418/875-2122; www.sepaq.com/duchesnay) is a resort in the town of Ste-Catherine-de-la-Jacques-Cartier; and **Parc Mont Ste-Anne** (© **888/827-4579** or 418/827-4561; www.mont-sainte-anne.com) is northeast of the city toward Charlevoix (p. 311).

During winter, the **HiverExpress** shuttle service picks up passengers at over a dozen hotels in the morning to take them to Parc Mont Ste-Anne and Station Stoneham (where Parc de la Jacques-Cartier is) and returns them to Québec City in later afternoon. Round-trip fare the same day is C$25 (US$25/£13). Call ☎ **418/525-5191** to make a reservation or ask if your hotel participates.

BIKING   Bike rentals are available in Lower Town; see p. 275. There's good riding along the river and up in Parliament Hill in the Parc des Champs-de-Bataille (Battlefields Park). Tourist information centers have bicycle trail maps and can point out other routes depending on your time and interests.

CAMPING   There are over 20 campgrounds in the greater Québec City area, some with as few as 25 individual campsites and others up to about 250 (one even has 703 sites). Most have showers and toilets available. One of the largest is in the **Parc Mont Ste-Anne** (see above). One of the smaller grounds, with 161 sites and chalet rentals, is **Camping La Loutre** (☎ **418/528-6868**) on Lac Jacques-Cartier in the park of the same name. The tourist site www.quebecregion.com has details.

CANOEING   The several lakes and rivers of **Parc de la Jacques-Cartier** (see above) are fairly easy to reach, yet still seem to be in the midst of virtual wilderness. Canoes are available to rent in the park itself. The **Station Touristique Duchesnay** resort (see above) is directly on the shores of Lac Saint-Joseph and has canoeing, kayaking, and pedal boats for rent.

CROSS-COUNTRY SKIING   In the city, the **Parc des Champs-de-Bataille (Battlefields Park)**, where the Carnaval de Québec establishes its winter playground during February, has a network of groomed cross-country trails. Equipment can be rented at the Discovery Pavilion at 835 av. Wilfrid-Laurier (☎ **418/648-2586**). The **Station Touristique Duchesnay** (see above) offers extensive trails on the grounds along with ski rentals. This is where the Ice Hotel is built each winter, making it well worth the trip out. There's also a spa, nightly accommodation, and a good bistro, Le Quatre-Temps, on the resort's campus. The **Association of Cross-Country Ski Stations** (www.rssfrq.qc.ca) has a list of maps and other options.

DOG SLEDDING 🏕️🏕️ *Kids*   **Aventure Inukshuk** (☎ **418/875-0770;** www.aventure inukshuk.qc.ca), at 143 route de Duchesnay in Ste-Catherine-de-la-Jacques-Cartier, in located in Station Touristique Duchesnay, near where the Ice Hotel is built. Guides show you how to lead a sled pulled by a team of dogs. Even on a 1-hour trip, you go deep into the hushed world of snow and thick woods, past rows of Christmas trees, and over a beaver pond. The company's 200-plus dogs work up an enormous cacophony of howls whenever a team of dogs is harnessed up and set to go. Overnight trips with camping are available. The 1-hour trip, which includes an additional half-hour of training, is C$87 (US$87/£43). Children ages 6 to 12 are half price, and ages 2 to 5 are free. It's expensive, especially for families, but the memory stays with you. Another firm providing similar experiences is **Aventures Nord-Bec** (☎ **418/889-8001;** www. aventures-nord-bec.com), at 4 chemin des Anémones in Stoneham. One and a half to 2 hours of dog sledding in addition to a 20-minute lesson costs C$83 adult (US$83/£41) and C$25 (US$25/£13) ages 5 to 11.

DOWNHILL SKIING   Foremost among the nearby downhill centers is **Mont Ste-Anne** (see above), with 65 trails (17 lit for night skiing), the largest total skiing surface in eastern Canada. In season, the Hiver Express shuttle service picks up from downtown hotels. Farther away—about an hour and a half north in the Charlevoix region—**Le Massif** is a mountain almost directly on the St. Lawrence River.

FISHING   Anglers can wet their lines in the river that flows through the **Parc de la Jacques-Cartier** (see above). The catches are mostly trout and salmon. Permits are required and can be purchased at many sporting-goods stores. Information on regulations for fishing is available from the **Minstère des Ressources naturelles et de la Faune** (© 866/248-6936; www.mrnf.gouv.qc.ca/faune).

GOLF   **Le Grand Vallon** (© 888/827-4579 or 418/827-4653; www.legrandvallon. com) at Parc Mont Ste-Anne, is an 18-hole, par 72 course with tree-lined stretches, wide open midcourse sections, four lakes, and 40 sand traps. Rates are C$36 to C$85 (US$36–US$85/£18–£42) and include golf cart, access to the driving range, and practice balls. Club rental is available.

ICE SKATING   In the wintertime, outdoor rinks with skate rentals are set up in the Place d'Youville just outside the Upper Town walls.

SWIMMING   Several hotels have pools, including **The Fairmont Le Château Frontenac, Manoir Victoria, Château Laurier,** and **Loews Le Concorde.** Even if you're not staying at the **Hilton Québec,** you can come for the Sunday brunch, which includes free admission to the year-round heated outdoor pool. A half-hour from the city, **Village Vacances Valcartier** is an all-season recreational center in St-Gabriel-de-Valcartier (1860 bd. Valcartier; © **418/844-1239**) with an immense wave pool and water slides (p. 295).

TOBOGGANING ⊛   An old-fashioned toboggan run is created every winter down a steep staircase at the south end of the Terrasse Dufferin. It runs nearly all the way to the Château Frontenac. Tickets are sold at a temporary booth adjacent and include the use of toboggans.

SPECTATOR SPORTS

Québec has not had a team in any of the major professional leagues since the NHL Nordiques left in 1995, but since 1999 it has been represented by the **Les Capitales de Québec (Québec City Capitales) baseball club** of the Northern League (www. capitalesdequebec.com). Home games are played in Stade Municipal (Municipal Stadium), 100 rue du Cardinal Maurice-Roy (© **418/521-2255**), not far beyond the St-Roch neighborhood. Tickets cost C$9 to C$16 (US$9–US$16/£4.50–£8).

8 Shopping

The compact size of Vieux-Québec makes it especially convenient for browsing and shopping. Much of the merchandise is generally of high quality.

   In the Upper Town, there are several art galleries deserving of attention, including the narrow pedestrian lane of **rue du Trésor.** Wander along **rue St-Jean,** both within and outside the city walls, and on **rue Garneau** and **Côte de la Fabrique,** which branch off the east end of St-Jean. For T-shirts, postcards, and other souvenirs, myriad shops line **rue St-Louis.** If you're heading to St-Roch to eat, build in time to stroll **rue St-Joseph**, which for a few blocks has new boutiques alongside cafes and restaurants.

   In the Lower Town, the **Quartier du Petit-Champlain,** offers many possibilities— clothing, souvenirs, gifts, household items, collectibles—and is avoiding (so far) the trashiness that often afflicts heavily touristed areas.

   Most stores are open Monday through Wednesday from 9 or 10am to 6pm, Thursday and/or Friday from 9am to 9pm, and Saturday from 9am to 5pm. Many stores are now also open on Sunday from noon to 5pm.

Indigenous crafts, handmade sweaters, and **Inuit art** are among the desirable items not seen everywhere else. An official igloo trademark identifies authentic Inuit (Eskimo) art. For Inuit artwork, which usually means carvings in stone or bone, expect to pay hundreds of dollars for even a relatively small piece.

Maple syrup products make sweet gifts, and **ice cider** *(cidre de glace)* and **ice wines** made in Québec province from apples and grapes left on trees and vines after the first frost can be had for around C$25 (US$25/£13). They are sold in duty-free shops at the border in addition to the state liquor stores (SAQ).

ANTIQUES

Antiques shops are proliferating along rue St-Paul in the Lower Town, near the new Espace 400ᵉ pavilion on the waterfront. Shops are filled with Québec country furniture, candlesticks, old clocks, Victoriana, Art Deco objects, and even the increasingly sought-after kitsch and housewares of the early post–World War II period.

ARTS & CRAFTS

Artisans du Bas-Canada Crafts predominate, all a little on the expensive side. There are plenty of fur hats, moccasins, lumberjack coats, jewelry, toy soldiers, soapstone carvings, and Canada-themed books. Perhaps a chess set of generals Montcalm and Wolfe, to relive the battle that took both men down? 30 Côte de la Fabrique, Upper Town. ✆ 418/692-2109.

Aux Multiples Collections Inuit and modern Canadian art are on offer in this gallery. The most appealing items, and those given prominence in display, are the Native Canadian carvings in stone, bone, and tusk. Prices are high, but competitive for merchandise of similar quality. Open daily. Check out, too, its sibling, the new private museum called **Galerie Brousseau et Brousseau,** nearby at 35 rue St-Louis (✆ 418/694-1828). 69 rue Ste-Anne (opposite the Hôtel-de-Ville), Upper Town. ✆ 418/692-1230.

Galerie d'Art du Petit-Champlain Featuring the superbly detailed carvings of Roger Desjardins, who applies his skills to meticulous renderings of waterfowl, this shop's inventory has been expanded to show lithographs, paintings, and some Inuit art. 88 1/2 rue du Petit-Champlain (near bd. Champlain), Lower Town. ✆ 418/692-5647.

BOOKS, MAGAZINES & NEWSPAPERS

Librairie du Nouveau Monde A wide variety of books, mostly in French, including the *Historical Guide to Québec,* by Yves Tessier (available in English), a good read about the city's past, filled with illustrations, photographs, and a foldout map. 103 rue St-Pierre (behind the Musée de la Civilisation), Lower Town. ✆ 418/694-9475.

Maison de la Presse Internationale This large store in the midst of the St-Jean shopping bustle stocks magazines, newspapers, and paperbacks from around the world. It's open daily at 7am (Sunday at 8am) until 11pm or midnight, and carries the *New York Times, Wall Street Journal,* and *International Herald Tribune.* There's another branch in the Place Québec, the mall between the Hilton and Radisson hotels on Parliament Hill. 1050 rue St-Jean (at the corner of rue Ste-Angèle), Upper Town. ✆ 418/694-1511.

CLOTHING

Fourrures du Vieux-Port The fur trade underwrote the development and exploration of Québec and the vast lands west, and it continues to be highly important to this day. This merchant has as good a selection as any, including knit furs and shearlings, along with designer coats by Christ, Louis Féraud, and Zuki, among others. 55 rue St-Pierre, Lower Town. ℂ **418/692-6686.**

La Maison Darlington The popular emporium in this ancient house comes on strong with both tony and traditional clothing for men and women produced by such makers as Ballantyne, Dale of Norway, and Geiger Austrian. Better still are the hand-smocked dresses produced by Québécois artisans for babies and little girls. 7 rue de Buade (near the Hôtel-de-Ville), Upper Town. ℂ **418/692-2268.**

FOOD

Marché du Vieux-Port By the water near the train station, this year-round market blossoms in spring and summer with farmers' bounty from Ile d'Orléans and beyond. In addition to fresh fruits and vegetables, you'll find relishes, jams, honey, meats, cheeses, and handicrafts. 160 Quai Saint-André (near Espace 400ᵉ), Lower Town. ℂ **418/692-2517.**

9 Québec City After Dark

Although Québec City doesn't have the volume of nighttime diversions of, say, Montréal, there is more than enough after-dark activity to occupy evenings during an average stay. Apart from theatrical productions, almost always in French, knowledge of the language is rarely necessary.

On Wednesdays and Saturdays from late July to mid-Aug, the city hosts a grand fireworks competition, **Les Grands Feux Loto-Québec,** at the scenic Montmorency Falls 15 minutes north of city center (p. 295).

Most bars and clubs stay open until 2 or 3am. Cover charges and drink minimums are rare in the bars and clubs that provide live entertainment. Mixed drinks aren't unusually expensive, but neither are they generously poured—many people stick to beer, usually Canadian.

THE PERFORMING ARTS

CLASSICAL MUSIC, OPERA & DANCE

The premier classical groups are **L'Orchestre Symphonique de Québec** (ℂ **418/643-8486;** www.osq.org), Canada's oldest symphony; the **Québec Opéra** (ℂ **418/529-0688;** www.operadequebec.qc.ca); and **Les Violons du Roy** (ℂ **418/692-3026;** www.violonsduroy.com). The orchestra and opera both play at the Grand Théâtre de Québec (see below). Les Violons du Roy is a string orchestra established in 1985 that features young musicians in the early stages of their careers. They perform at the Raoul-Jobin hall in the Palais Montcalm (see below).

CONCERT HALLS & PERFORMANCE VENUES

Many of the city's churches also host sacred and secular music concerts, as well as special Christmas festivities. Check for posters near or at the churches.

Colisée Pepsi Rock concerts by name acts on the order of Bob Dylan and Rush are held here, with events such as dog shows and wedding expositions filling in other days. The stadium is located in a park about a 10-minute drive northwest of Parliament Hill. 250 bd. Wilfrid-Hamel (ExpoCité), north of St-Roch. ℂ **418/691-7110.** www.expocite.com.

Grand Théâtre de Québec ★★★ Classical music concerts, opera, dance, jazz, klezmer, and theatrical productions are presented in two halls, one of them containing the largest stage in Canada. Visiting conductors, orchestras, and dance companies

Moments **Only in Québec City**

An after-dinner stroll and a lounge on a bench on **Terrasse Dufferin,** the board-walk next to the Château Frontenac, is gorgeously atmospheric. Ferries glide across the river below burnished by moon glow, and the stars haven't seemed this close since childhood.

often perform here when resident organizations are away. **L'Orchestre Symphonique de Québec** and the **Québec Opéra** perform here, and **The Trident Theatre** troupe does shows in French in the Salle Octave-Crémazie. 269 bd. René-Lévesque est (near av. Turn-bull), Parliament Hill. ℰ 418/643-8131. www.grandtheatre.qc.ca.

Kiosque Edwin-Bélanger *Value*   The bandstand at the edge of Battlefields Park is home to a summer music season, from about mid-June to late August. The outdoor performances are Thursday through Sunday evenings at 8pm and range from chorales and classical recitals to jazz, pop, and blues. Concerts are free. 390 av. de Bernières (at the Plains of Abraham), Parliament Hill. ℰ 418/648-4050.

Le Capitole   Shows at this historic 1,262-seat theater include dramatic productions and comedic performances in French, but the theater also hosts rock groups and occasional classical recitals. An ongoing production, from June to July, is the *Elvis Story.* 972 rue St-Jean (near Porte St-Jean), Parliament Hill. ℰ 800/261-9903 for tickets, or 418/694-4444 for information. www.lecapitole.com.

Palais Montcalm ✿   Reopened in 2007 after renovations, this venue in the centrally located Place D'Youville is home to the well-regarded **Les Violons du Roy.** The main performance space is the 979-seat Raoul-Jobin theater, which presents a mix of dance programs, classical music concerts, and plays. More intimate recitals and jazz groups are found in a 125-seat cafe/theater. 995 Place d'Youville (near Porte Saint-Jean), Parliament Hill. ℰ 418/641-6411 for tickets. www.palaismontcalm.htm.

THE CLUB & MUSIC SCENE
ROCK, FOLK, BLUES & JAZZ CLUBS

Québec City's **Festival d'Eté (Summer Festival)** (p. 296) brings more than 500 programs and some free jazz and folk shows to the city for about 2 weeks each July.

Bar Les Voûtes Napoléon   Down a flight of stairs tucked behind the outdoor cafes and away from the general bustle on the Grande-Allée, this amicable *boîtes à chansons* has music 7 nights a week starting at 10:30pm, and is always free. The stone arches and low ceiling give the front room a cavelike feel, with a postage stamp–size stage for the Québec singer-songwriters passing through town. 680 Grande-Allée, Parliament Hill. ℰ 418/640-9388.

Chez Son Père   A musical institution since 1960, Québécois music is featured on Fridays and Saturdays, with traditional French and contemporary folk music the other nights. The stage has the usual brick walls and sparse decor. During the school year there is a young, friendly college crowd, and at other times there are more tourists. 24 rue St-Stanislas (near rue St-Jean), Upper Town. ℰ 418/692-5308.

Largo *Finds*   This attractive restaurant-club, which opened in 2004, is one of a growing number of clubs and restaurants that are sprucing up rue St-Joseph in the St-Roch district. High ceilings and chandeliers give it an old-time class, while blonde-wood floors, clean angles, and contemporary art make it modern. There's jazz on Thursdays, Fridays, and Saturdays, starting at 8pm. Food prices are on the steep side, with main courses C$17 to C$39 (US$17–US$39/£8.50–£20). 643 rue St-Joseph est, St-Roch. ✆ 418/ 529-3111.

Pub St-Patrick   This Irish pub just keeps on getting on. Pints of Guinness are the steadiest pour, of course, and food is available, but the music of the Ould Sod is the big draw. For that, show up on Friday and Saturday after 9:30pm. 45 rue Couillard (near rue St-Jean), Upper Town. ✆ 418/694-0618.

Théâtre du Petit-Champlain   Québécois and French singers alternate with jazz and rock groups in this roomy cafe-theater. Have a drink on the patio before the show. Performances are usually Tuesday through Saturday. 68 rue du Petit-Champlain (near the funicular), Lower Town. ✆ 418/692-2631. www.theatrepetitchamplain.com.

DANCE CLUBS

Boudoir Lounge ✯   The hottest club so far in trendy St-Roch (and the bar of choice for much of the city's restaurant staff), Boudoir has two bars on the main floor and a disco downstairs. DJs work the fine sound systems in both rooms to 3am, with live jazz on Sundays and bands on Wednesdays. The dramatic decor includes a fire-place in the front. 441 rue du Parvis (at bd. Charest est). ✆ 418/524-2777.

Chez Dagobert   Long one of the top discos in Québec City, this three-story club has an arena arrangement on the ground floor for live bands, with raised seating around the sides. There's also a large dance floor and TV screens to keep track of sports events. The sound system is just a decibel short of bedlam. Things don't start until well after 11pm, and the party goes to 3am nightly. The crowd divides into students and their more fashionably attired older brothers and sisters, with a whole lot of eyeballing going on. 600 Grande-Allée est (near rue de la Chevrotiére), Parliament Hill. ✆ 418/522-0393.

Maurice   Successfully challenging **Chez Dagobert** (across the street and listed above) at the top rung of the nightlife ladder, this triple-tiered enterprise occupies a converted mansion at the thumping heart of the Grande-Allée scene. It includes a good restaurant (**VooDoo Grill**, p. 287), a couple of bars, and music that tilts toward Latin. In the wintertime, it builds a sidewalk-level "Icecothèque" with a bar made completely of ice and roaring music. Theme nights are frequent, and crowds of nearly 1,000 20- and 30-somethings are not unusual. 575 Grande-Allée est, Parliament Hill. ✆ 418/ 647-2000. www.mauricenightclub.com.

THE BAR & CAFE SCENE

In addition to the bars listed below, also stroll these three streets for nightlife: **rue St-Jean** in the Upper Town, the small **rue du Parvis** in St-Roch, and the strip of the **Grande-Allée** between Place Montcalm and Place George V, just beyond the St-Louis Gate of the old wall. There, a beery collegiate atmosphere can sometimes rule as the evening wears on, but early on, it's fun to sit and sip and watch.

Aviatic Club   A favorite for after-work drinks since 1945, this bar is located in the front of the city's restored train station. The theme is aviation (odd, given the venue), signaled by two miniature planes hanging from the ceiling. There's food, ranging from sushi to Tex-Mex, along with local and imported beers. 450 de la Gare-du-Palais (near rue St-Paul), Lower Town. ✆ 418/522-3555.

D'Orsay   Visitors who are well into their mortgages will want to keep this dark but chummy pub-bistro in mind. Most of the clientele is on the far side of 35, and they strike up conversations easily. In summer afternoons and evenings, music is piped onto the unassuming terrace out back. There is a full menu of conventional international dishes, from onion soup and fajitas to burgers and mussels. 65 rue de Buade (opposite Hôtel-de-Ville), Upper Town. ℂ 418/694-1582.

L'Astral ⦅ⶖ⦆   Spinning slowly above a city that twinkles below like tangled necklaces, this restaurant and bar atop the Hôtel Loews le Concorde unveils a breathtaking 360-degree panorama. Many people come for dinner at the high-quality restaurant, but you can also just come for drinks and the view. 1225 Cours Du General De Montcalm (at the Grande-Allée), Parliament Hill. ℂ 418/647-2222.

Le Pape-Georges ⦅*Finds*⦆   A cozy wine bar in a 325-year-old stone-and-beamed room. It features *chanson* (a French cabaret singing style), along with other music genres, usually Thursday through Sunday at 10pm. Light fare—plates of mostly Québec cheeses, assorted cold meats, and smoked salmon—is served. It's open from noon daily. Although it's in the middle of a tourist district, most of the patrons appear to be locals. 8 rue Cul-de-Sac (near bd. Champlain), Lower Town. ℂ 418/692-1320.

Saint Alexandre Pub ⦅ⶖ⦆   Roomy and sophisticated, this is one of the best-looking bars in town. It's done in British-pub style, with polished mahogany, exposed brick, and a working fireplace that's a particular comfort during the 8 cold months of the year. It serves 40 single-malt scotches and more than 200 beers, along with hearty victuals that complement the brews. Live music—rock, blues, sometimes jazz or Irish—is occasionally presented, usually Friday and Saturday nights, but check before planning your night around it. 1087 rue St-Jean (near St-Stanislas), Upper Town. ℂ 418/694-0015.

GAY BARS & CLUBS

The gay scene in Québec City is a small but vibrant one, centered in the Upper Town just outside the city walls, on **rue St-Jean** and the parallel **rue d'Aiguillon,** starting from where they cross **rue St-Augustin** and heading west.

Lesbians make up most of the clientele at the cute **Amour Sorcier Café Bar** at 789 Côte Ste-Geneviève (ℂ **418/523-3395**), but it gets a mixed crowd of women and men, gay and straight. There is a low-pressure bar inside the old building and a terrace out front for drinks and snacks. It's about 3 blocks west of Place d'Youville.

Le Drague Cabaret Club ("The Drag"), at 815 rue St-Augustin (ℂ **418/649-7212;** www.ledrague.com), just off rue St-Jean, has a cabaret and two dance rooms. The cabaret features drag shows on Sunday nights, with live shows, karaoke, country music dancing, and theater improv on other nights.

At the end of August, there's a 3-day gay fest, **Fête Arc-en-Ciel** (www.fete arcenciel.qc.ca). For information about current openings and happenings, look for *Être* magazine (**www.etremag.com**), often available at tourist offices.

---

10 Day Trips from Québec City: Ile d'Orléans, Ste-Anne Falls & More

Ile d'Orléans: 16km (10 miles) NE of Québec City; Montmorency Falls: 11km (7 miles) NE of Québec City; Ste-Anne-de-Beaupré: 33km (21 miles) NE of Québec City; Canyon Ste-Anne & Parc Mont Ste-Anne: 42km (26 miles) NE of Québec City

An excursion to Ile d'Orléans, Montmorency Falls, Ste-Anne-de-Beaupré, and Canyon Ste-Anne and its falls can be completed in a day, although it will admittedly be a breakfast-to-dark undertaking without much time to catch your breath. But the farthest of the four destinations is only 42km (26 miles) from Québec City.

Bucolic Ile d'Orléans, with its maple groves, orchards, farms, and 18th- and 19th-century houses, is an unspoiled mini-oasis. The waterfalls of both Montmorency and Canyon Ste-Anne are dazzling fun, especially in the spring when the winter thaws make them thunder. The shrine of Ste-Anne-de-Beaupré is a religious destination, with more than a million-and-a-half people making the pilgrimage each year to a complex that includes a church, a hillside station of the cross, a chapel, and a museum.

Although it is preferable to drive in this region, tour buses go to Montmorency Falls and the shrine of Ste-Anne-de-Beaupré, and circle the Ile d'Orléans. For more information, go to **www.quebecregion.com**.

ILE D'ORLEANS ✸✸

Ile d'Orléans was long inhabited by Native Indians and settled by the French as one of their first outposts of New France in the 17th century. Long isolated from the mainland, the island's 7,000 current residents keep a firm resistance to development, so far preventing it from becoming just another sprawling bedroom community. Many of the island's oldest houses are intact, and it remains a largely rural farming area.

Until 1935, the only way to get to Ile d'Orléans was by boat (in summer) or over the ice in sleighs (in winter). The highway bridge that was built that year has allowed the island's fertile fields to become Québec City's primary market-garden. During harvest periods, fruits and vegetables are picked fresh on the farms and trucked into the city daily. In mid-July, hand-painted signs posted by the main road announce *FRAISES: CUEILLIR VOUS-MEME* (STRAWBERRIES: YOU PICK 'EM). The same invitation is made during apple season, August through October. Farmers hand out baskets and quote the price, paid when the basket's full. Bring along a bag or box to carry away the bounty.

Thousands of migrating snow geese, ducks, and Canada geese stop by in April and May and again in late October. It's a spectacular sight when they launch themselves into the air in flapping hordes—so thick that they almost blot out the sun.

It's a short drive from Québec City to the island. Take Autoroute 440 east, in the direction of Ste-Anne-de-Beaupré. In about 15 minutes, the Ile d'Orléans bridge will be on the right. If you'd like a guide, **Maple Leaf Guide Services** (✆ **418/622-3677**) can provide one in your car or theirs.

While it's possible to bike over the bridge, it's not recommended; the sidewalk is narrow and precarious. But cyclists can park their cars at the tourist office for C$5 (US$5/£2.50) a day.

After arriving on the island, follow the "?" signs and turn right on Route 368 East toward Ste-Pétronille. The **Bureau d'Accueil Touristique** (✆ **418/828-9411; www.iledorleans.com**) is in the house on the right corner, and has a useful guidebook (C$1/US$1/50p). It's open daily late June to mid-October 8:30am to 7:30pm (till 8pm Fri–Sat), and the rest of the year Monday through Friday 9am to 5pm, Saturday 10am to 5pm, and Sunday 11am to 3pm. The *Québec City and Area Guide,* available from Québec City tourism offices, describes a short tour of Ile d'Orléans. A driving-tour CD can be rented at the tourist office, and cycling maps are available.

A coast-hugging road—Route 368, also called *chemin Royal* and, in a few stretches, *chemin de bout-de-l'île*—circles the island, which is 34km (21 miles) long and 8km (5 miles) wide. Another couple of roads bisect it. Farms and picturesque houses dot the east side, and abundant apple orchards enliven the west side.

There are six tiny villages, originally established as parishes, and each has a church as its focal point. Some are **stone churches** ✸ that date from the days of the French regime, a particular point of pride. It's possible to do a circuit of Ile d'Orléans in half

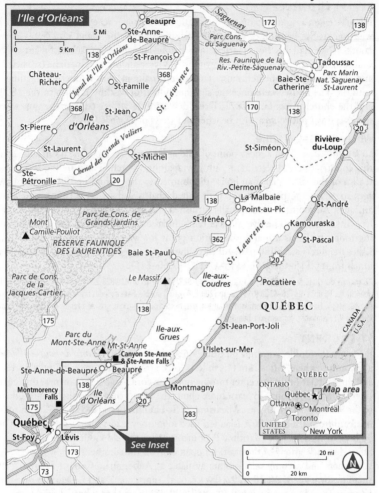

a day, but you can justify a full day if you eat a good meal, visit a sugar shack, do a little gallery hopping, or just skip stones from the beach. If you're strapped for time, loop around as far as St-Jean then drive across the island on Route du Mitan ("middle road"). You'll get to the bridge by turning left onto Route 368 West.

For much of the year you can meander at 40kmph (25 mph), pulling over only occasionally to let a car pass. There is no bike path, which means bikers share the narrow rural roads. Cars need to drive with care in the busiest summer months, and cyclists might want to avoid July or August.

Navigational note: Street numbers on the ring road chemin Royal start anew in each village, so that you could pass a 1000 chemin Royal in one stretch and then another 1000 chemin Royal a few minutes later. Be sure you know not just the number of your destination but which village it's in as well.

STE-PETRONILLE

If you've taken a right turn off the bridge, the first village reached on the counterclockwise tour is Ste-Pétronille. When the British occupied the island in 1759, General James Wolfe had his headquarters here before launching his successful attack on Québec City. The village is best known for its Victorian inn, **La Goéliche** (see below), and also claims the northernmost stand of **red oaks** in North America, dazzling in autumn. The houses were once the summer homes of wealthy English in the 1800s, and the church dates from 1871. Drive down to the water's edge at the inn, where there's a small public area with benches and views of Québec City.

Where to Stay & Dine

La Goéliche ⟨⟩   On a rocky point of land at the southern tip of Ile d'Orléans stands this country inn and restaurant with a wraparound porch. The building is a virtual replica of the 1880 Victorian house that burned to the ground in 1996, and it manages to retain the period flavor with tufted chairs, Tiffany-style lamps, and a few antiques. All rooms are individually furnished and face the water, and first-floor units have small terraces. The river slaps at the foundation of the glass-enclosed terrace dining room, which is a grand observation point for watching cruise ships and Great Lakes freighters steaming past. All three meals are served daily, with main courses at lunch from C$15–C$29 (US$15–US$29/£7.50–£15).

22 chemin du Quai, Ste-Pétronille, PQ G0A 4C0. © 888/511-2248 or 418/828-2248. Fax 418/828-2745. www. goeliche.ca. 16 units. C$128–$208 (US$128–US$208/£64–£104) double. Rate includes breakfast. Packages available. AE, DC, MC, V. Free parking. **Amenities:** Restaurant; bar; heated outdoor pool; golf and tennis nearby; babysitting. *In room:* Wi-Fi, minibar, coffeemaker, hair dryer.

ST-LAURENT

From Ste-Pétronille, continue on Route 368, which is called *chemin de bout-de-l'île* for a few minutes here. After 7km (4⅓ miles), you'll arrive at St-Laurent, founded in 1679 and once a boat-building center turning out ships for Glasgow ship owners that could carry up to 5,300 tons. To learn more about the town's maritime history, head down to the water and visit **Le Parc Maritime de St-Laurent** (© **418/828-9672**), an active boatyard from 1908 to 1967. Islanders used to journey across the river to Québec City by boat from here. The Maritime Park incorporates the old Godbout Boatworks and offers demonstrations of the craft. It's open daily in the summer.

Dinners and accommodations are available at **Auberge Le Canard Huppé,** 2198 chemin Royal (© **418/828-2292;** www.canard-huppe.com), and **Le Moulin de Saint-Laurent** ⟨⟩, 754 chemin Royal (© **888/629-3888;** www.moulinstlaurent.qc.ca). Le Moulin also has lunches in the summer on the shaded terrace beside a waterfall tumbling down a small hill.

ST-JEAN

St-Jean, 6km (3¾ miles) from St-Laurent, was home to sea captains. That might be why the houses in the village appear more luxurious than others on the island. The creamy yellow "Scottish brick" in the facades of several of the homes were ballast in boats that came over from Europe. The village church was built in 1734, and the walled cemetery is the final resting place of many fishermen and seafarers.

On the left as you enter St-Jean is the stately and well-preserved **Manoir Mauvide-Genest** ⟨⟩, 1451 chemin Royale (© **418/829-2630**). Jean Mauvide was a French surgeon who settled here in 1720. He went on to acquire much of the western part of the island and built this small estate in 1752, becoming one of the leading figures in the

New France. The manor house is unlike any other building on the island and is filled with authentic and reproduction furnishings of Mauvide's era; it's classified as an historic monument. Guided tours are available by reservation. The manor is open daily from 10am to 5pm May through November 1, and by reservation the rest of the year. Admission is C$5 (US$5/£2.50) for adults, C$2 (US$2/£1) for children under 12.

The manor also has a **restaurant** with an outdoor terrace and river views serving light meals—soups and salads, assorted pâtés and cheeses, smoked trout, a quiche du jour, antipasto plates—as well as formal repasts of three to five courses starting at C$14 (US$14/£7). It's open Tuesday through Sunday from 11:30am to well into the evening, depending on business. Call ✆ **418/829-2630** for reservations.

La Sucrerie Blouin, 2967 chemin Royal (✆ **418/829-2903**), is a *cabane à sucre* (a traditional "sugar shack"), where maple syrup is made and casual all-you-can-eat meals are available. A family of bakers who has lived on the island for 300 years runs this place and provides details on how the sap of a tree is turned into syrup.

If you're pressed for time, this is where you can pick up **Route du Mitan,** which crosses Ile d'Orléans from here to St-Famille on the northwest side of the island. Route du Mitan is marked with a small sign on the left just past the church in St-Jean. Even if you're continuing the full loop, a detour down the road offers a picturesque look at farmland and forest; return to St-Jean and proceed east on Route 368 to St-François.

ST-FRANÇOIS

The 9km (5⅔-mile) drive from St-Jean to St-François offers vistas of the Laurentian Mountains off to the left on the western shore of the river. Just past the village center of St-Jean, **Mont Ste-Anne** can be seen in the distance, its slopes scored by ski trails. The St. Lawrence River, a constant and mighty presence, is 10 times wider here than when it flows past Québec City, and can be viewed especially well from the town's observation tower.

After you've looped around the northern edge of the island, the road stops being Route 358 East and becomes Route 368 West.

STE-FAMILLE

Founded in 1661, Ste-Famille is the oldest parish on the island and 8km (5 miles) from St-François. Across the road from the triple-spired church (1743) is the convent of **Notre-Dame Congregation,** founded in 1685 by Marguerite Bourgeoys, one of Montréal's prominent early citizens.

Also here is the **Maison de nos Aïeux**, 3907 chemin Royal (✆ **418/829-0330**), a genealogy center with mini-movies about some of the island's oldest families and information about the island's history. It's open 10 months a year (closed Dec–Jan), daily in the summer from 10am to 6pm, and costs C$3 (US$3/£1.50). Adjacent is the **Parc des Ancêtres,** a riverside green space with picnic tables.

ST-PIERRE

When you reach St-Pierre, you're nearly back to where you started. The central attraction is the island's oldest church (1717). There's a large handicraft shop in the back, behind the altar (1695), which is even older than the church.

The orchard **Bilodeau** at 2200 chemin Royal (✆ **418/828-9316**) produces some of Ile d'Orléans's regular ciders and *cidre de glace,* or ice cider, an after-dinner drink made from apples left on the trees until after the first frost. Visitors can partake of samples, guided tours of the facility, apple picking in the fall, and a shop. It's open May through December and by appointment the rest of the year.

The **Buffet d'Orléans,** 1025 route Prévost (© **418/828-0013**), just at the bridge, is an old-time diner where the waitresses wear white skirts and black aprons and the bread comes wrapped in plastic. Try the *tourtière maison,* a homemade meat pie in a crust, served with two scoops of mashed potatoes and vegetables, for about C$10 ($10/£5). The restaurant is open daily 7am to 9pm year round, and to 11pm in the summer.

MONTMORENCY FALLS ★★

Back on the mainland, **Montmorency Falls,** which were named by Samuel de Champlain for his patron, the duke of Montmorency, are 83m (272 ft.) tall. That's 30m (98 ft.) higher than Niagara Falls—a boast no visitor is spared. They are, however, far narrower. On summer nights the plunging water is illuminated, and from late July to mid-August there is an international fireworks competition overhead 2 nights a week, **Les Grands Feux Loto-Québec** (p. 295). The yellow cast of the falls is from the high iron content of the riverbed.

GETTING THERE

BY BUS   Tour companies **La Tournée du Québec Métro** (© **800/672-5232** or 418/836-8687), **Old Québec Tours** (© **418/664-0460**), and **Dupont** (© **418/649-9226**) all have trips to the falls.

BY CAR   The falls and the parking lot are 11km (7 miles) northeast of Québec City, just off of Autoroute 440. If you miss the exit, you'll see the falls on your left and will be able to U-turn.

VIEWING THE FALLS

The waterfall is surrounded by the provincial **Parc de la Chute-Montmorency** (© **418/663-3330;** www.sepaq.com/chutemontmorency), where visitors can take in the view and have a picnic. The grounds are accessible year-round. In winter, it's a particularly impressive sight, as the freezing spray sent up by crashing water builds a mountain of white ice at the base called the *pain de sucre* (sugarloaf). It can grow as high as 30m (98 ft.) and attracts ice climbers.

There are several platforms to view the falls from, including a footbridge that spans the river just where it flows over the cliff. There also are stairs that ascend one side to nearly the top, and a cable car (not for the vertiginous) that runs from the parking lot off Autoroute 440 to a terminal above the falls near **Manoir Montmorency,** a villa that contains an interpretation center, a cafe-bar, and a restaurant.

The restaurant serves good quality lunches and dinners and a popular Sunday buffet brunch. Call © **418/663-3330** for meal reservations, which are suggested. The dining room and porch have a side view of the falls.

Admission to the falls is free, although parking costs C$9 (US$9/£4.50). Round-trip fares on the cable car cost C$8.25 (US$8.25/£4.10) for adults, C$4 (US$4/£2) for ages 6 to 16. The cable car operates every day from late April to late August, and on a limited schedule the rest of the year. Packages are available that include parking and cable rides.

STE-ANNE-DE-BEAUPRE

The village of Ste-Anne-de-Beaupré is centered around a two-spired basilica that is one of Canada's most famous shrines. The church has housing for temporary guests and a plot of land for RV campers.

Legend has it that French mariners were sailing up the St. Lawrence River in the 1650s when they ran into a terrifying storm. They prayed to their patroness, St. Anne, to save them, and when they survived they dedicated a wooden chapel to her on the north shore of the St. Lawrence, near the site of their perils. Not long afterward, a chapel laborer was said to have been cured of lumbago, the first of many documented miracles. Since that time, believers have made their way here to pay their respects to St. Anne, the mother of the Virgin Mary and grandmother of Jesus.

The route to the town is along the St. Lawrence River, which is tidal. At low tide, the beach is sometimes speckled with hundreds of birds pecking for food. You can see them behind the houses, gas stations, and garages that pepper the road.

GETTING THERE

BY BUS   La Tournée du Québec Métro (© 800/672-5232 or 418/836-8687) and **Old Québec Tours** (© 418/664-0460) both have tours that include Ste-Anne-de-Beaupré.

BY CAR   Autoroute 440 turns into Autoroute 40 at Montmorency Falls and then becomes Route 138 almost immediately. Continue on 138 to Ste-Anne-de-Beaupré. The town is 33km (21 miles) from Québec City and 22km (14 miles) from Montmorency Falls. The church and exit are visible from the road.

EXPLORING THE BASILICA

The towering **basilica** is the most recent building raised on this spot in St. Anne's honor. After the sailors' first modest wooden chapel was swept away by a flood in the 1600s, another chapel was built on higher ground. Floods, fires, and the ravages of time dispatched later buildings, until a larger structure was erected in 1887. In 1926, it, too, lay in ruins, gutted by fire. The present basilica is constructed in stone, following an essentially neo-Romanesque scheme, and was consecrated on July 4, 1976. Inside the front doors, look for the two columns dressed with racks of canes–presumably from people cured and no longer in need of assistance–that go 9m (30 feet) high.

In the summer, there is a daily candlelight procession at 8:15pm. The church and all of Ste-Anne-de-Beaupré are particularly busy on days of saintly significance: the first Sunday in May; mid- through late July; the fourth Sunday in August; and early September.

Other parts of the shrine include the **Way of the Cross,** lined with life-size bronze figures, on the hillside opposite the basilica; the **Scala Santa Chapel** (1891); the **Memorial Chapel** (1878), with a bell tower and altar from the late 17th and early 18th centuries, respectively; and the **Musée Sainte-Anne** (contributions accepted).

Also in the village is a building called the **Cyclorama,** which houses a 14m-high (46-ft.), 360-degree painting depicting old Jerusalem at the moment of Christ's crucifixion—"relive the sight," says the brochure. The Cyclorama is open from mid-April to October; admission is C$8 (US$8/£4) for adults, C$7 (US$7/£3.50) for seniors 65 and older, and C$5 (US$5/£2.50) for children 6 to 16.

WHERE TO STAY & DINE

Auberge La Camarine ⋒   This inn has a kitchen that is equaled by only a handful of restaurants in the region. The cuisine joins French, Italian, and Asian techniques and ingredients. Roasted pheasant and its salsa of caramelized apples is illustrative, and Québécois cheeses are offered for the meal's close. Guests have a choice of a four-course menu starting at C$28 (US$28/£14) or a degustation menu for C$60

(US$60/£30). Weekend brunches are C$18 (US$18/£9). While the locale on Route 138 isn't scenic, guest rooms blend antique and contemporary notions, and some have fireplaces and/or balconies.

10947 bd. Ste-Anne (Route 138), Beaupré, PQ G0A 1E0. ✆ 800/567-3939 or 418/827-5703. Fax 418/827-5430. www.camarine.com. 31 units. From C$95 (US$95/£48) double. Packages available. AE, DC, MC, V. **Amenities:** Restaurant; bistro-bar; access to nearby health club. *In room:* A/C (some rooms), TV.

CANYON STE-ANNE, STE-ANNE FALLS & PARC MONT STE-ANNE ⭑⭑

After Ste-Anne-de-Beaupré, Route 138 enters thick evergreen woods, and the busyness of urban life begins to slip away. A short drive off Route 138 is the deep gorge and powerful waterfall created by the Ste-Anne-du-Nord River. Unseen from the main road, the Canyon Ste-Anne and its falls are an exhilarating sight to experience. Nearby is the Parc Mont Ste-Anne, which surrounds an 800m-high (2,625-ft.) peak. Summertime invites camping, hiking, and biking (rentals available), while wintertime turns it into Québec City's busiest ski area.

GETTING THERE

BY BUS From about mid-November to the end of April, the **Hiver Express** (✆ 418/525-5191) shuttle service from Québec City carries passengers to a number of ski slopes, including Mont Ste-Anne, making it possible to stay in the city at night and ski the mountain by day. The cars or minivans are equipped to carry ski gear and the round-trip fare is C$25 (US$25/£13).

BY CAR Continue along Route 138 from Ste-Anne-de-Beaupré. To get to the Parc, follow the signs; the resort entrance is easy to spot from the highway. To get to the canyon and waterfalls, turn onto the secondary Route 360. The marked entrance is on the left. This area is about 42km (26 miles) from Québec City and about 9km (6 miles) from Ste-Anne-de-Beaupré.

VIEWING THE STE-ANNE FALLS ⭑⭑⭑

A dirt road from Route 360 leads through forest to a parking lot, picnic grounds, and a building containing a cafeteria, a shop, and the ticket booth. The falls are a 10-minute walk from the entrance, but an open-sided shuttle bus is available if you'd rather ride. The path ends at the top of the falls. There are trails that go down both sides of the falls, and three footbridges that go directly across the falls. The first is over the narrow river just before the water starts to drop. The second crosses right over the middle of the canyon; proximity to the unending thunder of water crashing over massive rocks is likely to induce vertigo in even the most stable of nerves. The final bridge is at the base of the gorge, just 9m (30 feet) above the water where it starts to flatten out again, and ends at an observation platform. Along both trails are platforms that jut over the water and have well-written information plaques.

The falls are 75m (246 ft.) high and at their most spectacular in the spring, when melt-off of winter snows bloats the rivers above and sends 100,000 liters (26,417 gallons) of water over *per second*. (The volume drops to 10,000 liters [2,642 gal.] Aug–Sept.) From 1904 to 1965 the river was used to float logs from lumbering operations, and part of the dramatic gorge was created by dynamiting in 1917, to cut down on the literal logjams. So voluminous is the mist coming from the crashing water that it creates a wall of mini-waterfalls on the side of the gorge. Management has wisely avoided commercial intrusions along the trails, letting the awe-inspiring natural beauty speak for itself.

There is an option for visitors to zip across the canyon directly over the water harnessed onto a cable wire (an extra fee, for the very brave-hearted only). Visitors who have difficulty walking can see the falls without going too far from the bus, and those who suffer acrophobia can stay on the side trails, strolling amid the hemlock and poplar trees and avoiding the bridges altogether.

Admission is C$10 (US$10/£5) adults, C$7.50 (US$7.50/£3.75) ages 13 to 17, C$4.50 (US$4.50/£2.25) ages 6 to 12. The site is open daily May through late October. Hours are 9am to 4:45pm, with an extra hour to 5:45pm from June 24 to Labour Day. It's closed the rest of the year. Confirm the hours, which are subject to change due to weather, by calling ℂ **418/827-4057.**

PARC MONT STE-ANNE ★★
Parc du Mont Ste-Anne (ℂ **888/827-4579** or 418/827-4561; www.mont-sainte-anne.com) is a wilderness resort surrounding an 800m-high (2,625-ft.) peak. An outdoor enthusiast's dream, in summer and early fall it offers camping, hiking, golfing, in-line skating, paragliding, and canyoning. It's well known for its huge network of trails for both **hard-core mountain biking** and milder day-tripping; bikes can be rented at the park. A panoramic gondola to the top of the mountain operates daily from mid-June to mid-October and on weekends for about a month on either end, weather permitting.

General admission to the park is C$8.85 (US$8.85/£4.45) for a family in a car. Gondola ticket prices are C$15 (US$15/£7.50) for adults, C$12 (US$12/£6) for ages 7 to 17, and C$13 (US$13/£6.50) for seniors, with a variety of family rates.

In winter, **skiing on Mont Ste-Anne** is terrifically popular. Just 40 minutes from Québec City, this is the region's largest and busiest mountain. There are 65 trails on three sides of the mountain, with a 625m (2,050-ft) vertical drop. At night, 17 trails are lit. Full-day lift tickets are C$55 (US$55/£27) for adults, C$45 (US$45/£22) for seniors, C$42 (US$42/£21) for ages 13 to 17, and C$29 (US$29/£15) for ages 7 to 12.

The park has the largest network of **cross-country ski trails** in Canada, at 212km (131 miles). There are seven heated rest huts, three of which can accommodate overnight guests. A day ticket is C$18 (US$18/£9) for adults, C$13 (US$13/£6.50) for seniors, C$12 (US$12/£6) for ages 13 to 17, and C$7 (US$7/£3.50) for children 7 to 12. The park also offers dog sledding, snowshoeing, snowmobiling, ice canyoning, and winter paragliding.

WHERE TO STAY & DINE
Château Mont Sainte-Anne ★ *(Kids)*   Tucked into the base of its namesake mountain, this resort opened in 1979 and continues to grow, with additional renovations in 2006. While the management is succeeding in its efforts to increase summer business, with two golf courses and a strong network of mountain biking trails, its real identity is as a ski center, with ski-in, ski-out accessibility at the base of the gondola lift. All rooms have either kitchenettes or full kitchens, and 40 have fireplaces. The menu in the main dining room is inventive for a mass feeding operation, and the bar provides satisfying pub grub. The hotel has a game room for young children and organizes family programs every day.

500 bd. Beau-Pré, Beaupré, PQ G0A 1E0. ℂ **866/900-5211** or 418/827-5211. Fax 418/827-5072. www.chateaumsa.ca. 240 units. From C$289 (US$289/£144) double in winter; from C$179 (US$179/£89) in summer. Children under 17 stay free in parent's room. Children ages 7–12 eat for half price; children 6 and under eat for free. Packages available. AE, DC, MC, V. Pets accepted in 10 units. **Amenities:** 2 restaurants; 1 bar/bistro; indoor and outdoor pools; outdoor hot tubs; golf; health club; spa; children's programs; game room; babysitting; laundry service; dry cleaning. *In room:* A/C, TV w/pay movies, Wi-Fi, kitchenette, fridge, coffeemaker, hair dryer.

11 Central Charlevoix: Baie-St-Paul, St-Irénée, & La Malbaie

Baie-St-Paul: 93km (58 miles) NE of Québec City; St-Irénée: 125km (78 miles) NE of Québec City; La Malbaie: 140km (87 miles) NE of Québec City

The Laurentians move closer to the shore of the St. Lawrence River as they approach what used to be called Murray Bay at the mouth of the Malbaie River. U.S. President William Howard Taft, who had a summer residence in the area, once said the air here was "as intoxicating as champagne, but without the morning-after headache."

In 1988, Charlevoix was named a UNESCO World Biosphere Reserve, a protected area for cross-disciplinary research into conservation. This was one of the first designated areas with a human population, and means development here is balanced against environmental concerns. Grand vistas over the St. Lawrence abound, and there are many farms in the area. The rolling, dark green mountains offer numerous places to hike and bike in the warm months and ski when there's snow.

Baie-St-Paul is an artists' colony, and good-to-memorable country inns dot the countryside up to La Malbaie. La Malbaie has a casino, a smaller offshoot of the one in Montréal. It's not unheard of, by the way, for the region to still have snow in May.

ESSENTIALS
GETTING THERE
BY CAR   Take Route 138 as far as Baie-St-Paul. Turn onto Route 362 to go into downtown Baie. To continue northeast, take either 138 or 362. Route 362 runs closer to the water and lets you visit St-Irénée on the way to La Malbaie.

VISITOR INFORMATION
Baie-St-Paul has a year-round **tourist office** on Route 138 (© **418/435-4160**), open daily from 8:30am to 7pm in the summer, and until 4:30pm in the winter. It's before the village and well marked from the highway (it's a sharp turn-off), and offers a grand vista of the river and town below. There are also offices throughout the region including one in La Malbaie directly on the water at 495 bd. de Comporté, Route 362 (© **800/667-2276** or 418/665-4454). That one is open daily until 9pm in the summer months, and 4:30pm off season. Regional information is also at **www.tourisme-charlevoix.com**.

BAIE-ST-PAUL & ISLE-AUX-COUDRES ★★
The first town of any size in Charlevoix, Baie-St-Paul is an attractive community of 7,365 that has had a reputation as an artists' retreat since the start of the 20th century. More than two dozen boutiques and galleries and a couple of small museums show the work of local painters and artisans. Given the setting, it isn't surprising that many of the artists are landscapists, but other styles and subjects are represented. Although some of their production is of the hobbyist level, much is highly professional. Options include the **Maison de René-Richard**, at 58 rue St-Jean-Baptiste (© **418/435-5571**), and **Carrefour culturel Paul-Médéric**, 4 rue Ambroise-Fafard (© **418/435-2540**).

For **bicycling**, pop off the mainland by taking the free 15-minute car ferry to the small island of **Isle-aux-Coudres**. Popular paths offer a 26km (16-mile) loop around the island. Single bikes, tandems, and quadricycles for two adults and two small children can be rented from **Centre Vélo-Coudres** (© **418/438-2118**). The island also has a smattering of boutiques and hotels. The ferry leaves from the town of St. Joseph-de-la-Rive, along Route 362 just east of Baie-St-Paul.

Foodies will want to consider a driving tour of the *circuit agroalimentaire*, a **tour of 11 working farms and shops.** They include **La Ferme Basque de Charlevoix,** 813 rue St-Edouard, St-Urbain (© **418/639-2246;** lafermebasque.ca), a small-scale family-run duck farm that makes foie gras sold throughout the province, and **La Maison d'Affinage Maurice Dufour,** 1339 blvd. Mgr-de-Lavel (Route 138), Baie-St-Paul (© **418/435-5692;** www.fromagefin.com), a fromagerie that makes the highly regarded artisanal cheese Le Ciel de Charlevoix and serves dinner Wednesdays through Sundays.

Many of Canada's elite skiers train at **Le Massif** (© **877/536-2774** or 418/632-5876; www.lemassif.com), the largest ski mountain in the area. It has 43 trails and gives skiers the illusion that they're heading directly into the adjacent St. Lawrence.

There are rumblings of a major project for the area. Daniel Gauthier, a founder of the Cirque du Soleil and the owner of Le Massif, has plans for a 150-room hotel, a rail station, a performance hall, and a market near downtown Baie-St-Paul. He also wants to refurbish a train line to allow travelers to get to the area without cars. As of this writing, none of these projects has broken ground yet.

A LOCAL MUSEUM

Centre d'Exposition   This brick-and-glass museum has three floors of work primarily by regional artists. Photography and Inuit sculptures are included, and temporary one-person and group shows are mounted throughout the year.

23 rue Ambroise-Fafard, Baie-St-Paul. © 418/435-3681. www.centredexpo-bsp.qc.ca. Admission C$4 (US$4/£2) adults, C$2.50 (US$2.50/£1.25) students, free for children 12 and under. Tues–Sun 11am–5pm, until 6pm in summer.

WHERE TO STAY & DINE

La Maison Otis ⊀   Slip into this rambling collection of connecting buildings as into a pair of favorite old jeans. Rooms with fireplaces, whirlpools, four-poster beds, and suites that sleep four are all available. A long porch fronts the colorful main street, and there's a small indoor pool. Meals are no sacrifice, served in a room with a stone fireplace. Smoked "Basque" fillet of duck with honeyed figs has been excellent in the past, as has leg of lamb steamed with garlic and cumin. Rates include dinner and breakfast; room-only rates are available for stays of more than 1 day. The hotel also runs the attached **Café des Artistes,** open all day, where the pizzas with wafer-thin crusts are exceptional. It does busy business with the town's local artists.

23 rue St-Jean-Baptiste, Baie-St-Paul, PQ G0A 1B0. © 800/267-2254 or 418/435-2255. Fax 418/435-2464. www.maisonotis.com. 30 units. C$182–C$355 (US$182–US$355/£91–£178) double. Rates include 5-course dinner and breakfast. Packages available. MC, V. Pets accepted. **Amenities:** 2 restaurants; bar; indoor pool; attached spa; sauna; free Wi-Fi in lobby and cafe; massage; babysitting. *In room:* A/C in 18 units, TV, Internet, coffeemaker, hair dryer, iron.

Le Saint-Pub BISTRO   This casual bistro is part of the town's MicroBrasserie. There's a small bar and dining area, and the kitchen serves up solid renditions of bar food, Québécois-style. House specialties are barbecue chicken for C$16 (US$16/£8) and a variety of foods cooked with beer (beer and onion soup, chocolate and stout pudding). The *traditionnel cigare au chou et sa sauce tomate* (ground pork wrapped in cabbage leaves with tomato sauce) is tasty. Five beers on tap and four in bottles are all made on-site. There's a patio in summer.

2 rue Racine, Baie-St-Paul. © 418/240-2332. Main courses C$16–C$25 (US$16–US$25/£8–£13). MC, V. Mon–Thurs 11:30am–2pm and 5–9pm; Fri–Sat 11:30am–9pm; Sun noon–8pm.

ST-IRENEE

From Baie-St-Paul, take Route 362 northeast toward La Malbaie. The air is scented by sea salt and rent by the shrieks of gulls, and Route 362 roller coasters over bluffs above the river, with wooded hills interrupted by narrow riverbeds. It can be treach-erous in the ice, though, so if you're heading straight to La Malbaie in the winter you might want to opt for the flatter Route 138, which runs more or less parallel.

In 32km (20 miles) is St-Irénée, a cliff-top hamlet of just 685 year-round residents. Apart from the setting, the best reason for dawdling here is the 60-hectare (148-acre) property and estate of **Domaine Forget** (© 888/336-7438 or 418/452-3535 for reservations; www.domaineforget.com). The facility is a performing arts center for music and dance and offers an international music festival and a music and dance academy. Concerts are staged in a 604-seat concert hall, with summertime Sunday musical brunches on an outdoor terrace with spectacular views of the river. The pro-gram emphasizes classical music with solo instrumentalists and chamber groups, but is peppered with jazz combos, dance recitals, and world music events. Most tickets are C$20 to C$35 (US$20–US$35/£10–£18).

From September to May, Domaine **rents its student dorms** to the general public. They're clean and well appointed, with cooking areas and beds for three to five peo-ple. They cost C$60 to C$90 (US$60–US$90/£30–£45), with discounts for longer stays, and include access to studio work areas.

Sea kayaking tours from a half-day to 4 days can be arranged through several com-panies in the area. **Katabatik** (© 800/453-4850 or 418/665-2332; www.katabatik.ca), based in La Malbaie, offers eco-touring that combines kayaking with information about the bays of the St-Lawrence estuary. A half-day tour is C$50 (US$50/£25) for adults, C$40 (US$40/£20) for children 14 to 17, and C$30 (US$30/£15) for children 9 to 13. Tours start in St-Irénée as well as other spots along the coast.

LA MALBAIE: POINTE-AU-PIC & CAP-A-L'AIGLE

From St-Irénée, Route 362 starts to bend west after 10km (6¼ miles), as the mouth of the Malbaie River starts to form. La Malbaie (or "Murray Bay," as it was called by the wealthy Anglophones who made this their resort of choice from the Gilded Age through the 1950s) is the collective name of five former municipalities: Pointe-au-Pic, Cap-à-l'Aigle, Rivière-Malbaie, Sainte-Agnès, and Saint-Fidèle. At its center is a small and scenic bay.

Inhabitants of the region justifiably wax poetic about their wildlife and hills and trees, the place "where the sea meets the sky." They also have something quite differ-ent to preen about these days, as well: a casino.

A CASINO & A MUSEUM

Casino de Charlevoix This is the second of Québec's gambling casinos (the first is in Montréal) and it is about as tasteful as such establishments get. Cherrywood pan-eling and granite floors enclose the ranks of more than 800 slot machines, a keno lounge, and over 20 tables, including blackjack, roulette, stud poker, and minibac-carat. Only soft drinks are allowed at the machines and tables, so players have to go to an adjacent bar to mourn (or celebrate) their losses. There is a dress code that keeps out sloppy ware. Parking is free.

183 av. Richelieu (follow the many signs). © 800/665-2274 or 418/665-5300. www.casino-de-charlevoix.com. Free admission (18 and over only). Daily 9am–3am on summer weekends; somewhat shorter hours other days.

Musée de Charlevoix Located on the Pointe-au-Pic Harbour, the museum fea-tures folk art, sculptures, and paintings by regional artists in both its permanent col-lection and frequent temporary exhibitions.

10 chemin du Havre (at the corner of Rte. 362). *C* 418/665-4411. Admission C$5 (US$5/£2.50) adults, C$4 (US$4/£2) seniors and students. June to mid-Oct daily 9am–5pm; mid-Oct to May Mon–Fri 10am–5pm, Sat–Sun 1–5pm.

WHERE TO STAY & DINE

The Fairmont Le Manoir Richelieu ✦✦ *Kids*   The grand resort of the region. Since 1899, there has been a hotel here, first serving the swells who summered in this aristocratic haven. After waves of renovations, the decor of this "castle on the cliff" is reminiscent of its posh heritage, with elegant Queen Anne furniture. Many rooms are at deluxe standards, with bathrobes, two or three phones, and easy Internet connections. The Fairmont Gold floor has a lounge serving complimentary breakfasts and evening hors d'oeuvres. The hotel offers spectacular views of the St. Lawrence River. A C$15-million, 4-year project molded the golf course into a glorious 27-hole expanse overlooking the St. Lawrence on one side and the hills of Charlevoix on the other. Guests include young couples, elderly folks who have been coming here since they were kids, gamers visiting the **Casino de Charlevoix** next door, and families who take advantage of the region's many child-friendly activities.

181 rue Richelieu, La Malbaie, PQ G5A 1X7. *C* 800/441-1414 or 418/665-3703. Fax 418/665-8131. www.fairmont. com. 405 units. Summer C$259 (US$259/£129) double; Nov–May C$159 (US$159/£79) double; suites from C$379 (US$379/£189). Packages available. AE, DC, MC, V. Valet parking C$19 (US$19/£9.50) with in/out privileges; self-parking for free. **Amenities:** 4 restaurants; bar; indoor and outdoor pools; golf; 3 tennis courts; health club; spa with 22 treatment rooms; Jacuzzi; sauna; watersports equipment; game room; concierge; business center; shopping arcade; limited room service; babysitting; laundry service; same-day dry cleaning; executive rooms. *In room:* A/C, TV w/pay movies, fax, high-speed Internet, minibar, coffeemaker, hair dryer, iron, safe.

La Pinsonnière ✦✦✦   It takes real confidence to close a property for 7 months to end up with 18 units—7 *fewer* than you had when you started. But the 2006 renovation of this long-time favorite property created six deluxe rooms (up from one) with spectacular river views, princely linens, private terraces, and spa bathrooms featuring oversize whirlpools, private saunas, or steam showers. The newer rooms are in contemporary, streamlined luxe decor, while the older ones are more classic Queen Anne. Each has a fireplace, either gas or wood. There is an on-site spa and an unspoiled beach at the end of the property. Dinners are C$68 (US$68/£34) and menus change daily. Wines are a particular point of pride here, evidenced by the impressive 12,000-bottle cellar with 750 different labels. La Pinsonnière was one of the first hostelries in Canada to be invited into the prestigious Relais & Châteaux organization.

124 rue St-Raphaël, La Malbaie (secteur Cap-à-l'Aigle), PQ G5A 1X9. *C* 800/387-4431 or 418/665-4431. Fax 418/665-7156. www.lapinsonniere.com. 18 units. C$285–C$485 (US$285–US$485/£143–243) double. Packages available. Minimum 2-night stay on weekends, 3 nights on holiday weekends. AE, MC, V. Pets accepted. **Amenities:** Restaurant; bar; heated indoor pool; tennis court; access to nearby health club; spa; sauna; concierge; limited room service; massage; babysitting; laundry service; dry cleaning; nature trail; beach. *In room:* A/C, TV, free Wi-Fi, free high-speed Internet, minibar, hair dryer, iron, safe.

12 Upper Charlevoix: St-Siméon, Baie Ste-Catherine & Tadoussac

St-Siméon: 173km (107 miles) NE of Québec City; Baie Ste-Catherine: 207km (129 miles) NE of Québec City; Tadoussac: 214km (133 miles) NE of Québec City.

St-Siméon is where travelers catch the ferry to the southern shore of the St. Lawrence. The northern end of Charlevoix, at Baie Ste-Catherine, is marked by the confluence of the Saguenay River and the St. Lawrence, and these waters attract a half dozen species of whales, many of which can be seen from shore mid-June through late

October. **Whale-watching cruises** are popular. Tadoussac is just across the Saguenay River and is the southernmost point of the tourist region called Manicouagan.

ESSENTIALS
GETTING THERE
BY CAR   Take Route 138 to reach the ferry at St-Siméon, and continue on 138 up to Baie Ste-Catherine. Tadoussac is across the Saguenay River. There is a free car ferry for the 10-minute crossing.

VISITOR INFORMATION
St-Siméon has a year-round **tourist office** at 494 rue St-Laurent, open daily between late June and Labour Day. Visit www.tourisme-charlevoix.com for more information.

ST-SIMÉON
After visiting La Malbaie, you have several options. You can return to Québec City the same way you came—it's only 140km (87 miles) away. You can continue up Route 138 for 33km (20 miles) to St-Siméon and cross the St. Lawrence River by ferry, landing at Rivière-du-Loup a little over an hour later and returning to Québec City along the river's south shore. If it's the summer season and you have more time—a full afternoon, or an extra day to stay overnight—consider continuing on to Baie-Ste-Catherine and Tadoussac to go on a whale-watching cruise. You also could simply soak in the striking views offered by the free ferry crossing at the Saguenay River, and then turn around and retrace your steps. (Note that in the winter and early spring, most of the few establishments between St-Siméon and Tadoussac are closed.)

To get to **the ferry in St-Siméon,** follow the signs that direct cars and trucks down to the terminal. Capacity is 100 cars; boarding is on a first-come, first-served basis. Departures vary substantially from month to month, so check at (2) **418/638-2856** or www.travrdlstsim.com. One-way fares are C$37 (US$37/£18) for a car, C$15 (US$15/£7.50) for each passenger age 12 to 64 years, less for seniors and children. Arrive at least 90 minutes before departure during the summer and holidays. Voyages take about an hour.

From late June to September, passengers may enjoy a bonus on the trip: That's when the **whales** are most active. They are estimated at more than 500 in number when pelagic (migratory) species join the resident minke and beluga. The ferry steams through the area they most enjoy, so summer sightings are an ever-present possibility.

BAIE STE-CATHERINE
For a better chance of seeing whales, continue northeast from St-Siméon on Route 138, arriving 30km (19 miles) later in Baie-Ste-Catherine (population 254), near the estuary of the Saguenay River. In season, companies offer cruises to see whales or cruise the majestic Saguenay Fjord.

The cruise companies use different sizes and types of watercraft, from powered inflatables called Zodiacs that carry 10 to 25 passengers to stately catamarans and cruisers that carry up to 500. The Zodiacs don't provide food, drink, or narration, while the larger boats have snack bars and naturalists onboard to describe the action. Zodiaks are more maneuverable, and get closer to the rolling and breaching behemoths.

Cruises are offered by **Croisières AML,** whose main office is in Québec City ((2) **800/563-4643** all year, 418/692-1159 in season; www.croisieresaml.com). From June to mid-October, they have up to six whale-watching departures daily. Fares for the 3-hour "Whales and Fjord" tours on the larger boats are C$57 (US$57/£28) for adults, C$52 (US$52/£26) for seniors and students, and C$25 (US$25/£13) for children 6 to 16. Two-hour Zodiac "Adventure" fares are C$52 (US$52/£26) for adults, C$47 (US$47/£23) for seniors and students, and C$37 (US$37/19) for children 6 to 16. Excursions of comparable duration and with similar fares are provided by **Group Dufour Croisières** (📞 800/463-5250; www.dufour.ca).

TADOUSSAC

From Baie Ste-Catherine, take the free 10-minute ferry, **Traverse Tadoussac** (📞 877/787-7483 or 418/235-4395), to get to Tadoussac, which sits directly on the water. The ferry crosses at the mouth of the dramatic Saguenay River, and palisades with evergreens poking out of rock walls rise sharply from both shores, the reason this area is often referred to as a fjord. Departure times vary according to season and demand, but in summer figure every 20 minutes from 8am to 8pm, and less frequently the other 12 hours and in low season.

Tadoussac is known as "The Cradle of New France." The oldest permanent European settlement north of Florida, it was established in 1600. Missionaries followed and stayed until the middle of the 19th century. The hamlet might have vanished soon after, had a resort hotel—now the **Hôtel Tadoussac,** below—not been built there in 1864. A steamship line brought vacationers from Montréal and points farther west and deposited them here for stays that often lasted all summer.

Apart from the hotel, just a few small support businesses, a marina, and some dozen small motels and B&Bs constitute the town. The sight of a beaver waddling up the hill from the ferry terminal in broad daylight is met with only mild interest. **Whale-watching** companies have departures from here as well as from Baie Ste-Catherine.

A WHALE CENTER

Centre d'Interprétation des Mammifères Marins   This small interpretation center, directly on the river's edge, offers information about whales, which can often be seen from the shores starting in mid-April each year. It offers a 15-minute film and whale experts on-site. It is run by the nonprofit GREMM, which is dedicated to scientific research on the marine mammals of the St. Lawrence. The center posts updates about whale activity at www.whales-online.net.

108 rue de la Cale Sèche (on the waterfront). 📞 418/235-4701. Admission C$8 (US$8/£4) adults, C$6 (US$6/£3) seniors, C$4 (US$4/£2) children 6–12. Family and group rates. Closed mid-October to mid-May.

WHERE TO STAY & DINE

Hôtel Tadoussac   The bright-red mansard roof of this sprawling hotel dominates the landscape of this small village. First established in 1864, the hotel's current building was erected in 1942. Balconies and a large front lawn overlook the river and the comings and goings of boats. Inside, the public spaces and bedrooms have a shambling, country-cottage appearance—there's no pretense of luxe here, although there is free Wi-Fi in the sprawling lobby. Maple furnishings and hand-woven rugs are all made in Québec. There is no air-conditioning, although all bedrooms have overhead fans and the 50 river-view rooms get a good breeze. Meals in the large dining room are perfectly adequate.

165 rue Bord de l'Eau, Tadoussac, PQ G0T 2A0. 📞 800/561-0718 or 418/235-4421. Fax 418/235-4607. www.hoteltadoussac.com. 149 units. C$154–C$239 (US$154–US$239/£77–£120) double. Children under 18 stay free in parent's room. Packages available. AE, DC, MC, V. Closed mid-Oct to early May. **Amenities:** 3 restaurants; bar; heated outdoor pool; tennis court; spa; children's programs; concierge; babysitting. *In room:* TV, coffeemaker, hair dryer, iron.

13 The Gaspé Peninsula ⭑⁄⭑

Riviére-du-Loup: 209km (130 miles) NE of Québec City; Grand Métis: 358km (222 miles) NE of Québec City; Matane: 411km (255 miles) NE of Québec City; Percé: 765km (475 miles) NE of Québec City.

The southern bank of the St. Lawrence River sweeps north, then eastward, and then back in towards itself, creating a thumb of land called the Gaspé Peninsula—Gaspésie in French. The Gaspé is the farthest end of the province and a primordial region heaped with aged, blunt hills covered with hundreds of square miles of woodlands. Over much of its northern perimeter, slopes fall directly into the sea.

The fishing villages in the coves cut from the coast are as sparsely populated as they've always been, with eagles and elk in the high grounds. Winter here is long and harsh, making the crystal days of summer precious. All that makes it the perfect place for hiking, biking, whale-watching, and fishing in near-legendary salmon streams.

A trip here will be a complete escape from the cities, and your destination is the village of **Percé** at the easternmost edge of the province, along the Gulf of St. Lawrence. It's here that you'll find **Rocher Percé**—Percé Rock, in English—the famed 470m-long (1,542-ft.) butte rising from the sea. It's an astounding sight that you may be tempted to walk up to at low tide.

ESSENTIALS
GETTING THERE
BY TRAIN Via Rail (© **888/842-7245**; www.viarail.ca) travels to the Gaspé region. It goes along the St. Lawrence River and then cuts inland and on to the southern shore of the peninsula. The train makes the trip three times a week, on Wednesdays, Fridays, and Sundays, and returns on Mondays, Thursdays, and Saturdays. From Montréal, the ride takes 16 hours. The Comfort Supersaver fare, with 5 days advance booking, is C$96 (US$96/£48) one-way. Rental cars in Gaspé can be arranged with **National** (© **418/368-1541**) or **Budget** (© **418/368-1610**).

BY CAR From Québec City, it's 765km (475 miles) to Percé, the furthest point on the peninsula, via the coastal Route 132 on the northern shore. This "north tour" is the most scenic route. Leave Québec City by crossing to the southern side of the St. Lawrence River and picking up Route 20 East. Route 20 turns into Route 132 in the Gaspé region. The underside of the peninsula, which you'll travel on if you continue on Route 132 after leaving Percé, is largely a flat coastal plain beside a regular shoreline.

VISITOR INFORMATION
The Québec Government's tourism office's website, **www.bonjourquebec.com**, is thorough and up-to-date. Click on "Explore" and then go to "Tourist Region/Gaspésie." Gaspé's regional tourism association (**www.tourisme-gaspesie.com**) has a number of brochures that they'll mail you. Note that as you move farther away from Québec City, the more difficult it becomes to find people who speak English. For a map of this region, see the "New Brunswick & the Gaspé Peninsula" map on p. 115.

GRAND METIS
After Riviére-du-Loup, 209km (130 miles) from Québec City, the country slowly grows more typically Gaspésien: bogs on the river side of the road yield bales of peat moss which are shipped to gardeners throughout the continent, while low rolling hills and fenced fields house dairy cattle. Along the roadside, hand-painted signs advertise

pain de ménage (homemade bread) and other baked goods for sale. At this point the two-lane highway has become 132 EST (east).

The region's largest city, Rimouski, is 108km (67 miles) past Riviére-du-Loup. Travelers not there on business are likely to pass on through. However, in the town of **Grand Métis,** 41km (25 miles) past Rimouski, you'll find the north shore's stellar attraction: the former Reford estate, now the **Jardins de Métis.**

A HORTICULTURAL WONDERLAND

Jardins de Métis ⚜   Also known as the Reford Gardens, these 40 acres near the Métis and St. Lawrence Rivers are home to over 3,000 species and varieties of native and exotic plants. The gardens were originally cultivated by Elsie Reford, a woman of such passion that even in Gaspé's relatively severe climate she was able to create a wonderland. Sections are laid out in the informal English manner and include a Blue Poppy Glade, Crabapple Garden, and Woodland Walk. There are shops, a small museum, and a busy garden cafe. Since 2000, an international garden festival has been hosted here each summer. It has a special focus on avant-garde design and runs June through September with gourmet dinners, art exhibitions, literary teas, musical brunches, and, of course, temporary gardens by contemporary international designers.

200 Rte. 132, Grand-Métis, PQ G0J 1Z0. ℂ **418/775-2222.** Fax 418/775-6201. www.jardinsmetis.com. C$16 (US$16/£8) adults, C$15 (US$15/£7.50) seniors, C$14 (US$14/£7) students, C$8 (US$8/£4) young adult, free for children under 14. June 2–Sept 30 daily 8:30am–5pm; last entrance 6pm July–Aug, with gates open until 8pm.

MATANE

About 55k (34 miles) past Grand Métis, the highway enters commercial **Matane.** This is about the halfway point to Percé and a logical place to stop for the night if you're trying to make the trip in 2 days. There are many motels and modest B&Bs called *gîtes.* The town's focal point is the Matane River, a thoroughfare for the **annual migration of spawning salmon.** They begin their swim up the Matane in June through a specially designed dam that facilitates their passage, continuing to September. Near the lighthouse is a seasonal **information bureau** (ℂ **877/762-8263**).

WHERE TO STAY

Riôtel Matane   Directly on the beach, this property is part of a small Gaspé chain. The best guest rooms are on the third floor and have ocean views, minibars, high-speed Internet access, and other big-city conveniences. The licensed dining room serves breakfast and dinner year round; Atlantic salmon from Matane is the house specialty.

250 av. du Phare Est, Matane, PQ G4W 3N4. ℂ **877/566-2651** or 418/566-2651. Fax 418/562-7365. www.riotel.com. 96 units. C$79–C$299 (US$79–C$299/£39–£149) double. Packages and Sept–May discounts available. AE, DC, MC, V. Free parking. **Amenities:** 2 restaurants; bar; heated outdoor pool in summer; tennis courts; exercise room; outdoor spa year-round; limited room service; dry cleaning. *In room:* TV, Internet (all units), Wi-Fi (72 units), coffeemaker, hair dryer, iron.

STE-ANNE-DES-MONTS & PARC DE LA GASPESIE

It takes 5 nonstop driving hours to get from Matane to Percé. There are frequent picnic grounds (look for signs announcing *Halte Municipale*), a couple of large nature preserves, and ample opportunities to sit by the water and collect driftwood. While towns along the way are smaller and more spread out, simple sustenance isn't a problem. Look for *casse-croûtes,* simple mobile roadside snack stands.

Ste-Anne-des-Monts is a small fishing town 87km (54 miles) past Matane, with a seasonal **tourist booth** (ℂ **418/763-7633**) on Route 132, 1km (½ mile) past the bridge. The town also has stores, gas stations, and other necessary services.

Rising higher inland here are the Chic-Choc Mountains, the northernmost end of the Appalachian range. Most of them are contained by the **Parc national de la Gaspésie** (© 418/763-7494; www.sepaq.com/pq/gas/en) and adjoining preserves just off Route 132. For a scenic detour, turn south onto Route 299 in Ste-Anne-des-Monts. The road climbs into the mountains, some of which are naked rock at the summits. After about 24km (15 miles), a welcome station provides information about the wilderness park. Back there, the rivers brim with baby salmon and speckled trout, and the forests and meadows sustain herds of moose, caribou, and deer. Return on Route 299 the way you came and continue on Route 132.

MONT-ST-PIERRE

After Ste-Anne, the highway becomes a narrow band crowded up to water's edge by sheer rock walls. Waterfalls spill along the cliffs alongside the road. Around a rocky point and down a slope, **Mont-St-Pierre,** 55km (34 miles) past Ste-Anne, is much like other Gaspésian villages except for the eye-catching striations in the rock of the mountain east of town. Due to its favorable updrafts, the site is regarded as nearly perfect for hang gliders, and for 10 days in July, the town hosts the **Fête du Vol-Libre (Hang-Gliding Festival).** Colorful gliders that loop and curve on air currents fill the sky, landing on sports grounds behind city hall. For more information, visit the village website at **www.mont-saint-pierre.ca**.

PARC NATIONAL FORILLON ⊛

Soon the road winds up through the mountains, down into valleys, and up again to the next rise. The settlements get smaller, but there are still roadside stands advertising fresh and smoked fish. Approaching the eastern edge of Canada, this is the part of the country known as Land's End.

About 120km (75 miles) past Mont-St-Pierre, there's an option to turn off Route 132 onto Route 197. This goes to Gaspé and Percé more directly, skipping the very eastern-most tip of the peninsula that you'll have to pay to drive through.

If you stay on Route 132, you'll soon reach the reception center for **Parc National Forillon** (© 418/368-5505; www.pc.gc.ca/forillon). Bilingual attendants can advise on park activities and regulations. Route 132 continues inside the park, whose 244 sq. km (94 sq. miles) of headlands capture a surprising number of the features characteristic of eastern Canada: rugged coastline, dense forests, colonies of seabirds, and abundance of wildlife. On the northern shore are sheer rock cliffs carved from the mountains by the sea, and on the south is the broad Bay of Gaspé. Hikers and campers from all over North America come for nature walks, beaches, picnicking, and overnight stays. The daily entrance fee in season is C$6.90 (US$6.90/£3.45) for adults, with reduced fees for children and family rates. Prices are lower in the off season. There are 367 campsites; four are open year-round, with others open mid-May through mid-October. Camping costs C$27 (US$27/£13) per night for a spot with electricity.

From within the park, you can pick up whale-watching cruises and sea kayaking excursions. **Croisières Baie de Gaspé** (© 418/892-5500; www.baleines-forillon. com) has 2½-hour cruises to get close to the seven species of whales in the region. Fares are C$45 (US$45/£22) for adults, C$40 (US$40/£20) for seniors and students, and C$20 (US$20/£10) for children, and park entrance fees must be paid in addition to fares. Reserve in advance.

GASPE

Shortly after the exit from the park is the village of Gaspé, protected from the ocean by a long, narrow bay. In 1534, Jacques Cartier stepped ashore here to claim the land for the king of France, erecting a wooden cross to mark the spot. Today the port is important economically because of the salmon rivers that empty into it. The principal attraction is the **Musée de la Gaspésie,** at Jacques Cartier Point on Route 132 (© **418/368-1534;** www.museedelagaspesie.ca), which endeavors to tell the story of Cartier's landing. It's open year-round daily June through October, and every day except Sunday the rest of the year.

PERCE ☞

About 62km (39 miles) past Gaspé, you'll wind around the hills toward Percé. From the road you'll see **Percé Rock**—Rocher Percé—and just farther in the ocean, **Bonaventure Island.**

The town of Percé isn't large, and except for a few quiet inland residential streets, it's confined to the main road running along the shore. The souvenir shops, snack bars, and motels that serve the summer tourists start to open by late May, and in high season there's a family-oriented beach-party ambience. People are so friendly and attentive, in fact, that you might wonder if you've grown a really cute second head.

Fishing was once the primary enterprise, with tourism as a sideline. With fish stocks dangerously depleted and with ever-harsher government restrictions, that relationship is reversed. The **Percé Information Touristique** office, at 142 Rte. 132 (© **418/782-5448;** www.rocherperce.com), is open daily in the summer season.

EXPLORING PERCE ROCK

Percé Rock ☞ is a massive butte that sits off the coast of Percé and is one of the natural highlights of the Québec province. Made of limestone, it is 470m long (1,542 ft.) and nearly 88m (289 ft.) tall at its highest point. It gets its name ("pierced rock") from an arch on its southern end that looks as if a giant needle has cut right through. At low tide, the rock can be reached by foot. Be careful, though: The village advises that because of falling rock you avoid walking directly alongside the monolith.

Just beyond the rock is **Parc national de l'Ile-Bonaventure-et-du-Rocher-Percé** ☞ (© **418/782-2240;** www.sepaq.com/pq/bon/en), a small bird sanctuary whose lure is its nearly 300,000 nesting birds. On the island are gannets, puffins, razorbills, black guillemots, kittiwakes, and over 200 other species. There are four trails totaling 15km (9 miles), observation decks, and, in warm months, an interpretation center staffed with naturalists. The center also has a modest cafe open June through September. The park is open year-round, although the visitor center is open only from May 28 to October 12. Entrance is C$3.50 (US$3.50/£1.75) adults, C$1.50 (US$1.50/75p) children 6 to 17, or free with Parcs Québec card.

To get to the island, 75-minute boat tours take visitors around Percé Rock and then on to the bird colony. Park wardens are often on board to answer questions, and the boats stop at the island to drop off and pick up visitors. Tours are available from **Les Bateliers de Percé** (© **877/782-2974**), **Les bateaux de croisières Julien Cloutier Enr** (© **877/782-2161**), and **Croisières Les Traversiers de l'Ile** (© **866/782-5526**). Trips are C$20 (US$20/£10) for adults, C$15 (US$15/£7.50) for students and seniors, and C$6 (US$6/£3) for children 6 to 12. The companies also offer whale-watching and sea-fishing cruises. They're open from mid-May to mid-October.

WHERE TO STAY & DINE

Hotels and restaurants are open in season, generally mid-May to mid-October. Business starts to tail off in mid-August, making it easier to find lodgings in the fall.

La Normandie 🔥   This small hotel facing Percé Rock is the class act of the town in style, service, dining, and facilities. All guest rooms have small sitting areas, and those facing the water have decks (room nos. 69–74 are tops). The kitchen is open for breakfast and lunch in season and is fairly ambitious, sending table d'hôte dinners (C$24–C$49/US$24–US$49/£12–£24) into a dining room with unobstructed views of the rock from every chair. Lobster, salmon, scallops, and trout are always on the card. Reserve ahead.

221 Rte. 132 ouest, C.P. 129, Percé, PQ G0C 2L0. ⓒ 800/463-0820 or 418/782-2112. Fax 418/782-2337. www.normandieperce.com. 45 units. C$75–C$219 (US$75–US$219/£37–£109) double. Packages available. AE, DC, MC, V. Closed mid-Oct to mid-May. **Amenities:** Restaurant; bar. *In room:* A/C, TV, hair dryer, iron.

WHERE TO DINE

La Maison du Pêcheur 🔥 *(Kids* SEAFOOD   It's close to sacrilegious to eat anything but fish here, within sight of the most important fishing grounds in the North Atlantic. So order up the cod cheeks, salmon in a maple-tinged sauce, or *L'assiette du Pêcheur,* a combination of fresh lobster, crab, scallops, and catch of the day. There are 15 choices of pizza, including options with squid or salmon. A cafe below the main room is open from 7:30am to midnight during the busiest months. Find the restaurant next to the town pier, behind the shops of the main street.

End of quai de Percé. ⓒ 418/782-5331. Table d'hôte dinner C$18–C$40 (US$18–US$40/£9–£20). AE, MC, V. June to mid-Oct daily 11:30am–2:30pm and 5:30–9:30pm.

9

Ottawa & Eastern Ontario

by Paul Karr

Ottawa might be the most underappreciated national capital east of Ulan Bator, even though on most counts it's an urban standard against which many North American cities would do well to measure themselves against. Ottawa's downtown is striking, to say the least: It sees more renovation and enlightened recycling of its 19th- and early-20th-century buildings happening every year. Its miles of tidy late-Victorian brick houses (with shops, restaurants, and homes) are characteristic of this city. The Gothic spires and towers of Parliament Hill look like the grand estate of an overachieving Scottish laird—with the voluptuous Gatineau Hills standing in for the Highlands. In spring, carpets of tulips and daffodils cloak residences and ministries, casting a visual fire against the deep greens of the city's parks.

Cutting a swath through it all? Only the Rideau Canal, a UNESCO World Heritage Site. It's a magnet for houseboats and cabin cruisers in summer, and a scene out of a Dutch painting in winter, when locals take to its ice on sleighs and skates; it's officially the world's largest skating rink. (You can look it up.)

Oh, yes, and everyone here speaks two languages. How's that for continental?

The real Ottawa is a far cry from the dour place one might expect before arriving. Befitting a national capital, it's kept spic-'n-span clean—men with pans and brooms constantly tend to the downtown gutters—and the streets are never choked with traffic. Ottawa, in fact, even possesses a certain romance in many of its

lanes, parks, and cul-de-sacs. See for yourself with a stroll down to Victoria Island: Look east, as the Ottawa River rushes past bluffs commanded by the Parliament building, and it doesn't take all that much imagination to summon up earlier days when fur traders, explorers, and enormous logs rolled down these rivers into what was then a clamorous lumber town. Developers and builders have yet to obscure the treasured vistas here. And, in this still most British of Canadian cities save perhaps Victoria, you can still watch troops of sentries swathed in scarlet tunics and black shakos marching to drum and bagpipe for the morning changing of the guard, each morning, just as they do at Buckingham Palace.

Certainly Ottawa was an unlikely candidate for Canada's capital when it was chosen as such in the mid-19th century. When the two provinces of Upper Canada (Ontario) and Lower Canada (Québec) were fused into the United Provinces of Canada, their rivalry was so bitter the legislature had been meeting alternately in Toronto and Montréal. No less than Queen Victoria herself settled that beef by selecting the village of Ottawa as the new national capital in 1858, no doubt hoping its location right on the Ontario-Québec border would smooth over differences between the French and English. Her choice wasn't met with much praise, at first: Essayist Goldwin Smith called it "a subarctic village, converted by royal mandate into a political cockpit." Other assessments weren't even that kind.

And for nearly a century, the city did indeed languish in a kind of thankless purgatory. (At least it managed to nurture a few rather colorful characters, including the man who was to become Canada's longest-serving prime minister, one William Lyon Mackenzie King; King is to said to have made Canadian decisions regarding World War II with the guidance of, among others, his dog, his deceased mother, and frequent consultations with his predecessor, Sir Wilfrid Laurier—who had passed away some 2 decades earlier.)

In the 1960s, either because of Canada's burgeoning nationalism or perhaps because the government simply wished to create a world-class capital, Ottawa slowly began to metamorphosize. The National Arts Centre was built, ethnic restaurants suddenly multiplied, the ByWard Market area and other historic buildings were rescued from the wrecking ball, and public parks and recreation areas were created. This process has continued into the present day with the recent addition of the wonderful National Gallery of Canada to the city's tableau. **Gatineau,** the large Québécois city directly across the river

(which was known as Hull until 2002), has been undergoing a similar transformation highlighted by the opening of the superb Museum of Civilization and the recently renamed Casino de Lac-Leamy. These twin cities are full of unexpected pleasures—you can watch the debates and pomp of parliamentary proceedings and take in a street scene from a sidewalk terrace, then ski, camp, or hike in true wilderness just 15 minutes away; that night, you can put your feet up before the fireplace of a rustic inn in the woods *or* lay down your head in a business hotel right in the heart of a truly international city.

After visiting Ottawa, you may wish to explore eastern Ontario for a few more days. **Kingston,** an appealing lakefront town, is the principal gateway to the **Thousand Islands** district of the St. Lawrence River. East from **Port Hope**—a worthy stop for antiques hounds—stretches the **Bay of Quinte** and **Quinte's Isle,** a tranquil region of farms, orchards, quaint villages, and riverside parks. Outside the usual tourist circuits, this area was settled by colonials loyal to the Crown who fled the American Revolution. Their descendants are still here today.

1 Essentials

GETTING THERE

BY PLANE **Ottawa International Airport** (✆ **613/248-2000;** www.ottawa-airport.ca), with the great airport code YOW, is about 20 minutes south of the city. **Air Canada** (✆ **888/247-2262;** www.aircanada.com) and its commuter subsidiary **Jazz** are the main airlines serving Ottawa, flying direct from Boston, New York, London, and Las Vegas, among other cities. Other airlines with direct flights include **US Airways** (✆ **800/428-4322;** www.usair.com) and **Northwest** (✆ **800/225-2525;** www.nwa.com), which fly in from the Midwestern U.S., and **Delta Connection** (✆ **800/221-1212;** www.delta.com), which flies to Atlanta and Cincinnati.

The **Airporter shuttle bus** (✆ **613/260-2359;** www.yowshuttle.com) operates between the airport and several downtown hotels for C$14 (US$14/£7) for adults and C$8 (US$8/£4) for ages 8 to 14, one-way—there are discounts for a second and third passenger in a group, and for round-trips. A **taxi** from the airport to the city costs about C$25 (US$25/£13). **Public buses** (known as OC Transpo bus; look for no. 97) to or from the airport cost C$3 (US$3/£1.50) one-way for adults, C$1.50 (US$1.50/75p) for ages 6 to 11; pick it up at post no. 14 outside the Level 1 Arrivals area.

Ottawa

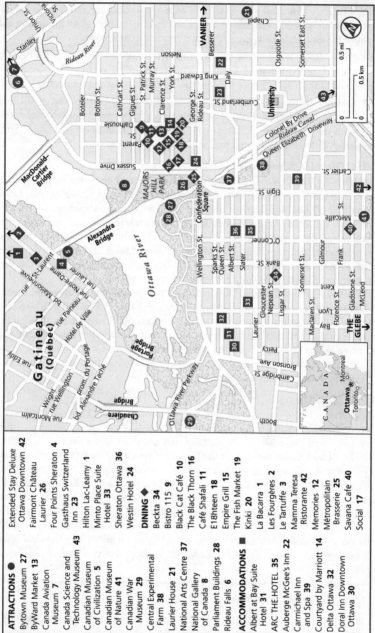

BY TRAIN   VIA Rail (© **888/842-7245;** www.viarail.ca) trains arrive at the Ottawa Station at 200 Tremblay Rd. (at blvd. St-Laurent), in the southeastern quadrant of the city. From here, buses and taxis connect to downtown.

BY BUS   Buses arrive at the **Ottawa Bus Terminal,** 265 Catherine St., between Kent and Lyon. **Greyhound Canada** (© **800/661-8747** or 613/238-6668; www. greyhound.ca) provides service to Montréal, Toronto, and western Canada.

BY CAR   Driving from New York, take Interstate 81 to Canada's Route 401 east, then continue to the new Route 416 north, which leads directly into the city. Coming from the west, come via Toronto on Route 401 east to Route 416 north. From Montréal, follow Route 17 west to Route 417.

VISITOR INFORMATION

TOURIST OFFICES   The most convenient place to gather answers and pick up maps and brochures is the **Capital Infocentre,** 90 Wellington St., across from Parliament Hill (© **800/465-1867** or 613/239-5000; www.canadascapital.gc.ca); it's open weekdays 8:30am to 8pm, weekends 9am to 5pm in summer and to 5pm daily in winter. The Info-Tent on Parliament Hill lawn behind the West Block is where you book free tours of Parliament. Mid-May to about the third week in June, hours are daily 9am to 5pm; the rest of June to Labour Day, it's open Monday through Friday 9am to 8pm and Saturday, Sunday, and holidays 9am to 5pm.

For details about the city of Gatineau and the surrounding rural region, contact **Outaouais Tourism,** 103 Laurier St., Gatineau, PQ J8X 3V8 (© **800/265-7822** or 819/778-2222; www.outaouais-tourism.ca). Summer hours are Monday through Friday 8:30am to 8pm and Saturday and Sunday 9am to 6pm; winter hours are Monday through Friday 8:30am to 5pm and Saturday and Sunday 9am to 4pm.

Another very useful Internet site related to Ottawa, run by a private concern, is located at **www.ottawakiosk.com**.

CITY LAYOUT

The **Ottawa River**—Canada's second longest, at more than 1,125km (700 miles) in length—curves around the northern edge of city. The compact downtown, where most of the major attractions are clustered, lies just south of the river.

The **Rideau Canal** sweeps past the National Arts Centre, cleaving downtown into two parts: Centretown and Lowertown. In **Centretown** are Parliament Hill, the Supreme Court, and the National Museum of Natural Sciences. In **Lowertown,** on the east side of the canal, are the National Gallery of Canada, ByWard Market, and (along Sussex Drive) the prime minister's residence, diplomats' row, and Rockcliffe Park. The area lying south of the Queensway, stretching west to Bronson and east to the canal, is known as the **Glebe,** and it harbors a number of popular restaurants and clubs, especially along Bank Street. North across the river, in the province of Québec, lies the city

---

Tips **Getting Oriented**

The main streets running east-west through Ottawa's city center are **Wellington, Laurier,** and **Somerset;** the **Rideau Canal** separates east from west (and Centretown from Lowertown); the main north-south streets are **Bronson, Bank,** and **Elgin.**

A Road by Any Other Name . . .

Finding your way around Ottawa on foot or by car can be bewildering to say the least, since streets have a habit of halting abruptly at a dead-end—then reappearing a few blocks farther on. Others change names several times. One main street begins in the west as Scott Street, changes to Wellington as it passes through downtown and in front of Parliament, changes again to Rideau, and finally becomes Montréal Road on the eastern fringes of town.

My advice? Three words: **Carry a map.** The information office provides a serviceable one. Ask for one at your hotel, too.

of **Gatineau,** the result of a recent merger that consolidated the city of Hull (where many national government offices are located) and four other suburban communities. It's reached via the Macdonald-Cartier and Alexandra bridges from the eastern end of town, or the Portage and Chaudière bridges from the western end of the city. At the end of the Alexandra Bridge stands the curvaceous Museum of Civilization, and nearby are some of the city's best French restaurants and liveliest nightlife action. North and east of Hull stretch the Gatineau Hills, with acres of parklands and ski country.

GETTING AROUND

Walking is easily the best way. The only public transportation is the 130-odd-route bus network operated by the **Ottawa-Carleton Regional Transit Commission (OC Transpo);** all routes converge downtown at the Rideau Centre, and they begin to close down at midnight. (There's no service at all 1–6am.) The no. 1 bus makes a fairly comprehensive tour of downtown. Using the bus is a bit complicated; rides require more than one ticket (for adult riders), and exact change must be used. An adult in-town ride (2 tickets) is C$3 (US$3/£1.50) for adults, C$1.50 (US$1.50/75p) for ages 6 to 11, free for children 5 and under. A C$6.60–$7.25 (US$6.60–US$7.25/£3.30–£3.65) **DayPass** allows unlimited travel on all routes. You can buy tickets at 300 retail outlets, such as at newsstands and at drugstores.

For more information about routes, where to buy tickets, and more, call © **613/ 741-4390** Monday through Friday 7am to 9pm, Saturday 8am to 9pm, and Sunday 9am to 6pm; or visit www.octranspo.com.

In Gatineau, buses are operated by the **Société de Transport de l'Outaouais** (© **819/770-3242**). Transfers between the two systems are obtainable when you pay your fare on the bus.

Taxis in Ottawa can be hailed on the street but can be found more readily in front of major hotels and important buildings. Or summon one by phone, something restaurant headwaiters are happy to do. One 24-hour company is **Blueline** (© **613/ 238-1111**), with more than 600 cabs. Fares are C$2.90 (US$2.90/£1.45) to start and about C$1.60 (US$1.60/80p) per kilometer after that; you also get charged for waiting in traffic, about C45¢ (US45¢/25p) per minute. Most drivers accept credit cards, usually MasterCard or Visa.

In summer, athletic young men (mostly university students—I think) pull passengers around the tourist districts in **rickshaws.** Fares are not fixed in the city; negotiate a good deal—*before* setting out.

You may not want to drive in Ottawa, although traffic isn't too bad except during rush hours, but a car is essential to explore the environs or continue elsewhere in

Canada. Rental agencies based in Ottawa include **Avis** (© **800/331-1212** or 613/ 739-3334), **Budget** (© **800/472-3325** or 613/521-4844), **Hertz** (© 800/654-**3001** or 613/521-3332), and **National Alamo** (© **800/227-7368** or 613/737-7023), all with offices at the airport and various downtown locations. However, you can save money by arranging for the rental before leaving home.

Parking will cost around C$4 (US$4/£2) for an hour, sometimes less, with about a C$20 (US$20/£10) maximum charge at many local garages. The best parking bets are the municipal parking lots, marked with a large green P in a circle.

When driving, remember that Ontario has a compulsory seat-belt requirement, and pay careful attention to the city's system of one-way streets, which often have three or four streets in a row going in the same direction, rather than alternating. The Queensway (Rte. 417)—a major expressway—cuts right through the city, adding to the confusion. The downtown entrance to this highway is at O'Connor Street; *exit* the highway at Kent Street if you want to reach downtown most quickly. Unlike in Montréal and New York, cars in Ottawa may turn right after first stopping for a red streetlight.

FAST FACTS: Ottawa

Area Code   The telephone area code for Ottawa is **613**; for Gatineau, **819**. You must now use area codes for *all* calls in Ottawa, local or long-distance; but if you're simply calling from Ottawa across the river to Gatineau, you don't need to dial "1." If you're calling farther afield in the provinces, dial "1" first.

Doctors/Dentists   There's a walk-in clinic, the **Family Medical Centre, 344** Slater St. (© 613/235-4140). Or check with the hotel front desk or with your consulate for the nearest doctor or dentist.

Embassies/High Commissions   The **U.S. Embassy** is in a large building at 490 Sussex Dr., north of Rideau Street (© **613/238-5335**). It's open Monday to Friday 8:30am to 5pm. The **British High Commission** is at 80 Elgin St. (© **613/237-1530**). The **Australian High Commission** is at 50 O'Connor St., Suite 710 (© **613/236-0841**), the **New Zealand High Commission** is at 99 Bank St., Suite 727 (© **613/238-5991**), and the **Irish Embassy** is at 130 Albert St., Suite 1105 (© **613/233-6281**).

Emergencies   Call © **911** for police, fire, or ambulance.

Hospital   Your best bet is the **Ottawa Hospital General Campus** at 501 Smyth Rd. (© **613/722-7000**).

Internet Access   Most of the major hotels in the city have business centers with computers to check your e-mail, and offer high-speed Internet access in-room as well. Many now also have wireless hot spots; ask when booking.

Liquor & Wine   The government controls liquor distribution, selling liquor and wine at certain LCBO stores and beer at others. Provincial liquor stores are generally open Monday through Saturday 10am to 6pm (to 9pm Thurs–Fri); Beer Store outlets are open Monday through Saturday noon to 8pm (to 9pm Thurs–Fri). The legal drinking age is 19 in Ottawa (and the rest of Ontario), but it's 18 across the river in Gatineau (because it's in Québec). There's a convenient liquor store downtown in the **Rideau Centre**, just inside the Rideau St. entrance (© **613/569-1879**).

Newspapers/Magazines A great variety of international publications, including the *New York Times,* the *Wall Street Journal,* and the *International Herald Tribune,* are sold at **Planet News,** 143 Sparks St. (*©* **613/232-5500**).

Police Call *©* **911.**

Post Office The most convenient post office is at 59 Sparks St., at Elgin Street (*©* **613/844-1545**), open Monday to Friday 8am to 6pm.

Taxes In Ontario, there's an 8% provincial sales tax (PST) plus the 5% national sales tax known as GST. However, there are a few exceptions to this rate: hotel stays are taxed at 5% (if you stay less than 30 days), plus the 5% GST, plus *another* city tax of 3% in the Ottawa area, for a total of 14%. Liquor is taxed at 10% and 12% at restaurants and liquor stores, respectively. Across the river in Québec, there's a 7.5% tax on food, liquor, merchandise, and accommodations, plus the 5% national sales tax (which is also taxed by the province).

Telephones The telephone system, operated by Bell Canada, works essentially the same as that in America. Pay phones are not exactly plentiful in Ottawa, but where present they generally accept coins and prepaid calling cards. All Bell Canada operators speak French and English.

Time Ontario and Québec are in the eastern time zone, the same as New York City. Daylight saving time is observed in summer, exactly as in the U.S.

2 Where to Stay

While a few reasonably priced rooms are available at in-town B&Bs, you'll have to look mostly to Ottawa's outer districts for truly inexpensive lodgings—primarily in motels. There are ample choices of midpriced to luxurious rooms, however, and an unusually large number of suite hotels in the city, intended primarily for businesspeople on long stays in the capital; these are ideal for families, because they usually sport full kitchens, plus enough bedding for four or more travelers. A few of the best are described below.

For additional choices, check the websites **www.all-hotels.com/canada** and **www.canadaselect.com**. Rates quoted below do not include the 5% Ontario hotel tax and 5% Canadian GST (sales tax) unless otherwise stated.

DOWNTOWN
VERY EXPENSIVE
ARC THE.HOTEL 🏨🏨   A former apartment house was converted into this hip boutique hotel, and it's been a successful transition; the place sports a multitude of cunning touches, large and small. The assured young staff stands ready to guide guests through their stays, and few details have been neglected: Champagne is poured at check-in, the evening bed turndown includes Godiva chocolates, rooms are stocked with Tazo teas and gourmet coffee. Your in-room safe is big enough for a laptop, use of the hotel's small business center is free, and all rooms include personalized business cards, Frette robes, mohair throws, minibars, two-line phones, and CD players (there's a library of discs available to guests). Shoeshines are free, too. A few steps up from the minimalist lobby is one of the city's best **restaurants** 🍴, bearing the same name as the

hotel. The kitchen here impresses with care and balance in preparation and ingredients, and service is gracious and efficient. Lunch and dinner are served daily.

140 Slater St. (between Metcalfe and O'Connor sts.), Ottawa, ON K1P 5H6. (℃) 800/699-2516 or 613/238-2888. Fax 613/238-0053. www.arcthehotel.com. 112 units. C$192–C$252 (US$192–US$252/£96–£126) double; from C$252 (US$252/£126) suite. AE, DC, MC, V. Valet parking C$18 (US$18/£9). **Amenities:** Restaurant; bar; fitness room; concierge; business center; limited room service; laundry service; dry cleaning. *In room:* A/C, TV, dataport, minibar, coffeemaker, hair dryer, safe.

The Fairmont Château Laurier ⍟⍟⍟ Built at the same time (1912) and in the same French Renaissance style as Québec City's famed Château Frontenac, the Laurier has long attracted royalty and celebrities to its ideal location beside the Rideau Canal at the east end of Parliament Hill. There was no stinting on materials or dimensions, as can be seen in the hotel's wide halls and acres of public lounges and lobbies. The spacious guest rooms are decorated with many Louis XV reproductions, and upper floors offer impressive views over the Ottawa River north to the Gatineau hills. A million-dollar overhaul has enhanced the dining experience in the redoubtable **Wilfrid's** ⍟, where there are terrace tables for alfresco dining in summer.

1 Rideau St. (at MacKenzie Ave.), Ottawa, ON K1N 8S7. (℃) 866/540-4410 or 613/241-1414. Fax 613/562-7030. www.chateaulaurier.com. 429 units. C$189–C$399 (US$189–US$399/£95–£200) double; C$369–C$2,500 (US$369–US$2,500/£185–£1,250) suite. Packages available. AE, DC, DISC, MC, V. Valet parking C$29 (US$29/£15); self-parking C$22 (US$22/£11). **Amenities:** 2 restaurants; lounge; large indoor pool; extensively equipped health club w/sauna; concierge; business center; shopping arcade; 24-hr. room service; in-room massage; babysitting; laundry service; dry cleaning; executive floors. *In room:* A/C, TV, dataport, minibar, coffeemaker, hair dryer, iron/ironing board, safe.

Westin Hotel ⍟⍟⍟ The atrium lobby and many guest rooms at Ottawa's centrally located Westin offer views over the canal toward Parliament Hill, and the hotel connects directly to both the Rideau Centre shopping complex and the Ottawa Congress Centre. Carefully furnished rooms contain oak furniture, brass lamps, and half-poster beds. The current "Heavenly" theme of the Westin chain is played to the hilt, especially on beds, which are heaped with down pillows, thick mattress covers, and clouds of comforters. Expect great dual showerheads, bath products, towels, and robes of Brazilian combed cotton in the bathrooms. Adult swimmers have the pool to themselves daily in the early-morning hours, and the fitness center is especially well outfitted with its whirlpool tub, saunas, and squash courts.

11 Colonel By Dr. (1 block south of Rideau St.), Ottawa, ON K1N 9H4. (℃) 800/228-3000 or 613/560-7000. Fax 613/234-5396. www.westin.com/ottawa. 495 units. Weekdays from C$199–C$389 (US$199–US$389/£100–£195) double and suite; weekends from C$169–C$249 (US$169–US$249/£85–£125) double and suite. AE, DC, MC, V. Valet parking C$28 (US$28/£14); self-parking C$15 (US$15/£7.50). Pets allowed. **Amenities:** 2 restaurants; lounge; indoor pool; fitness center; whirlpool; concierge; business center; 24-hr. room service; massage; babysitting; laundry service; dry cleaning. *In room:* A/C, TV, dataport, minibar, coffeemaker, hair dryer, iron/ironing board.

EXPENSIVE
Albert at Bay Suite Hotel ⍟⍟ *Kids Value* This Centretown hotel is one of my favorite secret digs in Ottawa, even if it is a bit off the beaten track in a neighborhood with nothing to do at night. In a converted apartment house, it's one of Ottawa's best buys for longer stay—and just as nice for a night or two, since all the customary conveniences of a conventional hotel are also in place. All the units are suites, and they're huge: the *smallest* have one bedroom and a sofa bed; a living room with terrace; two bathrooms; two TVs; and a full kitchen with appliances, dishes, and flatware. I've cooked many a meal here. The rooftop conceals a patio with picnic tables and lounge chairs. Free wireless high-speed Internet access is provided throughout, and parking is

in a garage right beneath the hotel (it's a bit tight). There's a popular "kid's club" daily during July and August, and the cooking facilities in each suite are great for families year-round. For provisions, there's a tiny 24-hour convenience store at street level, and for diners there's a decent restaurant and pub both on premises as well.

435 Albert St. (at Bay St.), Ottawa, ON K1R 7X4. ⓒ **800/267-6644** or 613/238-8858. Fax 613/238-1433. www.albert atbay.com. 197 units. C$100–C$149 (US$100–US$149/£50–£75) suite. Rates include continental breakfast. Weekend packages available. AE, DC, DISC, MC, V. Self-parking C$15 (US$15/£7.50). **Amenities:** Restaurant; bar; fitness center; whirlpool; sauna; children's program; secretarial services; business center; limited room service; babysitting; coin-op washers and dryers; dry cleaning. *In room:* A/C, TV, dataport, kitchen, fridge, coffeemaker, hair dryer, iron.

The Carmichael Inn and Spa 𝓕   Three blocks west of the Rideau Canal, this
fetching 1901 retreat served as a Supreme Court judge's residence and a convent before being converted to an inn. It's named after one of Canada's famed Group of Seven painters, and the decor recalls their art as well as their early-20th-century life and times. All guest rooms are queen-bedded, furnished in unique mixes of antiques and reproductions; some also have gas fireplaces. A variety of treatments and packages are available in the inn's spa, including herbal and mud wraps, hydrotherapy, aromatherapy, and reflexology. Before or after, guests can relax on couches in front of a marble fireplace or laze about in chairs on a veranda. This inn is extremely popular, so reserve both rooms and spa treatments at least a month in advance.

46 Cartier St. (at Somerset St.), Ottawa, ON K2P 1J3. ⓒ **877/416-2417** or 613/236-4667. Fax 613/563-7529. www.carmichaelinn.com. 11 units. Peak season C$149 (US$149/£75) double. Off-season rates discounted. Rates include continental breakfast. Weekend and spa packages available. AE, DC, MC, V. Free parking. **Amenities:** Spa; secretarial services; in-room massage; laundry service; dry cleaning. *In room:* A/C, TV, dataport, iron/ironing board.

Delta Ottawa 𝓕𝓕 *Kids*   This 1973 addition to a fine (and, in the U.S., still largely
unknown) Canadian chain has a sky-lit marble lobby with a fireplace in wintertime and island-style reception desks to give a personal welcome. The guest rooms come in a number of different configurations, all spacious and refreshingly decorated; a substantial number are big, 65 sq. m (700-sq.-ft.) one- or two-bedroom suites with kitchenettes, and more than half have balconies, too. All feature Nintendo systems, robes, and high-speed Internet access. While it's probably accurate to say that business clients rule the roost here during the work week, the hotel staff goes all out to make families feel welcome on the weekends: at check-in, kids receive bags of goodies, and parents can leave them to supervised play in the Children's Creative Centre (parents are even issued pagers in case of emergency). Another design highlight here is the 35m (115-ft.) indoor waterslide.

361 Queen St. (at Bay St.), Ottawa, ON K1R 7S9. ⓒ **877/814-7706** or 613/238-6000. Fax 613/238-2290. www.delta hotels.com. 328 units. C$129–C$229 (US$129–US$229/£65–£115) double, C$179–C$299 (US$179–US$299/£90–£150) suite; holiday rates higher. Packages available. AE, DC, MC, V. Self-parking C$21 (US$21/£11). Small pets accepted. **Amenities:** 3 restaurants; bar; indoor pool; exercise room; sauna; children's programs; game room; concierge; business center; limited room service; babysitting; coin-op washers and dryers; dry cleaning; executive rooms. *In room:* A/C, TV, dataport, minibar, coffeemaker, hair dryer, iron, safe.

Extended Stay Deluxe Ottawa Downtown 𝓕 *Value*   On a street which also
hosts several other suite hotels (possible alternatives if this one is full), there is isn't anything more you could ask of this hotel. Two adjoining apartment buildings comprise the property, which matches the big-name hotels in most areas (service, facilities) and surpasses them in several—including square footage and value. All of the one-bedroom suites have full-size kitchens, and even the smaller studio units have microwave ovens, refrigerators, and stoves; all of the sofas have pull-out beds (bring

the family). The least expensive rooms are classified as standard, and the upgraded section is "deluxe," but if you want a touch of luxury—including robes and wet bars—book one of the penthouse suites. Grocery deliveries can be arranged to your room, and there's a fitness center.

141 Cooper St. (east of Elgin St.), Ottawa, ON K2P 0E8. (C) 800/563-5634 or 613/236-7500. Fax 613/563-2836. 210 units. C$115–C$159 (US$115–US$159/£58–£80) double. AE, DC, MC, V. Self-parking C$11 (US$11/£5.50). Amenities: Restaurant; bar; exercise room; sauna; limited room service; coin-op washers and dryers; dry cleaning. In room: A/C, TV, dataport, kitchen, coffeemaker, hair dryer, iron/ironing board.

Minto Place Suite Hotel ★★   Reminding many guests of a luxury cruise ship, the high-rise Minto Place stacks more than 400 studio and one- and two-bedroom suites above a ground-floor shopping arcade. The upper-floor units have sweeping views, and all rooms have sofa beds and either kitchenettes or full kitchens; some even come with washers and dryers. Spacious living rooms are fully furnished with desks, two-line phones, and dining tables, and the hotel describes the suites' bathrooms as "spa-like." These great rooms cost no more than those in the many chain business hotels across the city; as a result, this is the best suite deal in town for your money. There's both a steakhouse and a casual Italian restaurant with a lounge on-site, as well.

185 Lyon St. N. (at Laurier.), Ottawa, ON K1R 7Y4. (C) 800/267-3377 or 613/232-2200. Fax 613/232-6962. www.mintosuitehotel.com. 417 units. C$135–C$250 (US$135–US$250/£68–£125) double and suite. Weekend discounts available. AE, DC, MC, V. Self-parking C$4–C$16 (US$4–US$16/£2–£8). Amenities: 2 restaurants; 2 bars; indoor pool; health club; Jacuzzi; sauna; children's programs (summer); secretarial services; shopping arcade; limited room service. In room: A/C, TV, dataport, kitchenette, fridge, coffeemaker, hair dryer, iron/ironing board.

Sheraton Ottawa ★   Business travelers know what to expect from a downtown Sheraton—a middle-of-everything location, fitness facilities, conference rooms, and spacious guest rooms with the usual electronics, including two phone lines, voice mail, and video games. This property meets those expectations, and the leisure traveler will enjoy it, too, if he or she has tired of the eccentricities of inns and boutique hotels. Almost half the rooms here are nonsmoking; extra amenities on the executive-level floors include larger rooms, bathrobes, high-speed Internet access, Nintendo PlayStations, and in-room fax machines. The lap pool and sauna are good bonuses, both housed in the hotel's impressive fitness center.

150 Albert St. (at O'Connor St.), Ottawa, ON K1P 5G2. (C) 800/489-8333 or 613/238-1500. Fax 613/238-8497. www.sheraton.com. 236 units. C$165–C$290 (US$165–US$290/£83–£145) double. Packages available. AE, DC, DISC, MC, V. Valet parking C$20 (US$20/£10). Pets accepted. Amenities: Restaurant; lounge; indoor pool; health club; sauna; children's programs; business center; limited room service; babysitting; laundry service; dry cleaning; executive rooms. In room: A/C, TV, dataport, coffeemaker, hair dryer, iron.

MODERATE
Auberge McGee's Inn   On a quiet street a few blocks from the University of Ottawa, this nonsmoking inn occupies a handsome Victorian with a steep dormer roof and an awning-protected entrance. Each guest room is distinctively decorated, often with touches reflective of the owner's Anglo-Peruvian upbringing. Unusually for a B&B, all rooms have fridges and some form of high-speed Internet access, and several—including the romantic, king-bedded Victorian Roses Suite—add double Jacuzzis and fireplaces, as well. Ample breakfasts are served each morning to guests, either in a high-ceilinged dining room or a sunny, windowed parlor. If you book an upper-floor room, remember that this three-floor inn has no elevator.

185 Daly Ave. (at Nelson St.), Ottawa, ON K1N 6E8. (C) 800/262-4337 or 613/237-6089. Fax 613/237-6201. www.mcgeesinn.com. 12 units. C$118–C$148 (US$118–US$148/£59–£74) double; C$184 (US$184/£92) suite. Rates

include full breakfast. AE, MC, V. Free parking. From downtown, take Laurier Ave. E. and turn left at Nelson St. **Amenities:** Nonsmoking rooms. *In room:* A/C, TV, dataport, fridge, coffeemaker, hair dryer, Jacuzzi (some units), fireplace (some units).

Courtyard by Marriott   Though this well-located building once housed a different hotel, it's now an entirely renovated facility, reopened in 1999. Like others in this popular business-hotel chain, this property is somewhere between an agreeable highway motel and a first-class hotel, with limited personal service but fairly complete facilities. Guest rooms are intentionally businesslike, featuring thoughtfully designed work areas and voice mail. Wireless high-speed Internet access is included and free, as well, as are morning papers and free coffee. The large parking lot adjoins, and all of ByWard Market lies just beyond.

350 Dalhousie St. (at York St.), Ottawa, ON K1N 7E9. (C) 800/341-2210 or 613/241-1000. Fax 613/241-4804. www.courtyard.com/yowcy. 183 units. C$169–C$199 (US$169–US$199/£85–£100) double. Rates include breakfast. AE, DC, MC, V. Parking C$12 (US$12/£6). **Amenities:** Restaurant; lounge; heated indoor pool; exercise room; whirlpool; secretarial services; 24-hr. room service; coin-op washers and dryers; laundry service; dry cleaning. *In room:* A/C, TV, dataport, coffeemaker, hair dryer, iron/ironing board.

INEXPENSIVE

Doral Inn Downtown Ottawa *(Value)*   Now flagged as part of the Travelodge chain, this is a good choice on the price-value scale: an amiable inn occupying an expanded brick town house characteristic of many of Ottawa's residential blocks. Guest rooms have brass bedsteads, floral wallpaper, desks, and armchairs. On the ground floor, two bay-windowed rooms serve as a lounge/sitting room and a breakfast area. Guests can use a nearby pool and fitness center for an extra charge. Note that children age 13 to 18 are charged as adults (about C$12/US$12/£6 per person beyond double occupancy).

486 Albert St. (at Bay St.), Ottawa, ON K1R 5B5. (C) 800/263-6725 or 613/230-8055. Fax 613/237-9660. www.doralinn.com. 40 units. C$125–C$169 (US$125–US$169/£63–£85) double; holiday rates higher. Rates include continental breakfast. Packages available. AE, DC, DISC, MC, V. Free parking. **Amenities:** Cafe; babysitting; coin-op laundry. *In room:* A/C, TV, dataport, fridge, coffeemaker, hair dryer.

Gasthaus Switzerland Inn *(R)*   East of the Rideau Centre and 2 blocks south of the ByWard Market area in a late-19th-century stone building, this B&B possesses the familiar hallmarks of red gingham and country pine associated with rural Swiss hospitality. There's a common sitting room, and guests have use of a garden (and its barbecue) in summertime. Puffy duvets cover the beds of the guest rooms, some of which have gas fireplaces. The place has upscaled a bit in recent years; the romantic honeymoon suites go over the top, for instance, with amenities such as king and queen poster beds, double Jacuzzis, CD players, Italian tiles, champagne, chocolates, and blended cotton-satin sheets. A full, Swiss-style breakfast buffet of breads, eggs, French toast, cheese, and cereal is served mornings. The three-floor inn is entirely nonsmoking, but there's no elevator—and the stairs are relatively steep. Ask for a room on the ground floor if your mobility is limited. Also think about parking in the nearby Rideau Centre or on the street (free, but not guaranteed safe) if you've brought a car, as the inn property only has room for a few cars.

89 Daly Ave. (at Cumberland St.), Ottawa, ON K1N 6E6. (C) 888/663-0000 or 613/237-0335. Fax 613/594-3327. www.gasthausswitzerlandinn.com. 22 units. C$118–C$168 (US$118–US$168/£59–£84) double; C$228–C$288 (US$228–US$288/£114–£144) suite. Rates include full breakfast. AE, DC, MC, V. Limited self-parking C$12 (US$12/£6). **Amenities:** Limited room service; laundry service. *In room:* A/C, TV, dataport, coffeemaker, hair dryer, Jacuzzi (some units), fireplace (some units).

> ## *Tips* An Outing on the Ottawa River
>
> For a break from city stress and traffic, drive east into Québec on Route 148 to Montebello. It takes only an hour, and you'll have access to golf, boating on the river, a wildlife park, and hiking, fishing, and canoeing in an unspoiled wilderness.

IN GATINEAU
MODERATE
Four Points by Sheraton and Conference Centre Gatineau ⭐ Directly opposite the Canadian Museum of Civilization, this shiny recent entry in the area's growing midpriced chain matches the offerings of many of its pricier competitors. While intended primarily to serve business travelers, families should be content here, if not thrilled. I will give management a gold star for restoring the rectory of the adjacent 19th-century Notre-Dame Church, now serving as an annex to the hotel.

35 rue Laurier, Gatineau, PQ J8X 4E9 ⓒ 800/567-9607 or 819/778-6111. Fax 819/778-3647. www.fourpoints.com. 201 units. C$90–C$140 (US$90–US$140/£45–£70) double; C$159–C$209 (US$159–US$209/£80–£105) suite. AE, DC, MC, V. Self-parking $10 (US$10/£5). **Amenities:** Restaurant; 2 bars; heated indoor pool; exercise room; children's programs; business center; limited room service; babysitting; laundry service; dry cleaning; executive rooms. *In room:* A/C, TV, dataport, fridge (some units), coffeemaker, hair dryer, iron/ironing board.

Hilton Lac-Leamy ⭐⭐ You will spot the silvery high-rise slab of this new Hilton property well before reaching it via exit 3 from Autoroute 5. The entry road sweeps past the casino and a theater before arriving right at the front door. A "wow" factor is invoked in the lobby by multicolored chandeliers that seem like surreal Venetian glass renditions of Medusa's hair. Guest rooms are less dramatic, but provide the expected comforts and a few extras, including video games, CD players, and morning newspapers. Most rooms look out onto wide Lake Leamy, which has a beach and small boats for rent. The chief attraction, of course, is Québec's third casino (see "Ottawa After Dark," later in this chapter), connected to the hotel via a corridor. That means you can eat, sleep, drink, dance, and lose more money than you ever intended without ever even setting a foot out of doors. If you're into that. The hotel is about a 10-minute drive from downtown Ottawa.

3 bd. du Casino, Gatineau, PQ J8Y 6X4. ⓒ 866/488-7888 or 819/790-6444. Fax 819/790-6408. www.hiltonlacleamy. com. 349 units. C$180–C$390 (US$180–US$390/£90–£195) double; C$270–C$2,500 (US$270–US$2,500/ £135–£1,250) suite. Packages available. AE, DC, MC, V. Covered valet parking C$15 (US$15/£7.50); outdoor self-parking free. **Amenities:** 2 restaurants; 2 bars; casino; heated indoor and outdoor pools; 2 tennis courts; health club; spa; children's programs; business center; salon; shopping arcade; 24-hr. room service; babysitting; laundry service; dry cleaning. *In room:* A/C, TV, dataport, minibar, coffeemaker, hair dryer, iron/ironing board, safe.

A RESORT IN NEARBY MONTEBELLO
The Fairmont Le Château Montebello ⭐⭐ A log palace constructed in the grand manner of the sprawling early-20th-century hideaways of the Alps and Rockies, this was an exclusive private resort until 1970, when it was converted to a hotel. Its most striking feature is the six-sided granite fireplace that occupies the center of the three-story lobby; the indoor pool is huge, as well. But what *really* amazes is the roster of activities available—including golf, clay shooting, guided nature walks and hikes, ice skating, cross-country skiing, curling, tennis, cycling, and kayaking. Much of this is undertaken on the adjacent Kenauk preserve, a protected natural environment of more

than 2,630 hectares (6,500 acres). After a day of exercise, hunger is addressed in several restaurants, where the food and service are better than expected.

392 rue Notre-Dame, Montebello, PQ J0V 1L0. © 866/540-4463 or 819/423-6341. Fax 819/423-1183. www.fairmont. com. 210 units. C$189–C$289 (US$189–US$289/£95–£145) double; C$468–C$688 (US$468–US$688/£234–£344) suite. Packages available. AE, DC, MC, V. Free parking. Amenities: 4 restaurants (2 in summer); 3 bars; indoor pool; 18-hole golf course; 8 tennis courts; health club; bike rental; kayak rental; children's programs; business center; salon; limited room service; massage; babysitting; laundry service; dry cleaning. In room: A/C, TV, dataport, minibar, coffeemaker, hair dryer, iron/ironing board.

3 Where to Dine

Ottawa has plenty of colorful ethnic restaurants, and plenty of expensive ones. Beyond that, try the street food. To experience a true Ottawa tradition, for instance, stop at the **Hooker's** stand at George and William streets in the center of ByWard Market and purchase a "beaver tail." Furry rodents aren't involved; *this* beaver tail is actually a deep-fried pastry about the size of a Ping-Pong paddle, served either sweet (with cinnamon and sugar or raspberry jam) or savory (with garlic butter, cheese, and scallions). It's tasty and cheap, and you'll feel somewhat like a local.

Nearby, and in commercial districts around town, step up to one of the rolling grill carts and order a hot Polish or German sausage cradled in a bun. Slather it with mustard and heap high with sauerkraut, pickles, peppers, and/or onions. Another inexpensive solution to the munchies is the proliferation of **chip wagons** found in parking lots and vacant spaces around the city, and out in the Ontario countryside. Similar to the *casse-croutes* of Québec, these carts or trucks serve limited menus of sandwiches, soft drinks, and french fries. For java, look for branches of the popular Ontario-based coffeehouse chain **Second Cup** at strategic locations around town; it often outdraws the inevitably close-by Starbucks.

CENTRETOWN
EXPENSIVE

Beckta ☆☆☆ CONTEMPORARY CANADIAN   Here's living proof that residents of the nation's capital are ready to embrace cooking transcending the beef and spaghetti houses that dominated the Ottawa dining scene not so very long ago. Owner Stephen Beckta has set a fine stage in several rooms of an old Victorian home, a fitting stage indeed for the works of Chef Michael Moffatt. Relying heavily on Canadian-caught, -raised, or -harvested items—British Columbian halibut, Alberta beef, Ontarian plums, Digby scallops, Québec fois gras—Moffatt reaches for extreme-foodie combinations like a pork trio incorporating smoked pork belly, braised hock, and blue-cheese spaetzle; bison *tartare* with horseradish crackers and a quail's egg; tuna sashimi with a piece of ginger tempura, black sesame oil, and honey-*yuzu* vinaigrette; and a fatty duck breast served with grilled peaches, pine mushrooms, polenta, and a carmelized foie gras sauce. These are ambitious plans, but there's not a misstep in the bunch. Desserts are amazingly creative and delicious, and even the bread is notches above the norm; the wine list, partly Canadian, is reasonably priced. Then there's the service, by a coed team of highly polished skills: there's no better group in town.

226 Nepean St. (between Kent and Bank). © 613/238-7063. Reservations strongly recommended. Main courses C$27–C$36 (US$27–US$36/£14–£18), 5-course tasting menu C$79 (US$79/£40). AE, DC, MC, V. Mon–Fri 5:30–10pm; Sat 5:30–10:30pm.

Mamma Teresa Ristorante ☆ CLASSIC ITALIAN   There was a real Mamma Teresa. Her son carries on her tradition in this handsome late-19th-century stone

Finds Bottoms Up . . . and Bombs Away

This side of the Big Briney, English country pubs don't get more authentic than the **Cheshire Cat** (© 613/831-2183), located at 2193 Richardson Side Rd. in the village of **Carp** (yes, really). Housed in an 1883 stone cottage with a wood-burning stove and horse brasses, it offers cool (never icy) draft bitter in dimpled mugs. You'll pick up snatches of Cockney slang among the regulars at the bar. A variety of sandwiches is available, as well as such traditional pub meals as Welsh rarebit, liver and bacon, steak-and-kidney pie, beer-and-beef stew, and shepherd's pie; there have also been some fancy recent additions such as steamed mussels, a shrimp Madras curry, and even (gasp) wraps. The beers are mostly British, along with a few Canadian microbrews. There's a special kids' menu, too, and on summer days the garden is a happy spot to idle. The kitchen is open Tuesday through Saturday 11:30am to 9pm and Sunday noon to 9pm; the bar is open to 11pm Sunday through Wednesday and to 1am Thursday through Saturday.

Reach Carp by first taking Route 417 west out of Ottawa to Route 5, then turning north and continuing to the village.

If you make the pilgrimage to the Cheshire Cat, don't miss one of the odder sights in Ontario nearby: the **Diefenbunker** 𝕜, just north of Carp center at 3911 Carp Rd. (© **613/839-0007**; www.diefenbunker.ca). Now designated as "Canada's Cold War museum," it's a four-story underground H-bomb shelter that was built during the earliest, most tension-filled days of confrontation between East and West. Canadian Prime Minister John Diefenbaker—a true character, who's worth a book in and of himself—ordered it built in secret between 1959 and 1961; the eerie, echoey labyrinth here was supposed to provide emergency shelter to key Canadian political and military figures, as well as the nation's gold reserves, in the unfortunate event of a nuclear attack. In 2006, the museum added two spectacular new permanent exhibitions: one very graphically archives the terrible physical toll (on structures *and* people) of nuclear weapons; the other is an exhibition about peacekeeping and peacekeepers around the world. There's perhaps no other museum so chilling on North American soil.

It's open year-round; tours are given at 2pm weekdays, and at 11am, 1pm, and 2pm weekends, and reservations are required. Admission is C$14 (US$14/£7) for adults, C$13 (US$13/£6.50) for seniors and students, and C$6 (US$6/£3) for children ages 6 to 17; families pay C$35 (US$35/£18). A sweater is recommended: Things can get pretty chilly underground when you're fighting a cold war.

---

house, which the restaurant has occupied since 1984 (and it opened 15 years earlier than that). The two floors require separate kitchens, since up to 325 meals are served nightly; patrons are more likely to depart with boxed leftovers than to finish one of these huge platters of pasta. Most of the pastas are made on premises, including lasagna, linguini, ravioli, pappardelle, and gnocchi. They arrive firm to the tooth and dressed in up to 30 different sauces. Special pride is taken in the penne Mamma

Teresa, a rich, earthy Bolognese sauce thick with porcini mushrooms. If you order the big antipasti plate for two, though, a pasta course may not be necessary—it contains grilled shrimp, crispy calamari, scallops, prosciutto with chunks of Parmesan, olives, and pickled hot peppers. Specific wines are suggested for each dish, and be sure to ask for the house-roasted bread to be brought to your table. Dessert? The zabaglione is lighter than air, a cake that shouldn't be skipped.

300 Somerset St. (near Bank St.). (C) 613/236-3023. Reservations recommended. Main courses C$15–C$35 (US$15–US$35/£7.50–£18). AE, DC, MC, V. Mon–Fri 11am–11pm; Sat–Sun 5–11pm.

MODERATE

Savana Cafe *Finds* CARIBBEAN/ASIAN FUSION Its tropical flavor, splashy Caribbean art, and peppery cuisine (a curious mixture of island cooking and pan-Asian) have kept this place superheated for more than 20 years. Lunches are pad Thai, spicy wraps, nothing out of the ordinary; but dinner shines. Start with the fabulous callaloo soup—the real thing, with okra, spinach, thyme, Scotch bonnet peppers, and lime. Main-course offerings might include jerked chicken, Cubana chicken (which is stuffed with bananas and cream cheese), lemony seafood soba (buckwheat) noodles, a Guatemalan-and-Thai spiced shrimp with vegetables and bananas, or lamb glazed with guava; you can order most of these dishes spiced mild, medium, or hot (and they mean *hot*) according to your preference. There are daily fish specials, as well. The bar and front terrace fill early each night with young to 40-ish professional types intent on unwinding with good rum concoctions, and in winter a fire in the hearth adds a welcoming touch.

431 Gilmour St. (between Bank and Kent). (C) 613/233-9159. Reservations recommended. Main courses C$9–C$11 (US$9–US$11/£4.50–£5.50) lunch, C$15–C$24 (US$15–US$24/£7.50–£12) dinner. AE, DC, MC, V. Mon–Fri 11:30am–3pm and 5–10pm; Sat 5–10pm.

LOWERTOWN & BYWARD MARKET AREA
EXPENSIVE

Black Cat Café *FUSION* News flash! Dining is fun again. Not a lot was invested in the decor of this two-room (plus terrace) storefront—wooden tables, some geometric patterns painted on the walls—but once the inventive food starts coming, you won't even notice or care. The chefs' new take on gazpacho one night, for instance, consisted of milk, almonds, and cut green grapes served in a tumbler—not a tomato in sight. Soup-sandwich-and-fries here might turn out to be a cup of lobster bisque, melted mascarpone between baguette croutons, and frites with five garnishes. Even the usual main courses take a couple of sidesteps from the norm, as with a beef tenderloin studded with olives or pistachios dressed with a scallion and juniper marmalade. Service is casual, and the waitstaff describe the novel preparations in as much detail as you need to figure out what's up. A bonus: There's a sign between the men's and women's restrooms declaring use is limited to 5 minutes. Find out why.

93 Murray St. (east of Parent Ave.) (C) 613/241-2999. Reservations recommended. Main courses C$21–C$34 (US$21–US$34/£11–£17). MC, V. Tues–Sat 5:30–10pm; Sun–Mon 5:30–9pm.

E18hteen *INTERNATIONAL* That's the way the management chooses to spell this chic restaurant's name. It's as consciously chic as it can be, with many mirrored surfaces, much chrome, and contemporary paintings of varying interest. Tall vases of lilies stand on glowing cubes beneath Italianate track lighting. Literary and design affectations aside, there's interesting and experimental food to sample here; black cod is painted with honey and ginger; a piece of seared Québec foie gras comes with caramelized pineapple, port sauce, and Szechwan peppercorns; oven-roasted ostrich (yes, ostrich) is served with enoki mushrooms and a cherry *gastrique;* the rib-eye comes with house-made barbecue sauce; and a butter-poached Nova Scotia lobster tail is paired with a beef tenderloin, tomato jam, and veal *jus.* Chef Matthew Carmichael is steadily improving things here, and DJs work hard each Friday and Saturday night spinning acid jazz and retro soul tunes in case you're just coming for drinks, the cool factor, and to see (and be part of) a scene.

18 York St. (near ByWard Market). ⓒ 613/244-1188. www.restaurant18.com. Reservations recommended. Main courses C$28–C$45 (US$28–US$45/£14–£23). Bar daily from 3:30pm; dinner daily 5–11:30pm.

MODERATE

Bistro 115 ⟨ FRENCH/ITALIAN   I'm not sure why this casual bistro (in a heritage house quietly set away from the most frenetic streets of ByWard Market) is called "115," because its address is no. 110. But I quibble. Lace tablecloths and a fireplace are inviting in winter, while the patio with its fountain, maple tree, and roof of trellised grapevines is an echo of sun-splashed Provence with a dash of Vermont thrown in for good measure. The seasonal menu changes weekly, but entrees usually include dependable main courses such as steak, *osso buco,* wine-steamed mussels, crispy duck leg confit, filet of salmon, cioppino, or grilled pork tenderloin. The weekend brunch is also a treat, but the very best deal of all is the weekday table d'hôte lunch, about C$17 (US$17/£8.50) for three courses. More than a dozen wines are available by the glass and half bottle here, as well.

110 Murray St. (east of Dalhousie St.). ⓒ 613/562-7244. Reservations recommended. Main courses C$11–C$16 (US$11–US$16/£5.50–£8) lunch, C$17–C$24 (US$17–US$24/£8.50–£12) dinner. AE, MC, V. Kitchen daily 11:30am–2pm and 5–9pm; lounge daily 11:30am–10pm.

The Black Thorn MEDITERRANEAN   This converted 19th-century brick house draws crowds to its fenced-in sidewalk terrace, a covered terrace in back with a courtyard fountain, and a small main dining room centered around an impressive mahogany bar. Hard to believe this used to be the workshop of a carriage maker, but it was. Today the kitchen turns out moderately creative food that includes healthy pizzas from a wood-burning oven (including versions with pepper, onion, pesto, or chicken toppings); tangerine-glazed chicken; salmon wrapped in pancetta; a grilled tenderloin with gorgonzola butter; and seafood linguini. There are a number of vegetarian dishes to choose from, as well, and a prix-fixe menu.

15 Clarence St. (west of Parent St.). ⓒ 613/241-0712. Reservations not accepted. Pizzas and other dishes C$13–C$29 (US$13–US$29/£6.50–£15). AE, MC, V. Sun–Tues 11am–midnight; Wed–Sat 11am–2am. Kitchen closes at 11pm daily.

Empire Grill ⟨ ECLECTIC   It doesn't attract the late-night restaurant chefs and staffers as it once did, but this popular New York–ish bistro/bar/club remains a desirable stop. The martinis are dry, the company congenial, the food piquant and mildly venturesome. You might find duck quesadillas or bruschetta for starters, then segue to the likes of Thai chicken curry, a duck breast dusted with cocoa, or Southwestern chicken and chipotle pasta with roasted vegetables. The bar, in a question-mark shape that encourages conversation, is ringed with tables, augmented with a warm-weather dining deck. Customers range from those barely over drinking age to well past retirement with no apparent social unease. A DJ works the turntables after late dinner, and they have live jazz Sundays 6 to 10pm.

47 Clarence St. (at Parent St.). ⓒ 613/241-1343. Reservations recommended in evening. Main courses C$14–C$32 (US$14–US$32/£7–£16). AE, DC, MC, V. Mon–Sat 11am–1:45am; Sun 11am–1am.

The Fish Market ⭐ *Finds* SEAFOOD   A market, a loft, a candlelit cellar, a private dining experience? Yes, yes, yes, and yes. In an 1875 heritage building on a prominent ByWard Market corner is this sprawling fish restaurant: The casual, inexpensive upstairs cafe Coasters stays open through the afternoon and offers pastas, pizzas, and fish and chips, while the basement tavern Vineyards features boutique wines and microbrews and live jazz. The main Fish Market dining room is enclosed by rough wood and brick, with nautical trappings and old advertising signs. Fish cooked without artifice is the most satisfying thing here, not to mention fastest out of the kitchen; the dauntingly large menu includes just about every marine creature available at the city docks on a given day, cooked to your preference. One platter incorporates a half lobster, Alaskan crab legs, two jumbo tiger shrimp, a smoked salmon filet, sea scallops, crabmeat-stuffed mushroom caps, onion rings, and rice pilaf. Yikes. Or fetch an order of all-you-can-eat mussels. They're proud of their wine list, too—the Alsatian Rieslings go well with many of these dishes.

54 York St. (at Byward St.). ℂ **613/241-3474.** Reservations not accepted. Main courses C$12–C$33 (US$12–US$33/£6–£17). AE, DC, MC, V. Mon–Fri 11:30am–2pm and 4:30–10pm; Sat 11:30am–2:30pm and 4:30–11pm; Sun 11:30am–3pm and 4:30–11pm.

Kinki ⭐⭐ SUSHI/ASIAN FUSION   Kinki features tables outside and inside, and sushi and cocktail bars in the back, and all of them are full most of the time. Just when the whole sushi phenomenon was starting to look a little tired, along come innovators like this to punch it up and make it actually seem sexy. The fish and associated cuisine here is fresh and sprightly; just check the sushi, maki, and nigiri portion of the menu, where diners get a chance to sample a wider range of tastes and combinations. Most come in two to four pieces, as does *maguro* (tuna) sashimi encrusted in spices. *Unakyu* (freshwater eel) is wrapped in rice with a cucumber dice, sweetish sauce, and sesame seeds. Non-sushi dishes are equally enticing—they might include grilled salmon with Thai red-curry sauce, spicy chicken with basil and green chile, or mango-dusted scallops. Sit at the bar, and if you seem sympathetic to the vibe, one of the sushi chefs may add a little something extra for you. DJs provide pumping background music most nights, too, to keep the mood ultrahip.

41 York St. (near Byward St.). ℂ **613/789-7559.** Reservations recommended. Main courses C$14–C$19 (US$14–US$19/£7–£9.50). AE, MC, V. Sun–Wed noon–1am; Thurs–Sat noon–2am.

Métropolitain Brasserie ⭐⭐ FRENCH BISTRO/SEAFOOD   This simulated brasserie is the latest undertaking of the same partners who have created a number of successful dining experiences around town, including the Empire Grill (see above). Not far from the big U.S. Embassy, this place deploys lavish amounts of tile and marble and pressed-tin ceiling panels, effectively evocative—but also surfaces that contribute to a high noise volume. Luckily that happy burble is due to happy diners and infectiously cheerful staff. While jollying the customers up, they transmit orders to the kitchen via PDAs; there are two bars in the two main rooms, one devoted to oysters and a bounteous *plateau de fruits de mer*—a tiered seafood platter of the sort that has already swept Manhattan by storm. They claim this is the city's largest raw bar, and I believe them. Well-executed bistro reliables on the card have included an earthy mushroom soup with chives and truffle oil, a crispy duck confit of two duck legs and frites cooked in duck fat, and "Grownup Mac and Cheese" using smoked bacon and Emmenthal. In the Parisian tradition, the brasserie is open from early morning until very late at night—late for Ottawa, anyway. It's located on the ground floor of a newish office building next to the Château Laurier.

700 Sussex Dr. (at Rideau St.) ℭ 613/562-1160. Reservations recommended. Main courses C$17–C$33 (US$17–US$33/£8.50–£17). AE, MC, V. Daily 8am–midnight.

Social 🏵 ECLECTIC/CANADIAN   Popular almost as soon as it opened, the tables in front, the striped half-moon banquettes in the rear, and the courtyard out back are fully occupied nightly at Social. New Brunswick native chef Stephen Mitton's philosophy is to incorporate elements from across the breadth of his wide country. Antipasto platters are fun, followed up by chargrilled Alberta steaks or lamb, B.C. halibut, and the like. A solid selection of reasonably priced wines is available by glass or bottle, including a number of Canadian selections, and given the youngish crowd it's also not surprising to find a DJ spinning subdued house and hip-hop at the black marble bar, nor jazz duets and trios playing during the week.

537 Sussex Dr. ℭ 613/789-7355. Reservations recommended. Main courses C$21–C$30 (US$21–US$30/£11–£15). AE, MC, V. Sun–Wed 11:45am–midnight; Thurs–Sat 11:45am–2am.

INEXPENSIVE

Café Shafali INDIAN   Less extravagant than many of its ethnic cousins around town, this shade of the ByWard Market culinary spectrum concentrates on what it puts on its tray (a tray that might resemble the one you brought through an elementary school cafeteria line). Butter chicken gets raves: The meat is cubed, roasted in a tandoor oven, then cooked with spices and garnished with almonds; the result is mild but flavorful. Vindaloos, on the other hand, made with vegetables, chicken, beef, lamb, or seafood, are as fiery with red-hot chiles as you'd expect. There isn't much to surprise regular fans of Indian food, but the preparation and service of the samosas, shrimp tikka, lamb masala, and so forth are more than competent; they'll even tell you what to expect—sweet, sour, hot, or medium spicy—before it hits the table. Lunch specials here are amazingly cost-effective, a range of combo platters lets you try multiple offers, and the house lassi (a mango-yogurt drink) is a good quaff while you leaf through the menu . . . as well as an effective fire extinguisher.

308 Dalhousie St. (between Clarence and York sts.) ℭ 613/789-9188. Reservations recommended on weekends. Main courses C$10–C$16 (US$10–US$16/£5–£8). Tues–Sat 11:30am–2:30pm and 5:30–10pm; Sun–Mon 6–10pm.

Memories BISTRO   Next door to the Black Thorn (see above), this popular cafe with sidewalk tables under an awning offers a menu of snacks and (mostly light) meals. The fixed-price lunch is composed of soup or salad plus a main course such as a Malaysian lamb curry. Ham-and-cheese sandwiches come with marinated mushrooms and Dijon mustard on a croissant, and there are salads, pita pizzas, soups, pâtés, and pastas. Weekend brunch brings the usual pastries, quiche, and eggs, as well as waffles with a choice of fruit toppings.

7 Clarence St. (east of Sussex St.). ℭ 613/241-1882. Reservations not accepted. Main courses C$9–C$13 (US$9–US$13/£4.50–£6.50). AE, MC, V. Sun–Mon 11am–11pm; Tues–Fri 11am–midnight; Sat 11am–1am.

GATINEAU & GATINEAU HILLS
VERY EXPENSIVE

La Baccara 🏵🏵🏵 FRENCH/CANADIAN FUSION   Few restaurants in eastern Canada can match the food or prices at La Baccara, which is tucked into a quiet corner on the third floor of the newish Casino du Lac-Leamy just outside Ottawa proper. This is your splurge night, if you're coming to Ottawa to do the town large. It has all the requisites: the harpist, views of the lake and the city skyline, upholstered armchairs, gold-velvet drapes, and a superbly professional staff bringing wonderful food from an open kitchen. And chef Serge Rourre's (formerly of the Ritz-Carlton in Montréal) menu more than delivers.

You'll find anything from Japanese-style beef tenderloin tataki (done French style, of course) to roasted milk-fed Québec piglet with maple and a tart chutney, from a rack of caribou in a crushed nut–and–juniper berry crust with wine-steeped figs in filo, to roasted lobster and scallops over pasta and cognac sauce; that's just a sampling. Desserts are nicely subtle here, with flavorings of berry, fruit, liqueur, and spice, rather than being overly heavy or sweet. The enormously knowledgeable sommelier will be happy to suggest a glass for every course from the 13,000-bottle cellar. If your bank balance and appetite move you, order from one of three prix-fixe menus, including an eight-course *menu gastronomique* which must be ordered by the entire table, but is sensational. Men must wear jackets, and women will want to wear their finest, too. This is a special place.

In the Casino du Lac-Leamy, Gatineau. © 819/772-6210. Reservations required. Main courses C$39–C$58 (US$39–US$58/£20–£29); prix-fixe menus C$60–C$115 (US$60–US$115/£30–£58). AE, DC, DISC, MC, V. Daily 5:30–11pm.

EXPENSIVE

Les Fougères ✶✶✶ NEW CANADIAN   This farmhouse restaurant fully justifies the 15-minute drive out into the country from downtown Ottawa; it might be creeping up into the ranks of one of the best in eastern Canada. A gourmet shop is attached to the restaurant, which has both inside rooms and a screened porch running around the back and side; gardens of herbs, vegetables, and edible flowers surround the property, some of which appear in dishes. Weekend brunches are understandably popular here, when twists on old Québec favorites appear such as a *tourtière* (meat pie) of duck and maple syrup or one of lamb, red pepper, and goat cheese. Other lunch items stress egg dishes and lovely salads.

But the kitchen gets truly serious at dinner—starting with soft-shell crabs or smoked venison, and moving on to grilled bison steaks with a sour cherry, horseradish, and port sauce and Yorkshire pudding; Baffin Island arctic char with organic prosciutto; a seafood curry with coconut fritters and chutney; broiled boar with mustard sauce and apples; or a *pot-au-feu* of local grain-fed chicken with lemon, caramelized onions, thyme, and soft Warwick cheese with vegetable ashes from Québec . . . all served over truffled fresh pasta made with Ontarian eggs. Finish with a dessert such as an apple tart with maple-syrup ice cream, a hazelnut dacquoise, a fig–pine nut cake seasoned with rosemary and served with Gorgonzola, chocolate-truffle tarts with crème fraîche and cassis compote, or a chocolate terrine with wine-poached plums. The wine list is well chosen, as well. In fact, all of it is amazing.

783 Rte. 105, Chelsea (at Scott). © 819/827-8942. Reservations recommended. Main courses C$11–C$25 (US$11–US$25/£5.50–£13) lunch, C$27–C$34 (US$27–US$34/£14–£17) dinner. AE, DISC, DC, MC, V. Mon–Fri 11am–9:30pm; Sat–Sun 10am–9:30pm.

Le Tartuffe ✶✶ FRENCH   It's almost a shock to find this nearly hidden town house restaurant near the Museum of Civilization, both for its out-of-the-way location and its inspired kitchen. The two dining rooms' capacity is doubled in summer by the addition of more tables on a shaded outdoors terrace; choices on the lunch and dinner fixed-price menus are unusually generous in both number and composition, and often employ Canadian meat, fish, and fowl. Lunch might take in seared veal liver or grilled leg of lamb; dinner's main courses could be pan-fried walleye tournedos with tapenade, a roasted chicken in cherry-cocoa sauce, boneless rabbit saddle, a grilled filet of Alberta beef with bordelaise sauce, or crusted pan-fried sweetbreads from Québec.

The service is genial and attentive. You can also order a la carte at lunch, though not at dinner. The restaurant is 2 blocks west of the museum on Laurier Street; turn right on rue Papineau, continuing to the corner of Notre-Dame de L'Ile.

133 rue Notre-Dame de L'Ile (at rue Papineau), Gatineau. ℂ **819/776-6424**. Reservations recommended. Prix-fixe lunch C$17–C$20 (US$17–US$20/£8.50–£10), dinner C$32–C$39 (US$32–US$39/£16–£20). AE, DC, MC, V. Mon–Fri 11:30am–2pm and 5:30–10pm; Sat 5:30–10pm.

4 Seeing the Sights

Most of Ottawa's major sights are clustered downtown, so it's not difficult to walk from one to another. But if you prefer **seeing the city by boat**—and the river, with the tableau of Parliament Hill above it, is surprisingly beautiful viewed this way—check out cruise-tour options which use the local waterways as "highways."

From May to October, **Paul's Boat Lines** (ℂ **613/225-6781** or 613/235-8409; www.paulsboatcruises.com)—no relation—offers two cruises. One begins from the marina in Gatineau (beside the Museum of Civilization) and proceeds along the Ottawa River, picking up additional passengers at the Ottawa Locks (located between Parliament Hill and The Fairmont Chateau Laurier hotel) 30 minutes later, continuing past all the major sights. It runs three to four times daily and lasts about 1½ hr. The other tour cruises the Rideau Canal, leaving from docks opposite the Arts Centre and proceeding down to the Experimental Farm and Carleton University and back; this tour operates five to seven times daily, and lasts about an hour and a quarter. The river trip costs C$18 (US$18/£9) for adults, C$16 (US$16/£8) for seniors and students, and C$9 (US$9/£4.50) for children age 5 to 15; discounts for families are available. The canal cruise costs C$16 (US$16/£8) for adults, C$14 (US$14/£7) for seniors and students, and C$9 (US$9/£4.50) for children.

An intriguing variation of this (that kids often love) is offered in an "amphi-bus" operated by **Lady Dive** (ℂ **613/223-6211** or 613/524-2221; www.amphibus.com). A covered, boat-shaped red vehicle lumbers around the major land-based sights of town, then eases into the river and continues cruising past the key waterside attractions. Find the bus (er, amphi-bus) at the corner of Sparks and Elgin Streets. It leaves on the 1-hour tours daily from May to mid-November from around 10:30am to 9pm in summer, with fewer departures in spring and fall (always call ahead to be sure). Fares for the ride are steep, about C$28 (US$28/£14) for adults, C$25 (US$25/£13) for seniors and students, C$19 (US$19/£9.50) for children ages 6 to 12, and C$9.50 (US$9.50/£4.75) for children ages 1 to 5, not including tax. Lady Dive also operates trolley and double-decker bus tours of the capital.

THE TOP ATTRACTIONS

Beyond the attractions described below, guided indoor tours of the Centre Block are offered on a daily schedule that varies throughout the year, while guided tours of the East Block are offered daily in July and August. Make reservations at the **Info-Tent** on Parliament Hill lawn behind the West Block. It's open from mid-May to Labour Day and distributes *Discover the Hill,* a free outdoor self-guiding booklet. Also check out the website **www.parliamenthill.gc.ca** to find out what's going on on "the Hill," and what sorts of tours are available.

PARLIAMENT HILL ✦✦✦

With their steeply pitched copper roofs, dormers, and towers, the buildings of Canada's Parliament are quite impressive, especially on first sighting from the river or road. In 1860, Prince Edward (later Edward VII) laid the cornerstone for these structures, which were finished in time to host the inaugural session of the first Parliament of the (then brand-new) Dominion of Canada in 1867. Entering through the south gate off Wellington Street, you pass the **Centennial Flame,** lit by Canadian Prime Minister Lester Pearson on New Year's Eve 1966 to mark the passing of 100 years since that historic event. On September 14, 2001, more than 100,000 visitors gathered on this same broad lawn in a day of remembrance after the terrorist attacks against the United States 3 days earlier.

THE BUILDINGS   Parliament is composed of three expansive structures—the **Centre Block,** straight ahead, and the flanking **West Block** and **East Block.** They form the core of Canadian political life, containing as they do both the House of Commons and the Senate. Sessions of the **House of Commons** can be observed as the 295 elected members debate in the handsome green chamber with the tall stained-glass windows. Parliament is usually in recess from late June to early September (and occasionally also out of session the rest of the year, including the Easter and Christmas holidays). Otherwise, the House normally sits on Mondays from 11am to 6:30pm, Tuesdays and Thursdays from 10am to 6:30pm, Wednesdays from 2 to 8pm, and Fridays from 10am to 4pm. The 104 appointed members of the **Senate** sit in an opulent red chamber with murals depicting Canadians fighting in World War I.

The imposing 92m (302-ft.) campanile dominating the Centre Block's facade is the **Peace Tower.** It houses a 53-bell carillon, a huge clock, an observation deck, and the Memorial Chamber, commemorating Canada's war dead—most notably the 66,650 who lost their lives in World War I. Stones from the deadliest battlefields are lodged in the chamber's walls and floors. Atop the tower is an 11m (36-ft.) bronze mast flying a Canadian flag. When Parliament is in session, this tower is lit. Going up the tower, most visitors notice something strange about the elevator: For the first 30m (98 ft.) of the journey it actually climbs at a 10-degree angle rather than straight up.

A 1916 fire destroyed the original Centre Block; only the Library at the rear was saved. A glorious 16-sided dome, supported outside by flying buttresses and paneled inside with Canadian white pine, features a marble statue of the young Queen Victoria and splendid carvings—gorgons, crests, masks, and hundreds of rosettes. The West Block, containing parliamentary offices, is closed to the public, but the East Block can be visited; it houses the offices of prime ministers, governors-general, and the Privy Council. Four historic rooms are on view: the original governor-general's office, restored to the period of Lord Dufferin (1872–78); the offices of Sir John A. Macdonald and Sir Georges-Etienne Cartier (the principal Fathers of Confederation); and the Privy Council Chamber, with its anteroom.

The grounds around the Centre Block are dotted with statues honoring such prominent figures as Queen Victoria, Sir Georges-Etienne Cartier, William Lyon Mackenzie King, and Sir Wilfrid Laurier. Behind the building is a promenade with sweeping views of the river. Here, too, is the old Centre Block's bell, which crashed to the ground shortly after tolling midnight on the eve of the 1916 fire. At the bottom of the cliff behind Parliament (accessible from the entrance locks on the Rideau Canal), a pleasant path leads along the Ottawa River.

CHANGING OF THE GUARD (Kids)   From late June to late August, a colorful half-hour ceremony is held each morning on the Parliament Hill lawn, weather permitting. Two historic regiments—the Governor-General's Foot Guards and the Canadian Grenadier Guards—compose the Ceremonial Guard. The parade of 125 soldiers in

Tips **You Say Reed-O, I Say Re-Dough . . .**

The main canal, shopping center, and waterfalls in Ottawa are all called Rideau. So is the province's main hiking trail. So who was this heroic, mysterious Rideau whose name has spread so far and wide? Some mustachioed horseback rider in black, who robbed from the rich and gave to the poor? Er, not quite. The name means "curtains" in French," and the explorer Samuel de Champlain first seems to have used the word to name the Rideau Falls that plunge around Green Island right in the heart of the capital city. Hmmm. Come to think of it, they *do* look like curtains. Now for the hard part: how do you say that? There's some debate, but one thing's for sure: don't ever say "Ride-O". That's *not* how you say it. French speakers (e.g., those with an 819 area code), tend to say "Re-DOUGH," treading lightly on the first syllable, which is more correct. Anglo speakers, on the other hand, tend to stress the first syllable a bit more, like "REED-oh." It's all good.

busbies and scarlet jackets assembles at Cartier Square Drill Hall (by the canal at Laurier Ave.) at 9:30am, then marches up Elgin Street to reach the hill at 10am. On arrival on the hill, the Ceremonial Guard splits, one division of the old guard positioned on the west side of the Parliament Hill lawn and two divisions of the new guard, or "duties," on the east side. Inspection of dress and weapons follows. The colors are then marched before the troops and saluted, the guards presenting arms. Throughout, sergeant-majors bellow unintelligible commands that prompt the synchronized stomp and clatter of boots and weapons. Finally, the outgoing guard commander gives the key to the guard room to the incoming commander, signifying the end of the process. The relieved unit marches back down Wellington Street to the beat of their drums and to the skirl of bagpipes.

SOUND & LIGHT SHOW   For years Canada's history has unfolded in a dazzling free half-hour display of sound and light against the dramatic backdrop of the Parliament buildings. From early July to early September, weather permitting, two performances are given each night, the early one in English, the later in French. There's bleacher seating for the free show. For details, contact the **National Capital Commission** at ② **800/465-1867** or 613/239-5000, or visit www.canadascapital.gc.ca. The commission also maintains an information kiosk at 90 Wellington St., across from Parliament Hill.

MORE MUST-SEES
Canada Aviation Museum 🏵🏵 *Kids*   This collection of more than 100 aircraft is one of the best of its kind in the world. In the main exhibit hall, a "Walkway of Time" traces aviation history from the start of the 20th century through the two world wars to the present. All the planes are either the real thing or full-size replicas, starting with the Silver Dart, a biplane built by a consortium headed by Alexander Graham Bell. It took off from the ice of Baddeck Bay, Nova Scotia, in February 1909, Canada's first powered flight. It flew for 9 minutes—not bad, considering it looks as though it were built out of bicycle parts and kites. The other sections are concerned with specific uses, including the amphibious craft of bush pilots (which are still critical for servicing

roadless areas of Canada) and the development of commercial, military, and naval aircraft from World War I through to the present jet age. Some examples are partially stripped of their outer skins to reveal their construction, and there are cockpit mock-ups with videos simulating takeoffs—a hit with kids.

11 Aviation Pkwy. at Rockcliffe Airport. © 613/993-2010. www.aviation.nmstc.ca. Admission C$6 (US$6/£3) adults, C$5 (US$5/£2.50) seniors and students, C$3 (US$3/£1.50) children 4–15, free for children under 4; free to all visitors after 4pm. May to Labour Day daily 9am–5pm (to 9pm Thurs); rest of the year Wed–Sun 10am–5pm (to 9pm Thurs). From Sussex Dr., take Rockcliffe Pkwy. and exit at the National Aviation Museum.

Canadian Museum of Civilization ★★★ (Kids)

Canadian Native architect Douglas Cardinal designed this visually arresting museum rising from the banks of the Ottawa River as though its curvilinear forms had been sculpted by wind, water, and glacier. It's Canada's most popular museum (by attendance), and deservedly so. The exhibits within tell the entire history of Canada, beginning with the **Grand Hall,** the high windows of which provide fine views of the skyline. Devoted to the "First Nations"—in this case, Native Canadian peoples of the west coast—the hall features a collection of huge totem poles and facades representing lodges. Behind these are small galleries of utensils, tools, weavings, and other artifacts. From there, take escalators to the third floor and its **Canada Hall.** Laid out in chronological order is the history of a nation from the arrival of Vikings. There are highly effective tableaux of shipboard life through the whaling period, too, with human-size models, moving images, and recorded shrieks of gulls and creaks of hawsers.

Replications of fortified settlements of 18th-century New France follow, on through the military past to the rise of cities, including a walk along an early-1900s street. On the second floor are a **Children's Museum** and a **Postal Museum,** but the principal attraction is the **CINEPLUS** theater, consisting of an IMAX screen and an OMNIMAX (dome-shaped) screen to propel viewers giddily into the action. There are a cafeteria and a restaurant, **Café du Musée** (© 819/776-7009) here, as well.

100 Laurier St., Gatineau. © 819/776-7000. www.civilization.ca. Admission C$10 (US$10/£5) adults, C$8 (US$8/£4) seniors and students, C$6 (US$6/£3) children 3–12, C$25 (US$25/£13) families. Free to all Thurs 4–9pm. Tickets to CINE-PLUS extra; combination museum and CINEPLUS tickets available. May–June daily 9am–6pm; July–Aug Sat–Wed 9am–6pm, Thurs–Fri 9am–9pm; Sept Fri–Wed 9am–6pm, Thurs 9am–9pm; Oct–Apr Tues–Sun 9am–5pm, Thurs till 9pm.

Canadian War Museum

There has been a war museum in the capital since 1880, in various places around town; this is the newest and grandest, opened in 2005. (You can buy a combination ticket to also enter the fine Canadian Museum of Civilization; see above). With intentional irony, it was designed by architect Raymond Moriyama, who was one of more than 20,000 Japanese-Canadians interned during World War II; the museum, occupying a windswept rise to the west of Parliament Hill, a bleak setting made even more so by the mausoleum-like sobriety of Moriyama's design. There is little drum beating here, which is a good thing, but it's also visually less compelling than the previous incarnation. Canada's long, often tragic military history is treated with respect yet never jingoism or glorification of combat in displays of uniforms, military equipment, and antique and modern weaponry. The exhibits begin from, well, the beginning: skirmishes within Native Canadian groups, their battles with early French and British explorers, and so on chronologically through the South African and world wars and the Cold War and its conflicts. The exhibits conclude with a depiction of the Canadian military's more recent role in peacekeeping missions.

1 Vimy Place. © 819/776-8600. www.warmuseum.ca. Admission C$10 (US$10/£5) adults, C$8 (US$8/£4) seniors and students, C$6 (US$6/£3) children 3–12, C$25 (US$25/£13) families. Combination tickets with Canadian Museum

of Civilization and CINEPLUS theaters available. Parking on-site C$1.75–C$10 (US$1.75–US$10/90p–£5). May–June daily 9am–6pm; July–Aug Sat–Wed 9am–6pm, Thurs–Fri 9am–9pm; Sept Fri–Wed 9am–6pm, Thurs till 9pm; Oct–Apr Tues–Sun 9am–5pm, Thurs 9am–9pm.

National Gallery of Canada 𝔾𝔾𝔾   Architect Moshe Safdie, famed for his Habitat apartment block and Musée des Beaux-Arts in Montréal, designed a rose-granite crystal palace that gleams from its promontory overlooking the Ottawa River. A dramatic long glass concourse leads to the Grand Hall, commanding glorious views of Parliament Hill. Natural light also fills the galleries, thanks to ingeniously designed shafts with reflective panels. The museum displays about 800 examples of Canadian art, just a sliver of the 10,000 or so works held in its permanent collection; one recommended way to take it all in is to go to the second floor and proceed down and counterclockwise. Among many highlights are Benjamin West's famous 1770 painting of General Wolfe's death at Québec; the fabulous Rideau Convent Chapel (1888), a rhapsody of wooden fan vaulting, cast-iron columns, and intricate carving created by architect/priest Georges Bouillon; the works of early Québécois artists such as Antoine Plamondon, Abbé Jean Guyon, and Frère Luc; Tom Thomson and the Group of Seven landscapists; and the Montréal Automatistes Paul-Emile Borduas and Jean-Paul Riopelle. The European masters are also represented, from Corot and Turner to Chagall and Picasso, and contemporary galleries feature pop art and minimalism, plus later abstract works, both Canadian and American.

Pause for a contemplative moment on the balcony of the central atrium looking down on a garden of triangular flower beds and a grove of trees that repeat the lines of the pyramidal glass roof. Each year, three or four major traveling exhibits are displayed, showcasing works by the likes of da Vinci, Michelangelo, and van Gogh. Other facilities here include two restaurants, a gift shop/bookstore, and an auditorium.

380 Sussex Dr. (at St. Patrick St.). 𝒞 613/990-1985. http://national.gallery.ca. Permanent collection C$6 (US$6/£3) adults, C$5 (US$5/£2.50) seniors and students, C$3 (US$3/£1.50) ages 12–19, C$12 (US$12/£6) family. Admission to special exhibitions extra; advance purchase recommended. May–Sept daily 10am–5pm (to 8pm Thurs); Oct–Apr Tue–Sun 10am–5pm (to 8pm Thurs). Guided tours daily at 2pm (Wed–Sun at 2pm in off season); register at information desk. Closed major holidays.

ADDITIONAL ATTRACTIONS

Billings Estate Museum   This imposing manse allows you to peer into the social life of the period running from 1829—when Braddish Billings, head of one of Ottawa's founding families, oversaw its construction—all the way up through to the 1970s, when the home was converted into a museum. Visitors can use the picnic area and stroll the 3-hectare (8-acre) grounds, an experience heightened when tea and scones are served on the lawn in summer up to 3 days a week (call ahead for current details of serving dates and times).

2100 Cabot St. 𝒞 613/247-4830. Admission C$4 (US$4/£2) adults, C$3.50 (US$3.50/£1.75) seniors, C$2.50 (US$2.50/£1.25) youth, C$11 (US$11/£5.50) family. Mid-May to Oct Wed–Sun noon–5pm. Go south on Bank St., cross the Rideau River at Billings Bridge and take Riverside East; turn right on Pleasant Park and right on Cabot.

Bytown Museum   Housed in Ottawa's oldest stone building (dating from 1827), this once served as the Commissariat for food and material during construction of the Rideau Canal; today, it displays the possessions of one Lieutenant-Colonel John By, the canal's builder and one of the early Ottawa's most influential citizens. Additional artifacts reflect the social history of the pioneer era of Bytown/Ottawa in three period rooms and a number of changing exhibits: In 2006, the museum featured the life and assassination of Confederation hero and original Parliamentarian Thomas D'Arcy McGee, including the first public showing of the revolver used to do the deed. The museum is beside the Ottawa Locks, between Parliament Hill and The Fairmont Château Laurier hotel.

540 Wellington St. (at Commissioner St.). (C) **613/234-4570.** www.bytownmuseum.com. Admission C$5 (US$5/£2.50) adults, C$3 (US$3/£1.50) seniors and students, C$1.50 (US$1.50/75p) children, C$12 (US$12/£6) families; Wed 5–8pm admission by donation. Apr to mid-May and Oct–Nov Mon–Fri 10am–2pm; mid-May to Sept daily 10am–5pm (late June to late Aug Wed to 8pm).

ByWard Market 🌟🌟🌟   This traditional farmers' market, established in 1826 by the ubiquitous John By (see the Bytown Museum, above), is one of Canada's oldest and largest public markets; By laid out George and York streets especially widely, so as to accommodate merchants bringing in their wares and create open space for public congregation. The market's vendors sell every manner of foods, plants, flowers, and produce around a central building housing two additional floors of ware and craft boutiques. During the summer, you can also snack at some 70 indoor and outdoor stand-up counters and cafes; watch a slice of the city's life go "By" over a beer or a glass of wine. The surrounding neighborhood is a mix of rehabilitated 19th-century brick buildings and contemporary structures, where street performers and balloon artists provide mild diversion—although someone seems to have rounded up and driven out the mimes (quietly, of course) who previously worked the crowds here. If you're simply trolling through for picnic items, ByWard Market Street is a good quick stop.

Area bounded by Sussex, Rideau, St. Patrick, and King Edward sts. (C) **613/562-3325.** www.byward-market.com. Individual shop and vendor hours vary; generally speaking, Mon–Sat 10am–6pm or 7pm, Sun 10am–5pm.

Canada Science and Technology Museum 🌟🌟 *Kids*   This hands-on science museum is pretty good—and science-minded kids will probably think it's off the charts. Interactive displays encourage visitor participation in demonstrations of such physical principles as viscosity, or to climb aboard a steam locomotive, launch a rocket from a mini–control room, observe the heavens in the evening through Canada's largest refracting telescope, watch chicks hatching, or walk through a Crazy Kitchen where everything seems normal—but the floor is tilted at a sharp angle. The permanent exhibits deal with Canada in space, land and marine transportation, communications, and all kinds of modern industrial and household technology, while temporary and traveling shows focus in on some aspect of science or technology history, such as a history of bicycles or food safety. An adjacent outdoor technology park features machines and devices from the windmill and lighthouse to radar and rocket. A popular new Virtual Voyage ride simulates two wild rides through outer space, using high-tech displays and special six-person pods that feel like they're flying right through the action on screen. These rides cost a bit extra, but are a thrill a minute.

1867 St. Laurent Blvd. (at Lancaster Rd.). (C) **866/442-4416** or 613/991-3044. www.science-tech.nmstc.ca. Admission C$6 (US$6/£3) adults, C$5 (US$5/£2.50) seniors and students, C$3 (US$3/£1.50) ages 4–14, C$14 (US$14/£7) family. Extra charge for Virtual Voyage space simulation attractions. May to Labour Day daily 9am–5pm; rest of the year Tues–Sun 9am–5pm. Appointments needed to enter observatory.

Canadian Museum of Nature 🌟 *Kids*   Seven permanent exhibit halls here trace the history of life on Earth, from its theoretical beginnings some 4,200 million years ago. A third-floor dinosaur hall is a popular highlight, with fossils, skulls, and the intact skeleton of a mastodon; an opposite gallery holds a variety of snails, bugs, spiders, and other creepy critters—some of them still alive. Down one floor are mineral

Finds A Scenic Drive

If you have brought a car to Ottawa or rented one after arrival, here's one picturesque way to see the town—I recommend that one co-pilot *reads* these directions aloud, while the other one does the actual driving. Don't try to do both at the same time. Begin by driving east along Wellington Street, past Parliament Hill and through Confederation Square. Pass the Château Laurier hotel (on your left), then turn left (north) onto Sussex Drive. Just after passing the imposing **American Embassy,** glorious views open up to your left over the river islands.

Proceed along Sussex Drive to St. Patrick Street, turning left into **Nepean Point Park.** Here, you share a fine river view with the park's statue of explorer Samuel de Champlain. Across the road is **Major's Hill Park,** between the Château Laurier and the National Gallery, where a noonday gun is fired off daily (though at 10am on Sun, to avoid disturbing church services). Return to Sussex Drive, continuing in the same direction. Just beyond the Macdonald-Cartier Bridge stands **Earnscliffe,** once the home of Sir John A. Macdonald (who was the first prime minister of the Dominion of Canada) and now the residence of the British high commissioner.

Farther along, Sussex Drive crosses the Rideau River, passing the contemporary **Ottawa City Hall** in the middle of Green Island near the Rideau Falls to your left. The parkway proceeds past the prime minister's house, shielded by trees at 24 Sussex Dr., and on to **Rideau Hall,** at no. 1, also known as Government House. It's the governor-general's residence. On the 35-hectare (86-acre) grounds here are scores of ceremonial trees planted by visiting dignitaries and heads of state, from Queen Victoria to John F. Kennedy, Richard Nixon, and Princess Diana. They're identified by nameplates at the bases of the trees. In summer, a brief changing-of-the-guard ceremony is held at noon at the main gate. Tours of the grounds and the interior public rooms are conducted daily in July and August and on weekends the rest of the year. For information, stop in at the **Visitor Centre,** open daily from around 9:30am to 5:30pm, or call (C) **613/991-4422.**

Continuing, the drive becomes **Rockliffe Driveway,** a beautiful route along the Ottawa River and through **Rockcliffe Park.** Where the road splits in the park, follow the right fork to Acacia Avenue to reach the **Rockeries,** where April blossoms herald the spring. If you wish, continue on Rockliffe Driveway to reach the **Canada Aviation Museum** (p. 344). Or simply continue on Acacia, which doubles back and connects once again with the Driveway, leading you right back to the city center.

galleries and exhibits of Canadian birds and large mammals preserved by taxidermy and placed in natural settings. Kids seem to enjoy the Discovery Den activity area.

240 McLeod St. (at Metcalfe). (C) **613/566-4700.** www.nature.ca. Admission C$5 (US$5/£2.50) per person, C$13 (US$13/£6.50) family, free for children under 3; free to all visitors Sat 9am–noon. May–Aug Fri–Tues 9am–6pm, Wed–Thurs 9am–8pm; Sept–Apr Tues–Sun 9am–5pm (to 8pm Thurs).

Laurier House This comfortable 1878 brick home—now a National Historic Site—is filled with mementos of the two Canadian prime ministers who lived here over a span of 50 years. From 1897 to 1919, it was occupied by Sir Wilfrid Laurier, Canada's seventh prime minister and the first French-Canadian elected to that office. He was followed by William Lyon Mackenzie King, who held the same post for 22 years and lived here from 1923 to 1950. King is said to have held séances in the library; on display is the crystal ball he supposedly coveted in London but couldn't afford—an American bought it for him when he overheard King speaking. A portrait of the King's mother is also here, in front of which he used to place a red rose daily, and you'll find a copy of the program Abraham Lincoln held on the night of his assassination plus copies of his death mask and hands. Lester B. Pearson's library has also been re-created, and holds the actual Nobel Peace Prize medal he won for his role in the 1956 Arab-Israeli dispute.

335 Laurier Ave. E. (at Chapel St.). © 613/992-8142. www.pc.gc.ca. Admission C$3.95 (US$3.95/£2) adults, C$3.45 (US$3.45/£1.75) seniors, C$1.95 (US$1.95/£1) ages 6–18, family C$9.90 (US$9.90/£4.95). Apr to mid-May Mon–Fri 9am–5pm; mid-May to early Oct daily 9am–5pm.

Royal Canadian Mounted Police Musical Ride *(Kids* The famous Musical Ride is not an amusement park attraction, but rather a mounted drill team who first performed in Regina back in 1878. The riders practice on horseback at the Canadian Police College, and the public is welcome to attend; tours of the stables are given daily in summer, less frequently the rest of the year. If you want to see the actual Ride, check ahead—the Ride is often touring Canada, especially during the summer months.

Rockcliffe RCMP Stables, 8900 St. Laurent Blvd. N. © 613/998-8199. At St. Laurent Blvd. N., take Sussex Dr. east past Rideau Hall and pick up Rockville Driveway; turn left at Sandridge Rd. and continue to the corner of St. Laurent.

GATINEAU PARK ★★

One of the star attractions in an Ottawa visit is **Gatineau Park,** which is across the river in Québec. It begins just 3km (2 miles) from Parliament, yet holds some 35,000 hectares (86,486 acres) of woodland and lakes, all named after the Québec notary-turned-explorer Nicolas Gatineau. This park was inaugurated in 1938, when the federal government bought up large tracts of land in the Gatineau Hills to put a halt to logging, development, and forest destruction in the region. Black bear, timber wolf, otter, marten, and raccoon are joined by white-tailed deer, beaver, and more than 100 species of birds. Also resident here, though rarely glimpsed, are lynx and wolverines . . . and cougars. One was spotted in the summer of 2007.

The park's facilities include 145km (90 miles) of **hiking trails** and supervised **swimming beaches** at Meech Lake, Lac Philippe, and Lac la Pêche. Canoes, kayaks, and rowboats can be rented at Lac Philippe and Lac la Pêche. Motorboats are only permitted on Lac la Pêche, where motors up to 10 horsepower may be used for fishing. Most of the park's lakes can be fished (if it's not allowed, it will be posted), too—a Québec license is required, and can be obtained at many of the convenience stores around the park.

Tips Man of Stone

In Ottawa's city parks and in front of some of its country mansions, visitors will spot rough-cut stone arrangements stacked to suggest standing men. These are "Inuksuk," originally created by the Inuit native people as directional aids.

> ## (Tips) Driving Miss Daisy . . . to Gatineau Park
>
> There are several routes to Gatineau Park by car from the city. It all depends on where you want to go. You can:
>
> - Cross one of the city's bridges over to Gatineau, then take boulevard Taché (Rte. 148) to the Gatineau Parkway, which leads to Kingsmere, Ski Fortune, and eventually Meech Lake.
> - Take Route 5 (the Autoroute de la Gatineau) north, taking Exit 12 for Old Chelsea, turning left, and proceeding 1km (½ mile) on Meech Lake Road to the Gatineau Park Visitor Centre.
> - To reach Lac Philippe, take Route 5 north out of Gatinteau and then Route 105 to the intersection of Route 366 west. Just before reaching Ste-Cecile-de-Masham, turn off to Lac Philippe; to reach Lac la Pêche, keep going along the Masham road to St-Louis-de-Masham and enter the park just beyond.

Camping facilities are at or near Lac Philippe, accessible by highways 5, 105, and 366; there are also 35 canoe camping sites at Lac la Pêche. For details on camping facilities, contact the **Gatineau Park Visitor Centre,** 33 Scott Rd., Chelsea, PQ J9B 1R5 (© **800/465-1867** or 819/827-2020; www.capitaleducanada.gc.ca/gatineau), or the **National Capital Commission,** 40 Elgin St., Suite 202, Ottawa, ON K1P 1C7. Reservations are vital.

In winter, hiking trails become **cross-country ski trails,** marked by numbers on blue plaques, with chalets along the way. Winter camping is available at Lac Philippe.

In the middle of the park is the former summer retreat of Mackenzie King, officially known as the "Mackenzie King Estate" but often simply called **Kingsmere.** While he was serving as Prime Minister for 22 years, King collected the architectural fragments on view at this estate, transported here from the Centre Block Parliament building after a 1916 fire and from London's House of Commons after the 1941 Blitz. Linger over a beverage and snack in a cottage converted to a tea room. It's open daily from 11am to 5pm spring through October. For reservations, call © **819/827-3405.**

MORE PARKS & GARDENS

The **Canada Agriculture Museum** and its core component, the **Central Experimental Farm,** on Prince of Wales Drive (© **613/230-3276**), don't form a traditional park, as is obvious by the name—but with its 500 hectares (1,236 acres), it qualifies as the largest green space of all. Though now surrounded by suburban Ottawa, the farm has livestock barns housing various breeds of cattle, pigs, chickens, sheep, and horses. (Milking time is usually 4pm.) The greenhouses shelter a noted chrysanthemum show every November, and there are also an ornamental flower garden and an arboretum with 2,000 varieties of trees and shrubs. You can ride in wagons drawn by brawny Clydesdales, weather permitting, and in winter there are sleigh rides.

Admission is C$6 (US$6/£3) for adults, C$5 (US$5/£2.50) for seniors and students, and C$3 (US$3/£1.50) for children ages 3 to 14. March through October, the agricultural museum, barns, and tropical greenhouse are open daily 9am to 5pm;

November through February, except Christmas and New Year's Day, the barns and tropical greenhouse are open but the museum's exhibits are closed.

Open all year, **Parc Oméga**, Route 323 North (Nord), Montebello (© **818/423-5487;** www.parc-omega.com), is a wildlife park near Gatineau Park. It changes dramatically by seasons, scarcely recognizable as the same park in summer that it was last winter. At the entrance, elk wait for one of the carrots purchased with your tickets, just a foreshadowing of the many animals you'll spot on your drive—most of which stroll right up to your car to take snacks from your hand. Among the most visible are whitetail deer, wapiti, bison, fallow deer, raccoons, and wild boar, all of which roam free. Kept in large enclosures are black bears, timber wolves, and raptors, including bald eagles. With luck, you might even see a reclusive moose.

A restaurant and picnic grounds are set above a pretty lake. From June to October, admission is C$16 (US$16/£8) for adults, C$11 (US$11/£5.50) for children ages 6 to 15, and C$6 (US$6/£3) for children ages 2 to 5. From November to May it costs only C$13 (US$13/£6.50) for adults, C$9 (US$9/£4.50) for children ages 6 to 15, and C$5 (US$5/£2.50) for children ages 2 to 5. You can enter from 9am to 5pm in high summer season, from 10am to 4pm the rest of the year.

ESPECIALLY FOR KIDS

Kids love the bands, rifles, and uniforms of the **Changing of the Guard** on Parliament Hill. The **Canada Aviation Museum** is a fantasyland for many, especially the mock-ups of cockpits where they can pretend to be pilots. Perennial favorites at the **Canadian Museum of Nature** include the dinosaurs, animals, and the Discovery Den, especially created for children. Kid-popular attractions at the **Canadian Museum of Civilization** include the Children's Museum, obviously, but also the CINEPLUS theater's IMAX movies.

Kids enjoy picnicking and getting close to the animals at the **Central Experimental Farm.** At the **Canada Science and Technology Museum,** the hands-on exhibits entertain while also teaching. Then there's the **Royal Canadian Mounted Police Musical Ride,** which practices at the Canadian Police College. All these attractions are described in detail earlier in this chapter.

When it's time to let off some steam, there's **canoeing** or **boating** at Dow's Lake, **biking** along the canal or **ice skating** on it, plus activities outside the city in Gatineau Park.

5 Special Events & Festivals

There's one thing you can say for sure about Canada: Canadians love winter. And not only NHL hockey; everything winter. On the first two weekends each February, **Winterlude** (© **613/239-5000;** www.capcan.ca/winterlude) takes over the city of Ottawa with parades, an ice-sculpture competition, fireworks, speed skating, snowshoe races, ice boating, curling, and more. One offbeat contest is a bed race on the frozen canal, while the most exciting event may be harness racing on ice.

But Ottawa's *biggest* annual event, surprisingly, is the **Canadian Tulip Festival** (© **613/567-5757** or 800/66-TULIP; www.tulipfestival.ca), which takes places over 2 weeks in mid-May. Suddenly the city comes ablaze with 200 varieties of tulips enlivening public buildings, monuments, embassies, homes, and driveways. (One of the best viewing points is at Dow's Lake.) The festival began in 1945, when the Netherlands sent 100,000 tulip bulbs to Canada in appreciation for the role Canadian

---

Fun Fact Born on Dutch Soil—in Ottawa?!

Queen Juliana of the Netherlands, who had spent the wartime years in Canada, arranged for an annual bulb presentation to celebrate the birth of her daughter, Princess Margriet, in Ottawa in 1943. To ensure the princess would still be born a Dutch citizen, the Canadian government designated her room in the Ottawa Civic Hospital as part of the Netherlands. Temporarily, of course.

---

troops played in liberating Holland. Today, festival events include fireworks, concerts, parades, and a flotilla on the canal.

Mid-June brings the **Festival Franco-Ontarien** (© 613/321-0102; www.ffo.ca), a 3-day celebration of Francophone Canada, featuring classical and other musical concerts, fashion shows, street performers, games and competitions, crafts, and French cuisine. Also in mid-June, the city is filled with the sounds of the **Ottawa Jazz Festival** (© 613/241-2633 or 888/226-4495; www.ottawajazzfestival.com). Local, national, and international artists give more than 125 performances at more than 20 venues.

Later, at the very end of June, the **R.C.M.P. Musical Ride Sunset Rides** take place, a day of performances of music and horsemanship, including jumping and dressage, as well as the ride itself; it's free, though donations are requested. In early June, the Canadian Museum of Nature holds a **Children's Festival,** an extravaganza of dance, mime, puppetry, and music.

On July 1, lots of Canadians flock to the city to celebrate **Canada Day** (© 800/465-1867; www.capcan.ca/canadaday)—basically, it's Canada's Fourth of July, with plenty of entertainment, including fireworks. The 2-week **Ottawa Chamber Music Festival** (© 613/234-8008; www.chamberfest.com), North America's largest, brings dozens of concerts to the city's churches in late July and early August.

On Labour Day weekend (late Aug and early Sept, same as in the U.S.), scores of brilliantly colored balloons fill the skies over Ottawa, while on the ground, people flock to musical events and midway rides during the **Gatineau Hot Air Balloon Festival** (© 819/243-2330; www.balloongatineau.com).

Some other major events in the region include the colorful **National Capital Dragon Boat Race Festival,** over 3 days in late June (© 613/238-7711; www.dragon boat.net), and the 10-day **Central Canada Exhibition** (© 613/237-7222; www. ottawasuperex.com) during mid-August, also known as the "Super Ex."

---

6 Outdoor Activities & Spectator Sports

OUTDOOR ACTIVITIES

BIKING Ottawans are enthusiastic cyclists, fully utilizing the more than 160km (100 miles) of bike paths running along the Ottawa and Rideau rivers and Rideau Canal, and through Gatineau Park; more miles are being added, too. A blue, black, and white cyclist logo marks all bikeways. From mid-April to the Canadian Thanksgiving (which occurs late in Oct), bicycles are available at **RentABike,** based at the east arch of the Plaza Bridge at 2 Rideau St. (© 613/241-4140). Town bikes, sport bikes, mountain bikes, and in-line skates are available, with standard bikes from C$9 (US$9/£4.50) per hour and performance bikes for an additional charge. Take the kids along in a bike trailer with two seats and a harness, if you like. The company will also provide maps of self-guided pathway tours around the city, as well as guided tours.

Bikes and in-line skates can also be rented at **Dow's Lake Marina Pavilion** (© 613/232-5278), located on the Rideau Canal at 1001 Queen Elizabeth Dr. The city's public transportation company, **OC Transpo,** has installed bicycle racks on the outside of more than 150 buses for the use of passengers with bikes; it's first come, first served. For details about specific routes on the system, call © **613/741-4390.**

BOATING/CANOEING   Rent paddleboats and canoes at the marina (© **613/232-1001**) at the **Dow's Lake Pavilion,** 1001 Queen Elizabeth Dr. The glass-and-steel complex, which looks like a flotilla of sails from a distance, has several restaurants and provides a welcome haven after a winter skate or a summer running or biking jaunt. Boats can also be rented in Gatineau Park at Lac la Pêche and Lac Philippe (© **819/827-2020**).

GOLF   The Ottawa metro region offers more than 60 courses in all, including the one on the premises of the **Château Montebello** in Québec (© **819/423-6341;** p. 334). Greens fees for 18 holes generally run C$25 to C$45 (US$25–US$45/ £13–£23), but are more expensive at resorts.

HIKING & NATURE WALKS   A band of protected wetlands and woodlands surrounds the capital on the Ontario side of the Ottawa River, and here you can find ideal hiking areas. Regional maps are available from the Capital Infocentre downtown at 14 Metcalfe St. Big **Gatineau Park** (© **819/827-2020**) couches impressive networks of hiking trails throughout its 35,000 hectares (86,487 acres); see "Gatineau Park," above. West of the city in the suburb of Kanata, **Riverfront Park** has nature trails along the Ottawa River. Over on the Québec side in the village of Luskville, a walking trail leads to **Luskville Falls**; it begins on the Chemin de Hôtel de Ville (which translates as "City Hall Road," if you're wondering).

Then there's the peaceful riverside **Rideau Trail** ⟪, running all the way from Ottawa to Kingston (see below): it's the area's major serious hiking trail, stretching some 390km (242 miles), including side trails. Though it doesn't present any huge gains or dips in altitude along its course, it's a nice extended stroll. Contact the Rideau Trail Association (© **613/545-0823;** www.rideautrail.org) for info and B&B listings along the way.

SKATING   From late December to late February (depending on the weather), the **Rideau Canal** ⟪ becomes the world's longest skating rink, stretching from the National Arts Centre to Dow's Lake and Carleton University; every morning the radio news reports ice conditions, and skating here is seriously romantic. Rent skates at several locations for C$12 to C$16 (US$12–US$16/£6–£8) per 2 hours. The canal is serviced with heated huts, sleigh rentals, boot-check and skate-sharpening services, concessions, and restrooms. In-line skates are available at the RentABike facility behind Château Laurier and from the pavilion at the Dow's Lake Marina.

SKIING   If you're serious about **cross-country skiing** on your trip to Ottawa, **Gatineau Park** is a splendid choice with its 185km (115 miles) or so of groomed trails. Even in downtown Ottawa, in fact, you can cross-country **ski the bike paths** paralleling the Eastern or Western parkways. Few visitors **downhill ski** the areas around Ottawa, however, mostly heading instead for Québec's sophisticated, excellent Laurentian resorts which lie only an hour or so to the east. (See "Outdoor Activities & Spectator Sports" in chapter 8.) Ski resorts around the capital are more compelling summer attractions, with their water parks and other family-friendly facilities. That said, check these out if you wish:

The Pride of Ottawa: The Rideau Canal

Built in the early 19th century under the leadership of Lt. Colonel John By, a civil and military engineer, the **Rideau Canal** was meant to bypass the Thousand Islands section of the St. Lawrence River, which was thought to be vulnerable to American attack in the tense atmosphere following the War of 1812. It was to connect Kingston with the Ottawa River, allowing the transportation of troops and supplies to Canada's capital and then onward to Montréal. Construction of the 198km (123-mile) canal began in 1826 and took just 6 years.

Beginning in Ottawa, the canal follows the course of the Rideau River to its summit on Upper Rideau Lake, which is connected to Newboro Lake; here, the canal descends the Cataraqui River through a series of lakes controlled by dams to Kingston. In Ottawa, a flight of eight locks allows boats to negotiate the 24m (79 ft.) difference in height between the artificially constructed section of the canal and the natural level of the Ottawa River—a sight not to be missed. You can observe this fascinating maneuver between Parliament Hill and Château Laurier.

I'm skipping over some history. The feared American invasion never materialized, railroads soon became the desired mode of travel and freight, and the swiftly outmoded canal was left to its own. Yet it has been miraculously reborn, over time, and it's a disused artifact no more; today, this is one of eastern Ontario's most impressive visual and recreational assets. In summer, walk or cycle along the canal paths or row a canoe or boat on a gentle journey before stopping at the canalside cafe at the National Arts Centre. You can even rent houseboats to navigate its entire length.

In winter, the canal becomes the world's longest (8km/5 miles) skating course, as families pile onto the ice with children perched on their backs and drawn on sleighs. Some locals even strap on skates and glide to and from work, briefcases in hand! And I'll wager you've never seen *that* before anywhere.

SWIMMING   Pools open to the public include those at **Carleton University** on Colonel By Drive, the University of Ottawa at 125 University Dr., and the YMCA-YWCA at 180 Argyle Dr. Lake swimming is available in **Gatineau Park, Meech Lake, Lac la Pêche,** and at **Lac Philippe.**

WHITE-WATER RAFTING   Enjoy the exhilaration of a day of white-water rafting and be back in your hotel bed that night. Outings are available from mid-May to September, depending on the river. **Owl Rafting** (© **613/646-2263** in summer, or 613/238-7238 in winter; www.owlrafting.com) offers white-water rafting trips within 90 minutes of the city, pounding over extensive rapids for the fit and adventurous and floating on gentler stretches for families. Prices start at around C$100 (US$100/£50) per person per day during the week, more on the weekends, meals included. Shorter trips of 2 hours are intended for families and are more cost effective.

SPECTATOR SPORTS

The **Ottawa Senators** (© 800/444-7367 or 613/599-0250; www.senators.com) won the NHL's Eastern Conference in 2007, so they're doing something right; their fans are, let's say, very devoted (note the scarlet-face-painted "Sens Army" members). The team plays at Scotiabank Place, west of the city center. Tickets mostly cost from C$30 to C$80 (US$30–US$80/£15–£40); call © 877/788-3267 or 613/599-3267.

7 Ottawa After Dark

Ottawa's culture and nightlife offerings aren't nearly up to those of Toronto or Montréal, extending mostly to the National Arts Centre, the bars and pubs of the ByWard Market and Elgin Street areas, and a few stray dance clubs. Still, there's certainly enough to occupy you for all the evenings of a long weekend.

The opening of the **Casino du Lac-Leamy**, 1 bd. du Casino (© 800/665-2274 or 819/772-2100; www.casino-du-lac-leamy.com), was big news to Ontarians; as a traveler, though, I'm frankly a bit baffled as to why anyone would spend time indoors gambling while on vacation. After all, this is hardly Vegas. If you can't resist, I will say this—it's both big and central. Less than 5km (3 miles) from Parliament Hill and open daily from 11am to 3am, the casino imposes a dress code (sorry, no bustiers, tank tops, caps, hats, jogging clothes, motorcycle boots, cutoffs, bicycle shorts, or beachwear). Both the exterior and the interior are dramatically landscaped with tropical plants, pools, and waterfalls, and there are more than 1,800 slot machines—plus 60 tables for playing blackjack, roulette, baccarat, and poker. Musical attractions in the Théâtre du Casino mostly take in headliners who were famous 40 years ago, and there are dance and musical revues to provide respite from losing.

The complex also provides two lounges and four restaurants to keep you in the building, including fine dining in La Baccara (p. 340), the popular buffet-style Banco, the seafood grill La Marina, and a poolside snack bar. You must be 18 to enter the casino, whose doors open daily at 9am and finally close at 4am (yes, 4 in the morning). Need wheels? Shuttles operate from Ottawa hotels to the casino for about C$10 (US$10/£5) per round-trip.

For Ottawa entertainment listings, pick up a copy of *Where,* a free guide often provided by hotels; *Ottawa* magazine; the hip and free *Ottawa X-Press* weekly newspaper; or the weekend edition of the *Ottawa Citizen,* the capital's daily paper.

THE PERFORMING ARTS

Canadian and international musical, dance, and theater artists—including the resident NAC Orchestra—perform at the expansive **National Arts Centre,** located at 53 Elgin St. at Confederation Square (© 866/850-ARTS or 613/947-7000; www.nac-cna. ca). The building, created by architect Fred Lebensold, is made of three interlocking hexagons beside the Rideau Canal, its terraces tendering views of Parliament Hill and the Ottawa River. There are three auditoriums: the European-style **Opera;** a 950-seat **Theatre** with an innovative apron stage; and the **Studio,** used for experimental works. The **National Arts Centre Orchestra** performs in seven or eight main concert series here each year. The center also offers classic and modern drama in English and French, and guided tours are also available. Ask for the free monthly *Calendar of NAC Events.* The NAC also owns a popular canalside restaurant, **Le Café** (© 613/594-5127; Mon–Sat year-round).

Augmenting the main events at the National Arts Centre, the ensemble at the **Great Canadian Theatre Company** (✆ **613/236-5196;** www.gctc.ca), presents contemporary drama and comedy with Canadian themes from September to May in a brand-new sparkling theater facility known as the **Irving Greenberg Theatre Centre.** It's located at 1233 Wellington St. W. (at Holland Ave.). Show tickets start at C$26 (US$26/£13).

MUSIC CLUBS

Nightlife used to close down at 1am (11pm Sun) in Ottawa, while it thumped on until the wee hours (3am) across the river in Gatineau—an accurate reflection of the tension between Canada's British proprietary and its Franco laissez-fairness. This created a kind of noisome, late-night stampede across the river; authorities on both sides of the river finally agreed it would just be best to synchronize closing regulations in both cities at 2am, and that's generally when it happens now.

Barrymore's Music Hall   This suitably disreputable-looking rock palace in a former cinema showcases bands with names like Dopamine, Buskerbash, Good Riddance, and Little Bones—plus some righteous AC/DC tribute bands. Open nightly, it presents a good mix of classic rock, alt-rock, folk, and house, switching on Sundays to "retro" '80s sounds spun by DJs. Covers vary but generally don't top C$15 (US$15/£7.50), though they may run as high as C$30 (US$30/£15) for bigger acts. 323 Bank St. ✆ 613/233-0307.

Full House   The upstairs lounge in this restaurant provides a playful atmosphere, as a singer/piano player holds court Thursdays through Saturdays from 5pm until 1am. The food ranges from onion soup to souvlaki. 337 Somerset St. W. ✆ 613/238-6734.

Mercury Lounge   Take the side door and head upstairs from The Collection/Bar 56 (see below) to find this lounge where jazz, soul, and world music get a sleek crowd of young professionals moving. The bands play on a stage at the street end of the room; limited seating is provided by velvet couches. This is as much a people-watching and networking spot as it is a place to hear music. Covers are C$8 (US$8/£4) and higher, much higher for top attractions. 56 Byward Market St. ✆ 613/789-5324.

The Rainbow   Live blues and bluesy rock energize this upstairs ByWard Market lounge nightly. The club has hosted such notable artists as k. d. lang and Buckwheat Zydeco; while the majority of acts aren't *that* famous, there's usually someone worth hearing. Cover charges run C$3 to C$15 (US$3–US$15/£1.50–£7.50), and there are sometimes free matinee shows. 76 Murray St. ✆ 613/241-5123.

Rasputin's   This is the place for acoustic folk, a New Agey vibe, and unpredictable open-mic nights. 696 Bronson Ave. ✆ 613/230-5102.

Vineyards   A wine bar and bistro in ByWard Market, this is one of the city's cozier subterranean hangouts, in a rusticated cellar with stone floors and checked tablecloths. Several house wines are featured every night, from among more than 60 varieties, and there's an ample roster of imported beers. Some nights bring live jazz, and light meals and snacks are available. 54 York St. ✆ 613/241-4270.

Zaphod Beeblebrox   Smaller and even more ragged than Barrymore's (see above), this ByWard Market club is open most nights, offering live underground, electronica, and alternative rock plus DJs. The cover varies, but is usually C$5 to C$10 (US$5–US$10/£2.50–£5). 27 York St. ✆ 613/562-1010.

Zoé's Lounge ⟨★⟩ Pianists and jazz combos enhance the gracious surroundings (plush carpeting, chandeliers) in this popular lounge secreted inside The Fairmont Château Laurier. The bar menu is fancy and excellent; afternoon tea is served daily; and Saturdays often bring dancing and live music. 1 Rideau St. ℂ **613/241-1425.**

BARS, PUBS & DISCOS

Ottawa has an abundance of English and Irish pubs of varying degrees of authenticity.

The Collection/Bar 56 A few steps up or down from the street, these are two martini bars with a DJ mixing house and fusion from around 9pm nightly. There's no food and no patio, yet this is a good place for conversation and relaxing after a long day of sightseeing. 56 ByWard Market St. ℂ **613/562-2384.**

D'Arcy McGee's ⟨★⟩ If this avowed Irish pub looks like just a little *too* authentic (albeit without smoke), that's because it is: The whole thing was shipped over from the Emerald Isle and reassembled. The etched and stained-glass panels, dark-wood partitions, and mosaic-tiled floor were installed in this vaguely Dublinesque building. Imported and domestic brews are on tap, as are single-malt scotches and Irish whiskey. Live Celtic music fills the place most nights, with some New World blues and rock squeezed in. In warm weather, tables wrap around the exterior. 44 Sparks St. (at Elgin St.). ℂ **613/230-4433.**

The Earl of Sussex Pub With a pronounced English flavor, this pub is just diagonally across from the U.S. Embassy. Wingbacks huddle around the fireplace and by the front windows. They have darts and boards, and live jazz on the weekend. In addition to daily chalkboard specials, menu standards include steak-and-kidney pie, liver and onions, bangers and mash, and Cornish pasties. There are about 30 ales, stouts, and lagers on draft. 431 Sussex Dr. ℂ **613/562-5544.**

Heart and Crown An Irish pub crammed nightly from the bar to the wraparound deck, Heart and Crown's principal attraction is live music, usually rousing Celtic tunes joined in with infectious enthusiasm by patrons who seem to know every word. Lots of English, Irish, and Canadian brews are on tap, with Harp and Guinness prominent. Expect soccer—sorry, football—on the tube. 67 Clarence St. ℂ **613/562-0674.**

Helsinki Lounge & Disco An upstairs cocktail bar/disco at the quiet end of George Street, this is a place for both martini-fueled conversations and partying down. Two fireplaces bracket the cocktail bar section, often staffed with Nordic beauties; they have tapas and small meals, and patrons can dance to pumping house, techno, and soul music. 15 George St. ℂ **613/241-2868.**

Maxwell's Bar This open-fronted destination has a shellfish bar, karaoke nights, and live bands many nights. Call ahead to be sure what's going on at a particular time. 340 Elgin St. ℂ **613/232-5771.**

Yuk Yuk's The local outpost of a Canadian national chain of comedy clubs showcases both familiar and unknown comics inside the Capitol Hill Hotel. Cover charges vary with the comic. 88 Albert St. ℂ **613/236-5233.**

GAY & LESBIAN BARS

Capital XTRA! is Ottawa's gay/lesbian news-and-events magazine, a source for up-to-date info on the local scene. For updated gay and lesbian activities and events, pick up a copy or log on to the magazine's website at www.xtra.ca. The last week of August brings the **Pride Festival** (© **613/421-5387;** www.prideottawa.com), celebrating Ottowa's large community of gay, lesbian, bisexual, and transgender residents.

The Lookout Bar   A ByWard Market gay standby, this large cocktail bar has nightly special events that ensure a large, regular turnout. The festivities continue through the weekend with DJs at the turntables and occasional karaoke. 41 York St. © **613/789-1624.**

8 Exploring Eastern Ontario: Kingston & Beyond

From the quiet village of **Port Hope,** 105km (65 miles) east of Toronto, the coast of Lake Ontario takes in the **Bay of Quinte** and **Quinte's Isle.** Once off the speedy main highway (Route 401), you'll discover a surprisingly tranquil region of farms and orchards that was mostly settled by United Empire Loyalists—British sympathizers who fled the impudent new republic to the south during and after the American Revolution. This region remains off the beaten track today, except to those in the know, who come to explore attractive villages; troll for antiques; or enjoy the beaches, dunes, and waterfront activities of the area's provincial parks. **Kingston,** an appealing lakefront city with a regular flea-and-farmers' market, is intriguing both architecturally and historically, and is the gateway to the mighty St. Lawrence River, the **Thousand Islands** region, and **St. Lawrence National Park.**

KINGSTON

A 2-hour drive from Ottawa and about 3 hours from Toronto (172km/107 miles southwest of Ottawa, 255km/158 miles northeast of Toronto), Kingston draws on more than 300 years of history—a history which included a brief tenure as capital of Canada. That rich heritage lingers in grand old limestone public buildings and private residences lining downtown's streets; the city has a gracious air. Four Martello towers that once formed a string of defense works guarding the waterways along the U.S.-Canadian border still stand, and a Christopher Wren–style St. Georges Church contains a Tiffany window.

The city stands at the confluence of Lake Ontario, the Rideau Canal, and the St. Lawrence Seaway. This position makes for remarkable scenery, best viewed by taking the free ferry to **Wolfe Island.** Ferries leave at frequent intervals for the sparsely populated island that doubles as a quiet offshore retreat of pronounced rural character. (See the box "A Journey into the Thousand Islands," below, for details about other seagoing sightseeing voyages.) A stroll along Kingston's **waterfront**, where there are many hotels and restaurants as well as marinas, pocket parks, gardens, and a maritime museum, is a must.

During the summer, **Confederation Park** at the harbor is the site of blues and buskers festivals, as well as frequent free concerts; in winter, you might catch a local hockey game. Three times a week, a farmers' market assembles behind City Hall in the refurbished **Market Square.** On Sundays, this space is transformed into a flea market with a few lingering produce stalls. It's all well worth exploring at your leisure.

ESSENTIALS

GETTING THERE   If you're driving from Ottawa, take Route 416 south to Route 401 (the Trans-Canada Hwy.), then drive west to Kingston. Or, with a little more time, take scenic Route 2 instead; Route 401 is an expressway, heavily trafficked and often stressful—if you're looking for relaxation, I'd avoid it if possible. From Toronto, you have little choice but to take Route 401 directly east to the Kingston exits.

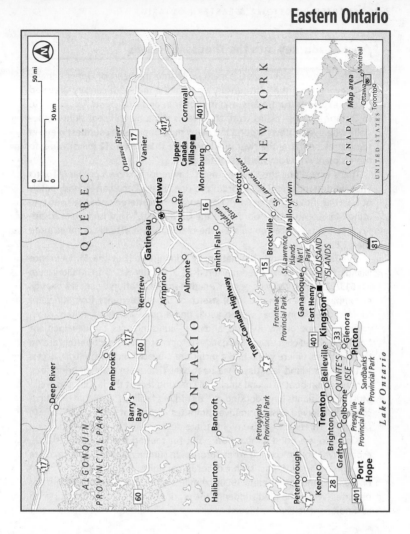

If you want to take public transit, several comfortable daily **VIA Rail** (© **888/VIA-RAIL**; www.viarail.ca) trains call at Kingston coming from Ottawa, Toronto, and Montréal.

VISITOR INFORMATION Stop by the handsome **Kingston Tourist Information Office** at 209 Ontario St. (© **888/855-4555** or 613/548-4415), housed inside the old railroad station on the waterfront across from City Hall. Its attendants can help you find lodging and sell tickets for the bus tours that start out front. Also consult the city's tourism website at **http://tourism.kingstoncanada.com**.

EXPLORING THE TOWN

Get a street map as soon as you arrive; this isn't one of those cities where a handy sign is available on every corner. A good way to get acquainted with the town is aboard the

Tips A Journey into the Thousand Islands

The St. Lawrence River was the main route into the heart of Upper Canada and beyond from the 17th century up until the mid–19th century. Traveled first by explorers, fur traders, and missionaries and later by settlers en route to Ontario and the plains west, the river is still a magnificent sight—especially wherever it flows around the many outcroppings of countless islets. In some stretches here, the river swells to more than 19km (12 miles) wide, so there's plenty of room for these interlopers.

That's why, along this stretch, the St. Lawrence is known primarily for its **Thousand Islands** region. According to one Native Canadian legend, petals of heavenly flowers fell to earth here and were scattered onto the river, creating Manitouana, the "Garden of the Great Spirit." That isn't quite so difficult to believe once you've seen the islands, which actually number more than 1,800.

The Thousand Islands are nationally administrated as the **St. Lawrence Islands National Park,** headquartered at 2 County Rd. 5 in Mallorytown (© 613/923-5261; www.pc.gc.ca). Canada's smallest national park is a beauty, encompassing an 80km (50-mile) stretch of the St. Lawrence from Kingston to Brockville. Along that stretch you'll find a good supply of motels, cabin colonies, campgrounds, RV sites, and boat-launching sites, but development has mostly been contained. The park's visitor center and headquarters are on the mainland, where you'll find a picnic area, beach, and nature trail; access to the park's island facilities is via boat only. (There are daily mooring fees, depending on boat size, and small daily parking fees at the landings as well.) Most of the islands have docking and picnicking facilities, available on a first-come, first-served basis; primitive campsites cost about C$15 (US$15/£7.50) per night. Three consecutive nights is the docking limit at each island.

Kingston is a good jumping-off point for touring the Thousand Islands, especially if you're coming from Toronto. In summer, **cruise boats** circulate through the islands, past such extraordinary sights as **Boldt Castle** ⋆, built on Heart Island in the early 1900s by millionaire George Boldt as a gift for his wife. (When she died suddenly, the work was abandoned, and it stands as a poignant relic of lost love.)

Confederation Tour Trolley (© 613/546-4453), a bus made to look like a streetcar. It leaves from in front of the Tourist Information Office (see above) every hour on the hour from mid-May to Labour Day 10am to 5pm (to 7pm July–Aug). The tour lasts 50 minutes and costs C$14 (US$14/£7) for adults and C$12 (US$12/£6) for seniors and youths. If you want to explore **Wolfe Island,** there's a free 25-minute trip aboard the car ferry from downtown Kingston; it departs frequently from the dock near the intersection of Queen and Ontario streets. Or, if you want to use the city as a starting point to some serious hiking, the **Rideau Trail** runs 390km (242 miles) along the Rideau canal from Kingston all the way to Ottawa. For details, contact the **Rideau Trail Association** at © 613/545-0823.

From Kingston Harbour at City Hall in May to mid-October, you can take a 3-hour cruise for C$28 (US$28/£14) adults and C$14 (US$14/£7) children ages 4–12 on the *Island Queen,* a triple-deck paddle wheeler; a lunch on the boat during the cruise costs extra. The 90-minute cruises (about C$20/US$20/ £10 for adults and C$10/US$10/£5 for children ages 4–12) aboard its sister boat, the *Island Belle,* take in the Kingston Harbour and waterfront. Both boats are used for 2-hour sunset cruises. Sunset dinner cruises of 3½ hours are also available. For details, call © **613/549-5544** or check the website **www.1000islandscruises.ca**.

From Kingston, you can also cruise the Rideau Canal or explore the Thousand Islands aboard a houseboat. Representative of the companies renting these types of watercraft is **Houseboat Holidays,** R.R. #3, Gananoque, ON K7G 2V5 (© **613/382-2842;** www.gananoque.com/hhl). Their houseboats sleep from 6 to 10 adults and come with fully equipped kitchens, hot and cold running water, and propane systems to provide heat and light. Weekly rentals on the canal system or on the river run from as little as C$900 up to C$2,000 (US$900–US$2,000/£450–£1,000), depending upon the time of year and the size of the vessel. Rentals are also available for weekends, long weekends, or for a minimum of 2 nights; you can rent from late April to mid-October.

From the waterfront in **Gananoque** in May to mid-October, the **Gananoque Boat Line** (© **888/717-4837** or 613/382-2144; www.ganboatline. com) offers cruises through the Thousand Islands. The longer cruise stops at the fantastical Boldt Castle. Note, though, that to visit the castle, which is in U.S. territory, you'll need either a valid passport or a birth certificate plus a picture ID (and a visa if you hail from many countries other than the U.S.). Call ahead for the cruise schedule. The same company operates group trips from **Ivy Lea,** leaving from west of the International Bridge on the Thousand Islands Parkway.

In fact, for a dramatic view of the islands from above, climb the **Skydeck Tower** on Hill Island (near Ivy Lea)—it rises 120m (394 ft.) above the river, and on clear days the reward is a sweeping 65km (40-mile) panoramic vista.

Kingston spent decades of its early years anticipating an attack that never came, the reason for its still-evident defenses. You can view some of these along the waterfront, where **Confederation Park** stretches from the front of the old 19th-century town hall down to the yacht basin. Several blocks west of the park is one of the city's finest Martello towers, built during the Oregon Crisis of 1846 to withstand possible naval bombardments. The moated, cylindrical **Murney Tower** (© **613/544-9925**) is now a museum where you can see the basement storage rooms, the barracks room, and the gun platform. Mid-May to Labour Day, it's open daily 10am to 5pm, charging C$3 (US$3/£1.50) per person or C$10 (US$10/£5) per family.

While exploring downtown or ambling along the waterfront, visit **City Hall** at 216 Ontario St. (© **613/546-4291**); free guided tours are offered weekdays from 10am to

4pm, weekends from 11am to 3pm. If there isn't enough time, at least take a look at the stained-glass windows upstairs in Memorial Hall, each one commemorating a World War I battle. It's open weekdays from around 8:30am until 4:30pm.

Agnes Etherington Art Centre On the campus of Queen's University, the center displays a fairly extensive, if somewhat disjointed, collection in seven galleries. The emphasis is Canadian, though it also gathers African sculpture and 16th- to 19th-century European masters. The center's heart is the original 19th-century home of benefactor Agnes Richardson Etherington (1880–1954), featuring three rooms furnished in period style.

University Ave. at Bader Lane. © 613/533-2190. Admission C$4 (US$4/£2) adults, C$2.50 (US$2.50/£1.25) seniors, free for students and children. Free to all Thurs. Tues–Fri 10am–4:30pm; Sat–Sun 1–5pm.

Bellevue House On July 1, 1867, the Canadian Confederation was proclaimed in Kingston's Market Square. One of the chief architects of that momentous political construction was Canada's first prime minister, Sir John A. Macdonald. Kingston was his home for most of his life, where Macdonald lived at Bellevue House as a young lawyer and rising member of Parliament. Now a National Historic Site, the building is a stucco-faced, vaguely Italianate villa with green trim and a red roof, jokingly referred to as the "Pekoe Pagoda" or the "Tea Caddy Castle" by some locals. Apple trees and hollyhocks fill the front yard, and costumed docents greet visitors. It has been restored to the period of 1848 to 1849, and there is indeed afternoon tea served here.

35 Centre St. © 613/545-8666. www.pc.gc.ca. Admission C$3.95 (US$3.95/£2) adults, C$3.45 (US$3.45/£1.75) seniors, C$1.95 (US$1.95/£1) children 6–15, C$9.90 (US$9.90/£4.95) families. Apr–May daily 10am–5pm; June to Labour Day daily 9am–6pm; day after Labour Day to Oct daily 10am–5pm.

Fort Henry Fort Henry, erected in 1812 and largely unchanged since its reconstruction in the 1830s, commands a high promontory overlooking the harbor and town. May 18 to August 31, the Fort Henry Guard and their goat mascot, David, perform 19th-century drills, musters, and parades. Regular programming includes music and marching displays by the fife-and-drum band, exhibitions of infantry drill, and mock battles of tall ships, many of them brought to a close with the firing of the garrison artillery and the lowering of the Union Jack. Parts of the fort—the officers' quarters, men's barracks, kitchens, and artisans' shops—have been restored to show the military way of life as it was around the year 1867. The most imposing events are the Sunset Ceremonies, elaborate military tattoos with martial music performed Wednesdays at 7:30pm in July and August. On those nights, an extra treat is a three-course dinner served in the officers' dining room followed by seatings in bleachers or in the balcony to view the Sunset Ceremonies.

On Rte. 2, just east of Kingston. © 613/542-9127. www.parks.on.ca/fort. Admission C$11 (US$11/£5.50) adults, C$9.75 (US$9.75/£4.90) seniors, C$8.50 (US$8.50/£4.25) students 13–18, C$5.50 (US$5.50/£2.75) children 5–12, C$2 (US$2/£1) children 2–4. Slight discounts in Sept. Sunset Ceremonies C$17 (US$17/£8.50) adults, C$16 (US$16/£8) seniors, C$14 (US$14/£7) students 13–18, C$11 (US$11/£5.50) children 5–12, C$2 (US$2/£1) children 2–4. Late May to Sept daily 10am–5pm.

Marine Museum of the Great Lakes Stop by the Maritime Museum to get a handle on the importance of shipping on the Great Lakes, which were critical in the development of central Canada. With model boats, memorabilia, vintage photos, and salvaged engines, the museum outlines the evolution from sailing in the 17th century to steamships in the 19th century, from the great schooners of the 1870s to today's bulk freighter carriers that still ply these waters. Moored at the far end of the museum is the 64m (210-ft.) *Alexander Henry*. A retired Coast Guard icebreaker, it can be toured, and it also functions as an offbeat **bed and breakfast** 🏠 with 25 simple, compact cabins available from around mid-May until Labour Day; double rates are C$95 to C$125 (US$95–US$125/£48–£63) per cabin, with many single bunks in shared rooms also available. Breakfast and museum admission are included.

55 Ontario St. ✆ 613/542-2261. www.marmuseum.ca. Admission C$6.50 (US$6.50/£3.25) adults, C$6 (US$6/£3) seniors and students, C$13 (US$13/£6.50) family. May–Sept daily 10am–4pm; off-season by appointment only.

Royal Military College Museum   The Royal Military College, which is Canada's West Point, sits across Navy Bay from Fort Henry. Its campus occupies the site of a Royal Navy dockyard that played a key role in the War of 1812. Though you can tour the grounds year-round, the museum, in a large Martello tower, is open only in summer. It houses displays about the college's history and Kingston's Royal Dockyard, plus the Douglas collection of small arms and weapons.

On Point Frederick. ✆ 613/541-6000, ext. 6664. Free admission. Late June to Labour Day daily 10am–5pm.

SIDE TRIPS TO FRONTENAC PROVINCIAL PARK & UPPER CANADA VILLAGE

Frontenac Provincial Park (✆ 613/376-3489), near Sydenham about 143km (89 miles) from Kingston and 72km (45 miles) from Ottawa, is a wilderness park with more than 182km (113 miles) of hiking trails exploring such intriguing areas as Moulton Gorge, the Arkon Lake bogs, and the Connor-Daly mine.

There are also terrific opportunities here to combine camping with self-propelled water journeys; an adventure might include sea kayaking among the Thousand Islands, for instance, with equipment supplied by a local outfitter. **Frontenac Outfitters** (✆ 613/376-6220 or 800/250-3174 from Ontario only) rents canoes, kayaks, paddles, life jackets, and car-top carriers for relatively modest fees, starting from C$25 (US$25/£13) per person per day. Both wooded and waterfront campsites are also available through the same outfitter, for C$25 (US$25/£13) per night (maximum of four campers per site). A program of guided tours through the region runs from about April to November.

About 50km (31 miles) east of Brockville along Route 2, just east of Morrisburg, is **Upper Canada Village** 🏠 (✆ 800/437-2233 or 613/543-4328; www.uppercanada village.com), Ontario's effort to preserve its pre-Dominion past—a kind of Williamsburg for Canada. This sprawling riverfront museum village makes a stab at representing frontier life in the 1860s, with some 40 brick-and-stone structures and interiors that have been accurately restored using hand-forged nails and wooden pegs. They appear as if they could still serve their purpose today, and they're occupied by costumed bilingual docents who answer questions while performing the chores and crafts of the day—sewing quilts, milling lumber, fashioning tinware, conducting church services, and the like. In the woolen mill, a waterwheel turns old machinery weaving wool into blankets; bellows wheeze and hammers clang against anvils in the blacksmith's shop; and the heady aroma of fresh bread drifts from a bake shop near the Willard's Hotel (which serves lunch and high tea). "True Canadian" draft horses draw both tour wagons and a barge along a carp-filled canal passing from the river to a small lake behind the village. History buffs and some kids will like it.

Admission to the village is C$17 (US$17/£8.50) for adults, C$16 (US$16/£8) for seniors, C$11 (US$11/£5.50) for students, C$7.50 (US$7.50/£3.75) for children ages 5 to 12, and C$2 (US$2/£1) for children ages 2 to 4; families traveling together get a 10% discount. It's open daily 9:30am to 5pm from mid-May to early October.

WHERE TO STAY

Several chain-style business hotels commandeer prime positions beside the harbor—the **Holiday Inn,** 2 Princess St. (© **800/465-4329** or 613/549-8400); the **Confederation Place Hotel** (a former Howard Johnson), 237 Ontario St. (© **888/825-4656** or 613/549-6300); and the **Radisson Kingston Harbourfront,** 1 Johnson St. (© **800/333-3333** or 613/549-8100). There's also a **Comfort Inn** at 1454 Princess St. (© **800/228-5150** or 613/549-5550.

Best Western Fireside Inn *(Finds)* It's not often I mark down a Best Western as a "find," but set aside preconceptions about motels on the interstate. The lounge off the lobby of *this* Best Western looks like a Yukon cabin, with log siding, a moose head, and wing chairs. Every room has a brick gas fireplace, Canadian pine furnishings, and a small fridge; some even have Jacuzzis. The small pool is actually nice. But the *real* draws here are the fantasy suites—spring for one, and your bed might be inside a real Rolls-Royce (the Lord and Lady suite), inside the basket of a 2½-story hot air balloon, or on a simulated Tranquility Moon Base. What a setting to make a memory! Lesser suites have whirlpools next to the fireplaces. Even the standard rooms trump most big-city hotels for comfort: They're equipped with four-posted canopy beds, marble bathrooms, puffy quilts, sofas, and shelves of old books. The hotel's Bistro Stefan fine-dining option is unexpectedly capable.

1217 Princess St., Kingston, ON K7M 3E1. © 800/567-8800 in Ontario and Québec, 800/528-1234 elsewhere, or 613/549-2211. Fax 613/549-4523. www.bestwestern.kingston.on.ca. 77 units. C$155–C$174 (US$155–US$174/ £78–£87) double; from C$220 (US$220/£110) suite. Suites rates include full breakfast on weekdays. AE, DC, MC, V. **Amenities:** Restaurant; lounge; heated outdoor pool; room service; laundry service; dry cleaning. *In room:* A/C, TV, dataport, fridge, coffeemaker, hair dryer, iron, safe.

Four Points by Sheraton Hotel & Suites *(★)* One of the youngest hotels in the city, Kingston's Four Points still has a whiff of new-hotel smell about it, undented by years of wear and tear. It's whisker clean and sturdy. The location is excellent, with great unobstructed views of town and lake from the upper floors, and staff are ever ready to help. The 47 suites have fridges and microwaves, and all have PlayStations and high-speed Internet access. Parking in the underground garage is complimentary.

285 King St. East, Kingston, ON K7L 3B1. © 888/478-4333 or 613/544-4434. Fax 613/548-1782. www.four points.com. 171 units. C$159–C$225 (US$159–US$225/£80–£113) double; from C$259 (US$259/£130) suite. AE, DC, MC, V. **Amenities:** Restaurant; bar; heated indoor pool; whirlpool; exercise room; business center; limited room service; coin-op washers and dryers; dry cleaning; sun deck. *In room:* A/C, TV, dataport, coffeemaker, hair dryer, iron, fridge (some units).

Frontenac Club Inn *(★★)* On one of the most attractive streets in town, lined with handsome 19th-century houses, this limestone building still manages to catch the eye. Erected in 1845 as a bank, it was made a private men's club in 1903 and a century later became an exemplary bed-and-breakfast. The large common rooms on the ground floor are furnished with oversize leather sofas and chairs, and the breakfast area is expanded onto a deck in summer. Bedrooms are on the second and third floors (though there is no elevator); they're uncommonly spacious, some with seating grouped around gas fireplaces, and a few even outfitted with Jacuzzis. Some rooms are named for guests of the former club—guys like Alexander Graham Bell, Carl Sandburg, and Prime Minister Mackenzie King (you might have heard of them.) Ambitious new construction has added bedrooms and meeting spaces, expanded the dining area, and created more parking space.

225 King St. E, Kingston, ON K7L 3A7. © 613/547-6167. www.frontenacclub.com. 13 units. C$149–C$209 (US$149–US$209/£75–£105) double. Rates include full breakfast. AE, MC, V. *In room:* A/C.

Hochelaga Inn & Spa ⚐ All the guest rooms are distinctively furnished in this 1870s Victorian, which has recently gone more upscale with the addition of a spa on the premises and Jacuzzis in more of the rooms. One favorite is no. 301, an oddly shaped space with love seat and a bed set on a diagonal, a large armoire, steps leading to an 11-sided tower with windows, and a stepladder reaching a tiny sitting area. Other rooms are furnished with oak pieces and wing chairs. Enjoy the sitting room with its carved ebony fireplace, or take a seat on the veranda facing the garden. The day spa features aromatherapy, massage, manicures, facials, and body treatments.

24 Sydenham St., Kingston, ON K7L 3G9. © 877/933-9433 or ©/fax 613/549-5534. www.hochelagainn.com. 21 units. C$115–C$205 (US$115–US$205/£58–£103) double. Rates include buffet breakfast. AE, MC, V. **Amenities:** Spa. *In room:* A/C, TV, dataport, hair dryer.

Hotel Belvedere Many regulars list this as their favorite midrange choice in Kingston. The mansard-roofed brick mansion sits in a residential district several blocks west of the downtown hubbub; all rooms have large beds and sitting areas, and a few have whirlpool baths, as well. Typical of the diversity of the decor is no. 204, with its tile-faced fireplace, tasseled curtains, and bed with a lace-embroidered coverlet. Relax in the elegant sitting room with a coal-burning fireplace and French windows opening onto a porch with tables and chairs and plants in classical urns; you can take your included continental breakfast either there or right in your own room.

141 King St. E., Kingston, ON K7L 2Z9. © 800/559-0584 or 613/548-1565. Fax 613/546-4692. www.hotel belvedere.com. 20 units. C$110–C$250 (US$110–US$250/£55–£125) double. Special weekend rates. Rates include continental breakfast. AE, DC, MC, V. **Amenities:** Bike rental; limited room service; babysitting; laundry service; dry cleaning. *In room:* A/C, TV, dataport.

WHERE TO DINE

For a quick snack, also check out the vendors' carts in front of the tourist office on Ontario Street. Here, juicy sausages are slit diagonally and heaped with a choice of fixings, which might include sauerkraut, relish, or hot-pepper slices.

Casa Dominico ⚐⚐ ITALIAN The front windows open in summer, a fireplace blazes in winter, and this upscale downtown rendezvous chatters blissfully away almost every night of the year. It also now has a more sophisticated look after renovations rearranged the floor plan and added tables and rich chocolate walls. You know what you're getting into when the server brings a basket of bread and pours a saucer of spiced extra-virgin olive oil for dipping: clearly, this isn't a red-sauce-and-spaghetti joint. Start with a half-portion of the monster Caesar salad. Main courses might run to free-range chicken in a cognac sauce, roasted salmon, citrusy tiger shrimp in a lobster sauce, seared tuna with foie gras, an oven-roasted chop with saltimbocca sauce, good lamb rib chops, or a grilled steak in mushrooms and Madeira, paired with Gorgonzola-flavored fries. Popular with large parties as well as amatory couples, it's noisy (in a happy way) and the food is worth it.

35 Brock St. © 613/542-0870. Reservations recommended. Main courses lunch C$10–C$18 (US$10–US$18/£5–£9), dinner C$15–C$34 (US$15–US$34/£7.50–£17). AE, MC, V. Mon–Sat 11:30am–2:30pm and 5–10pm (until 11pm Fri–Sat); Sun 5–10pm.

Chez Piggy ★★ *Finds* ECLECTIC   Just off Princess Street in a complex of renovated 19th-century buildings, this remains one of Kingstonians' favorite restaurants
despite the death of its flamboyant creator in 2002. Out front is a paved dining courtyard, and inside are a long bar with director's chairs and an upstairs dining room
enhanced by Tunisian rugs. Dinner possibilities include rack of venison, rib steaks,
duck leg confit, or any one of the half-dozen pastas; daily specials could include
teriyaki salmon or fried chorizo with black-bean cakes and eggs. This is also a good
place to put together a meal of several appetizers, given their globe-girdling charms
and ample portions; try the Vietnamese salad, heaping antipasto platter, or Calabrese
salad with sausage and grilled asparagus. Prix-fixe meals are offered nightly, and this
restaurant also runs a good bakery/bistro, Pan Chancho (see below).

68R Princess St. © 613/549-7673. Reservations recommended on weekends. Main courses C$9–C$18 (US$9–US$18/
£4.50–£9) lunch, C$14–C$30 (US$14–US$30/£7–£15) dinner. AE, DC, MC, V. Mon–Sat 11:30am–midnight; Sun
11am–midnight.

Kingston Brewing Company PUB FARE   Peer through the window behind the
bar at the huge brewing tanks in this, one of Ontario's first microbrew pubs. Beer, ales,
and a pleasant lager are produced here, the best known of which is Dragon's Breath
Ale—so rich it's almost syrupy. Locals come here for substantial victuals of the brewhouse kind: monster burgers, fat onion rings, pizzas, smoked beef and ribs, and charbroiled chicken wings with fiery barbecue sauce, as well as curries and pastas. There's
also a cheap—as well as politically correct, apparently—"ploughperson's lunch." All is
served at polished wood tables, in a rear courtyard, or on the covered sidewalk terrace.
A couple of TVs in the bar keep track of whatever games are on.

34 Clarence St. © 613/542-4978. Most items under C$12 (US$12/£6). AE, DC, MC, V. Mon–Sat 11am–2am; Sun
11:30am–1am.

Le Chien Noir ★ BISTRO/WINE BAR   Diners gather at this busy bar at the door,
where listed on the back mirror are more than 20 wines available by the glass. They
are then guided beneath fans and a stamped-tin ceiling to tables in back or even out
on a courtyard terrace with an awning. Some parts of the menu deviate from the traditional bistro card—such fare as onion soup, steak frites, mussels, and duck confit,
for instance—but you will find some innovative dishes. Execution is the chefs'
weapon—a precise and knowing touch applied to almost every dish. Expect such
choices as a red snapper paired with ratatouille and chorizo; PEI mussels in white
wine; a rack of lamb in a crust of cumin and garlic; or filet of salmon with a bright
green purée of mint and peas. They've even been known to impudently do an upscale
(!) version of *poutine*, an over-the-top take on that irrepressible Québécois comfort
food, with the fries scattered amongst shredded duck confit, brie, and a peppercorn-
and-cognac sauce—the latter replacing the usual cheese curds and beef gravy.

69 Brock St. © 613/549-5635. Reservations recommended. Main courses C$17–C$34 (US$17–US$34/£8.50–£17).
AE, DC, MC, V. Mon–Wed 11:30am–2pm and 5–10pm; Thurs–Sat 11:30am–11pm; Sun 11:30am–10pm.

Pan Chanco ★ *Value* ECLECTIC   There's no better way to ease into a Kingston day
than with a big glass of orange juice, fresh chocolate croissant, and a bowl of foamy
cafe au lait out beneath the trees on the terrace of this cafe/bakery/gourmet food store.
Put together a picnic lunch from offerings in the cold cases full of appetizing arrays of
prepared foods and from baskets of pastries, focaccia, baguettes, scones, and sourdough batards, all baked on the premises. Or eat in, choosing from plates of imported

and domestic cheeses or full meals that might start with *frites aioli,* taco salads, or mussels in butter sauce and continue on to smoked wild salmon with roasted beets or a Vietnamese shrimp cake with dragon noodles.

44 Princess St. ⓒ 613/544-7790. Main courses C$10–C$17 (US$10–US$17/£5–£8.50). AE, DC, MC, V. Mon–Sat 7am–7pm; Sun 7am–5pm.

Woodenheads Gourmet Pizza PIZZA/ITALIAN   A brick beehive oven at center stage underlines the status of what management calls its "gourmet pizza," and for once, that isn't hyperbole. These delectable pies have soft, lightly baked crusts with a variety of ingredients that dictate their classification as tomato, white, green, or in-between, in more than 30 combinations. Among the best are the Vesuvio, with tomatoes, bocconcini, marinated mushrooms, and blackened chicken; and the Loco, with chipotle salsa, cheddar cheese, smoked chicken, and balsamic-grilled red onion—if you like chicken on your pizza, that is. Patrons are even invited to create their own pies from a list of dozens of components. Yet this place is a lot *more* than pizza, too: tapas, panini, salads, and chicken dishes are all available, as well as some offbeat and surprisingly upscale offerings such as citrus-cured salmon seared rare and served over risotto; a shrimp-chicken crepe with lobster sauce; and Indian-spiced calamari rings.

192 Ontario St. ⓒ 613/549-1812. Main courses and pizzas C$6–C$17 (US$6–US$17/£3–£8.50). AE, MC, V. Daily 11:30am–midnight (but closing times are flexible).

10

Toronto

by Hilary Davidson

When I was growing up in Toronto in the 1980s, there were three little words that I dreaded. I heard them on a regular basis, almost daily sometimes, and they made me cringe. And while it's true that there are plenty of things that make an adolescent recoil, the phrase "world-class city" was my personal horror. It was a mantra that was repeated by Toronto politicians ad nauseam, and it ended up on other people's lips (my friends from Montréal found it endlessly amusing). The fact that local boosters had to prop up Toronto with a meaningless moniker made me wonder: If Toronto's so great, why do people sound like jerks when they say so?

Looking back now, it's easier to understand where those three little words came from. Have you been to Toronto? Chances are that even if you've never set foot in there, you've seen the city a hundred times over. Known for the past several years as "Hollywood North," Toronto has been a stand-in for international centers from European capitals to New York—but rarely does it play itself. Self-deprecating Torontonians embody a paradox: Proud of their city's architectural, cultural, and culinary charms, they are unsure whether it's all up to international snuff.

After spending a single afternoon wandering around Toronto, you might wonder why this is a question at all. The sprawling city boasts lush parks, renowned architecture, and excellent galleries. There's no shortage of skyscrapers, particularly in the downtown core. Still, many visitors marvel at the number of Torontonians who live in houses on tree-lined boulevards that are a walk or a bike ride away from work.

Out-of-towners can see the fun side of the place, but Torontonians aren't so sure. They recall the stuffiness of the city's past. Often called "Toronto the Good," it was a town where you could walk down any street in safety, but you couldn't get a drink on Sunday.

Then a funny thing happened on the way through the 1970s. Canada loosened its immigration policies and welcomed waves of Italians, Greeks, Chinese, Vietnamese, Jamaicans, Indians, Somalians, and others, many of whom settled in Toronto. Political unrest in Québec drove out Anglophones, many into the waiting arms of Toronto (that's how my Montréal friends arrived in Toronto in the first place). The city's economy flourished, which in turn gave its cultural side a boost.

Natives and visitors alike enjoy the benefits of this rich cultural mosaic. More than 7,000 restaurants are scattered across the city, serving everything from simple Greek souvlakia to Asian-accented fusion cuisine. Festivals such as Caribana and Caravan draw tremendous crowds to celebrate heritage through music and dance. Its newfound cosmopolitanism has made Toronto a key player on the arts scene, too. The Toronto International Film Festival in September and the International Festival of Authors in October draw top stars of the movie and publishing worlds. The theater scene rivals London's and New York's.

By any measure, Toronto is a great place to be. It has accomplished something rare, expanding and developing its daring side while holding on to its traditional strengths. The "world-class city" campaign may have been a world-class flop, but maybe that lingering insecurity is exactly what propels Toronto forward. It's a great place to visit, but watch out: You may just end up wanting to live here.

1 Essentials

GETTING THERE

BY PLANE   Most flights arrive at **Pearson International Airport,** in the northwest corner of metro Toronto, approximately 30 minutes from downtown. The trip usually takes 10 to 15 minutes longer during the weekday morning rush (7–9am) and evening rush (4–7pm). A few flights land at the **Toronto Island Airport,** a short ferry ride from downtown; if you're planning a trip to Montréal or Ottawa, check out **Porter Airlines** (✆ **888/619-8622** or 416/619-8622; www.flyporter.com), which offers daily flights from the island airport.

Pearson serves more than 50 airlines. In 2004, its long-awaited new terminal, officially named **Terminal 1,** opened to international traffic; however, it didn't open to U.S. flights until 2007. The other passenger terminal is the **Trillium Terminal 3.** Both terminals are airy and modern, with moving walkways, huge food courts, and many retail stores. For general airport information, including the lost and found department, call the **Greater Toronto Airport Authority** at ✆ 416/776-3000 (www.gtaa.com).

To get from the airport to downtown, take Highway 427 south to the Gardiner Expressway East. A **taxi** costs about C$46 (US$46/£23). A slightly sleeker way to go is by flat-rate **limousine,** which starts at C$50 (US$50/£25). Two limo services are **Aaroport** (✆ 416/745-1555) and **AirLine** (✆ 905/676-3210). You don't need a reservation. Most first-class hotels run their own **hotel limousine** services; check when you make your reservation.

The convenient **Airport Express bus** (✆ **905/564-6333**) travels between the airport, the bus terminal, and major downtown hotels—the Westin Harbour Castle, Fairmont Royal York, the Sheraton Centre Toronto, and the Delta Chelsea—every 20 to 30 minutes, from 4:55am to 12:55am. The adult fare is C$17 (US$17/£8.50) one-way, C$29 (US$29/£15) round-trip; children under 11 accompanied by an adult ride free (applies to two kids per adult). There is also a **GO Transit bus** (✆ **416/869-3200**) that at press time is picking up passengers at Terminal 1 and delivering them to the Yorkdale or York Mills subway stations. The fare is only C$4.05 (US$4.05/£2.05), but be warned—GO buses do not have under-floor luggage compartments. If you're traveling with only a carry-on bag, this bus can be a great option.

The cheapest way to go is by **bus and subway,** which takes about an hour. During the day, you have three options: the no. 192 "Airport Rocket" bus to Kipling station, the no. 58A bus to Lawrence West station, or the no. 307 bus to Eglinton West station. In the middle of the night, you can take the no. 300A bus to Yonge and Bloor. The fare of C$2.75 (US$2.75/£1.35) includes free transfer to the subway (which is available till 1:30am). All buses make stops at both terminals 1 and 3. It doesn't matter which bus you use; they all take roughly the same amount of time. (The Airport Rocket reaches the subway fastest, but the subway ride to downtown is twice as long as from the other stations.) For more information, call the **Toronto Transit Commission,** or TTC (✆ 416/393-4636).

Downtown Toronto

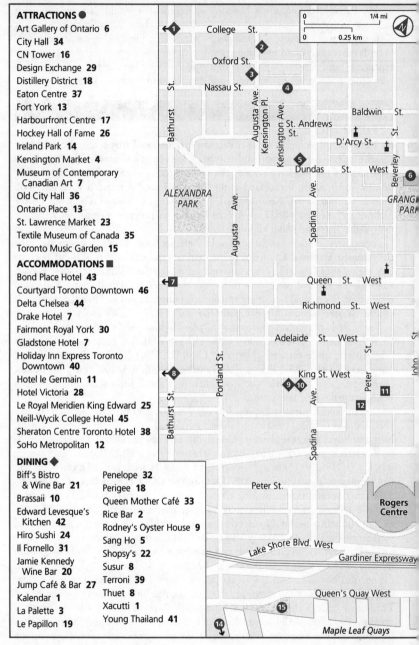

ATTRACTIONS ●
Art Gallery of Ontario **6**
City Hall **34**
CN Tower **16**
Design Exchange **29**
Distillery District **18**
Eaton Centre **37**
Fort York **13**
Harbourfront Centre **17**
Hockey Hall of Fame **26**
Ireland Park **14**
Kensington Market **4**
Museum of Contemporary
  Canadian Art **7**
Old City Hall **36**
Ontario Place **13**
St. Lawrence Market **23**
Textile Museum of Canada **35**
Toronto Music Garden **15**

ACCOMMODATIONS ■
Bond Place Hotel **43**
Courtyard Toronto Downtown **46**
Delta Chelsea **44**
Drake Hotel **7**
Fairmont Royal York **30**
Gladstone Hotel **7**
Holiday Inn Express Toronto
  Downtown **40**
Hotel le Germain **11**
Hotel Victoria **28**
Le Royal Meridien King Edward **25**
Neill-Wycik College Hotel **45**
Sheraton Centre Toronto Hotel **38**
SoHo Metropolitan **12**

DINING ◆
Biff's Bistro
  & Wine Bar **21**
Brassaii **10**
Edward Levesque's
  Kitchen **42**
Hiro Sushi **24**
Il Fornello **31**
Jamie Kennedy
  Wine Bar **20**
Jump Café & Bar **27**
Kalendar **1**
La Palette **3**
Le Papillon **19**
Penelope **32**
Perigee **18**
Queen Mother Café **33**
Rice Bar **2**
Rodney's Oyster House **9**
Sang Ho **5**
Shopsy's **22**
Susur **8**
Terroni **39**
Thuet **8**
Xacutti **1**
Young Thailand **41**

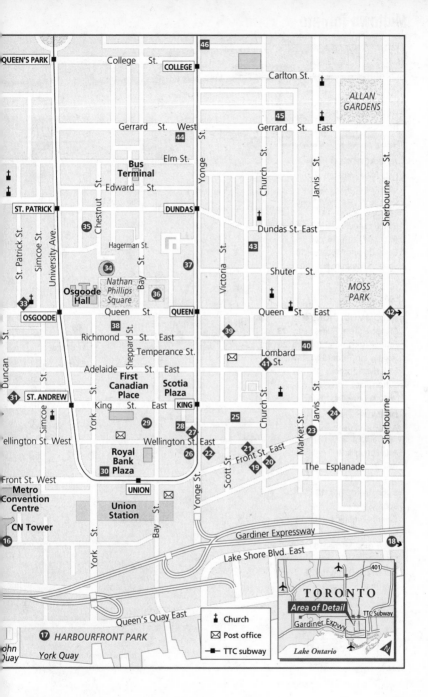

Midtown Toronto

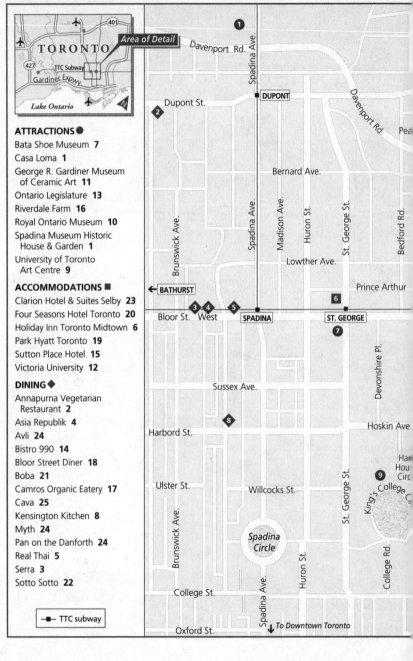

■— TTC subway

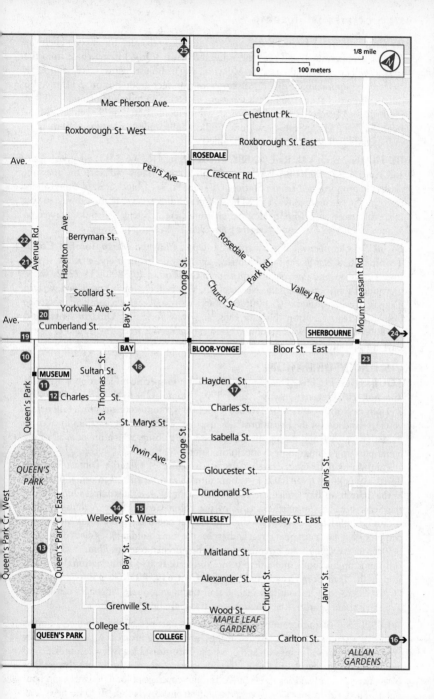

MacPherson Ave.

Roxborough St. West

Chestnut Pk.

Roxborough St. East

Ave.

Pears Ave.

ROSEDALE

Crescent Rd.

Avenue Rd.

Hazelton Ave.

Berryman St.

Rosedale

Park Rd.

Valley Rd.

Mount Pleasant Rd.

Scollard St.

Yorkville Ave.

Bay St.

Church St.

Yonge St.

Ave.

Cumberland St.

SHERBOURNE

BAY

BLOOR-YONGE

Bloor St.   East

Queen's Park

MUSEUM

Sultan St.

St. Thomas St.

Charles St.

Hayden St.

Charles St.

Isabella St.

St. Marys St.

Irwin Ave.

Yonge St.

Gloucester St.

Dundonald St.

**QUEEN'S
PARK**

Queen's Park Cr. West

Queen's Park Cr. East

Wellesley St. West

WELLESLEY

Wellesley St. East

Jarvis St.

Bay St.

Maitland St.

Alexander St.

Church St.

Jarvis St.

Grenville St.

Wood St.

*MAPLE LEAF
GARDENS*

College St.

Carlton St.

QUEEN'S PARK

COLLEGE

*ALLAN
GARDENS*

0   1/8 mile

0   100 meters

373

BY CAR   From the United States, you are most likely to enter Toronto via Highway 401, or via Highway 2 and the Queen Elizabeth Way (QEW) if you come from the west. If you come from the east via Montréal, you'll also use highways 401 and 2.

Here are approximate driving distances to Toronto: from Boston, 911km (566 miles); Buffalo, 155km (96 miles); Chicago, 859km (533 miles); Cincinnati, 806km (500 miles); Detroit, 379km (235 miles); Minneapolis, 1,564km (972 miles); Montréal, 545km (339 miles); New York, 797km (495 miles); Ottawa, 453km (281 miles); and Québec City, 790km (491 miles).

BY TRAIN   Both **VIA Rail** (© **888/VIA-RAIL** or 416/366-8411; www.viarail.ca) and **Amtrak** (© **800/USA-RAIL;** www.amtrak.com) trains pull into the massive, classically proportioned **Union Station,** 65 Front St. W., 1 block west of Yonge Street opposite the Fairmont Royal York. The station has direct access to the subway, so you can easily reach any Toronto destination from here. There is scheduled service to Montréal, Ottawa, Windsor, Niagara Falls, New York, and points west.

BY BUS   Out-of-town buses arrive and depart from the **Metro Toronto Coach Terminal,** 610 Bay St., at Dundas Street, and provide frequent and efficient service from Canadian and American destinations. **Greyhound** (© **800/231-2222;** www.greyhound.com) serves Buffalo, Niagara Falls, Windsor, Detroit, Ottawa, and western Canada; **Coach Canada** (© **800/461-7661;** www.coachcanada.com) offers service from Montréal, Kingston, Niagara Falls, and New York; and **Ontario Northland** (© **800/461-8558;** www.ontarionorthland.ca) has service from towns such as North Bay and Timmins.

VISITOR INFORMATION

TOURIST OFFICES   The best source for Toronto-specific information is **Tourism Toronto,** 207 Queens Quay W., Suite 590, Toronto, ON M5J 1A7 (© **800/499-2514** from North America, or 416/203-2600; www.torontotourism.com). Call before you leave and ask for the free information package, which includes sections on accommodations, sights, and dining. Better yet, visit the website, which provides all of the above plus up-to-the-minute events information.

For information about traveling in the province of Ontario, contact **Ontario Tourism** (© **800/ONTARIO;** www.ontariotravel.net), or visit its information center in the **Atrium on Bay** (street level) at 20 Dundas St. W.—it's just across Dundas from the Sears store at the northern edge of the Eaton Centre. (The Atrium's mailing address is 595 Bay St., but since the information booth is on the south side of the complex, they use a different street address for the same building.) It's open daily from 8:30am to 5pm; hours are extended during the summer, often to 8pm.

To pick up brochures and a map before you leave **Pearson International Airport,** stop by the **Transport Canada Information Centre** (© **905/676-3506** or 416/247-7678). There's one in each terminal. A staff fluent in a dozen languages can answer questions about tourist attractions, ground transportation, and more.

WEBSITES   **Toronto.com** (www.toronto.com), operated by the *Toronto Star,* offers extensive restaurant reviews, events listings, and feature articles. A couple of other great sources for local goings-on and news: the **Torontoist** blog (www.torontoist.com) and **blogTO** (www.blogto.com). If you love to shop, check out **SweetSpot** (www.sweetspot.ca) and for its extensive Toronto coverage of local designers and boutiques. The **Gridskipper** blog (www.gridskipper.com) covers some Toronto news, too.

CITY LAYOUT

Toronto is laid out in a grid . . . with a few interesting exceptions. **Yonge Street** (pronounced *Young*) is the main north-south street, stretching from Lake Ontario in the south well beyond Highway 401 in the north. Yonge Street divides western cross streets from eastern cross streets. The main east-west artery is **Bloor Street,** which cuts through the heart of downtown.

"Downtown" usually refers to the area from Eglinton Avenue south to the lake, between Spadina Avenue in the west and Jarvis Street in the east. Because this is such a large area, I have divided it into five sections. **Downtown West** runs from the lake north to College Street; the eastern boundary is Yonge Street. **Downtown East** goes from the lake north to Carlton Street (once College St. reaches Yonge, it becomes Carlton St.); the western boundary is Yonge Street. **Midtown** extends from College Street north to Davenport Road; the eastern boundary is Jarvis Street. **The Danforth/The East End** runs east Danforth Avenue; the western boundary is Broadview Avenue. **Uptown** is the area north of Davenport Road.

In Downtown West, you'll find many of the lakeshore attractions: Harbourfront, Ontario Place, Fort York, Exhibition Place, and the Toronto Islands. It also boasts the CN Tower, City Hall, the Four Seasons Centre for the Performing Arts, the Rogers Centre (formerly known as SkyDome), Chinatown, the Art Gallery of Ontario, and the Eaton Centre. Downtown East includes the Distillery District, the St. Lawrence Market, the Sony Centre (formerly the Hummingbird Centre), the St. Lawrence Centre for the Arts, and St. James' Cathedral. Midtown West contains the Royal Ontario Museum; the Gardiner Museum; the University of Toronto; Markham Village; and chic Yorkville, a prime area for shopping and dining. Midtown East/The East End features Riverdale Farm, the historic Necropolis, and Greektown. Uptown has traditionally been a residential area, but it's now a fast-growing entertainment area, too. Its attractions include the Sunnybrook park system and the Ontario Science Centre.

Toronto sprawls so widely that quite a few of its primary attractions lie outside the downtown core. These include the Toronto Zoo, Paramount Canada's Wonderland, and the McMichael Canadian Art Collection. Because these attractions require serious travel time and take up the better part of a day to see, you may want to give them a miss if you only have a short stay in the city.

There's also underground Toronto. You can walk from the Dundas subway station south through the Eaton Centre until you hit Queen Street, turn west to the Sheraton Centre, then head south. You'll pass through the Richmond-Adelaide Centre, First Canadian Place, and Toronto Dominion Centre, and go all the way (through the dramatic Royal Bank Plaza) to Union Station. En route, branches lead off to the stock exchange, Sun Life Centre, and Metro Hall. Additional walkways link Simcoe Plaza to 200 Wellington West and to the CBC Broadcast Centre. Other walkways run around Bloor Street and Yonge Street and elsewhere in the city. While its wide-ranging network makes this an excellent way to get around the downtown core when the weather is grim, the underground city has its own attractions, too. First Canadian Place in particular is known for hosting free lunch-hour lectures, opera and dance performances, and art exhibits; see www.fcpfirst.com.

2 Getting Around

The **Toronto Transit Commission,** or TTC (© **416/393-4636** for 24-hr. information; recordings available in 18 languages; www.city.toronto.on.ca/ttc), operates the subway, bus, streetcar, and light rapid transit (LRT) system.

Fares, including transfers to buses or streetcars, are C$2.75 (US$2.75/£1.35) or 10 tickets for C$23 (US$23/£12) for adults. Students age 13 to 19 with valid ID and seniors pay C$1.85 (US$1.85/95p) or 10 tickets for C$15 (US$15/£7.50), and children 12 and under pay C70¢ (US70¢/35p) or 10 tickets for C$5 (US$5/£2.50). You can buy a special day pass for C$9 (US$9/£4.50) that's good for unlimited travel for one person after 9:30am on weekdays and all day on weekends (at press time there has been talk of removing the weekday rush-hour restriction). There's also a weekly pass for C$32 (US$32/£16) for adults and C$26 (US$26/£13) for seniors, students, and children (there is no weekly pass for children under 12).

For surface transportation, you need a ticket, a token, or exact change. You can buy tickets and tokens at subway entrances and at authorized stores that display the sign TTC TICKETS MAY BE PURCHASED HERE. Bus drivers do not sell tickets, nor will they make change. Always obtain a free transfer *where you board the train or bus,* in case you need it. In the subways, use the push-button machine just inside the entrance. On streetcars and buses, ask the driver for a transfer.

THE SUBWAY   It's fast (especially compared with snarled surface traffic), clean, and very simple to use. There are two major lines—Bloor-Danforth and Yonge-University-Spadina—and one smaller line, Sheppard, in the northern part of the city. The Bloor Street east-west line runs from Kipling Avenue in the west to Kennedy Road in the east (where it connects with Scarborough Rapid Transit to Scarborough Centre and McCowan Rd.). The Yonge Street north-south line runs from Finch Avenue in the north to Union Station (Front St.) in the south. From there, it loops north along University Avenue and connects with the Bloor line at the St. George station. A Spadina extension runs north from St. George to Downsview station at Sheppard Avenue. The Sheppard line connects only with the Yonge line at Sheppard Station and runs east through north Toronto for just 6km (4 miles).

The LRT system connects downtown to Harbourfront. The fare is one ticket or token. It runs from Union Station along Queens Quay to Spadina, with stops at Queens Quay ferry docks, York Street, Simcoe Street, and Rees Street; then it continues up Spadina to the Spadina subway station. The transfer from the subway to the LRT (and vice versa) at Union Station is free.

The subway operates Monday through Saturday from 6am to 1:30am and Sunday from 9am to 1:30am. From 1am to 5:30am, the Blue Night Network operates on basic surface routes. It runs about every 30 minutes. For route information, pick up a "Ride Guide" at subway entrances or call © **416/393-4636.** Multilingual information is available. You can also use the automated information service at © **416/393-8663.**

BUSES & STREETCARS   Where the subway leaves off, buses and streetcars take over. They run east-west and north-south along the city's arteries. When you pay your fare (on bus, streetcar, or subway), always pick up a transfer so that you won't have to pay again if you want to transfer to another mode of transportation.

BY TAXI

As usual, this is an expensive mode of transportation. It's C$2.75 (US$2.75/£1.35) the minute you step in and C$1.30 (US$1.30/65p) for each additional kilometer.

The TTC Subway System

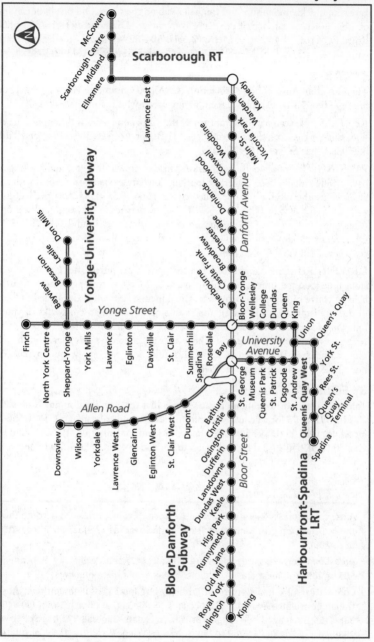

Fares can quickly mount up. You can hail a cab on the street, find one in line in front of a big hotel, or call one of the major companies—**Diamond** (© 416/366-6868), **Royal** (© 416/777-9222), or **Metro** (© 416/504-8294). If you experience problems with cab service, call the **Metro Licensing Commission** (© 416/392-3082).

BY CAR

The **Canadian Automobile Association (CAA),** 60 Commerce Valley Dr. E., Thornhill (© 905/771-3111), provides aid to any driver who is a member of AAA.

RENTALS   You can rent cars from any of the major companies at the airport. In addition, **Budget** has a convenient location at 141 Bay St. (© 416/364-7104), and **Tilden** is at 930 Yonge St. (© 416/925-4551).

PARKING   It's not fun finding parking in downtown Toronto, and parking lots have a wide range of fees. Generally speaking, the city-owned lots, marked with a big green P, are the most affordable. They charge about C$2 (US$2/£1) per half-hour, with a C$16 to C$20 (US$16–US$20/£8–£10) maximum between 7am and 6pm. After 6pm and on Sunday, the maximum rates drops to around C$8 (US$8/£4). Observe the parking restrictions—otherwise, the city will tow your car away, and it'll cost more than C$100 (US$100/£50) to get it back.

DRIVING RULES   A right turn at a red light is permitted after coming to a full stop, unless posted otherwise. The driver and front-seat passengers must wear seat belts; if you're caught not wearing one, you'll incur a substantial fine. The speed limit in the city is 50kmph (30 mph). You must stop at pedestrian crosswalks. If you are following a streetcar and it stops, you must stop well back from the rear doors so passengers can exit easily and safely. (Where there are concrete safety islands in the middle of the street for streetcar stops, this rule does not apply, but exercise care nonetheless.) Radar detectors are illegal.

BY FERRY

Toronto Parks and Recreation operates ferries that travel to the Toronto Islands. Call © 416/392-8193 for schedules and information. Round-trip fares are C$6 (US$6/£3) for adults, C$3.50 (US$3.50/£1.75) for seniors and students 15 to 19 (with valid ID), C$2.50 (US$2.50/£1.25) for children 3 to 14, and free for children 2 and under.

FAST FACTS: Toronto

American Express   There are several American Express offices in Toronto, but the most central is at Millenium Travel Canada Inc. at 77 Bloor St. W. (© 416/962-2200).

Area Code   Toronto's area codes are **416** and **647**; outside the city, the code is **905** or **289.** You must dial all 10 digits for all local phone numbers.

Consulates   All embassies are in Ottawa, but local consulates include: **Australian Consulate-General,** 175 Bloor St. E., Suite 314, at Church Street (© 416/323-1155; subway: Bloor-Yonge); **British Consulate-General,** 777 Bay St., Suite 2800, at College (© 416/593-1290; subway: College); and the **U.S. Consulate,** 360 University Ave. (© 416/595-1700; subway: St. Patrick).

Dentists For emergency services from 8am till midnight, call the **Dental Emergency Service** (ⓒ 416/485-7121). After midnight, your best bet is the **University Health Network,** which manages three downtown hospitals (ⓒ 416/340-3111). Otherwise, ask the front-desk staff or concierge at your hotel.

Doctors The staff or concierge at your hotel should be able to help you locate a doctor. You can also call the **College of Physicians and Surgeons,** 80 College St. (ⓒ 416/967-2626) or visit their website at www.cpso.on.ca (click "Doctor Search") for a referral. See also "Emergencies," below.

Emergencies Call ⓒ 911 for fire, police, or ambulance.

Hospitals In the downtown core, the **University Health Network** manages three hospitals: **Toronto General** at 200 Elizabeth St., **Princess Margaret** at 610 University Ave., and **Toronto Western** at 399 Bathurst St. The UHN has a central switchboard for all three (ⓒ 416/340-3111). Other hospitals include **St. Michael's,** 30 Bond St. (ⓒ 416/360-4000), and **Mount Sinai,** 600 University Ave. (ⓒ 416/596-4200). Also downtown is the **Hospital for Sick Children,** 555 University Ave. (ⓒ 416/813-1500). Uptown, there's **Sunnybrook Hospital,** 2075 Bayview Ave., north of Eglinton (ⓒ 416/480-6100). In the eastern part of the city, go to **Toronto East General Hospital,** 825 Coxwell Ave. (ⓒ 416/461-8272).

Liquor Laws The minimum drinking age is 19. Drinking hours are daily from 11am to 2am. The government is the only retail vendor. **Liquor Control Board of Ontario (LCBO)** stores sell liquor, wine, and some beers. They're open Monday through Saturday. Most are open from 10am to 6pm; some stay open evenings, and a few are open Sunday from noon to 5pm. The nicest shop is the **LCBO Summerhill,** 10 Scrivener Sq. (ⓒ 416/922-0403; subway: Summerhill). Built out of a former train station, this outpost hosts cooking classes, wines and spirits tastings, and party-planning seminars. Another good branch is at the **Manulife Centre,** 55 Bloor St. W. (ⓒ 416/925-5266). See www.lcbo.com for information about products and special in-store events.

Newspapers & Magazines The four daily newspapers are the *Globe and Mail,* the *National Post,* the *Toronto Star,* and the *Toronto Sun. Eye* and *Now* are free arts-and-entertainment weeklies. *Xtra!* is a free weekly targeted at the gay and lesbian community. In addition, many English-language ethnic newspapers serve Toronto's Portuguese, Hungarian, Italian, East Indian, Korean, Chinese, and Caribbean communities. *Toronto Life* is the major monthly city magazine; its sister publication is *Toronto Life Fashion. Where Toronto* is usually free at hotels and some Theater District restaurants.

Mail Postal services are available at convenience stores and drugstores. Almost all sell stamps, and many have a separate counter where you can ship packages from 8:30am to 5pm. Look for the sign in the window indicating such services. There are also post-office windows in **Atrium on Bay** (ⓒ 416/506-0911), in **Commerce Court** (ⓒ 416/956-7452), and at the **TD Centre** (ⓒ 416/360-7105).

Pharmacies One big chain is **Pharma Plus,** which has a store at 63 Wellesley St., at Church Street (ⓒ 416/924-7760). It's open daily from 8am to midnight. Other Pharma Plus branches are in College Park, Manulife Centre, Commerce Court, and First Canadian Place. The only 24-hour drugstore near downtown is **Shopper's Drug Mart** at 700 Bay St., at Gerrard Street West (ⓒ 416/979-2424).

Police In a life-threatening emergency, call ℂ **911**. For all other matters, contact the **Metro police**, 40 College St. (ℂ **416/808-2222**).

Safety As large cities go, Toronto is generally safe, but be alert and use common sense, particularly at night. The Yonge/Bloor, Dundas, and Union subway stations are favorites with pickpockets. In the downtown area, Moss Park is considered one of the toughest areas to police. Avoid Allan Gardens, Trinity-Bellwoods, and other parks at night.

Taxes The provincial retail sales tax is 8%; on accommodations, it's 5%. There is an additional 5% national goods-and-services tax (GST). The Canadian government suspended the GST Visitors' Rebate Program in 2007.

Time Toronto is on Eastern Standard Time, the same as New York, Boston, and Montréal. It's an hour ahead of Chicago.

3 Where to Stay

Whether you're seeking a historic hotel with old-world elegance or looking for all the conveniences of the office in your "home" away from home, you'll find a perfect place to stay in Toronto. The city's accommodations run the gamut from intimate boutique inns to large, comfortable convention hotels. Proximity to major attractions (such as the CN Tower, Harbourfront, the Rogers Centre, and the Eaton Centre) can cost a bundle. Even budget hotels charge more than C$150 (US$150/£75) a night in the high season, which runs from April to October. And remember to factor the 5% accommodations tax and the 5% GST into what you spend.

DOWNTOWN WEST
VERY EXPENSIVE

SoHo Metropolitan Hotel ✮✮✮   This gorgeous boutique hotel offers grown-up elegance at its most refined. The guest rooms are beautiful—a serene palette of neutral tones and blond wood make for a soothing setting. But more importantly, the SoHo Met's rooms make the best use of technology I've found in any Toronto hotel. It's as if the designers compiled a list of all of the most frustrating aspects about staying in a hotel room and resolved to fix them. Hate hopping into bed and then discovering you have to jump out again to turn out a light? All lights in the room can be controlled by switches right next to the headboard. Hate opening and closing curtains and drapes? All it takes here is the flick of another switch. Even better, another control will bring down a privacy screen that lets light in but shields you from view. The marble bathroom floor heats up at your command. The in-room safe is big enough for a laptop and has an outlet inside so that you can charge up your computer battery. There are no tatty DO NOT DISTURB signs; instead, another control panel lets you indicate your desire to be left alone, or request housekeeping as need be. And, of course, the telephones are cordless (it's a small thing but one I wish that other hotels would understand is important). The SoHo Met is also home to one of Toronto's best restaurants, Senses.

318 Wellington St. W., Toronto, ON M5V 3T4. ℂ **800/668-6600** or 416/599-8800. Fax 416/599-8801. www.metropolitan.com/soho. 89 units. From C$385 (US$385/£193) double. AE, DC, MC, V. Valet parking C$18 (US$18/£9); self-parking C$12 (US$12/£6). Subway: St. Andrew. **Amenities:** Restaurant; bar; health club; concierge; business center; 24-hr. room service; laundry service; dry cleaning. *In room:* A/C, TV, dataport, minibar, coffeemaker, hair dryer, iron, safe.

EXPENSIVE

The Fairmont Royal York ✦ Fairmont properties tend to the gigantic, and this historic hotel built by the Canadian-Pacific Railroad in 1929 is no exception. It has 1,365 guest rooms and suites, and 35 meeting and banquet rooms. The old-fashioned lobby is magnificent, and just sitting on a plush couch and watching the crowd is an event. Still, you have to decide whether you want to stay under the same roof with more than 1,000 others—business travelers, shoppers, tour groups, and convention-eers. Service is remarkably efficient but necessarily impersonal; the downtown loca-tion, across from Union Station and just steps from the Theatre District and the Sony Centre, is excellent. The guest rooms are furnished with antique reproductions, and there's generally not much spare space. If you're willing to spring for a Fairmont Gold room (the extra cost is well worth it, in my opinion), you'll stay on a private floor with superior, spacious rooms, separate check-in and concierge, a private lounge, and com-plimentary breakfast. The hotel pays particular attention to accessibility, making adap-tations to some guest rooms so that they are specially designed for wheelchair users, the hearing impaired, and the visually impaired. Every public area in the hotel is wheelchair-accessible.

100 Front St. W., Toronto, ON M5J 1E3. ℂ 800/441-1414. Fax 416/368-9040. www.fairmont.com/royalyork. 1,365 units. From C$229 (US$229/£115) double. Packages available. AE, DC, DISC, MC, V. Parking C$26 (US$26/£13). Sub-way: Union. Pets accepted. **Amenities:** 5 restaurants; 4 bars/lounges; skylit indoor pool; health club; spa (w/special packages for guests); Jacuzzi; sauna; concierge; business center; shopping arcade; salon; 24-hr. room service; babysit-ting; same-day laundry service/dry cleaning. *In room:* A/C, TV, dataport, minibar, coffeemaker, hair dryer, iron.

Hotel le Germain ✦✦ The Groupe Germain has become something of a legend in Québec for its excellent boutique hotels. Their first Toronto venture opened in spring 2003 to instant accolades. Located in Toronto's entertainment district, the Hotel le Germain has an elegant but slightly offbeat sensibility. The public spaces are magnificent: the vast lobby manages the amazing trick of being at once intimate and grand. The library lounge area boasts a fireplace, an espresso maker, a wall of objets d'art, and cozy white couches. Attention is paid to the smallest details, which explains why the elevators are "wrapped" in words of English and French poetry, and why the corridors are so broad (the Groupe Germain build this hotel from scratch, so they could do just what they pleased). The guest rooms are just as precise: the ceilings are high, the desk can be moved around to your liking (it's attached to the wall on one side), and the linens and robes are by Frette. My favorite feature, though, is the glass wall in every bathroom, which allows light in from the main room and makes every-thing feel more spacious (there are blinds for those who want their privacy, though).

30 Mercer St., Toronto, ON M5V 1H3. ℂ 866/345-9501 or 416/345-9500. Fax 416/345-9501. www.germain toronto.com. 122 units. From C$270 (US$270/£135) double. AE, DC, MC, V. Parking C$28 (US$28/£14). Subway: St. Andrew. **Amenities:** Restaurant; bar; health club; concierge; business center; 24-hr. room service; babysitting; laun-dry service; dry cleaning. *In room:* A/C, TV, dataport, minibar, coffeemaker, hair dryer, iron, safe.

MODERATE

Delta Chelsea ✦✦ *Kids Value* While not a budget hotel, the Delta Chelsea offers bang for the buck. Its downtown location draws heaps of tour groups and a smatter-ing of business travelers, its family-friendly facilities lure those with tykes, and its weekend packages pull in the cost-conscious. It's impossible for a hotel to be all things to all people, but the Delta Chelsea comes pretty close. Luxury seekers should look elsewhere, and backpackers won't be able to afford it, but the Delta Chelsea is talented at meeting the needs of many of those in between. This is a particularly good bet for young families. The guest rooms are bright and cheery; a few have kitchenettes, which is always a plus for family travel. On the Signature Club floor for business travelers, rooms have cordless speakerphones, faxes, well-stocked desks, and ergonomic chairs. The Delta Chelsea makes the most of its generous size, with features like the Corkscrew, a four-story indoor waterslide. What 8-year-old could resist? The hotel has got some grown-up amenities, too, such as the Bb33 Bistro and Brasserie, a two-in-one restaurant with a formal dining room and a fuss-free buffet room. There's also Deck 27, a lounge with a fantastic panoramic view of Toronto.

33 Gerrard St. W., Toronto, ON M5G 1Z4. © 800/243-5732 or 416/595-1975. Fax 416/585-4362. www.deltahotels. com. 1,590 units. From C$159 (US$159/£80) double. Extra person C$20 (US$20/£10). Children 17 and under stay free in parent's room. Weekend packages available. AE, DC, DISC, MC, V. Valet parking C$29 (US$29/£15); self-parking C$23 (US$23/£12). Subway: College. **Amenities:** 3 restaurants; 3 bars; 2 pools (1 for adults only); health club; Jacuzzi; sauna; children's center; billiards room; concierge; tour desk; business center; salon; babysitting; laundry service; dry cleaning. *In room:* A/C, TV, coffeemaker, hair dryer, iron.

The Drake Hotel 🎯🎯 *Finds*   The Drake opened in February 2004, and has already earned a following that includes some famous faces (the Black Eyed Peas and actress Heather Graham have stayed here). Part of the appeal is the hotel's rags-to-riches pedigree: The Drake was rescued by owner Jeff Stober, who injected C$6 million into creating a boutique hotel. The renovation is gorgeous. While the 19 guest rooms are mostly on the tiny side—they range from 14 to 36 sq. m (150–385 sq. ft.—they are cleverly designed and have good amenities (CD/DVD players and lovely linens, for example). The Drake's strength is in its public spaces, and for a property this small, it has an awful lot. There are a restaurant and bar, a rooftop lounge, and a cafe; an exercise studio for yoga classes and a massage room; and a performance venue, the Underground, that features live music. There are also works of art throughout the hotel. The Drake has been warmly welcomed by Toronto's arts community, and this is the one hotel in town where you're far more likely to meet city residents than visitors.

1150 Queen St. W., Toronto, ON M6J 1J3. © 416/531-5042. Fax 416/531-9493. www.thedrakehotel.ca. 19 units. From C$179 (US$179/£90) double. AE, MC, V. Subway: Osgoode, then streetcar west to Beaconsfield. **Amenities:** 2 restaurants; cafe; 2 bars; yoga studio; massage room. *In room:* A/C, TV, dataport, hair dryer, iron.

The Gladstone Hotel 🎯🎯 *Finds*   This Victorian red-brick hotel first opened its doors to guests in 1889; more recently, it was a grim flophouse. After a massive top-to-bottom renovation, the hotel relaunched itself as a chic place to stay in December 2005. The interior is notable for its decorative archways and high ceilings. Each guest room has been designed by a Canadian artist; the results range from the film-noir setting of the Parlour of Twilight, which channels the spirit of Raymond Chandler, to the riotous Red Room, a sumptuous confection of color, pattern, and texture. The view from the Rock Star Suite, located in the hotel's two-story tower, makes the downtown Toronto core look like a faraway metropolis. The Gladstone's co-owner, Christina Zeidler, is an artist, so it's no surprise that the property is beloved by Toronto's arts community. The hotel uses its public spaces as a rotating art gallery, and it is famous for its Wednesday-night drawing classes. The Melody Bar is widely regarded as the best place in Toronto for karaoke.

One caveat about the Gladstone: If you're a light sleeper, this may not be the place for you. The hotel has its original windows—which open to let air in—but they have single-pane glass. Earplugs are provided on the nightstand, but since the Gladstone is situated near railway tracks, this may not afford enough peace and quiet for everyone's liking.

1214 Queen St. W., Toronto, ON M6J 1J6. ✆ **416/531-4635**. Fax 416/539-0953. www.gladstonehotel.com. 51 units. From C$175 (US$175/£88) double. AE, MC, V. Subway: Osgoode, then streetcar west to Gladstone. **Amenities:** Restaurant; cafe; bar. *In room:* A/C, TV, dataport, hair dryer, iron, safe.

Sheraton Centre Toronto Hotel ★★ *Kids*   A convention favorite, the Sheraton is across the street from New City Hall, a block from the Eaton Centre, and a short stroll from the trendy restaurant and boutique area of Queen Street West. It's entirely possible to stay here and never venture outside—the Sheraton complex includes restaurants, bars, and a cinema, and the building connects to Toronto's underground city. If you long for a patch of green, the hotel provides that, too: The south side of the lobby contains a manicured garden with a waterfall. Am I making the place sound like a monolith? Well, it is. But it's an excellent home base for families because of its location and extensive list of child-friendly features, including a children's center and a huge pool. Most of the guest rooms in this skyscraper-heavy neighborhood lack a serious view, though as you near the top of the 46-story complex, the sights are inspiring indeed. Designed for business travelers, the Club Level rooms contain mini–business centers with a fax/printer/copier and two-line speakerphone.

123 Queen St. W., Toronto, ON M5H 2M9. ✆ **800/325-3535** or 416/361-1000. Fax 416/947-4854. www.sheraton toronto.com. 1,377 units. From C$179 (US$179/£90) double. Extra person C$20 (US$20/£10). 2 children 17 and under stay free in parent's room. Packages available. AE, DC, MC, V. Parking C$33 (US$33/£17). Subway: Osgoode. **Amenities:** 2 restaurants; bar; gigantic heated indoor/outdoor pool; health club; spa; Jacuzzi; sauna; children's center; concierge; tour desk; business center; shopping arcade; 24-hr. room service; babysitting; laundry service; dry cleaning. *In room:* A/C, TV, dataport, coffeemaker, hair dryer, iron.

INEXPENSIVE
Hotel Victoria ★★ *Value*   In a landmark downtown building near the Sony Centre and the Hockey Hall of Fame, the Victoria boasts the glamorous touches of an earlier age, such as crown moldings and marble columns in the lobby. It's Toronto's second-oldest hotel (built in 1909), but the facilities are upgraded annually. Because of its size, the 56-room hotel offers an unusually high level of personal service and attention, which you normally wouldn't expect in budget accommodations. Standard rooms are on the small side but are nicely put together; deluxe rooms are larger and have coffeemakers and minifridges. Another nice touch: complimentary high-speed wireless Internet access throughout the hotel.

56 Yonge St. (at Wellington St.), Toronto, ON M5E 1G5. ✆ **800/363-8228** or 416/363-1666. Fax 416/363-7327. www. toronto.com/hotelvictoria. 56 units. From C$119 (US$119/£60) double. Extra person C$15 (US$15/£7.50). Rates include continental breakfast. AE, DC, MC, V. Parking nearby from C$20 (US$20/£10). Subway: King. **Amenities:** Restaurant; access to nearby health club; babysitting; laundry service; dry cleaning. *In room:* A/C, TV, dataport, hair dryer, iron.

DOWNTOWN EAST
VERY EXPENSIVE
Le Royal Meridien King Edward ★★   At one time, the King Eddy was the only place in Toronto that Hollywood royalty, such as Liz Taylor and Richard Burton, would consider staying. In the 1980s, after many years of neglect, a group of local investors spent C$40 million to rescue it. The result recalls its former glory, with rosy marble columns and a glass-domed rotunda dominating the lobby. Although the guest rooms aren't what I'd call spacious—28 to 33 sq. m (300–355 sq. ft.) is standard—their uniformly high ceilings give them a sweeping grandeur that is unusual. The rooms are also charmingly appointed. Unlike rooms at many competitors, where you'd be hard-pressed to tell the difference among them, these guest rooms have been decorated with a personal touch. The bathrooms are particularly nice, with large marble tubs.

37 King St. E., Toronto, ON M5C 2E9. © 800/543-4300 or 416/863-9700. Fax 416/863-4102. www.starwoodhotels. com. 298 units. From C$249 (US$249/£125) double. AE, DC, MC, V. Parking C$30 (US$30/£15). Subway: King. Pets accepted. **Amenities:** 2 restaurants; bar; health club; Jacuzzi; sauna; concierge; 24-hr. room service; babysitting; laundry service; dry cleaning. *In room:* A/C, TV, fax, dataport, minibar, hair dryer, iron.

MODERATE

Courtyard Toronto Downtown 🏠 Anyone who knows the Marriott chain of hotels knows that its Courtyard hotels are usually out of the city center, not smack-dab in the middle of things. This bright and shiny property near Yonge and College is an exception, convenient both to the Financial District downtown and to the chic cafes and shops of Midtown—a claim few other hotels in the city can make. The lobby, with its double-sided fireplace, has a surprisingly intimate feel given the size of the hotel (truth be told, it's due to the fact that tour groups have a separate reception area). The guest rooms don't tend to be big, but they do have a lot of comforts, including windows that open, high-speed Internet access ports, and a second sink outside the bathroom. Ongoing refurbishments keep guest rooms looking fresh rather than lived-in. While Courtyards are generally regarded as business hotels, this one has family-friendly facilities such as a children's wading pool.

475 Yonge St. (1 block north of College St.), Toronto, ON M4Y 1X7. © 800/847-5075 or 416/924-0611. Fax 416/ 924-8692. www.courtyard.com/yyzcy. 575 units. From C$169 (US$169/£85) double. AE, DC, MC, V. Valet parking C$30 (US$30/£15). Subway: College. **Amenities:** 2 restaurants; bar; health club; tour desk; business center; limited room service; laundry service; dry cleaning. *In room:* A/C, TV, dataport, minibar, coffeemaker, hair dryer, iron, safe.

INEXPENSIVE

Bond Place Hotel 🏠 The location is right—a block from the Eaton Centre, around the corner from the Canon and Elgin theaters—and so is the price. Perhaps that's why this hotel tends to be popular with tour groups. (The fact that the staff speaks several European and Asian languages doesn't hurt, either.) The rooms are on the small side. Book as far in advance as you can; the hotel is usually packed, especially in summer.

65 Dundas St. E., Toronto, ON M5B 2G8. © 800/268-9390 or 416/362-6061. Fax 416/360-6406. www.bondplacehotel toronto.com. 287 units. From C$99 (US$99/£50) double. Extra person C$15 (US$15/£7.50). Weekend packages available. AE, DC, DISC, MC, V. Parking C$15 (US$15/£7.50). Subway: Dundas. **Amenities:** Restaurant; bar; concierge; tour desk; car-rental desk; limited room service; laundry service; dry cleaning. *In room:* A/C, TV, coffeemaker, hair dryer, iron.

Holiday Inn Express Toronto Downtown This is a no-frills hotel whose main selling point is its location, close to the Financial District and the Eaton Centre. It often offers special promotions, so be sure to ask. Rooms tend to be small, with standard amenities.

111 Lombard St. (between Adelaide and Richmond sts.), Toronto, ON M5C 2T9. © 800/228-5151 or 416/367-5555. Fax 416/367-3470. www.ichotelsgroup.com. 196 units. From C$125 (US$125/£63) double. Rates include continental breakfast. AE, DC, DISC, MC, V. Parking C$20 (US$20/£10). Subway: King or Queen. **Amenities:** Laundry service; dry cleaning. *In room:* A/C, TV, coffeemaker, hair dryer, iron.

Neill-Wycik College Hotel During the school year, this is a residence for nearby Ryerson Polytechnic University. Some students work here in the summer, when the Neill-Wycik morphs into a guesthouse. Travelers on tight budgets won't mind the minimalist approach—rooms have beds, chairs, desks, and phones, but no air-conditioning or TVs. Groups of five bedrooms share two bathrooms and one kitchen with a refrigerator and stove. It's less than a 5-minute walk to the Eaton Centre. The neighborhood is not as appealing as that around Victoria University at the University of Toronto, which offers a similar arrangement (p. 386).

96 Gerrard St. E. (between Church and Jarvis sts.), Toronto, ON M5B 1G7. ✆ **800/268-4358** or 416/977-2320. Fax 416/977-2809. www.neill-wycik.com. 300 units (none with private bathroom). C$56 (US$56/£28) double; C$64 (US$64/£32) family (2 adults plus children). MC, V. Closed Sept to early May. Limited parking nearby C$20 (US$20/£10). Subway: College. **Amenities:** Cafe; sauna; 24-hr. laundry room, 2 roof decks (on the 5th and 23rd floors); TV lounge.

MIDTOWN WEST
VERY EXPENSIVE

Four Seasons Hotel Toronto ★★ *(Kids)*   The Four Seasons is famous as the favored haunt of many visiting celebrities. The Rolling Stones call it home in Toronto, and during the Toronto International Film Festival every September, you can't get in here for love or money. The hotel, in the ritzy Yorkville district, has earned a reputation for offering fine service and complete comfort. Even small fries get the royal treatment: upon arrival, room service brings kids complimentary cookies and milk; the hotel also makes available bicycles and video games for them to borrow. The public areas are decorated like a French parlor, with marble floors and dramatic floral arrangements. Once you make it to your room, you'll find that while it may tend to be on the small side (a standard model is only about 30 sq. m/323 sq. ft.), it's well designed and easy on the eye. Corner rooms have charming balconies—all the better to appreciate street scenes. The formal dining room, Truffles, is a Toronto institution. The second-floor Studio Cafe is a favorite with the business crowd; its menu features many health-conscious, low-fat dishes. The Avenue bar is a perfect perch for people-watching, as it overlooks Yorkville Avenue.

21 Avenue Rd., Toronto, ON M5R 2G1. ✆ **800/268-6282** or 416/964-0411. Fax 416/964-2301. www.fourseasons. com/toronto. 380 units. From C$365 (US$365/£183) double. Weekend discounts and packages available. AE, DC, DISC, MC, V. Valet parking C$30 (US$30/£15). Subway: Bay. **Amenities:** 2 restaurants; 2 bars/lounges; indoor/outdoor pool; health club; Jacuzzi; bike rental; concierge; weekday courtesy limo to downtown; business center; 24-hr. room service; massage; babysitting; same-day laundry service/dry cleaning. *In room:* A/C, TV, dataport, minibar, hair dryer, iron, safe.

Park Hyatt Toronto ★★★   With its ongoing C$60-million renovations, the Park Hyatt has cemented its reputation for being the last word in luxe. It is, in my opinion, the very best hotel in Toronto at the moment, and it's where I'd choose to stay if price were no object. The location of the Park Hyatt is prime: It's in the posh Yorkville district, steps from the Royal Ontario Museum and the Bata Shoe Museum. The guest rooms in the North Tower are among the most generously proportioned in town— the *smallest* is 46 sq. m (500 sq. ft.). In the South Tower the guest rooms are smaller, but they are more individual—there are 90 rooms and 40 different room layouts. All rooms in both towers have free high-speed Internet access. A glamorous lobby dotted with Eastern-inspired objets d'art links the North and South towers. The ground-floor restaurant Annona is a treat for gourmets. The 18th-floor Roof Lounge is famous for attracting writers (author Mordecai Richler famously called the lounge the only civilized place in Toronto). Even if you're not a guest, you can book an appointment at the Stillwater Spa. One signature therapy is a Watsu-style massage, in which you float in a water-filled room while a therapist applies shiatsu moves—it's very soothing.

4 Avenue Rd., Toronto, ON M5R 2E8. ✆ **800/233-1234** or 416/925-1234. Fax 416/924-6693. www.parktoronto. hyatt.com. 346 units. From C$325 (US$325/£163) double. Weekend packages available. AE, DC, DISC, MC, V. Parking C$30 (US$30/£15). Subway: Museum or Bay. Pets accepted. **Amenities:** Restaurant; 2 bars; health club; spa; Jacuzzi; sauna; concierge; business center; 24-hr. room service; babysitting; laundry service; dry cleaning. *In room:* A/C, TV, fax, dataport, minibar, coffeemaker, hair dryer, iron, safe.

EXPENSIVE

The Sutton Place Hotel (*Ŕ*)   Although it towers over the intersection of Bay and Wellesley, the Sutton Place boasts the advantages of a small hotel—particularly detail-oriented, personalized service. In addition to hosting a galaxy of stars and celebrities, the hotel draws sophisticated business and leisure travelers in search of serious pampering. The emphasis is on sophistication—famous guests expect to be left alone, and management protects their privacy. In other words, no autograph seekers The hotel aims for European panache, littering the public spaces with antiques and tapestries. The spacious guest rooms are decorated in a similar, though scaled-down, style. A few suites have full kitchens. Not that you'd want to cook while you're here—the lovely ground-floor Accents restaurant serves Continental fare, and across the street, the star-studded Bistro 990 produces perfect French cuisine. One downside is that The Sutton Place stands alone in its neighborhood. It's about a 10-minute walk to attractions such as the Royal Ontario Museum and the Yorkville shopping district.

955 Bay St., Toronto, ON M5S 2A2. (*Ċ*) 800/268-3790 or 416/924-9221. Fax 416/924-1778. www.toronto.suttonplace. com. 294 units. From C$225 (US$225/£113) double. Extra person C$20 (US$20/£10). Children 17 and under stay free in parent's room. Weekend discounts available. AE, DC, MC, V. Valet parking C$28 (US$28/£14); self-parking C$20 (US$20/£10). Subway: Wellesley. Pets accepted. **Amenities:** Restaurant; bar; indoor pool; health club; sauna; concierge; business center; salon; 24-hr. room service; massage; babysitting; laundry service; dry cleaning. *In room:* A/C, TV, data-port, minibar, coffeemaker, hair dryer, iron, safe.

MODERATE

Clarion Hotel & Suites Selby (*Ŕ*) *(Finds)*   This hotel is one of Toronto's better-kept secrets. Ornate chandeliers, stucco moldings, and high ceilings make the 1890s Victorian building an absolute stunner. In a predominantly gay neighborhood, the Selby attracts gay and straight couples, as well as seniors (the latter group gets special discounts). All of the rooms now have private bathrooms, but only a few have an old-fashioned claw-foot tub. The staff is very friendly, and while there's no concierge, you receive plenty of recommendations for what to see and do. History buffs will love the fact that Ernest Hemingway lived here for a couple of years while he was on staff at the *Toronto Star* newspaper (and yes, there's a Hemingway suite).

592 Sherbourne St., Toronto, ON M4X 1L4. (*Ċ*) 800/4-CHOICE or 416/921-3142. Fax 416/923-3177. www.choice hotels.ca/hotels/hotel?hotel=CN534. 82 units. From C$120 (US$120/£60) double. Rates include continental break-fast. AE, DISC, MC, V. Parking C$10 (US$10/£5). Subway: Sherbourne. **Amenities:** Access to nearby health club; laundry room. *In room:* A/C, TV, dataport, coffeemaker, hair dryer, iron.

Holiday Inn Toronto Midtown *(Value)*   Considering this hotel's tony location—steps from Yorkville and several museums, including the Royal Ontario Museum—the price is hard to beat. The rooms are small but comfortable and outfitted with well-lit worktables. All rooms have free high-speed Internet access. However, there aren't many other amenities or services. This is a good home base for a leisure traveler who prizes location over other considerations. If you're not planning on hanging out a lot in your hotel room, it's a small trade-off to make for the price.

280 Bloor St. W. (at St. George St.), Toronto, ON M5S 1V8. (*Ċ*) 888/HOLIDAY or 416/968-0010. Fax 416/968-7765. ww.ichotelsgroup.com. 209 units. From C$140 (US$140/£70) double. Weekend and other packages available. AE, DC, DISC, MC, V. Parking C$22 (US$22/£11). Subway: St. George. **Amenities:** Restaurant; coffee shop; health club; limited room service; babysitting; laundry service; dry cleaning. *In room:* A/C, TV, dataport, coffeemaker, hair dryer, iron.

INEXPENSIVE

Victoria University (*Ŕ*) *(Value)*   This is a summer steal: You could not find a better deal in this part of town. From early May to late August, Victoria University (which is federated with the University of Toronto) makes its student accommodations available to travelers. Furnishings are simple—a bed (or two, in the twin rooms), desk, and chair are standard—but the surroundings are splendid. Many of the rooms are in Burwash Hall, a 19th-century building that overlooks a peaceful, leafy quad. All rooms are down the street from the Royal Ontario Museum, and up the street from Queen's Park. Guests are provided with linens, towels, and soap.

140 Charles St. W., Toronto, ON M5S 1K9. © 416/585-4524. Fax 416/585-4530. www.vicu.utoronto.ca. 700 units (none with private bathroom). C$60 (US$60/£30) single; C$80 (US$80/£40) double (2 twin beds). Rates include breakfast. Senior and student discounts available. MC, V. Closed Sept–Apr. Nearby parking C$20 (US$20/£10). Subway: Museum. **Amenities:** Tennis courts; access to fitness center w/Olympic-size pool; laundry room. *In room:* No phone.

4 Where to Dine

Dining out is nothing short of a passion in Toronto. It's not that residents are too lazy to cook, but we are spoiled by the embarrassment of edible riches in all parts of the city. The city is a restaurant-goer's nirvana for a wealth of reasons. For starters, there are more than 7,000 places to choose among. They represent cooking styles from any country or nationality you can name, making Toronto's culinary scene both eclectic and palate-teasing.

Meals are subject to the 8% provincial sales tax and to the 5% GST. In other words, tax and tip together can add 30% to your bill. Restaurants normally leave tipping to the diners' discretion unless there are six or more people at the table. The usual amount for good service is 15%, jumping to 20% at the pricier establishments. The price of a bottle of wine is generally quite high because of the tax on imports; get around it by ordering an Ontario vintage—local wines enjoy a rising international reputation. Remember that there is a 10% tax on alcohol. Checked items warrant C$1 (US$1/50p) per piece for the attendant.

DOWNTOWN WEST

This is where you will find Toronto's greatest concentration of great restaurants. **Little Italy,** which runs along **College Street,** and **Chinatown,** which radiates from **Spadina Avenue,** have more restaurants than any other parts of the city. King Street West is another hot spot for in-the-know gourmets.

VERY EXPENSIVE

Susur ✿✿✿ FUSION/VEGETARIAN   Susur is an absolute delight. For such a high-end establishment, its decor is refreshingly low-key, with stark white walls and oyster-pale upholstery warmed with colored lights. There is no pretension here, in either the ambience or the fine service. Named for chef Susur Lee, the restaurant serves stellar cuisine in the true fusion spirit, blending Asian and Western ingredients, cooking methods, and presentation. The menu changes frequently, with bold, savory offerings like rare venison loin with Gorgonzola-hawberry–red wine sauce (there's a vegetarian tasting menu, too). The cooking is complex, and the wine list, while pricey, has been put together with extreme care.

One more thing: If you can't get a reservation at Susur, you can still try its younger sibling, **Lee,** which is next door at no. 603 (© 416/504-7867). Funkier, louder, and far more casual than the first restaurant in the family (no reservations accepted), Lee serves up excellent tapas.

601 King St. W. ⓒ 416/603-2205. www.susur.com. Reservations required. Main courses C$29–C$48 (US$29–US$48/ £15–£24); prix-fixe tasting menu C$90 (US$90/£45). AE, MC, V. Mon–Sat 6–10pm. Subway: St. Andrew, then streetcar west to Bathurst St. and walk 1 block west to Portland St.

Thuet 🏂🏂 BISTRO   If you visited Centro uptown on a previous visit, you may already have sampled some of chef Marc Thuet's excellent cooking. His new spot is both a bistro and a bakery, and it allows the fourth-generation chef from Alsace to make use of some of his family secrets (some of the artisan bread-making recipes come from his ancestor Marcel Thuet, who was whipping up breads with a starter instead of yeast 200 years ago). The bistro's menu is hearty and rich, with entrees like a mille-feuille of yellowfin tuna, ocean trout, and foie gras, and an aged beef tenderloin with a ravioli of braised tripe. Don't be surprised if you're tempted to return to the bakery after you've eaten here—it's open Tuesday through Friday from 8:30am to 3pm, Saturday from 9am to 3pm, and Sunday from 9am to 4pm.

609 King St. W. ⓒ 416/603-2777. www.thuet.ca. Reservations required. Main courses C$30–C$40 (US$30–US$40/ £15–£20). AE, DC, MC, V. Thurs–Sat 6–10:30pm. Subway: St. Andrew, then streetcar west to Portland St.

EXPENSIVE

Brassaii 🏂 BISTRO/INTERNATIONAL   Named for the 1920s French photographer whose prints adorn the walls, Brassaii offers a picture-perfect setting. The long, cavernous dining room is decorated in dusky gray and black, and tall vases stand in the windows, each holding a single long-stemmed calla lily. Even on a street saturated with cool restaurants, Brassaii's excellent cooking and brilliant service stand out. While the menu frequently changes, it might include entrees such as braised duck atop lentils and spinach, or shoulder of lamb with chickpeas and tomato. The desserts are not to be missed, particularly the elegant apple crumble with berries and caramel ice cream. The wine list is substantial, and there are some very good vintages available by the glass. Still, my favorite drink here is the Brassaii martini, which blends a couple of types of fruit juice with 7-Up and vodka. I know it sounds bizarre, but it's a deliciously sweet drink.

461 King St. W. ⓒ 416/598-4730. www.brassaii.com. Reservations recommended. Main courses C$18–C$36 (US$18–US$36/£9–£18). AE, MC, V. Mon–Fri 7:30–11am and 11:30am–midnight; Sat 10am–2:30pm and 5:30pm–midnight; Sun 10am–3pm. Subway: St. Andrew, then streetcar west to Spadina Ave.

Jump Cafe & Bar 🏂🏂 AMERICAN   Jump is such a see-and-be-seen spot that you might suspect it's all show and no substance. Actually, the food is anything but an afterthought. To start, consider steamed mussels in ginger-and-coconut-milk broth or grilled tiger shrimps on Thai mango-peanut salad. The menu features dishes such as grilled 10-ounce New York black angus steak with Yukon gold fries, salsa, and mushroom gravy. The more adventurous have other choices, such as *osso buco* with spinach-and-lemon risotto. The wine list favors the New World, and there are a fair number of selections by the glass. Luxe desserts will set your diet back by about a month. Service is smooth, and the only complaint I could possibly make is that Jump never seems to settle down.

1 Wellington St. W. ⓒ 416/363-3400. www.jumpcafe.com. Reservations required. Main courses C$16–C$42 (US$16–US$42/£8–£21). AE, DC, MC, V. Mon–Fri 11:45am–midnight; Sat 5pm–midnight. Subway: King.

Xacutti 🏂🏂 INDIAN   There are a lot of reasons to love the beautifully executed cuisine of Xacutti (pronounced Sha-*koo*-tee), but I'll begin with the appetizers, which include galangal prawns in a lime-mint curry and baby greens in a kumquat vinaigrette. Mains range from cardamom-smoked lamb with mango chutney and ginger frites to pan-fried cod with new potatoes, spinach, and coconut-tomato curry. The weekend brunch menu is just as good, though it veers away from Indian food, serving up treats like blueberry pancakes with maple syrup and Devonshire cream or a wild mushroom–and–goat cheese omelet. The thoughtful service matches the cuisine.

503 College St. ℂ 416/323-3957. www.xacutti.com. Reservations strongly recommended for dinner; reservations not accepted for Sun brunch. Main courses C$20–C$37 (US$20–US$37/£10–£19). AE, DC, MC, V. Mon–Sat 6:30pm–midnight; Sun 10:30am–4pm. Subway: Queen's Park, then streetcar west to Palmerston.

MODERATE

Il Fornello ⊀ ITALIAN   Toronto has a wealth of Italian restaurants, but small local chain Il Fornello has become something of an institution. The restaurant serves up hearty pastas and pizzas to a happy crowd. Salads, like the Caesar and the excellent Roma (a mix of greens, goat cheese, walnuts, and roasted peppers), are available in half- and full-size portions. Pastas range from traditional fettuccine Alfredo to a lighter linguine with chicken, pesto, plum tomatoes, and pine nuts. In most cases, you can substitute rice pasta for wheat, a thoughtful option that makes Il Fornello a great option for anyone with a wheat allergy or celiac disease. The long list of thin-crust pizzas includes combinations like braised onion with Gorgonzola and fresh rosemary (pizzas can be made with gluten-free dough, too).

The King Street West location is right across the street from Roy Thomson Hall and down the block from the Royal Alexandra and Princess of Wales theaters (servers know to pick up the pace when you're watching the clock before a performance). Other branches are at Queen's Quay Terminal (ℂ **416/861-1028**), 576 Danforth Ave. (ℂ **416/466-2931**), Bayview Village (ℂ **416/227-1271**), and 1560 Yonge St., just north of St. Clair Avenue (ℂ **416/920-7347**).

214 King St. W. ℂ 416/977-2855. www.ilfornello.com. Reservations recommended for pre-theater dinners. Main courses C$12–C$24 (US$12–US$24/£6–£12). AE, DC, MC, V. Mon–Thurs 11:30am–10pm; Fri 11:30am–11pm; Sat 4:30–11pm. Subway: St Andrew.

La Palette ⊀ BISTRO   This is a terrific, offbeat addition to the Kensington Market neighborhood. It's so good, in fact, that you almost wonder why no one else ever thought of locating a classic French bistro on the edge of Chinatown. The 30-seat dining room is cozy and informal, with considerate, low-key service. The menu is classic, from ballantine of chicken stuffed with peppers and rice to lamb chops with a crusty coating of mustard and rosemary. If you're a dessert fiend like me, save room for the irresistible citron tart and dark-chocolate cake.

256 Augusta Ave. ℂ 416/929-4900. Reservations recommended. Main courses C$11–C$19 (US$11–US$19/£5.50–£9.50). AE, MC, V. Sun–Thurs 5:30–11pm; Fri–Sat noon–midnight. Subway: St. Patrick, then streetcar west to Augusta Ave.

Penelope GREEK   If you're in a rush to see a show at the Royal Alex, the Princess of Wales, or Roy Thomson Hall, come here for hearty food in a hurry. (And if you're seeing a show at the Sony Centre, check out the Penelope outpost across from it at 6 Front St. E.; ℂ **416/947-1159**.) Give the friendly staff an hour or less, and they will stuff you with spanakopita, moussaka, or souvlaki.

225 King St. W. ℂ 416/351-9393. www.peneloperestaurant.com. Reservations recommended for pre-theater dinner. Main courses C$11–C$25 (US$11–US$25/£5.50–£13). AE, DC, MC, V. Mon–Wed 11:30am–10pm; Thurs–Fri 11:30am–11:30pm; Sat 4:30–11:30pm. Subway: St. Andrew.

Rodney's Oyster House ⊀ SEAFOOD   Rodney has been providing Torontonians with fresh oysters for the past 2 decades. A favorite with the Financial District set, the restaurant is lively at all times of day (particularly the patio in good weather). The setting is as unpretentious as you could find: Think brick walls, rough-hewn wood booths and stools, and simply framed photographs. The main draw is the incredibly fresh oysters, and the lobster and salmon dishes are worth more than a look. While you're visiting, check out the Wall of Fame and its celebrity testimonials.

469 King St. W. 🕐 **416/363-8105.** Reservations recommended (reservations cannot be made for the patio except for groups of 10 or more). Main courses C$16–C$40 (US$16–US$40/£8–£20). AE, DC, MC, V. Mon–Sat 11am–1am. Subway: St. Andrew.

Sang Ho 🛪 CHINESE/SEAFOOD   There's no end of eateries in the eastern end of Chinatown, but Sang Ho is the one with the longest queue out front. The restaurant boasts not only a top-notch kitchen, but also a lovely dining room with several teeming aquariums. The regular menu of 100-plus dishes never changes, but wall-mounted boards list many daily specials. Seafood—shrimp, clams, or red snapper—is the obvious choice. Service is speedy and responsive. Try to go on a weeknight, when the waits are short.

536 Dundas St. W. 🕐 **416/596-1685.** Reservations not accepted. Main courses C$10–C$18 (US$10–US$18/£5–£9). MC, V. Sun–Thurs noon–10pm; Fri–Sat noon–11pm. Subway: St. Patrick.

INEXPENSIVE

Kalendar 🛪🛪 LIGHT FARE/VEGETARIAN   This has been a gem for years, serving sandwiches stuffed with portobello mushrooms, havarti, and roasted red peppers, and five "scrolls"—phyllo pastries filled with delights like artichoke hearts, eggplant, and hummus. The "nannettes" (pizzas) are baked nan breads topped with ingredients like smoked salmon, capers, and red onions. The ambience recalls a French bistro. In summer, the sidewalk patio is just the place to sit and watch the world.

546 College St. (just west of Bathurst St.). 🕐 **416/923-4138.** Main courses C$10–C$15 (US$10–US$15/£5–£7.50). MC, V. Mon–Fri 11am–midnight; Sat–Sun 11am–3pm. Subway: Queen's Park, then any streetcar west to Bathurst St.

Queen Mother Cafe 🛪 ASIAN/VEGETARIAN   Beloved by vegetarians, trend-hoppers, and reformed hippies, the Queen Mum is a Queen Street West institution with old-fashioned wooden furnishings and an underlit interior. The menu's lengthy descriptions are required reading. Ping Gai turns out to be chicken breast marinated in garlic, coriander, and peppercorns, served with lime sauce atop steamed rice. Bah Me Hang is egg noodles and stir-fried veggies in a spicy lime coriander sauce. In good weather, make for the garden patio at the back of the building.

208 Queen St. W. 🕐 **416/598-4719.** www.queenmothercafe.ca. Reservations accepted only for groups of 6 or more. Main courses C$13–C$18 (US$13–US$18/£7.50–£9). AE, MC, V. Mon–Sat 11:30am–1am; Sun noon–midnight. Subway: Osgoode.

Rice Bar (Value ASIAN/VEGETARIAN   Kensington Market has long been known as a place to buy food, thanks to its fresh produce stalls and small groceries, but in the past year it's become a dining destination, too. Rice Bar is easy to miss from the street, and inside the decor is strictly utilitarian (except for the floral pillowcases against the wall). Put that aside and focus on the food: The menu is designed around the notion of building your own meal in a bowl. You start with a selection of rice (basmati, jasmine, or wild), and add your choice of ingredients (all organic and additive-free). Service is on the slow side, but pleasant. The rice bowls come in several sizes, including the gargantuan Hungry Hungry Human. There are several house-designed bowls, too, including the much-loved Dragon Boat (rice noodles in a cilantro broth with tofu and kimchee).

319 Augusta Ave. ℂ **416/922-7423.** Rice bowls C$6–C$14 (US$6–US$14/£3–£7). MC, V. Tues–Sun 11am–10pm. Subway: Spadina, then streetcar south to College St.

DOWNTOWN EAST
VERY EXPENSIVE

Perigee ★★★ *Finds* ECLECTIC   This stunning restaurant is all about trust. From the moment you step inside—Perigee is located in a back alley at the southern end of the Distillery Historic District, and up one flight of stairs (I mention this because it's very hard to find on your first visit)—you can relax in the capable hands of the well-trained and thoughtful staff. All you need to do is decide whether you would like to try a five-, six-, or seven-course tasting menu. The staff will carefully note your preferences and aversions, and will ask a few questions (such as how you feel about sweetbreads or game meats) to gage how adventurous your palate is, and then you can sit back and enjoy. Perigee's kitchen is located at the center of the dining room, so you can watch the chefs at work if you choose. Wines can be paired with each course, or you can indulge in one of the delicious cocktails (go for the lychee martini). It's impossible to tell what will end up on your plate, but I can promise it will be creative, charmingly presented, and above all, delicious.

In the Distillery Historic District, 55 Mill St. (at Parliament St.). ℂ **416/364-1397.** www.perigeerestaurant.com. Reservations strongly recommended. Five-course prix-fixe menu C$90 (US$90/£45). AE, DC, MC, V. Tues–Sat 5–11pm. Subway: King, then streetcar east to Parliament St.

EXPENSIVE

Biff's Bistro & Wine Bar ★★ BISTRO   The same team that created a trio of excellent eateries (Jump, Canoe, and Auberge du Pommier) has come up with a classic bistro, with dishes priced somewhat lower than at the other establishments. The setting hits the right notes, with wood paneling and potted palms among the cozy-but-chic touches. The menu is equally fine, with pan-fried halibut covered with a second skin of thinly sliced potatoes, and traditional roast leg of lamb. The prime downtown location is a boon for Financial District types at lunch and theater-goers in the evening (the St. Lawrence and Sony centers are a stone's throw away).

4 Front St. E. (at Yonge St.). ℂ **416/860-0086.** www.biffsrestaurant.com. Reservations strongly recommended. Main courses C$21–C$34 (US$21–US$34/£11–£17). AE, DC, MC, V. Mon–Fri noon–2:30pm; Mon–Sat 5–10pm. Subway: Union or King.

Edward Levesque's Kitchen ★★★ BISTRO   Leslieville, once a no-man's land between Riverdale and the Beaches, is Toronto's hottest neighborhood (sorry, West Queen West), and Edward Levesque's Kitchen is one important reason why. This small, unpretentious bistro offers cooking so sophisticated and service so smooth that it caught the attention of the *New York Times.* I'm pleased to say that the accolades haven't changed a thing. The cooking is sublime, and while the menu changes constantly, you're in safe hands whether you choose grilled leg of Ontario lamb rubbed with cumin and garlic, or an asparagus, chive, and lemon risotto paired up with Atlantic salmon. This is an extremely popular place for brunch, and it's no mystery why when you try the frittata made with goat cheese and fresh rosemary (and since the restaurant won't take reservations for anything but dinner, go early!).

1290 Queen St. E. ℂ **416/465-3600.** www.edwardlevesque.ca. Reservations accepted only for dinner. Main courses C$21–C$28 (US$21–US$28/£11–£14). AE, MC, V. Wed–Fri 11am–3pm; Tues–Sat 6–10pm; Sat–Sun 9am–3pm; Sun 5:30–9pm. Subway: Queen, then streetcar east to Leslie St.

Hiro Sushi ⍟ JAPANESE/SUSHI   Widely regarded as the best sushi chef in the city, Hiro Yoshida draws a horde of Financial District types at lunch and mainly couples at dinner. The monochromatic setting is comfortably minimalist, and diners are encouraged to relax and leave their meal in Hiro's capable hands in true *omakase* style (choosing this five-course option costs C$60–C$75/US$60–US$75/£30–£38). The sushi varieties range from the expected to the inventive; you can also choose sashimi, tempura, and bento box combinations. Service can be rather slow. Forget the few wines listed in favor of sake or beer.

171 King St. E. ⓒ 416/304-0550. Reservations recommended. Main courses C$22–C$35 (US$22–US$35/£11–£18). AE, DC, MC, V. Tues–Fri noon–2:30pm; Tues–Sat 5:30–10:30pm. Subway: King.

MODERATE

Jamie Kennedy Wine Bar ⍟⍟⍟ *(Value* LIGHT FARE/TAPAS   Separate from the Jamie Kennedy Restaurant next door, my favorite wine bar is still one of the best bets in Toronto. The opening of the restaurant is great news for wine bar patrons, because it used to be necessary to arrive by 5:30pm to get a table here (and it's still advisable to show up early). Kennedy's innovative take on bistro cuisine is reminiscent of a tapas bar: All of the plates are small (with prices to match), and dishes include crisp Yukon gold frites, asparagus with poached egg and pine nuts, and tender duck confit with polenta. The staff is helpful and knowledgeable; ask about the difference between a glass of Ontario Riesling and a French sauvignon blanc, and you're likely to get a taste of each as well as an explanation.

9 Church St. ⓒ 416/362-1957. www.jkkitchens.com. Reservations not accepted. Small courses C$5–C$14 (US$5–US$14/£2.50–£7). AE, MC, V. Wine bar: Mon–Sat 11:30am–11pm; Sun 11am–11pm. Subway: King or Union.

Le Papillon QUEBECOIS   If you think crepes are simply for breakfast, stop by Le Papillon and think again. While you'll find many fruit-filled numbers, the best are savory crepes, which combine, for example, bacon, apples, and cheddar. Created from a mixture of white and buckwheat flour, the crepes make a satisfying lunch. For dinner, add some onion soup and a green salad, or go for *tourtière,* a traditional Québécois pie that includes beef, veal, *and* pork.

16 Church St. (between Front St. E. and Esplanade). ⓒ 416/363-3773. www.lepapillon.ca. Reservations recommended. Crepes and main courses C$10–C$25 (US$10–US$25/£5–£13). AE, DC, MC, V. Tues–Fri noon–2:30pm; Tues–Wed 5–10pm; Thurs 5–11pm; Fri 5pm–midnight; Sat 11am–midnight; Sun 11am–10pm. Subway: Union.

INEXPENSIVE

Shopsy's *(Kids* DELI   This Toronto institution has been in business for more than three-quarters of a century. Its large patio, festooned with giant yellow umbrellas, draws crowds for breakfast, lunch, dinner, and in between. This is where you go for heaping corned beef or smoked-meat sandwiches served on fresh rye, or for comfort foods like macaroni and cheese and chicken pot pie. Shopsy's also boasts one of the largest walk-in humidors in the city (which is not subject to the smoking crackdown).

33 Yonge St. ⓒ 416/365-3333. Reservations accepted only for groups of 6 or more. Main courses C$8–C$16 (US$8–US$16/£4–£8). AE, MC, V. Mon–Wed 6:30am–11pm; Thurs–Fri 6:30am–midnight; Sat 8am–midnight; Sun 8am–10pm. Subway: Union or King.

Terroni ITALIAN/LIGHT FARE   From its humble beginnings on Queen Street West, Terroni has grown into a local minichain. The setting is informal, with kitchen-style tables and chairs and a wall-mounted chalkboard with daily specials. The antipasti, salads, and pizzas, essentially the same at all three locations, are uniformly delightful. They range from the simplest margherita pizza (tomato, mozzarella, basil) to a gourmet salad of cooked oyster mushrooms drizzled with balsamic vinegar and served atop a bed of arugula. Other locations are at 720 Queen St. W. (© **416/504-0320**) and 1 Balmoral Ave. (© **416/925-4020**).

106 Victoria St. © 416/955-0258. Main courses C$10–C$18 (US$10–US$18/£5–£9). MC, V. Mon–Sat 9am–10pm. Subway: Queen.

Young Thailand ★★ *Value* THAI   Wandee Young was one of the first chefs to awaken Toronto's taste buds to the joys of Thai cuisine. That was more than 2 decades ago, and Young Thailand is still going strong. The large dining room contains a few Southeast Asian decorative elements, but it's the low-priced, high-quality cuisine that attracts the hip-but-broke and boomers alike. The all-you-can-eat buffet at lunch is always a mob scene (at C$11/US$11/£5.50, it's a steal). The dinner menu is a la carte, with popular picks like spiced chicken and bamboo shoots in coconut milk, satays with fiery peanut sauce, and the ever-present pad Thai. Soups tend to be sinus-clearing, and mango salads offer a sweet antidote.

81 Church St. (south of Lombard St.). © 416/368-1368. www.youngthailand.com. Reservations recommended. Main courses C$9–C$19 (US$9–US$19/£4.50–£9.50). AE, DC, MC, V. Mon–Thurs 11:30am–10pm; Fri 11:30am–11pm; Sat 5–11pm; Sun 5–10pm. Subway: Queen or King.

MIDTOWN WEST
VERY EXPENSIVE
Bistro 990 ★★★ FRENCH   Because Hollywood types frequent Toronto, it's no surprise to see the stars out for a night on the town. Bistro 990 is just across the street from the tony Sutton Place Hotel, so it attracts more than its fair share of big names. In any case, the Gallic dining room is charming, and the service is all-around attentive. The menu offers updated hors d'oeuvres, such as octopus and veggies in citrus marinade. Main dishes stick to *grand-mère's* recipes, like the satisfying roasted half chicken with garlicky mashed potatoes, and calves' liver in white-wine sauce. Sweets, such as the pineapple tarte tatin with kiwi coulis and blueberry ice cream, are made daily.

990 Bay St. (at St. Joseph). © 416/921-9990. Reservations required. Main courses C$26–C$44 (US$26–US$44/£13–£22). AE, DC, MC, V. Mon–Fri noon–3pm; Mon–Sat 5–10pm. Subway: Wellesley.

EXPENSIVE
Boba ★ FUSION   Stunning turn-of-the-20th-century houses abound in this part of town, and Boba happens to be in one of the most charming. Set back from the street, it has a front patio for summer dining. Inside, the pastel-hued walls and tasseled lampshades exude warmth, Provençal style. Boba is a scene every night, with a mix of dressed-up and dressed-down professionals table-hopping with abandon. What draws them is the inventive cuisine, which has turned co-chefs Barbara Gordon and Bob Bermann into local celebrities. One highlight is Gordon's wonderful Muscovy duck two ways, with the breast cooked rare and the leg braised. Grilled salmon is also just so, nicely mated with curried vegetable risotto. Desserts are overwhelming, particularly the Valrhona chocolate triangle with crème fraîche ice cream, raspberries, and berry coulis.

90 Avenue Rd. © 416/961-2622. www.boba.ca. Reservations recommended. Main courses C$23–C$36 (US$23–US$36/£12–£18). AE, DC, MC, V. Mon–Sat 5:45–10pm. Subway: Bay.

Sotto Sotto ★★ ITALIAN   Imagine the Bat Cave decorated by a Florentine, with aged frescoes, wall-mounted stonework, and wax-dripping candelabra. A few steps down from street level, this restaurant transports diners a world away. Tables are cheek by jowl, but the jovial suits and couples don't seem to mind. Efficient service lacks warmth, though the kitchen makes up for it. The menu leans to the lightweight, with a few irresistible creamy-sauced pastas. Main courses of meat or fish, like Cornish hen and swordfish, are nicely grilled. The risotto is lovely—just be warned that at least two people at the table must order it to have it served. There's a nice wine list, with many selections available by the glass.

116A Avenue Rd. (north of Bloor St.). © 416/962-0011. www.sottosotto.ca. Reservations required. Main courses C$17–C$42 (US$17–US$42/£8.50–£21). AE, DC, MC, V. Sun–Thurs 5:30–11pm; Fri–Sat 5pm–midnight. Subway: Bay or Museum.

MODERATE

Bloor Street Diner BISTRO/LIGHT FARE If you've shopped until you've dropped along Bloor Street West, this is just the place to grab a bite to eat and let your feet and your credit card recover. It's two restaurants in one: Le Café/Terrasse is an informal bistro that serves decent soups, salads, and sandwiches all day; La Rotisserie is a slightly more upscale dining room with heartier Provençal-style fare. Basics are what they do best. Try to snag a seat on the umbrella-covered patio overlooking Bay Street.

In the Manulife Centre, 55 Bloor St. W. © 416/928-3105. Main courses C$12–C$21 (US$12–US$21/£6–£11). AE, DC, MC, V. Daily 7am–1am. Subway: Bay or Yonge/Bloor.

Kensington Kitchen *(Kids* MEDITERRANEAN Drawing a crowd of regulars—students and profs—from the nearby University of Toronto, Kensington Kitchen is a perennial gem. The decor hasn't changed in years, with Oriental carpets covering the walls, a painted wood floor, and decorative objects scattered about. The tradition of big portions at small cost stays constant, too, with dishes like angel-hair pasta with heaps of shrimp, scallops, and mussels in tomato-coriander sauce; saffron paella with chicken and sausage; and Turkish-style braised lamb stuffed with raisins, eggplant, apricots, and figs. In clement weather, head to the rooftop patio, in the shade of a mighty Manitoba maple.

124 Harbord St. © 416/961-3404. Reservations recommended. Main courses C$11–C$18 (US$11–US$18/£5.50–£9). AE, DC, MC, V. Mon–Sat 11:30am–11pm; Sun 11:30am–10pm. Subway: Spadina, then LRT south to Harbord St.

Serra *(Finds* ITALIAN I've been dining at Serra since my student days at the University of Toronto. Back then, I loved it for its excellent food, friendly service, and reasonable prices. Guess what? It hasn't changed. This is an upscale-looking spot: The diners are casually chic, and Serra's look is sleek, with a wood-paneled bar in one corner and mahogany tables for two. The trattoria-worthy fare includes thin-crust pizza topped with olives, prosciutto, and goat cheese; light-sauced pasta dishes teeming with shrimp; and grilled focaccia sandwiches.

378 Bloor St. W. © 416/922-6999. www.serrarestaurant.com. Main courses C$12–C$25 (US$12–US$25/£6–£13). AE, DC, MC, V. Daily noon–11pm (no lunch on summer weekends). Subway: Spadina.

INEXPENSIVE

Annapurna Vegetarian Restaurant *(* INDIAN/VEGETARIAN The name pretty much says it all. This was one of the first vegetarian restaurants in Toronto, and it's still going strong after more than 25 years. I'm always suspicious of food that's billed as healthy—I'd rather have stuff that tastes good—but Annapurna's southern Indian satisfies on both fronts.

1085 Bathurst St. © 416/537-8513. Reservations not accepted. Main courses C$8–C$13 (US$8–US$13/£4–£6.50). MC, V. Mon–Tues and Thurs–Sat 11:30am–9pm; Wed 11:30am–6pm. Subway: Bathurst.

Asia Republik ★★ *Value* ASIAN/VEGETARIAN   A banner in front brags "Best Cheap Eats With Class"—and it's true. Inside, the cool, crisp lines of Scandinavian design mix with miniature Japanese plants for an upscale Zen ambience. The menu roams around Asia, offering up excellent renderings of pad Thai, Malaysian noodles, and Szechuan classics. There are some more creative entrees, too, like the soft-shell crab curry with ginger sticky rice, and the Vietnamese pork chop rubbed with lemon grass and spices. There's also a menu for vegetarians. If you're on a budget, you can't do better than Asia Republik's combo lunch: a meal that consists of a salad, spring roll, rice, and entree costs C$5.95 (US$5.95/£3).

372 Bloor St. W. ⓒ **416/921-6787.** Main courses C$8–C$13 (US$8–US$13/£4–£6.50). AE, MC, V. Mon–Thurs 11:30am–10pm; Fri 11:30am–11pm; Sat 1–11pm; Sun 1–10pm. Subway: Spadina.

Camros Organic Eatery ★ *Finds* LIGHT FARE/PERSIAN/VEGETARIAN Yonge and Bloor is a tough place to find a non-fast-food lunch. But this terrific little place is merely a block away. And while "healthy vegetarian fare" isn't something that gets my pulse racing, the Persian cooking at Camros is a big draw. Try the Adas Polo, a traditional rice dish with cinnamon and raisins, or the Gheymeh, a satisfying lentil stew. There's more to love about this place, including comprehensive ingredient lists to help people with food allergies, and takeout containers that are 100% biodegradable. If only it were open later!

25 Hayden St. ⓒ **416/960-0723.** www.camroseatery.com. Reservations not accepted. 2-item lunch combo C$5 (US$5/£2.50). MC, V. Mon–Fri 11:30am–7:30pm. Subway: Yonge/Bloor.

Real Thai ★★ THAI   Bloor Street west of Spadina Avenue is a solid bet for moderate to low-priced restaurants that serve excellent food. Even in this impressive company, Real Thai stands out. Its food is simply outstanding, and it serves the best green curry chicken I've tasted outside of Thailand. The menu favors spicy tastes, but the helpful, accommodating staff will get the kitchen to turn down the heat if that's your preference. There aren't a lot of choices for vegetarians here, but if you love seafood you're in luck.

350 Bloor St. W. ⓒ **416/924-7444.** Main courses C$7–C$12 (US$7–US$12/£3.50–£6). MC, V. Daily 11:30am–10:30pm. Subway: Spadina.

MIDTOWN EAST/THE EAST END

Just about everything *will* be Greek to you in the east end along Danforth Avenue. Known appropriately enough as Greektown, this is where to go for low-cost, delicious dining, or for a midnight meal—the tavernas along this strip generally stay open until the wee hours, even on weeknights.

EXPENSIVE

Myth ★★ GREEK/MEDITERRANEAN   Part trendy bar, part restaurant, this generous space is large enough to encompass both. The ambience is classical Greece meets MTV. Ornate oversize shields share space with a series of TVs running an endless loop of mythic movies. Who can pay attention to what's on the plate with so much going on? Fortunately, the food calls attention to itself. Starters, ranging from traditional spanakopita to tuna tartare with beet and taro-root chips, are impossible to ignore. Main courses, such as rabbit braised in port and cinnamon, or pizza topped with spiced lamb, zucchini, and onion purée, are just as demanding. As the night goes on, the crowd gathers at the bar, where a DJ starts spinning music at 11pm.

417 Danforth Ave. (between Logan and Chester). ℂ **416/461-8383**. Reservations recommended. Main courses C$18–C$27 (US$18–US$27/£9–£14). AE, MC, V. Mon–Wed 5–11pm; Thurs–Sun noon–11pm; bar open till 2am nightly. Subway: Chester.

MODERATE

Avli ⭐ GREEK   A white stucco archway contributes to the cavelike feel of the narrow street-level room, though the recent expansion to the second floor has created an airier place to dine. Always noisy, occasionally raucous, this taverna serves up some of the best food on the Danforth—nongreasy, thoughtfully prepared, and carefully seasoned. Meze starters are standard: *kopanisti* (spicy feta with peppers) and hummus for those who want cold food, grilled octopus and steamed mussels for those who like it hot. Main courses are standouts. The half chicken stuffed with cashews, dates, apples, and rice is exquisite, and the meat moussaka is the best around.

401 Danforth Ave. ℂ **416/461-9577**. www.avlirestaurant.com. Reservations recommended. Main courses C$15–C$22 (US$15–US$22/£7.50–£11). AE, DC, MC, V. Daily noon–midnight. Subway: Chester.

Pan on the Danforth ⭐ GREEK   To the best of my knowledge, Pan was a god of music, not of food. I must have mixed it up, because if he is the inspiration for this restaurant, he certainly knows his way around a kitchen. This long-established eatery updates classic Greek dishes with panache. Salmon is stuffed with mushrooms and spinach and wrapped in phyllo pastry, and a smoked baked pork chop comes with feta scalloped potatoes and zucchini relish. The well-chosen wine list favors the New World. The crowd is fairly sophisticated, which may explain the cryptic message over the bar: "You've done it already."

516 Danforth Ave. ℂ **416/466-8158**. www.panonthedanforth.com. Reservations accepted only for parties of 3 or more. Main courses C$14–C$30 (US$14–US$30/£7–£15). AE, MC, V. Sun–Thurs noon–11pm; Fri–Sat noon–midnight. Subway: Chester or Pape.

UPTOWN

This area is too large to be considered a neighborhood, stretching as it does from north of Davenport Road to Steeles Avenue. While it doesn't have the concentration of restaurants that the downtown area enjoys, it has a number of stellar options that make the trip north worthwhile.

VERY EXPENSIVE

Auberge du Pommier ⭐⭐ FRENCH   Don't have time to drop by your French country house this weekend? To the rescue comes Auberge du Pommier, a cozy château that exudes Provençal-style charm. Diners outfitted in business casual relax in the care of expert servers. The menu doesn't offer many surprises, but what it does, it does well. Appetizers set a high standard, with dishes like creamy lobster and white-bean soup, and baked artichokes stuffed with French goat cheese. Entrees, like pan-seared scallops with braised oxtail in a cabernet *jus*, keep up the pace.

4150 Yonge St. ℂ **416/222-2220**. www.aubergedupommier.com. Reservations recommended. Main courses C$30–C$43 (US$30–US$43/£15–£22). AE, DC, DISC, MC, V. Mon–Fri 11:30am–2:30pm; Mon–Sat 5–10pm. Subway: York Mills.

North 44 ⭐⭐⭐ INTERNATIONAL   This is the one restaurant that even people who've never set foot in Toronto have heard about. Its soft lighting and strategically situated mirrors wrap the dining room—and its occupants—in a lovely glow. The menu, which changes with the seasons, borrows from Mediterranean, American, and Asian sources. On the list of main courses, you might find grilled veal tenderloin with orange peppercorns, toasted barley, and root veggies, or roasted Muscovy duck breast with orange-soy marinade and foie gras. There are always a few pasta and pizza choices, such as caramelized squash ravioli with black-truffle essence. The desserts, like lemon meringue mille-feuille, are among the best in the city and are accompanied by a wide range of ice wines (a sweet dessert wine). The wine list is comprehensive, though most of the prices veer off into the stratosphere. What really sets North 44 apart is its seamless service. Don't like to be pampered? Stay away.

2537 Yonge St. ⓒ 416/487-4897. www.north44restaurant.com. Reservations required. Main courses C$39–C$54 (US$39–US$54/£20–£27). AE, DC, MC, V. Mon–Sat 5–11pm. Subway: Eglinton.

MODERATE

Cava 🌟🌟🌟 ECLECTIC   While I was sad to see Avalon finally close its doors in 2006 after an 11-year run, chef Chris McDonald has opened an extraordinary restaurant uptown. This small jewel of a dining room is hidden in an alleyway, so the trick is in finding it on a first visit. But the effort is worth it since Cava offers exquisite tapaslike plates and sparking wines at prices that will not break your budget. The menu does have its pricey side (you can have a flute of Nicolas Feuillatte champagne for C$20/US$20/£10), but if you stick with salt cod cake with chipotle cream, four oysters on the half-shell with tomatillo salsa, or 3-minute flank steak with chimchurri, you can't go wrong.

1560 Yonge St. ⓒ 416/979-9918. www.cavarestaurant.ca. Reservations strongly recommended. Tapas plates C$6–C$16 (US$6–US$16/£3–£8). AE, DC, MC, V. Mon–Fri noon–2pm; daily 5–10pm. Subway: St. Clair.

5 Seeing the Sights

First, the good news: Toronto has amazing sights to see and places to be that appeal to travelers of all stripes. The bad news? No matter how long your stay, you won't be able to fit everything in. Toronto is a sprawling city, and while downtown and midtown boast a sizable collection of attractions, some truly wonderful sights are in less accessible areas.

Another difficulty is that many attractions could take up a day of your visit. Ontario Place, Harbourfront, the Ontario Science Centre, and Paramount Canada's Wonderland all come to mind. That's not even mentioning the expansive parks, the arts scene, or the shopping possibilities. My best advice is to relax and bring a good pair of walking shoes. There's no better way to appreciate the kaleidoscopic metropolis that is Toronto than on foot.

THE TOP ATTRACTIONS
ON THE LAKEFRONT

Harbourfront Centre 🌟🌟 *Kids*   Back in 1972, the federal government took over a 38-hectare (94-acre) strip of waterfront land to preserve the vista. The abandoned warehouses and crumbling factories have yielded to a stunning urban playground that stretches over the old piers. **Queen's Quay,** at the foot of York Street, is the first stop you'll encounter on the LRT line from Union Station (you can also get there in 5 min. on foot walking south from Front St., but that requires you to go under the Gardiner Expwy., which I personally hate). From here, boats depart for harbor tours, and ferries leave for the Toronto Islands. In this renovated warehouse, you'll find the Premiere Dance Theatre and two floors of shops. To get something to eat, you can stay at Queen's Quay's casual Boathouse Grill or walk west to **York Quay**'s Lakeside Terrace restaurant. York Quay also boasts an art gallery and ever-changing art installations, and an information booth where you can pick up information on Harbourfront events. There's also the **Power Plant,** a contemporary art gallery, and behind it, the **Du Maurier Theatre Centre.** At the **Craft Studio,** you can watch artisans at work (you can also buy their works at **Bounty Contemporary Canadian Craft Shop**).

More than 4,000 events take place annually at Harbourfront, including the **Harbourfront Reading Series** in June and the **International Festival of Authors** in October. Other happenings include films, dance, theater, music, children's events, multicultural festivals, and marine events. Harbourfront is at its best in the summer, but it is a great destination for the whole family year-round.

235 Queens Quay W. ℂ 416/973-4000. www.harbourfrontcentre.com. Subway: Union, then LRT to Queen's Quay or York Quay.

Ontario Place ⭐ Kids   For all its space-age looks, this is really just a fun amusement park, much more thrilling than Centreville on Centre Island (see below), but nowhere near as cool as Paramount Canada's Wonderland (p. 401). From a distance, you'll see five steel-and-glass pods suspended on columns 32m (105 ft.) above the lake, three artificial islands, and a huge geodesic dome. The five pods contain a multimedia theater, a children's theater, a high-technology exhibit, and displays that tell the story of Ontario in vivid kaleidoscopic detail. The dome houses Cinesphere, where an 18m-by-24m (60-by-80-ft.) screen shows specially made IMAX movies year-round. Ontario Place has many attractions targeted at kids, starting with the **H2O Generation Station,** a gigantic "soft play" structure with twisting slides, towers, and walkways. The **Atom Blaster**—which claims to be Canada's largest foam-ball free-for-all—is fun for the whole family. Younger children will enjoy the new **MicroKids** play area with its ball pit, climbing platforms, and other tot-appropriate draws.

955 Lakeshore Blvd. W. ℂ 416/314-9811, or 416/314-9900 for recorded info. www.ontarioplace.com. Admission to grounds only starts at C$13 (US$13/£6.50) for ages 6 and over, C$6.75 (US$6.75/£3.35) for ages 4–5 and for seniors, free for children 3 and under; separate fees for rides and events (pricing varies by month). Play All Day pass C$49 (US$49/£25) for ages 4 and up. Mid-May to Labour Day daily 10am–dusk; evening events end and dining spots close later. Closed (except Cinesphere) early Sept to early May. Subway: Bathurst, then Bathurst Street streetcar south.

The Toronto Islands ⭐ Kids   In only 7 minutes, an 800-passenger ferry takes you to 245 hectares (605 acres) of island parkland crisscrossed by shaded paths and quiet waterways—a glorious spot to walk, play tennis, bike, feed the ducks, putter around in boats, picnic, or soak up the sun. Come here for the solitude or if you have kids. Of the 14 islands, the two major ones are **Centre Island** and **Ward's Island.** The first is the most popular with tourists; Ward's is more residential (about 600 people live in modest cottages on the islands). Originally, the land was a peninsula, but in the mid-1800s, a series of storms shattered the finger of land into islands.

On Centre Island, families enjoy **Centreville** (ℂ **416/203-0405;** www.centreisland.ca), an old-fashioned amusement park that's been in business since 1966. You'll find a turn-of-the-20th-century village complete with a Main Street; tiny shops; a firehouse; and the Far Enough Farm, where the kids can pet lambs, chicks, and other barnyard animals. The kids will also love trying out the antique cars, fire engines, old-fashioned train, authentic 1890s carousel, flume ride, and aerial cars. An all-day ride pass costs C$19 (US$19/£9.50) for those 4 ft. tall and under, C$28 (US$28/£14) for those over 4 ft.; a family pass for four is C$80 (US$80/£40). Centreville is open from 10:30am to 6pm daily mid-May through Labour Day and weekends in early May and September.

Lake Ontario. ⓒ 416/392-8193 for ferry schedules. Round-trip fare C$6 (US$6/£3) adults, C$3.50 (US$3.50/£1.75) seniors and children 15–19, C$2.50 (US$2.50/£1.25) children 3–14, free for children 2 and under. Ferries leave from docks at the bottom of Bay St. Subway: Union Station, then LRT to Queen's Quay.

DOWNTOWN
Art Gallery of Ontario 🔆
The AGO is in the midst of renovation mania, which will stretch into 2008 (at press time, there is no fixed date for its reopening). Toronto son Frank Gehry is reinventing the city's best art gallery, and his spectacular design will increase viewing space by 40%. The AGO's European collection ranges from the 14th century to the French Impressionists and beyond. Works by Pissarro, Monet, Boudin, Sisley, and Renoir fill an octagonal room. De Kooning's *Two Women on a Wharf* and Karel Appel's *Black Landscape* are just two of the modern pieces. There are several works of particular interest to admirers of the pre-Raphaelite painters, including one by Waterhouse. Among the sculptures, you'll find two beauties—Picasso's *Poupée* and Brancusi's *First Cry.* Even so, its Canadian collection has been the strongest. The paintings by the Group of Seven—which includes Tom Thomson, F. H. Varley, and Lawren Harris—are extraordinary. In addition, other galleries show the genesis of Canadian art from earlier to more modern artists. And don't miss the extensive collection of Inuit art.

Another reason to go: The **Henry Moore Sculpture Centre,** with more than 800 pieces (original plasters, bronzes, maquettes, woodcuts, lithographs, etchings, and drawings), is the largest public collection of his works. The artist gave them to Toronto because he was so moved by the citizens' enthusiasm for his work—public donations bought his sculpture *The Archer* to decorate Nathan Phillips Square at City Hall after politicians refused to free up money for it.

317 Dundas St. W. (between McCaul and Beverley sts.); temporary entrance is on McCaul St. ⓒ 416/977-0414. www.ago.net. Museum is closed for renovation; check website for information on its reopening. Subway: St. Patrick.

CN Tower 🔆 Kids
As you approach the city, whether by plane, train, or automobile, the first thing you notice is this slender structure. Glass-walled elevators glide up the 553m (1,814-ft.) tower, the tallest freestanding structure in the world. The elevators stop first at the 346m-high (1,135-ft.) Look Out level. (It takes just 58 seconds, so prepare for popping ears.) You can walk down one level to experience the Glass Floor, my favorite spot at the tower: Through it, you can see all the way down to street level (even as your heart drops into your shoes). As a bonus, if you wait long enough, you'll undoubtedly see some alpha males daring each other to jump on the glass. (They do, and no, it doesn't break—the glass can withstand the weight of 14 adult hippos. Now *that's* a sight I'd like to see. . .)

Above the Look Out is the world's highest public observation gallery, the Skypod, 447m (1,466 ft.) above the ground. From here, on a clear day you can't quite see forever, but the sweeping vista stretches to Niagara Falls, 161km (100 miles) south, and to Lake Simcoe, 193km (120 miles) north. Unless you're really taken with the tower, I wouldn't recommend it—the view from the Glass Floor is majestic enough for me. Atop the tower sits a 102m (335-ft.) antenna mast erected over 31 weeks with the aid of a giant Sikorsky helicopter. It took 55 lifts (and no hippos) to complete the operation.

301 Front St. W. ⓒ 416/868-6937. www.cntower.ca. Basic admission (Look Out and Glass Floor) C$21 (US$21/£11) adults, C$19 (US$19/£10) seniors, C$14 (US$14/£7) children 4–12; Total Tower Experience (includes Look Out, Glass Floor, Skypod, film, and 2 rides) C$32 (US$32/£16) all ages. Daily 9am–11pm (shorter hours in winter). Closed Dec 25. Subway: Union, then walk west on Front St.

The Distillery District ★★★   Although founded in 1832, it wasn't until 2003 that this 45-building complex was reinvented as a historic district (before that, the glorious buildings were best known for appearing in many period-piece movies). This was once the home of the Gooderham-Worts Distillery, which was Canada's largest distilling company in the 19th century. A miller named James Worts, who emigrated from Scotland in 1831, built the first building on the site, a windmill intended to power a grain mill (the millstone he brought with him is still on display). His brother-in-law, William Gooderham, soon joined him in the business. In 1834, Worts's wife died in childbirth, and in despair, Worts drowned himself in the mill's well. Gooderham took over the business and adopted Worts's son, who eventually joined the business.

The complex is an outstanding example of industrial design from the 19th century. Much of the construction here was done with that Victorian favorite, red brick; you'll see it in everything from the buildings to the streets themselves. One exception is the mill building, which was built out of stone and thus managed to survive an 1869 fire.

The Distillery District has launched an ambitious program of music, art, and food festivals throughout the year. A farmer's market takes place on Sundays in summer.

55 Mill St. ℂ 416/367-1800. www.thedistillerydistrict.com. Free admission. Subway: King, then streetcar east to Parliament St.

MIDTOWN

George R. Gardiner Museum of Ceramic Art ★★   Across the street from the ROM is Canada's only specialized ceramics museum. Its ambitious renovation, which was unveiled in June 2006, is regarded as a smash success. The C$20-million All Fired Up plan increased the museum's display space from 1,765 sq. m (19,000 sq. ft.) to 2,694 sq. m (29,000 sq. ft.) and allows far more of the vast—and growing—collection to be on display. The pre-Columbian department contains fantastic Olmec and Maya figures, and objects from Ecuador, Colombia, and Peru. The majolica collection includes spectacular 16th- and 17th-century salvers and other pieces from Florence, Faenza, and Venice, and a Delftware collection that includes fine 17th-century chargers. The 18th century is heavily represented by Continental and English porcelain: Meissen, Sèvres, Worcester, Chelsea, Derby, and other great names. Among the highlights are objects from the Swan Service—a 2,200-piece set that took four years (1737–41) to make—and an extraordinary collection of commedia dell'arte figures.

111 Queen's Park. ℂ 416/586-8080. www.gardinermuseum.on.ca. Admission C$12 (US$12/£6) adults, C$8 (US$8/£4) seniors, and C$6 (US$6/£3) students with ID, free for children 12 and under. Sat–Thurs 10am–6pm; Fri 10am–9pm. Closed Jan 1, Dec 25. Subway: Museum.

Royal Ontario Museum ★★★ (Kids   This is one of my favorite museums anywhere. The ROM (rhymes with "tom"), as it's affectionately called, is Canada's largest museum, with more than 6 million objects in its collections. And in 2008, many of those pieces will be back on display as the museum's ambitious renovation plan winds up. Called Renaissance ROM, this C$200-million project has added six new galleries overlooking Bloor Street West. Called the Michael Lee-Chin Crystal—after the generous donor who pledged C$30 million to build it—the galleries are encased inside an übermodern palace of jutting crystal prisms designed by Daniel Libeskind. Personally, the design plan brought to mind Superman's crystal palace at the North Pole, but now that the building is complete I have to admit that the spectacular crystal changes the face of Bloor Street West. (At press time, the ROM was busily moving its World Culture and Natural World galleries into the crystal. I can't wait to see how the dinosaurs look in their new home!)

100 Queen's Park. ℭ **416/586-8000**. www.rom.on.ca. Admission C$20 (US$20/£10) adults, C$17 (US$17/£8.50) seniors and students with valid ID, C$14 (US$14/£7) children 5–14, free for children 4 and under. Sat–Thurs 10am–6pm; Fri 10am–9:30pm. Closed Jan 1, Dec 25. Subway: Museum.

ON THE OUTSKIRTS
The McMichael Canadian Art Collection ℱ
In Kleinburg, 40km (25 miles) north of the city, the McMichael is worth a visit for the setting as well as the art. The collection occupies a log-and-stone gallery that sits amid quiet stands of trees on 40 hectares (100 acres) of conservation land. Specially designed for the landscape paintings it houses, the gallery is a work of art. The lobby has a pitched roof that soars 8m (26 ft.) on massive rafters of Douglas fir; throughout the gallery, panoramic windows look south over white pine, cedar, ash, and birch. The collection includes the work of Canada's famous circle of landscape painters, the Group of Seven, as well as David Milne, Emily Carr, and their contemporaries. An impressive collection of Inuit and contemporary Native Canadian art and sculpture is also on display. In addition, four galleries contain changing exhibitions of works by contemporary artists.

10365 Islington Ave., Kleinburg. ℭ **888/213-1121** or 905/893-1121. www.mcmichael.com. Admission C$15 (US$15/£7.50) adults, C$12 (US$12/£6) seniors and students with ID, free for children 5 and under. Daily 10am–4pm (the McMichael advises that you call ahead to confirm hours). Closed Dec 25. Parking C$5 (US$5/£2.50). By car: From downtown, take Gardiner Expwy. to Hwy. 427 north, follow it to Hwy. 7, and turn east. Turn left (north) at 1st light onto Hwy. 27. Turn right (east) at Major Mackenzie Dr. and left (north) at 1st set of lights to Islington Ave. and the village of Kleinburg. Or take Hwy. 401 to Hwy. 400 north. At Major Mackenzie Dr., go west to Islington Ave. and turn right. By bus: From Islington station, take bus no. 37 to Steeles Ave., then take the York Region Transit bus 13A to the museum driveway (it's about a 10-min. walk up the driveway from the bus stop); note that separate fares are required for the 2 buses; also, note that the 13A bus does not run on weekends, and offers only morning and evening service on weekdays.

Ontario Science Centre ℱℱℱ Kids
Possibly the best thing about growing up in Toronto was the frequent visits to the OSC. Wherever you look, there are things to touch, push, pull, or crank. Test your reflexes, balance, heart rate, and grip strength; surf the Internet; watch frozen-solid liquid nitrogen shatter into thousands of icy shards; study slides of butterfly wings, bedbugs, fish scales, or feathers under a microscope; tease your brain with a variety of optical illusions; land a spaceship on the moon; watch bees making honey; see how many lights you can light or how high you can elevate a balloon with your own pedal power. The fun goes on and on through the 10 exhibit halls and more than 800 interactive exhibits.

Another draw is the IMAX Dome theater, with a 24m (79-ft.) domed screen that creates spectacular effects. There are two eateries on-site: Galileo's Bistro, a buffet-style restaurant that serves alcohol, and Valley Marketplace, a cafeteria. More than a million people visit the OSC every year, so it's best to arrive promptly at 10am to see everything.

770 Don Mills Rd. (at Eglinton Ave. E.). ℭ **416/696-3127**, or 416/696-1000 for Omnimax tickets. www.ontario sciencecentre.ca. Admission C$17 (US$17/£8.50) adults, C$13 (US$13/£6.50) seniors and children 13–17, C$10 (US$10/£5) children 5–12, free for children 4 and under. Omnimax admission C$12 (US$12/£6) adults, C$9 (US$9/£4.50) seniors and children 13–17, C$8 (US$8/£4) children 5–12, free for children 4 and under. Combination discounts available. Daily 10am–5pm. Closed Dec 25. Parking C$8 (US$8/£4). Subway: Yonge St. line to Eglinton, then 34 Eglinton bus east to Don Mills Rd. By car: From downtown, take Don Valley Pkwy. to Don Mills Rd. exit and follow signs.

Paramount Canada's Wonderland ℱℱ Kids
Thirty minutes north of Toronto lies Canada's answer to Disney World. The 120-hectare (297-acre) park features more than 200 attractions, including 65 rides, a water park, a play area for tiny tots (KidZville), and live shows. Because the park relies on a local audience for most of its business, it introduces new attractions every year. One recent draw was the Paramount Hollywood Stunt Spectacular, a live show that was meant to make your jaw drop (and

it succeeded). Other top attractions include The Fly, a roller coaster designed to make every seat feel as though it's in the front car (the faint of heart can't hide at the back of this one!); Sledge Hammer, a "menacing mechanical giant" that stands 24m (79 ft.) tall and hurls riders through accelerated jumps and free-falls; Cliffhanger, a "super swing" that executes 360-degree turns and makes riders feel immune to gravity; and the Xtreme Skyflyer, a hang-gliding and skydiving hybrid that plunges riders 46m (151 ft.) in a free-fall. The roller coasters range from the looping, inverted Top Gun to the track-free suspended Vortex.

9580 Jane St., Vaughan. ℂ 905/832-7000 or 905/832-8131. www.canadas-wonderland.com. Pay-One-Price Pass-port (includes unlimited rides and shows but not parking, special attractions, or Kingswood Music Theater) C$48 (US$48/£24) adults and children over 48 inches tall, C$25 (US$25/£13) seniors and children aged 3 and up who are under 48 inches tall, free for children 2 and under. June 1–25 Mon–Fri 10am–8pm, Fri–Sat 10am–10pm; June 26 to Labour Day daily 10am–10pm; late May and early Sept to early Oct Sat–Sun 10am–8pm. Closed mid-Oct to mid-May. Parking C$10 (US$10/£5). Subway: Yorkdale or York Mills, then GO Express Bus to Wonderland. By car: From down-town, take Yonge St. north to Hwy. 400. Go north on Hwy. 400 to Rutherford Rd. exit and follow signs. By car from the north, exit at Major Mackenzie.

The Toronto Zoo 𝘈𝘈★ 𝘒𝘪𝘥𝘴 Covering 284 hectares (702 acres) of parkland, this unique zoological garden contains some 5,000 animals, plus an extensive botanical collection. Pavilions—including Africa, Indo-Malaya, Australasia, and the Ameri-cas—and outdoor paddocks house the plants and animals. One popular zoo attraction is at the **African Savanna** project. It re-creates a market bazaar and safari through Kesho (Swahili for "tomorrow") National Park, past such special features as a bush camp, rhino midden, elephant highway, and several watering holes. It also includes the **Gorilla Rainforest,** one of the most popular sights at the zoo—little wonder, as this is the largest indoor gorilla exhibit in North America. Another hit is Splash Island, a kids-only water park that includes a replica of a Canadian Coast Guard ship.

Ten kilometers (6 miles) of walkways offer access to all areas of the zoo. During the warmer months, the Zoomobile takes visitors around the major walkways to view the animals in the outdoor paddocks. The zoo has restaurants, a gift shop, first aid, and a family center. Visitors can rent strollers and wagons, and borrow wheelchairs. The African pavilion has an elevator for strollers and wheelchairs. There are ample parking and plenty of picnic areas with tables.

Meadowvale Rd. (north of Hwy. 401 and Sheppard Ave.), Scarborough. ℂ 416/392-5900. www.torontozoo.com. Admission C$20 (US$20/£10) adults, C$14 (US$14/£7) seniors, C$12 (US$12/£6) children 4–12, free for children 3 and under. Summer daily 9am–7:30pm; spring and fall daily 9am–6pm; winter daily 9:30am–4:30pm. Last admission 1 hr. before closing. Closed Dec 25. Parking C$8 (US$8/£4). Subway: Bloor–Danforth line to Kennedy, then bus 86A north (buses run daily in summer, but on weekdays only during the rest of the year). By car: From downtown, take Don Valley Pkwy. to Hwy. 401 east, exit on Meadowvale Rd., and follow signs.

MORE ATTRACTIONS
ARCHITECTURAL HIGHLIGHTS

Casa Loma 𝘈𝘈★ 𝘒𝘪𝘥𝘴 Every city has its folly, and Toronto has an unusually charm-ing one. It's complete with Elizabethan-style chimneys, Rhineland turrets, secret pas-sageways, an underground tunnel, and a mellifluous name: Casa Loma. Sir Henry Pellatt, who built it between 1911 and 1914, had a lifelong fascination with castles. He studied medieval palaces and gathered materials and furnishings from around the world, bringing marble, glass, and paneling from Europe, teak from Asia, and oak and walnut from North America. He imported Scottish stonemasons to build the massive walls that surround the 2.5-hectare (6-acre) site. It's a fascinating place to explore. Wander through the majestic Great Hall, with its 18m-high (60-ft.) hammer-beam ceiling; the Oak Room, where three artisans took 3 years to fashion the paneling; and the Conservatory, with its elegant bronze doors, stained-glass dome, and pink-and-green marble. The castle encompasses battlements and a tower; Peacock Alley, designed after Windsor Castle; and a 1,800-bottle wine cellar.

1 Austin Terrace. (𝆕 416/923-1171. www.casaloma.org. Admission C$12 (US$12/£6) adults, C$7.50 (US$7.50/£3.75) seniors and children 14–17, C$6.75 (US$6.75/£3.35) children 4–13, free for children 3 and under. Daily 9:30am–5pm (last entry at 4pm). Closed Jan 1, Dec 25. Subway: Dupont, then walk 2 blocks north.

City Hall 𝆕 An architectural spectacle, City Hall houses the mayor's office and the city's administrative offices. Daringly designed in the late 1950s by Finnish architect Viljo Revell, it consists of a low podium topped by the flying-saucer-shaped Council Chamber, enfolded between two curved towers. Its interior is as dramatic as its exterior. A free brochure detailing a self-guided tour of City Hall is available from its information desk; the tour can also be printed from the website below in French, Chinese, German, Italian, Japanese, Korean, Portuguese, and Spanish.

In front stretches **Nathan Phillips Square** (named after the mayor who initiated the project). In summer you can sit and contemplate the flower gardens, fountains, and reflecting pool (which doubles as a skating rink in winter), as well as listen to concerts. Here, you'll find Henry Moore's *The Archer* (formally, *Three-Way Piece No. 2*), purchased through a public subscription fund, and the Peace Garden, which commemorates Toronto's sesquicentennial in 1984. In contrast, to the east stands the **Old City Hall,** a green-copper-roofed Victorian Romanesque–style building.

100 Queen St. W. (𝆕 416/338-0338. www.city.toronto.on.ca/city_hall_tour/nps.htm. Free admission. Self-guided tours Mon–Fri 8:30am–4:30pm. Subway: Queen, then walk west to Bay.

Fort York 𝆕 *Kids* This base was established by Lieutenant Governor John Graves Simcoe in 1793 to defend "little muddy York," as Toronto was then known. Americans sacked it in April 1813, but the British rebuilt that same summer. Fort York was used by the military until 1880, and was pressed back into service during both world wars. You can tour the soldiers' and officers' quarters, clamber over the ramparts, and in summer, view demonstrations of drill, music, and cooking.

100 Garrison Rd., off Fleet St., between Bathurst St. and Strachan Ave. (𝆕 416/392-6907. www.fortyork.ca. Admission C$6 (US$6/£3) adults, C$3.25 (US$3.25/£1.60) seniors and children 13–18, C$3 (US$3/£1.50) children 6–12, free for children 5 and under. Free parking. Mid-May to Labour Day daily 10am–5pm; Sept to mid-May Mon–Fri 10am–4pm, Sat–Sun 10am–5pm. Subway: Bathurst, then streetcar no. 911 south.

Spadina Museum Historic House & Garden 𝆕 How do you pronounce "Spadina"? In the case of the avenue, it's Spa-*dye*-na; for this lovely landmark, it's Spa-*dee*-na. Why? Who knows! But if you want to see how the leading lights of the city lived in days gone by, visit the historic home of financier James Austin. The exterior is beautiful; the interior, even more impressive. Spadina House contains a remarkable collection of art, furniture, and decorative objects. The Austin family occupied the house from 1866 to 1980, and successive generations modified and added to the house and its decor. One caveat: The house has been used for film shoots, for which it suspends its regular admission hours, so call ahead to make sure it's open on the day you want to see it.

285 Spadina Rd. (𝆕 416/392-6910. Guided tour C$6 (US$6/£3) adults, C$5 (US$5/£2.50) seniors and children over 12, C$4 (US$4/£2) children 12 and under. Tues–Fri noon–4pm; Sat–Sun noon–5pm. Subway: Dupont.

MUSEUMS

Bata Shoe Museum 𝆕𝆕 Imelda Marcos—and anyone else obsessed with shoes (like, say, me!)—will love this museum, which houses the Bata family's 10,000-item collection. The building, designed by Raymond Moriyama, looks like a whimsical shoebox. The main gallery, "All About Shoes," traces the history of footwear. It begins with a plaster cast of some of the earliest known human footprints (discovered in Africa by anthropologist Mary Leakey), which date to 4 million B.C. You'll come across such specialty shoes as spiked clogs used to crush chestnuts in 17th-century France, Elton John's 12-inch-plus platforms, and Prime Minister Pierre Trudeau's well-worn sandals. One display focuses on Canadian footwear fashioned by the Inuit, while another highlights 19th-century ladies' footwear. The second-story galleries house changing exhibits, which have taken on some serious topics, such as a history of foot binding in China.

327 Bloor St. W. (at St. George St.). © 416/979-7799. www.batashoemuseum.ca. Admission C$12 (US$12/£6) adults, C$10 (US$10/£5) seniors, C$6 (US$6/£3) students with ID, C$4 (US$4/£2) children 5–14, free for children 4 and under. Free to all Thurs 5–8pm. Tues–Wed and Fri–Sat 10am–5pm; Thurs 10am–8pm; Sun noon–5pm. Subway: St. George.

Black Creek Pioneer Village *Kids*   The original pioneers on this land were Daniel and Elizabeth Strong, a newlywed couple in 1816 that cleared 40 hectares (100 acres) of wilderness for farming and built a log house in their spare time. Eventually a village developed around this site, and many of the existing buildings date from the 1860s. You can watch the authentically dressed villagers going about their chores, spinning, sewing, rail splitting, sheep shearing, and threshing. Visitors can enjoy the villagers' cooking, wander through the cozily furnished homesteads, visit the working mill, shop at the general store, or rumble past the farm animals in a horse-drawn wagon. The beautifully landscaped village has more than 30 restored buildings to explore. Special events take place throughout the year, from a great Easter egg hunt to Christmas by lamplight. The restaurant is open from 11am to 3pm and features a special children's menu.

1000 Murray Ross Pkwy. (at Steeles Ave. and Jane St.), Downsview. © 416/736-1733. www.blackcreek.ca. Admission C$12 (US$12/£6) adults, C$11 (US$11/£5.50) seniors and students 15 and up, C$8 (US$8/£4) children 5–14, free for children 4 and under. May–June Mon–Fri 9:30am–4:30pm, Sat–Sun and holidays 10am–5pm; July–Sept daily 10am–5pm; Oct–Dec Mon–Fri 9:30am–4pm, Sat–Sun and holidays 10am–4:30pm. Closed Jan–Apr, Dec 25. Parking C$6 (US$6/£3). Subway: Finch, then bus 60 west to Murray Ross Pkwy.

Design Exchange   Located in the old Stock Exchange Building, the Design Exchange—or DX, as it prefers to be known—has become an important Canadian design museum. It features work from disciplines as varied as architecture to fashion, and from landscape design to interactive media design. Note that the Resource Centre has been officially reopened, and its library-like collection of design books, magazines, and other materials can be viewed by appointment on Monday, Wednesday, and Friday afternoons.

234 Bay St. © 416/363-6121. www.dx.org. Admission C$5 (US$5/£2.50) adults, C$4 (US$4/£2) seniors and students with ID, free for children 13 and under. Mon–Fri 10am–5pm; Sat–Sun noon–5pm. Closed Jan 1, Dec 25. Subway: King.

Museum of Contemporary Canadian Art *★★*   MOCCA, as this museum is known, has relocated to the very hot Art & Design District on Queen Street West. Its growing collection includes works by Stephen Andrews, Genevieve Cadieux, Ivan Eyre, Betty Goodwin, Micah Lexier, Arnaud Maggs, and Roland Poulin, among many others. MOCCA's mandate has been widening in recent years, and that has made this gallery increasingly interesting. Some of the temporary exhibits have been real eye-openers, in particular one about tattoo art titled "Art for the Human Canvas"; tattoo art was also prominent in the 2006 exhibit "Sideshow" (the tagline for that show was

"If life is a circus, these cats are the freaks!" The line sums up the irreverence and playfulness of this museum).

952 Queen St. W., Toronto. (© 416/395-7430. www.mocca.toronto.on.ca. Free admission. Tues–Sun 11am–6pm. Closed for all statutory holidays. Subway: Osgoode, then streetcar west to Shaw St.

Textile Museum of Canada (⊛)   This fascinating museum is internationally recognized for its collection of more than 8,000 historic and ethnographic textiles and related artifacts. You'll find fine Oriental rugs, and cloth and tapestries from all over the world. One gallery presents the work of contemporary artists. The museum is small, so only a tiny portion of the collection is on display, but you'll always find a vibrant, interesting show.

55 Centre Ave. (© 416/599-5321. www.textilemuseum.ca. Admission C$10 (US$10/£5) adults, C$6 (US$6/£3) seniors, students, and children 5 and over, free for children 4 and under. Daily 11am–5pm (till 8pm Wed). Closed Jan 1, Dec 25. Subway: St. Patrick.

University of Toronto Art Centre (⊛ *Finds*)   This is a great find—and it's one that very few people outside the Toronto university community know about. You can enter the center from the University College quad, an Oxford-style cloistered garden that itself is a work of art. Inside, you'll find a gallery housing the Malcove Collection, which consists mainly of Byzantine art dating from the 14th to the 18th centuries. There are early stone reliefs and numerous icons from different periods. One of the Malcove's gems was painted by a German master in 1538: Lucas Cranach the Elder's *Adam and Eve*. The rest of the center is devoted to temporary exhibitions, which may display University College's large collection of Canadian art, or other special exhibits.

15 King's College Circle. (© 416/978-1838. www.utoronto.ca/artcentre. Admission C$5 (US$5/£2.50). Tues–Fri noon–5pm; Sat noon–4pm. Closed for all statutory holidays. Subway: St. George or Museum.

SPORTS HIGHLIGHTS

Air Canada Centre   This sports and entertainment complex is home to the Maple Leafs (NHL hockey) and the Raptors (NBA basketball). Longtime fans were crushed when the Leafs moved here in 1999 from Maple Leaf Gardens—the arena that had housed the team since 1931—but the Air Canada Centre has quickly become a fan favorite. Seating 18,700 for hockey, 19,500 for basketball, and 20,000 for concerts, the center was designed with comfort in mind. Seating is on a steeper-than-usual grade so that even the "nosebleed" sections have decent sightlines.

40 Bay St. (at Lakeshore Blvd.). (© 416/815-5500. www.theaircanadacentre.com. Subway: Union, then LRT to Queen's Quay.

Hockey Hall of Fame (⊛⊛ *Kids*)   Ice hockey fans will be thrilled by the artifacts collected here. They include the original Stanley Cup (donated in 1893 by Lord Stanley of Preston), a replica of the Montréal Canadiens' locker room, Terry Sawchuck's goalie gear, Newsy Lalonde's skates, and the stick Max Bentley used. You'll also see photographs of the personalities and great moments in hockey history. Most fun are the shooting and goalkeeping interactive displays, where you can take a whack at targets with a puck or don goalie gear and face down flying video pucks or sponge pucks.

In BCE Place, 30 Yonge St. (at Front St.). (© 416/360-7765. www.hhof.com. Admission C$13 (US$13/£6.50) adults, C$9 (US$9/£4.50) seniors and children 4–18, free for children 3 and under. Late June to Labour Day Mon–Sat 9:30am–6pm, Sun 10am–6pm; Sept to mid-June Mon–Fri 10am–5pm, Sat 9:30am–6pm, Sun 10:30am–5pm. Closed Jan 1, Dec 25. Subway: Union.

Rogers Centre ✦ This is home to the Toronto Blue Jays baseball team and the Toronto Argonauts football team. In 1989, the opening of this 53,000-seat stadium (known as SkyDome until 2005) was a gala event. The stadium represents an engineering feat, featuring the world's first fully retractable roof, which spans more than 3 hectares (7½ acres), and a gigantic video scoreboard. It is so large that a 31-story building would fit inside the complex when the roof is closed.

1 Blue Jays Way. ℂ 416/341-2770. www.rogerscentre.com. Subway: Union.

PARKS & GARDENS

Allan Gardens ✦ *Kids* Allan Gardens used to be down at the heels and seedy, but since the University of Toronto relocated its Botany Greenhouses here in 2004, this park has been infused with new life. This was actually Toronto's first civic park, created on the 4 hectares (10 acres) donated to the city by former mayor George William Allan. Originally called the Horticultural Gardens, the city renamed the park after Allan died in 1901. The stunning glass-domed Palm House conservatory dates back to 1910 and contains six greenhouses that cover 1,486 sq. m (15,995 sq. ft.). It has been joined by U of T's restored and renovated greenhouses, now called the Allan Gardens Children's Conservatory.

Between Jarvis, Sherbourne, Dundas, and Gerrard sts. ℂ 416/392-1111. Free admission. Daily dawn–dusk. Subway: Dundas.

High Park ✦ *Kids* This 161-hectare (398-acre) park in the far west of Midtown was surveyor and architect John G. Howard's gift to the city. He lived in Colborne Lodge, which still stands in the park. The grounds contain a large lake called Grenadier Pond (great for ice skating in wintertime); a small but exotic zoo (with peacocks, llamas, and bison, among others); a swimming pool; tennis courts; sports fields; bowling greens; and vast expanses of green for baseball, jogging, picnicking, bicycling, and more. But my favorite thing is the Dream in High Park, the annual Shakespearean offering, staged every summer (visit www.canstage.com for details).

1873 Bloor St. W., stretching south to the Gardiner Expwy. No phone. Free admission. Daily dawn–dusk. Subway: High Park.

Ireland Park ✦ *finds* In 1847, Toronto was a city of 20,000—until 38,000 Irish immigrants arrived that summer. On June 21, 2007, this memorial to the Irish Famine was opened at Eireann Quay by Mary McAleese, president of Ireland. The park was inspired by Rowan Gillespie's "Departure" series of famine figures, which stand on Dublin's Liffey quayside, depicting Irish emigrants looking out to sea. There are seven figures in Dublin and five in Toronto's new park, which seems appropriate given how many Irish perished on the journey. The figures in Ireland Park were also created by Gillespie, and they are called the "Arrival" series. There is also a memorial in the park to the more than 1,100 who died just after their arrival; their names will be inscribed in a limestone wall.

At Bathurst St. and Queen's Quay W., across from Bathurst Quay. ℂ 416/601-6906. www.irelandparkfoundation.com. Free admission. Daily dawn–dusk. Subway: Union, then LRT to Spadina and walk west to Bathurst.

Toronto Music Garden ✦✦✦ Toronto is a city of gardens, but this one along Toronto's waterfront is special. Cellist Yo-Yo Ma and landscape designer Julie Moir Messervy created the Toronto Music Garden to invoke Bach's First Suite for Unaccompanied Cello. Between 10am and 8pm, you can rent an audio guide to the music garden complete with commentary from Ma and Messervy, and snippets from the baroque work that inspired them (audio guides are C$5/US$5/£2.50 and are available at 539 Queen's Quay W.).

475 Queen's Quay W. (C) 416/338-0338. Free admission. Daily dawn–dusk. Subway: Union, then LRT to Spadina.

ESPECIALLY FOR KIDS

The city puts on a fabulous array of special events for children at **Harbourfront.** In March, the **Children's Film Festival** screens 40 entries from 15 countries. In April, **Spring Fever** celebrates the season with egg decorating, puppet shows, and more; on Saturday mornings in April, **cushion concerts** are given for the 5-to-12 set. In May, the **Milk International Children's Festival** brings 100 international performers to the city for a week of great entertainment. For additional information, call (C) **416/973-4000.** For the last 30 years, the **Lorraine Kimsa Theatre for Young People,** 165 Front St. E., at Sherbourne Street ((C) **416/862-2222**), has been entertaining youngsters. Its season runs from August to May. *Help! We've Got Kids* is an all-in-one directory for attractions, events, shops, and services appropriate for kids ages 12 and under in the greater Toronto area. Many of the listings are online at **www.helpwevegotkids.com**.

Here are Toronto's best venues, at least from a kid's point of view. Kids race to be the first at **Ontario Science Centre,** a paradise of hands-on games, experiments, and push-button demonstrations—800 of them. The kids can't wait to get on **Paramount Canada's Wonderland** roller coasters and daredevil rides. And don't forget to budget for video games. At **Harbourfront,** Kaleidoscope is an ongoing program of creative crafts, active games, and special events on weekends and holidays. There's also a pond, winter ice skating, and a crafts studio. At **Ontario Place,** the water slides, a huge Cinesphere, a futuristic pod, and other entertainment are the big hits at this recreational and cultural park. The **Toronto Zoo** is one of the best in the world, modeled after San Diego's—the animals in this 284-hectare (702-acre) park really do live in a natural environment.

Other venues address more specialized interests. Riding a ferry to the turn-of-the-20th-century amusement park **Centreville** on the **Toronto Islands** is part of the fun. Visit the **CN Tower** especially for the interactive simulator games and the terror of the glass floor. The top hits of the **Royal Ontario Museum** are the dinosaurs and the spooky bat cave. At **Fort York,** see reenactments of battle drills, musket and cannon firing, and musical marches with fife and drum. At the **Hockey Hall of Fame,** who wouldn't want the chance to tend goal against Mark Messier and Wayne Gretzky (with a sponge puck), and to practice with the fun and challenging video pucks? Go to **Black Creek Pioneer Village** for craft and other demonstrations. **Casa Loma**'s stables, secret passageway, and fantasy rooms really capture children's imaginations.

Riverdale Farm 🌟🌟   Idyllically situated on the edge of the Don Valley Ravine, this working farm located on 3 hectares (7½ acres) right in the city is a favorite with small tots. They enjoy watching the cows, pigs, turkeys, and ducks—and can get close enough to pet many animals, such as the rabbits. Because this really is a farm, you'll see all of the chores of daily life, such as horse grooming, cow- and goat-milking, egg collecting, and animal feeding. There's a farmer's market on-site every Tuesday from May to October.

201 Winchester St. (at Sumach St.). (C) 416/392-6794. Free admission. Daily 9am–5pm. Subway: Castle Frank, then bus 65 south on Parliament St. to Wellesley and walk 3 blocks east to Sumach.

6 Special Events & Festivals

Winter is a busy time. The **Chinese New Year** (depending on the lunar calendar, it falls in late Jan or early Feb) is ushered in with traditional and contemporary performances of Chinese opera, dancing, music, and more (for Harbourfront events, call © **416/ 973-4000;** for the Rogers Centre, call © **416/341-2770**). **Winterfest** (© **416/338- 0338**) is a 3-day celebration spread over various neighborhoods, and features ice-skating shows, snow play, midway rides, performances, and ice sculpting.

In late March and early April, there is the **Toronto Festival of Storytelling** at Harbourfront (© **416/973-4000;** www.storytellingtoronto.org), which features 60 storytellers imparting legends and fables from around the world.

May brings a couple of festivals. **Santé–The Bloor–Yorkville Wine Festival** (© **416/ 504-3977;** www.santewinefestival.net) is a 4-day gourmet extravaganza that brings together the award-winning Ontario vintages, food from the city's top-rated chefs, and live jazz. There's also the **Milk International Children's Festival** at Harbourfront. This is a 9-day celebration of the arts for kids—from theater and music to dance, comedy, and storytelling.

June boasts the **Harbourfront Reading Series** (© **416/973-4000;** www.readings. org), a festival that celebrates the best of Canadian literature. Top writers such as Anne Michaels and Barbara Gowdy flock here to read from their latest works. Alternative music fans flock to the **North by Northeast Music Festival** (© **416/469-0986;** www.nxne.com), a 3-day event that features rock and indie bands at 28 venues around Toronto. During the 3-day **Distillery Blues Festival** (in the Distillery Historic District), Toronto shows that it's got soul (www.distilleryblues.com). Toronto's multicultural diversity is celebrated at the **Toronto International Festival Caravan** (© **416/ 977-0466**), a 9-day event that features more than 40 themed pavilions, craft demonstrations, opportunities to sample authentic dishes, and traditional dance performances by 100 different cultural groups. The last week in June is **Gay and Lesbian Pride Celebration** (© **416/92-PRIDE** or 416/927-7433; www.pridetoronto.com), and the week of events, performances, symposiums, and parties culminates in an extravagant Sunday parade.

July's most important event is the 2-week **Caribana** celebration (© **416/465-4884;** www.caribana.com). Toronto's version of Carnival features traditional foods from the Caribbean and Latin America, ferry cruises, island picnics, children's events, concerts, and arts-and-crafts exhibits. It draws more than a million people from across North America and Britain. On the third weekend of July, there's the **Molson Indy** at the Exhibition Place Street circuit (© **416/922-7477;** www.molsonindy.com). This is one of Canada's major races on the Champ Car circuit.

August brings the **Canadian National Exhibition** at Exhibition Place (© **416/ 393-6000;** www.theex.com), locally known as "The Ex." One of the world's largest fairs, this 18-day extravaganza features midway rides, display buildings, free shows, and grandstand performers.

In September, Toronto is lit up by stars at the **Toronto International Film Festival** ⭐⭐⭐ (© **416/968-FILM;** www.tiffg.ca). Second only to Cannes, the 10-day festival features more than 250 films from 70 countries.

October boasts the **International Festival of Authors** at Harbourfront (© **416/ 973-4000;** www.readings.org). This renowned 11-day literary festival draws more than 100 authors from 25 countries to perform readings and on-stage interviews.

Among the literary luminaries who have appeared are Salman Rushdie, Margaret Drabble, Thomas Kenneally, Joyce Carol Oates, A. S. Byatt, and Margaret Atwood.

In November, there's fun for the whole family at the **Royal Agricultural Winter Fair and Royal Horse Show** at Exhibition Place (© **416/393-6400;** www.royalfair. org). This 12-day show is the largest indoor agricultural and equestrian competition in the world; the horse show is traditionally attended by a member of the British royal family. There's also the **Santa Claus Parade** (© **416/249-7833;** www.thesantaclaus parade.com), which has been a favorite with kids since 1905, with its marching bands, magical floats, and clowns. It's usually the third Sunday of November so that jolly St. Nick can avoid driving his reindeer through slushy snow.

In December, there's the **Canadian Aboriginal Festival** at SkyDome (© **519/751-0040;** www.canab.com). More than 1,500 Native American dancers, drummers, and singers attend this weekend celebration. There are also literary readings, an arts-and-crafts marketplace, and traditional foods to savor.

Contact **Tourism Toronto** (© **800/499-2514** or 416/203-2600; www.toronto tourism.com) for additional information on festivals and events.

7 Outdoor Activities & Spectator Sports

Toronto residents love the great outdoors, whatever the time of year. In summer, you'll see people cycling, boating, and hiking; in winter, there's skating, skiing, and snowboarding. So make like a native and enjoy the city's vast expanse of parkland.

For additional information on facilities in the parks, golf courses, tennis courts, swimming pools, beaches, and picnic areas, call **Metro Parks** (© **416/392-8186**) or **City Parks** (© **416/392-1111**). Also see "Parks & Gardens," above.

OUTDOOR ACTIVITIES

BEACHES The **Beaches** is the neighborhood along Queen Street East from Coxwell Avenue to Victoria Park. It has a charming boardwalk that connects several beaches, starting at **Ashbridge's Bay Park,** which has a sizable marina. **Woodbine Beach** connects to **Kew Gardens Park** and is a favorite with sunbathers and volleyball players. Woodbine also boasts the **Donald D. Summerville Olympic Pool.** Snack bars and trinket sellers line the length of the boardwalk.

Personally, I prefer the beaches on the **Toronto Islands.** The ones on **Centre Island,** always the busiest, are favorites with families because of nearby attractions like **Centreville.** The beaches on **Wards Island** are much more secluded. They're connected by the loveliest boardwalk in the city, with masses of fragrant flowers and raspberry bushes along its edges. **Hanlan's Point,** also in the islands, is Toronto's only nude beach.

BOATING/CANOEING The **Harbourfront Canoe and Kayak School,** 283A Queens Quay W. (© **800/960-8886** or 416/203-2277; www.paddletoronto.com), rents canoes and kayaks; call ahead if you are interested in taking private instruction. You can also rent canoes, rowboats, and pedal boats on the **Toronto Islands** just south of Centreville.

CROSS-COUNTRY SKIING Just about every park in Toronto becomes potential cross-country skiing territory as soon as snow falls. Best bets are Sunnybrook Park and Ross Lord Park, both in North York. For more information, call **Toronto Parks and Recreation** (© **416/392-8186;** www.city.toronto.on.ca/parks). Serious skiers interested in day trips to excellent out-of-town sites like Horseshoe Valley can call **Trakkers Cross Country Ski Club** (© 416/763-0173; www.trakkers.ca), which also rents equipment.

CYCLING With biking trails through most of the city's parks and more than 29km (18 miles) of street bike routes, it's not surprising that Toronto has been called one of the best cycling cities in North America. Favorite pathways include the **Martin Goodman Trail** (from the Beaches to the Humber River along the waterfront); the **Lower Don Valley** bike trail (from the east end of the city north to Riverdale Park); **High Park** (with winding trails over 160 hectares/395 acres); and the **Toronto Islands,** where bikers ride freely, without fear of cars. For advice, call the **Ontario Cycling Association** (© 416/426-7416) or **Toronto Parks and Recreation** (© 416/392-8186).

Bike lanes are marked on College/Carlton streets, the Bloor Street Viaduct leading to the Danforth, Beverly/St. George streets, and Davenport Road. For an up-to-date list of bike-rental shops, contact the **Toronto Bicycling Network** (© 416/766-1985) or see the website at www.tbn.ca. One sure bet is **Wheel Excitement,** 249 Queens Quay W., Unit 110 (© 416/260-9000; www.wheelexcitement.ca). If you're interested in cycling with a group or want information about daily excursions and weekend trips, call the Toronto Bicycling Network.

GOLF Toronto is golf obsessed, as evidenced by its more than 75 public courses within an hour's drive of downtown. Here's information on some of the best:

- **Don Valley,** 4200 Yonge St., south of Highway 401 (© 416/392-2465). Designed by Howard Watson, this is a scenic par-71 course with some challenging elevated tees. The par-3 13th hole is nicknamed the Hallelujah Corner (it takes a miracle to make par). It's considered a good place to start your kids.
- **Humber Valley,** 40 Beattie Ave., at Albion Road (© 416/392-2488). The relatively flat par-70 course is easy to walk and gets lots of shade from towering trees. The three final holes require major concentration (the 16th and 17th are both par 5s).
- The **Glen Abbey Golf Club,** 1333 Dorval Dr., Oakville (© 905/844-1800). The championship course is one of the most famous in Canada. Designed by Jack Nicklaus, the par-73 layout traditionally plays host to the Canadian Open.

Travelers who are really into golf might want to consider a side trip to **Muskoka** (see chapter 12 for specifics). This area just 90 minutes north has some of the best golfing in the country at courses such as **Taboo** and the **Deerhurst Highlands.**

ICE SKATING & IN-LINE SKATING **Nathan Phillips Square** in front of City Hall becomes a free ice rink in winter, as does an area at Harbourfront Centre. Rentals are available on-site. Artificial rinks (also free) are in more than 25 parks, including Grenadier Pond in High Park—a romantic spot, with a bonfire and vendors selling roasted chestnuts. They're open from November to March. In summer, in-line skaters pack Toronto's streets (and sidewalks). Go with the flow and rent some blades from **Wheel Excitement** (see "Cycling," above).

JOGGING Downtown routes might include **Harbourfront** and along the lakefront, or through **Queen's Park** and the university. The **Martin Goodman Trail** runs 20km (12 miles) along the waterfront from the Beaches in the east to the Humber River in the west. It's ideal for jogging, walking, or cycling. It links to the **Tommy Thompson Trail,** which travels the parks from the lakefront along the Humber River. Near the Ontario Science Centre in the Central Don Valley, **Ernest Thompson Seton Park** is also good for jogging. Parking is available at the Thorncliffe Drive and Wilket

Creek entrances. These areas are generally quite safe, but you should take the same precautions you would in any large city.

SNOWBOARDING & SKIING   The snowboard craze shows no sign of abating, at least from January to March (or anytime there's enough snow on the ground). One popular site is the **Earl Bales Park,** Bathurst Street (just south of Sheppard Ave.), which offers rentals. The park also has an alpine ski center, which offers both equipment rentals and coaching. Call **Toronto Parks and Recreation** (© **416/392-8186**) for more information.

TENNIS   More than 30 municipal parks have free tennis facilities. The most convenient are the courts in High, Rosedale, and Jonathan Ashridge parks. They are open in summer only. At Eglinton Flats Park, west of Keele Street at Eglinton Avenue, six of the courts can be used in winter. Call the city (© **416/392-1111**) or Metro Parks (© **416/392-8186**) for additional information.

SPECTATOR SPORTS

AUTO RACING   The **Grand Prix of Toronto** (© **416/872-4639**; www.grandprix toronto.com)—better known by its old moniker, the **Molson Indy**—runs at the Exhibition Place Street circuit, usually on the third weekend in July.

BASEBALL   **Rogers Centre,** 1 Blue Jays Way, on Front Street beside the CN Tower, is the home of the **Toronto Blue Jays.** For information, contact the Toronto Blue Jays, P.O. Box 7777, Adelaide St., Toronto, ON M5C 2K7 (© **416/341-1000;** www. bluejays.ca). For tickets, call © **416/341-1234.**

BASKETBALL   Toronto's basketball team, the **Raptors,** has its home ground in the **Air Canada Centre,** 40 Bay St. at Lakeshore Boulevard. The NBA schedule runs from October to April. The arena seats 19,500 for basketball. For information, contact the **Raptors Basketball Club,** 40 Bay St. (© **416/815-5600;** www.nba.com/raptors). For tickets, call **Ticketmaster** (© **416/870-8000**).

FOOTBALL   Remember Kramer on *Seinfeld?* He would watch only Canadian football. Here's your chance to catch a game. **Rogers Centre,** 1 Blue Jays Way, is home to the **Argonauts** of the Canadian Football League. They play between June and November. For information, contact the club at © **416/341-2700** or visit www.argonauts. on.ca. For tickets, call **Ticketmaster** (© **416/870-8000**).

GOLF TOURNAMENTS   Canada's national golf tournament, the **Bell Canadian Open,** usually takes place at the **Glen Abbey Golf Club** in Oakville, about 40 minutes from the city (© **905/844-1800**). Most years, it runs over the Labour Day weekend.

HOCKEY   Hockey isn't Canada's national sport, believe it or not (that's lacrosse), but it's arguably the most popular. The **Air Canada Centre,** 40 Bay St., at Lakeshore Boulevard, is the home of the **Toronto Maple Leafs** (www.torontomapleleafs.com). Though the arena seats 18,700 for hockey, tickets are not easy to come by, because many are sold by subscription. The rest are available through **Ticketmaster** (© **416/ 870-8000**).

HORSE RACING   Thoroughbred racing takes place at **Woodbine Racetrack,** Rexdale Boulevard and Highway 427, Etobicoke (© **416/675-6110** or 416/675-7223). It's famous for the Queen's Plate (usually contested on the third Sun in June); the Canadian International, a classic turf race (Sept or Oct); and the North America Cup (mid-June). Woodbine also hosts harness racing in spring and fall.

SOCCER   When I was growing up in Toronto, the soccer team was the Toronto Blizzard (and I have to confess that I didn't notice when the team ceased to exist). Toronto's new soccer club, the **Toronto FC** (http://toronto.fc.mlsnet.com), is getting a lot more attention. It's the first non-U.S. team in the Major League Soccer League. They play at BMO Field at Exhibition Place; it was built for the FC and it holds 20,195 spectators. For tickets, call **Ticketmaster** (© **416/870-8000**).

TENNIS TOURNAMENTS   Canada's international tennis championships, the **AT&T Rogers Cup** (for women) and the **Montréal/Toronto Tennis Masters Series** (for men), are important stops on the pro tours. They attract stars like the Williams sisters to the National Tennis Centre at York University in August. The men's and women's championships alternate cities each year. In 2008, the women play in Montréal and the men in Toronto. For more information, call © **416/665-9777** or check **www.tenniscanada.com**.

8 Shopping

Toronto's major shopping districts are the **Bloor/Yorkville** area for designer boutiques and top-name galleries; **Queen Street West** for a funkier mix of fashion, antiques, and bookstores; and the **Eaton Centre,** which stands at 220 Yonge St.

Stores usually open at around 10am Monday through Saturday. From Monday to Wednesday, most stores close at 6pm; on Thursday and Friday, hours run to 8pm or 9pm; on Saturday, closings are quite early, usually around 6pm. Most stores are open on Sunday, though the hours may be restricted—11am or noon to 5pm is not unusual.

ANTIQUES

For fine antiques, head north from Bloor Street along Avenue Road until you reach Davenport Avenue, or walk north on Yonge Street from the Rosedale subway station to St. Clair Avenue. True bargain-hunters will gravitate to Leslieville, the stretch of Queen Street East between Carlaw and Coxwell with its many small antique shops, which often contain great finds that need a little bit of fixing up. (*An insider's tip:* Leslieville is where owners of some of the most glamorous antiques stores in town shop; they buy pieces here, fix them up, and sell them at uptown prices.)

Abraham's Antiques *Finds*   My husband hates it when I drag him into this kind of place. Abraham's looks like a pack rat's attic, and it smells like one too. But it's got great furniture, decorative items, and collectibles at reasonable prices—and Abraham is on-site if you feel like haggling. 635 Queen St. W. © **416/504-6210**. Subway: Osgoode, then streetcar west to Bathurst.

Putti ℛ   Two generously proportioned rooms hold grand (and grandly priced) European treasures old and new: dining sets, armoires, cushions, and china. A recent addition is the floral department, which features both fresh and dried flowers. *Victoria* magazine has featured this shop repeatedly. 1104 Yonge St. © **416/972-7652**. Subway: Rosedale.

ART

Bau-Xi Gallery   After viewing the masterworks at the Art Gallery of Ontario, you can head across the street and buy your own. Founded in 1965, Bau-Xi features contemporary works by artists from across the country. 340 Dundas St. W. © **416/977-0600**. Subway: St. Patrick.

Eskimo Art Gallery ⚐ This award-winning gallery has the largest collection of Inuit stone sculptures in Toronto. At any given time, it shows more than 500 pieces. 12 Queens Quay W. (opposite Westin Harbour Castle). ✆ 416/366-3000. www.eskimoart.com. Subway: Union, then LRT to Queen's Quay.

Sandra Ainsley Gallery ⚐ Specializing in glass sculpture, this renowned gallery represents Canadian, American, and international artists, including Dale Chihuly, Jon Kuhn, Peter Powning, Tom Scoon, Susan Edgerley, and David Bennett. In the Distillery District, 55 Mill St. ✆ 416/214-9490. www.sandraainsleygallery.com. Subway: King, then streetcar east to Parliament St.

Stephen Bulger Gallery ⚐ *Finds* Bulger gallery displays contemporary Canadian and international photography, both by established artists and up-and-comers (the gallery is one of the driving forces behind CONTACT, Toronto's Annual Celebration of Photography, which has launched many careers). 1026 Queen St. W. ✆ 416/504-0575. www.bulgergallery.com. Subway: Osgoode, then streetcar west to Ossington Ave.

BOOKS

Book City ⚐ *Value* For a small chain, Book City offers big discounts—many tomes are discounted by 10% to 30%. The selection of international magazines is particularly good. Book City also has branches at 663 Yonge St. (✆ 416/964-1167), 1950 Queen St. E. (✆ 416/698-1444), and 348 Danforth Ave. (✆ 416/469-9997). 501 Bloor St. W. ✆ 416/961-4496. Subway: Bathurst.

Indigo Books Music & More The chain dominates Toronto's bookstore scene. Indigo offers a wide selection of merchandise, tables and chairs to encourage browsing, special events, and a cafe. There are also locations at the Eaton Centre (✆ 416/591-3622) and at 2300 Yonge St., at Eglinton Avenue (✆ 416/544-0049). Manulife Centre, 55 Bloor St. W. ✆ 416/925-3536. www.indigo.ca. Subway: Yonge/Bloor or Bay.

Nicholas Hoare This delightful old-fashioned bookshop has the cozy feel of an English library, with hardwood floors, plush couches, and a fireplace. 45 Front St. E. ✆ 416/777-2665. Subway: Union.

University of Toronto Bookstore ⚐ *Finds* This is one of the best-stocked independent booksellers in town. They also host their own Reading Series, which has featured authors such as Ann-Marie MacDonald and Roddy Doyle; check the website for details about upcoming events. In the Koffler Centre, 214 College St. ✆ 416/978-7900. www.uoft bookstore.com. Subway: Queen's Park.

CHINA, SILVER & GLASS

William Ashley *Value* The last word in luxe, whether it be fine china, crystal, or silver. All of the top manufacturers are represented, including Waterford, Baccarat, Christofle, Wedgwood, and Lenox. The prices are almost always better than you'll find elsewhere. Manulife Centre, 55 Bloor St. W. ✆ 416/964-2900. www.williamashley.com. Subway: Bay.

DEPARTMENT STORES

The Bay The Hudson's Bay Company started out as a fur-trading business when the first French-speaking settlers came to Canada. Today, the Bay boasts excellent midrange selections of clothing and housewares. It schedules sales almost every week, though shoppers should be warned that winning the staff's attention somtimes requires patience. Of the several locations, here are the two best: (1) 176 Yonge St. (at Queen St.).

(C) 416/861-9111. Subway: Queen. (2) 2 Bloor St. E. (at Yonge St.). (C) 416/972-3333. www.thebay.com. Subway: Yonge/Bloor.

Sears   If you visited Toronto before 2000, you'll remember the gorgeous Eaton's department store, which anchored the Eaton Centre complex. Sears Canada bought it and opened this department store in its place. This is definitely more upscale than your average Sears. Eaton Centre. (C) 416/343-2111. Subway: Dundas.

FASHION

Brian Bailey 🥀   This Canadian designer creates glamorous gowns, cocktail dresses, and smart suits. The shop is located in an edgy neighborhood, but the look is classic and feminine. 878 Queen St. W. (C) 416/516-7188. Subway: Osgoode, then streetcar west to Shaw.

Eza Wear *Finds*   Design duo Susanne Langlois and Erin Murphy make many of their cool men's clothes from hemp, which looks as elegant as linen. 695 Queen St. W. (C) 416/975-1388. Subway: Osgoode, then streetcar west to Markham St.

Femme de Carriere   For a dose of Québécois savoir-faire, look no further than this elegant emporium. While the name translates into "career woman," the offerings range from shapely suits to evening-appropriate dresses and chic separates. Eaton Centre. (C) 416/595-0951. Subway: Queen.

Girl Friday   Local designer Rebecca Nixon creates feminine dresses, suits, and separates for her shop under the name Girl Friday. The store also carries pieces from hip labels Nougat and Dish, but I come here for Nixon's elegant but affordable pieces. 740 Queen St. W. (C) 416/364-2511. www.girlfridayclothing.com. Subway: Osgoode, then streetcar west to Claremont St.

Harry Rosen   This men's store carries the crème de la crème of menswear designers, including Hugo Boss, Brioni, and Versace. 82 Bloor St. W. (C) 416/972-0556. Subway: Bay.

Pam Chorley   These glamorous dresses, designed by shop owner Pam Chorley, are a tribute to playful femininity and whimsical imagination. Many of the fabrics are made for Chorley in Paris, and you won't find them anywhere else. 322 1/2 Queen St. W. (C) 416/351-8758. Subway: Osgoode.

Peach Berserk   Toronto designer (and local legend) Kingi Carpenter creates dramatically printed silk separates, dresses, and coats. Don't look for demure florals—prints range from bold martini glasses to the ironic "Do I Look Fat in This?" logo. 507 Queen St. W. (C) 416/504-1711. www.peachberserk.com. Subway: Osgoode, then streetcar west to Spadina.

Price Roman   The husband-and-wife team of Derek Price and Tess Roman produces sleek, tailored clothes with a sultry edge. 267 Queen St. W. (C) 416/979-7363. Subway: Osgoode.

Roots   This is one Canadian retailer that seems to be universally loved. The clothes are casual, from hooded sweats to fleece jackets, and there's a good selection of footwear. Don't overlook the tykes' department, which has the same stuff in tiny sizes. Other locations include the Eaton Centre ((C) 416/593-9640). 95A Bloor St. W. (C) 416/323-9512. www.roots.ca. Subway: Bay.

FOOD

House of Tea   Visitors can drink in the heady scent of more than 150 loose teas. 1017 Yonge St. (C) 416/922-1226. Subway: Rosedale.

Kensington Market It's a very different scene at this market, bordered by Baldwin, Kensington, and Augusta avenues, and by Dundas Street to the south. Originally a Jewish community, it now borders on Chinatown. There are several Asian herbalists and grocers, as well as many West Indian and Middle Eastern shops. No phone. Subway: Spadina, then LRT to Baldwin St. or Dundas St. W.

SOMA Chocolatemaker The chocolate maker does all of his work on site, starting with roasting the raw cocoa beans. The results are breathtaking: chocolate bars (like the Dark Fire, with chiles, ginger, and vanilla, or the milk chocolate with dried cherries) simply melt in your mouth. In the Distillery District, 55 Mill St. (©️ **416/815-7662.** www.somachocolate.com. Subway: King, then streetcar east to Parliament St.

St. Lawrence Market A local favorite for fresh produce, it even draws people who live a good distance away. Hours are Tuesday to Thursday 9am to 7pm, Friday 8am to 8pm, Saturday 5am (when the farmers arrive) to 5pm. 92 Front St. E. (©️ **416/392-7219.** Subway: Union.

HEALTH & BEAUTY

M.A.C. M.A.C. was founded in Toronto and is now owned by Estée Lauder. This flagship store is perpetually packed, especially on weekends, but if you call ahead you can schedule an appointment for a makeup lesson. In addition to cosmetics, the store carries skin- and hair-care supplies. 89 Bloor St. W. (©️ **416/929-7555.** www.maccosmetics.com. Subway: Bay.

Noah's Noah's boasts aisle after aisle of vitamins and dietary supplements, organic foods and "natural" candies, skin-care and bath products, and books and periodicals. The staff is well informed and helpful. A smaller but more centrally located outlet is at 667 Yonge St. (at Bloor; (©️ **416/969-0220**). 322 Bloor St. W. (©️ **416/968-7930.** Subway: Spadina.

HOUSEWARES & FURNISHINGS

Bergo You will find the most cutting-edge international design represented here (Bergo has an especially notable collection of German and Danish pieces). There's also some architecturally inspired jewelry and watches by Frank Gehry. Prices veer to the high side, but that's no surprise, is it, *liebchen*? In the Distillery District, 55 Mill St. (©️ **416/861-1821.** www.bergo.ca. Subway: King, then streetcar east to Parliament St.

Umbra I've long been a fan of Umbra's überstylish yet affordable designs, so the opening of its first retail outpost in 2007 is huge news. The Toronto flagship store is a 650-sq.-m (7,000-sq.-ft.) bi-level wonder that includes an expansive range of products, some furniture, and a space where you can watch members of the design team at work. 165 John St. (©️ **416/599-0088.** www.umbra.com. Subway: Osgoode.

JEWELRY

Birks Among the silver, crystal, and china is an extensive selection of top-quality jewelry, including exquisite pearls and knockout diamond engagement rings. There are Birks branches at the Eaton Centre ((©️ **416/979-9311**) and at First Canadian Place ((©️ **416/363-5663**). At the Manulife Centre, 55 Bloor St. W. (©️ **416/922-2266.** Subway: Bay.

Trove I'm a magpie at heart, and this fabulous store carries all sorts of sparkly wonders that make my eyes pop and heart go a-flutter. Trove also stocks accessories, including handbags, hats, and scarves. 793 Bathurst St. (at Bloor St. W.) (©️ **416/516-1258.** Subway: Bathurst.

TOYS

Kidding Awound   Wind-up gadgets are the specialty here—hundreds of 'em. There are also some antique toys (which you won't let the kids near) and gag gifts. 91 Cumberland St. ℂ 416/926-8996. Subway: Bay.

Science City   Kids and adults alike will love this tiny store filled with games, puzzles, models, kits, and books—all related to science. Whether your interest is astronomy, biology, chemistry, archaeology, or physics, you'll find something here. Holt Renfrew Centre, 50 Bloor St. W. ℂ 416/968-2627. Subway: Yonge/Bloor.

WINE

In Ontario, Liquor Control Board of Ontario (LCBO) outlets and small boutiques at upscale grocery stores sell wine; no alcohol is sold at convenience stores. There are LCBO outlets all over the city, and prices are the same at all of them. The loveliest shop downtown is at the **Manulife Centre,** 55 Bloor St. W. (ℂ 416/925-5266). Other locations are at 20 Bloor St. E. ℂ 416/368-0521); the **Eaton Centre** (ℂ 416/979-9978); and **Union Station** (ℂ 416/925-9644). **Vintages** stores have a different name, but they're still LCBO outlets. Check out the one at **Hazelton Lanes** (ℂ 416/924-9463) and at **Queen's Quay** (ℂ 416/864-6777).

9 Toronto After Dark

Toronto has a vital and varied nightlife scene. Renowned local artists and troupes include the Canadian Stage Company, the Canadian Opera Company, the National Ballet of Canada, Soulpepper, the Tafelmusik Baroque Orchestra, and the Toronto Symphony Orchestra. You can catch major Broadway shows or a performance by one of the many small theater companies that make Toronto one of the leading theater centers in North America. For additional entertainment, there are enough bars, clubs, cabarets, comedy clubs, and other entertainment to keep anyone spinning.

For local happenings, check *Where Toronto* (you can probably find a copy in your hotel room) and *Toronto Life* (www.torontolife.com), as well as the *Globe and Mail* (www.globeandmail.ca), the *Toronto Star* (www.thestar.com), the *Toronto Sun* (www.fyitoronto.com), and the two free weekly papers, *Now* and *Eye*. Events of particular interest to the gay and lesbian community are listed in *Xtra!,* another free weekly. The **Torontoist** blog (www.torontoist.com) is also a great source for upcoming performances.

For almost any theater, music, or dance event, you can buy tickets from **Ticketmaster** (ℂ 416/870-8000; www.ticketmaster.ca). Ticketmaster also runs the **T.O. Tix** booth (www.totix.ca), which sells half-price day-of-performance tickets. Cash and credit cards are accepted; all sales are final. T.O. Tix is open Tuesday to Friday from noon to 7:30pm and on Saturday from noon to 6pm; the booth is closed Sunday and Monday. T.O. Tix is currently located in Yonge-Dundas Square, which is just across the street from the Eaton Centre.

THE PERFORMING ARTS

The major performing-arts venues include **Massey Hall,** 178 Victoria St. (ℂ 416/593-4828; subway: Queen), which is a Canadian musical landmark, hosting a variety of musical programming from classical to rock. The **Sony Centre,** 1 Front St. E. (ℂ 416/872-2262; subway: King or Union), presents national and international theater, music, and dance companies (the theater's naming rights were snapped up by

Sony in 2007, so it may have a new name by the time you arrive in Toronto). The **Four Seasons Centre for the Performing Arts,** 145 Queen St. W. (© **416/363-6671;** subway: Osgoode) opened to wide acclaim in 2006; it is now home to the Canadian Opera Company and the National Ballet of Canada. The **Distillery District,** 55 Mill St. (© **416/367-1800**), is now home to the Dancemakers and Native Earth troupes.

Roy Thomson Hall, 60 Simcoe St. (© **416/593-4828;** subway: St. Andrew), is the premier concert hall and home to the Toronto Symphony Orchestra, which performs here September to June. The **St. Lawrence Centre,** 27 Front St. E. (© **416/366-7723;** subway: King or Union), hosts musical and theatrical events and is home to the CanStage Theatre Company in the Bluma Appel Theatre and to Music Toronto and public debates in the Jane Mallett Theatre. And then there's the **Premiere Dance Theatre,** 207 Queen's Quay W. (© **416/973-4000;** subway: Union, then LRT to York Quay), home to a leading contemporary dance season featuring local companies—the Toronto Dance Theatre, the Danny Grossman Dance Company, and other Canadian and international companies including the Desrosiers Dance Theatre.

OPERA

The **Canadian Opera Company** (© **800/250-4653** or 416/363-6671; www.coc.ca) is Canada's largest opera company. Its 2007–08 season included productions of *Tosca, The Barber of Seville, The Marriage of Figaro,* and *Don Carlos.* Its home is the Four Seasons Centre for the Performing Arts. Toronto has a wealth of other opera companies too, including **Opera Atelier** (© **416/703-3767;** www.operaatelier.com), which produces Baroque period operas; **Tapestry New Opera Works** (© **416/537-6066;** www.tapestrynewopera.com) produces original Canadian works; and **Queen of Puddings Musical Theatre** (© **416/203-4149;** www.queenofpuddingsmusictheatre.com) is famous for its provocative take on chamber opera.

CLASSICAL MUSIC

The **Toronto Symphony Orchestra** (© **416/593-4828;** www.tso.on.ca) performs everything from classics to new Canadian works at Roy Thomson Hall from September to June. In June and July, the symphony puts on free concerts at outdoor venues throughout the city. The world-renowned **Toronto Mendelssohn Choir** also performs at Roy Thomson Hall (© **416/598-0422;** www.tmchoir.org). This choir, which was founded in 1895, performs the great choral works not only of Mendelssohn, but also of Bach, Handel, Elgar, and others. Its most famous recording, though, is undoubtedly the soundtrack from Spielberg's film *Schindler's List.*

The **Tafelmusik Baroque Orchestra** (© **416/964-6337;** www.tafelmusik.org), which has been celebrated in England as "the world's finest period band," plays on authentic period instruments. Concerts featuring the works of Bach, Handel, Telemann, Mozart, and Vivaldi are given at **Trinity-St. Paul's United Church,** 427 Bloor St. W., and also at **Massey Hall,** 178 Victoria St.

DANCE

Perhaps the most beloved and famous of Toronto's cultural icons is the **National Ballet of Canada** (© **866/345-9595** or 416/345-9595; www.nationalballet.ca). English ballerina Celia Franca launched the company in Toronto in 1951; in 2005, legendary ballerina Karen Kain became its artistic director. The company performs at the Four Seasons Centre in the fall, winter, and spring; tours internationally; and makes summer

Landmark Theatres

The following major theatres all offer guided tours, usually for a charge of C$5 (US$5/£2.50) or less; call ahead for schedules.

Canon Theatre   This glamorous building (formerly the Pantages Theatre), which first opened in 1920, has been restored to the tune of C$18 million; it was originally a silent film house and vaudeville theater. Recent productions have included *The Producers* and *Wicked*. 244 Victoria St. ☎ 416/872-2222. www.mirvish.com. Subway: Dundas.

The Elgin and Winter Garden Theatres   These two historic landmark theaters first opened their doors in 1913, and they have been restored to their original gilded glory. The downstairs Elgin is the larger of the pair, seating 1,500 and featuring a lavish domed ceiling and gilded decoration on the boxes and proscenium. The 1,000-seat Winter Garden possesses a striking interior adorned with hand-painted frescoes. Suspended from its ceiling and lit with lanterns are more than 5,000 branches of beech leaves, which were harvested, preserved, painted, and fireproofed. 189 Yonge St. ☎ 416/872-5555 for tickets, or 416/314-2871 for tour info. Subway: Queen.

Princess of Wales Theatre   This spectacular 2,000-seat state-of-the-art theater was built for the production of *Miss Saigon* and has a stage that was large enough to accommodate the landing of the helicopter in that production. In 2006, the world premiere of the stage adaptation of the epic *The Lord of the Rings* opened here. 300 King St. W. ☎ 416/872-1212. www.mirvish.com. Subway: St. Andrew.

Royal Alexandra Theatre   When shows from Broadway migrate north, they usually head for the Royal Alex. Tickets are often snapped up by subscription buyers, so your best bet is to call or write ahead of time to the theater at the address below. The Royal Alex itself is a magnificent spectacle: Constructed in 1907, it's a riot of plush reds, gold brocade, and baroque ornamentation. 260 King St. W., Toronto, ON M5V 1H9. ☎ 416/872-1212. www.mirvish.com. Subway: St. Andrew.

appearances before enormous crowds at the open theater at Ontario Place. Its repertoire includes the classics (you can always count on *The Nutcracker* every December) and works by luminaries like George Balanchine.

Toronto Dance Theatre (☎ 416/973-4000; www.tdt.org), the city's leading contemporary-dance company, burst onto the scene in 1972, bringing an inventive spirit and original Canadian dance to the stage. The **Danny Grossman Dance Company** (☎ 416/973-4000; www.dannygrossman.com) is revered for its athleticism, theatricality, humor, and passionate social vision. The company performs both new works and revivals of modern-dance classics.

THEATRE

While it may seem that Toronto favors big-budget musicals—*The Lion King* and *Mamma Mia!* both played here for what felt like forever—many excellent smaller companies also exist. Many of the smaller troupes have no permanent performance space, so they move from venue to venue. The best time to capture the flavor of Toronto's theater life is during the **Fringe Festival** (© 416/534-5919; www.fringe toronto.com), usually held for 12 days starting in late June or early July. In July and August, try to catch the **Dream in High Park** (© 416/368-3110; www.canstage. com). It mounts stunning productions of Shakespearean or Canadian plays from the CanStage Company in an outdoor setting.

The **CanStage Company** (© 416/368-3110) performs comedy, drama, and musicals in the St. Lawrence Centre, and also presents free summer Shakespeare performances in High Park. **Soulpepper** (© 416/866-8666; www.soulpepper.ca) is an artist-founded classical repertory company that presents theatrical masterpieces. The highly respected—and award-winning—group has recently staged Gogol's *The Government Inspector,* Mamet's *American Buffalo,* and Shakespeare's *King Lear.* Since 1970, the experimental **Factory Theatre,** 125 Bathurst St. (© 416/504-9971; www.factory theatre.ca), has been a home to Canadian playwriting, showcasing the best new authors, as well as established playwrights. The **Tarragon Theatre,** 30 Bridgman Ave., near Dupont and Bathurst (© 416/536-5018; www.tarragontheatre.com), opened in 1971 and continues to produce original works by such famous Canadian literary figures as Michael Ondaatje, Michel Tremblay, and Judith Thompson. It's a small, intimate theater. **Theatre Passe Muraille,** 16 Ryerson Ave. (© 416/504-7529; www. passemuraille.on.ca), started in the late 1960s when a pool of actors began experimenting and improvising original Canadian material. Set in another warehouse, there's a main space seating 220, and a back space for 70. Take the Queen Street streetcar to Bathurst. **Buddies in Bad Times,** 12 Alexander St. (© 416/975-8555; www. artsexy.ca), is Canada's premier gay theater. Its cutting-edge reputation has been built by American Sky Gilbert. In addition to plays that push out social boundaries, the theater also operates a popular bar and cabaret called Tallulah's.

COMEDY CLUBS

Toronto must be one heck of a funny place. That would explain why a disproportionate number of comedians, including Jim Carrey and Mike Myers, hail from the city. Check out new local talent at **Second City** , 56 Blue Jays Way (© 416/343-0011; www.secondcity.com), which has been and still is the cauldron of Canadian comedy. If you enjoy *Saturday Night Live* or *SCTV,* you'll love the improvisational comedy of Second City. Dan Aykroyd, John Candy, Bill Murray, Martin Short, Mike Myers, Andrea Martin, and Catherine O'Hara all got their start here.

Other top comedy clubs include **Yuk-Yuk's,** 2335 Yonge St. (© 416/967-6425; www.yukyuks.com), and **The Laugh Resort,** at the Holiday Inn on King at 370 Kings St. W. (© 416/364-5233; www.laughresort.com).

LIVE MUSIC VENUES

C'est What? This casual spot offers 28 draft beers—including the perennially popular Homegrown Hemp Ale and the Chocolate Ale—and a broad selection of single malts. Half pub and half performance space, C'est What? has hosted the likes of Jewel, Barenaked Ladies, and Rufus Wainwright before they hit the big time. 67 Front St. E. © 416/867-9499. www.cestwhat.com. Cover up to–C$10 (US$10/£5). Subway: Union.

El Mocambo This rock-'n'-roll institution was where the Rolling Stones rocked in the '70s, Elvis Costello jammed in the '80s, and Liz Phair mesmerized in the '90s. It has played peek-a-boo in recent years—it regularly closes and reopens and once even relocated to another site. Maybe that's why its current headliners include acts like Vendetta Red and DREDG (of course, I'll be eating my words about them one day . . .). Its Spadina Avenue digs are open again, and because they've gone through a top-to-toe reno, maybe they'll stay open this time. 464 Spadina Ave. ☏ 416/968-2001. Cover up to C$15 (US$15/£7.50). Subway: Spadina, then streetcar south to College St.

Healey's This downtown spot is owned by rock/blues guitarist Jeff Healey. Tuesday is Open Jam night, but on any other evening you'll hear rock, blues, and soul. Healey himself is on stage every Thursday night with different musicians, and on Saturday afternoons he plays jazz with his house band between 4 and 7pm (and there's no cover for the "Jazz Matinee"). 178 Bathurst St. ☏ 416/703-5882. www.jeffhealeys.com. Cover up to C$10 (US$10/£5). Subway: Osgoode.

The Horseshoe Tavern This old, traditional venue has showcased the sounds of the decades: blues in the '60s, punk in the '70s, New Wave in the '80s, and everything from ska to rockabilly to Celtic to alternative rock in the '90s. It's the place that launched Blue Rodeo, The Tragically Hip, The Band, and Prairie Oyster, and staged the Toronto debuts of The Police and Hootie & the Blowfish. It attracts a cross section of 20- to 40-year-olds. 368 Queen St. W. ☏ 416/598-4753. Cover up to C$15 (US$15 /£7.50). Subway: Osgoode.

Lee's Palace Versailles this ain't. Still, that hasn't deterred the crème de la crème of the alternative-music scene. Red Hot Chili Peppers, The Tragically Hip, and Alanis Morissette have performed here. Despite the graffiti grunge, Lee's does boast the best sight lines in town. The audience is young and rarely tires of slam dancing in the mosh pit in front of the stage. 529 Bloor St. W. ☏ 416/532-1598. www.leespalace.com. Cover up to C$20 (US$20/£10). Subway: Bathurst.

The Mod Club Theatre This is one of Toronto's best live music venues. The Mod Club is co-owned by Mark Holmes, the frontman for the '80s band Platinum Blonde (c'mon, you remember them, right? "Standing in the Dark" . . . "Situation Critical" . . . "Sad Sad Rain" . . .). In any case, Holmes is the DJ when the concert hall morphs into a dance club after hours. They book top-notch acts here, including The Killers, the Tragically Hip, and Amy Winehouse. 722 College St. ☏ 416/588-4MOD. Cover up to C$15 (US$15/ £7.50); sometimes higher prices for concerts. Subway: College Park, then streetcar west to Crawford St.

The Rex This watering hole has been drawing jazz fans since it opened in 1951. Admittedly, the decor hasn't changed much since the old days, but the sounds you'll find here are cutting edge. The Rex lures top local and international talent; Tuesday is the weekly jam night. 194 Queen St. W. ☏ 416/598-2475. Cover up to C$10 (US$10/£5). Subway: Osgoode.

The Rivoli Currently, this is the club for an eclectic mix of performances, including grunge, blues, rock, jazz, comedy, and poetry reading. Holly Cole launched her career here, Tori Amos made her Toronto debut in the back room, and The Kids in the Hall still consider it home. Shows begin at 8pm and continue until 2am. Upstairs, there are a billiards room and an espresso bar. 332 Queen St. W. ☏ 416/597-0794. Cover up to C$15 (US$15/£7.50). Subway: Osgoode.

Supermarket Kensington Market is famous for its grocery stores, so maybe it's appropriate that this new club is playing on the name. It does offer a wide assortment of live jazz, funk, soul and reggae. Earlier in the evening, Supermarket is an Asian fusion restaurant, and it occasionally hosts author readings and art events. 268 Augusta

St. ✆ **416/840-0501.** www.supermarkettoronto.com. Cover up to C$10 (US$10 /£5). Subway: Spadina then streetcar south to College St.

The Underground   In the basement of the Drake Hotel, this venue was designed with flexibility in mind. It's a good thing, too, because the performers who appear here range from local and visiting musical acts to burlesque artists. At the Drake Hotel, 1150 Queen St. W. ✆ **416/531-5042.** Cover up to C$15 (US$15/£7.50). Subway: Osgoode, then streetcar west to Beaconsfield.

DANCE CLUBS

Dance clubs come and go at an alarming pace in Toronto. My suggestions below are perennials, so they're almost certainly going to be around when you visit. That means that they're not on the cutting edge, so if you're looking for a hot, hip scene, be sure to check out the club listings in the free weekly *Now* or at **www.martiniboys.com** or **www.torontolife.com** for the latest and greatest. Some things stay constant, though. Most clubs don't have much of a dress code, though "no jeans" rules are not uncommon. And remember, it's always easier to get in earlier rather than later in the evening, when lines start to form.

Afterlife   Formerly the Limelight, this is truly the club that won't die. People in their early 20s have been coming in from the suburbs forever to dance, play pool, and lounge, and they show no signs of stopping. No jeans. 250 Adelaide St. W. ✆ **416/593-6126.** Cover C$10 (US$10/£5). Subway: St. Andrew.

Guvernment   This gigantic club has existed, in one incarnation or another, for more than 2 decades. It has survived because it really does offer something for everyone. There's a crazy long line to get in, but it does move along—and this isn't a pretentious place, so everyone gets in. There are several dance floors inside, plus two patios. The music ranges from progressive house to trance, with some hip-hop and disco thrown in for good measure. 131 Queen's Quay E. ✆ **416/869-0045.** Cover C$10–C$15 (US$10–US$15/£5–£7.50). Subway: Osgoode.

This Is London   While I've got my doubts about the name, I still think that this club is an interesting addition to the local scene (and I'm partial to the wood-burning fireplace in the foyer). It's more sophisticated and less frenzied than most of its peers—you might even manage a conversation. It reminds me of an old-fashioned gentleman's club with its Oriental rugs and comfortable armchairs, though the dance floor is pretty hot. *A word to the wise:* This is a very dressy place—go glam or go home. 364 Richmond St. W. ✆ **416/351-1100.** Cover C$20 (US$20/£10). Subway: Osgoode.

THE BAR SCENE
BARS & LOUNGES

Barrio   The Leslieville neighborhood has changed dramatically since the march to gentrification began, but this charming lounge has been here for 6 years. It serves up a long list of martinis (try the Porn Star, a blend of vodka, raspberry, and Sprite), and microbrews. 890 Queen St. E. ✆ **416/572-0600.** Subway: Queen, then streetcar east to Logan Ave.

Foundation Room   Half the fun with subterranean clubs is knowing how to find them. But the Foundation Room has far more to recommend it: The room is decked out in glorious Moroccan style, with plush lounges, hammered brass chandeliers, and plenty of mirrors. The vibe is very sexy—and the pomegranate martinis are delicious. 19 Church St. ✆ **416/364-8368.** Subway: Union.

Sutra   This intimate Little Italy bar has a subtly sexy vibe. The long slim space somehow manages not to feel claustrophobic. The heady cocktail of soft jazz music and champagne-infused drinks will leave you shaken *and* stirred. 612 College St. ℂ 416/537-8755. Subway: Queen's Park, then any streetcar west to Clinton St.

HOTEL BARS

Some of the best bars are located in hotels. **Accents,** at the Sutton Place, 955 Bay St. (ℂ 416/924-9221), boasts a pianist and a great selection of wines by the glass. The **Consort Bar,** at the King Edward Hotel, 37 King St. E. (ℂ 416/863-9700), is a wonderfully clubby, old-fashioned bar. The **Library Bar,** at the Fairmont Royal York, 100 Front St. W. (ℂ 416/863-6333), specializes in "fishbowl" martinis. **The Roof,** at the Park Hyatt, 4 Avenue Rd. (ℂ 416/924-5471), is an old literary haunt, with comfortable couches in front of a fireplace and excellent drinks; the view from the outdoor terrace is splendid—it's one of the best in the city.

OTHER BARS & PUBS

The **Brunswick House,** 481 Bloor St. W. (ℂ 416/964-2242; subway: Spadina or Bathurst)—affectionately known as the Brunny House by University of Toronto students—has been described as a cross between a German beer hall and an English north-country workingmen's club. At the other end of the spectrum is the tony **Irish Embassy,** 49 Yonge St. (ℂ 416/866-8282; subway: King), which fills up after the closing bell rings at the Toronto Stock Exchange. **Smokeless Joe's,** 125 John St. (ℂ 416/728-4503; subway: St. Andrew), has the longest list of beers of any bar in the city. The **Mill Street Brew Pub** in the Distillery District (ℂ 416/681-0338; subway: King, then streetcar east to Parliament St.) has an ever-changing list of microbrews, though its famous Tankhouse Pale Ale is a perennial.

WINE BARS

The name **Sottovoce,** 537 College St. (ℂ 416/536-4564; subway: Queen's Park, then streetcar west), must be some kind of in joke, because the decibel level here is outrageous. This wine bar is still a great find, not least because it serves up some truly inspired focaccia sandwiches and salads. The basement of the restaurant **Centro,** 2472 Yonge St. (ℂ 416/483-2211; subway: Eglinton), is an upscale wine bar. A well-dressed crowd drops by for the convivial atmosphere, the gourmet pizzas and pastas, and the extensive selection of wines, which includes more than 600 varieties from around the globe.

GAY & LESBIAN BARS

A popular spot for cruising, **Crews,** 508 Church St. (ℂ 416/972-1662; subway: Wellesley), is a complex with two patios. Friday and Saturday nights are for drag shows, too. The adjoining **Tango** bar draws a lesbian crowd; it hosts Tuesday and Sunday night karaoke. A friendly and very popular local bar, **Woody's,** 467 Church St., south of Wellesley (ℂ 416/972-0887; subway: Wellesley), is frequented mainly by men, but welcomes women. Next door is **Sailor,** 465 Church St. (ℂ 416/972-0887; subway: Wellesley), a bar and restaurant that boasts a Sunday night drag show. **El Convento Rico,** 750 College St. (ℂ 416/588-7800; subway: Queen's Park, then streetcar west), is one club that draws a substantial hetero contingent that comes out just to watch the fabulous drag queens—and don't be surprised if you encounter a bachelorette party in progress.

11

Southwestern Ontario

by Hilary Davidson

This lush, temperate region brushes up against three Great Lakes, making for some of the best farmland in Canada. A mix of Carolinian forests, rolling hills, and fertile plains, the southwestern corner of the province can claim more rare flora and fauna than anywhere else in the country. This also explains the burgeoning wine country in the Niagara region, which is home to several of Canada's award-winning vintners. Niagara-on-the-Lake is famed for its excellent theater festival, the Shaw, and Niagara Falls is one of the natural wonders of the world.

Southwestern Ontario attracted many of Canada's early pioneers. Different ethnic groups built their own towns, and these early influences are still felt today in local traditions and celebrations. Scots built towns such as Elora, Fergus, and St. Marys; the Germans, Kitchener-Waterloo; the Mennonites, Elmira and St. Jacobs; and the English Loyalists, Stratford and London. This cultural heritage feeds festivals such as Oktoberfest, the Highland Games, and the Mennonite quilt sale, but the biggest draw is the world-famous theater festival at Stratford. This region is also home to Hamilton, Ontario's fourth-largest city, which boasts both historic sites and spectacular botanical gardens.

1 Exploring the Region

The main attractions of the southwestern Ontario region—Niagara-on-the-Lake, Niagara Falls, and Stratford—are all within a 2-hour drive from Toronto. But if you're driving across the Canada-U.S. border, you can see some of the sights on the way to the big city.

ESSENTIALS

VISITOR INFORMATION Contact **Ontario Tourism** (*©* **800/ONTARIO;** www.ontariotravel.net) or visit its Toronto travel information center in the Atrium on Bay (street level) at 20 Dundas St. W.—it's just across Dundas from the Sears store at the northern edge of the Eaton Centre. (The Atrium's mailing address is 595 Bay St., but since the information booth is on the south side of the complex, they use a different street address for the same building.) It's open daily from 8:30am to 5pm; hours are extended during the summer, often to 8pm. Another good resource is the **Southern Ontario Tourism Organization** (*©* **800/267-3399;** http://soto.on.ca), which has a travel-planning booklet, an e-mail newsletter, and an informative website.

TOURIST OFFICES In addition to the Atrium on Bay location, you can find a **Travel Information Centre** in **Niagara Falls,** 5355 Stanley Ave. (*©* **905/358-3221**) and in **St. Catharines,** on the QEW as you head north from Niagara Falls (*©* **905/684-6354**). There are two information centers in **Windsor:** one is just east of the

Ambassador Bridge at 1235 Huron Church Rd. (© **519/973-1310**) and the other by the Detroit/Windsor Tunnel at 110 Park St. E. (© **519/973-1338**).

GETTING THERE

The Rainbow Bridge connects Niagara Falls with its New York State counterpart. Niagara-on-the-Lake is easily accessible from the QEW heading north out of Niagara Falls, and it's a scenic drive on the QEW around Lake Ontario on the way up to Toronto. This route also takes you past the city of Hamilton, which is well worth a stop for its botanical gardens and historic castle.

Windsor sits across from Detroit on the Canadian side of the border. From here, visitors can travel along either Highway 401 east or the more scenic Highway 3 (called the Talbot Trail, which runs from Windsor to Fort Erie), stopping along the way to visit some major attractions on the Lake Erie shore. Northeast of Windsor lies London, and from London it's an easy drive to Stratford. From Stratford, visitors can turn west to Goderich and Bayfield on the shores of Lake Huron or east to Kitchener-Waterloo and then north to Elmira, Elora, and Fergus.

THE GREAT OUTDOORS

Ontario's 260 provincial parks offer a staggering array of opportunities for outdoor recreation. Regulations about stays in provincial parks were overhauled in 2005, so even if you've visited before, you'll do well to familiarize yourself with the new rules at www.ontarioparks.com. One of the main changes is that all Ontario parks are now classified as either premium, middle, or low—a reference to a park's level of popularity, and to the fees it charges. Staying 1 night in a premium park can cost C$36 (US$36/£18) per person, whereas a low park would be more in the C$22 (US$22/£11) range (there are discounts for seniors and people with disabilities in all parks). The daily in-season entry fee for a vehicle stars at C$7.50 (US$7.50/£3.75). To make a park reservation, contact **Ontario Parks Reservations,** P.O. Box 25099, 370 Stone Rd. W., Guelph, ON, N1G 4T4 (© **888/668-7275;** www.ontarioparks.com); a reservation in any provincial park costs C$12 (US$12/£6).

BIKING   The South Point and Marsh trails in **Rondeau Provincial Park,** near Blenheim (© **519/674-1750**), are great for cycling.

BIRD-WATCHING   Point Pelee National Park, southeast of Windsor (© **519/322-2365;** www.pc.gc.ca), is one of the continent's premier bird-watching centers. The spring and fall migrations are spectacular; more than 300 species of birds can be spotted here. In late summer, it's also the gathering place for flocks of monarch butterflies, which cover the trees before taking off for their migratory flight down south. Located at the southernmost tip of Canada, which juts down into Lake Erie at the same latitude as northern California, it features some of the same flora—white sassafras, sumac, black walnut, and cedar.

Another good bird-watching outpost is the **Jack Miner Bird Sanctuary,** Road 3 West, 3km (2 miles) north of Kingsville off Division Road (© **877/289-8328** or 519/733-4034; www.jackminer.com). The famed naturalist established the sanctuary to protect migrating Canada geese, and the best time to visit is late October and November when thousands of migrating waterfowl stop over.

BOATING, CANOEING & KAYAKING   Companies offering trips on the Grand River include the **Heritage River Canoe & Kayak Company,** 73 Oakhill Dr., Brantford (© **866/462-2663** or 519/758-0761; www.heritageriver.com), and **Canoeing**

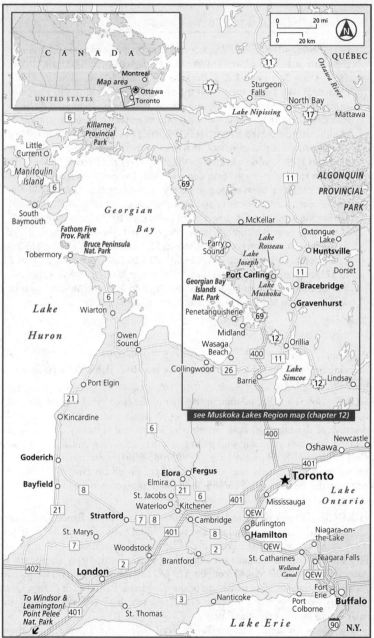

Southern Ontario

CANADA

UNITED STATES

Map area

Montreal
Ottawa
Toronto

QUÉBEC

Ottawa River

Sturgeon Falls
North Bay
Mattawa

Lake Nipissing

Killarney Provincial Park

Little Current

Manitoulin Island

South Baymouth

ALGONQUIN

PROVINCIAL

PARK

Georgian Bay

McKellar

Parry Sound

Lake Rosseau

Lake Joseph

Oxtongue Lake

Huntsville

Dorset

Port Carling

Lake Muskoka

Bracebridge

Georgian Bay Islands Nat. Park

Gravenhurst

Penetanguishene

Midland

Orillia

Fathom Five Prov. Park

Bruce Peninsula Nat. Park

Tobermory

Wasaga Beach

Lake Simcoe

Wiarton

Collingwood

Barrie

Lindsay

Lake

Huron

Owen Sound

see Muskoka Lakes Region map (chapter 12)

Port Elgin

Newcastle

Oshawa

Goderich

Elora
Fergus

Toronto

Lake

Ontario

Bayfield

Elmira

St. Jacobs

Waterloo
Kitchener

Mississauga

Stratford

Cambridge

Burlington

St. Marys

Hamilton

Niagara-on-the-Lake

Woodstock

Brantford

St. Catharines

Niagara Falls

Welland Canal

London

Fort Erie

Buffalo

To Windsor & Leamington/ Point Pelee Nat. Park

Nanticoke

Port Colborne

St. Thomas

Lake Erie

N.Y.

Finds   The Real Uncle Tom's Cabin

Off Highway 401 between Windsor and London is one of the most interesting visitor sites in southwestern Ontario: **Uncle Tom's Cabin Historic Centre,** 29251 Uncle Tom's Rd., R.R. 5, Dresden (© **519/683-2978;** www.uncletoms cabin.org). The center focuses on the life of Josiah Henson, who was born in slavery in Maryland in 1789, and escaped via the Underground Railroad into Canada in 1830. Henson and a group of ex-slaves, Quakers, and other abolitionists purchased 80 hectares (198 acres) of land in 1841, where they established a vocational school, the British American Institute for Fugitive Slaves. In 1849, Henson narrated his life story to Harriet Beecher Stowe, who went on to publish *Uncle Tom's Cabin* in 1852. The center includes an interpretive center, a theater, and a gallery, as well as the sawmill and the smokehouse built by Henson and his colleagues. One of the gallery's most fascinating exhibits is the collection of quilts used by the Underground Railroad; these carried elaborate, coded designs that helped lead many slaves to freedom. Admission is C$6.25 (US$6.25/£3.15) for adults, C$5.25 (US$5.25/£2.65) for seniors and students, C$4.50 (US$4.50/£2.25) for children ages 6 to 12, and free for kids 5 and under. The center is open mid-May through mid-October from Tuesday to Saturday 10am to 4pm and Sunday noon to 4pm, as well as Mondays in July and August 10am to 4pm.

the Grand, 3734 King St. E., Kitchener (© **877/896-0290** or 519/896-0290; www. canoeingthegrand.com). There are also canoe rentals in **Point Pelee National Park** (© **519/322-2371**).

GOLF   Golf is a major pastime in this part of the country; check out the Ontario listings and reviews on Golf Canada (www.golfcanada.com) to get some sense of the diversity of the offerings, both in terms of design and difficulty. In southwestern Ontario, you can't go wrong with golfing in the Niagara region. The **Royal Niagara Golf Club** in Niagara-on-the-Lake (© **905/685-9501;** www.royalniagara.com) features three 9-hole courses, and south of Niagara Falls off the Niagara Parkway, **Legends on the Niagara** (© **866/465-3642;** www.niagaralegends.com) also has three courses, including two 18-hole courses.

HIKING   Canada's oldest and most famous hiking trail, the **Bruce Trail,** starts in Queenston in Niagara-on-the-Lake and runs 782km (486 miles) up north to Tobermory at the top of the Bruce Peninsula. Hikers can enjoy as much of the trail as they like, but my favorite section runs along the Niagara Escarpment. The **Bruce Trail Association** (© **800/665-4453** or 905/529-6821; www.brucetrail.org) has 40 hiking routes on its website, all of which can be downloaded as PDFs free of charge. Ontario Tourism's website contains a wealth of information about different sections of the mighty trail (www.ontariotravel.net).

The 60km (37-mile) **Thames Valley Trail** follows the Thames River through London, past the University of Western Ontario and into farmlands all the way to St. Mary's. For information, contact **Thames Valley Trail Association** (© **519/645-2845;** www.thamesvalleytrail.org).

The 124km (77-mile) **Grand Valley Trail** follows the Grand River from Dunnville, north through Brantford, Paris, and farmlands around Kitchener-Waterloo to the Elora Gorge (see "Elora & Fergus: The Elora Gorge & More," later in this chapter), connecting with the **Bruce Trail** at Alton. For information, contact the Grand Valley Trails Association (✆ 519/576-6156; www.gvta.on.ca).

SWIMMING   The Elora Gorge is a favorite swimming spot; the conservation area includes a 1-hectare (2½-acre) lake with two beach areas; contact the Grand River Conservation Authority (✆ 866/900-4722 or 519/846-9742; www.grandriver.ca) for details. Swimming is also very popular at **Rondeau Provincial Park** (✆ 519/674-1750), which is located on Lake Erie (off Hwy. 21 near Blenheim); lots of other water-sports are available here as well.

2 Niagara-on-the-Lake & Niagara Falls

130km (81 miles) SE of Toronto

Only 1½ hours from Toronto, Niagara-on-the-Lake is one of the best preserved and prettiest 19th-century villages in North America. Handsome clapboard-and-brick period houses border the tree-lined streets. It's the setting for one of Canada's most famous events, the **Shaw Festival.** The town is the jewel of the **Ontario wine region.**

Less than a half-hour drive from Niagara-on-the-Lake is **Niagara Falls,** which was for decades the region's honeymoon capital (I say this in an attempt to explain its end-less motels, each with at least one suite that has a heart-shaped pink bed). While the falls truly are a sight that shouldn't be missed, you may want to stay at an inn in Nia-gara-on-the-Lake and come to Niagara Falls for a day trip. By the way, the drive along the **Niagara Parkway** is a delight: With its endless parks and gardens, it's an oasis for nature-lovers (see "Along the Niagara Parkway," later in this chapter).

ESSENTIALS

GETTING THERE   Niagara-on-the-Lake is best seen by **car.** From Toronto, take the Queen Elizabeth Way (signs read QEW) to Niagara via Hamilton and St. Catharines, and exit at Highway 55. The trip takes about 1½ hours.

Amtrak and **VIA** (✆ 416/366-8411) operate **trains** between Toronto and New York, but they stop only in Niagara Falls and St. Catharines, not in Niagara-on-the-Lake. Call ✆ 800/361-1235 in Canada or **800/USA-RAIL** in the United States. From either place, you'll need to rent a car. Rental outlets in St. Catharines include **National Tilden,** 162 Church St. (✆ 905/682-8611), and **Hertz,** 404 Ontario St. (✆ 905/682-8695). In Niagara Falls, **National Tilden** is at 4523 Drummond Rd. (✆ 905/374-6700).

VISITOR INFORMATION   The **Niagara-on-the-Lake Chamber of Commerce,** 153 King St. (P.O. Box 1043), Niagara-on-the-Lake, ON L0S 1J0 (✆ 905/468-4263; www.niagaraonthelake.com), provides information and can help you find accommodations. It's open Monday through Friday from 9am to 5pm, and Saturday and Sunday from 10am to 5pm.

For Niagara Falls travel information, contact **Niagara Falls Tourism** at (✆ 800/56-FALLS; www.niagarafallstourism.com), or the **Niagara Parks Commission** (✆ 905/356-2241; www.niagaraparks.com). **Information centers** are open daily in summer from 9am to 6pm at Table Rock House and the Maid of the Mist Plaza.

Tips Biking through Wine Country

Driving through Niagara-on-the-Lake by car is a delight, but many would argue that the region is best viewed by bicycle. As of 2007, Via Rail is offering a **Toronto-Niagara Bike Train** throughout the summer. It has a bike cargo car, and you can hop aboard—for C$59 (US$59/£30) per person—and get to Niagara Falls in less than 2 hours. From there, you can bike to your hotel (if you're a light traveler), or arrange for pickup for an extra fee. See www.biketrain.ca for more details.

THE SHAW FESTIVAL

The Shaw celebrates the dramatic and comedic works of George Bernard Shaw and his contemporaries, but it also features new works by Canadian playwrights. From April to October, the festival offers a dozen plays in the historic **Court House,** the exquisite **Shaw Festival Theatre,** and the **Royal George Theatre.** Recent performances have included *The Circle, The Invisible Man, Gypsy,* and Shaw's *Saint Joan* and *Arms and the Man.*

Free chamber concerts take place Sunday at 11am. Chats introduce performances on Friday evenings in July and August, and question-and-answer sessions follow Tuesday-evening performances.

The Shaw announces its festival program in mid-January. Tickets are difficult to obtain on short notice, so try to book at least a month in advance. Prices range from C$45 to C$95 (US$45–US$95/£23–£48). For more information, contact the **Shaw Festival,** P.O. Box 774, Niagara-on-the-Lake, ON L0S 1J0 (© **800/511-7429** or 905/468-2172; www.shawfest.com).

EXPLORING NIAGARA-ON-THE-LAKE

Niagara-on-the Lake is small, and most of its attractions are along one main street (Queen St.), making it easy to explore on foot.

Fort George National Historic Park *Ϝ* *Ƙids*   The fort played a central role in the War of 1812: It was headquarters for the British Army's Centre Division. The division was comprised of British regulars, local militia, Runchey's corps of former slaves, and Native forces. The fort was destroyed by American artillery fire in May 1813. After the war it was partially rebuilt, but it was abandoned in 1828 and not reconstructed until the 1930s. You can view the guardroom (with its hard plank beds), the officers' quarters, the enlisted men's quarters, and the sentry posts. The self-guided tour includes interpretive films. Those who believe in ghosts take note: The fort is one of Ontario's favorite "haunted" sites: reported sightings include a soldier patrolling its perimeter and a young damsel who appears in an 18th-century mirror (ghost-hunting tours are available throughout the summer and in Oct).

Niagara Pkwy. © **905/468-6614.** www.parkscanada.ca or www.friendsoffortgeorge.ca. Admission C$11 (US$11/£5.50) adults, C$9 (US$9/£4.50) seniors, C$5.50 (US$5.50/£2.75) children 6–16, free for children 5 and under. Apr 1–Oct 31 daily 10am–5pm.

Niagara Historical Society Museum   More than 20,000 artifacts pertaining to local history make up this collection. They include many possessions of United Empire Loyalists who first settled the area at the end of the American Revolution.

Niagara-on-the-Lake

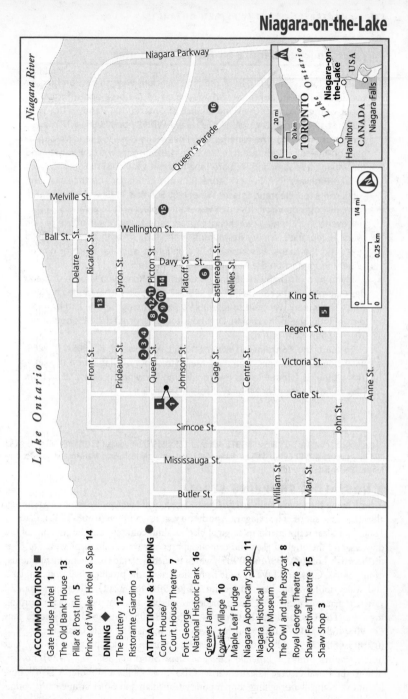

Tips **Touring Niagara-on-the-Lake Wineries**

Visiting a local winery is one of the most delicious ways to pass an hour or two in this region (pun intended). For maps of the area and information about vintners, contact the **Wine Council of Ontario,** 110 Hanover Dr., Suite B-205, St. Catharines, ON L2W 1A4 (© **888/5-WINERY** or 905/684-8070; www.winesofontario.org). The wineries listed below are close to the town of Niagara-on-the-Lake. Tours are free. Prices for tastings vary with the winery and the wine you're sampling, but are usually about C$10 (US$10/£5).

Take Highway 55 (Niagara Stone Rd.) out of Niagara-on-the-Lake, and you'll come to **Hillebrand Estates Winery** (© **905/468-7123**; www.hillebrand.com), just outside Virgil. It's open year-round, plays host to a variety of special events (including a weekend concert series), and even offers bicycle tours. Hillebrand's Winery Restaurant, with views of both the barrel-filled cellar and the Niagara Escarpment, is a delightful spot for lunch or dinner. Winery tours start on the hour daily from 10am to 6pm.

If you turn off Highway 55 and go down York Road, you'll reach **Château des Charmes,** west of St. David's (© **905/262-5202**; www.chateaudescharmes.com). The winery was built to resemble a French manor house, and its architecture is unique in the region. One-hour tours are given daily. It's open from 10am to 6pm year-round.

To reach the **Konzelmann Winery,** 1096 Lakeshore Rd. (© **905/935-2866**; www.konzelmannwines.com), take Mary Street out of Niagara-on-the-Lake. This vintner is famous for its award-winning ice wines. It offers tours from May to late September Monday through Saturday.

43 Castlereagh St. (at Davy). © 905/468-3912. Admission C$5 (US$5/£2.50) adults, C$3 (US$3/£1.50) seniors, C$2 (US$2/£1) students with ID, C$1 (US$1/50p) children 5–12. May–Oct daily 10am–5pm; Mar–Apr and Nov–Dec daily 1–5pm; Jan–Feb Sat–Sun 1–5pm.

A NOSTALGIC SHOPPING STROLL

A stroll along the town's main artery, Queen Street, will take you by some entertaining, albeit touristy, shops. The **Niagara Apothecary,** at no. 5 (© **905/468-3845**), dates to 1866. Gold-leaf script marks its original black-walnut counters and the contents of the drawers, and the original glass and ceramic apothecary ware is on display. At no. 13 is the **Scottish Loft** (© **905/468-0965**), which is filled with tartans, Celtic memorabilia, candy, books, CDs, and DVDs (aside from the tartans, the products hail from England and Wales, too). **Maple Leaf Fudge,** no. 14 (© **905/468-2211**), offers more than 20 varieties that you can watch being made on marble slabs. At no. 16 is a charming toy store, **The Owl and the Pussycat** (© **905/468-3081**). At no. 35 is **Greaves Jam** (© **905/468-7331**), run by fourth-generation jam makers. **Irish Design,** at no. 38 (© **905/468-7233**), sells hand-knit sweaters, traditional gold and silver jewelry, and other treasures from the Emerald Isle. The **Shaw Shop** (© **800/511-7429**), no. 79, next to the Royal George Theatre, carries GBS memorabilia and more. A Dansk outlet and several galleries selling contemporary Canadian and other ethnic crafts round out the mix.

JET-BOATING THRILLS

Jet boat excursions leave from the dock across from 61 Melville St. at the King George III Inn. Don a rainsuit, poncho, and life jacket, and climb aboard. The boat takes you out onto the Niagara River for a trip along the stonewalled canyon to the whirlpool downriver. The ride starts slow but gets into turbulent water. Trips, which operate from May to October, last an hour and cost C$56 (US$56/£28) for adults and C$47 (US$47/£24) for children 13 and under. Reservations are required. Call the **Whirlpool Jet Boat Company** at ✆ **888/438-4444** or 905/468-4800, or visit **www.whirlpool jet.com**.

WHERE TO STAY IN NIAGARA-ON-THE-LAKE

In summer, hotel space is in high demand, but don't despair if you're having trouble nailing down a room. Contact the chamber of commerce, which provides an accommodations-reservations service. Note that the same company, Vintage Inns, owns several of the hotels in town. (Vintage Inns is known for buying upscale properties and making them even more luxurious.) Or you could opt for one of the 120 bed-and-breakfasts around town. The **Niagara-on-the-Lake Chamber of Commerce** (✆ **905/468-4263**; www.niagaraonthelake.com) provides information about them and can help you find a place to stay. The prices listed below are for the peak summer season; deep discounts are available at all of these properties in early spring, late fall, and winter.

Gate House Hotel ✿ Unlike many of the Canadiana-influenced lodgings in town, the Gate House Hotel is decorated in cool, clean-lined Milanese style. Guest rooms have a marbleized look and are accented with ultramodern black lamps, block-marble tables, leatherette couches, and bathrooms with sleek Italian fixtures. The effect is quite glamorous. The Gate House's eatery, Ristorante Giardino, serves northern Italian cuisine and is one of the best places to dine in town.

142 Queen St. (P.O. Box 1364), Niagara-on-the-Lake, ON L0S 1J0. ✆ 905/468-3263. www.gatehouse-niagara.com. 10 units. From C$175 (US$175/£88) double. AE, MC, V. Free parking. **Amenities:** Restaurant; concierge. *In room:* A/C, TV, hair dryer.

The Old Bank House ✿ Beautifully situated down by the river, this two-story Georgian was built in 1817 as the first branch of the Bank of Canada. In 1902, it hosted the prince and princess of Wales, and today it is a charming bed-and-breakfast inn. Several tastefully decorated units have private entrances; one is the charming Garden Room, which also has a private trellised deck. Several of the rooms have private balconies. Eight units have a refrigerator and coffee or tea supplies. The most expensive suite accommodates five in two bedrooms. The extraordinarily comfortable sitting room (open to all guests) holds a fireplace and eclectic antique pieces.

10 Front St. (P.O. Box 1708), Niagara-on-the-Lake, ON L0S 1J0. ✆ 877-468-7136 or 905/468-7136. www.old bankhouse.com. 9 units. C$195 (US$195/£98) double. Rates include breakfast. AE, MC, V. Free parking. **Amenities:** Jacuzzi. *In room:* A/C, no phone.

Pillar & Post Inn The discreetly elegant Pillar & Post is a couple of blocks from the maddening crowds on Queen Street. This is one of the most sophisticated accommodations in town, complete with the 100 Fountain Spa offering the latest in deluxe treatments and a Japanese-style, warm mineral-spring pool, complete with cascading waterfall (spa packages are available). The light, airy lobby boasts a fireplace, lush plantings, and comfortable seating. The style is classic Canadiana: The spacious rooms all contain old-fashioned furniture, Windsor-style chairs, a pine cabinet (with a color

TV tucked inside), and historical engravings. In the back is a secluded pool. Some rooms facing the outdoor pool on the ground level have bay windows and window boxes.

48 John St. (at King St.), Niagara-on-the-Lake, ON L0S 1J0. © 888/669-5566 or 905/468-2123. Fax 905/468-1472. www.vintageinns.com. 123 units. From C$255 (US$255/£128) double. AE, DC, MC, V. Free parking. **Amenities:** 2 dining rooms; wine bar; indoor and outdoor pools; spa; Jacuzzi; sauna; bike rental; concierge; business center; dry cleaning. *In room:* A/C, TV, dataport, minibar, hair dryer, safe.

Prince of Wales Hotel & Spa 🏰🏰   The Prince of Wales still reigns as Niagara-on-the-Lake's most luxurious hotel. This place has it all: a central location across from the lovely gardens of Simcoe Park; full recreational facilities, including an indoor pool; a luxurious spa; lounges, bars, and restaurants; and attractive rooms, beautifully decorated with antiques or reproductions. It has a lively atmosphere yet retains the elegance and charm of a Victorian inn. Bathrooms have bidets, and most rooms have minibars. The hotel's original section was built in 1864. All rooms are nonsmoking.

6 Picton St., Niagara-on-the-Lake, ON L0S 1J0. © 888/669-5566 or 905/468-3246. Fax 905/468-5521. www.vintage inns.com. 114 units. From C$275 (US$275/£138) double. Packages available. AE, DC, DISC, MC, V. Free self-parking. Pets accepted. **Amenities:** Dining room; cafe; bar; lounge; indoor pool; health club; spa; Jacuzzi; bike rental; concierge; business center; 24-hr. room service; massage; dry cleaning. *In room:* A/C, TV, dataport, hair dryer, iron, safe.

ALONG THE WINE ROUTE
Inn on the Twenty and the Vintage House 🏰   On the grounds of the Cave Spring Cellars, one of Niagara's best wineries, these modern accommodations consist entirely of handsome suites. Each has an elegantly furnished living room with a fireplace, and a Jacuzzi in the bathroom. Seven are duplexes—one of them, the deluxe loft, has two double beds on its second level—and five are single-level suites with high ceilings. All of the suites are nonsmoking. The inn's eatery, On the Twenty Restaurant & Wine Bar (p. 433), is across the street. Its spa offers a full range of services for men and women, and has special packages for couples. Next door to the inn is the **Vintage House,** an 1840 Georgian mansion; it contains three suites, all with private entrances, for those who want to feel that they're in a secluded hideaway.

3845 Main St., Jordan, ON L0R 1S0. © 800/701-8074 or 905/562-5336. www.innonthetwenty.com. 30 units. From C$259 (US$259/£130) suite. AE, DC, MC, V. Free parking. From QEW, take Jordan Rd. exit south; at 1st intersection, turn right onto 4th Ave., then right onto Main St. **Amenities:** Restaurant; nearby golf course; health club; concierge. *In room:* A/C, TV, dataport, coffeemaker, hair dryer, iron.

WHERE TO DINE
IN TOWN
In addition to the listings below, don't forget the very fine dining rooms at the **Gate House Hotel,** the **Pillar & Post,** and the **Prince of Wales,** all listed above.

The stylish **Shaw Cafe and Wine Bar,** 92 Queen St. (© 905/468-4772), serves lunch and light meals, and has a patio. The **Epicurean,** 84 Queen St. (© 905/468-3408), offers hearty soups, quiches, sandwiches, and other fine dishes in a sunny, Provence-inspired dining room. Service is cafeteria style. Half a block off Queen Street, the **Angel Inn,** 224 Regent St. (© 905/468-3411), is a delightfully authentic English pub. For an inexpensive down-home breakfast, go to the **Stagecoach Family Restaurant,** 45 Queen St. (© 905/468-3133). It also serves basic family fare, such as burgers, fries, and meatloaf, but it doesn't accept credit cards. **Niagara Home Bakery,** 66 Queen St. (© 905/468-3431), is the place to stop for chocolate-date squares, cherry squares, croissants, cookies, and individual quiches.

The Buttery ✷ CANADIAN/ENGLISH/CONTINENTAL   The Buttery has been a dining landmark for years. At its weekend Henry VIII feasts, "serving wenches" bring food and wine while "jongleurs" and "musickers" entertain. The meal consists of "five removes"—courses involving broth, chicken, roast lamb, roast pig, sherry trifle, syllabub, and cheese, all washed down with a goodly amount of wine, ale, and mead.

19 Queen St. ✆ 905/468-2564. www.thebutteryrestaurant.com. Reservations strongly recommended; required for Henry VIII feast. Henry VIII feast C$55 (US$55/£28); main courses C$26 (US$26/£13). MC, V. Apr–Nov daily 11am–11pm; Dec–Mar Sun–Thurs 11am–7:30pm. Afternoon tea year-round daily 2–5pm.

IN NEARBY ST. CATHARINES

Café Garibaldi ✷ ITALIAN   This relaxed spot is a favorite among locals. It serves Italian staples such as *zuppa di pesce* and veal scaloppine; homemade lasagna is the most requested dish. The wine list features the local vintners' goods and some fine bottles from Italy.

375 St. Paul St., St. Catharines. ✆ 905/988-9033. Reservations recommended for dinner. Main courses C$18–C$28 (US$18–US$28/£9–£14). AE, DC, MC, V. Tues–Sat 11:30am–2:30pm and 5:30–10pm. From QEW, exit at Ontario St., follow DOWNTOWN sign to St. Paul St. and turn left.

Wellington Court ✷✷ CONTINENTAL   In an Edwardian town house with a flower trellis, the three candlelit dining rooms here are adorned with mirrors, lithographs, and photographs. The menu features daily specials along with such items as beef tenderloin in shallot-and-red-wine reduction; roast capon with a bacon, leek, and goat-cheese tart; and grilled sea bass with cranberry vinaigrette. Not surprisingly, given the location, the wine list is filled with excellent Niagara bottles.

11 Wellington St., St. Catharines. ✆ 905/682-5518. www.wellington-court.com. Reservations recommended. Main courses C$22–C$30 (US$22–US$30/£11–£15). MC, V. Tues–Sat 11:30am–2:30pm and 5–9:30pm. From QEW, exit at Lake St., turn left, follow to Wellington Ave., turn left, follow for 1 block, turn right.

ALONG THE WINE ROAD

Hillebrand Estates Winery Restaurant ✷ CONTINENTAL   This dining room is light and airy, and its floor-to-ceiling windows offer views over the vineyards to the distant Niagara Escarpment, or of wine cellars bulging with oak barrels. The food is excellent. The seasonal menu might feature such dishes as poached arctic char with shellfish ragout, or prosciutto-wrapped pheasant breast atop linguine tossed with mushrooms, roasted eggplant, and shallot. The starters are equally luxurious. Try roasted three-peppercorn pear served warm with salad greens, pine nuts, and Parmesan slivers, or the spiced goat cheese–and–grilled portobello "sandwich" with walnuts and endive. In case the food isn't enticing enough (and it should be), the restaurant also hosts special events throughout the year, many featuring jazz musicians.

Hwy. 55, between Niagara-on-the-Lake and Virgil. ✆ 905/468-7123. www.hillebrand.com. Reservations strongly recommended. 3-course prix-fixe menu from C$52 (US$52/£26). AE, MC, V. Daily noon–11pm (closes earlier in winter).

On the Twenty Restaurant & Wine Bar ✷ CANADIAN   This restaurant is a favorite among foodies. The gold-painted dining rooms cast a warm glow. The cuisine features ingredients from many local producers, giving On the Twenty a small-town feel. Naturally, there's an extensive selection of Ontario wines, including some wonderful ice wines to accompany such desserts as lemon tart and fruit cobbler. On the Twenty Restaurant is associated with Inn on the Twenty (p. 432), across the street.

At Cave Spring Cellars, 3836 Main St., Jordan. ✆ 905/562-7313. www.innonthetwenty.com. Reservations recommended. Main courses C$33–C$41 (US$33–US$41/£17–£21). AE, DC, MC, V. Daily 11:30am–3pm and 5–10pm.

Moments **The Falls by Night**

Don't miss seeing the falls after dark. Twenty-two xenon gas spotlights, each producing 250 million candlepower of light, illuminate them in shades of rose pink, red magenta, amber, blue, and green. Call ℭ **800/563-2557** (in the U.S.) or ℭ **905/356-6061** for schedules. The show starts around 5pm in winter, 8:30pm in spring and fall, and 9pm in summer. In addition, from July to early September, free fireworks start at 10pm every Friday.

Vineland Estates 𝕽𝕽 CONTINENTAL   This inspired eatery serves some of the most innovative food along the wine trail. On warm days, you can dine on a deck under a spreading tree or stay in the airy dining room. Start with a plate of seasoned mussels in a ginger broth. Follow with a Canadian Angus tenderloin with a risotto of truffles and morel mushrooms, or go for pan-seared sweetbreads with a celeriac-and-potato mash and confit of mushrooms glazed with ice wine. For dessert, try the wonderful tasting plate of Canadian farm cheeses, including Abbey St. Benoit blue Ermite; sweet-tooths can indulge in the hard-to-resist maple-walnut cheesecake in a biscotti crust.

3620 Moyer Rd., Vineland. ℭ **888/846-3526** or 905/562-7088. www.vineland.com. Reservations strongly recommended. Main courses C$34–C$40 (US$34–US$40/£17–£20). AE, MC, V. Daily noon–2:30pm and 5:30–9pm.

SEEING NIAGARA FALLS

The falls are the seventh natural wonder of the world. The most exciting way to see them is from the decks of the ***Maid of the Mist*** 𝕽𝕽, 5920 River Rd. (ℭ **905/358-5781;** www.maidofthemist.com). The sturdy boat takes you right in—through the turbulent waters around the American Falls; past the Rock of Ages; and to the foot of the Horseshoe Falls, where 34.5 million imperial gallons of water tumble over the 54m-high (177-ft.) cataract each minute. You'll get wet, and your glasses will mist, but that won't detract from the thrill. Boats leave from the dock on the parkway just down from the Rainbow Bridge. Trips operate daily from mid-May to mid-October. Fares are C$14 (US$14/£7) for adults and C$8.60 (US$8.60/£4.30) for children 6 to 12, free for children 5 and under.

Go down under the falls using the elevator at **Table Rock House,** which drops you 46m (151 ft.) through solid rock to the tunnels and viewing portals of the **Journey Behind the Falls** (ℭ **905/354-1551**). You'll receive—and appreciate—a rain poncho. Admission is C$10 (US$10/£5) for adults, C$6 (US$6/£3) for children 6 to 12, free for children 5 and under.

You can ride the external glass-fronted elevators 159m (522 ft.) to the top of the **Skylon Tower Observation Deck,** 5200 Robinson St. (ℭ **905/356-2651;** www.skylon. com). The observation deck is open daily from 8am to midnight from June to Labour Day; hours vary in other seasons, so call ahead. Adults pay C$12 (US$12/£6), children 12 and under C$6 (US$6/£3).

For a different view of Niagara Falls, stop by the **IMAX Theater,** 6170 Buchanan Ave. (ℭ **905/358-3611;** www.imaxniagara.com). You can view the raging, swirling waters in *Niagara: Miracles, Myths, and Magic,* shown on a six-story-high screen. Admission is C$12 (US$12/£6) for adults and students, C$9.50 (US$9.50/£4.75) for seniors, C$8.50 (US$8.50/£4.25) for children 4 to 12. I consider this a lot of money

Niagara Falls

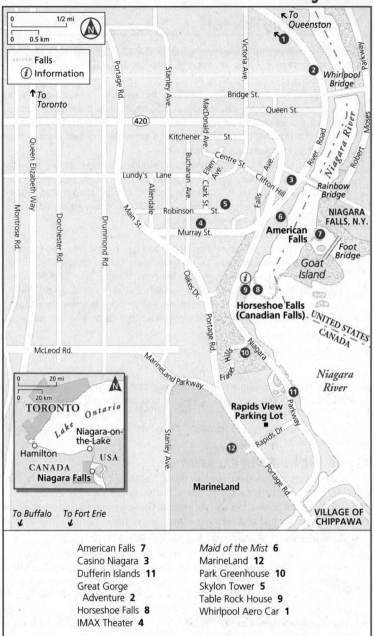

American Falls **7**

Casino Niagara **3**

Dufferin Islands **11**

Great Gorge
  Adventure **2**

Horseshoe Falls **8**

IMAX Theater **4**

Maid of the Mist **6**

MarineLand **12**

Park Greenhouse **10**

Skylon Tower **5**

Table Rock House **9**

Whirlpool Aero Car **1**

Kids A Family Adventure

If you're looking for something to keep the kids amused, visit **Marine-Land** ⟨, 7657 Portage Rd. (© **905/356-9565**; www.marinelandcanada.com). At the aquarium-theater, King Waldorf, the walrus mascot, presides over performances by killer whales, dolphins, and sea lions. Friendship Cove, a 4.5-million-gallon breeding and observation tank, lets the little ones see killer whales up close. Another aquarium features displays of freshwater fish. At the small wildlife display, children enjoy petting and feeding the deer and seeing bears and Canadian elk.

Marineland also has theme-park rides, including a roller coaster, a Tivoli wheel (a fancy Ferris wheel), Dragon Boat rides, and a fully equipped playground. The big thriller is Dragon Mountain, a roller coaster that loops, double-loops, and spirals through 305m (1,000 ft.) of tunnels. You can picnic or eat at one of the three restaurants.

In summer, admission is C$39 (US$39/£20) for adults and children 10 and over, C$32 (US$32/£16) for children 5 to 9, and free for children 4 and under. Marineland is open daily July and August from 9am to 6pm; mid-April to mid-May and September to early October from 10am to 4pm; and mid-May to June from 10am to 5pm (closed mid-October through mid-Apr). Rides open in late May and close the first Monday in October. In town, drive south on Stanley Street and follow the signs; from the QEW, take the McLeod Road exit.

to pay for a movie that is only 45 minutes long. Still, I'm an IMAX fan, and, I have to admit, the film looks great; also, if you see a second feature, it will cost only C$6 (US$6/£3) per person.

The falls are also exciting in winter, when the ice bridge and other formations are quite remarkable.

ALONG THE NIAGARA PARKWAY ⟨

The Niagara Parkway, on the Canadian side of the falls, is a gem. Unlike the American side, it abounds with natural wonders, including vast expanses of parkland. You can drive along the 56km (35-mile) parkway all the way from Niagara-on-the-Lake to Niagara Falls on the parkway, taking in attractions en route. Here are the major ones:

- The **White Water Walk,** 4330 River Rd. (© **905/374-1221**): The scenic boardwalk runs beside the raging white waters of the Great Gorge Rapids. Stroll along and wonder how it must have felt to challenge this mighty torrent, where the river rushes through the narrow channel at an average speed of 35kmph (22 mph). Admission is C$7.50 (US$7.50/£3.75) for adults, C$6.50 (US$6.50/£3.25) for children 6 to 12, free for children 5 and under. It's open daily from 9am to 5pm.

- The **Whirlpool Aero Car** (© **905/354-5711**): This red-and-yellow cable-car contraption whisks you on a 1,097m (3,600-ft.) jaunt between two points in Canada. High above the Niagara Whirlpool, you'll enjoy excellent views of the surrounding landscape. Admission is C$10 (US$10/£5) for adults, C$6 (US$6/£3) for children

6 to 12, free for kids 5 and under. Open daily May to the third Sunday in October, ride hours are from 10am to 4:30pm.

- The **Niagara Parks Botanical Gardens and School of Horticulture** (© 905/356-8119): Stop here for a free view of the vast gardens and a look at the **Floral Clock**, which contains 25,000 plants in its 12m-diameter (39-ft.) face. The **Butterfly Conservatory** is also in the gardens. In this lush tropical setting, more than 2,000 butterflies (50 international species) float and flutter among such nectar-producing flowers as lantanas and pentas. The large, bright-blue, luminescent morpho butterflies from Central and South America are particularly gorgeous. Interpretive programs and other presentations take place in the auditorium and two smaller theaters. The native butterfly garden outside attracts the more familiar swallowtails, fritillaries, and painted ladies. Admission is C$10 (US$10/£5) for adults, C$6 (US$6/£3) for children 6 to 12, free for children 5 and under. The school opens at 9am daily. It closes at 8pm in May and June; 9pm in July and August; 6pm in March, April, September, and October; and 5pm November through February. It's closed December 25.

- **Queenston Heights Park:** This is the site of a famous War of 1812 battle, and you can take a walking tour of the battlefield. Picnic or play tennis (for C$6/US$6/£3 per hour) in the shaded arbor before moving to the **Laura Secord Homestead,** Partition Street, Queenston (© 905/262-4851). This heroic woman threaded enemy lines to alert British authorities to a surprise attack by American soldiers during the War of 1812. Her home contains a fine collection of Upper Canada furniture from the period, plus artifacts recovered from an archaeological dig. Stop at the candy shop and ice-cream parlor. Tours run every half-hour. Admission is C$4 (US$4/£2), free for children age 5 and under. The homestead is open late May through Labour Day weekdays from 9am to 3:30pm and weekends from 11am to 5pm.

Niagara Parkway Commission Restaurants

The Niagara Parkway Commission has commandeered the most spectacular scenic spots, where it operates reasonably priced dining outlets. They serve traditional family-style food at lunch and dinner, and do not accept reservations. **Table Rock Restaurant** (© 905/354-3631) and **Victoria Park Restaurant** (© 905/356-2217), on the parkway right by the falls, are both pleasant, if crowded. **Diner on the Green** (© 905/356-7221) is also on the parkway, at the Whirlpool Golf Course near Queenston. But the star of the Niagara Parkway Commission's eateries is **Queenston Heights** (14275 Niagara Pkwy.; © 905/262-4274). Set in the park among firs, cypresses, silver birches, and maples, the open-air balcony affords a magnificent view of the lower Niagara River and the rich fruit-growing land through which it flows. Or you can sit under the cathedral ceiling in a room where the flue of the stone fireplace reaches to the roof. Dinner options might include filet of Atlantic salmon with Riesling-chive hollandaise, prime rib, or grilled pork with apples and cider–Dijon mustard sauce. If nothing else, go for a drink on the deck and enjoy the terrific view.

- Fruit farms, like **Kurtz Orchards** (© 905/468-2937), and wineries such as the **Inniskillin Winery,** Line 3, Service Road 66 (© 905/468-3554 or 905/468-2187): You'll find peaches, apples, pears, nectarines, cherries, plums, and strawberries at Kurtz; you can tour the 32 hectares (79 acres) on a tractor-pulled tram. Inniskillin is open daily from 10am to 6pm June to October, and Monday through Saturday from 10am to 5pm November through May. The self-guided free tour has 20 stops that explain the winemaking process. A free guided tour, offered daily in summer and Saturday only in winter, begins at 2:30pm.

- **Old Fort Erie,** 350 Lakeshore Rd., Fort Erie (© 905/871-0540): It's a reconstruction of the fort that was seized by the Americans in July 1814, besieged later by the British, and finally blown up as the Americans retreated across the river to Buffalo. Guards in period costume stand sentry duty, fire the cannons, and demonstrate drill and musket practice. The fort is open daily from 10am to 5pm from the first Saturday in May to mid-September, and weekends only to Canadian Thanksgiving (U.S. Columbus Day). Admission is C$8.50 (US$8.50/£4.25) for adults, C$4.50 (US$4.50/£2.25) for children 6 to 12, free for children 5 and under.

3 Hamilton

75km (47 miles) SW of Toronto

A couple of years ago, a friend of mine asked for recommendations on where to go on a day trip around Toronto. When I suggested Hamilton, she was surprised. She's a lifelong Toronto resident, and she had never been there. Moreover, she'd never thought about going there. Hamilton may be Ontario's most-overlooked city, and it's a shame. Situated on a landlocked harbor spanned at its entrance by the Burlington Skyway's dramatic sweep, Hamilton has long been nicknamed "Steeltown" for its industrial roots. Since the early 1990s, however, Hamilton has been making a name for itself with its ever-expanding list of attractions. It takes roughly an hour to drive here from Toronto, and a day trip here is time well spent for the whole family.

ESSENTIALS

GETTING THERE   Hamilton is easy to reach by car. From Toronto, take the Queen Elizabeth Way (signs read QEW) to Hamilton. The drive will take about an hour. **GO (Government of Ontario) Transit** is a commuter train that connects Toronto and Hamilton. Call © 800/438-6646 or 416/869-3200 for information, or check out www.gotransit.com. The **John C. Munro Hamilton International Airport** (© 905/679-8359; www.hamiltonairport.com) has long been popular with cargo carriers and is now a hub for WestJet. In 2007, **flyglobespan** began service to Hamilton, connecting the city to 13 U.K. destinations, including London (via Gatwick), Birmingham, Liverpool, Manchester, Belfast, Edinburgh, and Glasgow; visit **www.fly globespan.ca** for details.

VISITOR INFORMATION   The Tourism **Hamilton Information Centre** is at 34 James St. S., Hamilton, ON L8P 2X8 (© 800/263-8590 or 905/546-2666; www.tourismhamilton.com). It has a wealth of information about what to see and do, as well as where to dine and sleep. Its year-round hours run from Monday to Friday 9am to 5pm.

EXPLORING HAMILTON

Hamilton's downtown core is best explored on foot, but you will need a car to visit attractions in the outlying areas (such as the African Lion Safari).

African Lion Safari 🦁🦁 *Kids*   Just a half-hour drive northwest of Hamilton, you'll find a mirror image of a traditional zoo: At the African Lion Safari, visitors remain caged in their cars or in a tour bus while the animals roam wild and free. The 300-hectare (741-acre) wildlife park contains rhinos, cheetahs, lions, tigers, giraffes, zebras, vultures, and many other species. In addition to the safari, the cost of admission covers other attractions, like the cruise aboard the *African Queen,* during which a tour guide will take you around the lake and point out local inhabitants like spider monkeys, crested macaques, and ring-tailed lemurs. A train will take you through a forest populated by snapping turtles, among other wildlife.

The park has several baby Asian elephants, and the elephant-bathing event, which occurs daily, will particularly fascinate the kids. The Pets' Corner is filled with frisky otters and pot-bellied pigs. There are several play areas for children as well, including the Misumu Bay water park (bring bathing suits!).

Safari Rd., Cambridge. ℂ **800/461-WILD** or 519/623-2620. www.lionsafari.com. Admission C$27 (US$27/£14) adults, C$24 (US$24/£12) seniors, C$22 (US$22/£11) children 3–12, free for children 2 and under; rates are discounted in spring and fall. Late June to Labour Day daily 10am–5:30pm; mid-Apr to late June and early Sept to mid-Oct daily 9am–4pm. Closed mid-Oct to mid-Apr.

Art Gallery of Hamilton 🎨   This art gallery first opened in 1914, but it was only when it reopened its doors in 2005 that it became one of Hamilton's greatest attractions. After a major renovation that cost more than C$18 million, the AGH is a gorgeous place to visit, with one of the most comprehensive collections of Canadian art in the country, as well as notable holdings of European and American works. The overhaul came as the result of the gallery's receiving one of the largest bequests in Canadian history—the Joey and Toby Tannenbaum Collection, which included 211 works of 19th-century art from Europe. Now when you visit, you can see a great range of works, from Jules-Elie Delaunay's astonishing *Ixion Plunged into Hades* to Alex Colville's *Horse and Train* (two of my favorites). The renovation also helped shape areas such as the open-air Irving Zucker Sculpture Garden, a green, serene space that can also be viewed from the Sculpture Atrium inside the gallery.

123 King St. W. ℂ **905/527-6610.** www.artgalleryofhamilton.com. Admission C$12 (US$12/£6) adults, C$10 (US$10/£5) students & seniors, C$5 (US$5/£2.50) children 6–17, free for children 5 and under. Tues–Wed noon–7pm; Thurs–Fri noon–9pm; Sat–Sun noon–5pm; closed Mon except on most civic holidays. Closed Jan 1, Dec 25–26.

Canadian Warplane Heritage Museum   If you're an aircraft buff like my dad, you'll love this interactive museum that charts the course of Canadian aviation from the beginning of World War II to the present. Visitors can climb into the cockpits of World War II trainer crafts or a CF-100 jet fighter. The most popular attractions are the flight simulators, which allow aspiring pilots to test their skills (my favorite part). There are also short documentary films, photographs, and other memorabilia. The aircraft on display include rarities like the Avro Lancaster bomber and the deHavilland Vampire fighter jet. The collection also includes a variety of military and transport craft.

9280 Airport Rd. (at the John C. Munro Hamilton International Airport), Mount Hope. ℂ **877/347-3359** or 905/670-3347. www.warplane.com. Admission C$10 (US$10/£5) adults, C$9 (US$9/£4.50) seniors and youths 13–17, C$6 (US$6/£3) for children 6–12, free for children 5 and under. Daily 9am–5pm. Closed Jan 1, Dec 25.

Dundurn National Historic Site 🏛🏛   This site comprises two big attractions: **Dundurn Castle** and the **Hamilton Military Museum.** First, let's get something straight: Dundurn isn't really a castle, but a very grand manor house. But it does afford a glimpse of the opulent life as it was lived in southern Ontario in the mid–19th century. Costumed interpreters "living" in 1855 guide you through the house and tell vivid stories of what life was like there—for both the aristocrats and the servants.

Sir Allan Napier MacNab, premier of the United Canadas in the mid-1850s and a founder of the Great Western Railway, built Dundurn between 1832 and 1835; Queen Victoria knighted him for the part he played in the Rebellion of 1837. The 35-plus-room mansion has been restored and furnished in the style of 1855. The gray stucco exterior, with its classical Greek portico, is impressive enough, but inside, from the formal dining rooms to Lady MacNab's boudoir, the furnishings are rich. The museum contains a fascinating collection of Victoriana. In December, the castle is decorated splendidly for a Victorian Christmas.

The Hamilton Military Museum is on the grounds of Dundurn Castle. For those who are interested, it traces Canadian military history from the War of 1812 through World War I. Admission is included when you buy a ticket for Dundurn Castle.

Dundurn Park, York Blvd. (C) 905/546-2872. Admission C$10 (US$10/£5) adults, C$8 (US$8/£4) seniors and students with ID, C$5 (US$5/£2.50) children 6–14, free for children 5 and under. Victoria Day to Labour Day daily 10am–4pm; the rest of the year Tues–Sun noon–4pm. Closed Jan 1, Dec 25–26.

Hamilton Museum of Steam and Technology (Kids)   One of the things I like best about Hamilton is the city's pride in its industrial roots. This museum is a case in point. It explains—and celebrates—the technology that made urban life possible in the Victorian age. This museum has preserved two 14m (45-ft.) tall, 63,503kg (70-ton) steam engines that first pumped clean water to Hamilton (the stone-and-cast-iron Romanesque building that houses them is a gorgeous example of 19th-century public-works architecture as well). The waterworks were built to protect Hamilton from the deadly cholera outbreaks and fires that destroyed so many cities in that era. The museum also hosts a series of exhibits and special events, which let you do things like ride on a mini-version of a steam-powered train.

900 Woodward Ave (at the QEW). (C) 905/546-4797. Admission C$6 (US$6/£3) adults, C$5 (US$5/£2.50) seniors and students 13–17, C$4 (US$4/£2) children 6–12, free for children 5 and under. June 1 to Labour Day Tues–Sun 11am–4pm; the rest of the year Tues–Sun noon–4pm. Closed Jan 1, Dec 25–26.

Royal Botanical Gardens (Finds)   Situated just north of the city, the Royal Botanical Gardens spread over 1,214 glorious hectares (3,000 acres). The Rock Garden features spring bulbs in May, summer flowers in June to September, and chrysanthemums in October. The Laking Garden blazes during June and July with irises, peonies, and lilies. The arboretum fills with the heady scent of lilac from the end of May to early June, and the exquisite color bursts of rhododendrons and azaleas thereafter. The Centennial Rose Garden is at its best late June through mid-September.

The gardens host many festivals during the year, including the Mediterranean Food & Wine Festival in February, the popular Ontario Garden Show in early April, the Tulip Festival in May, the Rose Society Show in June, and the Japanese Flower Society Show in September.

Should you work up an appetite while strolling the grounds, the on-site dining options include the Gardens Café, which is open year-round, and the Rock Garden Tea House or the Turner Pavilion (both open throughout the summer).

680 Plains Rd. W., Burlington (C) 905/527-1158. www.rbg.ca. Admission C$8 (US$8/£4) adults, C$6 (US$6/£3) seniors and children 13–18, C$3 (US$3/£1.50) children 5–12, free for children 4 and under. Daily 9:30am–dusk. Closed Jan 1, Dec 25.

WHERE TO STAY

Because Hamilton is so close to Toronto, it's easy to make a day trip here and back, rather than pulling up stakes and spending the night here. However, if you do want to stay in the area, several well-known chains have hotels here, including **Sheraton** (© **800/514-7101** or 905/529-5515), **Ramada** (© **800/2RAMADA** or 905/528-3451), and **Comfort Inn** (© **877/424-6423** or 905/560-4500).

WHERE TO DINE

The suggested restaurants in St. Catharines and Welland, such as **Café Garibaldi** and **Wellington Court** (p. 433), are just a short drive away from Hamilton. However, Hamilton has a few restaurants worth checking out, too.

La Cantina ITALIAN   This is really two restaurants in one. A dining room serves up plates of veal scaloppini in a dry Marsala sauce, and seared ostrich medallions cooked with pinot noir. The casual pizzeria features more than 20 varieties of pizza, including the traditional Quattro Stagione (four seasons) with prosciutto, artichokes, olives, and mozzarella. This is a very popular spot, so try to make a reservation or arrive early, especially at lunch. If you're very lucky, you might just secure a seat in the restaurant's garden patio.

60 Walnut St. S., Hamilton. © **905/521-8989.** Reservations recommended. Main courses C$12–C$26 (US$12–US$26/£6–£13). AE, MC, V. Tues–Thurs 11:30am–10pm; Fri 11:30am–11pm; Sat 5–11pm.

Perry's Restaurant INTERNATIONAL   This casual family-style restaurant has a large menu that has something for everyone. It borrows from a range of cuisines, including Italian, French, Mexican, Greek, and American. Offerings include chicken souvlakia, rack of ribs, hearty sandwiches, and fish and chips. There are also lighter options, such as salads, soups, and chicken fingers. There's a sunny patio at the front of the restaurant, too.

1088 Main St. W., Hamilton. © **905/527-3779.** Main courses C$8–C$15 (US$8–US$15/£4–£7.50). MC, V. Daily 11:30am–1am.

4 London: A Family-Friendly Town

195km (121 miles) SW of Toronto

If you're driving into Canada from the U.S. Midwest, consider stopping in this pretty university town that sits on the Thames River—particularly if you have kids in tow.

ESSENTIALS

GETTING THERE   If you're driving, London is about 192km (120 miles) from Detroit via Highway 401, 110km (68 miles) from Kitchener via Highway 401, 195km (121 miles) from Niagara Falls via QEW, highways 403 and 401, and 65km (40 miles) from Stratford via 7 and 4. Direct flights from Toronto, Ottawa, and Detroit arrive at **London International Airport** (© **519/452-4015;** www.londonairport.on.ca). **VIA Rail** (© **888/VIA-RAIL** or 416/366-8411; www.viarail.ca) operates a Toronto-Brantford-London-Windsor route and also, in conjunction with **Amtrak** (© **800/USA-RAIL;** www.amtrak.com), a Toronto-Kitchener-Stratford-London-Sarnia-Chicago route. Both offer several trains a day. The VIA Rail station in London is at 197 York St. (© **519/434-2149**). **Greyhound** (© **800/231-2222;** www.greyhound.ca) provides service from Toronto, Detroit, Buffalo, and other Canadian and American destinations.

VISITOR INFORMATION   Contact **Tourism London, ☎ 800/265-2602** or 519/661-5000, or visit www.londontourism.ca. There are two information centers in London, one at 696 Wellington Rd. S. and the other one downtown at 267 Dundas St. Both are open 8:30am to 4:30pm on weekdays and from 10am to 5pm on Saturdays, but only the downtown location is open Sunday (10am–5pm).

SPECIAL EVENTS & FESTIVALS   The 10-day **Western Fair** (☎ **800/619-4629** or 519/438-7203; www.westernfair.com), held in September, is a major draw for the whole family. Traditionally, the **London International Air Fest** (www.londonairshow.com) ushers in the summer season each June, but it has been suspended for the past couple of years; there are plans to bring it back, so check the website for updates.

EXPLORING LONDON

Banting House National Historic Site
Sir Frederick G. Banting won the Nobel Prize for his discovery of insulin, and this museum is dedicated to his life and work as a doctor and as an artist. There are displays about his medical research at the University of Toronto, his years as a soldier, and his drawings. The museum is operated by the Canadian Diabetes Association.

442 Adelaide St. N. ☎ 519/673-1752. Admission C$4 (US$4/£2) adults, C$3 (US$3/£1.50) seniors and children 5–12, free for kids 4 and under. Tues–Sat noon–4pm. Closed Dec. 21–Jan 5 and public holidays.

Fanshawe Pioneer Village *(Kids)*
The Pioneer Village is a complex comprised of 25-plus buildings where you can see craft demonstrations (such as broom making and candle dipping), enjoy wagon rides, and imagine what life was like during the 18th century. In **Fanshawe Park** (☎ **519/451-2800**), there's a large pool and beach at the 6km (4-mile) long lake.

In Fanshawe Park (entrance off Fanshawe Park Rd., east of Clarke Rd.). ☎ 519/457-1296. www.fanshawepioneer village.ca. Admission C$5 (US$5/£2.50) adults, C$4 (US$4/£2) seniors and students, C$3 (US$3/£1.50) children 3–12; free for children 2 and under. Village: May 1–Nov 30 Wed–Sun 10am–4:30pm; Dec 1–20 daily 10am–4:30pm.

London Regional Children's Museum *(Kids)*
This interactive museum for kids occupies several floors of an old school building. In every room, children can explore, experiment, and engage their imaginations. For example, on "The Street Where You Live," kids can dress up in firefighters' uniforms, don the overalls of those who work under the streets, and assume the role of a dentist, doctor, or construction worker. Some rooms contrast how people lived long ago with how they live today. More up-to-the-minute experiences can be enjoyed at the photosensitive wall, the zoetrobe, or in the kitchen where children can see exactly how the appliances work. It's a fun place for children and adults.

21 Wharncliffe Rd. S. ☎ 519/434-5726. www.londonchildrensmuseum.ca. Admission C$5 (US$5/£2.50) all ages, free for children under 2. Year-round Tues–Sun 10am–5pm; Mon June–Aug and holidays. Closed Dec 25–26, Jan 1.

Museum of Ontario Archaeology
Affiliated with the University of Western Ontario, the museum contains artifacts from various periods of Native Canadian history—projectiles, pottery shards, effigies, turtle rattles, and more. The most evocative exhibit is the on-site reconstruction of a 500-year-old Attawandaron village. Behind the elm palisades, longhouses built according to original specifications and techniques have been erected on the 2 hectares (5 acres) where archaeological excavations are taking place.

1600 Attawandaron Rd. (off Wonderland Rd. N., just south of Hwy. 22). © **519/473-1360**. www.uwo.ca/museum. Admission C$4 (US$4/£2) adults, C$3.25 (US$3.25/£1.65) seniors and students, C$2 (US$2/£1) children 5–12, C$10 (US$10/£5) families, free for children 4 and under. May 1 to Labour Day daily 10am–4:30pm; Sept (after Labour Day) to Dec Tues–Sun 10am–4:30pm; Jan–Apr Sat–Sun 1–4pm.

Storybook Gardens ✶ *Kids*   The Storybook Gardens has evolved from its roots as a park with a storybook theme. The main attractions are now the Slippery's Great Escape water park, Pirate's Island (complete with towers, slides, and lookout points), and Storybook Valley with its seals and otters. Special daily events include the seal feeding at 3:30pm, and a variety of live entertainment. There's also a conservation area that is currently being developed.

Off Commissioners Rd. W. © **519/661-5770**. www.storybook.london.ca. Admission C$7.50 (US$7.50/£3.75) adults, C$6.50 (US$6.50/£3.25) seniors, C$5 (US$5/£2.50) youths and children, free for children under 2. May to Labour Day daily 10am–8pm; day after Labour Day to early Oct Mon–Fri noon–6pm, Sat–Sun 11am–6pm; between early Oct and Apr hours vary greatly, so call ahead.

WHERE TO STAY

London is less than a half-hour's drive away from Stratford, so it's easy to stay there for the theater festival and detour into London for a day. Personally, I prefer the accommodations in Stratford, although I make an exception for the property below.

Delta London Armouries Hotel   Built into the facade of a castlelike armory, this hotel is an impressive example of architectural conservation and conversion. The armory's 3.5m (11-ft.) thick walls, built in 1905, form the building's main floor and base, and above the crenellated turrets and ramparts soars a modern glass tower. Inside, the well-equipped rooms are furnished with Federal reproductions. A recent renovation has freshened up both the guest rooms and the fitness facilities. There are a variety of packages on offer here on any given week, including several family-friendly options.

325 Dundas St., London, ON N6B 1T9. © **877/814-7706** or 519/679-6111. www.deltahotels.com. 245 units. From C$120 (US$120/£60) double. Extra person C$15 (US$15/£7.50). Children under 18 stay free in parent's room. AE, DC, DISC, MC, V. Valet parking C$12 (US$12/£6); self-parking C$7.50 (US$7.50/£3.75). **Amenities:** Restaurant; lounge; pool; exercise room; children's activity center; squash court. *In room:* A/C, TV, minibar.

WHERE TO DINE

I'm going to level with you: No one comes to London for the food. I have relatives who live here and who will probably shoot me for saying this, but I've never had a memorable meal in this town. What you will find is an assortment of child-friendly restaurants with thoughtful waitstaffs. But if you're looking for something gourmet, head to Stratford.

Mongolian Grill ASIAN *Kids*   This is cooking as performance art. Diners assemble their own meal-in-a-bowl with raw ingredients ranging from chicken to shrimp, broccoli to bok choy, and ginger to coriander. The bowl is presented to the cooks, who labor at a huge wheel-shaped grill that sizzles and steams. The young cooks know how to put on a good show, though I couldn't get past wondering how they could stand the intense heat, which hovers around 600°F (315°C). Note that there is a separate menu for children.

645 Richmond St. **519/645-6400**. Main courses $8–$12 (US$8–US$12/£4–£6). AE, DC, MC, V. Daily noon–2:30pm and 5–10:30pm.

5 Goderich & Bayfield

220km (137 miles) W of Toronto

Goderich shamelessly bills itself as Canada's prettiest town. It is postcard perfect, so perhaps its boast is on the mark. The town's most striking feature is the central octagonal space with the Huron County Courthouse at its hub. Another highlight is the **Historic Huron Gaol,** with walls 5.5m (18 ft.) high and .5m (2 ft.) thick. Goderich has won numerous prizes for its flower gardens, a local point of pride. **Goderich Tourism** (📞 800/280-7637 or 519/524-6600; www.goderich.ca) operates a visitor center at 91 Hamilton St., which is open daily. For information about the town's lovely architecture—and efforts to preserve it—contact **Heritage Goderich** (📞 519/524-8344; www.goderich.ca/heritage).

Bayfield is no slouch in the beauty stakes, either. This lovely, well-preserved 19th-century town is about 20km (13 miles) from Goderich and 65km (40 miles) from Stratford. Once a major grain-shipping port, it became a quiet backwater when the railroad passed it by. Today, the main square, High Street, and Elgin Place are part of a Heritage Conservation District. Bayfield's Chamber of Commerce (📞 866/565-2499 or 519/565-2499; www.villageofbayfield.com) handles tourism inquiries.

WHERE TO STAY & DINE

Benmiller Inn & Spa ★★   The heart of the inn is the original wool mill, which dates from 1877, and now contains the dining room, bar, reception, and 12 guest rooms. When it became an inn in 1974, many mechanical parts were refashioned into decorative objects—mirrors made from pulley wheels, lamps from gears. Rooms feature barn-board siding, desks, floor lamps, heated ceramic tile in the bathrooms, and handmade quilts. The 18 rooms in Gledhill House, the original mill-owner's home, are generously proportioned, while the four suites have fireplaces and Jacuzzis. There are more rooms in the River Mill, which is attached to the building containing the swimming pool, whirlpool, and running track. The brick patio overlooking the gardens is a pleasant place to sit and look at the totem pole, brought from British Columbia. Spa day packages start at C$165 (US$165/£83). The elegant dining room serves up dishes such as teriyaki-glazed Atlantic salmon and rack of New Zealand lamb. It's open daily for lunch and dinner.

R.R. 4, Goderich, ON N7A 3Y1. 📞 800/265-1711 or 519/524-2191. www.benmiller.on.ca. 57 units. From C$169 (US$169/£85) double. Rates include breakfast; some packages include dinner. AE, DC, MC, V. **Amenities:** Restaurant; indoor pool; spa; sauna; billiards room; table tennis; cross-country ski trails. *In room:* A/C, TV.

The Little Inn at Bayfield ★   The inn, originally built in 1832, has been thoroughly modernized, but it still holds its traditional charm. The older rooms in the main building are small and have only showers, but they are comfortably furnished with oak or sleigh beds. Rooms in the newer section are larger and feature platform beds and modern furnishings. The suites are located across the street in the old carriage house; they have platform beds, pine hutches, and feature whirlpool bathrooms, propane-gas fireplaces, and verandas. Also in the carriage house is the new Sapphire Spa, which offers everything from sports massage to a chocolate body wrap.

The Little Inn's popular restaurant is open for lunch and dinner 7 days a week; its innovative menu includes the likes of smoked pork tenderloin in a walnut-horseradish-ale cream sauce.

Main St., P.O. Box 100, Bayfield, ON N0M 1G0. © **800/565-1832** or 519/565-2611. www.littleinn.com. 28 units. From C$195 (US$195/£98) double. Special packages available. AE, DC, MC, V. **Amenities:** Restaurant; spa; concierge; room service; babysitting; dry cleaning/laundry service. *In room:* A/C, TV, hair dryer, iron.

6 Stratford & the Stratford Festival ★/★

149km (93 miles) W of Toronto

The grand Stratford Festival has humble roots. The idea of a theater was launched in 1953, when director Tyrone Guthrie lured the great Sir Alec Guinness to the stage here. Whether Sir Alec knew the "stage" was set up in a makeshift tent is another question, but his acclaimed performance gave the festival the push—and press—it needed to become an annual tradition. Since then, the Stratford Festival has grown to become one of the most famous in North America, and its four theaters (no more tents!) have put this charming and scenic town on the map. While visitors will notice the Avon River and other sights named in honor of the Bard, they may not realize that Stratford has another claim to fame: It's home to one of Canada's best cooking schools, which makes dining at many of the spots in town a delight.

ESSENTIALS

GETTING THERE   Driving from Toronto, take Highway 401 west to Interchange 278 at Kitchener. Follow Highway 8 west onto Highway 7/8 to Stratford.

For me, nothing beats the train. Stratford is a small and very walkable town, so unless you're planning to tour the surrounding area, call **VIA Rail** (© **800-VIA-RAIL** or 416/366-8411; www.viarail.ca). Canada's national rail company operates several trains daily along the Toronto-Kitchener-Stratford route. The toll-free number works within North America; if you're traveling from overseas, you can book your rail travel in advance through one of Via's general sales agents. There's a long list of local agents on www.viarail.ca, and they cover the United Kingdom, Australia, New Zealand, Hong Kong, Japan, France, and several other countries.

VISITOR INFORMATION   For first-rate visitor information, go to the **Visitors Information Centre** by the river on York Street at Erie. From May to early November, it's open Sunday through Wednesday from 9am to 5pm, and Thursday through Saturday from 9am to 8pm. At other times, contact **Tourism Stratford,** 47 Downie St., Stratford, ON N5A 1W7 (© **800/561-SWAN** or 519/271-5140; www.city.stratford.on.ca).

EXPLORING THE TOWN

Stratford was founded in 1832, and much of its historic heart has been preserved. Ninety-minute **guided tours of Stratford** take place Monday through Saturday in July and August, and on Saturday only in May, June, September, and October. They leave at 9:30am from the Visitors' Information Centre by the Avon River and are free of charge (call ahead to confirm). The visitors' booth also has maps available for self-guided tours.

Paddleboat, kayak, and canoe rentals are available at the **Boathouse,** behind and below the information booth. It's open daily from 9am until dusk in summer. Contact **Avon Boat Rentals,** 40 York St. (© **519/271-7739**). There's also a boat, the *Juliet III,* that offers scenic half-hour tours.

Past the Orr Dam and the 90-year-old stone bridge, through a rustic gate, lies a very special park, the **Shakespearean Gardens.** In the formal English garden, where a sundial measures the hours, you can relax and contemplate the herb and flowerbeds and the tranquil river lagoon, and muse on a bust of Shakespeare by Toronto sculptor Cleeve Horne. For a picnic-friendly patch of green, visit **Queen's Park,** a stone's throw from the Festival Theatre. It has tall, shady trees and a great view of the swans on the Avon.

Stratford also has a fine art museum, the **Gallery Stratford,** 54 Romeo St. (© **519/ 271-5271;** www.gallerystratford.on.ca). It's in a historic building on the fringes of Confederation Park. Since it opened in 1967, its focus has been on Canadian artists. Its hours change with the seasons, but mid-May through late September, it's open from 9am to 5pm (call ahead for hours during other times of year). Admission is approximately C$5 (US$5/£2.50) for adults, C$4 (US$4/£2) for seniors and students 13 and up, and free for children 12 and under (note that admission prices change with the special exhibits on display).

A COUPLE OF EXCURSIONS FROM STRATFORD

Only half an hour or so from Stratford, the twin cities of **Kitchener** and **Waterloo** have two drawing cards: the **Farmer's Market** and the famous 9-day **Oktoberfest.** The cities still have a German-majority population (of German descent and often German speaking), and many citizens are Mennonites. On Saturday, starting at 6am, you can sample shoofly pie, apple butter, birch beer, summer sausage, and other Mennonite specialties at the market in the Market Square complex, at Duke and Frederick streets in Kitchener. For additional information, contact the **Kitchener–Waterloo Area Visitors and Convention Bureau,** 2848 King St. E., Kitchener, ON N2A 1A5 (© **519/748-0800;** www.kwtourism.ca). It's open from 9am to 5pm weekdays only in winter, daily in summer. For Oktoberfest information, check out www.oktoberfest.ca; call © **888/294-HANS** or 519/570-HANS; or write to **K-W Oktoberfest,** P.O. Box 1053, 17 Benton St., Kitchener, ON N2G 4G1.

Eight kilometers (5 miles) north of Kitchener is the town of **St. Jacobs.** It has close to 100 shops in venues such as a converted mill, silo, and other factory buildings. For those interested in learning more about the Amish-Mennonite way of life, the **Meetingplace,** 33 King St. (© **519/664-3518**), shows a short film about it (daily in summer, weekends only in winter). Ironically enough, there's also a **St. Jacobs Outlet Mall** (surely not run by the Amish!), filled with discounted Levi's jeans, Paderno cookware, Liz Claiborne and Jones New York clothing, Cadbury's chocolate, and Royal Doulton giftware. It's at 25 Benjamin Rd., and it is open Monday through Friday from 9:30am to 9pm, Saturday 8:30am to 6pm, and Sunday noon to 5pm (closed Jan 1 and Dec 25). Call © **519/888-0138** for more information.

WHERE TO STAY

When you book your theater tickets, you can book your accommodations at no extra charge. Options range from guest homes for as little as C$50 (US$50/£25) to first-class hotels charging more than C$200 (US$200/£100). Call the **Stratford Festival Accommodation Bureau** at © **800/567-1600** for information (note that some accommodations are open only to festival-goers, and these can be booked only through the Accommodation Bureau). You can also get information about where to stay from **Tourism Stratford** at © **800/561-SWAN.** Rooms in Stratford are most expensive in June, July, and August; it's easier to get a discount from fall to spring.

Stratford

ATTRACTIONS ●
Avon Boat Rentals **12**
Avon Theatre **11**
Confederation Park **2**
Festival Theatre **3**
Gallery Stratford **1**
Shakespearean
  Gardens **13**
Studio Theatre **11**
Tom Patterson Theatre **7**

DINING ◆
Bentley's **6**
The Church **9**
Keystone Alley Cafe **10**
The Old Prune **5**
Rundles **8**
38 Restaurant **14**

ACCOMMODATIONS ■
Bentley's/Annex Inn **6**
Festival Inn **4**
The Swan Motel **15**

ⓘ Information
✉ Post office

Bentley's/Annex Room Inn 🕭   For location, you can't beat this spot. Bentley's enjoys an excellent location at the center of town. The rooms are charming duplex suites with efficiency kitchens. Period English furnishings and attractive drawings, paintings, and costume designs on the walls make for a pleasant ambience. Five units have skylights. The Annex Room Inn is in a separate building that is just a few steps away. Its rooms are described as "executive" status, and they really are—airy and bright and very elegantly decorated. Many of the rooms have a gas fireplace and a stereo system—and all have whirlpool tubs.

99 Ontario St., Stratford, ON N5A 3H1. ℂ **800/361-5322** or 519/271-1121. www.bentleys-annex.com. 13 units. Bentley's doubles start at C$175 (US$175/£88) Apr to mid-Nov, C$95 (US$95/£48) mid-Nov to Mar; Annex doubles start at C$225 (US$225/£113). Extra person C$20 (US$20/£10). AE, DC, MC, V. Free parking. **Amenities:** 2 restaurants. *In room:* A/C, TV, kitchen, fridge, coffeemaker, hair dryer.

Festival Inn   The Festival Inn sits outside town off highways 7 and 8, on 8 hectares (20 acres) of landscaped grounds. This is the largest full-service hotel in Stratford. The place has an Old English air, with stucco walls, Tudor-style beams, and high-backed red settees in the lobby. Tudor style prevails throughout the large, motel-style rooms. All have wall-to-wall carpeting, matching bedspreads, floor-to-ceiling drapes, and reproductions of old masters on the walls. Some units have charming bay windows with sheer curtains, and all rooms in the main building, north wing, and annex have refrigerators. The indoor pool has an outdoor patio.

1144 Ontario St. (P.O. Box 811), Stratford, ON N5A 6W1. © **800/463-3581** or 519/273-1150. Fax 519/273-2111. www.festivalinnstratford.com. 182 units. From C$160 (US$160/£80) double. Children under 16 stay for free in parent's room. AE, DC, MC, V. Free parking. **Amenities:** Dining room; coffee shop; indoor pool; Jacuzzi; sauna. *In room:* A/C, TV, fridge, coffeemaker.

The Swan Motel 🏖 *(Value*   I don't know what "motel" means to you, but to me, it normally sounds like an unprepossessing place to stop that's right by a highway. Well, the Swan is indeed 2 miles from downtown Stratford, but its grounds are completely luxurious. This property has been run by the same family for more than 40 years, and it has a warm, gracious atmosphere. The rooms are uniformly nonsmoking, and they are simply but pleasantly arranged. The grounds are the real drawing card, with the romantic Victorian gazebo, beds of perennial flowers, and outdoor pool. It's far enough from the center of town that I don't recommend staying here unless you're driving, but if you have a car, the Swan is a lovely place to retreat to.

Downie St. S., 3765 Perth Rd. 112, Stratford, ON N5A 6S3. © **519/271-6376.** Fax 519/271-0682. www.swanmotel.ca. 24 units. From C$96 (US$96/£48) double. Extra person C$15 (US$15/£7.50). Rates include continental breakfast. AE, DC, MC, V. Free parking. No children. **Amenities:** Outdoor pool. *In room:* A/C, TV, fridge, hair dryer.

WHERE TO DINE

Bentley's   CANADIAN/ENGLISH   Bentley's is *the* local watering hole and a favorite theater-company gathering spot. The popular pastime is darts, but you can also watch TV. In summer, you can sit on the garden terrace and enjoy the light fare—grilled shrimp, burgers, gourmet pizza, fish and chips, shepherd's pie, and pasta dishes. The dinner menu features more substantial meals, including lamb curry, sirloin steak, and salmon baked in white wine with peppercorn-dill butter. The bar offers 16 drafts on tap.

99 Ontario St. © **519/271-1121.** www.bentleys-annex.com. Reservations not accepted. Main courses C$10–C$20 (US$10–US$20/£5–£10). AE, DC, MC, V. Daily 11:30am–1am.

Finds **An Open-Air Art Gallery**

Museums are grand, but who wants to spend a glorious summer day indoors? Thanks to the **Art in the Park** (© 519/272-0429; www.artintheparkstratford. com), you can have both. On Wednesdays, Saturdays, and Sundays from June to September, regional artists gather at Lakeside Drive and Front Street, and put on a show from 9am to 5pm, weather permitting. The artists and artisans work in various media, so you'll find paintings, sculptures, ceramics, jewelry, and glass, among other things. While many of the works are for sale, this isn't just a market: The artists are selected through a juried process, and they are required to demonstrate their medium as part of their display.

Tips The Play's the Thing

On July 13, 1953, *Richard III,* starring Alec Guinness, was staged in a huge tent. From that modest start, Stratford's artistic directors have built on the radical, but faithfully classic, base established by Tyrone Guthrie to create a repertory theater with a glowing international reputation.

Stratford has four theaters. The **Festival Theatre,** 55 Queen St., in Queen's Park, has a dynamic thrust stage. The **Avon Theatre,** 99 Downie St., has a classic proscenium stage. The **Tom Patterson Theatre,** Lakeside Drive, is an intimate 500-seat theater. The newest venue is the **Studio Theatre,** an intimate 278-seat space for experimental works.

World famous for its Shakespearean productions, the festival also offers classic and modern theatrical masterpieces. Recent productions have included *The Sound of Music, Private Lives,* and *Who's Afraid of Virginia Woolf?* Offerings from the Bard have included *The Merchant of Venice, Twelfth Night,* and *Macbeth.* Among the company's famous alumni are Dame Maggie Smith, Sir Alec Guinness, Sir Peter Ustinov, Alan Bates, Christopher Plummer, Irene Worth, and Julie Harris. Present company members include Lucy Peacock, Cynthia Dale, Martha Henry, and Brian Bedford.

In addition to attending plays, visitors may enjoy the "Celebrated Writers Series," which features renowned authors (some of whom have penned works performed at the Stratford Festival). The list of speakers has included Margaret Atwood, Michael Ondaatje, Joyce Carol Oates, and Rohinton Mistry. All lectures take place on Sunday mornings at the Tom Patterson Theatre or the Studio Theatre, and they cost C$25 (US$25/£13) per person; tickets are available from the box office.

The season usually begins in May and continues through October, with performances Tuesday through Sunday nights and matinees on Wednesday, Saturday, and Sunday. Ticket prices range from C$26 to C$97 (US$26–US$97/ £13-£49), with special prices for students and seniors. For tickets, call ⓒ **800/567-1600;** visit www.stratfordfestival.ca; or write to the Stratford Festival, P.O. Box 520, Stratford, ON N5A 6V2. Tickets are also available in the United States and Canada at Ticketmaster outlets. The box office opens for mail and fax orders in late January; telephone and in-person sales begin in late February.

The Church ☞☞ CONTINENTAL   The Church is simply stunning. The organ pipes and the altar of the 1873 structure are intact, along with the vaulted roof, carved woodwork, and stained-glass windows. Fresh flowers and elegant table settings further enhance the experience. In summer, there's a special four-course fixed-price dinner menu and an after-theater menu. Among the selection entrees, you might find caribou with port-and-blackberry sauce, cabbage braised in cream with shallots and glazed chestnuts, or lobster salad with green beans, new potatoes, and truffles scented with caraway. Desserts are equally exciting—try charlotte of white-chocolate mousse with summer fruit and dark-chocolate sauce, or nougat glace with kiwi sauce. To dine here during the festival, make reservations in March or April when you buy your tickets. The upstairs Belfry Bar is a popular pre- and post-theater gathering place.

70 Brunswick St. (at Waterloo St.). ℂ 519/273-3424. www.churchrestaurant.com. Reservations required. Main courses C$38–C$52 (US$38–US$52/£19–£26); 5-course prix-fixe menu C$85 (US$85/£43). AE, DC, MC, V. The Church: Tues–Sat 5–8:30pm; Sun 11:30am–1:30pm; off-season hours vary. The Belfry: Tues–Sat 11:30am–midnight; off-season hours vary.

Keystone Alley Cafe 🛪 ASIAN/CONTINENTAL   The food here is better than at some pricier competitors. Theater actors often stop in for lunch—perhaps a sandwich, such as the maple-grilled chicken-and-avocado club, or a main dish such as cornmeal-crusted Mediterranean tart. At dinner, entrees range from breast of Muscovy duck with stir-fried Asian vegetables and egg noodles in honey-ginger sauce, to escalopes of calves' liver accompanied by garlic potato purée and creamed Savoy cabbage with bacon. The short wine list is reasonably priced.

34 Brunswick St. ℂ 519/271-5645. Reservations recommended. Main courses C$17–C$27 (US$17–US$27/£8.50–£14). AE, DC, MC, V. Mon–Sat 11:30am–2:30pm; Tues–Sat 5–9pm.

The Old Prune 🛪 CONTINENTAL   Situated in a lovely Edwardian home, the Old Prune has three dining rooms and an enclosed garden patio. Former Montréalers, the proprietors demonstrate Québec flair in both decor and menu. The menu changes constantly because the dishes are based on what's fresh and what's in season (much of the produce comes from the region's organic farms). Appetizers might include outstanding house-smoked salmon with lobster potato salad topped with Sevruga caviar, or refreshing tomato consommé with saffron and sea scallops. Among the main courses, you might find Perth County pork loin grilled with tamari and honey glaze and served with shiitake mushrooms, pickled cucumbers, and sunflower sprouts; steamed bass in Napa cabbage with curry broth and lime leaves; or rack of Ontario lamb with smoky tomatillo–chipotle pepper sauce. Desserts, such as rhubarb-strawberry Napoleon with vanilla mousse, are always inspired.

151 Albert St. ℂ 519/271-5052. www.oldprune.on.ca. Reservations required. 3-course prix-fixe dinner C$71 (US$71/£35). AE, MC, V. Wed–Sun 11:30am–1pm; Tues–Sat 5–9pm; Sun 5–7:45pm. Call for winter hours.

Rundles 🛪 INTERNATIONAL   Rundles provides a premier dining experience in a serene dining room overlooking the river. Proprietor Jim Morris eats, sleeps, thinks, and dreams food, and Chef Neil Baxter delivers the exciting, exquisite cuisine to the table. The prix-fixe dinner offers palate-pleasing flavor combinations. Appetizers might include shaved fennel, arugula, artichoke, and Parmesan salad, or warm seared Québec foie gras. Among the five main dishes might be poached Atlantic salmon garnished with Jerusalem artichokes, wilted arugula, and yellow peppers in a light carrot sauce; or pink roast rib-eye of lamb with ratatouille and rosemary aioli. My dessert

---

Stratford Bed & Breakfasts

Stratford has an extraordinary wealth of bed-and-breakfast options. While they're not cheap in the high season, they can give you the chance to live in a Victorian or Edwardian mansion, at least for a weekend. For more information on the bed-and-breakfast scene, contact **Tourism Stratford** (ℂ **800/561-SWAN** or 519/271-5140; www.city.stratford.on.ca). Many of the B&B options are listed online—with photographs—at www.bbcanada.com.

Finds Shopping in Stratford

I know, we're all here for the theater scene, but don't miss out on Stratford's excellent shopping options. If you were expecting touristy, overpriced, and kitschy, you're in for a pleasant surprise. Many of the stores downtown sell clothing and housewares that rival what you'll see in the best boutiques in Toronto. Prices tend to be quite reasonable. Here are some of my favorite spots.

- **For housewares:** You'll find both locally made cranberry glass and objects from Indonesia and Uzbekistan at **Watson's Chelsea Bazaar,** 84 Ontario St. (© 519/273-1790). **White Oleander,** 136 Ontario St. (© 519/271-5616), sells lovely linens, bedding, and tableware. Everything at **Pariscope,** 21 York St. (© 519/271-3316), is French imported or French inspired. The venerable **Bradshaws,** 129 Ontario St. (© 519/271-6283), has been in business since 1895 selling crystal and china.

- **For clothing: Elizabeth Noel,** 26 Ontario St. (© 519/273-4506), sells beautiful dresses and other ladylike pieces, many of which are by Canadian labels such as Sweet Chemise. **The Green Room,** 40 Ontario St. (© 519/271-3240), is actually several rooms, all jam-packed with clothing and accessories.

- **For gift items:** The fair-trade company **Ten Thousand Villages,** 14 Ontario St. (© 519/272-0700), sells crafts, jewelry, housewares, and toys from artisans in developing countries. **The Wanderer,** 17 Market Place (© 519/271-0410), stocks wall-hangings, carvings, and semiprecious jewelry.

- **For eclectic tastes:** One of the most interesting stores in Stratford is **The Great Dame,** 96 Downie St. (© 519/275-3000), which sells sweet-smelling toiletries from Europe and a house line, Lily Josephine, that I prefer (the Blood Orange bath products are irresistible). Owner Janet Hill also sells her own artwork here, glamorous paintings of—what else?—great dames. Another wonderful find is **Gallery Indigena,** 69 Ontario St. (© 519/271-7881; www.galleryindigena.com), which sells works of art by the Inuit, Iroquois, Cree, Plains, Woodland, and North Pacific Coast peoples. In business for more than 3 decades, the gallery hosts several "Meet the Artist" events throughout the summer, and it ships artwork all over the world.

choice would be glazed lemon tart and orange sorbet, but hot mango tart with pineapple sorbet is also a dream.

9 Cobourg St. © 519/271-6442. www.rundlesrestaurant.com. Reservations required. 3-course prix-fixe dinner C$78 (US$78/£39). AE, DC, MC, V. Apr–Oct Sat–Sun 11:30am–1:15pm; Tues and Sat 5–7pm; Wed–Fri 5–8:30pm. Closed Nov–Mar.

38 *Finds* CANADIAN   Put together some young Stratford-trained chefs. Add top-notch ingredients sourced from local growers and other Canadian sources. Throw in a laid-back, funky setting that includes a sunny patio. That's the recipe behind 38.

This fun, friendly bistro is a relative newcomer to the Stratford scene, first opening its doors in 2004. Appetizers range from fingerling potato skins with bacon, parmigiano-reggiano, crème fraîche, and an ancho barbecue sauce (yum) to seared foie gras with a sultana raisin compote and micro greens salad (swoon). The mains keep up the pace with offerings like seared B.C. chinook salad with an artichoke-asparagus salad, or the crisp duck confit with an orange-tamari vinaigrette. The short wine list is well chosen and well priced, and everything sold by the bottle is available by the glass, too.

38 Erie St. © 519/271-0321. Reservations recommended. Main courses C$14–C$20 (US$14–US$20/£7–£10). AE, DC, MC, V. Wed–Mon 11:30am–2:30pm and 5:30–9pm.

A NEARBY PLACE TO STAY

Langdon Hall ★★ This elegant house stands at the head of a curving, tree-lined drive. Eugene Langdon Wilks, a great-grandson of John Jacob Astor, completed it in 1902. It remained in the family until 1987, when its transformation into a small country-house hotel began. Today, Langdon Hall is a Relais & Châteaux property, and its 81 hectares (200 acres) of lawns, gardens, and woodlands make for an ideal retreat. The main house, of red brick with classical pediment and Palladian-style windows, has a beautiful symmetry. Throughout, the emphasis is on comfort rather than grandiosity. The luxurious on-site spa offers a complete range of treatments. Most rooms surround the cloister garden. Each room is individually decorated; most have fireplaces. The furnishings consist of handsome reproduction antiques, mahogany wardrobes, ginger-jar porcelain lamps, and armchairs upholstered with luxurious fabrics. The property has a croquet lawn and cross-country ski trails. The light, airy dining room serves fine regional cuisine. Main courses run C$32 to C$45 (US$32–US$45/£16–£23). Tea is served on the veranda, and there's a bar.

R.R. 3, Cambridge, ON N3H 4R8. © 800/268-1898 or 519/740-2100. Fax 519/740-8161. www.langdonhall.ca. 49 units. From C$259 (US$259/£130) double. Rates include full breakfast. AE, DC, MC, V. Free parking. From Hwy. 401, take Exit 275 south, turn right onto Blair Rd., follow signs. Pets accepted. **Amenities:** Dining room; bar; outdoor pool; tennis courts; health club; spa; Jacuzzi; sauna; billiard room; concierge; business center; 24-hr. room service; babysitting; dry cleaning. *In room:* A/C, TV, dataport, coffeemaker, hair dryer, iron.

7 Elora & Fergus: The Elora Gorge & More

115km (71 miles) W of Toronto

If you're driving from Toronto, take Highway 401 west to Highway 6, drive north to Highway 7 east, then get back on Highway 6 north and take it into Fergus. From Fergus take Highway 18 west to Elora.

Elora has always been a special place. To the Natives, the gorge was a sacred site, home of spirits who dwelt within the great cliffs. Early explorers and Jesuit missionaries also wondered at the natural spectacle, but it was Scotsman William Gilkinson who put the town on the map in 1832 when he purchased 5,700 hectares (14,085 acres) on both sides of the Grand River and built a mill and a general store, and named it Elora, after the Ellora Caves in India.

Most of the houses that the settlers built in the 1850s stand today. You'll want to browse the stores along picturesque Mill Street. For real insight into the town's history, pick up a walking-tour brochure from the tourist booth on Mill Street.

The **Elora Gorge** is a 140-hectare (346-acre) park on both sides of the 20m (66-ft.) limestone gorge. Nature trails wind through it. Overhanging rock ledges, small caves, a waterfall, and the evergreen forest on its rim are some of the gorge's scenic delights. The park (© **519/846-9742**) has camping and swimming facilities, plus picnic areas and playing fields. It's a favorite with rock climbers. Located just west of Elora at the junction of the Grand and Irvine rivers, it is open from May 1 to October 15 from 10am to sunset. For information, contact the **Grand River Conservation Authority** (© **866/900-4722** or 519/846-9742; www.grandriver.ca).

An additional summer attraction is the **Elora Festival**, a 3-week music celebration held from mid-July to early August. For more information, contact the **Elora Festival** (© **888/747-7550** or 519/846-0331; www.elorafestival.com).

Fergus (pop. 7,500) was founded by Scottish immigrant Adam Ferguson. There are more than 250 fine old 1850s buildings to see—examples of Scottish limestone architecture—including the foundry, which now houses the Fergus market. The most noteworthy Fergus event is the **Fergus Scottish Festival**, which includes Highland Games, featuring pipe-band competitions, caber tossing, tug-of-war contests, Highland dancing, and the North American Scottish Heavy Events, held usually on the second weekend in August. For more information on the games, contact **Fergus Scottish Festival and Highland Games** (© **866/871-9442** or 519/787-0099; www.fergusscottishfestival.com).

WHERE TO STAY & DINE

Breadalbane Inn 🖈🖈 Located in the heart of Fergus, the inn's main house is an excellent example of 1860s architecture. The stone imported from Scotland is complemented by intricate ironwork, walnut banisters, and newel posts. It was built by the Honorable Admiral Ferguson as a residence, but also served as a nursing home and rooming house before it was converted into a charming country hotel. Guest rooms are all extremely comfortable and elegantly furnished with early Canadian-style furniture. The deluxe suites (four of which are located in the Coach House) boast fireplaces and Jacuzzi tubs. This is a romantic spot, so it's no shocker to discover that the Breadalbane offers several romantic-getaway packages; but it also offers a learn-to-fly-fish package, too.

The Breadalbane dining room is proudly formal, with its polished dark-wood tables set with Royal Doulton china. The cooking—think venison with a lingonberry sauce, or beef strip loin with a shallot-mushroom marmalade—is sublime. Prices range from C$24 to C$32 (US$24–US$32/£12–£16). There's also the Fergusson Room for true Scottish pub fare.

487 St. Andrew St. W., Fergus, ON N1M 1P2. © **888/842-2825** or 519/843-4770. www.breadalbaneinn.com. 13 units. From C$185 (US$185/£93) double. Rates include continental breakfast. AE, MC, V. **Amenities:** Restaurant; bar.

Elora Mill Inn This inn is located in a former gristmill that was built in 1870 and operated until 1974. This explains both its rustic charm and its idyllic view of the Grand River and the Elora Gorge itself. Each guest room is uniquely furnished with a mix of antiques and pieces by local artisans. (Modern conveniences—such as televisions—are hidden from view in armoires). Some rooms in adjacent buildings are duplexes and have decks and river views. Many inn rooms have gorge views, and some units have fireplaces. All rooms are designated nonsmoking.

The dining room is a treat: While the menu is relatively short, it features tasty entrees like the shellfish *pot-au-feu*. It's open daily for lunch and dinner.

77 Mill St. W., Elora, ON N0B 1S0. © **866/713-5672** or 519/846-9118. www.eloramill.com. 32 units. From C$190 (US$190/£95) double. Rates include breakfast. AE, DC, MC, V. **Amenities:** Restaurant. *In room:* A/C, TV.

12

North to Ontario's Lakelands & Beyond

by Hilary Davidson

If southern Ontario is marked by its sprawling cities and picturesque towns, the northern part of the province is remarkable for its vast wilderness. You'll be struck by the rugged beauty of the landscape, the forests of old-growth pine, and the thousands of lakes in the region. The most popular destinations are **Georgian Bay, Algonquin Provincial Park,** and the cottage country of **Huronia** and the **Muskoka Lakes.**

1 Exploring the Region

On weekends, many Torontonians head north to the cottage or to a resort to unwind. But if you want to explore the whole region, drive out from Toronto via Highway 400 north to Barrie. At Barrie, you can either turn west to explore Georgian Bay, the Bruce Peninsula, and Manitoulin Island or continue due north to the Muskoka Lakes, Algonquin Provincial Park, and points farther north.

ESSENTIALS

VISITOR INFORMATION Contact **Ontario Tourism** (© **800/ONTARIO;** www. ontariotravel.net), which operates 18 Travel Information Centres throughout Ontario. If you're beginning your trip in Toronto, visit the information center at the Atrium on Bay (street level) at 20 Dundas St. W.—it's just across Dundas from the Sears store at the northern edge of the Eaton Centre. (The Atrium's mailing address is 595 Bay St., but since the information booth is on the south side of the complex, they use a different street address for the same building.) It's open daily from 8:30am to 5pm; hours are extended during the summer, often to 8pm.

There are also Ontario Tourism **Travel Information Centres** in Barrie (21 Mapleview Drive at Highway 400; © **705/725-7280**), Sault Ste. Marie (261 Queen St. W.; © **705/945-6941**), and Fort Frances (400 Central Ave.; © **807/274-7566**).

Those who are interested in exploring Northern Ontario's rich Native culture should contact the **Northern Ontario Native Tourism Association** (© **866/844-0497** or 807/623-0497; www.nonta.net).

THE GREAT OUTDOORS

In the parts of northern Ontario covered by this chapter, you'll find plenty of terrific places to canoe, hike, bike, or fish. Some 260 provincial parks in Ontario offer ample opportunities for outdoor recreation. Regulations about stays in provincial parks were overhauled in 2005, so even if you've visited before, you'll do well to familiarize yourself with the new rules at **www.ontarioparks.com**. One of the main changes is that all Ontario parks are now classified as either "premium," "middle," or "low"—a reference to a park's level of popularity, and to the fees it charges. Staying 1 night in a premium park can cost C$36 (US$36/£18) per person, whereas a "low" park would be more in the C$22 (US$22/£11) range (there are discounts for seniors and people with disabilities in all parks). The daily in-season entry fee for a vehicle stars at C$7.50 (US$7.50/£3.75). To make a park reservation, contact Ontario Parks Reservations, P.O. Box 25099, 370 Stone Rd. W., Guelph, ON, N1G 4T4 (© 888/668-7275; www. ontarioparks.com); a reservation in any provincial park costs C$12 (US$12/£6).

Ontario Parks uses Google maps on its website. Detailed topographic maps (vital for extended canoeing or hiking trips) can no longer be obtained from the **Canada Map Office;** however, the government bureau does list on its website more than 900 outlets in Canada, the U.S., and overseas where the maps can be purchased. See http://maps.nrcan.gc.ca for details.

BIKING You'll find networks of biking and hiking trails in the national and provincial parks. Contact the individual parks directly for more information. One good route is the **Georgian Cycle and Ski Trail,** running 32km (20 miles) along the southern shore of Georgian Bay from Collingwood via Thornbury to Meaford. The **Bruce Peninsula** and **Manitoulin Island** also offer good cycling opportunities. In the Burk's Falls–Magnetawan area, the **Forgotten Trail** has been organized along old logging roads and railroad tracks. For details, contact the **Georgian Triangle Tourist Association,** 30 Mountain Rd., Collingwood, ON L9Y 5H7 (© **888/227-8667** or 705/445-7722; www.georgiantriangle.org).

CANOEING & KAYAKING Northern Ontario is a canoeist's paradise. You can enjoy exceptional canoeing in **Algonquin, Killarney,** and **Quetico provincial parks;** along the rivers in the **Temagami** (Lady Evelyn Smoothwater Provincial Park) and **Wabakimi** regions; along the **Route of the Voyageurs** in Algoma Country (Lake Superior Provincial Park); and along the rivers leading into James Bay, such as the **Missinaibi. Killbear Provincial Park, Georgian Bay,** and **Pukaskwa National Park** also are good places to paddle.

Around Parry Sound and Georgian Bay, canoeing and kayaking trips are arranged by the **White Squall Paddling Centre,** R.R. 1, 53 Carling Bay Rd., Nobel, ON P0G 1G0 (© **705/342-5324;** www.whitesquall.com). Its offerings range from half-day paddling clinics to 4-day trips. In Algonquin Provincial Park, several outfitters serve park visitors, including **Algonquin Outfitters,** Oxtongue Lake (R.R. 1), Dwight, ON P0A 1H0 (© **705/635-2243;** www.algonquinoutfitters.com), and **Opeongo Outfitters,** P.O. Box 123, Whitney, ON K0J 2M0 (© **800/790-1864** or 613/637-5470; www.opeongooutfitters.com). In the Georgian Bay area, **Killarney Outfitters,** on Highway 637, 5km (3 miles) east of Killarney (© **800/461-1117** or 705/287-2828; www.killarneyoutfitters.com), offers canoe and kayak rentals. Around the Quetico area, contact **Canoe Canada Outfitters,** Box 1810, 300 O'Brien St., Atikokan, ON P0T 1C0 (© **807/597-6418;** www.canoecanada.com).

North of Thunder Bay is excellent land for camping, fishing, hunting, and canoeing in the Wabakimi Wilderness Park, with plenty of scope for beginners, intermediates, and advanced paddlers. Contact **Mattice Lake Outfitters** (© **800/411-0334** or 807/583-2483; www.matticelake.com) for excursions that run between 3 and 9 days. For other outfitters, call the **Northern Ontario Tourist Outfitters Association** (© **705/472-5552;** www.noto.net).

Note: In most provincial parks, you must register with park authorities and provide them with your route.

FISHING   Ontario is one of the world's largest freshwater fishing grounds, with more than 250,000 lakes and 96,000km (60,000 miles) of rivers supporting more than 140 species. The northern area covered in this chapter is the province's best fishing region. Before you go, check out the **Fish Ontario!** website (www.fishontario. com) for the latest information. In summer, on **Manitoulin Island,** fishing for Chinook, coho, rainbow, lake trout, perch, and bass is excellent in Georgian Bay or any of the island lakes—**Mindenmoya, Manitou, Kagawong,** and **Tobacco,** to name a few. Trips can be arranged through **Timberlane Lodge** (© **800/890-4177** or 705/ 377-4078; www.timberlane.ca).

Around **Nipissing** and **North Bay,** there's great fishing for walleye, northern pike, smallmouth bass, muskie, whitefish, and perch. In addition to these, the **Temagami** region offers brook, lake, and rainbow trout. You can find more remote fishing in the **Chapleau** and **Algoma** regions, the **James Bay Frontier,** and north of **Lake Superior.**

Some outfitters will rent lakeside log cabins equipped with a propane stove and refrigerator and motorboat to go along with it. One outfitter to contact is **Mattice Lake Outfitters** (see above). For additional suggestions, contact **Ontario Tourism** or the **Northern Ontario Tourist Outfitters Association** (see above).

Note: You must follow fishing limits and regulations. Canadian residents need to acquire an Outdoors Card before they can get a fishing license; contact the **Ministry of Natural Resources** (© **800/387-7011;** www.mnr.gov.on.ca). Residents of other countries can obtain a fishing license without this added requirement; call © **800/ 667-1940** for information.

GOLF   For a golf getaway, Muskoka is the perfect place to be. The greens here truly are different: Muskoka is located on the **Canadian Shield,** a bedrock layer just a few feet below the surface. The granite thwarted farmers who tried to work the land, but it makes an excellent setting for golfers. The landscape is filled with natural rock outcroppings, and the golf courses take full advantage. Not only does the locale make for a stunning landscape, but it heightens the challenge. Some of the area's top-rated golf courses—such as **Taboo** and the Mark O'Meara Course at **Grandview**—have banded together to create the **Muskoka Golf Trail,** with design-your-own package plans that allow you to stay at one resort but golf at the others (otherwise competition for tee times can be tough). Call © **800/465-3034** or 905/755-0999, or visit www.ultimategolf.ca for details. For general information about all of the courses in Muskoka, including the spectacular **Deerhurst Highlands,** visit www.teeingitup.com/ontario.

Barrie has two exceptional courses—the **National Pines Golf and Country Club** (© **800/663-1549** or 705/431-7000) and the **Horseshoe Resort** golf course (© **800/ 461-5627** or 705/835-2790; www.horseshoeresort.com). Collingwood offers the scenic **Cranberry Resort** course (© **800/465-9077**). In the Huronia region, there's the **Bonaire Golf and Country Club** (© **888/266-2473** or 705/835-3125; www.bonaire golf.com), in the town of Coldwater.

HIKING   The region is a hiker's paradise. The **Bruce Trail,** starting at Queenston, runs for 782km (486 miles), crossing the Niagara escarpment and Bruce Peninsula and ending up in Tobermory. The Bruce Trail Association publishes a map you can get from sporting-goods stores specializing in outdoor activities. In the Bruce Peninsula National Park are four trails, three linked to the Bruce Trail. There's also a hiking trail around Flowerpot Island in Fathom Five National Park.

Manitoulin Island is popular with hikers, particularly the **Cup and Saucer Trail.** South of Parry Sound, hikers can follow the 66km (41-mile) **Seguin Trail,** which meanders around several lakes. In the Muskoka region, trails abound in **Arrowhead Provincial Park** at Huntsville and the Resource Management Area on Highway 11, north of Bracebridge, and in **Algonquin Park.** Algonquin is a great choice for an extended backpacking trip, along the Highland Trail or the Western Uplands Hiking Trail, which combines three loops for a total of 170km (105 miles).

You can do a memorable 7- to 10-day backpacking trip in **Killarney Provincial Park** on the 97km (60-mile) La Cloche Silhouette Trail, which takes in some stunning scenery. **Sleeping Giant Provincial Park** has more than 81km (50 miles) of trails. The Kabeyun Trail provides great views of Lake Superior and the 245m-high (804-ft.) cliffs of the Sleeping Giant. And the **Pukaskwa National Park** offers a coastal hiking trail between the Pic and Pukaskwa rivers along the northern shore of Lake Superior.

For additional hiking information, see the park entries in section 7, "Some Northern Ontario Highlights: Driving along Highways 11 & 17," later in this chapter.

HORSEBACK RIDING   On Manitoulin Island, **Honora Bay Riding Stables,** R.R. 1, Little Current, ON P0P 1K0 (© **705/368-2669;** www.hbrstable.com), offers riding lessons, trail rides, and overnight excursions. Near Sault Ste. Marie, **Cedar Rail Ranch,** R.R. 3, 428 Wharncliffe Rd., Thessalon (© **705/842-2021**), offers both hourly and overnight trail rides with stops for swimming breaks along the route.

SKIING & SNOWMOBILING   Ontario's largest downhill-skiing area is the **Blue Mountain Resorts** in Collingwood. In the Muskoka region, there's downhill skiing at **Hidden Valley Highlands** (© **800/398-9555** or 705/789-1773; www.skihidden valley.on.ca). Up north around Thunder Bay, try **Loch Lomond** (© **807/475-7787**) or **Mount Baldy** (© **807/683-8441**).

You can cross-country ski at **Kamview Nordic Centre** (© **807/625-5075**) and in provincial parks such as **Sleeping Giant** and **Kakabeka Falls.**

One of the top destinations is the **Parry Sound** area, which has an extensive network of cross-country ski trails and more than 1,047km (650 miles) of well-groomed snowmobiling trails. There are nine snowmobiling clubs in the area, and the **Chamber of Commerce** (© **705/746-4213**) can put you in touch with them. For details on cross-country skiing, contact the **Georgian Nordic Ski and Canoe Club,** Box 42, Parry Sound, ON P2A 2X2 (© **888/866-4447** or 705/746-5067; www.georgian nordic.com), which permits day use of its ski trails.

You'll also find groomed cross-country trails at **Sauble Beach** on the Bruce Peninsula and in many of the provincial parks farther north. Along the mining frontier, contact the **Porcupine Ski Runners** at © **705/360-1444** (www.porcupineskirunners. com) in Timmins.

2 From Collingwood/Blue Mountain to Tobermory/ Bruce Peninsula National Park

Nestled at the base of Blue Mountain, **Collingwood** is the town closest to Ontario's largest skiing area. Collingwood first achieved prosperity as a Great Lakes port and shipbuilding town that turned out large lake carriers. Many mansions and the Victorian main street are reminders of those days. And just east of Blue Mountain sweep 14km (9 miles) of golden sands at **Wasaga Beach.**

North beyond Collingwood stretches the **Bruce Peninsula National Park,** known for its limestone cliffs, wetlands, and forest. From Tobermory, you can visit an underwater national park.

ESSENTIALS

GETTING THERE   If you head west from Barrie, northwest from Toronto, you'll go along the west Georgian Bay coast from Collingwood up to the Bruce Peninsula. Driving from Toronto, take Highway 400 to Highway 26 west.

VISITOR INFORMATION   For information, contact the **Georgian Triangle Tourist Association** (© 888/227-8667 or 705/445-7722; www.georgiantriangle.org).

BLUE MOUNTAIN SKI TRAILS, SLIDES, RIDES & MORE

In winter, skiers flock to **Blue Mountain Resort,** at R.R. 3, Collingwood (© 705/445-0231; www.bluemountain.ca). Ontario's largest resort has 16 lifts, 98% snowmaking coverage on 35 trails, and three base lodges. In addition, there are three repair, rental, and ski shops, a ski school, and day care. Lift rates are C$50 (US$50/£25) daily.

In summer, you can take advantage of the so-called "Green Season" attractions. These include tennis, golfing, and mountain biking; there's also a private beach on the shores of Georgian Bay that's a 10-minute ride by shuttle from the resort. Blue Mountain offers many programs for kids, ranging from tennis camp to weekend scavenger hunts on the beach.

My own favorite spot in Collingwood is the **Scenic Caves Nature Adventures,** P.O. Box 215, Collingwood, ON L9Y 3Z5 (© 705/446-0256; www.sceniccaves.com). The area was carved out by glaciers during the Ice Age and today is one of Canada's UNESCO biosphere reserves. The caves are set into limestone cliffs, and offer unique sights—including the "chilling" Ice Cave, a natural refrigerator that boasts icicles even on the hottest days of summer. The lush Fern Cavern is another don't-miss spot. The caves were once home to the Huron village of Ekarenniondi, and you can still see the famous worshiping rock that souls were said to pass on their way to the afterlife.

BRUCE PENINSULA NATIONAL PARK

Bruce Peninsula National Park, Box 189, Tobermory, ON N0H 2R0 (© 519/596-2233 or 519/596-2263; www.pc.gc.ca), features limestone cliffs, abundant wetlands, quiet beaches, and forest sheltering more than 40 species of orchids, 20 species of ferns, and several insectivorous plants. About 100 species of bird also inhabit the park. Three campgrounds (one trailer, two tent) offer 242 campsites (no electricity).

The **Bruce Trail** winds along the Georgian Bay Coastline, while Route 6 cuts across the peninsula; both end in Tobermory. It's one of Ontario's best-known trails, stretching 782km (486 miles) from Queenston in Niagara Falls to Tobermory. The most rugged part of the trail passes through the park along the Georgian Bay shoreline. **Cypress Lake Trails,** from the north end of the Cyprus Lake campground, provide access to the Bruce Trail and lead to cliffs overlooking the bay. You can use canoes and manpowered craft on Cyprus Lake. The best swimming is at **Singing Sands Beach** and **Dorcas Bay,** both on Lake Huron on the west side of the peninsula. Winter activities include cross-country skiing, snowshoeing, and snowmobiling.

AN UNDERWATER NATIONAL PARK

From Tobermory, you can visit an underwater national park, the **Fathom Five National Marine Park,** P.O. Box 189, Tobermory, ON N0H 2R0 (© 519/596-2233;

www.pc.gc.ca), where at least 21 known shipwrecks lie waiting for diving exploration around the 19 or so islands in the park. The most accessible is **Flowerpot Island,** which you can visit by tour boat to view its weird and wonderful rock pillar formations. Go for a few hours to hike and picnic. Six campsites are available on the island on a first-come, first-served basis. Boats leave from Tobermory harbor.

WHERE TO STAY

Beild House Country Inn & Spa 🌸 *Beild* is the Scottish word for shelter, but this charming inn is anything but basic. The stately Edwardian house dates from 1909, and its public spaces are warmed by two fireplaces and decorated with folk art, quill boxes from Manitoulin, and sculptures. Guest rooms are individually furnished with elegant pieces (one contains a bed once owned by the duke and duchess of Windsor). The five third-floor rooms have canopied beds and fireplaces. The hotel offers a sumptuous breakfast and a five-course dinner that's even more so, with such dishes as Georgian Bay trout on spinach with herbed beurre blanc, and pork tenderloin with grilled apples and a port wine glaze.

64 Third St., Collingwood, ON L9Y 1K5. ℂ **888/322-3453** or 705/444-1522. Fax 705/444-2394. www.beildhouse. com. 11 units. From C$280 (US$280/£140) double. Rates include breakfast. AE, MC, V. **Amenities:** Restaurant; spa. *In room:* A/C.

Blue Mountain Resort 🌸 *Kids* Stay here right at the mountain base and you can beat the winter lift lines. In summer, the resort boasts access to a private beach, which is 10 minutes away by shuttle. The real reason to stay at Blue Mountain is its unbeatable selection of activities—it's impossible to be bored here. Guest rooms are on the smallish side and are simply furnished in a country style. You can also rent one- to three-bedroom condos, either slopeside or overlooking the fairway. This is an excellent choice for families—Blue Mountain has a great deal to offer kids.

R.R. 3, Collingwood, ON L9Y 3Z2. ℂ **705/445-0231.** www.bluemountain.ca. 95 units. From C$149 (US$149/£75) double. From C$179 (US$179/£90) condo. Special packages available. AE, MC, V. **Amenities:** Dining room; 2 lounges; outdoor and indoor pools; 18-hole golf course; 12 tennis courts; squash courts; fitness center; spa; mountain-bike and kayak rental; children's programs. *In room:* A/C, TV.

WHERE TO DINE

Alphorn Restaurant *Kids* SWISS Bratwurst, Wiener schnitzel, chicken Ticino, and cheese fondue are just some of the favorites served at this casual, chalet-style restaurant. It's popular with families, and my only caveat is to go early as the place is crowded winter and summer. Save room for the Swiss crepes with chocolate and almonds.

Hwy. 26 W., Collingwood. ℂ **705/445-8882.** Reservations not accepted. Main courses C$14–C$22 (US$14–US$22/ £7–£11). AE, MC, V. Mon–Fri 4–10pm; Sat–Sun 4–10:30pm (summer also daily 11:30am–3pm).

Spike & Spoon Bistro & Gallery 🌸 CONTINENTAL This longtime favorite is under new management, and a few changes have been made as a result. The Spike & Spoon's menu is shorter than it used to be, and an art gallery has been added to the second floor (a charming addition). The setting is still grand—the restaurant is in an elegant mid-19th-century redbrick house that once belonged to a Chicago millionaire—and seasonal dishes are still prepared with fresh ingredients and herbs grown out back.

637 Hurontario St. ℂ **705/446-1629.** Reservations recommended. Main courses C$16–C$26 (US$16–US$26/ £8–£13). MC, V. Tues–Sat noon–2:30pm; Tues–Sun 6–10pm.

3 Manitoulin Island: A Spiritual Escape

Manitoulin Island, named after the Great Indian Spirit Gitchi Manitou, is for those who seek a quiet, remote, and spiritual place, where life is slow.

ESSENTIALS

GETTING THERE   By road, you can cross over the swing bridge connecting Little Current to Great Cloche Island and via Highway 6 to Espanola. You can also reach the island via the **Chi-Cheemaun ferry,** which transports people and cars from Tobermory to South Baymouth on a 1¾- to 2-hour trip. Ferries operate early May to mid-October, with four departures a day in summer. One-way fare is C$14 (US$14/£7) for adults and C$7.05 (US$7.05/£3.50) for children ages 5 to 11; an average-size car costs C$31 (US$31/£16) one-way, and bicycles cost C$6.10 (US$6.10/£3.05). For information, call **Owen Sound Transportation Company** (© 800/265-3163 or 519/376-6601; www.ontarioferries.com) or the **Tobermory Terminal** (© 519/596-2510). Reservations are strongly recommended during the summer, but plan carefully: You can make a reservation on the first and last ferries of the day for no fee, but there is an additional C$20 (US$20/£10) charge for the two ferry trips in the middle of the day.

VISITOR INFORMATION   Contact the **Manitoulin Tourism Association,** P.O. Box 119, Little Current, ON P0P 1K0 (© **705/368-3021;** www.manitoulintourism. com), open daily late April to late October 10am to 4pm, or stop by the **information center** just past the swing bridge in Little Current, which is open daily May through September 10am to 4pm.

EXPLORING THE ISLAND

Native peoples have lived on this land for centuries, and you can visit the **Ojibwa Indian Reserve,** occupying the large peninsula on the island's eastern end. It's home to about 2,500 people of Odawa, Ojibwa, and Potawotami descent; the area was never ceded to the government. The reserve isn't a tourist attraction but may appeal to anyone genuinely interested in modern life on a reservation. Summer weekends are filled with powwows, with the **Wikwemikong Annual Competition Powwow** in early August being one of the biggest draws. The island has long been a haven for artists, and you call visit some in their studios, such as jewelry designer **Ursula Hettmann,** 3 Dominion Rd., Spring Bay (© 705/377-4265; www.hettmannstudio.com). One gallery worth a visit is the **Perivale Gallery,** 1320 Perivale Rd. E., Spring Bay (© 705/377-4847), open the May holiday to mid-September daily 10am to 6pm. Owners Sheila and Bob McMullan scour the country searching for the remarkable artists and craftspeople whose work they display in their log-cabin gallery overlooking Lake Kagawong. Glass, sculpture, paintings, engravings, fabrics, and ceramics fill the space. From Spring Bay, follow Perivale Road east for about 3km (2 miles); turn right at the lake and keep following the road until you see the gallery on the right.

Although there are several communities on the island, the highlights are scenic and mostly outside their perimeters, such as the **Mississagi Lighthouse,** at the western end outside Meldrun Bay. Follow the signs that'll take you about 6km (4 miles) down a dirt road past the limestone/dolomite quarry entrance (from which materials are still shipped across the Great Lakes) to the lighthouse. From late May through Labour Day, you can see how the light keeper lived in this isolated area before the advent of electricity. Its dining room—the Foghorn—is also open in summer. From the light-house, several short trails lead along the shoreline.

The island is great for hiking, biking, bird-watching, boating, cross-country skiing, and just plain relaxing. Charters also operate from Meldrun Bay. You'll find golf courses in Mindemoya and Gore Bay. Fishing is excellent either in Georgian Bay or in the island's lakes and streams. You can arrange trips through **Timberlane Lodge** (© 800/890-4177 or 705/377-4078; www.timberlane.ca). May through October, **Honora Bay Riding Stables,** R.R. 1, Little Current, ON P0P 1K0 (© 705/368-2669; www.hbrstable.com), 27km (17 miles) west of Little Current on Highway 540, offers trail rides.

There are several nature trails on the island. Among the more spectacular is the **Cup and Saucer Trail,** starting 18km (11 miles) west of Little Current at the junction of Highway 540 and Bidwell Road. Also off Highway 540 lies the trail to **Bridal Veil Falls** as you enter the village of Kagawong. Halfway between Little Current and Man-itowaning, stop at **Ten Mile Point** for the view over the North Channel, dotted with 20,000 islands. The best beach with facilities is at **Providence Bay** on the island's south side.

WHERE TO STAY

Your best bet is to seek out one of the island's bed-and-breakfasts, which will most likely be plain and simple but clean. Contact **Manitoulin Tourism Association,** Box 119, Little Current, ON P0P 1K0 (© 705/368-3021; www.manitoulintourism.com). One standout is the **Queen's Inn,** a B&B located in a grand 1880 house that is filled with Victorian antiques (© 705/282-0665; www.thequeensinn.ca).

Rockgarden Terrace Resort and the Shaftesbury Inn   The Rockgarden Ter-race is a family resort on the rocks above Lake Mindemoya, long known for its Bavar-ian flair. Its accommodations are mostly motel-style units furnished in contemporary style, but there are also four log cabin–style suites. The dining room seems like an Aus-trian hunting lodge, with trophies displayed on the oak-paneled walls and a cuisine featuring German-Austrian specialties such as Wiener schnitzel, sauerbraten, goulash, and beef rolladen. The newly opened Shaftesbury Inn is a different experience alto-gether: Its nine guest rooms are in a sprawling house that dates back to 1884. The byword here is romance.

R.R. 1, Spring Bay, ON P0P 2B0. © 705/377-4652. www.rockgardenresort.on.ca. 18 motel units, 4 chalet suites, 9 guest rooms. From C$102 (US$102/£51) per person, including breakfast and dinner. Weekend and weekly packages available. MC, V. **Amenities:** 3 restaurants; lounge; outdoor pool; nearby golf course; Jacuzzi; sauna; bike rental; fish-ing pier. *In room:* TV.

WHERE TO DINE

The food on the island is simple and homey. In summer, the **Foghorn Restaurant** at the **Mississagi Lighthouse** overlooking Meldrun Bay is arguably the most scenic spot (note that it's open only from late May through Labour Day). For more sophisticated palate-pleasers, go to the **Rockgarden Terrace Resort** (© 705/377-4642) near Spring Bay. In Little Current, one of the nicest casual spots on the island for break-fast, lunch, or dinner is the **Anchor Inn Bar & Grill,** 1 Water St. (© 705/368-2023). While the menu carries a wide range of dishes, the specialty here is local seafood, so you'll find plenty of whitefish, rainbow trout, and arctic char. Open year-round (except for the patio, which is open June–Sept), the Anchor Inn serves meals daily from 7am to 11pm.

4 Along Georgian Bay: Midland & Parry Sound

MIDLAND

Midland is the center for cruising through the thousands of beautifully scenic Georgian Islands, and **30,000 Island Cruises** (© **705/549-7795;** www.georgianbaycruises. com) offers 3-hour cruises following the route of Brele, Champlain, and La Salle up through the inside passage to Georgian Bay. May to Canadian Thanksgiving (U.S. Columbus Day), boats usually leave the town dock twice a day. Fares are C$18 (US$18/£9) for adults, C$16 (US$16/£8) for seniors, C$8 (US$8/£4) for children ages 5 to 14, free for children 4 and under.

Midland lies 53km (33 miles) east of Barrie and 145km (90 miles) north of Toronto. If you're driving from Barrie, take Highway 400 to Highway 12W to Midland.

EXPLORING THE AREA

See the box below for details on **Sainte-Marie Among the Hurons.** Across from the Martyrs' Shrine, the **Wye Marsh Wildlife Centre** (© **705/526-7809;** www.wyemarsh. com) is a 60-hectare (148-acre) wetland/woodland site offering wildlife viewing, guided and self-guided walks, and canoe excursions in the marsh. A floating boardwalk cuts through the marsh, fields, and woods, where trumpeter swans have been reintroduced into the environment and now number 40 strong. Reservations are needed for the canoe trips (call the number above) offered in July and August and occasionally September. In winter, cross-country skiing and snowshoeing are available. For information, visit the website. Admission is C$10 (US$10/£5) for adults, C$6.50 (US$6.50/£3.25) for students, seniors and kids, and free for children 3 and under. The center is open daily 9am to 5pm year-round, but is closed on Dec. 25.

In town, **Freda's,** in an elegant home at 342 King St. (© **705/526-4851**), serves excellent Continental cuisine. Just down the street at no. 249 King St. is **Riv Bistro** (© **705/526-9432**), which offers Mediterranean cooking and plenty of seafood.

EN ROUTE TO THE MUSKOKA LAKES: ORILLIA

Traveling to the Muskoka Lakeland region, you'll probably pass through **Orillia** (from Barrie, take Hwy. 11). Here you can visit Canadian author/humorist **Stephen Leacock**'s summer home (50 Museum Dr.; © **705/329-1908;** www.leacockmuseum. com), a green-and-white mansard-roofed and turreted structure with a central balcony overlooking the beautiful lawns and garden sweeping down to the lake. The interior is filled with heavy Victorian furniture and mementos of this Canadian Mark Twain, author of 35 volumes of humor, including *Sunshine Sketches of a Little Town,* which caricatured many of the residents of Mariposa, a barely fictionalized version of Orillia. Admission is C$5 (US$5/£2.50) for adults, C$4 (US$4/£2) for seniors, C$3 (US$3/£1.50) for students, and C$2 (US$2/£1) for children ages 3 to 12. It's open weekdays from 9am to 5pm; closed on legal holidays.

GEORGIAN BAY ISLANDS NATIONAL PARK

The park consists of 59 islands in Georgian Bay and can be reached via water taxi from Honey Harbour, a town north of Midland right on the shore. (As you're taking Hwy. 400 north, branch off to the west at Port Severn to reach Honey Harbour.) Hiking, swimming, fishing, and boating are the name of the game in the park. In summer and on weekends and holidays, the boaters really do take over—but it's a quiet retreat weekdays, late August, and off-season. The park's center is on the largest island, **Beausoleil,** with camping and other facilities. For more information, contact the Superintendent,

The Tragic Tale of Sainte-Marie Among the Hurons

Midland's history dates from 1639, when Jesuits established here a fortified mission, **Sainte-Marie Among the Hurons,** to bring Christianity to the Huron tribe. However, the mission retreat lasted only a decade, for the Iroquois, jealous of the Huron-French trading relationship, stepped up their attacks in the area. By the late 1640s, the Iroquois had killed thousands of Hurons and several priests and had destroyed two villages within 10km (6 miles) of Sainte-Marie. Ultimately, the Jesuits burned down their own mission and fled with the Hurons to Christian Island, about 32km (20 miles) away. But the winter of 1649 was harsh, and thousands of Hurons died. In the end, only a few Jesuits and 300 Hurons were able to make the journey back to the relative safety of Québec. The Jesuits' mission had ended in martyrdom. It was 100 years before the Native Canadians in the region saw Europeans again, and those newcomers spoke a different language.

Today, local history is recaptured at the **mission** (© 705/526-7838), 8km (5 miles) east of Midland on Highway 12 (follow the HURONIA HERITAGE signs). The blacksmith stokes his forge, the carpenter squares a beam with a broad-axe, and the ringing church bell calls the missionaries to prayer, while a canoe enters the fortified water gate. A film depicts the life of the mission-aries. Special programs given in July and August include candlelight tours and a 1½-hour canoeing trip (at extra cost). Admission is C$11 (US$11/£5.50) for adults, C$9.75 (US$9.75/£4.80) for seniors and students, C$8.50 (US$8.50/£4.25) for youths 6-12, and free for children 5 and under (all prices are slightly discounted in early May and in the fall after Labour Day). From April 30 to November 2, it's open daily 10am to 5pm.

Just east of Midland on Highway 12 rise the twin spires of the **Martyrs' Shrine** (© 705/526-3788), a memorial to the eight North American martyr saints. As six were missionaries at Sainte-Marie, this imposing church was built on the hill overlooking the mission, and thousands make pilgrimages here each year. The bronzed outdoor stations of the cross were imported from France. Admission is C$3 (US$3/£1.50) per person, free for children 9 and under.

Georgian Bay Islands National Park, Box 28, Honey Harbour, ON P0E 1E0 (© 705/756-2415; www.pc.gc.ca).

THE PARRY SOUND AREA

Only 225km (140 miles) north of Toronto and 161km (100 miles) south of Sudbury, the Parry Sound area is the place for active vacations. For details, contact the **Parry Sound Area Chamber of Commerce,** 70 Church St. (© 705/746-4213; www.parry soundchamber.ca), which is open daily from 10am to 4pm.

There's excellent canoeing and kayaking; if you need an outfitter, contact **White Squall Paddling Centre,** R.R. 1, 53 Carling Bay Rd., Nobel, ON P0G 1G0 (© 705/342-5324; www.whitesquall.com), which offers both day trips and multiday excursions. Run by **30,000 Island Cruise Lines,** 9 Bay St., Parry Sound, ON P2A 1S4

Fun Fact **Bright Lights in the Wilderness**

While most visitors to northern Ontario are drawn by the peaceful expanses of wilderness, increasing numbers are gravitating to the **Casino Rama,** R.R. 6, Rama, L0K 1T0 (✆ 888/817-7262 or 705/329-3325; www.casino-rama.com), the 18,000-sq.-m (195,000-sq.-ft.) state-of-the-art casino just east of Orillia. Open 24 hours, the casino boasts more than 2,100 slot machines and 109 gaming tables. There are also three full-service restaurants, a food arcade, and a lounge with live entertainment (headliners include Michael Bolton, Jewel, the Barenaked Ladies, and that Vegas perennial Wayne Newton). So when all that peace and quiet starts getting to you, you know where to turn.

(✆ 705/549-3388; www.georgianbaycruises.com), the *Island Queen* cruises through the 30,000 islands for 3 hours. It leaves the town dock once or twice a day ; fares are C$18 (US$18/£9) for adults, C$16 (US$16/£8) for seniors, C$8 (US$8/£4) for children ages 5 to 14, and free for children 4 and under.

And there are many winter diversions as well—loads of cross-country ski trails and more than 1,000km (621 miles) of well-groomed snowmobiling trails. For details on cross-country skiing, contact the **Georgian Nordic Ski and Canoe Club,** Box 42, Parry Sound, ON P2A 2X2 (✆ 888/866-4447 or 705/746-5067; www.georgian nordic.com), which permits day use of their ski trails.

Nature lovers will head for **Killbear Provincial Park,** P.O. Box 71, Nobel, ON P0G 1G0 (✆ 705/342-5492, or 705/342-5227 for reservations), farther north up Highway 69; it offers 1,600 hectares (3,954 acres) set in the middle of 30,000 islands. There are plenty of watersports—swimming at a 3km (2-mile) beach on Georgian Bay, snorkeling or diving off Harold Point, and fishing for lake trout, walleye, perch, pike, and bass. The climate is moderated by the bay, which explains why trillium, wild leek, and hepatica bloom. Among the more unusual fauna are the Blandings and Map turtles that inhabit the bogs, swamps, and marshes.

There are three **hiking trails,** including 3.5km (2.2-mile) Lookout Point, leading to a commanding view over Blind Bay to Parry Sound; and the Lighthouse Point Trail, crossing rocks and pebble beaches to the lighthouse at the peninsula's southern tip. There's also **camping** at 883 sites in seven campgrounds.

WHERE TO STAY

The inn below is exquisite and expensive, but there are other places to stay in the area. The **Parry Sound & District Bed and Breakfast Association** (www.parrysoundbb. com) has detailed listings on its website. And at the edge of Otter Lake, the modest, family-oriented **Resort Tapatoo,** Box 384, Parry Sound, ON P2A 2X5 (✆ 705/378-2208), rents cottages, rooms, and suites and offers boating, windsurfing, waterskiing, canoeing, fishing, and swimming in an indoor pool. Rates start at C$100 (US$100/£50).

Inn at Manitou ✿✿ The Inn at Manitou is a stunner. Everything about the foyer glows; the space is opulently furnished in French style with elegant touches of chinoiserie. Beyond the foyer and a sitting area, a veranda stretches around the building's rear, with wicker and bamboo chairs overlooking the tennis courts. To the foyer's left is the very inviting Tea Room with a view of the lake. A steep staircase leads down to the swimming and boating dock. The accommodations are up the hill in several cedar lodges overlooking the lake. The standard rooms are small and simple; the deluxe units contain fireplaces, small sitting areas, and private sun decks, while the luxury rooms feature sizable living rooms with fireplaces, whirlpool baths, saunas, and private decks.

Downstairs in the main building is the Club Lounge nightclub, a billiard room, and an open-to-view wine cellar, filled with fine vintages, where twice-weekly wine tastings are held. The resort's cuisine is renowned and is part of the reason the Relais & Châteaux organization awarded the property the distinguished Gold Shield. At dinner, a casual three-course bistro menu and a more elaborate four-course gourmet menu are offered along with a special spa menu. Afterward, you can retire to the Tea Room for coffee, petit fours, and truffles.

McKellar, ON P0G 1C0. ℂ 800/571-8818 or 705/389-2171. Fax 705/389-3818. www.manitou-online.com. 35 units, 1 3-bedroom country house, 1 4-bedroom country house. From C$295 (US$295/£148) per person double. Rates for country houses start at C$1,200 (US$1,200/£600). Rates include breakfast, lunch, afternoon tea, and dinner. Special packages available; special musical, cooking, and other events scheduled. AE, MC, V. Closed late Oct to early May. **Amenities:** Restaurant; bar; outdoor heated pool; nearby golf course; instructional golfing range; 20 tennis courts; spa; bikes, sailboats, and canoes; concierge; room service (7am–11pm); babysitting; dry cleaning. *In room:* A/C, TV, minibar, hair dryer, iron, safe.

5 The Muskoka Lakes: A Land of Resorts ⍟

Just a 90-minute drive north of Toronto, the Muskoka region has been a magnet for visitors since the 19th century. While the area proved futile for farming (it's located on the Canadian Shield, where you need dig only a foot or two in some places to come up against sheets of granite), its more than 1,600 lakes, unspoiled wilderness, and laid-back attitude made it an excellent place for a retreat. In the past decade, Muskoka's charms have expanded to include excellent golf courses, soothing spas, and top-notch restaurants. While the region is at its most popular in summer, when families congregate at the resorts and Hollywood celebrities such as Goldie Hawn and Tom Hanks lounge at their lakefront "cottages," this is a great area to visit at any time of the year.

Once accessible only by the water, Muskoka is still a boater's dream. The region also has several towns of note: Gravenhurst, Bracebridge, Port Carling, Huntsville, and Bala. Located a few kilometers apart, these communities date back to the 1850s, when logging was Muskoka's primary industry. Filled with historic sites and more modern attractions, it's well worth devoting a day or two to explore them (fortunately, they are all easily reachable by car these days).

ESSENTIALS

GETTING THERE You can drive from the south via Highway 400 to Highway 11, from the east via highways 12 and 169 to Highway 11, and from the north via Highway 11. It's about 160km (100 miles) from Toronto to Gravenhurst, 15km (9 miles) from Gravenhurst to Bracebridge, 25km (16 miles) from Bracebridge to Port Carling, and 34km (21 miles) from Bracebridge to Huntsville. **VIA Rail** (ℂ 416/366-8411; www.viarail.ca) services Gravenhurst, Bracebridge, and Huntsville from Toronto's Union Station. An airport about 18km (11 miles) from Gravenhurst is used mainly for small aircraft. Several other landing strips and a helicopter-landing pad are at the Deerhurst Resort in Huntsville.

VISITOR INFORMATION For information on the region, contact **Muskoka Tourism,** on Highway 11 at Severn Bridge, R.R. 2, Kilworthy, ON P0E 1G0 (ℂ **800/267-9700** or 705/689-0660; www.discovermuskoka.ca).

> ### Tips Finding a B&B
>
> If you don't want to pay resort rates or restrict yourself to staying at an American Plan resort, contact the **Muskoka Bed and Breakfast Association,** 175 Clairmont Rd., Gravenhurst, ON P1P 1H9 (© **705/687-4511;** www.bbmuskoka.com), which represents 28 or so B&Bs throughout the area.

EXPLORING THE TOWNS

Both Gravenhurst and Huntsville are lovely towns that are well worth a visit. They are scenic, but they also have enough shops, restaurants, and public spaces to make them interesting. Unless you have kids, there's not much of a reason to linger in Bracebridge.

GRAVENHURST

Gravenhurst is Muskoka's first town—the first you reach if you're driving from Toronto and the first to achieve town status (in 1887 at the height of the logging boom).

The **Norman Bethune Memorial House** is the restored 1890 birthplace of Dr. Norman Bethune, 235 John St. N. (© **705/687-4261**). In 1939, this surgeon, inventor, and humanitarian died tending the sick in China during the Chinese Revolution. Tours of the historic house include a modern exhibit on Bethune's life. A visitor center displays gifts from Chinese visitors, and an orientation video is shown. In summer, the house is open daily from 10am to 4pm June through October, weekdays only from 1 to 4pm November through May. Admission is C$3.50 (US$3.50/£1.75) adults and C$2 (US$2/£1) for children 6 to 16, free for children 5 and under.

Sailing is one of Muskoka's greatest summer pleasures. Gravenhurst is home to the Muskoka Fleet, which includes a lovingly restored coal-powered 1887 steamship, the **RMS *Segwun.*** There are a variety of cruising options available, such as the 1-hour tour; a 2½-hour lunch cruise; and a 4-hour late-afternoon tour of **Millionaire's Row,** where you can be dazzled by the real estate as well as the natural beauty of the region. Reservations are required for all of the tours; call © **705/687-6667** or visit **www.realmuskoka.com** for more information. Prices start at C$16 (US$16/£8) adults and C$9.50 (US$9.50/£4.75) for children for tours.

Year-round, there are theater performances at the **Gravenhurst Opera House** (© **705/687-5550**), which celebrates its 107th anniversary in 2008. In summer only, there are shows at the **Port Carling Community Hall** (© **705/765-5221**). For either, tickets usually cost between C$15 and C$30 (US$15–US$30/£7.50–£15).

BRACEBRIDGE: SANTA'S WORKSHOP

Halfway between the equator and the North Pole, **Bracebridge** bills itself as Santa's summer home, and **Santa's Village** (© **705/645-2512;** www.santasvillage.ca) is an imaginatively designed fantasyland full of delights: pedal boats and bumper boats on the lagoon, a roller-coaster sleigh ride, a Candy Cane Express, a carousel, and a Ferris wheel. At Elves' Island, kids can crawl on a suspended net and over or through various modules—the Lunch Bag Forest, Cave Crawl, and Snake Tube Crawl. Rides, water attractions, and roving entertainers are all part of the fun. Mid-June through Labour Day, it's open daily from 10am to 6pm. Admission is C$20 (US$20/£10) ages 5 and up, C$16 (US$16/£8) for seniors and children 2 to 4, and free for children under 2.

The Muskoka Lakes Region

PORT CARLING

As waterways became the main means of transportation in the region, **Port Carling** grew into the hub of the lakes. It became a boat-building center when a lock was installed connecting Lakes Muskoka and Rosseau, and a canal between Lakes Rosseau and Joseph opened all three to navigation. The **Muskoka Lakes Museum** on Joseph Street (*©* **705/765-5367**) captures the flavor of this era. July and August, it's open Monday through Saturday from 10am to 5pm and Sunday noon to 4pm; June, September, and October, hours are Tuesday through Saturday from 10am to 4pm and Sunday from noon to 4pm. Admission is C$3.50 (US$3.50/£1.75) adults and C$2.50 (US$2.50/£1.25) seniors and students.

HUNTSVILLE

Since the late 1800s, lumber has been the name of the game in Huntsville, and today it's Muskoka's biggest town, with major manufacturing companies. You can see some of the region's early history at the **Muskoka Heritage Place,** which includes **Muskoka Pioneer Village,** 88 Brunel Rd. (*©* **705/789-7576;** www.muskokaheritageplace.org). It's open daily from 11am to 4pm from mid-May to mid-October. Admission is C$10 (US$10/£5) adults, C$7 (US$7/£3.50) children 3 to 12, and free for children 2 and under. Muskoka Heritage Place also features the **Portage Flyer Steam Train.** Once

---

Fun Fact **The Shania Connection**

The Deerhurst has many charms to recommend it, and whether or not you stay there, you must check out its excellent song-and-dance stage show. Now in its 26th year, it's famous in part because the phenomenally talented Shania Twain performed in it for 3 years (1988–1990). Twain has kept up her connection with the Deerhurst since, even having her wedding there. In 2002, she brought Katie Couric and a NBC film crew to reminisce about her days on its stage. Twain continues to visit the resort—and when she does, she always checks out the show. Every summer, the show is different, but it is always a pleasure to see.

---

part of the world's smallest commercial railway, it ran from 1904 till 1958. Now it has been reborn as a tourist attraction, and you can ride its scenic route from Tuesday to Saturday for C$5 (US$5/£2.50) for adults and C$3 (US$3/£1.50) for kids.

Robinson's General Store on Main Street in Dorset (© **705/766-2415**) is so popular, it was voted Canada's best country store. Wood stoves, dry goods, hardware, pine goods, and moccasins—you name it, it's here.

WHERE TO STAY

Muskoka is famous for its lakes, but also for its resorts. While I normally like to wander from place to place when I travel to a particular area, I honestly think I could just stay put at one of the resorts here and be completely entertained for a week. Bed-and-breakfast and country-inn choices also abound. Contact **Muskoka Tourism** (© **800/267-9700** or 705/689-0660; www.discovermuskoka.ca).

RESORTS

Deerhurst Resort ★★★ *Kids*   The Deerhurst is an excellent spot for a family vacation, though it's also very popular with conference groups. This stunning resort complex rambles over 320 hectares (791 acres), and it boasts an array of amenities that boggles the mind: two 18-hole golf courses (part of the Muskoka Golf Trail) and a golf academy; a full-service Aveda spa; seemingly endless kilometers of nature trails for hiking (or snowmobiling or cross-country skiing in winter); canoeing, kayaking, and all manner of watersports; an ambitious musical revue than runs all summer; and horseback riding. (Note that most of the activities, including golf, the spa, and skiing, are available to visitors not staying at the resort.)

The accommodations here are spread out among several buildings on the property. They range from high-ceilinged hotel rooms in the Terrace and Bayshore buildings to fully appointed one-, two-, or three-bedroom suites, many with fireplaces and/or whirlpools. The suites come with extras like CD players, TVs, and VCRs; some have full kitchens with microwaves, dishwashers, and washer/dryers. The most expensive suites are the three-bedroom units on the lake. One major draw is the top-notch Aveda spa, which has some of the most talented therapists I've ever encountered.

1235 Deerhurst Dr., Huntsville, ON P1H 2E8. © **800/461-4393** or 705/789-6411. Fax 705/789-2431. www.deerhurst resort.com. 388 units. Summer from C$229 (US$229/£115) double; rest of the year from C$139 (US$139/£70) double. AE, DC, DISC, MC, V. Free parking. Take Canal Rd. off Hwy. 60 to Deerhurst Rd. **Amenities:** 2 restaurants; 2 bars; 2 indoor pools and 3 outdoor pools; 2 18-hole golf courses; tennis courts; 3 squash courts; racquetball court; indoor sports complex; spa; 11 Jacuzzis; sauna; children's programs; concierge; business center; limited room service; laundry service; dry cleaning. *In room:* A/C, TV, dataport, minibar, hair dryer.

Delta Grandview Resort ᗢ *(Kids)*   If the Deerhurst is for the folks on the fast track, the Delta Grandview is for those looking for a more measured pace. This smaller resort retains the natural beauty and contours of the original farmstead even while providing the latest resort facilities. Eighty accommodations are traditional hotel-style rooms, but most units are suites in a series of buildings, some down beside the lake and others up on the hill with a lake view. The main dining room, the Rosewood Inn, is located in one of the resort's original buildings and overlooks Fairy Lake. Snacks are served in summer at the Dockside Restaurant right on the shores of the lake. In summer, the free Kidzone program provides supervision—and plenty of fun—for kids 4 to 12 daily from 8am to 4pm. That way, adults can spend the day on the Mark O'Meara golf course.

939 Hwy. 60, Grandview Drive, Huntsville, ON P1H 1Z4. (℃) **888/778-5050** or 705/789-4417. Fax 705/789-1674. www.deltahotels.com. 123 units. Summer from C$190 (US$190/£95) double; rest of the year from C$110 (US$110/£55) double. Seasonal discounts available. AE, MC, V. Free parking. **Amenities:** 2 restaurants; indoor and outdoor pools; 18-hole and 9-hole golf courses; 3 tennis courts; health club; children's programs; babysitting. *In room:* A/C, TV.

Taboo Resort ᗢᗢᗢ *(Kids)*   Near the town of Gravenhurst in the southern Muskoka region, Taboo stands out for its sleek sophistication in a bucolic setting. Known until May 2003 as Muskoka Sands, the resort's new name may conjure up images of a hedonistic adults-only retreat. The truth is anything but: Taboo is a family-friendly zone, with a kids' club that schedules activities for every day of the week during the high season in summer. But the fact that the resort is so willing to take care of the children means that many adults can soak up spa treatments or dine at one of the on-site restaurants without a second thought.

Taboo is best known for its golf course, which Mike Weir (the 2003 Masters champion) calls his home course. The course is a major stop on the Muskoka Golf Trail. The Golf Academy can help those who want to improve their game. Another reason to come to Taboo is the excellent dining at Elements Restaurant, Culinary Theatre & Lounge (p. 470).

One of my favorite things about Taboo is that every single room, large and small alike, has its own deck or balcony. While all of the sophisticated offerings at the resort are excellent, nothing beats taking in the utterly serene and beautiful setting it enjoys.

Muskoka Beach Rd., R.R. 1, Gravenhurst, ON P1P 1R1. (℃) **800/461-0236** or 705/687-2233. Fax 705/687-7474. www.tabooresort.com. 157 units. Summer from C$295 (US$295/£148) double; rest of the year from C$150 (US$150/£75) double. AE, MC, V. Free parking. **Amenities:** 2 restaurants; bar; 1 indoor and 3 outdoor pools; 2 golf courses (18-hole and 9-hole); 5 tennis courts; squash court; health club; spa (in-room treatments also available); Jacuzzi; sauna; children's programs; game room; concierge; business center; limited room service; laundry service; dry cleaning. *In room:* A/C, TV, hair dryer.

Windermere House Resort ᗢ   The appearance of the house brings you into the 1870s, with its stone-and-clapboard facade and romantic turrets. (The truth is, the original building was destroyed by fire in 1996 and was rebuilt according to its original 1870s design in 1997.) It overlooks well-manicured lawns that sweep down to Lake Rosseau. Out front stretches a broad veranda furnished with Adirondack chairs and geranium-filled window boxes. Rebuilding allowed the guest rooms to enjoy modern conveniences (including air-conditioning) while retaining a traditional, homey look. Most of the rooms have gorgeous views (the best look over the lake), and a few have balconies or walkout decks.

Off Muskoka Rte. 4 (P.O. Box 68), Windermere, ON P0B 1P0. (℃) **800/461-4283** or 705/769-3611. Fax 705/769-2168. www.windermerehouse.com. 78 units. From C$220 (US$220/£110) double in summer; seasonal discounts available. Rates include breakfast. Weekly rates also available. AE, MC, V. Free parking. **Amenities:** Restaurant; lounge; outdoor pool; golf course; tennis courts; children's programs; limited room service; laundry service; dry cleaning. *In room:* A/C, TV, minibar.

COUNTRY INNS

Inn at the Falls 🔆 *Finds*   This attractive "inn" is actually a group of seven Victorian houses on a quiet cul-de-sac overlooking Bracebridge Falls and the Muskoka River. The inviting gardens are filled with delphiniums, peonies, roses, and spring flowers, plus there's an outdoor heated pool. The guest rooms are individually decorated, with antiques and English chintz. Some units have fireplaces, Jacuzzis, and balconies; others have views of the falls. The Fox & Hounds is a popular local gathering place at lunch or dinner. In winter, the fire crackles and snaps, but in summer, the terrace is filled with flowers and umbrella-shaded tables. The more elegant Carriage Room serves upscale Continental fare. It's a perfect getaway-from-it-all spot, so I try to ignore the fact that the Inn now has Wi-Fi access. . . .

1 Dominion St., P.O. Box 1139, Bracebridge, ON P1L 1V3. ℂ 877/645-9212 or 705/645-2245. Fax 705/645-5093. www.innatthefalls.net. 42 units. From C$120 (US$120/£60) double. Extra person C$16 (US$16/£8). Rates include breakfast. AE, DC, MC, V. Free parking. **Amenities:** 2 restaurants; outdoor pool; nearby golf course. *In room:* TV.

Severn River Inn *Value*   The Severn River Inn (19km/12 miles north of Orillia and 14km/9 miles south of Gravenhurst) occupies a 1906 building that has served as a general store, post office, telephone exchange, and boardinghouse. The guest rooms are individually furnished with pine and oak pieces, brass beds, floral-patterned fabrics, flouncy pillows, and quilts. The suite contains a sitting room and the original old bathtub and pedestal sink (this is the only room with a bathtub—the others all have showers only). The intimate restaurant, with a Victorian ambience, is candlelit at night. In summer, the screened-in porch and outdoor patio overlooking the river are favored dining spots. The menu features contemporary Continental cuisine.

Cowbell Lane off Hwy. 11 (P.O. Box 100), Severn Bridge, ON P0E 1N0. ℂ 705/689-6333. Fax 705/689-2691. www.severnriverinn.com. 10 units. From C$70 (US$70/£35) double; from C$120 (US$120/£60) minisuite. Rates include breakfast. MC, V. Free parking. **Amenities:** Restaurant; lounge; nearby golf course. *In room:* A/C.

WHERE TO DINE

Eclipse 🔆🔆 CANADIAN/INTERNATIONAL   Recently renovated and remodeled, Eclipse remains a Muskoka favorite. With an expansive lake view, this spacious dining room with a soaring ceiling of Douglas fir beams is a blend of fine dining and casual Muskoka charm. Open for breakfast and dinner, the restaurant has a lengthy menu with plenty of vegetarian options, so it's relatively easy to please different tastes. My favorite appetizer is the baked phyllo pastry filled with forest mushrooms and goat cheese, but the Sizzle—the signature dish—is the most popular (tiger shrimp sautéed in garlic, dried chiles, and white wine, and baked under mozzarella). Entrees run the gamut from breast of pheasant filled with wild rice and cranberries to a rack of lamb rubbed with fresh herbs and sourdough crumbs and served with apple-maple compote. The wine list is just as interesting as the menu. There are 300 selections, which sounds daunting, though the well-informed staff can help you choose.

1235 Deerhurst Dr., Huntsville, ON P1H 2E8. ℂ 705/789-6411. www.deerhurstresort.com. Reservations recommended. Main courses C$27–C$36 (US$27–US$36/£14–£18). AE, DC, MC, V. Daily 7–11am and 5–11pm.

Elements Restaurant, Culinary Theatre & Lounge 🔆🔆🔆 *Finds* CANADIAN/ FUSION   It's strange to think that some Torontonians are coming to Muskoka to eat, given the big city's impressive culinary pedigree. But the chefs here have cooked at some of Toronto's famous kitchens, so perhaps it's no wonder that Elements is

Rest, Relax, Recharge

Northern Ontario is deservedly famous for outdoor activities like skiing, boating, hiking, and biking. But a growing segment of the tourist trade is coming for another reason altogether: spas. Getting away from it all in these parts no longer automatically means going on an ice-fishing expedition; it could just as easily involve a hot-stone massage. The spas listed below offer almost all of their services to both sexes. For more information, including a free directory, contact the **Spas Ontario** association at © **800/990-7702** or visit the website at **www.spasontario.com**. Here are two of the best:

Deerhurst Resort (p. 468): The Deerhurst thoughtfully provides children's programs, so you can drop off the tykes before you go for your aromatherapy massage or Ancient Dead Sea Mud Wrap. The emphasis here is on total relaxation, and with all of the delicious products and scents, it's impossible to resist. The Deerhurst was one of the founding members of Spas Ontario, and the standards at the spa are excellent. The highly trained therapists are particularly talented at working out those inevitable golf-induced kinks.

Taboo Resort (p. 469): This is the choice for those who want to lie in the lap of luxury—and get a Swedish or reflexology massage while they're at it. The name of the newly built spa is Indulgence, which seems terribly appropriate. The list of services is comprehensive, and includes facials, manicures, pedicures, waxing, and, of course, massage. There are also several tempting body treatments, such as the Cranberry-Maple Body Polish, which includes a maple-sugar exfoliating scrub, a cranberry-infused whirlpool bath, and a rubdown with cranberry moisturizer (mmm . . .).

attracting gourmets from far and wide. The restaurant's floor-to-ceiling windows face west, so that you can take in the glorious sunset over the lake. Its a la carte menu includes wonders like Nova Scotia lobster with charred-corn-and-crab bread pudding.

The Culinary Theatre offers a unique experience. Only 30 seats are available at a time for this culinary school/live cooking show mix. Guests participate by selecting ingredients. Each meal—consisting of tasting menus of three, five, or seven courses—is cooked as you watch.

Muskoka Beach Rd., R.R. 1, Gravenhurst, ON P1P 1R1. © **705/687-2233**. www.tabooresort.com. Reservations strongly recommended. Main courses C$29–C$45 (US$29–US$45/£15–£23); tasting menus start at C$90 (US$90/£45). AE, DC, MC, V. Daily 6–10pm.

3 Guys and a Stove ♠ ⓚⁱᵈˢ INTERNATIONAL   This is a family restaurant with a special menu for kids. But don't let the unpretentious atmosphere and the casual name fool you—the cooking is *very* fine. The curried pumpkin–and–sweet potato soup is an absolute must-have when it's on the menu; the spicy chicken stew is another surefire winner. This restaurant is also a terrific choice for vegetarians: the list of pasta and rice main-course dishes is substantial, and includes gems like the shitake and button-mushroom risotto with sweet onions and garlic.

143 Hwy. 60, Huntsville. © **705/789-1815**. www.3guysandastove.com. Main courses C$13–C$38 (US$13–US$38/£6.50–£19). AE, MC, V. Daily 11am–9:30pm.

6 Algonquin Provincial Park: Canoeing, Fishing & More

Immediately east of Muskoka lie **Algonquin Provincial Park**'s 7,770 sq. km (3,000 sq. miles) of wilderness—a haven for the naturalist, camper, and fishing and sports enthusiast.

ESSENTIALS

GETTING THERE   The main access points (West Gate and East Gate) are on Highway 60, east of Huntsville.

VISITOR INFORMATION   Algonquin's excellent **Visitor Centre** on Highway 60 at Km 43 (© **705/633-5572**) is open daily from 9am to 9pm from late June through Labour Day, and from 10am to 4pm or 6pm during the rest of the year. The center features exhibits about the park's history, a bookstore, a restaurant, and a gallery of Algonquin art. Inside the East Gate, at Km 54.5, is the **Algonquin Logging Museum.** It's open daily from 9am to 5pm from mid-May through early October; during the rest of the year, only its outdoor exhibits along an easy-to-walk 1.3km (.8-mile) trail are accessible.

FEES   Regulations about stays in provincial parks were overhauled in 2005, so even if you've visited Algonquin, you'll need to familiarize yourself with the new rules at **www.ontarioparks.com.** Day-use fees are C$13 (US$13/£6.50) per vehicle, but camping and other fees vary depending on the date you're visiting, the ages of the people in your group, and other factors. You can call © **888/ONT-PARK** to make a reservation (reservation fee of C$12/US$12/£6 required).

EXPLORING THE PARK

Algonquin Park is an especially memorable destination for the canoeist, with more than 1,610km (1,000 miles) of **canoe routes** for paddling. One of Canada's largest provincial parks, it served as a source of inspiration for the famous Group of Seven artists. Algonquin Park is a sanctuary for moose, beaver, bear, and deer, and offers camping, canoeing, backpacking trails, and plenty of fishing for speckled, rainbow, and lake trout and smallmouth black bass (more than 230 lakes have native brook trout and 149 have lake trout).

Among the **hiking trails** is the 2.4km (1.5-mile) self-guided trail to the 100m-deep (328-ft.) Barron Canyon on the park's east side. In addition, there are 16 day trails. The shortest is the 1km (.6-mile) **Hardwood Lookout Trail,** which goes through forest to a fine view of Smoke Lake and the surrounding hills. Other short walks are the 1.5km (1-mile) **Spruce Bog Boardwalk** and the **Beaver Pond Trail,** a 2km (1.2-mile) walk with good views of two beaver ponds.

For longer backpacking trips, the **Highland Trail** extends from Pewee Lake to Head, Harness, and Mosquito lakes for a round-trip of 35km (22 miles). The **Western Uplands Hiking Trail** combines three loops for a total of 169km (105 miles), beginning at the Oxtongue River Picnic Grounds on Highway 60. The first 32km (20-mile) loop will take 3 days; the second and third loops take longer. There's also a **mountain bike trail.**

Fall is a great time to visit—the maples usually peak in the last week of September. Winter is wonderful, too; you can **cross-country ski** on 80km (50 miles) of trails. Three trails lie along the Highway 60 corridor with loops ranging from 5km (3 miles) to 24km (15 miles). Mew Lake Campground is open in winter, and you can rent skis at the west gate. Spring offers the best **trout fishing** and great **moose viewing** in May and June. During summer, the park is most crowded, but it's also when park staff lead expeditions to hear the timber wolves howling in response to naturalists' imitations. More than 250 **bird species** have been recorded in the park, including the rare gray jay, spruce grouse, and many varieties of warbler. The most famous bird is the common loon, found nesting on nearly every lake.

WHERE TO STAY & DINE

There are eight **campgrounds** along Highway 60. The most secluded sites are at **Canisbay** (248 sites) and **Pog Lake** (281 sites). **Two Rivers** and **Rock Lake** have the least secluded sites; the rest are average. Four remote wilderness campgrounds are set back in the interior: **Rain Lake** with only 10 sites; **Kiosk** (17 sites) on Lake Kioshkokwi; **Brent** (28 sites) on Cedar Lake, great for pickerel fishing; and **Achray** (39 sites), the most remote site on Grand Lake, where Tom Thomson painted many of his great landscapes (the scene that inspired his Jack Pine is a short walk south of the campground). Call the **Visitor Centre** (✆ **705/633-5572**) for details.

Arowhon Pines ⚐   Located 8km (5 miles) off Highway 60 down a dirt road, Arowhon guarantees you total seclusion and serenity. The cabins are dotted around the pine forests surrounding the lake, and each is furnished uniquely with assorted Canadian pine antiques; they vary in layout but all have bedrooms with private bathrooms and sitting rooms with fireplaces. You can opt for a private cottage or one containing anywhere from 2 to 12 bedrooms and sharing a communal sitting room with a stone fireplace. Sliding doors lead onto a deck. There are no TVs or phones—just the sound of the loons, the gentle lap of the water, the croaking of the frogs, and the sound of oar paddles cutting the smooth surface of the lake. You can swim in the lake or canoe, sail, row, or windsurf. At the heart of the resort is a hexagonal dining room beside the lake with a spacious veranda. A huge fireplace is at the room's center. The food is good, with fresh ingredients, and there's plenty of it. No alcohol is sold in the park, so if you wish to have wine with dinner you'll need to bring your own (the staff will uncork it free of charge).

Algonquin Park, ON P1H 2G5. ✆ **866/633-5661**, 705/633-5661 in summer, or 416/483-4393 in winter. www. arowhonpines.ca. 50 units. From C$189 (US$189/£95) per person double. A 15% service charge is automatically added to the bill. Rates include all meals. MC, V. **Amenities:** Dining room; 2 tennis courts; sauna; free use of canoes, sailboats, and kayaks; hiking trails. *In room:* Hair dryer.

Killarney Lodge   The Killarney isn't as secluded as Arowhon (the highway is still visible and audible), but it too has charm. The pine-log cabins, with decks, stand on a peninsula jutting out into the Lake of Two Rivers. Furnishings include old rockers, country house–style beds, desks, chests, and braided rugs. A canoe comes with every cabin. Home-style meals are served in an attractive rustic log dining room. You can relax in the log cabin lounge warmed by a woodstove.

Algonquin Park, ON P1H 2G9. ✆ **866/473-5551**, 705/633-5551 in summer, or 416/482-5254 in winter. www.killarney lodge.com. 26 cabins. From C$159 (US$159/£80) per person double. Rates include all meals. MC, V. Closed mid-Oct to mid-May. Enter the park on Hwy. 60 from either Dwight or Whitney. **Amenities:** Dining room; lounge; watersports equipment rentals.

7 Some Northern Ontario Highlights: Driving along Highways 11 & 17

From the Muskoka region, **Highway 11** winds up toward the province's northernmost frontier via North Bay, Kirkland Lake, Timmins (using Rte. 101), and Cochrane before sweeping west to Nipigon. There it links up briefly with **Highway 17,** the

Northern Ontario

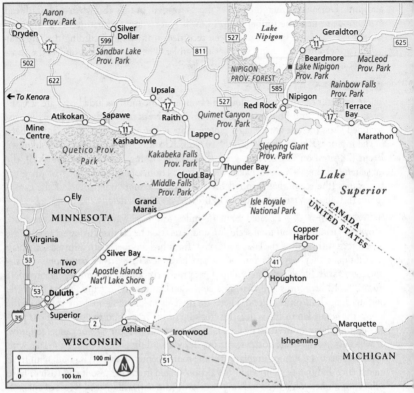

route traveling the northern perimeters of the Great Lakes from North Bay via Sudbury, Sault Ste. Marie, and Wawa, to Nipigon. At Nipigon, highways 11 and 17 combine and lead into Thunder Bay. They split again west of Thunder Bay, with Highway 17 taking a more northerly route to Dryden and Kenora and Highway 11 proceeding via Atikokan to Fort Frances and Rainy River.

TRAVELING HIGHWAY 11 FROM HUNTSVILLE TO NORTH BAY, COBALT & TIMMINS

From Huntsville, Highway 11 travels north past **Arrowhead Provincial Park** (© 705/789-5105), with close to 400 campsites. The road heads through the town of Burk's Falls, at the head of the Magnetawan River, and the town of South River, the access point for **Mikisew Provincial Park** (© 705/386-7762), with sandy beaches on the shore of Eagle Lake.

From South River, the road continues to **Powassan,** famous for its excellent cedar-strip boats. Stop in at B. Giesler and Sons to check out these reliable specimens. The next stop is **North Bay,** on the northeast shore of Lake Nipissing. The town originated on the northern Voyageurs route traveled by fur traders, explorers, and missionaries. Noted for its nearby hunting and fishing, North Bay became world famous in 1934, when the Dionne quintuplets were born in nearby Corbeil; their original home is now a local museum.

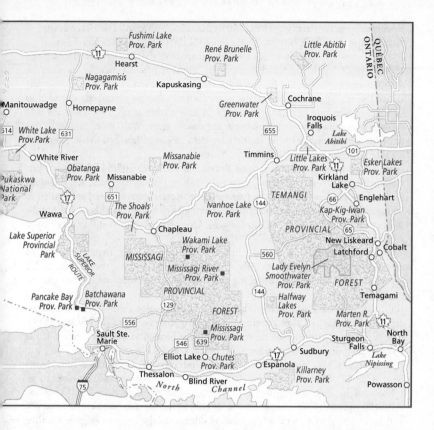

From North Bay, Highway 11 continues north toward New Liskeard. Along the route, you'll pass **Temagami,** at the center of a superb canoeing region. Its name is Ojibwa for "deep waters by the shore." The region is also associated with the legendary figure Grey Owl, who first came to the area in 1906 as a 17-year-old named Archie Belaney. Archie had always dreamed of living in the wilderness among the Indians; eventually he learned to speak Ojibwa and became an expert in forest and wilderness living. He abandoned his original identity and name, renamed himself Grey Owl, married an Indian woman, and became accepted as a Native trapper. He subsequently published a series of books that quickly made him a celebrity.

Finlayson Point Provincial Park (© **705/569-3205**) is on Lake Temagami. The small park—only 94 hectares (232 acres)—is a great base for exploring the lake and its connecting waterways. Steep rugged cliffs, deep clear waters dotted with 1,300 islands, and magnificent stands of tall pines along its shore make for an awesome natural display. The park offers 113 secluded campsites (many on the lakeshore), plus canoeing, boating, swimming, fishing, hiking, and biking.

Lady Evelyn Smoothwater Provincial Park is 45km (28 miles) northwest of Temagami and encompasses the highest point of land in Ontario Maple Mountain and Ishpatina Ridge. Waterfalls are common along the Lady Evelyn River, with Helen Falls cascading more than 24m (79 ft.). White-water skills are required for river travel. There are no facilities. For details, contact District Manager, **Temagami District,** Ministry of Natural Resources, P.O. Box 38, Temagami, ON P0H 2H0 (© **705/569-3205**).

The next stop is **Cobalt,** which owes its existence to the discovery of silver here in 1903. Legend has it that blacksmith Fred LaRose threw his hammer at what he thought were fox's eyes, but he hit one of the world's richest silver veins. Cobalt was also in the ore; hence the name of the town. By 1905 a mining stampede extended to Gowganda, Kirkland Lake, and Porcupine. A little farther north, **New Liskeard** is at the northern end of Lake Timikaming at the mouth of the Wabi River. Strangely, this is a dairy center, thanks to the "Little Clay Belt," a glacial lake bed that explains the acres of farmland among the rock and forest.

Even farther north, **Kap-kig-iwan Provincial Park** (© **705/544-2050**) lies just outside **Englehart,** also the name of the river rushing through the park, and is famous for its "high falls," which give the park its name. Recreational facilities are limited to 64 campsites and self-guided trails. Farther along Highway 11, **Kirkland Lake** is the source for more than 20% of Canada's gold. One original mine is still in production after more than half a century.

At **Iroquois Falls,** a town on the Abitibi River, it's said some Iroquois once raided the Ojibwa community near the falls. After defeating the Ojibwa, the Iroquois curled up to sleep in their canoes tied along the riverbank. But when the Ojibwa cut the canoes loose, the Iroquois were swept over the falls to their deaths. From Iroquois Falls, you can take Route 101 southwest to **Timmins.** Along the way you'll pass the access road to **Kettle Lakes Provincial Park,** 896 Riverside Dr. (© **705/363-3511**). The park's name refers to the depressions that are formed as a glacier retreats. It has 137 camping sites, five trails, three small beaches, and 22 lakes to fish and enjoy.

In Timmins, you can take the **Timmins Underground Gold Mine Tour,** James Reid Road (© **800/387-8466** or 705/360-8500; www.timminsgoldminetour.com). Discovered by Benny Hollinger in 1909, it produced more than C$400 million (US$400 million/£$200 million) worth of gold in its day. You don helmets, overalls, and boots and grab a torch before walking down into the mine to observe a scaling bar, slusher, mucking machine, and furnace at work and to view the safety room to which the miners rushed in the event of a rockfall. At the surface is a panoramic view from the Jupiter Headframe and ore samples to be inspected along the Prospector's Trail. Admission is C$19 (US$19/£9.50) for adults, C$17 (US$17/£8.50) for students, and C$8 (US$8/£4) for surface tours only. In July and August, tours are offered daily at 9:30am, 11:30am, 1:30pm, and 3pm. During the rest of the year, two tours are offered each day, though it's essential to call ahead as the Timmins Underground center isn't open every day.

Adjacent to the gold mine is a center dedicated to a more recent—but just as valuable—Timmins export: Shania Twain. The country-pop singer's hometown has dedicated a **Shania Twain Centre,** 220 Algonquin Blvd. E. (© **800/387-8466** or 705/360-8510; www.shaniatwaincentre.com), which opened in June 2001. Filled with memorabilia detailing the star's climb, this is really just for devoted fans—particularly those willing to shell out good money to see displays such as Shania's suede parka. Admission is C$9 (US$9/£4.50) for adults and C$7 (US$7/£3.50) for students and seniors. A combined ticket with the gold mine is C$23 (US$23/£12) for adults and C$20 (US$20/£10) for students and seniors. It is open daily 10am to 5pm.

For additional city information, contact the **Tourism Timmins,** 220 Algonquin Blvd. E. (© **800/387-8466** or 705/360-2619; www.tourismtimmins.com). Hours are daily from 10am to 4pm June through August, and noon to 3pm during the rest of the year.

COCHRANE: STARTING POINT OF THE *POLAR BEAR EXPRESS*

Back on Highway 11, the next stop is **Cochrane,** at the junction of the Canadian National Railway and the Ontario Northland Railway. From here, the famous *Polar Bear Express* ⚓ departs to Moosonee and Moose Factory, making one of the world's great railroad/nature excursions. The train travels 4½ hours, 300km (186 miles) from Cochrane along the Abitibi and Moose rivers (the latter, by the way, rises and falls 2m/6½ ft. twice a day with the tides) to Moosonee on James Bay, gateway to the Arctic.

Your destination, **Moosonee** and **Moose Factory,** on an island in the river, will introduce you to frontier life—still challenging, though it's easier today than when Native Cree and fur traders traveled the rivers and wrenched a living from the land 300 years ago. You can take the cruiser *Polar Princess* or a freighter-canoe across to Moose Factory (site of the Hudson's Bay Company, founded in 1673) and see the 17th-century Anglican church and other sights. If you stay over, you can also visit **Fossil Island,** where you can see 350-million-year-old fossils in the rocks, and the **Shipsands Waterfowl Sanctuary,** where you may see rare birds, including the Gyrfalcon.

Trains operate the end of June to Labour Day, but tickets are limited because priority is given to the excursion passengers. Round-trip fares are C$90 (US$90/£45) for adults and C$45 (US$45/£23) for children ages 2 to 11. Various 3-day/2-night and 4-day/3-night packages are also offered from North Bay and Toronto. Contact **Ontario Northland** (© 800/268-9281 or 705/272-5338, ext. 28; www.polarbearexpress.ca). From June to Labour Day, you'll need to make lodging reservations well in advance.

For information, contact the **Corporation of the Town of Cochrane** (© 705/272-4361; www.town.cochrane.on.ca).

WHERE TO STAY

The accommodations in this area are low key—think motels and B&Bs. To see the available options, contact the **James Bay Frontier Travel Association** (© 800/461-3766 or 705/360-1989; www.jamesbayfrontier.com).

EN ROUTE FROM COCHRANE TO NIPIGON

From Cochrane, Highway 11 loops farther north past the turnoff to **Greenwater Provincial Park** (© 705/272-6335). This 5,350-hectare (13,220-acre) park has good camping (90 sites in three campgrounds), swimming, boating (rentals available), hiking, and fishing on 26 lakes. One of the park's more challenging trails goes along Commando Lake. Spectacular views of the northern lights are an added attraction.

Highway 11 continues west past **Rene Brunelle Provincial Park** (© 705/367-2692) and **Kapuskasing,** where General Motors has its cold-weather testing facility, to **Hearst,** Canada's "Moose Capital," at the northern terminus of the Algoma Central railway. It continues all the way to **Lake Nipigon Provincial Park** (© 807/887-5000) on the shores of Lake Nipigon. The lake is famous for its black-sand beaches. Facilities include 60 camping sites, boat rentals, and self-guided trails.

The nearby town of **Nipigon** stands on Lake Superior at the mouth of the Nipigon River. It's where the world-record brook trout, weighing 6.5 kilograms (15 lb.), was caught. At this point highways 17 and 11 join and run all the way into Thunder Bay.

TRAVELING HIGHWAY 17 ALONG THE PERIMETER OF THE GREAT LAKES

Instead of traveling north from North Bay up Highway 11 to explore the northern mining frontier, you could choose to take Highway 17 along the perimeter of the Great Lakes. I consider this the more scenic and interesting route.

SUDBURY

The road travels past Lake Nipissing through Sturgeon Falls to **Sudbury,** a nickel-mining center. With a population of 160,000, this is northern Ontario's largest metro area, a rough-and-ready mining town with a landscape so barren that U.S. astronauts were trained here for lunar landings.

Sudbury's two major attractions are **Science North,** 100 Ramsey Lake Rd. (© 705/522-3701, or 705/522-3700 for recorded info; www.sciencenorth.ca) and the **Dynamic Earth** (formerly the Big Nickel Mine), 122 Big Nickel Rd. (© 705/522-3701; http://dynamicearth.ca). The more impressive of the two is **Science North,** which occupies two giant stainless-steel snowflake-shaped buildings dramatically cut into a rock outcrop overlooking Lake Ramsey. You can conduct experiments such as simulating a hurricane, monitoring earthquakes on a seismograph, or observing the sun through a solar telescope. In addition to the exhibits, a 3-D film/laser experience, *Shooting Star,* takes you on a journey 5 billion years into the past, charting the formation of the Sudbury Basin. A performance in another theater tells the story of naturalist Grey Owl. There's also a water playground (kids can play and adults can build a sailboat), space-exploration and weather command centers, and a fossil-identification workshop. It's open daily May and June 9am to 5pm and July to Canadian Thanksgiving (U.S. Columbus Day) 9am to 6pm; call ahead for winter hours (usually 10am–4pm). **Dynamic Earth** explores life under the surface of our planet. The 9m (30-ft.) replica of a Canadian nickel remains from this destination's former life as the Big Nickel Mine. It's open daily March through April 10am to 4pm, May through June 9am to 5pm, and July through Labour Day 9am to 6pm. Admission to both Science North and Dynamic Earth is C$40 (US$40/£20) for adults and C$30 (US$30/£15) for seniors and children. Admission to Science North only is C$18 (US$18/£9) for adults, and C$15 (US$15/£7.50) for students and seniors. Admission to Dynamic Earth only is C$16 (US$16/£8) for adults and C$13 (US$13/£6.50) for seniors and children. (The dual admission is more expensive because it also includes admission to an IMAX film and some other promotions.)

For further information on Sudbury, contact **Sudbury Tourism** (© 877-304-8222 or 705/523-5587; www.sudburytourism.ca).

Where to Stay

Your best bets for lodgings are the chains—**Best Western,** 151 Larch St. (© 705/673-7801); the **Comfort Inn,** which has two locations in town: 2171 Regent St. S. (© 705/522-1101) and 440 Second St. (© 705-560-45022); or **Howard Johnson,** 50 Brady St. (© 705/675-5602).

A CROWN JEWEL: KILLARNEY PROVINCIAL PARK

Less than an hour's drive southwest of Sudbury is **Killarney Provincial Park** (© 705/287-2900), called the "crown jewel" of the province's park system. This 48,479-hectare (119,795-acre) park on the north shore of Georgian Bay, accessible only on foot or by canoe, features numerous lakes and a fabulous range of quartzite ridges. More than 100 species of birds breed here, including kingfishers and loons on the lakes in summer. Four members of the Group of Seven painted in the region: Frank Carmichael, Arthur Lismer, A. Y. Jackson, and A. J. Casson. The park has 122 campsites at the George Lake campground near the entrance.

Killarney is a paradise for the canoeist (rentals are available in the park). Compared to Algonquin Park, it's much quieter—you have to cross only one lake to find total privacy at Killarney, while at Algonquin you may have to canoe across three lakes. Three hiking trails loop from the campground and can be completed in 3 hours.

For a more ambitious backpacking tour, the park's **La Cloche Silhouette Trail** winds for more than 97km (60 miles) through forest and beaver meadows past crystal-clear lakes. The trail's main attraction is Silver Peak, towering 370m (1,214 ft.) above Georgian Bay and offering views of 81km (50 miles) on a clear day. This is a serious undertaking; it'll take 7 to 10 days to complete the whole trail.

The best fishing is in Georgian Bay; sadly, acid rain has killed off most of the fish in the lakes.

DRIVING WEST FROM SUDBURY

From Sudbury, it's 305km (189 miles) west along Highway 17 to Sault Ste. Marie, or the Soo, as it's affectionately called. At Serpent River, you can turn off north to the town of Elliot Lake, which is near **Mississagi Provincial Park** (© **705/848-2806**) and the river of the same name. The park has 90 campsites and swimming and offers some fine canoeing. Hikers will find short self-guided trails as well as trails from 6km to 16km (3.7–10 miles) long.

Continuing along Highway 17, bordering the North Channel, will bring you past the access point to **Fort St. Joseph National Park** (© **705/941-6203**) on St. Joseph Island (between Michigan and Ontario) and into the Soo, 305km (190 miles) west of Sudbury.

SAULT STE. MARIE

The highlights of any visit to **Sault Ste. Marie** are the **Soo locks,** the **Agawa Canyon Train,** and the **Bon Soo,** one of North America's biggest winter carnivals, celebrated in late January and early February. There's an **Ontario Tourism Information Centre** at 261 Queen St. W. (© **705/945-6941**).

The **Soo,** at the junction of lakes Superior and Huron, actually straddles the border. The twin cities, one in Ontario and the other in Michigan, are separated by the St. Marys River rapids and now are joined by an international bridge. The Northwest Fur Trading Company founded a post here in 1783, building a canal to bypass the rapids from 1797 to 1799. That canal was replaced later by the famous **Soo locks**—four on the American side and one on the Canadian. The locks are part of the St. Lawrence Seaway system, enabling large international cargo ships to navigate from the Atlantic along the St. Lawrence to the Great Lakes. Lake Superior is about 7m (23 ft.) higher than Lake Huron, and the locks raise and lower the ships. You'll find a viewing station at both sets of locks. June to about October 10, you can take a 2-hour cruise through the lock system daily at a cost of C$26 (US$26/£13) for adults, C$21 (US$21/£11) for youths, and C$13 (US$13/£6.50) for children. For information, contact **Lock Tours Canada** (© **877/226-3665** or 705/253-9850; www.locktours.com).

The Algoma Central Railway, which operates the **Agawa Canyon Tour Train** ⊛, was established in 1899. The Canadian artists known as the Group of Seven used to shunt up and down the track in a converted boxcar they used as a base camp for canoe excursions into the wilderness. Today, the tour train takes you on a 184km (114-mile) trip from the Soo to the Agawa Canyon, where you can enjoy a 2-hour stop to view the waterfalls, walk the nature trails, or enjoy a picnic. The train snakes through a vista of deep ravines and lakes, hugging the hillsides and crossing gorges on skeletal trestle bridges. The most spectacular time to take the trip is mid-September to mid-October, when the fall foliage is at its best, but it's a magical trip at any time of year. In the fall, fares are at their highest—C$85 (US$85/£43) for adults, C$53 (US$53/£27) for youths ages 5 to 18, and C$28 (US$28/£14) for children 4 and under. In other seasons there are substantial discounts, though in some cases there are also changes to the schedule (the winter train only stops for a few minutes in the canyon, so it's a shorter voyage). For information, contact the **Algoma Central Railway** (© 800/242-9287 or 705/946-7300; www.agawacanyontourtrain.com).

The surrounding area offers great fishing, snowmobiling, cross-country skiing, and other sports opportunities. Contact **Tourism Sault Ste. Marie** (© 800/461-6020 or 705/759-5432; www.saulttourism.com) for information.

Where to Stay

Whatever you do, make your reservations in advance. If you're taking the Algoma Train, the most convenient hotel is the **Quality Inn Bay Front,** 180 Bay St. (© 705/945-9264), across from the train station. You can also try the other chains: the **Holiday Inn,** 208 St. Marys River Dr., on the downtown waterfront (© 705/949-0611), or **Comfort Inn,** 333 Great Northern Rd. (© 705/759-8000). The **Best Western,** 229 Great Northern Rd. (© 705/942-2500), has great facilities for families—a waterslide, bowling, indoor golf, and more.

LAKE SUPERIOR PROVINCIAL PARK

Alona and Agawa bays are in **Lake Superior Provincial Park** ⊛ (© 705/856-2284). The 1,550-sq.-km (598-sq.-mile) park, one of Ontario's largest, offers the haunting shoreline and open waters of Longfellow's "Shining Big-Sea Water," cobble beaches, rugged rocks, and limitless forests. Dramatic highlights include rock formations such as Lac Mijinemungshing, the Devil's Chair, and Old Woman Bay. At the park's east end, the Algoma Central Railway provides access to the park along the Agawa River. At Agawa Rock, you can still see traces of the early Ojibway people—there are centuries-old paintings depicting animals and scenes from their legends.

The magnificent scenery has attracted artists for years, including the Group of Seven. Among the most famous paintings of the park are Frank Johnston's *Canyon and Agawa,* Lawren Harris's *Montreal River,* A. Y. Jackson's *First Snows,* and J. E. H. MacDonald's *Algoma Waterfall and Agawa Canyon.* As for wildlife, you may see moose as well as caribou, which once were common here and have been reintroduced along the coast areas and offshore islands. More than 250 bird species have been identified here; about 120 types nest in the area.

Some 269 camping sites are available at three **campgrounds.** The largest, at Agawa Bay, has a 3km (2-mile) beach. Crescent Lake, at the southern boundary, is the most basic, while Rabbit Blanket Lake is well located for exploring the park's interior.

The park has eight canoe routes, ranging in length from 3km to 56km (2–35 miles) and range in difficulty from easy to challenging, with steep portages and white water. Rentals are available at the campgrounds, but outfitter services are limited. Contact **Township of Wawa Tourism** (© 800/367-9292, ext. 260, or 705/856-2244, ext. 260; www.wawa.cc/tourism.aspx).

Fun Fact **Where Winnie-the-Pooh Was Born**

On Highway 17, 98km (61 miles) from Wawa, is **White River,** birthplace of Winnie-the-Pooh. In 1916, Winnipeg soldier Harry Colebourne, on his way to Europe from his hometown, bought a mascot for his regiment here and named it Winnie. When he shipped out from London, he couldn't take the bear cub, so it went to the London Zoo, where it became the inspiration for A. A. Milne's classic character. Just outside White River are the spectacular **Magpie High Falls.**

The 11 **hiking trails** range from short interpretive trails to rugged overnight trails up to 55km (34 miles) long. The most accessible is the **Trapper's Trail,** featuring a wetlands boardwalk from which you can watch beaver, moose, and great blue heron. The 16km (10-mile) **Peat Mountain Trail** leads to a panoramic view close to 150m (492 ft.) above the surrounding lakes and forests. The 26km (16-mile) **Toawab Trail** takes you through the Agawa Valley to the 25m (82-ft.) Agawa Falls. The **Orphan Lake Trail** is popular due to its moderate length and difficulty, plus its panoramic views over the Orphan and Superior lakes, a pebble beach, and Baldhead Falls. The **Coastal Trail,** along the shoreline, is the longest at 55km (34 miles), stretching from Sinclair Cove to Chalfant Cove, and will take 5 to 7 days to complete. The fall is the best time to hike, when the colors are amazing and the insects are few.

In winter, though there are no formal facilities or services provided, you can cross-country ski, snowshoe, and ice-fish at your own risk.

WAWA & THE CHAPLEAU GAME RESERVE

From the park, it's a short trip into **Wawa,** 230km (143 miles) north of the Soo, the site of the famous salmon derby. Wawa serves as a supply center for canoeists, fishermen, and other sports folks.

East of Wawa is some of Ontario's best canoeing and wildlife viewing (especially moose and waterfowl) in **Chapleau-Nemegosenda River Provincial Park**—200km (124 miles) northeast of the Soo and 100km (62 miles) west of Timmins. It's accessible from Chapleau or by Emerald Lake on Highway 101 to Nemegosenda Lake. There are no facilities, and hunting is not permitted. Nonresidents need a permit to camp, costing C$10 (US$10/£5) per person per night. For additional info, contact the **Ministry of Natural Resources Northeast Zone,** 190 Cherry St., Chapleau, ON P0M 1K0 (✆ 705/864-1710, ext. 214; www.ontarioparks.com).

PUKASKWA NATIONAL PARK

Southwest of White River on the shores of Lake Superior is Ontario's only national park in the wilderness, **Pukaskwa National Park,** Hattie Cove, Heron Bay, ON P0T 1R0 (✆ 807/229-0801; www.pc.gc.ca/pukaskwa), reached via Highway 627 from Highway 17. The interior is accessible only on foot or by boat.

In this 1,878-sq.-km (725-sq.-mile) park survives the most southerly herd of **woodland caribou**—only 40 of them. Lake Superior is extremely cold, and for this reason rare arctic plants are also found here. **Hattie Cove** is the center of most park activities and services, including a 67-site campground, a series of short walking trails, access to three sand beaches, parking facilities, and a visitor center.

The 60km (37-mile) **Coastal Hiking Trail** winds from Hattie Cove south to the North Swallow River and requires proper planning and equipment (camping areas are every half- to a full-day's hike apart). A 15km (9-mile) day hike along this trail can be taken to the White River Suspension Bridge. There are also backcountry trails. In winter, cross-country skiers can use 6km (4 miles) of groomed trails or hazard the fast slopes and sharp turns created by the topography. Snowshoers are welcome, too.

CANOEING THE WHITE & PUKASKWA RIVERS

The White and Pukaskwa rivers offer white-water adventure. You can paddle the easily accessed **White River** any time during the open-water season. Many wilderness adventurers start from nearby **White Lake Provincial Park** and travel 4 to 6 days to the mouth of the White River and then paddle about an hour north on Lake Superior to Hattie Cove.

The **Pukaskwa River** is more remote, more difficult (with rugged and long portages and a 260m/853-ft. drop between the headwaters at Gibson Lake and the river mouth at Lake Superior), and navigable only during the spring runoff. The best place to start is where the river crosses Highway 17 near Sagina Lake and paddle to Gibson Lake via Pokei Lake, Pokei Creek, and Soulier Lake. Otherwise, you'll have to fly in from White River or Wawa.

Outfitters include **Naturally Superior Adventures,** R.R. 1 Lake Superior, Wawa ON P0S 1K0 (© **800/203-9092** or 705/856-2939; www.naturallysuperior.com).

MORE PROVINCIAL PARKS

From White River, it's 270km (168 miles) to **Nipigon** and **Nipigon Bay,** offering fine rock, pine, and lake vistas. It's another 12km (7½ miles) to **Ouimet Canyon Provincial Park** (© **807/977-2526**), at the location of a spectacular canyon 100m (330 ft.) deep, 150m (492 ft.) wide, and 1.5km (1 mile) long. When you stand on the edge of the canyon and gaze out over the expanse of rock and forest below, you can sense the power of the forces that shaped, built, and split the earth's crust and then gouged and chiseled this crevasse—one of eastern Canada's most striking canyons. The park is for day use only.

About 25km (16 miles) on, the next stop is **Sleeping Giant Provincial Park** (© **807/977-2526**), named after the rock formation the Ojibwa Indians say is Nanabosho (the Giant), turned to stone after disobeying the Great Spirit. The story goes that Nanabosho, who had led the Ojibwa to the north shore of Lake Superior to save them from the Sioux, discovered silver one day, but fearing for his people, he told them to bury it on an islet at the tip of the peninsula and keep it a secret. But vanity got the better of one of the chieftains, who made silver weapons for himself. Subsequently, he was killed in battle against the Sioux. Shortly afterward, Nanabosho spied a Sioux warrior leading two white men in a canoe across Lake Superior to the source of the silver. To keep the secret, he disobeyed the Great Spirit and raised a storm that sank and drowned the white men. For this, he was turned into stone.

Take Route 587 south along the Sibley Peninsula, which juts into the lake. Among the park's natural splendors are bald eagles, wild orchids, moose, and more than 190 species of birds. Facilities include 168 campsites at Marie Louise Campground plus about 40 interior sites. There's a beach at the campground.

The trail system consists of three self-guided nature trails, three walking trails, and a network of about 70km (43 miles) of hiking trails, including the 2-day Kabeyun

Trail, which originates at the Thunder Bay lookout and follows the shoreline south to Sawyer Bay. The park has great cross-country skiing with 30km (19 miles) of trails.

THUNDER BAY

Just before you enter Thunder Bay, stop and honor Terry Fox at the **Monument and Scenic Lookout.** Not far from this spot he was forced to abandon his heroic cross-Canada journey to raise money for cancer research. To access the remote **Wabakimi region,** take Route 527 north just east of Thunder Bay. It'll take you to Armstrong, the supply center for this wilderness region.

From the port city of **Thunder Bay**—an amalgam of Fort William and Port Arthur—wheat and other commodities are shipped out via the Great Lakes all over the world. Fifteen grain elevators still dominate the skyline. You can't really grasp the city's role and its geography unless you take the **Harbor Cruise.** Other highlights include **Fort William Historical Park** (© 807/473-2344; www.fwhp.ca), about 16km (10 miles) outside the city on the Kaministiquia River. From 1803 to 1821, this reconstructed fort was the headquarters of the North West Fur-Trading Company, which was later absorbed by the Hudson's Bay Company. At press time, the fort was closed for extensive repairs due to flooding in 2006, but is expected to reopen in May 2008.

Where to Stay

For hotel, motel, and B&B accommodations, contact the **North of Superior Tourism Association** at © 800/265-3951 or visit www.nosta.on.ca. Your best bets are the chains: **Best Western,** 655 Arthur. St. W. (© 807/577-4241); **Super 8 Motel,** 439 Memorial Ave. (© 807/344-2612); and the **Valhalla Inn,** 1 Valhalla Inn Rd. (© 807/ 577-1121; www.valhallainn.com).

FROM THUNDER BAY TO FORT FRANCES/RAINY RIVER VIA HIGHWAY 11

From Thunder Bay, it's 480km (298 miles) along the Trans-Canada Highway to **Kenora.** Several provincial parks line the route.

Kakabeka Falls Provincial Park, 435 James St. S., Suite 221, Thunder Bay (© 807/473-9231), with its fantastic 40m (131-ft.) high waterfall, is 29km (18 miles) along the Trans-Canada Highway. The gorge was carved out of the Precambrian Shield when the last glaciers melted, and fossils dating back 1.6 billion years have been found here. The park has several nature trails, plus safe swimming at a roped-off area above the falls. Two campgrounds provide 166 sites. In winter, there are 13km (8 miles) of groomed cross-country ski trails.

Atikokan is the gateway to **Quetico Provincial Park** 🔍 (© 807/597-2737), primarily a wilderness canoeing park. The 4,662-sq.-km (1,800-sq.-mile) park has absolutely no roads and only two of the six entrance stations are accessible by car (those at French Lake and Nym Lake, both west of Thunder Bay). Instead, there are miles of interconnecting lakes, streams, and rivers with roaring white water dashing against granite cliffs. It's one of North America's finest canoeing areas. **Dawson Trail Campgrounds,** with 133 sites at French Lake, is the only accessible site for car camping. Extended hikes are limited to the 13km (8-mile) trip to Pickerel Lake; there are also six short trails in the French Lake area (three interpretive). The park can be skied, but there are no groomed trails. Also in the park on some rocks near Lac la Croix you can see 30 ancient pictographs representing moose, caribou, and other animals, as well as hunters in canoes.

Fort Frances is an important border crossing to the United States and the site of a paper mill. Here you'll find an **Ontario Travel Information Centre** at 400 Central Ave. (© **807/274-7566**) at the Minnesota border. Another 90km (56 miles) will bring you to **Rainy River** at the extreme western point of Ontario across from Minnesota. The district abounds in lake-land scenery, much of it in **Lake of the Woods Provincial Park,** R.R. 1, Sleeman (© **807/488-5531**), 43km (27 miles) north of Rainy River. This shallow lake has a 169m-long (554-ft.) beach and is good for swimming and water-skiing. In spring you can fish for walleye, northern pike, and large- and smallmouth bass. You can rent canoes and boats in nearby Morson. The park has 100 campsites as well as a couple of easy nature trails to hike.

Almost due north of Thunder Bay via Route 527 lies **Wabakimi Provincial Park,** which has some fine canoeing and fishing. It's accessible from Armstrong.

FROM THUNDER BAY TO KENORA VIA HIGHWAY 17

Instead of taking Highway 11 west from Thunder Bay as described above, you can take Highway 17, which follows a more northerly route. Just follow 17 where it branches off at Shabaqua Corners, about 56km (35 miles) from Thunder Bay. Continue northwest to **Ignace,** the access point for two provincial parks.

At Ignace, turn off onto Highway 599 to **Sandbar Lake** (© **807/934-2995,** or 807/934-2233 for local Natural Resources office), which offers more than 5,000 hectares (12,355 acres) of forest with nine smaller lakes plus the large one from which it takes its name. The park's most notable inhabitants are the painted turtle (whose tracks you can often see in the sand), the spotted sandpiper, the loon, the common merganser, and several species of woodpecker. The campground has 75 sites; the beach has safe swimming; and there are several short and long canoe routes plus several hiking trails, including the 2km (1.2-mile) **Lookout Trail,** which begins on the beach.

Turtle River Provincial Park is a 120km (75-mile) long waterway from Ignace to Mine Centre. The canoe route begins on Agimak Lake at Ignace and follows a series of lakes into the Turtle River, ending on Turtle Lake just north of Mine Centre. The park also includes the famous log castle built by Jimmy McQuat in the early 1900s on White Otter Lake. Follow Highway 599 farther north to the remote Albany and Apawapiskat rivers, which drain into James Bay.

Back on Highway 17 from Ignace, it's another 40km (25 miles) to the turnoff on Highway 72 to **Ojibway Provincial Park** (© **807/737-2033**), which has only 45 campsites but offers swimming, boating, and self-guided trails. Back on Highway 17, it's only a short way beyond Highway 72 to **Aaron Provincial Park** (© **807/938-6534,** or 807/223-3341 for Natural Resources office), where you'll find close to 100 campsites, facilities for boating and swimming, plus some short nature trails. Nearby Dryden is the supply center for Aaron.

From Dryden, it's about 43km (27 miles) to Vermilion Bay, where Route 105 branches off north to Red Lake, the closest point to one of the province's most remote provincial parks, **Woodland Caribou** (© **807/727-2253**). Offering superb fishing, the 450,000-hectare (1,111,974-acre) park has no facilities except picnic tables and boat rentals nearby. It's home to one of the largest herds of woodland caribou south of the Hudson Bay lowlands. It's also inhabited by black bear, great blue heron, osprey, and bald eagles. There are 1,600km (994 miles) of canoe routes. Contact the **Northern Ontario Tourist Outfitters Association** (© **705/472-5552;** www.noto.net) for details on fly-in camps. Back on Highway 17 from Vermilion Bay, it's only 72km (45 miles) until the road links up with Highway 71 outside Kenora, just shy of the Manitoba border. West of Kenora there's a **Visitors Information Centre** on Highway 17 at the Manitoba border

WHERE TO STAY & DINE NEAR KENORA

Totem Lodge   At the end of Long Bay on Lake of the Woods, this lodge caters to outdoor enthusiasts and families who come for the fishing and hunting. The main lodge is an A-frame featuring a dining room, a lounge, and decks with umbrella-shaded tables overlooking the water. The timber-and-stone decor is appropriately rustic. The cabins have full modern bathrooms, beds with Hudson's Bay blankets, fireplaces, and screened-in porches or outdoor decks, plus cooking facilities. Rooms above the boathouse lack cooking facilities but do have refrigerators. Management will arrange fly-out fishing trips for guests. Fish-cleaning facilities and freezer service are available on-site.

Box 180, Sioux Narrows, ON P0X 1N0. ⟨⟩ **800/668-6836** or 807/226-5275. www.totemresorts.com/totem.html. 27 cabins, 3 units. C$180 (US$180/£90) per person per night. All meals included in rate. Weekly and special packages available. MC, V. Access is off Hwy. 71, 2km (1 mile) north of Sioux Narrows. **Amenities:** Dining room; 5m (16-ft.) fishing boats; canoes; Windsurfers. *In room:* A/C, TV, coffeemaker.

Wiley Point Lodge   This lodge is accessible only by boat and therefore offers more of a wilderness experience. This is first and foremost a fishing lodge, with trout, walleye, bass, and muskie being the principal lures for visitors. (Spring and fall bear hunts are also offered, as well as more traditional hunting.) The main lodge has eight suites, plus there are seven cabins (two- or three-bedroom), all with full bathroom, refrigerator, and screened-in porch. The lodge contains a dining room, lounge, and deck overlooking the lake.

Box 180, Sioux Narrows, ON P0X 1N0. ⟨⟩ **800/668-6836** or 807/226-5275. www.totemresorts.com/wiley.html. 8 units, 7 cabins. Fishing packages C$220 (US$220/£110) per person per night based on 2 per boat (this includes boat, gas, and bait). Hunting packages also available. MC, V. **Amenities:** Dining room; lounge; exercise room; hot tub; sauna; game room; beach w/diving raft; paddleboats; Windsurfers.

13

Manitoba & Saskatchewan

by Bill McRae

Visitors don't exactly flock to central Manitoba and Saskatchewan, but that can be a plus if you like unpopulated, wide-open spaces. Located where the northern Great Plains meet the southern reaches of the subarctic boreal forests, these two provinces boast miles of fertile farmland, beautiful wilderness and parkland, and an almost infinite chain of lakes, making them terrific choices for fishing, canoeing, wildlife-watching, and more.

Manitoba is famous for its friendly people, who not only brave long, harsh winters but also till the southern prairie lands in summer, making the region a breadbasket for the nation and the world. Along the southern border outside Winnipeg, wheat, barley, canola, sunflowers, and flax wave at the roadside, the horizon is limitless, and grain elevators pierce the skyline. Beyond the province's southern section, punctuated by Lake Winnipeg

and Lake Manitoba, stretches one of the last wilderness frontiers, a paradise for anglers and outdoors enthusiasts of all sorts. Here you'll find many of the province's thousands of lakes, which cover about 20% of Manitoba (the province is sometimes claimed to have 100,000 lakes). You'll also see polar bears and beluga whales and hear the timber wolves cry on the lonesome tundra surrounding the Hudson Bay port of Churchill.

Five times the size of New York State, with a population of a little over a million, **Saskatchewan** produces about 55% of Canada's wheat. Here you'll find a hunting and fishing paradise in the northern lakes and forests; several summer playgrounds (including Prince Albert National Park and 31 provincial parks); and the cities of Regina, the capital, and Saskatoon, a progressive university city.

1 Exploring the Provinces

The **Trans-Canada Highway** (Hwy. 1) cuts across the southern part of both provinces. In Manitoba, you can stop along Highway 1 at Whiteshell Provincial Park in the east. You can return to the highway or visit the shores of Lake Winnipeg at Grand Beach Provincial Park and then head south via Selkirk and Lower Fort Garry to Winnipeg, the provincial capital. From Winnipeg, you can take the train north to Churchill to explore the tundra around Hudson Bay. On your return to Winnipeg, you can pick up Highway 1 again and drive west across the province, stopping for a detour to Riding Mountain National Park or to Spruce Woods Provincial Park before exiting into Saskatchewan.

Highway 1 leads from Manitoba to Regina, with a stop perhaps at Moose Mountain Provincial Park along the way. From Regina, it's a 2½-hour or so drive to Saskatoon, and about another 2½-hour drive to Prince Albert National Park (you can stop

Manitoba

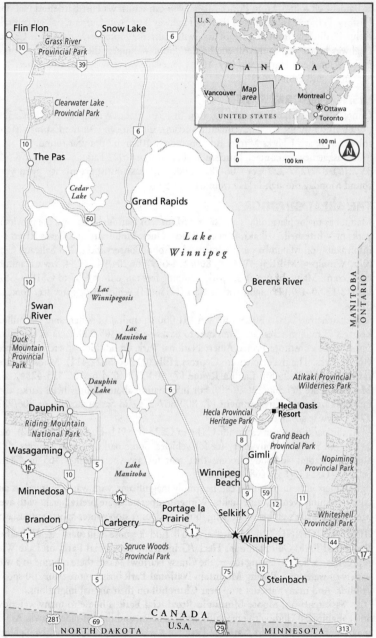

Flin Flon
Snow Lake
`6`
`10`
Grass River Provincial Park
`39`

Clearwater Lake Provincial Park

`10`

`6`

The Pas

Cedar Lake

`60`
Grand Rapids

Lake Winnipeg

`10`

Lac Winnipegosis

Swan River

Duck Mountain Provincial Park

Lac Manitoba

Dauphin Lake

Berens River

MANITOBA
ONTARIO

Atikaki Provincial Wilderness Park

Dauphin

Riding Mountain National Park

Wasagaming
`16`

Minnedosa

`5`
`10`

Lake Manitoba

`6`

Hecla Provincial Heritage Park

Hecla Oasis Resort

Grand Beach Provincial Park

`8`
Gimli

Winnipeg Beach

`9`
`59`
`12`
`11`

Nopiming Provincial Park

`16`

Brandon
`1`
Carberry
Portage la Prairie
`1`

Selkirk

★ **Winnipeg**

Whiteshell Provincial Park

`44`

`10`
`5`
Spruce Woods Provincial Park

`75`
`12`
Steinbach

`1`
`17`

`281`
`69`

CANADA
U.S.A.

NORTH DAKOTA

`29`

MINNESOTA

`313`

Inset map

U.S.

C A N A D A

Vancouver
Map area
Montreal
✪ Ottawa
Toronto

UNITED STATES

0   100 mi
0   100 km

at Batoche en route). From Prince Albert, you can return via Fort Battleford National Historic Park to Saskatoon and then to Highway 1 at Swift Current, or you can take Route 4 directly from Battleford to Swift Current. From here, the Trans-Canada Highway heads west to the Alberta border. From Winnipeg, the other driving option is the Yellowhead Highway (Hwy. 16), a four-lane expressway that runs directly to Saskatoon and Edmonton.

VISITOR INFORMATION

Contact **Travel Manitoba,** 155 Carlton St., 7th Floor, Winnipeg, MB R3C 3H8 (© **800/665-0040;** www.travelmanitoba.com). Or you can visit the **Explore Manitoba Centre** at 21 Forks Market Rd., open daily 10am to 6pm year-round.

In Saskatchewan, contact **Tourism Saskatchewan,** 1922 Park St., Regina, SK S4P 3V7 (© **877/237-2273** or 306/787-2300; www.sasktourism.com); it's open year-round Monday through Friday from 8am to 5pm.

THE GREAT OUTDOORS

Manitoba's major playgrounds are **Riding Mountain National Park** and the provincial parks of **Whiteshell, Atikaki, Spruce Woods, Duck Mountain,** and **Grass River.** For information on Manitoba parks contact **Manitoba Conservation,** 200 Saulteaux Crescent, Winnipeg, MB R3J 3W3 (© **800/214-6497** or 204/945-6784; www.manitoba parks.com). Manitoba provincial parks camping fees range from C$7 to C$18 (US$7–US$18/£3.50–£9) per night, with a C$6 (US$6/£3) vehicle/park entry fee, good for 3 days.

Saskatchewan boasts 80,290 sq. km (31,000 sq. miles) of water, and 1.2 million hectares (3 million acres) are given over to parks—nearly 405,000 hectares (1 million acres) alone constitute Prince Albert National Park. In addition, there are 34 provincial parks. The major ones are **Cypress Hills** (© 306/662-5411), **Moose Mountain** (© 306/577-2600), **Lac La Ronge** (© 800/772-4064 or 306/425-4234), and **Meadow Lake** (© 306/236-7680). For information about all provincial parks, contact **Saskatchewan Environment** (© 800/667-2757 in Saskatchewan, or 306/787-2700; www.se.gov.sk.ca/saskparks).

At the parks, you can camp for C$11 to C$24 (US$11–US$24/£5.50–£12), plus a C$7 (US$7£3.50) daily entry fee for vehicles. Some parks, such as Cypress Hills, also have cabins and lodge rooms that rent for anywhere from C$65 to C$135 (US$65–US$135/£33–£68) a night.

Summers in both provinces can be simply magnificent, with warm sunny days and cool refreshing evenings and nights. Winter temperatures are pretty harsh, with average highs usually well below freezing, but that doesn't stop winter-sports enthusiasts.

BIRD-WATCHING   In Manitoba, you'll find a goose sanctuary at **Whiteshell Provincial Park.** Gull Harbour's **Hecla/Grindstone Provincial Park,** on Lake Winnipeg, has a wildlife-viewing tower; the Grassy Narrows Marsh there is home to a wide variety of waterfowl. **Riding Mountain National Park** boasts more than 200 species of birds. And many varieties stop near **Churchill** on their annual migrations.

In Saskatchewan, **Moose Mountain Provincial Park** is home to many waterfowl and songbirds, including the magnificent blue heron and the red-tailed hawk. As you may expect, **Prince Albert National Park** has a wide variety of bird life; the highlight is an enormous colony of white pelicans at Lavallee Lake. And there's even a waterfowl park right in the middle of downtown **Regina,** where you can see more than 60 species. A naturalist is on duty weekdays.

Saskatchewan

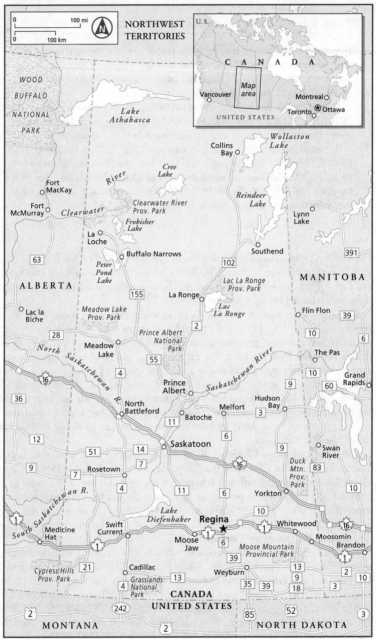

> ### *Tips* Farm & Ranch Vacations on the Prairies
>
> There's no better way to really get the feel of the prairies than to stay on a farm or ranch. Contact the **Manitoba Country Vacations Association,** Box 93, Minto, MB R0K 1M0 (© 866/201-0440 or 204/776-2176; www.country vacations.mb.ca), for details about farm accommodations. Rates average C$75 (US$75/£38) per day and C$450 (US$450/£225) per week for adults and C$25 (US$25/£13) per day and C$150 (US$150/£75) per week for children— a very reasonable price for such an exciting authentic experience.
>
> In Saskatchewan, farm vacations average C$60 to C$75 (US$60–US$75/ £30–£38) for a double bed and a real farm breakfast (additional meals can be arranged). The **Saskatchewan Bed and Breakfast Association,** Box 694, Lumsden, SK S0G 3C0 (© 306/731-2646; www.bbsask.ca), has many rural members that also offer hands-on farm and ranch activities.

CANOEING   In Manitoba, the best places to canoe are Riding Mountain National Park, Whiteshell Provincial Park, Woodland Caribou Provincial Park, Atikaki Provincial Park (on the Bloodvein River), and the chain of lakes around Flin Flon, which is right on the border between the two provinces.

Saskatchewan is one of the world's great wilderness canoe areas. Half of the province is covered by forest and one-eighth is water. The Precambrian Shield in northern Saskatchewan provides the setting for an adventurer's paradise. **Prince Albert National Park** has some fine canoeing, and plenty of other northern water routes offer a challenge to both novice and expert. Some 55 canoe routes have been mapped, traversing terrain that hasn't changed since the era of explorers and fur traders. You can get to all but three of the routes by road. Various outfitters will supply tents, camping equipment, and canoes; look after your car; and transport you to your trip's starting point. Most are in either Flin Flon or Lac La Ronge, 400km (248 miles) north of Saskatoon.

Horizons Unlimited Churchill River Canoe Outfitters in Missinipe, near La Ronge, Saskatchewan (Box 1110, La Ronge, SK S0J 1L0; © 306/635-4420; www. churchillrivercanoe.com), offers a selection of packages. Canoes and kayaks go for around C$35 (US$35/£18) per day, or they can outfit you for a multiday wilderness expedition. You can also rent cabins from C$33(US$33£17) per person per night, with a C$95 to C$210 (US$95–US$210/£48–£105) per cabin nightly minimum. The **Canoe Ski Discovery Company,** 1618 9th Ave. N., Saskatoon, SK S7K 3A1 (© 306/653-5693; www.canoeski.com), offers several canoeing and cross-country skiing wilderness eco-tours in Prince Albert National Park, in Lac La Ronge Provincial Park, and along the Churchill and Saskatchewan rivers. The trips last 2 to 12 days. Prince Albert National Park canoe packages include 2-day, 1-night trips from C$350 (US$350/£175), to 4-day, 3-night excursions for C$750 (US$750/£375), and are led by qualified eco-interpreters. For additional information, contact **Tourism Saskatchewan,** 1922 Park St., Regina, SK S4P 3V7 (© 877/237-2273 or 306/787-2300; www.sasktourism.com), or **Canoe Saskatchewan** (www.canoesaskatchewan. rkc.ca).

FISHING   The same clear, cold northern lakes that draw canoeists hold out the chance of catching walleye, northern pike, four species of trout, and arctic grayling. Licenses are required in both provinces.

Since Manitoba has strong catch-and-release and barbless-hook programs, the number of trophy fish is high. The province is also known as the North American mecca for channel catfish, particularly along the Red and Bloodvein rivers. Good fishing abounds in **Whiteshell, Duck Mountain,** the lake chains around **The Pas** and **Flin Flon,** and in fly-in areas up north. For a selection of outfitters, contact the **Manitoba Lodges and Outfitters Association,** Box 399, Beausejour, MB R0E 0C0 (© **204/268-1968;** www.mloa.com).

In Saskatchewan, **La Ronge, Wollaston,** and **Reindeer** are just a few of the lakes so densely inhabited by northern pike and walleye that you can practically pluck them from the clear waters. More than 300 northern outfitters—both fly-in and drive-in camps—offer equipment, accommodations, and experienced guides to take you to the best fishing spots. Rates for packages vary—commonly in the range of C$1,000 to C$3,000 (US$1,000–US$3,000/£500–£1,500) per person per week, including transportation, meals, boat, guide, and accommodations. Contact the **Saskatchewan Outfitters Association,** 3700 2nd Ave. W., Prince Albert, SK S6W 1A2 (© **306/763-5434;** www.soa. ca). A boat and motor will cost about C$120 to C$250 (US$120–US$250/£60–£125) per day, and guide services run about C$80 to C$150 (US$80–US$150/£40–£75) per day. For further information, contact **Tourism Saskatchewan,** 1922 Park St., Regina, SK S4P 3V7 (© **877/237-2273** or 306/787-2300; www.sasktourism.com).

WILDLIFE VIEWING   Manitoba's **Riding Mountain National Park** is a prime destination for wildlife enthusiasts, who may be able to spot moose, coyote, wolf, lynx, black bear, beaver, and more—even a bison herd. **Grass River Provincial Park** is home to moose and woodland caribou. Churchill, in the far northern part of the province, is a fantastic place for viewing polar bears. During the summer, you can also see white beluga whales in the mouth of the Churchill River.

In Saskatchewan, **Prince Albert National Park** is the place to be; you'll be able to spot and photograph moose, elk, caribou, shaggy bison, lumbering black bears, and more. It'll come as no surprise that moose live in **Moose Mountain Provincial Park,** where their neighbors include deer, elk, beaver, muskrat, and coyote. You can also spot adorable black-tailed prairie dogs in **Grasslands National Park.**

2 Winnipeg: Capital of Manitoba ★★

572km (355 miles) E of Regina, 697km (433 miles) NW of Minneapolis, 235km (146 miles) N of Grand Forks

Tough, sturdy, muscular, midwestern—that's Winnipeg, Manitoba's capital. The history of its rich architecture—brick warehouses, quarried stone banks, railroad depots, and grain elevators—all testify to its historical role as a distribution-and-supply center, first for furs and then for agricultural products. It's a toiling city where about 680,000 inhabitants sizzle in summer and shovel in winter.

That's one side. The other is a city and populace that have produced a symphony orchestra that triumphed in New York, the first Royal ballet company in the British Commonwealth, and a theater-and-arts complex worthy of any national capital.

As a hard-working city in the midst of the prairies, Winnipeg has a lot in common with Chicago. Although a smaller city, Winnipeg also has a long history of immigrant assimilation and, due to its cultural mix, an extremely rich restaurant scene.

ESSENTIALS

GETTING THERE   **Winnipeg International Airport** (© **204/987-9402;** www.
waa.ca) is only about 20 minutes west-northwest of the city center (allow 30–40 min.
in rush hours). You can get from the airport to downtown by taxi for C$20 to C$25
(US$20–US$25/£10–£13), or by city bus on **Winnipeg Transit** (© **204/986-5700;**
www.winnipegtransit.com) for C$2 (US$2/£1). Buses run to Portage and Garry about
every 15 minutes during the day and every 22 minutes during the night.

The **VIA Rail** train depot is at 123 Main St., where it intersects Broadway. For VIA
Rail information, call © **888/842-7245** in Canada, 800/561-3949 in the U.S., or
204/943-3578 in Winnipeg, or go online to www.viarail.ca.

VISITOR INFORMATION   Contact **Travel Manitoba,** 155 Carlton St., 7th
Floor, Winnipeg, MB R3C 3H8 (© **800/665-0040** or 204/945-3777; www.travel
manitoba.com). You can also visit the **Explore Manitoba Centre** next to the Forks
Market, open daily 10am to 6pm year-round. For specific Winnipeg information,
contact **Destination Winnipeg,** 279 Portage Ave., Winnipeg, MB R3B 2B4 (© **800/
665-0204** or 204/943-1970; www.tourism.winnipeg.mb.ca), open Monday through
Friday 8:30am to 4:30pm, or the **Tourism Winnipeg InfoCentre** at the Winnipeg
International Airport (© **204/982-7543**), open daily 8am to 9:45pm.

CITY LAYOUT   A native Winnipegger once said to me, "I still can't get used to
the confined and narrow streets in the east." When you see Portage and Main, each
40m (131 ft.) wide (that's 9m/30 ft. off the width of a football field), and the eerie
flatness that means no matter where you go, you can see where you're going, you'll
understand why.

The **Forks**—the site of the original Winnipeg settlement, at the junction of the
Red and Assiniboine rivers—remains a hub of the city, with its historic warehouses
converted to shops and restaurants and the ample riverside green space dedicated to
festivals and concerts. Northeast of the Forks is the city's most famous corner, **Portage
and Main**—the focus of the city's high-rise commercial district. This intersection is
also known as the historic site of the 1919 General Strike, and has the reputation as
the windiest spot in Canada (it has to do with the way the business towers funnel the
prevailing winds).

The Red River runs north-south, as does Main Street; the Assiniboine River and
Portage Avenue run east-west. Going north on Main from the Portage-Main junction
will bring you to the City Hall, the Exchange District, the Manitoba Centennial Centre (including the Manitoba Theatre Centre), the Manitoba Museum, and on into the
North End, once a mosaic of cultures and still dotted with bulbous Ukrainian church
domes and authentic delis.

From Portage and Main, if you go 6 blocks west along Portage (a major shopping
district) and 2 blocks south, you'll hit the Convention Centre. From here, going 1
block south and 2 blocks west brings you to the Legislative Building, the art gallery,
and south, just across the Assiniboine River, trendy Osborne Village.

On the east side of the Red River, across the Provencher Bridge, is the old French-
Canadian settlement of St. Boniface. Boulevarde Provencher is the main commercial
street through St. Boniface, while avenue Taché runs along the riverfront and past the
ruined facade of the Roman Catholic cathedral.

GETTING AROUND   The **City of Winnipeg Transit System,** 421 Osborne St.
(© **204/986-5700;** www.winnipegtransit.com) offers two forms of bus transport. In

Winnipeg

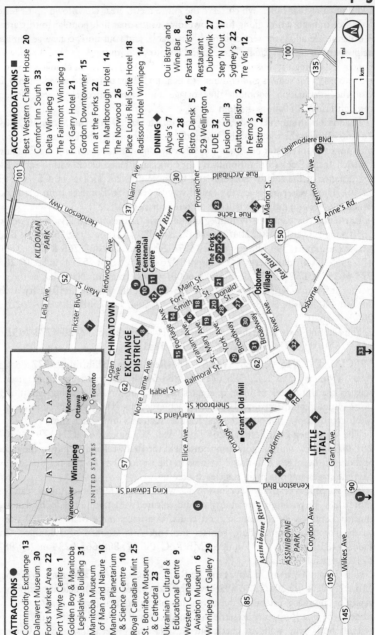

addition to regular buses, which serve the entire metro area, Downtown Spirit buses offer free transportation along four downtown routes that link popular tourist areas. A brochure detailing the service is readily available, and your hotel concierge can also help you navigate the system. There is no Downtown Spirit bus service on Sundays or holidays. For regular buses, you need C$2 (US$2/£1) in exact change (C$1.65/US$1.65/85p for seniors and children) to board. Call for route and schedule info, or visit the information booth in the Portage and Main concourse, open Monday through Friday 8:30am to 4:30pm.

In addition, in summer and early fall, the **Splash Dash Water Bus Service** (© 204/783-6633) plies the waters of the Red and the Assiniboine rivers. Departing every 10 minutes or so, the water bus links a number of tourist areas, including the Exchange District, Taché Dock (for St. Boniface), the Forks, and Hugo Dock, within easy walking distance of the trendy Corydon and Osborne districts. Tickets are C$3 (US$3/£1.50). These water buses are the easiest way to get to St. Boniface from the Forks, which is otherwise rather a challenge on public transport.

Car-rental companies in Winnipeg include **Avis,** at the airport, 234 York Ave., or 1350 King Edward St. (© **204/956-2847,** 204/989-7521, or 204/956-2847); **Budget,** at the airport, 593 Ellice Ave., or 1355 Regent Ave. (© **800/268-8900,** or 800/472-3355 in Canada); **Hertz,** at the airport, 276 Colony St., or 1577 Erin St. (© **204/925-6625,** 204/925-6600, or 204/925-6600; www.hertz.com); **National,** at the airport or at five in-town locations (© **204/925-3531** at the airport); and **Thrifty,** at the airport, 420 Kensington St., or 112 Garry St. (© **204/949-7608,** 204/949-7622, or 204/949-7620).

You can find taxis at the downtown hotels. Try **Duffy's Taxi** (© **204/772-2451** or 204/775-0101) or **Unicity Taxi** (© **204/925-3131**).

SPECIAL EVENTS & FESTIVALS The **Red River Exhibition,** 3977 Portage Ave., Winnipeg, MB R3K 2ES (© **204/888-6990;** www.redriverex.com), usually starting the third week of June, celebrates the city's history, showcasing agricultural, horticultural, commercial, and industrial achievements. There are also a midway, a photography show, and other themed features such as a lumberjack show.

The **Winnipeg Folk Festival,** 264 Taché Ave., Winnipeg, MB R2H 1Z9 (© **204/231-0096;** www.winnipegfolkfestival.ca), held the first weekend of July, is the oldest and one of the largest folk-music festivals in the world. Over 85 acts perform on five daytime stages and one main stage each evening.

Folklorama, a Festival of Nations, is a 2-week cultural festival in August featuring more than 35 pavilions celebrating ethnic culture, with traditional food, dancing, music, costumes, entertainment, and crafts. It attracts more than 400,000 guests yearly. For more information, contact the Folk Arts Council of Winnipeg, 2nd Floor—183 Kennedy St., Winnipeg, MB R3C 1S6 (© **800/665-0234** or 204/982-6210; www.folklorama.ca).

The 10-day **Festival du Voyageur,** Le Rendez-Vous at 768 Taché Ave., Winnipeg, MB R2H 2C4 (© **204/237-7692;** www.festivalvoyageur.mb.ca), held in mid-February in St. Boniface, celebrates the adventures of the original French *voyageurs,* or fur traders, the first Europeans to settle in Canada, as well as French Métis culture.

Film buffs may want to check out the National Screen Institute of Canada's **FilmExchange** film festival, running for over a week in early March. Screening only Canadian films, this festival is striving to become what the Sundance festival is for the

U.S. For more information, contact the **National Screen Institute—Canada,** 206–70 Arthur St., Winnipeg, MB R3B 1G7 (℗ **800/952-9307** or 204/956-7800; www.nsi-canada.ca/filmexchange).

EXPLORING THE CITY
THE TOP ATTRACTIONS

The Forks ✦✦   At the junction of the Red and Assiniboine rivers is the Forks National Historic Site, which has been a trade and meeting place for over 5,000 years. First Natives, then fur traders and settlers found this river confluence a propitious place for settlement. The area was redeveloped in the late 1980s when the old Canadian National rail yard was redeveloped into the bustling **Forks Market** and festival grounds (℗ **204/957-7618;** www.theforks.com). A major draw is the fresh food market and an abundance of inexpensive market restaurants in the historic rail warehouses—this is a good spot to come for lunch or a light supper. A number of shops and boutiques offer gifts and housewares, while street musicians and magicians entertain.

Other Forks attractions include the **Oodena Celebration Circle,** a shallow, bowl-like platform surrounded by a set of astronomically arranged metal structures that look like fanciful sci-fi creatures, commemorating the region's First Nations people; and **Festival Park Stage,** the site of summer concerts. The **Manitoba Children's Museum** (℗ **204/924-4000**) and the new **Manitoba Theatre for Young People** (℗ **204/947-0394**) are both here at the Forks as well. In summer, you can stroll on the river walks along the Red and Assiniboine rivers, picnic by the riverside, and catch water buses to other parts of the city; in winter, there's free public skating on outdoor artificial ice or along groomed river trails. Free Downtown Spirit buses connect The Forks to the rest of downtown Winnipeg from beside Forks Market.

At the confluence of the Red and Assinboine rivers, behind the Via Rail Station at 123 Main St. ℗ 204/942-6302. www.theforks.com. Free admission to parks and markets. Forks Market open July 1 to Labour Day Mon–Sat 9:30am–9pm, Sun 9:30am–6:30pm; day after Labour Day to June 30 daily 9:30am–6:30pm (Fri till 9pm).

Exchange District   Just north of the famous corner of Portage and Main is the historic Exchange District, the best-preserved turn-of-the-20th-century district in North America. Now a national historic site, the area encompasses over 30 city blocks, featuring unparalleled examples of terra-cotta and cut-stone architecture. In recent years, the area has been in great demand as a backdrop for movie production by filmmakers from across the continent. The Exchange District is also home to many of Winnipeg's best art galleries. Check out the **Plug In Gallery,** 286 McDermott Ave. (℗ **204/942-1043;** www.plugin.org), and **Artspace Inc.,** 425–100 Arthur St. (℗ **204/947-0984**), a six-story building that houses 23 arts organizations including several galleries, publishers, and art studios. For more information on things to do and places to go in the Exchange District, pick up the widely available and free Exchange District visitors guide from any tourist office.

The **Exchange District Business Improvement Zone** or **BIZ** (for contact information see below) offers guided walking tours of historic sites in the Exchange District—including the interiors of some buildings—from June 1 to Labour Day, weather permitting. Tours begin at the Exchange District Info Centre in Old Market Square (King St. and Bannatyne Ave.), daily at 10am and 2pm, lasting roughly 1½ to 2 hours each. The cost is C$6 (US$6/£3) for adults, C$5 (US$5/£2.50) for seniors and students.

Bounded by Portage, Main, Bannatyne and Princess sts. Free admission. For information, contact Exchange District Business Improvement Zone (BIZ) at ℗ 204/942-6716. www.exchangedistrict.org.

Manitoba Museum ⭐ *Kids* This museum is a fascinating place, with galleries depicting local history, culture, and geology through life-size exhibits such as a buffalo hunt, prehistoric creatures, pioneer life, pronghorn antelope, tepees, sod huts, and log cabins. In the Urban Gallery, you can walk down a 1920s Winnipeg street past typical homes and businesses of the era. The Boreal Forest Gallery depicts Manitoba's most northerly forested region. You can climb aboard the *Nonsuch*, a full-size replica of the 17th-century ketch that returned to England in 1669 with the first cargo of furs out of Hudson Bay. One wing is dedicated to the Hudson's Bay Company—with over 10,000 artifacts and artworks from a private archive that the company began amassing in 1920.

In the Manitoba Centennial Centre, 190 Rupert Ave. ⓒ **204/956-2830**, or 204/943-3139 for recorded info. www. manitobamuseum.mb.ca. Admission C$8 (US$8/£4) adults; C$6.50 (US$6.50/£3.25) seniors, students, and youths 3–17; C$27 (US$27/£14) families. AE, MC, V. Victoria Day to Labour Day daily 10am–6pm; the rest of the year Tues–Fri 10am–4pm, Sat–Sun and holidays 11am–5pm.

Manitoba Planetarium & Science Gallery *Kids* The planetarium, part of the Manitoba Museum (see above), offers shows in its 280-seat Star Theatre exploring everything from cosmic catastrophes to the reality of UFOs. The Science Gallery is a hands-on science gallery containing close to 100 interactive exhibits explaining a gamut of phenomena in all realms of science.

In the Manitoba Centennial Centre, 190 Rupert Ave. ⓒ **204/943-2830**, or 204/956-3139 for recorded info. www. manitobamuseum.mb.ca. Planetarium or Science Gallery C$6.50 (US$6.50/£3.25) adults; C$5 (US$5/£2.50) seniors, students, and youths 3–17; free for children under 3; C$20 (US$20/£10) families. AE, MC, V. Planetarium shows daily mid-May to Labour Day Thurs, Sat–Sun, and holidays; the rest of the year, call for show times. Science Gallery Victoria Day to Labour Day daily 10am–6pm; rest of the year Tues–Fri 10am–4pm, Sat–Sun and holidays 11am–5pm.

Royal Canadian Mint A producer of currency for countries worldwide, one in four people in the world carry coins made in Winnipeg's mint. The process of making money is mind-boggling, and the tour offered here will prove it to you. Dies are produced; a roof crane lifts 1,818-kilogram (4,000-lb.) strips of bronze and nickel; three 150-ton presses stamp out up to 8,800 coin blanks per minute; and coining presses turn out up to 18,000 coins per hour to the telling machines that count the number for bagging. The whole process represents an extraordinary engineering feat streamlined by conveyor belts and an overhead monorail.

520 Lagimodière Blvd. ⓒ **204/983-6429**. www.mint.ca. Admission weekdays C$5 (US$5/£2.50) adults, C$3 (US$3/ £1.50) children 4–15, families C$13 (US$13/£6.50); weekends C$3.50 (US$3.50/£1.75) adults, C$2 (US$2/£1) children 4–15, C$10 (US$10/£5) families. Tours given regularly during listed hours, or by appointment. Victoria Day to Labour Day daily 9am–5pm, the rest of the year Mon–Fri 9am–5pm. Take Main St. south over the Assiniboine/Red rivers, turn left onto Marion St., and then right onto Lagimodière. You'll see the mint rise up just beyond the Trans-Canada Hwy. (Rte. 135).

Ukrainian Cultural & Educational Centre (Oseredok) The Oseredok, or Ukrainian Centre, one of the largest such institutions in North America, conserves the artifacts and heritage of the Ukrainian people. The art gallery and museum feature changing exhibits on such subjects as 18th-century icons, embroidery, weaving, painted eggs, woodcarving, ceramics, clothing, and other folk arts. The gift shop stocks traditional and contemporary folk arts and crafts. There's also an extensive library, and guided tours of the museum are available on request.

184 Alexander Ave. E. (at the corner of Main and the Disraeli Fwy.). ⓒ **204/942-0218**. www.oseredok.org. Donations requested. Mon–Sat 10am–4pm; July–Aug also Sun 1–4pm.

Taste of France across the River: The Historic District of St. Boniface

Across the river in **St. Boniface,** a street becomes a *rue* and a hello becomes *bonjour.* Here you'll find the largest French-speaking community in western Canada, dating from 1783, when Pierre Gaultier de Varennes established Fort Rouge at the junction of the Red and Assiniboine rivers. The junction became the center of a thriving fur trade for the North West Company, which rivaled and challenged the Hudson's Bay Company. A basilica built in 1819 was dedicated to Boniface, and in 1846, four Grey Nuns arrived and began their ministry, by establishing the area's first hospital.

The original basilica was replaced in 1908 by a beautiful stone church that was subsequently destroyed by a fire in 1968. The massive Gothic arches remain, and cradled within the shell of the old building is the new basilica, built in 1972. In front of the cathedral, the cemetery is the resting place of Louis Riel, whose grave is marked by a replica of a Red River cart. Riel, leader of the Métis uprising and president of the provincial government formed from 1869 to 1870, tried to prevent the transfer of the Red River settlement to Canada. For walking tours of St. Boniface—including the summer-only "In Riel's Footsteps," a 90-minute theatrical tour of the cemetery, with actors playing the roles of some of Manitoba's most interesting and noteworthy historical characters—contact the **Riel Tourism Bureau** (© **866/808-8338;** www.tourismeriel.com).

Winnipeg Art Gallery ✦✦   A distinctive triangular building of local Tyndall stone, the Winnipeg Art Gallery houses one of the world's largest collections of contemporary Inuit art. Other collections focus on historic and contemporary Canadian art, as well as British and European artists. The decorative art collections feature works by Canadian silversmiths and studio potters, while the photography collection contains more than 200 works by André Kertész and represents other 20th-century photographers, such as Diane Arbus and Irving Penn. You'll always find a number of interesting rotating exhibits on display, as well. The penthouse restaurant overlooks the fountain and flowers in the sculpture court.

300 Memorial Blvd. © 204/786-6641. www.wag.mb.ca. Admission C$6 (US$6/£3) adults, C$4 (US$4/£2) students and seniors, C$3 (US$3/£1.50) youths 6–12, C$15 (US$15/£7.50) families. Tues–Sun 11am–5pm (till 9pm Thurs).

MORE ATTRACTIONS

Commodity Exchange   Organized in 1887 as a grain exchange, the Commodity Exchange is the only exchange in Canada that trades in agricultural commodities. Once, this was the heart and soul of Winnipeg, the world's premier grain market until World War II. Today, it has about 240 members and 77 companies registered for trading privileges. It's best to come around 9:30am or right near closing at 12:55pm, when you're more likely to see some feverish action on the floor.

On the 4th floor of the Commodity Exchange Tower, 400–360 Main St. © 204/925-5000. www.wce.ca. Free viewing gallery open Mon–Fri 9:30am–1:15pm. Tours for groups at 9:10am and 12:50pm daily, but call ahead to arrange.

Dalnavert Museum   Just 2 blocks east of the Legislative Building (see below) stands the Victorian home built in 1895 for Hugh John Macdonald, the only son of Canada's first prime minister and one of Manitoba's premiers. It's a fine example of a late-Victorian gingerbread house with a wraparound veranda and the latest innovations of the time—electric lighting, indoor plumbing, central hot-water heating, and walk-in closets—opulently decorated and full of heirloom objects. The new "green" visitors center offers a well-stocked gift shop.

61 Carlton St. (between Broadway and Assiniboine Ave.). ✆ 204/943-2835. www.mhs.mb.ca. Admission C$5 (US$5/£2.50) adults, C$4 (US$4/£2) seniors, C$3 (US$3/£1.50) ages 5–17, C$12 (US$12/£6) families, free for children 4 and under. MC, V. Wed–Fri 10am–5pm; Sat 11am–6pm; Sun noon–4pm.

Fort Whyte Centre   About 15 minutes from downtown, some old cement quarries have been converted into lakes at Fort Whyte Centre and now serve as a feature-packed environmental educational facility. A 929-sq.-m (10,000-sq.-ft.) interpretive center houses Manitoba's largest indoor aquarium, which displays local freshwater species such as the northern pike and walleye. Outside, you can view a herd of 25 bison on a 28-hectare (70-acre) prairie field, as well as a prairie dog town. There are also self-guided nature trails, bike paths, waterfowl gardens, a restaurant, and a gift shop.

1961 McCreary Rd., Fort Whyte. ✆ 204/989-8355 or 204/989-8350 for recorded info. www.fortwhyte.org. Admission C$6 (US$6/£3) adults, C$5 (US$5/£2.50) seniors, C$4 (US$4/£2) students and children over 3. MC, V. Mon–Fri 9am–5pm; Sat–Sun 10am–5pm. Extended evening hours June–Oct.

The Golden Boy & Manitoba Legislative Building   There he stands, 73m (240 ft.) above ground atop the Legislative Building's dome, clutching a sheaf of wheat under his left arm and holding aloft in his right arm an eternally lit torch symbolizing the spirit of progress. French sculptor Charles Gardet created his 5-ton, 4m (13-ft.) bronze statue during World War I. The building, a magnificent classical Greek structure, was designed in 1919 by British architect Frank Worthington Simon. The building's focal point is the Legislative Chamber, where the 57 members of Manitoba's legislative assembly meet.

450 Broadway. ✆ 204/945-5813. July to Labour Day free tours given hourly daily 9am–6pm; by reservation at other times for groups of 10 or more. Self-guided tours year-round daily 8am–8pm. 2-hr. visitor parking on grounds.

St. Boniface Museum & Cathedral   The religious, historic, and cultural home to many of western Canada's French-speaking Catholics was St. Boniface, established in 1818. The museum in the old convent house of the Grey Nuns is one of the oldest oak log structures in North America, and it tells the story of the region's early Francophone settlers, with a sharp focus on the story of Louis Riel, the messianic Métis leader who was instrumental in the establishment of both Manitoba and Saskatchewan. Also on the grounds is St. Boniface Cathedral. All that remains of the historic stone structure are portions of the walls and the noble facade—a fire in 1968 destroyed the rest of the structure. The current cathedral was rebuilt within the original walls.

494 av. Taché. ✆ 204/237-4500. Admission C$5 (US$5/£2.50) adults, seniors and children C$3 (US$3/£1.50), free for children under 6, C$12 (US$12/£6) families. Mon–Sat 9am–5pm; Sun noon–4pm. Closed major holidays.

Western Canada Aviation Museum (Kids)   Among the dozens of historic flying treasures at the Western Canada Aviation Museum is Canada's first helicopter, designed and test flown between 1935 and 1939. There's also a plane-flight simulator, and the Spaceways exhibit, which includes a space-flight simulator, is a great kid's favorite. The museum is both fun and educational, as you are able to interact with real airplanes and learn about the history and technology of flight, from early plane designs to spacecraft and everything in between.

958 Ferry Rd. © 204/786-5503. www.wcam.mb.ca. Admission C$7.50 (US$7.50/£3.75) adults, C$5 (US$5/£2.50) seniors and students 13 and older, C$3 (US$3/£1.50) children 3–12, C$18 (US$18/£9) family. Mon–Fri 9:30am–4:30pm; Sat 10am–5pm; Sun noon–5pm. Closed Dec 25–26, Jan 1, Good Friday.

PARKS & GARDENS

Comprising 160 hectares (395 acres) for playing, picnicking, or biking, **Assiniboine Park,** at 2355 Corydon Ave., contains a miniature railway, duck pond, English garden (which opens in June), and conservatory. In winter, you can go skating on the pond or tobogganing. The park also contains a 40-hectare (99-acre) zoological park (see "Especially for Kids," below). Art lovers will also want to visit the **Leo Mol Sculpture Garden** (© 204/986-6531) to see his works and visit the **Leo Mol Schoolhouse Studio.** The park is open daily dawn to dusk. The elegant **Tavern in the Park** (© 204/896-7275) offers lunch 11:30am to 2:30pm (C$8–C$14/US$8–US$14/£4–£7) and dinner 5 to 9:30pm (C$16–C$37/US$16–US$37/£8–£19) Tuesday through Sunday. Reservations are suggested. The free **Pavilion Gallery** (© 204/888-5466) houses a permanent collection of works by three Manitoba artists. And the new outdoor **Lyric Theatre** (© 204/888-5466, ext. 5) provides free entertainment in summer with performances by the Winnipeg Symphony, the Royal Winnipeg Ballet, local jazz combos, and so on. In late August, this theater hosts the **Winnie the Pooh Festival**—the famous A. A. Milne character was inspired by a bear named Winnipeg, brought to London by a Canadian Army lieutenant from Winnipeg during World War I as a military mascot.

Kildonan Park is quite delightful, with landscaped gardens, picnic spots, biking paths, outdoor swimming, and wading pools, as well as a restaurant and dining room overlooking a small artificial lake. Also look for the Witch's House from *Hansel and Gretel* in the park. Rainbow Stages musicals are performed here in July and August.

CRUISES & A STEAM-TRAIN EXCURSION

During summer, the cruise ships **MS *River Rouge*** and **MS *Paddlewheel Queen*** depart from their dock at Water and Gilroy at the foot of the Provencher Bridge on a variety of cruises, including a sunset dinner-dance cruise beginning at 7pm and a moonlight version on weekends leaving at 10pm. Both cost C$18 (US$18/£9) for adults, C$16 (US$16/£8) for seniors and C$8.25 (US$8.25/£4.15) for children under 11. Two-hour sightseeing trips costing C$17 (US$17/£8.50) for adults, C$15 (US$15/£7.50) for seniors, and C$8.25 (US$8.25/£4.15) for children under 11, depart at 1pm and provide fine views of the city from the Red and Assiniboine rivers. Fares cover the cruises only; drinks and meals are extra. For details, contact **Paddlewheel River Rouge Tours,** P.O. Box 3930, Postal Station B, Winnipeg, MB R2W 5H9 (© 204/944-8000; www.paddlewheelcruises.com).

A 1900 steam-era train, the ***Prairie Dog Central,*** takes you on a 2½-hour, 58km (36-mile) round-trip from Winnipeg north on the Oak Point line. En route, you get a feel for the prairie and what the late-19th-century immigrants might've seen when they arrived. The train operates every weekend from mid-May to September and some Wednesdays in August, September, and October, plus the first Monday in July, August, and September. Basic fares depend on whether the engine is steam or diesel, and range from C$22 (US$22/£11) adult, C$17 (US$17/£8.50) children on the diesel train to C$27 (US$27/£14) adult, C$22 (US$22/£11) children on the steam train. For details, contact the **Vintage Locomotive Society** (© **204/832-5259;** www.pdcrailway.com). You can also call © **204/253-2787** to purchase tickets from Ticketmaster.

ESPECIALLY FOR KIDS

At the Forks, the **Manitoba Children's Museum** (© **204/956-1888;** www.childrens-museum.com) has participatory exhibits for 2- to 13-year-olds. There are several themed galleries, including Under the Big Top, where kids can run away to the circus and devise a show of their very own; and the TV studio, where they can create their own television shows, as performers or as technicians. Admission is C$6.25 (US$6.25/£3.15) adults, C$5.75 (US$5.75/£2.90) seniors, C$6.75 (US$6.75/£3.40) children ages 2 to 17, and free for children under 2. The museum is open Sunday through Thursday from 9:30am to 4:30pm, Friday and Saturday 9:30am to 8pm. Call for holiday hours. The museum's closed for 4 days following Labour Day, on Christmas and the following 2 days, and on Easter Sunday.

Assiniboine Park, 2355 Corydon Ave., is a great place to picnic or play. Its top attraction, however, is the 40-hectare (99-acre) zoo (© **204/982-0660;** www.zoosociety.com) where 1,700 animals of 325 species—including bears, red pandas, tigers, zebras, bison, and moneys—are kept in as natural an environment as possible. Some exotic species on display are snow leopards, ruffed lemurs, and Irkutsk lynx. Many spectacular birds live and breed in the Tropical House. A special Discovery Centre with a barnful of young farm animals is fun. March through October, admission is C$4.25 (US$4.25/£2.15) adults, C$4 (US$4/£2) seniors, C$2.75 (US$2.75/£1.40) youths ages 13 to 17, and C$2.25 (US$2.25/£1.15) children ages 2 to 12; November through February, it's C$3.75 (US$3.75/£1.90) adults, C$3.50 (US$3.50/£1.75) seniors, C$2.15 (US$2.15/£1.10) youths ages 13 to 17, and C$1.60 (US$1.60/80p) children ages 2 to 12; The park is open daily dawn to dusk with the zoo open daily 10am to dusk (July–Aug from 9am). To get there, take Portage Avenue west, exit onto Route 90 south, and then turn right onto Corydon.

The **Manitoba Theatre for Young People,** in the CanWest Global Performing Arts Centre at Forks Market (© **204/947-0394,** or 204/942-8898 for the box office; www.mtyp.ca), presents plays for children and teens. The season runs October through May, and tickets start at C$13 (US$13/£6.50).

SHOPPING & ROAMING

Several areas in Winnipeg are known for their shops, galleries, and cafes and make good destinations for those spending a few days in town, to get a better feel for the city and its diversity. These areas are: **Academy Road,** trending toward upscale shops and appealing to a middle-age and older crowd; **Corydon Avenue,** or Little Italy, known for its restaurants as well as plenty of boutiques, second-hand and curio shops, and galleries; **Osborne Village,** on Osborne Street, the city's most densely populated area, catering to the young and fashion-minded; the **Exchange District,** as described earlier, the most historic part of town, with many shops, galleries, restaurants, and clubs; the **Wolseley** area (aka the "Granola Belt"), particularly along Westminster Avenue, with shops catering to ecological and spiritual interests, plus bakeries and cafes; and **China-town,** between James and Logan avenues west of Main Street, where you can find excellent restaurants, visit herbalists and import shops, and view some beautiful architecture.

SPAS

Ten Spa, 222 Broadway (© **204/946-6520;** www.tenspa.ca), provides a world-class spa experience atop the Fort Gary Hotel. The C$3-million, 929-sq-m (10,000-sq.-ft.)

facility is the result of 3 years of research at many of the world's foremost spas. Ten Spa offers a full range of aesthetic treatments and state-of-the-art steam rooms, with aroma- and light therapy, a variety of mud baths, scrubs, and massage and body treatments, as well as a co-ed hamam, a modern reinterpretation of the traditional Turkish bath. The full hamam treatment (C$150/US$150/£75) is a 2-hour journey that includes a salt scrub, steam bath on a marble slab with foot and scalp massage, full body exfoliation, and olive oil soap scrub-down finished with a flexibility massage. The entire Ten Spa is beautifully designed, its tasteful modern aesthetic in distinction to the Victorian splen- dor found in the rest of the Fort Garry Hotel.

WHERE TO STAY
EXPENSIVE

Delta Winnipeg *(Kids)*   The massive 17-story Delta Winnipeg, right downtown, is connected by a skywalk to the Convention Centre. Totally renovated in 2002, the Delta focuses on corporate business travelers but offers lots of extras for families. Delta's Premier rooms, all with king-size beds, are great for business travelers or for anyone that needs to keep in touch while traveling, with high-speed Internet access, wireless phones, and the option of in-room printers. Two secure executive floors offer concierge service plus other luxuries such as a private lounge with breakfast buffet, afternoon hors d'oeuvres, and honor bar. Standard rooms are large and beautifully fur- nished—all rooms have balconies. Throughout, deep rich colors and quality furniture make your stay restful and comfortable. The Delta also offers access to a private health club with full fitness facilities and a large indoor pool. Poolside family suites open onto the pool and sleep six comfortably. The **Elephant and Castle Pub** is open for all-day dining, as well as billiards, and the **Blaze Bistro and Lounge** offers notable contemporary cuisine based on Manitoba-produced ingredients.

350 St. Mary's Ave., Winnipeg, MB R3C 3J2. *©* **888/311-4990** or 204/942-0551. Fax 204/943-8702. www.delta winnipeg.com. 393 units. C$129–C$349 (US$129–US$349/£65–£175) double. Children under 18 stay free in parent's room. AE, DC, DISC, MC, V. Valet parking C$16 (US$16/£8); heated self-parking C$11 (US$11/£5.50). **Amenities:** Restaurant; bar; lounge; indoor, outdoor, wading pools; fitness center; Jacuzzi; sauna; concierge; business center; gift shop; 24-hr. room service; babysitting; laundry service; same-day dry cleaning; nonsmoking rooms; executive-level rooms. *In room:* A/C, TV, high-speed Internet access, coffeemaker, hair dryer, iron.

The Fairmont Winnipeg *&*   Don't let looks deceive—at the corner of Portage and Main rises the Fairmont, whose graceless concrete facade disguises a stylish luxury hotel: The lobby is a study in understated chic, a savvy aesthetic that extends to many of the hotel guest rooms. If it's in the budget, step up to the Fairmont Deluxe rooms, Suites, or Gold rooms, which were completely refurbished in 2003. Stocked with lots of extras (the two-room suites have five phones and two TVs), these rooms feature all- new furniture with walls and upholstery in muted, restful colors. Standard rooms are also comfortable (though they march to a different aesthetic) and offer a choice of two doubles or one queen-size bed. Wheelchair-accessible rooms are also available. The Fairmont is attached to an underground arcade with shops and services, and offers an indoor pool and an extensive selection of exercise equipment. The opulent **Velvet Glove Restaurant** features luxurious dining amid gilt-framed portraits, wood panel- ing, and brass torchières.

2 Lombard Place, Winnipeg, MB R3B 0Y3. *©* **800/441-1414** or 204/957-1350. Fax 204/949-1486. www.fairmont. com. 340 units. C$169–C$599 (US$169–US$599/£85–£300) double. Weekend packages available. C$20 (US$20/£10) additional person. AE, DC, DISC, MC, V. Valet parking C$20 (US$20/£10); self-parking C$13 (US$13/£6.50). Small pets allowed, add C$25 (US$25/£13). **Amenities:** Restaurant; lounge; indoor pool; fitness center; Jacuzzi; sauna; steam

room; concierge; business center; shopping arcade; 24-hr. room service; babysitting; laundry service; same-day dry cleaning. *In room:* A/C, TV w/pay movies, minibar, coffeemaker, hair dryer, iron.

Fort Garry Hotel ☺☺ If you love grand historic hotels, the Fort Garry is the lodging for you. Built in 1913, the Fort Garry was for decades the city's most opulent hotel. With its towering château style, it was designed to mirror New York's Plaza Hotel. The Fort Garry boasts an elegant lobby and handsome dining rooms and lounges, and the ballrooms are classics of early-20th-century grandeur. For a hotel of this vintage, rooms are spacious and exquisitely furnished with top-flight linens, feather-top beds and pillows, and luxury soaps and lotions. Forget the cheap coffeemaker and stale coffee usually found in hotel rooms; the Fort Garry offers complimentary (and freshly brewed) coffee, tea, cookies, apples, and newspapers delivered to guest rooms whenever required. The quality amenities, exemplary service, and the overall sense of elegance make this a memorable stay. The new and luxurious **Ten Spa** has taken over the entire 10th floor of the hotel and in addition to treatments and massage, offers a hammam, or Turkish bath.

222 Broadway Ave., Winnipeg, MB R3C 0R3. ℂ **800/665-2351** or 204/942-8251. Fax 204/956-2351. www.fortgarry hotel.com. 246 units. C$129–C$179 (US$129–US$179/£65–£90) double. Parking C$11 (US$11/£5.50). **Amenities:** Restaurant; lounge; fitness center w/indoor pool, whirlpool, and steam room; spa; concierge; 24-hr. room service; laundry service; all nonsmoking rooms. *In room:* A/C, TV w/pay movies, high-speed wireless Internet access, hair dryer, iron.

Inn at the Forks ☺ This new hotel overlooks the Forks, the confluence of the Assiniboine and Red rivers, once the heart of a fur-trading community and now a lively market and arts venue. The Inn at the Forks is not just new, it's modern—the decor is sleekly contemporary with light earth-tone colors and lively carpets. Guest rooms are thoughtfully furnished, with high-end linens and works by local artists, which add warmth and focus. The bathrooms feature glass countertops and upscale amenities. If you're here to work, guest rooms have large desks and leather office chairs. For more room, step up from the standard or deluxe rooms to a silver-level room—for C$20 (US$20/£10) or so, you'll get a second TV and a parlor area. The **Riverstone Spa** offers upscale pampering and aesthetic treatments, plus massage, hydrotherapy, and a menu of treatments for men. The **Current Restaurant,** open for three meals daily, serves innovative regional cuisine.

75 Forks Market Rd., Winnipeg, MB, R3C 0A2. ℂ **877/377-4100** or 204/942-6555. www.innforks.com. 115 units. From C$144 (US$144/£72) double; from C$279 (US$279/£140) suites. Free parking. **Amenities:** Restaurant; lounge; full spa; limited room service. *In room:* A/C, TV w/pay movie channels, wireless and wired high-speed Internet access, coffeemaker, hair dryer, iron.

Radisson Hotel Winnipeg ☺ Winnipeg's tallest hotel, the 29-story Radisson completed a C$6-million renovation in 2003, and offers very pleasant and thoughtfully equipped guest rooms with great views over the city. The King Suites and business-class rooms are especially nice, with king-size beds, a large desk, and an ergonomic office chair. In addition to a full business center, the 13th floor has a large tiled pool, fitness room, two saunas, and an open-air patio. The Peak Bistro offers three meals a day. The Radisson is the most centrally located hotel in Winnipeg—within easy walking distance of most tourist and business destinations.

288 Portage Ave. (at Smith St.), Winnipeg, MB R3C 0B8. ℂ **800/333-3333** or 204/956-0410. Fax 204/947-1129. www.radisson.com/winnipegca. 272 units. Weekdays C$144–C$164 (US$144–US$164/£72–£82) double. Weekend packages available. AE, DC, DISC, MC, V. Valet or self-parking, maximum C$12 (US$12/£6) per day. **Amenities:** Restaurant; lounge; indoor pool; golf course nearby; exercise room; Jacuzzi; sauna; children's center; concierge; tour

and activities desk; business center; 24-hr. room service; babysitting; laundry service; same-day dry cleaning. *In room:* A/C, TV, dataport, complimentary high-speed Internet, coffeemaker, hair dryer, iron.

MODERATE

In addition to the following choices, you may want to look at any of seven newer **Canad Inns** (*©* **888/33-CANAD;** www.canadinns.com) hotels, locally owned and operated by the Canad Corporation, which also operates many clubs, casinos, and even a record label in town. Many of these places tend toward a Las Vegas–like atmosphere, with casinos in the lobbies, theme rooms, and common areas. If that's your style, the hotels are reasonably affordable, very new, and offer plenty of amenities.

Best Western Charter House Centrally located a block from the Convention Centre, the Charter House undertook a complete renovation in 2002. A third of the rooms are designed for business travelers, with king-size beds, lots of work space and a large desk, and a separate sitting area. Rooms are comfortably outfitted, and half have balconies. Facilities include the **Rib Room** steakhouse, a lively pub with pool tables and fast food, and exercise equipment.

330 York Ave. (at Hargrave St.), Winnipeg, MB R3C 0N9. *©* 800/782-0175 or 204/942-0101. Fax 204/956-0665. www.bwcharterhouse.com. 86 units. C$109–C$159 (US$109–US$159/£55–£80) double. Extra person C$10 (US$10/£5). Children under 17 stay free in parent's room. Weekend rates, senior and AAA discounts available. AE, DC, DISC, MC, V. Parking C$5 (US$5/£2.50) nightly. **Amenities:** Restaurant; lounge and gaming room; exercise room; free shuttle service to/from airport, train and bus stations; business center; room service (7am–11pm); coin laundry room; same-day dry cleaning; executive-level rooms; rooms for those w/limited mobility. *In room:* A/C, TV w/pay movies, free high-speed Internet, coffeemaker, hair dryer, iron.

The Marlborough Hotel *(Value* Built in 1914, the Marlborough retains its vaulted ceilings, Tiffany chandeliers, English stained-glass windows, and exquisite walnut-paneled dining room from a more opulent era. As part of a newly completed C$2-million remodel, all guest rooms have been fully renovated, with several expanded into very large suites. The rooms boast all new beds, pillow-top mattresses, and 27-inch flatscreen TVs. The updating also converted an adjoining building into a conference center, making the Marlborough the largest convention hotel facility in Winnipeg, though the very moderate prices make this an attractive lodging for the general traveler. The Marlborough also features a new indoor pool, waterslide, and complimentary fitness center. At least, glance in at the faux-medieval Olde Normandy coffee shop and sumptuous Churchill's Dining Room, where the British prime minister indeed once dined.

331 Smith St. (at Portage), Winnipeg, MB R3B 2G9. *©* 800/667-7666 or 204/942-6411. Fax 204/942-2017. www. themarlborough.ca. 148 units. C$79–C$145 (US$79–US$145/£40–£73) double. Children under 18 stay free in parent's room. Special weekend rates, senior and AAA discounts available. AE, MC, V. Parking $6. Pets allowed. **Amenities:** Restaurant; lounge; indoor pool; waterslide; fitness facility; hot tub; courtesy limo; limited room service; coin-op laundry; valet laundry service; dry cleaning. *In room:* A/C, TV w/pay-per-view movies, dataport, free wireless Internet access, coffeemaker, hair dryer, iron.

The Norwood Although you can't tell by looking at this large, modern building across the Red River from the Forks district in St. Boniface, the Norwood is Manitoba's oldest family-owned and -operated hotel, dating from 1885. Bearing no resemblance to its original wooden structure, this is a comfortable and clean hotel with plenty of standard amenities, including high-speed Internet access, in even its basic rooms. Executive suites add full living rooms and refrigerators. For dining, you can choose between the Jolly Friar restaurant and the Wood Tavern & Grill pub.

112 Marion St. (at av. Taché), Winnipeg MB R2H 0T1. © **888/888-1878** or 204/233-4475. Fax 204/231-1910. www. norwood-hotel.com. 52 units. From C$104 (US$104/£52) double. Senior and AAA discounts available. AE, DC, MC, V. Free parking. **Amenities:** Restaurant; bar; room service (7am–9pm); same-day dry cleaning; rooms for those w/limited mobility. *In room:* A/C, TV, dataport, coffeemaker, hair dryer, iron.

Place Louis Riel Suite Hotel ⭐⭐ (Kids)   In the heart of downtown is a friendly, all-suite hotel with excellent, personalized service. Always a top hotel pick, the PLR, as it's known by the locals, is now even better. The entire hotel has undergone a massive C$15-million renovation (completed in 2008) that practically rebuilt the hotel from the inside out. Guests may not notice the new room configurations, but they will notice the sumptuous new fixtures, luxury linens, and granite and leather accents. Built as an apartment building, the Place Louis Riel has a great many room types, ranging from studios to one- and two-bedroom suites, all with full kitchens. Courtesy of the new renovation and communicating doors, corner units can expand to include two kitchens, four TVs, two bathrooms and five beds—perfect for a large family traveling together. All rooms feature original Native Canadian art from area artists. For convenience, a laundromat, grocery store, and restaurant and lounge are on the ground floor. This is a pet- and kid-friendly hotel.

190 Smith St. (at St. Mary's Ave.), Winnipeg, MB R3C 1J8. © **800/665-0569** or 204/947-6961. Fax 204/947-3029. www.placelouisriel.com. 294 units. C$79–C$140 (US$79–US$140/£40–£70) double; C$140–C$175 (US$140–US$175/£70–£88) for premier floor double. Extra person C$10 (US$10/£5). Children under 17 stay free in parent's room. Weekend rates, senior and AAA discounts available. AE, DC, MC, V. Parking C$6 (US$6/£3). Pets allowed with C$10 (US$10/£5) fee per day. **Amenities:** Restaurant; bar; exercise room; tour and activities desk; business center; room service (6:30am–10:30pm); coin-op laundry; laundry service; same-day dry cleaning; nonsmoking rooms; executive-level rooms; 4 rooms for those w/limited mobility. *In room:* A/C, TV w/pay movies, high-speed Internet access, kitchen, fridge, coffeemaker, hair dryer, iron.

WHERE TO DINE

An excellent place for a good Mediterranean restaurant (or a funky bar or eclectic shopping) is along **Corydon Avenue,** south of downtown across the Assiniboine River. Known as **Little Italy,** the area was settled by Italian immigrants and still has a continental feel, with lots of cafes and good people-watching. Many of the restaurants have outdoor courtyard seating in summer. Likewise, the **Osborne Village** area, just south of the Assiniboine River on Osborne Street, is another nucleus of pubs and trendy, casual restaurants. Note that most independent chef-owned restaurants are closed on Sundays, and many are closed on Monday.

EXPENSIVE

Amici ⭐⭐ CONTINENTAL/ITALIAN   With a new chef at the helm, Amici remains at the pinnacle of sublime northern Italian cuisine. You have your choice of 20 or more antipasti (appetizers); try gnocchi with herbed-brie cream sauce with thinly sliced beef tenderloin for a wonderful combination of flavor and texture. Entrees include traditional but highly refined Italian classics such as veal scallopini stuffed with asparagus and other richly flavored meat, chicken and fish classics, plus more innovative Italian-influenced dishes such as roasted veal chops on straw potatoes with fig and Marsala glaze, or pistachio-crusted salmon with citrus and saffron cream. The menu changes regularly, but the ingredients are always fresh and the preparations top-notch. For a casual drink and less formal meal, Amici is also home to Bombolini's wine bar, downstairs.

326 Broadway Ave. © **204/943-4997.** www.amiciwpg.com. Reservations recommended. Main courses C$18–C$42 (US$18–US$42/£9–£21). AE, MC, V. Mon–Fri 11:30am–2pm; Mon–Sat 5–10pm.

529 Wellington STEAKS/SEAFOOD   Situated in a lushly renovated, grand old stone-faced mansion—once home to the family of Winnipeg businessman and mayor, J. H. Ashdown—529 Wellington serves up steaks, chops, and seafood in an elegant setting. Worthy starters include maple-smoked steelhead salmon or a salad of fire-roasted peppers with shaved garlic, herbs, and chèvre. Entrees include prime-graded Canadian beef, or any of a number of fresh seafood choices, ranging from Atlantic salmon or lobster to sushi-grade ahi tuna. To top things off, the award-winning wine list features about 400 selections.

529 Wellington Crescent. © 204/487-8325. www.wowhospitality.ca. Reservations recommended. Main courses C$28–C$42 (US$28–US$42/£14–£21). Mon–Fri 11:30am–11pm; Sat 5–11pm; Sun 5–10pm. Take Broadway/Hwy. 1 west, then go left/south on Maryland St., cross the Assiniboine, and turn left on Wellington Crescent.

Gluttons Bistro 🍷🍷 INTERNATIONAL   Very much Winnipeg's restaurant of the moment, Gluttons is a small bistro attached to an upscale gourmet market. Gluttons rose to national prominence when chef/owner Makoto Ono, then 28, was named the Canadian Culinary Champion in the 2007 Gold Medal Plates competition. Now a pilgrammage destination for serious foodies, the restaurant serves a daily changing, four-course prix-fixe menu, with two appetizers (one cold, one hot), main course, and dessert. Appetizers may include fois gras with port syrup or venison carpaccio, and main courses have featured seared sea scallops with cinnamon red-wine reduction, poached lobster with marinated chantrelles and burnt-butter mayonnaise, or porcini-crusted beef tenderloin. If you can't afford dinner here (with the suggested wine pairings and tip, dinner can edge toward $100 a person) or can't get reservations, try lunch, when the chef's prodigious gifts shine in an a la carte menu.

842 Corydon Ave. © 204/475-5714. Reservations required. 4-course prix-fixe menu C$56 (US$56/£28), matching wine flight C$36 (US$36/£18). AE, MC, V. Tues–Sat 11:30am–2pm and 5:30–10pm.

Restaurant Dubrovnik 🍷 CONTINENTAL   Dubrovnik offers a romantic setting for fine Continental cuisine and Eastern European specialties. It occupies a beautiful Victorian brick town house with working fireplaces, leaded-glass windows, and an enclosed veranda. Each dining area is decorated tastefully with a few plants and colorful gusle (beautifully carved musical instruments, often inlaid with mother-of-pearl). Start with artichoke-and–porcini mushroom ravioli with red-bell-pepper coulis or exquisite little sandwiches of lobster and mango. Main courses are very refined—Muscovy duck breast is served with sour cherries and pomegranate glaze, while roasted squab comes with foie gras, baked apple, figs, and a glaze of port. Finish with a coffee Dubrovnik (sljivovica—plum brandy— with Kruskovac pear liqueur, coffee, whipped cream, and chopped walnuts).

390 Assiniboine Ave. © 204/944-0594. Reservations recommended. Main courses C$19–C$40 (US$19–US$40/ £9.50–£20). AE, MC, V. Mon–Fri 11am–2pm; Mon–Sat 5–11pm.

Step 'N Out ECLECTIC   Located in St. Boniface, at the end of the Provencher Bridge, this classy but campy restaurant is noted for its unique setting—it's just the spot for an upbeat dinner with someone special. The restaurant is richly decorated, with a huge collection of vintage miniature shoes, photos of Hollywood stars, and lots of plants and twinkling lights, all the better to highlight the superlative food. The handwritten menu, brought to diners on a chalkboard, changes weekly to ensure that seasonal products take center stage. Everything served here is handcrafted, from appetizers such as escargot and spinach-stuffed prawns to Moroccan-spiced beef over chilled asparagus. The chef's Australian roots show through in dishes such as grilled duck breast served with wild mushrooms and Woolloomooloo chutney.

157 Provencher Blvd. ℂ 204/956-7837. Reservations required. Main courses C$22–C$36 (US$22–US$36/£11–£18). AE, DC, MC, V. Mon–Fri 11am–2pm; Mon–Sat 5–9pm.

Sydney's ECLECTIC   Not so long ago, going out for a multicourse dinner meant out-of-control portions and formal dining according to rules laid down 200 years ago in Paris. However, the prix-fixe menu at Sydney's approaches multicourse dining from the perspective of an upscale, very global tapas bar. For a single price, diners choose a sequence of five courses from an ambitiously large and international menu. Menus change about once a month to reflect what's seasonal, as well as what's cutting edge (the kitchen is very responsive to the latest food trends). Because portions are tapas-size, you won't end up stuffed (and the table buried in plates), and you are able to devise your own formula to assemble a unique series of flavors.

For starters, a Napoleon of candied pears with brie drizzled with cognac syrup awakens the palate. After a palate-cleansing sorbet, the main course may be rosemary-and-black-mustard-crusted rack of lamb with cabernet and espresso sauce, or 3 Little Pigs (pork tenderloin stuffed with a bacon and pork sausage finished with Calvados white-balsamic reduction). The red-brick warehouse at the Forks serves as historic backdrop for this very up-to-date cuisine. The lunch menu is served a la carte.

The Forks Market, 2nd floor. ℂ 204/942-6075. Reservations recommended. 5-course menu C$48 (US$48/£24). AE, DC, MC, V. Tues–Fri 11:30am–2pm; Mon–Sat 5pm–midnight.

MODERATE

Bistro Dansk DANISH   This warm chalet-style bistro serves up northern European comfort food. Main courses include seven superlative Danish specialties, such as *frikadeller* (Danish meat patties, made from ground veal and pork, served with red cabbage and potato salad), and *aeggekage* (a Danish omelet with bacon, garnished with tomatoes and green onions, and served with home-baked Danish bread). At lunch, specialties include nine or so open-face sandwiches, served on homemade rye or white bread.

63 Sherbrook St. (near Wolseley Ave.). ℂ 204/775-5662. Reservations recommended. Main courses C$8–C$14 (US$8–US$14/£4–£7). AE, MC, V. Mon–Sat 11am–3pm; Tues–Sat 5–9:30pm.

FUDE ℛ REGIONAL/CONTEMPORARY   A restaurant with a stated philosophy is usually to be avoided, but when your server summarizes the culinary thinking behind FUDE, it's encouraging. As much as possible, all food is made in-house (for instance, all the breads and desserts), and ingredients are sourced in Manitoba. Beyond this, the philosophy goes, eating FUDE ought to be fun! FUDE's culinary zing comes from its sophisticated forays into world cuisine. The menu is divided into sections: Flat, for pizza; Twisted, for pasta; and Comfort, for entrees such as pork loin with huckleberry gravy, and the house specialty, grilled chicken breast with choco-late–chipotle pepper sauce. In summer, diners can sit on the second-floor deck above bustling Osborne Street, just south of downtown. FUDE is a splendid example of the cuisine alchemy popular in Winnipeg.

99 Osborne St. (upstairs). ℂ 204/284-3833. Reservations recommended. Main courses C$17–C$30 (US$17–C$30/£8.50–£15). AE, DC, MC, V. Mon–Thurs 5–10pm; Fri–Sat 5–11pm.

Fusion Grill ℛ INTERNATIONAL/CANADIAN   This is a hip and fun place serving up some of Winnipeg's best nontraditional cuisine. Begin by getting into a different mindset with the "Soup of Tomorrow," featured daily. Then the fusion experience begins. Tantalizing starters may include a crispy tiger prawn dumplings with garlic-sesame noodles and sweet soy dipping sauce, or white-truffle perogies with duck sausage and walnut cream. Daily changing entrees may include pan-seared pork tenderloin with morel mushrooms, black-spruce jelly, celery-walnut-fig relish and wild-berry compote. Fusion Grill is a fun and exciting place—prepared to be wowed.

550 Academy Rd. (near Lanark St.). © 204/489-6963. www.fusiongrill.mb.ca. Reservations recommended. Main courses C$20–C$36 (US$20–US$36/£10–£18). AE, DC, V, MC. Tues–Sat 11:30am–2pm and 5:30–10pm. From Portage Ave./Rte. 85/Hwy. 1 west, left on Maryland St., cross the Assiniboine where it becomes Academy Rd.

In Ferno's Bistro ✦ FRENCH   In Ferno's Bistro is a popular and bustling restaurant—with lots of patio seating—in the heart of St. Boniface. While the menu preserves the hallmarks of classic French and French-Canadian bistro cooking—three preparations of mussels and frites, onion soup *grantinee,* and a creamy veal *grandmère* fricassee—it's the more contemporary dishes that truly stand out. Stylized but not precious, an appetizer such as chicken pot stickers with creamy sweet-chile sauce and a salad robed in mango-chutney dressing is an explosion of flavors and textures, as is salmon ceviche with thin slices of white onion and lemon. The house specialty, braised lamb shank with maple syrup and balsamic-vinegar reduction, is another great combo of flavors. However, it's the extensive list of seasonal specials that should guide your choice of main courses. For food of this quality, the prices are very reasonable.

312 Des Meurons St. © 204/262-7400. Reservations recommended. Main courses C$12–C$27 (US$12–US$27/£6–£14). AE, MC, V. Mon–Thurs 11am–11pm; Fri–Sat 11am–midnight.

Oui Bistro and Wine Bar ✦ FRENCH   Simultaneously old world and contemporary, Oui Bistro has the elegance and sophistication of a classic French dining room but with updated food and friendly, energetic service. In a historic Exchange District storefront, Oui Bistro is a jewel box of Belle Epoque mirrors, golden drapes and deep-blue walls, but this is no food museum. Chef Tristan Foucault dusts off classic French cooking to rediscover the fresh tastes and textures behind the great standards of Gallic cooking. Salt cod fritters are drizzled with chive oil, and seared foie gras appears on cinnamon pound cake, topped with apple compote and garnished with a fig and port reduction. Main courses include all your French favorites—mussels prepared three ways, beef bourguignon, cassoulet with house-made duck confit and garlic sausages—but enlivened with lighter preparations and the best of local ingredients.

283 Bannatyne Ave. © 204/989-7700. Reservations recommended. C$12–C$29 (US$12–US$29/£6–£15). AE, MC, V. Tues–Thurs 11:30am–2:30pm and 5–10pm; Fri 11:30am–2:30pm and 5–11pm; Sat 5–11pm.

Pasta la Vista ✦ ITALIAN   You might think that Pasta la Vista's location, across from a major hotel and the Winnipeg convention center, would lead to a by-the-numbers Italian eatery. But you'd be wrong. Pasta la Vista offers new twists on traditional Italian dishes and a bustling yet comfortable atmosphere. Pasta dishes range from traditional favorites such as lasagna and penne with sausage to more adventurous Flurry of Curry (mango-and-pineapple curry sauce with chicken) to Black Magic, with squid-ink pasta and shellfish with chile sauce. Rotisserie chicken is a stand-out entry, as are a handful of Italian and Asian roast meat and vegetable dishes. In season, the Magic Mushroom special, woodland mushroom ravioli with Marsala cream sauce topped with crispy threads of potato and beet, is a knockout. Then there are the wood-fired pizzas to seduce the taste buds when nothing else seems quite right. Pasta la Vista is a fun and lively place to meet friends for drinks and dinner.

66–333 St. Mary Ave. © **204/956-2229.** www.wowhospitality.ca. Reservations recommended. Main courses C$9–C$25 (US$9–US$25/£4.50–£13). AE, DC, MC, V. Mon–Sat 11am–11pm; Sun 4–10 pm.

Tre Visi ITALIAN   This Exchange District restaurant has a tiny dining room but a big reputation as serving the city's best traditional Italian food. Tre Visi seems like a transplant from New York, with studied, expert service and a menu that doesn't expand the boundaries of Italian cooking but instead delivers expertly prepared classics. All the details are exactly right: Spaghetti puttanesca is pungent with a touch of heat; *saltimbocca alla romana,* the traditional veal scaloppini topped with sage leaves and proscuitto, is both moist and crispy. Gnocchi is one of the house specialties, served with either pesto cream or deep, rich tomato sauce. The walls glow with creamy golden colors, the better to display the mural-like paintings that flank the always-bustling dining room.

173 McDermott Ave. © **204/949-9032.** Reservations required. Main courses C$13–C$28 (US$13–US$28/£7.50–£14). AE, MC, V. Mon–Wed 11:30am–2:30pm and 5–9pm; Thurs–Fri 11:30am–2:30pm and 5–10pm; Sat 5–10pm.

INEXPENSIVE

The **Forks Market** area is filled with inexpensive food stalls and places for a quick bit to eat. Also, both the **Portage Place** (on Portage Ave. between Vaughan and Carlton sts.) and **cityplace** shopping centers (at Graham Ave. and Donald St.) have large food courts.

Alycia's *(Value* UKRAINIAN   Famed as one of the late comedian John Candy's favorite restaurants, Alycia's is the ultimate place for comfort food, and lets you sample Winnipeg's Ukrainian culture gastronomically. The atmosphere is homey and warm, bedecked with Ukrainian knickknacks and art, and the place is often full of Ukrainian diners. The menu prominently features pierogies, potato-and-cheese stuffed dumplings, which can be pan-fried or boiled (Alycia's pumps out a 12,000 a day!) Alycia's menu also features many North American standards, including plenty of sandwiches on the lunch menu. Prices are extremely reasonable, and the service is quick and friendly.

559 Cathedral Ave. (at McGregor). © **204/582-8789.** Main courses C$5–C$11 (US$5–US$11/£2.50–£5.50). AE, DC, MC, V. Mon–Fri 8am–8pm; Sat 9am–8pm. Go north on Hwy. 52 to Cathedral Ave., and turn left.

WINNIPEG AFTER DARK

THE PERFORMING ARTS   The **Manitoba Centennial Centre,** 555 Main St. (© **204/956-1360**), is a complex that includes the Centennial Concert Hall (home to the Royal Winnipeg Ballet, the Winnipeg Symphony, and the Manitoba Opera). Nearby are the Manitoba Theatre Centre, the Warehouse Theatre, and Pantages Playhouse Theatre.

Other spaces offering frequent concerts and performances include the **Winnipeg Art Gallery** (© **204/786-6641;** www.wag.mb.ca), with blues/jazz, chamber music, and contemporary music groups; and the **Pantages Playhouse Theatre,** 180 Market Ave. E. (© **204/989-2889;** www.pantagesplayhouse.com).

The world-renowned **Royal Winnipeg Ballet** ⊛, 380 Graham Ave., at Edmonton Street (© **204/956-2792** for the box office; www.rwb.org), was founded in 1939 by two British immigrant ballet teachers, making it North America's second-oldest ballet company (after San Francisco's). By 1949, it was a professional troupe, and in 1953, it was granted a royal charter. Today, its repertoire includes both contemporary and classical works, such as Ashton's *Thais, Giselle,* and *Sleeping Beauty.* The company performs at the Centennial Concert Hall, usually for a week in October, November,

December, March, and May. Tickets are C$24 to C$68 (US$24–US$68/£12–£34), with discounts for students, seniors, and children.

The **Winnipeg Symphony Orchestra,** 555 Main St. (© **204/949-3950,** or 204/ 949-3999 for the box office; www.wso.mb.ca), was established in 1947. The orchestra's prestige has attracted guest artists such as Itzhak Perlman, Isaac Stern, Tracey Dahl, and Maureen Forrester. The season usually runs September to mid-May, and tickets are C$25 to C$49 (US$25–US$49/£13–£25).

The **Manitoba Opera,** 380 Graham Ave. (© **204/942-7479,** or 204/957-7842 for the box office; www.manitobaopera.mb.ca), features a season of two or three operas each year at the Centennial Concert Hall, with performances in February and April, and possibly November. English subtitles are used. Tickets range from C$30 to C$99 (US$30–US$99/£15–£50).

THEATER   You can enjoy theater in the park at the **Rainbow Stage,** in Kildonan Park at 2021 Main St. (© **204/989-5261** or 204/989-0888 for tickets; www.rainbow stage.net), Canada's largest and oldest continuously operating outdoor theater. The theater group actually presents two musical classics, running about 3 weeks each, one in the summer at Kildonan and one in mid-winter at the Pantages Playhouse Theatre (see above). On the banks of the Red River, the outdoor Rainbow Stage is easily accessible by bus or car.

The **MTC Warehouse,** at 140 Rupert Ave. at Lily (© **204/943-4849,** or 204/ 942-6537 for the box office; www.mtc.mb.ca), presents more cutting-edge, controversial plays in an intimate 300-seat theater. Its four-play season generally runs mid-October to mid-May, and tickets are C$13 to C$60 (US$13–US$60/£6.50–£30). Recent offerings have included a production of *Hamlet* starring Keanu Reeves.

The **Prairie Theatre Exchange,** 3rd level, Portage Place, 393 Portage Ave. (© **204/942-7291,** or 204/942-5483 for the box office; www.pte.mb.ca), also offers about six productions from October to April, and provides the most serious alternative to MTC shows. A recent season featured *The Glass Menagerie* and Virginia Woolf's *A Room of One's Own.* Standard ticket prices are about C$32 (US$32/£16) for adults, C$22 (US$22/£11) for seniors and students. Some less expensive shows run at the end of the season.

CASINOS   The tropical-themed **Club Regent,** 1425 Regent Ave. (© **888/957-4652** or 204/957-2700; www.clubregent.com), offers slots, electronic blackjack, bingo, poker, keno, and breakopen games, plus traditional bingo and the Fountain of Fortune, a series of progressive slot machines. Huge, walk-through aquariums and two live music stages add to the diversions. The club is open Monday through Saturday 10am to 3am and Sunday noon to 3am.

The Grand Railway Hotel–themed **McPhillips Station,** 484 McPhillips St. (© **204/957-3900;** www.clubregent.com) is your other major casino option in town, featuring many of the same gaming choices as at the Club Regent (both are operated and regulated by the Manitoba Lotteries Corporation). The side show here is the Millennium Express multimedia theater presentation, a quasi-time-travel ride and show taking you back into Manitoba's past. McPhillips Station operates during the same hours as its sister casino, and both have restaurants and gift shops.

DANCE CLUBS   Country-western dance bars used to be a large part of the nightlife in Winnipeg, but the scene is rapidly changing. Even the **Palomino Club,** 1133 Portage Ave. (© **204/722-0454**), once the best place to sample line dancing, mostly features classic rock. **Silverado's,** 2100 McPhillips St., in the Canad Inn Garden City

(© **204/633-0024**), has three floors of dancing to country bands and rock acts, plus DJ-spun dance-floor hits.

The dance club scene has really exploded in Winnipeg with the opening of several new upscale clubs in the past few years; a small sampling follows. **The Empire,** at 436 Main St., near Portage Ave. (© **204/943-3979**), features a Roman-themed dance floor in a historic bank building. In the Exchange District, **Alive,** 140 Bannatyne (© **204/989-8080**), has both DJs and live bands, and attracts a slightly more mature crowd—you'll feel comfortable even if you're over 30. As dance clubs can be ephemeral, you may want to check out the latest news when you visit town; see *Uptown Magazine*'s website at **www.uptownmag.com** to search the latest club information and listings.

SIDE TRIPS FROM WINNIPEG

LOWER FORT GARRY NATIONAL HISTORIC SITE   The oldest intact stone fur-trading post in North America is **Lower Fort Garry** (© **877/534-3678** or 204/785-6050; www.pc.gc.ca), only 32km (20 miles) north of Winnipeg on Highway 9. Built in the 1830s, Lower Fort Garry was an important Hudson's Bay Company transshipment and provisioning post. Within the walls of the compound are the governor's residence; several warehouses, including the fur loft; and the Men's House, where male employees lived. Outside the compound are company buildings—a blacksmith's shop, the farm manager's home, and so on. The fort is staffed by costumed volunteers who make candles and soap; forge horseshoes, locks, and bolts; and generally demonstrate the ways of life of the 1850s. In a lean-to beside the fur-loft building stands an original York boat; hundreds of these once traveled the waterways from Hudson Bay to the Rockies and from the Red River to the Arctic carrying furs and trading goods.

Mid-May through Labour Day, the site is open daily from 9am to 5pm. Admission is C$7.15 (US$7.15/£3.60) for adults, C$5.90 (US$5.90/£2.95) for seniors, C$3.45 (US$3.45/£1.75) for youths ages 6 to 16, C$18 (US$18/£9) for families, and free for children under 6. Call **Beaver Bus Lines** (© **204/989-7007**), to get a charter bus from downtown Winnipeg to Lower Fort Garry.

STEINBACH MENNONITE HERITAGE VILLAGE   About 48km (30 miles) outside Winnipeg is the **Steinbach Mennonite Heritage Village** ☞ (© **204/326-9661;** www.mennoniteheritagevillage.com), 2.5km (1½ miles) north of Steinbach on Highway 12, south off Highway 1, east from town. This 16-hectare (40-acre) museum complex is worth a detour. Between 1874 and 1880, about 7,000 Mennonites migrated here from the Ukraine, establishing settlements such as Kleefeld, Steinbach, Blumenort, and others. Between 1922 and 1926, many moved to Mexico and Uruguay when Manitoba closed all unregistered schools, but they were replaced by another surge of emigrants fleeing the Russian Revolution. Their community life is portrayed here in a complex of about 20 buildings. In the museum, dioramas display daily life and community artifacts, such as woodworking and sewing tools, sausage makers, clothes, medicines, and furnishings. Elsewhere in the complex, you can view a windmill grinding grain, ride in an ox-drawn wagon, watch a blacksmith at work, or view any number of homes, agricultural machines, and more. In summer, a restaurant serves Mennonite food—a full meal of borscht, thick-sliced homemade brown bread, coleslaw, pierogies, and sausage, plus rhubarb crumble, all at reasonable prices.

The village is open Monday through Saturday May and September 10am to 5pm; hours during June, July, and August are 10am to 6pm. On Sunday, the gates don't open until noon. October to April, the museum is open Monday through Friday

10am to 4pm. Admission is C$8 (US$8/£4) for adults, C$6 (US$6/£3) for seniors and students 13 to 22, C$2 (US$2/£1) for children aged 6 to 12, and C$20 (US$20/£10) for families.

3 Whiteshell Provincial Park & Lake Winnipeg

WHITESHELL PROVINCIAL PARK ✪

Less than a 2-hour drive east of Winnipeg (144km/89 miles) lies a network of a dozen rivers and more than 200 lakes in the 2,590-sq.-km (1,000-sq.-mile) **Whiteshell Provincial Park** (© 204/369-5246). Among the park's natural features are Rainbow and Whitemouth falls; a lovely lily pond west of Caddy Lake; West Hawk Lake, Manitoba's deepest lake, created by a meteorite; and a goose sanctuary (best seen mid-May to July, when the goslings are about). You can also view petroforms, stone arrangements fashioned by an Algonquin-speaking people to communicate with the spirits. In fall, you can witness an ancient ritual—First Nations Canadians harvesting wild rice. One person poles a canoe through the rice field while another bends the stalks into the canoe and knocks the ripe grains off with a picking stick.

In July and August, the **Manitoba Naturalists Society,** headquartered at 401–63 Albert St. in Winnipeg (© **204/943-9029;** www.manitobanature.ca), operates wilderness programs and other workshops at their cabin on Lake Mantario. There are six self-guided trails, plus several short trails you can complete in less than 2 hours. For serious backpackers, the **Mantario Trail** is a 3- to 6-day hike over 60km (37 miles) of rugged terrain. There are also all-terrain biking trails. You can choose among one of several canoe routes, including the Frances Lake route, which covers 18km (11 miles) of pleasant paddling with 12 beaver-dam hauls and three portages, and takes about 6 hours. There is swimming at Falcon Beach; scuba diving in West Hawk Lake; and sailing, windsurfing, water-skiing, and fishing in other places.

Horseback riding is offered at **Falcon Beach Ranch** (© **877/949-2410** or 204/349-2410; www.falconbeachranch.com). In winter, there is downhill skiing, cross-country skiing, snowmobiling, snowshoeing, and skating. Most recreational equipment, including skis, canoes, snowshoes, and fishing gear, is available from the **Falcon Trails Resort** (© **204/349-8273;** www.trails.falcontrails.biz), which also rents lakeside cabins.

Within the park, Falcon Lake is the center of one of Canada's most modern recreational developments, including various resorts with tennis courts, an 18-hole par-72 golf course, hiking trails, horseback riding, fishing, canoeing, and skiing. Most park resorts and lodges charge C$125 to C$200 (US$125–US$200/£63–£100) for a double per night, with weeklong rates for groups of four in two-bedroom cabins. Most resorts offer recreational equipment rentals. Camping facilities abound. For more info, call the park at © **204/369-5246** or contact **Travel Manitoba,** Dept. SV2, 155 Carlton St., 7th Floor, Winnipeg, MB R3C 3H8 (© **800/665-0040** or 204/945-3777; www.travelmanitoba.com).

LAKE WINNIPEG

The continent's seventh largest lake, **Lake Winnipeg** is 425km (264 miles) long, and its shores shelter some interesting communities and attractive natural areas. At its southern end, **Grand Beach Provincial Park** (© **204/754-2212**) has white-sand beaches backed by 10m-high (33-ft.) dunes in some places. This is a good place to swim, windsurf, and sail. There are three self-guided nature trails. Campsites are available in summer only.

About 97km (60 miles) north of Winnipeg, on the western shore, the farming-and-fishing community of **Gimli** is the hub of Icelandic culture in Manitoba. Established over a century ago as the capital of New Iceland, it had its own government, school, and newspapers for many years. It still celebrates an Icelandic festival known as Islendingadagurinn on the first long weekend in August (© **204/642-7417;** www. icelandicfestival.com).

Hecla Island, 165km (102 miles) northeast of Winnipeg, was once a part of the Republic of New Iceland and home to a small Icelandic-Canadian farming-and-fishing community. Today it's the site of **Hecla/Grindstone Provincial Park** (© **204/ 378-2945**). Open year-round, it's an excellent place to hike (with five short trails), golf, fish, camp, bird-watch, canoe, swim, windsurf, play tennis (two courts), cross-country ski, snowshoe, or snowmobile and toboggan. Camping is available in summer. Photographers and wildlife enthusiasts appreciate the park's wildlife-viewing tower and the **Grassy Narrow Marsh,** which shelters many species of waterfowl. There are a campground and 17 cabins available. For campground and cabin reservations at all provincial parks, call © **888/482-2267** or go to www.gov.mb.ca/natres/ parks/reservations. Another option is the Resort Hecla (see below).

WHERE TO STAY IN GULL HARBOUR

Hecla Oasis Resort   The former Gull Harbour Resort, located on the shores of Lake Winnipeg within Hecla Provincial Park, reopened in 2008 after a C$15-million redevelopment that updated, upgraded, and expanded the offerings of this well-loved institution. In addition to updating the entire resort, the remodel introduces a family indoor and outdoor water park, a full-service day spa and wellness center, biologist-led eco- and adventure tours, a pet spa and culinary studio, and the Hecla Oasis Learning Centre. These join the resort's three restaurants, comfortable rooms, and one of Manitoba's top championship golf courses, along with hiking and biking trails, beaches, and tennis courts. There are plenty of wintertime activities also, including cross-country skiing, snowmobiling, snowshoeing, and kiteboarding, with future plans for an Icelandic Family Winter Park.

Box 789, Riverton MB R0C 2R0. © **800/267-6700.** www.heclaoasis.com. 90 units. C$189–C$450 (US$189–US$450/ £95–£225) double. Extra person is C$30 (US$30/£15). Children under 12 stay free in parent's room. Specials and packages available year-round. AAA/CAA discounts available. AE, DC, MC, V. **Amenities:** 3 restaurants; indoor and outdoor waterparks; golf course; fitness center; mineral pools; sports equipment rental; bike rental. *In room:* A/C, plasma TV, high-speed Internet access, microwave, fridge, electronic safe.

4 West along the Trans-Canada Highway to Spruce Woods Provincial Park & Brandon

About 67km (42 miles) west of Portage la Prairie, before reaching Carberry, turn south on Highway 5 to **Spruce Woods Provincial Park,** Box 900, Carberry, MB R0K 0H0 (© **204/827-8850** in summer, or 204/834-8800). The park's unique and most fragile feature is **Spirit Sands,** a 5-sq.-km (2-sq.-mile) tract of open, blowing sand dunes that are the remains of the once-wide Assiniboine Delta. Only a few hardy creatures—including the prairie skink (Manitoba's only lizard), hognose snake, Bembix wasp, and one type of wolf spider—live here. The rest of the park is forest and prairie grasslands inhabited by herds of wapiti (elk).

There's camping at **Kiche Manitou** as well as at hike-in locations. The park is on the Assiniboine River canoe route, which starts in Brandon and ends north of Holland. You can rent canoes at Pine Fort IV in the park. The park's longest trail is the

40km (25-mile) **Epinette Trail,** but its most fascinating is the **Spirit Sands/Devil's Punch Bowl,** accessible from Highway 5. It loops through the dunes and leads to the Devil's Punch Bowl, which was carved by underground streams. There are also bike and mountain-bike trails; swimming at the campground beach; and in winter, cross-country skiing, skating, tobogganing, and snowmobiling.

Brandon is Manitoba's second-largest city, with a population of about 45,000. This university town features the **Art Gallery of Southwestern Manitoba** at 710 Rosser Ave. (© **204/727-1036;** http://agsm.ca); the **B. J. Hales Museum of Natural History** on the Brandon University campus (© **204/727-7307;** http://flinflon. brandonu.ca/bjhales), with mounted specimens of birds and mammals. Another worthy attraction is the **Commonwealth Air Training Plan Museum** at the airport (© **204/727-2444;** www.airmuseum.ca), with historical aircraft and artifacts from Royal Canadian Air Force training schools of World War II.

5 Riding Mountain National Park & Duck Mountain Provincial Park

RIDING MOUNTAIN NATIONAL PARK ★★

About 248km (154 miles) northwest of Winnipeg, **Riding Mountain National Park,** Wasagaming, MB R0J 2H0 (© **800/707-8480** or 204/848-7275), is set in the highlands atop a giant wooded escarpment sheltering more than 260 species of birds, plus moose, wolf, coyote, lynx, beaver, black bear, and a bison herd at Lake Audy.

The park has more than 400km (249 miles) of **hiking trails.** Twenty are short, easily accessible, and easy to moderate in difficulty; another 20 are long backcountry trails. Call the number above for more info. You can ride many trails on mountain bike and horseback and can rent both bikes and horses in Wasagaming.

You can rent canoes and other boats at **Clear Lake Marina** (© **204/867-7298**). As for **fishing,** northern pike is the main game fish and specimens up to 14 kilograms (30 lb.) have been taken from Clear Lake. Rainbow and brook trout populate Lake Katherine and Deep Lake. The park also has one of the province's best **golf courses** (© **204/848-4653;** www.clearlakegolfcourse.com); greens fees are between C$40 and C$44 (US$40–US$44/£20–£22). In winter, there's **ice fishing** and **cross-country skiing** (call the park for permits and information).

The **visitor center** is open daily in summer 9am to 9pm. For information, contact the park (see above). The park is easily accessed from Brandon, about 95km (59 miles) north along Highway 10. Entry is C$7 (US$7/£3.50) for adults and C$17 (US$17/ £8.50) for families; multiday passes are also available.

WHERE TO STAY

In Wasagaming, you can stay at five park **campgrounds** or in motel and cabin accommodations for anywhere from about C$80 to C$180 (US$80–US$180/£40–£90) for a double. Wasagaming also has six tennis courts, lawn-bowling greens, a children's playground, and a log-cabin movie theater in the **Wasagaming Visitor Centre** beside Clear Lake. There are also a dance hall, picnic areas with stoves, and a band shell down by the lake for Sunday-afternoon concerts. At the lake itself, you can rent boats and swim at the main beach.

Wasagaming Campground has more than 500 sites, most unserviced. Facilities include showers and toilets, kitchen shelters, and a sewage-disposal station nearby. Rates range from C$26 to C$36 (US$26–US$36/£13–£18) for full service in the summer. Other outlying campgrounds (93 sites) are at **Moon Lake, Lake Audy, Whirlpool,** and **Deep Lake.** None of these is serviced. For reservations, call © **800/ 707-8480.** Outlying campgrounds are C$15 (US$15/£7.50), site only. Backcountry camping is also available with a permit. Advance reservations (© **877/737-3783;** www.pccamping.ca) are strongly recommended.

Elkhorn Resort Hotel & Conference Centre   This year-round lodge is on the edge of Wasagaming with easy access to Riding Mountain, overlooking quiet fields and forest. Guest rooms are large, comfortable, and nicely appointed with modern pine furnishings; some have fireplaces and private balconies. At the ranch's common room, you can join a game of bridge or cribbage in the evening. In summer, facilities include a riding stable, and there's a lake nearby for water activities; winter pleasures include sleigh rides, cross-country skiing, outdoor skating, and tobogganing. Also on the property are several fully equipped two- and three-bedroom chalets (with fireplaces, toasters, dishwashers, microwaves, and balconies with barbecues) designed after Quonsets.

Mooswa Dr. E., Clear Lake, MB R0J 1N0. © 866/ELKHORN or 204/848-2802. Fax 204/848-2109. www.elkhorn resort.mb.ca. 57 units. Mid-May to Sept and late Dec to Jan 1 C$140–C$225 (US$140–US$225/£70–£113) lodge room double, from C$300 (US$300/£150) chalet; Oct to late Dec and Jan 2 to mid-May C$110–C$140 (US$110–US$140/ £55–£70) lodge room double, from C$280 (US$280/£140) chalet. Weekly chalet rates available. Extra person in lodge C$15 (US$15/£7.50). Children under 17 stay free in parent's room. AE, DC, DISC, MC, V. **Amenities:** Restaurant; indoor pool; golf course; tennis courts; exercise room; Jacuzzi; sauna; bike rental; children's center; activities desk; room service; massage; babysitting; coin-op laundry. *In room:* TV/DVD, dataport, fridge, coffeemaker, hair dryer, iron.

DUCK MOUNTAIN PROVINCIAL PARK

Northwest of Riding Mountain via Highway 10, off Route 367, **Duck Mountain Provincial Park** (© **204/734-3429**) is popular for fishing, camping, boating, hiking, horseback riding, and biking. **Baldy Mountain,** near the park's southeast entrance, is the province's highest point at 831m (2,727 ft.). **East Blue Lake** is so clear the bottom is visible at 9 to 12m (30–40 ft.).

For accommodations in Duck Mountain, the place to stay is **Wellman Lake Lodge,** Box 249, Minitonas, MB R0L 1G0 (© **888/525-5896** or 204/525-4422; www. wellmanlakelodge.com), which has seven cabins starting at C$115 (US$115/ £58) for two. All are modern and winterized, with full bathrooms and well-equipped kitchenettes, plus a covered deck with picnic table. Two have fireplaces or pellet stoves. Full services for anglers and hunters are offered. There's also a beach for swimming. There are three campgrounds in Duck Mountain that offer various levels of service.

6 On to the Far North & Churchill, the World's Polar Bear Capital ⊛⊛

The best way to explore the north is aboard **VIA Rail's** *Hudson Bay* on a 2-night, 1-day trip from Winnipeg to Churchill, via **The Pas,** a mecca for fishing enthusiasts, and the mining community of Thompson. You can also drive to Thompson and take the train from there. No other land route has yet penetrated this remote region, which is covered with lakes, forests, and frozen tundra. The train leaves Winnipeg at about 8:45pm and arrives about 36 hours later in Churchill. A round-trip ticket price can vary considerably depending on time of year, but a double-bedroom sleeper will typically cost around C$1,750 (US$1,750/£875) for two—be aware that sleeping compartments on this route are often booked well in advance due to block booking by tour operators. If you're okay sleeping in reclining seats or a multiberth cabin, two can travel round-trip by train for as little as C$1,150 (US$1,150/£575), 7-day advance purchase, in economy class any time of year. For more information, contact your travel agent or **VIA Rail** (© 888/VIA-RAIL or 800/561-8630; www.viarail.ca). You can also fly into Churchill on **Calm Air** (© 800/839-2256; www.calmair.com).

If you're up this way in late winter, The Pas hosts the annual **Northern Manitoba Trappers' Festival** ✶ (© 204/623-2912; www.trappersfestival.com), with world-championship dog-sled races, ice fishing, beer fests, moose calling, and more. It's usually held the third week in February.

EXPLORING THE AREA

Churchill is the polar-bear capital of the world. To the south and east of the city lies one of the largest polar bear maternity denning sites. The area was placed under government protection in 1996 when the **Wapusk National Park** was established. Visit October to early November to see these awesome creatures. The area is also a vital habitat for hundreds of thousands of waterfowl and shorebirds. More than 200 species, including the rare Ross Gull, nest or pass through on their annual migration. In summer, white beluga whales frolic in the mouth of the Churchill River, and you can sight seals and caribou along the coast. You can also see the aurora borealis from here. For additional info, contact **Parks Canada**, Box 127, Churchill, MB R0B 0E0 (© 888/748-2928 or 204/675-8863; www.pc.gc.ca).

From Churchill, a number of outfitters offer polar bear and other arctic wildlife viewing tours. Special "bear buggies" take you out onto the tundra to the polar bear denning sites where you can safely watch and photograph these magnificent creatures. A week-long tour, beginning and ending in Winnipeg and inclusive of all lodging and airfare, costs between C$3,200 and C$5,400 (US$3,200–US$5,400/£1,600–£2,700), depending on types of activities and hotels. Go to the **Churchill Chamber of Commerce** website at www.churchillmb.net/~cccomm and follow the links for more information, as the pricing information is quite complex.

One local Churchill outfitter with an excellent reputation and a number of tour options is **Great White Bear Tours, Inc.,** Box 91, Churchill, MB R0B 0E0 (© 866/765-8344 or 204/675-2781; www.greatwhitebeartours.com). **Churchill Nature Tours,** P.O. Box 429, Erickson, MB R0J 0P0 (© 204/636-2968; www.churchillnaturetours.com) offers several polar bear and other wildlife-viewing safari packages that include lodging in Churchill's Aurora Inn. The lodges afford excellent viewing of wildlife and the northern sky. All packages include a helicopter nature-viewing tour, plus plenty of trips out for bear viewing in tundra vehicles. Naturalists lead the tours, and you'll be sure to see plenty of other tundra wildlife. Trips last a total of 6 or 8 days, and include return airfare from Winnipeg and 2 night's lodging at an airport hotel.

Churchill, population around 1,100, is a grain-exporting terminal, and grain elevators dominate its skyline. You can watch the grain being unloaded from grain cars onto ships—25 million bushels of wheat and barley clear the port in only 12 to 14 weeks of frantic nonstop operation. You can also take a boat ride to **Prince of Wales Fort** (© 204/675-8863; www.pc.gc.ca). Construction of this partially restored, large stone fort was started in 1730 by the Hudson's Bay Company and took 40 years. Yet after all that effort, Gov. Samuel Hearne and 39 clerks and tradesmen surrendered the fort to the French without resistance in 1782, when faced with a possible attack by three French ships. From here you can observe beluga whales. June 1 to November 10, the park is open daily 1 to 5pm and 6 to 9pm. Admission to the grounds is free, though there are C$8 (US$8/£4) fees for guided tours or special interpretive programs.

Cape Merry, at the mouth of the Churchill River, is also an excellent vantage point for observing beluga whales and is a must for birders (it's open continuously June–Aug). The town's **Visitor Centre** is open daily mid-May to mid-November, weekdays only otherwise. For Churchill information, contact the **Churchill Chamber of Commerce,** Box 176, Churchill, MB R0B 0E0 (© **888/389-2327** or 204/675-2022; www.churchill.ca). In town, the **Eskimo Museum,** 242 Laverendrye St. (© **204/675-2030**), has a collection of fine Inuit carvings and artifacts. In the summer (June to mid-Nov), it's open Monday from 1 to 5pm and Tuesday through Saturday from 9am to noon and 1 to 5pm, and in winter (mid-Nov to May), the hours are Monday through Saturday from 1 to 4:30pm; the museum is closed Sundays and statutory holidays. Admission is free, but donations are welcome.

North of The Pas are two provincial parks. The first is **Clearwater Lake Provincial Park** (no phone), at the junction of highways 10 and 287; the lake lives up to its name because the bottom is visible at 11m (36 ft.). It offers great fishing, plus swimming, boating, hiking, and camping. The second is **Grass River Provincial Park** (no phone), on Highway 39, a wilderness home to woodland caribou, moose, and plenty of waterfowl. The Grass River is good for fishing and canoeing.

WHERE TO STAY

The **Aurora Inn,** 24 Bernier St. (© **888/840-1344** or 204/675-2071; www.aurora-inn.mb.ca) is one of Churchill's newest hotels, featuring 19 spacious, split-level loft suites with fully equipped kitchens, plus three smaller standard rooms. Suite doubles go for C$195 (US$195/£98) during peak polar bear viewing season (Oct–Nov), and C$139 (US$139/£70) or C$115 (US$115/£58) in shoulder or off seasons, respectively. The **Polar Inn & Suites,** 153 Kelsey Blvd. (© **877/POLAR-33** or 204/675-8878; www.polarinn.com), offers standard rooms plus one-bedroom apartments and kitchenette suites with fridges and coffeemakers for C$114 to C$210 (US$114–US$210/£57–£105). The **Lazy Bear Lodge** (© **204/675-2969;** www.lazybearlodge.com) is a newer, log cabin–type hotel with 32 spacious rooms, a restaurant, and free shuttle; rates range from C$125 to C$250 (US$125–US$250/£63–£125).

7 Regina: Capital of Saskatchewan

257km (160 miles) SE of Saskatoon, 572km (355 miles) W of Winnipeg, 788km (490 miles) E of Calgary

Originally named "Pile O' Bones" after the heap of buffalo skeletons the first settlers found (Native Canadians had amassed the bones in the belief they would lure the vanished buffalo back again), the city of **Regina** (pronounced Re-*jeye*-na) has Princess Louise, daughter of Queen Victoria, to thank for its more regal name. She named the city in her mother's honor in 1882 when it became the capital of the Northwest Territories. Despite the barren prairie landscape and the infamous Regina mud, the town grew.

Today, the provincial capital of Saskatchewan has a population of about 200,000 and remains true to its agrarian roots, but has developed a sophisticated veneer, with excellent hotels, good restaurants, and quite interesting attractions.

ESSENTIALS

GETTING THERE   There is no passenger rail service to Regina. The closest rail connections are in Saskatoon.

Regina Airport (www.yqr.ca) is west of the city, only 15 minutes from downtown. It is served largely by **Air Canada** affiliates (© 888/247-2262), **Northwest** (© 800/225-2525), and **WestJet** (© 800/538-5696).

The Regina **bus station** is downtown at 2041 Hamilton St. (© **306/787-3340**). Greyhound as well as Saskatchewan Transportation Company (www.stcbus.com) buses—which are the dominant public transport service in the province—use the station.

If you're **driving,** the Trans-Canada Highway passes just south of Regina.

VISITOR INFORMATION Contact **Tourism Saskatchewan,** 1922 Park St., Regina, SK S4P 3V7 (© **877/237-2273** or 306/787-2300; www.sasktourism.com), open Monday through Friday 8am to 5pm. For on-the-spot Regina info, contact **Tourism Regina,** P.O. Box 3355, Regina, SK S4P 3H1 (© **800/661-5099** or 306/789-5099; www.tourismregina.com), or visit the **Visitor Information Centre,** Highway 1 East, just east of the city and west of CKCK-TV; it's open summer (mid-May to Labour Day) weekdays 8am to 7pm and weekends or holidays 10am to 6pm, and winter weekdays only 8am to 5pm.

CITY LAYOUT The two main streets are **Victoria Avenue,** which runs east-west, and **Albert Street,** which runs north-south. South of the intersection lies the **Wascana Centre.** Most of the downtown hotels stretch along Victoria Avenue between Albert Street on the west and Broad Street on the east. The RCMP barracks are to the north and west of the downtown area. **Lewvan Drive** and **Ring Road** together encircle the city.

GETTING AROUND **Regina Transit,** 333 Winnipeg St. (© **306/777-7433;** www.reginatransit.com), operates nine bus routes that make it easy to get around. For schedules and maps, go to the **Transit Information Centre** at 2124 11th Ave., at the Cornwall Centre, open weekdays 7am to 9pm and Saturday 9am to 4pm. Fares are C$2.10 (US$2.10/£1.05) for adults, C$1.60 (US$1.60/80p) for students. Exact fare is required.

Each of the following car-rental agencies also have bureaus at the airport: **Avis,** 665 Broad St. (© **306/757-5460** or 306/757-1653); **Budget,** 505 McIntyre St. (© **800/527-0700** in the U.S., or 800/267-6810 in Saskatchewan); **Hertz,** 601 Albert St. (© **306/791-9131** or 306/791-9139); **National,** 789 Broad St. (© **306/757-5757** or 306/791-9808); and **Thrifty,** 1975 Broad St. (© **306/352-1000** or 306/525-1000).

You can most easily find **taxis** at downtown hotels. From downtown to the airport, the cost is about C$12 (US$12/£6). **Regina Cab** (© **306/543-3333**) is the most used service.

SPECIAL EVENTS & FESTIVALS During the first week of June, **Mosaic** (© **306/757-9550**) celebrates the city's multiethnic population. Special passports entitle you to enter pavilions and experience the food, crafts, customs, and culture of each group. Regina's **Buffalo Days,** P.O. Box 167, Exhibition Park, Regina, SK S4P 2Z6 (© **888/734-3975** or 306/781-9200; www.buffalodays.ca), usually held the end of July into the first week in August, recalls the time when this noble beast roamed the west. Throughout the city, businesses and individuals dress in Old West style, while the fairgrounds sparkles with a midway, grandstand shows, big-name entertainers, livestock competitions, and much more.

TOP SIGHTS

While **Casino Regina** is described below as a gaming destination (see "Regina After Dark," later), even nongamblers will be interested in this impressive gambling establishment. Right downtown, it incorporates Regina's original Canadian National rail terminal from 1911 and features antique rail cars in its dining room and a Vegas-style show lounge; admission is free.

Government House This elegant structure was built in 1891 as home to the British lieutenant governor, the queen's representative who served as head of government for the entire Northwest Territories—which at the time included all of western and northern Canada except British Columbia. Tours of the elegant stone manor are led by costumed docents, who take visitors through 14 period rooms, including government chambers, living areas, ballroom, and conservatory, plus manicured gardens.

4607 Dewdney Ave. ℂ **306/787-5773**. www.gr.gov.sk.ca/govhouse. Free admission. Tues–Sun 10am–4pm. Tours every half-hour.

Legislative Building This splendid, stately edifice built from 1908 to 1912 boasts 30 kinds of marble in the interior. Check out the mural *Before the White Man Came,* depicting Native people in the Qu'Appelle Valley preparing to attack a herd of buffalo on the opposite shore. See also the Legislative Assembly Chamber, the 400,000-volume library, and the art galleries in the basement and on the first floor.

2405 Legislative Dr. ℂ **306/787-5358**. www.legassembly.sk.ca. Free admission. Tours daily every half-hour 8am–5pm in winter (Sept–May), 8am–9pm in summer (Victoria Day to Labour Day). Tours can be arranged through the visitor services office. On sessional nights, tours available 6–9pm. Groups please call ahead.

Mackenzie Art Gallery The art gallery's approximately 1,600 works concentrate on Canadian artists, particularly such Saskatchewan painters as James Henderson and Inglis Sheldon-Williams; contemporary American artists; and 15th- to 19th-century Europeans who are represented with paintings, drawings, and prints.

3475 Albert St., T.C. Douglas Bldg. ℂ **306/584-4250**. www.mackenzieartgallery.ca. Free admission. Mon–Wed 10am–5:30pm; Thurs–Fri 10am–9pm; Sat 10am–5:30pm; Sun and holidays 11am–5:30pm.

RCMP Training Academy & Heritage Centre 🅰🅰 This is the primary training facility for the Royal Canadian Mounted Police, or the Mounties, who function as both Canada's national police and the country's version of the FBI. Tours of the training grounds and academy are offered Monday to Friday at 1:30pm. In addition to visiting the **chapel**—the oldest building in Regina—you can watch fledgling Mounties strut their stuff during **Sergeant Major's Parade,** which normally takes place around 12:45pm Monday to Friday. The schedule is tentative, so call before you go. In July and early August, the **Sunset Retreat Ceremony**—an event that dates from the RCMP's roots—takes place on Tuesdays just after 6:30pm; it's an exciting 45-minute display of horsemanship by the Mounties accompanied by pipe and bugle bands.

In addition to these activities, the RCMP Heritage Centre, opened in 2007, traces the fascinating history of the Royal Canadian Mounted Police since 1874, when they began the Great March West to stop liquor traffic and enforce the law in the Northwest Territories. In six different galleries, the museum documents the lives of the early Mounties and pioneers using replicas, newspaper articles, artifacts, uniforms, weaponry, and mementos to illustrate the Mounties' role in the 1885 Riel Rebellion, the Klondike Gold Rush, the Prohibition era, world wars I and II, the 1935 Regina labor riot, and the capture of the mad trapper (who was pursued in arctic temperatures for 54 days in 1931–32). In addition to the main exhibits, the RCMP Heritage Centre offers an impressive 27-minute multimedia presentation called "Tour of Duty"—it's definitely worth seeing.

The Trial of Louis Riel

Louis Riel was tried and hanged in Regina in 1885. Bitter arguments have been fought between those who regard Riel as a patriot and martyr and those who regard him as a rebel. Whatever the opinion, Riel certainly raises some extremely deep and discomforting questions. As G. F. Stanley, professor of history at the Royal Military College, Kingston, has written, "The mere mention of his name bares those latent religious and racial animosities which seem to lie so close to the surface of Canadian politics." Riel has gained some official respect from the Anglo-European community in recent years; in his honor, the Saskatchewan government has renamed Highway 11 from Prince Albert to Regina the **Louis Riel Trail.**

Even though he took up the cause of the mixed-blood population of the west, French-speaking Canadians often regarded Riel as a martyr and English-speaking Canadians damned him as a madman. Written by John Coulter, *The Trial of Louis Riel* is a play based on the actual court records of the historical trial. It's presented Wednesday through Friday at the MacKenzie Art Gallery over a month between July and August. Nothing if not provocative, the play raises such issues as language rights, prejudice, and justice that still resound. Tickets are C$12 (US$12/£6) for adults, C$11 (US$11/£5.50) for seniors and students, and C$9 (US$9/£4.50) for children ages 12 and under. For information or reservations, call (C) 306/728-5728.

Off Dewdney Ave. W. (C) 306/780-5838. www.rcmpheritagecentre.com. Admission to RCMP National Heritage Centre C$12 (US$12/£6) adult, C$10 (US$10/£5) senior and youths 13–17, C$6 (US$6/£3) children 6–12, C$3 (US$3/£1.50) children 3–5. Free admission to the grounds and the Sunset Retreat Ceremony. Heritage Centre Tues–Sun 10am–4:30pm, until 8pm on Sunset Retreat Ceremony nights.

Royal Saskatchewan Museum *(Kids)*   This museum focuses on the province's anthropological and natural history, displaying a life-size mastodon and a robotic dinosaur that comes roaring to life, plus other specimens. The museum is organized into three galleries: the Life Sciences; the Earth Sciences, which features Saskatchewan geologic history; and First Nations, which tells the stories of the province's indigenous peoples. A video cave, a sand table, and dinosaur-size board games are all found in the interactive Paleo Pit. The Apperley Place gift shop offers, among other things, traditional Native art and Saskatchewan crafts.

College Ave. and Albert St. (C) 306/787-2815. www.royalsaskmuseum.ca. Free admission, with suggested donations of C$2 (US$2/£1) adults and C$5 (US$5/£2.50) family. May to Labour Day daily 9am–5:30pm; day after Labour Day to Apr daily 9am–4:30pm. Closed Dec 25.

Saskatchewan Science Centre *(Kids)*   The Saskatchewan Science Centre is home to the Powerhouse of Discovery and the Kramer IMAX Theatre. The first houses more than 80 thought-provoking and fun hands-on exhibits demonstrating basic scientific principles, ranging from a hot-air balloon that rises three stories in the central mezzanine to exhibits where you can test your strength, reaction time, and balance. The Kramer IMAX Theatre shows films on a five-story screen accompanied by thrilling six-channel surround-sound. Call for show times (most are in the afternoon).

Winnipeg St. and Wascana Dr. ℭ **800/667-6300** or 306/522-4629. www.sasksciencecentre.com. Admission to Powerhouse of Discovery C$7 (US$7/£3.50) adults, C$5 (US$5/£2.50) seniors and youth 6–13, C$3 (US$3/£1.50) children 3–5; free for children under 3. IMAX theater C$7 (US$7/£3.50) adults, C$5 (US$5/£2.50) seniors and youth 6–13, C$3.75 (US$3.75/£1.90) children 5 and under. Combination tickets C$12 (US$12/£6) adults, C$9 (US$9/£4.50) seniors and youths 6–13, C$6 (US$6/£3) children 3–5, C$3.75 (US$3.75/£1.90) children under 3. MC, V. Tues–Fri 9am–6pm; Sat–Sun 10am–6pm; holiday Mon 9am–5pm.

Wascana Centre   This 930-hectare (2,300-acre) park in the city center—one of the largest urban parks in North America—contains its own **waterfowl park,** frequented by 60 or more species of marsh and water birds. There's a naturalist on duty Monday to Friday 9am to 4pm. Another delightful spot is **Willow Island,** a picnic island reached by a small ferry from the overlook west of Broad Street on Wascana Drive. In winter, ice skaters take to the park's central lake and cross-country skiers navigate its snowy trails.

The center also contains the domed Saskatchewan Legislative Building, the University of Regina, the Royal Saskatchewan Museum, the MacKenzie Art Gallery, and the Saskatchewan Centre of the Arts. Also in the park stands the **Diefenbaker Homestead,** the unassuming one-story log home of John Diefenbaker, Canada's prime minister from 1957 to 1963. Diefenbaker helped his father build the three-room house, which was moved here from Borden, Saskatchewan, and it's furnished in pioneer style with some original family articles. It's open daily 9am to 6pm, Victoria Day through Labour Day; admission is free.

Wascana Place, the headquarters building for the **Wascana Centre Authority** (ℭ **306/522-3661;** www.wascana.sk.ca), provides public information. You can get a fine view from its fourth-level observation deck. Victoria Day through Labour Day, it's open daily 9am to 6pm; winter hours are Monday to Saturday 9:30am to 5:30pm.

WHERE TO STAY
EXPENSIVE
Delta Regina Hotel   Location, location, location. Conveniently located downtown in the Saskatchewan Trade and Convention Centre, the Delta Regina is linked by skyways to the Cornwall Centre and the Casino Regina. Corner Premier rooms offer lots of light, plus plenty of living and working space, while Signature Club rooms offer luxury touches such as granite-tiled bathrooms, king-size beds, and a Jacuzzi tub, plus access to a private lounge. Standard guest rooms are nicely appointed with a choice of two double or one queen-size bed, an easy chair, and a small work desk. The hotel also has a waterworks recreation complex with a three-story indoor waterslide and whirlpool. Also on-site is the casual Summerfield's Dining Room and a nonsmoking lounge.

1919 Saskatchewan Dr., Regina, SK S4P 4H2. ℭ **877/814-7706** or 306/525-5255. Fax 306/781-7188. www. deltaregina.com. 274 units. C$150–C$210 (US$150–US$210/£75–£105) double. Extra person C$15 (US$15/£7.50). Children under 18 stay free in parent's room. Weekend, senior, and package rates available. AE, DC, DISC, MC, V. Adjacent parking C$5 (US$5/£2.50). **Amenities:** Restaurant; lounge; indoor pool and 3-story waterslide; golf course nearby; fitness center; Jacuzzi; business center; limited room service; same-day dry cleaning; nonsmoking rooms. *In room:* A/C, TV, dataport, complimentary high-speed Internet, coffeemaker, hair dryer, iron.

Holiday Inn Express Hotel and Suites   Located downtown and near the conference center and casino, the Holiday Inn Express (formerly the venerable Chelton Hotel) is a newly renovated all-suite hotel with the largest standard rooms in Regina. All rooms have a sitting area; kitchen area with fridge, microwave, and coffeemaker; a dining table; a separate work desk; and two TVs. One- and two-bedroom suites are even larger. The hotel also has a guest business center and fitness room. For the size, comfort, and location, these very comfortable rooms are an excellent value.

1907 11th Ave., Regina, SK S4P 0J2. © **800/667-9922** in Canada, or 306/569-4600. Fax 306/569-3531. www.hi express.com. 78 units. C$117–C$142 (US$117–US$142/£59–£71) double. Rates include continental breakfast and local phone calls. Weekend rates, seniors and AAA discounts available. AE, DC, MC, V. Free parking. **Amenities:** Restaurant; lounge; fitness center. *In room:* A/C, TV, dataport, free wireless Internet access, fridge, coffeemaker, hair dryer, iron.

Hotel Saskatchewan Radisson Plaza 🌟🌟 The historic hotel's elegant old-world lobby and solid limestone exterior look as if they belong in London—except the Hotel Saskatchewan is more beautifully maintained and comfortable than many of the classic hotels it resembles. Built as a regal railroad hotel in 1927, the hotel is filled with opulence, from the gilt moldings and luxury carpets to the spacious specialty suites literally designed for royalty. Standard guest rooms are large for a hotel of this vintage— most have walk-in closets—and have quality furnishings. Business-class rooms—on corners for extra light—are even larger and outfitted with king-size beds, large business desks, and ergonomic chairs. Plaza Club guests have extra amenities such as feather duvets and luxury-level furniture, plus access to the wonderful Plaza Clubroom, a fantastic sitting room and private lounge that looks like a drawing room for Edwardian aristocrats. The Essence of EnVogue spa offers a selection of beauty treatments.

Needless to say, there aren't many hotels like this in Regina, and even if you don't stay here, consider stopping by for a meal—Sunday brunch is C$22 (US$22/£11)— or a drink in Monarch's Lounge, a lovely formal room with a fireplace and carved beams. On weekends, the Victoria Tea Room is open for traditional afternoon tea.

2125 Victoria Ave. (at Scarth St.), Regina, SK S4P 0S3. © **800/333-3333** or 306/522-7691. Fax 306/522-8988. www.hotelsask.com. 224 units. C$119–C$209 (US$119–US$209/£60–£105) double. Extra person C$15 (US$15/ £7.50). Children under 12 stay free in parent's room. Group, senior, and package rates offered. AE, DC, MC, V. **Amenities:** Restaurant; fitness center; spa; whirlpool and steam room; room service; executive-level rooms; rooms for those w/limited mobility. *In room:* A/C, TV, complimentary high-speed Internet, minibar, coffeemaker, hair dryer, iron.

Ramada Hotel & Convention Centre 🌟 Completely renovated in 2003, the Ramada offers very comfortable rooms, conference facilities, and lots of extras for both corporate and leisure travelers. Standard rooms come with two double beds and a full range of amenities, while the business-class rooms occupy the hotel's top two floors, both secured. These rooms offer king-size beds, large work desks, and adjustable office chairs, plus a sitting area with overstuffed easy chairs. The suites at the Ramada are exceptional—junior suites are very large, light filled, and homelike, while seven executive suites are practically apartments (one occupies two stories). The spa area features cascading multilevel pools, exercise equipment, and a deck.

1818 Victoria Ave., Regina, SK S4P 0R1. © **800/272-6232** or 306/569-1666. Fax 306/352-6339. www.ramada.ca. 233 units. C$102–C$142 (US$102–US$142/£51–£71) double; from C$215 (US$215/£108) suite. Children under 18 stay free in parent's room. Weekend packages, senior and AAA discounts available. AE, DC, MC, V. Parking C$5 (US$5/£2.50). Some pets allowed. **Amenities:** Restaurant; lounge; bar; indoor pool; exercise room; Jacuzzi; sauna; children's center; salon; room service; coin-op laundry; same-day dry cleaning; rooms for those w/limited mobility. *In room:* A/C, TV w/pay movies, free wireless Internet access, coffeemaker, hair dryer, iron.

Regina Inn 🌟 Completely renovated in 2004, the Regina Inn provides stylish and comfortable rooms at moderate prices, right in the center of the city. The large Platinum level rooms come with high-speed Internet, multiple phones, and other perks for business travelers—such as granite-countered bathrooms. Additionally, there are Jacuzzi suites, while Gold-level rooms feature a queen-size bed and a working desk. Standard Silver rooms are simpler, but still very pleasant and spacious. Nearly all rooms have balconies. All in all, a good value for very high quality. The hotel offers the botaniCa all-day cafe and drinks in a stone-flanked lounge, complete with water-fall.

1975 Broad St., Regina, SK S4P 1Y2. (℃) 800/667-8162 in Canada, or 306/525-6767. Fax 306/352-1858. www.regina inn.com. 235 units. C$124–C$144 (US$124–US$144/£62–£72) double. Extra person C$10 (US$10/£5). Children under 18 stay free in parent's room. Weekend and other packages, and group and senior rates available. AE, DC, DISC, MC, V. **Amenities:** Restaurant; lounge; fitness center; car-rental desk; room service; executive-level rooms; rooms for those w/ limited mobility. *In room:* A/C, TV w/cable and pay movies, high-speed Internet, coffeemaker, hair dryer, iron.

INEXPENSIVE
HI Regina—Turgeon International Hostel (ℜ)   Regina is fortunate to have one of Canada's best youth hostels, located in a handsome 1907 town house adjacent to the Wascana Centre. Accommodations are in dorms with three or four bunks; the top floor has two larger dorms, and each dorm has access to a deck. Downstairs is a comfortable sitting room worthy of any inn, with couches in front of the oak fireplace and plenty of magazines and books. The basement contains an impeccably clean dining and cooking area with electric stoves. Picnic tables are available in the backyard.

2310 McIntyre St., Regina, SK S4P 2S2. (℃) 306/791-8165. Fax 306/721-2667. www.hihostels.ca. 29 beds. Bunks C$21 (US$21/£11) members, C$26 (US$26/£13) nonmembers; private rooms C$35–C$55 (US$35–US$55/£18–£28) members, C$40–C$60 (US$40–US$60/£20–£30) nonmembers. Group rates available. MC, V. Limited street parking. Closed Dec 25–Jan 31. Lights out at 11:30pm. **Amenities:** Tour and activities desk; coin-op laundry; free Internet access. *In room:* A/C, no phone.

WHERE TO DINE
In addition to the places below, try **Neo Japonica,** 2167 Hamilton St., at 14th Avenue ((℃) **306/359-7669**), for good Japanese cuisine; it's open Monday through Friday 11am to 1:30pm, Sunday through Thursday 5 to 9:30pm, Friday and Saturday 5 to 10:30pm. Although this is beef country, the **Heliotrope Whole Food Vegetarian Restaurant,** 2204 McIntyre St. ((℃) **306/569-3373**), serves good ethnic vegan cooking prepared from organic produce. It's open Monday through Friday 11am to 3pm and 5 to 9pm, and Saturday 5 to 9pm.

Cathedral Village Free House PUB   This spacious and atmospheric pub features a number of local ales, and also serves exceptional pub fare. In addition to standards such as burgers and wood-fired pizza, this popular institution offers specialties such as fire-roasted chicken with a choice of three sauces and local pickerel with lemon sauce. Just the spot for a drink and a casual meal.

2062 Albert St. (℃) **306/359-1661.** Reservations not accepted. Main courses C$8–C$22 (US$8–US$22/£4–£11). AE, MC, V. Daily 11:30am–11pm.

Crave Kitchen & Wine Bar (ℜ) NEW CANADIAN   Located downtown in the historic, once-private Assiniboia Club House, Crave updates the ornate 1925 setting with excellent modern cuisine, wild colors, and moody neon lights. The menu is rather confusing (graphic design trumps comprehension), but it boils down to a selection of multicultural tapas, with most main courses reflecting aspirations toward Plains-inspired cuisine with feints to Orientalia. The Caesar salad is very tasty, and the Goucho Salad, with grilled steak piled high over cherry tomatoes and avocado slices, and dressed with chimichurro dressing, is a delight. At dinner, you can choose from wood-fired pizzas or steaks, duckmeat noodle bowls, East Indian butter chicken, and Pacific salmon with chardonnay broth. In warm weather, you can dine on the outdoor patio, and on weekends there's frequently live music and DJs.

1925 Victoria Ave. ℭ 306/525-8777. Reservations recommended. Main courses C$15–C$32 (US$15–US$32/£7.50–£16). AE, MC, V. Mon–Wed 11am–midnight; Thurs–Sat 11am–2am.

Creek in Cathedral Bistro ☞☞ CONTINENTAL   The Cathedral neighborhood of Regina is just west of the downtown core, and has the reputation of being the city's most artsy enclave. It's not surprising that this bustling restaurant is one of the area's most noteworthy and innovative restaurants. The frequently changing menu is a bit hard to characterize, but the menu features up-to-date preparations that feature Prairie foods (and fresh seafood) dressed in French and Continental preparations. A roast chicken breast is dressed with Saskatoon berry–Calvados reduction and served with local wild-mushroom risotto, and almond-cumin-crusted halibut cheeks come with lime beurre blanc. In good weather, the outdoor patio here is one of the most popular see-and-be-seen spots in the city.

3414 13th Ave. ℭ 306/352-4448. Reservations recommended. Main courses C$23–C$28 (US$23–US$28/£12–£14). MC, V. Mon–Thurs 11am–2pm and 5–9pm; Fri 11am–2pm and 5–10pm; Sat 10am–2pm and 5–10pm.

Crushed Grape Wine and Food Bar MEDITERRANEAN   West of downtown, in an older residential neighborhood, is this popular night spot, with a specialty of matching cheese and wine—though this is also an excellent restaurant for French- and Italian-influenced meals. The menu isn't huge—in fact, the various entries are simply identified as The Pork, The Chicken, The Fish, and so on, with seasonal selections changing from week to week—but preparations are excellent (think pork loin on a bed of fresh spring-bean cassoulet), so you don't need an extensive menu as long as the chosen dishes are as good as this. And if nothing else pleases, simply make a meal of the abundant cheeses and well-selected wines.

2118 Robinson St. ℭ 306/352-9463. Reservations recommended. Main courses C$14–$26 (US$14–US$26/£7–£13). MC, V. Tues and Wed 4–9pm; Thurs–Sat 11:30am–10pm; Sun 4–9pm.

Diplomat Steak House ☞☞ CANADIAN   You wouldn't know from the modern redbrick exterior, but this old-style steakhouse is a longtime favorite of Regina movers and shakers. Inside, the Diplomat has the well-aged patina of a London club. Around the room hang portraits of eminent-looking Canadian prime ministers, with lots of dark wood and a fireplace and lounge upfront. The sizable menu's main attractions are the steaks—20-ounce porterhouse, 18-ounce T-bone, and more, all cut from AAA Canadian Angus beef—along with rack of lamb, barbecued ribs, and other traditional favorites. Tableside preparations are another specialty—this is your chance for a perfectly prepared steak Diane. In addition, you'll find such specialties as grilled salmon with horseradish and whiskey sauce; and Chicken Neptune, grilled chicken breast topped with crabmeat, asparagus, and a cheddar-cheese sauce. The Diplomat has over 200 wines to complement your meal. If you're planning on splurging on an ultimate steakhouse dinner, this is the place to do it.

2032 Broad St. ℭ 306/359-3366. Reservations recommended. Main courses C$19–C$46 (US$19–US$46/£9.50–£23). AE, DC, MC, V. Mon–Fri 11am–2pm; Mon–Sat 4pm–midnight.

REGINA AFTER DARK

The focus of the city's cultural life is the Conexus Arts Centre (formerly **Saskatchewan Centre of the Arts),** on the southern shore of Wascana Lake (ℭ **800/667-8497,** or 306/525-9999 for the box office; www.saskcentreofthearts.com). With two theaters and a large concert hall, the center is home to the **Regina Symphony Orchestra** and features many other performance companies. Ticket prices vary depending on the show. The box office at 200 Lakeshore Dr. (© **306/525-9999**) is open Monday through Saturday 10am to 6pm.

Late September to early May, the **Globe Theatre,** Old City Hall, 1801 Scarth St. (© **306/525-6400;** www.globetheatrelive.com), a theater-in-the-round, presents six plays. Productions run the gamut from classics (Shakespeare, Molière, Shaw, and others) to modern dramas, musicals, and comedies. Tickets are C$33 to C$38 (US$33–US$38/ £17–£19). Box office hours are Monday through Saturday 10am to 5pm.

The **Casino Regina,** 1880 Saskatchewan Dr., at Broad Street (© **800/555-3189** or 306/565-3000; www.casinoregina.com), is very impressive. Seven blocks long and incorporating the city's original rail station, Casino Regina has over 35 gaming tables to go with its more than 600 slots, as well as a restaurant and live-show theater, and is open daily 9am to 4am (closed Christmas). The top live music venue in Regina is **The Distrikt,** 1326 Hamilton St. (© **306/359-8223** information line), offering national and local bands, three bars, a large dance floor, and three outdoor decks.

Across the tracks from downtown is the old railway warehouse district, now being revived as an arts and clubs area. Centering on Dewdney Avenue between Albert and Broad streets, this district offers travelers a number of pubs and nightclubs. The **SOHO Nightclub** at 2300 Dewdney Ave. (© **306/359-7771**) has a lively cocktail bar plus an outdoor deck in summer. On weekends, local DJs give the downstairs club on an electric vibe. Of the many pubs in the area, check out **Bushwakker Pub and Brewing Company,** 2206 Dewdney Ave. (© **360/359-7276;** www.bushwakker. com), with 30 beers and ales brewed on-site to go with standard pub fare. **The Crooked Cue,** 2288 Dewdney Ave. (© **306/585-6500**), is a billiards hall with full dining and lounge facilities.

A couple of other pubs with an Irish flavor, popular in Regina, are **O'Hanlon's,** 1947 Scarth St. (© **306/566-4094**); and **McNally's,** at 2226 Dewdney Ave. (© **306/ 522-4774;** www.mcnallys-tavern.com), which also features live music.

8 Saskatchewan Highlights along the Trans-Canada Highway

MOOSE MOUNTAIN PROVINCIAL PARK & WEST TO REGINA

Just across the Manitoba/Saskatchewan border at Whitewood, you can turn south down Highway 9 to **Moose Mountain Provincial Park** (© **306/577-2600**); it's also accessible from highways 16 and 13. About 106km (66 miles) southeast of Regina, this 388-sq.-km (150-sq.-mile) park is dotted with lakes and marshes. The park harbors a variety of waterfowl and songbirds—blue-winged teal, red-necked duck, blue heron, red-tailed hawk, ovenbird, rose-breasted grosbeak, and Baltimore oriole—and animals, including deer, elk, moose, beaver, muskrat, and coyote.

In summer, park rangers lead guided hikes. The Beaver Youell Lake and the Wuche Sakaw trails are also easy to follow. You can hike or bike along the **nature trails;** swim at the **beach** south of the main parking lot and at several of the lakes; cool off at the superfun **giant waterslides** on Kenosee Lake, which include an eight-story freefall slide (mid-May to Labour Day); **golf** at the 18-hole course; go **horseback riding;** or play **tennis.** In winter, the park has more than 56km (35 miles) of **cross-country ski trails** and more than 120km (75 miles) of **snowmobiling trails.**

The modern, comfortable **Kenosee Inn,** Box 1300, Carlyle, SK S0C 0R0 (© **306/ 577-2099;** www.kenoseeinn.com), offers 30 rooms and 23 cabin accommodations (with air-conditioning, TV, and phone) overlooking Kenosee Lake in the park. Facilities include a restaurant, bar, indoor pool, and hot tub. High-season rates are C$89

(US$89/£45) for a double room, C$99 (US$99/£50) for a one-bedroom cabin, and C$135–C$150 (US$135–US$150/£68–£75) for a two-bedroom cabin. Off-season rates are available. The park also has two **campgrounds.**

MOOSE JAW

Moose Jaw gained notoriety as Canada's rum-running capital; it was known as "Little Chicago" in the 1920s. Today, some restored buildings still retain the underground tunnels used for the illicit trade. **The Tunnels of Moose Jaw** (© **306/693-5261;** www.tunnelsofmoosejaw.com) provides two guided tours of the tunnels, one detailing the "Chicago Connection"—including stories of Al Capone beating the heat up north—and the other, "Passage to Fortune," telling the story of Chinese immigrants who came to Moose Jaw looking for economic opportunity through work in the tunnels. There's also a small museum archive of documents and pictures from Moose Jaw's heyday, located at Tunnels Central, 18 Main St. N. Individual tours costs C$13 (US$13£6.50) for adults, C$10 (US$10/£5) for seniors, C$9.50 (US$9.50/£4.75) for youths 13 to 18, and C$6.50 (US$6.50/£3.25) for children 6 to 12; there are discounts if you take both tours on the same day. Tours are generally offered every half-hour Monday to Friday 10am to 4:30pm, Saturday 10am to 5:30pm, and Sunday noon to 4:30pm.

The **Moose Jaw Art Museum, Gallery & Historical Museum,** 461 Langdon Crescent, in Crescent Park (© **306/692-4471;** www.mjmag.ca), has a fine collection of Cree and Sioux beadwork and clothing, plus plenty of contemporary art and history exhibits. It's open daily noon to 5pm; admission is by donation. Moose Jaw is also known for its 39 outdoor murals depicting aspects of the city's heritage. For information, call **Murals of Moose Jaw** at © **306/693-4262,** or visit www.citymoosejaw.com for a detailed list of the murals.

The **Western Development Museum**'s **History of Transportation** branch, at 50 Diefenbaker Dr., by the intersection of highways 1 and 2 (© **306/693-5989;** www.wdm.ca), showcases the roles that air, rail, land, and water transportation played in opening up the West. One gallery pays tribute to the Snowbirds, Canada's famous air-demonstration squadron. A new exhibit lays out the various threads of history that led to the founding of Saskatchewan, using costumed automatons. Museum admission is C$8.50 (US$8.50/£4.25) for adults, C$7.50 (US$7.50/£3.75) for seniors, C$5.75 (US$5.75/£2.90) for students, C$2 (US$2/£1) for children 6–12, and C$19 (US$19/£9.50) for families; preschoolers enter free. **Wakamow Valley** (© **306/692-2717**), which follows the course of the river through town, includes six parks with walking and biking trails, canoeing, and skating facilities. Free guided walking tours are available to groups on request.

If you stop in Moose Jaw, the place to stay is the **Temple Gardens Mineral Spa Hotel and Resort,** 24 Fairford St. E. (© **800/718-7727** or 306/694-5055; www.templegardens.sk.ca), offering 96 rooms and 24 spa suites with private mineral-water Jacuzzis. It's a full-facility resort with special mineral pools where you can take the waters. The spa offers a full range of body treatments. The hotel also links to **Casino Moose Jaw** (© **306/694-3888;** www.casinomoosejaw.com). Rates are C$139 to C$159 (US$139–US$159/£70–£80) for a double and C$229 (US$229/£115) and up for spa Jacuzzi suites.

For more information, contact **Tourism Moose Jaw,** 450 Diefenbaker Dr., Moose Jaw, SK S6H 4P2 (© **866/693-8097;** www.citymoosejaw.com).

SWIFT CURRENT, CYPRESS HILLS INTERPROVINCIAL PARK & FORT WALSH

Swift Current, Saskatchewan's base for western oil exploration and a regional trading center for livestock and grain, is 167km (104 miles) west along the Trans-Canada Highway from Moose Jaw. It's known for its **Frontier Days** in June and **Old Tyme Fiddling Contest** in September. From Swift Current, it's about another 201km (125 miles) to the Alberta border. For more information about Swift Current, contact **Tourism Swift Current,** 1703 22nd Ave. NE, Swift Current, SK S9H 5B7 (✆ **306/778-9174;** www.tourismswiftcurrent.ca).

Straddling the border is **Cypress Hills Interprovincial Park,** P.O. Box 850, Maple Creek, SK S0N 1N0 (✆ **306/662-5411;** www.cypresshills.com), and the **Fort Walsh National Historic Site** (see below). En route to Cypress Hills, off the Trans-Canada Highway, is **Maple Creek,** a thoroughly western cow town with many heritage store-fronts on the main street. On the Saskatchewan side, the provincial park is divided into a Centre Block, off Route 21, and a West Block, off Route 271. Both blocks are joined by Gap Road, which is impassable when wet. The park's core is in the Centre Block, where there are six campgrounds; an outdoor pool; canoe, row/paddleboat, and bike rentals; a 9-hole golf course; tennis courts; a riding stable; and swimming at the beach on Loch Leven. In winter there are 24km (15 miles) of **cross-country skiing trails.** Entry to the park costs C$7 (US$7/£3.50); camping in the summer costs C$11 to C$24 (US$11–US$24/£5.50–£12).

The **Cypress Park Resort Inn** (✆ **306/662-4477;** www.cypressresortinn.com) offers nice hotel-style rooms for C$75 to C$135 (US$75–US$135/£38–£68), as well as cabins starting at C$69 (US$69/£35) and condominium accommodations from C$99 to C$169 (US$99–US$169/£50–£85) in high season; off-season rates are also available. The resort features amenities such as an indoor pool and full-service dining room.

Fort Walsh National Historic Site, Box 278, Maple Creek, SK S0N 1N0 (✆ **306/298-2645;** www.pc.gc.ca), can be accessed from Route 271 or directly from the park's West Block via gravel and clay roads. Built in 1875, the fort's soldiers tried to contain local Native tribes and the many Sioux who sought refuge after the Battle of Little Bighorn in 1876, as well as keep out American criminals seeking sanctuary. It was dismantled in 1883. Today, the reconstruction consists of five buildings and a trading post staffed with folks in period costume. Victoria Day to Labour Day, it's open daily 9:30am to 5:30pm. Admission is C$9.15 (US$9.15/£4.60) for adults, C$7.90 (US$7.90/£3.95) for seniors, C$4.45 (US$4.45/£2.25) for youths ages 6 to 16, free for children under 6, and C$20 (US$20/£10) for families. There are additional fees for various presentations or scheduled events.

GRASSLANDS NATIONAL PARK

About 121km (75 miles) south of Swift Current along the U.S. border stretches **Grasslands National Park,** P.O. Box 150, Val Marie, SK S0N 2T0 (✆ **360/298-2257;** www.pc.gc.ca)—2 blocks of protected land separated by about 27km (17 miles). On this mixed prairie and grassland, there's no escape from the sun and the wind. The **Frenchman River** cuts deep into the West Block, where you can spot pronghorn antelope. Black-tailed **prairie dogs,** which bark warnings at intruders and reassure each other with kisses and hugs, also make their home here. In the East Block, the open prairie is broken with coulees and the adobe hills of the Killdeer Badlands, so called because of their poor soil.

Although the park doesn't have facilities, there are two self-guided **nature trails,** and you can also climb to the summit of **70 Mile Butte** and no-trace camp. The **information center** (℡ **306/298-2257**) is in Val Marie at the junction of Highway 4 and Centre Street (closed weekends in winter).

9 Saskatoon: The Progressive City on the Plains

257km (160 miles) NW of Regina, 524km (326 miles) SE of Edmonton

Saskatoon (pop. about 230,000) retains a distinctly western air, with cowboys and horse trailers as numerous as flame-haired University of Saskatchewan students on its downtown streets. It's not a glitzy place, but there's a lot more going on here than you'd think from the surface.

The university provides Saskatoon with its economic clout, as it is one of North America's top bioscience research centers. This seemingly remote city on the edge of Canadian prairies is at the center of today's world of agribusiness. In addition, much of the city's recent wealth has come from the surrounding mining region that yields potash, uranium, diamonds, petroleum, gas, and gold; nearby Key Lake is the world's most productive uranium mine. In fact, in 2007 Saskatoon had Canada's most dynamic economy, according to research reported in the Toronto *Globe and Mail.*

Scenically, Saskatoon possesses some distinct natural advantages. The South Saskatchewan River cuts a swath through the city. Spanned by several graceful bridges, its park-lined banks are great for strolling, biking, and jogging.

ESSENTIALS

GETTING THERE   **Saskatoon John G. Diefenbaker Airport** (℡ **306/975-8900;** www.yxe.ca) is served primarily by Air Canada (℡ **888/247-2262**), Northwest (℡ **800/447-4747**), and WestJet (℡ **877/952-4638**).

VIA Rail (℡ **888/VIA-RAIL;** www.viarail.ca) trains arrive in the west end of the city on Chappel Drive.

If you're **driving,** Highway 16 (the Yellowhead Hwy.) leads to Saskatoon from the east or west. From Regina, Route 11 leads northwest to Saskatoon.

VISITOR INFORMATION   From mid-May to the end of August, a booth is open at Avenue C North at 47th Street. Otherwise, contact **Tourism Saskatoon,** 6–305 Idylwyld Dr. N., Saskatoon, SK S7L 0Z1 (℡ **800/567-2444** or 306/242-1206; www.tourismsaskatoon.com). Summer hours for both are Monday to Friday 8:30am to 7pm and Saturday and Sunday 10am to 7pm; winter hours for the Tourism Saskatoon office, in the old CP Railway Station at Idylwyld and 24th Street, are Monday through Friday 8:30am to 5pm.

CITY LAYOUT   The South Saskatchewan River cuts a diagonal north-south swath through the city. The main downtown area lies on the west bank; the **University of Saskatchewan** and the long neon sign–crazed **8th Street** dominate the east bank. Streets are laid out in a numbered grid system—22nd Street divides north- and south-designated streets; **Idylwyld Drive** divides, in a similar fashion, east from west. **First Street** through **18th Street** lie on the river's east side; **19th Street** and up are situated on the west bank in the downtown area. **Spadina Crescent** runs along the river's west bank, where you'll find such landmarks as the Delta Bessborough Hotel, the Ukrainian Museum, and the art gallery.

GETTING AROUND   You may need to use transportation only when you visit the University of Saskatchewan and the Western Development Museum. **Saskatoon Transit System,** 301–226 23rd St. E. (© 306/975-3100; www.city.saskatoon.sk.ca/org/transit), operates buses to all city areas Monday through Saturday 6am to 12:30am and Sunday 9:15am to 9pm for an exact-change fare of C$2.25 (US$2.25/£1.15) for adults, C$1.70 (US$1.70/85p) for high school students, and C$1.35 (US$1.35/70p) for grade-school students.

Car-rental companies include **Avis,** 2625 Airport Dr. or 114–2301 Avenue C N. (© 306/652-3434); **Budget,** at the airport or three in-town locations in Saskatoon (© 800/844-7888); **Hertz,** at the airport (© 306/373-1161); **National,** at the airport or Avenue C N. (© 306/665-7703 or 306/664-8771); and **Thrifty,** at the airport or 143 Robin Crescent (© 306/244-8000). Try **Saskatoon Radio Cab Ltd.** (© 306/242-1221), which runs taxis and six-passenger minivans; or **United/Blueline Taxi** (© 306/652-2222), which also operates a limousine to the airport or VIA Rail for C$15 (US$15/£7.50) from downtown hotels.

SPECIAL EVENTS & FESTIVALS   The 8-day **Saskatoon Exhibition** (P.O. Box 6010, Saskatoon, SK S7K 4E4; © 888/931-9333 or 306/931-7149; www.saskatoonexhibition.ca), usually held the second week of August, provides some grand agricultural spectacles, such as the threshing competition in which steam power is pitted against gas—sometimes with unexpected results—and the tractor-pulling competition, when standard farm tractors are used to pull a steel sled weighted down with a water tank. The pay-one-price admission of C$10 (US$10/£5) for adults and C$7 (US$7/£3.50) for youths ages 11 to 15 (children under 11 go free with an adult) lets you in all the entertainments—a craft show, talent competitions, thoroughbred racing, midway, and Kidsville, which features clowns, games, and a petting zoo. Parking is C$5 (US$5/£2.50).

In mid-August, the **Saskatoon Folkfest** (© 306/931-0100; http://saskatoon.com/folkfest) celebrates the city's many ethnic groups through food, displays, and performances; admission is C$12 (US$12/£6) for adults, and children under 12 go free if accompanied by an adult.

EXPLORING THE CITY

An excellent introduction to the city comes from exploring the **Meewasin Valley Trail system** that follows the banks of the South Saskatchewan River through the downtown area. Particularly pleasant is the west bank of the river, with the massive Delta Bessborough Hotel rising like a French château above parklands and the river.

The **University of Saskatchewan** (© 306/966-4343; www.usask.ca) occupies a dramatic 1,030-hectare (2,545-acre) site overlooking the South Saskatchewan River across from downtown and is attended by some 20,000 students. The actual campus buildings are set on 145 hectares (358 acres) while the rest of the area is largely given over to the university farm and experimental plots. The **University Observatory** (© 306/966-6429; open Sat evenings after dusk) houses the Duncan telescope. The **Little Stone Schoolhouse** (© 306/966-8384), built in 1887, served as the city's first school and community center. It's open May 1 to Labour Day, Monday through Friday 9:30am to 4:30pm, and Saturday and Sunday noon to 4:30pm; admission is by donation. You can arrange special tours of the research farm and many of the colleges. Contact the Office of Communications, University of Saskatchewan (© 306/966-6607; www.usask.ca/communications). To get there, take bus no. 7 or 19 from downtown at 23rd Street and 2nd Avenue.

Mendel Art Gallery 𝒜 Along the north bank of the South Saskatchewan River, just a short walk from downtown, is the Mendel Art Gallery. Housed in a striking modern building, the gallery has collected over 5,000 works of art in different media, including paintings, sculpture, prints, and drawings of national importance. The collection began with a representative grouping of early-20th-century Canadian works, but the focus now extends to a vital and very compelling collection of works by contemporary Saskatchewan artists.

950 Spadina Crescent E. ℂ 306/975-7610. www.mendel.ca. Free admission. Daily 9am to 9pm (closed Dec 25).

Ukrainian Museum of Canada Also on the north riverbank near downtown is this museum of Ukranian culture. Reminiscent of an early-1900s Ukrainian home in western Canada, this museum preserves Ukrainian heritage in clothing, linens, tools, books, photographs, documents, wooden folk art, ceramics, *pysanky* (Easter eggs), and other treasures and art forms brought from the homeland by Ukrainian immigrants to Canada.

910 Spadina Crescent E. ℂ 306/244-3800. www.umc.sk.ca. C$3 (US$3/£1.50) adults, C$2 (US$2/£1) seniors, and C$1 (US$1/50p) children 6–12. Victoria Day to Labour Day Mon–Sat 10am–5pm and Sunday 1–5pm; closed Mon during the rest of the year.

Wanuskewin Heritage Park 𝒜𝒜 This park is built around the archaeological discovery of 21-plus Northern Plains Indian precontact sites. Walking along its trails, you'll see archaeological digs in progress, habitation sites, stone cairns, tepee rings, bison jumps, and other trace features of this ancient culture. At the amphitheater, First Nations performers present dance, theater, song, and storytelling; at the outdoor activity area, you can learn how to build a tepee, bake bannock, tan a hide, or use a travois (a transportation device). The exhibit halls feature computer-activated displays and artifacts, multimedia shows exploring the archaeology and culture of the Plains peoples, and a fascinating collection of contemporary Native Canadian art.

R.R. 4, 5km (3 miles) north of Saskatoon off Hwy. 11 and Warman Rd. ℂ 306/931-6767. www.wanuskewin.com. Admission C$8.50 (US$8.50/£4.25) adults, C$7.50 (US$7.50/£3.75) seniors, C$5 (US$5/£2.50) students 6–18, free for children under 6, C$27 (US$27/£14) families. Victoria Day to Labour Day daily 9am–8pm; the rest of the year, daily 9am–5pm. Follow bison signs as you near the park.

Western Development Museum The energetic years of Saskatchewan settlement are vividly portrayed by Boomtown 1910, an authentic replica of prairie community life in that year. When you step onto the main street of Boomtown, the realities of an earlier age flood your senses. Browse through the shops, crammed with the unfamiliar goods of days gone by; savor the past through the mysterious aromas that permeate the drugstore; step aside as you hear the clip-clop of a passing horse and buggy; or wander down to Boomtown Station drawn by the low wail of an approaching steam locomotive. The museum truly comes to life during "Pion-Era" in July, when volunteers in authentic costume staff Boomtown and pieces of vintage equipment are pressed into service once again.

2610 Lorne Ave. S. ℂ 306/931-1910. www.wdm.ca. C$8.50 (US$8.50/£4.25) adults, C$7.50 (US$7.50/£3.75) seniors, C$5.75 (US$5.75/£2.90) students, C$2 (US$2/£1) for children 6–12, preschoolers free, and C$19 (US$19/£9.50) families. Daily 9am–5pm; closed Mon Jan–Mar. Take Idylwyld Dr. south to the Lorne Ave., exit and follow Lorne Ave. south until you see the museum on the right. Bus: 1 from the 23rd St. Bus Mall between 2nd and 3rd aves.

SHOPPING
For Canadian merchandise, stop in at **The Trading Post,** 226 2nd Ave. S. (ℂ **800/ 653-1769** or 306/653-1769), which carries Inuit soapstone carvings, Native Canadian

art, Cowichan sweaters, mukluks, beadwork, and more. Some galleries showing local artists that are worth browsing include the **Prairie Pottery,** 150B 2nd Ave. N. (© 306/242-8050; www.prairiepottery.com); Darrell Bell Gallery, 317–220 3rd Ave S. (© 306/955-5701; www.darrellbellgallery.com); the **Collector's Choice Art Gallery,** 625D 1st Ave. N. (© 306/665-8300); and the **Handmade House Handcraft Store,** 710 Broadway Ave. (© 306/665-5542), which specializes in crafts.

WHERE TO STAY

A hotel just north of downtown, and within walking distance of restaurants and shopping, the **Holiday Inn Express Hotel & Suites,** 315 Idylwyld Dr. N. (© **800/465-4329** or 306/384-8844; www.hiexpress.com), may be your hotel if you're looking for modern easy-in, easy-out rooms (C$129–C$149/US$129–US$149/£65–£75 double). It features a pool, complimentary breakfast, and extra-clean rooms.

Delta Bessborough ⭐⭐⭐   There are few hotels in Canada where dramatic location, superb historic architecture, and exceptional hospitality come together so magnificently as the Delta Bessborough. Built in the 1930s to resemble a French château, the towering, turreted hotel dominates the Saskatoon skyline and the parklands along the South Saskatchewan River. A complete renovation of the hotel interior completed in 2003 celebrates the hotel's gracious past while thoroughly updating systems and facilities—this is one of western Canada's great luxury hotels.

Signature Club rooms are large and graciously furnished with feather duvets, handsome furniture, mobile phones, and high-speed Internet access, plus access to a private lounge. Standard rooms are equally large and luxurious, though without the business-traveler extras. Be sure to peek inside the hotel's magnificent ballrooms on the third floor, especially the Versailles-like Adam Ballroom. Facilities also include a full health club with a small pool and spa with beauty and fitness treatments. The Samurai Japanese Steakhouse offers delicious tableside teppanyaki grill preparations.

601 Spadina Crescent E., Saskatoon, SK S7K 3G8. © **800/268-1133** or 306/244-5521. Fax 306/665-7262. www.deltahotels.com. 225 units. C$189–C$209 (US$189–US$209/£95–£105) double. Extra person C$10 (US$10/£5). Children under 18 stay free in parent's room. Weekend packages available. AE, DC, MC, V. Valet or self-parking C$6 (US$6/£3) per day. **Amenities:** 2 restaurants; lounge; indoor pool; fitness center; Jacuzzi; sauna; business center. *In room:* A/C, TV w/video games, dataport, free high-speed Internet, coffeemaker, hair dryer, iron.

Hilton Garden Inn Saskatoon Downtown *(Value)*   This modern hotel has a very convenient location, right downtown opposite the Midtown Plaza shopping complex and TCU Place. Standard family rooms come with two queen beds or one king-size bed, while larger business rooms have a king-size bed plus a work desk; all rooms offer high-speed Internet access. This is a very affordable option for downtown lodging.

90 22nd St. E. (at 1st Ave.), Saskatoon, SK S7K 3X6. © **877/782-9444** or 306/244-2311. www.saskatoon.stayhgi.com. 180 units. From C$109 (US$109/£55) double. AE, MC, V. Free parking. **Amenities:** Restaurant; lounge; indoor heated pool; Jacuzzi; room service. *In room:* A/C, TV w/pay movies, free wired and wireless high-speed Internet access, coffeemaker, hair dryer, iron.

Radisson Hotel Saskatoon ⭐   Rising above the city and the river, the Radisson is a busy corporate and convention hotel with a wide variety of room types, all freshly remodeled and redecorated in 2007 with soft earth tones, new furniture, and luxury linens. Standard rooms come with two queen-size beds—ask for a corner room, which offer more room and light. The executive suites occupy the hotels top floors, and offer lots of extras such as business desks, dining tables, couches and chairs, and superlarge bathrooms with Jacuzzis. Aroma Mediterranean Resto Bar offers drinks and fine dining, and guests enjoy a three-story recreation complex with multistory waterslides.

405 20th St. E., Saskatoon, SK S7K 6X6. © 800/333-3333 or 306/665-3322. Fax 306/665-5531. www.radisson. com/saskatoonca. 291 units. C$129–C$169 (US$129–US$169/£65–£85) double. Extra person C$10 (US$10/£5). Children under 16 stay free in parent's room. Senior and CAA/AAA discounts available. AE, DC, MC, V. Parking C$10 (US$10/£5). **Amenities:** Aroma Restaurant; lounge; indoor water park including pool; fitness center; Jacuzzi; sauna; room service (6:30am–11pm); same-day dry cleaning; executive-level rooms. *In room:* A/C, TV, free high-speed Internet, coffeemaker, hair dryer, iron.

Sheraton Cavalier 𝒦𝒦 *Kids*   This handsome hotel offers a lot in the way of luxury and facilities in an excellent downtown location overlooking the Saskatchewan River. All rooms were refurbished in 2007, with all new beds and furnishings; lobby and meeting room renovations were completed in 2003. The rooms are stylishly decorated with a sleek contemporary look, with soft forest colors, handsome furniture, and plush upholstery and linens. The top-of-the-line suites are very cosmopolitan, some with two stories and hardwood floors. Business-club rooms come with king-size beds, granite bathroom counters, in-room printers, and telecommunication extras, plus a private club room with complimentary breakfast. Traveling families will love the extensive indoor water park, with two large waterslides, swimming pool, children's wading pool, and hot tubs.

612 Spadina Crescent E. © 800/325-3535 or 306/652-6770. http://sheratoncavalier.com/saskatoon. 249 units. C$169 (US$169/£85) double; C$249 (US$249/£125) 1-bedroom suite. AE, MC, V. Heated parking C$8 (US$8/£4). **Amenities:** 2 restaurants; bar; pool complex; fitness center; limited room service; laundry service. *In room:* A/C, TV w/pay movies, dataport, minibar, coffeemaker, hair dryer, iron.

WHERE TO DINE

Barking Fish Tavern TAPAS/ECLECTIC   It seems a little odd to call this smart and bustling restaurant and cocktail lounge a tavern, but who's quibbling over nomenclature? The Barking Fish is very popular with Saskatoon's downtown professionals and young and trendy students, who gather here for cocktails, tapas, and imaginative dining in hip yet comfortable surroundings (the large, hat-box-like lights are especially cool). Choose a house specialty martini and sample such tapas as pan-seared scallops with spicy chorizo sausage, or ahi tuna three ways (seared, tartare, and sushi-rolled); or stay for dinner and dine on steaks, lobster ravioli, linguini vongole with smoked tuna, or braised beef ribs with spicy maple glaze.

154 2nd Avenue S. © 306/665-2220. Reservations recommended. Main courses C$12–C$22 (US$12–US$22/ £6–£11). MC, V. Mon–Thurs 11:30am–midnight; Fri–Sat 11:30am–2am.

Ivy's Dining & Lounge CONTEMPORARY CANADIAN 𝒦𝒦   Located in the fast-changing warehouse area just north of the city center, Ivy's is a swank restaurant that design-wise manages to be industrial and warm at the same time. A stylized waterfall and fireplace take the chill off the dark and slightly formal dining room and bar, with the result that you feel you're welcomed into a very comfortable, stylish cave (you may need to ask for extra light to read the menu). Food is equally modern, even cheeky (at lunch, you have the option of a fried baloney sandwich). More tempting is the Thai Chicken Martini, consisting of satay skewers served in a martini glass filled with rice noodles and chile-lime dipping sauce, and main courses such as seared venison loin and cherry brandy demi-glace, or chicken breast stuffed with fig and apple and served with five-grape port sauce. Pasta and wood-fired pizza are also offered, as well as a fine selection of salads (for example, caramelized pear and tangerine segments atop micro greens with a candied orange vinaigrette). The bar, with its atmospheric pools of light, makes a great spot for a cocktail and appetizer.

24th St. E. and Ontario Ave. ⓒ 306/384-4444. www.ivydiningandlounge.com. Reservations recommended. Main courses C$16–C$32 (US$16–US$32/£8–£16). AE, MC, V. Mon–Fri 11am–2pm and 4–11pm; Sat 4pm–midnight; Sun 5–9pm.

John's Prime Rib STEAKHOUSE   Every Canadian city has a traditional, well-loved steakhouse that serves as an epicenter for local movers and shakers and as a place to gather for celebrations. For Saskatoon, John's has served this role admirably for over 30 years. With an old-fashioned, linen-and-crystal decor, it's the place to go for steaks, rack of lamb, fresh fish, roast duck with cinnamon-cranberry compote, pheasant breast with wild mushrooms, steak Diane, and, of course, prime rib.

401 21st St. E. ⓒ 306/244-6384. www.johnssaskatoon.com. Reservations recommended. Main courses C$22–C$53 (US$22–US$53/£11–£27). AE, DC, MC, V. Mon–Fri 11am–11:30pm; Sat 4:30–11:30pm.

St. Tropez Bistro CONTINENTAL   This little dining room is a favorite down-town spot for French- and Cajun-influenced meals at the right price and with just the right touch of cozy formality. Although the menu is small, it packs a lot of flavor. For dinner, you can choose from a variety of pastas, stir-fries, seafood, or dishes such as a peppercorn filet mignon or blackened chicken. For dessert, you might try the triple-chocolate mousse pie or daily cheesecake.

238 2nd Ave. S. ⓒ 306/652-1250. Reservations recommended. Main courses C$14–C$28 (US$14–US$28/£7–£14). AE, MC, V. Sun–Thurs 5–10pm; Fri–Sat 5–11pm.

Saskatoon Station Place GREEK/STEAKHOUSE   This is a restaurant with a lot of thematic convergence going on. The dining room faces into a real vintage rail dining car, and the decor reflects a nostalgia for the golden age of rail. However, about half the menu (the better half?) is Greek, with excellent souvlaki and grilled ribs. Otherwise, a good selection of steaks and seafood is available if the Greek and rail themes don't charm. This is a nice place to come for a drink and nibbles.

221 Idylwyld Dr. N. ⓒ 306/244-7777. Reservations recommended. Main courses C$15–C$21 (US$15–US$21/£8–£11). AE, DC, MC, V. Mon–Thurs 10:30am–midnight; Fri–Sat 10:30am–12:30am; Sun 10am–11pm.

Simon's British Flavours ⭑⭑ BRITISH   British fine dining may seem like an oxy-moron after your last trip to the United Kingdom, but at Simon's—a spare, well-lit dining room in downtown Saskatoon—you'll enjoy modern British-influenced food that's more in the style of the celebrity English chefs that overpopulate TV's Food Network. It's no longer culinary news to use classic French or Italian techniques with fresh Canadian ingredients to create a regionally focused cuisine; it's far rarer to encounter British cookery as a catalyst to transform local foods. But that's the alchemy at Simon's. An Angus rib-eye steak is served with Scotch whisky cream sauce; a terrine of elk, chicken, and smoky bacon comes with cranberry chutney; and slow-cooked lamb shank is glazed with honey and rosemary and served with "bubble and squeak," a type of York-shire pudding. Of course, there are traditional British favorites here, such as shepherd's pie and fish and chips, and from 2:30 to 5pm, afternoon tea is served.

240 22nd St. E. ⓒ 306/477-4468. www.simonsbritishflavours.com. Reservations recommended. Main courses C$14–C$28 (US$14–US$28/£7–£14). MC, V. Mon–Thurs 11:30am–9pm; Fri–Sat 11:30am–10pm.

Spadina Freehouse ⭑ PUB FARE   Bright and lively, and—for many travelers—right on the city's most important corner, the Spadina Freehouse combines the best features of a youthful brewpub and a casual but exciting restaurant. Wood-fired pizzas are the choice for light meals, while a selection of salads, stir-fries, steaks, roast chicken, and fish provide options for diners seeking cuisine. One night's special left satisfying memories: grilled beef tenderloin with a cabernet and portobello-mushroom sauce, served with braised fennel. Excellent, cheerful service.

608 Spadina Crescent E. (𝘊 **306/668-1000**. www.spadinafreehouse.com. Main courses C$7–C$21 (US$7–US$21/ £3.50–£11). AE, DC, MC, V. Daily 11:30am–11pm.

SASKATOON AFTER DARK

The **TCU Place,** 35 22nd St. E. (𝘊 **800/970-7328,** or 306/938-7800 for tickets; www.tcuplace.com), provides a superb 2,003-seat theater for much of what there is, with a range of shows. The **Saskatoon Symphony** (𝘊 **306/665-6414;** www.saskatoon symphony.org) regularly performs during a September-to-April season. Tickets for adults are C$18 to C$50 (US$18–US$50/£9–£25).

The leading local theater company, the **Persephone Theatre** (𝘊 **306/384-2126** or 306/384-7727 for the box office; www.persephonetheatre.org), will move to its brand-new theater space sometime in 2008; check the website for details. Persephone offers six shows per fall-to-spring season (dramas, comedies, and musicals); tickets are C$25 to C$32 (US$25–US$32/£13–£16). **Shakespeare on the Saskatchewan,** 602–245 3rd Ave. S., Saskatoon, SK S7K 1M4 (𝘊 **306/653-2300** or 306/652-9100 for the box office; www.shakespeareonthesaskatchewan.com), produces the Bard in two tents overlooking the river from July to mid-August. Three Shakespeare plays are performed, plus a special Festival Frolics during the season. Tickets are C$27 (US$27/ £14) for adults, C$22 (US$22/£11) for seniors and students, with discounts for previews and matinees.

For quiet drinking and conversation, you can't beat **Stovin's Lounge** in the **Delta Bessborough Hotel,** 601 Spadina Crescent E. (𝘊 **306/244-5521**). For a more pub-like atmosphere, try the **O'Shea's Irish Pub,** 222 2nd Ave. S. (𝘊 **306/384-7444**), within easy walking distance from local hotels. The **Marquis Downs** racetrack, in the Prairieland Park Exhibition Centre at the corner of Ruth Street and St. Henry Avenue (𝘊 **306/242-6100**), is open for live and simulcast racing. The live season goes mid-May to mid-October. The racetrack has a lounge, cafeteria, and terrace dining overlooking the paddock and home stretch. Admission is free. The other place to wager is the **Emerald Casino,** also at Prairieland Park (𝘊 **306/683-8840**), where you can play five or so table games. It opens at 5:30pm weekdays and at 2pm weekends. Take the Ruth Street exit off Idylwyld Freeway.

SIDE TRIPS FROM SASKATOON

In addition to the national historic parks listed below, visitors looking for a little healthful rejuvenation may want to consider a trip to the resort town of **Manitou Beach** near Watrous, about an hour's drive southeast of Saskatoon on the transcontinental Yellowhead Highway 16 and Saskatchewan Highway 2. On the shores of **Little Manitou Lake,** the **Manitou Springs Resort and Mineral Spa,** Box 610, Watrous, SK S0K 4T0 (𝘊 **800/667-7672** or 306/946-2233; www.manitousprings. ca), offers guests an opportunity to soak in heated pools of the lake's mineral-rich waters, a composition found only here, in eastern Europe, and in Israel's Dead Sea. The water contains magnesium, carbonate, sulphate, potassium, mineral salts, sodium, calcium, iron, silica, and sulfur, all combining to give it a high specific gravity. This property offers increased buoyancy to bathers so that they float in it effortlessly. In addition to its mineral spring pools, the resort complex offers guests a variety of therapeutic services, including massages, reflexology, and body wraps, as well as an exercise facility. Guests can visit for the day or stay in a 60-room lodge with an upscale dining room.

FORT BATTLEFORD NATIONAL HISTORIC SITE   About 138km (86 miles), a 1½-hour drive, northwest of Saskatoon on Highway 16, **Fort Battleford** (© 306/ 937-2621; www.pc.gc.ca) served as the headquarters for the Northwest Mounted Police from 1876 to 1924. Outside the interpretative gallery, a display relates the role of the mounted police from the fur-trading era to the events that led to the rebellion of 1885. You'll see a Red River cart, the type used to transport police supplies into the west; excerpts from the local *Saskatchewan Herald;* a typical settler's log-cabin home, which is amazingly tiny; articles of the fur trade; and an 1876 Gatling gun.

Inside the palisade, the Visitor Reception Centre shows two videos about the 1885 Uprising and the Cree People. From there, proceed to the Guardhouse (1887), containing a cell block and the sick-horse stable (1898), and the Officers Quarters (1886), with police documents, maps, and telegraph equipment.

Perhaps the most interesting building is the Commanding Officer's Residence (1877), which, even though it looks terribly comfortable today, was certainly not so in 1885 when nearly 100 women took shelter in it during the siege of Battleford. Admission is C$7.15 (US$7.15/£3.60) for adults, C$5.90 (US$5.90/£2.95) for seniors, C$3.45 (US$3.45/£1.75) for students, and C$18 (US$18/£9) for families. It's open Victoria Day through Labour Day daily from 9am to 5pm.

BATOCHE NATIONAL HISTORIC SITE 𝄞   In spring 1885, the Northwest Territories exploded in an armed uprising led by the Métis Louis Riel and Gabriel Dumont. Trouble had been brewing along the frontier for several years. The Métis were demanding food, equipment, and farming assistance that had been promised to them in treaties. The settlers were angry about railway development and protective tariffs that meant higher prices for the equipment and services they needed.

The Métis were the offspring of the original French fur traders, who had intermarried with the Cree and Saulteaux women. Initially, they'd worked for the Hudson's Bay and North West companies, but when the two companies merged, many were left without work and returned to buffalo hunting or became independent traders with the Indians in the west. When Riel was unable to obtain guarantees for the Métis in Manitoba from 1869 to 1870, even when he established a provisional government, it became clear the Métis would have to adopt the agricultural ways of the whites to survive. In 1872, they moved westward and established the settlement at **Batoche** along the South Saskatchewan River; but they had a hard time acquiring legal titles and securing scrip, a certificate that could be exchanged for a land grant or money from the British authorities. The French-speaking Métis complained to the British government but received no satisfactory response. So they called on Riel to lead them in what became known as the Northwest Rebellion.

Of the rebellion's five significant engagements, the Battle of Batoche was the only one the British government forces decisively won. From May 9 to May 12, 1885, fewer than 300 Métis and Indians led by Riel and Dumont defended the village against the Northwest Field Force commanded by Gen. Frederick Middleton and numbering 800. On the third day, Middleton succeeded in breaking through the Métis lines and occupying the village. Dumont fled to the United States but returned and is buried at the site; Riel surrendered, stood trial, and was executed (see the box "The Trial of Louis Riel" on p. 519).

At the park, you can view four battlefield areas. It'll take 4 to 6 hours to walk to all four areas, 2½ hours to complete areas 1 and 2. For more information, contact **Batoche National Historic Site,** P.O. Box 999, Rosthern, SK S0K 3R0 (© **306/423-6227;** www.pc.gc.ca). Admission is C$7.15 (US$7.15/£3.60) for adults, C$5.90 (US$5.90/£2.95) for seniors, C$3.45 (US$3.45/£1.75) for students, and C$18 (US$18/£9) for families; special events and presentations may cost extra. Early May through September, Batoche is open daily 9am to 5pm. The site is about an hour from Saskatoon via Highway 11 to 312 to 225.

10 Prince Albert National Park: A Jewel of the National Park System ★

The 400,000-hectare (1 million-acre) wilderness area of Prince Albert National Park, 240km (149 miles) north of Saskatoon and 91km (57 miles) north of the town of Prince Albert, is one of the jewels of Canada's national park system. Its terrain is astoundingly varied, since it lies at the point where the great Canadian prairie grasslands give way to the pristine evergreen forests of the north. Here you'll find clear, cold lakes, ponds, and streams created thousands of years ago as glaciers receded. It's a hilly landscape, forested with spruce, poplar, and birch.

The park offers outdoor activities from canoeing and backpacking to nature hikes, picnicking, swimming, and great wildlife viewing. You can see and photograph moose, caribou, elk, black bear, bison, and loons. (The moose and caribou tend to wander through the forested northern part of the park, while the elk, bison, and deer graze on the southern grasslands.) Lavallee Lake is home to Canada's second-largest white-pelican colony.

In the 1930s, this park's woods and wildlife inspired famed naturalist Grey Owl, an Englishman adopted by the Ojibwe who became one of Canada's pioneering conservationists and most noted naturalists. For 7 years, he lived in a simple one-room cabin called Beaver Lodge on Ajawaan Lake; many hikers and canoeists make a pilgrimage to see his cabin and nearby grave site.

Entry fees are C$6.90 (US$6.90/£3.45) for adults, C$5.90 (US$5.90/£2.95) for seniors, and C$3.45 (US$3.45/£1.75) for children ages 6 to 16, and C$18 (US$18/£9) families. The park is open year-round, but many campgrounds, motels, and facilities are closed after October. A handful of winter campsites are open for ice fishers or cross-country skiers on the more than 150km (93 miles) of trails.

The town of **Waskesiu Lake,** which lies on the shores of the lake of the same name, is the supply center and also has accommodations. Open all year, the **Hawood Inn** (© **877/441-5544** or 306/663-5911; www.hawood.com) is a great choice, an elegant lodge with a serene backwoods atmosphere, very comfortable rooms (from C$95/US$95/£48), and fine dining. At the **Visitor Service Centre** at park headquarters in Waskesiu, you'll find an 18-hole golf course, tennis courts, bowling greens, and a paddle wheeler that cruises Waskesiu Lake. The staff can tell you about the weather and the condition of the trails; check in with them before undertaking any serious canoe or backcountry trip. The park's **Nature Centre** (© **306/663-4512**) presents an audiovisual program called "Up North" daily in July and August.

More than 30% of the park's surface is water, making a canoe or kayak a great way to navigate and explore this nearly roadless area. **Canoeing** routes wind through much of the park through a system of interconnected lakes and rivers. Canoes can be rented at three lakes, including Lake Waskesiu, and paddled along several routes, including the

Bagwa and Bladebone routes. **CanoeSki Discovery Company** (© **306/653-5693;** www.canoeski.com), a Parks Canada licensed outfitter, offers a selection of multiday canoe adventures into the heart of the park. The trips are led by naturalists and certified canoeing guides, including some especially for families and birders. Canoe packages include 2-day, 1-night trips from C$350 (US$350/£175), to 4-day, 3-night trips for C$750 (US$750/£375). There's also terrific fishing in the park, but anglers must have a national-park fishing license available for sale at the information center.

The park has 10 short **hiking trails,** plus four or so longer trails for backpackers, ranging from 10km to 41km (6.2–25 miles). Several easier ones begin in or near Waskesiu, though the best begin farther north. From the northwest shore of Lake Kingsmere, you can pick up the 20km (12-mile) trail leading to Grey Owl's cabin. The park offers six **campgrounds,** two with more than 100 sites and two with fewer than 30. They fill up fast on summer weekends; rates are C$15 to C$33 (US$15–US$33/£7.50–£17). The information office in Waskesiu issues backcountry camping permits to backpackers and canoeists.

For additional info, contact **Prince Albert National Park,** P.O. Box 100, Waskesiu Lake, SK S0J 2Y0 (© **306/663-4522;** www.pc.gc.ca).

14

Alberta & the Rockies

by Bill McRae

Stretching from the Northwest Territories to Montana in the south, flanked by the Rocky Mountains in the west and Saskatchewan in the east, Alberta is a big, beautiful, empty chunk of North America. At 661,188 sq. km (255,286 sq. miles), the province has just over 3 million inhabitants.

Culturally, Alberta is a beguiling mix of big-city swagger and affluence and rural Canadian sincerity. Its cities, Calgary and Edmonton, are models of modern civic pride and hospitality; in fact, a behavioral survey recently named Edmonton Canada's friendliest city.

Early settlers came to Alberta for its wealth of furs; the Hudson's Bay Company established Edmonton House on the North Saskatchewan River in 1795. The Blackfeet, one of the West's most formidable Indian nations, maintained control of the prairies until the 1870s, when the Northwest Mounted Police arrived to enforce the white man's version of law and order. Open-range cattle ranching prospered on the rich grasslands, and agriculture is still the basis of the rural Alberta economy. Vast oil reserves were discovered in the 1960s, introducing a tremendous 40-year boom.

More than half the population lives in Edmonton and Calgary, leaving the rest of the province a tremendous amount of breathing room and unspoiled scenery.

The Canadian Rockies rise to the west of the prairies and contain some of the finest mountain scenery on earth. Between them, Banff and Jasper national parks preserve much of this mountain beauty, but vast and equally spectacular regions of the Rockies, as well as portions of the nearby Columbia and Selkirk mountain ranges in British Columbia, are protected by other national and provincial parks.

All this wilderness makes outdoor activity Alberta's greatest draw. Hiking, biking, and pack trips on horseback have long pedigrees in the parks, as does superlative skiing—the Winter Olympics were held in Calgary in 1988. Outfitters throughout the region offer white-water and float trips on mighty rivers; and calmer pursuits such as fishing and canoeing are also popular.

In addition, some of Canada's finest and most famous hotels are in Alberta. The incredible mountain lodges and châteaux built by early rail entrepreneurs are still in operation, offering unforgettable experiences in luxury and stunning scenery. These grand hotels established a standard of hospitality that's observed by hoteliers across the province. If you want a more rural experience, head to one of Alberta's many guest ranches, where you can saddle up, poke some doggies, and enjoy a steak barbecue.

1 Exploring the Province

It's no secret that Alberta contains some of Canada's most compelling scenery and out-door recreation. Mid-June through August, this is a very busy place; Banff is generally acknowledged to be Canada's single most popular destination for foreign travelers. A little planning is essential, especially if you're traveling in summer or have specific destinations or lodgings in mind.

Skiers should know that heavy snowfall closes some mountain roads in winter. However, major passes are maintained and usually remain open. Highways 3, 1, and 16 are open year-round, though it's a good idea to call to check road conditions. You can inquire locally or call **Travel Alberta** (© 800/661-8888; www.travelalberta.com) or the **Alberta Motor Association** (© 403/474-8601; www.ama.ab.ca). If you're a member of AAA or CAA, call their information line (© 800/642-3810). Always carry traction devices such as tire chains in your vehicle, plus plenty of warm clothes and a sleeping bag if you're planning winter car travel.

VISITOR INFORMATION

For information about the entire province, contact **Travel Alberta,** Box 2500, Edmonton, AB T5J 2Z4 (© 800/252-3782; www.travelalberta.com). Be sure to ask for a copy of the accommodations guide (**www.explorealberta.com** has many listings also), as well as the excellent *Traveler's Guide* and a road map. There's a separate guide for campers, which you should ask for if you're considering camping at any point during your trip.

Alberta has no provincial sales tax. There's only the 5% goods and services tax (GST), plus a 5% accommodations tax.

THE GREAT OUTDOORS

Banff and Jasper national parks have long been Alberta's center of mountain recreation. If you're staying in Banff, Jasper, or Lake Louise, you'll find that outfitters and recreational rental operations in these centers are pretty sophisticated and professional: They make it easy to get outdoors and have an adventure. Most hotels offer a concierge service that can arrange activities; for many, you need little or no advance registration. Shuttle buses to more distant activities are usually available as well.

You don't even have to break a sweat to enjoy the magnificent scenery—hire a horse and ride to the backcountry or take an afternoon trail ride. Jasper, Banff, and Lake Louise have gondolas to lift you from the valley floor to the mountaintops. Bring a picnic or plan a ridge-top hike. If you're not ready for white water, the scenic cruises on Lake Minnewanka and Maligne Lake offer a more relaxed waterborne adventure.

BACKPACKING Backcountry trips through high mountain meadows and remote lakes provide an unforgettable experience; Banff Park alone has 3,059km (1,900 miles) of hiking trails.

BIKING Both Banff and Jasper provide free maps of local mountain-bike trails; the **Bow Valley Parkway** 𝕲 between Banff and Lake Louise and **Parkway 93A** 𝕲 in Jasper Park are both good less trafficked roads for road biking. Bike rentals are easily available nearly everywhere in the parks.

ROCK CLIMBING, ICE CLIMBING & MOUNTAINEERING The sheer rock faces on **Mount Rundle** near Banff and the **Palisades** near Jasper are popular with climbers, and the area's many waterfalls become frozen ascents for ice climbers in

Alberta

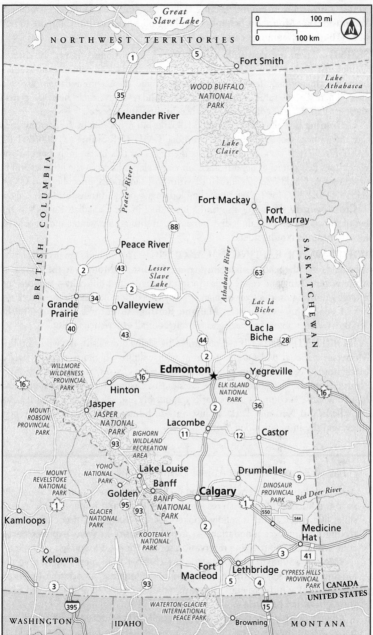

winter. Instruction in mountaineering skills, including rock climbing, is offered by **Yamnuska Inc. Mountain School,** a climbing outfitter based in Canmore (© **403/ 678-4164;** www.yamnuska.com).

SKIING   There are **downhill** areas at Banff, Lake Louise, Jasper, Nakiska and Golden. At its best, skiing is superb here: The snowpack is copious, the scenery is beautiful, the après-ski festivities are indulgent, and the accommodations are world-class. There's good value in an Alberta ski holiday—lift tickets here are generally cheaper than those at comparable ski areas in the United States.

Heli-skiing isn't allowed in the national parks but is popular in the adjacent mountain ranges near Golden in British Columbia. **CMH Heli-Skiing** (© **800/661-0252** or 403/762-7100; www.cmhski.com) is the leader in this increasingly popular sport, which uses helicopters to deposit skiers on virgin slopes far from the lift lines and runs of ski resorts. CMH offers 7- and 10-day trips to 12 locations; prices begin at C$5,414 (US$5,414£2,707) for 1 week, including lodging, food, and transport from Calgary.

Cross-country skiers will also find a lot to like in the Canadian Rockies. A number of snowbound mountain lodges remain open throughout winter and serve as bases for adventurous Nordic skiers.

WHITE-WATER RAFTING & CANOEING   The Rockies' many glaciers and snowfields are the source of mighty rivers. Outfitters throughout the region offer white-water rafting and canoe trips of varying lengths and difficulty—you can spend a single morning on the river or plan a 5-day expedition. Jasper is central to a number of good white-water rivers; **Maligne Rafting Adventures Ltd.** (© **780/852-3370;** www.mra.ab.ca) has packages for rafters of all experience levels.

WILDLIFE VIEWING   If you're thrilled by seeing animals in the wild, the Rocky Mountain national parks are all teeming with wildlife—bighorn sheep, grizzly and black bears, deer, mountain goats, moose, coyotes, lynxes, wolves, and more. See "Introducing the Canadian Rockies," later in this chapter, for warnings about how to handle wildlife encounters in the parks responsibly and safely. Aside from the Rockies, **Elk Island National Park** ✦, just outside Edmonton, harbors the tiny pygmy shrew and the immense wood buffalo.

Tips A Word (or Two) About Lodging

Accommodations are very tight throughout the province in summer, especially so in the Rockies. Make room reservations for Banff and Jasper as early as possible; likewise, Calgary is solidly booked for the Stampede. If you are having trouble finding accommodations, search the website at **www.explorealberta. com**, which offers an online reservation service for most lodgings.

B&Bs are abundant in Alberta and are cheaper than most hotels. If you're looking for a B&B, try the **Alberta Bed and Breakfast Association** (www.bb alberta.com), which provides listings of member inspected and approved B&Bs throughout the province.

Alberta is rich with hostels as well, especially in the Rocky Mountain national parks, where they're often the only affordable lodging option. Hostels run by **Hostelling International Canada** (www.hihostels.ca) in Alberta welcome guests of all ages.

Getting a Taste of the Old West at a Guest Ranch

Alberta has been ranch country for well over a century, and the Old West lifestyle is deeply ingrained in its culture. Indulge in a cowboy fantasy and spend a few days at one of the province's many historic guest ranches.

At Seebe, in the Kananaskis Country near the entrance to Banff National Park, are a couple of the oldest and most famous guest ranches. **Rafter Six Ranch** (© **888/267-2624** or 403/673-3622; www.raftersix.com), with its beautiful log lodge, can accommodate up to 60. The original Brewster homestead was transformed in 1923 into the **Brewster's Kananaskis Guest Ranch** (© **800/691-5085** or 403/673-3737; www.kananaskisguestranch.com). Once a winter horse camp, the **Black Cat Guest Ranch** (© **800/859-6840** or 780/865-3084; www.blackcatguestranch.ca) near Hinton is another long-established guest ranch in beautiful surroundings.

At all these historic ranches, horseback riding and trail rides are the main focus, but other western activities, such as rodeos, barbecues, and country dancing, are usually on the docket. Gentler pursuits, such as fishing, hiking, and lolling by the hot tub, are equally possible. Meals are usually served family-style in the central lodge, while accommodations are either in cabins or in the main lodge. A night at a guest ranch usually ranges from C$110 to C$200 (US$110–US$200/£55–£100) and includes a ranch breakfast. Full bed-and-board packages are available for longer stays. There's usually an additional hourly fee for horseback riding.

Homestays at smaller working ranches are also possible. Here you can pitch in and help your ranch-family hosts with their work or simply relax. For a stay on a real mom-and-pop farm or ranch, obtain a list of members from **Alberta Country Vacations Association** (© **403/722-3053**; www.alberta countryvacation.com).

2 Calgary: Home of the Annual Stampede (★(★

303km (188 miles) S of Edmonton, 788km (490 miles) W of Regina, 512km (318 miles) NW of Great Falls

Calgary dates only from the summer of 1875, when a detachment of the Northwest Mounted Police reached the confluence of the Bow and Elbow rivers. The solid log fort they built had attracted 600 settlers by the end of the year. Gradually, the lush prairie lands around the settlement drew tremendous beef herds, many of them from over-grazed U.S. ranches in the south. Calgary grew into a cattle metropolis and a large meat-packing center. When World War II ended, the placid city numbered barely 100,000.

The oil boom erupted in the late 1960s, and in 1 decade the pace and complexion of the city changed utterly. In 1978 alone, C$1 billion worth of construction was added to the skyline, creating office high rises, hotel blocks, walkways, and shopping centers so fast even locals weren't sure what was around the corner. In the mid-1990s, the oil market heated up again, and Alberta's pro-business political climate tempted national companies to build their headquarters here. With world oil prices at all-time highs, Calgary continues to boom in the 21st century, and building cranes continue to dominate the skyline.

In February 1988, Calgary was the site of the Winter Olympics, giving it the opportunity to roll out the welcome mat on a truly international scale. The city outdid itself in hospitality, erecting a whole network of facilities, including the Canada Olympic Park, by the Trans-Canada Highway, some 15 minutes west of downtown.

Calgary, with a population of one million, has an imposing skyline boasting dozens of business towers topping 40 stories. Despite this, the city doesn't seem urban. With its many parks and convivial populace, Calgary retains the atmosphere of a much smaller, friendlier town.

ESSENTIALS

GETTING THERE BY PLANE   **Calgary International Airport** (www.calgary airport.com) lies 16km (10 miles) northeast of the city. The airport is served by **Air Canada** (© 800/372-9500), **Delta** (© 800/221-1212), **American Airlines** (© 800/433-7300), **United** (© 800/241-6522), **Continental** (© 800/525-0280), and **Northwest** (© 800/447-4747), among others. An air shuttle service to and from Edmonton is run almost hourly by Air Canada.

Cab fare to downtown hotels comes to around C$35 (US$35/£18). The **Airporter bus** (© **403/531-3909**) takes you downtown for C$15 (US$15£7.50).

GETTING THERE BY TRAIN   The nearest **VIA Rail** station is in Edmonton (see "Edmonton: Capital of Alberta," later in this chapter). You can, however, take a scenic train ride to/from Vancouver/Calgary on the **Rocky Mountaineer,** operated by the **Great Rocky Mountaineer Railtours** (© **800/665-7245** or 604/606-7245; www. rockymountaineer.com). The lowest-priced tickets begin at C$889 (US$889/£445) for 2 days of daylight travel, which includes four meals and overnight accommodation in Kamloops; many other packages are available.

GETTING THERE BY BUS   **Greyhound** buses (© **800/661-8747** or 403/260-0877; www.greyhound.ca) link Calgary with most other points in Canada, including Banff and Edmonton, as well as towns in the United States. The depot is at 877 Greyhound Way SW, west of downtown near the corner of 9th Avenue SW and 16th Street SW.

GETTING THERE BY CAR   From the U.S. border in the south, Highway 2 runs to Calgary. The same excellent road continues north to Edmonton (via Red Deer). From Vancouver in the west to Regina in the east, take the Trans-Canada Highway.

VISITOR INFORMATION   The downtown **Visitor Service Centre** is at the base of Calgary Tower at 101 9th Ave. SW (© **800/661-1678** or 403/263-8510; www. tourismcalgary.com). There's also a tourist office at the airport. Send written requests to **Tourism Calgary,** 200 238 11th Ave. SE, Calgary, AB T2G 0X8.

CITY LAYOUT   Central Calgary lies between the Bow River in the north and the Elbow River to the south. The two rivers meet at the eastern end of the city, forming **St. George's Island,** which houses a park and the zoo. South of the island stands Fort Calgary, birthplace of the city. The Bow River makes a bend north of downtown, and in this bend nestles **Prince's Island Park** and **Eau Claire Market.** The Canadian Pacific Railway tracks run between 9th and 10th avenues, and **Central Park** and **Stampede Park,** scene of Calgary's greatest annual festival, stretch south of the tracks. Northwest, across the Bow River, is the **University of Calgary's** lovely campus. The airport is northeast of the city.

Calgary

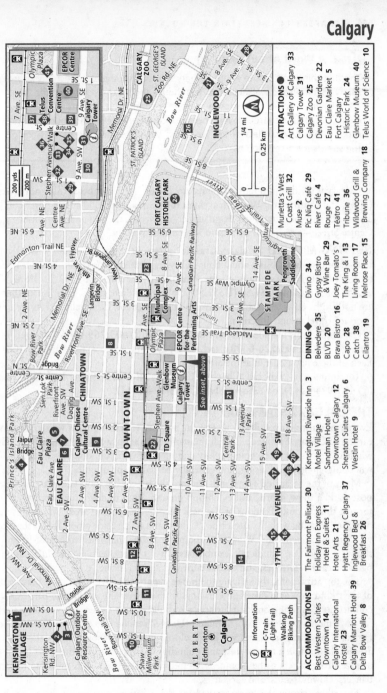

ATTRACTIONS ●
Art Gallery of Calgary **33**
Calgary Tower **31**
Calgary Zoo **25**
Devonian Gardens **22**
Eau Claire Market **5**
Fort Calgary
  Historic Park **24**
Glenbow Museum **40**
Telus World of Science **10**

Murieta's West
  Coast Grill **32**
Muse **2**
Pic Niq Café **29**
River Café **4**
Rouge **27**
Teatro **41**
Tribune **36**
Wildwood Grill &
  Brewing Company **18**

DINING ◆
Belvedere **35**
BLVD **20**
Brava Bistro **16**
Capo **28**
Catch **38**
Cilantro **19**

Divino **34**
Gypsy Bistro
  & Wine Bar **29**
Joey Tomato's **7**
The King & I **13**
Living Room **17**
Melrose Place **15**

ACCOMMODATIONS ■
Best Western Suites
  Downtown **14**
Calgary International
  Hostel **23**
Calgary Marriott Hotel **39**
Delta Bow Valley **8**

The Fairmont Palliser **30**
Holiday Inn Express
  Hotel & Suites **11**
Hotel Arts **21**
Hyatt Regency Calgary **37**
Inglewood Bed &
  Breakfast **26**

Kensington Riverside Inn **3**
Motel Village **1**
Sandman Hotel
  Downtown Calgary **12**
Sheraton Suites Calgary **6**
Westin Hotel **9**

i Information
CK C-Train
  (Light rail)
  Walking/
  Biking Path

Tips   **A Word About Walking**

The first thing you'll note about Calgary is how long the east-west blocks are. Allow 15 minutes to walk 5 blocks. You should also make good use of the "Plus-15" system, a series of enclosed walkways connecting downtown buildings 4.5m (15 ft.) above street level. These walkways enable you to shop in living-room comfort, regardless of the weather. Watch for the little "+15" signs on the streets for access points.

Calgary is divided into four segments: **northeast** (NE), **southeast** (SE), **northwest** (NW), and **southwest** (SW), with avenues running east-west and streets north-south. The north and south numbers begin at Centre Avenue, the east and west numbers at Centre Street—a recipe for confusion if ever there was one.

GETTING AROUND   Calgary Transit System (© **403/276-1000;** www.calgary transit.com) operates buses and a light-rail system called the C-Train. You can transfer from the light rail to buses on the same ticket. The ride costs C$2.50 (US$2.50/£1.25) for adults and C$1.50 (US$1.50/75p) for children; the C-Train is free (buses are not) in the downtown stretch between 10th Street and City Hall. Tickets are only good for travel in one direction.

Car-rental firms include **Avis,** 211 6th Ave. SW (© **403/269-6166**); **Budget,** 140 6th Ave. SE (© **403/226-0000**); and **Hertz,** 227 6th Ave. SW (© **403/221-1681**). Each of these has a bureau at the airport.

To summon a taxi, call **Checker Cabs** (© **403/299-9999**), **Red Top Cabs** (© **403/974-4444**), or **Yellow Cabs** (© **403/974-1111**).

THE CALGARY STAMPEDE ☆☆☆

Every year during July, Calgary puts on the biggest, wildest, woolliest western fling on earth: the Calgary Stampede. To call the stampede a show would be a misnomer. The whole city participates by going mildly crazy for the occasion, donning western gear, whooping, hollering, dancing, and generally behaving uproariously.

Many of the organized events spill out into the streets, but most take place in Stampede Park, a show, sports, and exhibition ground south of downtown that was built for just this purpose. Portions of the park become amusement areas, whirling, spinning, and rotating with the latest rides. Other parts are set aside especially for the kids, who romp through Kids' World and the petting zoo. Still other areas host livestock shows, a food fair, handicraft exhibitions, an art show, lectures, an international bazaar, a casino, lotteries, and entertainment on several stages.

The top attractions, though, are the **rodeo events,** the largest and most prestigious of their kind in North America. Cowboys from all over the world take part in such competitions as riding bucking broncos and bulls, roping calves, and wrestling steers for prize money totaling C$1.75 million (US$1.75 million/£875,000). At the world-famous **Chuckwagon Race,** you'll see old-time western cook wagons thundering around the track in a fury of dust and pounding hooves. At night, the arena becomes a blaze of lights when the Stampede Grandstand takes over with precision-kicking dancers, clowns, bands, and spectacles.

The whole city is absolutely packed for the occasion, not just to the rafters but way out into the surrounding countryside. Reserving accommodations well ahead is essential—as many months ahead of your arrival as you can possibly foresee. Some downtown watering holes even take reservations for space at the bar; that should give you an idea of how busy Calgary gets.

The same advice applies to reserving tickets for Stampede events. Tickets begin at C$27 (US$27£14) but go up from there, depending on the event, the seats, and whether the event takes place in the afternoon or evening. For mail order bookings, contact the **Calgary Exhibition and Stampede,** P.O. Box 1060, Station M, Calgary, AB T2P 2K8 (© **800/661-1767;** www.calgarystampede.com).

FAST FACTS: Calgary

American Express The office at 421 7th Ave. SW (© **403/261-5982**) is open Monday through Friday 9am to 5pm.

Area Code Calgary's area code is **403.**

Doctors If you need nonemergency medical attention, check the phone number for the closest branch of **Medicentre,** a group of walk-in clinics open daily 7am to midnight.

Drugstores Check the phone book for **Shoppers Drug Mart,** which has more than a dozen stores in Calgary, most open till midnight. The branch at the Chinook Centre, 6455 Macleod Trail S. (© **403/253-2424**), is open 24 hours.

Emergency For medical, fire, or crime emergencies, dial © **911.**

Hospitals If you need medical care, try **Foothills Hospital,** 1403 29th St. NW (© **403/670-1110**).

Newspapers Calgary's two dailies, the *Calgary Herald* (www.calgaryherald. com) and the *Calgary Sun* (www.calgarysun.com), are both morning papers. *Ffwd* (www.ffwdweekly.com) is a youth-oriented newsweekly and a good place to look for information on the local music and arts scene.

Police The 24-hour number is © **403/266-1234.** Dial © **911** in emergencies.

Post Office The main post office is at 207 9th Ave. (© **403/974-2078**). Call © 403/292-5434 to find other branches.

Time Calgary is on Mountain Standard Time, the same as Edmonton and Denver, and it observes daylight saving time.

EXPLORING CALGARY
THE TOP ATTRACTIONS

Calgary Tower   Reaching 762 steps or 190m (623 ft.) into the sky, this Calgary landmark is topped by an observation terrace offering unparalleled views of the city and mountains and prairies beyond. The high-speed elevator whisks you to the top in just 63 seconds. A stairway from the terrace leads to the cocktail lounge, where you can enjoy drinks and a panoramic vista. Photography from up here is fantastic. The **Panorama Restaurant** (© **403/508-5822**) is the near-mandatory revolving restaurant.

9th Ave. and Centre St. SW. © **403/266-7171.** www.calgarytower.com. Elevator ride C$13 (US$13£6.50) adults, C$11 (US$11/£5.50) seniors, C$9 (US$9/£4.50) youths 6–17, C$5 (US$5/£2.50) children 5 and under. June 15–Sept 15 daily 7am–11pm (last lift 10:30pm); Sept 16–June 14 daily 9am–11pm (last lift 9pm). LRT: 1st St. E.

Calgary Zoo, Botanical Garden & Prehistoric Park ⭐ *Kids* Calgary's large and thoughtfully designed zoo resides on St. George's Island in the Bow River. The Calgary Zoo comes as close to providing natural habitats for its denizens as is technically possible. You'll particularly want to see the troop of majestic lowland gorillas and the African warthogs. The flora and fauna of western and northern Canada are on display in the Botanical Garden, and there's an amazing year-round tropical butterfly enclosure as well. Adjoining the zoo is the Prehistoric Park, a three-dimensional textbook of ancient dinosaur habitats populated by 22 amazingly realistic replicas—these imposing reproductions will give Barney-loving children something to think about. Call to inquire about special summer events, such as Thursday Jazz Nights and free interpretive talks called "Nature Tales."

1300 Zoo Rd. NE. ✆ 403/232-9300. www.calgaryzoo.ab.ca. Admission C$18 (US$18/£9) adults, C$16 (US$16/£8) seniors, C$12 (US$12/£6) youths 13–17, C$10 (US$10/£5) children 3–12. From Labour Day to April 30, all rates reduced by C$2 (US$2/£1). Daily 9am–5pm. LRT: Zoo station.

Canada Olympic Park *Kids* This lasting memento of Calgary's role as host of the 1988 Winter Olympics stands in Olympic Park, which was the site for ski jumping, luge, and bobsledding during the games. Exhibits include the world's largest collection of Olympic souvenirs, such as the torch used to bring the flame from Greece; costumes and equipment used by the athletes; superb photographs; and a gallery of all medal winners. The reason that the park is still an exciting destination is the activities and lessons available. In winter, both adults and children can take downhill and cross-country ski lessons, learn to ski jump or snowboard, or get an introduction to snow skating. More exciting are the opportunities to ride a bobsled down the Olympic track or to take a zip line off the ski jump tower—harnessed onto a cable system, reaching speeds between 120 and 140kmph (75–90 mph) before launching 500m (1,610 ft.) with a vertical drop of more than 100m (328 ft.) will get the adrenaline pumping for road-trip weary teenagers (C$49/US$49/£25). Other summer activities include a mountain-bike course and chairlift rides up to the ski-jump tower.

88 Canada Olympic Park Rd. SW. ✆ 403/247-5452. www.coda.ab.ca. Admission C$10 (US$10/£5) per person, C$35 (US$35/£18) per family; separate fees for activities and lessons. Summer daily 8am–9pm; off season daily 8am–5pm. Take Hwy. 1 west.

Eau Claire Market & Prince's Island Park Eau Claire Market is part of a car-free pedestrian zone north of downtown on the banks of the Bow River that links to lovely Prince's Island Park, a bucolic island in the Bow River lined with paths, shaded by cottonwood trees, and populated by hordes of Canada geese. This is where much of downtown Calgary comes to eat, drink, shop, sunbathe, jog, and hang out in good weather. The market itself no longer offers a lot for the traveler except for a few eateries (better options are the pubs in the plaza outside the market) though it remains busy with a four-screen cinema and an **IMAX theater** (✆ **403/974-4629**), with its five-story domed screen.

Near 2nd Ave. SW and 3rd St. SW. ✆ 403/264-6450. Free admission. Market building open 9am–9pm; shops and restaurants have varying hours. LRT: 3rd St. W.

Fort Calgary Historic Park ⭐⭐ *Kids* On the occasion of the city's centennial in 1975, Fort Calgary became a public park of 16 hectares (40 acres), spread around the ruins of the original Mounted Police stronghold. In 2001, volunteers completed a replica of the 1888 barracks using traditional methods and building materials. The

Interpretive Centre captures the history of Calgary, from its genesis as a military fort to the beginnings of 20th-century hegemony as an agricultural and oil boomtown. Kids can do time in the 1875-era jail, or dress up as a Mountie. There are a number of interesting videos and docent-led displays; always in focus are the adventures and hardships of the Mounties a century ago. The rigors of their westward march and the almost unbelievable isolation these pioneer troopers endured now seems incredible.

If all this history whets your appetite, cross the Elbow River on 9th Avenue and head to the Deane House. This historic home was built by a Fort Calgary superintendent nearly 100 years ago and is now the **Deane House Restaurant** operated by Fort Calgary (✆ **403/269-7747**), open Monday through Friday from 11am to 3pm, Saturday and Sunday from 10am to 3pm.

750 9th Ave. SE. ✆ **403/290-1875**. www.fortcalgary.ab.ca. Admission C$11 (US$11/£5.50) adults, C$10 (US$10/£5) seniors and postsecondary students, C$7 (US$7/£3.50) youths 7–17; C$5 (US$5/£2.50) children 3–6. Daily 9am–5pm. LRT: Bridgeland.

Glenbow Museum 🏆🏆 One of the country's finest museums, the Glenbow is a must for anyone with an interest in the history and culture of western Canada. What sets it apart from other museums chronicling the continent's Native cultures and pioneer settlement is the excellence of its interpretation. Especially notable is the third floor, with its vivid evocation of Native cultures—particularly of the local Blackfeet—and compelling descriptions of western Canada's exploration and settlement. You'll enjoy the brief asides into whimsy, such as the display of early washing machines. Other floors contain displays of West African carvings, gems and minerals, and a cross-cultural look at arms and warfare.

130 9th Ave. SE (at 1st St.). ✆ **403/268-4100**. www.glenbow.org. Admission C$14 (US$14/£7) adults, C$10 (US$10/£5) seniors, C$12 (US$12/£6) postsecondary students, C$9 (US$9/£4.50) youths 7–17, children under 6 free. Daily 9am–5pm (Thurs to 9pm). LRT: 1st St. E.

Telus World of Science 🇰🇮🇩🇸 Formerly known as the Calgary Science Centre, this museum features a fascinating kid-oriented combination of exhibitions, a planetarium, films, laser shows, and live theater, all under one roof. The hands-on, science-oriented exhibits change, but always invite visitors to push, pull, talk, listen, and play. The 360-degree Discovery Dome Theatre offers a number of filmed presentations that engulf the senses.

701 11th St. SW. ✆ **403/221-3700**. www.calgaryscience.ca. Admission (exhibits and star shows) C$15 (US$15/£7.50) adults, C$12 (US$12/£6) children 3–17, children under 3 free, C$49 (US$49/£25) families. Mon–Thurs 9:45am–4pm; Fri 9:45am–5pm; Sat, Sun, and holidays 10am–5pm. LRT: 10th St. W.

MORE ATTRACTIONS

Art Gallery of Calgary This contemporary art gallery, housed in two recently renovated downtown buildings, places a special emphasis on the contribution of local and regional talent and is a good place to see Calgary's contribution to the modern-art scene. National and regional shows also travel to the Art Gallery.

117 8th Ave. SW. ✆ **403/770-1350**. www.artgallerycalgary.org. Admission C$5 (US$5/£2.50) adults, C$2.50 (US$2.50/£1.25) seniors and students, children under 6 free. Tues–Sat 10am–5pm. LRT: 1st St. E.

Devonian Gardens These indoor gardens are a patch of paradise in downtown, especially in the chill of winter. Laid out in natural contours with 1.5km (1 mile) of pathways and a central stage for musical performances, they contain 20,000 plants (a mix of native Alberta and tropical plants), a reflecting pool, sun garden, children's playground, sculpture court, and water garden. The Devonian Gardens, encompassing 1 hectare (2½-acres) and rising three stories, is one of the world's largest indoor parks.

8th Ave. and 3rd St. SW, 4th floor. © 403/268-3830. Free admission. Daily 9am–9pm. LRT: 3rd St. W.

Fish Creek Provincial Park   On the outskirts of town but easily accessible, Fish Creek Park is one of the largest urban parks in the world—actually, a kind of metropolitan wildlife reserve. Spreading over 1,175 hectares (2,900 acres), it provides a sheltered habitat for a vast variety of animals and birds. You can learn about them by joining in the walks and slide presentations given by park interpreters.

Canyon Meadows Dr. and Macleod Trail SE. © 403/297-5293. http://tprc.alberta.ca/parks/fishcreek. Bus: 78 or 83.

Military Museums   Formerly the Museum of the Regiments, this complex has newly expanded and when fully complete in 2008, will include seven museums situated on 5.3 hectares (13 acres), encompassing 9,662 sq. m (104,000 sq. ft.) of viewing area dedicated to Canadian Forces' history and heritage. As the largest military museum in western Canada, the Military Museums focus on the story of four famous Canadian regiments from the early 1900s to today. A series of lifelike miniature and full-size displays re-create scenes from the Boer War in 1900 to World War II; contemporary peacekeeping operations are also depicted. You also see videos, weapons, uniforms, medals, and photographs relating the history of the regiments and hear the actual voices of the combatants describing their experiences.

4520 Crowchild Trail SW (at Flanders Ave.). © 403/974-2850. http://themilitarymuseums.ca. Admission C$6 (US$6/£3) adults, C$4 (US$4/£2) seniors, C$3 (US$3/£1.50) students and children 7–17, free for military personnel and veterans. Daily 9:30am–4pm. Bus: 20 to Flanders Ave., then 1 block south.

TOURS & EXCURSIONS

Brewster Transportation (© 877/791-5500; www.brewster.ca), in conjunction with Gray Line Bus Lines (© 800/661-4919; www.grayline.ca), offers a wide variety of bus tours. In addition to a 4-hour Calgary tour for C$50 (US$50/£25), destinations include Banff, Lake Louise, Jasper, the Columbia Icefields, and Waterton Lakes.

Hammer Head Scenic Tours (© 403/260-0940; www.hammerheadtours.com) has 9-hour tours to the Drumheller badlands and the Royal Tyrrell Museum for C$90 (US$90/£45). Once weekly, the company runs its van to Head-Smashed-In Buffalo Jump for C$97 (US$97/£49).

SHOPPING

SHOPPING DISTRICTS OF NOTE

The main shopping district is downtown along **8th Avenue SW,** between 5th and 1st streets SW. The lower part of 8th Avenue has been turned into a pedestrian zone called the **Stephen Avenue Mall.** Major centers lining 8th Avenue between 1st and 4th streets include the Hudson's Bay Company and Holt Renfrew. Check out **Art Central,** 100 7th Ave. SW, a visual-arts complex with over 30 artists' studios and galleries. A hip hangout for the young at heart, **Kensington Village** is just northwest of downtown across the Bow River, centered at 10th Street NW and Kensington Road. Crowded between the ubiquitous coffeehouses are bike shops and trendy boutiques. The stretch of **17th Avenue SW** between 4th and 10th streets SW has developed a mix of specialty shops, boutiques, cafes, and bars that makes browsing a real pleasure.

Mountain Equipment Co-op, 830 10th Ave. SW (© 403/269-2420; www.mec.ca), is the largest outdoors store in Calgary, with everything from kayaks to ice axes. Come here before you head to the backcountry. If you like the look of pearl-snap shirts and the cut of Wranglers jeans, head to **Riley & McCormick,** 209 8th Ave. SW (© **403/262-1556**), one of Calgary's original western-apparel stores. If you're looking for cowboy boots, **Alberta Boot Company,** 614 10th Ave. SW (© **403/263-4605;** www.alberta boot.com), is Alberta's only remaining boot manufacturer.

The **Inglewood** neighborhood, south of downtown on 9th Avenue SE, is filled with antiques stores.

WHERE TO STAY

Finding inexpensive lodging in Calgary can be difficult. The city's booming economy means that many of the older hotels that once offered perfectly pleasant but moderately priced accommodations have gentrified. If you enjoy B&Bs, try the **Bed and Breakfast Association of Calgary** (www.bbcalgary.com), which has several dozen listings for Calgary. The newly relocated **Calgary International Hostel** (p. 552) is an option for budget travelers. The many hotels in **Motel Village** (see below), which link to the city center via the C-Train, are another option; you can often find these rooms at discount hotel websites.

DOWNTOWN
Very Expensive
The Fairmont Palliser ✦✦✦   This is the classiest address in all of Calgary. Opened in 1914 as one of the Canadian Pacific Railroad hotels, the Palliser is Calgary's landmark historic hotel. The vast marble-floored lobby, surrounded by columns and lit by gleaming chandeliers, is the very picture of Edwardian sumptuousness. You'll feel like an Alberta cattle king in the Rimrock Dining Room, with vaulted ceilings, period murals, a massive stone fireplace, and hand-tooled leather panels on teak beams. The lounge bar looks like a gentlemen's West End club. Guest rooms are sumptuously furnished and large for a hotel of this vintage while Fairmont Gold suites come with their own concierge and a private lounge with complimentary breakfast, drinks, and hors d'oeuvres.

133 9th Ave. SW, Calgary, AB T2P 2M3. © 800/441-1414 or 403/262-1234. Fax 403/260-1260. www.fairmont.com. 405 units. C$169–C$399 (US$169–US$399/£85–£200) double; from C$209–C$889 (US$209–US$889/£105–£445) suite. AE, DC, DISC, MC, V. Valet parking C$32 (US$32/£16). **Amenities:** Restaurant; bar; indoor pool; health club and spa; concierge; business services; salon; 24-hr. room service; babysitting; laundry service; same-day dry cleaning; concierge-level rooms. *In room:* A/C, TV, dataport, minibar, coffeemaker, hair dryer, iron.

Hyatt Regency Calgary ✦   Downtown's most upscale hotel, the Hyatt is linked to the Telus Convention Centre and is convenient to shopping and arts venues. Guest rooms are large, measuring roughly 37 sq. m (400 sq. ft.), with comfy furniture and great views. Suites are truly spacious, with most of the comforts of home. All rooms come with high-speed Internet access and two-line speakerphones, just the thing for the busy traveler. The hotel's Stillwater Spa is a full-service day spa, with a combination of massage and hydrotherapies, body wraps, and beauty treatments for both men and women. The fitness center and saline pool, located on the 18th floor, offers majestic views across the city skyline to the Rockies. The Hyatt flanks historic Stephen Avenue; and rather than leveling the 1890s stone storefronts, the Hyatt cleverly incorporates them into the hotel's facade. Original art worth C$2 million (US$2 million/£1 million) is on display in the hotel lobby and corridors.

700 Center St. SE, Calgary, AB T2G 5P6. © 800/233-1234 or 403/717-1234. Fax 403/537-4444. www.calgary.hyatt. com. 355 units. From C$179 (US$179/£90) traditional guest room; from C$1,500 (US$1,500/£750) Regency Club suite. AE, DC, DISC, MC, V. Valet and self-parking based on availability. **Amenities:** Restaurant; lounge; indoor pool, Jacuzzi,

sauna; StayFit health club; Stillwater Spa; concierge; business center; 24-hr. room service; laundry service; same-day dry cleaning. *In room:* A/C, TV, wired or wireless high-speed Internet, coffeemaker, hair dryer, iron, laptop safe.

Sheraton Suites Calgary ✦   The Sheraton Suites overlooks the Eau Claire Market area, just steps away from both the Bow River Greenway and downtown business towers. As an all-suite hotel, the Sheraton offers large and thoughtfully designed rooms that put luxury and business ease foremost. Guest rooms are decorated with a striking modern aesthetic, with quality and notably comfortable furniture, plus easy access to all the high-tech tools necessary to get work done, including high-speed Internet access. The built-in cabinetry makes it feel very homelike, as do the Prairie-influenced art, houseplants, and two TVs found in all rooms. Corner king suites are especially nice, with a huge bathroom, tiled shower, and Jacuzzi tub.

255 Barclay Parade SW, Calgary AB T2P 5C2. © **888/784-8370** or 403/266-7200. Fax 403/266-1300. www.sheraton suites.com. 323 suites. C$169–C$469 (US$169–US$469/£85–£235) double. Extra person C$30 (US$30/£15). AE, DC, DISC, MC, V. Valet parking C$27 (US$27/£14). **Amenities:** 2 restaurants; lounge; indoor pool; water slide; exercise room; in-suite spa services; Jacuzzi; sauna; concierge; business center; salon; 24-hr. room service; babysitting; laundry service. *In room:* A/C, TV w/games and movie channels, dataport, fridge, microwave, coffeemaker, hair dryer, iron, safe.

Westin Hotel ✦✦ *Kids*   The Westin completed a C$6-million renovation in 2007, with upgraded rooms and a new lobby. Despite its anonymous business-hotel exterior, most guest rooms have a subtle western feel that's reflected in the mission-style furniture, sunny colors, and period photos. Beautiful barn-wood breakfronts and lowboys (built especially for the hotel by local artisans) add another patina of history. For business travelers, 126 rooms have been redesigned in a more contemporary style and with special features such as flat-screen TVs and all the technology to help a business traveler multi-task, such as large glass-topped working desks and two-line phones. While standard rooms are very comfortable, corner rooms come with balconies. For extra quiet, request one of the Tower rooms, which are normally reserved for business travelers.

The hotel rolls out the welcome mat for kids, with a "kids' club" offering children's furniture, babysitting, and a children's menu—and games and special treats from room service. Special needs are anticipated, from strollers to room-service delivery of fresh diapers. Even dogs, which are welcome, have specialty beds!

320 4th Ave. SW, Calgary, AB T2P 2S6. © **800/937-8461** or 403/266-1611. Fax 403/233-7471. www.westin.com/calgary. 525 units. C$149–C$489 (US$149–US$489/£75/£245) double. Extra person C$30 (US$30/£15). AE, DC, DISC, MC, V. Self-parking C$15 (US$15/£7.50), valet parking C$29 (US$29/£15). **Amenities:** 2 restaurants; bar; coffee shop; panoramic roof-top indoor pool; health club and spa; sauna and whirlpool; concierge; business center; 24-hr. room service; laundry service; same-day dry cleaning. *In room:* A/C, TV, dataport, high-speed Internet access, minibar, coffeemaker, hair dryer, iron, safe.

Expensive

Best Western Suites Downtown   This well-maintained older hotel is an excellent value. The rooms are quite large, some almost apartment-size, and are fitted with quality furniture; some come with efficiency kitchens. It's located between downtown and trendy 17th Avenue.

1330 8th St. SW, Calgary, AB T2R 1B3. © **800/981-2555** or 403/228-6900. Fax 403/228-5535. www.bestwestern suitescalgary.com. 123 units. C$139–C$159 (US$139–US$159/£70–£80) junior suite; C$159–C$189 (US$159–US$189/£80–£95) 1-bedroom suite. Extra person C$10 (US$10/£5). Senior, weekly, and monthly rates available. AE, DISC, MC, V. Free parking. **Amenities:** Restaurant; Jacuzzi; laundry service. *In room:* A/C, TV, dataport, kitchenette, coffeemaker, hair dryer.

Calgary Marriott Hotel ✦   The Marriott is about as central as things get in Calgary: Linked to the convention center and convenient to the goings-on at the Centre for the Performing Arts and the Glenbow Museum, the Marriott is also connected via skywalk with Palliser Square, Calgary Tower, and loads of downtown shopping. Its large guest rooms received a total makeover in 2005 and are subtly decorated and outfitted with niceties such as windows that open, lots of mirrors, high-speed Internet access, and desks set up for business travelers. The even larger, tasteful suites are worth the extra money—especially the French Parlour suites, with lots of room to decompress. Yes, it's a convention hotel—but a lot nicer than the stereotype, and an excellent choice for leisure travelers.

110 9th Ave. SE (at Centre St.), Calgary, AB T2G 5A6. ℂ 800/228-9290 or 403/266-7331. Fax 403/269-1961. www.calgarymarriott.com. 384 units. C$119–C$259 (US$119–US$259/£60–£130) double; C$279–C$359 (US$279–US$359/£140–£180) suites. Extra person C$20 (US$20/£10). Weekend packages available. AE, DC, DISC, MC, V. Valet parking C$24 (US$24/£12) per day; self-parking C$18 (US$18/£9). **Amenities:** 2 restaurants; lounge; indoor pool; exercise room; Jacuzzi; sauna; concierge; business center; limited room service; same-day dry cleaning. *In room:* A/C, TV, dataport, high-speed Internet, fridge, microwave, coffeemaker, hair dryer, iron.

Hotel Arts 🏨🏨   The long-time Holiday Inn just south of downtown Calgary has recently undergone a C$10-million renovation/upgrade, emerging as Hotel Arts, a one-of-a-kind boutique hotel that's a redoubt of contemporary chic style. The remodel increased the size of guest rooms and brought in such features as 42-inch plasma TVs, upscale linens, and luxury soaps and lotions; the lobby is filled with briskly modern visual art. Guest-room decor is both swank and dramatic: Chocolate-brown walls, blue-velvet curtains, and strikingly modern furniture and lighting provide lots of pizzazz; all rooms have balconies. If you're weary of identical corporate hotels but require excellent service and amenities, Hotel Arts is for you. For special occasions, you can't go wrong with the Jacuzzi suites, with massive bathrooms and walk-in two-person tubs, or the pool suites, which overlook the hotel's pool courtyard, one of the top cocktail scenes for Calgary's beautiful people. Both Hotel Arts' restaurants, Raw Bar and St. Germain, are among the city's finest.

119 12th Ave. SW, Calgary, AB T2R 0G8. ℂ 800/661-9378 or 403/266/4611. Fax 403/237-0978. www.hotelarts.ca. 185 units. From C$129 (US$129/£65) double. AE, DISC, DC, MC, V. C$18 (US$18/£9) valet parking. **Amenities:** 2 restaurants; heated outdoor pool w/licensed patio; fitness room; concierge; 24-hr. room service; same-day dry-cleaning service; event space for private bookings. *In room:* A/C, flat-screen plasma TV; high-speed Internet, coffeemaker, hair dryer, iron.

Sandman Hotel Downtown Calgary *(Value)*   This hotel on the west end of downtown is one of Calgary's best deals. The Sandman is conveniently located on the free rapid-transit mall, just west of the main downtown core. The standard rooms are a good size, but the real winners are the very large corner units, which feature small kitchens and great views. The Sandman is a popular place with corporate clients, due to its central location, good value, and high-speed Internet access. It also boasts a complete fitness facility. Its private health club, available free to guests, has a lap pool, three squash courts, aerobics, and weight-training facilities.

888 7th Ave. SW, Calgary, AB T2P 3J3. ℂ 800/726-3626 or 403/237-8626. Fax 403/290-1238. www.sandman hotels.com. 301 units. From C$135 (US$135/£68) double. Children under 16 stay free in parent's room. AE, DC, DISC, MC, V. Parking C$12 (US$12/£6). **Amenities:** Restaurant; bar; indoor pool; health club; concierge; business center; limited room service; laundry service; same-day dry cleaning. *In room:* A/C, TV, dataport, fridge, microwave, coffeemaker, hair dryer, iron.

INGLEWOOD

Inglewood Bed & Breakfast 🏨 *(Finds)*   It's a great location: minutes from downtown, on a quiet residential street backed up to a park and the swift waters of the Bow

River. The Inglewood is a rambling modern structure in Queen Anne style built as a B&B. The three guest rooms are simply but stylishly furnished with handmade pine furniture and antiques; all have private bathrooms. Two of the turret rooms have great views over the river. If in Calgary with a family or on an extended stay, ask about the suite, with full kitchen facilities, a fireplace, and TV. Both owners are professional chefs, so expect an excellent breakfast.

1006 8th Ave. SE, Calgary, AB T2G 0M4. © **403/262-6570.** www.inglewoodbedandbreakfast.com. 3 units. C$90–C$135 (US$90–US$135/£45/£68) double. Rates include breakfast. MC, V. Free parking. *In room:* TV/VCR.

KENSINGTON

Kensington Riverside Inn ★★ *(Finds* Discriminating travelers, look no further. Just across the Bow River from downtown is the hip Kensington neighborhood, with lots of boutique shops, pubs, coffee shops and restaurants, a quick 5 minutes from the city center on the C-Train (Kensington is the first stop north of the river). Facing downtown across the river is the Kensington Riverside Inn, a beautifully furnished small boutique hotel that's a cross between a luxurious country inn and a hip urban getaway. Each of the expansive guest rooms has a balcony or patio, plus fireplace and high-quality furniture and linens. All of the rooms are uniquely decorated, but expect uniformly top-notch furnishings and service. Morning brings a coffee tray and newspaper to your door, and rates also include a full cooked breakfast. In 2008, the inn will open a small, exclusive restaurant with contemporary cuisine.

1126 Memorial Dr. NW, Calgary, AB T2N 3E3. © **877/313-3733** or 403/228-4442. Fax 403/228-9608. www.kensington riversideinn.com. 19 rooms. C$319–C$419 (US$319–US$419/£160–£210 double). Rates include parking. **Amenities:** Restaurant; bar; video/DVD library; private meeting room. *In room:* A/C, TV/DVD, wireless Internet access, coffeemaker, hair dryer, iron.

MOTEL VILLAGE

Northwest of downtown, Motel Village is a triangle of more than 20 large motels, plus restaurants, stores, and gas stations, forming a self-contained hamlet near the University of Calgary. Enclosed by Crowchild Trail, the Trans-Canada Highway, and Highway 1A, the village is arranged so that most of the costlier establishments flank the highway; the cheaper ones lie off Crowchild Trail, offering a wide choice of accommodations in a small area with good transportation connections. If you're driving and don't want to deal with downtown traffic, just head here to find a room.

Except during the Stampede, you'll be able to find a vacancy without reservations; on C-Train, use either Lions Park or Banff Park stops. Use discount hotel websites such as Travelocity to find deals here. Your favorite chain hotels are located here, including **Comfort Inn Calgary Motel Village,** 2369 Banff Trail NW (© **800/228-5150** or 403/289-2581); **Best Western Village Park Inn,** 1804 Crowchild Trail NW (© **888/774-7716** or 403/289-4645); **Travelodge North,** 2304 16th Ave. NW (© **800/578-7878** or 403/289-0211); and the **Quality Inn University,** 2359 Banff Trail NW (© **800/661-4667** or 403/289-1973).

BUDGET OPTIONS

Calgary International Hostel The 120 beds at the Calgary hostel are the city's most affordable lodgings—but there are reasons beyond economy to stay here. The hostel is on the edge of downtown, convenient to bars and restaurants along Stephen Avenue and theaters near the performing-arts center. Facilities include two family rooms, a common area, and a small convenience store.

520 7th Ave. SE, Calgary, AB, T2G 0J6. (*C*) **403/269-8239.** Fax 403/283-6503. www.hihostels.ca. 120 beds. Members C$26 (US$26/£13) single; nonmembers C$30 (US$30/£15) single. MC, V. Free parking. **Amenities:** Free wireless Internet access; coin-op laundry; self-catering kitchen.

CAMPING

The **Calgary West Campground,** on the Trans-Canada Highway West (Box 10, Site 12, SS no. 1), Calgary, AB T2M 4N3 ((*C*) **403/288-0411;** www.cmy.ab.ca), allows tents and pets. Facilities include washrooms, toilets, laundry, a dumping station, hot showers, groceries, and a pool. The price for full hookup with two people is C$41 (US$41/£21) per night; tent sites are C$29 (US$29/£15) per night.

WHERE TO DINE

Calgary has very stylish and exciting restaurants. The city is going through an unparalleled period of prosperity, and the citizenry's average age is around 30. Put these two factors together and you've got the ingredients for a vibrant bar and restaurant scene. The hot spots for dining and revelry are downtown along Stephen Avenue area (that is, 8th Ave. between 2nd St. SE and 4th St. SW), much of it a bustling pedestrian mall; the long 17th Avenue strip with an abundance of small independent restaurants; and the Kensington area, across the Bow River from downtown, with a number of upbeat dining choices in a tony shopping district. In addition, several formal, chef-owned restaurants with outsized local reputations have set down roots in Inglenook, just south of downtown.

DOWNTOWN
Expensive

Belvedere ✿✿✿ NEW CANADIAN   The very stylish Belvedere is one of the most impressive of Calgary's restaurants. The dining room exudes a darkly elegant, 1930s atmosphere. The menu blends traditional favorites with stand-up-and-take-notice preparations. Foie gras frequently appears as an appetizer, perhaps seared with fig brioche and caramalized shallot purée. Main courses feature local meats and seasonal produce; favorite main courses include free-range pheasant breast with confit pheasant ravioli and fennel broth, Meursault wine–poached lobster, and roast duck with blood-orange sauce. Vegetarians have the option of a seasonal tasting platter. The bar is a quiet and sophisticated spot for a drink.

107 8th Ave. SW. (*C*) **403/265-9595.** Reservations recommended. Main courses C$31–C$42 (US$31–US$42/£16–£21). AE, DC, MC, V. Mon–Fri 11:30am–10pm; Sat 5:30–10pm.

Catch ✿ SEAFOOD   Calgary's top seafood restaurant has hooked a kreel-full of awards under the direction of chef Brad Horen (including 2006 Canadian National Chef of the Year), so forget that Calgary is landlocked and explore the remarkable cooking at this two-story dining room in the Calgary Hyatt. The main floor is dedicated to cocktails, light dining, and an oyster bar, while the upscale second floor is reserved for fine dining. There, selections change daily, based on what's fresh and available, but expect innovative, even startling preparations. A dish like fennel butter–poached lobster with smoked sweetbreads, apricot foam, and fava bean and chanterelle mushroom cassoulet could drive a serious foodie to gastronomic delirium. Quality lamb, steaks, and beef tenderloin are also available, often matched with seafood as reborn surf-and-turf extravaganzas.

100 8th Ave SE. (*C*) **403/206-0000.** www.catchrestaurant.ca. Reservations recommended. Main courses oyster bar C$12–C$37 (US$12–US$37/£6–£19), dining room C$32–C$52 (US$32–US$52/£16–£26); 6-course tasting menu

C$110 (US$110/£55). AE, MC, V. Oyster bar Mon–Fri 11:30am–10pm, Sat 4:30–10pm; dining room Mon–Sat 5:30–9:30pm.

Murietta's West Coast Grill REGIONAL CANADIAN   Just around the corner from the vibrant Stephen Avenue restaurant scene, Murietta's is a popular and stylish bar and dining room that combines the best of historic and contemporary Calgary. Located on the second story of the 1890s Alberta Hotel, Murietta's huge bar is a favorite watering hole for urban professionals, and the art-filled, two-story stone-walled dining room is the place for Alberta steaks and local lamb, pork, and game. For appetizers, choose fresh oysters or tuna tartare, and if excellent, locally sourced red meat's not your thing, Murietta's offers a daily changing selection of fresh fish with a choice of sauces—perhaps spicy maple-ginger sauce on seared wild Pacific salmon.

808 1st St. SW. ℭ 403/269-7707. Reservations recommended. Main courses C$16–C$42 (US$16–US$42/£8–£21). AE, DC, MC, V. Mon–Wed 11am–midnight; Thurs 11am–1am; Fri–Sat 11am–2am; Sun 4–10pm.

River Café ✮✮✮ NEW CANADIAN   If you have one meal in Calgary, it should be here. To reach the aptly named River Café, it takes a short walk through the Eau Claire Market area, then over the footbridge to lovely Prince's Island Park in the Bow River. On a lovely summer evening, the walk is a plus, as are the restaurant's lovely parkside decks (no vehicles hurtling by). The River Cafe has an elegant fishing lodge atmosphere, and the seasonal menu (which reads like a very tasty adventure novel for gourmets) features products from small Alberta farms and ranches, and includes smoked fish and game and hearth-baked breads. There's a wide range of appetizers and light dishes—many vegetarian—as well as pizzalike flat breads topped with zippy cheese, vegetables, and fruit. An excellent choice for a shared appetizer is the fish-and-game platter, with house-made cured meats and preserved vegetables. Specialties from the grill may include braised pheasant breast with mustard spaetzle, black-cherry oil, and roasted apple.

Prince's Island Park. ℭ 403/261-7670. www.river-cafe.com. Reservations recommended. Main courses C$36–C$50 (US$36–US$50/£18–£25). AE, MC, V. Mon–Fri 11am–11pm; Sat–Sun 10am–11pm. Closed Jan.

Téatro ✮✮✮ ITALIAN   Located in the historic Dominion Bank building just across from the Centre for the Performing Arts, Téatro delivers the best "new Italian" cooking in Calgary, courtesy of chef Dominique Moussu. The high-ceilinged dining room is dominated by columns and huge panel windows, bespeaking class and elegance. The extensive menu is based on "Italian market cuisine," featuring what's seasonally best and freshest, which is then cooked skillfully and simply to preserve natural flavors. The handmade pastas are marvelous, ranging from agnolotti stuffed with braised lamb shoulder served with chestnuts and robed in red-wine sauce, to papparadella tossed with minced sea lettuce (a brisk and briny northern Atlantic seaweed) and anchovy butter. Main courses, which feature Alberta beef, veal, and seafood, are prepared with flair and innovation; prime Alberta beef tenderloin is served with white-truffle soufflé and a single, decadent fois gras ravioli. The broad, marble-topped bar is a marvelous spot for a drink. Service is extremely professional, but friendly without undue formality.

200 8th Ave. SE. ℭ 403/290-1012. www.teatro-rest.com. Reservations recommended. Main courses C$22–C$49 (US$22–US$49/£11–£25). AE, DC, MC, V. Mon–Fri 11:30am–11pm; Sat 5pm–midnight; Sun 5–10pm.

Tribune ✮ REGIONAL CANADIAN   Along historic Stephens Avenue there are plenty of period-looking bars and restaurants, though perhaps the Tribune (housed in a former newspaper office) most successfully updates the turn-of-the-20th-century venerability with contemporary style and juju. The sandstone walls contrast marvelously with dark wood and deep-red upholstery of the bar (main floor) and restaurant (lower level). The menu features full-flavored and up-to-date interpretations of Alberta meats and fresh seafood. Bison daube is a very rich stew, redolent of red wine and served with house-made truffled pasta. Lamb shoulder is coddled in olive oil until falling-apart tender, and served with arugula and white beans al fiasco (in a flask). The wine list is very impressive, a League of Nations roundup of intriguing vintages.

118 8th Ave. SW. ✆ 403/269-3160. www.thetribunerestaurant.ca. Reservations recommended. Main courses C$24–C$50 (US$24–US$50/£12–£25). AE, MC, V. Mon–Thurs 5–10pm; Fri–Sat 5–11pm.

Moderate

Divino 𝒜𝒜 BISTRO   This estimable bar and restaurant calls itself a "wine and cheese bistro," and while a casual spot for a drink and cheese platter is welcome on busy Stephen Avenue, Divino offers a lot more. This bustling, stylish gathering spot offers intriguing light entrees from sandwiches—lamb confit melt with fig jam—to pasta (cannelloni filled with lobster and chanterelles) in addition to full-flavored and satisfying main courses such as roast chicken with herb-mustard gnocchi. And whether you start or end your meal with cheese, you'll appreciate a choice of over two dozen cheeses ordered from a sushi-style checklist. A class act.

113 8th Ave. SW. ✆ 403/234-0403. Reservations recommended. Main courses C$12–C$30 (US$12–US$30/£6–£15). AE, DC, MC, V. Daily 11am–11pm.

Gypsy Bistro & Wine Bar BISTRO   A small jewel box of a restaurant, the Gypsy Bistro is in the historic Grain Exchange building, and features deep-red walls, odd nooks and crannies, and a soft-focus bordello ambience. The menu is extensive and Mediterranean-focused. For light appetites, there's a broad selection of pizzas, entree salads, and specialty sandwiches, such as a lamb and dried-cranberry burger. The Gypsy is also the spot for a chic, low-key dinner, with main courses such as roast lamb with lavender-honey mustard and pancetta-wrapped salmon. The wine list is beguiling and the service friendly—this is the perfect spot for leisurely dinner and conversation.

817 1st St. SW. ✆ 403/263-5869. Reservations recommended. Main courses C$13–C$29 (US$13–US$29/ £6.50–£15). AE, MC, V. Daily 11am–10pm.

Joey Tomato's ITALIAN   Located in the popular Eau Claire Market complex, the lively Joey Tomato's serves Italian/Asian fusion cooking to throngs of appreciative Calgarians. And no wonder it's often packed with the city's young and tanned: The food is really good, the prices moderate (by the city's standards), and there's a lively bar scene. What more could you want? Thin-crust pizzas come with zippy, cosmopolitan choices such as tandoori chicken. Pasta dishes are just as unorthodox, with dishes such as linguini and smoked chicken, jalapeño, cilantro, and lime-cream sauce. The wide-ranging menu includes steaks, fresh fish, and stir-fried veggies. It's a fun, high-energy place to eat, and the food is always worth trying.

208 Barclay Parade SW. ✆ 403/263-6336. Reservations not accepted. Main courses C$9–C$25 (US$9–US$25/ £4.50–£13). AE, MC, V. Sun–Thurs 11am–midnight; Fri–Sat 11am–1am.

The King & I THAI   This restaurant was the first to introduce Thai cuisine to Calgary, and it still ranks high. Chicken, seafood, and vegetables predominate—one of the outstanding dishes is chicken filet sautéed with eggplant and peanuts in chile-bean sauce. For more seasoned palates, there are eight regional curry courses, ranging from mild to downright devilish.

820 11th Ave. SW. ℂ **403/264-7241**. Main courses C$7–C$20 (US$7–US$20/£3.50–£10). AE, MC, V. Mon–Thurs 11:30am–10:30pm; Fri 11:30am–11:30pm; Sat 4:30–11:30pm; Sun 4:30–9:30pm.

Pic Niq Café ⍟ BISTRO   The Pic Niq is as casual and enjoyable as it sounds—an intimate little wine bar and bistro that's perfect for both a quick pre-event meal or a full dinner. You can assemble a meal from the selection of small plates—such as the trio of Canadian smoked salmon—or indulge in made-to-share dishes such as one of the specialty pizzas or pork tenderloin with Calvados. Or if time and appetite allow, make a night of it and order main courses such as five-spice duck confit or boar bacon cassoulet. Pic Niq is upstairs from Beat Niq, a popular jazz bar.

811 1st St. SW. ℂ **403/263-1650**. Reservations required. Main courses C$19–C$33 (US$19–US$33£10–£17). AE, MC, V. Mon–Fri 11am–2pm; Tues 5–9pm; Wed–Sat 5–10pm.

Inexpensive

There are dozens of inexpensive restaurants in **Chinatown,** not all Chinese; check out Vietnamese and Thai options. Dim sum is widely available and inexpensive. There's also a **food court** in the TD Square mall at 8th Avenue and 3rd Street SW.

ON 17TH AVENUE

Roughly between 4th Street SW and 10th Street SW, 17th Avenue is home to many casual restaurants and bistros (and the scene has recently edged south along 4th Street SW). Take a cab or drive over and walk the busy cafe-lined streets, perusing the menus; the restaurants listed below are just the beginning.

A good place to get a feel for the avenue is **Melrose Place,** 730 17th Ave. SW (ℂ **403/228-3566**), a bar/restaurant that has the best deck seating in the area (sit by the street or by a waterfall).

BLVD ⍟ MEDITERRANEAN   If basic black is your color, and the club scene is your ideal, then you'll love BLVD, a chic eatery, cocktail lounge and night club just south of 17th Avenue. The name BLVD pays homage to the restaurant's large outdoor seating and drinking zone on one of the hippest corners in this most hip of Calgary enclaves. Get past the velvet ropes and into the swank all-black-with-red-Lucite-chairs dining room; while many come here to drink and see and be seen, early in the evening you'll be in the minority of customers who come here to eat. The Mediterranean-influenced food is outstanding. For appetizers, try the excellent caramel prawns, or move on to one of the notable pasta dishes: pappardelle pasta in preserved lemon cream sauce is tossed with seared chicken breast, oven-dried cherry tomatoes and crispy threads of fried leek. Seared thyme-and-sesame-crusted lamb sirloin teamed with grilled fresh apricots and almond-studded tabouleh is a gastronomic revelation. Roast golden beet salad topped with pistachios and thin slices of fennel is not only delicious, but looks great with the decor.

1800 4th St. SW. ℂ **403/244-2583**. www.blvdlounge.com. Reservations recommended. Main courses C$18–C$48 (US$18–US$48/£9–£24). AE, MC, V. Mon–Wed 11am–midnight; Thurs–Fri 11am–2am; Sat 4pm–2am.

Brava Bistro ⍟⍟ NEW CANADIAN   Brava began as an offshoot of a successful catering company, and has now evolved from fine dining house to a Mediterranean-style bistro. Happily, the food is as good as ever. In the relaxed, beautifully lit dining room, you can try a variety of dishes, from elegant appetizers and boutique pizzas to traditional main courses with contemporary zest. For an appetizer, try lobster gnocchi or chipotle prawns with beefsteak tomatoes. Among the entrees, the sautéed salmon with beets and horseradish is deliciously complex and colorful, while the homey rotisserie chicken or beef ribs with creamy polenta are tempting when comfort food feels more appropriate. The wine list is large and well priced.

723 17th Ave. SW. ℂ 403/228-1854. www.bravabistro.com. Reservations recommended. Main courses C$16–C$28 (US$16–US$28/£8–£14). AE, DC, MC, V. Mon–Wed 11:30am–3pm and 5–10pm; Thurs–Sat 11:30am–3pm and 5pm–midnight; Sun 5–10pm.

Cilantro INTERNATIONAL   Cilantro has a forlorn stucco storefront that would look New Mexican if it weren't on an urban strip of 17th Avenue. The walls hide a tucked-away garden courtyard with a veranda bar. The food here is eclectic with feints toward California and Santa Fe. You can snack on sandwiches, house-made pasta, or salads such as spinach in creamy tarragon vinaigrette with crispy pancetta, fresh figs, toasted pecans, and goat cheese. Or have a full meal of roasted free-range chicken with merlot demi-glace or grilled sea bass with grilled peppers and citrus–ancho chile sauce. The wood-fired pizzas—with mostly Mediterranean ingredients—are great for lunch. The food is always excellent, and the setting casual and friendly.

338 17th Ave. SW. ℂ 403/229-1177. Reservations recommended on weekends. Main courses C$9–C$30 (US$9–US$30/£4.50–£15). AE, DC, MC, V. Mon–Thurs 11am–10pm; Fri 11am–11pm; Sat 5–11pm; Sun 5–10pm.

Living Room CONTEMPORARY   This popular new restaurant is the antithesis of a small-plates tapas bar. Located in a heritage home fronting onto 17th Avenue, with tables inside and on a lovely shaded patio (heated by outdoor fireplaces in chilly weather), the Living Room specializes in "contemporary interactive cuisine," which translates as those classics of French, Italian, and Canadian cooking meant to be shared. Most beguiling are the many dishes designed for two: double-size portions of fondues, whole roast chicken, rack of lamb, bouillabaisse, double-cut prime rib, and lobster Newburg. Of course, individual portions are also served, though in the same spirit of contemporary interactive dining; a six-course chef's tasting menu (C$85/US$85/£43) lets the chef showcase what's absolutely up to the moment. Local produce and meats are featured; the rack of local lamb with almond-and-cranberry-mustard crust is a standout.

514 17th Ave. SW. ℂ 403/228-9830. Reservations recommended. Main courses C$20–C$42 (US$20–US$42/£10–£21). MC, V. Tues–Fri 11:30am–2:30pm and 5pm–midnight; Sat–Mon 5pm–midnight.

Wildwood Grill & Brewing Company ✦ BREWPUB   A few blocks south of 17th Avenue's street scene is this nouveau hunting lodge–style brewpub. Don't think pub grub—though you can get a good burger here—because Wildwood Grill offers high-end cuisine to match their house-made ales. In addition to pasta, wood-fired pizza (lemon-thyme chicken with goat cheese is a delicious choice), and upscale standards such as chicken breast sautéed with thyme and truffles, the pub specializes in game dishes. Caribou scaloppine with sour cherry–ginger sauce is a standout for adventurous meat eaters. In good weather, the covered patio is a great spot to sample the brewery's excellent drafts.

2417 4th St SW. ℂ 403/228-0100. Reservations recommended. Main courses C$13–C$36 (US$13–US$36/£7–£18). AE, MC, V. Mon–Thurs 11am–midnight; Fri 11am–2am; Sat 5–11pm; Sun 5–10pm.

INGLEWOOD

Capo ✦ ITALIAN   Just a short drive or cab ride south of downtown is Capo, one of the most lauded new restaurants in Calgary. Chef Guiseppe di Gennaro worked his way up through a handful of other Calgary restaurants, finally moving to Inglewood and his own very modern and stylish dining room in 2006. The huzzahs were almost immediate, garnering several national accolades and drawing foodies from near and far to sample Capo's updated but tradition-based Italian cuisine. A standout is the pillowy ricotta gnocchi, served with lobster, onion sprouts, white truffles, and a touch of tomato. The house specialty is roasted pheasant breast, served with morel mushrooms, parsnip purée, and a reduction of Muscat wine and rosemary. The dining room is tiny, seating just 35, so reservations are a must; on weekends, there are two seatings, 5:30 and 8:30pm, so plan ahead.

1420 9th Ave. SE. © 403/264-2276. www.caporestaurant.ca. Reservations required. Main courses C$20–C$39 (US$20–US$39/£10–£20). AE, MC, V. Mon–Sat 5:30–10pm; Wed–Fri 11:30am–2pm.

Rouge FRENCH   Located in a historic home, Rouge serves upscale French cuisine in a quiet, almost rural setting. In summer, the dining room extends into the shaded yard, where the bustle of Calgary feels far away. The menu emphasizes contemporary French cuisine zestily translated to western Canada. Diners have a choice of a la carte selections or the chef's six-course tasting menu (C$95/US$95/£48). For appetizers, try the silky and savory "surf and turf" scallop with oxtail, or seared fois gras with pear soufflé. Roast sable fish is served with saffron and pancetta beurre blanc, and candied breast of duck comes with garlic caramel and lavender risotto.

1240 8th Ave. SE. © 403/531-2767. www.rougecalgary.com. Reservations recommended. Main courses C$18–C$40 (US$18–US$40/£9–£20). MC, V. Mon–Sat 5:30–10pm; June–Aug and Dec also Mon–Fri 11:30am–2pm.

KENSINGTON

Muse ℱ FRENCH   Appropriately situated in the trendy Kensington neighborhood, Muse serves very up-to-date and stylish food based on French cooking, but deconstructed and reimagined as an extravagant dining adventure. There's playfulness and urbanity to the food, and it seems clear that the cooks are having fun in the kitchen. Start your meal with truffled beef tenderloin and avocado tartare, a fois gras Sauternes jelly sandwich, or a creamy bowl of sweet corn and cumin soup. Main courses are complex creations that verge temptingly on decadence: Potato lobster lasagna features buttery lobster between thin layers of Yukon gold potatoes, topped with seared scallops and flying fish roe; mint-and-rosemary marinated lamb strip loin is grilled and served with breaded lamb rillettes and sweet-pea risotto. The dining room is a three-story maze curved around an atrium; the various levels and nooks only add to the sense of discovery.

107 10th St. NW. © 403/670-6873. www.muserestaurant.ca. Reservations recommended. Main courses C$22–C$42 (US$22–US$42/£11–£21). AE, MC, V. Daily 5–10pm.

CALGARY AFTER DARK
THE PERFORMING ARTS   The sprawling **EPCOR Centre for the Performing Arts,** 205 8th Ave. SE (© 403/294-7455; www.epcorcentre.org), houses the Jack Singer Concert Hall, home of the **Calgary Philharmonic Orchestra** (© 403/571-0849; www.cpo-live.com); the Max Bell Theatre, home of **Theatre Calgary** (© 403/294-7440; www.theatrecalgary.com); and the Martha Cohen Theatre, home of **Alberta Theatre Projects** (© 403/294-7402; www.atplive.com).

An acoustic marvel, **Jubilee Auditorium,** 14th Avenue and 14th Street NW, on the Southern Alberta Institute of Technology campus (© 403/297-8000; www.jubilee auditorium.com), is located high on a hill with a panoramic view of downtown Calgary.

> **(Tips** **Summer Jazz & Shakespeare**
>
> From late June to late July, the **Calgary Jazz Festival** (© 403/249-1119; www.calgaryjazz.com) brings nearly 50 jazz bands and artists to Calgary, presenting live music in a variety of venues in Calgary, including outdoor concerts at Eau Claire Market and on Stephen Avenue Mall.
>
> Early July through mid-August, **Shakespeare in the Park** (© 403/240-6374) presents the Bard's works Thursday through Saturday at 7pm at Prince's Island Park in the Bow River. Admission is free (donations are appreciated, though).

The **Calgary Opera** (© 403/262-7286; www.calgaryopera.com) and the **Alberta Ballet** (© 403-254-4222; www.albertaballet.com) both stage performances here.

Calgary loves dinner theater, and **Stage West,** 727 42nd Ave. SE (© 403/243-6642; www.stagewestcalgary.com), puts on polished performances as well as delectable buffet fare. Tickets for evening performances and dinner start at C$84 (US$84/£42). Performances are Tuesday through Sunday.

THE CLUB & BAR SCENE Cover charges at most clubs are C$5 to C$10 (US$5–US$10/£2.50–£5) for live music. Pick up a copy of *Ffwd* (www.ffwdweekly.com) for up-to-date listings.

Eau Claire Market is the home of the **Garage** (© 403/262-67620), a hip warehouse-of-a-bar for playing billiards and listening to loud indie rock. A number of pubs and late-night watering holes are just outside the market on the Barclay Parade plaza. Check out **Barleymill Neighbourhood Pub,** 201 Barclay Parade SW (© 403/290-1500), an oldsy-worldsy pub plunked down in the plaza across from the Eau Claire Market.

If you're just looking for a convivial drink, **Bottlescrew Bill's Old English Pub,** 1st Street and 10th Avenue SW (© 403/263-7900), is a great choice. This friendly neighborhood pub is just on the edge of downtown, has lots of outdoor seating, and pours Alberta's widest selection of microbrewed beers.

If you're looking for dance clubs, head south of downtown. **Warehouse Nightclub,** 731 10th Ave. SW (© 403/264-0535), offers straightforward rock with Calgary's top DJs. **Hi-Fi Club,** 219 10th Ave. SW (© 403/263-5222), offers more alternative music and occasional live music and entertainment. **Broken City**, 613 11th Ave. SW (© 403/262-9976), is a hipster hangout with live local bands on Tuesdays, Thursdays, and Saturdays.

Put on your cowboy boots and swing your partner out to **Ranchman's,** 9615 Macleod Trail S. (© 403/253-1100), the best country-western dance bar in the city. Free swing and line dance lessons are usually offered on Sunday afternoons; call to confirm.

Calgary isn't really a jazz town, but there's one good club to check out: **Beat Niq Jazz & Social Club,** downstairs at the Bistro Piq Niq, 811 1st St. SW (© 403/263-1650; www.beatniq.com) has great atmosphere and the best of local bands.

Twister Element, 1006 11th Ave. SW (© 403/802-0230), is Calgary's largest gay bar and dance club. It has both a dance floor and a downstairs piano bar. It's at the center of the city's small gay bar area.

CASINO Calgary has several legitimate casinos whose proceeds go wholly to charities. None impose a cover. Located across from the Stampede grounds, the **Elbow**

River Inn Casino, 1919 Macleod Trail S. (© **403/266-4355**), offers Las Vegas–style gaming plus a poker variation called Red Dog.

ON THE TRAIL OF DINOSAURS IN THE ALBERTA BADLANDS ⭐⭐

The Red Deer River slices through Alberta's rolling prairies east of Calgary, revealing underlying sedimentary deposits that have eroded into badlands. These expanses of desertlike hills, strange rock turrets, and banded cliffs were laid down about 75 million years ago, when this area was a low coastal plain in the heyday of the dinosaurs. Erosion has incised through these deposits spectacularly, revealing a vast cemetery of Cretaceous life. Paleontologists have excavated here since the 1880s, and the Alberta badlands have proved to be one of the most important dinosaur-fossil sites in the world. Two separate areas have been preserved and developed for research and viewing.

Royal Tyrrell Museum of Palaeontology ⭐⭐   North of Drumheller, and about 145km (90 miles) northeast of Calgary, this is one of the world's best paleontology museums and educational facilities. It offers far more than just impressive skeletons and life-size models, though it has dozens of them. The entire fossil record of the earth is explained, era by era, with an impressive variety of media and educational tools. You walk through a prehistoric garden, watch numerous videos, use computers to "design" dinosaurs for specific habitats, watch plate tectonics at work, and see museum technicians preparing fossils. The museum is also a renowned research facility where scientists study all forms of ancient life.

Radiating out from Drumheller and the museum are a number of interesting side trips. Pick up a map from the museum and follow an hour's loop drive into the badlands along North Dinosaur Trail. The paved road passes two viewpoints over the badlands and crosses a free car-ferry on the Red Deer River before returning to Drumheller along the South Dinosaur Trail. A second loop passes through Rosedale to the south, past a ghost town, hoodoo formations, and a historic coal mine.

P.O. Box 7500, Drumheller, AB T0J 0Y0. © **888/440-4240** or 403/823-7707. Fax 403/823-7131. www.tyrrellmuseum.com. Admission C$10 (US$10/£5) adults, C$8 (US$8/£4) seniors, C$6 (US$6/£3) youths 7–17, C$30 (US$30/£15) families. Mid-May to Sept daily 9am–9pm; Oct to mid-May Tues–Sun 10am–5pm.

Dinosaur Provincial Park ⭐   In Red Deer River Valley near Brooks, about 225km (140 miles) east of Calgary and 193km (120 miles) southeast of Drumheller, this park contains the world's greatest concentration of fossils from the late Cretaceous period. More than 300 complete dinosaur skeletons have been found in the area, which has been named a World Heritage Site. Park excavations continue from early June to late August, based out of the Field Station of the Royal Tyrrell Museum. Much of the park is a natural preserve, with access restricted to guided interpretive bus tours and hikes. Space on these tours is limited, so be prepared to be flexible with your choices. "Rush" tickets are sold at 8:30am for that day's events (maximum four tickets per person). Reservations are strongly encouraged in July and August. May through August, lab tours run so that you can view fossil preparation.

Five self-guiding trails and two outdoor fossil displays are also available. Facilities at the park include a campground, a picnic area, and a service center.

P.O. Box 60, Patricia, AB T0J 2K0. © **403/378-4342** or 403/378-4344 for tour reservations. Fax 403/378-4247. www.tprc.alberta.ca/parks/dinosaur. Fees for bus tours and hikes. Advance tickets C$8 (US$8/£4) adults, C$6 (US$6/£3) youths 7–17, C$25 (US$25/£13) family; rush tickets C$6.50 (US$6.50/£3.25) adults, C$4.50 (US$4.50/£2.25) youths 7–17, C$20 (US$20/£10) family; advance or rush free for children under 7. Lab tours C$2 (US$2/£1) adults, C$1 (US$1/50p) youths. Tours daily mid-May to Labour Day; weekends Labour Day to mid-Oct.

DAY TRIPS FROM CALGARY: THE OLD WEST

The Old West isn't very old in Alberta. If you're interested in the life and culture of the cowboy and rancher, drive through the ranch country along the foothills of the Rockies and stop at the historic Bar U Ranch. This short side trip into the Old West is just a short detour on the way from Calgary to the Rocky Mountains.

Bar U Ranch National Historic Site ✶✶ An hour southwest of Calgary is this well-preserved and still-operating cattle ranch that celebrates both past and present traditions of the Old West. Tours of the ranch's 35 original buildings (some date from the 1880s) are available; a video of the area's ranching history is shown in the interpretive center. Special events include displays of ranching activities and techniques; since this is a real ranch, you might get to watch a branding or roundup.

Follow Hwy. 22 south from Calgary to the little community of Longview. ⓒ **403/395-2212.** www.pc.gc.ca. Admission C$7.15 (US$7.15/£3.60) adults, C$5.90 (US$5.90/£2.95) seniors, C$3.45 (US$3.45/£1.75) for children, C$18 (US$18/£9) families. Late May to early Oct daily 10am–6pm.

3 Southern Alberta Highlights

South of Calgary, running through the grain fields and prairies between Medicine Hat and Crowsnest Pass in the Canadian Rockies, Highway 3 roughly parallels the U.S.-Canadian border. This rural connector links several smaller Alberta centers and remote but interesting natural and historic sites.

MEDICINE HAT & CYPRESS HILLS PROVINCIAL PARK

Medicine Hat, 291km (180 miles) southeast of Calgary, is at the center of Alberta's vast natural-gas fields. To be near this inexpensive source of energy, a lot of modern industry has moved to Medicine Hat, making this an unlikely factory town surrounded by grain fields. In the early 1900s, the primary industry was fashioning brick and china from the local clay deposits. Consequently, the town's old downtown is a showcase of handsome frontier-era brick buildings; take an hour and explore the historic city center, flanked by the South Saskatchewan River.

Cypress Hills Provincial Park, 81km (50 miles) south of Medicine Hat, is 316 sq. km (122 sq. miles) of highlands—outliers of the Rockies—that rise 450m (1,500 ft.) above the flat prairie grasslands. In this preserve live many species of plants and animals, including elk and moose, usually found in the Rockies.

LETHBRIDGE

East of Fort Macleod, 105km (65 miles) north of the U.S. border and 216km (134 miles) southeast of Calgary, Lethbridge is a delightful garden city and popular convention site (it gets more annual hours of sunshine than most places in Canada). Lethbridge started out as Fort Whoop-Up, a notorious trading post that traded whiskey to the Plains Indians in return for buffalo hides and horses. The post boomed during the 1870s, until the Mounties arrived to bring order. Today, Lethbridge is a pleasant prairie city and Alberta's third largest, with a population of 66,000. For details, contact the **Lethbridge Visitor Centre,** 2805 Scenic Dr., Lethbridge, AB T1K 5B7 (ⓒ **800/661-1222** or 403/320-1222), open daily from 9am to 5pm.

Lethbridge has two good art centers that display regional and touring art. The **Southern Alberta Art Gallery,** 601 3rd Ave. S. (ⓒ **403/327-8770;** www.saag.ca), has a number of changing art shows throughout the year; the gift shop is a good place to go for local crafts. It's open Tuesday through Saturday from 10am to 5pm and Sunday from 1 to 5pm. The **Bowman Arts Centre,** 811 5th Ave. (© **403/327-2813**), is housed in an old school and is the fine-arts hub of Lethbridge, with studios, classes, offices for arts organizations, and two galleries featuring the works of area artists; it's open Monday through Friday from 9am to 9pm and Saturday from 10am to 4pm.

The **Sir Alexander Galt Museum and Archives,** at the west end of 5th Avenue S. (© **403/320-4258;** www.galtmuseum.com), is an excellent regional museum located in a historic former hospital. Exhibit galleries focus on the local Native culture, the city's coal-mining past, and the role of immigrants in the region's growth. Two galleries are devoted to the works of regional artists. The back windows of the museum overlook the impressive Oldman River Valley with its natural park systems. It's open daily from 10am to 6pm (till 4:30 in off season); admission is C$5 (US$5/£2.50) adult, C$4 (US$4/£2) senior and postsecondary students, C$3 (US$3/£1.50) youths 7–17, children 6 and under free, and families C$12 (US$12/£6).

The city's heritage as a frontier whiskey-trading center is commemorated at the **Fort Whoop-Up Interpretive Centre** (© **403/329-0444;** www.fortwhoopup.com) in Indian Battle Park (follow 3rd Ave. S. toward the river). A replica of the fort—built by Montana-based traders of buffalo skins and whiskey in the 1870s—stands in the park, with costumed docents providing horse-drawn carriage tours, interpretive programs, and historic reenactments. Mid-May to September, it's open Tuesday through Sunday from 10am to 5pm; the rest of the year, it's open Tuesday through Friday from 10am to 4pm and Sunday from 1 to 4pm. Admission is C$7 (US$7/£3.50) for adults, C$6 (US$6/£3) for seniors, C$5 (US$5/£2.50) for students, and free for children under 6.

The pride of Lethbridge is the **Nikka Yuko Japanese Garden** (© **403/328-3511;** www.nikkayuko.com) in Henderson Lake Park on Mayor Mangrath Drive, east of downtown. Its pavilion and dainty bell tower were built by Japanese artisans without nails or bolts. The garden is one of the largest Japanese gardens in North America; Japanese-Canadian women in kimonos give tours and explain the philosophical concepts involved in Japanese garden design. From July 1 to Labour Day, the gardens are open daily 9am to 8pm; early May to late June and after Labour Day to early October, it's open daily 9am to 5pm. Admission is C$7 (US$7/£3.50) for adults, C$5 (US$5/£2.50) for seniors, C$4 (US$4/£2) for youths ages 6 to 17, and free for children under 6.

WHERE TO STAY & DINE

Heritage House B&B   This wonderful B&B will come as an architectural surprise: In an otherwise early-1900s neighborhood, this Art Deco jewel really stands out. Considered one of the finest examples of International Art Moderne in the province, the house is a designated Provincial Historic Site. The interior retains the look of the 1930s, including some original wall murals. The comfortable guest rooms are spacious and share a bathroom and a half.

1115 8th Ave. S., Lethbridge, AB T1J 1P7. © **403/328-3824.** Fax 403/328-9011. www.ourheritage.net/bb.html. 2 units, neither with private bathroom. C$80 (US$80/£40) double. Rates include breakfast. No credit cards. *In room:* TV, no phone.

Ramada Hotel & Suites *(Kids)*   One of the nicest lodgings in Lethbridge, the Ramada is designed to attract business travelers, but vacationers will also find it a very comfortable place to stay. If the kids are along, it may be hard to convince them to leave the indoor water park with its two water slides and a wave pool.

2375 Mayor Magrath Dr. S., Lethbridge, AB T1K 7M1. ☎ **888/298-2054** or 403/380-5050. Fax 403/380-5051. www.
ramada.ca. 119 units. C$149–C$159 (US$149–US$159/£75–£80) double. AE, DC, DISC, MC, V. **Amenities:** Pool; exercise room; Jacuzzi; business center; convenience store. *In room:* A/C, TV, dataport, fridge, microwave, coffeemaker, hair
dryer, iron.

WHERE TO DINE

For breakfast pastries or lunchtime sandwiches, the **Penny Coffee House,** 331 5th St.
S. (☎ **403/320-5282**), is a friendly hangout open Monday to Saturday 7am to 10pm
and Sunday 9am to 5pm. **Douro's Pizza, Steakhouse and Lounge,** 2433 Fairway
Plaza Rd. S. (☎ **403/327-3067**), has tasty Greek food plus steaks and pizza, and is
open daily from 5 to 11pm. With good food and a lively atmosphere, **Coco Pazzo,**
1264 3rd Ave. S. (☎ **403/329-8979**), is probably one of the best places to eat in town,
with a menu focusing on pizza and specialties from the wood-fired oven; it's open
daily from 11am to midnight. For steaks and pasta, you can't go wrong at **La Bella
Notte,** 402 2nd Ave. S. (☎ **403/331-3319**), a handsome dining room in a vintage fire
station. It's open weekdays for lunch and nightly for dinner.

FORT MACLEOD

Fort Museum of the North West Mounted Police Forty-four kilometers (27
miles) west of Lethbridge stands what was in 1873 the western headquarters of the
Northwest Mounted Police. Named after Colonel James Macleod, the redcoat commander who brought peace to Canada's west, the reconstructed Fort Macleod is now
a provincial park and is still patrolled by Mounties in their traditional uniforms.

The fort is filled with fascinating material on the frontier period. Among its treasured documents is the rule sheet of the old Macleod Hotel, written in 1882: "All
guests are requested to rise at 6am. This is imperative as the sheets are needed for
tablecloths. Assaults on the cook are prohibited. Boarders who get killed will not be
allowed to remain in the house." The fort grounds also contain the Centennial Building, a museum devoted to the history of the local Plains Indians. A highlight of visiting the fort in summer is the **Mounted Patrol Musical Ride** at 10am, 11:30am, 2pm,
and 3:30pm, with eight horseback Mounties performing a choreographed equestrian
program to music.

219 25th St., Fort Macleod, AB T0L 0Z0. ☎ 403/553-4703. www.nwmpmuseum.com. Admission C$7.50 (US$7.50/
£3.75) adults, C$6.50 (US$6.50/£3.25) seniors, C$5.50 (US$5.50/£2.75) youths 12–17, C$4.50 (US$4.50/£2.25) children 6–11, free for children under 6. May 1 to Victoria Day and day after Labour Day to Canadian Thanksgiving
Wed–Sun 10am–4pm; Victoria Day to June 30 daily 9am–5pm; July 1 to Labour Day daily 9am–5pm.

Head-Smashed-In Buffalo Jump 𝕣𝕣 One of the most interesting sights in
southern Alberta, and a World Heritage Site, is the curiously named Head-Smashed-
In Buffalo Jump. This excellent interpretive center/museum is built into the edge of a
steep cliff over which the First Nations peoples used to stampede herds of bison, the
carcasses then providing them with meat, hides, and horns. The multimillion-dollar
facility tells the story of these ancient harvests by means of films and Native Canadian
guide-lecturers. Other displays illustrate and explain the traditional life of the prairie-
dwelling Natives in precontact times and the ecology and natural history of the northern Great Plains. Hiking trails lead to undeveloped jump sites.

Fort Macleod, AB T0L 0Z0. ☎ 403/553-2731. www.head-smashed-in.com. C$9 (US$9/£4.50) adults, C$8 (US$8/£4)
seniors, C$5 (US$5/£2.50) children 7–17. Daily 9am–6pm in summer; 10am–5pm in winter. Spring Point Rd., 19km
(12 miles) west of Fort Macleod on Hwy. 2.

4 Waterton Lakes National Park ⟨⋆⟩

In the southwestern corner of the province, Waterton Lakes National Park is linked with Glacier National Park in neighboring Montana; together these two beautiful tracts of wilderness compose Waterton-Glacier International Peace Park. Once the hunting ground of the Blackfeet, 526-sq.-km (203-sq.-mile) Waterton Park contains superb mountain, prairie, and lake scenery and is home to abundant wildlife.

During the last ice age, the park was filled with glaciers, which deepened and straightened river valleys; those peaks that remained above the ice were carved into distinctive thin, finlike ridges. The park's famous lakes also date from the Ice Ages; all three of the Waterton Lakes nestle in glacial basins.

The park's main entrance road leads to **Waterton Townsite,** the only commercial center, with a number of hotels, restaurants, and tourist facilities. Other roads lead to more remote lakes and trail heads. Akamina Parkway leads from the townsite to Cameron Lake, glimmering beneath the crags of the Continental Divide. At the small visitor center, you can rent canoes; this is a great spot for a picnic. Red Rock Parkway follows Blackiston Creek past the park's highest peaks to Red Rock Canyon. From here, three trails lead up deep canyons to waterfalls.

The most popular activity in the park is the **Inter-Nation Shoreline Cruise** (⟨© **403/859-2362;** www.watertoninfo.com/m/cruise.html), which leaves from the townsite and sails Upper Waterton Lake past looming peaks to the ranger station at Goat Haunt, Montana, in Glacier Park. The tour boat operates from June 1 through early October. In the high season, from the last weekend of June through August, there are five tour boat departures daily, with two or three daily in the shoulder seasons (check the website for exact schedules). Only during the high season does the boat land in Montana. The cruise usually takes just over 2 hours, including the stop in Montana. The price is C$30 (US$30/£15) for adults, C$15 (US$15/£7.50) for youths ages 13 to 17, and C$10 (US$10/£5) for children ages 4 to 12.

For more information, contact the **Waterton Park Chamber of Commerce and Visitors Association,** P.O. Box 5599, Waterton Lakes National Park, AB T0K 2M0 (⟨© **403/859-5133** summer, or 403/859-2224 winter; www.pc.gc.ca and www.discover waterton.com). The per-day park entry fee is C$6.90 (US$6.90/£3.45) for adults, C$5.90 (US$5.90/£2.95) for seniors, and C$3.45 (US$3.45/£1.75) for children.

WHERE TO STAY

Kilmorey Lodge   Beloved by oft-returning guests, the Kilmorey is a rambling old lodge from the park's heyday. One of the few lodgings that has direct lake views, it offers small but elegantly appointed rooms. Expect down comforters, antiques, squeaky floors, and loads of character and charm. The Lamp Post is one of Waterton's most acclaimed restaurants; also on-site are the Gazebo Café and the Ram's Head Lounge.

P.O. Box 100, Waterton Park, AB T0K 2M0. ⟨© 888/859-8669 or 403/859-2334. Fax 403/859-2342. www.kilmorey lodge.com. 23 units. C$129–C$252 (US$129–US$252/£65–£126) double. Extra person C$20 (US$20/£10). Children under 16 stay free in parent's room. AE, DC, DISC, MC, V. **Amenities:** Fine-dining restaurant; outdoor cafe; bar. *In room:* Hair dryer, no phone.

Prince of Wales Hotel *⟨Overrated⟩*   Built in 1927 by the Great Northern Railway, this beautiful mountain lodge, perched on a bluff above Upper Waterton Lake, is reminiscent of the historic resorts in Banff. Rooms have been renovated, though many are historically authentic in that they're rather small. Operated by the same dilatory Greyhound/Dial Soap consortium that manages the historic lodges in Glacier

National Park in Montana, the Prince of Wales is in need of some serious reinvestment. You'll want to at least visit this landmark for the view and perhaps for a meal at the Garden Court restaurant. Historic-monument status aside, however, there are better places to stay than this handsome doyen—until someone who values these grand lodges pries them away from Greyhound.

P.O. Box 33, Waterton Lakes National Park, AB T0K 2M0. ✆ **403/859-2231**. Fax 403/859-2630. www.princeofwales waterton.com. In off season, contact Glacier Park Inc. Central Reservations, P.O. Box 2025, Columbia Falls, MT 59912, ✆ 406/892-2525. 86 units. C$265–C$345 (US$265–US$345/£133/£173) double. Extra person C$15 (US$15/£7.50). Children under 12 stay free in parent's room. AE, MC, V. Closed late Sept to early June. **Amenities:** 2 restaurants; 2 bars; nonsmoking rooms.

Waterton Lakes Lodge ✿   This classy complex sits on 1.5 hectares (4 acres) in the heart of Waterton Townsite. The 80 rooms are in nine separate lodgelike buildings that flank a central courtyard. There are three types of accommodations: large standard rooms with queen-size beds; deluxe rooms with two queen-size beds and a sofa bed, a gas fireplace, a two-person shower, and a jetted tub; and kitchenette units with all the features of deluxe rooms plus a dining area and kitchen. All are decorated with an environmental theme and appointed with handsome pine furniture. The Wildflower Dining Room, the Good Earth Deli, and the Wolf's Den Lounge are part of the resort complex. Also on the property are a guest and community sports facility, with a large pool, fitness center, and spa. Winter sports and cross-country ski rentals are available.

P.O. Box 4, Waterton Park, AB T0K 2M0. ✆ **888/985-6343** or 403/859-2150. Fax 403/859-2229. www.watertonlakes lodge.com. 80 units. C$180–C$225 (US$180–US$225/£90–£113) double. Extra person C$20 (US$20/£10). Off-season rates available. AE, MC, V. Closed Nov–Apr. **Amenities:** 2 restaurants; bar; health club w/pool; fitness center and spa; coin-op laundry; nonsmoking rooms. *In room:* A/C, TV, dataport, fridge, coffeemaker, hair dryer.

5 Introducing the Canadian Rockies

Few places in the world are more dramatically beautiful than the Canadian Rockies. Banff and Jasper national parks are famous for their mountain lakes, flower-spangled meadows, spirelike peaks choked by glaciers, and abundant wildlife. Nearly the entire spine of the Rockies—from the U.S. border north for 1,127km (700 miles)—is preserved as parkland or wilderness.

That's the good news. The bad news is that this Canadian wilderness, the flora and fauna that live in it, and the lovers of solitude who come here, are going to need all this space as the Rockies become more popular. More than five million people annually make their way through Banff National Park. But it seems that Draconian measures such as limiting visitors are, as of yet, brought up only in order to be dismissed. Advance planning for a trip to the Canadian Rockies is absolutely necessary if you're going to stay or eat where you want or if you want to evade the swarms of visitors that throng the parks in summer.

ESSENTIALS

Canada's Rocky Mountain parks include Jasper and Banff, which together comprise 17,519 sq. km (6,764 sq. miles); the provincial parklands of the Kananaskis Country and Mount Robson (the latter is in British Columbia); and Yoho and Kootenay national parks to the west in British Columbia.

GETTING THERE   The parks are traversed by one of the finest highway systems in Canada, plus innumerable nature trails leading to more remote valleys and peaks. The two "capitals," Banff and Jasper, lie 287km (178 miles) apart, connected by Highway

The Canadian Rockies

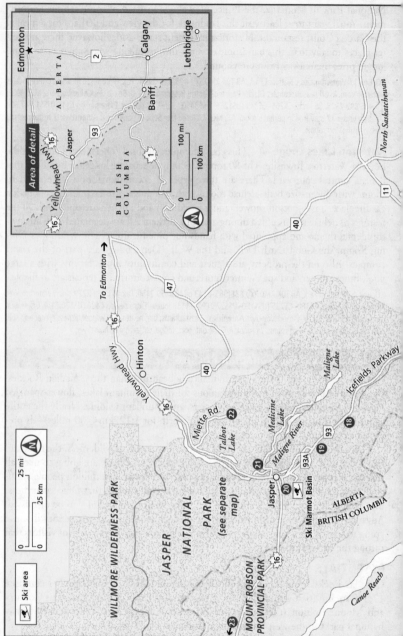

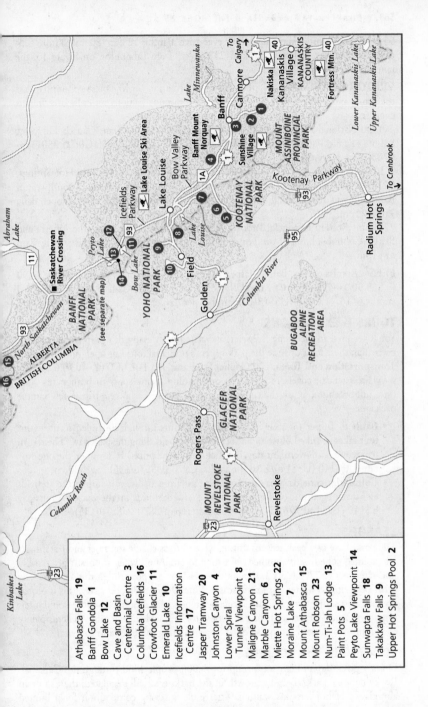

Athabasca Falls **19**
Banff Gondola **1**
Bow Lake **12**
Cave and Basin
Centennial Centre **3**
Columbia Icefields **16**
Crowfoot Glacier **11**
Emerald Lake **10**
Icefields Information
Centre **17**
Jasper Tramway **20**
Johnston Canyon **4**
Lower Spiral
Tunnel Viewpoint **8**
Maligne Canyon **21**
Marble Canyon **6**
Miette Hot Springs **22**
Moraine Lake **7**
Mount Athabasca **15**
Mount Robson **23**
Num-Ti-Jah Lodge **13**
Paint Pots **5**
Peyto Lake Viewpoint **14**
Sunwapta Falls **18**
Takakkaw Falls **9**
Upper Hot Springs Pool **2**

93, one of the most scenic routes you'll ever drive. Banff is 128km (80 miles) from Calgary via Highway 1; Jasper, 375km (233 miles) from Edmonton on Route 16, the famous Yellowhead Highway.

VISITOR INFORMATION   For visitor information on Kananaskis Country, and the Banff and Jasper national parks, see the respective sections on each later in this chapter.

Yoho National Park Visitor Centre is located just off the Trans-Canada Highway, 83km (51 miles) northwest of Banff (P.O. Box 99, Field, BC V0A 1G0; ℭ **250/343-6783;** www.pc.gc.ca), and is open daily 9am to 4pm.

Kootenay National Park Visitor Centre, 7556 Main St. E., Radium Hot Springs, BC V0A 1M0 (ℭ **250/347-9505;** www.pc.gc.ca), is 134km (83 miles) southwest of Banff, but you drive through the park to get to the Visitor Centre, which is open daily 9am to 5pm.

Mount Robson Provincial Park (ℭ **250/566-4325**) is just across the Alberta and British Columbia border from Jasper and is open May through September daily 7am to 11pm.

FEES   Admission to Banff, Jasper, Yoho, and Kootenay parks costs C$8.90 (US$8.90/£4.45) adult, C$7.65 (US$7.65/£3.85) seniors, C$4.45 (US$4.45/£2.25) youths 6–16, or C$18 (US$18/£9) families per day.

TOURS & EXCURSIONS

You'll get used to the name Brewster, associated with many things in these parts. In particular, these folks operate the park system's principal tour-bus operation. **Brewster Transportation and Tours,** 100 Gopher St., Banff, AB T0L 0C0 (ℭ **403/762-6767;** www.brewster.ca), covers most of the outstanding scenic spots in both parks. Call for a full brochure, or ask the concierge at your hotel to arrange a trip. A few sample packages:

- **Banff to Jasper** (or vice versa): Some 9½ hours through unrivaled scenery, this tour takes in Lake Louise and a view of the icefield along the parkway. (The return trip requires an overnight stay, not included in the price.) In summer, the one-way fare is C$140 (US$140/£70) for adults, C$70 (US$70/£35) for children.
- **Columbia Icefields:** On this 9½-hour tour from Banff, you stop at the Icefields Centre and get time off for lunch and a Snowcoach ride up the glacier. Adults pay C$140 (US$140/£70) in summer; children pay C$70 (US$70/£35).

SEASONS

The parks have two peak seasons during which hotels charge top rates and restaurants are jammed. The first is summer (mid-June to late Aug), when it doesn't get terribly hot, rarely above 77°F (25°C), though the sun's rays are powerful at this altitude. The other peak time is winter, the skiing season from December to February; this is probably the finest skiing terrain in all Canada. March to May is decidedly off season: Hotels offer bargain room rates, and you can choose the best table in any eatery. There's plenty of rain in the warmer months, so don't forget to bring some suitable rainwear.

LODGING IN THE ROCKIES

On any given day in high season, up to 60,000 people wind through the Canadian Rocky national parks. Because growth in the parks is strictly regulated, there's not an abundance of hotel rooms waiting. The result is strong competition for a limited number of very expensive rooms. Adding to the squeeze is the fact that many hotels

> **Tips Reserve Far Ahead**
>
> If you're reading this on the day you plan to arrive in Banff, Jasper, or Lake Louise and haven't yet booked your room, start worrying. Most hotels are totally booked for the season by July 1. To avoid disappointment, reserve your room as far in advance as you know your travel dates. If you are having trouble locating a room, or simply don't want to deal with the hassle, contact **Rocky Mountain Reservations** (© 877-902-9455; www.rockymountainreservations.com) for a free hotel and activities booking service.

have 80% to 90% of their rooms reserved for coach tours in summer. To avoid disappointment, particularly if you want to stay in one of the landmark hotels, *reserve your room as far in advance as possible.*

On the other hand, if you don't mind uncertainty and are traveling with a laptop, the advent of discount hotel websites opens up possibilities for those who want to gamble on last-minute room availability. Using sites such as Travelocity—or just type in the name of your favorite hotel into a browser and marvel at the number of websites ready to sell you discounted rooms—you can take the chance that top-ranked hotels will have last-minute cancellations to sell over the Internet. In high season, the savings can be up to 50%, though there is no guarantee that you'll get the hotel or room type that you want.

Also, even if you plan to focus on Banff activities during your holiday, consider staying in Canmore, a thriving town just east of the Banff park boundary. Canmore offers abundant hotel rooms at lower cost than central Banff, which is only 20 minutes away by car. The facilities—and the views—are just as fine as in Banff.

Regarding price, it seems that lodgings can ask for and get just about any rate they want in high season. For the most part, hotels are well kept up in the parks, but few would justify these high prices anywhere else in the world. Knowing that, there are a few choices. You can decide whether or not to splurge on one of the world-class hotels here, actually only a bit more expensive than the midrange competition. Camping is another good option, because the parks have dozens of campgrounds with varying levels of facilities. There are also a number of hostels throughout the parks.

In the off season, prices drop dramatically, often as much as 50%. Most hotels offer ski packages in winter, as well as other attractive getaway incentives. Ask about any special rates, especially at the larger hotels.

PARK WILDLIFE & YOU

The parklands are swarming with wildlife, with some animals meandering along and across highways and hiking trails, within easy camera range. However tempting, **don't feed the animals and don't touch them!** For starters, you can be fined up to C$500 (US$500/£250) for feeding any wildlife. There's also the distinct possibility you may end up paying more than cash for disregarding this warning.

It isn't easy to resist the blithely fearless bighorn sheep, mountain goats, elk, soft-eyed deer, and lumbering moose you meet. (You'll have very little chance of meeting the coyotes, lynx, and occasional wolves, since they give humans a wide berth.) But the stuff you feed them can kill them. Bighorns get accustomed to summer handouts of bread, candy, potato chips, and marshmallows when they should be grazing on the high-protein vegetation that'll help them survive through the winter.

Moose involve additional dangers. They've been known to take over entire picnics after being given an initial snack, chase off the picnickers, and eat up everything in sight—including cutlery, dishes, and the tablecloth.

Portions of the parks may sometimes be closed to hikers and bikers during elk calving season. A mother elk can mistake your recreation for an imminent attack on her newborn; or an unsuspecting hiker could frighten a mother from her calf, separating the two for good. Pay attention to—and obey—postings at trail heads.

Bears pose the worst problems. The parks contain two breeds: the big grizzly, standing up to 2m (6½ ft.) on its hind legs, and the smaller black bear, about 1.5m (5 ft.) long. The grizzly spends most of the summer in high alpine ranges, well away from tourist haunts. As one of North America's largest carnivores, its appearance and reputation are awesome enough to make you beat a retreat on sight. But the less formidable black bear is a born clown with tremendous audience appeal and takes to human company like a squirrel. The black bear's cuddly looks and circus antics, plus its knack for begging and rummaging through garbage cans, tend to obscure the fact that these are wild animals: powerful, faster than a horse, and completely unpredictable.

Hiking in bear country (and virtually all parkland is bear country) necessitates certain precautions—ignore them at your peril. Never hike alone and never take a dog along. Dogs often yap at bears, then when the animal charges, they run toward their owners for protection, bringing the pursuer with them. Use a telephoto lens when taking pictures. Bears in the wild have a set tolerance range that, when encroached upon, may bring on an attack. Above all, never go near a cub. The mother is usually close by, and a female defending her young is the most ferocious creature you'll ever face—and possibly the last.

6 Kananaskis Country & Canmore

Kananaskis Country is the name given to three Alberta provincial parks on the Rocky Mountains' eastern slope, southeast of Banff National Park. Once considered only a gateway region to more glamorous Banff, the Kananaskis has developed into a recreation destination on a par with more famous brand-name resorts in the Canadian Rockies.

Located just west of the Kananaskis and just outside the eastern boundary of Banff National Park, **Canmore** is a sprawl of condominium and resort developments in a dramatic location beneath the soaring peaks of Three Sisters Mountain. Only 20 minutes from Banff, Canmore has become the time-share capital of the Rockies, but the scenery is magnificent and the accommodations generally much less expensive and considerably less overbooked than those in Banff.

Weather is generally warmer and sunnier here, which is conducive to great golf: The championship course at **Kananaskis** is considered one of the best in North America.

When the 1988 Olympics were held in Calgary, the national park service wouldn't allow the alpine ski events to be held in the parks. Nakiska, in the Kananaskis, became the venue instead, vaulting this ski area to international prominence.

The main road through Kananaskis Country is Highway 40, which cuts south from Highway 1 at the gateway to the Rockies and follows the Kananaskis River. Kananaskis Village, a collection of resort hotels and shops, is the center of activities in the Kananaskis and is convenient to most recreation areas. Highway 40 eventually climbs up to 2,206m (7,238-ft.) Highwood Pass, the highest pass in Alberta, before looping around to meet Highway 22 south of Calgary.

For information on Kananaskis and Canmore, contact **Kananaskis Country** (© **866/432-4322;** www.kananaskisvalley.com) or the **Barrier Lake Visitor Information Centre,** Box 32, Exshaw, AB G0L 2C0 (© **403/673-3985**). The **Travel Alberta Visitor Information Centre,** at the Bow Valley Trail exit off Highway 1 at Canmore (© **403/678-5277**), also has lots of information.

ADVENTURE SPORTS

It's the excellent access to outdoor activities that makes Canmore and the Kananaskis such a prime destination. From its offices at 20 Lincoln Park (corner of Lincoln Park and Bow Valley Trail) off Exit 91 from the Trans-Canada Highway, **Canmore Rafting Centre & Mirage Adventure Tours** (© **888/312-7238** in western Canada, or 403/678-4919; www.canmoreraftingcentre.com) represents most local outfitters. You'll find bike trips, trail rides, rafting, hiking, and sightseeing tours on offer. Mirage also rents cross-country skis and equipment.

DOWNHILL SKIING   Kananaskis gained worldwide attention when it hosted the alpine ski events for the Winter Olympics in 1988, and skiing remains a primary attraction in the area. At **Nakiska** (© **800/258-7669** or 403/591-7777; www.skinakiska. com), skiers can follow in the tracks of past Winter Olympians. A second ski area, **Fortress Mountain** (© **800/258-7669** or 403/591-7108; www.skifortress.com), is 19km (12 miles) south of Kananaskis Village (call ahead to confirm that Fortress has received its latest operating permit; the ski area experienced lease difficulties in 2007). Although overshadowed by Nakiska's Olympic reputation, Fortress Mountain offers an escape from the resort crowd and features overnight accommodations in an on-site dormitory. Both areas offer terrain for every age and ability, and are open from early December to mid-April. Adult lift tickets cost C$55 (US$55/£28) at Nakiska, C$43 (US$43/£22) at Fortress; tickets are completely transferable between the two areas.

CROSS-COUNTRY SKIING & MORE   The **Canmore Nordic Centre** 🎿, south of town off Spray Lakes Road (1988 Olympic Way, Canmore, AB T1W 2T6; © **403/ 678-2400**), was developed for the Olympics' cross-country skiing competition, though the facility is now open year-round. Today, it's administered as an all-season provincial park. In winter, the center offers 70km (43 miles) of scenic cross-country trails, plus the on-site **Trail Sports** shop (© **403/678-6764**) for rentals, repairs, and sales. In summer, hikers and mountain bikers take over the trails, and Trail Sports offers bike rentals, skill-building courses, and guided rides.

GOLF   Kananaskis features four championship golf courses and one of Canada's premier golf resorts. **Kananaskis Country Golf Course** 🎿 boasts two 18-hole, par-72 courses set among alpine forests and streams, and featuring water hazards on 20 holes, 140 sand traps, and 4 tee positions. Kananaskis is rated among the top courses in Canada. For information, contact **Golf Kananaskis,** Kananaskis Country Golf Course, P.O. Box 1710, Kananaskis Village, AB T0L 2H0 (© **877/591-2525** or 403/ 591-7272; www.kananaskisgolf.com). Greens fees are C$85 (US$85/£43).

Near Canmore, the 18-hole **Canmore Golf Course** is right along the Bow River at 2000 8th Ave. (© **403/678-4785;** www.canmoregolf.net). Greens fees are C$75 (US$75/£38).

The Les Furber–designed **SilverTip Golf Course** 🎿 (© **403/678-1600;** www. silvertipresort.com) is an 18-hole, par-72 course high above Canmore, off SilverTip Drive. You'll look eye-to-eye with the Canadian Rockies here. Boasting a length of 7,300 yards, the course has sand bunkers on all holes, and water on eight. Greens fees range from C$125 to C$175 (US$125–US$175/£63–£88). Also at Canmore is the **Stewart Creek Golf Club** (© **877/993-4653**; www.stewartcreekgolf.com), with 18 holes, 32 bunkers, and a beautiful location below the Three Sisters peaks. The course measures 7,150 yards and incorporates natural lakes, streams, and even historic mine entrances. Greens fees range from C$105 to C$175 (US$105–US$175/£53–£88), and include use of a golf cart.

HORSEBACK TRIPS   The Kananaskis is noted for its dude ranches (see "Guest Ranches," below), which offer a variety of horseback adventures from short trail rides to multiday pack trips. A 2-hour guided ride will generally cost C$60 to C$75 (US$60–US$75/£30–£38). In addition, **Boundary Ranch,** just south of Kananaskis Village on Highway 40 (© **877/591-7177** or 403/591-7171; www.boundaryranch. com), offers a variety of trail rides including a horseback lunch excursion.

RAFTING   The Kananaskis and Bow rivers are the main draw here. In addition to a range of half-day (C$49–C$85/US$49–US$85/£25–£43), full-day (C$119/US$119/ £60), and 2-day (C$259/US$259/£130) white-water trips, there are excursions that combine a half-day of horseback riding with an afternoon of rafting (C$145/US$145/ £73). Contact **Canmore Rafting Centre,** above, for information.

WHERE TO STAY

Kananaskis is a major camping destination for families in Calgary, and the choice of **campgrounds** is wide. There's a concentration of campgrounds at Upper and Lower Kananaskis lakes, some 32km (20 miles) south of Kananaskis Village. A few campgrounds are scattered nearer to Kananaskis Village, around Barrier Lake and Ribbon Creek. For a full-service campground with RV hookups, go to **Mount Kidd RV Park** (© **403/591-7700**) just south of the Kananaskis golf course.

KANANASKIS VILLAGE

Kananaskis was the site of the international G8 Summit in 2002, so you may well stay in a room once graced by a world leader. There's no more than a stone's throw between the hotels, and to a high degree, public facilities are shared among all the lodgings.

Delta Lodge at Kananaskis ⚘   This resort hotel consists of two separate buildings that face each other across a pond at the center of Kananaskis Village. The lodge is the larger building, with a more rustic facade, a shopping arcade, and a number of drinking and dining choices. Its guest rooms are large and well furnished; many have balconies and some have fireplaces. The Signature Club service rooms are in the smaller—and quieter—of the two lodge buildings. Rooms here are generally more spacious than those in the lodge, and even more sumptuously furnished. Additionally, the Signature Club rooms include deluxe continental breakfast, afternoon hors d'oeuvres, honor bar, and full concierge service. The new Summit Spa and Fitness Centre provides health and beauty treatments for both men and women.

Kananaskis Village, AB T0L 2H0. © **800/268-1133** or 403/591-7711. Fax 403/591-7770. www.deltalodgeat kananaskis.ca. 321 units. C$259–C$349 (US$259–US$349/£130–£175) double. Ski/golf package rates and discounts available. AE, DC, MC, V. Parking C$12 (US$12/£6); valet parking C$16 (US$16/£8). **Amenities:** 4 restaurants; bar; indoor pool; golf courses nearby; tennis courts; health club; complete spa w/saltwater pool, whirlpool, and beauty treatments; bike rental; concierge; tour desk; business center; wireless Internet access in all public areas; shopping arcade; limited room service; babysitting; laundry service; dry cleaning; concierge-level rooms. *In room:* A/C (Signature Club), TV/VCR w/pay movies, high-speed Internet access, minibar, fridge, coffeemaker, hair dryer, iron.

Executive Resort at Kananaskis   This handsome, wood-fronted hotel offers newly renovated rooms with lush new linens and upscale furnishings. All of the smoke- and pet-free rooms have balconies or patios, and most suites have a gas fireplace. The hotel offers a wide variety of room types, including many loft units that can sleep up to six. There are mountain views from practically every room.

2 Terrace Dr., P.O. Box 10, Kananaskis Village, AB T0L 2H0. © **888/591-7501** or 403/591-7500. Fax 403/591-7893. www.executivehotels.net/kananaskis. 91 units. C$159–C$249 (US$159–US$249/£80–£125) double. AE, MC, V. Paid underground heated parking; free surface parking. **Amenities:** Restaurant; pub; tennis courts; exercise room; business center; room service; laundry service. *In room:* TV w/pay movies, wireless high-speed Internet, fridge, coffeemaker, hair dryer, iron, personal safe.

Kananaskis Wilderness Hostel   This is a great place for a recreation-loving traveler on a budget. The hostel is located at the Nakiska ski area, within walking distance of Kananaskis Village, and is close to 60 mountain-biking, hiking, and cross-country trails. Area outfitters offer special discounts to hostel guests. The hostel has a common room with a fireplace and four private family rooms.

At Nakiska Ski Area. © **866/762-4122** or 403/670-7580 for reservations, or 403/591-7333 for the hostel itself. www.hihostels.ca. 47 beds. C$21 (US$21/£11) members; C$25 (US$25/£13) nonmembers. MC, V. **Amenities:** Laundry. *In room:* No phone.

CANMORE

About half of the hotel development in Canmore dates from the 1988 Olympics, and the rest dates from—oh, the last 15 minutes. Canmore is presently going through an intense period of growth, with new lodgelike hotels and timeshare developments springing out of the forest like mushrooms. To a large degree, this is due to the restrictions on development within the national parks to the west: Hoteliers, outfitters, and other businesses designed to serve the needs of park visitors find Canmore, right on the park boundary, a much easier place to locate than Banff. As a result, Canmore is booming, and is now a destination in its own right.

The main reason to stay in Canmore is the price of hotel rooms. Rates here are between a half and a third lower than in Banff, and the small downtown area is blossoming with interesting shops and good restaurants. The hotels listed below are, in relative terms, the older properties in Canmore. Built for the Olympics, they generally have more facilities than today's batch of hotels. Older—though still perfectly pleasant—Canmore hotels can represent especially good deals on discount hotel websites.

For a complete list of B&Bs, contact the **Canmore–Bow Valley B&B Association,** P.O. Box 8005, Canmore, AB T1W 2T8 (www.bbcanmore.com).

Best Western Pocaterra Inn ⚘   One of the nicest of the hotels along the Bow Valley Trail strip is the Pocaterra Inn. All rooms are spacious and come with gas fireplaces, and lots of thoughtful niceties. The King suites on the top floor are especially spacious and have grand views of the Rockies. Free wireless high-speed Internet service is available throughout the hotel, and there's a complimentary Internet kiosk in the lobby.

1725 Mountain Ave., Canmore, AB T1W 2W1. © **888/678-6786** or 403/678-4334. Fax 403/678-3999. www.pocaterra inn.com. 83 units. C$249–C$269 (US$249–US$269/£125–£135) double. Children under 18 stay free in parent's room. Rates include continental breakfast. AE, DISC, MC, V. **Amenities:** Indoor pool w/waterslide; exercise room; whirlpool; sauna; coin-op laundry. *In room:* A/C, TV, high-speed Internet access, fridge, microwave, coffeemaker, hair dryer.

Chateau Canmore ⚘   You can't miss this enormous complex along the hotel strip. Like a series of 10 four-story conjoined chalets, the all-suite Chateau Canmore offers some of the largest rooms in the area. The accommodations are decorated in a comfortable rustic style, while the lobby and common rooms look like they belong in a log lodge. Each standard suite has a fireplace and separate bedroom, while the deluxe one- or two-bedroom suites add a living room and dining area. Just like home, but with a better view.

1720 Bow Valley Trail, Canmore, AB T1W 2X3. ⓒ **800/261-8551** or 403/678-6699. Fax 403/678-6954. www. chateaucanmore.com. 93 units. C$119–C$199 (US$119–US$199/£60–£100) double. AE, DC, DISC, MC, V. **Amenities:** Dining room; lounge; indoor pool; health club; spa; outdoor hot tub; sauna. *In room:* A/C, TV, complimentary wireless Internet access, fridge, microwave, toaster, coffeemaker, hair dryer.

Falcon Crest Lodge ⓒⓒ
This beautifully equipped hotel is one of Canmore's newest, and is about a mile from the downtown core. The rooms here may be brand new, but they don't have the build-'em-by-the-hundreds anonymity that can become so tedious in mass-constructed condo developments. There are four room types: The deluxe, usually with two queen beds, is pleasant but just a bit tight, though it does have a kitchenette. Step up to the studio or one-bedroom for lots of space, a full kitchen and fireplace; for larger families or groups, there are also two-bedroom units. All rooms have balconies. All in all, a delightful place to stay.

190 Kananaskis Way, Canmore, Alberta T1W 3K5. ⓒ **866/609-3222** or 403/678-6150. Fax 403/678-6148. www.falcon crestlodge.ca. 70 units. C$179–C$239 (US$179–US$239/£90–£120) double. AE, MC, V. Free parking. **Amenities:** Restaurant; lounge; exercise room; 2 outdoor hot tubs. *In room:* A/C, TV/DVD player, high-speed Internet access, kitchen or kitchenette, coffeemaker, hair dryer, iron, fireplace.

Fire Mountain Lodge ⓒⓒ
One of the nicest of the many condo developments that have sprouted in Canmore in the last 5 years is the Fire Mountain Lodge. Its location is away from the busy railway tracks that form the backyard for many Canmore hotels, yet it's within easy driving distance of downtown restaurants and shopping. The standard two-story units are beautifully furnished: On the main floor is a fully equipped granite-countered kitchen, dining area, living room with fireplace, guest bathroom and deck, while on the loft level you'll find two bedrooms, full bathrooms, and a balcony (the units are also available in one-bedroom configurations). If you're traveling with a family or group and want extra space, or are going to be in Canmore a few days and want a full kitchen, these condo units are highly recommended. Pets are welcome.

121 Kananaskis Way, Canmore, AB, T1W 2X2. ⓒ **866/740-3473** or 403/609-9949. Fax 403/609-8204. www.fire mountain.ca. 24 units. From C$315 (US$315/£158) double. AE, MC, V. Free parking. **Amenities:** Exercise facilities; outdoor hot tub. *In room:* A/C, TVs/DVD players, CD player, high-speed Internet access, full kitchen w/dining table, coffeemaker, hair dryer, iron, fireplace, washer and dryer.

Paintbox Lodge ⓒ
One of the few lodgings in Canmore's charming town center, the Paintbox Lodge is a small and luxurious boutique inn that mingles rustic mountain charm and refined sophistication. The lodge offers seven guest rooms in the main building and a two-bedroom suite with a full kitchen in a separate lodge, all just steps from the Bow River and the lively cafes and shops of Canmore.

701 Mallard Alley, Canmore, AB T1W 2A2. ⓒ **888/678-3100** or 403/609-0482. Fax 403/609-0481 www.paintbox lodge.com. 8 units. C$199–C$259 (US$199–US$259/£100–£130) double. AE, MC, V. *In room:* TV w/movie channels, CD player, high-speed Internet access, minibar, fridge, coffeemaker, hair dryer, 2-person soaker tubs.

Radisson Hotel and Conference Centre Canmore
This vast complex is Canmore's largest hotel and also serves as the town's convention center. With all of the functions and services offered here, it's almost a self-contained community. There are two styles of accommodations: standard guest rooms in the main building, all with balconies and quality furnishings, or luxury lodge rooms, most with kitchenettes and fireplaces. A few two-bedroom lodge units with full kitchens are available as well (call for rates).

511 Bow Valley Trail, Canmore, AB T1W 1N7. © 800/333-3333 or 403/678-3625. Fax 403/678-3765. www.radisson.com/canmoreca. 224 units. C$169–C$219 (US$169–US$219/£85–£110) double. AE, DC, DISC, MC, V. **Amenities:** Restaurant; bar; indoor pool; exercise room; hot tub; sauna; car-rental desk; limited room service; babysitting; laundry service; same-day dry cleaning (weekdays only). *In room:* A/C, TV w/pay movies, high-speed Internet access, coffeemaker, hair dryer, iron.

Guest Ranches

Brewster's Kananaskis Guest Ranch ✿ The Brewsters were movers and shakers in the region's early days, playing a decisive role in the formation of Banff and Jasper national parks. They were also the first outfitters (and transport providers) in the parks. The original family homestead from the 1880s was transformed into a guest ranch in 1923. Located right on the Bow River near the mouth of the Kananaskis River, the original lodge buildings now serve as common areas; an 18-hole golf course occupies a former horse pasture. The 33 guest rooms, in chalets and cabins, are fully modern, each with full bathroom facilities. Activities include horseback riding, river rafting, canoeing, hiking, and more. Long-distance 2- and 4-day backcountry horseback rides are a specialty, and backcountry campsites have rustic log cabins for sleeping accommodations.

30 min. east of Banff on Hwy. 1. P.O. Box 340, Exhaw, AB T0L 2C0. © 800/691-5085 or 403/673-3737. Fax 403/673-2100. www.kananaskisguestranch.com. C$98–C$114 (US$98–US$114/£49–£57) double. Rates include dinner and breakfast. MC, V. **Amenities:** Restaurant; bar w/the ranch's only TV; 15-person Jacuzzi.

Rafter Six Ranch Resort An old-time guest ranch with a long pedigree, this full-service resort is located in a meadow right on the banks of the Kananaskis River and accommodates visitors in an especially inviting old log lodge (with restaurant, barbecue deck, and lounge). Comfortable lodging is provided in the historic lodge, in various sizes of log cabins, and in large chalets that sleep up to six and have full kitchens. All rooms have private bathrooms. Casual horseback and longer pack trips are offered, as well as raft and canoe trips. Seasonal special events might include rodeos, country dances, and hay or sleigh rides. The ranch is open year-round.

P.O. Box 6, Seebe, AB T0L 1X0. © 888/267-2624 or 403/673-3622. Fax 403/673-3961. www.raftersix.com. 60 rooms. C$110–C$250 (US$110–US$250/£55–£125) double in the lodge; C$125–C$250 (US$125–US$250/£63–£125) double in the cabins and chalets. 3- and 4-day recreation packages available. AE, MC, V. **Amenities:** Restaurant; bar; outdoor pool; Jacuzzi; playground.

WHERE TO DINE

The dining rooms at both **Rafter Six Ranch Resort** and **Brewster's Kananaskis Guest Ranch** (see "Guest Ranches," above) are open to nonguests with reservations. Pub dining in Canmore is also noteworthy; most pubs have pleasant garden patios. **Grizzly Paw Pub,** 622 Main St. (© **403/678-9983**), makes its own excellent ales and serves good food. The **Rose and Crown,** 749 Railway Ave. (© **403/678-5168**), overlooking the river, wins for the best deck.

Crazyweed Kitchen ✿✿ CONTEMPORARY CANADIAN Crazyweed began as a little lunch spot in downtown Canmore that was part health-food cafeteria and part international ethnic-food diner. After winning accolades for its fresh and well-crafted cooking, Crazyweed took the big step and moved into a brand-new building between downtown Canmore and Highway 1, where it's now open for both lunch and dinner. The dining room departs from the dark and woodsy look usually favored in the Canadian Rockies, with lots of windows, white walls, and modern art. The food is equally contemporary, with locally sourced ingredients enhanced with a touch of Asian, Italian, or Mexican zing. The menu is divided into small and large plates, tempting full-flavored dishes like fresh fig salad with crispy prosciutto, grilled shrimp with mango and mint salsa, and beef tenderloin in Korean spices with house-made potato "ruffles." Service is excellent; this is easily one of the new best restaurants in the Canadian Rockies.

1600 Railway Ave. (© 403/609-2530. Reservations required. Main courses C$26–C$36 (US$26–US$36/£13–£18). MC, V. Daily noon–10pm.

Murrieta's Bar & Grill 𝒢𝒢 STEAKHOUSE/SEAFOOD   Residing a floor above Canmore's busy main street, Murrieta's is a stylish and lively steakhouse and bar with attractive lodge decor and a soaring 7m (24-ft.) cathedral ceiling. The food is lofty as well. In addition to steak and chops, Murrieta's offers a broad selection of fresh fish and seafood, the grilled shrimp with vanilla-saffron sauce is outstanding, and for a break from beef, try the chile-roasted pork rib-eye with red-onion marmalade. On Friday and Saturday nights, the bar features live jazz.

200–737 Main St. (© 403/609-9500. www.murrietas.ca. Reservations recommended. Main courses C$12–C$38 (US$12–US$38/£6–£19). AE, MC, V. Mon–Thurs 11am–11pm; Fri–Sat 11am–1am; Sun 11am–10pm.

Quarry Bistro 𝒢𝒢 CONTINENTAL   This friendly, informal spot offers intriguing cooking based on French and Italian classics but translated into New Canadian vernacular by chef David Wyse. Using local and organic ingredients, Wyse creates a seasonal cuisine that's sophisticated but low key. Wild mushroom–and–lemon thyme ravioli makes an excellent appetizer, and one evening's special, a grilled organic pork chop with fresh crabapple-tarragon relish, was full of fall flavors. It sounds unlikely, but the house-made blueberry-basil sorbet is delightful. This bright and lively spot is right on Main Street, with a few streetside tables.

718 Main St. (© 403/678-6088. Reservations recommended. Main courses C$14–C$32 (US$14–US$32/£7–£16). MC, V. Mon–Fri 11:30am–2:30pm and 5–10pm; Sat–Sun 9:30am–2:30pm and 5–10pm.

Tapas Restaurant 𝒢 SPANISH/PORTUGUESE   Many restaurants use the term *tapas* to refer to finger food and appetizers from just about any cuisine, forgetting that tapas are supposed to be Spanish. There's no such mistake here: Tapas Restaurant serves up over 40 authentically Spanish and Portuguese favorites, including chile and cilantro mussels escabeche, Calabasino fritters (with zucchini, mint and feta cheese), and an amazing Piri Piri, with chile-grilled chicken, watermelon slices, sheep's cheese, olives, and mint. The restaurant also focuses on dishes to be shared by two, including Cataplana, a Portuguese pork and seafood stew served in a copper pot. Three kinds of paella are also served for duo diners. With the scent of garlic and sausage in the air, you might just believe you're in Seville.

633 10th St. (© 403/609-0583. Reservations recommended. Tapas C$5–C$12 (US$5–US$12/£2.50–£6); main courses for 2 C$30–C$40 (US$30–US$40/£15–£20). AE, MC, V. Summer daily 8am–11pm; winter daily 5:30–11pm.

Wood Steakhouse & Lounge CANADIAN   This handsome log restaurant on the busiest corner of downtown Canmore was a longtime favorite under the name Sherwood House. With its new identity came a few changes: a sandblast to brighten up the venerable log interior and an update to the furnishings and menu. While steaks and chops remain the mainstay, the new menu ventures beyond grilled meats to include Parma-ham wrapped shrimp, wasabi-crusted salmon with Asian slaw, and forest mushroom tagliatelle. There's something for everyone, but what makes this one of Canmore's favorite gathering spots is the wonderful landscaped deck and beautiful views onto the Rockies. In summer, there's no better place to spend the afternoon. In winter, you'll enjoy the traditional lodge building with its cozy fireplace.

832 Main St. © **403/678-3404.** Reservations recommended. Main courses C$18–C$42 (US$18–US$42/£9–£21). AE, MC, V. Daily 11am–midnight.

7 Banff National Park: Canada's Top Tourist Draw ★★★

Banff is Canada's oldest national park, founded in 1885 as a modest 26-sq.-km (10-sq.-mile) reserve by the country's first prime minister, Sir John A. Macdonald. The park is now 6,641 sq. km (2,564 sq. miles) of incredibly dramatic mountain landscape, glaciers, high morainal lakes, and rushing rivers. Its two towns, Lake Louise and Banff, are both splendid counterpoints to the wilderness, with beautiful historic hotels, fine restaurants, and lively nightlife.

If there's a downside to all this sophisticated beauty, it's that Banff is incredibly popular—it's generally considered Canada's number-one tourist destination. About five million people visit Banff yearly, with the vast majority squeezing in during June, July, and August.

Happily, the wilderness invites visitors to get away from the crowds and from the congestion of the developed sites. Banff Park is blessed with a great many outfitters who make it easy to get on a raft, bike, or horse and find a little mountain solitude. Alternatively, consider visiting the park off season, when prices are lower, the locals are friendlier, and the scenery is just as stunning.

For more information on the park, contact **Banff National Park,** P.O. Box 900, Banff, AB T1L 1K2 (© **403/762-1550;** www.pc.gc.ca).

SPORTS & OUTDOOR ACTIVITIES IN THE PARK

Lots of great recreational activities are available in Banff National Park, so don't just spend your vacation shopping the boutiques on Banff Avenue. Most day trips require little advance booking—a day in advance is usually plenty—and the easiest way to find a quick adventure is just to ask your hotel's concierge to set one up. Multiday rafting and horseback trips do require advance booking, because places are limited and keenly sought after. There are many more outfitters in Banff than the ones I list, but the offerings and prices below are typical of what's available.

BIKING   The most popular cycling adventure in the Canadian Rockies is the 287km (178-mile) trip between Banff and Jasper along the Icefields Parkway, one of the world's most magnificent mountain roads. Most cyclists will need 3 days to make the trip, spending the nights at the numerous and charming hostels found along this amazing mountain road.

If you're fit and ready for a high-elevation ride, but don't want to bother with the logistics yourself, consider signing on with a bike-touring outfitter. Among the dozens of tour operators in the area, **Canusa Cycle Tours** (© **800/938-7986** or 403/703-5566; www.canusacycletours.com) offers 6-day supported trips starting at C$1,000 (US$1,000/£500).

If you'd prefer a self-guided tour, simply rent a bike in Banff or Lake Louise and pedal along the Bow Valley Parkway—Highway 1A—between Banff and Lake Louise, which makes an easy day trip for the average cyclist.

FISHING   **Banff Fishing Unlimited** (© **403/762-4936;** www.banff-fishing.com) offers a number of fly-fishing expeditions on the Bow River as well as lake fishing at

Lake Minnewanka. All levels of anglers are accommodated, and packages include part- or whole-day trips.

GOLF   The **Banff Springs Golf Course** ✦ (© **403/762-6801**) rolls out along the Bow River beneath towering mountain peaks. One of the most venerable courses in Canada, and one of the most expensive, it offers 27 holes of excellent golf. Although associated with the resort hotel, the course is open to the public.

HELICOPTER TOURS   If you'd like to see the beautiful scenery of the Canadian Rockies from the air, contact **Alpine Helicopters** (© **403/678-4802;** www.alpine helicopter.com), which operates out of Canmore. This company's flights over the Rockies start at C$95 (US$95/£48) per person with a minimum of two passengers.

HIKING   One of the great virtues of Banff is that many of its most scenic areas are easily accessible by day hikes. The park has more than 80 maintained trails, ranging from interpretive nature strolls to long-distance expeditions (you'll need a permit if you plan to camp in the backcountry). For a good listing of popular hikes, pick up the free "Banff/Lake Louise Drives and Walks" brochure.

One of the best day hikes in the area is up **Johnston Canyon** ✦, 24km (15 miles) north of Banff on Highway 1A. This relatively easy hike up a limestone canyon passes seven waterfalls before reaching a series of jade-green springs known as the Inkpots. Part of the fun of this trail is the narrowness of the canyon—the walls are more than 30m (98 ft.) high, but only 5.5m (18 ft.) across; the path skirts the cliff face, tunnels through walls, and winds across wooden footbridges for more than 1.5km (1 mile). The waterfalls plunge down through the canyon, soaking hikers with spray; watch for black swifts diving in the mist. The hike through the canyon to Upper Falls takes 1½ hours; all the way to the Inkpots will take at least 4 hours.

It's easy to strike out from **Banff Townsite** and find any number of satisfying short hikes. Setting off on foot can be as simple as following the paths along both sides of the Bow River. From the west end of the Bow River Bridge, trails lead east to Bow Falls, past the Banff Springs Hotel to the Upper Hot Springs. Another popular hike just beyond town is the **Fenlands Trail,** which begins past the train station and makes a loop through marshland wildlife habitat near the Vermillion Lakes.

Two longer trails leave from the Cave and Basin Centennial Centre. The **Sundance Trail** follows the Bow River for nearly 5km (3 miles) past beaver dams and wetlands, ending at the entrance to Sundance Canyon. Keen hikers can continue up the canyon another 2.5km (1.5 miles) to make a loop past Sundance Falls. The Marsh Loop winds 2.5km (1.5 miles) past the Bow River and marshy lakes.

If you'd prefer a guided hike, Parks Canada offers several hikes daily. Ask at the Banff Information Centre or check the chalkboard outside to find out what hiking options are available. Some walks are free, while others (like the popular evening Wildlife Research Walks) charge a small fee; both require preregistration. For informa- tion and preregistration, call © **403/762-9818.**

HORSEBACK RIDING   See Banff on horseback with **Warner Guiding and Out- fitting** (© **800/661-8352** or 403/762-4551; www.horseback.com) multiday trail rides, which start at C$686 (US$686/£343) for a 3-day lodge-to-lodge trip and peak at C$1,377 (US$1,377/£689) for a 6-day backcountry tenting trip, explore some of the most remote areas of the park. Some rides climb up to backcountry lodges, which serve as base camps for further exploration; other trips involve a backcountry circuit,

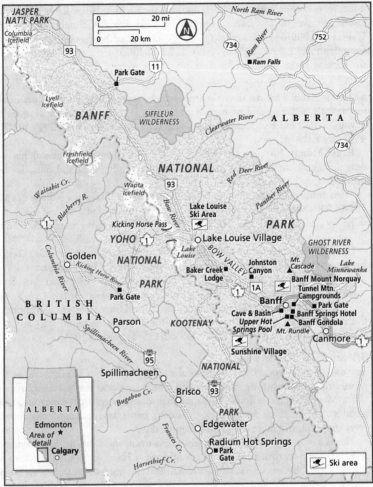

with lodging in tents. Shorter day rides are also offered from two stables near the townsite. A morning ride with brunch goes for C$97 (US$97/£49).

Operating out of Lake Louise, **Timberline Tours** (© 888/858-3388 or 403/522-3743; www.timberlinetours.ca) offers day trips to some of the area's more prominent beauty sites, starting at C$55 (US$55/£28) for 90 minutes of riding. Three- to ten-day pack trips are also offered.

RAFTING & CANOEING Family float trips on the Bow River just below Banff are popular 2-hour diversions, available from **Canadian Rockies Rafting Company** (© 877/226-7625 or 403/678-6535; www.rafting.ca). Trips are C$50 (US$50/£25) for adults and C$45 (US$45/£23) for seniors and children ages 9 to 16, with free pickup at Banff and Canmore hotels. Longer, more challenging trips on area rivers are also available.

For serious white water, the closest option is the **Kicking Horse River** ❀, past Lake Louise just over the Continental Divide near Field, British Columbia. **Hydra River Guides** (© **800/644-8888** or 403/762-4554; www.raftbanff.com) offers transport from Banff and Lake Louise (an extra C\$20/US\$20/£10), then a 2½-hour run down the Kicking Horse through Class IV rapids. Trips go for C\$99 (US\$99/£50), which includes gear and a barbecue lunch.

SKIING   Banff Park has three ski areas, which together have formed a partnership for booking, ticketing and promotional purposes. For information on all of the following, contact **Ski Banff/Lake Louise,** Box 1085, Banff, AB T0l 0C0 (© **403/762-4561;** www.skibig3.com).

Banff Mount Norquay (© **403/762-4421;** www.banffnorquay.com) has twin runs just above the town of Banff. They cater to family skiing and offer day care, instruction, and night skiing.

Skiers must ski or take a gondola to the main lifts at **Sunshine Village** (© **403/762-6500;** www.skibanff.com) and the Sunshine Inn, a ski-in, ski-out hotel. Sunshine, located 15 minutes west of Banff off Highway 1, receives more snow than any ski area in the Canadian Rockies (more than 9m/30 ft. per year!).

Lake Louise Ski Area (© **800/258-SNOW** in North America, or 403/552-3555) has been named the most scenic ski resort in North America by *Ski* magazine. It's also one of the largest in Canada, with 4,200 skiable acres and 113 named runs. Snowmaking machines keep the lifts running from November to early May.

A single lift pass allows skiers unlimited access to all three resorts (and free rides on shuttle buses between the ski areas). Passes for 3 days (minimum) start at C\$231 (US\$231/£116) for adults and C\$69 (US\$69/£35) for youths 13–17.

BANFF TOWNSITE ❀❀❀

Few towns in the world boast as beautiful a setting as Banff. The mighty Bow River courses right through town, while massive mountain blocks rear up on Banff's outskirts. Mount Rundle, a finlike mountain that somehow got tipped over on its side, parades off to the south. Mount Cascade rises up immediately north of downtown. In every direction, still more craggy peaks fill the sky.

This is a stunning, totally unlikely place for a town, and Banff has been trading on its beauty for more than a century. The Banff Springs Hotel was built in 1888 as a destination resort by the Canadian Pacific Railroad. As outdoor-recreation enthusiasts began to frequent the area for its scenery, hot springs, and access to fishing, hunting, climbing, and other activities, the little town of Banff grew up to service their needs.

While the setting hasn't changed since the early days of the park, the town certainly has. Today, the streets of Banff are lined with exclusive boutiques; trendy cafes spill out onto the sidewalks; and bus after bus filled with tourists choke the streets. Japanese, English, French, and German visitors are very much in evidence. There's a vital and cosmopolitan feel to the town; just don't come here expecting a bucolic Alpine village—Banff in summer is a very busy place.

ESSENTIALS

GETTING THERE   If you're flying into Calgary and heading straight to Banff, call and reserve a seat on the **Banff Airporter** (© **403/762-3330;** www.banffairporter.com). Vans depart from Calgary Airport roughly every 2 hours; a one-way ticket costs C\$55 (US\$55/£28).

Banff Town

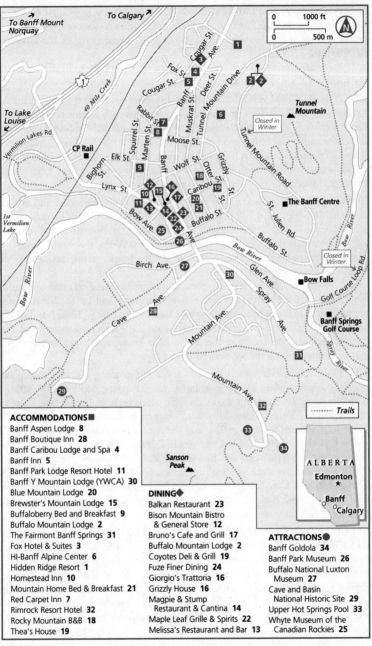

To Banff Mount Norquay

To Calgary

To Lake Louise

40 Mile Creek

CP Rail

1st Vermilion Lake

Cougar St.

Fox St.

Cougar St.

Banff Ave.

Deer St.

Tunnel Mountain Drive

Tunnel Mountain

Closed in Winter

Rabbit St.

Squirrel St.

Marten St.

Elk St.

Bighorn St.

Moose St.

Banff Ave.

Wolf St.

Otter St.

Grizzly St.

Tunnel Mountain Road

The Banff Centre

Lynx St.

Caribou St.

Buffalo St.

St. Julien Rd.

Bow Ave.

Buffalo St.

Bow River

Birch Ave.

Glen Ave.

Closed in Winter

Bow Falls

Cave Ave.

Ave.

Spray Ave.

Mountain Ave.

Golf Course Loop Rd.

Banff Springs Golf Course

Mountain Ave.

Spray River

Sanson Peak

Trails

0   1000 ft
0   500 m

N

ALBERTA

Edmonton ★

Banff ○
Calgary ○

ACCOMMODATIONS ■
Banff Aspen Lodge **8**
Banff Boutique Inn **28**
Banff Caribou Lodge and Spa **4**
Banff Inn **5**
Banff Park Lodge Resort Hotel **11**
Banff Y Mountain Lodge (YWCA) **30**
Blue Mountain Lodge **20**
Brewster's Mountain Lodge **15**
Buffaloberry Bed and Breakfast **9**
Buffalo Mountain Lodge **2**
The Fairmont Banff Springs **31**
Fox Hotel & Suites **3**
HI-Banff Alpine Center **6**
Hidden Ridge Resort **1**
Homestead Inn **10**
Mountain Home Bed & Breakfast **21**
Red Carpet Inn **7**
Rimrock Resort Hotel **32**
Rocky Mountain B&B **18**
Thea's House **19**

DINING ◆
Balkan Restaurant **23**
Bison Mountain Bistro
  & General Store **12**
Bruno's Cafe and Grill **17**
Buffalo Mountain Lodge **2**
Coyotes Deli & Grill **19**
Fuze Finer Dining **24**
Giorgio's Trattoria **16**
Grizzly House **16**
Magpie & Stump
  Restaurant & Cantina **14**
Maple Leaf Grille & Spirits **22**
Melissa's Restaurant and Bar **13**

ATTRACTIONS ●
Banff Goldola **34**
Banff Park Museum **26**
Buffalo National Luxton
  Museum **27**
Cave and Basin
  National Historic Site **29**
Upper Hot Springs Pool **33**
Whyte Museum of the
  Canadian Rockies **25**

581

Greyhound (© **800/661-8747** or 403/260-0877; www.greyhound.ca) operates **buses** that pass through Banff on the way from Calgary to Vancouver. One-way fare between Banff and Calgary is C$23 (US$23/£12). The depot is at 100 Gopher St. (© **403/762-6767**).

If you're **driving,** the Trans-Canada Highway takes you right to Banff's main street; the town is 129km (80 miles) west of Calgary.

VISITOR INFORMATION The **Banff Information Centre,** at 224 Banff Ave., houses both the Banff Tourism Bureau and a national-park information center. Contact the office at P.O. Box 1298, Banff, AB T1L 1B3 (© **403/762-8421;** www.banff lakelouise.com). The center is open daily June 15 through October 15 from 9am to 9pm and the rest of the year from 9am to 5pm. Be sure to ask for the *Official Visitors Guide,* which is packed with information about local businesses and recreation. For information on the park, go to **www.pc.gc.ca**.

TOWN LAYOUT Getting your bearings is easy. The **Greyhound and Brewster Bus Depot** is located at 327 Railway Ave. (© **403/762-1091**). The main street—Banff Avenue—starts at the southern end of town at the Bow River and runs north until it's swallowed by the Trans-Canada Highway. Along this broad, bright, and bustling thoroughfare, you'll find most of Banff's hotels, restaurants, stores, office buildings, and nightspots.

Just beyond the river stands the park administration building amid a beautifully landscaped garden. Here the road splits: **Banff Springs Hotel** and the **Banff Gondola** are to the left; to the right are the **Cave and Basin Hot Springs,** Banff National Park's original site. At the northwestern edge of town is the old railroad station, and a little farther northwest the road branches off to Lake Louise and Jasper. In the opposite direction, northeast, is the highway going to Calgary.

GETTING AROUND Banff offers local bus service along two routes designed to pass through downtown and by most hotels. Service on the **Banff Bus** (© **403/760-8294**) is pretty informal, but there's generally a bus every half-hour. One route runs from the Banff Springs Hotel down Banff Avenue to the northern end of town; the other runs between the train station and the Banff Hostel on Tunnel Mountain; the fare is C$1 (US$1/50p). The bus operates in summer only.

For a taxi, call **Banff Taxi and Limousine** (© **403/762-4444**).

For a rental car, contact **National,** at Caribou and Lynx streets (© **403/762-2688**), or **Banff Rent A Car,** 204 Lynx St. (© **403/762-3352**), for a less expensive but reliable vehicle. Avis, Budget, and Hertz also have offices in Banff. Reserve well in advance as cars are frequently sold out.

SPECIAL EVENTS & FESTIVALS The **Banff Centre,** St. Julien Road (© **800/413-8368** or 403/762-6300; www.banffcentre.ca), is a remarkable year-round institution devoted to the arts and entertainment in the widest sense. From June to August, the center hosts the **Banff Summer Arts Festival** ⟨, offering a stimulating mixture of drama, opera, jazz, ballet, classical and pop music, and the visual arts. Highlights include the International String Quartet Competition, with 10 world-class quartets vying for a cash prize and a national tour, and the Digital Playgrounds series, which brings performance artists to the stage. Tickets for some of the events cost from pay-what-you-can to C$25 (US$25/£13); a great many are absolutely free. In November, the center is home to the **Festival of Mountain Films.** Find out what's currently on by getting the program at the Banff Tourism Bureau or by checking out the Banff Centre's website.

EXPLORING BANFF

Banff Gondola ⚐   Apart from helicopter excursions (see above), the best way to get an overall view of Banff's landscape is this high-wire act (formerly the Sulphur Mountain Gondola). In 8 minutes, the enclosed gondolas lift you 700m (2,297 ft.) from the valley floor up to the top of Sulphur Mountain, at 2,281m (7,484 ft.). Up here, at the crest of the mountains behind Banff, the panoramas are stunning. Trails lead out along the mountain ridges; hike back to the bottom of the mountain, or spend the day exploring the subarctic zone along the mountaintop. Also at the upper terminal are two restaurants, a snack bar, and gift shop. Lines to get on the gondola can be very long in summer; if you are set on riding up to the high country, try to go as early as possible.

The lower terminal is 6km (4 miles) southeast of town on Mountain Ave. ℰ 403/762-5438. www.banffgondola. com. Admission C$25 (US$25/£13) adults, C$13 (US$13/£6.50) children 6–15. May 1 to Labour Day 7:30am–9pm; check website for off-season schedule.

Banff Park Museum   Housed in a lovely wood-lined building dating from 1903, this museum beside the Bow River Bridge is largely a paean to taxidermy, but there's a lot to learn here about the wildlife of the park and how the various ecosystems interrelate. The real pleasure, though, is the rustic, lodge-style building, now preserved as a National Historic Site.

Banff Ave. and Buffalo St. ℰ 403/762-1558. Admission C$4 (US$4/£2) adults, C$3.50 (US$3.50/£1.75) seniors, C$2 (US$2/£1) youths 6–16, C$10 (US$10/£5) families. Mid-May to late Sept daily 10am–6pm, rest of year 1–5pm. Closed Dec 25–26, Jan 1.

Buffalo Nations Luxton Museum   Housed in a log fort south of the Bow River, just across the bridge from downtown Banff, this museum is devoted to the history of the First Nations peoples of the Canadian Rockies and Northern Plains. It offers realistic dioramas, tepees, a sun-dance exhibit, artifacts, and ornaments.

1 Birch Ave. ℰ 403/762-2388. Admission C$8 (US$8/£4) adults, C$6 (US$6/£3) seniors and students, C$2.50 (US$2.50/£1.25) children 6–12. Late May to Sept daily 11am–5pm; Oct to mid-May daily 1–5pm.

Cave and Basin National Historic Site ⚐   Although most people now associate Banff with skiing or hiking, in the early days of the park, travelers streamed in to visit the curative hot springs. In fact, it was the discovery of the hot springs now preserved at this historic site that spurred the creation of the national park in 1888. During the 1910s, these hot mineral waters, which rise in a limestone cave, were piped into a rather grand natatorium. Although the Cave and Basin springs are no longer open for swimming or soaking, the old pool area and the original cave have been preserved; interpretive displays and films round out the experience.

1.5km (1 mile) west of Banff; turn right at the west end of the Bow River Bridge. ℰ 403/762-1566. Admission C$4 (US$4/£2) adults, C$3.50 (US$3.50/£1.75) seniors and students, C$2 (US$2/£1) children 6–12. May 15–Sept 30 daily 9am–6pm; Oct 1–May 14 Mon–Fri 11am–4pm, Sat–Sun 9:30am–5pm.

Lake Minnewanka Boat Tours   These very popular scenic and wildlife-viewing trips in glassed-in motor cruisers take place on Lake Minnewanka, a glacial lake wedged between two mountain ranges. These trips—usually 2 hours long—are among those excursions that nearly every visitor to Banff ends up taking, so unless you want to be part of a huge shuffling throng, try to go early in the day. Reservations are suggested. In high season, there are five sailings a day and buses leave from the bus station and from most hotels daily to meet these tours.

24km (15 miles) north of Banff. ℰ 403/762-3473. Fax 403/762-2800. www.minnewankaboattours.com. Tickets C$40 (US$40/£20) adults, C$20 (US$20/£10) children 5–11. Mid-May to early Oct.

Tips Off-Season Rates

All accommodations prices listed are for high season, which normally runs from mid-May to mid-October; nearly all hotels have a complex rate schedule with discounts for late fall, holidays, winter, late winter, and spring accommodations. Call for information on these reduced off-season rates, as well as for ski and other packages. If you're having trouble finding affordable lodgings in Banff, try properties in Canmore, located 20 minutes away (see "Kananaskis Country & Canmore," earlier in this chapter).

Upper Hot Springs Pool   If visiting the Cave and Basin makes you long for a soak in mountain hot springs, then drive up Mountain Avenue to this spa. In addition to the redesigned swimming pool filled with hot, sulfurous waters, you'll find a restaurant, snack bar, and home spa boutique. If you're looking more for a cure than a splash, try the adjacent **Upper Hot Springs Spa** (℗ **403/760-2500**) with a steam room, massage, plunge pools, and aromatherapy treatments.

At the top of Mountain Ave., 5km (3 miles) west of Banff. ℗ **403/762-1515**. Pool admission C$7.50 (US$7.50/£3.75) adults, C$6.50 (US$6.50/£3.25) seniors and children, C$23 (US$23/£12) families. Package spa treatments begin at C$145 (US$145/£73) and are open to adults only. Daily 9am–11pm with reduced hours in winter.

Whyte Museum of the Canadian Rockies   Part art gallery, part local-history museum, this is the only museum in North America that collects, exhibits, and interprets the history and culture of the Canadian Rockies. Two furnished heritage homes on the grounds are open in summer and stand as a memorial to the pioneers of the Rockies. Interpretive programs and tours are offered year-round. The Elizabeth Rummel Tea Room is open from mid-May to mid-October and serves light lunches, desserts, and coffee.

111 Bear St. ℗ **403/762-2291**. www.whyte.org. Admission C$6 (US$6/£3) adults, C$3.50 (US$3.50/£1.75) seniors and students, free for children under 5, C$15 (US$15/£7.50) family. Daily 10am–5pm.

SHOPPING

The degree to which you like the town of Banff will depend largely upon your taste for shopping. **Banff Avenue** is increasingly an open-air boutique mall, with throngs of shoppers milling around. Of course, you would expect to find excellent outdoor-gear and sporting-goods stores here, as well as the usual T-shirt and gift emporiums. What's more surprising are the boutiques devoted to Paris and New York designers, the upscale jewelry stores, and the high-end galleries. What's most surprising of all is that many visitors seem to actually prefer to while away their time in this masterpiece of nature called Banff by shopping for English soaps or Italian shoes. There are no secrets to shopping here: Arcade after arcade opens onto Banff Avenue, where you'll find everything you need. Quality and prices are both quite high.

WHERE TO STAY

Banff National Park offers hundreds of campsites within easy commuting distance of Banff. The closest are the three **Tunnel Mountain campgrounds** ✿, just past the youth hostel west of town. Two of the campgrounds are for RVs only and have both partial and full hookups (C$36/US$36/£18); the third has showers and is usually reserved for tenters (C$26/US$26/£13). For more information, call the park's visitor center (✆ **403/762-1500**). Campsites within the park cannot be reserved in advance.

Very Expensive

Banff Caribou Lodge & Spa   The Caribou, with its gabled green roof, outdoor patio, bay windows, and wooden balconies, has a western-lodge look that blends well with the alpine landscape. The interior is equally impressive, especially the vast lobby with slate-tile floor, peeled-log woodwork, and huge stone fireplace. The finely furnished bedrooms continue the western theme with rustic pine chairs and beds decked out with snug down comforters. The bathrooms are spacious; some of the rooms have balconies. New in 2007 is the Red Earth Spa, a full service spa (with a large fitness area adjacent) with aesthetic and massage treatments, a Vichy shower table, and a couples' treatment room. The Keg is a local favorite for steaks. Although it's not in the absolute center of town (about 10 min. on foot), a free shuttle bus ferries guests to destinations throughout Banff.

521 Banff Ave., Banff, AB T1L 1A4. ✆ 800/563-8764 or 403/762-5887. Fax 403/762-5918. www.bestofbanff.com/bcl. 195 units. From C$235 (US$235/£118) double; from C$300 (US$300/£150) suite. Up to 2 children under 16 stay free in parent's room. AE, DC, DISC, MC, V. Free heated parking. **Amenities:** Restaurant; bar; exercise room; 30-person indoor hot pool, steam room; sauna; concierge; limited room service. *In room:* TV w/pay movies, dataport, wireless Internet access, coffeemaker, hair dryer, iron.

Banff Park Lodge Resort Hotel and Conference Centre ✿   A handsome cedar-and-oak structure with a cosmopolitan air, the Banff Park Lodge is a quiet 1½ blocks off the town's main street, near the Bow River. Calm and sophisticated are the key words here: All rooms are soundproofed, and wild, après-ski cavorting isn't the norm, or even much encouraged. The lodge will feel like a tranquil retreat after a day in frantic Banff. The standard rooms are spacious and exceptionally well furnished, all with balconies. Most suites have a whirlpool, jetted tub, and fireplace. With its abundant ground-floor rooms and wide hallways, this lodging is popular with travelers with disabilities or mobility concerns.

222 Lynx St., Banff, AB T1L 1K5. ✆ 800/661-9266 or 403/762-4433. Fax 403/762-3553. www.banffparklodge.com. 211 units. C$275 (US$275/£138) double; from C$395 (US$395/£198) suite. Extra person C$20 (US$20/£10). Children 16 and under stay free in parent's room. Off-season and ski packages available. AE, DC, MC, V. **Amenities:** Formal and family restaurants; bar; indoor pool; access to nearby health club; spa; Jacuzzi; steam room; concierge; tour and activities desk; business center; shopping arcade; salon; room service (7am–midnight); babysitting; laundry service; same-day dry cleaning. *In room:* A/C, TV w/movie channels, dataport, coffeemaker, hair dryer, iron.

Brewster's Mountain Lodge ✿   All in all, for the comfort and convenience, this is one of the top picks in central Banff. This handsome lodgelike hotel, right in the heart of Banff, is operated by the Brewster family, which dominates much of the local recreation, guest ranching, and transportation scene. The modern hotel does its best to look rustic: Peeled log posts and beams fill the lobby and foyer, while quality pine furniture and paneling grace the spacious guest rooms. Wheelchair-accessible rooms are available. Although there's no fine dining in the hotel, you'll find plenty adjacent in central Banff. The Brewster affiliation makes it simple to take advantage of lodging and adventure packages involving horseback riding and hiking.

208 Caribou St., Banff, AB T1L 1C1. ✆ 888/762-2900 or 403/762-2900. Fax 403/762-2970. www.brewstermountain lodge.com. 73 units. From C$235 (US$235/£118) double. AE, MC, V. Self-parking C$10 (US$10/£5). **Amenities:** Restaurant; Jacuzzi; sauna; car-rental desk; same-day dry cleaning. *In room:* TV/VCR, high-speed Internet access, hair dryer, iron.

Buffaloberry Bed and Breakfast ✿ Newly built and centrally located, the Buffaloberry offers the hominess of a B&B with the upscale touches of a fine hotel. The inn was purpose built, so rooms are expansive and have large, beautifully fitted bathrooms, plus in-floor heating and soundproofed walls. The bedrooms, all with private bathrooms, have a relaxed formality with country touches in the furniture and fabrics. You'll also find the kind of extras that you'd expect at a hotel: turn-down service, bathrobes, slippers, pillow-top mattresses, and 800-thread-count linens. Guests share a two-story Great Room with woodburning fireplace, leather couches, loads of reading material, and a dining nook, where extravagant breakfasts begin the day for lucky guests. The friendly innkeepers are avid outdoorspeople and bird-watchers and are happy to share their experience.

417 Marten St. (Box 5443), Banff, AB T1L 1G5. ✆ **403762-3750**. Fax 403/762-3752. www.buffaloberry.com. 4 units. C$295 (US$295/£148) double. MC, V. Free underground heated parking. *In room:* TV/DVD, stereo, hair dryer, iron.

Buffalo Mountain Lodge ✿✿ The most handsome of the properties on Tunnel Mountain, 1.6km (1 mile) northeast of Banff, this is the perfect choice if you'd rather avoid the frenetic pace of downtown and yet remain central to restaurants and activities. Its quiet location and beautiful lodge make this a good alternative to equally priced hotels in the heart of town (the Banff Bus stops right out the front door). The lodge building itself is an enormous log cabin, right out of your fantasies. The lobby is supported by massive rafters and filled with Navajo-style carpets. A fieldstone fireplace dominates the lounge, while the restaurant (p. 591) overlooks the grounds. An enormous, 25-person hot tub sits between the lodge and the guest rooms.

Accommodations are scattered around the forested 3-hectare (8-acre) property. They range from one-bedroom suites with kitchens to the exceptionally handsome Premier rooms, which feature slate-tiled bathrooms with both claw-foot tubs and slate-walled showers. The pine-and-twig furniture lends a rustic look to the otherwise sophisticated decor. All units have fireplaces (wood is stacked near your door), DVD players, high-speed Internet access, balconies or patios, and beds made up with feather duvets. These are some of the most attractive rooms in Banff.

1.6km (1 mile) northeast of Banff on Tunnel Mountain Rd., P.O. Box 1326, Banff, AB T1L 1B3. ✆ **800/661-1367** or 403/762-2400. Fax 403/760-4492. www.buffalomountainlodge.com. 108 units. C$249 (US$249/£125) double; C$309 (US$309/£155) 1-bedroom apt. AE, MC, V. Follow Otter St. from downtown. **Amenities:** 2 restaurants; lounge; exercise room; Jacuzzi; steam room; laundry service; same-day dry cleaning. *In room:* TV, dataport, coffeemaker, hair dryer, iron.

The Fairmont Banff Springs ✿✿ Standing north of Bow River Falls like an amazing Scottish baronial fortress, the Banff Springs is one of the most beautiful and famous hotels in North America. Founded in 1888 as an opulent destination resort by the Canadian Pacific Railroad, this stone castle of a hotel is still the best address in Banff—especially so after the renovation of all guest rooms and a C$75-million face-lift that transformed many of the public and reception spaces. The Willow Stream spa is one of Canada's top spas, with 3,530 sq. m (38,000 sq. ft.) devoted to treatment, relaxation, and fitness. This venerable hotel doesn't offer the largest rooms in Banff, but the amenities are superlative. Expect sumptuous linens, fancy soaps and lotions, real art, and quality furniture. With the views, the spa, and the near pageantry of service, this is still the most amazing resort in an area blessed with beautiful accommodations.

405 Spray Ave. (P.O. Box 960), Banff, AB T1L 1J4. ✆ **800/441-1414** or 403/762-2211. Fax 403/762-5755. www. fairmont.com. 778 units. C$369–C$589 (US$369–US$589/£185–£295) double; C$539–C$839 (US$539–US$839/£270–£420) suite. AE, DC, DISC, MC, V. Valet parking C$29 (US$29/£15); self-parking C$22 (US$22/£11). **Amenities:**

12 dining outlets; 4 lounges; Olympic-size pool; the famed Banff Springs golf course; 4 tennis courts; the Willow Stream Spa; hot tubs; bike and ski rental; concierge; tour and activities desk; business center; shopping arcade; 24-hr. room service; babysitting; laundry service; same-day dry cleaning; horseback riding; bowling center. *In room:* A/C, TV/VCR w/pay movies and video games, high-speed Internet access, coffeemaker, hair dryer, iron.

Rimrock Resort Hotel 🕊   If you seek modern luxury and great views, this is your hotel. From its roadside lobby entrance, the enormous, stunningly beautiful Rimrock drops nine floors down a steep mountain slope, affording tremendous views from nearly all of its rooms. Aiming for the same quality of architecture and majesty of scale as venerable older lodges, the Rimrock offers a massive glass-fronted lobby that's lined with cherry wood, tiled with unpolished limestone flooring, and filled with inviting chairs and Oriental rugs. The stone fireplace, open on two sides, is so large that staff members step inside it to ready the kindling. Guest rooms are large and well appointed with handsome furnishings; some have balconies. Standard rooms are all the same size; their prices vary only depending on the view. The suites are truly large, with balconies, wet bars, and cozy couches.

300 Mountain Ave. (5km/3 miles south of Banff), P.O. Box 1110, Banff, AB T1L 1J2. 𝓒 **800/661-1587** or 403/762-3356. Fax 403/762-1842 4132. www.rimrockresort.com. 346 units. C$400–C$550 (US$400–US$550/£200–£275) double; C$550–C$1,300 (US$550–US$1,300/£275–£650) suite. AE, DC, DISC, MC, V. Valet parking C$18 (US$18/£9); C$10 (US$10/£5) self-parking in heated garage. C$25 (US$25/£13) Resort Package includes valet parking, wireless Internet, and access to business center and fitness center. **Amenities:** 2 restaurants; 2 bars; pool; squash court; gym; hot tub; 24-hr. concierge; 24-hr. business center; boutiques; 24-hr. room service; massage; babysitting; laundry service; same-day dry cleaning. *In room:* A/C, TV w/pay movies and video games, dataport, minibar, coffeemaker, hair dryer, iron.

Thea's House 🕊   The most upscale and elegant bed-and-breakfast in Banff, Thea's is a modern home that was designed as a B&B. Just a 2-minute walk from downtown, this striking log-and-stone structure boasts 8m (26-ft.) ceilings, antiques and exquisite artwork, and discreet and friendly service. Guest rooms are all very large and beautifully outfitted, with vaulted pine ceilings, fir floors, rustic pine and antique furniture, fireplaces, sitting areas, cassette and CD players, and private balconies. All guests have access to a lounge area with a stocked minibar and refrigerator and a coffee and tea service; a full breakfast is included in the rates. Ski packages are also available. "Elegant Alpine" is how Thea's describes itself, and you'll have no trouble imagining yourself in a fairy-tale mountain lodge. It is the perfect spot for a romantic getaway.

138 Otter St. (Box 1237), Banff, AB T1L 1B2. 𝓒 **403/762-2499.** Fax 403/762-2496. www.theashouse.com. 3 units. C$250–C$275 (US$250–US$275/£125–£138) double. 3-night minimum stay in summer and winter holidays. Rates include full breakfast. MC, V. **Amenities:** Complimentary health club pass available; bike rental. *In room:* TV/DVD, stereo, hair dryer, iron, gas fireplace.

Expensive

Banff Aspen Lodge 🕊 *Value*   Located a 5-minute walk from downtown, the Banff Aspen is a very well-maintained motel that offers reasonably good value for the dollar—remember, this is Banff. Rooms are quite large and pleasantly decorated, all with twin vanities and king- or queen-size beds. Some are divided into two sleeping areas by the bathroom, a great configuration for families or groups. Most units have balconies or patio access.

401 Banff Ave., Banff, AB T1L 1A9. 𝓒 **877/886-6660** or 403/762-4401. Fax 403/762-5905. www.banffaspenlodge.com. 89 units. C$166–C$238 (US$166–US$238/£83–£119) double. Rates include continental breakfast. AE MC, V. **Amenities:** Hot tub; sauna; steam room; wireless Internet access; gift shop; coin-op laundry. *In room:* TV, wireless Internet access, coffeemaker, hair dryer, iron, kettle.

Banff Boutique Inn   Formerly the Pensione Tannenhof, this rambling historic home in a quiet neighborhood is just an 8-minute stroll along the Bow River from downtown. The original structure was constructed in the 1940s by a Calgary businessman with a large family, and the built-in hominess still shows through. Most rooms are quite large, with a mix of bed configurations, making this a good choice for families, who are welcome. Two rooms have fireplaces, and all have either en suite or private bathrooms. In a separate chalet at the back of the inn are two large rooms each with two queen beds, both with a fireplace and jetted tub. All have been updated, repainted, and refurnished in 2007. The home's original living room, an expansive room with fireplace and comfy couches, is a great place to relax and trade stories with other travelers.

121 Cave Ave. (P.O. Box 1870), Banff, AB T1L 1B7. (€ **403/762-4636.** Fax 403/762-5660. www.banffboutiqueinn. com. 10 units. C$150–C$300 (US$150–US$300/£75–£150) double. Extra person C$20 (US$20/£10). Rates include full breakfast. MC, V. **Amenities:** Jacuzzi; sauna; coin-op laundry. *In room:* Plasma TV.

Banff Inn   One of the newer accommodations in Banff, the Banff Inn is a very handsome, mountain lodge–like structure. Like most of the other hotels along the Banff Avenue strip, the illusion of the lodge ends at the lobby—rooms are comfortable, nicely furnished, and identical to corporate hotel rooms across North America, except that some units have private balconies and fireplaces. Facilities include a breakfast-only coffee shop and heated underground parking. The Banff Inn is located about a mile from downtown. The inexpensive Banff Bus has a stop right outside the hotel, with frequent transport to the city center.

P.O. Box 1018, 501 Banff Ave., Banff, AB T1L 1A9. (€ **800/667-1464** or 403/762-8844. Fax 403/762-4418. www. banffinn.com. 99 units. C$169–C$202 (US$169–US$202/£85–£101) double. Extra person C$15 (US$15/£7.50). Children under 13 stay free in parent's room. Early-bird specials available. AE, MC, V. **Amenities:** Breakfast room; Jacuzzi; sauna. *In room:* A/C, TV, hair dryer.

Fox Hotel & Suites   This new hotel along Banff Avenue offers a stylized take on the country lodge aesthetic so prevalent in Banff—and it offers the town's most notable hot pool, an underground grotto inspired by the original Cave and Basin hot springs that were responsible for Banff's founding. The Fox has a stylish lobby, complete with a waterfall, paneled-wood walls, and Mission-style furniture, and, as the staff will remind you, quite possibly the nicest Chili's restaurant on the planet.

There are a bewildering number of room types and suites, in part because the units can be configured to the individual needs of groups and families. Bedrooms can be rented as simple hotel rooms, or they can be opened up to adjacent rooms to form larger multibedroom suites that can sleep up to eight. Suites come with handsome efficiency kitchens and living rooms with quality furniture, fireplaces and stone counters—and depending on your needs, up to two bedrooms. The individual bedrooms can be small if rented without the kitchen and living room suites, but that's not an issue if you're in Banff to get outdoors. And if you step up to a full suite, you've got Banff's newest rooms and more space than most urban apartments; the loft suites are especially nice.

461 Banff Ave. (Box 1070) Banff, AB T1L 1B1. (€ **800/661-8310** or 403/760-8500. Fax 403/762-4763. www.best ofbanff.com/fox. 116 units. C$174–C$399 (US$174–US$399/£87–£200) double. AE, MC, V. Free parking. **Amenities:** Restaurant; lounge; grotto hot pool. *In room:* A/C, TV/DVD, stereo/MP3 player hookup, coffeemaker, iron.

Hidden Ridge Resort   Up on Tunnel Mountain, a 5-minute drive above downtown Banff, is a collection of condo developments of various ages and levels of sophistication. These properties are popular because they are out of the busy center of Banff and they offer large units that can accommodate large families and groups. One collection, Hidden Ridge Resort, is undergoing a renovation and general spiffing-up, but offers some excellent deals for travelers who want self-catering accommodations. Condos range from one-bedroom units with king beds to two-bedroom condos with lofts that comfortably sleep eight—even before opening out the sofa bed. All units have full maplewood kitchens with granite counters, stone fireplace, dining area, living room, and balcony or patio. Added features include a giant outdoor hot tub, a covered barbecue area available to all guests, and incredible views onto Mount Rundle.

901 Hidden Ridge Way, Banff, AB T1L 1H8 📞 800/661-1372 or 403/762-3544. www.bestofbanff.com/hrr. 94 units. C$199–C$239 (US$199–US$239/£100–£120) double. AE, MC, V. Free parking. **Amenities:** Hot tub; barbecue. *In room:* TV, kitchen, coffeemaker, hair dryer.

Moderate

Blue Mountain Lodge
This rambling place east of downtown began its life in 1908 as a boardinghouse. As you may expect in an older building constructed at the edge of the wilderness, the bedrooms were never exactly palatial to begin with—and when the rooms were redesigned to include private bathrooms, they got even smaller. That's the bad news. The good news is that the lodge is full of charm and funny nooks and crannies. Those small rooms just mean that you'll be spending time with new friends in the lounge and common kitchen. Sound familiar? The owner admits that guests refer to the Blue Mountain Lodge as an upscale hostel, and it's an accurate characterization. Whatever you call it, it's one of the least expensive and friendliest places to stay in central Banff. Breakfast is served buffet-style, or you can cook up some eggs on your own. Many guests here are avid outdoorsy types, making this a great place to stay if you're on your own and would appreciate meeting other people to hike with. The staff is young, friendly, and eager to help you get out on the trails.

137 Muskrat St. (Box 2763), Banff, AB T1L 1C4. 📞 403/762-5134. Fax 403/762-8081. www.bluemtnlodge.com. 10 units. From C$119–C$179 (US$119–US$179/£60–£90) double. Extra person C$10 (US$10/£5). Rates include continental breakfast and afternoon hot beverages and homemade cookies. Extended-stay discounts available. MC, V. Free off-street parking. *In room:* TV.

Homestead Inn *(Value)*
One of the best lodging deals in Banff is the Homestead Inn, only a block from all the action on Banff Avenue. Though the amenities are modest compared to upscale alternatives, the rooms are tastefully furnished and equipped with armchairs and stylish bathrooms. Factor in the free downtown parking and this well-maintained older motel seems all the more enticing.

217 Lynx St., Banff, AB T1L 1A7. 📞 800/661-1021 or 403/762-4471. Fax 403/762-8877. www.homesteadinnbanff.com. 27 units. C$139 (US$139/£70) double. Extra person C$10 (US$10/£5). Children under 12 stay free in parent's room. AE, MC, V. **Amenities:** Family restaurant. *In room:* TV, fridge, hair dryer, coffeemaker.

Mountain Home Bed & Breakfast *(★)*
If you're looking for a bit of historic charm coupled with modern comforts, this excellent B&B may be it. It was originally built as a tourist lodge in the 1940s, and then served as a private home for years before being restored and turned back into a guesthouse. The present decor manages to be evocative without being too fussy. The bedrooms are airy and nicely furnished with quality furniture and antiques; all have an en suite bathroom and telephone. Especially nice is the cozy Rundle Room, with its own slate fireplace. Breakfast is a full cooked meal with homemade baked goods. Downtown Banff is just a 2-minute walk away.

129 Muskrat St. (P.O. Box 272), Banff, AB T1L 0A4. 📞 403/762-3889. Fax 403/762-3254. www.mountainhomebb.com. 3 units. C$135–C$175 (US$135–US$175/£68–£88) double. Extra person C$20 (US$20/£10). Rates include full breakfast. MC, V. *In room:* TV/VCR w/pay movies, dataport, wireless Internet access, hair dryer, iron.

Red Carpet Inn *Value*   A handsome brick building with a balcony along the top floors, the Red Carpet Inn is located along the long, hotel-lined street leading to downtown. Well maintained and more than adequately furnished, this is one of the best deals in Banff. Guest rooms are furnished with easy chairs and desks. There's no restaurant, but an excellent one is right next door. The entire facility is shipshape and very clean—just the thing if you don't want to spend a fortune.

425 Banff Ave., Banff, AB T1L 1B6. © 800/563-4609 or 403/762-4184. Fax 403/762-4894. www.banffredcarpet.com. 52 units. C$140–C$175 (US$140–US$175/£70–£88) double. Rates include continental breakfast. AE, MC, V. Free parking. **Amenities:** Hot tub. *In room:* A/C, TV, free wireless Internet access, fridge, coffeemaker, hair dryer.

Rocky Mountain B&B *Kids* *Value*   A former boardinghouse converted into a B&B, this pleasant and rambling inn offers comfortable, clean, and cozy rooms and a location just a few minutes from downtown. Accommodations have a mix of private and shared bathrooms. Four units have kitchenettes. Families are welcome.

223 Otter St. (Box 2528), Banff, AB T1L 1C3. ©/fax 403/762-4811. www.rockymtnbb.com. 10 units. C$100–C$160 (US$100–US$160/£50–£80) double. Extra person C$15 (US$15/£7.50). Rates include breakfast. MC, V. Closed Dec 1–April 30. *In room:* TV.

Inexpensive
Banff Y Mountain Lodge (YWCA) *Value*   The YWCA is a bright, modern building with good amenities, just across the Bow River bridge from downtown. The Y welcomes both genders—singles, couples, and family groups—with accommodations in private or dorm rooms. Some units have private bathrooms. On-site are a guest laundry and an assembly room with a TV.

102 Spray Ave. (P.O. Box 520), Banff, AB T1L 1A6. © 800/813-4138 or 403/760-3207. Fax 403/760-3202. www.ymountainlodge.com. 80 beds, 43 private rooms. C$31 (US$31/£16) bunk in dorm room (linens included); C$80–C$160 (US$80–US$160/£40–£80) double. MC, V. Free parking. **Amenities:** Restaurant; common room w/TV; Internet terminal; coin-op laundry; lockers.

HI-Banff Alpine Centre   With a mix of two-, four-, and six-bed rooms, this hostel is the most pleasant budget lodging in Banff. Couple and family rooms are available. Facilities include a recreation room, kitchen, laundry, and lounge with fireplace. Meals are available at the Cougar Pete's Kitchen and Lookout; there's also an on-site pub. Reserve at least a month in advance for summer stays.

On Tunnel Mountain Rd., 1.6km (1 mile) west of Banff (P.O. Box 1358), Banff, AB T1L 1B3. © 866/762-4122 or 403/760-7580. Fax 403/762-3441. www.hihostels.ca. 216 beds. C$30 (US$30/£15) members; C$34 (US$34/£17) nonmembers. Private rooms available. MC, V. **Amenities:** Restaurant; access to health club across the street; bike rental; activities desk; free wireless Internet access; coin-op laundry. *In room:* No phone.

WHERE TO DINE
Food is generally good in Banff, although you pay handsomely for what you get. The difference in price between a simply okay meal in a theme restaurant and a nice meal in a classy dining room can be quite small. Service is often indifferent, as many restaurant staff members have become used to waiting on the in-and-out-in-a-hurry tour-bus crowds. An abundance of eateries line Banff Avenue, and most hotels have at least one dining room. The following recommendations are just a sample of what's available in a very concentrated area.

Expensive
Bison Mountain Bistro & General Store CANADIAN   This recently opened two-story restaurant in downtown Banff has developed a loyal following for its "Rocky Mountain comfort food." On the ground floor is the "general store," a small deli with

a good selection of meats and cheeses plus a variety of canned house-made pickles and relishes to purchase as gifts; this is a good spot for a lunchtime sandwich. The atmosphere changes as you climb the stairs to the dining room, dominated by an open kitchen and cathedral ceilings, with a pleasant side deck. As you'd expect in a restaurant named Bison, game meat reigns. At lunch, there's a choice of beef, bison, and elk burgers in addition to a smoked bison pizza, though for those interested in sources of protein that didn't start off as wildlife, there are lighter dishes. On the evening menu, in addition to steaks, chops, and lamb dishes, are seared scallops and locally smoked bacon served with stewed navy beans and tomato-leek fondue, plus roast chicken suprêmes with creamed potatoes and preserved peach *jus*.

211 Bear St. © **403/762-5550**. www.thebison.ca. Main courses C$19–C$34 (US$19–US$34/£10–£17). Mon–Fri 11am–9pm; Sat–Sun 10am–3pm and 6–9pm.

Buffalo Mountain Lodge ★★ NEW CANADIAN   One of the most pleasing restaurants in Banff, the dining room at the Buffalo Mountain Lodge occupies half of the lodge's soaring, three-story lobby, set in a quiet wooded location just outside town. As satisfying as all this is to the eye and the spirit, the food here is even more notable. The chef brings together the best of regional ingredients—Alberta beef, lamb, pheasant, venison, trout, and B.C. salmon—and prepares each in a seasonally changing, contemporary style. Roasted wild salmon with rhubarb maple compote and citrus couscous was one evening's standout. The fireplace-dominated bar is a lovely place for an intimate cocktail.

1.5km (1 mile) west of Banff on Tunnel Mountain Rd. © **403/762-2400**. www.buffalomountainlodge.com. Reservations recommended on weekends. Main courses C$22–C$48 (US$22–US$48/£11–£24). AE, DC, MC, V. Daily 6–10pm.

Fuze Finer Dining ★★ INTERNATIONAL   This welcome addition to the Banff dining scene brings together bold flavors and sophisticated preparations. While "fuze" suggests fusion cuisine, in fact most preparations are updates on French cooking, though a number of tempting dishes reflect Asian influences. Start your meal with Masala prawns with mango in a pappadum basket or a fricassee of escargot and oyster mushrooms. Or slurp up some bivalves from the oyster bar. Butter-poached lobster comes with pesto risotto and tomato marmalade, and Alberta beef tenderloin is served with foie gras, oxtails, and truffled Madeira sauce. The dining room is chic and modern; a lighter menu is available in the lounge.

110 Banff Ave. (2nd floor). © **403/760-0853**. www.fuzedining.com. Reservations recommended. Main courses C$27–C$39 (US$27–US$39/£14–£20). AE, MC, V. Mon–Sat 4:30–10pm; Sun 10:30am–2pm and 4:30–10pm.

Grizzly House FONDUE   Grizzly House has nothing to do with bears except a rustic log-cabin atmosphere. The specialty here is fondue—from cheese to hot chocolate, and everything in between, including seafood, rattlesnake, frogs' legs, alligator, and buffalo fondue. Steaks and game dishes are the Grizzly's other specialty. The setting is frontier Banff, not the Swiss shtick you may expect from a fondue palace, and the fare excellent.

207 Banff Ave. © **403/762-4055**. Fax 403/762-4359. http://banffgrizzlyhouse.com. A la carte fondue for 2 C$27–C$80 (US$27–US$80/£14–£40). AE, MC, V. Daily 11:30am–midnight.

Maple Leaf Grille & Spirits ★★★ NEW CANADIAN   This excellent restaurant serves innovative cuisine based on Canadian produce and meats, particularly game. For regionally focused fine dining, the Maple Leaf is tops in Banff. The dining rooms

and bar, all wood-paneled with river-rock columns, occupy two stories in the very center of Banff, and are linked by a long open staircase. The seasonally changing menu features whimsical game meat "sliders"—three bite-size burgers made from elk, bison, and venison meat, while the game meat platter, piled with house-made pâtés and cured meats, Canadian cheeses, and pickled vegetables, is a more traditional starter. The highly recommended house specialty is seared organic bison tenderloin, wrapped with double-smoked bacon and sprinkled with local blue-cheese crumbles. Vegetarians aren't forgotten: Eggplant with forest mushroom ragout is a hearty match for any of the meat dishes. The 600-vintage-strong wine list, winner of a Best of the Best award from *Wine Spectator* magazine, is equally impressive.

137 Banff Ave. (C) 403/760-7680. www.banffmapleleaf.com. Reservations recommended. C$17–C$42 (US$17–US$42/£8.50–£21). AE, MC, V. Daily 11am–11pm, limited menu until 2am.

Moderate

Balkan Restaurant GREEK   You'll find this airy blue-and-white dining room up a flight of stairs, with windows overlooking the street below. The fare consists of reliable Hellenic favorites, well prepared and served with a flourish; pasta and steaks are available as well. The Greek platter for two consists of a small mountain of beef souvlaki, ribs, moussaka, lamb chops, tomatoes, and salad. If you're dining alone, you can't do better than the *lagos stifado* (rabbit stew) with onions and red wine.

120 Banff Ave. (C) 403/762-3454. Reservations recommended. Main courses C$12–C$25 (US$12–US$25/£6–£13). AE, MC, V. Daily 11am–11pm.

Coyotes Deli & Grill *&* SOUTHWEST/MEDITERRANEAN   One of the few places in Banff where you can find lighter, healthier food that's also delicious, Coyote's is an attractive bistrolike restaurant with excellent contemporary Southwestern cuisine. There's a broad selection of vegetarian dishes, as well as fresh fish, grilled meats, and multiethnic dishes prepared with an eye to spices and full flavors. At the deli you can pick up the makings for a picnic and head to the park. This is a very popular place, so go early or make reservations if you don't want to stand in line.

206 Caribou St. (C) 403/762-3963. Reservations recommended. Main courses C$14–C$25 (US$14–US$25/£7–£13). AE, DC, MC, V. Daily 7:30am–11pm.

Giorgio's Trattoria ITALIAN   Giorgio's is a cozy eatery with an Italian country-inn theme. Giorgio's serves authentic old-country specialties at reasonable prices. Entrees range from pizza with smoked salmon, to *osso buco* and Genoa fish stew. Don't miss the *gnocchi alla piemontese* (potato dumplings in meat sauce).

219 Banff Ave. (C) 403/762-5114. Reservations accepted for groups of 8 or more. Main courses C$12–C$26 (US$12–US$26/£6–£13). MC, V. Daily 5–10pm.

Magpie & Stump Restaurant & Cantina *&* MEXICAN   The false-fronted Magpie & Stump doesn't really match up architecturally with the rest of smart downtown Banff—and neither does the food and atmosphere, thank goodness. The food here is traditional Mexican and Tex-Mex, done up with style and heft: Someone in the kitchen sure knows how to handle a tortilla. This isn't high cuisine, just well-prepared favorites such as enchiladas, tamales, tacos, and the like. Barbecued ribs and chicken are also delicious. Meals are well priced compared to those elsewhere in town, and you won't leave hungry. The interior looks like a dark and cozy English pub, except for the buffalo heads and cactus plants everywhere—along with a lot of Southwest kitsch. The Cantina is a good place for a lively late-night drink, as the town's young summer waitstaff likes to crowd in here to unwind with an after-shift beverage—usually a beer served in a jam jar.

203 Caribou St. ℭ 403/762-4067. Reservations accepted for groups of 10 or more. Main courses C$10–C$24 (US$10–US$24/£5–£12). AE, MC, V. Daily noon–2am.

Inexpensive

If you're really on a budget, you'll probably get used to the deli case at **Safeway,** at Martin and Elk streets, as even inexpensive food is costly here. There's also a food court in the basement of **Cascade Plaza mall,** at Banff and Wolf streets. Other favorites for cheap and quick food include **Evelyn's Coffee Bar,** 201 Banff Ave. (ℭ 403/762-0352), for great home-baked muffins and rolls; the **Jump Start Coffee and Sandwich Place,** 206 Buffalo St. (ℭ 403/762-0332), which offers sandwiches, soup, salads, pastries, and picnics to go; and **Aardvark Pizza,** 304a Caribou St. (ℭ **403/762-5500**), open daily to 4am for all-day and all-night pizza.

Bruno's Cafe and Grill CANADIAN   Named for Bruno Engler, a famed outdoor guide and photographer, Bruno's serves burgers, pizza, wraps, and hearty Canadian-style entrees—all best washed down with locally brewed draft beer. This cozy and casual little joint is open late, a rarity in Banff.

304 Caribou St. ℭ **403/762-8115**. Reservations not accepted. Main courses C$8–C$15 (US$8–US$15/£4–£8). MC, V. Daily 7am–1am.

Melissa's Restaurant and Bar CANADIAN   Banff's original hostelries weren't all as grand as the Banff Springs Hotel. There was also the Homestead Inn, established in the 1910s, with its much-loved restaurant, Melissa's. The original hotel has been replaced with a more modern structure, but the half-timbered cabin that houses Melissa's remains. The food has been updated a bit in the last century, but old-fashioned, traditionally Canadian foods still dominate the menu. Breakfasts are famed, especially the apple hotcakes. Lunch and dinner menus feature burgers, sandwiches, local trout, and steaks.

218 Lynx St. ℭ **403/762-5511**. Reservations recommended. Main courses C$8–C$27 (US$8–US$27/£4–£14). AE, MC, V. Daily 7am–10pm.

BANFF AFTER DARK

Most of Banff's larger hotels and restaurants offer some form of nightly entertainment. However, for a more lively selection, head to downtown's Banff Avenue.

One of the best spots is the legendary **Wild Bill's Saloon,** 203 Banff Ave. (ℭ **403/762-0333**), where you can watch tourists in cowboy hats learning to line dance. Alt-rock bands dominate on Monday and Tuesday evenings; Wednesday through Saturday, it's all country rock, all the time. The venerable **Rose and Crown Pub,** 202 Banff Ave. (ℭ **403/762-2121**), used to be the only place to hear live music in Banff. It's still one of the best. Bands range from Celtic to folk to rock. In summer, sit on the rooftop bar and watch the stars. Popular with foreign tourists, **The Barbary Coast,** 119 Banff Ave. (ℭ **403/762-4616**), is a California-style bar and restaurant that features live music among the potted plants. Bands range from '80s cover bands to light jazz.

It took the ultracool cocktail lounge format awhile to reach Banff, but here it is: **Aurora,** 110 Banff Ave. (ℭ **403/760-5300**). Dance nightly to DJ-spun rock while sipping something delicious in a martini glass. Banff's most popular dance club, **HooDoo Lounge,** 137 Banff Ave. (ℭ **403/762-8434**), is in the basement of the old King Eddy Hotel. DJs spin the tunes while young white-water guides chat and dance with impressionable young tourists. Thursday night is ladies' night.

LAKE LOUISE ✿✿✿

Deep-green Lake Louise, 56km (35 miles) northwest of Banff and surrounded by snowcapped mountains, is one of the most famed beauty spots in a park renowned for its scenery. The village in the valley below the lake has developed into a resort destination in its own right. Lake Louise boasts one of the largest ski areas in Canada and easy hiking access to the remote high country along the Continental Divide.

The lake may be spectacular, but probably as many people wind up the road to Lake Louise to see its most famous resort, the Fairmont Chateau Lake Louise. Built by the Canadian Pacific Railroad, the Chateau is, along with the Banff Springs Hotel, one of the most celebrated hotels in Canada. More than just a lodging, this storybook castle—perched a mile high in the Rockies—is the center of recreation, dining, shopping, and entertainment for the Lake Louise area.

In case you were wondering, there's a reason the water in Lake Louise is so green: The stream water that tumbles into the lake is filled with minerals, ground by the glaciers that hang above the lake. Sunlight refracts off the glacial "flour," creating vivid colors. You'll want to at least stroll around the shore and gawk at the glaciers and the massive Chateau. The gentle **Lakeshore Trail** follows the northern shore to the end of Lake Louise. If you're looking for more exercise and even better views, continue on the trail as it begins to climb. Now called the **Plain of Six Glaciers Trail** ✿, it passes a teahouse 5km (3 miles) from the Chateau, and is open in summer only, on its way to a tremendous viewpoint over Victoria Glacier and Lake Louise.

SEEING THE SIGHTS

The **Lake Louise Summer Sightseeing Lift** (© **403/522-3555**) offers a 14-minute ride up to 2,088m (6,850 ft.) on Mt. Whitehorn, midway up the Lake Louise Ski Area. From here, the views of Lake Louise and the mountains along the Continental Divide are magnificent. Hikers can follow one of many trails into alpine meadows, visit the Wildlife Interpretation Centre, or join a free naturalist-led walk to explore the delicate ecosystem. Round-trip on the lift costs C$24 (US$24/£12) for adults, C$22 (US$22/£11) for seniors and students, and C$12 (US$12/£6) for children ages 6 to 15. The lift operates from mid-May to mid-September. At the base, the Lodge of Ten Peaks offers buffet dining: ride-and-dine packages are available.

To many visitors, **Moraine Lake** ✿✿ is even more beautiful than Lake Louise, its more famous twin. Ten spirelike peaks, each over 3,000m (9,843 ft.) high, rise precipitously from the shores of this tiny gem-blue lake. It's an unforgettable sight, and definitely worth the short 13km (8-mile) drive from Lake Louise. A trail follows the lake's north shore to the mountain cliffs. There's also the Moraine Lake Lodge, which offers accommodations, meals, and canoe rentals.

WHERE TO STAY

Baker Creek Lodge ✿   Secluded and rustic, Baker Creek Lodge offers log-built lodge, cabin, and chalet accommodations just off the quiet Bow Valley Parkway (Hwy. 1A). This very charming, family-owned lodge resort sits right on the banks of Baker Creek amid firs and pines, and is the perfect destination for families who want their memories of Banff to be of mountains and woods, not the shopping precincts of Banff Townsite. Accommodations range from top-of-the-line one-bedroom Trapper's Cabins with wood-burning fireplace, double Jacuzzi, and a gas barbecue on the porch, to a selection of large chalets and suites that can comfortably sleep six. Call ahead and discuss your needs with the staff, as there are a number of room configurations; all have fireplaces, full or efficiency kitchens, decks, and locally built pine furniture.

Highway 1A, 15km (9 miles) east of Lake Louise, P.O. Box 66, Lake Louise, AB T0L 1E0. (© 403/522-3761. Fax 403/522-2270. www.bakercreek.com. 33 units. C$255–C$365 (US$255–US$365/£128–£183) double; C$220–C$330 (US$220–US$330/£110–£165) suite. Reduced off-season rates. AE, MC, V. **Amenities:** Restaurant; lounge; gym; steam room; sauna. *In room:* Kitchen, coffeemaker, fireplace, no phone.

Deer Lodge   The Chateau Lake Louise isn't the only historic lodge at the lake. Built in the 1920s, the original Deer Lodge was a teahouse for the early mountaineers who came to the area to hike (the original tearoom is now the Mount Fairview Dining Room and bar, offering Northwest cuisine). Although Lake Louise itself is a 3-minute stroll away, the charming Deer Lodge features a sense of privacy and solitude that the busy Chateau can't offer. Choose from three eras of rooms, all of which are unfussy and comfortable: small, basic rooms in the original lodge; larger rooms in the newer Tower Wing; and Heritage Rooms, the largest rooms in the newest wing. The handsome common rooms, particularly the bar and the log-and-stone sitting room, will create memories.

109 Lake Louise Dr., Lake Louise (P.O. Box 1598), Banff, AB T0L 0C0. (© 800/661-1595 or 403/522-3747. Fax 403/522-4222. www.deerlodgelakelouise.com. 73 units. C$185–C$265 (US$185–US$265/£93–£133) double. AE, MC, V. **Amenities:** Restaurant; lounge; rooftop Jacuzzi; sauna; coin-op laundry; dry cleaning. *In room:* TV.

The Fairmont Chateau Lake Louise 🌲🌲🌲   The Chateau Lake Louise is one of the best-loved hotels in North America—and one of the most expensive. If you want to splurge on only one place in the Canadian Rockies, make it this one—you won't be sorry.

This massive, formal structure is blue-roofed and turreted, furnished with Edwardian sumptuousness and alpine charm. Built in stages over the course of a century by the Canadian Pacific Railroad, the entire hotel was remodeled and upgraded in 1990, and now stays open year-round. The cavernous grand lobby, with its curious figurative chandeliers, gives way to a sitting room filled with overstuffed chairs and couches; these and other common areas overlook the Chateau's gardens and the deep blue-green lake in its glacier-hung cirque. The guest rooms' marble-tiled bathrooms, crystal barware, and comfy down duvets are indicative of the attention to detail and luxury you can expect here. The Chateau can sometimes feel like Grand Central Station—so many guests and so many visitors crowding into the hotel. But the guest rooms are truly sumptuous and the service highly professional. New construction in 2003 added a conference center and additional guest rooms to the Chateau.

Lake Louise, AB T0L 1E0. (© 800/441-1414 or 403/522-3511. Fax 403/522-3834. www.fairmont.com. 513 units. High season C$499–C$649 (US$499–US$649/£250–£325) double. Rates vary depending on whether you want a view of the lake or mountains. Off-season rates and packages available. Children under 17 stay free in parent's room. AE, DC, DISC, MC, V. Parking C$20 (US$20/£10) per day. **Amenities:** 9 restaurants in high season, including the exquisite Fairview Room and the jolly Walliser Stube Wine Bar (p. 597); 2 bars; indoor pool; exercise room; health club; Jacuzzi; sauna; bike and canoe rental; concierge; tour desk; business center; shopping arcade; salon; 24-hr. room service; massage; babysitting; laundry service; same-day dry cleaning; concierge-level rooms. *In room:* A/C, TV, dataport, minibar, coffeemaker, hair dryer, iron.

Lake Louise Inn   The Lake Louise Inn stands in a wooded 3-hectare (8-acre) estate at the base of the moraine, 7 driving minutes from the fabled lake. You'll stay in a room with forest all around and snowcapped mountains peering over the trees outside your window. The inn consists of five different buildings—a central lodge with pool, whirlpool, steam room, restaurant, bar, and lounge, and four additional lodging units.

There are five different room types, starting with standard units with double beds. The superior queen and executive rooms in Building Five are the newest and nicest, with pine-railed balconies and sitting areas. For families, the superior lofts are capable of sleeping up to eight, with two bathrooms, full kitchen, living room and fireplace, and two separate bedrooms and a fold-out couch—just the ticket for a big group.

210 Village Rd. (P.O. Box 209), Lake Louise, AB T0L 1E0. © 800/661-9237 or 403/522-3791. Fax 403/522-2018. www.lakelouiseinn.com. 232 units. High season C$179–C$278 (US$179–US$278/£90–£139) double. AE, DC, MC, V. Free parking. **Amenities:** Restaurant; bar; pool; Jacuzzi; sauna; business center; coin-op laundry. *In room:* TV, high-speed Internet access, fridge, microwave, coffeemaker, hair dryer.

Moraine Lake Lodge   The only lodging at beautiful Moraine Lake is this handsome lakeside lodge. The original building houses eight basic rooms, each with two double beds. In the newer Wenkchemna Wing are six rooms with queen-size beds and fireplaces. The cabins contain either one king-size or two twin beds, plus a sunken seating area with fireplace. One suite is available as well, with a fireplace, Jacuzzi, king-size bed, and views over the lake. All accommodations are simply but nicely furnished with pine furniture. The dining room is open for three meals daily and serves excellent Northwest cuisine. Room rates include use of canoe rentals and naturalist presentations.

13km (8 miles) south of Lake Louise at Moraine Lake (Box 70), Banff, AB T0L 0C0. © 403/522-3733. Fax 403/522-3719. www.morainelake.com. 33 units. C$449–C$499 (US$449–US$499/£225–£250) double; C$559 (US$559/£280) suite; C$549 (US$549/£275) cabin. AE, MC, V. Open June to early Oct only. **Amenities:** 2 restaurants; bar; canoe rental; concierge. *In room:* Hair dryer, no phone.

Post Hotel 🎖🎖🎖   Discreetly elegant and beautifully furnished, this wonderful log hotel with a distinctive red roof began its life in 1942 as a humble ski lodge. Between 1988 and 1993, new owners completely rebuilt the old lodge, transforming it into one of the most luxurious getaways in the Canadian Rockies; in fact, the Post Hotel is one of only a few properties in western Canada that has been admitted into the Relais & Châteaux network. The entire lodge is built of traditional log-and-beam construction, preserving the rustic flavor of the old structure and of its mountain setting. The public rooms are lovely, from the renowned dining room (preserved intact from the original hotel) to the arched, two-story, wood-paneled library (complete with rolling track ladders and river-stone fireplace).

Accommodations throughout are beautifully furnished with rustic pine pieces and rich upholstery. Most units have stone fireplaces, balconies, and whirlpool tubs. Due to the rambling nature of the property, there are a bewildering 14 different layouts available. Families will like the "N" rooms, as each has a separate bedroom with queen-size bed, a loft with queen-size and twin beds, a fireplace, and balconies. The "F" units are fantastic, featuring a huge tiled bathroom with both shower and Jacuzzi, a separate bedroom, a large balcony, and a sitting area with couch, river-stone fireplace, and daybed. Amenities include a notably attractive glass-encased pool facility and a full-service spa. Hospitality and service here are top-notch.

P.O. Box 69, Lake Louise, AB T0L 1E0. © 800/661-1586 or 403/522-3989. Fax 403/522-3966. www.posthotel.com. 98 units. High season C$335–C$440 (US$335–US$440/£168–£220) double; C$570–C$825 (US$570–US$825/£285–£413) suite; C$380–C$715 (US$380–US$715/£190–£358) cabin. AE, MC, V. Closed mid Oct to late Nov. **Amenities:** Restaurant (see below); 2 bars; indoor pool; Jacuzzi; sauna; massage; babysitting; laundry service; dry cleaning. *In room:* TV/VCR, high-speed Internet access, hair dryer, iron, safe.

WHERE TO DINE
Lake Louise Station STEAKS/SEAFOOD   This handsome and historic log building served as the Lake Louise train station for nearly a century, before rail service

ceased in the 1980s. Guests now dine in the old waiting room, or enjoy a quiet drink in the old ticketing lobby. Two dining cars sit on the sidings beside the station and are open for fine dining in the evening. The most popular dish is rib-eye steak with whiskey-and–green peppercorn sauce, though fresh tuna loin with warm pineapple and coconut sauce provides a delicious change of pace.

200 Sentinel Rd. ⓒ **403/522-2600.** Reservations recommended on weekends. Pizzas C$15 (US$15/£7.50); steaks and seafood C$16–C$32 (US$16–US$32/£8–£16). AE, MC, V. Daily 11:30am–midnight.

Post Hotel Dining Room 𝍏𝍏𝍏 INTERNATIONAL   Let's face it: Your trip through the Canadian Rockies is costing you a lot more than you planned. But don't start economizing on food just yet, because the Post Hotel offers some of the finest dining in western Canada. The food was famous long before the rebuilding and renovation of the old hotel, but in recent years, the restaurant has maintained such a degree of excellence that it has won the highly prized endorsement of the French Relais & Châteaux organization; the 1,800-bottle wine list received the "Grand Award" from *Wine Spectator,* one of only four Canadian restaurants to win such an honor.

Guests dine in a long, rustic room with wood beams and windows looking out onto glaciered peaks. The menu focuses on full-flavored meat and fish preparations. For an appetizer, you might try Pacific marlin carpaccio with heirloom tomato tartar and three mustard sauces, and as a main course buffalo strip loin with blackberry–maple syrup butter and corn fritters. Desserts are equally imaginative. Service is excellent, as is the very impressive wine list: With 30,000 bottles in the cellar, there are even some good values discreetly hidden in the mostly French selection.

In the Post Hotel, Lake Louise. ⓒ **403/522-3989.** www.posthotel.com. Reservations required. Main courses C$30–C$52 (US$30–US$52/£15–£26). AE, MC, V. Daily 7–11am, 11:30am–2pm, and 5–10pm.

Walliser Stube Wine Bar 𝍏 SWISS   While the Chateau Lake Louise operates four major restaurants, including the formal Fairview Room, the most fun and relaxing place to eat is the Walliser Stube, a small dining room that serves excellent Swiss-style food and some of the best fondue ever. The back dining room is called the Library, and is indeed lined with tall and imposing wood cases and rolling library ladders. Happily, the cases are filled with wine, not books. A meal in the Walliser Stube is an evening's worth of eating and drinking, as the best foods—a variety of fondues and raclettes—make for convivial and communal dining experiences. The cheese fondue, C$33(US$33/£17) for two, is fabulous. Raclettes are another communal operation, involving heat lamps that melt chunks of cheese until bubbly; the aromatic, molten result is spread on bread. If hot cheese isn't your thing, the Walliser Stube also offers more traditional meat and chicken preparations. It's all great fun in a great atmosphere—go with friends and have a blast.

In Chateau Lake Louise. ⓒ **403/522-1817.** Reservations required. Main courses C$18–C$36 (US$18–US$36/ £9–£18); fondues for 2 C$33–C$48 (US$33–US$48/£17–£24). AE, DISC, MC, V. Daily 5–11:30pm.

THE ICEFIELDS PARKWAY 𝍏𝍏𝍏

Between Lake Louise and Jasper winds one of the most spectacular mountain roads in the world. Called the Icefields Parkway, the road climbs through three deep river valleys; beneath soaring, glacier-notched mountains; and past dozens of hornlike peaks shrouded with permanent snowfields. Capping this 287km (178-mile) route is the **Columbia Icefields,** a massive dome of glacial ice and snow straddling the top of the continent. From this mighty cache of ice—the largest nonpolar ice cap in the world—flow the Columbia, the Athabasca, and the North Saskatchewan rivers.

Although you can drive the Icefields Parkway in 3 hours, plan to take enough time to stop at eerily green lakes, hike to a waterfall, and take an excursion up onto the Columbia Icefields. There's also a good chance that you'll see wildlife: ambling bighorn sheep, mountain goats, elks with huge shovel antlers, and mama bears with cubs—all guaranteed to halt traffic and set cameras clicking.

After Lake Louise, the highway divides: Highway 1 continues west toward Golden, British Columbia, while Highway 93 (the Icefields Pkwy.) continues north along the Bow River. **Bow Lake,** the river's source, glimmers below enormous **Crowfoot Glacier;** when the glacier was named, a third "toe" was more in evidence, lending a resemblance to a bird's claw. Roadside viewpoints look across the lake at the glacier. **Num-Ti-Jah Lodge,** on the shores of Bow Lake, is a good place to stop for lunch and to take some photographs; this venerable lodge also offers lodging in traditional guest rooms.

The road mounts Bow Summit and drops into the North Saskatchewan River drainage. Stop at the **Peyto Lake Viewpoint** and hike up a short but steep trail to glimpse this startling blue-green body of water. The North Saskatchewan River collects its tributaries at the little community of Saskatchewan River Crossing; thousands of miles later, the Bow and Saskatchewan rivers will join and flow east through Lake Winnipeg to Hudson Bay.

The parkway then begins to climb up in earnest toward the Sunwapta Pass. Here, in the shadows of 3,490m (11,450-ft.) **Mount Athabasca,** the icy tendrils of the **Columbia Icefields** come into view. However impressive these glaciers may seem from the road, they're nothing compared to the massive amounts of centuries-old ice and snow hidden by mountain peaks; the Columbia Icefields cover nearly 518 sq. km (200 sq. miles) and are more than 760m (2,500 ft.) thick. From the parkway, the closest fingers of the ice field are **Athabasca Glacier,** which fills the horizon to the west of the **Columbia Icefields Centre** (✆ 780/852-7032), a recently rebuilt lodge with a restaurant open from 8am to 10pm and double rooms starting at C$235 (US$235/£118). The **Icefields Information Centre** (✆ 780/852-7030), a park service office that answers questions about the area, stands beside the lodge. It's open May 1 to June 14 daily from 9am to 5pm, June 15 to September 7 daily from 9am to 6pm, and September 8 to October 15 daily from 9am to 5pm. It is closed October 16 to April 30.

From the **Brewster Snocoach Tours** ticket office (✆ 403/762-6735), specially designed buses with balloon tires take visitors out onto the face of the glacier. The 90-minute excursion includes a chance to hike the surface of Athabasca Glacier. The Snowcoach Tour is C$38 (US$38/£19) for adults and C$19 (US$19/£10) for children. If you don't have the time for the tour, you can drive to the toe of the glacier and walk up onto its surface. Use extreme caution when on the glacier; tumbling into a crevasse can result in broken limbs or even death.

From the Columbia Icefields, the parkway descends steeply into the Athabasca River drainage. From the parking area for **Sunwapta Falls,** travelers can choose to crowd around the chain-link fence and peer at this turbulent falls, or take the half-hour hike to equally impressive but less crowded Lower Sunwapta Falls. **Athabasca Falls,** farther north along the parkway, is another must-see. Here, the wide and powerful Athabasca River constricts into a roaring torrent before dropping 25m (82 ft.) into a narrow canyon. A mist-covered bridge crosses the chasm just beyond the falls; a series of trails lead to more viewpoints. The parkway continues along the Athabasca River, through a landscape of meadows and lakes, before entering the Jasper Townsite.

WHERE TO STAY

Facilities are few along the parkway. Hikers and bikers will be pleased to know that there are **rustic hostels** at Mosquito Creek, Rampart Creek, Hilda Creek, Beauty Creek, Athabasca Falls, and Mount Edith Cavell. Reservations for all Icefields Parkway hostels can be made by calling © **866/762-4122.** A shuttle runs between the Calgary International Hostel and hostels in Banff, Lake Louise, and along the Icefields Parkway to Jasper. You must have reservations at the destination hostel to use the service. Call © **403/283-5551** for more information.

Simpson's Num-Ti-Jah Lodge   Many Rocky Mountain hotels are newly constructed to look vintage—Num-Ti-Jah Lodge is the real thing. Sitting on the edge of Bow Lake, with a view of glaciers and soaring peaks to rival that at Lake Louise, this beloved lodge with a bright red roof had its beginnings when pioneering outfitter Jimmy Simpson stood on this site in 1898 and vowed one day to "build a shack here." Over the next 50 years, Simpson and his family did just that, though the handsome log-and-stone lodge now presiding over this astonishing vista is quite a bit more than a shack.

Num-Ti-Jah Lodge (from a First Nation word for pine marten) breathes frontier tradition with its huge stone fireplaces, stuffed moose heads and antlers on the log walls, and cozy library and lounge areas amply supplied with comfy chairs and couches. Num-Ti-Jah is best for those who appreciate the heritage of a traditional lodge: Some will be charmed; others will consider this roughing it. Don't expect upscale guest rooms; though they are clean and nicely furnished, they are authentic to the period in which they were built. All but five rooms have private bathrooms. The dining room is a wonderful spot for lunch, and three-course dinners are available for C$60 (US$60/£30) in addition to a la carte dining.

40km/25 miles north of Lake Louise on Hwy. 93, P.O. Box 39, Lake Louise AB T0L 1E0. © **403/522-2167.** Fax 403/522-2425. www.num-ti-jah.com. 25 units. C$195–C$300 (US$195–US$300/£98–£150) double. Extra person C$15 (US$15/£7.50). MC, V. Closed mid-Oct to early Dec. **Amenities:** Restaurant; lounge with pool table; gift shop. *In room:* No phone.

8 Jasper National Park: Canada's Largest Mountain Park ★★

Jasper, Canada's largest mountain park, was established in 1907. Slightly less busy than Banff to the south, Jasper Park attracts a much more outdoors-oriented crowd, with hiking, biking, climbing, horseback riding, and rafting the main activities. Sure, there is shopping and fine dining in Jasper, but it's not the focus of activity, as in Banff. Travelers seem a bit more determined and rugged-looking, as if they've just stumbled in from a long-distance hiking trail or off the face of a rock—certainly there's no shortage of outdoor recreation here.

For more information on the park, contact **Jasper National Park,** P.O. Box 10, Jasper, AB T0E 1E0 (© **780/852-6176;** www.pc.gc.ca).

SPORTS & OUTDOOR ACTIVITIES IN THE PARK

The **Jasper Adventure Centre,** 604 Connaught Dr. (© **800/565-7547** in western Canada, or 780/852-5595; www.jasperadventurecentre.com), is a clearinghouse of local outfitters and guides. White-water rafting and canoeing trips, horseback rides, guided hikes, and other activities can be arranged out of this office, which is open June 1 to October 1 daily from 9am to 9pm.

A number of shops rent most of the equipment you'll need. Mountain bikes, canoes and rafts, tents, fishing gear, and skis are available for rent from **On-Line Sport and Tackle,** 600 Patricia St. (© 780/852-3630), which can also set you up on guided rafting and fishing trips. Snowboards, cross-country ski equipment, and more bikes are available from **Freewheel Cycle,** 618 Patricia St. (© 780/852-3898).

FISHING   Currie's Guiding (© 780/852-5650; www.curriesguidingjasper.com), conducts fishing trips to beautiful Maligne Lake; the cost is C$149 (US$149/£75) per person (min. 2 people) for an 8-hour day. Tackle, bait, boat, and lunch are included. Ask about special single and group rates. Patricia and Pyramid lakes, north of Jasper, are more convenient to Jasper-based anglers who fancy trying their luck at trout fishing.

GOLF   The 18-hole course at **Jasper Park Lodge** ✿ (© 780/852-6090), east of Jasper Townsite, is one of the most popular and challenging courses in the Rockies, with 73 sand traps and other, more natural hazards—such as visiting wildlife. *Score* magazine ranked this the best golf course in Alberta.

HIKING   Overnight and long-distance hikers will find an abundance of backcountry trails around Jasper, reaching into some of the most spectacular scenery in the Canadian Rockies. Day hikers have fewer, but still good, choices.

The complex of trails around **Maligne Canyon** ✿ makes a good choice for a group, as there are a number of access points (across six different footbridges). The less keen can make the loop back and meet fellow hikers (after getting the car) farther down the canyon. Trails ring parklike Beauvert and Annette lakes (the latter is wheelchair accessible), both near Jasper Park Lodge. Likewise, Pyramid and Patricia lakes just north of town have loop trails but more of a backcountry atmosphere.

The brochure "Day Hikers' Guide to Jasper National Park" details dozens of hikes throughout the park. It costs C$1 (US$1/50p) at the visitor center. Several outfitters lead guided hikes; contact **Friends of Jasper National Park** (© 780/852-4767) or **Walk and Talks Jasper** (© 780/852-4945; www.walksntalks.com) for a selection of half- and full-day hikes.

If you plan on riding the Jasper Tramline to the top of Whistler's Peak, consider hiring naturalist Anne Williams of **Wild Routes** (© 403/852-5788; wildroutes@ incentre.net) to provide a natural history guided hike to the alpine meadows. In addition to learning to identify birds and plants, you'll learn about the fascinating sex life of wildflowers. A 3-hour tour is C$60 (US$60/£30).

HORSEBACK RIDING   One of the most exhilarating experiences the park can offer is trail riding. Guides take your riding prowess (or lack of it) into account and select trails slow enough to keep you mounted. The horses used are steady, reliable animals not given to sudden antics. For a short ride, call **Pyramid Stables** (© 780/852-7433), which offers 1- to 3-hour trips (C$40–C$85/US$40–US$85/£20–£43) around Pyramid and Patricia lakes.

Long-distance trail rides take you into the backcountry. **Skyline Trail Rides** (© 888/582-7787 or 780/852-4215; www.skylinetrail.com) offers a number of short day trips costing roughly C$40 (US$40/£20) per hour, as well as 3- to 4-day trips to a remote, albeit modernized, lodge. Sleigh rides are offered in winter.

RAFTING   Jasper is the jumping-off point for float and white-water trips down several rivers. A raft trip is a good option for that inevitable drizzly day, as you're going to get wet anyway. The mild rapids (Class II–III) of the wide Athabasca River make a

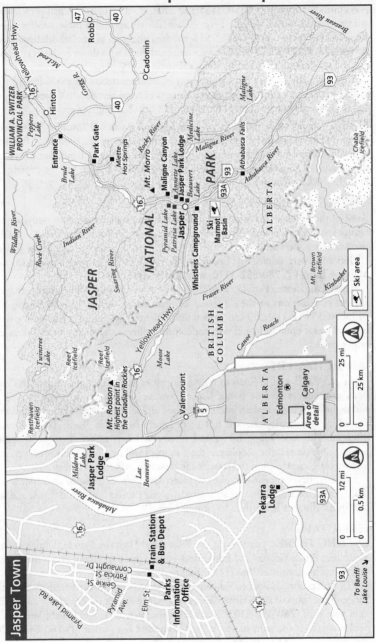

good introductory trip (C$55/US$55/£28 adult, children under 13 half price), while wilder runs down the Maligne River (Class III) will appeal to those needing something to brag about (C$85/US$85/£43, children under 13 half price). **Maligne River Adventures** (ⓒ 780/852-3370; www.mra.ab.ca) offers trips down both rivers, as well as a 3-day wilderness trip on the Kakwa River (Class IV-plus).

Trips generally include most equipment and transportation. Jasper is loaded with rafting outfitters; a stroll along the main streets of town reveals a half-dozen options. Or just ask your hotel concierge for advice and help booking a trip.

SKIING Jasper's downhill ski area is **Ski Marmot Basin** (ⓒ 780/852-3816; www. skimarmot.com), located 19km (12 miles) west of Jasper on Highway 93. Marmot is generally underrated as a ski resort; it doesn't get the crowds of Banff, nor does it get the infamous Chinook winds. The resort has 52 runs and seven lifts, and rarely any lines. Lift tickets start at C$63 (US$63/£32).

GETTING AROUND THE PARK

Some of the principal outfitters and guides also offer transportation to outlying park beauty spots. Leaving from Jasper, organized tours of the park's major sites—notably the Athabasca snowfields (C$110/US$110/£55) and a Maligne Lake cruise (C$60/US$60/£30)—are offered by **Brewster** (ⓒ 780/852-3332; www.brewster.ca) and **Maligne Tours** (ⓒ 780/852-3370; www.malignelake.com).

Beyond the Beaten Path (ⓒ 780/852-5650; www.jasperbeyondthebeatenpath.com) also offers excursions to these popular destinations, as well as trips to Miette Hot Springs (C$55/US$55/£28) and more intimate sightseeing, photography, wildlife viewing, and picnic options. In addition, the company offers a shuttle service for hikers and rafting parties.

JASPER TOWNSITE

Jasper isn't Banff, and to listen to most residents of Jasper, that's just fine with them. Born as a railroad division point, Jasper Townsite lacks its southern neighbor's glitz and slightly precious air of an internationalized alpine fantasyland. Instead, it gives off a lived-in, community-oriented feel that's largely lacking in Banff. The streets are thronged with avid young hikers and mountain bikers rather than the shopping hordes. Chances are, the people you meet in town will be a little muddy or wet, as if they've just gotten in from the river or the mountain. Chances are they have.

However, development is rapidly approaching: New nightclubs, restaurants, and shops geared toward tourists are springing up along Patricia Street, and that sound you hear in the distance is the thunder of tour buses.

ESSENTIALS

GETTING THERE   Jasper is on the Yellowhead Highway System, linking it with Vancouver, Prince George, and Edmonton—and is therefore an important transportation hub. The town is 287km (178 miles) northwest of Banff.

VIA Rail connects Jasper to Vancouver and Edmonton with three trains weekly; the Skeena line connects with Prince George and Prince Rupert on the Pacific coast. The train station (ⓒ 780/852-4102) is at the town center, along Connaught Street. Also headquartered at the train station is the **Greyhound** bus station (ⓒ 780/852-3926) and **Brewster Transportation** (ⓒ 780/852-3332), which offers express service to Banff, as well as a large number of sightseeing excursions.

VISITOR INFORMATION   For information on the townsite, contact **Jasper Tourism and Commerce,** P.O. Box 98, Jasper, AB T0E 1E0 (© **780/852-3858;** www.jaspercanadianrockies.com).

TOWN LAYOUT   Jasper Townsite is much smaller than Banff. The main street, **Connaught Drive,** runs alongside the Canadian National Railway tracks, and is the address of the majority of Jasper's hotels. **Patricia Street,** a block west, is quickly becoming the boutique street, with new shops and cafes springing up. Right in the center of town, surrounded by delightful shady gardens, is the **Parks Information Offices** (© **780/852-6146**). The post office is at the corner of Patricia and Elm streets. At the northern end of Connaught and Geike streets, about .5km (¼ mile) from downtown, is another complex of hotels.

GETTING AROUND   For a rental car, contact **National,** 607 Connaught Dr. (© **780/852-1117**). Call a taxi at © **780/852-5558** or 780/852-3600.

EXPLORING JASPER & ENVIRONS

Just northeast of Jasper, off the Jasper Park Lodge access road, the Maligne River drops from its high mountain valley to cut an astounding canyon into a steep limestone face on its way to meet the Athabasca River. The chasm of **Maligne Canyon** is up to 46m (150 ft.) deep at points, yet only 3m (10 ft.) across; the river tumbles through the canyon in a series of powerful waterfalls. A sometimes-steep trail follows the canyon down the mountainside, bridging the gorge six times. Interpretive signs describe the geology. In summer, a teahouse operates at the top of the canyon.

An incredibly blue mountain lake buttressed by a ring of high-flying peaks, **Maligne Lake** is 45 minutes east of Jasper, and is one of the park's great beauty spots. Maligne is the largest glacier-fed lake in the Rockies, and the second largest in the world. The Native Canadians, who called the lake Chaba Imne, had a superstitious awe of the region. White settlers didn't discover Maligne until 1908.

Today, droves of tour buses go to the "hidden lake," and the area is a popular destination for hikers, anglers, trail riders, and rafters. No matter what else they do, most visitors take a **boat cruise to Spirit Island,** at the head of the lake. The 90-minute cruise leaves from below the Maligne Lake Lodge, an attractive summer-only facility with a restaurant, bar, and gift shop (but no lodging). Cruise tickets cost C$43 (US$43/£22) for adults, C$22 (US$22/£11) for kids 6 to 12.

Maligne Lake waters are alive with rainbow and eastern brook trout, and the Maligne Lake Boathouse is stocked with licenses, tackle, bait, and boats. Guided **fishing** trips include equipment, lunch, and hotel transportation, with half-day excursions starting at C$180 (US$180/£90) per person for two or more, or C$319 (US$319/£160) solo. You can rent a boat, canoe, or sea kayak to ply the waters. All facilities at Maligne Lake, including lake cruises, fishing, trail rides, and a white-water raft outfitter that offers trips down three Jasper Park rivers, are operated by **Maligne Tours** (www.malignelake.com). Offices are located at the lake, next to the lodge in Jasper at 626 Connaught Dr. (© **780/852-3370**) and at the Jasper Park Lodge (© **780/852-4779**). Maligne Tours also operates a shuttle bus between Jasper and the lake.

Downstream from Maligne Lake, the Maligne River flows into **Medicine Lake.** This large body of water appears regularly every spring, grows 8km (5 miles) long and 18m (59 ft.) deep, and then vanishes in fall, leaving only a dry gravel bed through the winter. The reason for this annual wonder is a system of underground drainage caves.

The First Nations locals believed that spirits were responsible for the lake's annual disappearance, hence the name.

Jasper Tramway ⚲★ This aerial gondola tour starts at the foot of Whistler's Mountain, 6km (4 miles) south of Jasper off Highway 93. Each car takes 30 passengers (plus baby carriages, wheelchairs, and the family dog) and hoists them 2km (1¼ miles) up to the 2,250m (7,382-ft.) summit in a breathtaking sky ride. At the upper terminal, you'll step out into alpine tundra, the region above the tree line where some flowers take 25 years to blossom. A wonderful picnic area carpeted with mountain grass is alive with squirrels. You'll also see the "whistlers"—actually hoary marmots—that the mountain is named for. Combo tickets that include meals at the upper terminal's Treeline Restaurant are also available.

Off Hwy. 93, south of Jasper. ℂ 780/852-3093. www.jaspertramway.com. Tickets C$25 (US$25/£13) adults, C$13 (US$13/£6.50) children. Mid-April to mid-May and late Aug to mid-Oct. 10am–5pm; mid-May to late June 9:30am–6:30pm; late June to late Aug 9am–8pm. Cars depart every 10–15 min. Closed mid-Oct to mid-Apr.

Miette Hot Springs The hot mineral-water pools are only one reason to make the side trip to Miette Hot Springs. The drive is also one of the best wildlife-viewing routes in the park. Watch for elk, deer, coyotes, and moose en route. The springs can be enjoyed in a beautiful swimming pool or in two soaker pools (one is wheelchair accessible), surrounded by forest and an imposing mountain backdrop. Campgrounds and an attractive lodge with refreshments are nearby.

60k (37 miles) northeast of Jasper off Hwy. 16. ℂ 780/866-3939. Admission C$6.25 (US$6.25/£3.15) adults, C$5.25 (US$5.25/£2.65) children and seniors, C$18 (US$18/£9) families. June 22–Sept 9 daily 8:30am–10:30pm; May 11–June 21 and Sept 10–Oct 8 daily 10:30am–9pm.

SHOPPING

Weather can be unpredictable in Jasper. If it's raining, you can while away an afternoon in the town's shops and boutiques—the town is especially rich in shops for outdoor gear and recreation clothing. In Jasper itself, Patricia Street and Connaught Drive contain most of the high-quality choices. A number of galleries feature Inuit and Native arts and crafts: Check out **Our Native Land,** 601 Patricia St. (ℂ **780/852-5592**). The arcade at the Jasper Park Lodge, called the **Beauvert Promenade,** has a number of excellent clothing and gift shops.

WHERE TO STAY

As in Banff, there's a marked difference in rates between high season and the rest of the year, so if you can avoid the June-to-September crush, you may save up to 50%. All prices listed below are for high season. Call for off-season rates, as they usually follow a complex price structure. Reserve well in advance if possible.

If you find the prices too astronomical in Jasper, or just can't find a room, consider staying east of the park near Hinton (see below).

Very Expensive

Chateau Jasper Once the top (and most expensive) hotel in Jasper Townsite, the Chateau Jasper has gone through some upheavals in the last couple years, in the form of changed ownership and delayed maintenance. There's good news: Chateau Jasper has changed hands again, and is under new local ownership and is receiving a face-lift and some well-deserved attention to upkeep. The basics have always been good here: The guest rooms are large and comfortably furnished, and the indoor pool area is a jewel. With room rates reduced about 25% from their highs 2 years ago, this is good value for your lodging dollar.

96 Geikie St., Jasper, AB T0E 1E0. © 800/852-7737 or 780/852-5644. Fax 780/852-4860. www.mpljasper.com. 119 units. From C$225 (US$225/£113) double. AE, DC, DISC, MC, V. Parking C$8 (US$8/£4) per day. **Amenities:** Restaurant; bar; indoor pool; Jacuzzi; concierge; limited room service; babysitting; laundry service; same-day dry cleaning. *In room:* A/C, TV, high-speed Internet access, coffeemaker, hair dryer, safe.

The Fairmont Jasper Park Lodge ⨁
Jasper's most exclusive lodging, the Jasper Park Lodge was built by the Canadian Pacific Railroad and has an air of luxury and gentility, but with a more woodsy feel—sort of like an upscale summer camp. The hotel's wooded, elk-inhabited grounds—over 360 hectares! (900 acres)—are located along Lac Beauvert, about 8km (5 miles) east of Jasper proper. The central lodge's lofty great room offers huge fireplaces to snuggle by. Accommodations are very comfortable, though a bit hard to characterize, as there are a wide variety of cabins, lodge rooms, chalets, and cottages available—all from different eras, all set amid the forest. It's a good idea to call and find out what suits your budget and needs. Groups can opt for one of the wonderful housekeeping cabins, some of which have up to eight bedrooms.

P.O. Box 40, Jasper, AB T0E 1E0. © 800/441-1414 or 780/852-3301. Fax 780/852-5107. www.fairmont.com. 446 units. C$399–C$449 (US$399–US$449/£200–£225) double; from C$554 (US$554/£277) suite. AE, DC, DISC, MC, V. Free parking. **Amenities:** 9 restaurants, including the 4-star Edith Cavell Dining Room and the Moose's Nook Northern Grill (p. 611); 3 lounges; heated outdoor pool; one of Canada's finest golf courses (Jasper Park Lodge Golf Course); tennis courts; health club; canoe, paddle-boat, and bike rentals; children's center; concierge; tour desk; business center; shopping arcade; 24-hr. room service; babysitting; laundry service; same-day dry cleaning; horseback riding. *In room:* TV w/pay movies, dataport, high-speed Internet access, coffeemaker, hair dryer, iron.

Jasper Inn Alpine Resort ⨁
The Jasper Inn, on the northern end of town but set back off the main road, is one of the nicest lodgings in town. Rooms are available in three different buildings and in many configurations. If you're looking for good value, look past the standard units (which are perfectly nice, mind you); instead, fork over C$18 (US$18/£9) more and reserve a spacious suite with fireplace and kitchen. Even nicer are the rooms in the separate Maligne Suites building, which come with marble-and-granite bathrooms, fireplaces, Jacuzzis, and balconies. Two-bedroom chalet-style rooms can sleep up to seven.

98 Geikie St. (P.O. Box 879), Jasper, AB T0E 1E0. © 800/661-1933 or 780/852-4461. Fax 780/852-5916. www.jasperinn.com. 143 units. C$243–C$248 (US$243–US$248/£122–£124) double; C$255–C$413 (US$255–US$413/£128–£207) suite. Extra person C$15 (US$15/£7.50). Children 17 and under stay free in parent's room. AE, DC, MC, V. Free parking. **Amenities:** Restaurant; small indoor pool; Jacuzzi; sauna; babysitting; coin-op laundry and laundry service. *In room:* TV, dataport, fridge, microwave, hair dryer.

Lobstick Lodge ⨁ᴷⁱᵈˢ
The Lobstick Lodge is a longtime favorite for the discerning traveler with an eye to value, with some of the largest standard units in Jasper. Even more impressive are the huge kitchen units, which come with a full kitchen, a sitting room with sofabed and easy chairs, plus a separate bedroom with either two doubles or a king-size bed. As large as most apartments, these kitchen units are perfect for families and go fast—reserve early. King suites are also large and very comfortably furnished. A complete remodel of the hotel was completed in 2003.

96 Geikie St. (P.O. Box 1200), Jasper, AB T0E 1E0. © 888/852-7737 or 780/852-4431. Fax 780/852-4142. www.lobsticklodge.com. 139 units. C$221 (US$221/£111) double; C$243 (US$243/£122) kitchen unit. Children under 15 stay free in parent's room. AE, DC, MC, V. Free parking. **Amenities:** Restaurant; lounge; indoor pool; 3 Jacuzzis; 2 saunas. *In room:* TV, dataport, coffeemaker, hair dryer, iron.

Marmot Lodge 𝓡 At the northern end of Jasper's main street, the Marmot Lodge offers pleasant rooms in three different buildings. One building contains large kitchen units with fireplaces, living area, and separate bedrooms with two queen-size beds or a king-size bed. These units are deservedly popular with families—ask for units with balconies off the back and you may see elk grazing on the back lawn. The building facing the street offers smaller, less expensive rooms; the third building features very large deluxe units. All are comfortable according to a relaxing, unfussy aesthetic that's restful after a day of sightseeing.

86 Connaught Dr., Jasper, AB T0E 1E0. ⓒ 800/661-6521 or 780/852-4471. Fax 780/852-3280. www.marmotlodge. com. 107 units. C$235 (US$235/£118) double; from C$255 (US$255/£128) kitchen unit. Children under 15 stay free in parent's room. AE, DC, MC, V. **Amenities:** Restaurant; lounge; indoor pool; Jacuzzi; sauna. *In room:* TV w/pay movies, coffeemaker, hair dryer.

Sawridge Inn and Conference Centre 𝓡𝓡 The three-story lobby of this hotel is large and airy, opening onto a central atrium lit with skylights and filled with tropical plants. The Sawridge is the classiest of all the Jasper Townsite hotels—the entire hotel was renovated in 2003, and offers large and beautifully furnished rooms. Half the rooms (most with one queen-size bed) overlook the junglelike atrium, which also contains the restaurant, lounge, and pool. The other rooms (most with two queen-size beds) overlook the town and offer large private balconies as well. The king-size bed corner suites are truly large, with two balconies and a jetted tub. New at the Sawridge is the European Beauty and Wellness Centre, a day spa with a selection of beauty, aromatherapy, and massage treatments. The Sawridge, on the northern edge of Jasper, is unique in that it's owned by the Sawridge Cree Indian Band.

82 Connaught Dr. (P.O. Box 2080), Jasper, AB T0E 1E0. ⓒ 888/729-7343 or 780/852-5111. Fax 780/852-5942. www. sawridge.com. 153 units. C$245–C$280 (US$245–US$280/£123–£140) double; C$320–C$380 (US$320–US$380/ £160–£190) suites. AE, DC, DISC, MC, V. **Amenities:** Restaurant; lounge; indoor pool; day spa; Jacuzzi; sauna; business center; room service (7am–10pm); coin-op laundry; dry-cleaning service. *In room:* A/C, TV w/movie channels, high-speed Internet, coffeemaker, fridge, hair dryer, robes.

Expensive

If you are really just looking for a motel room, Jasper has a few standard motor lodges to accommodate your needs. The **Maligne Lodge,** on the western edge of Jasper at 900 Connaught Dr. (ⓒ 800/661-1315 or 780/852-3143), offers an indoor pool, restaurant, lounge, and clean unfussy rooms starting at C$190 (US$190/£95) double.

Becker's Chalets 𝓡 This attractive log-cabin resort offers a variety of lodging options in freestanding chalets, set in a glade of trees along the Athabasca River. While the resort dates from the 1940s and retains the feel of an old-fashioned mountain retreat, most of the chalets have been built in the last 10 years, and thus are thoroughly modernized. Cabins come in a wide variety of sizes and styles, ranging from one-room cottages to four-bedroom chalets, with everything in between. Most cabins come with river-stone fireplaces and kitchens. My favorite? Ask for a deluxe one-bedroom log chalet (C$185/US$185/£93) and live your log-cabin fantasies. The dining room at Becker's is also one of Jasper's best.

Hwy. 95, 5km (3 miles) south of Jasper (P.O. Box 579), Jasper, AB T0E 1E0. ⓒ 780/852-3779. Fax 780/852-7202. www.beckerschalets.com. 118 chalets. C$155–C$185 (US$155–US$185/£78–£93) 1-bedroom cabin; C$180–C$250 (US$180–US$250/£90–£125) 2-bedroom cabin; C$220–C$390 (US$220–US$390/£110–£195) 3-bedroom cabin. AE, MC, V. Closed early Oct to May. **Amenities:** Restaurant; babysitting; coin-op laundry; playground. *In room:* TV, fridge, coffeemaker, hair dryer, no phone.

Patricia Lake Bungalows   If you're looking for a bit of lakefront solitude and comfortable, unfussy lodgings, these cottages and motel rooms on Patricia Lake, just 10 minutes from downtown Jasper, are highly recommended. Lodgings are in a mix of vintage one-bed cottages, motel rooms, newly built suites, and a log cabin—something for every budget. Most of the cottages and all of the suites have kitchens; many have fireplaces.

7km (4 miles) west of Jasper (P.O. Box 657), Jasper AB T0E 1E0. © 888/499-6848 or 780/852-3560. Fax 780/ 852-4060. www.patricialakebungalows.com. 38 units. C$85–C$150 (US$85–US$150/£43–£75) motel units; C$160– C$175 (US$160–US$175/£80–£88) cottage; C$210 (US$210/£105) log cabin; C$250–C$285 (US$250–US$285/ £125–£143) suite. MC. V. Closed Nov–April. **Amenities:** Hot tub; bike rentals; boat rentals; laundry facilities; barbecues; playground. *In room:* Some kitchens, coffeemakers, no phones.

Tekarra Lodge ✦   Just east of Jasper, this venerable log-cabin resort is situated above the confluence of the Miette and Athabasca rivers. Accommodations are in the lodge or in vintage cabins that can sleep from two to seven people; the lodge room rates include breakfast. The log cabins are nicely furnished (all with kitchens and private bathrooms), but it's the location that really sets Tekarra apart. Just far enough from the bustle of Jasper, off a quiet road in the forest, it offers the kind of charm that you dream of in a classic mountain-cabin resort. One of Jasper's best restaurants is located in the lodge, making this a great place for a family seeking solitude yet access to good food. Pets welcome.

1.5km (1 mile) east of Jasper off Hwy. 93A (P.O. Box 669), Jasper AB T0E 1E0. © 888/962-2522 or 780/852-3058. Fax 780/852-4636. www.maclabhotels.com. 52 units. C$175 (US$175/£88) lodge room; C$199–C$250 (US$199– US$250/£100–£125) cabin double. 2-night minimum for cabins in summer. Extra person C$10 (US$10/£5). Rates for lodge rooms include continental breakfast. AE, DC, MC, V. Closed early Oct to May. **Amenities:** Restaurant; bar; bike rental; coin-op laundry. *In room:* Kitchen, coffeemaker, hair dryer, no phone.

Moderate

In high season, it seems that nearly half the dwellings in Jasper let rooms, B&B-style; contact **Jasper Home Accommodation Association,** P.O. Box 758, Jasper, AB T0E 1E0 (www.stayinjasper.com), for a full list and booking service. B&Bs listed with the local visitor association have little signs in front; if you arrive early enough in the day, you can comb the streets looking for a likely suspect. Note that B&Bs here are much less grand than those in Banff, and less expensive as well. Double-occupancy accommodations are in the C$60-to-C$90 (US$60–US$90/£30–£45) range at most homes. You'll need to pay cash for most.

Athabasca Hotel *Value*   This hotel's lobby is like a hunting lodge, with a stone fireplace and trophy heads of deer and elk. A gray-stone corner building with a homey, old-fashioned air, the Athabasca was built in 1929, and has long served as one of Jasper's principal gathering spots. Each guest room offers a mountain view, although only half have private bathrooms; while rooms are small, the furnishings are simple and tasteful. The place is really quite pleasant—it's the very image of venerable Canadian charm—and one of the few good values in Jasper.

510 Patricia St., Jasper, AB T0E 1E0. © 877/542-8422 or 780/852-3386. Fax 780/852-4955. www.athabascahotel. com. 61 units (39 with private bathroom). C$99 (US$99/£50) double with shared bathroom, C$159–C$175 (US$159–US$175/£80–£88) double with private bathroom. AE, DC, MC, V. **Amenities:** Restaurant; 2 bars; concierge; room service (7am–11pm). *In room:* TV, dataport, hair dryer.

Austrian Haven   This large home in a quiet residential section of Jasper offers two very comfortable and spacious suites that are essentially full apartments. The large family suite offers two queen beds, living room, kitchen, and dining area. The honeymoon suite is opulently decorated, and has a king bed, cozy down duvet, and private sunroom with outstanding views. Both suites have private bathrooms, fridges, microwaves, TVs and VCRs, and private entrances. Both suites share a mountain-view deck with barbecue.

812 Patricia St. (Box 1856), Jasper, AB T0E 1E0. (℃ 780/852-4259. Fax 780/852-4259. www.austrianhaven.ca. 2 units. C$130–C$150 (US$130–US$150/£65–£75) double. Rates include continental breakfast. Cash and traveler's checks only. **Amenities:** Barbecue deck. *In room:* TV/VCR, fridge, microwave, toaster, coffeemaker.

Inexpensive

Two Hostelling International **hostels,** both reachable at P.O. Box 387, Jasper, AB T0E 1E0 (℃ **780/852-3215;** www.hihostels.ca), are the best alternatives for the budget traveler. Advance reservations are strongly advised in summer. The 80-bed **Jasper International Hostel,** on Skytram Road, 6km (4 miles) west of Jasper, charges C$23 (US$23/£12) for members and C$28 (US$28/£14) for nonmembers. The closest hostel to Jasper, it's open year-round. Two family rooms, a barbecue area, indoor plumbing, hot showers, and bike rentals are available. In winter, ask about ski packages. The **Maligne Canyon Hostel,** off Maligne Lake Road, 18km (11 miles) east of Jasper, sleeps 24; rates are C$18 (US$18/£9) for members and C$23 (US$23/£12) for nonmembers. This convenient hostel is just above the astonishing Maligne Canyon. Facilities include a self-catering kitchen and dining area.

In & Around Hinton

Just east of the park gate in and near Hinton are a number of options that offer high-quality accommodations at significantly lower prices than you'll find in Jasper. Downtown Jasper is a 30- to 45-minute drive away from the choices listed below.

Hinton has a number of motel complexes with standard, no-nonsense rooms. The **Best Western White Wolf Inn,** 828 Carmichael Lane (℃ **800/220-7870** in Canada, or 780/865-7777), has 42 air-conditioned rooms, most with kitchenettes. The **Black Bear Inn,** 571 Gregg Ave. (℃ **888/817-2888** or 780/817-2000), features an exercise room, hot tub, and restaurant. The **Crestwood Hotel,** 678 Carmichael Lane (℃ **800/ 661-7288** or 780/865-4001), has a pool and restaurant. Doubles at these motels cost between C$120 and C$150 (US$120–US$150/£60–£75).

Mountain Splendour Bed & Breakfast   The spacious rooms at this large, modern home are outfitted with private bathrooms, tables and chairs, and English-theme decor. The largest of the three rooms is the English Garden Suite, a comfortable space with a private deck, fireplace, and large bathroom with Jacuzzi, separate shower, and cathedral ceilings. Guests can lounge by the fireplace or watch TV in the light, airy living room, which has picture windows framing a view of Jasper Park.

P.O. Box 6544, 17 Folding Mountain Village, Jasper East, AB T7V 1X8. (℃ **780/866-2116.** Fax 780/866-2117. www. mountainsplendour.com. 3 units. C$149–C$179 (US$149–US$179/£75–£90) double. Rates include breakfast. MC, V. **Amenities:** Jacuzzi. *In room:* TV, hair dryer, iron.

Overlander Mountain Lodge ✦   The Overlander is a historic lodge on the edge of Jasper National Park. The original lodge building houses the Stone Peak Restaurant, a handsome fine-dining room and bar with tremendous views of the Rockies, plus cozy guest rooms with queen-size or twin beds. A newer wing features rooms with gas fireplaces and jetted tubs. The fourplex cabins have two double beds and gas fireplace. Most of the chalets, which are scattered in the forest behind the lodge, contain a fireplace or wood-burning stove, full kitchen, washer/dryer, and patio. Accommodations throughout have private bathrooms and are decorated handsomely and furnished with country flair. The dining room serves notably tasty international and regional cuisine, with specialties of rack of lamb, venison, and fish. The Overlander's staff is friendly and helpful. This property offers excellent value and makes a charming base for exploring the park.

1km (½ mile) from Jasper Park East Gate (Box 6118), Hinton, AB T7V 1X5. © 877/866-2330 or 780/866-2330. Fax 780/866-2332. www.overlandermountainlodge.com. 29 units. C$175–C$230 (US$175–US$230/£88–£115) lodge room; C$175 (US$175/£88) cabin room; C$330 (US$330/£165) 2-bedroom chalet; C$410 (US$410/£205) 3-bedroom chalet. AE, MC, V. **Amenities:** Restaurant; lounge; horseback riding; hiking trails. *In room:* Coffeemaker, hair dryer, no phone.

Suite Dreams B&B
A modern, wheelchair-accessible home built as a B&B, Suite Dreams offers large, comfortable rooms with lots of natural light in a quiet, forested setting. Each room is decorated according to a horticultural theme and features art from several generations of the owner's talented family. All units have private bathrooms, and one can sleep up to four. The spacious living room has a fireplace. The backyard features 100 yards of golf greens. The hostess is happy to make specialty breakfasts for guests with dietary restrictions.

Box 6145 (Lot 3134 Maskuta Estates), Hinton, AB T7V 1X5. © 780/865-8855. Fax 780/865-2199. www.suitedream. com. 4 units. From C$105 (US$105/£53) double. Extra person C$20 (US$20/£10). Rates include full breakfast. MC, V. **Amenities:** Golf greens. *In room:* TV/VCR, fridge.

Wyndswept Bed & Breakfast ⌨
This excellent B&B has a hostess who will make you feel like family. The main-floor guest rooms have private bathrooms, robes, hair dryers, handmade soaps, kettles, and other extras. The suite, which gives out onto a deck, measures 110 sq. m (1,184 sq. ft.) and has a full kitchen, large bathroom, and sitting area; it can sleep up to five. Guests have access to a computer and fax machine. Breakfast is delicious and substantial—there's even a dessert course. Chances are good you'll see wildlife while here: Bears, coyotes, wolves, and deer have all been spotted from the deck. The owner will outfit you with a Wyndswept backpack upon arrival that contains books about hiking, wildlife, mosquito spray, Band-Aids, and other incidentals that make your stay more comfortable and interesting—items that you won't need to purchase for your stay.

4km (2½ miles) east of Jasper Park gates (Box 2683), Hinton, AB T7V 1Y2. © 780/866-3950. Fax 780/866-3951. www. wyndswept.com. 3 units. C$165–C$199 (US$165–US$199/£83–£100) double. Extra person C$35 (US$35/£18). MC, V. *In room:* A/C, TV w/movie channels, dataport, coffeemaker, hair dryer, iron.

A Local Guest Ranch
Black Cat Guest Ranch
This venerable and historic wilderness retreat was established in 1935 by the Brewsters. The ranch boasts a superb mountain setting just outside the park boundaries in the foothills, with the Rockies filling up the western horizon. The rustic two-story lodge, built in 1978—guests don't stay in the original old cabins—offers 16 unfussy units, each with private bathroom, large windows, and an unspoiled view of the crags in Jasper Park across a pasture filled with horses and chattering birds. There's a large central fireplace room with couches, easy chairs, and game tables scattered about. Three home-cooked meals per day, served family-style by the friendly, welcoming staff, are available for C$41 (US$41/£21) adult, C$31 (US$31/£16) kids per day. Activities include hiking, horseback riding, canoe rentals, murder-mystery weekends, and fishing. The ranch staff will meet your train or bus at Hinton.

56km (35 miles) northeast of Jasper. P.O. Box 6267, Hinton, AB T7V 1X6. *©* **800/859-6840** or **780/865-3084.** Fax 780/865-1924. www.blackcatguestranch.ca. 16 units. C$110 (US$110/£55) per person, based on double occupancy. MC, V. **Amenities:** Large outdoor hot tub.

CAMPING

There are 10 campgrounds in Jasper National Park. You need a special permit to camp anywhere in the parks outside the regular campgrounds—a regulation necessary due to fire hazards. Contact the parks information office (*©* **780/852-6176**) for permits. The campgrounds range from completely unserviced sites to those providing water, power, sewer connections, laundry facilities, gas, and groceries. The closest to Jasper Townsite is **The Whistlers,** up the road toward the gondola, providing a total of some 700 campsites for C$22 to C$36 (US$22–US$36/£11–£18).

WHERE TO DINE
Expensive
Andy's Bistro ✸ CONTINENTAL/CANADIAN   This resourceful little restaurant's dining room looks like a wine cellar, and indeed the wine list is noteworthy. The food is classic Continental with a sprinkling of New World specialties thrown in for spice. Starters may feature baked brie jubilee—with sour-cherry sauce—and black-olive toast. Main courses range from grilled salmon and asparagus, with a creamy strawberry-and–white vermouth sauce, to pork tenderloin festooned with fresh Chanterelle mushrooms and roast garlic. Though the menu may seem highbrow, the atmosphere is casual and friendly—one communal table for six is saved for first-come, first-served diners.

606 Patricia St. *©* **780/852-4559.** www.andysbistro.com. Reservations recommended. Main courses C$19–C$27 (US$19–US$27/£9.50–£14). MC, V. Mid-May to mid-Oct daily 5–11pm; mid-Oct to mid-May Tues–Sat 5–11pm.

Becker's Gourmet Restaurant FRENCH/CANADIAN   Although the name's not very elegant, it's highly descriptive. This inventive restaurant serves what could only be termed gourmet food, observing the mandate to serve what's fresh and local without turning the menu into a list of endangered game animals. Samples include apricot-glazed rack of lamb, milk-poached veal tenderloin, and shrimp, scallops and oyster mushrooms grilled in a banana leaf. The dining room is an intimate log-and-glass affair that overlooks the Athabasca River.

At Becker's Chalets, Hwy. 93, 5km (3 miles) south of Jasper. *©* **780/852-3779.** Reservations required. Main courses C$18–C$40 (US$18–US$40/£9–£20). MC, V. Daily 8–11am and 5:30–10pm.

Fiddle River Seafood ✸ SEAFOOD   This rustic-looking retreat has panoramic windows facing the Jasper railroad station and the mountains beyond. The specialty here is fresh fish, though a number of pasta dishes and red-meat entrees will complicate your decision-making process. While there are plenty of good selections on the menu, Fiddle River offers as many daily specials (presented at the table on an easel-propped blackboard). At least 8 or 10 fresh fish and seafood specials are featured, including oysters and several preparations of Pacific salmon. A recent favorite was pan-roasted crab cakes scented with sherry and turmeric and served with chipotle mayonnaise. For "landlubbers," as the menu denotes the non–fish eaters, there are also excellent steaks: a peppered rib-eye is served with blue-cheese demi-glace. The wine list is short but interesting.

620 Connaught Dr. *©* **780/852-3032.** Reservations required. Main courses C$18–C$38 (US$18–US$38/£9–£19). AE, MC, V. Daily 5–10pm.

Moose's Nook Northern Grill ⚘ CANADIAN   This atmospheric restaurant off the great room of the Jasper Park Lodge features "Canadiana" specialties. With equal parts tradition and innovation, the Moose's Nook offers hearty presentations of native meats, fish, and game. Grilled duck breast is served with figs and celery root, and venison loin comes with a sauce of wild mushrooms and leeks. Lighter appetites will enjoy the vegetarian cabbage rolls.

In the Fairmont Jasper Park Lodge, 8km (5 miles) east of Jasper. ✆ **780/852-6052**. Reservations recommended. Main courses C$24–$40 (US$24–US$40/£12–£20). AE, DISC, MC, V. Daily 6–9pm.

Tekarra Lodge Restaurant STEAK/INTERNATIONAL   This local favorite offers excellent international cuisine, as well as steaks and other intriguing dishes such as rack of lamb with macadamia-nut crust, pan-seared chicken with roast grapes and Pacific Rim bouillabaisse. Lighter dishes such as salads and pastas are also available. The charming lodge dining room is one of Jasper's hidden gems; the service is friendly, and the fireplace-dominated room intimate.

Hwy. 93A, 1.6km (1 mile) east of Jasper (call for directions). ✆ **780/852-3058**. Reservations recommended on weekends. Main courses C$22–C$56 (US$22–US$56/£11–£28). AE, DC, MC, V. Daily 5:30–10pm.

Moderate

Denjiro Japanese Restaurant JAPANESE   Denjiro's is a slice of Japan, complete with sushi bar, karaoke lounge, intimate ozashiki booths, shoeless patrons, soft Asian mood music, and service that's both fast and impeccable. The place has a studied simplicity that goes well with the traditional Japanese fare served: sushi, sashimi, tempura, teriyaki, and bento.

410 Connaught Dr. ✆ **780/852-3780**. Reservations recommended. Most items C$8–C$22 (US$8–US$22/£4–£11). AE, MC, V. Mid-May to mid-Oct daily noon–2:30pm and 5–10:30pm; mid-Oct to mid-May daily 5–10pm.

Jasper Brewing Company BREWPUB   A welcome addition to Jasper's youthful eating and nightlife scene, this new brewpub made its debut on Food Network's *Opening Soon* series. All the attention has made this a very popular place, though the excellent ales and food—upscale pub grub with a Creole twist—are reason enough to make this your home away from home while in Jasper.

624 Connaught Dr. ✆ **780/852-4111**. Main courses C$10–C$26 (US$10–US$26/£5–£13). MC, V. Daily 11am–midnight.

Something Else INTERNATIONAL/PIZZA   Something Else is accurately named: Folded together here are a good Greek restaurant and a pizza parlor, to which a high-quality Canadian-style restaurant has been added. Stir in a Creole bistro. In short, if you're with a group that can't decide where to eat, this is the place to go. Prime Alberta steaks, fiery Louisiana jambalaya and mesquite chicken, Greek saganaki and moussaka, an array of 18 pizzas—no matter what you choose, it's all well prepared and fresh, and the welcome is friendly.

621 Patricia St. ✆ **780/852-3850**. Main courses C$15–C$24 (US$15–US$24/£7.50–£12). AE, DC, MC, V. Daily 11am–11pm.

Inexpensive

For muffins and sandwiches, coffee, desserts, soups, and salads, go to **Soft Rock Cafe,** 632 Connaught Dr. (✆ **780/852-5850**), in the Connaught Square Mall. You can go online or check your e-mail at one of its computers. Another casual spot is **Spooner's Coffee Bar,** upstairs at 610 Patricia St. (✆ **780/852-4046**), with a juice bar, coffee drinks, burritos, soups, sandwiches, and other deli items.

Jasper Pizza Place PIZZA One of Jasper's most popular eateries, the redesigned Pizza Place agreeably combines the features of an upscale boutique pizzeria with a traditional Canadian bar. The excellent thin-crust pizzas are baked in a 1000°F wood-fired oven, and come in some very unusual—some would say unlikely—combinations. If you're not hungry for pizza, you'll also find inexpensive pasta, burgers, and even the French-Canadian specialty *poutine*. The bar side of things is lively, with pool tables and a crowd of summer resort workers on display.

402 Connaught Dr. ℂ 780/852-3225. Pizza C$7–C$18 (US$7–US$18/£3.50–£9). MC, V. Daily 11am–11pm.

JASPER AFTER DARK

Nearly all of Jasper's nightlife can be found in the bars and lounges of the hotels, motels, and inns. **O'Shea's,** Athabasca Hotel, 510 Patricia St. (ℂ **780/852-3386**), is a longtime favorite party den, usually just called the Atha'B, or simply The B. It caters to a young clientele with its changing lineup of Top 40 bands, dance floor, and movies shown on the large-screen TV. O'Shea's is in action Monday to Saturday until 2am. If it's a straightforward and straight-head party scene that you're looking for, consider the **D'ed Dog Bar and Grill,** 404 Connaught Dr. (ℂ **780/852-3351**). This is where the young river and hiking guides who work in Jasper every summer gather to compare exploits by shouting above the din of country rock. Jasper's hottest club for music, **Pete's On Patricia,** upstairs at 614 Patricia St. (ℂ **780/852-6262**), presents live alternative and blues bands.

It's a little bit anomalous—Jasper's most exclusive and expensive hotel providing shelter for one of Jasper's most popular 20-something hangouts. **Tent City** is a youthful gathering place in the bowels of the Jasper Park Lodge, where you'll find billiards, loud music, and a preponderance of the JPL's 650 employees.

You may think of most basement bars as dank and airless, but pleasant **Downstream Bar,** 620 Connaught Dr. (ℂ **780/852-9449**), is a friendly place for a late-evening drink, and you won't feel out of place if you're not 25 and totally tan.

9 Edmonton: Capital of Alberta ⟨★⟩

303km (188 miles) N of Calgary, 524km (326 miles) NW of Saskatoon

Edmonton, Alberta's capital city, is located on the banks of the North Saskatchewan River, which cuts a deep wooded valley through the city. It's a civilized city of one million citizens that's known for its summer festivals and easy-going friendliness.

Established as a fur-trading post in 1786, Edmonton grew in spurts, following a boom-and-bust pattern as exciting as it was unreliable. The railroad arrived in 1912 bringing homestead farmers, many from eastern Europe. While Edmonton initially boomed as the market center for these emigrant farm communities, the farm economy went bust during the droughts and Great Depression of the 1930s. During World War II, the boom came in the form of the Alaska Highway, with Edmonton as the material base and temporary home of 50,000 American troops and construction workers.

The ultimate boom, however, gushed from the ground in February 1947, when oil was discovered southwest of the city. Edmonton soon found itself the capital not just of Alberta but of the Canadian oil industry. Today the city is filled with gleaming office towers and other monuments to wealth—enormous shopping centers, a wonderful park system, and excellent arts performance facilities.

Edmonton

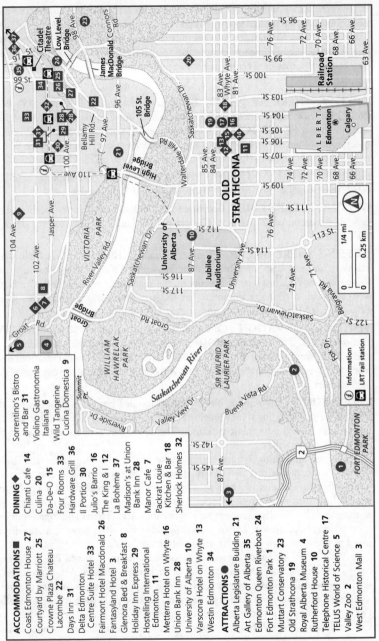

ACCOMMODATIONS ■
Coast Edmonton House **27**
Courtyard by Marriott **25**
Crowne Plaza Chateau
Lacombe **22**
Days Inn **31**
Delta Edmonton
Centre Suite Hotel **33**
Fairmont Hotel Macdonald **26**
Fantasyland Hotel **3**
Glenora Bed & Breakfast **8**
Holiday Inn Express **29**
Hostelling International
Edmonton **11**
Metterra Hotel on Whyte **16**
Union Bank Inn **28**
University of Alberta **10**
Varscona Hotel on Whyte **13**
Westin Edmonton **34**

DINING ◆
Chianti Cafe **14**
Culina **20**
Da-De-O **15**
Four Rooms **33**
Hardware Grill **36**
Il Portico **30**
Julio's Barrio **16**
The King & I **12**
La Bohème **37**
Madison's at Union
Bank Inn **28**
Manor Cafe **1**
Packrat Louie
Kitchen & Bar **18**
Sherlock Holmes **32**
Sorrentino's Bistro
and Bar **31**
Violino Gastronomia
Italiana **6**
Wild Tangerine
Cucina Domestica **9**

ATTRACTIONS ●
Alberta Legislature Building **21**
Art Gallery of Alberta **35**
Edmonton Queen Riverboat **24**
Fort Edmonton Park **1**
Muttart Conservatory **23**
Old Strathcona **19**
Royal Alberta Museum **4**
Rutherford House **10**
Telephone Historical Centre **17**
TELUS World of Science **5**
Valley Zoo **2**
West Edmonton Mall **3**

ⓘ Information
Ⓔ LRT rail station

However, the combination of oil industry workers and provincial bureaucrats don't exactly make for a scintillating civic culture, and despite the youthful energy of 17,000 University of Alberta students, Edmonton lacks the spark you'd expect of a city of this size. It's ironic—and somehow symptomatic—that a city with over 200 years of history considers a shopping center its proudest monument.

ESSENTIALS

GETTING THERE BY PLANE **Edmonton International Airport** (℗ 800/ 268-7134; www.edmontonairports.com) is served by **Air Canada** (℗ 800/372-9500) and **Northwest** (℗ 800/447-4747), among other airlines. The airport lies 29km (18 miles) south of the city on Highway 2, about 45 minutes away from city center. By cab, the trip costs about C$45 (US$45/£23); by Airporter bus, C$15 (US$15/£7.50).

GETTING THERE BY TRAIN The **VIA Rail** (℗ 800/561-8630 or 780/422-6032; www.viarail.ca) station is at 104th Avenue and 100th Street.

GETTING THERE BY BUS **Greyhound** (℗ 780/413-8747; www.greyhound.ca) buses link Edmonton to points in Canada and the United States from the depot at 10324 103rd St.

GETTING THERE BY CAR Edmonton straddles Highway 16, the Yellowhead Highway, an east-west interprovincial highway that links western Manitoba and Prince Rupert, B.C. Just west of Edmonton, the Yellowhead joins to the Alaska Highway. Highway 2 connects Edmonton to Calgary, which is a 3-hour drive south. Edmonton is 515km (320 miles) north of the U.S. border.

VISITOR INFORMATION Contact **Edmonton Tourism,** 9990 Jasper Ave. NW, Edmonton, AB T5J 1N9 (℗ 800/463-4667 or 780/496-8400; www.edmonton. com). There are also visitor centers located at city hall and at Gateway Park, both open from 9am to 6pm, and on the Calgary Trail at the southern edge of the city, open from 9am to 9pm.

CITY LAYOUT The winding **North Saskatchewan River** flows right through the heart of the city, dividing it into roughly equal halves. Most of this steep-banked valley has been turned into public parklands. The downtown business district is on the north bank of the valley.

The street numbering system begins at the corner of 100th Street and 100th Avenue, which means that downtown addresses have five digits and that suburban homes often have smaller addresses than businesses in the very center of town. Downtown Edmonton's main street is **Jasper Avenue** (actually 101st Ave.), running north of the river. The "A" designations you'll notice for certain streets and avenues downtown add to the confusion: They're essentially old service alleys between major streets, many of which are now pedestrian areas with sidewalk cafes.

At 97th Street, on Jasper Avenue, rises the massive pink **Canada Place,** the only completely planned government complex of its kind in Canada. Across the street is the **Edmonton Convention Centre,** which stair-steps down the hillside to the river.

Beneath the downtown core stretches a network of pedestrian walkways—called **Pedways**—connecting hotels, restaurants, and malls with the library, city hall, and Citadel Theatre. These Pedways not only avoid the surface traffic, but are also climate-controlled—important in winter.

At the northern approach to the High Level Bridge stand the buildings of the **Alberta Legislature.** Across the bridge, to the south, is **Old Strathcona,** a bustling neighborhood of cafes, galleries, and hip shops that's now a haven for Edmonton's more alternative population. The main arterial through Old Strathcona is **Whyte Avenue,** or 82nd Avenue. Running south from here is 104th Street, which becomes the **Calgary Trail** and leads to the airport. Just west of Old Strathcona, and the source of much of the city's youthful energy, is the **University of Alberta.**

West of downtown, Jasper Avenue shifts and twists to eventually become Stony Plain Road, which passes near **West Edmonton Mall,** the world's largest shopping and entertainment center, before merging with Highway 16 on its way to Jasper National Park.

GETTING AROUND   Edmonton Transit (© 780/496-1611) operates the buses and the LRT (Light Rail Transit). This electric rail service connects downtown with Northlands Park to the north and the University of Alberta to the south. The LRT and buses have the same fares: C$2.50 (US$2.50/£1.25) for adults and C$2.25 (US$2.25/£1.15) for seniors and children; a day pass goes for C$7.50 (US$7.50/ £3.75). Monday through Friday from 9am to 3pm, downtown LRT travel is free between Churchill, Central, Bay, Corona, and Grandin stations.

In addition to the following downtown locations, **National,** 10133 100A St. NW (© 780/422-6097); **Budget,** 10016 106th St. (© 780/448-2000); and **Hertz,** 10815 Jasper Ave. (© 780/423-3431), all have bureaus at the airport.

Call **CO-OP Taxi** (© 780/425-2525 or 780/425-8310) for a ride in a driver/owner-operated cab.

FAST FACTS: Edmonton

American Express The office at 10180 101st St., at 102nd Avenue (© 780/421-0608; LRT: Corona), is open Monday to Friday from 9am to 5pm.

Area Code Edmonton's area code is © 780.

Doctors If you need nonemergency medical care while in Edmonton, check the phone book for the closest branch of **Medicentre,** which offers walk-in medical services daily.

Emergency For fire, medical, or crime emergencies, dial © 911.

Hospitals The closest hospital with emergency service to downtown Edmonton is the **Royal Alexandra Hospital,** 10240 Kingsway Ave. (© 780/477-4111; bus: 9).

Newspapers The *Edmonton Journal* (www.edmontonjournal.com) and *Edmonton Sun* (www.edmontonsun.com) are the local daily papers. Arts, entertainment, and nightlife listings can be found in the weekly *See* (www.see magazine.com).

Pharmacies **Shoppers Drug Mart** has more than a dozen locations in Edmonton, most open till midnight. One central location is 8210 109th St. (© 780/ 433-2424; bus: 6).

Post Office The main post office is at 103A Avenue and 99th Street (LRT: Churchill).

Time Edmonton is on Mountain Standard Time, the same as Calgary and Denver, and it observes daylight saving time.

SPECIAL EVENTS & FESTIVALS

Edmonton promotes itself as "the Festival City," and in summer almost every weekend brings another celebration. The citywide **Jazz City International Festival** (© 780/432-7166; www.edmontonjazz.com) takes over most music venues in Edmonton during the last week of June and first week of July.

The summer's biggest shindig is **Capital City Exposition,** AKA Capital EX, (© 888/800-7275 or 780/471-7210; www.capitalex.ca), formerly Klondike Days. Capital EX has shed the previous event's gold-rush trappings and focuses instead on midway rides, live music performances, and shopping promotions. Most events take place at Northlands Park, northeast of the city at 75th St. and 118th Ave.

The **Edmonton Folk Music Festival** (© 780/429-1899; www.efmf.ab.ca) is the largest folk-music festival in North America. Held in early August, it brings in musicians from around the world, from the Celtic north to Indonesia, plus major rock stars playing "unplugged." All concerts are held outdoors.

For 11 days in mid-August, Old Strathcona is transformed into a series of stages for the renowned Edmonton international **Fringe Theatre Festival** (© 780/448-9000; www.fringetheatreadventures.ca). Only Edinburgh's fringe festival is larger than Edmonton's—more than 150 troupes attend from around the world, as does an audience of over 600,000. The festival has 12 indoor theater stages and two outdoor stages, offering more than 1,000 individual performances; when one show ends, another begins on the same stage an hour later. In addition to the hubbub of actors and theater, the Fringe Theatre Festival also plays host to food and crafts booths, beer tents, and innumerable buskers and street performers.

EXPLORING THE CITY
THE TOP ATTRACTIONS

Fort Edmonton Park (Ⓚ (Kids)   Fort Edmonton Park is a complex of townscapes that reconstructs four distinct eras of Edmonton's history. Perhaps most interesting is the complete reconstruction of the old Fort Edmonton fur-trading post from the turn of the 19th century. This vast wooden structure is a warren of rooms and activities: Blacksmiths, bakers, and other docents ply their trades. On 1885 Street, you'll see frontier Edmonton, complete with saloons, general store, and Jasper House Hotel, which serves hearty pioneer meals. On 1905 Street, the agricultural boom years of the early 20th century are celebrated, when Edmonton thronged with new immigrants and was named provincial capital. On 1920 Street, sip an old-fashioned ice-cream soda at Bill's confectionery and see the changes wrought in the rural west by World War I. You can ride streetcar no. 1, a stagecoach, or a steam locomotive between the various streets. As an open-air museum, the park is very impressive; the variety of activities and services here make this a great family destination.

If Fort Edmonton will appeal to your family, consider spending a night at the park's **Hotel Selkirk,** a handsome replica of a 1910s hotel, but with all modern comforts (© 888/962-2522 or 780/496-7227; www.hotelselkirk.com).

On Whitemud Dr. at Fox Dr. © 780/496-8787. www.edmonton.ca/fort. Admission C$13 (US$13/£6.50) adults, C$9.75 (US$9.75/£4.90) seniors and youths, C$6.50 (US$6.50/£3.25) children, C$39 (US$39/£20) families. Late June to early Sept daily 10am–6pm; call for off-season hours. LRT to University Station, then bus no. 32.

Old Strathcona (ⅩⅩ)   This historic district used to be a separate township, but was amalgamated with Edmonton in 1912 and still contains some of the best-preserved landmarks in the city. It's best seen on foot, guided by the brochures given out at the

Old Strathcona Foundation, 10324 82nd Ave., fourth floor (② **780/433-5866**). It's easy to spend an afternoon here, just wandering the shops, sitting at streetside cafes, and people-watching. This is hipster-central for Edmonton, where students, artists, and the city's alternative community come to hang out. In addition, if you're looking for good value in restaurants or for the city's prime spot for pubs and nightlife, Old Strathcona is ground zero: Come take in the sometimes rowdy evening scene. Be sure to stop by the **Old Strathcona Farmers Market** (② **780/439-1844**), at 83rd Avenue and 103rd Street, an open-air market with fresh produce, baked goods, and local crafts. It's open Saturday year-round, plus Tuesday and Thursday afternoons in summer.

Around 82nd Ave., between 103rd and 105th sts. Bus: 46 from downtown.

Royal Alberta Museum ⚡ *(Kids* Expertly curated, this 18,500-sq.-m (99,132-sq.-ft.) modern museum displays Alberta's natural and human history in three permanent galleries. The Wild Alberta exhibit represents Alberta's diverse natural history with astonishingly lifelike dioramas and interactive displays utilizing computers, microscopes, and other hands-on tools. The Gallery of Aboriginal Culture tells the 11,000-year story of Alberta's First Nations inhabitants, incorporating artifacts, film, interactive media, and Native interpreters; it's one of Canada's foremost exhibits on Native culture. The Natural History Gallery has fossils, minerals, and a live-bug room.

12845 102nd Ave. ② 780/453-9100. Fax 780/454-6629. www.royalalbertamuseum.ca. Admission C$10 (US$10/£5) adults, C$8 (US$8/£4) seniors, C$7 (US$7/£3.50) students, C$5 (US$5/£2.50) youths 7–17, free for children under 7, C$28 (US$28/£14) families; Sat–Sun half-price admission 9–11am. Daily 9am–5pm. Bus: 1.

West Edmonton Mall *(Kids* You won't find many shopping malls mentioned in this book, but the West Edmonton Mall is something else: Guinness Book of World Records recognizes this as the world's largest shopping mall. Although it contains 800 stores and services, including 110 eateries, it looks and sounds more like a large slice of Disneyland that has somehow broken loose and drifted north. The locals modestly call it the "Eighth Wonder of the World." More theme park than mall, it encompasses 480,000 sq. m (5.2 million sq. ft.)—that's 48 city blocks—and houses the world's largest indoor amusement park, including a titanic roller coaster, bungee-jumping platform, and enclosed wave-lake, complete with beach. It has a regulation-size National Hockey League ice rink, 21 (count 'em, 21) movie theaters, a lagoon with performing sea lions, and several fabulous adventure rides (one of them by submarine to the "ocean floor"). In the middle of it all, an immense fountain with 19 computer-controlled jets weaves and dances in a musical performance.

Of course, you can shop here, too, and some of Edmonton's most popular restaurants are located in the mall. Roll your eyes all you want, but do go. You have to see the West Edmonton Mall to believe it.

8882 170th St. ② 800/661-8890 or 780/444-5200. www.westedmontonmall.com. Bus: 10.

MORE ATTRACTIONS
Alberta Legislature Building The Alberta Legislature rises on the site of the early trading post from which the city grew. Surrounded by lovingly manicured lawns, formal gardens, and greenhouses, it overlooks the river valley. The seat of Alberta's government was completed in 1912; it's a stately Edwardian structure open to the public throughout the year. Free conducted tours tell you about the functions of provincial lawmaking: who does what, where, and for how long.

109th St. and 97th Ave. ② 780/427-7362. www.assembly.ab.ca. Free tours daily every hour 9am–4pm, Sat–Sun and holidays noon–5pm. LRT: Grandin.

Art Gallery of Alberta Formerly the Edmonton Art Gallery, this is an institution in transition. The longtime gallery on Churchill Square is undergoing a major restructuring, and in the interim the AGA is mounting shows and displaying works from its permanent collection at Enterprise Square, 10230 Jasper Ave. (formerly the Hudson Bay Building). Operated in collaboration with the University of Alberta, the Enterprise Square gallery offers 1,022 sq. m (11,000 sq. ft.) of newly renovated gallery space, as well as studio classrooms and an art-and-gift storefront. Meanwhile, the old gallery on Churchill Square has been gutted to make way for a postmodern, architecturally daring exhibition hall and art center designed by Los Angeles architect Randall Stout. The expanded gallery, with a price tag of C$48 million, is due to open in 2009.

2 Sir Winston Churchill Sq. © 780/422-6223. www.artgalleryalberta.com. Admission C$10 (US$10/£5) adults, C$7 (US$7/£3.50) seniors and students, C$5 (US$5/£2.50) children 6–12, free for children under 6. Free admission for all Thurs 4–8pm. Mon–Fri 10:30am–5pm (Thurs till 8pm); Sat–Sun and holidays 11am–5pm. LRT: Churchill.

Edmonton Queen Riverboat Moored just outside the convention center, this riverboat plies the North Saskatchewan River as it runs through the city's many parks. A number of packages are offered, usually the cruise itself or a meal package that includes lunch or dinner.

9734 98th Ave. © 780/424-2628. www.edmontonqueen.com. Cruise only C$18 (US$18/£9); meal packages from C$48 (US$48/£24). Call for hours. Bus: 12 or 45.

Muttart Conservatory Each of four pavilions that look like I. M. Pei pyramids house a sampling of plants from different climatic zones. One has desert air and shows flowering cacti and their relatives, while another features tropical palms and orchids. The temperate zone includes a cross-section of plants from this global region. The fourth pyramid features changing ornamental displays of plants and blossoms. For good measure, there's also the Treehouse Cafe.

Off James MacDonald Bridge at 98th Ave. and 96A St. © 780/496-8755. www.edmonton.ca/muttart. Admission C$9 (US$9/£4.50) adults, C$6.75 (US$6.75/£3.40) seniors and youths 13–17, C$4.50 (US$4.50/£2.25) children 3–12, free for childen 2 and under. Mon–Fri 9am–5:30pm; Sat–Sun and holidays 11am–5:30pm. Bus: 51.

Rutherford House The home of Alberta's first premier, Alexander Rutherford, this lovingly preserved Edwardian gleams with polished silver- and gilt-framed oils. Around 1915, this mansion was the magnet for the social elite of the province; today, guides dressed in period costumes convey some of the spirit of the times. There's also a charming restaurant/tearoom, the **Arbour** (© **780/422-2697**), open daily from 11:30am to 4pm.

11153 Saskatchewan Dr., on the campus of the University of Alberta. © 780/427-3995. Admission C$4 (US$4/£2) adults, C$3 (US$3/£1.50) seniors and youths, C$12 (US$12/£6) families. Summer daily 9am–5pm; winter Tues–Sun noon–5pm. LRT: University.

Telephone Historical Centre North America's largest museum devoted to the history of telecommunications is located in the 1912 Telephone Exchange Building. Multimedia displays tell the history of words over wire and hints at what your modem will get up to next.

10440 84th Ave. © 780/433-1010. www.telephonehistoricalcentre.com. Admission by donation. Mon–Fri 10am–4pm. Bus: 44.

ESPECIALLY FOR KIDS

TELUS World of Science—Edmonton ★ *Kids* This is one of the most advanced facilities of its kind in the world. It contains, among other wonders, an **IMAX theater**

((C) **780/493-4250**), the largest planetarium theater in Canada, high-tech exhibits (including a virtual-reality showcase and a display on robotics), and an observatory open on clear afternoons and evenings. Exhibits include a journey through the human body (including the Gallery of the Gross!) and Mystery Avenue, where young sleuths can collect clues at a crime scene, then analyze them at a crime lab.

11211 142nd St., Coronation Park. (C) **780/451-3344**. www.odyssium.com. Admission C$13 (US$13/£6.50) adults, C$11 (US$11/£5.50) seniors and youths 13–17, C$10 (US$10/£5) children 4–12, C$48 (US$48/£24) families. Summer daily 10am–9pm; winter Sun–Thurs and holidays 10am–5pm, Fri–Sat 10am–9pm. Bus: 17 or 22. Free parking.

Valley Zoo *Kids*   Edmonton's small zoo is home to over 400 animals, including 20 endangered species, including Siberian tigers and snow leopards. Young children will like the pony and train rides, while older kids will be fascinated by falconry demonstrations.

In Laurier Park, 13315 Buena Vista Rd. (C) **780/496-6911**. Admission C$8.50 (US$8.50/£4.25) adults, seniors and students, C$6.25 (US$6.25/£3.15) children under 13, C$25 (US$25/£13) families. Summer daily 9:30am–8pm; winter daily 9:30am–4pm. Bus: 12.

SHOPPING

There are more shops per capita in Edmonton than in any other city in Canada. Go for it! See the **West Edmonton Mall** (p. 617).

DOWNTOWN   Most of the downtown shops are in a few large mall complexes; all are linked by the Pedway system, which gives pedestrians protection from summer heat and winter cold. The largest is **Edmonton City Centre** with 170 stores; it shares the block with the Hudson's Bay Company, and is across 102nd Avenue from **Holt Renfrew** department store. All of the above face 102nd Avenue, between 103rd and 100th streets.

OLD STRATHCONA   If you don't like mall shopping, then wandering the galleries and boutiques along **Whyte Avenue** (aka 82nd Ave.) may be more your style. One of the few commercial areas of Edmonton that retain historic structures, Old Strathcona is trend-central for students and bohemians. Shop for antiques, gifts, books, crystals, and crafts. Or pick up a souvenir tattoo. Be sure to stop by the **Farmers Market** at 103rd Street and 102nd Avenue.

HIGH STREET   This small district, running from 102nd to 109th avenues along 124th Street, has Edmonton's greatest concentration of art galleries, housewares shops, boutiques, and bookstores. It has great restaurants, too.

WHERE TO STAY

For B&Bs, try the **Alberta Bed and Breakfast Association** (www.bbalberta.com).

VERY EXPENSIVE

Delta Edmonton Centre Suite Hotel   This all-suite establishment forms part of the upscale City Centre shopping complex in the heart of downtown. Without having to stir out of doors, you can access 170 shops in the mall, plus movie theaters and an indoor putting green. Four other malls are connected to the hotel via Pedway. Three-quarters of the windows look into the mall, so you can stand behind the tinted one-way glass (in your pajamas, if you like) and watch the shopping action outside. Most units are deluxe executive suites, each with a large sitting area (with TV and wet bar) and separate bedroom (with another TV and a plate-glass wall looking into the mall). If you need lots of room, or have work to do in Edmonton, these very spacious rooms are just the ticket.

10222 102nd St., Edmonton, AB T5J 4C5. (800/661-6655 or 780/429-3900. Fax 780/428-1566. www.deltahotels. com. 169 units. C$212–C$379 (US$212–US$379/£106–£190) standard room; C$264–C$404 (US$264–US$404/ £132–£202) deluxe suite. Ask about summer family discounts, weekend packages, and special rates for business travelers. AE, DC, MC, V. Parking C$20 (US$20/£10) per day; valet parking C$24 (US$24/£12) per day. **Amenities:** Restaurant; bar; exercise room; Jacuzzi; sauna; concierge; business center; room service; coin-op laundry and laundry service; same-day dry cleaning. *In room:* A/C, TV w/pay movies, dataport, coffeemaker, hair dryer, iron.

The Fairmont Hotel Macdonald ★★★

From the outside, with its limestone facade and gargoyles, the Mac looks like a feudal château—it's no wonder that this is where Queen Elizabeth II stays when she's in town. Originally opened in 1915, the palatial Hotel Macdonald has undergone a masterwork of sensitive renovation and restoration. Signature elements such as the deep tubs, brass door plates, and paneled doors were kept intact, and important additions such as new plumbing were installed. Everything, including the service, is absolutely top-notch.

Rooms are beautifully furnished with luxurious upholstery, feather duvets, and original art. Rooms are large, and many have vistas across the river valley. Business-class suites each have a sitting area with a couch and two chairs, and a handy dressing area off the bathroom with a vanity table. Executive suites have two TVs and telephones, with a separate bedroom and a large sitting area. The eight specialty suites, which take up the entire seventh and eighth floors, are simply magnificent. Even pets get special treatment: a gift bag of treats and a map of pet-friendly parks. Needless to say, there aren't many hotels like this in Edmonton, or in Canada for that matter. As I rode the elevator, a guest broke the silence with the completely voluntary and effusive statement: "This is a *great* hotel."

10065 100th St., Edmonton, AB T5J 0N6. (800/441-1414 or 780/424-5181. Fax 780/429-6481. www.fairmont.com. 199 units. High season C$299–C$499 (US$299–US$499/£150–£200) deluxe standard room; C$399–C$899 (US$399– US$899/£200–£450) premier suite. Weekend and off-season discounts available. AE, DC, DISC, MC, V. Parking C$26 (US$26/£13) per day. **Amenities:** Restaurant; lounge; indoor pool; squash court; health club and spa; concierge; business center; 24-hr. room service; babysitting; laundry service; same-day dry cleaning; concierge-level rooms. *In room:* A/C, TV/VCR w/pay movies, dataport w/high-speed Internet access, minibar, coffeemaker, hair dryer, iron.

Fantasyland Hotel (Kids)

From the outside, this solemn tower at the end of the huge West Edmonton Mall reveals little of the wildly decorated rooms found within. Fantasyland is a cross between a hotel and Las Vegas: It contains a total of 116 themed rooms decorated in 12 different styles (as well as 238 large, well-furnished regular rooms). Theme rooms aren't just a matter of subtle touches; these units are exceedingly clever, very comfortable, and way over the top. Take the Truck Room: Your bed is located in the back end of a real pickup, the pickup's bench seats fold down into a child's bed, and the lights on the vanity are real stoplights. In the Igloo Room, a round bed is encased in a shell that looks like ice blocks; statues of sled dogs keep you company, and the walls are painted with amazingly lifelike arctic murals. The dog sleds even become beds for children. The themes continue, through the Canadian Rail Room (train berths for beds), the African Room, and more. All theme rooms come with immense four-person Jacuzzis and plenty of amenities.

It's not all fantasy here, though. The nontheme rooms are divided into superior rooms, with either a king-size or two queen-size beds, and executive rooms, with a king-size bed and Jacuzzi. The hotel's restaurant is quite good; of course, you have all-weather access to the world's largest mall and its many eateries as well.

17700 87th Ave., Edmonton, AB T5T 4V4. (800/737-3783 or 780/444-3000. Fax 780/444-3294. www.fantasyland hotel.com. 355 units. C$239–C$369 (US$239–US$369/£120–£185) double. Extra person C$10 (US$10/£5). Weekend and off-season packages available. AE, MC, V. Free parking. **Amenities:** Restaurant; bar; exercise room; concierge;

24-hr. room service; babysitting; laundry service; same-day dry cleaning. *In room:* A/C, TV w/pay movies, fax, data-port, wireless Internet, fridge, coffeemaker, hair dryer, iron.

Westin Edmonton 🌟🌟 Located in the heart of the downtown shopping and entertainment district, this modern hotel offers some of the city's largest and most comfortable rooms—the beds feature custom mattresses designed for near-perfect support, and showers have dual shower heads. Throughout the hotel, the rooms are decorated with a clean, contemporary look right out of *Architectural Digest.* Standard rooms come with one king-size bed or two double beds, while deluxe rooms are designed for business travelers, and come with two phone lines, wireless Internet, and other telecom upgrades, in addition to upgraded amenities. Suites are gracious and large, with separate bedrooms, large dressing room, and bathroom, and a very swank sitting room with black-leather furniture. These stylish and comfortable rooms will quickly take the pain out of both business and leisure travel.

10135 100th St., Edmonton, AB T5J 0N7. 📞 800/228-3000 or 780/426-3636. Fax 780/428-1454. www.thewestin edmonton.com. 413 units. C$214–C$329 (US$214–US$329/£107–£165) double. AE, DC, DISC, MC, V. Parking C$16 (US$16/£8) per day; valet parking C$21 (US$21/£11) per day. **Amenities:** 2 restaurants; lounge; indoor pool; exercise room; Jacuzzi; sauna; concierge; business center; 24-hr. room service; babysitting; laundry service. *In room:* A/C, TV, dataport, minibar, fridge, coffeemaker, hair dryer, iron.

EXPENSIVE

Coast Edmonton House This is a great alternative to pricier downtown hotels: With a great location right above the North Saskatchewan River, the all-suite hotel has one of the best views in Edmonton. Each suite comes with a full kitchen and dining area, bedroom, separate sitting area with foldout couch, balcony, and two phones; most offer free high-speed Internet access. Edmonton House is within easy walking distance of most downtown office areas and public transport.

10205 100th Ave., Edmonton, AB T5J 4B5. 📞 800/661-6562 or 780/420-4000. Fax 780/420-4008. www.coast hotels.com. 305 units. C$145–C$205 (US$145–US$205/£73–£103) 1-bedroom suite. Extra person C$15 (US$15/£7.50). Weekend packages and weekly/monthly rates available. AE, DC, MC, V. Parking C$5 (US$5/£2.50). **Amenities:** Restaurant; lounge; indoor pool; exercise room; business center; limited room service. *In room:* TV, dataport, kitchen, fridge, microwave, coffeemaker, hair dryer, iron.

Courtyard by Marriott 🌟 *Finds* Don't let the name fool you—this is anything but a could-be-anywhere business hotel. Located downtown on the cliff edge of the North Saskatchewan River, with vistas over City Centre and the breadth of the valley, this Courtyard (formerly the Warwick) must have the best views in the entire chain. The structure was built as an apartment building before conversion into a hotel, meaning that no two rooms are the same and many are very large; the two-bedroom, two-bathroom units are literally family-size. Rooms are comfortable and well furnished—business travelers will like the large work desks, a real office chair, and free high-speed Internet access—but it's the setting and facilities at this hotel that really stand out. Edmontonians have voted the three-tiered bar and restaurant patio—cantilevered hundreds of feet above the river—the city's top spot for outdoor drinks and dining.

One Thornton Court (99th St. and Jasper Ave.), Edmonton, AB T5J 2E7. 📞 866/441-7591 or 780/423-9999. Fax 780/423-9998. 177 units. C$129–C$199 (US$129–US$199/£65–£100) double. Parking C$19 (US$19/£9.50) per day. **Amenities:** Restaurant; lounge; fitness center; business center; laundry service. *In room:* A/C, TV, fridge, coffeemaker, hair dryer, iron.

Crowne Plaza Chateau Lacombe Centrally located downtown, the Crowne Plaza, a round 24-story tower sitting on the edge of a cliff overlooking the North Saskatchewan River, possesses some of the city's best views (best seen from **La Ronde,**

the hotel's revolving restaurant; p. 624). The nicely furnished standard rooms aren't huge, though the wedge-shaped design necessitates that they are broadest toward the windows, where you'll spend time looking over the city. The Crowne Plaza's Sleep Advantage program focuses on extra-high-quality linens and pillows, plus interesting extras such as relaxation CDs and aromatherapeutic lavender atomizers for the sheets. For just a C$30 (US$30/£15) upgrade, executive suites offer twice the square footage of standard rooms, with a full living room with foldout bed—a sweet deal.

10111 Bellamy Hill, Edmonton, AB T5J 1N7. ℂ 800/661-8801 or 780/428-6611. Fax 780/425-5564. www.chateau lacombe.com. 307 units. From C$149 (US$149/£75) double. Extra person C$10 (US$10/£5). Weekend packages available. AE, DC, DISC, MC, V. Parking C$8 (US$8/£4) per day. **Amenities:** Revolving fine-dining restaurant; lounge; cafe; exercise room; business center; room service; laundry service. *In room:* A/C, TV, CD player, wireless Internet access, coffeemaker, hair dryer, iron.

Glenora Bed & Breakfast ℛ

Located in the heart of the artsy High Street district, just west of downtown, the Glenora occupies the upper floors of a 1912 heritage apartment building that has been converted to B&B accommodations. While lots of care has been taken to retain the period character and charm of the rooms, the rooms have been thoroughly updated—all but three have private bathrooms, and some have full kitchen facilities. Most appealing is the happy mix of unique period furnishings and snappy interior design—absolutely every room is unique. There are five styles of rooms, from simple bedroom units with shared bathrooms to one-bedroom apartment suites with kitchens. Included is free parking and access to a handsome Edwardian common room and a second-story deck. Complimentary breakfast is offered in an adjacent restaurant, and two of Edmonton's top restaurants are a block away. The Glenora is an excellent value and fun to boot. It's a great option if you're weary of anonymous chain motels.

12327 102nd Ave. NW, Edmonton, AB T5N 0I8. ℂ 877/453-6672 or 780/488-6766. Fax 780/488-5168. www.glenora bnb.com. 18 units. C$90–C$175 (US$90–US$175/£45–£88) double; specialty room packages available. Rates include continental breakfast. AE, MC, V. **Amenities:** Restaurant and bar downstairs; access to nearby health club; coin-op laundry. *In room:* TV/VCR, dataport, minibar, coffeemaker, hair dryer, iron.

Holiday Inn Express *Value*

This convenient hotel in a wooded neighborhood setting is tucked between downtown and the legislature building—a 5-minute walk will get you to shopping or lobbying. Although rooms aren't huge, they are newly remodeled and a good alternative to expensive hotels nearby. Nearly all rooms have balconies and free high-speed Internet access, and lots of cafes and pubs are within walking distance.

10010 104th St., Edmonton, AB T5J 0Z1. ℂ 877/423-4656 or 780/423-2450. Fax 780/425-1783. www.hiexdowntown. com. 140 units. From C$122 (US$122/£61) double. Rates include continental breakfast. AE, DISC, MC, V. Parking C$5 (US$5/£2.50). **Amenities:** Indoor pool; fitness center; whirlpool; business center; laundry. *In room:* A/C, TV, CD player, coffeemaker, hair dryer, iron.

Metterra Hotel on Whyte ℛℛ

The lively Old Strathcona neighborhood, filled with students and artists, now boasts a unique and stylish hotel. The Metterra is a redesigned former office building transformed into a swank boutique hotel, with a style that's contemporary and sleek but with homey warmth. The lobby sets the tone, with striking art, two-story rundlestone wall, and waterfall, while the guest rooms are large, with contemporary and Indonesian art adding a touch of humor and funk to the sleek modern decor. Some rooms offer a fireplace; others feature that ultimate of comfort, a La-Z-Boy recliner. Rooms are all unique, reflecting the fact that this wasn't built as a hotel, including top floor suites, with two balconies and more space than most apartments. Rates include a continental breakfast and an afternoon wine-and-cheese tasting. The Metterra is not a typical out-of-the-box business hotel, and thank goodness for it, but it offers all the features and services that sophisticated business and leisure travelers require, including high-speed wireless Internet access. The Metterra is also central for great nightlife and dining in Edmonton's hippest neighborhood.

10454 82nd Ave., Edmonton, AB, T6E 4Z7. (C) 866/465-8150 or 780/465-8150. Fax 780/465-8174. www. metterra.com. 98 rooms. From C$175 (US$175/£88) double. Rates include deluxe continental breakfast. AE, MC, V. Free valet parking. *In room:* A/C, TV, dataport, high-speed Internet, coffeemaker, hair dryer, iron, bathrobe.

Union Bank Inn 🏵🏵   If you're tired of unmemorable business hotels, this is a wonderful choice. The stylish Union Bank, built in 1910, now houses an elegant restaurant and intimate boutique hotel with each unique heritage guest room displaying its own charming style, rich colors, furniture, and fabrics. Joining the original inn are 20 contemporary business-class rooms in a new addition—each equally idiosyncratic and uniquely designed. All units, however, have the same amenities, including fireplaces, voice mail, feather duvets, and upscale toiletries. The older rooms vary in layout and aren't incredibly big; if you're in town with work to do, ask for one of the newer and larger units. Service is very friendly and professional. The restaurant/bar, Madison's, is a great place to meet friends (p. 625).

10053 Jasper Ave., Edmonton, AB T5J 1S5. (C) 800/423-3601 or 780/423-3600. Fax 780/423-4623. www.unionbank inn.com. 34 units. C$189–C$399 (US$189–US$399/£95–£200) double. Rates include full breakfast and in-room afternoon wine-and-cheese service. AE, DC, MC, V. Free parking. **Amenities:** Restaurant; bar; exercise room; access to nearby health club; business center; limited room service; same-day dry cleaning. *In room:* A/C, TV, dataport, fridge, hair dryer, iron, fireplace.

Varscona Hotel on Whyte *Value*   A sister boutique hotel to the boldly contemporary Metterra just down the street, the Varscona offers the same excellent quality of lodging and service but with a choice of more traditional hotel rooms. All rooms are nicely appointed and reflect a 2007 update of the decor; the real values here are the one-bedroom suites, with work desk, efficiency kitchen, dining room, Bose CD player, and sitting area. Old Strathcona shopping, dining, and nightlife are just outside your door.

8208 106th St., Edmonton, AB, T6E 6R9. (C) 866/465-8150 or 780/434-6111. Fax 780/439-1195. www.varscona. com. 89 rooms. From C$155 (US$155/£78) double. Rates include deluxe continental breakfast and afternoon wine and cheese. AE, MC, V. Free valet parking. *In room:* A/C, TV, dataport, high-speed Internet access, coffeemaker, hair dryer, iron, bathrobe.

INEXPENSIVE

Days Inn *Value*   For the price, this is one of downtown Edmonton's best deals. Located just 5-minute's walk from the city center, the motor inn has everything you need for a pleasant stay, including comfortably furnished rooms and easy access to public transport. If all you need for a night or two is a clean and basic room in a convenient location, this is a top choice.

10041 106th St., Edmonton, AB T5J 1G3. (C) 800/267-2191 or 780/423-1925. Fax 780/424-5302. www.daysinn.ca. 76 units. From C$98 (US$98/£49) double. Senior, AAA, and corporate discounts available. AE, DC, DISC, MC, V. Free parking. **Amenities:** Restaurant; bar; limited room service; coin-op laundry; same-day dry cleaning. *In room:* A/C, TV, dataport, wireless Internet, coffeemaker, hair dryer, iron.

Hostelling International Edmonton   Well located near the university in the lively Old Strathcona neighborhood, this pleasant hostel has shared kitchen facilities and spacious common rooms. Some family rooms are available and check-in is at 3pm.

10647 81st Ave. ⓒ **780/988-6836.** Fax 780/988-8698. www.hihostels.ca. 88 beds. Members C$24–C$28 (US$24–US$28/£12–£14); nonmembers C$28–C$32 (US$28–US$32/£14–£16). MC, V. **Amenities:** Self-catering kitchen; bike rental; coin-op laundry.

University of Alberta   In May through August, dormitory rooms in Lister and Schäffer Halls at the University of Alberta are thrown open to visitors. Some are standard bathroom-down-the-hall dorm rooms, single or twin, while others are single or twins with private washroom. In addition, the university has recently opened a number of hotel-style guest rooms with private bathrooms (C$95/US$95/£48). The university is right on the LRT line and not far from trendy Old Strathcona.

87th Ave. and 116th St. ⓒ **780/492-4281.** Fax 780/492-0064. C$39 (US$39/£20) single without private bathroom, C$49 (US$49/£25) twin without private bathroom; C$50 (US$50/£25) single with private bathroom, C$55 (US$55/£28) twin with private bathroom. MC, V. Parking C$5 (US$5/£2.50) per day. **Amenities:** Food service nearby; coin-up laundry.

WHERE TO DINE

Edmonton has a vigorous dining scene, with hip new eateries joining traditional steak and seafood restaurants. In general, fine dining is found downtown and on High Street, close to the centers of politics and business. Over in Old Strathcona, south of the river, are trendy—and less expensive—cafes and bistros.

DOWNTOWN
Expensive

Hardware Grill ✸✸✸ NEW CANADIAN   This is easily one of western Canada's most exciting restaurants. The building may be historic (and within walking distance of most downtown hotels), but there's nothing antique about the dining room. Postmodern without being stark, the room is edged with glass partitions, and exposed pipes and ducts are painted a smoky rose. There are as many appetizers as entrees, making it tempting to graze through a series of smaller dishes. Bison carpaccio is served with Québec Migneron cheese, and hand-cut potato gnocchi are dressed in morel cream and shaved black truffle. But it's hard to resist entrees such as plank-roasted salmon with fresh corn relish, grilled lamb tenderloin with chokecherry sauce, or Alberta beef tenderloin with chorizo-gratin potatoes.

9698 Jasper Ave. ⓒ **780/423-0969.** www.hardwaregrill.com. Reservations recommended. Main courses C$28–C$48 (US$28–US$48/£12–£24). AE, DC, MC, V. Mon–Fri 11:30am–2pm; Mon–Thurs 5–9:30pm; Fri–Sat 5–10pm. Closed 1st week of July.

La Bohème FRENCH   La Bohème consists of two small, lace-curtained dining rooms in a historic building northeast of downtown (at the turn of the 20th century, this structure was a luxury apartment building—the upper floors are now available as B&B accommodations). The cuisine is French, of course, and so is the wine selection, with a particular accent on Rhône Valley vintages. There's a wide selection of appetizers and light dishes, including a number of intriguing salads. The entrees are hearty, classically French preparations of lamb, chicken, and seafood. The restaurant also features daily changing vegetarian entrees. Desserts are outstanding.

6427 112th Ave. ⓒ **780/474-5693.** www.laboheme.ca. Reservations required. Main courses C$24–C$35 (US$24–US$35/£12–£18); table d'hôte menu C$70 (US$70/£35). AE, MC, V. Tues–Sun 4:30–11pm; Fri 11:30am–2:30pm; Sun 10:30am–2:30pm.

La Ronde ✸ REGIONAL CANADIAN   On the 24th floor of the Crowne Plaza Chateau Lacombe, the revolving La Ronde offers the best views of any restaurant in Edmonton. The Alberta-focused menu also puts on quite a show; chef Jasmin Kobajica is passionate about local organic meats and produce, and his menu is rich in Alberta-raised beef, lamb, and game prepared with a focus on indigenous flavors. Local bison rib-eye is served with prairie mushrooms and wheat-berry potato cake, while pork medallions are served with native black-currant *jus*. The intensely regional focus of the menu makes a brilliant contrast to the ever-changing, revolving vista of office towers and river valley.

10111 Bellamy Hill. (C) 780/428-6611. Reservations required. Main courses C$26–C$35 (US$26–US$35/£13–£18). AE, MC, V. Daily 5:30–11pm; Sun 10:30am–2pm.

Madison's at Union Bank Inn NEW CANADIAN   One of the loveliest dining rooms and casual cocktail bars in Edmonton is Madison's. Once an early-20th-century bank, the building's formal architectural details remain, but they share the light and airy space with modern art and excellent food. The menu is up-to-date, bridging Continental European cooking with regional Canadian ingredients. The menu features grilled and roast fish and meats, plus pasta dishes, and interesting salads (one special featured rose petals, baby lettuce, and shaved white chocolate). For meat eaters, beef tenderloin with mushroom-shallot compote and Guinness hollandaise is a standout, while lighter appetites will enjoy intriguing combinations such as pepper-crusted tuna carpaccio with Nicoise salsa and avocado-cucumber sorbet.

10053 Jasper Ave. (C) 780/423-3600. Reservations recommended. Main courses C$29–C$37 (US$29–US$37/£15–£19). AE, MC, V. Mon–Thurs 7–10am, 11am–2pm, and 5–10pm; Fri 7–10am, 11am–2pm, and 5–11pm; Sat 8–11am and 5–11pm; Sun 8–11am and 5–8pm.

Red Ox Inn NEW CANADIAN   Just a quick drive or taxi ride from downtown, the Red Ox Inn has a real neighborhood feel—and with just 15 tables, this intimate restaurant is bound to remain an insider's favorite. Not a lot of money has been spent on decor; in fact, the dining room, with black booths, white walls, and gleaming hardwood floors, is almost austere. The Red Ox keeps its focus on the food, producing subtly delicious dishes based on quality regional produce, meats, and fresh fish. Grilled chile prawns are served with crisp corn and scallion dumplings and chipotle-mayonnaise dipping sauce. An autumn night's special was leek-wrapped local pickerel stuffed with shrimp mousse served in a pool of red-beet beurre blanc, a masterpiece of delicate flavors and startling visual élan. The Red Ox serves serious cuisine, but in a very relaxed and comfortable atmosphere.

9420 91st St. (C) 780/465-5727. www.theredoxinn.com. Reservations recommended. Main courses C$26–C$34 (US$26–US$34/£13–£17). MC, V. Tues–Sun 5–10pm.

Sorrentino's Bistro and Bar ITALIAN   This upscale branch of a local chain is a good addition to the downtown scene. The sophisticated dining room is a popular meeting place for the captains of the city's business and social life. At lunch, you can order from the menu or choose sauces and noodles from a pasta buffet. The daily appetizer table features grilled vegetables, salads, and marinated anchovies. Entrees range from risotto to wood-fired pizza to imaginative choices such as tournedos of salmon and scallops.

10162 100th St. (C) 780/424-7500. www.sorrentinos.com. Reservations recommended. Main courses C$23–C$35 (US$23–US$35/£12–£18). AE, DC, MC, V. Mon–Fri 11:30am–2:30pm; Mon–Sat 5–11pm.

Moderate/Inexpensive

Four Rooms FUSION   You'll be glad to discover this externally unassuming restaurant and watering hole on the flank of Edmonton City Centre mall. If you're staying downtown and can't face the meat fest that most high-end restaurants serve as upscale regional cuisine, then this comfortable, easy-on-the-pocket restaurant with friendly and professional service is for you. The menu is a hybrid of Asian and North American cooking with lots of appetizers, salads, and tapas coming in under 10 bucks. Confit duck pot stickers, chicken enchiladas, beef bulgogi, and seared tuna salad are all delicious—and not *too much food*. The same high quality and diversity extends through the main courses. Thursday through Saturday you can catch live jazz in the lounge.

137 Edmonton City Centre East (102nd Ave. and 100A St.). ℂ 780/426-4767. Reservations recommended on weekends. Main courses C$18–C$32 (US$18–US$32/£9–£16). MC, V. Mon–Thurs 11am–midnight; Fri 11am–2am; Sat noon–2am; Sun 5pm–midnight.

Il Portico ☆☆ ITALIAN   A popular Italian restaurant among locals, Il Portico has a wide menu of well-prepared traditional but updated dishes. With excellent selections of grilled meats, pastas, and pizza, it's one of those rare restaurants where you want to try everything. Pear, fig, and frisee salad with Gorgonzola cheese is delicious, and gnocchi with Italian sausage, picholine olives, and smoked mozzarella is a delightful composition of textures and flavors. Service is impeccable, and the wine list one of the best in the city: Remarkably, the staff will open any bottle on the list (except reserve bottles) if you buy a half-liter. The dining room is nicely informal but classy; in summer, a lovely Tuscan-style courtyard offers alfresco dining.

10012 107th St. ℂ 780/424-0707. www.ilportico.ca. Reservations recommended on weekends. Main courses C$16–C$31 (US$16–US$31/£8–£16). AE, DC, DISC, MC, V. Mon–Fri 11:30am–2:30pm; Mon–Sat 5:30–10:30pm.

Sherlock Holmes ENGLISH   The Sherlock Holmes is a tremendously popular English-style pub with local and regional beers on tap (as well as Guinness) and a very good and well-executed bar menu. The pub is housed in a charming Tudor-style building with a picket fence around the outdoor patio, completely surrounded by high-rise towers. The menu has a few traditional English dishes—fish and chips, steak-and-kidney pie—but there's a strong emphasis on new pub grub—the tandoori chicken–and–goat cheese quesadilla is excellent.

10012 101A Ave. ℂ 780/426-7784. www.thesherlockholmes.com. Reservations not accepted. Main courses C$7–C$15 (US$7–US$15/£3.50–£7.50). AE, MC, V. Daily 11:30am–1am.

Wild Tangerine Cucina Domestica ☆ FUSION   Wild Tangerine is one of many new restaurants springing up in the former rail yards—now condo eruption—just west of downtown. This very hip and colorful restaurant offers updated and addictive versions of traditional Asian cuisine—the flavors and textures are as bright and crisp as the decor. The five-spice octopus salad with peppers, taro, and lotus root with a citrus dressing is an explosion of color and flavor. Shrimp lollipops with wasabi yogurt start the meal off with a bang. The jocular owner wanders from table to table. Besides the friendly welcome and the wonderful and affordable food, the green tea–based cocktails are ample reason for a return visit.

10393 112th St. (entrance on 104th Ave.). ℂ 780/429-3131. www.wildtangerine.com. Reservations not accepted. Main courses C$12–C$18 (US$12–US$18/£6–£9). AE, MC, V. Mon–Thurs 11:30am–10pm; Fri 11:30am–11:30pm; Sat 5–11:30pm.

HIGH STREET
Manor Cafe INTERNATIONAL   Housed in a stately home amid gardens, the Manor Cafe offers one of the most fashionable outdoor dining patios in Edmonton. This longtime Edmonton favorite offers fusion and international cuisine, ranging from Italian pastas—Manor Pasta with chicken, spinach, goat cheese, and tomato-gin-cream

sauce is the signature dish—to a delicious Moroccan curry to traditional Wiener schnitzel. The food is eclectic, but always delicious.

10109 125th St. (C) 780/482-7577. www.manorcafe.com. Reservations recommended on weekends. Main courses C$20–C$39 (US$20–US$39/£10–£20). AE, MC, V. Daily 11am–2pm and 5–9pm.

Violino Gastronomia Italiana ITALIAN   Violino, located along High Street's gallery row in a 1913 heritage home, offers nouveau Italian fine dining with an emphasis on fresh, stylish ingredients. There's a large selection of appetizers for starters or light dining, including a trio of fois gras preparations. Pasta dishes are especially tempting, including tiger-stripped agnolotti with lobster, scallops, artichoke hearts and goat cheese, or pear and pecorino cheese ravioli with reduced cream and a drizzle of port. The house specialty is *biftecca fiorentina,* a grilled T-bone steak for two. The dining room exudes a certain version of luxe, with floor-length brocaded curtains, velvet upholstered chairs, and granite-tiled walls. In summer there is alfresco dining on a quiet shady deck.

10133 125th St. (C) 780/757-8701. Reservations recommended on weekends. Main courses C$23–C$38 (US$23–US$38/£12–£19). AE, MC, V. Mon–Fri 11am–2:30pm and 5–10:30pm; Sat 5–10:30pm.

OLD STRATHCONA

Chianti Cafe (Value) ITALIAN   Chianti is a rarity among Italian restaurants: very good and very inexpensive. Pasta dishes begin at C$8 (US$8/£4) and run to C$12 (US$12/£6) for fettuccine with scallops, smoked salmon, curry, and garlic; even veal dishes (over half a dozen are offered) and seafood specials barely top C$16 (US$16/£8). Chianti is located in a handsomely remodeled post office building; the restaurant isn't a secret, so it can be a busy and fairly crowded experience.

10501 82nd Ave. (C) 780/439-9829. www.chianticafe.ca. Reservations required. Main courses C$8–C$20 (US$8–US$20/£4–£10). AE, DC, DISC, MC, V. Daily 11am–11pm.

Culina (C)(C) INTERNATIONAL   A few blocks north of Old Strathcona's busy Whyte Avenue is Culina, an intimate and coolly retro dining room with intriguing but casual fine dining. The cooking here is a celebration of international flavors, without the muddied tastes so common with fusion cooking or the assertive exoticism of many global menus. Instead, this is what comfort food would taste like if the whole world were your neighborhood. Grilled white salmon is glazed with honey, almonds, and goat cheese, and sirloin steak is topped with an unexpectedly rich and flavorful sauce of blue cheese and chocolate. At lunch, there's no better appetite quencher than the House Sandwich, grilled zucchini, spinach, cream cheese, and pickled peppers on house-made bread. Sunday is "family night" when there's a three-course chef's choice dinner (C$24/US$24/£12) served family style. All meats are from local Alberta farms and ranches, and fish is line-caught.

9914 89th Ave. (C) 780/437-5588. www.culina.ca. Reservations recommended. Main courses C$16–C$23 (US$16–US$23/£8–£12). MC, V. Mon–Fri 9am–3pm and 5–10pm; Sat 10am–3pm and 5–11pm; Sun 5–8pm.

Da-De-O CAJUN/SOUTHERN   This New Orleans–style diner is authentic right down to the low-tech, juke-box-at-your-table music system. The food is top-notch, with good and goopy po' boy sandwiches, fresh oysters, and five kinds of jambalaya. Especially good is the Louisiana Linguine, with crawfish and clams in basil cream. Relax in a vinyl booth, listen to Billie Holiday, and graze through some crab fritters.

10548A 82nd Ave. (C) 780/433-0930. www.dadeo.ca. Reservations not accepted. Main courses C$10–C$16 (US$10–US$16/£5–£8). AE, MC, V. Mon–Tues and Thurs–Sat 11:30am–11pm; Sun noon–10pm.

Julio's Barrio MEXICAN   If you like Tex-Mex food, it's worth a detour to Julio's—in Canada, south-of-the-border cooking normally takes on quite a different meaning. This very lively restaurant and watering hole is a great place to snack on several light dishes while quaffing drinks with friends. The food ranges from enchiladas and nachos to sizzling shrimp fajitas. The atmosphere is youthful, high energy, and minimalist-hip: no kitschy piñatas or scratchy recordings of marimba bands here.

10450 82nd Ave. ℂ 780/431-0774. Reservations not accepted. Main courses C$9–C$19 (US$9–US$19/£4.50–£9.50). AE, MC, V. Mon–Wed 11:45am–11pm; Thurs 11:45am–midnight; Fri–Sat noon–1am; Sun noon–11pm.

The King & I ⊛ THAI   This member of a well-respected Alberta chain is the place for excellent, zesty Thai food, which can be a real treat after the beef-rich cooking of western Canada. Many dishes are vegetarian, almost a novelty in Alberta. Various curries, ranging from mild to sizzling, and rice and noodle dishes are the house specialties. For a real treat, try the lobster in curry sauce with asparagus.

8208 107th St. ℂ 780/433-2222. Main courses C$12–C$25 (US$12–US$25/£6–£13). AE, MC, V. Mon–Thurs 11:30am–10:30pm; Fri 11:30am–11:30pm; Sat 4:30–11:30pm.

Packrat Louie Kitchen & Bar ⊛⊛ ITALIAN   Bright and lively, this very popular bistro has a somewhat unlikely name, given that it's one of the best casual Italian trattorie in Edmonton. Menu choices range from specialty pizzas to fine entree salads—I loved the seared goat-cheese salad with mushrooms, pumpkin seeds, and smoked-pear dressing—to grilled meats, chicken, and pasta. Most dishes cast an eye toward light or healthy preparations without sacrificing complexity. Grilled salmon is dressed with maple-sage–brown butter sauce, and served over a warm salad of spinach, basil leaves, and dried cranberries; pork rib-eye is topped with blueberry-pepper sauce.

10335 83rd Ave. ℂ 780/433-0123. www.packratlouie.com. Reservations recommended on weekends. Main courses C$20–C$40 (US$20–US$40/£10–£20). MC, V. Tues–Sat 11:30am–11:30pm.

EDMONTON AFTER DARK

Tickets to most events are available through **Ticketmaster** (ℂ 780/451-8000). For listings of current happenings, check the Friday arts section of the *Edmonton Journal* (www.edmontonjournal.com) or the alternative weekly *See* (www.seemagazine.com).

THE PERFORMING ARTS   A masterpiece of theatrical architecture, the **Citadel Theatre**, 9828 101A Ave. (ℂ 780/426-4811; www.citadeltheatre.com), looks like a gigantic greenhouse and takes up the entire city block adjacent to Sir Winston Churchill Square. It houses five different theaters, workshops and classrooms, a restaurant, and a magnificent indoor garden with a waterfall. The Citadel is one of the largest, busiest theaters in Canada.

Home to the **Edmonton Opera** (ℂ 780/424-4040; www.edmontonopera.com) and the **Alberta Ballet** (ℂ 780/428-6839; www.albertaballet.com), the **Northern Alberta Jubilee Auditorium**, 11455 87th Ave. (ℂ 780/427-2760; www.jubileeauditorium.com), also plays host to traveling dance troupes, Broadway shows, and other acts that require a large stage and excellent acoustics.

THE CLUB & BAR SCENE   The flashy, upscale country-and-western scene is very popular in Edmonton, and the hottest country-dance bar in town is the **Cook County Saloon**, 8010 103rd St. (ℂ 780/432-2665).

An Edmonton institution, the **Sidetrack Café** ⊛, 10333 112th St. (ℂ 780/421-1326), is a holdover from the '60s, when live music was a way of life. This venerable club on the wrong side of the tracks sees a real variety of bands, from Australian rock to west coast punk to progressive jazz. For something uniquely Edmonton without the twang, check out the versatile Sidetrack Café.

It may not look like much (and that's usually a good sign), but the popular **Blues on Whyte,** 10329 82nd Ave. (© **780/439-5058**), in the vintage Commercial Hotel in Old Strathcona, is Edmonton's best blues club.

Downtown, the **New City**, 10081 Jasper Ave. (© **780/429-2582**), is a youthful hangout with something different every night, from live bands to DJs to drag shows. In Old Strathcona, the **Backroom Vodka Bar,** 10324 82nd Ave. (© **780/436-4418**), offers a similarly lively mix of live music, DJs, and performance. You'll find plenty of other nightclubs and music scenes along 82nd Avenue in Old Strathcona.

Looking for Edmonton's gay and lesbian scene? Start your investigation of the city's lively gay life at **The Roost,** 10345 104th St. (© **780/426-3150**), with dancing and cocktails, or **Buddy's,** 11725 Jasper Ave. (© **780/488-6636**), with dancing nightly and drag shows on Wednesday.

SIDE TRIPS FROM EDMONTON

Elk Island National Park ⚑
One of Canada's most compact and prettiest national parks, Elk Island protects a prairie lake ecosystem, one of Canada's most endangered biosystems, and is the home and roaming ground to North America's largest and smallest mammals—the wood buffalo and the pygmy shrew (a tiny creature half the size of a mouse but with the disposition of a tiger). The park has hiking trails, campgrounds, golf courses, a lake, and a sandy beach.

On the Yellowhead Hwy., 32km (20 miles) east of Edmonton. © **780/992-5790.** www.pc.gc.ca. Admission C$6.90 (US$6.90/£3.45) adults, C$5.90 (US$5.90/£2.95) seniors, C$3.45 (US$3.45/£1.75) youths, or C$17 (US$17/£8.50) per family or group.

Reynolds Alberta Museum
Located 40 minutes south of Edmonton off Highway 2, the Reynolds Alberta is a science-and-technology museum with specialties in transport, industry, and agricultural engineering. The collection of vintage cars, bicycles, and period farm equipment is especially impressive, and there are hands-on activities to keep children busy. Adjoining the museum is Canada's Aviation Hall of Fame, with a hangar full of vintage airplanes.

2km (1¼ miles) west of Wetaskiwin on Hwy. 13. © **800/661-4726** or 780/361-1351. www.machinemuseum.net. Admission C$9 (US$9/£4.50) adults, C$7 (US$7/£3.50) seniors, C$5 (US$5/£2.50) youths 7–17, or C$20 (US$20/£10) families. Mid-May to Sept 1 daily 10am–5pm; Sept 2 to mid-May Tues–Sun 10am–5pm.

Ukrainian Cultural Heritage Village ⚑
This open-air museum has 30 restored historic buildings arranged in an authentic setting; the adjacent fields and pastures are planted and harvested according to period techniques. You'll learn what life was like for Ukrainian pioneers in the 1892-to-1930 era through costumed interpreters who re-create the daily activities of the period. The village and interpretive center are definitely worth the drive, especially in midsummer, when you can watch laborers in horse-drawn wagons gathering hay and harvesting grain.

25 min. east of Edmonton on Yellowhead Hwy. 16. © **780/662-3640.** Admission C$8 (US$8/£4) adults, C$7 (US$7/£3.50) seniors, C$4 (US$4/£2) children 7–17, free for children 6 and under, C$20 (US$20/£10) families. Mid-May to Labour Day daily 10am–6pm; day after Labour Day to mid-Oct weekends only 10am–6pm.

15

Vancouver

by Donald Olson

If you really want to understand Vancouver, stand at the edge of the Inner Harbour (the Canada Place cruise-ship terminal makes a good vantage point) and look around you. To the west you'll see Stanley Park, one of the world's largest urban parks, jutting out into the waters of Burrard Inlet. To the north, just across the inlet, rise snowcapped mountains. To the east, right along the water, is the low-rise brick-faced Old Town. And almost everything else you see lining the water's edge will be a new glass-and-steel high-rise tower. As giant cruise ships glide in to berth, floatplanes buzz in and out, and your ears catch a medley of foreign tongues, you may wonder just where on earth you are. Vancouver is majestic and intimate, sophisticated and completely laid-back, a bustling, prosperous city that somehow, almost miraculously, manages to combine its contemporary, urban-centered consciousness with the free-spirited magnificence of nature on a grand scale.

Vancouver is probably one of the "newest" cities you'll ever visit, and certainly it's one of the most cosmopolitan. There's a youthfulness, too, a certain Pacific Northwest chic (and cheek) that comes from being used in so many movies that Vancouver is sometimes called "Hollywood North." I can guarantee you that part of your trip will be spent puzzling out what makes it so unique, so livable and lovable, what gives it such a buzz. Nature figures big in that equation, but so does enlightened city planning and the diversity of cultures. Vancouver is a place where people *want* to live. It's a place that awakens dreams and desires.

The city's history is in its topography. Thousands of years ago a giant glacier sliced along the foot of the coast range, carving out a deep trench and piling up a gigantic moraine of rock and sand. When the ice retreated, water from the Pacific flowed in and the moraine became a peninsula, flanked on one side by a deep natural harbor (on Burrard Inlet) and on the other by a river of glacial meltwater (today called the Fraser River). Vast forests of fir and cedar covered the land and wildlife flourished. The First Nations tribes that settled in the area developed rich cultures based on cedar and salmon.

Some 10,000 years later, a surveyor for the Canadian Pacific Railroad (CPR) came by, took in the peninsula, the harbor, and the river, and decided he'd found the perfect spot for the CPR's new Pacific terminus. He kept it quiet, as smart railway men tended to do, until the company had bought up most of the land around town. Then the railway moved in, set up shop, and the city of Vancouver was born.

Working indoors, Vancouverites have seemingly all fallen in love with the outdoors. And why shouldn't they? Every terrain needed for every kind of outdoor pursuit—hiking, in-line skating, mountain biking, downhill and cross-country skiing, kayaking, windsurfing, rock climbing, parasailing, snowboarding—is right there in their backyard: ocean, rivers, mountains, islands, sidewalks. The international resort town of Whistler, which will take center stage during the Winter Olympics in 2010, is just 2 hours north of downtown Vancouver. And when Vancouverites aren't skiing or kayaking, they're drinking coffee or eating out. In the past decade or so, Vancouver has become one of the top restaurant cities in the world, bursting with an incredible variety of cuisines and making an international name for itself with its unique Pacific Northwest cooking.

The rest of the world has taken notice of the blessed life people in these parts lead. Surveys routinely rank Vancouver as one of the 10 best cities in the world to live. It's also one of the 10 best to visit, according to *Condé Nast Traveler.* And in 2003, the International Olympic Committee awarded Vancouver the right to host the 2010 Olympic Winter Games. Heady stuff, particularly for a spot that less than 25 years ago was routinely derided as the world's biggest mill town.

1 Essentials

GETTING THERE

BY PLANE   **Vancouver International Airport** (© 604/207-7077; www.yvr.ca) is 13km (8 miles) south of downtown Vancouver on uninhabited Sea Island. Daily direct flights between major U.S. cities and Vancouver are offered by **Air Canada** (© 888/247-2262; www.aircanada.com); **Alaska Airlines** (© 800/252-7522; www.alaskaair.com); **American Airlines** (© 800/433-7300; www.aa.com); **Continental** (© 800/231-0856; www.continental.com); **Frontier Airlines** (© 800/432-1359; www.frontierairlines.com): **Northwest Airlines** (© 800/447-4747; www.nwa.com); and **United Airlines** (© 800/241-6522; www.united.com). Direct flights on major carriers serve 33 cities in North America, including Denver, Phoenix, Dallas, New York, Houston, Minneapolis, Reno, and San Francisco; 12 cities in Asia; and 3 cities in Europe.

For domestic travelers within Canada, there are fewer options. **Air Canada** (© 888/247-2262) operates flights to Vancouver and Victoria from all major Canadian cities, connecting with some of the regional airlines. Cheaper and reaching farther all the time is the no-frills airline **WestJet** (© 888/WEST-JET or 800/538-5696; www.westjet.com), which operates regular flights from Vancouver and Victoria to Prince George, Kelowna, Edmonton, Calgary, Toronto, Montréal, Ottawa, Halifax, and farther afield.

Direct flights between London and Vancouver are offered by **Air Canada** (© 0871/220-1111; www.aircanada.com) and the no-frills **Zoom** (© 866/359-9666 in North America, or 0870/213-266 in U.K.; www.flyzoom.com). Other major carriers serving London (United, Continental, British Airways) make stops in the U.S. before continuing on to Vancouver. **Air Canada** (© 0871/220-1111; www.aircanada.com) also flies to Vancouver from Sydney, Australia, and Auckland, New Zealand.

Tourist information kiosks on Level 2 of the main and international arrival terminals (© 604/207-0953) are open daily from 8am to 11pm. In 2007, two new **Plaza Premium Lounges** (www.plaza-ppl.com) opened in the domestic and international terminals. The lounges are available to all passengers regardless of airline, travel class, or membership programs. The domestic terminal lounge is located post-security and features comfortable seating, runway views, business services, Wi-Fi, and refreshments for a C$25 (US$25/£13) entrance fee. The Plaza Premium Lounge at the international terminal features all of the above, as well as napping stations and showers, for a C$30 (US$30/£15) entrance fee. Lounges are open daily from 6am to 11:30pm.

Vancouver

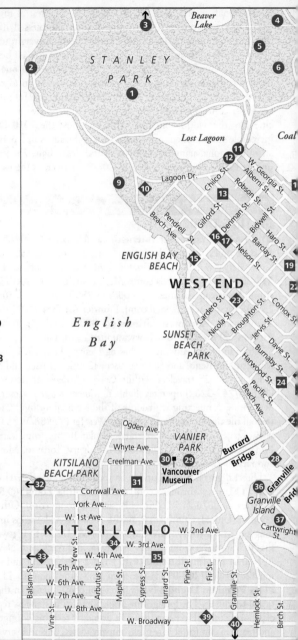

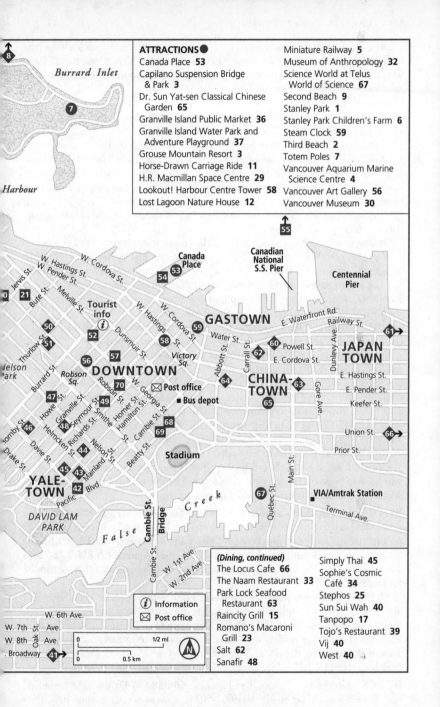

ATTRACTIONS ●

Canada Place **53**
Capilano Suspension Bridge & Park **3**
Dr. Sun Yat-sen Classical Chinese Garden **65**
Granville Island Public Market **36**
Granville Island Water Park and Adventure Playground **37**
Grouse Mountain Resort **3**
Horse-Drawn Carriage Ride **11**
H.R. Macmillan Space Centre **29**
Lookout! Harbour Centre Tower **58**
Lost Lagoon Nature House **12**
Miniature Railway **5**
Museum of Anthropology **32**
Science World at Telus World of Science **67**
Second Beach **9**
Stanley Park **1**
Stanley Park Children's Farm **6**
Steam Clock **59**
Third Beach **2**
Totem Poles **7**
Vancouver Aquarium Marine Science Centre **4**
Vancouver Art Gallery **56**
Vancouver Museum **30**

Burrard Inlet

Harbour

Canada Place
Canadian National S.S. Pier
Centennial Pier

W. Cordova St.
W. Hastings St.
W. Pender St.
Jervis St.
Bute St.
Melville St.
Tourist info
W. Hastings
W. Cordova St.
GASTOWN
E. Waterfront Rd.
Railway St.
Thurlow St.
Dunsmuir St.
Water St.
Powell St.
E. Cordova St.
JAPAN TOWN
E. Hastings St.
Burrard St.
Robson Sq.
DOWNTOWN
Victory Sq.
Abbott St.
Carrall St.
Dunlevy Ave.
Gore Ave.
E. Pender St.
Keefer St.
Nelson Park
Robson St.
W. Georgia St.
Post office
Bus depot
CHINA-TOWN
Howe St.
Granville St.
Seymour St.
Smithe St.
Homer St.
Hamilton St.
Cambie St.
Union St.
Prior St.
Hornby St.
Helmcken St.
Richards St.
Nelson St.
Beatty St.
Stadium
Main St.
VIA/Amtrak Station
Davie St.
YALE-TOWN
Mainland St.
Pacific Blvd.
Bridge
Creek
Québec St.
Terminal Ave.
DAVID LAM PARK
False
Cambie St.
Cambie St.
W. 1st Ave.
W. 2nd Ave.

ⓘ Information
✉ Post office

W. 6th Ave.
W. 7th Ave.
W. 8th Ave.
Oak St.
Broadway

0   1/2 mi
0   0.5 km

(Dining, continued)
The Locus Cafe **66**
The Naam Restaurant **33**
Park Lock Seafood Restaurant **63**
Raincity Grill **15**
Romano's Macaroni Grill **23**
Salt **62**
Sanafir **48**
Simply Thai **45**
Sophie's Cosmic Café **34**
Stephos **25**
Sun Sui Wah **40**
Tanpopo **17**
Tojo's Restaurant **39**
Vij **40**
West **40**

Drivers heading into Vancouver take the Arthur Laing Bridge, which leads directly to Granville Street, the most direct route to downtown. The **YVR Airporter** (© 604/ 946-8866; www.yvrairporter.com) provides **airport bus service** to downtown Vancouver's major hotels and cruise-ship terminal. It leaves from Level 2 of the main terminal every 15 minutes daily from 6:30am until midnight. Fares for the 30-minute ride across the Granville Street Bridge into downtown Vancouver are C$13 (US$13/ £6.50) for adults (C$20/US$20/£10 round-trip); C$10 (US$10/£5) for seniors (C$20/ US$20/£10 round-trip); C$6 (US$6/£3) for children (C$12/US$12/£6 round-trip); and C$26 (US$26/£13) for families (2 adults, 2 children; C$40/US$40/£20 round-trip). Bus service to the airport leaves from selected downtown hotels every half-hour between 5:35am and 10:55pm. Scheduled pickups serve the bus station, cruise-ship terminal, Four Seasons, Hotel Vancouver, Georgian Court, Sutton Place, and others. Ask the bus driver on the way in or ask your hotel concierge for the nearest pickup stop and time.

Getting to and from the airport with **public transit** is much slower and requires at least one transfer, but it costs less. Public buses are operated by **Translink** (© 604/ 953-3333; www.translink.bc.ca). If you wish to travel into town this way, catch bus no. 424 at ground level of the domestic terminal; it will take you to Airport Station. From there, bus no. 98B will take you into downtown Vancouver. B.C. Transit fares are C$3.25 (US$3.25/£1.65) during peak hours, and C$2.25 (US$2.25/£1.10) on weekends and after 6:30pm. You must have the exact fare because drivers do not make change. Transfers are free in any direction within a 90-minute period.

The average **taxi** fare from the airport to a downtown Vancouver hotel is approximately C$25 (US$25/£13) plus tip, but the fare can run up to C$40 (US$40/£20) if the cab gets stuck in traffic. **LimoJet** (© 604/273-1331; www.limojetgold.com) offers flat-rate stretch-limousine service at C$39 (US$39/£19) per trip (not per person) to the airport from any downtown location, plus tip, for up to three people (C$45/US$45/£23 for up to six passengers). The drivers accept all major credit cards; reserve in advance.

Most major **car-rental firms** have airport counters and shuttles.

Canada Line, a new light-rail hookup from Vancouver International Airport, is scheduled to begin operation in 2009; visitors will be able to board the train at the airport and arrive downtown or in Yaletown in 22 minutes.

BY TRAIN   VIA Rail Canada, 1150 Station St., Vancouver (© 888/842-7245; www.viarail.ca), connects with Amtrak at Winnipeg, Manitoba. From there, you travel on a spectacular route that runs between Calgary and Vancouver. Lake Louise's beautiful alpine scenery is just part of this enjoyable journey. **Amtrak** (© 800/872-7245; www.amtrak.com) has regular service from Seattle, though buses are often substituted for trains on this line.

The main **Vancouver railway station** is at 1150 Station St., near Main Street and Terminal Avenue just south of Chinatown. You can reach downtown Vancouver from there by cab for about C$10 (US$10/£5). One block from the station is the SkyTrain Main Street Station, providing quick access to the downtown area. A one-zone Sky-Train ticket (covering the city of Vancouver) costs C$3.25 (US$3.25/£1.65) during peak hours, and C$2.25 (US$2.25/£1.10) on weekends and after 6:30pm.

BY BUS   Greyhound Canada Bus Lines (© 604/482-8747; www.greyhound.ca) and **Pacific Coach Lines** (© 604/662-8074; www.pacificcoach.com) have their terminals at the Pacific Central Station, 1150 Station St. Pacific Coach Lines provides service between Vancouver and Victoria. The cost is C$73 (US$73/£37) round-trip, which includes the ferry ride. Pacific Coach Lines will pick up passengers from most downtown hotels; call (C) **604/662-8074** to reserve.

BY CAR   You'll probably be driving into Vancouver along one of two routes. **U.S. Interstate 5** from Seattle becomes **Highway 99** when you cross the border at the **US-BC Peace Arch border crossing.** The 210km (130-mile) drive from Seattle takes about 2½ hours. Expect to wait anywhere from 15 minutes to over an hour to get through Passport and Immigration Control. There's a **Tourist Info Centre,** 356 Hwy. 99, Surrey, located just north of the border crossing. On the Canadian side of the border you'll drive through the cities of White Rock, Delta, and Richmond, pass under the Fraser River through the George Massey Tunnel, and cross the Oak Street Bridge. The highway ends there and becomes Oak Street, a very busy urban thoroughfare heading toward downtown. Turn left at the first convenient major arterial (70th Ave., 57th Ave., 49th Ave., 41st Ave., 33rd Ave., 16th Ave., and 12th Ave. will all serve) and proceed until you hit the next major street, which will be Granville Street. Turn right on Granville Street. This street heads directly into downtown Vancouver on the Granville Street Bridge.

    Trans-Canada Highway 1 is a limited-access freeway running all the way to Vancouver's eastern boundary, where it crosses the Second Narrows bridge to North Vancouver. When traveling on Highway 1 from the east, exit at Cassiar Street and turn left at the first light onto Hastings Street (Hwy. 7A), which is adjacent to Exhibition Park. Follow Hastings Street 6.4km (4 miles) into downtown. When coming to Vancouver from Whistler or parts north, take Exit 13 (the sign says TAYLOR WAY, BRIDGE TO VANCOUVER) and cross the Lions Gate Bridge into Vancouver's West End.

BY SHIP & FERRY   The **Canada Place** cruise-ship terminal at the base of Burrard Street ((C) **604/665-9085;** www.portvancouver.com) is a city landmark. Topped by five eye-catching white Teflon sails, Canada Place Pier juts out into Burrard Inlet at the edge of the downtown financial district. **Princess Cruises, Holland America, Royal Caribbean, Crystal Cruises, Norwegian Cruise Lines, World Explorer Majesty Cruise Line,** and **Hanseatic, Seabourn,** and **Carnival** cruise lines dock at Canada Place and the nearby Ballantyne Pier to board passengers headed for Alaska via British Columbia's Inside Passage. They carry over 1.7 million passengers annually on their nearly 350 Vancouver-Alaska cruises. Public-transit buses and taxis greet new arrivals, but you can also easily walk to many major hotels.

    BC Ferries ((C) **888/223-3779** in B.C. only, or 250/386-3431; www.bcferries.com) has three routes operating between Vancouver and Vancouver Island. See "Getting There" in chapter 16's Victoria section for more information.

VISITOR INFORMATION
TOURIST OFFICES & PUBLICATIONS   The **Vancouver Touristinfo Centre,** 200 Burrard St. ((C) **604/683-2000;** www.tourismvancouver.com), is your single-best travel information source about Vancouver and the North Shore. An incredibly helpful and well-trained staff provides information, maps, and brochures, and can help you with all your travel needs, including hotel, cruise-ship, ferry, bus, and train reservations. There's also a **half-price ticket office** (Tickets Tonight) for same-day shows and events in Vancouver. The Touristinfo Centre is open daily from 8:30am to 6pm.

If you're driving, there's a Touristinfo Centre at 356 Hwy. 99, Surrey, located just north of the **US-BC Peace Arch border crossing.** Visitors arriving by ship will find a Touristinfo Centre at the **Canada Place Cruise Ship Terminal,** 999 Canada Place. Both of these are walk-in offices (no phone).

The free weekly tabloid *Georgia Straight* (© **604/730-7000;** www.straight.com), found all over the city in cafes, bookshops, and restaurants, provides up-to-date schedules of concerts, lectures, art exhibits, plays, recitals, and other happenings. The glossy city magazine *Vancouver* (© **604/877-7732**) is loaded with information and attitude. "VanMag," as it's also known, is available on newsstands and on the Web at **www.vanmag.com.** The free guide called *Where Vancouver* (© **604/736-5586;** www.where.ca) is available in many hotels and lists attractions, entertainment, upscale shopping, and fine dining. It also has good maps.

CITY LAYOUT

With four different bodies of water lapping at its edges and mile after mile of shoreline, Vancouver's geography can seem a bit convoluted. That's part of the city's charm, of course, and visitors normally don't find it too hard to get their bearings. Think of the downtown peninsula as being like an upraised thumb on the mitten-shaped Vancouver mainland. Stanley Park, the West End, Yaletown, and Vancouver's business and financial center are located on the "thumb," which is bordered to the west by English Bay, to the north by Burrard Inlet, and to the south by False Creek. The mainland part of the city, the mitten, is mostly residential, with a sprinkling of businesses along main arterial streets. Both mainland and peninsula are covered by a simple rectilinear street pattern.

MAIN ARTERIES & STREETS

On the downtown peninsula, there are four key **east-west streets. Robson Street** starts at BC Place Stadium on Beatty Street, flows through the West End's more touristed shopping district, and ends at Stanley Park's Lost Lagoon on Lagoon Drive. **Georgia Street**—far more efficient for drivers than the pedestrian-oriented Robson—runs from the Georgia Viaduct on the eastern edge of downtown, through Vancouver's commercial core; it then carries on through Stanley Park and over the Lions Gate Bridge to the North Shore. Three blocks north of Georgia is **Hastings Street,** which begins in the West End, runs east through downtown, and then skirts Gastown's southern border as it runs eastward to the Trans-Canada Highway. **Davie Street** starts at Pacific Boulevard near the Cambie Street Bridge, travels through Yaletown into the West End's more residential shopping district, and ends at English Bay Beach.

Three **north-south downtown streets** will get you everywhere you want to go in and out of downtown. Two blocks east of Stanley Park is **Denman Street,** which runs from West Georgia Street at Coal Harbour to Beach Avenue at English Bay Beach. This main West End thoroughfare is where locals dine out. It's also the shortest north-south route between the two ends of the Stanley Park Seawall.

Eight blocks east of Denman is **Burrard Street,** which starts near the Canada Place Pier and runs south through downtown, crosses the Burrard Street Bridge, and then forks. One branch, still **Burrard Street,** continues south and intersects West 4th Avenue and Broadway Avenue before ending at West 16th Avenue on the borders of Shaughnessy. The other branch becomes **Cornwall Avenue,** which heads west through Kitsilano, changing its name to **Point Grey Road** and then **Northwest Marine Drive** before entering the University of British Columbia campus.

Granville Street starts near the Waterfront Station on Burrard Inlet and runs the entire length of downtown, crosses the Granville Bridge to Vancouver's West Side, and carries on south across the breadth of the city before crossing the Arthur-Laing Bridge to Vancouver International Airport.

On the mainland portion of Vancouver, the city's east-west roads are successively numbered from 1st Avenue at the downtown bridges to 77th Avenue by the banks of the Fraser River. By far, the most important east–west route is **Broadway** (formerly 9th Ave.), which starts a few blocks from the University of British Columbia (UBC) and extends across the length of the city to the border of neighboring Burnaby, where it becomes the **Lougheed Highway.** In Kitsilano, **West 4th Avenue** is also an important east-west shopping and commercial corridor. Intersecting with Broadway at various points are a number of important north-south commercial streets, each of which defines a particular neighborhood. The most significant of these streets are (from west to east) **Macdonald Street** in Kitsilano, **Granville Street, Cambie Street, Main Street,** and **Commercial Drive.**

FINDING AN ADDRESS   In many Vancouver addresses, the suite or room number precedes the building number. For instance, 100–1250 Robson St. is Suite 100 at 1250 Robson St.

In downtown Vancouver, Chinatown's **Carrall Street** is the east-west axis from which streets are numbered and designated. Westward, numbers increase progressively to Stanley Park; eastward, numbers increase approaching Commercial Drive. For example, 400 W. Pender would be 4 blocks from Carrall Street heading toward downtown; 400 E. Pender would be 4 blocks on the opposite side of Carrall Street. Similarly, the low numbers on north-south streets start on the Canada Place Pier side and increase southward in increments of 100 per block (the 600 block of Thurlow St. is 2 blocks from the 800 block) toward False Creek and Granville Island.

Off the peninsula the system works the same, but **Ontario Street** is the east-west axis. Also, all east-west roads are avenues (for example, 4th Ave.), while streets (for example, Main St.) run exclusively north-south.

THE NEIGHBORHOODS IN BRIEF

DOWNTOWN Most of Vancouver's commercial and office space is found in a square patch starting at Nelson Street and heading north to the harbor, with Homer Street and Burrard Street forming the east and west boundaries respectively. Many of the city's best hotels are also found in this area, clustering near Robson Square and the water's edge. The most interesting avenues for visitors are Georgia, Robson, and Granville streets. **Georgia Street** is where you'll find the Vancouver Art Gallery (p. 666), the Coliseum-shaped Vancouver Public Library, and the Pacific Centre regional shopping mall. **Robson Street** is Trend Central, crammed with designer boutiques, restaurants, and cafes. Rapidly gentrifying **Granville Street** is the home of bars, clubs, theaters, pubs, and restaurants (along with one or two remaining porn shops to add that touch of seedy authenticity).

THE WEST END This was Vancouver's first upscale neighborhood, settled in the 1890s by the city's budding class of merchant princes. All the necessities of life are contained within the West End's border, especially on **Denman** and **Robson streets:** great cafes, good nightclubs, bookshops, and some of the best restaurants in the city. That's part of what makes it such a sought-after address, but it's also the little things, like the street trees, the mix of high-rise condos and sturdy old Edwardians, and the way that, in the midst of such an urban setting, you now and again stumble on a view of the ocean or the mountains.

GASTOWN The oldest section of Vancouver, Gastown has a charm that shines through the souvenir shops and panhandlers. It can be seedy—druggies and winos hang out around its fringes—but it's recently become home to some great new restaurants and stores. It's worth visiting because it's the only section of the city that has the feel of an old Victorian town—the buildings stand shoulder to shoulder, and cobblestones line the streets. The current Gastown was built from scratch just a few months after an 1886 fire wiped out the entire city. It's the place to look for a new and experimental art gallery, a young fashion designer setting up shop, or a piece of beautiful, hand-carved First Nations art in one of the galleries along **Water** and **Hastings** streets.

CHINATOWN Even though much of Vancouver's huge Asian population has moved out to Richmond, Chinatown remains a kick because it hasn't become overtly touristy. The low-rise buildings in this lively community are painted in bright colors, and sidewalk markets abound. For the tens of thousands of Cantonese-speaking Canadians who live in the surrounding neighborhoods, Chinatown is simply the place they go to shop. For visitors, the fun is to simply wander, look, and taste.

YALETOWN & FALSE CREEK NORTH Vancouver's former meat-packing and warehouse district, Yaletown has been converted to an area of apartment lofts, nightclubs, restaurants, high-end furniture shops, and a fledgling multimedia biz. It's a relatively tiny area, and the main streets of interest are **Mainland, Hamilton,** and **Davie.** For visitors, it features some interesting cafes and patios, some high-end shops, and a kind of gritty urban feel. This old-time authenticity provides an essential anchor to the brand-new bevy of towers that has arisen in the past 10 years on **Pacific Boulevard** along the north edge of False Creek (an area called False Creek North). The two neighborhoods are slowly melding into one wonderful whole.

GRANVILLE ISLAND Part crafts fair, part farmers market, part artist's workshop, part mall, and part industrial site,

Granville Island seems to have it all. Some 25 years ago, the federal government decided to try its hand at a bit of urban renewal, so they took this piece of industrial waterfront and redeveloped it into . . . well, it's hard to describe. One of the most enjoyable ways to experience the Granville Island atmosphere is to head down to the **Granville Island Public Market,** grab a latte (and perhaps a piece of cake or pie to boot), then wander outside to enjoy the view of the boats, the buskers, and the children endlessly chasing flocks of squawking seagulls.

KITSILANO   Once Canada's Haight-Ashbury, with coffeehouses, head shops, and lots of incense and long hair, Kitsilano has become thoroughly yuppified. Nowadays, it's a fun place to wander. There are great bookstores and trendy furniture and housewares shops, lots of consignment clothing stores, snowboard shops, coffee everywhere, and lots of places to eat (every third storefront is a restaurant). The best parts of Kitsilano are the stretch of **West 4th Avenue** between Burrard and Balsam streets, and **West Broadway** between Macdonald and Alma streets. Oh, and **Kits Beach,** of course, with its fabulous heated saltwater swimming pool.

COMMERCIAL DRIVE   Known as "The Drive" to Vancouverites, Commercial Drive is the 12-block section from Venables Street to East 6th Avenue. The Drive has a less glitzy, more down-to-earth, fading counterculture feel to it. It's an old immigrant neighborhood that, like everyplace else in Vancouver, has been rediscovered. The first wave of Italians left old-fashioned, delightfully tacky cafes such as **Calabria,** 1745 Commercial Dr. (© **604/253-7017**), and **Caffe Amici,** 1344 Commercial Dr. (© **604/255-2611**). More recent waves of Portuguese, Hondurans, and Guatemalans have also left their mark. And lately, lesbians, vegans, and artists have moved in—the kind of folks who love to live in this kind of milieu; think Italian cafe next to the Marxist bookstore across from the vegan deli selling yeast-free Tuscan bread. After the relentless see-and-be-seen scene in the West End, it's nice to come out to The Drive for a bit of unpretentious fun.

SHAUGHNESSY   Distances within Shaugnessy aren't conducive to a comfortable stroll, but Shaughnessy is a great place to drive or bike, especially in the spring when trees and gardens are blossoming. Designed in the 1920s as an enclave for Vancouver's budding elite, this is Vancouver's Westmount or Nob Hill. It takes a little bit of driving around to find your way in; it's an effort worth making, however, if only to see the stately homes and monstrous mansions. To find the neighborhood, look on the map for the area of curvy and convoluted streets between Cypress and Oak streets and 12th and 32nd avenues. The center of opulence is the Crescent, an elliptical street to the southwest of Granville and 16th Avenue.

RICHMOND   Twenty years ago, Richmond was mostly farmland with a bit of sleepy suburb. Now it's Asia West, an agglomeration of shopping malls geared to the new—read: rich, educated, and successful—Chinese immigrant. The residential areas of the city are not worth visiting (unless tract homes are your thing), but malls like the **Aberdeen Mall** or the **Yao Han Centre** are something else. It's like getting into your car in Vancouver and getting out in Singapore.

STEVESTON   Steveston, located at the southwest corner of Richmond by the mouth of the Fraser River, once existed for nothing but salmon. Fishermen set out from its port to catch the migrating sockeye, and returned to have the catch cleaned and canned. Much of that history is reprised in the **Gulf of Georgia Cannery National Historic Site,** near the wharf at Bayview Street and 4th Avenue (℡ **604/664-9009**). Since the fishery was automated long ago, Steveston's waterfront has been fixed up. There are public fish sales, charter trips up the river or out to the Fraser delta, and, above all, a laid-back, small-town atmosphere.

PUNJABI MARKET India imported. Most of the businesses on this 4-block stretch of Main Street, from 48th up to 52nd Avenue, are run by and cater to Indo-Canadians, primarily Punjabis. The area is best seen during business hours, when the fragrant scent of spices wafts out from food stalls, and the sound of Hindi pop songs blares from hidden speakers. Young brides hunt through sari shops or seek out suitable material in discount textile outlets. Frontier Cloth House, 6695 Main St. (℡ 604/325-4424), specializes in richly colored silk saris, shawls, fabrics, and costume jewelry.

2 Getting Around

BY PUBLIC TRANSPORTATION

The **Translink** (℡ **604/521-0400;** www.translink.bc.ca) system includes electric buses, SeaBus catamaran ferries, and the magnetic-rail SkyTrain. It's an ecologically friendly, highly reliable, and inexpensive system that allows you to get everywhere, including the beaches and ski slopes. Regular service runs daily from 5am to 2am.

Schedules and routes are available at the Touristinfo Centre, at major hotels, online, and on buses. Pick up a copy of *Discover Vancouver on Transit* at one of the Touristinfo Centres (see "Visitor Information," above). This publication gives transit routes for many city neighborhoods, landmarks, and attractions, including numerous Victoria sites.

FARES Fares are the same for the buses, SeaBus, and SkyTrain. A one-way, one-zone fare (which includes everything in central Vancouver) costs C$2.25 (US$2.25/£1.10). A two-zone fare—C$3.25 (US$3.25/£1.65)—is required to travel to nearby suburbs such as Richmond or North Vancouver, and a three-zone fare—C$4.50 (US$4.50/£2.25)—is required for travel to the far-off edge city of Surrey. After 6:30pm on weekdays and all day on weekends and holidays, you can travel anywhere in all three zones for C$2.25 (US$2.25/£1.10). **DayPasses,** good on all public transit, cost C$8 (US$8/£4) for adults and C$6 (US$6/£3) for seniors, students, and children. They can be used for unlimited travel on weekdays or weekends and holidays.

Keep in mind that drivers do not make change, so you need the exact fare, or a valid transit pass. Pay with cash or buy tickets and passes from ticket machines at stations, Touristinfo Centres, both SeaBus terminals, convenience stores, drugstores, and outlets displaying the FAREDEALER sign; most of these outlets also sell a transit map showing all routes.

BY SKYTRAIN The SkyTrain is a computerized, magnetic-rail train that services 20 stations along its 35-minute trip from downtown Vancouver east to Surrey through Burnaby and New Westminster. An extension, the Millennium line, opened in 2002. Not really of interest to most visitors, but those venturing off past Vancouver's Commercial Drive will find new stations at Broadway, Renfrew, and Rupert as well as new stations in New Westminster, towards Coquitlam.

BY SEABUS The SS *Beaver* and SS *Otter* catamaran ferries annually take more than 700,000 passengers, cyclists, and wheelchair riders on a scenic 12-minute commute between downtown's Waterfront Station and North Vancouver's Lonsdale Quay. On weekdays, a SeaBus leaves each stop every 15 minutes from 6:15am to 6:30pm, then every 30 minutes until 1am. SeaBuses depart on Saturdays every half-hour from 6:30am to 12:30pm, then every 15 minutes until 7:15pm, then every half-hour until 1am. On Sundays and holidays, runs depart every half-hour from 8:30am to 11pm. Note that the crossing is a two-zone fare on weekdays until 6:30pm.

BY BUS   Some key routes to keep in mind if you're touring the city by bus: **no. 5** (Robson St.), **no. 2** (Kitsilano Beach–downtown), **no. 50** (Granville Island), **no. 35** or **135** (to the Stanley Park bus loop), **no. 240** (North Vancouver), **no. 250** (West Vancouver–Horseshoe Bay), and buses **no. 4** or **10** (UBC–Exhibition Park via Granville St. downtown). From June until the end of September, the **Vancouver Parks Board** operates a bus route through Stanley Park stopping at 14 points of interest. Call (C) **604/257-8400** for details on the free service or contact (C) **604/953-3333** for general public transportation information.

BY TAXI

Cab fares start at C$2.45 (US$2.45/£1.25) and increase at a rate of C10¢ every 71m (233 ft.) or fraction thereof. In the downtown area, you can expect to travel for less than C$10 (US$10/£5) plus tip. Taxis are easy to find in front of major hotels, but flagging one down can be tricky. Most drivers are usually on radio calls. But thanks to built-in satellite positioning systems, if you call for a taxi, it usually arrives faster than if you go out and hail one. Call for a pickup from **Black Top** ((C) **604/731-1111**), **Yellow Cab** ((C) **604/681-1111**), or **MacLure's** ((C) **604/731-9211**).

BY CAR

Vancouver has nowhere near the almost-permanent gridlock of northwest cities such as Seattle, but the roads aren't exactly empty either. Fortunately, if you're just sightseeing around town or heading up to Whistler (a car is unnecessary in Whistler), public transit and cabs should see you through. However, if you're planning to visit the North Shore mountains or pursue other out-of-town activities, then by all means rent a car or bring your own. Gas is sold by the liter; speeds and distances are posted in kilometers. The speed limit in the city is 50kmph (31 mph); highway speed limits vary from 90kmph to 110kmph (56 mph–68 mph).

RENTALS   Rates vary widely depending on demand and style of car. If you're over 25 and have a major credit card, you can rent a vehicle from **Avis,** 757 Hornby St. ((C) **800/879-2847** or 604/606-2868); **Budget,** 501 W. Georgia St. ((C) **800/472-3325** or 604/668-7000); **Enterprise,** 585 Smithe St. ((C) **800/736-8222** or 604/688-5500); **Hertz Canada,** 1128 Seymour St. ((C) **800/263-0600** or 604/606-4711); **National/Tilden,** 1130 W. Georgia St. ((C) **800/387-4747** or 604/685-6111); or **Thrifty,** 1015 Burrard St. or 1400 Robson St. ((C) **800/847-4389** or 604/606-1666). These firms all have counters and shuttle service at the airport as well. To rent a recreational vehicle, contact **Go West Campers,** 1577 Lloyd Ave., North Vancouver ((C) **800/661-8813** or 604/987-5288; www.go-west.com).

PARKING   All major downtown hotels have guest parking; either in-house or at nearby lots, rates vary from free to C$28 (US$28/£14) per day. There's public parking at **Robson Square** (enter at Smithe and Howe sts.), the **Pacific Centre** (Howe and Dunsmuir sts.), and **The Bay** department store (Richards near Dunsmuir St.). You'll also find larger **parking lots** at the intersections of Thurlow and Georgia, Thurlow and Alberni, and Robson and Seymour streets.

Metered **street parking** isn't impossible to come by, but it may take a trip or three around the block to find a spot. Rules are posted on the street and are strictly enforced. (Drivers are given about a 2-min. grace period before their cars are towed away when the 3pm no-parking rule goes into effect on many major thoroughfares.) Unmetered parking on side streets is often subject to neighborhood residency requirements: Check the signs. If you park in such an area without the appropriate sticker on your windshield, you'll get ticketed, then towed. If your car is towed away or you need a towing service and aren't a CAA or an AAA member, call **Unitow** (✆ **604/251-1255**) or **Busters** (✆ **604/685-8181**).

SPECIAL DRIVING RULES   Canadian driving rules are similar to those in the United States. Stopping for pedestrians is required even outside crosswalks. Seat belts are required. Children under 5 must be in child restraints. Motorcyclists must wear helmets. It's legal to turn right at a red light after coming to a full stop unless posted otherwise. Unlike in the United States, however, daytime headlights are mandatory. Though photo radar is no longer used in B.C. (the new government got elected partially on its pledge to eliminate the hated system), photo-monitored intersections are alive and well. If you run through a red light, you may get an expensive picture of your vacation from the police. Fines start at C$100 (US$100/£50).

AUTO CLUB   Members of the American Automobile Association (AAA) can get assistance from the **Canadian Automobile Association (CAA),** 999 W. Broadway, Vancouver (✆ **604/268-5600,** or for road service 604/293-2222; www.caa.ca).

BY BIKE

Vancouver's a great place to bike. There are plenty of places to rent a bike along Robson and Denman streets near Stanley Park. A trip around the **Stanley Park Seawall** 𝕬𝕬𝕬 is one of Vancouver's premier sightseeing experiences. Bike routes are designated throughout the city. Paved paths crisscross through parks and along beaches, and new routes are constantly being added. Helmets are mandatory and riding on sidewalks is illegal except on designated bike paths.

You can take your bike on the SeaBus anytime at no extra charge. All of the West Vancouver blue buses (including the bus to the Horseshoe Bay ferry terminal) can carry two bikes, first come, first served, and free of charge. In Vancouver, only a limited number of suburban routes allow bikes on the bus: bus no. 351 to White Rock, bus no. 601 to South Delta, bus no. 404 to the airport, and the 99 Express to UBC. For more information, see "Bicycling & Mountain Biking," later in this chapter.

BY MINIFERRY

Crossing False Creek to Vanier Park or Granville Island on one of the blue miniferries is cheap and fun. The **Aquabus** (✆ **604/689-5858;** www.theaquabus.com) docks at the south foot of Hornby Street, the Arts Club on Granville Island, Yaletown at Davie Street, Science World, and Stamp's Landing. Ferries operate daily from 6:40am to 9pm (8:30pm in winter), as frequently as every 15 to 30 minutes. One-way fares are C$2.50 to C$5 (US$2.50–US$5/£1.25–£2.50) for adults and C$1.25 to C$3 (US$1.25–US$3/60p–£1.50) for seniors and children. A day pass costs C$12 (US$12/£6) for adults, C$11 (US$11/£5.50) for seniors, and C$8 (US$8/£4) for children.

FAST FACTS: Vancouver

Area Codes The telephone area code for the lower mainland, including greater Vancouver and Whistler, is **604**. The area code for Vancouver Island, the Gulf Islands, and the interior of the province is **250**.

Business Hours Vancouver **banks** are open Monday through Thursday from 10am to 5pm and Friday from 10am to 6pm. Some banks, like Canadian Trust, are also open on Saturdays. **Stores** are generally open Monday through Saturday from 10am to 6pm. Last call at the city's **restaurant bars** and **cocktail lounges** is 2am.

Consulates The **U.S. Consulate** is at 1075 W. Pender St. (© **604/685-4311**). The **British Consulate** is at 800–1111 Melville St. (© **604/683-4421**). The **Australian Consulate** is at 1225–888 Dunsmuir St. (© **604/684-1177**). Check the Yellow Pages for other countries.

Dentist Most major hotels have a dentist on call. **Vancouver Centre Dental Clinic,** Vancouver Centre Mall, 11–650 W. Georgia St. (© **604/682-1601**), is another option. You must make an appointment. The clinic is open Monday through Wednesday 8:30am to 6pm, Thursday 8:30am to 7pm, and Friday 9am to 6pm.

Doctor Hotels usually have a doctor on call. **Vancouver Medical Clinics,** Bentall Centre, 1055 Dunsmuir St. (© **604/683-8138**), is a drop-in clinic open Monday through Friday 8am to 4:45pm. Another drop-in medical center, **Carepoint Medical Centre,** 1175 Denman St. (© **604/681-5338**), is open daily from 9am to 9pm.

Emergencies Dial © **911** for fire, police, ambulance, and poison control.

Hospitals **St. Paul's Hospital,** 1081 Burrard St. (© **604/682-2344**), is the closest facility to downtown and the West End. West Side Vancouver hospitals include **Vancouver General Hospital Health and Sciences Centre,** 855 W. 12th Ave. (© **604/875-4111**), and **British Columbia's Children's Hospital,** 500 Oak St. (© **604/875-3163**). In North Vancouver, there's **Lions Gate Hospital,** 231 E. 15th St. (© **604/988-3131**).

Internet Access Most hotels have Wi-Fi hot spots, in-room Internet access, or guest computers or business centers with computer access. Free Internet access is available at the Vancouver **Public Library** Central Branch, 350 W. Georgia St. (© **604/331-3600**). **Cyber Space Internet Café,** 1741 Robson St. (© **604/684-6004**), and **Internet Coffee,** 1104 Davie St. (© **604/682-6668**), are both open until at least 1:30 a.m.

Liquor Laws The legal drinking age in British Columbia is 19. Spirits are sold only in government liquor stores, but beer and wine can be purchased from specially licensed, privately owned stores and pubs. LCBC (Liquor Control of British Columbia) stores are open Monday through Saturday from 10am to 6pm, but some are open to 11pm.

Newspapers & Magazines The two local papers are the *Vancouver Sun* (www.vancouversun.com), published Monday through Saturday, and *The Province* (www.canada.com/theprovince/index.html), published Sunday through

Friday mornings. The free weekly entertainment paper, *The Georgia Straight* (www.straight.com), comes out on Thursday. *Where Vancouver,* a shopping/tourist guide, can be found in your hotel room or at Tourism Vancouver.

Pharmacies **Shopper's Drug Mart,** 1125 Davie St. (© **604/685-6445**), is open 24 hours. Several Safeway supermarket pharmacies are open late; the one on Robson and Denman is open until midnight.

Police For emergencies, dial © **911.** Otherwise, the **Vancouver City Police** can be reached at © **604/717-3535.**

Post Office The **main post office** (© **800/267-1177**) is at West Georgia and Homer streets (349 W. Georgia St.). It's open Monday through Friday from 8am to 5:30pm. You'll also find post office outlets in Shopper's Drug Mart and 7-11 stores.

Restrooms Hotel lobbies are your best bet for downtown facilities. The shopping centers like Pacific Centre and Sinclair Centre, as well as the large department stores like the Bay, also have restrooms.

Safety Overall, Vancouver is a safe city and violent-crime rates are quite low. However, property crimes and crimes of opportunity (such as items being stolen from unlocked cars) occur frequently, particularly downtown. Vancouver's Downtown East Side, between Gastown and Chinatown, is a troubled neighborhood and should be avoided at night.

Taxes Hotel rooms are subject to a 10% tax. The **provincial sales tax (PST)** is 7% (excluding food, restaurant meals, and children's clothing). For specific questions, call the **B.C. Consumer Taxation Branch** (© **604/660-4524**).

Most goods and services are subject to a 5% **federal goods and services tax (GST).**

Time Zone Vancouver is in the Pacific time zone, as are Seattle and San Francisco. Daylight saving time applies April through October.

Weather Call © **604/664-9010** or 604/664-9032 for weather updates; dial © **604/666-3655** for marine forecasts. Each local ski resort has its own snow report line. Cypress Ski area's is © **604/419-7669;** Whistler/Blackcomb's is © **604/687-7507** (in summer it also provides events listings for the village).

3 Where to Stay

The past few years have seen a lot of activity in the Vancouver hotel business. The building boom associated with Expo '86 was followed by a flush of new hotel construction and renovation in the late '90s, right up to 2008, when three new hotels are scheduled to open. There are lots of rooms and lots of choices, from world-class luxury hotels to moderately priced hotels and budget B&Bs and hostels.

Most of the hotels are in the downtown area or in the West End. Central Vancouver is small and easily walkable, so in both these neighborhoods you'll be close to major sights, services, and nightlife.

Remember that quoted prices don't include the 10% **provincial accommodations tax** or the 5% **goods and services tax (GST).**

Reservations are highly recommended June through September and during holidays. If you arrive without a reservation or have trouble finding a room, call **Super Natural British Columbia's Discover British Columbia** hot line at (C) **800/435-5622** or **Tourism Vancouver**'s hot line at (C) **604/683-2000**. Both organizations will make free reservations using their large database of hotels, hostels, and B&Bs.

DOWNTOWN & YALETOWN

Downtown, which includes Vancouver's financial district, the area around Canada Place convention center and cruise-ship terminal, and the central shopping/business area around Robson Square, is buzzing during the day but pretty quiet at night. All downtown hotels are within 5 to 10 minutes' walking distance of shops, restaurants, and attractions. Hotels in this area lean more toward luxurious than modest, a state of affairs reflected in their prices. *One thing to note:* Downtown hotels on south Granville Street offer central location without the high price tag, but the area they're in is not very attractive and it's a prime hangout for panhandlers. It's not dangerous, but you shouldn't book there unless you have a reasonable tolerance for the tattooed and the pierced. Yaletown, a hip area of reconverted warehouses, is loaded with clubs and restaurants.

VERY EXPENSIVE

The Fairmont Hotel Vancouver ★★ A landmark in the city since it first opened in 1939, and located directly across from busy Robson Square and the Vancouver Art Gallery, the grande dame of Vancouver hotels has been completely brought up to 21st-century standards but retains its very old-fashioned, traditional elegance. The rooms are spacious, quiet, and comfortable, if not particularly dynamic in layout or finish. The bathrooms gleam with marble floors and sinks, and the solid tubs are those that you just don't find anywhere anymore. The courtyard suites feature a large, luxuriously furnished living room, separated from the bedroom by glass French doors. A state-of-the-art spa features day packages and a la carte treatments including body scrubs and wraps.

900 W. Georgia St., Vancouver, BC V6C 2W6. (C) 800/441-1414 or 604/684-3131. Fax 604/662-1929. www.fairmont. com. 556 units. High season C$349–C$535 (US$349–US$535/£175–£267) double; low season C$298–C$442 (US$298–US$442/£149–£221) double. Children under 18 stay free in parent's room. AE, DC, DISC, MC, V. Parking C$25 (US$25/£13). **Amenities:** 2 restaurants; bar; indoor pool; health club; excellent spa; Jacuzzi; sauna; concierge; tour desk; car rental; business center; shopping arcade; salon; 24-hr. room service; massage; babysitting; laundry service; same-day dry cleaning; nonsmoking rooms; Fairmont Gold executive-level rooms; rooms for those w/limited mobility; rooms for hearing-impaired guests. *In room:* A/C, TV w/pay movies, dataport, minibar, coffeemaker, hair dryer, iron/ironing board.

Four Seasons Hotel ★★ *Kids* For nearly 30 years now, the Four Seasons has reigned as one of Vancouver's top hotels. The hotel is favored by international business travelers who expect impeccable service and a full array of services—everything from complimentary shoe shines to a car service. The Four Seasons also caters to families with excellent children's amenities (including child-size bath robes and cookies and milk on arrival). From the outside, this huge high-rise hotel across from the Vancouver Art Gallery is rather unappealing. But the elegant lobby opens up into a spacious garden terrace and the appealingly large, light-filled rooms offer interesting views of downtown with glimpses of the mountains. The marble bathrooms are particularly well done. For a slightly larger room, reserve a deluxe corner room with wraparound floor-to-ceiling windows. One of the glories of this hotel is its health club with an enormous heated pool, half indoors and half outdoors, on a terrace right in the

Bed & Breakfast Registries

If you prefer to stay in a B&B, **Vancouver Bed & Breakfast,** 4390 Frances St., Burnaby, BC V5C ZR3 (© **604/298-8815;** www.vancouverbandb.bc.ca), specializes in matching guests with establishments that best suit their needs. **Canada-West Accommodations,** P.O. Box 86607, North Vancouver, BC V7L 4L2 (© **800/ 561-3223** or 604/990-6730; www.b-b.com) is another good agency to try. **Beachside Vancouver Bed & Breakfast Registry,** 1180 Renton Place, West Vancouver, BC V7S 2K7 (© **800/563-3311** or 604/922-7773) specializes in high-end B&Bs in the lower mainland.

heart of downtown. In 2004, *Travel + Leisure* magazine voted the Four Seasons one of the top 10 hotels for value in Canada.

791 W. Georgia St., Vancouver, BC V6C 2T4. © **800/332-3442** in the U.S. or 604/689-9333. Fax 604/844-6744. www.fourseasons.com/vancouver. 376 units. Nov–Apr C$230–C$520 (US$230–US$520/£115–£260) double; May–Oct C$350–C$790 (US$350–US$790/£175–£395) double. AE, DC, MC, V. Parking C$26 (US$26/£13). **Amenities:** 2 restaurants; bar; indoor and heated outdoor pool; outstanding exercise room; sauna; concierge; car rental; business center; shopping arcade; 24-hr. room service; massage; babysitting; laundry service; same-day dry cleaning; nonsmoking rooms; rooms for those w/limited mobility. *In room:* A/C, TV/VCR, Wi-Fi, minibar, hair dryer, iron/ironing board, safe.

Opus Hotel ☆☆☆   If you want to stay in a hip, happening, luxury hotel, try the Opus—it opened in 2002 and in 2005, *Condé Nast Traveler* voted it one of the world's top 100 hotels. It's the only hotel in Yaletown, the trendiest area in the city for shopping, nightlife, and dining. Each room is furnished according to one of five "personalities," with its own layout, color, and flavor. Everything is done well here, and the luscious room colors are eye candy if you're tired of blah hotel interiors. Bathrooms are fitted with high-design sinks and soaker tubs or roomy showers (or both). For the best views, book one of the corner suites on the seventh floor.

The cool Opus Bar serves an international tapas menu, and on weekends becomes one of Yaletown's late-night see-and-be-seen scenes (be forewarned: this area of Yaletown is Club Central, and can be noisy until the wee hours; book a Courtyard Room if you don't want to be disturbed). Opus's top-notch restaurant, Elixir, serves modern French bistro food. A complimentary car service is available to take you to cruise-ship terminals or any downtown location. *Note:* Until mid-2008, part of Davie Street, right outside the hotel, is closed off for construction of the new Canada Line light-rail system. Highest prices below are for suites.

322 Davie St., Vancouver, BC V6B 5Z6. © **866/642-6787** or 604/642-6787. Fax 604/642-6780. www.opushotel.com. 96 units. May–Oct C$429–C$1,800 (US$429–US$1,800/£214–£900) double; Nov–Apr C$349–C$1,300 (US$349–US$1,300/£175–£650) double. Children 17 and under stay free in parent's room. AE, DC, MC, V. Valet parking C$25 (US$25/£13). **Amenities:** Restaurant; bar; fitness center; complimentary bicycles; concierge; complimentary car service; 24-hr. room service; laundry service; dry cleaning; nonsmoking rooms. *In room:* A/C, TV w/pay movies, Wi-Fi, minibar, coffeemaker, hair dryer, iron/ironing board, safe, robes.

Pan Pacific Hotel Vancouver ☆☆☆   Since its completion in 1986, this 23-story luxury hotel atop Canada Place, with its cruise-ship terminal and convention center, has become a key landmark on the Vancouver waterfront. Guest rooms begin on the ninth floor, above a huge lobby with a wall of glass overlooking the mountains and the harbor. Despite its size, the hotel excels in comfort and service, and it provides spectacular views (note, however, that construction of the massive new addition to

Canada Place is going on just below the hotel on the west side). Book a deluxe Harbor and Mountain room, and you can wake to see the sun glinting off the mountains of the North Shore, floatplanes taking off from Burrard Inlet, and cruise ships arriving and departing just below your window. The rooms are spacious and comfortable, with large picture windows, contemporary furnishings, and a soothing palette of colors. Bathrooms are large and luxurious. Guests have free use of a heated outdoor pool and Jacuzzi overlooking the harbor. In 2005, the hotel opened its outstanding new health club (daily use fee). Café Pacifica puts on one of the best breakfast buffets in Vancouver and is open for casual meals all day; the Five Sails Restaurant, open for dinner only, is the hotel's fine-dining option.

300–999 Canada Place, Vancouver, BC V6C 3B5. © **800/937-1515** in the U.S. or 604/662-8111. Fax 604/685-8690. www.panpacific.com. 504 units. May–Oct C$490–C$640 (US$490–US$640/£245–£320) double, C$640–C$2,200 (US$640–US$2,200/£320–£1,100) suite; Nov–Apr C$390–C$480 (US$390–US$480/£195–£240) double, C$480–C$2,000 (US$480–US$2,000/£240–£1,000) suite. AE, DC, DISC, MC, V. Valet parking C$27 (US$27/£14). **Amenities:** 2 restaurants; bar; outdoor heated pool; squash court; health club; spa; Jacuzzi; sauna; concierge; business center; shopping arcade; 24-hr. room service; babysitting; laundry service; same-day dry cleaning; nonsmoking floors. *In room:* A/C, TV w/pay movies, dataport w/high-speed Internet, minibar, coffeemaker, hair dryer, iron/ironing board, safe.

Wedgewood Hotel ✮✮✮ If you're searching for a romantic, sophisticated hotel with superb service, spacious rooms, fine detailing, a good restaurant, a full-service spa, and a central downtown location, you can't do any better than the Wedgewood. One of the things that makes the award-winning Wedgewood so distinctive is that it's independently owned (by Greek-born Eleni Skalbania), and the owner's elegant personal touch is evident throughout. All 83 units are spacious and have balconies (the best views are those facing the Vancouver Art Gallery and Law Court; avoid the rooms that look out over the back of the hotel). Furnishings and antiques are of the highest quality, and the marble-clad bathrooms with deep soaker tubs and separate walk-in Roman showers are simply the best. Bacchus, the cozy hotel restaurant, serves a fairly traditional menu of fish, pasta, and meat.

845 Hornby St., Vancouver, BC V6Z 1V1. © **800/663-0666** or 604/689-7777. Fax 604/608-5349. www.wedgewood hotel.com. 83 units. C$400–C$600 (US$400–US$600/£200–£300) double; C$500–C$1,500 (US$500–US$1,500/£250–£750) suite. AE, DC, MC, V. Valet parking C$20 (US$20/£10). **Amenities:** Restaurant; small weight room; spa; concierge; business center; complimentary Wi-Fi; 24-hr. room service; laundry service; dry cleaning; executive-level rooms. *In room:* A/C, TV/VCR w/pay movies, CD player, dataport w/high-speed Internet, minibar, coffeemaker, hair dryer, iron/ironing board, safe.

MODERATE

Georgian Court Hotel ✮ *Value* This modern, 14-story brick hotel dating from 1984 is extremely well located, just a block or two from BC Place Stadium, GM Place Stadium, the Queen Elizabeth Theatre, the Playhouse, and the Vancouver Public Library. You can walk to Robson Square in about 10 minutes. The guest rooms are relatively large, nicely decorated, and have good-size bathrooms. And while the big-time celebs are usually whisked off to the glamorous top hotels, their entourages often stay at the Georgian Court, as it provides all the amenities and business-friendly extras such as two phones in every room, brightly lit desks, and complimentary high-speed Internet access, a service that other hotels almost always charge for.

773 Beatty St., Vancouver, BC V6B 2M4. © **800/663-1155** or 604/682-5555. Fax 604/682-8830. www.georgian court.com. 180 units. May–Oct 15 C$199–C$249 (US$199–US$249/£100–£125) double; Oct 16–Apr C$150–C$195 (US$150–US$195/£75–£98) double. AE, DC, MC, V. Parking C$9 (US$9/£4.50). **Amenities:** Restaurant; bar; health club; Jacuzzi; sauna; concierge; business center; limited room service; babysitting; laundry service; dry cleaning; nonsmoking rooms. *In room:* A/C, TV, dataport w/high-speed Internet, minibar, hair dryer, iron/ironing board.

Moda Hotel *Finds* Situated downtown, across from the Orpheum Theatre and close to the clubs in the Granville Street entertainment district, the Moda offers lots of style and excellent value. The hotel, located in a 1908 heritage building, reopened its doors in 2007 after receiving a major makeover from Vancouver's acclaimed interior designer Alda Pereira. Rooms and suites feature a sleek, tailored, European look with dramatic colors, luxury beds and linens, flatscreen televisions, nice tiled bathrooms with bath/shower, and double-glazed windows to dampen the traffic noise from Granville. The only thing the refurbers couldn't change was the slant in some of the old floors. For years, this hotel was called The Dufferin and catered to a mostly gay clientele; it's still super gay-friendly, but anyone with a bit of adventure and a taste for something out of the ordinary will enjoy a stay here. Suites offer an extra half-bath, corner locations with more light, and upgraded amenities.

900 Seymour St., Vancouver, BC V6B 3L9. © **604/683-4251.** Fax 604/683-4256. www.modahotel.ca. 57 units. C$119–C$229 (US$119–US$229/£60–£115) double; C$219–C$289 (US$219–US$289/£110–£145) suite. AE, DC, DISC, MC, V. **Amenities:** 2 restaurants; bar. *In room:* A/C, TV, dataport w/high-speed Internet, hair dryer.

INEXPENSIVE

Hostelling International Vancouver Downtown Hostel Located in a converted nunnery, this modern curfew-free hostel is an extremely convenient base of operations from which to explore downtown and the adjacent West End. The beach is a few blocks south; downtown is a 10-minute walk north. Most beds are in quad dorms, with a limited number of doubles and triples available. Except for two rooms with a private bathroom, all bathroom facilities are shared. Rooms and facilities are accessible for travelers with disabilities. There are common cooking facilities, as well as a rooftop patio and game room. The hostel is extremely busy in the summertime, so book ahead. There's free shuttle service to the bus/train station and Jericho Beach.

1114 Burnaby St. (at Thurlow St.), Vancouver, BC V6E 1P1. © **888/203-4302** or 604/684-4565. Fax 604/684-4540. www.hihostels.ca. 68 units (44 4-person shared rooms, 24 double or triple private rooms). Bed C$25 (US$25/£13) IYHA members, C$28 (US$28/£14) nonmembers; double C$62 (US$62/£31) members, C$68 (US$68/£34) nonmembers. Annual adult membership C$35 (US$35/£17). MC, V. Limited free parking. **Amenities:** Bike rental; game room; activities desk; coin laundry. *In room:* No phone.

The Kingston Hotel *Value* An affordable downtown hotel is a rarity for Vancouver; but if you can do without the frills, the Kingston offers a clean, safe, inexpensive place to sleep and a complimentary continental breakfast to start your day. You won't find a better deal anywhere, and the premises have far more character than you'll find in a cookie-cutter motel. The Kingston is a Vancouver version of the kind of small budget B&B hotels found all over Europe. Just 9 of the 55 rooms have private bathrooms and TVs. The rest have hand basins and the use of shared showers and toilets on each floor. In 2004, the hotel added a new lobby, breakfast room, pub-restaurant, and garden patio. The premises are well kept, the location is central so you can walk everywhere. The staff is friendly and helpful, and if you're just looking for a place to sleep and stow your bags, you'll be glad you found this place.

757 Richards St., Vancouver, BC V6B 3A6. © **888/713-3304** or 604/684-9024. Fax 604/684-9917. www.kingston hotelvancouver.com. 55 units, 9 with private bathroom. C$65–C$75 (US$65–US$75/£33–£38) double with shared bathroom; C$85–C$145 (US$85–US$145/£43–£73) double with private bathroom. Rates include continental breakfast. AE, MC, V. Parking C$20 (US$20/£10) across the street. **Amenities:** Restaurant; bar; sauna; coin laundry; nonsmoking rooms. *In room:* TV (in units with private bathrooms), no phone.

YWCA Hotel/Residence *Value* Built in 1995, this attractive 12-story residence next door to the Georgian Court Hotel is an excellent choice for travelers on limited budgets. Bedrooms are simply furnished; some have TVs. There are quite a few reasonably priced restaurants nearby (but none in-house). Three communal kitchens are available for guests' use, and all rooms have minifridges. (There are a number of grocery stores nearby.) The Y has three TV lounges and free access to the best gym in town at the nearby co-ed YWCA Fitness Centre.

733 Beatty St., Vancouver, BC V6B 2M4. © 800/663-1424 or 604/895-5830. Fax 604/681-2550. www.ywcahotel. com. 155 units, 53 with private bathroom. C$59–C$77 (US$59–US$77/£30–£39) double with shared bathroom; C$76–C$137 (US$76–US$137/£38–£68) double with private bathroom. Week-long discounts available. AE, MC, V. Parking C$10 (US$10/£5). **Amenities:** Access to YWCA facility; coin laundry; nonsmoking rooms. *In room:* A/C, TV, dataport, fridge, hair dryer.

THE WEST END

The West End is green, leafy, and residential, a neighborhood of high-rise apartment houses, beautifully landscaped streets, and close proximity to Coal Harbor, Stanley Park, and the best beaches. When downtown gets quiet at night, the West End starts hopping. There are dozens of restaurants, cafes, and bars along Robson and Denman streets.

EXPENSIVE

The Listel Hotel ★★ *Finds*   What makes the Listel unique is its artwork. Hallways and suites on the top two Gallery floors are decorated with original pieces from the Buschlen Mowatt Gallery (Vancouver's pre-eminent international gallery) or, on the Museum floor, with First Nations artifacts from the UBC anthropology museum. The interior of this boutique hotel is luxurious without being flashy. Rooms feature top-quality bedding and handsome furnishings. The roomy upper-floor suites facing Robson Street, with glimpses of the harbor and the mountains beyond, are the best bets here. Rooms at the back are quieter but face the alley and nearby apartment buildings. All the rooms and bathrooms were refurbished in 2007. In the evenings, you can hear live jazz at O'Doul's, the hotel's restaurant and bar; during the Vancouver International Jazz Festival in late June, it's the scene of late-night jam sessions with world-renowned musicians. The Listel is located right at the western end of the Robson Street shopping and restaurant strip; you can walk downtown or to Stanley Park in 10 minutes.

1300 Robson St., Vancouver, BC V6E 1C5. © 800/663-5491 or 604/684-8461. Fax 604/684-7092. www.thelistel hotel.com. 129 units. May–Sept C$260–C$320 (US$260–US$320/£130–£160) standard to gallery room double, C$520 (US$520/£260) suite; Oct–Apr C$180–C$240 (US$180–US$240/£90–£120) standard to gallery room double, C$340 (US$340/£170) suite. AE, DC, DISC, MC, V. Parking C$26 (US$26/£13). **Amenities:** Restaurant; bar; exercise room; whirlpool; concierge; free Internet access in lobby; limited room service; same-day laundry service and dry cleaning; executive-level rooms. *In room:* A/C, TV w/pay movies, iPod docking station, dataport w/high-speed Internet, Wi-Fi, minibar, coffeemaker, hair dryer, iron/ironing board, newspaper.

Pacific Palisades Hotel ★★★ *Finds*   Walk into the Pacific Palisades lobby and you know right away that this is not just another standard-issue hotel. Sherbet yellows and apple greens with pastel-colored fabrics, bright splashes of color, and whimsical touches make the hotel bright and welcoming to the young and the young at heart (the ubiquitous rock music playing in the lobby can be upbeat or annoying, depending on your mood and musical tastes). Guest rooms, spread out over two towers dating from 1969, are spacious, airy, and equipped with kitchenettes (with minibar items priced at corner-store prices). The one-bedroom suites boast large living/dining rooms and balconies. A few other perks that make this hotel a worthwhile choice are the complimentary afternoon wine tasting in the attached art gallery, the complimentary yoga program, the kid-friendly atmosphere, the large indoor pool and fitness rooms, and the fact that pets stay free. Plus, you're right on trendsetting Robson Street, minutes from beaches, shopping, cafes, and restaurants. Zin is a cool spot for a drink and dinner.

1277 Robson St., Vancouver, BC V6E 1C4. ⓒ **800/663-1815** or 604/688-0461. Fax 604/688-4374. www.pacific palisadeshotel.com. 233 units. C$150–C$425 (US$150–US$425/£75–£213) double. AE, DC, DISC, MC, V. Valet parking C$26 (US$26/£13). **Amenities:** Restaurant; bar; indoor lap pool; excellent health club; spa services; Jacuzzi; sauna; concierge; business center; limited room service; babysitting; coin laundry and laundry service; same-day dry cleaning; nonsmoking rooms; basketball court; yoga program. *In room:* A/C, TV, dataport w/high-speed Internet, kitchenette, minibar, fridge, coffeemaker, hair dryer, iron/ironing board.

Westin Bayshore Resort & Marina 🌟🌟🌟 *(Kids)*   This is the only resort hotel in Vancouver that has its own marina in case you want to arrive by boat, and the views from all but a handful of its rooms are stunning. Perched on the water's edge overlooking Coal Harbour marina and Stanley Park on one side, and Burrard Inlet and the city on the other, the Bayshore is an easy stroll from Canada Place Pier, Robson Street, and downtown. Rooms in the original 1961 building have been refurbished with classic-looking decor and floor-to-ceiling windows that open wide. In the newer tower, the rooms are a bit larger and have narrow, step-out balconies. The bathrooms in both buildings are nicely finished but fairly small. The circular, heated outdoor pool is reputedly the largest in North America; there's a second indoor pool plus a full gym. This family-friendly hotel provides children with their own welcome package. Like other Westins, the Bayshore is completely nonsmoking and features the aptly named "Heavenly" beds.

1601 Bayshore Dr., Vancouver, BC V6G 2V4. ⓒ **800/937-8461** or 604/682-3377. Fax 604/687-3102. www.westin bayshore.com. 510 units. C$330–C$390 (US$330–US$390/£165–£195) double; C$550–C$695 (US$550–US$695/ £275–£347) suite. Children under 18 stay free in parent's room. AE, DC, MC, V. Valet parking C$23 (US$23/£12); self-parking C$20 (US$20/£10). **Amenities:** 2 restaurants; bar; indoor and outdoor pool; health club; full-service spa; Jacuzzi; sauna; concierge; business center; shopping arcade; 24-hr. room service; babysitting; laundry service; same-day dry cleaning; nonsmoking hotel. *In room:* A/C, TV w/pay movies, dataport w/high-speed Internet, minibar, coffeemaker, hair dryer, iron/ironing board, safe.

MODERATE

Barclay House 🌟 *(Finds)*   The Barclay House, located on one of the West End's quiet maple-lined streets just a block from historic Barclay Square, opened as a bed-and-breakfast in 1999. Built in 1904 by a local developer, this beautiful house can be a destination on its own. The elegant parlors and dining rooms are perfect for lounging on a rainy afternoon or sipping a glass of complimentary sherry before venturing out for dinner in the trendy West End. On a summer day, the front porch, with its wooden Adirondack chairs, is a cozy place to read. All rooms are beautifully furnished in Victorian style; a number of the pieces are family heirlooms. Modern conveniences such as CD players, TV/VCRs, and luxurious bathrooms blend in perfectly. The penthouse offers skylights, a fireplace, and a claw-foot tub; the south room contains a queen-size brass bed and an elegant sitting room.

1351 Barclay St., Vancouver, BC V6E 1H6. ⓒ **800/971-1351** or 604/605-1351. Fax 604/605-1382. www.barclay house.com. 5 units. C$175–C$245 (US$175–US$245/£88–£123) double. MC, V. Free parking. **Amenities:** Access to nearby fitness center; concierge; nonsmoking rooms. *In room:* TV/VCR w/pay movies, video library, CD player, Wi-Fi, fridge, hair dryer, iron/ironing board.

Blue Horizon *(Value)*   This 31-story high-rise built in the 1960s has a great location on Robson Street, just a block from the trendier Pacific Palisades and the tonier Listel Hotel (see above for both). It's cheaper than those places and has views that are just as good if not better, but it lacks their charm and feels bit like a high-rise motel. The rooms are fairly spacious, though, and every room is on a corner with wraparound windows, which maximizes the light and the view; every room has a small balcony, too. In 2000, the hotel renovated all its guest rooms, giving them a clean, contemporary look. Bathrooms are on the small side and have tubs with showers. Superior rooms and penthouse suites on the 15th to 30th floors offer breathtaking views looking north towards the mountains or west towards English Bay. If you're ecology-minded, book a room on the "Green Floor," which features energy-efficient lighting, low-flow showerheads, and recycling bins. The entire hotel is nonsmoking.

1225 Robson St., Vancouver, BC V6E 1C3. ℂ 800/663-1333 or 604/688-1411. Fax 604/688-4461. www.bluehorizon hotel.com. 214 units. C$109–C$199 (US$109–US$199/£54–£99) double; C$119–C$219 (US$119–US$219/£60–£110) superior double; C$199–C$329 (US$199–US$329/£100–£165) penthouse suite. Children under 16 stay free in parent's room. AE, DC, MC, V. Self-parking C$14 (US$14/£7). **Amenities:** Restaurant; indoor pool; exercise room; Jacuzzi; sauna; concierge; same-day dry cleaning; nonsmoking hotel. *In room:* A/C, TV w/pay movies, free high-speed Internet, mini-bar, fridge, coffeemaker, hair dryer, iron/ironing board, safe.

Coast Plaza Hotel & Suites 𝒦

Built originally as an apartment building, this 35-story hotel atop Denman Place Mall attracts a wide variety of guests, from business travelers and tour groups to film and TV actors. They come for the large rooms, the affordable one- and two-bedroom suites, and the fabulous views of English Bay. The two-bedroom corner suites are bigger than most West End apartments, and boast spectacular panoramas. The spacious one-bedroom suites and standard rooms feature floor-to-ceiling windows and walk-out balconies; about half the units have full kitchens. Furnishings are plain and comfortable, if a little dated. Though there's a good-size heated pool, it's in a basement room that is not particularly appealing.

1763 Comox St., Vancouver, BC V6G 1P6. ℂ 800/663-1144 or 604/688-7711. Fax 604/688-5934. www.coast hotels.com. 269 units. C$179–C$219 (US$179–US$219/£90–£110) double; C$219–C$299 (US$219–US$299/£110–£150) suite. AE, DC, DISC, MC, V. Valet parking C$8 (US$8/£4). **Amenities:** Restaurant; bar; indoor pool; complimentary access to Denman Fitness Centre in mall below; Jacuzzi; sauna; concierge; free downtown shuttle service; business center; shopping arcade; 24-hr. room service; babysitting; coin laundry; same-day dry cleaning; nonsmoking rooms. *In room:* A/C, TV, dataport w/high-speed Internet, minibar, fridge, coffeemaker, hair dryer, iron/ironing board.

Sunset Inn & Suites 𝒦 (𝒱alue (𝒦ids

Just a couple of blocks from English Bay on the edge of the residential West End, the Sunset Inn offers roomy accommodations in a great location for a reasonable price. Units are either studios or one-bedroom apartments, and come with fully equipped kitchens and dining areas. Like many other hotels in this part of town, the Sunset Inn started life as an apartment building, which means that the rooms are larger than your average hotel room, and all have balconies. The view gets better on the higher floors, but the price remains the same, so book early and request an upper floor. For those traveling with children, the one-bedroom suites have a separate bedroom and a pullout couch in the living room. Most of the rooms have recently been redone to look upscale, but the finishes are faux and the furniture is oddly unyielding. Still, the beds are comfy, the staff is helpful and friendly, and the location is great for this price.

1111 Burnaby St., Vancouver, BC V6E 1P4. ℂ 800/786-1997 or 604/688-2474. Fax 604/669-3340. www.sunsetinn. com. 50 units. C$99–C$229 (US$99–US$229/£50–£115) studio; C$109–C$299 (US$109–US$299/£55–£150) 1-bedroom suite. Children under 12 stay free in parent's room. Weekly rates available. AE, DC, MC, V. Free parking. **Amenities:** Small exercise room; coin laundry; nonsmoking rooms. *In room:* TV, free Wi-Fi, kitchen, coffeemaker, iron/ironing board.

West End Guest House 𝒦 (𝒻inds

A heritage home built in 1906, the West End Guest House is a handsome example of what the neighborhood looked like before concrete towers and condos replaced the original Edwardian homes in the early 1950s. Decorated with early-20th-century antiques and a serious collection of vintage photographs of Vancouver taken by the original owners, this is a calm respite from the hustle and bustle of the West End. The seven guest rooms feature feather mattresses, down duvets, and your very own resident stuffed animal. The Grand Queen Suite, an attic-level bedroom with a brass bed, fireplace, sitting area, claw-foot bathtub, and skylights, is the best and most spacious room; no. 7 is quite small. Owner Evan Penner pampers his guests with a scrumptious breakfast and serves iced tea and sherry in the afternoon (on the back second-floor balcony in the summer). Throughout the day, guests have access to a pantry stocked with home-baked munchies and refreshments.

1362 Haro St., Vancouver, BC V6E 1G2. (℃) **888/546-3327** or 604/681-2889. Fax 604/688-8812. www.westend guesthouse.com. 9 units. C$89–C$295 (US$89–US$295/£45–£148) double. Rates include full breakfast. AE, DISC, MC, V. Free off-street parking. **Amenities:** Complimentary bikes; business center; laundry service. *In room:* TV/DVD, Wi-Fi, hair dryer.

INEXPENSIVE

Buchan Hotel   Built in 1926, this three-story building is tucked away on a quiet tree-lined residential street in the West End, less than 2 blocks from Stanley Park and Denman Street and 15 minutes by foot from the business district. Like the Kingston (p. 648) downtown, this is a small European-style budget hotel that doesn't bother with frills or charming decor; unlike the Kingston, it isn't a B&B, so you won't get breakfast. The Standard rooms are quite plain; be prepared for cramped quarters and tiny bathrooms, half of which are shared. The best rooms in the house are the Executive rooms. These four front-corner rooms are nicely furnished and have private bathrooms. The hotel also offers in-house bike and ski storage as well as a reading lounge.

1906 Haro St., Vancouver, BC V6G 1H7. (℃) **800/668-6654** or 604/685-5354. Fax 604/685-5367. www.buchan hotel.com. 60 units, 30 with private bathroom. C$48–C$78 (US$48–US$78/£24–£39) double with shared bath; C$73–C$98 (US$73–US$98/£36–£49) double with private bath; C$110–C$135 (US$110–US$135/£55–£68) executive room. Children 12 and under stay free in parent's room. Weekly rates available. AE, DC, MC, V. Limited street parking available. **Amenities:** Lounge; coin laundry. *In room:* TV, hair dryer and iron available on request, no phone.

THE WEST SIDE

Right across False Creek from downtown and the West End is Vancouver's West Side. If your agenda includes a Granville Island shopping spree, exploration of the laid-back Kitsilano neighborhood, time at Kits Beach, visiting the fabulous Museum of Anthropology and famed gardens on the University of British Columbia campus, and strolls through the sunken garden at Queen Elizabeth Park, or if you require close proximity to the airport without staying in an "airport hotel," you'll find cozy B&Bs and hotels in this area of Vancouver.

EXPENSIVE

Granville Island Hotel (⭐ *Finds*   One of Vancouver's best-kept hotel secrets, this hotel is tucked away on the edge of Granville Island in a unique waterfront setting that's just a short stroll from theaters, galleries, and the fabulous Granville Island public market. Rooms in the original wing are definitely fancier, so book these if you can, but the new wing is fine, too. Rooms are fairly spacious with traditional, unsurprising decor and large bathrooms with soaker tubs; some units have balconies and great views out over False Creek. The best rooms and views are in the Penthouse suites, located in the new wing. If you don't have a car, the only potential drawback to a stay here is the location. During the daytime when the False Creek ferries are running, it's a quick ferry ride to Yaletown. After 10pm, however, you're looking at a C$10 to C$15 (US$10–US$15/£5–£7.50) cab ride or an hour walk. That said, there's a reasonable amount happening on the island after dark, and the hotel's waterside restaurant and brewpub are wonderful hang-out spots with outdoor seating.

1253 Johnston St., Vancouver, BC V6H 3R9. ℂ 800/663-1840 or 604/683-7373. Fax 604/683-3061. www.granville islandhotel.com. 85 units. Oct–Apr C$160 (US$160/£80) double, C$350 (US$350/£175) penthouse; May–Sept C$240 (US$240/£120) double, C$450 (US$450/£225) penthouse. AE, DC, DISC, MC, V. Parking C$8 (US$8/£4). **Amenities:** Restaurant; brewpub; access to nearby tennis courts; small fitness room with Jacuzzi and sauna; concierge; tour desk; car-rental desk; business center; limited room service; massage; babysitting; laundry service; same-day dry cleaning; nonsmoking rooms. *In room:* A/C, TV w/pay movies, dataport w/high-speed Internet, minibar, coffeemaker, hair dryer, iron/ironing board.

MODERATE

Camelot Inn ★ *Finds*   This handsome 1906 house is one of the nicest and most romantic B&Bs in Vancouver. Surrounded by old trees and located just 2 blocks from the nicest stretch of 4th Avenue in Kitsilano, and a 10-minute walk from Kits Beach, the Edwardian-era house is full of gorgeous period details (lots of wood) and decorated in an age-appropriate style. Three guest rooms are located on the second floor and two lovely studios with separate entrances are tucked away in the back. The Camelot Room features a huge sleigh bed and large Jacuzzi tub beneath a leaded bay window. The somewhat smaller Eden Room sports a queen bed, antiques, and a bathroom with large soaker tub. The Camay Room, the smallest, is nice and bright and features a queen bed but only a large shower. The Latvian-born innkeepers serve a very good breakfast. Unusual attention to detail is a hallmark of this find.

2212 Larch St., Vancouver, BC V6K 3P7. ℂ 604/739-6941. www.camelotinnvancouver.com. 5 units. May–Sept C$159–C$189 (US$159–US$189/£80–£95) double; Oct–Apr C$120–C$140 (US$120–US$140/£60–£70) double. Summer rates include full breakfast. MC, V. Street parking. *In room:* TV, kitchenette, no phone.

Chocolate Lily ★ *Finds Kids*   If you're looking for a self-catered place to stay, this attractive, Craftsman-style house in a quiet Kitsilano neighborhood is a real find. Two self-contained suites with private entrances and patios allow you to come and go as you please. The location is wonderful, just minutes from all the splash of Kits Beach and the dash of Kits shopping (you don't need a car; public transporation can get you downtown in minutes). The suites are small but carefully designed (a sofa in each makes into an extra bed) and furnished in a comfortable Northwest style. Both units have kitchenettes; the rear unit has only a shower. Breakfast is not served, but you're given a basket of fruit and baked goods upon arrival. In high season a 3-day minimum stay is required; there are special rates for longer stays.

1353 Maple St., Vancouver, BC V6M 1G6. ℂ 866/903-9363 or 604/731-9363. www.chocolatelily.com. 2 self-catered suites. C$95–C$165 (US$95–US$165/£48–£83). MC, V. Free parking. *In room:* TV, DVD player (in 1 unit), high-speed Internet, kitchenette w/microwave, toaster oven, coffeemaker.

INEXPENSIVE

The University of British Columbia Conference Centre ★ *Value*   The University of British Columbia is in a pretty, forested setting on the tip of Point Grey—a convenient location if you plan to spend a lot of time in Kitsilano or at the university itself. If you don't have a car, it's a half-hour bus ride from downtown. Although these are student dorms most of the year, rooms are usually available. The rooms are very nice, but don't expect luxury. The 17-story Walter Gage Residence offers comfortable accommodations, many on the upper floors with sweeping views of the city and ocean. One-bedroom suites here come equipped with private bathrooms, kitchenettes, TVs, and phones. Each studio suite has a twin bed; each one-bedroom suite features a queen bed; the six-bedroom Tower suites—a particularly good deal for families—feature one double bed and five twin beds. The West Coast Suites, renovated in 2007, offer the most appealing accommodations, and at a very appealing price.

5961 Student Union Blvd., Vancouver, BC V6T 2C9. (C) **604/822-1000.** Fax 604/822-1001. www.ubcconferences. com. About 1,900 units. Gage Towers units available May 10–Aug 26; Pacific Spirit Hostel units available May 15–Aug 19; West Coast Suite units (adjacent to the Gage Residence) available year-round. Gage Towers: C$89 (US$89/£45) studio; C$119 (US$119/£60) 1-bedroom suite. Pacific Spirit Hostel: C$56 (US$56/£28) double; C$99 (US$99/£50) studio suite with private bathroom. West Coast Suites: C$159 (US$159/£80) suite. AE, MC, V. Parking C$5 (US$5/£2.50). Bus: 4, 17, or 99. **Amenities** (nearby on campus): Restaurant; cafeteria; pub; Olympic-size pool; tennis courts; weight room; sauna for C$5 (US$5/£2.50) per person; video arcade; laundry. *In room:* A/C, TV, hair dryer.

THE NORTH SHORE

The North Shore cities of North and West Vancouver are pleasant and lush; staying here offers easy access to the North Shore mountains and their attractions, including the Capilano Suspension Bridge and the ski slopes on Mount Seymour, Grouse Mountain, and Cypress Bowl. The disadvantage is that there is little or no nightlife, and if you want to take your car into Vancouver, there are only two bridges, and during rush hours they're painfully slow.

Lonsdale Quay Hotel   Directly across the Burrard Inlet from the Canada Place Pier, the moderately priced Lonsdale Quay Hotel sits at the water's edge above the Lonsdale Quay Market at the SeaBus terminal. An escalator rises from the midst of the market's food, crafts, and souvenir stalls to the hotel's front desk on the third floor. Some rooms have unique harbor and city views, but others have wedge-shaped concrete balconies and feel closed in. This is a good location if you're exploring North Vancouver: The hotel is only 15 minutes by bus or car from Grouse Mountain Ski Resort and Capilano Regional Park.

123 Carrie Cates Court, North Vancouver, BC V7M 3K7. (C) **800/836-6111** or 604/986-6111. Fax 604/986-8782. www.lonsdalequayhotel.com. 70 units. C$90–C$169 (US$90–US$169/£45–£85) double. Senior discount available. AE, DC, DISC, MC, V. Parking C$7 (US$7/£3.50); free on weekends and holidays. SeaBus: Lonsdale Quay. **Amenities:** 2 restaurants; small exercise room; spa; bike rental; concierge; limited room service; babysitting; laundry service; same-day dry cleaning. *In room:* A/C, TV, dataport, minibar, coffeemaker, hair dryer, iron/ironing board.

4 Where to Dine

Foodies, take note: Vancouver is one of North America's top dining cities, right up there with New York, San Francisco, and any other food capital you can think of. Vancouverites dine out more frequently than residents of any other Canadian city, and outstanding meals are available in all price ranges and in many different cuisines, with a preponderance of informal Chinese, Japanese, Vietnamese, and Thai restaurants. Sushi lovers are in heaven here because superlative sushi is available all over for a fraction of what you'd pay south of the Canadian border. There are also top restaurants that for preparation, taste, and presentation of Pacific Northwest cuisine can compete with the best anywhere.

"Buy local, eat seasonal" is the mantra of all the best restaurateurs in Vancouver, and they take justifiable pride in the bounty of local produce, game, and seafood available to them. Once less than palatable, British Columbian wines are now winning international acclaim to rival vintages from California, Australia, France, and Germany. The big wine-producing areas are in the Okanagan Valley (in southern British Columbia's dry interior) and on southern Vancouver Island.

There's no provincial tax on restaurant meals in British Columbia, but venues add the 5% federal **goods and services tax (GST)**. Restaurant hours vary. Lunch is typically served from noon to 1 or 2pm; Vancouverites begin dining around 6:30pm, later in summer. Reservations are recommended at most restaurants and are essential at the city's top tables.

DOWNTOWN & YALETOWN
VERY EXPENSIVE

Blue Water Café and Raw Bar ✦✦✦ SEAFOOD   Since opening in the fall of 2000, Blue Water Café in Yaletown has become one of Vancouver's hottest restaurants. If you had to describe this busy, buzzy place in one word, it would be *fresh,* as in fresh, seasonal seafood; only the best from sustainable and wild fisheries makes it onto the menu. If you love sushi, the raw bar under the direction of Yoshihio Tabo offers up some of the city's best Japanese-style sushi and sashimi. Frank Pabst, the restaurant's executive chef, creates his dishes in another large open kitchen. For starters, try a medley of Kushi oysters with various toppings, a sushi platter, or smoked sockeye salmon terrine with salmon caviar, crème fraîche, and red-onion relish. Main courses depend on whatever is in season: It might be spring salmon, halibut, Dungeness crab, and flying squid served with couscous, chickpeas, green onions, tomatoes, and harissa vinaigrette, or B.C. sablefish caramelized with soy and sake. The desserts are fabulous, everything from homemade sorbet to warm dark Cuban chocolate cake. A masterful wine list and an experienced sommelier assure fine wine pairings.

1095 Hamilton St. (at Helmcken) ☎ **604/688-8078.** www.bluewatercafe.net. Reservations recommended. Main courses C$30–C$46 (US$30–US$46/£15–£23). AE, DC, MC, V. Daily 5pm–midnight. Valet parking: C$8 ($8/£4). Bus: 2.

C ✦✦✦ SEAFOOD/PACIFIC NORTHWEST   Since opening in 1997, the popularity of this trendsetter hasn't flagged for a moment. The waterside location on False Creek is sublime, opening out to a passing parade of boats and people on the seawall; the dining room is a cool white space with painted steel and lots of glass. Ingredients make all the difference here: The chef and his highly knowledgeable staff can tell you not only where every product comes from, but also the name of the boat or farm. Expect exquisite surprises and imaginative preparations. For appetizers, fresh B.C. oysters with a tongue-tickling saffron anise cream and juices of jalapeño and cucumber, or watercress salad with sablefish and scallop sausage. Mains are artfully created; for example, grilled ultrarare albacore tuna sits atop creamy couscous with charred lemon and caper condiments. For a really memorable dining experience, give chef Robert Clark a chance to show off and order the nine-course sampling menu as you watch the sun set over the marina. Excellent wine pairings, too.

1600 Howe St. ☎ **604/681-1164.** www.crestaurant.com. Reservations recommended. Main courses C$35–C$48 (US$35–US$48/£18–£24); sampling menu C$120 (US$120/£60). AE, DC, MC, V. Daily 5:30–11pm; Mon–Fri 11:30am–2:30pm (May to Labour Day). Valet parking C$7 (US$7/£3.50). Bus: 1 or 2.

EXPENSIVE

Chambar Belgian Restaurant ✦✦ *Finds* BELGIAN   One of Vancouver's favorite restaurants since it opened in 2004, Chambar occupies an intriguing space in a kind of no man's land on lower Beatty Street between Yaletown and Gastown. Michelin-trained chef Nico Scheuerman and his wife Karri have worked hard to make the place a success, and plenty of plaudits have come their way. The menu features small plates and large plates. Small choices might include mussels cooked in white wine, bacon, and cream (or with fresh tomatoes); halibut and candied-ginger beignet; or green and white asparagus salad. Main courses feature market-fresh options such as *waterzooi* (bouillabaisse) with prawns, scallops, mussels, and halibut, or a tagine of braised lamb shank with honey. For dessert, try the classic Belgian chocolate mousse or the hot mocha soufflé. Chambar specializes in Belgian beers, some 25 varieties in bottles and on tap.

562 Beatty St. © 604/879-7119. www.chambar.com. Reservations recommended. Small plates C$10–C$20 (US$10–US$20/£5–£10); main courses C$23–C$28 (US$23–US$28/£12–£14); 3-course set menu C$50 (US$50/£25). AE, MC, V. Daily 5:30–11pm. Bus: 5 or 17.

Coast ✿✿✿ *Finds* SEAFOOD/INTERNATIONAL   This dashing Yaletown restaurant opened in May 2004 and quickly became a culinary and people-watching spot of note. The dining room is a handsomely designed affair with two levels, lots of light wood, and a special "community table" around an induction cooking surface, so lucky diners can watch chef Jeremy Atkins prepare their culinary teasers. The concept at Coast is to offer an extensive variety of fresh (and nonendangered) seafood from coasts around the world. For starters you might have ahi tuna sashimi and avocado salad, or a wild white sea-tiger-prawn cocktail. Then, from the grill, you could order Hawaiian ahi tuna, wild B.C. salmon, Indian Ocean tiger prawns, or hand-harvested scallops from Newfoundland. Or, for a reasonably priced splash, try the signature seafood platter (C$68/US$68/£34) with lobster, mussels, crab roll, crab cocktail, prawns, oysters, and smoked salmon. The cooking is just right for every dish, never overdone or underdone, never overwhelming the fish, and a joy for the taste buds. Accompany your meal with a recommended wine from Coast's large cellar.

1257 Hamilton St. © 604/685-5010. www.coastrestaurant.ca. Reservations recommended. Main courses C$18–C$33 (US$18–US$33/£9–£17). AE, DC, MC, V. Daily 4:30–11pm. Bus: 1 or 22.

Il Giardino di Umberto Ristorante ✿✿ ITALIAN   Restaurant magnate Umberto Menghi started this small restaurant, tucked away in a yellow heritage house at the bottom of Hornby Street, about 3 decades ago. Today, it still serves some of the best Italian fare in town, and has one of the prettiest garden patios. A larger restaurant now adjoins the original house, opening up into a spacious and bright dining room that re-creates the ambience of an Italian villa. The menu leans toward Tuscany, with dishes that emphasize pasta and game. Entrees usually include classics such as *osso buco* with saffron risotto, and that Roman favorite, spaghetti carbonara. A daily list of specials makes the most of seasonal fresh ingredients, often offering outstanding seafood dishes. The wine list is comprehensive and well chosen.

1382 Hornby St. (between Pacific and Drake). © 604/669-2422. Fax 604/669-9723. www.umberto.com. Reservations recommended. Main courses C$15–C$35 (US$15–US$35/£7.50–£18). AE, DC, MC, V. Mon–Fri 11:30am–3pm and 6–11pm; Sat 6–11pm. Closed holidays. Bus: 1 or 22.

MODERATE
Bin 941 Tapas Parlour ✿ TAPAS/CASUAL   Still booming after 8 years, Bin 941 remains the place for trendy tapas dining. True, the music's too loud and the room's too small, but the food that alights on the bar or the eight tiny tables is delicious and fun to eat, and the wine list is great. Look especially for local seafood offerings such as scallop and tiger prawn tournedos. Sharing is unavoidable in this sliver of a bistro, so come prepared for socializing. The original model was so successful that a second

Bin, dubbed Bin 942, opened at 1521 W. Broadway (© **604/673-1246**). The tables start to fill up at 6:30pm at both spots, and by 8pm, there's a long line of the hip and hungry.

941 Davie St. © **604/683-1246**. www.bin941.com. Reservations not accepted. All plates are C$15 (US$15/£7.50). MC, V. Daily 5pm–1:30am. Bus: 4, 5, or 8.

Sanafir 𝕲𝕲 *Finds* INTERNATIONAL   Influenced by the exotic dining and decor found along the Silk Road, Sanafir provides a memorable dining experience that's opulent, fun, and doesn't cost a fortune. The first-floor dining room is loud and buzzily exciting, but parties can also drink and dine upstairs while reclining on pillows in spaces hung with sexy harem-style draperies. The tapas-style plates come in three of five possible Silk Road variations: Asian, Mediterranean, Middle Eastern, Indian, or North African. And the trio of tastes costs only C$14 (US$12/£6). So, say you order the scallops, your three-dish tapas plate might contain a seared Indian five-spice scallop with mango chutney, sautéed scallops wrapped in lettuce with a hoison glaze, and a gently poached scallop over a kasha and sumac salad in a fennel-scented phyllo cup. Larger chef's specials are also available, such as the super-rich oxtail cappelletti with white-truffle cream, parmagiano reggiano, and shaved black truffle. The show-off interior and the quality of the food makes this a destination restaurant worth trying. There's no sign, but look for the most glamorous place on gentrifying Granville Street, and you'll be there.

1026 Granville St. (at Nelson). © **604/678-1049**. Reservations recommended. Tapas C$14 (US$14/£7); chef's specials C$17 (US$17/£8.50). AE, DC, MC, V. Daily from 5pm. Bus: 4 or 7.

Simply Thai 𝕲 THAI   At this small Thai restaurant in the trendy heart of Yaletown, you can watch chef and owner Siriwan in the open kitchen as she cooks up a combination of northern and southern Thai dishes with some fusion sensations. The appetizers are perfect finger foods: *Gai satay* features succulent pieces of grilled chicken breast marinated in coconut milk and spices and covered in a peanut sauce, while the delicious *cho muang* consists of violet-colored dumplings stuffed with minced chicken. Main courses run the gamut of Thai cuisine: noodle dishes and coconut curries with beef, chicken, or pork, as well as a good number of vegetarian options. Don't miss the *tom kha gai,* a deceptively simple-looking soup; Siriwan creates a richly fragrant coconut milk–based broth that balances the delicate flavors of the lemon grass and other spices with mushrooms and chicken. The set menu is a good way to sample a bit of everything.

1211 Hamilton St. © **604/642-0123**. Reservations recommended on weekends. Main courses C$13–C$26 (US$13–US$26/£6.50–£13); set menu C$40 (US$40/£20). AE, DC, MC, V. Mon–Fri 11:30am–3pm and 5–10:30pm; Sat–Sun 5–10:30pm. Bus: 2.

GASTOWN & CHINATOWN
EXPENSIVE
The Cannery 𝕲 SEAFOOD   At least some of the pleasure of eating at the Cannery comes from the adventure of finding the place. (Drive or take a cab because it's impossible to get there on foot or by public transportation.) Hop over the railroad tracks, thread your way past a harbor security checkpoint, pass container terminals and fish-packing plants, and there it is—a timber-framed rectangular building hanging out over the waters of Burrard Inlet. The interior, with its exposed beams and seafaring memorabilia, adds to the Cannery's charm, but many come here for the amazing view, one of the best in Vancouver. You'll find good, solid, traditional seafood here, with

ever-changing specials to complement the fresh, wild salmon, halibut, and Dungeness crab. Famous dishes include salmon Wellington (salmon, shrimp, and mushrooms baked in a puff pastry), smoked Alaskan black cod, and roasted mussels. Meat lovers can get a grilled New York steak or Alberta beef tenderloin. Chef Frederic Couton has been getting more inventive lately, but when an institution founded in 1971 is still going strong, no one's ever *too* keen to rock the boat. The wine list is stellar, and the desserts are wonderfully inventive.

2205 Commissioner St. (near Victoria Dr.). (℃ **877/254-9606** or 604/254-9606. www.canneryseafood.com. Reservations recommended. Main courses C$23–C$40 (US$23–US$40/£11–£20). AE, DC, DISC, MC, V. Mon–Fri 11:30am–2:30pm and 5:30–9pm; Sat 5–9:30pm; Sun 5–9pm. Closed Dec 24–26. From downtown, head east on Hastings St., turn left on Victoria Dr. (2 blocks past Commercial Dr.), then right on Commissioner St.

MODERATE

Park Lock Seafood Restaurant *(Kids)* CHINESE/DIM SUM If you've never done dim sum, this large, second-floor dining room in the heart of Chinatown is a good place to give it a try, even though you'll have to listen to schlocky country-and-western music while you dine. From 8am to 3pm daily, waitresses wheel little carts loaded with Chinese delicacies past the tables. When you see something you like, you point and ask for it. The final bill is based upon how many little dishes are left on your table. Dishes include spring rolls, *hargow* (shrimp dumplings), and *shumai* (steamed shrimp, beef, or pork dumplings), prawns wrapped in fresh white noodles, small steamed buns, sticky rice cooked in banana leaves, curried squid, and lots more. Parties of four or more are best—that way you get to try each other's food.

544 Main St. (at E. Pender St., on the 2nd floor). (℃ **604/688-1581**. Reservations recommended. Main courses C$10–C$25 (US$10–US$25/£5–£12); dim sum dishes C$3–C$7 (US$3–US$7/£1.50–£3.50). AE, MC, V. Mon–Thurs 7:30am–4pm; Fri–Sun 7:30am–4pm and 5–9:30pm. Bus: 19 or 22.

INEXPENSIVE

Incendio *(Finds)* PIZZA If you're looking for something casual and local that won't be full of other tourists reading downtown maps, this little Gastown hideaway is great. The 22 pizza combinations are served on fresh, crispy crusts baked in an old wood-fired oven. Pastas are homemade. The wine list is decent; the beer list is inspired. And there's a patio. Much to the delight of Kitsilano residents, a second location with a slightly larger menu opened next to the 5th Avenue movie theater at 2118 Burrard (℃ **604/736-2220**).

103 Columbia St. (℃ **604/688-8694**. Main courses C$11–C$24 (US$11–US$24/£5.50–£12). AE, MC, V. Mon–Thurs 11:30am–3pm and 5–10pm; Fri 11:30am–3pm and 5–11pm; Sat 5–11pm; Sun 4:30–10pm. Closed Dec 23–Jan 3. Bus: 1 or 8.

Salt *(*) CHARCUTERIE The location of this new dining spot in Gastown might put some visitors off, and single women will probably be uncomfortable walking along the horribly named Blood Alley alone at night. And that's really a shame, because Salt is unique, and a wonderful place to get a good, inexpensive meal. The room is long and minimalistically modern, with an enormous communal dining table made from an 800-year-old spruce tree. There's no kitchen per se because Salt serves only cured meats and artisan cheeses plus a daily soup, a couple of salads, and grilled meat and cheese sandwiches. For the tasting plate you mix and match three of the meats and cheeses listed on the blackboard. Salt serves beer, several good wines, and a selection of whiskeys. There are no street numbers on Blood Alley, so look for the salt shaker flag over the doorway. Try it for lunch if you're in Gastown.

Blood Alley, Gastown. © **604/633-1912**. Tasting plates C$15 (US$15/£7.50), soup C$6 (US$6/£3). AE, MC, V. Daily noon–midnight. Bus: 1 or 8.

THE WEST END

CinCin ★★★ MODERN ITALIAN   Vancouverites in need of great Italian food frequent this second-story restaurant on Robson Street. The spacious dining room, done in a rustic Italian-villa style, surrounds an open kitchen built around a huge wood-fired oven and grill; the heated terrace is an equally pleasant dining and people-watching spot. The food at CinCin is exemplary, and if you're in the mood to sample a bit of everything, I'd recommend the fabulous five-course tasting menu. The dishes change monthly, but the tasting menu might begin with fresh buffalo mozzarella with rosso bruno tomatoes, go on to tortelli pasta stuffed with ricotta and chard, followed by wood-roasted fish and shellfish in fennel broth, and then venison loin served with chestnut and sweet garlic tortellini, after which a chestnut crème brulee arrives. Mouth-watering a la carte possibilities include mushroom-dusted sablefish cooked in the wood-fired oven, ahi tuna and beef tenderloin from the wood grill, and a delicious pizza with prosciutto, asparagus, fontina cheese, roasted garlic, and rosemary. The award-winning wine list is extensive, as is the selection of wines by the glass. Service is excellent.

1154 Robson St. © **604/688-7338**. www.cincin.net. Reservations recommended. Main courses C$19–C$44 (US$19–US$44/£9.50–£22); tasting menu C$78 (US$78/£39). AE, DC, MC, V. Mon–Fri 11:30am–2:30pm and 5–11pm; Sat–Sun 5–11pm. Bus: 5 or 22.

The Fish House in Stanley Park ★★ SEAFOOD/PACIFIC NORTHWEST/AFTERNOON TEA   Reminiscent of a more genteel era, this green clapboard clubhouse dating from 1929 is surrounded by green lawns and ancient cedar trees, and looks out over English Bay (in the summer, try for a table on the veranda). Inside, you'll find a warm, comfortable clubhouse atmosphere and wonderfully friendly service. You can enjoy a traditional afternoon tea, Sunday brunch, or come for a memorable lunch or dinner. The lunch and dinner menus feature fresh B.C. oysters and shellfish, fresh seasonal fish, and signature dishes such as maple-glazed salmon, flaming prawns (done at your table with ouzo), and a seafood cornucopia. The wine list is admirable, the desserts sumptuous. Guests have been enjoying chef Karen Barnaby's cooking since 1993; in addition to her signature standbys, she often creates special theme menus and offers a reasonably priced three-course set dinner menu monthly.

8901 Stanley Park Dr. © **877/681-7275** or 604/681-7275. www.fishhousestanleypark.com. Reservations recommended. Main courses C$17–C$30 (US$17–US$30/£8.50–£15); 3-course set menu C$30 (US$30/£15); afternoon tea C$24 (US$24/£12). AE, DC, DISC, MC, V. Mon–Sat 11:30am–10pm; Sun 11am–10pm; afternoon tea daily 2–4pm. Closed Dec 24–26. Bus: 1, 35, or 135.

Joe Fortes Seafood and Chop House ★★★ SEAFOOD   Named after the burly Caribbean seaman who became English Bay's first lifeguard, Joe Fortes is the best place to come if you're hankering for top-of-the-line fresh seafood served the "old-fashioned" way, without a lot of modern culinary intrusions. The downstairs dining room evokes a kind of turn-of-the-20th-century saloon elegance, but if the weather's fine, try for a table on the rooftop patio. Stick with the seafood because it's what they do best. The waiters will inform you what's just come in and where it's from. Although Joe's is adding more fusion elements to boost the novelty, you can ask for your fish selection to be simply grilled or sautéed. My personal recommendation is that you sample the seasonal oysters (Joe Fortes has the best oyster bar in Vancouver) and/or order the trio of grilled fresh fish or the famous seafood tower, which comes with an iced assortment of marinated mussels, poached shrimp, grilled and chilled scallops, marinated calamari, tuna sashimi, Manila clams, Dungeness crab, and local beach oysters. Heavy on the white, the wine list is gargantuan and includes some wonderful pinots from the Okanagan Valley.

777 Thurlow St. (at Robson). (𝐂 604/669-1940. www.joefortes.ca. Reservations recommended. Main courses C$27–C$45 (US$27–US$45/£14–£23). AE, DC, DISC, MC, V. Daily 11am–10:30pm (brunch Sat–Sun 11am–4pm). Bus: 5.

Raincity Grill ✹✹✹ PACIFIC NORTHWEST   This restaurant, which opened on English Bay in 1990, is a gem—painstaking in preparation, arty in presentation, and yet completely unfussy in atmosphere. Raincity Grill was one of the very first restaurants in Vancouver to embrace the "buy locally, eat seasonally" concept. The menu focuses on seafood, game, poultry, and organic vegetables, all of it from British Columbia and the Pacific Northwest. The room is long, low, and intimate—perfect for romantic dining.

To sample a bit of everything, I recommend the seasonal tasting menu, a bargain at C$60 (US$60/£30), or C$89 (US$89/£45) with wine pairings. One recent tasting menu included organic chicken leg with Yukon potato confit; roasted Berkshire pork belly with sunroot and candied kanbocha squash; duck breast with braised endive, beets, and celeriac; and fennel seed and honey panna cotta—all of it made with ingredients found within 100 miles of the restaurant. The wine list is huge and, in keeping with the restaurant's philosophy, sticks pretty close to home. From May to Labour Day, Raincity opens a takeout window on Denham Street, where you can get a gourmet sandwich, salad, and sweet to go for C$10 (US$10/£5).

1193 Denman St. (𝐂 604/685-7337. www.raincitygrill.com. Reservations recommended. Main courses C$17–C$33 (US$17–US$33/£8.50–£16). AE, DC, MC, V. Mon–Fri 11:30am–2:30pm and 5–10:30pm; Sat–Sun 10:30am–3pm (brunch) and 5–10:30pm. Bus: 1 or 5.

MODERATE

Hapa Izakaya ✹ JAPANESE   Dinner comes at almost disco decibels in Robson Street's hottest Japanese "eat-drink place" (the literal meaning of Izakaya), where chefs call out orders, servers shout acknowledgements, and the maitre d' and owner keep up a running volley to staff about the (often sizable) wait at the door. The menu features inventive nontraditional dishes such as bacon-wrapped asparagus, *negitori* (spicy tuna roll), and fresh tuna belly chopped with spring onions and served with bite-size bits of garlic bread. For non–raw fish eaters, there are inventive appetizers and meat dishes and a scrumptious Korean hot pot. The crowd is about a third expat Japanese, a third Chinese (both local and expat), and a third well-informed Westerners. The service is fast and obliging, and the price per dish is very reasonable. Success has spawned a second location in Kitsilano at 1516 Yew St. ((𝐂 **604/738-4272**).

1479 Robson St. (𝐂 604/689-4272. Reservations not accepted 6–8pm. Main courses C$8–C$14 (US$8–US$14/£4–£7). AE, MC, V. Sun–Thurs 5:30pm–midnight; Fri–Sat 5:30pm–1am. Bus: 5.

Romano's Macaroni Grill (𝘒𝘪𝘥𝘴 FAMILY STYLE/ITALIAN   It's almost worth eating here just to see the interior. Housed in a stone mansion built in 1900 by sugar baron B. T. Rogers, Romano's is a fun and casual chain restaurant with an Italian-influenced menu. This isn't high-concept Italian; the food is simple, understandable, and reliably good. The pastas are definitely favorites. The children's menu features lasagna, mac and cheese, spaghetti with meatball, and tasty pizzas. In the summer it's fun to dine outside on the beautiful garden patio, but the stunning interior, filled with handcrafted wood detailing and stained glass, is pretty amazing.

1523 Davie St. (℃) 604/689-4334. Reservations recommended. Main courses C$15–C$23 (US$15–US$23/£7.50–£12); children's courses C$4.95 (US$4.95/£2.45). AE, DC, MC, V. Mon–Thurs noon–10pm; Fri–Sat noon–11pm. Bus: 5.

Tanpopo (*Value*) JAPANESE   Occupying the second floor of a corner building on Denman Street, Tanpopo has a partial view of English Bay, a large patio, and a huge menu of hot and cold Japanese dishes. But the line of people waiting 30 minutes or more every night for a table are here for the all-you-can-eat sushi. The unlimited fare includes the standards—makis, tuna and salmon sashimi, California and B.C. rolls— as well as cooked items such as tonkatsu, tempura, chicken kara-age, and broiled oysters. The quality here is okay, probably a bit above average for an all-you-can-eat place. There are a couple of secrets to getting seated. You might try to call ahead, but they only take an arbitrary percentage of reservations for dinner each day. Otherwise, you can ask to sit at the sushi bar.

1122 Denman St. (℃) 604/681-7777. Reservations recommended for groups. Main courses C$7–C$20 (US$7–US$20/ £3.50–£10); all-you-can-eat sushi C$25 (US$25/£13) for dinner, C$14 (US$14/£7) for lunch. AE, DC, MC, V. Daily 11:30am–10pm. Bus: 5.

INEXPENSIVE

Banana Leaf ✴ MALAYSIAN   One of the city's best spots for Malaysian food, Banana Leaf is just a hop and a skip from English Bay. The menu includes inventive specials such as mango and okra salad, delicious south Asian mainstays such as *gado gado* (a salad with hot peanut sauce), *mee goreng* (fried noodles with vegetables topped by a fried egg) and occasional variations such as an assam curry (seafood in hot and sour curry sauce) that comes with okra and tomato. For dessert, don't pass up on *pisang goring*—fried banana with ice cream. The small room is tastefully decorated in dark tropical woods; the rather unadventurous wine list features a small selection of inexpensive reds and whites. Service is very friendly. There's another location at 820 W. Broadway ((℃) 604/731-6333).

1096 Denman St. (℃) 604/683-3333. www.bananaleaf-vancouver.com. Main courses C$10–C$20 (US$10–US$20/ £5–£10). AE, MC, V. Sun–Thurs 11:30am–10pm; Fri–Sat 11:30am–11pm. Bus: 5.

Stephos (*Value*) GREEK   A fixture on the Davie Street dining scene, Stephos has been packing them in since Zorba was a boy. The cuisine is simple Greek fare at its finest and cheapest. Customers line up outside for a seat amid Greek travel posters, potted ivy, and whitewashed walls (the average wait is about 10–15 min., but it could be as long as 30 min., as once you're inside, the staff will never rush you out the door). Order some pita and dip (hummus, spicy eggplant, or garlic spread) while you peruse the menu. An interesting appetizer is the *avgolemono* soup, a delicately flavored chicken broth with egg and lemon, accompanied by a plate of piping hot pita bread. When choosing a main course, keep in mind that portions are huge. The roasted lamb, lamb chops, fried calamari, and a variety of souvlakia are served with rice, roast potatoes, and Greek salad. The beef, lamb, or chicken pita comes in slightly smaller portions served with fries and *tzatziki*.

1124 Davie St. (℃) 604/683-2555. Reservations accepted for parties of 5 or more. Main courses C$6–C$11 (US$6–US$11/£3–£5.50). AE, MC, V. Daily 11am–11:30pm. Bus: 5.

THE WEST SIDE
VERY EXPENSIVE

Tojo's Restaurant ⭐⭐⭐ JAPANESE   Tojo's is considered Vancouver's top Japanese restaurant, the place where celebs come to dine on the best sushi in town. It's expensive, but the food is absolutely fresh, inventive, and, boy, is it good. In 2007, the restaurant relocated to a stunning new 604 sq. m (6,500-sq.-ft.) space designed by sculptor/architect Colin Kwok. An underlying Japanese sensibility pervades everything, from subtle colors to custom-designed chairs. The main area wraps around Chef Tojo and his sushi chefs with a giant curved maple sake bar and an adjoining sushi bar. Tojo's ever-changing menu offers such specialties as sea urchin on the half shell, herring roe, lobster claws, tuna, crab, and barbecue eel. The best thing to do is go for the Chef's Arrangement—tell them how much you're willing to spend (per person), and let the good times roll.

1133 W. Broadway. ℂ 604/872-8050. www.tojos.com. Reservations required. Main courses C$16–C$30 (US$16–US$30/£8–£15); sushi/sashimi C$8–C$28 (US$8–US$28/£4–£14); Chef's Arrangement C$50–C$100 (US$50–US$100/£25–£50). AE, DC, MC, V. Mon–Sat 5–10pm. Closed Christmas week. Bus: 9.

EXPENSIVE

West ⭐⭐⭐ FRENCH/PACIFIC NORTHWEST   I wasn't surprised when West won the Best Restaurant Award from *Vancouver* magazine in 2005, 2006, and 2007. Every meal I've had here has been memorable. This is a restaurant where details matter, high standards reign, and cooking is a fine art, yet it's not stuffy or stiff. You'll want to dress up, though, and you'll want to linger over your food, prepared by executive chef David Hawksworth.

The credo at West is deceptively simple: "True to our region, true to the seasons." What that means is that fresh, organic, locally harvested seafood, game, and produce are transformed into extraordinary creations. The menu changes three to four times a week, but first courses might include caramelized scallops with apple-curry vinaigrette or a ravioli of quail; for a main course you might find fennel-and-pepper-crusted yellowfin tuna with watermelon radish and miso mustard; honey-and-clove-braised pork cheeks; or lamb with wild mushrooms and sage-and–confit garlic gnocchi. For the ultimate dining experience, try one of the seasonal tasting menus, a multicourse progression through the best the restaurant has to offer; there's also an early bird menu served until 6pm. A carefully chosen wine list includes a selection of affordable wines by the glass and half-bottle. If you're really into cooking, reserve one of the two "chef tables" adjacent to Chef Hawksworth's bustling kitchen.

2881 Granville St. ℂ 604/738-8938. www.westrestaurant.com. Reservations recommended. Main courses C$17–C$44 (US$17–US$44/£8.50–£22); tasting menus C$78–C$129 (US$78–US$129/£39–£65); early prix-fixe menu until 6pm C$45 (US$45/£23). AE, DC, MC, V. Mon–Fri 11:30am–2:30pm and 5:30–11pm; Sat–Sun 5:30–11pm. Bus: 8.

MODERATE

Aurora Bistro ⭐⭐ PACIFIC NORTHWEST   How nice to discover a top-notch restaurant with fine food and great service at reasonable prices! Aurora opened in 2003 with a "back-to-the-basics" philosophy, allowing ingredients to speak for themselves rather than masking them with complicated sauces or combining too many tastes. The menu is divided into small, medium, and large plates. You might want to start with a country-style pork pâté or blue-cheese tart, and then try sweet potato gnocchi or root beer–braised bison short ribs. What you find on the menu will be seasonal and sustainable. All wines are from B.C. A pleasant, lower-key experience in Vancouver's overheated restaurant scene.

2420 Main St. ✆ 604/873-9944. www.aurorabistro.ca. Reservations recommended. Main courses C$25–C$27 (US$25–US$27/£12–£14). MC, V. Daily 5:30–10:30pm. Bus: 3, 8, or 19.

Vij 🌟🌟🌟 INDIAN   Vij doesn't take reservations and there's a line outside his door every single night. Patrons huddled under Vij's violet neon sign are treated to complimentary tea and *papadums* (a thin bread made from lentils). Inside, the decor is as warm and subtle as the seasonings, which are all roasted and ground by hand, then used with studied delicacy. The menu changes monthly, though some of the more popular entrees remain constants. Recent offerings included coconut curried chicken and saffron rice and marinated pork medallions with garlic-yogurt curry and *nan* (flat bread). Vegetarian selections abound, including curried vegetable rice pilaf with cilantro cream sauce and Indian lentils with *nan* and *raita* (yogurt-mint sauce). The wine and beer list is short but carefully selected. And for teetotalers, Vij has developed a souped-up version of the traditional Indian chai, the chaiuccino.

1480 W. 11th Ave. ✆ 604/736-6664. Reservations not accepted. Main courses C$20–C$26 (US$20–US$26/£10–£13). AE, DC, MC, V. Daily 5:30–10pm. Closed Dec 24–Jan 8. Bus: 8 or 10.

INEXPENSIVE

The Naam Restaurant 🌟 *Kids* VEGETARIAN   Back in the '60s, when Kitsilano was Canada's hippie haven, the Naam was tie-dye central. Things have changed since then, but Vancouver's oldest vegetarian and natural-food restaurant still retains a pleasant granola feel, and it's open 24/7. The decor is simple, earnest, and welcoming, and includes well-worn wooden tables and chairs, plants, an assortment of local art, and a nice garden patio. There's live music every night. The brazenly healthy fare ranges from all-vegetarian burgers, enchiladas, and burritos to tofu teriyaki, Thai noodles, and a variety of pita pizzas. The sesame spice fries are a Vancouver institution. And though the Naam is not quite vegan, they do cater to the anti-egg-and-cheese crowd with specialties like the macrobiotic Dragon Bowl of brown rice, tofu, peanut sauce, sprouts, and steamed vegetables.

2724 W. 4th Ave. ✆ 604/738-7151. www.thenaam.com. Reservations accepted on weekdays only. Main courses C$5–C$12 (US$5–US$12/£2.50–£6). AE, MC, V. Daily 24 hr. Live music every night 7–10pm. Bus: 4 or 22.

Sophie's Cosmic Café *Kids* FAMILY STYLE/AMERICAN   Sophie's is easily identifiable by the giant silver knife and fork bolted to the storefront. Inside, every available space has been crammed with toys and knickknacks from the 1950s and '60s. So, understandably, children are inordinately fond of Sophie's. Crayons and coloring paper are always on hand. The menu is simple: pastas, burgers and fries, great milkshakes, and a few classic Mexican dishes. The slightly spicy breakfast menu is hugely popular with Kitsilano locals; lines can stretch to half an hour or more on Sunday mornings.

2095 W. 4th Ave. ✆ 604/732-6810. www.sophiescosmiccafe.com. Main courses C$5–C$17 (US$5–US$17/£2.50–£8.50). MC, V. Daily 8am–9:30pm. Bus: 4 or 7.

THE EAST SIDE
EXPENSIVE

Sun Sui Wah 🌟🌟 *Kids* CHINESE/DIM SUM/SEAFOOD   One of the most elegant and sophisticated Chinese restaurants in town, the award-winning Sun Sui Wah is well known for its seafood. Fresh and varied, the catch of the day can include fresh crab, rock cod, geoduck, scallops, abalone, oyster, prawns, and more. Pick your own from the tank or order from the menu if you'd rather not meet your food eye-to-eye before it's cooked. Dim sum is a treat, with the emphasis on seafood. Just point and choose. There are plenty of other choices for meat lovers and vegetarians, though they will miss out on one of the best seafood feasts in town. There's a second location in Richmond at 102 Alderbridge Place, 4940 No. 3 Rd. (© **604/273-8208**).

3888 Main St. © 604/872-8822. www.sunsuiwah.com. Main courses C$11–C$50 (US$11–US$50/£5.50–£25). AE, DC, MC, V. Daily dim sum 10:30am–3pm; dinner 5–10:30pm. Bus: 3.

MODERATE

The Locus Café CASUAL/SOUTHWESTERN   Even if you arrive by your lonesome, you'll soon have plenty of friends because the Locus is a cheek-by-jowl kind of place, filled with a friendly, funky crowd of artsy Mount Pleasant types. A big bar dominates the room, overhung with "swamp-gothic" lacquer trees and surrounded by a tier of stools with booths and tiny tables. The cuisine originated in the American Southwest and picked up an edge somewhere along the way, as demonstrated in the roasted half-chicken with a cumin-coriander crust and sambuca citrus demi-glace. Keep an eye out for fish specials, such as grilled tomba tuna with a grapefruit and mango glaze. The pan-seared calamari makes a perfect appetizer. Bowen Island brewery provides the beer, so quality's high. Your only real problem is catching the eye of the busy bartender.

4121 Main St. © 604/708-4121. Reservations recommended. Main courses C$9–C$15 (US$9–US$15/£4.50–£7.50). MC, V. Mon–Sat 11am–1:30am; Sun 11am–midnight. Bus: 3.

THE NORTH SHORE

The Beach House at Dundarave Pier ☆ PACIFIC NORTHWEST   The Beach House offers a panoramic view of English Bay from its waterfront location. Diners on the heated patio get more sunshine, but they miss out on the rich interior of this restored 1912 teahouse. The food is consistently good—innovative, but not so experimental that it leaves the staid West Van burghers gasping for breath. Appetizers include soft-shell crab tempura with salt-and-fire jelly; spicy calamari with ginger; and a salad of crab, shrimp, avocado, and tomato. Entrees have included espresso-crusted pork tenderloin with risotto, pan-fried halibut with artichoke puree, and grilled prawns and scallops. The wine list is award-winning.

150 25th St., West Vancouver. © 604/922-1414. www.atthebeachhouse.com. Reservations recommended. Main courses C$18–C$36 (US$18–US$36/£9–£18). AE, DC, MC, V. Daily 11am–10pm. Bus: 255 to Ambleside Pier.

5 Exploring Vancouver

A city perched on the edge of a great wilderness, Vancouver offers unmatched opportunities for exploring the outdoors. But within the city limits, Vancouver is intensely urban, with buzzy sidewalk cafes and busy shopping streets. The forest of high-rises ringing the central part of the city reminds some visitors of New York or Shanghai, and Chinatown inevitably invites comparisons to San Francisco. But comparisons with other places begin to pall as you come to realize that Vancouver is entirely its own creation: a young, self-confident, sparklingly beautiful city like no other place on earth.

THE TOP ATTRACTIONS
DOWNTOWN & THE WEST END

Canada Place ☆☆   If you've never been to Vancouver, this is a good place to orient yourself and see some of what makes B.C.'s largest city so special. (Or you may arrive here on a cruise ship, in which case this will be your first introduction to Vancouver.)

With its five tall Teflon sails and bowsprit jutting out into Burrard Inlet, Canada Place is meant to resemble a giant sailing ship. Inside it's a convention center on one level and a giant cruise-ship terminal below, with the Pan Pacific Hotel (p. 646) perched on top. Around the perimeter there's a promenade with plaques at regular intervals explaining the sights and providing historical tidbits. A huge expansion to add more convention space and additional docking facilities is currently underway. You can walk all the way around on a pedestrian promenade that offers wonderful views across Burrard Inlet to the North Shore peaks and toward nearby Stanley Park. Continue around the promenade, and you'll get great city views and be able to see the older, low-rise buildings of Gastown, where Vancouver began. Bus sightseeing tours begin here, there's a giant-screen **IMAX Theatre** (© **604/682-IMAX**), and the Tourism Vancouver Touristinfo Centre is right across the street.

Canada Place at the end of Burrard St. Promenade daily 24 hr. Bus: 1 or 5.

Stanley Park ☆☆☆ *Kids*   The green jewel of Vancouver, Stanley Park is a 400-hectare (988-acre) rainforest jutting out into the ocean from the edge of the busy West End. Exploring the second-largest urban forest in Canada is one of Vancouver's quintessential experiences. In 2006, however, portions of Stanley Park were damaged by a windstorm that felled thousands of trees and left some big gaps in the forest canopy.

The park, created in 1888, is still filled with towering western red cedar and Douglas fir, manicured lawns, flower gardens, placid lagoons, and countless shaded walking trails that meander through it all. The famed **seawall** ☆☆☆ runs along the waterside edge of the park, allowing cyclists and pedestrians to experience the magical interface of forest, sea, and sky. One of the most popular free attractions in the park is the **collection of totem poles** ☆☆☆ at Brockton Point, most of them carved in the 1980s to replace the original ones that were placed in the park in the 1920s and 1930s. The area around the totem poles features open-air displays on the Coast Salish First Nations and a small gift shop/visitor information center.

The park is home to lots of wildlife, including beavers, coyotes, bald eagles, blue herons, cormorants, trumpeter swans, brant geese, ducks, raccoons, skunks, and gray squirrels imported from New York's Central Park decades ago and now quite at home in the Pacific Northwest. (No, there are no bears.) For directions and maps, brochures, and exhibits on the nature and ecology of Stanley Park, visit the **Lost Lagoon Nature House** (© **604/257-8544;** 10am–7pm July 1 to Labour Day; weekends only outside this period; free admission). On Sundays they offer Discovery Walks of the park. Equally nature-focused but with way more wow is the **Vancouver Aquarium** ☆☆ (see below). There's also the **Stanley Park's Children's Farm** (© **604/257-8530**), a petting zoo with peacocks, rabbits, calves, donkeys, and Shetland ponies. Next to the petting zoo is **Stanley Park's Miniature Railway** ☆ (© **604/257-8531**), a diminutive steam locomotive that pulls passenger cars on a circuit through the woods.

Of the three restaurants located in the park, the best is **The Fish House at Stanley Park** (p. 659), where you can have lunch, afternoon tea, or dinner. For swimmers, there's **Third Beach** and **Second Beach,** the latter with an outdoor pool beside English Bay. For kids there's a free **Spray Park** near Lumberman's Arch, where they can run and splash through various water-spewing fountains. Perhaps the best way to explore the park is to rent a bike (p. 676) or in-line skates, and set off along the seawall. If you decide to walk, remember there's a free summer shuttle bus that circles the park every 15 minutes, allowing passengers to alight and descend at most of the park's many attractions. There's also a wonderful **horse-drawn carriage ride** ☆☆ that begins near Lost Lagoon. For a complete listing of attractions, operating hours, admission fees, and a post-storm restoration report, check the website.

Stanley Park. © 604/257-8400. www.city.vancouver.bc.ca/parks. Free admission; charge for individual attractions. Parking entire day C$5 (US$5/£2.50) summer; C$3 (US$3/£1.50) winter. Park does not close. Bus: 23, 35, or 135; free "Around the Park" shuttle bus circles the park at 15-min. intervals from June 13–Sept 28 (visitors can get off and on at 14 points of interest).

Vancouver Aquarium Marine Science Centre 🐟🐟 *Kids*   One of North America's largest and best, the Vancouver Aquarium houses more than 8,000 marine species. In the icy-blue arctic Canada exhibit, you can see beluga whales whistling and blowing water at unwary onlookers. Human-size freshwater fish inhabit the Amazon rainforest gallery, while overhead, an hourly rainstorm is unleashed in an atrium that houses three-toed sloths, brilliant blue and green poison tree frogs, and piranhas. Regal angelfish glide through a re-creation of Indonesia's Bunaken National Park coral reef, and blacktip reef sharks menacingly scour the Tropical Gallery's waters. (Call for the shark and sea otter feeding times.) The Pacific Canada exhibit is dedicated to sea life indigenous to B.C. waters, including the Pacific salmon and the giant Pacific octopus.

On the Marine Mammal Deck, there are sea otters, Steller sea lions, beluga whales, and a Pacific white-sided dolphin. During regularly scheduled shows, the aquarium staff explains marine mammal behavior while working with these impressive creatures.

For a substantial extra fee (C$150/US$150/£75 per person; C$210/US$210/£105 adult and one child age 8–12), you can have a behind-the-scenes Beluga Encounter, helping to feed these giant white cetaceans, then head up to the Marine Mammal deck to take part in the belugas' regular training session. Beluga encounters are available daily from 9 to 10:30am, with extra encounters on weekends between 2 and 4pm. On the more reasonably priced Trainer Tours (C$25–C$35/US$25–US$35/£13–£18 per person; C$40–C$50/US$40–US$50/£20–£25 adult and one child age 8–12), you go on a 45-minute behind-the-scenes tour, helping an aquarium trainer prepare the daily rations for and then feeding the sea otters or harbor seals. Trainer Tours are available daily but times vary. Call © **800/931-1186** to reserve all of these programs ahead of time. Children must be 8 or older to participate. *Note:* If you have younger children, I recommend the sea otters; Steller sea lions are enormous and sometimes ill-tempered.

Stanley Park. © 604/659-FISH. www.vanaqua.org. Admission C$20 (US$20/£10) adults; C$15 (US$15/£7.50) seniors, students, and youths 13–18; C$12 (US$12/£6) children 4–12; free for children 3 and under. Summer daily 9:30am–7pm; winter daily 10am–5:30pm. Bus: 135; "Around the Park" shuttle bus June–Sept only. Parking C$6 (US$6/£3) summer, C$3 (US$3/£1.50) winter.

Vancouver Art Gallery 🐟🐟   Designed as a courthouse by B.C.'s leading early-20th-century architect Francis Rattenbury (the architect of Victoria's Empress Hotel and the Parliament buildings), and renovated into an art gallery by B.C.'s leading late-20th-century architect Arthur Erickson, the VAG is an excellent stop to see what sets Canadian and west coast art apart from the rest of the world. There is an impressive collection of paintings by B.C. native **Emily Carr** 🐟🐟🐟, as well as examples of a unique Canadian art style created during the 1920s by members of the "Group of Seven," which included Vancouver painter Fred Varley. The VAG also hosts rotating exhibits of contemporary sculpture, graphics, photography, and video art from around the world. Geared to younger audiences, the Annex Gallery offers rotating presentations of visually exciting educational exhibits.

750 Hornby St. © **604/662-4719** or 604/662-4700. www.vanartgallery.bc.ca. Admission C$20 (US$20/£10) adults; C$15 (US$15/£7.50) seniors; C$14 (US$14/£7) students; C$6.50 (US$6.50/£3.25) children 5–12; C$49 (US$49/£25) family; Tues 5–9pm by donation. Daily 10am–5:30pm (Tues and Thurs until 9pm). SkyTrain: Granville. Bus: 3.

THE WEST SIDE

Granville Island ✿✿✿ *Kids*   Almost a city within a city, Granville Island is a good place to browse away a morning, an afternoon, or a whole day. You can wander through a busy public market jammed with food stalls, shop for crafts, pick up some fresh seafood, enjoy a great dinner, watch the latest theater performance, rent a yacht, stroll along the waterfront, or simply run through the sprinkler on a hot summer day; it's all there and more. If you only have a short period of time, make sure you spend at least part of it in the **Granville Island Public Market** ✿✿✿, one of the best all-around markets in North America.

Once a declining industrial site, Granville Island started transforming in the late 1970s when the government encouraged new, people-friendly developments. Maintaining its original industrial look, the former warehouses and factories now house galleries, artist studios, restaurants, and theaters; the cement plant on the waterfront is the only industrial tenant left. Access to Granville Island is by Aquabus from the West End, Yaletown, or Kitsilano (see "By Miniferry," in "Getting Around," earlier in this chapter; the Aquabus drops you at the public market) or by foot, bike, or car across the bridge at Anderson Street (access from W. 2nd Ave.). Avoid driving over on weekends and holidays—you'll spend more time trying to find a parking place than in the galleries. Check the website for upcoming events or stop by the information center, behind the Kids Market.

Located on the south shore of False Creek, under the Granville St. Bridge. For studio and gallery hours and other information about Granville Island, contact the information center at © **604/666-5784**. www.granville-island.net. Public market daily 9am–7pm. Bus: 50.

H. R. MacMillan Space Centre ✿ *Kids*   In the same building as the Vancouver Museum, the space center and observatory has hands-on displays and exhibits that will delight budding astronomy buffs and their parents (or older space buffs and their children). Displays are highly interactive: In the Cosmic Courtyard, you can try designing a spacecraft or maneuvering a lunar robot. Or, punch a button and get a video explanation of the *Apollo 17* manned-satellite engine that stands before you. The exciting **Virtual Voyages Simulator** ✿✿ takes you on a voyage to Mars—it's a thrilling experience for adults and kids. In the GroundStation Canada Theatre, video presentations explore Canada's contributions to the space program and space in general. The StarTheatre shows movies—many of them for children—on an overhead dome. The Planetarium Star Theatre features exciting laser shows in the evening.

1100 Chestnut St., in Vanier Park. © **604/738-7827**. www.hrmacmillanspacecentre.com. Admission C$15 (US$15/£7) adults; C$11 (US$11/£5.50) seniors, students, children 5–18; C$7 (US$7/£3.50) children under 5; C$45 (US$45/£22) families (up to 5, maximum 2 adults). Evening laser shows C$11 (US$11/£5.50) each. Tues–Sun 10am–5pm; evening laser shows Thurs 9:30pm, Fri–Sat 9:30pm and 10:45pm. Closed Dec 25. Bus: 22.

Museum of Anthropology ✿✿✿   This isn't just any old museum. In 1976, architect Arthur Erickson created a classic Native post-and-beam-style structure out of poured concrete and glass to house one of the world's finest collections of west coast Native art.

Enter through doors that resemble a huge, carved, bent-cedar box. Artifacts from different coastal communities flank the ramp leading to the Great Hall's **collection of**

360 Degrees of Vancouver

The most popular (and most touristed) spot from which to view Vancouver's skyline and surrounding topography is high atop the space needle observation deck at the **Lookout!, Harbour Centre Tower** ⊛, 555 W. Hastings St. (© **604/ 689-0421**). It's a great place for first-time visitors who want a panorama of the city. The glass-encased Skylift whisks you up 166m (545 ft.) to the rooftop deck in less than a minute. The 360-degree view is remarkable (yes, that is Mt. Baker looming above the southeastern horizon), but the signage could be a lot better. Skylift admission is C$13 (US$13/£6.50) for adults, C$11 (US$11/£5.50) for seniors, C$9 (US$9/£4.50) for students and youth 11 to 17, C$6 (US$6/£3) children 4 to 10, and free for children under 4. It's open daily in summer from 8:30am to 10:30pm and in winter from 9am to 9pm, and tickets are valid for the entire day.

---

totem poles. Haida artist Bill Reid's touchable cedar bear and sea wolf sculptures sit at the Cross Roads; Reid's masterpiece, *The Raven and the First Men,* is worth the price of admission all by itself. The huge carving in glowing yellow cedar depicts a Haida creation myth, in which Raven—the trickster—coaxes humanity out into the world from its birthplace in a clamshell. Some of Reid's fabulous jewelry creations in gold and silver are also on display.

The **Masterpiece Gallery**'s argillite sculptures, beaded jewelry, and hand-carved ceremonial masks lead the way to the Visible Storage Galleries, where more than 15,000 artifacts are arranged by culture. You can open the glass-topped drawers to view small treasures and stroll past larger pieces housed in tall glass cases.

Also at the museum is the somewhat incongruous Koerner Ceramics Gallery, a collection of European ceramics that—while interesting—is really only there because old man Koerner had the money to endow the wing to hold his collection.

After visiting the galleries, take a walk around the grounds behind the museum. Overlooking Point Grey are two **longhouses** built according to the Haida tribal style, resting on the traditional north-south axis. Ten hand-carved totem poles stand in attendance along with contemporary carvings on the longhouse facades. *Note:* You might want to combine your visit to the Museum of Anthropology with the nearby UBC Botanical Garden and Nitobe Japanese Garden (p. 672).

6393 NW Marine Dr. (at Gate 4). © **604/822-5087.** www.moa.ubc.ca. Admission C$9 (US$9/£4.50) adults; C$7 (US$7/£3.50) seniors, students, children 6–18; free for children under 6; free Tues 5–9pm. Summer Wed–Mon 10am–5pm, Tues 10am–9pm; winter Wed–Sun 11am–5pm, Tues 11am–9pm. Closed Dec 25–26. Bus: 4 or 99 (10-min. walk from UBC bus loop).

Science World at Telus World of Science ⊛ (Kids)
Science World is impossible to miss: It's the big blinking geodesic dome (built for Expo '86 and now partnered with Telus, a telephone company, hence the branded name) on the eastern end of False Creek. Inside, it's a hands-on scientific discovery center where you and your kids can light up a plasma ball, walk through a 160-sq.-m (1,722-sq.-ft.) maze, wander through the interior of a camera, create a cyclone, watch a zucchini explode as it's charged with 80,000 volts, stand inside a beaver lodge, play in wrist-deep magnetic liquids, create music with a giant synthesizer, and watch mind-blowing three-dimensional slide and laser shows as well as other optical effects. Science World is loaded with first-rate adventures for kids from toddler age to early teens; you'll want to spend

at least a couple of hours here. Throughout the day, special shows, many with nature themes, are presented in the OMNIMAX Theatre—a huge projecting screen equipped with surround sound.

1455 Quebec St. (©) 604/443-7443. www.scienceworld.ca. Admission C$16 (US$16/£8) adults; C$13 (US$13/£6.50) seniors, students; C$11 (US$11/£5.50) children 4–17; free for children under 4; C$54 (US$54/£27) family pass for 6 related people. Combination tickets additional C$5 (US$5/£2.50) for OMNIMAX film. Sept–June Mon–Fri 10am–5pm, Sat–Sun 10am–6pm; July–Aug daily 10am–6pm; holidays 10am–6pm. SkyTrain: Main Street–Science World.

Vancouver Museum   Located in the same building as the H. R. MacMillan Space Centre (see above), the Vancouver Museum is dedicated to the city's history, from its days as a Native settlement and European outpost to its 20th-century maturation into a modern urban center. The exhibits have been remounted and revitalized to make them more interesting to the casual visitor. Of most importance here is the wonderful collection of First Nations art and artifacts. Hilarious, campy fun abounds in the 1950s Room, where a period film chronicles "Dorothy's All-Electric Home." Next to this is another fun, and socially intriguing, room devoted to Vancouver's years as a hippie capital, with film clips, commentary, and a replica hippie apartment.

1100 Chestnut St. (©) 604/736-4431. www.vanmuseum.bc.ca. Admission C$10 (US$10/£5) adults; C$8 (US$8/£4) seniors; C$6 (US$6/£3) youths 4–19. Daily 10am–5pm (Thurs till 9pm); closed Mon Sept–Apr. Bus: 22, then walk 3 blocks south on Cornwall Ave. Boat: Granville Island Ferry to Heritage Harbour.

GASTOWN & CHINATOWN
Dr. Sun Yat-sen Classical Chinese Garden ⊛   This small reproduction of a Classical Chinese Scholar's garden truly is a remarkable place, but to get the full effect it's best to take the free guided tour. Untrained eyes will only see a pretty pond surrounded by bamboo and funny shaped rocks. The engaging guides, however, can explain this unique urban garden's Taoist yin-yang design principle, in which harmony is achieved through dynamic opposition. To foster opposition (and thus harmony) in the garden, Chinese designers place contrasting elements in juxtaposition: Soft moving water flows across solid stone; smooth swaying bamboo grows around gnarled immovable rocks; dark pebbles are placed next to light pebbles in the floor. Moving with the guide, you discover the symbolism of intricate carvings and marvel at the subtle, ever-changing views from covered serpentine corridors. This is one of two Classical Chinese gardens in North America (the other is in Portland, Oregon) created by master artisans from Suzhou, the garden city of China.

578 Carrall St. (©) 604/689-7133. www.vancouverchinesegarden.com. C$8.75 (US$8.75/£4.40) adults; C$7 (US$7/£3.50) seniors and students; free children 5 and under; C$20 (US$20/£10) family pass. Free guided tour included. May–June 14 and Sept daily 10am–6pm; June 15–Aug daily 9:30am–7pm; Oct–Apr Tues–Sun 10am–4:30pm. Bus: 19 or 22.

Steam Clock (Kids)   A quirky urban timepiece and one of Vancouver's most inexplicably popular tourist draws, the Steam Clock at Water and Cambie Streets gives a steamy rendition of the Westminster Chimes every 15 minutes, drawing its power from the city's underground steam-heat system. A plaque on the base of the clock explains the mechanics of it all.

Water and Cambie St. Admission free.

NORTH VANCOUVER & WEST VANCOUVER
Capilano Suspension Bridge & Park ⊛   Vancouver's first and oldest tourist trap (built in 1889), this attraction still works—mostly because there's still something inherently thrilling about walking across a narrow, shaky walkway, 69m (226 ft.)

Finds **The *Other* Suspension Bridge**

Lynn Canyon Park, in North Vancouver between Grouse Mountain and Mount Seymour Provincial Park on Lynn Valley Road, offers a free alternative to the overpriced Capilano Suspension Bridge. True, the **Lynn Canyon Suspension Bridge** ✷ is both shorter and a little lower than Capilano (see above), but the waterfall and swirling whirlpools in the canyon below add both beauty and a certain fear-inducing fascination. Plus, it's free.

The park in which the bridge is located is a gorgeous 247-hectare (610-acre) rainforest of cedar and Douglas fir, laced throughout with walking trails. It's also home to an **Ecology Centre** (3663 Park Rd.; ✆ **604/981-3103**), which presents natural history films, tours, and displays that explain the local ecology. Staff members lead frequent walking tours. The center is open daily from 10am to 5pm (Oct–May Sat–Sun noon–4pm). The park itself is open from 7am to 7pm in spring and fall, 7am to 9pm in summer, and 7am to dusk in winter; it's closed December 25 and 26 and January 1. There is a cafe in the park that serves sit-down and takeout meals. To get there, take the SeaBus to Lonsdale Quay, then transfer to bus no. 229; by car, take the Trans-Canada Highway (Hwy. 1) to the Lynn Valley Road exit (about a 20-min. drive from downtown), and follow Lynn Valley Road to Peters Road, where you turn right.

---

above a canyon floor, held up by nothing but a pair of tiny cables. Set in a beautiful 8-hectare (20-acre) park about 15 minutes from downtown, the suspension bridge itself is a 135m-long (443-ft.) cedar-plank and steel-cable footbridge, which sways gently above the Capilano River. Visitors nervously cross above kayakers and salmon shooting the rapids far below. A new attraction called **"Treetops Adventure"** features more bridges and walkways, only these are attached to giant tree trunks 24m (80 ft.) above the rainforest floor.

In addition to the bridge, there's a **carving center** where Native carvers demonstrate their skill; an exhibit describing the region's natural history; guides in period costume who recount Vancouver's frontier days; and a pair of overpriced and poorly serviced restaurants. Though it's quite well done, it's hard to justify the exorbitant entrance fee and the summer crowds can be off-putting.

3735 Capilano Rd., North Vancouver. ✆ **604/985-7474.** www.capbridge.com. Admission winter/summer C$24–C$27 (US$24–US$27/£12–£14) adults; C$22–C$25 (US$22–US$25/£11–£13) seniors; C$19–C$21 (US$19–US$21/£9.50–£11) students; C$14–C$16 (US$14–US$16/£7–£8) youths 13–16; C$7.50–C$8.50 (US$7.50–US$8.50/£3.75–£4.25) children 6–12; free for children under 6. Hours change monthly, but generally May–Sept daily 8:30am–dusk, Oct–Apr daily 9am–5pm. Closed Dec 25. Bus: 246 from downtown Vancouver or 236 from Lonsdale Quay SeaBus terminal. Car: Hwy. 99 north across Lions Gate Bridge to Exit 14 on Capilano Rd.

Grouse Mountain ✷✷ *Kids* Once a local ski hill, Grouse Mountain has developed into a year-round mountain recreation park that claims to be the number-one attraction in Vancouver. It's fun if you're sports-minded or like the outdoors; if not, you might find it disappointing. Located only a 15-minute drive from downtown, the **SkyRide gondola** ✷✷ transports you to the mountain's 1,110m (3,642-ft.) summit.

(Hikers can take a near vertical trail called the Grouse Grind.) On a clear day, the **view** ⊛⊛⊛ from the top is the best around: You can see the city and the entire lower mainland, from far up the Fraser Valley east across the Gulf of Georgia to Vancouver Island.

In the lodge, **Theater in the Sky** ⊛ shows wildlife movies. Outside, in the winter, you can ski and snowboard (26 runs, 13 runs for night skiing/snowboarding; drop-in ski lessons available), go snowshoeing, skate on the highest outdoor rink in Canada, take a brief "sleigh ride" (behind a huge snow-cat), and the kids can play in a special snow park. In warmer weather, you can wander forest trails, take a scenic chair ride, enjoy a lumberjack show or "Birds in Motion" demonstrations, visit the Refuge for Endangered Wildlife, or ride on the mountainbike trails. Most of these activities are included in the rather exorbitant price of your Skyride ticket; you have to pay extra for a lift ticket and equipment rentals. Additional activities include helicopter tours and tandem paragliding. There are casual and fine-dining options, and a Starbucks, in the lodge.

6400 Nancy Greene Way, North Vancouver. ⓒ **604/984-0661.** www.grousemountain.com. SkyRide C$30 (US$30/£15) adults; C$28 (US$28/£14) seniors; C$17 (US$17/£8.50) youths 13–18; C$11 (US$11/£5.50) children 5–12; free children 4 and under. Full day ski-lift tickets C$45 (US$45/£23 adults, C$35 (US$35/£18) senior and youth, C$20 (US$20/£10) children, C$125 (US$125/£63) family (2 adults, 2 children under 18). SkyRide free with advance Observatory Restaurant reservation. Daily 9am–10pm. Bus: 232, then transfer to bus no. 236. SeaBus: Lonsdale Quay, then transfer to bus no. 236. Car: Hwy. 99 north across Lions Gate Bridge, take North Vancouver exit to Marine Drive, then up Capilano Rd. for 5km (3 miles). Parking C$3 (US$3/£1.50) for 2 hrs in lots below SkyRide.

VANCOUVER'S PLAZAS & PARKS
OUTDOOR PLAZAS

Unlike many cities, Vancouver's great urban gathering places stand not at the center but on the periphery, on two opposite sides of the **seawall** that runs around Stanley Park: **English Bay,** on the south side of Denman Street, and **Coal Harbour,** on the northern, Burrard Inlet side, are where Vancouverites go to stroll and be seen. On warm sunny days, these two areas are packed. Another waterside gathering spot is **Canada Place** (p. 664), which serves as the city's cruise-ship terminal (as well as a huge convention center with a giant hotel on top for good measure).

Designed by architect Arthur Erickson to be Vancouver's central plaza, **Robson Square**—downtown, between Hornby and Howe streets from Robson to Smithe streets—has never really worked. The square, which anchors the north end of the Provincial Law Courts complex designed by Erickson in 1972, suffers from a basic design flaw: It's sunk one story below street level, making it difficult to see and to access. The Law Courts complex, which sits on a higher level, raised above the street, is beautifully executed with shrubbery, cherry trees, sculptures, and a triple-tiered waterfall, but Robson Square below is about as appealing as a drained swimming pool. Just opposite Robson Square, however, the steps of the **Vancouver Art Gallery** are a great people place, filled with loungers, political agitators, and old men playing chess. It just goes to show you that grandiose urban theory and urban design, especially back in the 1970s, didn't always take the human element into account.

Library Square—a few blocks east from Robson Square at the corner of Robson and Homer streets—is an example of a new urban space that does work. It's been popular with locals since it opened in 1995. People sit on the steps, bask in the sunshine, read, harangue passersby with half-baked political ideas, and generally seem to enjoy themselves.

PARKS & GARDENS

Park and garden lovers are in heaven in Vancouver. The wet, mild climate is ideal for gardening, and come spring the city blazes with blossoming cherry trees, rhododendrons, camellias, azaleas, and spring bulbs. Roses are a favorite summer bloom. You'll see gardens everywhere, and urban gardens with fountains have been incorporated into most of the city's new development. Nature is part of the scheme here. For general information about Vancouver's parks, call ℂ **604/257-8400** or try www.parks. vancouver.bc.ca. For information on **Stanley Park,** the queen of them all, see p. 665.

The University of British Columbia on the West Side has two lovely gardens: the **UBC Botanical Garden,** one of the largest living botany collections on the west coast, and the sublime **Nitobe Japanese Garden.**

In Chinatown, the **Dr. Sun Yat-sen Classical Chinese Garden** (p. 669) is a small, tranquil oasis in the heart of the city, built by artisans from Suzhou, China; right next to it, accessed via the Chinese Cultural Centre on Pender Street, is the pretty (and free) **Dr. Sun Yat-sen Park,** with a pond, walkways, and plantings.

On the West Side, **Queen Elizabeth Park**—at Cambie Street and West 33rd Avenue—sits atop a 150m-high (492-ft.) extinct volcano and is the highest urban vantage point south of downtown, offering panoramic views in all directions (although leafy deciduous trees now block some of the best views). Along with the Rose Garden in Stanley Park, it's Vancouver's most popular location for wedding-photo sessions, with well-manicured gardens and a profusion of colorful flora. There are areas for lawn bowling, tennis, pitch-and-putt golf, and picnicking. The **Bloedel Conservatory** (ℂ **604/257-8584**) stands next to the park's huge sunken garden, an amazing reclamation of an abandoned rock quarry. A 42m-high (138-ft.) domed structure, the conservatory houses a tropical rainforest with more than 100 plant species as well as free-flying tropical birds. Admission to the conservatory is C$4.25 (US$4.25/£2.15) for adults, with discounts for seniors and children. Take bus no. 15 to reach the park.

VanDusen Botanical Gardens ⚘, 5251 Oak St., at West 37th Avenue (ℂ **604/ 878-9274;** www.vandusengarden.org), is located just a few blocks from Queen Elizabeth Park and the Bloedel Conservatory. In contrast to the flower fetish displayed by Victoria's famous Butchart Gardens (p. 703), Vancouver's 22-hectare (54-acre) botanical garden concentrates on whole ecosystems. From trees hundreds of feet high down to the little lichens on the smallest of damp stones, the gardeners at VanDusen attempt to re-create the plant life of an enormous number of different environments. Depending on which trail you take, you may find yourself wandering through the Southern Hemisphere section, the Sino-Himalayan garden, or the northern California garden where giant sequoias reach for the sky. Should all this tree gazing finally pall, head for the farthest corner of the garden where you'll find a devilishly difficult Elizabethan garden maze. Admission April through September is C$7.75 (US$7.75/£3.90) adults, C$5.50 (US$5.50/£2.75) seniors, C$5.75 (US$5.75/£2.90) youth 13 to 18, C$4 (US$4/£2) children 6 to 12, free for children under 6, C$18 (US$18/£9) families. Admission is about C$2 (US$2/£1) less from October through March. The gardens are open daily 10am to dusk. Take bus no. 17.

Adjoining UBC on the city's west side at Point Grey, **Pacific Spirit Regional Park,** called the **Endowment Lands** by long-time Vancouver residents, is the largest green space in Vancouver. Comprising 754 hectares (1,863 acres) of temperate rainforest, marshes, and beaches, the park includes nearly 35km (22 miles) of trails ideal for hiking, riding, mountain biking, and beachcombing.

Across the Lions Gate Bridge, there are six provincial parks that delight outdoor enthusiasts year-round. Good in winter or for those averse to strenuous climbing is the publicly maintained **Capilano River Regional Park,** 4500 Capilano Rd. (© **604/ 666-1790**), surrounding the Capilano Suspension Bridge & Park (p. 669). Hikers can follow a gentle trail by the river for 7km (4/25 miles) down the well-maintained **Capilano trails** to the Burrard Inlet and the Lions Gate Bridge, or about a mile upstream to **Cleveland Dam,** which serves as the launching point for white-water kayakers and canoeists.

The **Capilano Salmon Hatchery,** on Capilano Road (© **604/666-1790**), is on the river's east bank about a half a kilometer (⅓ mile) below the Cleveland Dam. Approximately two million Coho and Chinook salmon are hatched annually in glass-fronted tanks connected to the river by a series of channels. You can observe the hatching fry (baby fish) before they depart for open waters, as well as the mature salmon that return to the Capilano River to spawn. Admission is free, and the hatchery is open daily from 8am to 7pm (until 4pm in the winter). Drive across the Lions Gate Bridge and follow the signs to North Vancouver and the Capilano Suspension Bridge. Or take the SeaBus to Lonsdale Quay and transfer to bus no. 236; the trip takes less than 45 minutes.

Eight kilometers (5 miles) west of the Lions Gate Bridge on Marine Drive West, West Vancouver, is **Lighthouse Park** *ƒƒ*. This 74-hectare (183-acre) rugged-terrain forest has 13km (8 miles) of groomed trails and—because it has never been clear-cut—some of the largest and oldest trees in the Vancouver area. One of the paths leads to the 18m (59-ft.) **Point Atkinson Lighthouse,** on a rocky bluff overlooking the Strait of Georgia and a fabulous view of Vancouver. It's an easy trip on bus no. 250. For information about other West Vancouver parks, call © **604/925-7200** weekdays.

Driving up-up-up the mountain from **Lighthouse Park** will eventually get you to the top of **Cypress Provincial Park.** Stop halfway at the scenic viewpoint for a sweeping vista of the Vancouver skyline, the harbor, the Gulf Islands, and Washington State's Mount Baker, which peers above the eastern horizon. The park is 12km (7½ miles) north of Cypress Bowl Road and the Highway 99 junction in West Vancouver. Cypress Provincial Park has an intricate network of trails maintained for hiking during the summer and autumn and for downhill and cross-country skiing during the winter (see "Outdoor Activities & Spectator Sports," below).

Rising 1,430m (4,692 ft.) above Indian Arm, **Mount Seymour Provincial Park,** 1700 Mt. Seymour Rd., North Vancouver (© **604/986-2261**), offers another view of the area's Coast Mountains range. The road to this park roams through stands of Douglas fir, red cedar, and hemlock. Higher than Grouse Mountain, Mount Seymour has a spectacular view of Washington State's Mount Baker on clear days. It has challenging hiking trails that go straight to the summit, where you can see Indian Arm, Vancouver's bustling commercial port, the city skyline, the Strait of Georgia, and Vancouver Island. The trails are open all summer for hiking; during the winter, the paths are maintained for skiing, snowboarding, and snowshoeing (see "Outdoor Activities & Spectator Sports," below). Mount Seymour is open daily from 7am to 10pm.

ESPECIALLY FOR KIDS

Pick up copies of the free monthly newspapers *B.C. Parent* (www.bcparent.com), and *West Coast Families; West Coast Families'* centerfold, "Fun in the City," and event calendar, list everything currently going on, including **CN IMAX** shows at Canada Place Pier, **OMNIMAX** (© **604/443-7443**) shows at Science World at Telus World of

Science, and free children's programs. Both publications are available at Granville Island's Kids Market and at neighborhood community centers throughout the city.

To give kids (and yourself) an overview of the city, you can take the fun trolley tour offered by **Vancouver Trolley Company** (© **888/451-5581** or 604/801-5515; www. vancouvertrolley.com). Gas-powered trolleys run along a route through Downtown, Chinatown, the West End, and Stanley Park.

Stanley Park 愛愛愛 (p. 665) offers a number of attractions for children.

Also in Stanley Park, the **Vancouver Aquarium Marine Science Centre** 愛愛 (p. 666) has sea otters, sea lions, whales, and numerous other marine creatures, as well as many exhibits geared toward children. Right in town, **Science World at Telus World of Science** (p. 668) is a hands-on kids' museum where budding scientists can get their hands into everything.

A trip to **Granville Island** 愛愛愛 by Aquabus will delight kids, and there are a couple of specific kids' places they'll really enjoy. Granville Island's **Kids Market,** 1496 Cartwright St. (© **604/689-8447**), is open daily from 10am to 6pm. Playrooms and 28 shops filled with toys, books, records, clothes, and food are all child-oriented. At **Granville Island's Water Park and Adventure Playground,** 1496 Cartwright St., kids can really let loose with movable water guns and sprinklers. They can also have fun on the water slides or in the wading pool. The facilities are open during the summer daily (weather permitting) from 10am to 6pm. Admission is free; changing facilities are nearby at the False Creek Community Centre (© **604/257-8195**).

Greater Vancouver Zoo, 5048 264th St., Aldergrove (© **604/856-6825;** www. greatervancouverzoo.com), located 48km (30 miles) east of downtown Vancouver (about a 45-min. drive), is a lush 48-hectare (119-acre) reserve filled with lions, tigers, jaguars, ostriches, elephants, buffalo, elk, antelope, zebras, giraffes, a rhino, hippos, and camels; 124 species in all. The zoo also has food service and a playground. It's open daily 9am to 4pm from October to March; 9am to 7pm from April to September. Admission is C$16 (US$16/£8) for adults, C$13 (US$13/£6.50) for seniors and children 3 to 15, and free for children under 3. Take the Trans-Canada Highway to Aldergrove, Exit 73; parking is C$3 (US$3/£1.50) per day.

The prospect of walking high above the rushing waters is the main draw at the **Capilano Suspension Bridge & Park** or the **Lynn Canyon Suspension Bridge** (p. 670).

A whale-watching excursion is one of the most exciting adventures you can give a kid. See "Wildlife-Watching" in "Outdoor Activities & Spectator Sports," below, for information.

6 Special Events & Festivals

The first event of the year is the annual **New Year's Day Polar Bear Swim** at English Bay Beach; thousands of hardy citizens show up in elaborate costumes to take a dip in the icy waters of English Bay. On the second Sunday in January, the **Annual Bald Eagle Count** takes place in Brackendale, about an hour's drive north of Vancouver on the Sea to Sky Highway. The count starts at the Brackendale Art Gallery (© **604/ 898-3333**).

In late January or early February (dates change yearly), the **Chinese New Year** is celebrated with 2 weeks of firecrackers, dancing dragon parades, and other festivities. **The Vancouver Playhouse International Wine Festival** (www.playhousewinefest.com) in late March or early April (dates change yearly) is a major wine-tasting event featuring the latest international vintages. The **Vancouver Sun Run** (www.sunrun.com), in April, is Canada's biggest 10K race, featuring 40,000 runners, joggers, and walkers who race through 10 scenic kilometers. The run starts and finishes at BC Place Stadium.

During the **Vancouver International Jazz Festival** (© 604/872-5200; www.jazz vancouver.com) in late June and early July, more than 800 international jazz and blues players perform at 25 venues around town. Running July to September, the **Bard on the Beach Shakespeare Festival** in Vanier Park (© 604/739-0559; www.bardonthe beach.org) presents Shakespeare's plays in a tent overlooking English Bay. On **Canada Day,** July 1, Canada Place Pier hosts an all-day celebration including music and dance and an evening fireworks display over the harbor to top off the entertainment. The second or third weekend in July brings the **Vancouver Folk Music Festival** (© 604/ 602-9798; www.thefestival.bc.ca). International folk music is played outdoors at Jericho Beach Park. During the **HSBC Celebration of Light** (www.celebration-of-light. com), three international fireworks companies compete for a coveted title by launching their best displays rigged to explode in time to accompanying music over English Bay Beach. Don't miss the grand finale on the fourth night. In the last week of July and first week of August, the **Vancouver International Comedy Festival** (http://comedyfest.com) features comedians from all over Canada and the United States performing at a variety of venues around town.

On B.C. Day (the first Sun in Aug) the **Vancouver Pride Parade** (© 604/687-0955; www.vancouverpride.ca), a huge gay- and lesbian- parade, covers a route along Denman and Davie streets, beginning at noon and caps off the weeklong Pride Week festivities. In August, the **Abbottsford International Air Show** (© 604/852-8511; www.abbotsfordairshow.com) features barnstorming stuntmen and precision military pilots flying everything from Sopwith Camels to VTOLs and Stealth Bombers. Mid-August to Labour Day, the **Pacific National Exhibition** (© 604/253-2311; www. pne.bc.ca) offers everything from big-name entertainment to a demolition derby, livestock demonstrations, logger sports competitions, fashion shows, and North America's finest all-wooden roller coaster.

Every October, the **Vancouver International Film Festival** (© 604/685-0260; www.viff.org) features 250 new works, revivals, and retrospectives, representing filmmakers from 40 countries. All December, the **Christmas Carol Ship Parade** (www. carolships.org) lights up Vancouver Harbour; harbor cruise ships decorated with colorful Christmas lights sail around English Bay while on-board guests sip cider and sing Christmas carols.

7 Outdoor Activities & Spectator Sports

Vancouver is definitely an outdoors-oriented city and just about every imaginable sport has an outlet within the city limits. Downhill and cross-country skiing, snowshoeing, sea kayaking, fly-fishing, hiking, paragliding, and mountain biking are just a few of the options. Activities that can be enjoyed in the vicinity include rock climbing, river rafting, and heli-skiing. An excellent resource for outdoor enthusiasts is **Mountain Equipment Co-op,** 130 W. Broadway (© 604/872-7858; www.mec.ca). The MEC's retail store has a knowledgeable staff, the co-op publishes an annual mail-order catalog, and you can find useful outdoor activities information on the website.

OUTDOOR ACTIVITIES

BEACHES   Only 10% of Vancouver's annual rainfall occurs during June, July, and August; 60 days of summer sunshine is not uncommon. **English Bay Beach** ⟨★★⟩, at the end of Davie Street off Denman Street and Beach Avenue, is a great place to see sunsets. The bathhouse dates to the turn of the 20th century, and a huge playground slide is mounted on a raft just off the beach every summer.

On **Stanley Park**'s western rim, **Second Beach** ⟨★⟩ is a short stroll north from English Bay Beach. A playground, a snack bar, and an immense heated oceanside **pool** ⟨★⟩ (© 604/257-8370), open from May to September, makes this a convenient and fun spot for families. Admission to the pool is C$4.85 (US$4.85/£2.45) for adults, C$3.40 (US$3.40/£1.70) for seniors, C$3.65 (US$3.65/£1.80) for youths 13 to 18, and C$2.45 (US$2.45/£1.25) for children 6 to 12. Farther along the seawall, due north of Stanley Park Drive, lies secluded **Third Beach.** Locals tote along grills and coolers to this spot, a popular place for summer-evening barbecues and sunset watching.

South of English Bay Beach, near the Burrard Street Bridge, is **Sunset Beach** ⟨★⟩. Running along False Creek, it's actually a picturesque strip of sandy beaches filled with enormous driftwood logs that serve as windbreaks and provide a little privacy for sunbathers and picnickers. There's a snack bar, a soccer field, and a long, gently sloping grassy hill for people who prefer lawn to sand.

On the West Side, **Kitsilano Beach** ⟨★★★⟩, along Arbutus Drive near Ogden Street, is affectionately called Kits Beach. It's an easy walk from the Maritime Museum and the False Creek ferry dock. If you want to do a saltwater swim but can't handle the cold, head to the huge (135m/443-ft.-long) heated (77°F/25°C) **Kitsilano pool** ⟨★★⟩. Admission is the same as for Second Beach pool, above.

Farther west on the other side of Pioneer Park is **Jericho Beach** (Alma St. off Point Grey Rd.). This is another local after-work and weekend social spot. **Locarno Beach,** off Discovery Street and Northwest Marine Drive, and **Spanish Banks,** Northwest Marine Drive, wrap around the northern point of the UBC campus and University Hill. (Be forewarned that beachside restrooms and concessions on the promontory end abruptly at Locarno Beach.) Below UBC's Museum of Anthropology is **Point Grey Beach,** a restored harbor defense site. The next beach is **Wreck Beach** ⟨★★★⟩— Canada's largest nude beach. You get down to Wreck Beach by taking the very steep Trail 6 on the UBC campus near Gate 6 down to the water's edge. Extremely popular with locals and maintained by the Wreck Beach Preservation Society, Wreck Beach is also the city's most pristine and least developed sandy stretch. It's bordered on three sides by towering trees.

For information on any of Vancouver's many beaches, call © 604/738-8535 (summer only).

BICYCLING & MOUNTAIN BIKING   Cycling in Vancouver is fun, amazingly scenic, and very popular. Cycling maps are available at most bicycle retailers and rental outlets. Some West End hotels offer guests bike storage and rentals. Daily rentals run around C$15 to C$40 (US$15–US$40/£7.50–£20), helmets and locks included. Popular shops that rent city and mountain bikes, child trailers, child seats, and in-line skates (protective gear included) include **Spokes Bicycle Rentals & Espresso Bar,** 1798 W. Georgia St. (© 604/688-5141; www.spokesbicyclerentals.com), at the corner of Denman Street at entrance to Stanley Park; **Alley Cat Rentals,** 1779 Robson St., in the alley (© 604/684-5117); and **Bayshore Bicycle and Rollerblade Rentals,**

745 Denman St. (© **604/688-2453;** www.bayshorebikerentals.ca). *Note:* Be advised that wearing a helmet is mandatory, and one will be included in your bike rental.

The most popular cycling path in the city runs along the **seawall** ★★★ around the perimeter of Stanley Park, although portions of this might be closed in 2008 because of the restoration work following the December 2006 windstorm. Another popular route is the **seaside bicycle route,** a 15km (9⅓-mile) ride that begins at English Bay and continues around False Creek to the University of British Columbia. Serious mountain bikers also have a wealth of world-class options within a short drive from downtown Vancouver. The trails on **Grouse Mountain** (p. 670) are some of the lower mainland's best.

BOATING   With thousands of miles of protected shoreline along British Columbia's west coast, boaters enjoy some of the finest cruising grounds in the world. Explore the many inlets, passages, and islands. You can rent powerboats for a few hours or up to several weeks at **Bonnie Lee Boat Rentals,** 1676 Duranleau St., Granville Island (© **866/933-7447** or 604/290-7441; www.bonnielee.com). Rates for a 5.8m (19-ft.) sport boat with 115 horsepower motor begin at C$55 (US$55/£28) per hour (plus C$7/US$7/£3.50 insurance fee and fuel), or C$350 (US$350/£175) for an 8-hour package. **Jerry's Boat Rentals,** Granville Island (© **604/644-3256**), is just steps away and offers similar deals.

CANOEING & KAYAKING   Both placid, urban False Creek and the incredibly beautiful 30km (19-mile) North Vancouver fjord known as Indian Arm have launching points that can be reached by car or bus. Prices range from about C$40 (US$40/£20) per 2-hour minimum rental to C$70 (US$70/£35) per 5-hour day for single kayaks and about C$60 (US$60/£30) for canoe rentals. Customized tours range from C$75 to C$150 (US$75–US$150/£37–£75) per person.

Ecomarine Ocean Kayak Centre, 1668 Duranleau St., Granville Island (© **888/425-2925** or 604/689-7575; www.ecomarine.com), has 2-hour, daily and weekly kayak rentals, as well as courses and organized tours. The company also has an office at the **Jericho Sailing Centre,** 1300 Discovery St., at Jericho Beach (© **604/222-3565**). In North Vancouver, **Deep Cove Canoe and Kayak Rentals,** 2156 Banbury Rd. (at the foot of Gallant St.), Deep Cove (© **604/929-2268;** www.deepcovekayak.com), is an easy starting point for anyone planning an Indian Arm run. It offers hourly and daily rentals of canoes and kayaks, as well as lessons and customized tours.

Lotus Land Tours, 2005–1251 Cardero St. (© **800/528-3531** or 604/684-4922; www.lotuslandtours.com), runs guided kayak tours on Indian Arm that come with hotel pickup, a barbecue salmon lunch, and incredible scenery. The wide, stable kayaks are perfect for first-time paddlers. One-day tours cost C$155 (US$155/£78) for adults, C$114 (US$114/£57) for children.

ECO-TOURS   **Lotus Land Tours** (see "Canoeing & Kayaking," above) runs guided kayak tours on Indian Arm. From late November to the end of January, this small local company also offers unique float trips on the Squamish River to see the large concentration of bald eagles up close. **Rockwood Adventures** (© **888/236-6606** or 604/980-7749; www.rockwoodadventures.com) has 4-hour **guided walks of the North Shore rainforest** ★, complete with a trained naturalist, stops in Capilano Canyon and at the Lynn Canyon Suspension Bridge (p. 670), and lunch. Cost is C$75 (US$75/£37) for adults, C$66 (US$66/£33) for seniors and students, and C$60 (US$60/£30) for children 6 to 11.

FISHING   With the Pacific Ocean to the west and an intricate river and lake system throughout the province, British Columbia has long been one of North America's best fishing destinations. Five species of salmon, rainbow and Dolly Varden trout, steelhead, and sturgeon abound in the local waters around Vancouver. To fish, anglers over the age of 16 need a **nonresident saltwater or freshwater license.** Licenses are available provincewide from more than 500 vendors, including tackle shops, sporting-goods stores, resorts, service stations, marinas, charter boat operators, and department stores. Saltwater (tidal waters) fishing licenses cost C$7.50 (US$7.50/£3.75) for 1 day, C$20 (US$20/£10) for 3 days, and C$33 (US$33/£16) for 5 days. Fly-fishing in national and provincial parks requires special permits, which you can get at any park site for a nominal fee. Permits are valid at all Canadian parks.

The *B.C. Tidal Waters Sport Fishing Guide, B.C. Sport Fishing Regulations Synopsis for Non-Tidal Waters,* and the *B.C. Fishing Directory and Atlas,* available at many tackle shops, are good sources of information. The *Vancouver Sun* prints a daily **fishing report** in the B section that details which fish are in season and where they can be found. Another good source of general information is the **Fisheries and Ocean Canada** website (www.pac.dfo-mpo.gc.ca).

Hanson's Fishing Outfitters, 102–580 Hornby St. (𝒞 **604/684-8988;** www.hansons-outfitters.com), and **Granville Island Boat Rentals,** 1696 Duranleau St. (𝒞 **604/682-6287**), are outstanding outfitters. **Bonnie Lee Fishing Charters Ltd.,** 1676 Duranleau St., Granville Island 𝒞 **604/290-7447;** www.bonnielee.com), is another reputable outfitter and also sells fishing licenses.

GOLF   Golf is a year-round sport in Vancouver. With five public 18-hole courses, half a dozen pitch-and-putt courses in the city, and dozens more nearby, golfers are never far from their love. For discounts and short-notice tee times at more than 30 Vancouver-area courses, contact the **A-1 Last Minute Golf Hot Line** (𝒞 **800/684-6344** or 604/878-1833; www.lastminutegolfbc.com).

A number of excellent public golf courses, maintained by the **Vancouver Board of Parks and Recreation** (𝒞 **604/280-1818** to book tee times; www.city.vancouver.bc.ca/parks), can be found throughout the city. **Langara Golf Course,** 6706 Alberta St., around 49th Avenue and Cambie Street (𝒞 **604/713-1816**), built in 1926 and recently renovated and redesigned, is one of the most popular golf courses in the province. Depending on the course, summer greens fees range from C$24 to C$55 (US$24–US$55/£12–£28) for an adult, with discounts for seniors, youths, and off-season tee times.

The public **University Golf Club,** 5185 University Blvd. (𝒞 **604/224-1818**), is a great 6,560-yard, par-71 course with a clubhouse, pro shop, locker rooms, bar and grill, and sports lounge.

Leading private clubs are situated on the North Shore and in Vancouver. Check with your club at home to see if you have reciprocal visiting memberships with one of the following: **Capilano Golf and Country Club,** 420 Southborough Dr., West Vancouver (𝒞 604/922-9331); **Marine Drive Golf Club,** West 57th Avenue and Southwest Marine Drive (𝒞 604/261-8111); **Seymour Golf and Country Club,** 3723 Mt. Seymour Pkwy., North Vancouver (𝒞 604/929-2611); **Point Grey Golf and Country Club,** 3350 SW Marine Dr. (𝒞 604/261-3108); and **Shaughnessy Golf and Country Club,** 4300 SW Marine Dr. (𝒞 604/266-4141). Greens fees range from C$42 to C$75 (US$42–US$75/£21–£37).

HIKING   Great trails for hikers of all levels run through Vancouver's dramatic environs. Good trail maps are available from **International Travel Maps and Books,** 539 Pender St. (© **604/687-3320;** www.itmb.com), which also stocks guidebooks and topographical maps. You can pick up a local trail guide at any bookstore.

If you're looking for a challenge without a longtime commitment, hike the aptly named **Grouse Grind** from the bottom of **Grouse Mountain** (p. 670) to the top; then buy a one-way ticket down on the Grouse Mountain SkyRide gondola.

For a bit more scenery with a bit less effort, take the Grouse Mountain SkyRide up to the **Grouse chalet** and start your hike at an altitude of 1,100m (3,609 ft.). The trail north of **Goat Mountain** is well marked and takes approximately 6 hours round-trip, though you may want to build in some extra time to linger on the top of Goat and take in the spectacular 360-degree views of Vancouver, Vancouver Island, and the snowcapped peaks of the Coast Mountains.

Lynn Canyon Park, Lynn Headwaters Regional Park, Capilano River Regional Park, Mount Seymour Provincial Park, Pacific Spirit Park, and **Cypress Provincial Park** (see "Exploring Vancouver," earlier in this chapter) have good, easy to challenging trails that wind up through stands of Douglas fir and cedar and contain a few serious switchbacks. Pay attention to the trail warnings posted at the parks (some have bear habitats), and always remember to sign in with the park service at the start of your chosen trail.

ICE SKATING   The highest ice-skating rink in Canada is located on **Grouse Mountain** (p. 670). In the city, the **West End Community Centre,** 870 Denman St. (© **604/257-8333**), rents skates at its enclosed rink, open October through March. Another option is the **Kitsilano Ice Rink,** 2690 Larch St. (© **604/257-6983;** www. vancouverparks.ca), open from October to June. The enormous **Burnaby 8 Rinks Ice Sports Centre,** 6501 Sprott, Burnaby (© **604/291-0626**), is the Vancouver Canucks' official practice facility. It has eight rinks, is open year-round, and offers lessons and rentals. Call ahead to check hours for public skating at all these rinks.

IN-LINE SKATING   All over Vancouver you'll find lots of locals rolling along beach paths, streets, park paths, and promenades. If you didn't bring a pair of blades, try **Bayshore Bicycle and Rollerblade Rentals,** 745 Denman St. (© **604/688-2453;** www.bayshorebikerentals.com). Rentals run C$5 (US$5/£2.50) per hour or C$20 (US$20/£10) for 8 hours. For information on in-line skating lessons and group events, visit www.inlineskatevancouver.com.

JOGGING   Local runners traverse the **Stanley Park seawall** 👟👟👟 and the paths around **Lost Lagoon** and **Beaver Lake.** If you're a dawn or dusk runner, take note that this is one of the world's safer city parks. However, if you're alone, don't tempt fate—stick to open and lighted areas. Other prime jogging areas in the city are **Kitsilano Beach, Jericho Beach,** and **Spanish Banks** (for more information, see "Beaches," above); all of them offer flat, well-maintained running paths along the ocean.

The **Sun Run** in April and the **Vancouver International Marathon** in May attract runners from around the world. Contact the **Vancouver International Marathon Society,** 1601 Bayshore Dr., in the Westin Bayshore Hotel (© **604/872-2928;** www.vanmarathon.bc.ca), or the **Vancouver Sun Run,** 655 Burrard St. (© **604/689-9441;** www.sunrun.com), for information.

PARAGLIDING   In North Vancouver, **First Flight Paragliding** (© 604/988-1111; www.first-flight.ca) offers tandem flights June through September from the peak of Grouse Mountain at C$190 (US$190/£95) for 1 hour, lift ticket to the summit of Grouse Mountain not included. The actual flight takes approximately 20 minutes.

SAILING   Trying to navigate a sailboat in the unfamiliar straits around Vancouver is unwise and unsafe unless you enroll in a local sailing course before attempting it. Knowing the tides, currents, and channels is essential, and you won't be able to rent a sailboat without this basic navigational and safety knowledge. Multiday instruction packages sometimes include guided Gulf Island cruises.

   Cooper Boating Centre, 1620 Duranleau St. (© 604/687-4110; www.cooper boating.com) offers chartered cruises, boat rentals, and sail-instruction packages.

SKIING & SNOWBOARDING   World-class skiing lies outside the city at the **Whistler/Blackcomb Ski Resort,** 110km (68 miles) north of Vancouver. However, you don't have to leave the city to get in a few runs. It seldom snows in the city's downtown and central areas, but Vancouverites can ski before work and after dinner at the three ski resorts in the North Shore mountains. In 2010, these local mountains will play host to the freestyle and snowboard events in the Winter Olympics.

   Grouse Mountain Resort, 6400 Nancy Greene Way, North Vancouver (© 604/984-0661; snow report 604/986-6262; www.grousemountain.com), is about 3km (1¾ miles) from the Lions Gate Bridge and overlooks the Burrard Inlet and Vancouver skyline. Four chairs, two beginner tows, and two T-bars take you to 24 alpine runs. The resort has night skiing, special events, instruction, and a spectacular view, as well as a 90m (295-ft.) half pipe for snowboarders. Though the area is small, all skill levels are covered, with two beginner trails, three blue trails, and five black-diamond runs, including Coffin and Inferno, which follow the east slopes down from 1,230 to 750m (4,035–2,461 ft.). Rental packages and a full range of facilities are available. Lift tickets good for all-day skiing are C$45 (US$45/£23) for adults, C$35 (US$35/£18) for seniors and youths, C$20 (US$20/£10) for children 5 to 12, and free for children under 4. These lift prices are in addition to your gondola ride up to the summit.

   Mount Seymour Provincial Park, 1700 Mt. Seymour Rd., North Vancouver (© 604/986-2261; snow report 604/986-3999; www.mountseymour.com), has the area's highest base elevation; it's accessible via four chairs and a tow. Lift tickets are C$39 (US$39/£20) all day for adults, C$27 (US$27/£14) for seniors, C$32 (US$32/£16) for youths 12 to 19, and C$16 (US$16/£8) for children 6 to 11. Nighttime skiing from 4 to 10pm costs less. In addition to day and night skiing, the facility offers snowboarding, snowshoeing, and tobogganing along its 22 runs. There are also 26km (16 miles) of cross-country trails. Mount Seymour has one of western Canada's largest equipment rental shops. Shuttle service is available during ski season from various locations on the North Shore, including the Lonsdale Quay SeaBus. For more information, call © 604/953-3333.

   Cypress Bowl, 1610 Mt. Seymour Rd. (© 604/926-5612; snow report 604/419-7669; www.cypressmountain.com), has the area's longest vertical drop (525m/1,722 ft.), challenging ski and snowboard runs, and 16km (10 miles) of track-set cross-country ski trails (including 5km/3.1 miles set aside for night skiing). Full-day lift tickets are C$43 to C$47 (US$43–US$47/£22–£24) for adults, with reduced rates for youths, seniors, and children. Cross-country full-day passes are C$16 (US$16/£8) for adults, with reduced rates for youths, seniors, and children. Snowshoe tours and excellent introductory ski packages are available. *Note:* Cypress will be home to the 2010

Olympics freestyle skiing (moguls and aerials), snowboarding (half pipe and parallel giant slalom), and brand-new ski cross events. In winter 2008 Cypress will open nine new runs for intermediate and expert skiers and snowboarders, accessed by a new quad chairlift. A new day lodge is under construction and is set to open for the winter 2008–09 season.

SWIMMING & WATERSPORTS   Vancouver's midsummer saltwater temperature rarely exceeds 65°F (18°C). If you've really got a hankering to have a saltwater swim, there are **heated outdoor pools** at both **Kitsilano Beach** 🐟🐟🐟 and **Second Beach** 🐟 (see "Beaches," earlier in this chapter). You can also take to the water at public aquatic centers.

The **Vancouver Aquatic Centre,** 1050 Beach Ave., at the foot of Thurlow Street (© **604/665-3424**), has a heated, 50m (164-ft.) Olympic pool, saunas, whirlpools, weight rooms, diving tanks, locker rooms, showers, child care, and a tot pool. Adult admission is C$4.85 (US$4.85/£2.45) for adults, C$2.45 (US$2.45/£1.25) children 2-12. The new, coed **YWCA Fitness Centre,** 535 Hornby St. (© **604/895-5777;** www.ywcavan.org), in the heart of downtown, has a six-lane, 25m (82-ft.), ozonated (much milder than chlorinated) pool, steam room, whirlpool, conditioning gym, and aerobic studios. A day pass is C$16 (US$16/£8) for adults.

TENNIS   The city maintains 180 outdoor hard courts that have a 1-hour limit and accommodate patrons on a first-come, first-served basis from 8am until dusk. Local courtesy dictates that if people are waiting, you surrender the court on the hour. (Heavy usage times are evenings and weekends.) With the exception of the Beach Avenue courts, which charge a nominal fee in summer, all city courts are free.

Stanley Park has four courts near Lost Lagoon and 17 courts near the Beach Avenue entrance, next to the Fish House Restaurant. During the summer season (May–Sept), six courts are taken over for pay tennis and can be prebooked by calling © **604/605-8224. Queen Elizabeth Park**'s 18 courts service the central Vancouver area, and **Kitsilano Beach Park**'s 🐟 10 courts service the beach area between Vanier Park and the UBC campus.

WHITE-WATER RAFTING   A 2½-hour drive from Vancouver, on the wild Nahatlatch River, **Reo Rafting,** 845 Spence Way, Anmore (© **800/736-7238** or 604/461-7238; www.reorafting.com), offers some of the best guided white-water trips in the province, at a very reasonable price. One-day packages—including lunch, all your gear, and 4 to 5 hours on the river—start at C$109 (US$109/£55) for adults. Multiday trips and group packages are available, and they can provide transportation from Vancouver.

Only a 1½-hour drive from the city is **Chilliwack River Rafting** (© **800/410-7238;** www.chilliwackriverrafting.com), which offers half-day trips on the Chilliwack River and in the even hairier Chilliwack Canyon. The cost is C$89 (US$89/£45) for adults and C$69 (US$69/£35) for children.

WILDLIFE-WATCHING   Vancouver is an internationally famous stop for naturalists, eco-tourists, pods of orca whales, and thousands of migratory birds, so bring your camera, binoculars, and bird-spotting books. Salmon, bald eagles, herons, beavers, and numerous rare, indigenous marine and waterfowl species live in the metropolitan area.

Orcas, or killer whales, are the largest mammals to be seen in the waters around Vancouver. Three orca pods (families), numbering about 80 whales, return to this area every year to feed on the salmon returning to spawn in the Fraser River starting in May and continuing into October. The eldest female leads the group; the head of one pod is thought to have been born in 1911. From April to October, daily excursions offered by **Vancouver Whale Watch,** 12240 2nd Ave., Richmond (© **604/274-9565;** www. vancouverwhalewatch.com), focus on the majestic killer whales plus Dall's porpoises, sea lions, seals, eagles, herons, and other wildlife. The cost is C$105 (US$105/£53) per person. The same adult rates apply at **Steveston Seabreeze Adventures,** 12551 No. 1 Rd., Richmond (© **604/272-7200;** www.seabreezeadventures.ca), but the price for seniors is C$89 (US$89/£45) and for children it's C$59 (US$59/£30). Both companies offer a shuttle service from downtown Vancouver.

Thousands of migratory birds following the Pacific Flyway rest and feed in the Fraser River delta south of Vancouver, especially at the 340-hectare (840-acre) **George C. Reifel Bird Sanctuary,** 5191 Robertson Rd., Westham Island (© **604/946-6980;** www.reifelbirdsanctuary.com), which was created by a former bootlegger and wetland-bird lover. The sanctuary is wheelchair accessible and open daily from 9am to 4pm. Admission is C$4 (US$4/£2) for adults and C$2 (US$2/£1) for seniors and children.

The **Richmond Nature Park,** 1185 Westminster Hwy. (© **604/718-6188**), was established to preserve the Lulu Island wetlands bog. It features a nature house with educational displays and a boardwalk-encircled duck pond. On Sunday afternoons, knowledgeable guides give free tours and acquaint visitors with this unique environment. Admission is by donation.

During the winter, thousands of bald eagles—in fact, the largest number in North America—line the banks of the **Squamish, Cheakamus,** and **Mamquam** rivers to feed on spawning salmon. To get there by car, take the scenic **Sea-to-Sky Highway** (Hwy. 99) from downtown Vancouver to Squamish and Brackendale; the trip takes about an hour. Contact **Squamish & Howe Sound Visitor Info Centre** (© **604/ 892-9244;** www.squamishchamber.bc.ca) for more information.

The annual summer salmon runs attract more than bald eagles. Tourists also flock to coastal streams and rivers to watch the waters turn red with leaping coho and sockeye. The salmon are plentiful at the **Capilano Salmon Hatchery** (p. 673), **Goldstream Provincial Park** (p. 728), and numerous other fresh waters.

WINDSURFING   Windsurfing is not allowed at the mouth of False Creek near Granville Island, but you can bring a board to **Jericho** and **English Bay beaches** 😻 or rent one there. Equipment sales, rentals (including wet suits), and instruction can be found at **Windsure Windsurfing School,** 1300 Discovery St., at Jericho Beach (© **604/224-0615;** www.windsure.com). Rentals start at about C$18 (US$18/£9) per hour, wet suit and life jacket included.

SPECTATOR SPORTS

Spectators and participants will find plenty of activities in Vancouver. You can get schedule information on all major events at Tourism Vancouver's **Touristinfo Centre,** 200 Burrard St. (© **604/683-2000;** www.tourismvancouver.com). You can also get information and purchase tickets from Ticketmaster at the **Vancouver Ticket Centre,** 1304 Hornby St. (© **604/280-4444;** www.ticketmaster.ca), which has 40 outlets in the greater Vancouver area. Popular events such as Canucks games and the Vancouver Indy can sell out weeks or months in advance, so it's a good idea to book ahead.

FOOTBALL   The Canadian Football League's **B.C. Lions** (© **604/589-7627;** www.bclions.com) play their home and Grey Cup championship games (in good seasons) in the 60,000-seat **B.C. Place Stadium,** 777 Pacific Blvd. S. (at Beatty and

7777777777777777777

Robson sts.). Canadian football differs from its American cousin: It's a three-down offense game on a field that's 10 yards longer and wider. Some of the plays you see will have NFL fans leaping out of their seats in surprise. Tickets for individual games are available from Ticketmaster (© **604/280-4639;** www.ticketmaster.ca); prices run C$27 to C$70 (US$27–US$70/£14–£35).

HOCKEY   The National Hockey League's **Vancouver Canucks** play at **General Motors Place** (otherwise known as GM Place, or the Garage), 800 Griffith's Way (© **604/899-4600;** event hot line 604/899-7444; www.canucks.com). Tickets are C$33 to C$94 (US$33–US$94/£17–£47); they're difficult to obtain because the season tends to sell out in advance, but some individual seats are made available for every home game.

HORSE RACING   Thoroughbreds run at **Hastings Park Racecourse,** Exhibition Park, East Hastings and Cassiar streets (© **604/254-1631;** www.hastingspark.com), from mid-April to October. Post time varies; call ahead or check the website for the latest schedule if you want to place a wager. There is a decent restaurant there, so you can make a full evening or afternoon of dining and racing.

RUNNING   The **Vancouver Sun Run** in April and the **Vancouver International Marathon** (Canada's largest) in May attract thousands of runners from around the world and even more spectators. Contact the **Vancouver International Marathon Society** (© **604/872-2928;** www.vanmarathon.bc.ca), or the **Vancouver Sun Run,** 655 Burrard St. (© **604/689-9441;** www.sunrun.com), for information.

SOCCER   The American Professional Soccer League's **Vancouver Whitecaps** (© **604/899-9283**) play at Swangard Stadium (© **604/435-7121;** www.whitecaps fc.com) in Burnaby. Admission is normally C$21 to C$42 (US$21–US$42/£11–£21).

8 Shopping

THE SHOPPING SCENE
Blessed with a climate that seems semitropical in comparison to the rest of Canada, Vancouverites tend to do their shopping on the street, browsing from one window to the next, on the lookout for something new. **Robson Street** is the spot for high-end fashions. The 10-block stretch of **Granville Street** from 6th Avenue up to 16th Avenue is where Vancouver's old money comes to shop for classic men's and women's fashions, housewares, and furniture. **Water Street** in **Gastown** features knickknacks, antiques, cutting-edge furniture, First Nations art, and funky basement retro shops. **Main Street** from 19th Avenue to 27th Avenue means antiques, and lots of 'em. **Granville Island,** a rehabilitated industrial site beneath the Granville Street Bridge, is one of the best places to pick up salmon and other seafood. It's also a great place to browse for crafts and gifts.

SHOPPING A TO Z
ANTIQUES   The **Vancouver Antique Centre,** 422 Richards St. (© **604/669-7444;** Bus: 20), contains 15 shops, specializing in everything from china, glass, Orientalia, and jewelry to military objects, sports, toys, and watches. **Uno Langmann Ltd.,** 2117 Granville St. (© **604/736-8825;** www.langmann.com; bus: 4), caters to upscale shoppers, specializing in European and North American paintings, furniture, and silver.

BOOKS Since 1957, the locally owned chain **Duthie Books,** 2239 W. 4th Ave., Kitsilano (© **604/732-5344;** bus: 4), has been synonymous with good books in Vancouver. **Chapters,** 788 Robson St. (© **604/682-4066;** bus: 5), is pleasant and well planned, with little nooks and comfy benches in which to browse at length; there are other locations around town. **Little Sister's Book & Art Emporium,** 1238 Davie St. (© **604/669-1753;** www.littlesistersbookstore.com; bus: 1), is the West End bookstore with the largest selection of lesbian, gay, bisexual, and transgender books, videos, and magazines. **International Travel Maps,** 552 Seymour St. (© **604/687-3320;** www.itmb.com; bus: 4), has the best selection of travel books, maps, charts, and globes.

CAMERA Located near the food court of the downtown Pacific Centre mall, **Lens & Shutter,** 8700 W. Georgia St. (© **604/684-4422;** www.lensandshutter.com; bus: 4), can provide excellent film and camera advice, repairs, and sales.

DEPARTMENT STORES From the establishment of its early trading posts during the 1670s to its modern coast-to-coast chain, **The Bay** (Hudson's Bay Company), 674 Granville St. (© **604/681-6211;** www.hbc.com; bus: 4), has built its reputation on quality goods. You can still buy a Hudson's Bay woolen "point" blanket (the colorful stripes originally represented how many beaver pelts each blanket was worth in trade), but you'll also find wares from Tommy Hilfiger, Polo, DKNY, Ellen Tracy, Anne Klein II, and Liz Claiborne.

FASHION Many well-known international designers have boutiques in Vancouver, mostly scattered around Robson, Hastings, and Burrard streets.

For something uniquely west coast, don't miss the one-of-a-kind First Nations designs of **Dorothy Grant,** 250–757 W. Hastings St. (© **604/681-0201;** www.dorothygrant.com; bus: 4). Grant's exquisitely detailed Haida motifs are appliquéd onto coats, leather vests, jackets, caps, and accessories. The clothes are gorgeous and collectible. **Dream,** 311 W. Cordova St. (© **604/683-7326;** bus: 1), is one of the few places to find the early collections of local designers. **Zonda Nellis Design Ltd.,** 2203 Granville St. (© **604/736-5668;** www.zondanellis.com; bus: 4), offers imaginative hand-woven separates, sweaters, vests, soft knits, and a new line of hand-painted silks.

FIRST NATIONS ART You'll find First Nations art in abundance in Vancouver. **Images for a Canadian Heritage,** 164 Water St. (© **604/685-7046;** www.imagesforcanada.com; bus: 1), is a government-licensed First Nations art gallery, featuring traditional and contemporary works. **Hill's Native Art,** 165 Water St. (© **504/686-4249;** www.hillsnativeart.com; bus: 1), established in 1946 and claiming to be North America's largest Northwest coast Native art gallery, sells moccasins, ceremonial masks, Cowichan sweaters, wood sculptures, totem poles (priced up to C\$35,000/US\$35,000/£17,500), silk-screen prints, soapstone sculptures, and gold, silver, and argillite jewelry. The **Lattimer Gallery,** 1590 W. 2nd Ave. (© **604/732-4556;** www.leonalattimer.com; bus: 4), presents museum-quality displays of ceremonial masks, totem poles, argillite sculptures, and gold and silver jewelry.

FOOD At **Chocolate Arts,** 2037 W. 4th Ave. (© **604/739-0475;** bus: 4), the works are of such exquisite craftsmanship that they're sometimes a wrench to eat. Look for the all-chocolate diorama in the window—it changes every month or so. **Murchie's Tea & Coffee,** 970 Robson St. (© **604/669-0783;** www.murchies.com; bus: 5), is a Vancouver institution. You'll find everything from Jamaican Blue Mountain and Kona coffees to Lapsing, Souchong, and Kemun teas. **The Lobsterman,**

1807 Mast Tower Rd. (© 604/687-4531; www.lobsterman.com; bus: 50), is one of the city's best spots to pick up seafood. Salmon and other seafood can be packed for air travel. And the **Salmon Village,** 779 Thurlow St. (© **604/685-3378;** www. salmonvillage.com; bus: 4), specializes in salmon of all varieties.

GIFTS For a good range of basic souvenirs, try **Canadian Impressions at the Station,** 601 Cordova St. (© **604/681-3507;** bus: 1). The store carries lumberjack shirts, Cowichan sweaters, T-shirts, and other trinkets.

JEWELRY Opened in 1879, **Henry Birk & Sons Ltd.,** 698 W. Hastings St. (© **604/669-3333;** bus: 7), has a long tradition of designing and creating beautiful jewelry and watches and selling jewelry to international designers. On Granville Island, **The Raven and the Bear,** 1528 Duranleau St. (© **604/669-3990;** bus: 50), is a great spot to shop for west coast Native jewelry.

MALLS & SHOPPING CENTERS The **Pacific Centre Mall,** 700 W. Georgia St. (© **604/688-7236;** bus: 7), is a 3-block complex containing 200 shops and services, including Godiva, Benetton, Crabtree & Evelyn, and Eddie Bauer. For more upscale shopping, try the **Sinclair Centre,** 757 W. Hastings St. (© **604/659-1009;** www.sinclaircentre.com; bus: 7), which houses elite shops such as Armani, Leone, and Dorothy Grant, as well as smaller boutiques, art galleries, and a food court.

SHOES John Fluevog of **John Fluevog Boots & Shoes Ltd.,** 837 Granville St. (© **604/688-2828;** www.fluevog.com; bus: 4), has an international following for his under-C$200 (US$200/£100) urban and funky creations. You'll find outrageous platforms and clogs, and experiments for the daring footwear fetishist.

SPORTING GOODS Everything you'll ever need for the outdoors is at **Mountain Equipment Co-op,** 130 W. Broadway (© 604/872-7858; www.mec.ca; bus: 9).

TOYS The **Kids Only Market,** Cartwright Street, Granville Island (© **604/689-8447;** www.kidsmarket.ca; bus: 50), is a 24-shop complex that sells toys, games, computer software, and books for kids.

WINE **Marquis Wine Cellars,** 1034 Davie St. (© **604/684-0445;** www.marquis-wines.com; bus: 1), carries a full range of British Columbian wines as well as a large international selection, and has a very knowledgeable staff.

9 Vancouver After Dark

For the best overview of Vancouver's nightlife, pick up a copy of the weekly tabloid, the *Georgia Straight* (www.georgiastraight.com). The Thursday edition of the *Vancouver Sun* contains the weekly entertainment section *Queue.* The monthly *Vancouver* magazine is filled with listings and strong views about what's really hot in the city. Check out their website at www.vanmag.com. Or get a copy of *Xtra! West* (www.xtra.ca), the free gay and lesbian biweekly tabloid, available in shops and restaurants throughout the West End.

The **Alliance for Arts and Culture,** 100–938 Howe St. (© 604/681-3535; www.allianceforarts.com), is a great information source for all performing arts, literary events, and art films. The office is open Monday through Friday from 9am to 5pm.

Ticketmaster (Vancouver Ticket Centre), 1304 Hornby St. (© **604/280-3311;** www.ticketmaster.ca), has 40 outlets in the Vancouver area. Half-price tickets for same-day shows and events are available at the **Tickets Tonight** (www.ticketstonight.ca) kiosk (Tues–Sat 11am–6pm) in the **Vancouver Touristinfo Centre,** 200 Burrard St.

(© **604/684-2787** record events info). The Touristinfo Centre is open from May to Labour Day daily from 8am to 6pm; the rest of the year, it's open Monday through Saturday from 8:30am to 5pm.

Three major Vancouver theaters regularly host touring performances: the **Orpheum Theatre,** 801 Granville St. (© **604/665-3050;** bus: 7); the **Queen Elizabeth Theatre,** 600 Hamilton St. (© **604/665-3050;** bus: 5); and the **Vancouver Playhouse,** in the Queen Elizabeth Theatre complex (© **604/873-3311;** www.vancouverplayhouse.com). They share a website at **www.vancouver.ca/theatres**. On the campus of UBC, the **Chan Centre for the Performing Arts,** 6265 Crescent Rd. (© **604/822-2697;** www.chancentre.com), hosts a winter concert series; its acoustics are the best in town.

THE PERFORMING ARTS

Theater isn't only an indoor pastime here. There's an annual summertime Shakespeare series called **Bard on the Beach,** in Vanier Park (© **604/737-0625;** www.bardonthebeach.org; bus 22). You can also bring a picnic dinner to Stanley Park and watch **Theatre Under the Stars** (© **604/687-0174;** www.tuts.bc.ca; bus: 35), which features popular musicals and light comedies. For more original fare, don't miss **Vancouver's Fringe Festival** (© **604/257-0350;** www.vancouverfringe.com). The Fringe features more than 500 innovative and original shows each September.

The **Arts Club Theatre Company** presents live theater in two venues, the Granville Island Stage at the Arts Club Theatre, 1585 Johnston St. (bus: 50), and the Stanley Theatre, 2750 Granville St. (bus: 8). For information on both theaters, call © **604/687-1644** or head online to **www.artsclub.com**.

In a converted early-1900s church, the **Vancouver East Cultural Centre** (the "Cultch" to locals), 1895 Venables St. (© **604/251-1363;** www.vecc.bc.ca; bus: 20), hosts avant-garde theater productions, children's programs, and art exhibits.

OPERA The first-rate **Vancouver Opera,** 500–845 Cambie St. (© **604/683-0222;** www.vancouveropera.ca; bus: 17), alternates between less performed or new works and older, more popular favorites. English supertitles projected above the stage help audiences follow the stories.

CLASSICAL MUSIC The **Vancouver Symphony,** 601 Smithe St. (© **604/876-3434;** www.vancouversymphony.ca; bus: 7), presents a number of series: great classical works, light classics, modern classics and ethnic works, popular and show tunes, and music geared toward school-age children. Other classical groups in town include the **Vancouver Bach Choir,** 805–235 Keith Rd., West Vancouver (© **604/921-8012;** www.vancouverbachchoir.com); the **Vancouver Cantata Singers,** 5115 Keith Rd., West Vancouver (© **604/921-8588;** www.cantata.org); and the **Vancouver Chamber Choir,** 1254 W. 7th Ave. (© **604/738-6822;** www.vancouverchamberchoir.com).

DANCE The **Scotiabank Dance Centre,** 677 Davie St. (© **604/606-6400;** www.thedancecentre.com), provides a new focus point for the Vancouver dance community. For fans of modern and original dance, the time to be here is early July, when the **Dancing on the Edge Festival** (© **604/689-0691;** www.dancingontheedge.org) presents 60 to 80 envelope-pushing original pieces over a 10-day period. **Ballet British Columbia,** 502–68 Water St. (© **604/732-5003;** www.balletbc.com; bus: 4), is a young company that strives to present innovative works.

COMEDY & LIVE-MUSIC CLUBS Performers with the **Vancouver Theatre-Sports League** (© **604/687-1644;** www.vtsl.com) rely on a basic plot supplemented by audience suggestions the actors take and improvise on, often to hilarious results. Performances are in the Arts Club Theatre, 1585 Johnston St., Granville Island (bus: 50).

The old-style suspended hard-wood dance floor makes the **Commodore Ballroom,** 868 Granville St. (© 604/739-7469; www.commodoreballroom.com), the best place in Vancouver to catch a midsize band—be it R&B, jazz, blues, hip-hop, or pop. For folk, the **WISE Hall,** 1882 Adanac (© 604/254-5858; bus: 20), is the place to be. And for blues, go to the smoky, sudsy old **Yale Hotel,** 1300 Granville St. (© 604/ 681-9253; www.theyale.ca; bus: 4).

BARS, PUBS & LOUNGES   **Lift,** 333 Menchions Mews (© 604/689-5438), built on piers behind the Westin Bayshore Resort, is one of Vancouver's nicest glamour hot spots, offering dramatic views and luxe features such as an illuminated onyx bar. Popular younger-crowd bar-lounges in hoppin' Yaletown include **Afterglow,** 350 Davie St. (© 604/642-0577), and **Opus Bar,** 50 Davie St. (© 604/642-0577), in the trend-setting Opus Hotel. More romantic and less noisy, with piano music instead of high-decibel rock, is **Bacchus Lounge** in the Wedgewood Hotel, 845 Hornby St. (© 604/608-5319), a hot spot for professional powerbrokers. In Gastown, **The Irish Heather,** 217 Carrall St.(© 604/688-9779), is a pleasant Irish pub with numerous nooks and crannies, some of the best beer in town, and a menu that does a lot with the traditional Emerald Isle spud. **The Shark Club Bar and Grill,** 180 W. Georgia St. (© 604/687-4275; bus: 5), is the city's premier sports bar. If you're looking for a brew pub, **Steamworks Pub & Brewery,** 375 Water St. (© 604/689-2739; bus: 7), is your best bet. Choose from a dozen in-house beers, from dark Australian-style ales to light, refreshing wheat lagers. **The Yaletown Brewing Company,** 1111 Mainland St. (© 604/688-0039; bus: 2), also offers good home-brewed fare. Vancouver's best spot for late-night jazz and jam sessions is **O'Douls** in the Listel Hotel, 1300 Robson St. (© 604/684-8461).

DANCE CLUBS   Who knows how long they will be around? At press time, these were among the hottest dance floors in Vancouver. Downtown, **Au Bar,** 674 Seymour St. (© 604/648-2227), is packed with beautiful people milling from bar to dance floor to bar (there are two) and back again. **Balthazar,** 215 Bidwell St. at Davie (© 604/689-8822), in a funky Spanish Revival building with a seedy past as a bordello, offers martinis, wine, and tapas till the wee hours (2am), plus two small dance floors each with its own DJ; the crowd in this West End lounge is a little older and dresses the part. **Caprice,** 965 Granville St. (© 604/681-2114), has an upstairs lounge, with a fireplace, a big-screen TV showing old movies, and doors opening onto a patio; downstairs, The Nightclub is a large room with a funky semicircular glowing blue bar, big comfy wall banquettes, a secluded circular passion pit in one corner, and a medium-size dance floor.

The Cellar, 1006 Granville St. (© 604/605-4350), has a small dance floor and a DJ who mostly spins Top 40, but patrons are far less interested in groovin' than they are in meeting other Cellar dwellers, a process facilitated by a wall-length message board upon which pickup lines are posted. Wine snobs will feel right at home at **Crush Champagne Lounge,** 1180 Granville St. (© 604/684-0355), where a professional sommelier will help you make your wine selection; the drink list also includes a large selection of sexy champagne cocktails and by-the-glass bubblies. The lounge has a small dance floor and the music is mellow R&B, soul, classic lounge, and jazz. A former movie theater, **The Plaza Club,** 881 Granville St. (© 604/646-0064), makes a great nightclub with its high ceilings and spacious dance floor. Lineups start early at this popular club, which features different club nights (hip-hop, reggae) and DJs spinning Top 40 tunes on Friday and Saturday. It may be venerable, but the line of limos outside **Richard's on Richards,** 1036 Richards St. (© **604/687-6794**), attests to the fact that Dick's is still hot; inside there are two floors, four bars, a laser-light system, and lots of DJ'ed dance tunes and concerts.

GAY & LESBIAN BARS   The "Gay Village" is in the West End, particularly on Davie and Denman streets. Many clubs feature theme nights and dance parties, drag shows are ever popular, and every year in early August, as Gay Pride nears, the scene goes into overdrive. The **Gay Lesbian Transgendered Bisexual Community Centre,** 2–1170 Bute St. (© **604/684-5307;** www.lgtbcentrevancouver.com), has information on the current hot spots, but to find out what's *au courant* it's easier just to pick up a free copy of *Xtra West!,* available in most downtown cafes.

Reflecting the graying and—gasp!—mellowing of Vancouver's boomer-age gay crowd, the hottest hangout for gays is the **Fountain Head,** 1025 Davie St. (© **604/ 687-2222**), a pub located in the heart of the city's gay ghetto on Davie Street. The Head offers excellent microbrewed draft, good pub munchies, and a pleasant humming atmosphere till the morning's wee hours.

The Lotus Hotel, 455 Abbott St. (© **604/685-7777**), once among the most disreputable of Gastown gay bars, was given a face-lift and is now home to three separate bars and lounges, all with a largely but not exclusively gay clientele. Downstairs, the Lotus Lounge is one of the hottest house music venues in town, particularly on Straight Up Fridays with an all-female DJ team on the turntables. Lick, on the main floor, is a hot lesbian bar. The third venue, also on the main floor, is Honey, a comfortable restaurant/lounge where a mixed crowd gathers for cocktails or beers. On most nights, the DJs keep the music on a mellow, conversational level. However, on Saturdays, decibels go up significantly when the Queen Bee review, a New York–style cabaret drag show, fills the house.

A multilevel dance club with five floors and three bars, **Numbers,** 1042 Davie St. (© **604/685-4077**), hasn't changed much over the years: Extroverts hog the dance floor while admirers look on from the bar above. Great sound and lights. On the second floor, carpets, wood paneling, pool tables, darts, and a lower volume of music give it a neighborhood pub feel. **The Odyssey,** 1251 Howe St. (© **604/689-5256**), is the hottest and hippest gay/mixed dance bar in town; shows vary depending on the night.

16

Victoria & British Columbia

by Bill McRae & Donald Olson

British Columbia runs the length of Canada's west coast, from the Washington border to the Alaskan panhandle. Roughly 947,800 sq. km (365,948 sq. miles), it's more than twice the size of California, though the population (4.3 million) is less than half of that of Los Angeles.

British Columbia's outstanding feature is its variety of scenery, climates, and cultures. While most residents live in the greater Vancouver and **Victoria** areas in the southwest, along a coast dotted with islands, beachfront communities, modern cities, and belts of rich farmland, just a few hours' drive to the north or east on any of B.C.'s mostly two-lane highways, the communities are tiny, the sparse population is scattered, and the land is alternately towering forest, fields of stumps left by timber harvests, high alpine wilderness, and even desert. Between these extremes are the areas covered in this chapter.

1 Exploring the Province

There's more to British Columbia than Vancouver's urban bustle. In fact, the other Vancouver—**Vancouver Island**—is 90 minutes from the city by ferry. On Vancouver Island is the province's capital, **Victoria.** It's a lovely seaport city that's proud of its British roots, lavish Victorian gardens, and picturesque port. It's also the ideal place to begin exploring the entire island, which stretches more than 450km (280 miles) from Victoria to the northwest tip of Cape Scott. Along the way plan to visit the island's wild west coast at Tofino and view sea life at Campbell River.

It's only a 121km (75-mile) drive from Vancouver to North America's most popular ski resorts at Whistler and Blackcomb mountains. Whistler will be the site of the skiing competition for the 2010 Winter Olympics, and recent years have seen lots of improvements to an already stellar resort. Whistler is also a popular summer getaway, offering great fishing, excellent mountain-biking and hiking trails, and world-class golf.

Travel inland to interior B.C. and leave the maritime climate behind you. In the Okanagan and Thompson river valleys, the landscape turns more arid and mountainous—perfect for orchards and vineyards. The Okanagan is one of Canada's premier wine-growing areas, and its deep glacial lakes and warm summer temperatures provide a sunny golf-and-beach playground for visitors from across Canada.

VISITOR INFORMATION

TOURIST OFFICES Contact **Tourism British Columbia** (© **800/HELLO-BC** or 604/683-2000; www.hellobc.com), and the **Tourism Association of Vancouver Island** (203–335 Wesley St., Nanaimo, BC V9R 2T5 (© **250/754-3500;** www.vancouverisland.travel) for details about travel in the province. Contact the individual

Southern British Columbia

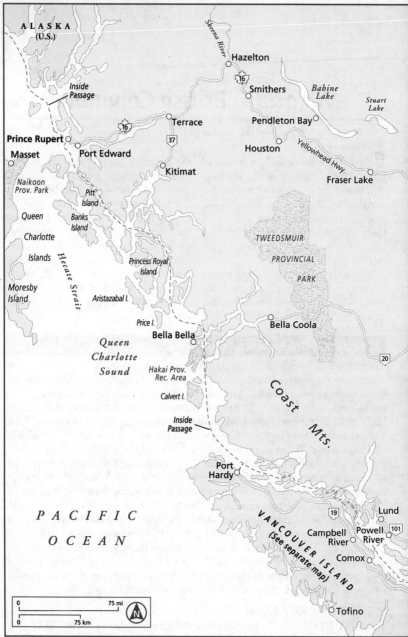

ALASKA (U.S.)

Inside Passage

Prince Rupert

Masset

Naikoon Prov. Park

Queen Charlotte Islands

Moresby Island

Hecate Strait

Pitt Island

Banks Island

Princess Royal Island

Aristazabal I.

Price I.

Port Edward

Kitimat

Terrace

Sheena River

Hazelton

Smithers

Babine Lake

Stuart Lake

Pendleton Bay

Houston

Fraser Lake

Yellowhead Hwy.

TWEEDSMUIR PROVINCIAL PARK

Bella Bella

Bella Coola

Queen Charlotte Sound

Hakai Prov. Rec. Area

Calvert I.

Inside Passage

PACIFIC OCEAN

Coast Mts.

Port Hardy

VANCOUVER ISLAND (See separate map)

Campbell River

Powell River

Lund

Comox

Tofino

0   75 mi
0   75 km

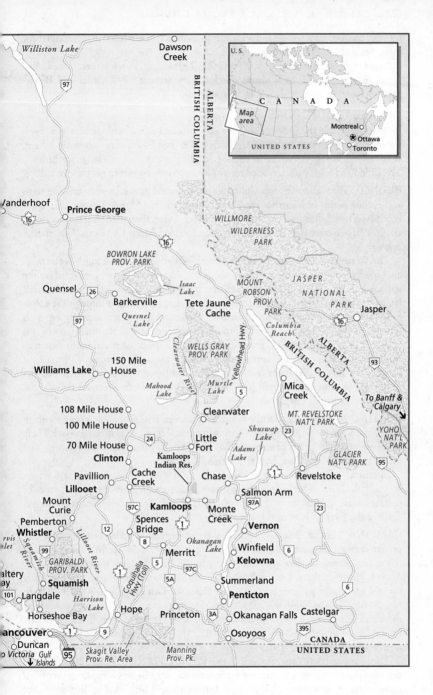

regional tourism associations and Visitor Information Centres listed in this chapter for more detailed local information.

Another excellent information site online is **Tourism BC** at **www.travel.bc.ca**. And if you plan to head off to Whistler, check out the website for **Whistler and Blackcomb Resorts** at **www.whistlerblackcomb.com**.

THE GREAT OUTDOORS

It's hard to believe the province's variety of sports and other outdoor activities. Even the most cosmopolitan British Columbians spend their leisure time mountain biking, windsurfing, skiing, or hiking in the surrounding mountains, rivers, and meadows. The varied and largely uninhabited terrain seems to lure visitors to get close to nature.

BIKING   Throughout British Columbia are countless marked mountain-bike trails and cycling paths. In **Victoria,** the 13km (8-mile) Scenic Marine Drive has an adjacent paved path following Dallas Road and Beach Drive, then returning to downtown via Oak Bay Avenue (see "Victoria: Victorian England Meets Canadian Wilderness," below).

The ski runs on the lower elevations of both **Whistler and Blackcomb mountains** are transformed into mountain-bike trails during summer. Bikes are permitted on the gondola ski lift, allowing you to reach the peaks where the winding marked trails begin. From here, experts, intermediates, and novices barrel down through the colorful alpine slopes. June to September, bike challenges take place regularly on both mountains (see "Whistler: One of North America's Premier Ski Resorts," later in this chapter). In town, the **Valley Trail** offers 20km (12 miles) of paved paths that pass through residential areas and around alpine lakes. Next to the Chateau Whistler Golf Course, the **Lost Lake Trails** feature numerous unpaved alternative routes that fan out from the main lakeside trail (see "Whistler: One of North America's Premier Ski Resorts," later in this chapter).

BOATING & SAILING   While you're in **Victoria,** take a leisurely cruise south to Sooke Harbour or up the Strait of Georgia in a rental boat or a skippered vessel. There are many outfitters at the **Brentwood Bay** and **Oak Bay marinas** (see "Victoria: Victorian England Meets Canadian Wilderness," below).

In central B.C., the **Okanagan Valley** lakes lure boaters, houseboaters, and watersports enthusiasts. Whether you're into water-skiing, fishing, jet-skiing, or house- or pleasure boating, local marinas offer full-service rentals (see "The Okanagan Valley: A Taste of the Grape," later in this chapter).

CAMPING   British Columbia's national parks, provincial parks, marine parks, and private campgrounds are generally filled during summer weekends. Most areas are first come, first served, so stake your claim early in the afternoon (for weekends, arrive by Thurs). However, April 1 to September 15 you can book a provincial park campsite up to 3 months in advance by contacting **Discover Camping** (*©* **800/689-9025** in North America or 604/689-9025; www.discovercamping.ca). It's open Monday through Friday 7am to 9pm and Saturday and Sunday 9am to 5pm. There's a nonrefundable service fee of C$6.50 (US$6.50/£3.25), and reservations can be confirmed only with MasterCard or Visa.

The provincial park campgrounds charge C$9 to C$22 (US$9–US$22/£4.50–£11) per site. There's a 2-week maximum for individual campsite stays. Facilities vary from rustic (walk-in or water-access) to basic (pit toilets and little else) to luxurious (hot showers, flush toilets, and sani-stations). All provincial drive-in campgrounds offer precut-wood piles, grill-equipped fire pits, bear-proof garbage cans, pumped well water, and well-maintained security. The rustic wilderness campgrounds provide minimal services—a covered shelter or simply a cleared patch of ground and little else.

CANOEING & KAYAKING You'll quickly discover why sea kayakers rate **Vancouver Island's west coast** one of the world's best places to paddle. Novice and intermediate paddlers launch from Tofino to explore the marine wilderness of **Clayoquot Sound.** Surf kayakers are drawn to the tidal swells that crash along the shores of **Long Beach,** part of Pacific Rim National Park. And the **Broken Island Group**'s many islands offer paddlers an excellent site for overnight expeditions amid the rugged beauty of the outer coast.

In **Whistler,** paddlers are treated to an exhilarating stretch of glacial waters that runs behind the village itself. Some savvy kayakers and canoeists call it the "River of Dreams" (see "Whistler: One of North America's Premier Ski Resorts," later in this chapter).

CLIMBING Off Valleyview Road, east of Penticton in the Okanagan Valley, **Skaha Bluffs** has more than 400 bolted routes set in place. For info about organized climbing trips throughout the province, contact the **Federation of Mountain Clubs of BC,** 1367 W. Broadway, Vancouver, BC V6H 4A9 (© **604/737-3053;** www.mountain clubs.org).

FISHING Numerous fishing packages depart from the **Victoria** docks, where charters run to the southern island's best catch-and-release spots for salmon, halibut, cutthroat, and lingcod. Year-round sportfishing for salmon, steelhead, trout, Dolly Varden char, halibut, cod, and snapper lures anglers to the waters near **Port Alberni** and **Barkley Sound.** Nearby **Long Beach** is great for bottom fishing (see "Vancouver Island's West Coast: Tofino & Long Beach," later in this chapter).

On Vancouver Island's east coast, **Campbell River** is the home of **Painter's Lodge.** A favorite Hollywood getaway for over 70 years, it has entertained Bob Hope, John Wayne (who was a frequent guest), and Goldie Hawn (see "Vancouver Island's East Coast: Parksville to Campbell River & Quadra Island," later in this chapter).

Whistler's **Green River** and nearby **Birkenhead Lake Provincial Park** have runs of steelhead, rainbow trout, Dolly Varden char, cutthroat, and salmon that attract sport anglers from around the world (see "Whistler: One of North America's Premier Ski Resorts," later in this chapter).

GOLFING Considering **Victoria**'s British heritage and its lush rolling landscape, it's no wonder golf is a popular pastime. The three local courses offer terrain—minus thistles—similar to Scotland's, too (see "Victoria: Victorian England Meets Canadian Wilderness," below).

There are also a number of outstanding layouts in central **Vancouver Island,** including an 18-hole course designed by golf legend Les Furber. The **Morningstar** championship course is in Parksville. The **Storey Creek Golf Club** in Campbell River also has a challenging course design and great scenic views (see "Vancouver Island's East Coast: Parksville to Campbell River & Quadra Island," later in this chapter). There are 9- and 18-hole golf courses in the **Okanagan Valley,** including the **Gallagher's Canyon Golf & Country Club** in Kelowna and **Predator Ridge** in Vernon (see "The Okanagan Valley: A Taste of the Grape," later in this chapter). Visitors to **Whistler** can tee off at the **Chateau Whistler Golf Course,** at the base of Blackcomb Mountain, or at the **Nicklaus North** golf course on the shore of Green Lake (see "Whistler: One of North America's Premier Ski Resorts," later in this chapter).

(Moments Three Trips of a Lifetime

Each of the following trips, within striking distance of Vancouver and Victoria, takes you to a place like no other on earth.

Kayaking Clayoquot Sound ✿✿ In 1993, environmentalists from across the province and around the world arrived in British Columbia to protect this pristine fjord on the west coast of Vancouver Island. More than 1,000 were arrested before the government and logging companies gave in and agreed to leave Clayoquot (pronounced *Kla*-kwat) Sound's temperate old-growth rainforest intact. This trip involves paddling a kayak for 2 or 3 days through the protected waters of the sound, from the funky former fishing village of Tofino to a natural hot-springs bath near a Native village of the Hesquiaat people. Along the way, you'll see thousand-year-old trees, glaciers, whales, and bald eagles.

Three companies in Tofino can set you up with a kayak: **Pacific Kayak,** 606 Campbell St. (℃ **250/725-3232;** www.tofino-bc.com/pacifickayak); the **Tofino Sea Kayaking Company,** 320 Main St. (℃ **250/725-4222;** www.tofino-kayaking.com); and **Remote Passages,** 71 Wharf St. (℃ **800/666-9833** or 250/725-3330; www.remotepassages.com). Sea kayaking isn't hard, and the great advantage of a trip on Clayoquot Sound is that it's entirely in sheltered inshore waters, though the scenery and the feeling are those of being in a wide-open wilderness. If you're tentative about kayaking on your own, many companies, like the three above, can set you up on a guided trip.

The preferred route leaves Tofino and travels through the protected waters of Clayoquot Sound up to the natural Hot Springs Cove. From there you can fly back—strapping your kayak to the floats of the plane—or retrace your route to Tofino. Whichever way you go, save some time and money for a memorable meal at The Pointe Restaurant in the Wickaninnish Inn (p. 746); after a week in the wilderness, the food here will seem sublime.

Sailing through the Great Bear Rain Forest ✿✿✿ If you look at a map of British Columbia, you'll see, about halfway up the west coast, an incredibly convoluted region of mountains, fjords, bays, channels, rivers, and inlets. There are next to no roads here—the geography's too intense. Thanks to that isolation, this is also one of the last places in the world where grizzly

HIKING The boardwalked **South Beach Trail** near Tofino provides a contemplative stroll through a Sitka-spruce temperate rainforest, as does the **Big Cedar Trail** on Meares Island. The trails following **Long Beach** allow hikers a close-up glimpse of the marine life that inhabits the tidal pools in the park's many quiet coves (see "Vancouver Island's West Coast: Tofino & Long Beach," later in this chapter). At Whistler, **Lost Lake Trails'** 30km (19 miles) of marked trails around creeks, beaver dams, blueberry patches, and lush cedars are ideal for biking, Nordic skiing, or just quiet strolling and picnicking. The **Ancient Cedars** area of Cougar Mountain above Whistler's Emerald Estates is an awe-inspiring grove of towering old-growth cedars and Douglas firs.

bears are still found in large numbers, not to mention salmon, large trees, killer whales, otters, and porpoises. But to get there, you'll need a boat. And if you have to take a boat, why not take a 100-year-old fully rigged 28m (92-ft.) sailing schooner?

Run by an ex-park ranger, **Maple Leaf Adventures,** Box 8845, 28 Bastion Sq., Victoria, BC V8W 3Z1 (© **888/599-5323** or 250/386-7245; www.maple leafadventures.com), runs a number of trips to this magic area. Owner Kevin Smith is extremely knowledgeable and normally brings along a trained naturalist to explain the fauna (especially the whales, dolphins, and grizzlies). The trips vary from 6 to 13 days and from C$1,950 (US$1,950/£975) to C$6,250 (US$6,250/£3,125), covering territory from the midcoast to the Queen Charlotte Islands (Haida Gwaii) to the coasts of Alaska. All include gourmet meals (more than you could ever eat) and comfortable but not luxurious accommodations aboard Kevin's beautiful schooner, the *Maple Leaf.*

Horse Trekking on the Chilcotin Plateau 🌟🌟 The high plateau country of the B.C. interior boasts some of the most impressive scenery in the west. Soaring peaks rise above deep valleys, and mountain meadows come alive with flowers that bloom for just a few weeks in high summer. The advantages to taking in this territory on horseback are that the horse's feet get sore, not yours; if you come across a grizzly, you've got some height on him; and horses can carry far more and far better food.

While dude ranches abound in both Canada and the States, there's one key difference to certain British Columbia outfits. It's called a guide-outfitter tenure—one company is granted exclusive rights to run guided tours through that section of wilderness. In B.C., the territories are typically 5,000 sq. km (1,930 sq. miles), all high-country wilderness where you likely won't meet another horse team. One of the guide outfitters closest to Vancouver is the **Chilcotin Holidays Guest Ranch,** Gun Creek Road, Gold Bridge, BC V0K 1P0 (© **250/238-2274;** www.chilcotinholidays.com). Their trips run 4 to 7 days, with costs of C$989 to C$1,742 (US$989–US$1,742/£495–£871), and involve encounters with wildflowers, bighorn sheep, grizzlies, and wolves.

Whistlers' **Singing Pass Trail** is a 4-hour moderately difficult hike winding from the top of Whistler Mountain down to the village via the Fitzsimmons Valley. North of Whistler, **Nairn Falls Provincial Park** features a gentle 1.5km (1-mile) trail leading to a stupendous view of the icy-cold Green River as it plunges 60m (197 ft.) over a rocky cliff into a narrow gorge. There's also an incredible view of Mount Currie peaking over the treetops.

HORSEBACK RIDING   You can take an afternoon ride along a wooded trail near Victoria's Buck Mountain. In Whistler, there are riding trails along the Lillooet River near Pemberton (see "Whistler: One of North America's Premier Ski Resorts," later in this chapter).

RAFTING Whistler's **Green River** offers novices small rapids and views of snow-capped mountains for their first rafting runs (see "Whistler: One of North America's Premier Ski Resorts," later in this chapter).

SKIING & SNOWBOARDING **Whistler Mountain,** with a 1,524m (5,000-ft.) vertical and 100 marked runs, is the cream of the province's ski resorts. **Blackcomb Mountain,** which shares its base with Whistler, has a 1,600m (5,249-ft.) vertical and also has 100 marked runs. Ski passes are good for both mountains. **Helicopter skiing** makes another 100-plus runs accessible on nearby glaciers. **Lost Lakes Trails** are converted into miles of groomed cross-country trails, as are the **Valley Trail System, Singing Pass,** and **Ancient Cedars** (see "Whistler: One of North America's Premier Ski Resorts," later in this chapter).

Cross-country and powder skiing are the **Okanagan Valley**'s main winter attractions. **Big White Ski Resort** gets an annual average of 5.5m (18 ft.) of powder and has more than 20km (12 miles) of cross-country trails. **Apex Resort** maintains 56 downhill runs and extensive cross-country trails. Nearby **Crystal Mountain** caters to intermediate and novice downhill skiers and snowboarders (see "The Okanagan Valley: A Taste of the Grape," later in this chapter).

WILDLIFE-WATCHING Whether you're in search of the 20,000 **Pacific gray whales** that migrate to **Vancouver Island**'s west coast (see "Vancouver Island's West Coast: Tofino & Long Beach," later in this chapter), or the orcas and salmon off Campbell River, there are land-based observation points and numerous knowledgeable outfitters who can guide you to the best nature and bird-spotting areas the island has to offer.

If you take the ferry cruise up the **Inside Passage,** you have a great opportunity to spot **orcas, Dall porpoises, salmon, bald eagles,** and **sea lions.**

2 Victoria: Victorian England Meets Canadian Wilderness ★★★

In an Arcadian parkland of oak and fir at the edge of a natural harbor, Victoria spent the better part of the 20th century in a reverie, looking back to its glorious past as an outpost of England at the height of the Empire. It was a busy trading post and booming colonial city in the 19th century, but Victoria's lot began to fade soon after Vancouver was established in the 1880s. When its economy finally crashed early in the 20th century, shocked Victorians realized they were looking at a future with nothing much to live on but some fabulous Tudor and Victorian architecture, a beautiful natural setting, and a carefully cultivated sense of Englishness. So they decided to market that.

So successful was the sales job that the Victorians themselves began to believe they inhabited a little patch of England. They began growing elaborate rose gardens, which flourished in the mild Pacific climate, and cultivated a taste for afternoon tea with jam and scones. For decades, the reverie continued unabated. But the Victorians proved flexible enough to accommodate some changes as well. Early on it was discovered that few in the world shared the English taste for cooking, so Victoria's restaurants branched out into seafood and ethnic and fusion cuisines. And lately, as visitors have shown themselves more interested in exploring the natural world, Victoria has quietly added whale-watching and mountain-biking trips to its traditional tours on London-style double-decker buses. The result is that Victoria is now the only city in the world where you can zoom out on a Zodiac in the morning to see a pod of killer whales and make it back in time for a lovely afternoon tea with all the trimmings.

ESSENTIALS
GETTING THERE

Victoria, the capital of British Columbia, sits at the southeastern corner of Vancouver Island. You can get there by plane, boat, or (once you're on Vancouver island) train.

BY PLANE   Victoria International Airport (© **250/953-7500;** www.victoria airport.com) is near the Sidney ferry terminal, 22km (14 miles) north of Victoria off the Patricia Bay Highway (Hwy. 17).

Air Canada (© **888/247-2262** or 800/661-3936; www.aircanada.com) and **Horizon Air** (© **800/547-9308;** www.horizonair.com) offer direct connections from Seattle, Vancouver, Portland, Calgary, Edmonton, Saskatoon, Winnipeg, and Toronto. Canada's low-cost airline **WestJet** (© **888/WEST-JET;** www.westjet.com) offers flights to Victoria from Kelowna, Calgary, Edmonton, and other destinations; WestJet service now extends to a few U.S. cities as well. **Delta Airlines** (© **800/241-4141;** www.delta.com) offers a direct flight to Victoria from Salt Lake City.

Commuter airlines, including floatplanes that land in Victoria's Inner Harbour, provide service to Victoria from Vancouver and destinations within B.C. They include **Air B.C.** (can be reached through Air Canada at © 888/247-2262); **Harbour Air Sea Planes** (© **604/274-1277** in Vancouver, or 250/384-2215 in Victoria; www.harbourair.com); and **West Coast Air** (© **800/347-2222;** www.westcoastair.com).

In addition to serving B.C. destinations, **Kenmore Air** (© **800/543-9595;** www.kenmoreair.com) and **Helijet Airways** (© **800/665-4354;** www.helijet.com) offer 35-minute flights between Seattle and Victoria.

The **Akal Airporter shuttle bus** (© **250/386-2525;** www.victoriaairporter.com) makes the trip downtown in about a half-hour. Buses leave every 30 minutes daily from 4:30am to midnight; the fare is C$15 (US$15/£7.50) one-way; C$10 (US$10/£5) per person for groups of three or more. Drop-offs are made at most hotels and bed-and-breakfasts, and pickups can be arranged as well. A limited number of hotel courtesy buses also serve the airport. A cab ride into downtown Victoria costs about C$45 (US$45/£23) plus tip. **Empress Cabs** and **BlueBird Cabs** (see "Getting Around," below) make airport runs.

Several **car-rental** firms have desks at the airport, including **Avis** (© **800/879-2847** or 250/656-6033; www.avis.com), **Budget** (© **800/668-9833** or 250/953-5300; www.budgetvictoria.com), **Hertz** (© **800/654-3131** or 250/656-2312; www.hertz.com), and **National** (© **800/227-7368** or 250/656-2541; www.nationalcar.com). If you're driving from the airport, take Highway 17 south to Victoria; it becomes Douglas Street as you enter downtown.

BY TRAIN   VIA Rail (© **888/842-7245** in Canada; www.viarail.ca) has a Vancouver Island sightseeing train, the *Malahat,* that travels once a day (in either direction) between Courtney and Victoria, with stops in Chemainus, Nanaimo (where you can connect to the Horseshoe Bay–Nanaimo Ferry), Parksville, or Qualicum Beach. The *Malahat* departs Victoria's **E&N Station,** 450 Pandora Ave. (near the Johnson St. Bridge) at 8:15am, arrives in Courtney at 12:50pm, departs Courtney in the other direction at 1:30pm, and arrives back in Victoria at 6pm.

BY BUS   The **Victoria Bus Depot** is at 700 Douglas St., behind The Fairmont Empress hotel. **Pacific Coach Lines** (© **604/662-8074;** www.pacificcoach.com) provides service between Vancouver and Victoria with daily departures between 5:45am and 7:45pm. Pacific Coach Lines will pick up passengers from the Vancouver cruise-ship terminal and from most downtown hotels. Pacific Coach Lines also offers an Island Excursion Program, departing downtown Vancouver at 9am on the Harbour Lynx high-speed passenger ferry for Nanaimo. After a sightseeing tour and a day or overnight visit to Victoria, make your return to Victoria via BC Ferries. For more information, call © **604/662-8074** or visit www.pacificcoach.com. **Island Coach Lines** (© **250/385-4411;** www.victoriatours.com) has daily scheduled runs to Nanaimo, Port Alberni, Campbell River, and Port Hardy.

BY FERRY   BC Ferries (© **888/223-3779** in B.C. only, or 250/386-3431; www.bcferries.com) has three routes operating between Vancouver and Vancouver Island. The one-way fare in peak season is C$12 (US$12/£6) for adults, C$6.40 (US$6.40/£3.20) for children 5 to 11, and C$39 (US$39/£20) per car. Children under 5 ride free. In the summer, it is advisable to reserve a space when traveling with a vehicle, especially on long weekends and to and from the Gulf Islands.

The most direct route between Vancouver and Victoria is the **Tsawwassen–Swartz Bay ferry,** which runs every 2 hours between 7am and 9pm. The crossing takes 95 minutes. Driving distance from Vancouver to Tsawwassen is about 20km (12 miles). Take Hwy. 99 from Vancouver until it merges with Hwy. 17 from Tsawwassen near the George Massey Tunnel. B.C. Transit (see "Getting Around," below) has regular bus service from Vancouver to Tsawwassen and from Swartz Bay to Victoria.

The **Mid-Island Express** operates between Tsawwassen and Duke Point, just south of Nanaimo. The 2-hour crossing runs eight times daily between 5:15am and 10:45pm.

The **Horseshoe Bay–Nanaimo ferry** has eight daily sailings, leaving Horseshoe Bay near west Vancouver and arriving 95 minutes later in Nanaimo. To reach Horseshoe Bay from Vancouver, take the Trans-Canada Highway (Hwy. 1) east and then take Exit 13 (Taylor Way) to the Lions Gate Bridge and then Trans-Canada Highway (Hwy. 1) to the marked exit for Horseshoe Bay ferries.

VISITOR INFORMATION

TOURIST OFFICES & MAGAZINES   On the Inner Harbour's wharf, across from The Fairmont Empress hotel, is the **Tourism Victoria Visitor Centre,** 812 Wharf St. (© **250/953-2033;** www.tourismvictoria.com). If you didn't reserve a room before you arrived, you can go to this office or call its **reservations hot line** (© **800/663-3883** or 250/953-2033) for last-minute bookings at hotels, inns, and B&Bs. The center is open daily, September to June 15 from 9am to 5pm and June 16 through August from 9am to 8:30pm.

For details on the entertainment and nightlife scene, pick up a copy of *Monday* magazine (© **250/382-6188;** www.mondaymag.com), available free in cafes around the city.

CITY LAYOUT

Victoria is on the southeastern tip of Vancouver Island, across the Strait of Juan de Fuca from Washington state's snow-capped Olympic Peninsula. The areas of most interest to visitors, including the **downtown** and **Old Town,** lie along the eastern edge of the **Inner Harbour.** (North of the Johnson St. Bridge is the **Upper Harbour,** which is almost entirely industrial.) A little farther east, the **Ross Bay** and **Oak Bay** residential areas around Dallas Road and Beach Drive reach the beaches along the open waters of the Strait of Juan de Fuca.

Victoria

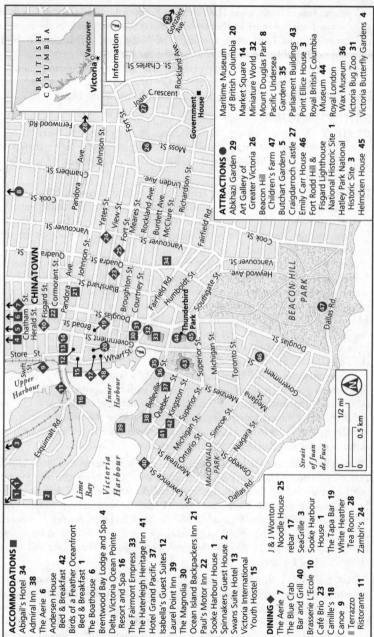

Information (i)

ATTRACTIONS ●

Abkhazi Garden **29**
Art Gallery of
 Greater Victoria **26**
Beacon Hill
 Children's Farm **47**
Butchart Gardens **5**
Craigdarroch Castle **27**
Emily Carr House **46**
Fisgard Lighthouse
 National Historic Site **1**
Fort Rodd Hill &
 Hatley Park National
 Historic Site **1**
Helmcken House **45**

Maritime Museum
 of British Columbia **20**
Market Square **14**
Miniature World **32**
Mount Douglas Park **8**
Pacific Undersea
 Gardens **35**
Parliament Buildings **43**
Point Ellice House **3**
Royal British Columbia
 Museum **44**
Royal London
 Wax Museum **36**
Victoria Bug Zoo **31**
Victoria Butterfly Gardens **4**

ACCOMMODATIONS ■

Abigail's Hotel **34**
Admiral Inn **38**
The Aerie **6**
Andersen House
 Bed & Breakfast **42**
Birds of a Feather Oceanfront
 Bed & Breakfast **1**
The Boathouse **6**
Brentwood Bay Lodge and Spa **4**
Delta Victoria Ocean Pointe
 Resort and Spa **16**
The Fairmont Empress **33**
The Haterleigh Heritage Inn **41**
Hotel Grand Pacific **37**
Isabella's Guest Suites **12**
Laurel Point Inn **39**
The Magnolia **30**
Ocean Island Backpackers Inn **21**
Paul's Motor Inn **22**
Sooke Harbour House **1**
Spinnakers Guest House **2**
Swans Suite Hotel **13**
Victoria International
 Youth Hostel **15**

DINING ◆

The Aerie **7**
The Blue Crab
 Bar and Grill **40**
Brasserie L'Ecole **10**
Café Brio **23**
Camille's **18**
Canoe **9**
Il Terrazzo
 Ristorante **11**
J & J Wonton
 Noodle House **25**
rebar **17**
SeaGrille **3**
Sooke Harbour
 House **1**
The Tapa Bar **19**
White Heather
 Tea Room **28**
Zambri's **24**

Victoria's central landmark is **The Fairmont Empress** hotel on Government Street, right across from the Inner Harbour wharf. If you turn your back to the hotel, the downtown and Old Town are on your right, while the provincial **Legislative Buildings** and the **Royal BC Museum** are on your immediate left.

Government Street goes through Victoria's main downtown shopping-and-dining district. **Douglas Street,** running parallel to Government Street, is the main business thoroughfare as well as the road to Nanaimo and the rest of the island.

GETTING AROUND

BY FOOT   Victoria is a great city for walking. Strolling along the Inner Harbour's pedestrian walkways and streets is a pleasant and popular activity. The terrain is predominantly flat, and, with few exceptions, Victoria's points of interest are accessible in less than 30 minutes on foot.

BY BUS   The **Victoria Regional Transit System (B.C. Transit),** 520 Gorge Rd. (© **250/382-6161;** www.bctransit.com), operates 40 bus routes through greater Victoria as well as the nearby towns of Sooke and Sidney. Buses run to both the Butchart Gardens and the Vancouver Ferry Terminal at Sidney. Regular service on the main routes runs daily from 6am to just past midnight.

Schedules and routes are available at the Tourism Victoria Visitor Info Centre (see "Visitor Information," above), where you can pick up a copy of the *Victoria Rider's Guide* or *Discover Vancouver on Transit: Including Victoria.* Popular Victoria bus routes include **no. 2** (Oak Bay), **no. 5** (downtown, James Bay, Beacon Hill Park), **no. 14** (Victoria Art Gallery, Craigdarroch Castle, University of Victoria), **no. 61** (Sooke), **no. 70** (Sidney, Swartz Bay), and **no. 75** (Butchart Gardens).

Fares are calculated on a per-zone basis. One-way single-zone fares are C$2.25 (US$2.25/£1.15) for adults and C$1.40 (US$1.40/70p) for seniors and children 5 to 13; two zones cost C$3 (US$3/£1.50) and C$2.25 (US$2.25/£1.15), respectively. Transfers are good for travel in one direction only, with no stopovers. A **DayPass,** C$7 (US$7/£3.50) for adults and C$4 (US$4/£2) for seniors and children 5 to 13, covers unlimited travel throughout the day. You can buy passes at the Tourism Victoria Visitor Centre (see "Visitor Information," above), convenience stores, and ticket outlets throughout Victoria displaying the FAREDEALER sign.

BY FERRY   Crossing the Inner, Upper, and Victoria harbors by one of the blue 12-passenger **Victoria Harbour Ferries** (© **250/708-0201;** www.victoriaharbourferry.com) is scenic and fun. May through September, the ferries to The Fairmont Empress hotel, Coast Harbourside Hotel, and Ocean Pointe Resort hotel run about every 15 minutes daily from 9am to 8:15pm. In March, April, and October, ferry service runs daily 11am to 5pm. November through February, the ferries run only on sunny weekends 11am to 5pm. The cost per hop is C$4 (US$4/£2) for adults and C$1.50 (US$1.50/75p) for children.

BY CAR   Traffic is light by U.S. standards, largely because the downtown core is so pedestrian-friendly there's no point in using a car. Gas is sold by the liter; speeds and distances are posted in kilometers.

Car-rental agencies in Victoria include the following: **Avis,** 1001 Douglas St. (© **800/879-2847** or 250/386-8468; bus no. 5 to Broughton St.); **Budget,** 757 Douglas St. (© **800/268-8900** or 250/953-5300); **Hertz,** 655 Douglas St., in the Queen

Victoria Inn (☎ **800/263-0600** or 250/360-2822); and **National,** 767 Douglas St. (☎ **800/227-7368** or 250/386-1312). The latter three agencies can be reached on the no. 5 bus to the Convention Centre.

Metered **street parking** is readily available in the downtown area, but be sure to feed the meter because rules are strictly enforced. Unmetered parking on side streets is rare. All major downtown hotels have guest parking, with rates from free to C$25 (US$25/£13) per day. There are parking lots at **View Street** between Douglas and Blanshard streets, **Johnson Street** off Blanshard Street, **Yates Street** north of Bastion Square, and **the Bay** on Fisgard at Blanshard Street.

BY BIKE   Biking is the easiest way to get around the downtown and beach areas. There are bike lanes throughout the city and paved paths along parks and beaches. Helmets are mandatory, and riding on sidewalks is illegal, except where bike paths are indicated. You can rent bikes starting at C$7 (US$7/£3.50) per hour and C$24 (US$24/£12) per day (lock and helmet included) from **Cycle B.C.,** 747 Douglas St. (☎ **250/380-2453;** www.cyclebc.com).

BY TAXI   Within the downtown area, you can expect to travel for less than C$10 (US$10/£5), plus tip. It's best to call for a cab; drivers don't always stop on city streets for flag-downs, especially when it's raining. Call for a pickup from **Empress Cabs** (☎ **250/381-2222;** www.empresstaxi.com) or **BlueBird Cabs** (☎ **250/382-4235;** www.taxicab.com).

BY PEDAL-CAB   You get to sit while an avid bicyclist with thighs of steel pedals you anywhere you want to go for C$1 (US$1/50p) per minute. You'll see these two- and four-seater bike cabs along the Inner Harbour, in front of the Empress Hotel, at the base of Bastion Square, or you can call **Kabuki Kabs** (☎ **250/385-4243;** www.kabukikabs.com) for 24-hour service.

SPECIAL EVENTS & FESTIVALS

So many flowers bloom during the temperate month of February in Victoria and the surrounding area that the city holds an annual **Flower Count** (☎ **250/383-7191** for details). Toward the end of May, thousands of yachts sail into Victoria Harbor during the **Swiftsure Yacht Race** (☎ **250/953-2033;** www.swiftsure.org). In late June, the **Jazz Fest International** (☎ **250/388-4423;** www.vicjazz.bc.ca) brings jazz, swing, bebop, fusion, and improv artists from around the world.

The provincial capital celebrates **Canada Day** (July 1) with events centered around the Inner Harbour, including music, food, and fireworks. The August **First Peoples Festival** (☎ **250/384-3211**) highlights the culture and heritage of the Pacific Northwest First Nations tribes with dances, performances, carving demonstrations, and heritage displays at the Royal British Columbia Museum. The **Royal Victoria Marathon** (☎ **250/658-4520;** www.royalvictoriamarathon.com), an annual October race, attracts runners from around the world (half-marathon course available, too). In November, the **Great Canadian Beer Festival** (☎ **250/952-0360;** www.gcbf.com) features samples from the province's best microbreweries. And Victoria rings in the New Year with **First Night** (☎ **250/380-1211**), a family-oriented New Year's Eve celebration with free performances at many downtown venues.

FAST FACTS: Victoria

Area Code The telephone area code for all of Vancouver Island, including Victoria and most of British Columbia, is **250.**

Dentist Most major hotels have a dentist on call. **Cresta Dental Centre,** 3170 Tillicum Rd., at Burnside Street in the Tillicum Mall (*©* **250/384-7711;** bus no. 10), is open Monday through Friday 8am to 9pm, Saturday 8am to 5pm, and Sunday 11am to 5pm.

Doctor Hotels usually have doctors on call. The **Tillicum Medical Centre,** 3170 Tillicum Rd. at Burnside Street (*©* **250/381-8112;** bus no. 10 to Tillicum Mall), accepts walk-in patients daily 9am to 9pm.

Emergencies Dial *©* **911** for fire, police, ambulance, and poison control.

Hospitals Local hospitals include the **Royal Jubilee Hospital,** 1900 Fort St. (*©* **250/370-8000;** emergency 250/370-8212), and the **Victoria General Hospital,** 1 Hospital Way (*©* **250/727-4212;** emergency 250/727-4181). You can get to both hospitals on bus no. 14.

Internet Access Open late in the heart of the old town is Stain Internet Café, 609 Yates St. (*©* **250/382-3352**), open daily 10am to 2am. Closer to the Legislature, try the James Bay Coffee and Books, 143 Menzies St. (*©* **250/386-4700**), open daily from 7:30am to 10pm.

Pharmacies **Shopper's Drug Mart,** 1222 Douglas St. (*©* **250/381-4321;** bus no. 5 to View St.), is open Monday through Friday 7am to 8pm, Saturday 9am to 7pm, and Sunday 9am to 6pm.

Police Dial *©* **911.** The **Victoria City Police** can also be reached by calling *©* **250/995-7654.**

Post Office The **main post office** is at 714 Yates St. (*©* **250/953-1352**), bus no. 5 to Yates Street.

Safety Crime rates are quite low in Victoria, but transients panhandle throughout the downtown areas. The most common crimes are property crimes, which are often preventable with a few common-sense precautions.

Weather Check the local forecast at **www.weather.com.**

SEEING THE SIGHTS
THE TOP ATTRACTIONS

Abkhazi Garden *Finds* It's a bit out of the way, about 5 minutes east of downtown by car, but if you're a nature lover, you'll love discovering this .4-hectare (1-acre) jewel box of a garden and the romantic story behind its creation. The wealthy Marjorie Pemberton-Carter met Russian Prince Nicholas Abkhazi in Paris in the 1920s, but they didn't meet again until 1946, by which time both had endured incarceration in prisoner-of-war camps (she in Shanghai as a British National, he in Germany). They wed, moved to Victoria, and set about creating a landscape garden that takes full advantage of a dramatic site that contains quiet woodland, rocky slopes, and lovely vistas. The rhododendron woodland includes treelike plants more than 100 years old. The modernist summerhouse the Abkhazis built first has been lovingly restored, as has the small, charming house where they eventually lived. The house is used as a tearoom and gift shop. Allow 1 hour.

1964 Fairfield Rd. (© 250/598-8096. www.abkhazi.com. Admission C$10 (US$10/£5) adults, C$7.50 (US$7.50/£3.75) seniors and students, free for children under 12, C$35 (US$35/£17) families. Daily 11am–5pm; tea room daily 11:30am–4pm. Bus: 1 to Fairfield Rd. and Foul Bay.

Art Gallery of Greater Victoria

Housed in a combination of contemporary exhibition space and a historic 19th-century mansion called Gyppeswick, the Art Gallery of Greater Victoria features a permanent collection of more than 15,000 objets d'art drawn from Asia, Europe, and North America, though the gallery's primary emphasis is on Canada and Japan. The permanent **Emily Carr exhibit** 🛠 integrates Carr's writings, works from the gallery collection, and images from the British Columbia provincial archives to create a compelling portrait of this preeminent Victoria artist. Allow 1½ hours.

1040 Moss St. (© 250/384-4101. www.aggv.bc.ca. Admission C$12 (US$12/£6) adults, C$10 (US$10/£5) seniors and students, C$2 (US$2/£1) children 6–17. Daily 10am–5pm (Thurs until 9pm). Closed holidays. Bus: 11, 14, or 22.

British Columbia Aviation Museum 🛠

A must for plane buffs, or for anyone with an interest in the history of flight. Located adjacent to Victoria International Airport, this small hanger is crammed to bursting with a score of original, rebuilt, and replica airplanes. The collection ranges from the first Canadian-designed craft ever to fly (a bizarre kitelike contraption) to World War I–vintage Nieuports and Tiger Moths, to floatplanes and Spitfires and slightly more modern water bombers and helicopters. Thursdays you can watch the all-volunteer crew in the restoration hangar working to bring these old craft back to life. Allow 1 hour.

1910 Norseman Rd., Sidney. (© 250/655-3300. www.bcam.net. Admission C$7 (US$7/£3.50) adults, C$5 (US$5/£2.50) seniors, C$3 (US$3/£1.50) students, free for children under 12. Summer daily 10am–4pm; winter daily 11am–3pm. Closed Dec 25, Jan 1. Bus: Airport.

Butchart Gardens 🛠🛠🛠

These internationally acclaimed gardens were created after Robert Butchart exhausted the limestone quarry near his Tod Inlet home, about 22km (14 miles) from Victoria. His wife, Jenny, gradually landscaped the deserted eyesore into the resplendent **Sunken Garden,** opening it for public display in 1904. A **Rose Garden, Italian Garden,** and **Japanese Garden** were added. As the fame of the 20-hectare (50-acre) gardens grew, the Butcharts also transformed their house into an attraction. The gardens—still in the family—now display more than a million plants throughout the year. As impressive as the numbers is the sheer perfection of each garden—gardeners will be amazed.

Evenings in summer, the gardens are beautifully illuminated with a variety of softly colored lights. June through September, musical entertainment is provided free Monday through Saturday evenings. You can even watch fireworks displays on Saturdays in July and August. A very good lunch, dinner, and afternoon tea are offered in the Dining Room Restaurant in the historic residence; afternoon and high teas are also served in the Italian Garden (reservations strongly recommended). Allow 2 to 3 hours; in peak summer months you'll experience less congestion in the garden if you come very early or after 3pm.

800 Benvenuto Ave., Brentwood Bay. (© **866/652-4422** or 250/652-4422; dining reservations 250/652-8222. www.butchartgardens.com. Admission June 15–Sept C$25 (US$25/£13) adults, C$13 (US$13/£6.50) youths 13–17, C$3 (US$3/£1.50) children 5–12, free for children under 5; admission prices reduced in spring, fall, and winter. Daily 9am–sundown (call or visit website for seasonal closing times); visitors can remain in gardens for 1 hr. after gate

closes. Bus: 75 or the Gray Line shuttle from the Victoria Bus Station (runs late Apr to Sept); C$14 (US$14/£7) round-trip. For shuttle departure times, call 🕿 800/663-8390 or 250/388-6539. Take Blanshard St. (Hwy. 17) north toward the ferry terminal in Saanich, then turn left on Keating Crossroads, which leads directly to the gardens—about 20 min. from downtown Victoria; it's impossible to miss if you follow the trail of billboards.

Craigdarroch Castle 🏰 What do you do when you're the richest man in British Columbia, when you've clawed, scraped, and bullied your way up from indentured servant to coal baron and merchant prince? You build a castle, of course, to show 'em all what you're worth. Located in the highlands above Oak Bay, Robert Dunsmuir's home, built in the 1880s, is a stunner. The four-story, 39-room Highland-style castle is topped with stone turrets and chimneys and filled with the opulent Victorian splendor you'd expect from an arriviste who finally arrived—detailed woodwork, Persian carpets, stained-glass windows, paintings, and sculptures. The nonprofit society that runs Craigdarroch does an excellent job showcasing the castle. You're provided with a self-tour booklet, and volunteer docents are happy to provide further information. To tour the castle takes from 30 minutes to an hour. The castle also hosts many events throughout the year, including theater performances, concerts, and dinner tours.

1050 Joan Crescent (off Fort St.). 🕿 250/592-5323. www.craigdarrochcastle.com. Admission C$12 (US$12/£6) adults, C$11 (US$11/£5.50) seniors, C$3.75 (US$3.75/£1.90) children 5–12, free for children under 5. June 15 to Labour Day daily 9am–7pm; day after Labour Day to June 14 daily 10am–4:30pm. Closed Dec 25, 26, and Jan 1. Bus: 11 to Joan Crescent. Take Fort St. out of downtown, just past Cook, and turn right on Joan Crescent.

Fort Rodd Hill & Fisgard Lighthouse National Historic Site Perched on an outcrop of volcanic rock, the **Fisgard Lighthouse** has guided ships toward Victoria's sheltered harbor since 1873. The light no longer has a keeper (the beacon has long been automated), but the site itself has been restored to its 1873 appearance. Two floors worth of exhibits in the light keepers' house recount stories of the lighthouse, its keepers, and the terrible shipwrecks that gave this coastline its ominous moniker "the graveyard of the Pacific."

Adjoining the lighthouse, **Fort Rodd Hill** is a preserved 1890s coastal artillery fort that—though in more than half a century it never fired a shot in anger—still sports camouflaged searchlights, underground magazines, and its original guns. Audiovisual exhibits bring the fort to life with the voices and faces of the men who served at the outpost. Displays of artifacts, room re-creations, and historic film footage add to the experience. Allow 1 to 2 hours.

603 Fort Rodd Hill Rd. 🕿 250/478-5849. Admission C$4 (US$4/£2) adults, C$3 (US$3/£1.50) seniors, C$2 (US$2/£1) children 6–16, C$10 (US$10/£5) families, free for children under 6. Mar–Oct daily 10am–5:30pm; Nov–Feb daily 9am–4:30pm. No public transit.

Hatley Park National Historic Site 🏰 Craigdarroch Castle (see above) was built during the 1880s to serve as Scottish coal-mining magnate Robert Dunsmuir's home. In 1908, Dunsmuir's son James built his own palatial manse, Hatley Castle, on a 226-hectare (565-acre) waterfront estate about 25 minutes from Victoria. The younger Dunsmuir reportedly commissioned architect Samuel Maclure with the words "Money doesn't matter, just build what I want."

The impressive castle, built of local stone in a hybrid Norman-Tudor fantasy style, belongs to Royal Roads University but is open to visitors on guided tours from mid-May to Labour Day (the not-very-interesting museum down in the basement is open year-round). As you're shown around the castle, you have to use your imagination, since all the furniture was sold in 1937 (much of it is now in Craigdarroch Castle) and the rooms are either empty or filled with office modules and equipment. The paneling and wood floors are truly remarkable, though. The surrounding estate features several lovely heritage gardens, including the tranquil Japanese Garden, designed almost a century ago by the Japanese architect Isaburo Kishida, who also designed the Japanese Gardens at Butchart Gardens. Allow 1 to 2 hours; I'd recommend that you take the 1-hour tour.

Royal Roads University, 200 Sooke Rd., Colwood. © 250/391-2511. www.hatleypark.ca. 1-hr castle tour and garden access C$17 (US$17/£8.50) adults, C$16 (US$16/£8) seniors, C$11 (US$11/£5.50) youth 13-17, C$9 (US$9/£4.50) children 6–12; gardens only C$9 (US$9/£4.50) adults, C$8 (US$8/£4) seniors, C$6 (US$6/£3) youth 13-17, C$27 (US$27/£14) family (5 members). Mid-May to Aug castle tours daily 10am–4pm (Sat–Sun until 3:15pm), museum and gardens 10am–8pm; Sept–Apr gardens and museum daily 10am–5pm. From Victoria, take Government St. north for about 2km (1¼ miles), turn left onto Gorge Rd. (Hwy. 1A) and follow about 20km (12 miles); turn left onto Sooke Rd. (Hwy. 14A) and look for signs to Royal Roads University or Hatley Park National Historic Site.

Maritime Museum of British Columbia
Housed in the former provincial courthouse, this museum is dedicated to recalling B.C.'s rich maritime heritage. The displays do a good job of illustrating maritime history, from the early explorers to the fur trading and whaling era to the days of grand ocean liners and military conflict. There's also an impressive collection of ship models and paraphernalia—uniforms, weapons, gear—along with photographs and journals. The museum also shows films in its Vice Admiralty Theatre. Allow 1 hour.

28 Bastion Sq. © 250/385-4222. www.mmbc.bc.ca. Admission C$8 (US$8/£4) adults, C$5 (US$5/£2.50) seniors, C$3 (US$3/£1.50) students, C$2 (US$2/£1) children 6–11, C$20 (US$20/£10) families, free for children under 6. Daily 9:30am–4:30pm. Closed Dec 25. Bus: 5 to View St.

Miniature World Kids
It sounds cheesy—hundreds of dolls and miniatures and scenes from old fairy tales. And yet Miniature World—inside The Fairmont Empress hotel (the entrance is around the corner)—is actually kinda cool. You walk in and you're plunged into darkness, except for a moon, some planets, and a tiny spaceship flying up to rendezvous with an orbiting mother ship. This is the most up-to-date display. Farther in are re-creations of battle scenes, fancy 18th-century dress balls, a miniature CPR railway running all the way across a miniature Canada, a three-ring circus, and scenes from Mother Goose and Charles Dickens stories. Better yet, most of these displays do something: The train moves at the punch of a button and the circus rides whirl around and light up as simulated darkness falls. Allow 1 hour to see it all.

649 Humboldt St. © 250/385-9731. www.miniatureworld.com. Admission C$9 (US$9/£4.50) adults, C$8 (US$8/£4) youths, C$7 (US$7/£3.50) children 4–12, free for children under 4. Summer daily 8:30am–9pm; fall/winter daily 9am–5pm; spring daily 9am–7pm. Bus: 5, 27, 28, or 30.

Pacific Undersea Gardens
Savvy locals aren't very keen on the sight of this conspicuous white structure floating in the Inner Harbour, and those with some knowledge of Vancouver Island's marine environment will tell you that many of the creatures on display here are not indigenous to these waters, but your kids might enjoy a visit—or they might not, since the place is dark and kind of scary for little ones. A gently sloping walkway leads down to a glass-enclosed viewing area. Every hour, on the hour, there's an underwater show in which a diver catches and—thanks to a microphone hook-up—explains a variety of undersea fauna. One of the star attractions is a remarkably photogenic octopus (reputedly the largest in captivity). Injured seals and orphaned seal pups are cared for in holding pens alongside the observatory as part of a provincial marine-mammal rescue program. Allow 1 hour.

490 Belleville St. ℂ 250/382-5717. www.pacificunderseagardens.com. Admission C$9.50 (US$9.50/£4.75) adults, C$8.50 (US$8.50/£4.25) seniors, C$7.50 (US$7.50/£3.75) youths 12–17, C$5.50 (US$5.50/£2.75) children 5–11, free for children under 5. Sept–Mar daily 10am–5pm; Apr–May daily 10am–6pm; June–Aug daily 9am–8pm. Bus: 5, 27, 28, or 30.

Parliament Buildings (Provincial Legislature) ⊛ Designed by 25-year-old Francis Rattenbury and built between 1893 and 1898 at a cost of nearly C$1 million, the Parliament Buildings (also called the Legislature) are an architectural gem. The 40-minute tour comes across at times like an eighth-grade civics lesson, but it's worth it to see the fine mosaics, marble, woodwork, and stained glass. And if you see a harried-looking man surrounded by a pack of minicam crews, it's likely just another B.C. premier getting hounded out of office by the aggressive and hostile media: Politics is a blood sport in B.C.

501 Belleville St. ℂ 250/387-3046. www.protocol.gov.bc.ca. Free admission. Late May to Labour Day daily 9am–5pm; Sept to late May 9am–5pm Mon–Fri. Tours offered every 20 min. in summer (up to 23 times a day). In winter hours call ahead for the tour schedules as times vary due to school-group bookings. No tours noon–1pm.

Royal BC Museum ⊛⊛⊛ *Kids* One of the world's best regional museums, the Royal BC has a mandate to present the land and the people of coastal British Columbia. The second-floor **Natural History Gallery** showcases the coastal flora, fauna, and geography from the ice age to the present; it includes dioramas of a temperate rainforest, a seacoast, and (particularly appealing to kids) a life-size woolly mastodon. The third-floor **Modern History Gallery** presents the recent past, including historically faithful re-creations of Victoria's downtown and Chinatown. On the same floor, the **First Peoples Gallery** ⊛⊛⊛ is an incredible showpiece of First Nations art and culture with rare artifacts used in day-to-day Native life, a full-size re-creation of a longhouse, and a hauntingly wonderful gallery with totem poles, masks, and artifacts. The museum also has an **IMAX theater** showing an ever-changing variety of large-screen movies.

On the way out (or in), be sure to stop by **Thunderbird Park,** beside the museum, where a cedar longhouse (Mungo Martin House, named after a famous Kwakiutl artist) houses a workshop where Native carvers work on new totem poles. To see and experience everything takes 3 to 4 hours.

675 Belleville St. ℂ 888/447-7977 or 250/387-3701. www.royalbcmuseum.bc.ca. Admission C$14 (US$14/£7) adults; C$9.50 (US$9.50/£4.75) seniors, students, and youths; free for children under 6; C$38 (US$38/£19) family of 4. IMAX C$11 (US$11/£5.50) adults, C$9.50 (US$9.50/£4.75) seniors, students, C$8.75 (US$8.75/£4.40) seniors, C$5 (US$5/£2.50) children. Oct–May daily 9am–5pm; June–Sept Sun–Thurs 9am–5pm, Fri–Sat 9am–10pm; IMAX daily 9am–8pm. Closed Dec 25 and Jan 1. Bus: 5, 28, or 30.

Royal London Wax Museum *Overrated* I've never understood why one of Victoria's most beautiful classical buildings, right on the waterfront, had to be used for a wax museum. And a pretty cheesy wax museum at that, with figures that often look more like old store mannequins than the people they're based on. Inside, you can see the same dusty royal family you already get too much of on television and other insignificant royals from times past. But there are other figures, too—everyone from Buddha to Charlie Chaplin, Marilyn Monroe, and Goldie Hawn (the most recent addition). It's doubtful even your kids will much enjoy it, except, of course, for the gory Chamber of Horrors.

470 Belleville St. ℂ 877/929-3228 or 250/388-4461. www.waxmuseum.bc.ca. Admission C$10 (US$10/£5) adults, C$9 (US$9/£4.50) seniors, C$7 (US$7/£3.50) students 13 and older, C$5 (US$5/£2.50) children 6–12, free for children under 6. Daily 9:30am–5pm. Bus: 5, 27, 28, or 30.

Victoria Butterfly Gardens ☆ *Kids*   This is a great spot for kids, nature buffs, or anyone who just likes butterflies. Hundreds of exotic colorful butterflies flutter freely through this lush tropical greenhouse as you're provided with an ID chart and set free to roam around. Species present range from the tiny Central American Julia (a brilliant orange butterfly about 3 in. across) to the Southeast Asian Giant Atlas Moth (mottled brown and red, with a wingspan approaching a foot). Other butterflies are brilliant blue, yellow, or a mix of colors and patterns. Naturalists are on hand to explain butterfly biology, and there's a display where you can see the beautiful creatures emerge from their cocoons. Allow 1 to 2 hours. Please note that the gardens are closed from November to February.

1461 Benvenuto Ave. (P.O. Box 190), Brentwood Bay. ☎ 877/722-0272 or 250/652-3822. www.butterflygardens. com. Admission C$11 (US$11/£5.50) adults, C$10 (US$10/£5) seniors and students, C$5.75 (US$5.75/£2.80) children 5–12, free for children under 5. Mar to mid-May daily 9:30am–4:30pm; mid-May to Sept daily 9am–5:30pm; Sept–Oct daily 9:30am–4:30pm. Closed Nov–Feb. Bus: 75.

ARCHITECTURAL HIGHLIGHTS & HISTORIC HOMES

Perhaps the most intriguing downtown edifice isn't a building at all but a work of art. The walls of **Fort Victoria,** which once covered much of downtown, have been demarcated in the sidewalk with bricks bearing the names of original settlers and fur traders. Look in the sidewalk on Government Street at the corner of Fort Street.

Most of the retail establishments in Victoria's Old Town area are housed in 19th-century shipping warehouses that have been carefully restored. You can take a **self-guided tour** of these buildings, most of which were erected between the 1870s and 1890s and whose history is recounted on easy-to-read outdoor plaques. The majority of the restored buildings are between Douglas and Johnson streets from Wharf Street to Government Street. The most impressive structure once contained a number of shipping offices and warehouses but is now the home of a 45-shop complex known as **Market Square,** 560 Johnson St./255 Market Sq. (☎ 250/386-2441; bus: 6).

Some of the British immigrants who settled Vancouver Island during the 19th century built magnificent estates and mansions. In addition to architect Francis Rattenbury's crowning turn-of-the-20th-century achievements—the provincial **Parliament Buildings,** 501 Belleville St. (completed in 1898), and the opulent **Fairmont Empress hotel,** 721 Government St. (completed in 1908)—you'll enjoy a visit to **Craigdarroch Castle** (p. 704).

Helmcken House, 610 Elliot St. Sq. (☎ 250/361-0021), is the oldest house in B.C. on its original site. Dr. John Sebastian Helmcken, a surgeon with the Hudson's Bay Company, set up house here in 1852 when he married the daughter of Governor Sir James Douglas. Originally a three-room log cabin, the house was built by Helmcken and expanded as both the prosperity and size of the family grew. It still contains its original furnishings, imported from England. Helmcken went on to become a statesman and helped negotiate the entry of British Columbia as a province into Canada. From May to September, the house is open daily 10am to 5pm. Admission is C$5 (US$5/£2.50) for adults, C$4 (US$4/£2) for seniors and students, and C$3 (US$3/£1.50) for children.

Point Ellice House ☆, 2616 Pleasant St. (☎ 250/380-6506), was the summer gathering place for much of Victoria's Victorian elite. From mid-May to mid-September, it's open for 30-minute guided tours daily noon to 5pm; admission is the same as for Carr House, above. Point Ellice is also one of the better spots for afternoon tea (see

Finds **Emily Carr, Visionary from Victoria**

Victoria was the birthplace of one of British Columbia's most distinguished early residents, the painter and writer Emily Carr (1871–1945). Though trained in the classical European tradition, Carr developed her own style in response to the powerful landscapes of the Canadian west coast. Eschewing both marriage and stability, she spent her life traveling the coast, capturing the landscapes and Native peoples in vivid and striking works.

In addition to visiting the great collection of Carr's paintings at the Art Gallery of Greater Victoria (p. 703), you can visit the **Emily Carr House** ⟨★, 207 Government St. (⟨© **250/383-5843;** www.emilycarr.com), where she was born. The house has been restored to the condition it would have been in when Carr lived there. In addition, many of the rooms have been hung with reproductions of her art or quotations from her writings. From June to Labour Day, the house is open daily 11am to 4pm; May and September it's open the same hours but closed Sunday and Monday. On Fridays and Saturdays from June to August, a local actress portrays Emily Carr and regales visitors with Carr family stories. Admission is C$5 (US$5/£2.50), C$10 (US$10/£5) for special events. The Vancouver Art Gallery (p. 666) also has a major collection of Carr's hauntingly evocative paintings.

"Taking Afternoon Tea" on p. 726). The easiest way to reach the house is by harbor ferry from in front of The Fairmont Empress.

PARKS & GARDENS

The 62-hectare (153-acre) **Beacon Hill Park** (bus: 11) stretches from Southgate Street to Dallas Road between Douglas and Cook streets. Stands of indigenous Garry oaks (found only on Vancouver Island, Hornby Island, and Salt Spring Island) and manicured lawns are interspersed with floral gardens and ponds. Hike up Beacon Hill to get a clear view of the Strait of Georgia, Haro Strait, and Washington's Olympic Mountains. The children's farm (see below), aviary, tennis courts, lawn-bowling green, putting green, cricket pitch, wading pool, playground, and picnic area make this a wonderful place to spend a few hours with the family.

Government House, the official residence of the Lieutenant Governor, is at 1401 Rockland Ave. (bus: 1), in the Fairfield residential district. The house itself is closed to the public, but the formal gardens are open and well worth a wander. Round back, the hillside of Garry oaks is one of the last places to see what the area's natural fauna would've looked like before European settlers arrived. At the front, the rose garden is sumptuous.

Just outside downtown, **Mount Douglas Park** offers great views of the area, several hiking trails, and—down at the waterline—a picnic/play area with a trail leading to a good walking beach.

About 45 minutes southwest of town, **East Sooke Park** ⟨★ is a 1,400-hectare (3,459-acre) microcosm of the west coast wilderness: jagged seacoast, Native petroglyphs, and hiking trails up to a 270m (886-ft.) hilltop. Access is via the Old Island Highway and East Sooke Road.

ESPECIALLY FOR KIDS

Nature's the thing for kids in Victoria. At the **Beacon Hill Children's Farm,** Circle Drive, Beacon Hill Park (© **250/381-2532;** bus: 11), kids can ride ponies; pet goats, rabbits, and other barnyard animals; and even cool off in the wading pool. Mid-March to September, the farm is open daily 10am to 5pm. Admission is by donation.

For a new take on this old concept, visit the **Victoria Butterfly Gardens** (p. 707). Closer to town and two shades creepier than the Butterfly Gardens is the **Victoria Bug Zoo,** 1107 Wharf St. (© **250/384-BUGS;** www.bugzoo.bc.ca; bus: 6), home to praying mantises and giant African cockroaches, along with knowledgeable guides who can bring the bugs out and let you or your kids handle and touch them. Admission is C$8 (US$8/£4) for adults, C$6 (US$6/£3) for seniors, C$7 (US$7/£3.50) students, C$5 (US$5/£2.50) for children 3 to 16, and free for children under 3; it's open Monday through Saturday 9:30am to 5pm, Sundays 11am to 5:30pm.

ORGANIZED TOURS

BUS TOURS   Gray Line of Victoria, 700 Douglas St. (© **800/663-8390** or 250/ 388-6539; www.grayline.ca), conducts a number of tours of Victoria and Butchart Gardens. The 1½-hour "Grand City Tour" costs C$21 (US$21/£11) for adults and C$10 (US$10/£5) for children ages 5 to 11. There are daily departures throughout the year, usually at 12:30 and 2:30pm. For other tours, check the website.

SPECIALTY TOURS   Victoria Harbour Ferries, 922 Old Esquimalt Rd. (© **250/ 708-0201;** www.victoriaharbourferry.com), offers a terrific 45-minute **harbor tour** ⚡ for C$20 (US$20/£10) adults, C$18 (US$18/£9) seniors, and C$10 (US$10/£5) for children under 12. Harbor tours depart from seven stops around the Inner Harbour every 15 or 20 minutes daily 10am to 5:30pm (May–Sept daily 9am–8pm). If you wish to stop for food or a stroll, you can get a token good for reboarding at any time during the same day. A 50-minute **Gorge Tour** ⚡ takes you to the gorge opposite the Johnson Street Bridge, where tidal falls reverse with each change of the tide. The price is the same as for the harbor tour; June through September, gorge tours depart from the dock in front of The Fairmont Empress every half-hour from 9am to 8:15pm; at other times the tours operate less frequently, depending on the weather. The ferries are 12-person, fully enclosed boats, and every seat is a window seat.

Heritage Tours and Daimler Limousine Service, 713 Bexhill Rd. (© **250/474- 4332;** www.islandnet.com/~daimler), guides you through the city, Butchart Gardens, and Craigdarroch Castle in a six-passenger British Daimler limousine. Rates start at C$75 (US$75/£37) for the Daimler per hour per vehicle (not per person). Also available are stretch limos that seat 8 to 10 people, starting at C$85 (US$85/£42) per hour per vehicle.

The bicycle-rickshaws operated by **Kabuki Kabs,** 613 Herald St. (© **250/385- 4243;** www.kabukikabs.com), can usually be found on the causeway in front of The Fairmont Empress or hailed in the downtown area. Prices for a tour are C$1 (US$1/ 50p) per minute for a two-person cab.

Tallyho Horse-Drawn Tours, 2044 Milton St. (© **250/383-5067;** www.tallyho tours.com), has conducted tours of Victoria in horse-drawn carriages and trolleys since 1903. Horse-drawn trolley and carriage excursions start at the corner of Belleville and Menzies streets. Fares for the trolley are C$15 (US$15/£7.50) for adults, C$11 (US$11/£5.50) for students, C$8 (US$8/£4) for children 17 and under. Trolley tours operate daily every 30 minutes 9am to 3pm during summer. An assortment of private carriage tours (maximum six people) are available throughout the year and in the summer from 10am to 10pm; cost runs from C$40 (US$40/£20) for 15 minutes, or C$200 (US$200/£100) for an hour and 30 minutes.

To get a bird's-eye view of Victoria, take a 30-minute tour with **Harbour Air Seaplanes,** 1234 Wharf St. (℗ **800/665-0212** or 250/384-2215; www.harbour-air.com). Rates are C$99 (US$99/£50) per person. For a romantic evening, try the "Fly and Dine" to Butchart Gardens deal; C$215 (US$215/£108) per person includes the flight to the gardens, admission, dinner, and a limousine ride back to Victoria.

Fresh Air Tours Ltd. (℗ **877/868-7790;** www.freshairtours.com) offers year-round scenic sightseeing minicoach and cycling tours to Victoria's highlights, wineries, the Butchart Gardens, the town of Sidney, Salt Spring Island, All Fun Recreation Park waterslides, and seasonal tours such as the Halloween pumpkin patch and Christmas lights. The company provides complimentary hotel pickup and drop-off; on cycling tours, bicycles, helmets and support van are provided.

WALKING TOURS **Victoria Bobby Walking Tours** (℗ **250/995-0233;** www. walkvictoria.com) offers a leisurely story-filled walk around Old Town with a former English bobby as guide. Tours depart at 11am daily, May through September 15, from the Visitor Information Centre on the Inner Harbour; cost is C$15 (US$15/£7.50) per person.

The **Old Cemetery Society of Victoria** (℗ **250/598-8870;** www.oldcem.bc.ca) runs regular cemetery tours throughout the year. Particularly popular are the slightly eerie **Lantern Tours of the Old Burying Ground** ✪, which begin at the Cherry Bank Hotel, 845 Burdett St., at 9pm nightly in July and August. The tour costs C$5 (US$5/£2.50) per person.

Discover the Past (℗ **250/384-6698;** www.discoverthepast.com) organizes interesting year-round walks; in the summer, **Ghostly Walks** explores Victoria's haunted Old Town, Chinatown, and historic waterfront; tours depart from the front of the Visitor Info Centre on Friday and Saturday at 7:30pm from October to May, and nightly at 7:30 and 9:30pm from June to September. The cost is C$12 (US$12/£6) adults, C$10 (US$10/£5) seniors and students, C$8 (US$8/£4) children 6 to 10, and C$30 (US$30/£15) for families. Check the website for other walks.

The name says it all for **Walkabout Historical Tours** (℗ **250/592-9255;** www. walkabouts.ca). Charming guides lead tours of The Fairmont Empress, Victoria's Chinatown, Antique Row, Old Town Victoria, or will help you with your own itinerary. The Empress Tour costs C$10 (US$10/£5) and begins at 10am daily in the Empress Tea Lobby. Other tours have different prices and starting points.

The **Victoria Heritage Foundation,** #1 Centennial Square (℗ **250/383-4546;** vhf@pinc.com), offers the excellent free pamphlet *James Bay Heritage Walking Tour.* The well-researched pamphlet (available at the Visitor Info Centre or from the Victoria Heritage office) describes a self-guided walking tour through the historic James Bay neighborhood.

OUTDOOR ACTIVITIES

Mountain biking, eco-touring, in-line skating, Alpine and Nordic skiing, parasailing, sea kayaking, canoeing, tidal-water fishing, fly-fishing, diving, and hiking are popular in and around Victoria.

BIKING The 13km (8-mile) **Scenic Marine Drive** bike path begins at Dallas Road and Douglas Street, at the base of Beacon Hill Park. The paved path follows the walkway

---

Tips **Suiting Up for the Outdoors**

In the sections below, specialized rental outfitters are listed for each activity.
Sports Rent, 3–1950 Government St. (© **250/385-7368**), is a great general equipment and watersports rental outlet. Its entire inventory, including rental rates, is
online at **www.sportsrentbc.com**.

---

along the beaches before winding up through the residential district on Beach Drive. It
eventually turns left and heads south toward downtown Victoria on Oak Bay Avenue.
The **Inner Harbour pedestrian path** has a bike lane for cyclists who want to take a
leisurely ride around the entire city seawall. The new **Galloping Goose Trail** (part of the
Trans-Canada Trail) runs from Victoria west through Colwood and Sooke all the way up
to Leechtown. If you don't want to bike the whole thing, there are numerous places to
park along the way, as well as several places where the trail intersects with public transit.
Call **BC Transit** at © 250/382-6161 to find out which bus routes take bikes.

Bikes and child trailers are available by the hour or day at **Cycle BC Rentals,** 747 Douglas St. (year-round) or 950 Wharf St. (May–Oct) (© **250/885-2453;** www.cyclebc.ca).
Rentals run C$7 (US$7/£3.50) per hour and C$24 (US$24/£12) per day, helmets and
locks included.

BIRDING   The **Victoria Natural History Society** runs regular weekend birding
excursions. Their **event line** at © **250/479-2054** lists upcoming outings and gives
contact numbers.

BOATING   Kayaks, canoes, rowboats, and powerboats are available from **Great
Pacific Adventures,** 811 Wharf St. (© **877/733-6722** or 250/386-2277; www.great
pacificadventures.com).

CANOEING & KAYAKING   **Ocean River Sports,** 1437 Store St. (© **800/909-
4233** or 250/381-4233; www.oceanriver.com), can equip you with everything from a
single kayak, a double kayak, and a canoe to life jackets, tents, and dry-storage camping gear. Rental costs for a single kayak range from C$25 (US$25/£13) per hour to
C$70 (US$70/£35) per day. Multiday and weekly rates are also available. The company also offers numerous **guided tours** ✿ of the Gulf Islands and the B.C. west
coast. For beginners, there's the guided 4½-hour "Explore Tour" of the coast around
Victoria or Sooke for C$95 (US$95/£48). There's also a guided 3-day/2-night "Expedition" trip to explore the nearby Gulf Islands for C$595 (US$595/£298).

Blackfish Wilderness Expeditions (© **250/216-2389;** www.blackfishwilderness.
com) offers a number of interesting kayak-based tours such as the kayak/boat/hike
combo, where you boat to the protected waters of the Discovery Islands, hike around
one of the islands, and kayak to get a better look at the pods of resident killer whales
that roam the waters around Victoria. Day tours start at C$70 (US$70/£35) per person.

FISHING   Saltwater fishing's the thing out here, and unless you know the area, it's
best to take a guide. **Adam's Fishing Charters** (© **250/370-2326;** www.adamsfishing
charters.com) is located on the Inner Harbour down below the Visitor Info Centre.
Chartering a boat and guide starts at C$95 (US$95/£47) per hour per boat, with a
minimum of 5 hours.

To fish, you need a nonresident saltwater fishing license. Licenses for saltwater fishing (including the salmon surcharge) cost C$14 (US$14/£7) for 1 day for nonresidents

and C$12 (US$12/£6) for B.C. residents. Tackle shops sell licenses, have details on current restrictions, and often carry copies of the *B.C. Tidal Waters Sport Fishing Guide* and *B.C. Sport Fishing Regulations Synopsis for Non-Tidal Waters*. Independent anglers should also pick up a copy of the *B.C. Fishing Directory and Atlas*. **Robinson's Sporting Goods Ltd.,** 1307 Broad St. (© **250/385-3429**), is a reliable source for information, recommendations, lures, licenses, and gear. For the latest fishing hot spots and recommendations on tackle and lures, check out **www.sportfishingbc.com.**

GOLFING   The **Cedar Hill Municipal Golf Course,** 1400 Derby Rd. (© **250/595-3103;** www.golfcedarhill.com), the busiest course in Canada, is an 18-hole public course 3km (1¾ miles) from downtown Victoria. It's open on a first-come, first-served basis; daytime greens fees are C$38 (US$38/£19) and twilight fees (after 3pm) are C$23 (US$23/£12). Golf clubs can be rented for C$15 (US$15/£7.50). The **Cordova Bay Golf Course,** 5333 Cordova Bay Rd. (© **250/658-4075;** www.cordova baygolf.com), is northeast of the downtown area. Designed by Bill Robinson, the 18-hole course features 66 sand traps and some tight fairways. Greens fees are C$50 to C$79 (US$50–US$79/£25–£40) depending on day and season; twilight fees range from C$30 to C$49 (US$30–US$49/£15–£25). The **Olympic View Golf Club,** 643 Latoria Rd. (© **250/474-3673;** www.golfbc.com/courses/olympic_view), is one of the top 35 golf courses in Canada. Amid 12 lakes and a pair of waterfalls, this 18-hole, 6,414-yard course is open daily year-round. Daytime greens fees, depending on day and season, are C$65 to C$75 (US$65–US$75/£33–£38) and twilight fees are C$30 to C$40 (US$30–US$40/£15–£20). Power carts cost an additional C$30 (US$30/£15).

The new star of Vancouver Island golf courses, and the most expensive to play, is the 18-hole, 7,212-yard, par 72 course designed by Jack Nicklaus and his son for **Westin Bear Mountain Golf Resort & Spa,** 1376 Lynburne Pl. (© **888/533-2327** or 250/744-2327 tee time bookings). Golf carts (included with fee) and collared shirts (blue jeans not permitted) are mandatory on this upscale, mountaintop course that features breathtaking views and a spectacular 19th hole for recreational betting. Non-member greens fees, depending on when you reserve and the time you play, range from C$65 to C$130 (US$65–US$130/£33–£65).

You can call **Last Minute Golf Hot Line** at © 800/684-6344 for substantial discounts and short-notice tee times. **Island Links Hot Line** at © 866/266-GOLF acts as a booking agent for courses around Vancouver Island and will provide transportation from your hotel to the course.

HIKING   Goldstream Provincial Park (30 min. west of downtown along Hwy. 1; p. 728) is a tranquil site for a short hike through towering cedars and past clear, rushing waters. The hour-long hike up **Mount Work** provides excellent views of the Saanich Peninsula and a good view of Finlayson Arm. The trail head is a 30- to 45-minute drive. Take Highway 17 north to Saanich, then take Highway 17A (the W. Saanich Rd.) to Wallace Drive, turn right on Willis Point Drive, and right again on the Ross-Durrance Road, looking for the parking lot on the right. There are signs along the way. Equally good, though more of a scramble, is the hour-plus climb up **Mount Finlayson** in Gowland-Tod Provincial Park (take Hwy. 1 west, get off at the Millstream Rd. exit, and follow Millstream Rd. north to the very end).

The very popular **Sooke Potholes** trail wanders up beside a river to an abandoned mountain lodge. Take Highway 1A west to Colwood, then Highway 14A (the Sooke Rd.). When you reach Sooke, turn north on the Sooke River Road, and follow it to the park. For a taste of the wild and rocky west coast, hike the oceanside trails in beautiful

East Sooke Regional Park 𝅘𝅥𝅘𝅥. Take Hwy. 14A west, turn south on Gillespie Road, and then take East Sooke Road.

For serious backpacking, go 104km (65 miles) west of Victoria on Highway 14A to Port Renfrew and the challenging **West Coast Trail** 𝅘𝅥𝅘𝅥𝅘𝅥, extending 77km (48 miles) from Port Renfrew to Bamfield in a portion of **Pacific Rim National Park** 𝅘𝅥𝅘𝅥𝅘𝅥 (p. 738). This trail was originally established as a lifesaving trail for shipwrecked sailors. Plan a 7-day trek if you want to cover the entire route; reservations are required, so call ⓒ **604/663-6000.** The newer, less challenging 48km (30-mile) long **Juan de Fuca Marine Trail** 𝅘𝅥𝅘𝅥 connects Port Renfrew and the Jordan River.

Island Adventure Tours (ⓒ **866/812-7103;** www.islandadventuretours.com) offers a number of options for folks wanting to explore the outdoors. There are 6-hour guided **rainforest walks** for C$95 (US$95/£47) or a full-day hike including transportation and lunch. For the deluxe Juan de Fuca experience, sign up for a 3-day, fully catered backpacking trip along the rugged West Coast Trail for C$499 (US$499/£250).

PARAGLIDING   Vancouver Island Paragliding (ⓒ 250/886-4165; www.viparagliding.com) offers tandem paraglide flights. The pilot steers; you hang on and enjoy the adrenaline rush. Flights last around 25 minutes. They also offer 1-day training courses that allow you to take off on your own.

SAILING   One of the most exciting ways to explore the Strait of Juan de Fuca is aboard the *Thane,* a 16m (53-ft.) sailing ship that offers 3-hour sail tours of the Strait 𝅘𝅥𝅘𝅥 for C$60 (US$60/£30) per person. The vessel is moored in front of The Fairmont Empress. Daily summer sailings leave at 9am, 1, and 5pm. Guests are welcome to bring along a picnic. For information, contact the **SV *Thane*** (ⓒ **877/788-4263** or 250/885-2311; www.eco-correct.com).

WATERSPORTS   The **Crystal Pool & Fitness Centre,** 2275 Quadra St. (ⓒ **250/ 361-0732**), is Victoria's main aquatic facility. The 50m (164-ft.) lap pool; children's pool; diving pool; sauna; whirlpool; and steam, weight, and aerobics rooms are open Monday through Friday 5:30am to 11pm, Saturday 6am to 6pm, and Sunday 9am to 4pm. Drop-in admission is C$4.75 (US$4.75/£2.90) for adults, C$3.75 (US$3.75/ £1.90) for seniors and students, C$2.50 (US$2.50/£1.25) for children 6 to 12, and free for children under 6.

WHALE-WATCHING   The waters surrounding the southern tip of Vancouver Island teem with orcas (killer whales), as well as harbor seals, sea lions, bald eagles, and harbor and Dall porpoises. All whale-watching companies basically offer the same tour; the main difference comes in the equipment they use: Some use a 12-person Zodiac, where the jolting ride is almost as exciting as seeing the whales, whereas others take a larger, more leisurely craft. Both offer excellent platforms for seeing whales. In high season (June to Labour Day), most companies offer several trips a day. Always ask if the outfitter is a "responsible whale-watcher"—that is, doesn't go too close to disturb or harass the whales.

Seafun Safaris Whale Watching, 950 Wharf St. (ⓒ **877/360-1233** or 250/360-1200; www.seafun.com), is just one of many outfits offering whale-watching tours in Zodiacs and covered boats. Adults and kids will learn a lot from the naturalist guides, who explain the behavior and nature of the orcas, gray whales, sea lions, porpoises, cormorants, eagles, and harbor seals encountered along the way. Fares are C$99 (US$99/£50) for adults and C$69 (US$69/£35) for children.

Other reputable companies include **Prince of Whales,** 812 Wharf St. (℃ **888/ 383-4884** or 250/383-4884; www.princeofwhales.com), just below the Visitor Info Centre, and **Orca Spirit Adventures** (℃ **888/672-ORCA** or 250/383-8411; www. orcaspirit.com), which departs from the Coast Harbourside Hotel dock.

SHOPPING

Victoria has dozens of little specialty shops that appeal to every taste and whim, and because the city is built to such a pedestrian scale, you can wander from place to place seeking out whatever treasure it is you're after. Nearly all the areas below are within a short walk of the Empress hotel.

ANTIQUES   Many of the best stores are in **Antique Row,** a 3-block stretch on Fort Street between Blanshard and Cook streets. Though farthest from downtown, **Faith Grant's Connoisseur Shop Ltd.,** 1156 Fort St. (℃ **250/383-0121;** bus: 1 or 10), is also the best. Other shops on the row that are worth poking your nose into are **Jeffries and Co. Silversmiths,** 1026 Fort St. (℃ **250/383-8315;** bus: 1 or 10); **Romanoff & Company Antiques,** 837 Fort St. (℃ **250/480-1543;** bus: 1 or 10); and for furniture fans, **Charles Baird Antiques,** 1044A Fort St. (℃ **250/384-8809;** bus: 1 or 10).

ARTS & CRAFTS   **Starfish Glassworks,** 630 Yates St. (℃ **250/388-7827**), is both a glassblowing artists' studio, where you can watch pieces being created, and a gallery where contemporary glass pieces are sold.

A DEPARTMENT STORE & SHOPPING MALL   **The Bay Centre,** between Government and Douglas sts., off Fort and View sts. (℃ **250/389-2228;** bus: 1, 5, or 30) formerly known as the Eaton Centre, is named after its new anchor store, the **Hudson's Bay Company** (℃ **250/385-1311**). Canada's oldest department store sells everything from housewares to fashions to cosmetics and of course the trendy Hudson's Bay woolen point blankets. The rest of the complex houses a full shopping mall, disguised as a block of heritage buildings, with three floors of shops and boutiques offering fashions, china and crystal, housewares, gourmet foods, and books.

FASHION   **Breeze,** 1150 Government St. (℃ **250/383-8871**), is a high-energy fashion outlet that carries a number of affordable and trendy lines for women, plus accessories. **Hughes Ltd.,** 564 Yates St. (℃ **250/381-4405**) is a local favorite for contemporary women's fashions. **The Plum Clothing Co.,** 1298 Broad St. (℃ **250/ 381-5005**), features quality dressy casuals. For men's fashions, try **British Importers,** 1125 Government St. (℃ **250/386-1496;** bus: 1, 5, or 30).

FOOD   **Rogers' Chocolates,** 913 Government St. (℃ **250/384-7021;** http://rogers chocolates.com), is a Victoria institution housed in an appropriately old-fashioned shop loaded with tempting treats that will satisfy even a discerning chocoholic. **Murchies,** 1110 Government St. (℃ **250/383-3112**), offers many specialty teas, including the custom-made Empress blend, served at The Fairmont Empress hotel's afternoon tea.

JEWELRY   Ian MacDonald of **MacDonald Jewelry,** 618 View St. (℃ **250/382- 4113;** bus: 1 or 2), designs and crafts all his own jewelry, which makes for some interesting creations. At the **Jade Tree,** 606 Humboldt St. (℃ **250/388-4326;** bus: 1, 5, or 30), you'll find jewelry crafted from British Columbia jade into necklaces, bracelets, and other items.

NATIVE ART   All the coastal tribes are represented in the **Alcheringa Gallery,** 665 Fort St. (℃ **250/383-8224;** bus: 1 or 2), along with a significant collection of pieces from Papau New Guinea. **Cowichan Trading Ltd.,** 1328 Government St. (© 250/383-0321; bus: 1, 5, or 30), sells a mix of T-shirts and gewgaws in addition to fine Cowichan sweaters, masks, and fine silver jewelry. **Hill's Native Art,** 1008 Government St. (© 250/385-3911; bus: 1, 5, or 30), features traditional Native art, including wooden masks and carvings, Haida argillite, and silver jewelry.

OUTDOOR CLOTHES & EQUIPMENT   **Ocean River Sports,** 1824 Store St. (© 250/381-4233; bus: 6), is a good spot for outdoor clothing and camping equipment.

WHERE TO STAY

Victoria has been welcoming visitors for well-nigh 100 years, so it knows how to do it with style. You'll find a wide choice of fine accommodations in all price ranges, most in the Old Town or around the Inner Harbour. But you don't have to limit yourself to Victoria proper. A 20-minute or half-hour drive north, east, or west takes you to all manner of marvelous resorts and inns, some on the ocean, some next to quiet bays and harbors, and some perched on mountaintops. Reservations are absolutely essential in Victoria May through September. If you arrive without a reservation and have trouble finding a room, **Tourism Victoria** (© 800/663-3883 or 250/382-1131) can make reservations for you at hotels, inns, and B&Bs.

INNER HARBOUR
Very Expensive

Delta Victoria Ocean Pointe Resort and Spa 🜲🜲 *Kids*   The "OPR," located across the Johnson Street Bridge on the Inner Harbour's north shore, is a big, bright, modern hotel with commanding views of downtown, the Legislature, The Fairmont Empress, and the busy harbor itself. You'll see this view as you enter the grand lobby with its two-story-tall windows. The rooms here are nice and big, and so are the bathrooms. The decor, like the hotel itself, is a blend of contemporary and traditional. The prime-view rooms face the Inner Harbour; rooms with a "working harbor" view look out over a less interesting industrial mixed-use scene. A few extra dollars buys a few extra perks, like breakfast and evening hors d'oeuvres in the third-floor Signature Lounge. All guests have use of the big indoor pool, a really good whirlpool, and a fully equipped gym with racquetball and tennis courts. Lots of guests come for the new spa, one of the best in Victoria. Like all the Delta hotels, OPR is very kid-friendly.

45 Songhees Rd., Victoria, BC V9A 6T3. © 800/667-4677 or 250/360-2999. Fax 250/360-1041. www.deltavictoria.com. 242 units. C$119–C$499 (US$119–US$499/£60–£250) double; C$349–C$999 (US$349–US$999/£175–£500) suite. Children under 17 stay free in parent's room. AE, DC, MC, V. Underground valet parking C$14 (US$14/£7). Bus: 24 to Colville. **Amenities:** Restaurant/lounge; indoor pool; outdoor tennis courts; health club; full-service spa; Jacuzzi; sauna; concierge; 24-hr. business center; 24-hr. room service; babysitting; same-day dry cleaning; nonsmoking rooms; executive-level rooms; rooms for those w/limited mobility. *In room:* A/C, TV/VCR w/pay movies, Internet, minibar, coffeemaker, hair dryer, iron/ironing board, safe.

The Fairmont Empress 🜲🜲   Francis Rattenbury's 1908 harborside creation is the most famous landmark on the Victoria waterfront. When you see it, you'll instantly think that you'd love to stay here. Think twice, however, before throwing down the plastic. The hotel's 256 standard rooms (called Fairmont rooms) cost more and offer less than you can find elsewhere in the city. They're small rooms with smaller bathrooms, and offer little in the way of view. For some, the hotel's fabulous location and the building itself, as well as its first-class amenities—large pool, good weight room, luxurious Willow Stream spa, lounge, restaurant, tea lobby, and so on—or just the aura of being in the Empress makes up for this lack of personal space. The 80 Deluxe rooms are bigger, and many of them have a view of the harbor. If you don't stay here, you may want to stop by for afternoon tea (see "Taking Afternoon Tea," p. 726).

721 Government St., Victoria, BC V8W 1W5. ⓒ 800/441-1414 or 250/384-8111. Fax 250/381-4334. www.fairmont. com/empress. 477 units. C$179–C$569 (US$179–US$569/£90–£285) double; C$319–C$1,519 (US$319–US$1,519/ £160–£760) suite. AE, DC, DISC, MC, V. Underground valet parking C$19 (US$19/£9.50). Bus: 5. **Amenities:** 2 restaurants; bar/lounge; tearoom (p. 726); indoor pool; high-quality health club; spa; Jacuzzi; sauna; concierge; business center; shopping arcade; limited room service; in-room massage; babysitting; laundry service; same-day dry cleaning; nonsmoking rooms; executive-level rooms; rooms for those w/limited mobility. *In room:* TV w/pay movies, Internet, hair dryer, iron/ironing board.

Hotel Grand Pacific 🏝🏝 On Victoria's bustling Inner Harbour, directly across the street from the Port Angeles–Victoria ferry dock, the Grand Pacific is more luxurious than the Delta Ocean Pointe, and has rooms that are generally more spacious than those at The Fairmont Empress. Like those other two hotels on the Inner Harbour, the Grand Pacific has its own spa; its health club is better than the others, and features a huge ozonated indoor pool. All rooms have balconies and are attractively and comfortably furnished. Standard rooms face the Olympic Mountains and Ogden Point or, for a bit more money, the Inner Harbour; bathrooms are on the small side. Suites provide the best views, overlooking the harbor and the Empress. The fabulous luxury suites feature huge bathrooms, fireplaces, and several balconies. Fine dining options include the informal Pacific Restaurant and the Mark.

463 Belleville St., Victoria, BC V8V 1X3. ⓒ 800/663-7550 or 250/386-0450. Fax 250/380-4473. www.hotelgrand pacific.com. 304 units. C$152–C$286 (US$152–US$286/£76–£143) double; C$212–C$390 (US$212–US$390/£106– £195) suite. AE, DC, DISC, MC, V. Self-parking free; valet parking C$10 (US$10/£5). Bus: 30 to Superior and Oswego sts. **Amenities:** 2 restaurants; cafe; bar; indoor pool; squash courts; superior health club; full-service spa; Jacuzzi; concierge; tour desk; business center; 24-hr. room service; massage; babysitting; laundry service; same-day dry cleaning; nonsmoking rooms. *In room:* A/C, TV w/pay movies, Internet, minibar, coffeemaker, hair dryer, iron/ironing board, safe.

Expensive

Andersen House Bed & Breakfast 🏝 The art and furnishings in Andersen House are drawn from the whole of the old British Empire and a good section of the modern world beyond. The 1891 house has the high ceilings, stained-glass windows, and ornate fireplaces typical of the Queen Anne style, but the art and decorations are far more eclectic. Each room has a unique style: The sun-drenched Casablanca room on the top floor, for example, boasts Persian rugs, a four-poster queen bed, and a boxed window seat. All rooms have private entrances and come with books, CD players and CDs, and complimentary high-speed Wi-Fi access; all feature soaker tubs or two-person Jacuzzis.

301 Kingston St., Victoria, BC V8V 1V5. ⓒ 877/264-9988 or 250/388-4565. Fax 250/388-4502. www.andersen house.com. 4 units. C$125–C$275 (US$125–US$275/£63–£138) double. Rates include breakfast. MC, V. Free off-street parking. Bus: 30 to Superior and Oswego sts. Children under 12 not accepted. **Amenities:** Jacuzzi; nonsmoking rooms. *In room:* TV/VCR, free Wi-Fi, coffeemaker, hair dryer, iron/ironing board.

The Haterleigh Heritage Inn 🏝 Haterleigh innkeeper Paul Kelly is a font of information, on Victoria in general and on this lovingly restored 1901 home in particular. With his wife, Elizabeth, he runs this exceptional B&B that captures the essence of Victoria's romance with a combination of antique furniture, original stained-glass windows, and attentive personal service. The rooms feature high arched ceilings, large windows, sitting areas, and large bathrooms, some with hand-painted tiles and Jacuzzi tubs. On the top floor, the cozy Angel's Reach room features a big four-poster bed. The second-floor Secret Garden room has a small balcony with views of the Olympic mountain range. The Day Dreams room downstairs is the dedicated honeymoon suite. A full gourmet breakfast with organic produce is served family style at 8:30am. There's also complimentary sherry in the drawing room each evening.

243 Kingston St., Victoria, BC V8V 1V5. © 866/234-2244 or 250/384-9995. Fax 250/384-1935. www.haterleigh. com. 7 units. C$135–C$340 (US$135–US$340/£68–£170) double. Rates include full breakfast. MC, V. Free parking. Bus: 30 to Superior and Montreal sts. **Amenities:** Jacuzzi; free Internet. *In room:* Hair dryer.

Laurel Point Inn ✹✹✹   The three stars are for the newly refurbed and utterly gorgeous South Wing suites, featuring stylish, contemporary furnishings; Asian artwork; balconies overlooking a Japanese garden; shoji-style sliding doors; and luxurious marble bathrooms with deep soaker tubs and glassed-in showers. This art-filled, resort-style hotel occupies a prettily landscaped promontory jutting out into the Inner Harbour, and consists of the original north wing and the newer south wing designed by noted Vancouver architect Arthur Erickson in 1989. The overall design reflects the elegant simplicity of Japanese artistic principals and is a refreshing change from the chintz and florals found in so many Victoria hotels. Rooms in the older north wing are fine—with good beds, pocket balconies (every room in the hotel has a water view), and nice bathrooms—but the south wing is where you want to be. The hotel is in the process of a total remodel to be completed in 2008.

680 Montreal St., Victoria, BC V8V 1Z8. © 800/663-7667 or 250/386-8721. Fax 250/386-9547. www.laurelpoint.com. 200 units. C$124–C$264 (US$124–US$264/£62–£132) double; C$204–C$394 (US$204–US$394/£102–£197) suite. Children under 18 stay free in parent's room. AE, DC, DISC, MC, V. Free secure parking. Bus: 30 to Montreal and Superior sts. **Amenities:** Restaurant; bar; indoor pool; whirlpool; complimentary access to YMCA facilities; concierge; business center; 24-hr. room service; babysitting; same-day dry cleaning; nonsmoking rooms; rooms for those w/limited mobility; free lobby Wi-Fi. *In room:* A/C, TV, dataport w/free high-speed Internet, coffeemaker, hair dryer, iron/ironing board, safe, free local calls.

Moderate

Admiral Inn *(Value) (Kids)*   The family-operated Admiral is in a three-story building on the Inner Harbour, near the Washington-bound ferry terminal and close to restaurants and shopping. The combination of clean, comfortable rooms and reasonable rates attracts young couples, families, seniors, and other travelers in search of a harbor view at a price that doesn't break the bank. The rooms are pleasant and comfortably furnished, a bit motel-like, with small bathrooms and balconies or terraces. The more expensive rooms come with a kitchenette with a small fridge and stove. The suites come with full kitchens. Some units can sleep up to six (on two double beds and a double sofa bed). The owners provide sightseeing advice as well as extras like free bicycles, free local calls, and an Internet terminal in the lobby.

257 Belleville St., Victoria, BC V8V 1X1. © 888/823-6472 or ©/fax 250/388-6267. www.admiral.bc.ca. 29 units. C$99–C$219 (US$99–US$219/£49–£110) double; C$129–C$249 (US$129–C$249/£65–£125) suite. Children under 12 stay free in parent's room. Rates include continental breakfast. AE, DC, MC, V. Free parking. Bus: 5 to Belleville and Government sts. **Amenities:** Complimentary bikes; coin laundry; dry cleaning; nonsmoking rooms; complimentary Internet access. *In room:* A/C, TV, kitchen/kitchenette (in some units), fridge, coffeemaker, hair dryer, iron/ironing board.

Spinnakers Guest House ✹ *(Value)*   This bed-and-breakfast-style guesthouse offers good accommodations at a moderate price. There are two separate buildings, owned and operated by the same local entrepreneur who runs Spinnakers Brewpub. The 1884 heritage building on Catherine Street is the more luxurious. Rooms here feature queen beds, lovely furnishings, in-room Jacuzzis, fireplaces, high ceilings, and lots of natural light. The four Garden Suites units on Mary Street are really self-contained apartments, with separate bedrooms and full kitchens, perfect for longer stays or for families. Guests at both buildings get an in-room breakfast. The waterfront location is a 10- to 20-minute walk from downtown; the harbor ferry stops nearby.

308 Catherine St., Victoria, BC V9A 3S3. © 877/838-2739 or 250/384-2739. Fax 250/384-3246. www.spinnakers. com. 11 units. C$129–C$249 (US$129–US$249/£65–£125) double. Rates include breakfast. AE, DC, MC, V. Free parking. Bus: 24 to Catherine St. **Amenities:** Nonsmoking rooms. *In room:* Kitchen (some units), fireplace (some units), Jacuzzi.

DOWNTOWN & OLD TOWN
Expensive
Abigail's Hotel 🏨🏨 A Tudor-style mansion in a residential neighborhood just east of downtown, Abigail's began life in the 1920s as a luxury apartment house before being converted to a boutique hotel. If you like small, personalized, bed-and-breakfast hotels, you'll enjoy this impeccably maintained property. Everything is done well here, and the quality is high throughout. In the original building, some of the 16 rooms are bright and sunny and beautifully furnished, with pedestal sinks and goose-down duvets. Others feature soaker tubs and double-sided fireplaces, so you can relax in the tub by the light of the fire. The six Celebration Suites in the Coach House are more luxurious. Recent renovations added Italian marble bathrooms, new furniture, and a new spa. Abigail's chef prepares a multicourse gourmet breakfast served in the sunny breakfast room, on the patio, or in your room.

906 McClure St., Victoria, BC V8V 3E7. © 866/347-5054 or 250/388-5363. Fax 250/388-7787. www.abigailshotel. com. 23 units. C$139–C$450 (US$139–US$450/£70–£225) double. Rates include full breakfast. AE, MC, V. Free parking. Bus: 1 to Cook and McClure sts. Children under 10 not accepted. **Amenities:** Concierge; dry cleaning; afternoon appetizers. *In room:* A/C, TV (in some rooms), dataport w/high-speed Internet, Wi-Fi, hair dryer, iron/ironing board, Jacuzzi (in some rooms), fireplace (in some rooms).

The Magnolia 🏨🏨 A boutique hotel in the center of Victoria, the Magnolia was completed in 1999 and offers a taste of luxury at a reasonable price. The small lobby, with a fireplace, chandelier, and overstuffed chairs, has a clubby Edwardian look. The room decor manages to be classic without feeling frumpy, with high-quality linen, down duvets, and quality furnishings. The spacious marble bathrooms are perhaps the best in Victoria, with walk-in showers and deep soaker tubs. The windows extend floor to ceiling, letting in lots of light, but there are really no great views in this hotel. The needs of business travelers are kept in mind: Work desks are large and well lit with dataports and high-speed Internet access. Local calls are complimentary. The Diamond Suites on the sixth and seventh floors feature a sitting room with fireplace. The hotel has a good restaurant, a fine microbrewery, and a full-service Aveda spa. If you want a small downtown hotel with personalized service and fine finishes, this is a good choice.

623 Courtney St., Victoria, BC V8W 1B8. © 877/624-6654 or 250/381-0999. Fax 250/381-0988. www.magnoliahotel. com. 63 units. C$169–C$329 (US$169–US$329/£85–£165) double. Rates include continental breakfast. AE, DC, MC, V. Valet parking C$15 (US$15/£7.50). Bus: 5. **Amenities:** Restaurant; bar; access to nearby health club; spa; concierge; limited room service; laundry service; same-day dry cleaning; executive-level rooms. *In room:* A/C, TV w/pay movies, dataport, Internet, minibar, fridge, coffeemaker, hair dryer, iron/ironing board.

Moderate
Isabella's Guest Suites 🏨 *Finds* Two suites located above Willy's bakery provide affordable, fun, and surprisingly stylish accommodations in the heart of the city. The front suite is a large, elegantly furnished studio with a bed/sitting room that opens into a dining room and full kitchen. Bright colors and cheerful accents, upscale rustic furniture, high ceilings, large windows, and plenty of space make this a great home

base for exploring Victoria. The second unit, a one-bedroom suite, overlooks the alley and patio of Il Terrazzo restaurant. The living room is painted in bright red, which goes surprisingly well with the wood floors and funky furniture. Both units have king beds and are nonsmoking. Breakfast is included and served at the bakery. Parking is free, and you have your own front door.

537 Johnson St., Victoria, BC V8W 1M2. ✆ **250/595-3815.** Fax 250/381-8415. www.isabellasbb.com. 2 units. C$150–C$195 (US$150–US$195/£75–£98) double. Rates include continental breakfast. Free parking. Bus: 5. *In room:* A/C, TV, full kitchen, hair dryer, iron/ironing board.

Swans Suite Hotel ☆☆ *Kids*   In 1988, this heritage building was turned into a hotel, restaurant, brewpub, and nightclub. Located near the Johnson Street Bridge, it's now one of Old Town's best-loved buildings, and just minutes from Bastion Square, Chinatown, and downtown. Like any good boutique hotel, Swans is small, friendly, and charming. The suites are large and many are split level, featuring open lofts and huge exposed beams. All come with fully equipped kitchens, dining areas, living rooms, queen-size beds, and original artwork. The two-bedroom suites are like little town houses; they're great for families, accommodating up to six comfortably. Swan's Brew Pub is one of the most popular in the city and features live entertainment nightly. One potential drawback to this otherwise fine hotel is that there's a homeless shelter across the street.

506 Pandora St., Victoria, BC V8W 1N6. ✆ **800/668-7926** or 250/361-3310. Fax 250/361-3491. www.swanshotel.com. 30 units. C$179–C$199 (US$179–US$199)/£90–£99) studio; C$219–C$359 (US$219–US$359/£110–£180) suite. Children under 12 stay free in parent's room. AE, DC, DISC, MC, V. Parking C$12 (US$12/£6). Bus: 23 or 24 to Pandora Ave. **Amenities:** Restaurant; brewpub; limited room service; laundry room; same-day dry cleaning. *In room:* TV, Wi-Fi, kitchen, coffeemaker, hair dryer, iron/ironing board.

Inexpensive
Ocean Island Backpackers Inn ☆ *Value*   This is one of the best spots in Victoria for pleasant and inexpensive lodging, and it's located right downtown, just a few blocks from Bastion Square and the Inner Harbour. All sorts of travelers make their way to this hostel (an alternative to the Hostelling International network), from families with children to on-the-go seniors and young adults with global wanderlust. There's a big, comfy lounge/common area with all kinds of stuff going on, including live music and open-mic evenings. You can buy cheap meals and snacks, use the kitchen, or kick back with a beer or glass of wine. In addition to the dorm rooms, there are 60 private rooms, in various configurations, including some with their own bathrooms. The staff here goes out of its way to help guests make the most of their time in Victoria and on Vancouver Island, including arranging day trips to out of the ordinary places.

791 Pandora Ave., Victoria, BC V8W 1N9. ✆ **250/385-1785.** Fax 250/385-1780. www.oceanisland.com. 50 units. C$19–C$24 (US$19–US$24/£9.50–£12) dorm bed; C$25–C$68 (US$25–US$68/£13–£34) private room (some with private bath). MC, V. Parking C$5 (US$5/£2.50). Bus: 70 to Pandora Ave. and Douglas St. **Amenities:** Restaurant; lounge; tour desk; coin laundry; coin Internet; Wi-Fi; free bike/luggage storage. *In room:* TV (in some rooms), Wi-Fi.

Paul's Motor Inn *Value*   Sometimes nothing but an inexpensive motor inn or motel will do, and that's where Paul's comes in. It's been around for ages, it's very well maintained, and it's within walking distance to downtown. The rooms are pleasant for what they are, and much nicer than those in many motel chains. The staff here is friendly and helpful and there's an above-average restaurant. Clean and cheerful all around.

1900 Douglas St., Victoria, BC V8T 4R8. ✆ **866/333-7285.** www.paulsmotorinn.com. 78 units. C$59–C$104 (US$59–US$104/£30–£52) double. AE, DC, DISC, MC, V. Free parking. Bus: 30 to Douglas and Chatham sts. **Amenities:** Restaurant; coin laundry; fax/copying services. *In room:* TV, Internet, fridge, coffeemaker.

Victoria International Youth Hostel   The location is perfect—right in the heart of Old Town. In addition, this hostel has all the usual accouterments, including two kitchens (stocked with utensils), a dining room, a TV lounge, a game room, a common room, a library, laundry facilities, an indoor bicycle lockup, 24-hour security, and hot showers. The dorms are on the large side (16 people to a room), showers are shared and segregated by gender, and a couple of family rooms are available (one of which has a private toilet). There's an extensive ride board, and the collection of outfitter and tour information rivals that of the tourism office. The front door is locked at 2:30am, but you can make arrangements to get in later.

516 Yates St., Victoria, BC V8W 1K8. (C) **888/883-0099** or 250/385-4511. Fax 250/385-3232. www.hihostels.ca. 104 beds. HI/YHA members C$18–C$21 (US$18–US$21/£9–£11) dorm bed; C$40–C$52 (US$40–US$52/£20–£26) private room; nonmembers pay C$3 (US$3/£1.50) extra for dorm bed, C$8 (US$8/£4) extra for private room. Wheelchair-accessible unit available. MC, V. Parking on street. Bus: 70 from Swartz Bay ferry terminal. **Amenities:** Lounge; game room; laundry facilities; kitchens; free Wi-Fi.

OUTSIDE THE CENTRAL AREA
Expensive
The Aerie 𝒜𝒜𝒜   On a forested mountain slope high above a fjord about half an hour from town, this Mediterranean-inspired villa enjoys a spectacular outlook. A member of the prestigious Relais & Châteaux, the Aerie is one of the most luxurious retreats you'll find on Vancouver Island, though some may find the European-inspired decor and design a bit over the top. Accommodations are in three separate buildings, including the newly completed Villa Cielo, which offers the most amazing views of all. All rooms include big comfortable beds with top-quality linen, and all but the lowest-priced Deluxe rooms include a soaker tub for two (sometimes right in the middle of the room). As you move into the master and residence suites, you get private decks and fireplaces. An on-site full-service spa offers a variety of aesthetic treatments. Dining is an integral part of the experience, and The Aerie restaurant (p. 725) is among the best on the island. A full breakfast is included in the room rate.

600 Ebedora Lane (P.O. Box 108), Malahat, BC V0R 2L0. (C) **800/518-1933** or 250/743-7115. Fax 250/743-4766. www.aerie.bc.ca. 29 units. C$195–C$295 (US$195–US$295/£98–£148) double; C$300–C$565 (US$300–US$565/£150–£283) suite. Rates include breakfast. AE, DC, MC, V. Free parking. Take Hwy. 1 north, turn left at the Spectacle Lake turnoff, take the first right, and follow the winding driveway. **Amenities:** Restaurant; bar; small indoor pool; tennis courts; small weight room; full spa; indoor and outdoor Jacuzzis; concierge; 24-hr. room service; laundry service; dry cleaning; all nonsmoking rooms. *In room:* A/C, TV, dataport, free Wi-Fi, minibar, coffeemaker, hair dryer, iron/ironing board.

The Boathouse 𝒜𝒜𝒜 *(Finds)*   There's nothing else like it on Vancouver Island, and I can almost guarantee that you'll fall in love with this tiny, secluded cottage—a former boathouse—set on pilings over Saanich Inlet on Brentwood Bay. The only passersby you're likely to encounter are seals, bald eagles, otters, herons, and raccoons, plus the occasional floatplane flying in. The converted boathouse is at the end of a very long flight of stairs behind the owner's home (if you have mobility issues, this is not the place for you). Outside, there's a waterside porch; inside are a queen bed, a dining table, a kitchen area with a small refrigerator and toaster oven, an electric heater, and a reading alcove with a stunning view all the way up Finlayson Arm. Toilet and shower facilities are in a separate bathhouse, 17 steps back uphill. All the makings for a delicious continental breakfast are delivered in the evening. Just below the boathouse is a floating dock—which doubles as a great sun deck—with a small dinghy reserved for the exclusive use of guests.

746 Sea Dr., Brentwood Bay, Victoria, BC VM8 1B1. (©) **866/654-9370** or 250/652-9370. www.bctravel.com/boat house.html. 1 unit. C$215 (US$215/£108) double with continental breakfast; C$195 (US$195/£97) double without breakfast. 2-night minimum. AE, MC, V. Free parking. Closed Oct–Feb. Bus: 75 to Wallace Dr. and Benvenuto Ave. No children under 18. *In room:* Fridge, coffeemaker, hair dryer, iron/ironing board.

Brentwood Bay Lodge & Spa ⭐⭐⭐ *Finds*   Located on a pristine inlet about 20 minutes north of downtown Victoria, just minutes from Butchart Gardens, this contemporary timber-and-glass lodge offers the best of everything, including a fabulous spa, boat shuttle to Butchart Gardens, and all manner of eco-adventures, including kayaking, scuba diving, fishing, and boat trips through the surrounding waters. This is a place where every detail has been carefully considered and beautifully rendered. The rooms feature handcrafted furnishings, gas fireplaces, luxurious bathrooms with soaker tubs and body massage showers, balconies, and king beds fitted with the highest-quality Italian linens. The SeaGrille dining room (p. 727) offers seasonal menus focusing on foraged and organic local ingredients, plus a wine-tasting bar with a selection of fine wines from the resort's award-winning cellar. You can also dine in the casual Marine Pub. The hotel has its own marina and is a licensed PADI (Professional Association of Diving Instructors) dive center—the fjord on which it sits is considered one of the best diving spots in the world. The Essence of Life spa offers fresh Pacific seaweed, herb, ocean salt, and other treatments in a tranquil environment. Breakfast is delivered to your room.

849 Verdier Ave. on Brentwood Bay, Victoria, BC V8M 1C5. (©) **888/544-2079** or 250/544-2079. Fax 250/544-2069. www.brentwoodbaylodge.com. 33 units. C$179–C$419 (US$179–US$419/£90–£210) double; C$369–C$699 (US$369–US$699/£184–£350) suite. Rates include continental breakfast. AE, DC, MC, V. Free parking. Take Pat Bay Hwy. north to Keating Crossroads, turn left (west) to Saanich Rd., turn right (south) to Verdier Ave. **Amenities:** Restaurant; pub; heated outdoor pool; full-service spa; Jacuzzi; concierge; 24-hr. room service; laundry service; dry cleaning. *In room:* A/C, TV/DVD, free Wi-Fi, minibar, coffeemaker, hair dryer, iron/ironing board.

Sooke Harbour House ⭐⭐⭐   This quirkily distinctive inn/restaurant, located right on the ocean at the end of a sand spit about 30km (19 miles) west of Victoria, has earned an international reputation (voted second-best country inn *in the world* by *Gourmet* magazine in 2000) thanks to the care lavished on the guests by owners Frederique and Sinclair Philip and their attentive staff. Frederique looks after the sumptuous rooms, each furnished and decorated according to a particular Northwest theme. Thanks to some clever architecture, all the rooms are awash in natural light and have fabulous ocean views. In addition, all have wood-burning fireplaces and sitting areas, all but one have sun decks, and most have Jacuzzis or soaker tubs. The other half of the Harbour House's reputation comes from the outstanding restaurant (p. 725). Breakfast (served in your room) and a picnic lunch is included in the room rate. This is the most environmentally conscious hotel on Vancouver Island, with its own bioreactor to process waste water for reuse in the gardens, and biopermeable parking areas.

1528 Whiffen Spit Rd., Sooke, BC V0S 1N0. (©) **800/889-9688** or 250/642-3421. Fax 250/642-6988. www.sooke harbourhouse.com. 28 units. C$175–C$575 (US$175–US$575/£88–£288) double. Rates include full breakfast and picnic lunch (no picnic lunch weekdays Nov–Apr). MC, V. Free parking. Take the Island Hwy. (Hwy. 1) to the Sooke/Colwood turnoff (junction Hwy. 14); follow Hwy. 14 to Sooke; about 1.6km (1 mile) past the town's only traffic light, turn left onto Whiffen Spit Rd. **Amenities:** Restaurant; nearby golf course; access to nearby health club; spa; sauna; limited room service; babysitting; laundry service; nonsmoking rooms. *In room:* Wi-Fi, CD player, minibar, fridge, coffeemaker, hair dryer, iron/ironing board.

Moderate
Birds of a Feather Oceanfront Bed & Breakfast   Located on an oceanfront lagoon 20 minutes west of Victoria, this quiet, eco-friendly B&B run by Annette

Moen and Dieter Gerhard is super for bird-watchers and nature lovers. The lagoon is on the Pacific Flyway and attracts thousands of migratory birds and other wildlife. The three guest rooms, in their own separate wing, are furnished with Arts & Crafts–inspired beds and comfy leather chairs; they all have a good-sized bathroom, kitchen, gas fireplace, and patio area with views of the water. The Honeymoon Suite is flooded with light on two sides; the family room has two levels with a spiral staircase.

206 Portsmouth Dr., Victoria, BC V9C 1R9. ✆ 800/730-4790 or 250/391-8889. www.birdsofafeather.ca. 3 units; C$145–C$210 (US$145–US$210/£73–£105) double. Rates include full breakfast. AE, MC, V. From Victoria take Hwy. 1 to exit 10 (Colwood/View Royal), turn left at Knob Hill St., left on Ocean Blvd., right on Lagoon Rd. right on Heatherbell, right on Portsmouth Dr. **Amenities:** Complimentary bikes, canoes, kayaks; nonsmoking rooms. *In room:* TV/DVD, Wi-Fi, kitchen w/fridge, microwave, tea/coffeemaker, hair dryer.

Inexpensive
University of Victoria Housing, Food, and Conference Services (Value One of the best deals going is found at the University of Victoria, when classes aren't in session and summer visitors are welcomed. All rooms have single or twin beds and basic furnishings, and there are bathrooms, pay phones, and TV lounges on every floor. Linens, towels, and soap are provided. The suites are an extremely good value—each has four bedrooms, a kitchen, a living room, and 1½ bathrooms. For C$5 (US$5/£2.50) extra per day, you can make use of the many on-campus athletic facilities. Each of the 28 buildings has a coin laundry. The disadvantage, of course, is that the U. Vic. campus is a painfully long way from everywhere—the city center is about a half-hour drive away.

P.O. Box 1700, Sinclair at Finerty Rd., Victoria, BC V8W 2Y2. ✆ 250/721-8395. Fax 250/721-8930. www.hfcs.uvic.ca. 898 units. May–Aug C$48 (US$48/£24) single; C$58 (US$58/£29) twin; C$185 (US$185/£93) suite (sleeps 4 people). Rates include full breakfast and taxes. MC, V. Parking C$5 (US$5/£2.50). Closed Sept–Apr. Bus: 4 or 14 to University of Victoria. **Amenities:** Indoor pool; access to athletic facilities; coin laundry; nonsmoking rooms.

WHERE TO DINE
The dining scene in Victoria isn't nearly as sophisticated as Vancouver's, but more and more attention is being paid to the glories of fresh local produce. Good wines are now produced in the Cowichan Valley, and cheesemakers on Salt Spring Island are producing some delicious cheeses. Though the city isn't as mad about multicourse "tasting menus" as Vancouver, there's still plenty to taste. The city offers a cornucopia of culinary styles from around the world. Note that the touristy restaurants along Wharf Street serve up mediocre food for folks they know they'll never have to see again. One lingering aspect of English cuisine is the delicious custom of afternoon tea. American visitors in particular should give it a try. For the best places to try, see "Taking Afternoon Tea" on p. 726. Most restaurants close at 10pm, especially on weekdays. Reservations are strongly recommended for prime sunset seating during summer.

THE INNER HARBOUR & THE OLD TOWN
Expensive
The Blue Crab Bar and Grill 🎣 SEAFOOD One of Victoria's best bets for seafood, the Blue Crab combines excellent fresh ingredients and straightforward preparation. It also has a great view—floatplanes slip in and out while you're dining, little ferries chug across the harbor, and the sun sets slowly over the Sooke Hills. Like other top-end restaurants in town, the Crab sources much of its ingredients locally, but you might also find scallops from Alaska or lamb from New Zealand. For lunch or dinner you can find tasty offerings such as seafood chowder or a smoked salmon and crab sandwich. The award-winning wine list (*Wine Spectator* Award of Excellence

2003–05) features mid-range and top-end vintages, drawn mostly from B.C., Washington, and California. The service is deft and obliging.

146 Kingston St., in the Coast Hotel. ⓒ 250/480-1999. www.bluecrab.ca. Reservations recommended. Main courses C$25–C$34 (US$25–US$34/£13–£17). AE, DC, MC, V. Daily 6:30am–10pm (dinner from 5pm). Bus: 30 to Erie St. or harbor miniferry to Coast Hotel.

Brasserie L'Ecole 🦐🦐 FRENCH   In the overheated world of food fashion, it's so refreshing to find simple French bistro fare deftly prepared and served at amazingly reasonable prices. Honesty is what's on offer at this warm, comfortable restaurant, the brainchild of longtime Victoria chef Sean Brenner. L'Ecole's menu changes daily, depending entirely on what comes in fresh from Victoria's hinterland farms. Preparation is simple, no big reductions or complicated *jus,* just shellfish, local fish, meats with red-wine sauces, and fresh vegetables with vinaigrettes. Quality is excellent; L'Ecole has won a bevy of awards in its few short years on the scene. The wine list is small, with no hugely expensive vintages, but has good straightforward wine to match the excellent food. Very satisfying in every way.

1715 Government St. ⓒ 250/475-6262. www.lecole.ca. Reservations recommended. Main courses C$19 (US$19/£9.50). AE, MC, V. Tues–Sat 5:30–11pm.

Café Brio 🦐🦐🦐 PACIFIC NORTHWEST/ITALIAN   Having just celebrated its 10th anniversary, Café Brio remains one of Victoria's best and buzziest spots for casual but top-flight dining. The Tuscan-influenced cuisine strongly reflects the seasons, fresh local meats and produce, and Pacific seafood. The menu changes daily, but appetizers always include locally harvested oysters, a wonderful house-made paprika sausage, and a delicious charcuterie plate (the chef makes all his charcuterie on the premises). For entrees choose from handmade pasta (such as fresh herb-ricotta agnolotti), roasted or poached wild fish, or a "local farm plate." The wine list is excellent, with an impressive selection of B.C. and international reds and whites. The service is deft, friendly, and knowledgeable, and the kitchen stays open as long as guests keep ordering.

944 Fort St. ⓒ 250/383-0009. www.cafe-brio.com. Reservations recommended. Main courses C$17–C$30 (US$17–US$30/£8.50–£15). AE, MC, V. Daily 5:30–9:30pm.

Camille's 🦐🦐🦐 PACIFIC NORTHWEST   The most romantic of Victoria's restaurants, Camille's is also one of the very best. Tucked away in two rooms beneath the old Law Chambers, its decor contrasts white linen with century-old exposed brick, stained-glass lamps, and candlelight. Chef and owner David Mincey was one of the founders of a Vancouver Island farm cooperative that brings local farmers together with local restaurants, so you're usually dining on foods found within a 100-mile radius of the restaurant. The ever-changing menu displays Mincey's love for cheeky invention and the seasonal bounty of Vancouver Island. To sample a bit of everything try the five-course tasting menu, a fantastic bargain at C$50 (US$50/£25), C$75 (US$75/£37) with wine pairings. The reasonable and extensive wine list comes with liner notes that are amusing and informative. A meal here is a quiet, memorable occasion abetted by the professionalism of the staff.

45 Bastion Sq. ⓒ 250/381-3433. www.camillesrestaurant.com. Reservations recommended. Main courses C$24–C$34 (US$24–US$34/£12–£17). AE, MC, V. Tues–Sun 5:30–10pm.

Moderate
Canoe 🦐 PUB GRUB/PACIFIC NORTHWEST   What was once a Victorian power station is now one of the loveliest and liveliest brewpub restaurants in Victoria,

with a fabulous outdoor patio overlooking the harbor toward the Johnson Street Bridge and an industrial-inspired interior with massive masonry walls and heavy timber crossbeams. Casual Canoe is popular because it basically has something for every taste, and everything is very tasty. The kitchen offers intriguing variations on standard pub fare and bar snacks, including thin-crust pizzas (but with grilled lamb or chile prawns) and classic burgers. Head upstairs for finer fare such as premium top sirloin steak or seafood curry masala. The ingredients for every dish are fresh and local, the beer is excellent, and there's also a small, select, award-winning wine list.

450 Swift St. ℂ 250/361-1940. www.canoebrewpub.com. Reservations recommended for weekend dinner and Sun brunch. Main courses C$11–C$32 (US$11–US$32/£5.50–£16); pub fare and bar snacks C$6–C$17 (US$6–US$17/£3–£8.50). AE, MC, V. Daily 11am–midnight.

Il Terrazzo Ristorante ⭐⭐ ITALIAN   This charming spot in a converted heritage building off Waddington Alley is always a top contender for Victoria's best Italian restaurant. You can be assured of a good meal here. The northern Italian cooking includes wood-oven-roasted meats, fish and pizzas as well as homemade pastas. There's an emphasis on fresh produce and local seafood, with appetizers such as artichokes stuffed with salmon and crabmeat drizzled with a light lemon-cream sauce, and entrees like salmon crusted with almond and black pepper and baked in the wood-burning oven, or a fabulous rack of lamb. The mood is bustling and upbeat; there's an atmospheric courtyard furnished with flowers, marble tables, wrought-iron chairs, and heaters. The wine list is enormous, with some 1,200 vintages. Service is friendly and helpful.

555 Johnson St., off Waddington Alley. ℂ 250/361-0028. www.ilterrazzo.com. Reservations recommended. Main courses C$19–C$37 (US$19–US$37/£9.50–£19). AE, MC, V. Mon–Sat 11:30am–3pm (Oct–Apr no lunch on Sat); daily 5–10pm. Bus: 5.

The Tapa Bar (Finds) TAPAS   The perfect meal for the commitment shy, tapas are small and flavorful plates that you combine together to make a meal. Tapas to be sampled in this warm and welcoming spot include fried calamari, palm hearts, and grilled portobello mushrooms. Whatever else you order, however, don't pass up on the *gambas al ajillo*—shrimp in a rich broth of garlic. The martini list is likely longer than the list of wines, but between the two there's enough joy juice to keep the room buzzing till the witching hour.

620 Trounce Alley. ℂ 250/383-0013. Tapas plates C$7–C$15 (US$7–US$15/£3.50–£7.50). AE, MC, V. Mon–Thurs 11:30am–11pm; Fri–Sat 11:30am–midnight; Sun 11am–10pm.

Zambri's ⭐ (Finds) ITALIAN   This little deli-restaurant in a strip mall off Yates Street has earned numerous accolades for its honest and fresh Italian cuisine served in an unpretentious, no-nonsense style. The lunch menu, served cafeteria style, includes daily pasta specials and a handful of entrees such as fresh rockfish or salmon. In the evenings, the atmosphere is slightly more formal with table service and a regularly changing a la carte menu. Menu items veer from penne with sausage and tomato to pasta with chicken liver pâté or peas and Gorgonzola. Many diners come for the three-course dinner (C$40–C$45/US$40–US$45/£20–£23).

110-911 Yates St. ℂ 250/360-1171. Reservations not accepted. Lunch C$8–C$14 (US$8–US$14/£4–£7); dinner main courses C$22–C$25 (US$22–US$25/£11–£13). MC, V. Tues–Sat 11:30am–2:30pm and 5–9pm.

Inexpensive

J&J Wonton Noodle House ⭐ (Finds) CHINESE   This place doesn't go overboard on the atmosphere (it's perfectly pleasant), and you won't find better noodles anywhere in Victoria. The kitchen is glassed in so you can watch the chefs spinning out noodles. Lunch specials—which feature different fresh seafood every day—are good and cheap, so expect a line of locals at the door. If you miss the specials, noodle soups, chow mein, and other dishes are also quick, delicious, and inexpensive. Dinner is pricier.

1012 Fort St. ℂ 250/383-0680. Main courses C$11–C$16 (US$11–US$16/£5.50–£8); lunch specials C$6–C$13 (US$6–US$13/£3–£6.50). MC, V. Tues–Sat 11am–2pm and 4:30–8:30pm. Bus: 5.

rebar *(Kids)* VEGETARIAN   Even if you're not hungry, it's worth dropping in here for a juice blend—say grapefruit, banana, melon, and pear with bee pollen or blue-green algae for added oomph. If you're hungry, then rejoice: rebar is the city's premier dispenser of vegetarian comfort food. Disturbingly wholesome as that may sound, rebar is not only tasty, but fun, and a great spot to take the kids for brunch or breakfast. The room—in the basement of an 1890s heritage building—is bright and funky, with loads of cake tins glued to the walls. The service is friendly and casual. The food tends toward the simple and wholesome, including quesadillas, omelets, and crisp salads. Juices are still the crown jewels, with more than 80 blends on the menu.

50 Bastion Sq. ℂ 250/361-9223. www.rebarmodernfood.com. Main courses C$7.50–C$16 (US$7.50–US$16/£3.75–£8). AE, MC, V. Mon–Thurs 8:30am–9pm; Fri–Sat 8:30am–10pm; Sun 8:30am–3:30pm. Reduced hours in the winter. Bus: 5.

OUTSIDE THE CENTRAL AREA
Very Expensive
The Aerie *(★★★)* FRENCH   The dining room of this Relais & Châteaux hotel (p. 720) enjoys a breathtaking view over Finlayson Inlet, the Strait of Juan de Fuca, and, on a clear day, the Olympic Mountains. The room itself is decorated with a 14-carat gold-leaf ceiling, crystal chandeliers, and a large open-hearth fireplace. As for the food—well, eating at this award-winning restaurant is definitely a culinary event. Chef Christophe Letard's creations combine west coast freshness with unmistakably French accents. Guests choose from a la carte selections or a seven-course Discovery Tasting menu. A recent tasting menu included sautéed spot prawns from Finlayson Arm, steamed halibut pavé, and Cowichan Valley duck breast. Excellent wine pairings, featuring many local vintages, help to make meals even more memorable. The service is impeccable.

600 Ebedora Lane, Malahat. ℂ 800/518-1933 or 250/743-7115. www.aerie.bc.ca. Reservations required. Main courses C$36–C$42 (US$36–US$42/£18–£21); tasting menu C$100 (US$100/£50). AE, DC, MC, V. Daily noon–3pm and 5:30–8:30pm; Sun brunch noon–2pm. Take Hwy. 1 to the Spectacle Lake turnoff; take the 1st right and follow the winding driveway.

Sooke Harbour House *(★★★)* PACIFIC NORTHWEST   The dining room of this celebrated restaurant/hotel (p. 721) offers spectacular waterfront views of Sooke Harbour, a relaxed atmosphere, and some of the best and most inventive food in Canada. Dishes on the daily-changing, seasonally adjusted menu are prepared with care, imagination, and flair. Ingredients are resolutely local (many come from the inn's own organic garden or from the ocean at the Harbour House's doorstep). Depending on the season, dishes might include grilled flounder with hazelnut, arugula and cheese pesto or grilled pork tenderloin with a red-wine meat-stock reduction and dried cherry and thyme compute. The presentation is always interesting, and the staff is knowledgeable and professional. The wine cellar is extensive (one of the best in Canada), and the pairings are particularly well chosen. There is a four-course set menu, but for the best of everything, and the most memorable meal, order the Gastronomical Menu.

Moments Taking Afternoon Tea

Okay, so it's expensive and touristy. Go anyway. Though the caloric intake at a top-quality tea can be substantial, it's really more about the ritual than the potential weight gain. For that reason, you don't want to go to just any old teahouse. Note that in summer it's a good idea to book at least a week ahead, if not longer.

If you want the best experience and can afford the price, head to **The Fairmont Empress** &&&, 721 Government St. (© **250/384-8111**; bus no. 5 to the Convention Centre), where tea is served in the Tea Lobby, a busy and beautifully ornate room at the front of the hotel. Price depends on the time and season, and runs from C$38 to C$55 (US$38–US$55/£19–£28). For that, you'll be pampered with fresh berries and cream; sandwiches of smoked salmon, cucumber, and carrot and ginger; and scones with strawberry preserves and thick Jersey cream. Even the tea is a special house blend. When you leave, you'll receive a gift of 10 bags to brew at home. There are seatings every 15 minutes four times a day starting at noon, 1:30, 3, and 4:30pm; reservations are essential.

More affordable, less crowded, and just as historic is tea on the lawn of **Point Ellice House**, 2616 Pleasant St. (© **250/380-6506**), where the cream of Victoria society used to gather in the early 1900s. On the Gorge waterway, Point Ellice is just a 5-minute trip by ferry from the Inner Harbour, or take bus no. 14 to Pleasant Street. Afternoon tea costs C$22 (US$22/£11) and includes a half-hour tour of the mansion and gardens, plus the opportunity to play a game of croquet. Hours are daily 10am to 4pm (tea served 11am–4pm) May through the first Monday of September; phone ahead for Christmas hours. If you want your tea in a historic garden setting, head over to **Abkhazi Garden** (p. 702), 1964 Fairfield Rd. (© **250/598-8096**; by car or bus no. 1 from downtown), where tea is served daily in the small, modernist house built by Prince and Princess Abkhazi.

With impeccably maintained gardens as a backdrop, "Afternoon Tea at the Gardens" at the **Butchart Gardens Dining Room Restaurant** &&&, 800 Benvenuto Ave. (© **250/652-4422**; bus no. 75), is a memorable experience. Sitting inside the Butchart mansion and looking out over the flowers, you can savor this fine tradition for C$25 (US$25/£13) per person. Tea is served daily noon to 5pm year-round; reservations recommended. Call ahead for winter hours.

What the **White Heather Tea Room** &&, 1885 Oak Bay Rd. (© **250/595-8020**), lacks in old-time atmosphere, it more than makes up for with the sheer quality and value of the tea, and the charm of proprietress and tea mistress Agnes. What's more, there are numerous options on offer, all of them less expensive than a similar experience at The Empress. For those feeling not so peckish, there's the Wee Tea at C$12 (US$12/£6). For those a little hungrier, there's the Not So Wee Tea at C$16 (US$16/£8). For the borderline starving, there's the Big Muckle Great Tea for Two at C$37 (US$37/£18). The White Heather is open Tuesday through Saturday 10am to 5pm.

1528 Whiffen Spit Rd., Sooke. ⓒ **800/889-9688** or 250/642-3421. www.sookeharbourhouse.com. Reservations required. Set menus C$75–C$100 (US$75–US$100/£37–£50). MC, V. Daily 5:30–9pm. Take the Island Hwy. to the Sooke/Colwood turnoff (Junction Hwy. 14); continue on Hwy. 14 to Sooke; about 2km (1¼ mile) past the town's only traffic light, turn left onto Whiffen Spit Rd.

Moderate

SeaGrille 🐾 PACIFIC NORTHWEST   The dining room of beautiful Brentwood Bay Lodge (p. 721), about a 20-minute drive north of Victoria, is all warm wood with giant windows overlooking Saanich Inlet. The food prepared here emphasizes fresh, seasonal seafood such as seared B.C. salmon or halibut and king crab risotto. There are also steaks, chops, and chicken breast, plus a vegetarian special. You can also order from the more casual pub menu, which includes thin-crust pizzas and staples such as fish and chips and a halibut burger.

In Brentwood Bay Lodge and Spa, 849 Verdier Ave., Brentwood Bay. ⓒ **888/544-2079** or 250/544-5100. www. brentwoodbaylodge.com. Reservations recommended. Main courses C$11–C$34 (US$11–US$34/£5.50–£17). AE, DC, MC, V. Daily 5–10pm. From Victoria, take Pat Bay Hwy. north to Keating Crossroads, turn left (west) to Saanich Rd., turn right (south) to Verdier Ave.

VICTORIA AFTER DARK

Victoria is never going to set the world on fire, but taken together the U Vic. students and the tourists and a small but dedicated cadre of Victoria revelers form a critical mass large enough to keep a number of small but steady reactions going in various parts of the city. You just have to know where to look. *Monday* magazine's (www. mondaymag.com) listings section provides near-comprehensive coverage of what's happening in town.

You can buy tickets and get schedules from the **Tourism Victoria Travel Visitor Centre,** 812 Wharf St. (ⓒ **800/663-3883** or 250/382-1131; bus: 5 or 30), open daily 9am to 5pm (summer till 9pm).

THE PERFORMING ARTS   The **Royal Theatre,** 805 Broughton St. (ⓒ **250/ 361-0820;** box office 250/386-6121; www.rmts.bc.ca; bus: 5 or 30), hosts events such as Victoria Symphony concerts, dance recitals, and touring stage plays. The box office is at the **McPherson Playhouse,** 3 Centennial Sq., at Pandora Avenue and Government Street (ⓒ **250/386-6121;** bus: 5 or 30), which is also home to Victoria's Pacific Opera and the Victoria Operatic Society. The box office is open Monday through Saturday from 9:30am to 5:30pm.

The **Belfry Theatre,** 1291 Gladstone St. (ⓒ **250/385-6815;** www.belfry.bc.ca; bus: 1 or 2), is a nationally acclaimed theatrical group that stages four productions October to April and a summer show in August. The **Victoria Fringe Festival** (ⓒ **888/FRINGE-2** or 250/383-2663; www.victoriafringe.com) presents short, inexpensive original fare at various venues from late August to mid-September.

The **Pacific Opera Victoria,** 1316B Government St. (ⓒ **250/385-0222;** www. pov.bc.ca; box office 250/386-6121; bus: 5 or 30), presents productions in October, February, and April. Performances are normally at the McPherson Playhouse and Royal Theatre. **The Victoria Operatic Society,** 798 Fairview Rd. (ⓒ **250/381-1021;** www.vos.bc.ca), stages old-time Broadway musicals and other popular fare year-round at the McPherson Playhouse.

The **Victoria Symphony Orchestra,** 846 Broughton St. (ⓒ **250/385-9771;** www. victoriasymphony.bc.ca; bus: 5 or 30), kicks off its season on the first Sunday of August with Symphony Splash, a free concert performed on a barge in the Inner Harbour. Regular performances begin in October and last to May.

LIVE-MUSIC CLUBS   **Legends,** 919 Douglas St. (© **250/383-7137;** bus: 5 or 30), is the live-music venue below street level in the Strathcona Hotel. It covers the gamut from Afro-pop to blues to zydeco. **Lucky,** 517 Yates St. (© **250/382-5825**), is currently the hottest spot in Victoria. This low cavernous space has a pleasantly grungy feel like Seattle's Pioneer Square. Lucky's DJs spin house and trance on the weekends, with bands often showing up earlier in the week. **Steamers,** 570 Yates St. (© **250/381-4340;** bus: 5 or 30), is the city's premium blues bar. Cover hovers around C$5 (US$5/£2.50).

LOUNGES, BARS & PUBS   A truly unique experience, the **Bengal Lounge** in the Empress hotel, 721 Government St. (© **250/384-8111;** bus: 5 or 30), is one of the last outposts of the old Empire, except the martinis are ice cold and jazz plays in the background (on weekends it's live in the foreground). A restaurant by day, **The Reef** (533 Yates St.; © **250/388-5375;** bus: 6) transforms into a funky reggae lounge after dark, with great martinis, good tunes, and a DJ thrown in now and again just to spice things up. **Canoe,** 450 Swift St. (© **250/361-1940;** bus: 6), is one of the most pleasant spots to go to hoist a pint after a long day's sightseeing. **Big Bad John's,** 919 Douglas St., in the Strathcona Hotel (© **250/383-7137;** bus: 5 or 30), is Victoria's only hillbilly bar—a low, dark warren of a place, with inches of discarded peanut shells on the plank floor and a crowd of drunk and happy rowdies.

Overlooking Victoria Harbour on the west side of the Songhees Point Development, **Spinnakers Brewpub,** 308 Catherine St. (© **250/386-BREW** or 250/386-2739; bus: 6 or harbor ferry), has one of the best views and some of the best beer in town. **Med Grill@Mosaic,** 1063 Fort St. (© **250/381-3417**), is a coolly contemporary bistro by day and turns into a loungy martini spot at night (happy hour nightly 9–10pm), when DJs spin mellow sounds. **Swans Pub,** 506 Pandora Ave. (© **250/ 361-3310**), is an enjoyable and convivial drinking spot in Swans Hotel, with a collection of Pacific Northwest and First Nations art and beer brewed on-site; there's live entertainment every night.

DANCE CLUBS   Most dance clubs are open Monday to Saturday to 2am and Sunday to midnight. **Sugar,** 858 Yates St. (© **250/920-9950**), open Thursday through Saturday, offers the chance to dance the night away under an old-fashioned disco ball; line-ups start at 10pm and DJs spin mostly hip-hop, house, and Top 40 tunes (C$3–C$6/US$3–US$6/£1.50–£3 cover Fri–Sat). The **One Lounge,** 1318 Broad St. (© **250/384-3557;** www.theonelounge.com), spins Top 40 dance tracks for a late-20s-to-early-30s crowd; the format depends on the night of the week (C$5/US$5/£2.50 cover on weekends). **The Red Jacket,** 751 View St. (© **250/384-2582**), opened in 2004 and quickly became the hoppin' hot spot thanks to a Friday night bash featuring some of Victoria's finest urban DJ talent.

GAY & LESBIAN BARS   **Hush,** 1325 Government St. (© **250/385-0566;** C$5/US$5/£2.50 cover on weekends), a gay but straight-friendly space, features top-end touring DJs.

A SIDE TRIP FROM VICTORIA: GOLDSTREAM PROVINCIAL PARK

The tranquil arboreal setting of Goldstream Provincial Park overflowed with prospectors during the 1860s gold-rush days. Trails take you past abandoned mine shafts and tunnels, as well as 600-year-old stands of towering Douglas fir, lodgepole pine, red cedar, indigenous yew, and arbutus trees. The **Gold Mine Trail** leads to Niagara Creek and the abandoned mine that was operated by Lt. Peter Leech, a Royal Engineer who

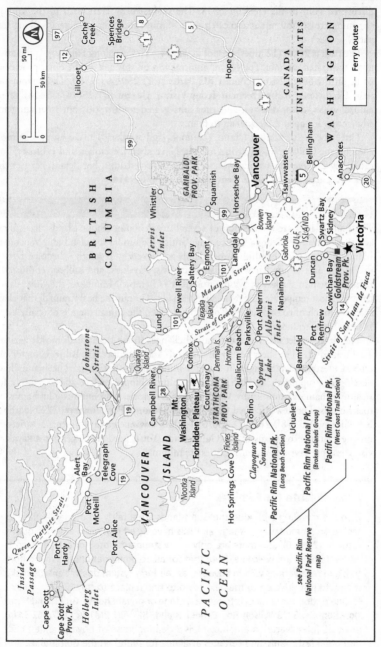

discovered gold in the creek in 1858. The **Goldstream Trail** leads to the salmon spawning areas. (You might also catch sight of mink and river otters racing along this path.)

The park is 20km (12 miles) west of downtown Victoria along Highway 1; the drive takes about half an hour. For general information on this and all the other provincial parks on the South Island, contact **BC Parks** at ✆ **250/391-2300.** Throughout the year, Goldstream Park's **Freeman King Visitor Centre** (✆ **250/478-9414**) offers guided walks, talks, displays, and programs geared toward kids but interesting for adults, too. It's open daily 9:30am to 6pm.

Three species of salmon (chum, Chinook, and steelhead) make **annual salmon runs** up the Goldstream River in October, November, December, and February. You can easily observe this natural wonder along the riverbanks. For details, contact the park's **Freeman King Visitor Centre** at ✆ **250/478-9414.**

3 The Gulf Islands

The Gulf Islands are a collection of several dozen mountainous islands that sprawl across the Strait of Georgia between the British Columbia mainland and Vancouver Island. While only a handful of the islands are served by regularly scheduled ferries, this entire area is popular with boaters, cyclists, kayakers, and sailboat enthusiasts. Lying in the rain shadow of Washington State's Olympic Mountains, the Gulf Islands have the most temperate climate in all of Canada, without the heavy rainfall that characterizes much of coastal British Columbia. In fact, the climate here is officially listed as semi-Mediterranean!

The past few decades have seen radical changes to the traditional, mostly agricultural, island life: The sheer beauty of the land- and seascapes, the balmy climate, and relaxed lifestyle have brought in a major influx of new residents. The islands have developed a reputation as both a countercultural hippie enclave and a getaway for wealthy urbanites from nearby Vancouver and Victoria, who build trophy homes on rocky bluffs. The newly formed **Gulf Islands National Park Reserve,** 2220 Harbour Rd., Sidney, BC V8L 2P6 (✆ **250/654-4000;** www.pc.gc.ca), protects a variety of unique marine ecosystems in the Gulf Islands. You'll need scuba gear or a kayak to visit these preserves, as visitor facilities are minimal.

Tips **A Note for Families**

If you're traveling with kids, the Gulf Islands are a fairly inhospitable place to secure accommodations. Nearly all B&Bs have listed minimum ages for guests (usually 12 or 16), and there are only a few standard motels or cottage resorts where families are welcome. Note that for all accommodations, it's mandatory to make reservations well in advance, as the ferry system doesn't exactly make it easy to just drive on to the next town to find a place to stay.

One option for families is to rent a cottage or private home. **Gulf Island Vacation Rentals,** 5402 Wilson Rd., Pender Island, BC V0N 2M1 (✆ **877/662-3414;** www.gulfislandvacationrentals.com), is a clearinghouse of private homes, bed-and-breakfast rooms, and cottages available for rental on the Gulf Islands.

ESSENTIALS
GETTING THERE
BY FERRY   BC Ferries (© 888/BCFERRY in B.C., or 250/386-3431; www.bcferries. bc.ca) operates five different runs to the southern Gulf Islands, from Tsawwassen on the British Columbia mainland, and from Swartz Bay, Crofton, and Nanaimo on Vancouver Island. Be aware that the ferries are not particularly large; to ensure that you make the one you want, arrive at least 15 minutes early (30 min. on summer weekends). You can make reservations on the routes from Tsawwassen, but not on the other runs.

There are separate fares for drivers, passengers, and vehicles, plus fees for bikes, kayaks, and canoes on most runs. Sample peak-season fares: a car and two passengers from Swartz Bay to Salt Spring Island, C$43 (US$43/£22); a single foot passenger, C$9 (US$9/£4.50).

If you are planning to visit several islands, consider purchasing a 4- or 7-day **Sail-Pass** (www.bcferries.com/sailpass) from BC Ferries, which can reduce both fares and confusion. The SailPass is a one-price ticket that allows you to travel along 20 ferry routes in southern B.C., including those routes servicing the Gulf Islands (except for travel along the Inside Passage routes or to the Queen Charlottes). The ticket includes passage for a vehicle plus two adults (more adults can be added to the ticket by paying more). A 4-day ticket is C$169 (US$169/£85), and a 7-day ticket is C$199 (US$199/£100), which, given normal use, will represent a savings of about one-third over regular fares. The only hitch is that you need to prepurchase the SailPass—you can't buy one at the ferry terminal. They can be ordered from the BC Ferry website above (allow a week for delivery) or purchased the same day from the **Tourism Vancouver Info Centre,** 200 Burrard St. (© **604/683-2000**), open Monday to Saturday 8:30am to 6:30pm; **Peace Arch Provincial Visitor Info Centre,** 356 Hwy. 99, Surrey (© **604/531-7352**), daily 9am to 5pm; and **Vancouver International Airport Visitor Info Centre** (© **604/207-0953**), daily 8am to midnight.

BY PLANE   A number of commuter airlines offer regular floatplane service from either Vancouver Harbour or Vancouver International Airport. One-way tickets to the islands usually cost C$79 to C$89 (US$79–US$89/£40–£45) per person, not a bad fare when you consider the time and hassle involved in taking a ferry. However, floatplanes are small and seats sell out quickly, so reserve ahead of time. Call **Harbour Air Seaplanes** (© **800/665-0212** or 604/688-1277; www.harbour-air.com), or **Seair Seaplanes** (© **800/447-3247** or 604/273-8900; www.seairseaplanes.com).

VISITOR INFORMATION
For general information on the Gulf Islands, contact **Tourism Vancouver Island,** Suite 203, 335 Wesley St., Nanaimo (© **250/754-3500;** www.vancouverisland.travel). Another good comprehensive resource is **www.gulfislands.com**.

SALT SPRING ISLAND
The largest of the Gulf Islands, Salt Spring is—to the outside world—a bucolic getaway filled with artists, sheep pastures, and cozy B&Bs. While this image is mostly true, Salt Spring is also a busy cultural crossroads: Movie stars, retirees, high-tech telecommuters, and hippie farmers all rub shoulders here. The hilly terrain and deep forests afford equal privacy for all lifestyles, and that's the way the residents like it.

With a year-round population of 10,000 residents, Salt Spring is served by three ferries, making it by far the easiest of the Gulf Islands to visit. Not coincidentally, Salt Spring also has the most facilities for visitors. The center of island life is **Ganges,** a little

---

Moments **The Mother of All Saturday Markets**

Not to be missed is **Market in the Park** ✸ (www.saltspringmarket.com), held April through October on Saturdays from 8am to 4pm in the Ganges' waterfront Centennial Park. The market brings together a lively mix of craftspeople, farmers, musicians, and bakers. It's great fun, and a good chance to shop for local products. As you might guess, the people-watching is matchless.

---

village with gas stations, grocery stores, and banks, all overlooking a busy pleasure-boat harbor. You can easily spend from an hour to most of a day poking around the art galleries, boutiques, and coffee shops here.

In fact, the island is famed across Canada as an artists' colony and many people visit expressly to see the studios of local artists and craftspeople. Stop by the visitor center for the **Studio Tour Map,** which pinpoints nearly 50 island artists—glass blowers, painters, ceramists, weavers, carvers, and sculptors, many of whom are available to visit.

KAYAKING   Island Escapades, 118 Natalie Lane (✆ **888/529-2567** or 250/537-2537; www.islandescapades.com), offers a 2-hour introduction to kayaking on the placid waters of Cusheon Lake, for C$45 (US$45/£23), with guided 3-hour ocean tours for C$60 (US$60/£30). **Sea Otter Kayaking,** 149 Lower Ganges Rd. (✆ **877/537-5678;** www.saltspring.com/kayaking), rents kayaks and canoes, starting at C$55 (US$55/£28) a day. Guided tours are C$55 (US$55/£28) for 3 hours. **Saltspring Kayaking,** 2923 Fulford-Ganges Rd. (✆ **250/537-4664;** www.saltspring.com/sskayak), offers rentals and 2-hour sunset harbor tours from C$38 (US$38/£19). They also offer 2-day guided tours of the new Gulf Islands National Park for C$275 (US$275/£138).

WHERE TO STAY

Ruckle Provincial Park, off Beaver Point Road (✆ **250/391-2300;** www.env.gov.bc.ca/bcparks), has 70 walk-in sites and eight reservable sites for C$14 (US$14/£7).

Hastings House Country Estate ✸✸   In the 1930s, an English couple built a replica of a 16th-century Sussex estate, now known as the Manor House, on the site of an old Hudson's Bay Company trading post. Almost all of the original structures have been converted into beautifully furnished accommodations. For example, the original Manor House now serves as the restaurant and library, with two guest suites on the second floor; the farmhouse contains two two-story suites; and the old trading post is now a cottage suite. Other guest rooms are in the old barn, a cottage, and in newly constructed Hillside suites.

While the rooms are full of character, what really sets Hastings House apart is its incredible 10-hectare (25-acre) setting. This charming inn is just east of Ganges, in a forested valley that drops directly onto Ganges Harbour.

The **Hastings House Dining Room** ✸✸ is easily the most elegant eating experience on Salt Spring, with both a four-course daily-changing chef's tasting menu (C$95/US$95/£48) and a seasonal a la carte menu.

160 Upper Ganges Rd., Salt Spring Island, BC V8K 2S2. ✆ **800/661-9255** or 250/537-2362. Fax 250/537-5333. www.hastingshouse.com. 18 units. From C$275 (US$275/£138) double. Extra person C$65 (US$65/£33) per night.

Weekly cottage rental available. Off-season 2-, 3-, and 5-night packages available. AE, MC, V. Closed mid-Nov to mid-Mar. Children must be 16 or older. **Amenities:** Restaurant; golf course and tennis courts nearby; spa including massage; free bikes and scooters; laundry service; dry cleaning, Wi-Fi access. *In room:* CD player, dataport, minibar, hair dryer, iron.

Old Farmhouse B&B ⓐⓐ   One of the best-loved accommodations in the Gulf Islands, the Old Farmhouse combines top-quality lodgings and great multicourse breakfasts. This Victorian-era homestead was built in 1894 amid 1.2 hectares (3 acres) of meadows and orchards—in fact, the enormous 500-year-old arbutus (or madrona) tree in the front yard may be the world's largest. The bedrooms are in a stylistically harmonious guesthouse adjoining the original farmhouse. Each room has a balcony or patio; the decor incorporates just the right country touches—floral wallpaper, wainscoted walls—without lapsing into Laura Ashley excess. The farm's old chicken house has been transformed into the charming Chateau de Poulet, a cozy one-bedroom suite with a king bed. The extensive meadows are perfect for lolling with a book or playing a game of croquet.

1077 N. End Rd., Salt Spring Island, BC V8K 1L9. ⓒ 250/537-4113. Fax 250/537-4969. www.oldfarmhouse.ca. 5 units. C$185 (US$185/£93) double. Rates include full breakfast. MC, V. Call to inquire about children and pets. **Amenities:** Common room; Internet access; nonsmoking facility. *In room:* Hair dryer, no phone.

WHERE TO DINE
Artist's Bistro ⓐ INTERNATIONAL   Alfresco waterfront dining is just one of the delights of Artist's Bistro. This classy restaurant combines Continental flair with Northwest fish and produce, resulting in an outstanding menu rich in temptation. Start with smoked salmon and avocado salad with horseradish dressing, or try Gambas Pil Pil—sizzling shrimp in garlic, hot peppers, and fresh herbs. Pork tenderloin Normandy is a fall favorite, served with apples in cider, brandy, and cream sauce. The bright dining room is festive in any season, and service is exceptional.

Grace Point Sq., Ganges. ⓒ 250/537-1701. www.artistsbistro.com. Reservations recommended. Main courses C$26–C$45 (US$26–US$45/£13–£23). MC, V. Wed–Mon 6–9pm. Above Ganges harbor near the intersection of Fulford Ganges Rd. and Purvis Rd.

Calvin's ⓐ CANADIAN   If you ask a local where to eat in Ganges, chances are he or she will recommend Calvin's, a friendly, bustling restaurant with good prices and flavorful food. Ingredients are fresh and local, like the island lamb available in multiple preparations. Wild fish is often featured on the broad menu that ranges from traditional schnitzel to Northwest bouillabaisse, a tangy tomato broth rich with salmon, mussels, clams, and halibut. Surprisingly, Calvin's is also a great spot for Thai food, as the Thai-born chef frequently offers Bangkok specialties. In good weather, deck seating overlooks the marina. The charmingly energetic Swiss owners will make you feel very welcome—if you want stuffy, formal service, this isn't your restaurant.

133 Lower Ganges Rd. ⓒ 250/538-5551. Reservations recommended. Dinner main courses C$16–C$28 (US$16–US$28/£8–£14). MC, V. Tues–Sat 11:30am–2pm and 5pm to closing.

GALIANO ISLAND
Galiano is perhaps the most physically striking of the Gulf Islands, particularly the mountainous southern shores. Mount Sutil, Mount Galiano, and the exposed cliffs above Georgeson Bay (simply called the Bluffs) rise above sheep-filled meadows, shadowy forests, and fern-lined ravines. **Active Pass,** the narrow strait that separates Galiano from Mayne Island, is another scenic high spot: All the ferry and much of the pleasure craft traffic between Vancouver and Victoria negotiates this turbulent, cliff-lined passage.

Watch the bustle of the boats and ferries from **Bellhouse Provincial Park,** a picnicking area at the end of Jack Road, or head to **Montague Harbour Provincial Park,** a beautiful preserve of beach and forest.

Galiano is the closest Gulf Island to Vancouver, and many of the properties here are second homes of the city's elite. The rural yet genteel feel of the island is perfect for a romantic getaway or a relaxing break from the hassles of urban life. However, don't come to Galiano looking for high-octane nightlife or boutique shopping. There isn't much of a town on the island, just a few shops and galleries at Sturdies Bay and several excellent inns and B&Bs.

VISITOR INFORMATION   Contact **Galiano Island Chamber of Commerce** (© **866/539-2233;** www.galianoisland.com). A seasonal information booth sits at the top of the ferry dock ramp.

HIKING   Several short hikes lead to Active Pass overlooks, including the trail to the top of 330m (1,083-ft.) Mount Galiano and the cliff-edge path in Bluffs Park. Bodega Ridge is a park about two-thirds of the way up the island, with old-growth forest, wildflowers, and views of the distant Olympic and Cascade mountain ranges.

KAYAKING   Home to otters, seals, and bald eagles, the gentle waters of Montague Harbour are a perfect kayaking destination. **Gulf Island Kayaking** (© **250/539-2442;** www.seakayak.ca) offers a variety of guided part- and whole-day trips, including a 3-hour sunset paddle for C$45 (US$45/£23). If you want to really get away, consider a custom multiday kayaking/camping trip. Gulf Island Kayaking also offers kayak rentals from its base at the Montague Harbour marina.

WHERE TO STAY & EAT

Galiano Oceanfront Inn & Spa ✦✦   Formerly the Galiano Lodge and one of the original accommodations on Galiano Island, the inn—with an unrestricted vista onto the harbor, the busy boat traffic on Active Passage, and the lighthouse on Mayne Island—is now a top destination in the Gulf Islands. Unique in the islands, the Galiano Inn is just a 5-minute stroll from the ferry dock, so guests can leave the car on the mainland. Galiano Inn also offers some of the largest and most comfortable rooms on the island. Each of the very plush rooms has a fireplace, a patio or balcony with stunning water views, and extras such as bathrobes and CD players. Rooms with king beds have Jacuzzi tubs, while others have soaker tubs. The **Atrevida Restaurant** ✦✦, with notable regional cuisine, is in a separate, even more stunning building filled with Northwest Native art; **Madrona del Mar Spa,** a complete beauty and wellness center, shares the waterfront building. A large garden courtyard with a fountain greets guests, while a new garden addition includes a koi pond, herb and vegetable beds for the restaurant, and outdoor treatment areas for the spa; a path leads to a small sandy beach.

134 Madrona Dr., Galiano Island, BC V0N 1P0. © **877/530-3939** or 250/539-3388. Fax 250/539-3338. www.galiano inn.com. 20 units. C$249–C$299 (US$249–US$299/£125–£150). Off-season rates available. Rates include full breakfast. MC, V. Free parking. **Amenities:** Restaurant; lounge; golf course nearby; spa; outdoor hot tub; kayaking/boat rentals nearby; tour/activities desk; courtesy limo; business center; British Columbia wine and gourmet shop; room service; laundry service; gardens; 1 room for those w/limited mobility. *In room:* CD player, Wi-Fi, minibar, fridge, coffeemaker, hair dryer.

Woodstone Country Inn ✦✦   A quintessential small country inn, Woodstone is one of the most refined lodgings on Galiano. It sits among fir trees overlooking a series of meadows, which serve as a de facto bird sanctuary. The entire inn is decorated with restrained but exquisite taste: You'll find not only the owner's collection of art from world travels but canvases from renowned local painters. Woodstone's architecture is such that all rooms are large and unique; many second-floor rooms also have dramatic dormered ceilings. All units have fireplaces, some have soaker tubs, and one is wheelchair accessible. Rooms on the main floor have small private patios. The **Wisteria Dining Room** ⭐⭐ is one of the top restaurants in the Gulf Islands, with a menu that blends classic French cuisine, vivid international flavors, and local produce, meats, and fish.

743 Georgeson Bay Rd., R.R. 1, Galiano Island, BC V0N 1P0. ℂ 888/339-2022 or 250/539-2022. Fax 250/539-5198. www.woodstoneinn.com. 12 units. C$129–C$209 (US$129–US$209/£65–£105) double. Rates include full breakfast and afternoon tea. Packages available. AE, MC, V. Closed Dec–Jan. Children should be 15 or older. **Amenities:** Restaurant; lounge; golf course nearby; concierge; tour/activities desk; business center; in-room massage. *In room:* Hair dryer, no phone.

MAYNE ISLAND

Bucolic Mayne Island is a medley of rock-lined bays, forested hills, and pastureland. Mayne was once a center of Gulf Island agriculture, noted for its apple and tomato production. Many of the island's early farmhouses remain, and a rural, lived-in quality is one of Mayne's most endearing features.

Miner's Bay is by default the commercial center of the island, though in most locales this somewhat aimless collection of homes and businesses wouldn't really qualify as a village. **Bennett Bay,** on the northeast coast, is the best swimming beach. **Campbell Bay,** just northwest, is another favorite pebble beach. **Dinner Bay Park** is lovely for a picnic.

On a sunny day, the grounds of the **Georgina Point Lighthouse** offer dramatic views. Located on the island's northern tip, this lighthouse juts into Active Pass and overlooks the southern shores of Galiano Island, less than a mile away.

VISITOR INFORMATION   Contact the **Mayne Island Community Chamber of Commerce,** Box 2, Mayne Island, BC V0N 2J0 (no phone; www.mayneisland chamber.ca).

HIKING   The roads on Mayne are usually quiet enough that they can also serve as paths for hikers. Those looking for more solitude should consider **Mount Parke Regional Park,** off Fernhill Road in the center of the island. The park's best views reward those who take the 1-hour hike to Halliday Viewpoint.

KAYAKING   **Mayne Island Kayak & Canoe Rentals** (ℂ 250/539-5599; www. maynekayak.com), at Seal Beach in Miner's Bay, rents kayaks and canoes for C$28 (US$28/£14) for 2 hours, or C$48 (US$48/£24) for a full day. The company will drop off kayaks at any of six launching points on the island, and, if you get stranded, will even pick up kayaks (and too-weary kayakers) from other destinations.

WHERE TO STAY & DINE

Oceanwood Country Inn ⭐⭐   This luxury property is one of the best places to stay in the Gulf Islands. A gem of understated elegance, it has an excellent restaurant, attentive staff, spacious rooms with sumptuous furnishings, and just the right blend of comfortable formality and relaxed hospitality. All but one of the rooms have magnificent views of Navy Channel and Saturna Island. The original inn's rooms are smaller and less expensive, yet still comfortable and beautifully outfitted; two have balconies. The rooms in the new wing are truly large, with private decks, two-person tubs, and fireplaces. The Wisteria Suite is a three-tiered unit with two baths, multiple decks, and an outdoor soaker tub.

The inn's public rooms are equally impressive. Facing the gardens are a comfortable living room and library, separated by a double-sided fireplace. The **Oceanwood Dining Room** ★★ is one of the most sophisticated places to eat on the Gulf Islands, presenting up-to-date, full-flavored cooking that unites the rich bounty of Northwest fish, meat, game, and produce in a daily-changing tableau of impressive tastes and texture

630 Dinner Bay Rd., Mayne Island, BC V0N 2J0. (☎ 250/539-5074. Fax 250/539-3002. www.oceanwood.com. 12 units. Mid-June to mid-Sept C$179–C$349 (US$179–US$349/£90–£175); mid-Sept to Oct 31 and Mar 2 to mid-June C$159–C$299 (US$159–US$299/£80–£150). Extra person C$25 (US$25/£13). Rates include full breakfast and after-noon tea. MC, V. Closed Nov 1 to Mar 1. **Amenities:** Restaurant; bar; golf course nearby; Jacuzzi; sauna; free bikes; in-room massage; nonsmoking facility. *In room:* Hair dryer, no phone.

THE PENDER ISLANDS

The Penders consist of North and South Pender islands, separated by a very narrow channel that's spanned by a one-lane bridge. North Pender is much more developed, though that's all relative out in the Gulf Islands.

Mount Norman Regional Park, which encompasses the northwest corner of South Pender Island, features hiking trails through old-growth forest to wilderness beaches and ridge-top vistas. Access to trails is just across the Pender Island bridge.

The extensive network of roads makes these islands good destinations for cyclists. Rentals are available at **Otter Bay Marina,** 2311 McKinnon Rd. ((☎ **250/629-3579**), where you'll also find **Mouat Point Kayaks,** 1615 Storm Crescent ((☎ **250/629-6767**). If beachcombing or sunning are more your style, try **Hamilton Beach** on the east side of North Pender, or **Medicine Beach** and the beaches along **Beaumont Marine Park,** both of which flank Bedwell Harbour.

VISITOR INFORMATION   The **Pender Island Visitor Info Centre,** 2332 Otter Bay Rd. ((☎/fax **250/629-6541**), is open from May 15 to September 2. Or check out the chamber of commerce website at www.penderislandchamber.com.

WHERE TO STAY

Poets Cove Resort and Spa ★★★   This very impressive new resort shows what a difference an investment of C$48 million can make. Poets Cove opened in 2004 on the former Bedwell Harbour Resort site, which served for many years as a rustic boat-ing lodge and the Canadian Customs office for U.S. and Canadian pleasure-boat traf-fic. The resort has emerged as a classy and sprawling complex that includes a 22-room Arts and Crafts–style lodge complete with upscale **Surussus Spa,** fitness center, ball-room, casual restaurant/pub, and fine-dining restaurant, plus 15 cottages and nine luxury apartment–like villas. Furnishings are top quality, and the attention to detail is exquisite. Lodge rooms have soaker tubs, tiled showers, fireplaces, and balconies with views over Bedwell Harbour, while the cottages and villas are spacious units (several boast three bedrooms) with full kitchens, fireplaces, balconies or decks, two bath-rooms, and—in addition to indoor soaker tubs—outdoor hot tubs in many.

The refined solitude makes it easy to forget that incredible recreation waits just out-side the door, but the kayak and charter boat rental at the activity center can help you remember. Or simply enjoy one of the two swimming pools (one for adults only). Poets Cove sets the gold standard for marina resorts in southwest British Columbia; you can't go wrong here. And the swank **Aurora** dining room ★★ combines excellent food, a romantic setting, and terrific views.

9801 Spalding Rd., S. Pender Island, BC V0N 2M3. (☎ **888/512-7638** or 250/629-2100. Fax 250/629-2110. www. poetscove.com. 46 units. From C$179 (US$179/£90) double lodge rooms; from C$349 (US$349/£175) 2-bedroom vil-las; from C$449 (US$449/£225) 3-bedroom villa; from C$369 (US$369/£185) 2-bedroom cottage; from C$519

(US$519/£260) 3-bedroom cottage. Extra person C$25 (US$25/£13). AE, MC, V. **Amenities:** Restaurant; bar; 2 pools; tennis court; fitness center; spa; sports-equipment rental; activity center; concierge; market; beer and wine store; coin-op laundry; marina. *In room:* TV/DVD, fridge, coffeemaker, hair dryer, iron, kettle.

WHERE TO DINE

Hope Bay Café 𝓡𝓡 NEW CANADIAN   Northeast of North Pender Island is Hope Bay, a tiny community perched above a rocky harbor. When the old general store at Hope Bay, open since 1903, burned down a few years ago, a group of island artists and merchants pooled resources to rebuild a new commercial center in this lovely waterfront spot. In the corner with the best views is the Hope Bay Café, a very pleasant, light-filled dining room whose informality veils some very serious and delicious cooking. It's a classic story: Big city–trained chef comes to small community and cooks fantastic food. Get here before the crowds do. While the printed menu is small and includes dishes such as Hope Bay Bouillabaisse and pork shoulder stuffed with apricots and leeks, the real attractions are the specials that vary seasonally as local ingredients become available. One evening's special, baked guinea hen with a gravy of wild mushrooms, fennel, and port, was superb.

4301 Bedwell Harbour Rd. (𝓒 250/629-6668. Main courses C$16–C$26 (US$16–US$26/£8–£13). MC, V. Wed–Sun 11am–3pm and 5–8pm.

SATURNA ISLAND

The most remote of the southern Gulf Islands, Saturna is both pristine and, compared with its neighbors, mostly vacant—it has only about 350 residents. Whereas other islands are best described as rural, Saturna is truly wild. It's not surprising that the new Gulf Islands National Park Reserve has its largest presence on Saturna: About half the island is now protected as reserve land.

Any visit to Saturna should include a stop at **Saturna Island Family Estate Winery** (𝓒 **877/918-3388** or 250/539-3521), a small, well-established winery in an extremely dramatic setting. Perched between massive cliffs and the sea, the setting is reminiscent of Corsica. The tasting room, open daily 11am to 4:30pm from May to October, is reached by a precipitous single track road with a 20% grade. The tasting room also offers soups and salads for lunch.

Its remoteness makes Saturna a favorite destination of outdoorsy types. The island boasts nice beaches, including Russell Reef, Veruna Bay, and Shell Beach at **East Point Park.** This park, with its still-active lighthouse, is a good spot to watch for orcas. Hikers can drive to **Mount Warburton Pike** 𝓡 and follow the **Brown Ridge Nature Trail.** Views from this craggy cliff-faced peak are astonishing, taking in southern Vancouver Island, the San Juan Islands, and the Olympic Peninsula. For more information, check out www.saturnatourism.com.

WHERE TO STAY & DINE

Saturna Lodge & Restaurant 𝓡𝓡   This well-established resort, which began its life as a 1940s boardinghouse, has been revamped into a very comfortable, upscale country inn. If your idea of an island getaway is seclusion and genteel comfort, this is your lodging. Set amid gardens, with views onto Boot Cove, the lodge has taken on a winery theme—each of the charming guest rooms is named for a wine or grape varietal. The top of the line is the Sauterne Room, a large suite with soaker tub, private deck, and king bed. Families will like the suite of ground-floor rooms with private entrances, where a twin-bed room and a queen room share a large bathroom. The attractive main-floor lounge overlooks the gardens and has a fireplace, small library, and television.

For most guests, the highlight of a stay here is a meal at **Saturna Lodge Restaurant.** The menu features Saturna Island lamb, local seafood, and organic produce. In good weather, the menu offers barbecued meats and fish from the outdoor grill. Three-course meals are C$39 (US$39/£20); a la carte selections are also available. There's a well-chosen wine list, featuring wines from Saturna and the other islands, as well as some from around British Columbia.

130 Payne Rd., Saturna Island, BC V0N 2Y0. © **866/539-2254** or 250/539-2254. Fax 250/539-3091. www. saturna.ca. 7 units. C$120–C$195 (US$120–US$195/£60–£98) double. Rates include breakfast. Special packages available. MC, V. Closed Jan–Feb. Pets allowed in 3 garden rooms for C$20 (US$20/£10) per night. **Amenities:** Restaurant; bar; Jacuzzi; free bikes; tour/activities desk; business center; nonsmoking facility. *In room:* TV/DVDs available, hair dryer, no phone.

4 Vancouver Island's West Coast: Tofino & Long Beach ★★★★

Vancouver Island's west coast is a magnificent area of old-growth forests, stunning fjords (called "sounds" in local parlance), rocky coasts, and long sandy beaches. And though **Pacific Rim National Park** (www.pc.gc.ca/pn-np/bc/pacificrim) was established back in 1971 as Canada's first marine park, it wasn't until 1993—when thousands of environmentalists gathered to protest the clear-cutting of old-growth forests in Clayoquot Sound—that the area really exploded into the people's consciousness. Tourism here has never looked back.

Driving out to Long Beach and Tofino is a bit of a slog. From Parksville, allow 3 hours to make the journey. Although the road is paved, some of it is very rough, winding, and narrow.

ESSENTIALS

VISITOR INFORMATION   Mid-March through October, the **Long Beach Visitor Information Centre,** about 1.5km (1 mile) from the Highway 4 junction to Tofino (© **250/725-3414;** www.tourismtofino.com), is open daily 10am to 6pm.

GETTING THERE   By Bus   Greyhound Vancouver Island Coach (© **250/ 388-5248**) operates regular daily service between Victoria and Tofino. The 6-hour trip, departing Victoria at 7:30am and arriving in Tofino at 2:35pm, costs C$61 (US$61/£31) to Tofino. The bus also stops in Nanaimo and can pick up passengers arriving from Vancouver on the ferry. The **Tofino Bus** (© **866/986-3466;** www. tofinobus.com) also offers daily bus service from Victoria and Vancouver to Tofino. A one-way ticket from Victoria to Tofino is C$64 (US$64/£32).

By Car   Tofino and Long Beach all lay near the end of Highway 4 on the west coast of Vancouver Island. From Nanaimo, take the Island Highway (Hwy. 19) north for 52km (32 miles). Just before the town of Parksville is a turnoff for Highway 4, which leads first to the midisland town of Port Alberni (38km/24 miles) and then to Tofino (135km/84 miles west of Port Alberni). The road is paved the whole way but gets windy and rough after Sproat Lake.

By Ferry   A 4½-hour ride aboard the **Alberni Marine Transportation** (© **250/ 723-8313;** www.ladyrosemarine.com) passenger ferry MV *Lady Rose* takes you from Port Alberni through Alberni Inlet to Ucluelet, 41km (26 miles) south of Tofino. It makes brief stops along the way to deliver mail and packages to solitary cabin dwellers along the coast and to let off or pick up kayakers bound for the Broken Islands Group. The *Lady Rose* departs three times a week to each destination from Alberni Harbour Quay's Angle Street. The fare to Ucluelet is C$32 (US$32/£16) one-way and C$64

Pacific Rim National Park Reserve

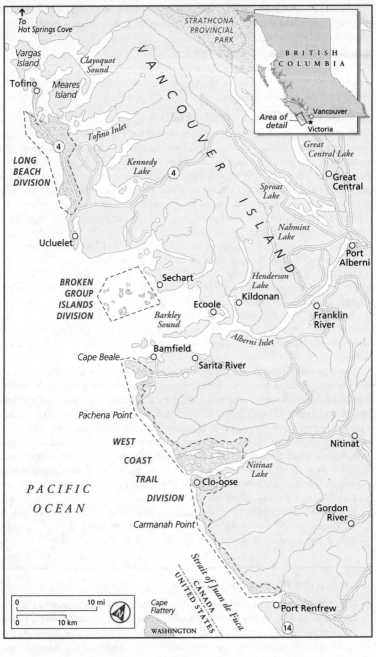

(US$64/£32) round-trip. The service operates in summer only; however, the same company offers year-round mail delivery trips to/from Port Alberni and Bamfield—check the website for details.

By Plane **Orca Airways** (© **888/359-6722** or 604/270-6722; www.flyorcaair.com) offers year-round flights between Vancouver International Airport and Tofino. **Sound Flight** offers air service between the Seattle area and Tofino (© **866/921-3474** or 425/254-8064; www.soundflight.net).

EXPLORING TOFINO & LONG BEACH

Pacific Rim National Park has three units, though only one, Long Beach ★★, is easily accessed by the average traveler. Long Beach is a stretch of coastal wilderness at the outer edge of a peninsula about halfway up Vancouver Island's western shore. The beach is more than 16km (10 miles) long, broken here and there by rocky headlands and islands and bordered by tremendous groves of cedar and Sitka spruce. The beach is popular with countless species of birds and marine life, and, lately, with wet-suited surfers as well. Hiking trails wind through coastal rainforests and mossy bogs. Per day entry to the park is C$6.90 (US$6.90/£3.45) for adults, C$5.90 (US$5.90/£2.95) seniors, C$3.45 (US$3.45/£1.75) youths, and C$17 (US$17/£8.50) families.

Two former fishing villages serve as entry points to Long Beach. The town of **Ucluelet** (pronounced You-*clue*-let, meaning "safe harbor" in the local Nuu-chah-nulth dialect) sits on the southern end of the Long Beach peninsula, on the edge of Barkely Sound. At the far-northern tip of the peninsula, **Tofino** (pop. 1,600) borders on beautiful Clayoquot Sound and is the center of the west coast eco-tourism business. It's a schizophrenic kind of town: Half is composed of eco-tourism outfitters, nature lovers, activists, and serious granolas; the other half is composed of loggers and fishers.

The reason for Tofino's popularity is not hard to fathom. Tofino offers incredible marine vistas at the end of a thin finger of land, battered by the Pacific to the west and lapped by Tofino Sound on the east. The town is notched with tiny bays and inlets, with a multitude of islands, many of them very mountainous, just offshore. Further east, the jagged, snow-capped peaks of Strathcona Park fill the horizon.

Tofino is becoming more crowded and subject to a particular brand of gentrification. On the beaches south of town, luxury inns serve the rarified demands of upscale travelers attracted to the area's scenery. There are more fine-dining restaurants and boutiques here than can possibly be justified by the town's size. Dining is as big a draw as sea kayaking for many Tofino visitors.

With all the bustle, it can be difficult at times to find solitude in what's actually still an amazingly beautiful and wild place. Accordingly, more people decide to avoid the crowds and visit Tofino in winter, to watch dramatic storms roll in from the Pacific.

Fun Fact **A Whale of a Festival**

About 20,000 Pacific gray whales migrate to this area annually. During the second week of March, the **Pacific Rim Whale Festival** (© **250/726-4641**; www.pacificrimwhalefestival.org) is held in Tofino and Ucluelet. Live crab races, the Gumboot Golf Tournament, guided whale-watching hikes, and a Native Indian festival are just a few of the events celebrating the annual whale migration.

OUTDOOR PURSUITS

FISHING Sportfishing for salmon, steelhead, rainbow trout, Dolly Varden char, halibut, cod, and snapper is excellent off the west coast of Vancouver Island. **Jay's Clayoquot Ventures** (© 888/534-7422 or 250/725-2700; www.tofinofishing.com) organizes fishing charters throughout the Clayoquot Sound area. Deep sea and both saltwater and freshwater flying-fishing excursions are offered. The company supplies all the gear, a guide, and a boat. Prices for inshore saltwater expeditions start at a minimum of C$95 (US$95/£48) per hour, with a minimum of 5 hours.

GUIDED NATURE HIKES Owned/operated by Bill McIntyre, former chief naturalist of Pacific Rim National Park, the **Long Beach Nature Tour Co.** (© 250/ 726-7099; www.oceansedge.bc.ca) offers guided beach walks, storm watching, land-based whale-watching tours, and rainforest tours customized to suit your group's needs.

HIKING In and around **Long Beach,** numerous marked trails 1km to 3.5km (.5 mile–2 miles) long take you through the thick temperate rain forest edging the shore. The **Gold Mine Trail** (about 3.5km/2 miles long) near Florencia Bay still has a few artifacts from the days when a gold-mining operation flourished here. The partially boardwalked **South Beach Trail** (less than 1.5km/1 mile long) leads through the moss-draped rainforest onto small quiet coves like Lismer Beach and South Beach, where you can see abundant life in the rocky tidal pools. The **Big Cedar Trail** (© 250/725-3233) on Meares Island is a 3.5km (2-mile) boardwalk path built in 1993 to protect the old-growth temperate rainforest. Maintained by the Tla-o-qui-aht Native Indian Band, the trail has a long staircase leading up to the Hanging Garden Tree, the province's fourth-largest western red cedar.

KAYAKING Perhaps the quintessential Clayoquot experience, and certainly one of the most fun, is to slip into a kayak and paddle out into the sound. For beginners, half-day tours to Meares Island (usually with the chance to do a little hiking) are an especially good bet. For rentals, lessons, and tours, try **Pacific Kayak,** 606 Campbell St., at Jamie's Whaling Station (© 250/725-3232; www.tofino-bc.com/pacifickayak). The **Tofino Sea-Kayaking Company,** 320 Main St., Tofino (© 800/863-4664 or 250/725-4222; www.tofino-kayaking.com), offers kayaking packages ranging from 4-hour paddles around Meares Island (from C$68/US$68/£34 per person) to weeklong paddling and camping expeditions. Instruction by experienced guides makes even your first kayaking experience a comfortable, safe, and enjoyable one.

Guides from the Nuu-chah-nulth First Nation also offer tours on ocean-going canoes. **Tla-ook Cultural Adventures** (© 877/942-2663 or 250/725-2656; www. tlaook.com) offer paddle trips with commentary by Native guides to Meares Island (C$64/US$64/£32 per person) and other Clayoquot Sound destinations. Daylong paddle excursions explore traditional hunting and fishing grounds and end with a salmon feast (C$140/US$140/£70) per person).

SURFING The big lashing waves that the Pacific delivers to Long Beach have become popular with surfers. A number of businesses have sprung up to address the needs of surfers, including **Pacific Surf School,** 440 Campbell St. (© 888/777-9961 or 250/725-2155; www.pacificsurfschool.com), which offers lessons and camps for beginners, plus rentals and gear sales. A 3-hour group lesson is C$79 (US$79/£40); private lessons are also available. **Live to Surf Inc.,** 1180 Pacific Rim Hwy. (© 250/ 725-4464; www.livetosurf.com), is Tofino's oldest surf shop, since 1984. It also has the largest selection of new and used boards, and offers lessons and advice on local

---

(Moments Walking the Wild Side: A Glimpse of First Nations Life

---

Clayoquot Sound is the traditional home of the Nuu-chah-nulth peoples. Accessed via water taxi, the **Walk the Wild Side Trail (© 888/670-9586)** runs along the south side of Flores Island from the village of Ahousat to Cow Bay. First Nation peoples have used this route for centuries to reach the wild beaches on the west side of the island. There's a C$75 (US$75/£38) fee for walking the trail, included in excursions from **Seaside Adventures (© 888/ 332-4252;** www.seaside-adventures.com). Most of the route follows sandy beaches, and trails cut across headlands to join with the next beach. For an extra C$45 (US$45/£23) you can hire a First Nations guide to accompany your group, though it's a good idea to be clear what kind of interpretation you're looking for. Some who have done the trail have reported incredible experiences and afterward were invited by elders to come to the village to celebrate a potlatch, while others have been foisted off on teenage boys more interested in playing with their two-way radios than looking at nature.

---

beaches. **Surfing Vancouver Island** (www.surfingvancouverisland.com/surf) is a helpful website that includes links to local surfing resources, plus photos of Canada's top surfers.

WHALE-WATCHING, BIRDING & MORE   A number of outfitters conduct tours through this region inhabited by gray whales, bald eagles, porpoises, bears, orcas, seals, and sea lions. In addition, **Hot Springs Cove,** accessible only by water, is a natural hot spring 67km (42 miles) north of Tofino. Take a water taxi, sail, canoe, or kayak up to Clayoquot Sound to enjoy swimming in the steaming pools and bracing waterfalls. A number of kayak outfitters and boat charters offer trips to the springs.

March through October, **Jamie's Whaling Station,** 606 Campbell St., Tofino, BC V0R 2Z0 (© **800/667-9913** or 250/725-3919; www.jamies.com), uses a 20m (66-ft.) power cruiser as well as a fleet of Zodiacs for tours to watch the gray whales. In addition to whale-watching and hot springs expeditions, **Seaside Adventures (© 888/ 332-4252** or 250/725-2292; www.seaside-adventures.com) offers bear-watching trips from May to September. Fares for both companies' expeditions generally start at C$80 (US$80/£40) per person for a 2- or 3-hour tour; customized trips can run as high as C$250 (US$250/£125) per person for a full day.

March through November, **Remote Passages,** Meares Landing, 71 Wharf St., Tofino, BC V0R 2Z0 (© **800/666-9833** or 250/725-3330; www.remotepassages.com), runs daily 2½-hour whale-watching tours in Clayoquot Sound on Zodiac boats, costing C$79 (US$79/£40) for adults and C$59 (US$59/£30) for children under 12. The company also conducts a 7-hour whale-watching/hot springs trip at C$110 (US$110/£55) for adults and C$89 (US$89/£45) for children under 12. Reservations are recommended.

For bird-watchers, the protected waters of Clayoquat Sound and the beaches of Pacific Rim National Park offer fantastic birding opportunities. **Just Birding (© 250/ 725-2520;** www.justbirding.com) offers a range of bird-watching adventures, from walking tours of the beaches to paddle trips to bald eagle habitat to boat tours for off-shore pelagic birding. Guided trips begin at C$79 (US$79/£40) per person.

RAINY-DAY ACTIVITIES

You can browse books at the **Wildside Booksellers and Espresso Bar,** Main Street (© 250/745-4222), or get a massage or salt glow at the **Ancient Cedars Spa** at the Wickaninnish Inn (© 250/725-3100).

You can also check out the galleries. The **Eagle Aerie Gallery,** 350 Campbell St. (© 250/725-3235), constructed in the style of a Native Indian longhouse, features the innovative work of Tsimshian artist Roy Henry Vickers. The **House of Himwitsa,** 300 Main St. (© 250/725-2017), is also owned/operated by First Nations artists. The quality and craftsmanship of the shop's artwork, masks, baskets, totems, gold and silver jewelry, and apparel are excellent. You can find the new-age side of Tofino in the **Reflecting Spirit Gallery,** 441 Campbell St. (© 250/725-4229), which offers medicine wheels, rocks, and crystals, as well as a great selection of Native art, carvings, woodcrafts, and pottery.

WHERE TO STAY

The 94 campsites on the bluff at **Green Point** are maintained by Pacific Rim National Park (© 250/726-7721). The grounds are full every day in July and August, and the average wait for a site is 1 to 2 days. Leave your name at the ranger station when you arrive to be placed on the list. You're rewarded for your patience with a magnificent ocean view, pit toilets, fire pits, pumped well water, and free firewood (no showers or hookups). Sites are C$17 to C$23 (US$17–US$23/£8.50–£12). The campground is closed October through March.

The **Bella Pacifica Resort & Campground,** 3.5km (2 miles) south of Tofino on the Pacific Rim Highway (P.O. Box 413), Tofino, BC V0R 2Z0 (© 250/725-3400; www.bellapacifica.com), is privately owned and has 165 campsites from which you can walk to Mackenzie Beach or take the resort's private nature trails to Templar Beach. Flush toilets, hot showers, water, laundry, ice, fire pits, firewood, and full and partial hookups are available. Rates are C$21 to C$46 (US$21–US$46/£11–£23) per two-person campsite. Reserve at least a month in advance for a summer weekend.

Best Western Tin-Wis Resort (Kids   The Tla-o-qui-aht First Nations band run this large, hotel-like lodge on MacKenzie Beach. All rooms are spacious, with oceanfront views, although more basic than you'll find at most other beachfront lodges. Options include queen loft units and deluxe king rooms with fireplaces, kitchenettes, and Jacuzzi tubs. Most units have sofa beds, making them a good choice for families.

1119 Pacific Rim Hwy., Box 380, Tofino, BC V0R 2Z0. © **800/661-9995** or 250/725-4445. Fax 250/725-4447. www.tinwis.com. 86 units. June 20–Oct 15 C$216–C$240 (US$216–US$240/£108–£120) double; C$360 (US$360/£180) executive suite. Substantially lower off-season rates. Senior, AAA, and group discounts available. AE, DC, DISC, MC, V. **Amenities:** Restaurant; lounge; well-equipped exercise room; large Jacuzzi. *In room:* TV, fridge, coffeemaker, hair dryer.

The Inn at Tough City (Finds   This is possibly Tofino's nicest small inn and certainly the quirkiest. Built in 1996 from salvaged and recycled material, it's filled with antiques, stained glass, and bric-a-brac; it sits right above the harbor just steps from the center of town. The rooms are spacious, and several feature soaker tubs, fireplaces, or both. The on-site restaurant features seafood and sushi and is open for dinner year-round; lunch in summer season only.

350 Main St., P.O. Box 8, Tofino, BC V0R 2Z0. © **877/725-2021** or 250/725-2021. Fax 250/725-2088. www.toughcity.com. 8 units. Mid-May to mid-Oct C$169–C$229 (US$169–US$229/£85–£115) double. Shoulder and off-season

discounts. AE, MC, V. Pets allowed for C$10 (US$10/£5). **Amenities:** Restaurant; in-room massage; laundry service; nonsmoking rooms. *In room:* TV, dataport, coffeemaker, hair dryer.

Long Beach Lodge Resort ✮✮✮ A contender for the title of Tofino's most upscale lodge is this extremely handsome log-and-stone resort perched above the waves on Cox Bay. The care and style that went into the building of the lodge and cottages is extraordinary—in fact, the Long Beach Lodge Resort was featured in *Architectural Digest* magazine. The architects and designers did a great job updating the usually rather heavy backcountry-lodge look, making the entire resort seem both timeless and comfortable modern.

The Great Room, filled with fine furniture and flanked by a huge granite fireplace and massive windows overlooking Cox Bay, is the heart of the lodge, serving as breakfast and lunch dining room, cocktail lounge and a comfortable living room for snoozing, reading and watching surfers. There are a number of lodging options, including lodge rooms (with less expensive rooms facing the forest, not the Pacific) and free-standing duplex cottages. All come with marvelous fir furniture, slate-floored bathrooms with soaker tubs and separate showers, bathrobes, and loads of rich decor (including original artwork); some rooms have fireplaces and balconies/patios. The cottages are 93 sq. m (1,000-sq.-ft.) dwellings with all the above, plus private hot tubs, a large sitting area with overstuffed couches and chairs, washer and dryer, and a full kitchen. The rate formula is rather complex, so check the website or call for exact rates for the date of your visit. The dining room here has quickly gained attention for its regional fine dining. Resort staff will help you put together outdoor activities and recreation.

1441 Pacific Rim Hwy., Box 897, Tofino, BC V0R 2Z0. ✆ **877/844-7873** or 250/725-2442. Fax 250/725-2402. www. longbeachlodgeresort.com. 60 units. Late June to Oct 1 C$299–C$569 (US$299–US$569/£150–£285) double; C$459 (US$459/£230) cottage. 3-night minimum cottage stay in high season. Lower shoulder and off-season rates; packages available. Extra person C$30 (US$30/£15). Some discounts available with 3-day minimum stays during shoulder and off season. AE, DC, MC, V. Pets allowed in some cottages. **Amenities:** Restaurant; fitness room; guest laundry; beautifully furnished lodge "great room" w/fireplace. *In room:* TV, DVD/CD player, fridge, coffeemaker, hair dryer, iron.

Middle Beach Lodge ✮✮ This beautiful lodge/resort complex is on a headland overlooking the ocean just south of Tofino. The rustic look was accomplished by using largely recycled beams and salvaged lumber, and as a result the lodge exudes a sense of venerability and history, despite its recent construction. Accommodations are in a variety of structures: a "beach house" with standard hotel rooms, two lodges (one family oriented, one adults only) with a mix of suites and guest rooms, and oceanfront cabins, some of which can sleep seven. Although most of the suites and cabins have decks, soaker or Jacuzzi tubs, gas fireplaces, CD players, and kitchenettes, it's a good idea to phone the lodge to discuss specific room features, as there are many subtle variations. All guests have access to two lofty common rooms overlooking the ocean. These are good spots to pour a coffee or something stronger and look out over the waves crashing in.

400 Mackenzie Beach Rd. (P.O. Box 100), Tofino, BC V0R 2Z0. ✆ **866/725-2900** or 250/725-2900. Fax 250/725-2901. www.middlebeach.com. 45 units, 19 cabins. C$140–C$200 (US$140–US$200/£70–£100) double; C$230–C$360 (US$230–US$360/£115–£180) suite; C$240–C$450 (US$240–US$450/£120–£225) cabin. 2-night minimum stay required Mar–Oct. Shoulder and off-season rates available. AE, MC, V. Children 12 and under not accepted at beach and some headlands accommodations. **Amenities:** Exercise room; tour desk; laundry service; nonsmoking facility. *In room:* TV/VCR (suites and cabins only), kitchenette, fridge, coffeemaker, no phone.

Red Crow Guest House ✮ While the Wickaninnish and other coastal lodges show you the wild, stormy west-facing side of Tofino, the Red Crow displays the kinder, subtler beauty on the peninsula's east side. By the sheltered waters of Jensen Bay, this pleasant Cape Cod–style home sits in 2.8 secluded hectares (7 acres) of old-growth forest. Two rooms are in the lower level of the house (with private entrances), opening out onto a fabulous view of the bay—perhaps best seen from the inn's outdoor hot tub. Rooms here are large and pleasant, with queen or king beds and 1920s-style furnishings. In addition, there's a charming two-bedroom garden cottage with full kitchen. Come here for the wildlife viewing (eagles, seals, and shorebirds) and stay for the breakfasts (the innkeeper is a professional chef). Guests have free use of canoes to explore offshore islands.

1084 Pacific Rim Hwy., Tofino, BC V0R 2Z0. ℂ 250/725-2275. Fax 250/725-3214. www.tofinoredcrow.com. 3 units. C$175–C$195 (US$175–US$195/£88–£98) double. Shoulder and off-season rates available. Extra person C$20 (US$20/£10). V. *In room:* CD player, fridge, coffeemaker, hair dryer, no phone.

Whalers on the Point Guesthouse   This modern hostel is one way to save money in an increasingly expensive town. Located downtown, with views of Clayoquot Sound, it offers both shared and private rooms; wheelchair-accessible rooms are available. The hostel offers discounted activities, arranged through local outfitters.

81 West St., Box 296, Tofino, BC V0R 2Z0. ℂ 250/725-3443. Fax 250/725-3463. www.tofinohostel.com. 55 beds. May–Sept double C$80 (US$80/£40), shared C$28–C$30 (US$28–US$30/£14–£15) per person; Oct–Apr double from C$50 (US$50/£25), shared C$22–C$24 (US$22–US$24/£11–£12) per person. Hostelling International member, off-season, multiday, and family discounts available. MC, V. **Amenities:** Kitchen, sauna; game room; coin-op laundry; Internet kiosk; kitchen; TV room. *In room:* No phone.

The Wickaninnish Inn 🐾🐾🐾   No matter which room you book at this beautiful inn of cedar, stone, and glass, you'll wake to a magnificent view of the untamed Pacific. The Wick, as it's affectionately known, is on a rocky promontory, surrounded by an old-growth spruce and cedar rainforest and the sprawling sands of Chesterman Beach. Perennially ranked as one of the top inns in North America, the Wick succeeds by blurring the distinction between outdoors and in through art, furnishings, architecture, and building materials. Rustic driftwood furniture, richly printed textiles, and local artwork highlight the rooms, each of which features a private balcony, oceanfront view, fireplace, down duvet, soaker tub and stone-lined shower, luxurious bath amenities, thick bathrobes, a CD player, a large-screen TV, and complimentary high-speed Internet access. Special occasion suites, particularly the Canopy Suite with custom-made furniture, "seashore" bathroom, and fiber-optic sky-scape of the summer solstice above the bed, are truly fantastic.

Wickaninnish On the Beach is a major expansion of the inn that adds a health-club facility and library to the resort, in addition to 30 more luxury-level guest rooms. Winter storm–watching packages have become so popular that the inn is nearly as busy in winter as it is in summer. The Pointe Restaurant (see below) is one of the top dining rooms in western Canada. The staff can arrange whale-watching, golfing, fishing, and diving packages. Affiliated with Aveda, the inn's Ancient Cedars Spa offers a host of packages and beauty and relaxation treatments. *Note:* Smoking is not permitted.

Osprey Lane at Chesterman Beach, P.O. Box 250, Tofino, BC V0R 2Z0. ℂ 800/333-4604 in North America or 250/725-3100. Fax 250/725-3110. www.wickinn.com. 75 units. From C$480 (US$480/£240) double. Special packages available year-round. Reduced shoulder and off-season rates. AE, DC, MC, V. Drive 5km (3 miles) south of Tofino toward Chesterman Beach to Osprey Lane. **Amenities:** Restaurant; bar; spa; concierge; in-room massage; babysitting; beach access; walking trail on-site; shuttle service available; rooms for those w/ limited mobility. *In room:* A/C, TV, CD player, dataport, Wi-Fi access, minibar, coffeemaker, hair dryer, iron.

WHERE TO DINE
IN TOFINO

If you're just looking for a cup of java and a snack, it's hard to beat the **Caffé Vincenté,** 441 Campbell St. (© **250/725-2599**), a touch of urban hip near the entrance to town. The cafe also does an excellent breakfast and lunch and serves afternoon dessert. The **Common Loaf Bakeshop,** 180 First St. (© **250/725-3915**), open 8am to 9pm, is locally famous as the gathering place for granola lovers, hippies, and other reprobates back when such things mattered in Tofino. At the "far" end of town, the Loaf offers excellent baked goods and a healthy lunch or dinner (soups and pizza) can be had for C$6 to C$11 (US$6–US$11/£3–£5.50).

The Pointe Restaurant ★ PACIFIC NORTHWEST   The famed restaurant at the Wickaninnish Inn is perched on the water's edge at Chesterman Beach, where a 280-degree view of the roaring Pacific is the backdrop to a dining experience that can only be described as pure Pacific Northwest. Under chef de cuisine Tim Cuff, the cooking has become even more regionally oriented, focusing on farm-fresh, organic Vancouver Island ingredients and the bounty (including Dungeness crab, spotted prawns, halibut, salmon, quail, lamb, and rabbit) of the very waters overlooked by the restaurant For long-time fans of The Pointe, a few of the inn's signature dishes remain on the new menu, including the Wickaninnish Potlatch, a chunky, fragrant stew of fish, shellfish, and vegetables simmered in a thick seafood broth. While most other seafood dishes are consistently exceptional, some of the menu's new dishes seem not just more local, but more earthbound, lacking the flair you'd expect at these prices. In addition to the seasonal a la carte menu is a menu influenced by the on-site Ancient Cedars Spa. Service is top-notch and the wine list wins awards from *Wine Spectator.*

The Wickaninnish Inn, Osprey Lane at Chesterman Beach. © **250/725-3100.** Reservations required. Main courses C$29–C$52 (US$29–US$52/£15–£26); 4-course gastronomic menu C$95 (US$95/£48). AE, MC, V. Daily 8am–9:30pm.

The RainCoast Café WEST COAST   This cozy restaurant, just off the main street, has developed a deserved reputation for some of the best—and best value—seafood and vegetarian dishes in town. There are a number of small plates, which you can assemble into a meal, many featuring local shrimp, oysters, and clams in innovative preparations. Main courses reflect an Asian influence. Thai bouillabaisse combines local fish and shellfish with a fragrant green-curry broth, while seared halibut nestles in pear-and-apple chutney. Start your meal off with the popular RainCoast Salad—smoked salmon, sautéed mushrooms, and chèvre on a bed of greens, with maple-balsamic vinaigrette.

120 Fourth St. © **250/725-2215.** www.raincoastcafe.com. Main courses C$15–C$30 (US$15–US$30/£7.50–£15). AE, MC, V. Daily 5:30–9:30pm.

Shelter ★★ PACIFIC NORTHWEST   You don't come here for the view; you come to this land-locked restaurant for the food. As one of the best of Tofino's new crop of restaurants, Shelter buys most of its fish and fresh ingredients directly from producers—right off the boat and right off the land. The result is cooking that's remarkable for its bright flavors and textures. The signature bouillabaisse is stuffed with local fish and shellfish and simmered in a fire-roasted tomato broth; a delicate halibut fillet surmounts a bed of double-smoked bacon lentils. Local low-alcohol white wines dominate the wine list, chosen to highlight the delicate flavors of fish and seafood. Just as there's no ocean view in the narrow, fireplace-warmed dining room, there's also no kitschy totem poles or wooden seagulls in fishing nets. Instead, a single, heraldic surfboard dominates the dining room, emblematic of the youthful energy of the Shelter's cooking style.

601 Campbell St. ℰ 250/725-3353. www.shelterrestaurant.com. Reservations recommended. Main courses C$16–C$27 (US$16–US$27/£8–£14). MC, V. Daily 5–10pm.

SOBO INTERNATIONAL This friendly, ambitious restaurant with "fresh food from here and there" got its start as a catering wagon in the Tofino Botanical Gardens, where it was discovered and written up by visiting journalists from the likes of the *New York Times*. In 2007, the catering wagon went into storage and SOBO moved into a real restaurant space in downtown Tofino. The food is still high quality and characterized by "We are the World" street-food eclecticism, but now you don't have to stand outdoors to order. As much as possible, all ingredients come from Vancouver Island. During the day, SOBO serves tasty but informal dishes such as smoked seafood chowder, wood-fired pizzas, soba noodle salad, and fish tacos, but weekend evenings bring a more formal dinner service and a more creative approach: Pan-seared local halibut is served with carrot and orange emulsion, and house-made pappardelle noodles is topped with duck confit, arugula, and Gorgonzola cheese. Considering the quality, the price is very fair, and you can't beat the friendly, youthful energy generated by the staff and kitchen.

311 Neill St. ℰ 250/725-2341. www.sobo.ca. Reservations recommended on weekends. Main courses C$20–C$24 (US$20–US$24/£10–£12). MC, V. Mon–Thurs 9am–5:30pm; Fri–Sun 9am–9pm.

5 Vancouver Island's East Coast: Parksville to Campbell River & Quadra Island

Vancouver Island's east coast is lined with long sandy beaches, world-class golf courses, and fishing resorts. Parksville and neighboring Qualicum Beach are longtime favorites for family vacations. With miles of beach for the kids and six local golf courses for the parents, these twinned towns are the perfect base for a relaxing vacation. Comox and Courtenay, 61km (38 miles) north, are another set of intergrown beach towns with access to great sea kayaking and tours to fossil digs. Campbell River (pop. 29,000), 46km (29 miles) farther north, is by far the most famous salmon-fishing center in British Columbia, with many long-established fishing resorts that have hosted everyone from the shah of Iran to John Wayne to Goldie Hawn.

ESSENTIALS

VISITOR INFORMATION For information on Qualicum Beach, contact the **Qualicum Beach Visitor Information Centre,** 2711 W. Island Hwy., Qualicum Beach, BC V9K 2C4 (ℰ 250/752-9532; www.qualicum.bc.ca). For information on Parksville and to get a free visitor's guide, contact the **Parksville Visitor Info Centre,** 1275 East Island Hwy., P.O. Box 99, Parksville, BC V9P 2G3 (ℰ 250/248-3613; www.chamber.parksville.bc.ca). For more information on the Comox/Courtenay area, contact the **Comox Valley Visitor Info Centre,** 2040 Cliffe Ave., Courtenay, BC V9N 2L3 (ℰ 888/357-4471 or 250/334-3234; www.discovercomoxvalley.com). The **Campbell River Visitor Info Centre** is at 1235 Shopper's Row, Campbell River, BC V9W 2C7 (ℰ 250/287-4636; www.campbellriverchamber.ca), or you can write for information to Box 400, Campbell River, BC V9W 5B6.

GETTING THERE **By Plane** The **Campbell River and District Regional Airport,** located south of Campbell River off Jubilee Parkway, has regularly scheduled flights on commuter planes to and from Vancouver and Seattle.

Comox Valley Regional Airport, north of Comox, welcomes daily flights from Vancouver, Calgary, and Edmonton. The airport is served by **Pacific Coastal Airlines** (✆ **800/663-2872;** www.pacific-coastal.com) and **WestJet** (✆ **877/952-4638;** www. westjet.com).

By Train   The **E&N Railiner** operates daily between Courtenay and Victoria, with stops in Parksville and Qualicum Beach.

By Bus   **Greyhound** (✆ **800/661-8747**) operates one bus daily with service from Victoria all the way to Port Hardy. There are three buses daily between Nanaimo Parksville, Qualicum Bay, Courtenay, and Campbell River. One-way fare from Nanaimo to Campbell River is C$25 (US$25/£13).

By Ferry   **BC Ferries** (✆ **888/724-5223** or 604/444-2890; www.bcferries.bc.ca) operates a 75-minute crossing from Powell River on the mainland to Little River, just north of Comox. The one-way fare is C$11 (US$11/£5.50) per passenger and C$34 (US$34/£17) per vehicle.

By Car   From Nanaimo, the Island Highway (Hwy. 19) links Parksville, Courtenay, and Campbell River with points north. Campbell River is 52km (32 miles) north of Courtenay and 266km (165 miles) north of Victoria.

EXPLORING THE EAST COAST

Parksville (pop. 9,576) and **Qualicum Beach** (pop. 6,874) are near the most popular beaches on Vancouver Island: Spending a week on the beach here is a family tradition for many B.C. families. Parksville claims to have the warmest ocean-water beaches in all Canada. **Rathtrevor Beach Provincial Park** is a popular place for swimming and sunbathing.

Facing each other across the Courtenay River Estuary, the twin towns **Comox** (pop. 11,847) and **Courtenay** (pop. 18,420) provide a bit of urban polish to a region rich in beaches, outdoor recreation, and dramatic land- and seascapes. The highlight of the **Courtenay District Museum & Paleontology Centre,** 207 Fourth St. (✆ **250/334-0686;** www.courtenaymuseum.ca), is a 12m (39-ft.) cast skeleton of an elasmosaur, a crocodile-like Cretaceous marine reptile. With four departures daily in July and August, the museum leads 3-hour **fossil tours** of its paleontology lab and to a local fossil dig; C$25 (US$25/£13) adults, C$20 (US$20/£10) seniors and students, C$15 (US$15/£7.50) children, or C$75 (US$75/£38) per family. Call ahead for reservations; tours also run on Saturdays April through June. Admission to the museum alone is by donation. Summer hours are Monday to Saturday 10am to 5pm and Sunday 12 to 4pm. Winter hours are Tuesday to Saturday 10am to 5pm.

The Museum at Campbell River (★, 470 Island Hwy. (✆ **250/287-3103;** www. crmuseum.ca), is worth seeking out. This large and captivating museum is devoted to carvings and artifacts from the local First Nations tribes; especially fine is the display of contemporary carved wooden masks. Also compelling is the sound-and-light presentation *The Treasures of Siwidi,* which uses masks to retell an ancient Native Indian myth. Another gallery houses a replica of a pioneer-era cabin and a collection of photos and tools from the early days of Vancouver Island logging. The 30-seat theater offers a couple of short films; one, *War of the Land Canoes,* is a 1914 documentary shot in local Native villages. The gift shop is one of the best places in Campbell River to buy authentic Native art and jewelry. The museum is open daily mid-May through September 10am to 5pm, and October through mid-May Tuesday to Sunday noon to

5pm. Admission is C$6 (US$6/£3) adults, C$4 (US$4/£2) students, C$15 (US$15/ £7.50) family, free for children under 6.

SPORTS & OUTDOOR ACTIVITIES

DIVING   The decommissioned **HMCS *Columbia*** was sunk in 1996 near the sea-life-rich waters of Seymour Narrows off the Quadra Island's west coast. For information on diving to this artificial reef and on other diving sites (with enticing names like Row and Be Damned, Whisky Point, Copper Cliffs, and Steep Island) in the Campbell River area, contact **Beaver Aquatics** (© **250/287-7652;** www.connected.bc.ca/~baquatics).

FISHING   Between Quadra Island and Campbell River, the broad Strait of Georgia squeezes down to a narrow mile-wide passage called Discovery Channel. All the salmon that entered the Strait of Juan de Fuca near Victoria to spawn in northerly rivers funnel down into this tight constriction, a churning waterway with 4m (13-ft.) tides.

However, fishing isn't what it once was in Campbell River, when tyee and coho salmon regularly tipped the scales at 34kg (75 lb.). Some salmon runs are now catch-and-release only, while others are open for limited catches; many fishing trips are now billed as much as wildlife adventures as hunting-and-gathering expeditions.

If you'd like to get out onto the waters and fish, be sure to call ahead and talk to an outfitter or the tourist center to find out what fish are running during your visit and if the seasons have been opened. Because of plummeting numbers of salmon and of recent treaties with the United States, the next few years will see even more greatly restricted fishing seasons in the waters off Vancouver Island. Don't be disappointed if there's no salmon fishing when you visit or if the salmon you hook is catch-and-release only. For one thing, there are other fish in the sea: Not all types of salmon are as threatened as the coho and tyee, and fishing is also good for halibut and other bottom fish. And if you really just want to get out on the water and have an adventure, consider a wildlife-viewing boat tour, offered by many fishing outfitters.

There are dozens of fishing guides in the Campbell River area, with a range of services that extend from basic to pure extravagance. Expect to pay around C$100 (US$100/£50) per hour for 4 to 5 hours of fishing with a no-frills outfitter. A flashier trip on a luxury cruiser can cost more than C$120 (US$120/£60) per hour. The most famous guides are associated with the Painter's Lodge and its sister property, April Point Lodge on Quadra Island. A few smaller fishing-guide operations include Coastal Wilderness Adventures © **866/640-1173** or 250/287-3427, www.coastwild.com) with both salt water and freshwater fly-fishing trips; **CR Fishing Village,** 260 Island Hwy. (© **250/287-3630;** www.fishingvillage.bc.ca); and **Coastal Island Fishing Adventures,** 663 Glenalan Rd. (© **888/225-9776** or 250/923-5831; www.coastal islandfishing.com), with operations in Campbell River and also at Gold River, on Vancouver Island's west coast.

You can also check out the info center's directory to fishing guides by following the links at www.campbellriverchamber.ca. Most hotels in Campbell River also offer fishing/ lodging packages; ask when you reserve.

GOLF   Greens fees at the following courses are C$50 to C$85 (US$50–US$85/ £25–£43) for 18 holes.

There are six courses in the Parksville–Qualicum Beach area, and more than a dozen within an hour's drive. Here are two favorites: The **Eagle Crest Golf Club,** 2035 Island Hwy. (© **250/752-6311**), is a 18-hole, par-71 course with an emphasis

The Inside Passage & Northern B.C.

Most of this chapter's towns and sights are geographically in British Columbia's midsection. By the time you reach **Prince Rupert** in northern B.C., however, you'll feel the palpable sense of being in the north: The days are long in summer and short in winter, and the spruce forestlands have a primordial character. First Nations peoples make up a greater percentage of the population here than in more southerly areas, and Native communities and heritage sites are common.

One of the most dramatic ways to reach northern British Columbia is by ferry. The BC Ferries **Inside Passage** route operates between Port Hardy, on Vancouver Island, and Prince Rupert, on the mainland; this 15-hour, 491km (305-mile) ferry run passes through mystical land- and seascapes, combining the best scenic elements of Norway's rocky fjords, New Zealand's majestic South Island, Chile's Patagonian range, and Nova Scotia's wild coastline, with excellent wildlife-viewing opportunities. Prince Rupert is a feisty little seaport on the northwestern edge of Canada, a perfect spot to explore deep-sea fishing, learn about ancient Native culture or perfect your sea kayaking skills. Inland from Prince Rupert, the Yellowhead Highway (Hwy. 16) follows the mighty Skeena and Bulkley rivers past First Nations villages and isolated ranches, finally reaching Prince George, the largest city in northern British Columbia. Prince George is also a transportation gateway.

If you're beguiled by what you read here, pick up a copy of *Frommer's British Columbia & the Canadian Rockies* for more extensive coverage of northern B.C.

THE INSIDE PASSAGE ✦✦   Fifteen hours may seem like a long time to be on a ferry. But you'll never get bored as the MV *Northern Adventure* noses its way through an incredibly scenic series of channels and calm inlets, flanked by green forested islands. Whales, porpoises, salmon, bald eagles, and sea lions line the route past the mostly uninhabited coastline. This BC Ferries run between Port Hardy and Prince Rupert follows the same route as expensive Alaska-bound cruise ships, but at a fraction of the cost. And in midsummer, with the north's long days, the trip is made almost entirely in daylight.

The ferry north from Port Hardy initially crosses a couple hours' worth of open sea—where waters can be rough—before ducking behind Calvert Island. Except for a brief patch of open sea in the Milbanke Sound north of Bella Bella, the rest of the trip follows a narrow, protected channel between the mainland and a series of islands.

The actual Inside Passage begins north of Bella Bella, as the ferry moves behind mountainous Princess Royal and Pitt islands. The passage between these islands and the mainland is very narrow—often less than a mile wide. The scenery is extraordinarily dramatic: Black cliffs drop thousands of feet directly into the channel, notched with hanging glacial valleys and fringed with forests. Powerful waterfalls shoot from dizzying heights into the sea. Eagles float along thermal drafts, and porpoises cavort in the ferry's wake. Even in poor conditions (the weather is very unpredictable here), this is an amazing trip.

Mid-May through September, the ferry crosses every other day, leaving Port Hardy (or southbound, Prince Rupert) at 7:30am and arriving in Prince Rupert (or Port Hardy) at 10:30pm. On board you'll find a cafeteria, snack bar, playroom, and gift shop. Midsummer one-way fares between Prince Rupert and Port Hardy are C$125 (US$125/£63) per adult car passenger or walk-on, C$300 (US$300/£150) for a normal-size vehicle; fuel surcharges are sometimes added. Reservations are mandatory. The ship's cabins rent for between C$75 and C$85 (US$75–US$85/£38–£43) for day use. Ferry service to/from Prince Rupert and Port Hardy continues at least once weekly the rest of the year, with somewhat lower fares, though the service runs over night, not the day, as in summer. See the BC Ferries website (www.bcferries. com) for dates and prices. From Prince Rupert, you can continue north to Skagway and other Alaska Panhandle destinations on the **Alaska Marine Highway System ferry** (© 800/642-0066), which docks at the same terminal.

WHERE TO STAY IN PORT HARDY   The night before the 15-hour Inside Passage ferry runs, Port Hardy is booked up and reservations are needed at most restaurants. If you are taking the ferry north in summer, you'll definitely need reservations the evening before the 7:30am departure; try the **Quarterdeck Inn**, 6555 Hardy Bay Rd. (© **877/902-0459** or 250/902-0455, www.quarterdeckresort.net), a pleasant hotel right on the fishing harbor with doubles from C$145 (US$145/£73).

WHERE TO STAY & DINE IN PRINCE RUPERT   One and a half kilometers (1 mile) from the ferry terminal, the **Park Avenue Campground,** 1750 Park Ave. (© **250/624-5861;** mailing address: Box 612, Prince Rupert, BC V8J 4J5), has 97 full-hookup and tenting sites. Facilities include a laundry, hot showers, flush toilets, a playground, mail drop, and pay phones. Make reservations in advance during summer because this campground is the best in the area. Rates are C$13 (US$13/£6.50) for tenters to C$26 (US$26/£13) for RVs.

Hotel options include **Coast Prince Rupert Hotel,** 118 Sixth St. (© **800/663-1144** or 250/624-6711; www.coasthotels.com), with well-maintained rooms right downtown for C$130 (US$130/£65) double; and the **Crest Hotel** ⋒, 222 First Ave. W. (© **800/663-8150** or 250/624-6771; www.cresthotel.bc.ca), which offers the best views in town, good dining, and beautifully furnished rooms for C$129–C$169 (US$129–US$169/£65–£85) double. Best dining bets include the **Breakers Pub** ⋒, 117 George Hills Way, on the Cow Bay Wharf (© **250/624-5990**), a popular pub with a harbor view and well-prepared international food; and **Cow Bay Café** ⋒, 205 Cow Bay Rd. (© **250/627-1212**), a homey place with lots of vegetarian options.

on shot making and accuracy; and the public **Morningstar Golf Club,** 525 Lowry's Rd. (© **250/248-8161**), is an 18-hole, 7,018-yard course with a par-72 rating.

One of the finest courses on Vancouver Island is the **Crown Isle Resort & Golf Community,** 339 Clubhouse Dr., Courtenay (© **888/338-8439** or 250/703-5050; www.crownisle.com). This lavish 18-hole links-style championship golf course has already hosted the Canadian Tour and Canadian Junior Men's Tournament. Because it was carved out of a dense forest, you may see wildlife grazing on the fairway and roughs at the **Storey Creek Golf Club,** Campbell River (© **250/923-3673**). Gentle creeks and ponds also wind through this course.

KAYAKING With the Courtenay Estuary and Hornby, Tree, and Denman islands an easy paddle away, sea kayaking is very popular in this area. In fact, you might consider it **Kayak Utopia,** which is the new business name used by **Comox Valley Kayaks,** 2020 Cliffe Ave., Courtenay and **Campbell River Kayaks,** 1620 Petersen Rd., Campbell River, (© **888/545-5595** or 250/334-2628; www.comoxvalleykayaks. com). Both locations offer rentals, lessons, and tours. A 2½-hour introductory lesson is C$39 (US$39/£20). A day trip to Tree Island goes for C$72 (US$72/£36). Rentals start at C$15 (US$15/£7.50) for 2 hours.

SKIING **Mount Washington Alpine Resort** ❅ (© **888/231-1499** or 250/338-1386; 250/338-1515 for snow report; www.mtwashington.bc.ca) is a 5-hour drive from Victoria and open year-round (for hiking or skiing, depending on the season). The summit reaches 1,588m (5,210 ft.), and the mountain averages 860cm (339 in.) of snow per year. A 505m (1,657-ft.) vertical drop and 60 groomed runs are served by eight lifts and a beginners' tow. Fifty-five kilometers (34 miles) of Nordic track-set and skating trails connect to Strathcona Provincial Park. The **Raven Lodge** has restaurants, equipment rentals, and locker rooms. Lift rates are C$56 (US$56/£28) for adults, C$46 (US$46/£23) for seniors and students, and C$30 (US$30/£15) for kids 7 to 12. Take the Strathcona Parkway 37km (23 miles) to Mount Washington, or use turnoff 130 from Inland Highway 19.

WHERE TO STAY & DINE
IN PARKSVILLE & QUALICUM BEACH

Tigh-Na-Mara Resort Hotel ❅❅❅ *Kids* This time-honored log-cabin resort just keeps getting better. Established in the 1940s on a forested waterfront beach (near Rathtrevor Beach Provincial Park), Tigh-Na-Mara has expanded over the years: more cottages, lodge-style rooms, and beautifully furnished condo-style suites with stunning ocean views, all log-built. Accommodations types include studio and one-bedroom lodge rooms, plus one- and two-bedroom cottages. If you're traveling with a group, the duplex cottages can be converted into a series of rooms large enough to sleep eight. The new oceanside condo units all have views as well as balconies or patios. All rooms and cottages at Tigh-Na-Mara have fireplaces and full bathrooms, and almost all have a kitchen. The cottages are comfortably lived in and homey, while the condos are new and lavish. New units are being added and older ones constantly renovated; 2007 saw the addition of flat-screen TVs, new furniture, new fitness facilities, and a renovation of the pool, hot tub, and sauna facilities. The new and very impressive **Grotto Spa** ❅❅ is the largest in the province and offers a mineral pool, body and massage treatments, plus a full line of aesthetic spa services: facials, waxing, manicures, and skin and hair care. Plus, the spa offers the spa-client-only Treetop Tapas and Grill, where friends and couples wine and dine in bathrobes after their treatments.

Families will especially appreciate the lengthy list of supervised child-friendly activities (many of them free), such as swimming lessons; babysitting (for a fee) is also available. The restaurant in the log-and-stone lodge serves an eclectic version of Northwest cuisine. There's a full children's menu, adjacent lounge, and Friday barbecues and dances in summer.

1155 Resort Dr., Parksville, BC V9P 2E5. © **800/663-7373** or 250/248-2072. Fax 250/248-4140. www.tigh-na-mara. com. 192 units. July–Aug C$199–C$359 (US$199–US$359/£100–£180) double. Rates vary throughout the year. Extra person C$8–C$15 (US$8–US$15/£4–£7.50). Weekly rates available. Varying minimum stays apply in midsummer, on holidays, and weekends. AE, DC, DISC, MC, V. Free parking. 1 pet allowed per cottage Sept–June, add C$2 (US$2/£1) per day. **Amenities:** Restaurant; bar; indoor pool and fitness facilities; golf courses nearby; unlit tennis court; full spa facilities; sauna; paddle boats; bike rental; children's programs; concierge; tour/activities desk (summer); car-rental desk; business center; babysitting; coin-op laundry; laundry service; dry cleaning; nonsmoking rooms. *In room:* TV/with on-demand movies, Wi-Fi access, fridge, coffeemaker.

IN COURTENAY

Kingfisher Oceanside Resort and Spa 🌟🌟   Located 7km (4½ miles) south of Courtenay, this long-established resort has modernized with an added bank of beachfront suites and a classy spa. The older motel units are large, nicely furnished rooms with balconies or patios, most with views of the pool and the Strait of Georgia. The newer one-bedroom suites are splendid, each with a full kitchen, two TVs, fireplace, and balcony that juts out over the beach; most suites have a two-person whirlpool tub in addition to a full bathroom with heated tile floors. Our favorite is no. 401, on the end of the building, with banks of windows on two sides. Two rooms are available for people with disabilities.

The **Kingfisher restaurant** is one of the best places to eat in Courtenay. The spa offers a wide selection of treatments and body work. Trained technicians offer thalassotherapy baths and wraps, massage, Reiki, and facials. Guests also have access to a steam cave. *Note:* Smoking is not permitted on the premises.

4330 Island Hwy. S, Courtenay, BC V9N 9R9. © **800/663-7929** or 250/338-1323. Fax 250/338-0058. www.kingfisher spa.com. 64 units. From C$170 (US$170/£85) double oceanview room; C$220 (US$220/£110) suite. Extra person C$25 (US$25/£13). Golf, ski, spa packages available. Senior discounts available. AE, DC, DISC, MC, V. Free parking. Pets allowed in some rooms, add C$25 (US$25/£13). **Amenities:** Restaurant; outdoor heated pool; golf course nearby; unlit tennis court; hot tub; oceanview fitness room; full-service spa; conference facilities; shuttle service; business center; Wi-Fi; laundry service; dry cleaning; nonsmoking rooms; executive-level rooms; 2 rooms for those w/limited mobility. *In room:* TV (suites have TV/DVD), fridge, coffeemaker, hair dryer.

IN CAMPBELL RIVER

Painter's Lodge Holiday & Fishing Resort 🌟🌟   This resort has been a favorite fishing hideaway for film stars such as John Wayne, Bob Hope, Goldie Hawn, and Kurt Russell. Once you see the awe-inspiring wooded coastal location, you'll understand why. Built in 1924 on a point overlooking the Discovery Passage, the lodge retains a rustic grandeur, with spacious rooms and suites decorated in natural wood and pastels. Four secluded, self-contained cottages nestled near the lodge are also available for rent. Guests can enjoy all three meals and cocktails in the **Legends Dining Room,** Tyee Pub (offering burgers and pub food), and Fireside Lounge. Amenities include guided fishing trips, and jogging and hiking trails around the grounds. The Painter's Lodge is also popular and well equipped for business conferences. Wheelchair-accessible rooms are available. *Note:* Guests are requested to smoke outside. Common areas are nonsmoking.

1625 McDonald Rd., Box 460, Campbell River, BC V9W 5C1. © **800/663-7090** or 250/286-1102. Fax 250/286-0158. www.painterslodge.com. 94 units. C$175–C$319 (US$175–US$319/£88–£160) double; from C$239–C$299

(US$239–US$299/£120–£150) cottage. Extra person C$12 (US$12/£6). Off-season discounts available. AE, DC, MC, V. Closed Nov–Mar. **Amenities:** Restaurant; pub; lounge; heated outdoor pool; golf course nearby; 2 unlit tennis courts; exercise room; Jacuzzi; bicycle, scooter, and kayak rentals; children's center; game room; tour and activities desk; car-rental desk; babysitting; laundry service; same-day dry cleaning; executive-level rooms. *In room:* A/C, TV, coffeemaker, hair dryer, iron.

6 Whistler: One of North America's Premier Ski Resorts

The premier ski resort in North America, according to *Ski* and *Snow Country* magazines, the **Whistler/Blackcomb complex** boasts more vertical, more lifts, and more varied ski terrain than any other on the continent. In winter, you can choose from downhill skiing, backcountry skiing, cross-country skiing, heli-skiing, snowboarding, snowmobiling, sleigh riding, and more. The area got the ultimate seal of approval from the International Olympic Committee in 2003 when it landed the opportunity to stage many of the Alpine events for the 2010 Winter Games. It's not a bad place in summer either, when visitors can indulge in rafting, hiking, golfing, and horseback riding.

And then there's **Whistler Village,** a resort town with a year-round population of 10,000—plus 115 hotels and lodgings and myriad restaurants—arranged around a central village street in a compact enough fashion you can park your car and remain a pedestrian for the duration of your stay.

ESSENTIALS

VISITOR INFORMATION   The **Whistler Visitor Info Centre,** easy to find on the Village Bus Loop at 4230 Gateway Dr., Whistler, BC V0N 1B4 (© **604/932-5522;** www.whistlerchamber.com), is open daily 9am to 5pm. **Tourism Whistler** is at the Whistler Conference Centre at 4010 Whistler Way, Whistler, BC V0N 1B0, open daily 9am to 5pm (© **877/991-9988** or 604/938-2769; www.tourismwhistler.com). Both offices can assist you with event tickets, reservations for recreation, and last-minute accommodations bookings.

GETTING THERE   **By Car**   Whistler is about a 2-hour drive from Vancouver along Highway 99, also called the Sea to Sky Highway. The drive is spectacular, winding along the edge of Howe Sound before climbing up through the mountains. Through 2009, you'll need to allow extra time for road construction while driving this extravagantly scenic route, as road crews are widening the road in advance of the 2010 Olympics. Before you depart, check **www.tourismwhistler.com** for updates on lane and road closures so you don't get stuck. Note that the highway may be closed on weekdays from 12:30 to 2:30pm, midnight to 2am, and 3 to 5am for blasting. Parking at the mountain is free for day skiers.

By Bus   **Whistler Express,** 8695 Barnard St., Vancouver (© **604/266-5386** in Vancouver, or 604/905-0041 in Whistler; www.perimeterbus.com), operates door-to-door bus service from Vancouver International Airport via 16 downtown Vancouver hotels (for registered guests) to over 25 lodgings in Whistler. Buses depart seven times daily in the summer and nine times in winter. The trip typically takes about 3 hours, though construction on the Sea to Sky Highway may delay the bus; one-way fares are C$67 (US$67/£34) for adults and C$45 (US$45/£23) for children. Kids under 5 ride free. Reservations are required year-round. **Greyhound,** Pacific Central Station, 1150 Station St., Vancouver (© **604/662-8051** in Vancouver, or 604/482-8747 in Whistler; www.greyhound.ca), operates service from the Vancouver Bus Depot to the

Whistler bus depot at 2029 London Lane. The trip takes about 2½ hours; one-way fares are C$18 (US$18/£9) for adults and C$10 (US$10/£5) for children ages 5 to 12. **Pacific Coach Lines** (*©* **800/661-1725** or 604/662-7575; www.pacificcoach. com) operates bus service from Vancouver International Airport to Whistler-area hotels for C$62 (US$62/£31) and C$32 (US$32/£16) children 5 to 11 one-way.

Snowbus (*©* **604/685-7669;** www.snowbus.ca) offers service to/from Whistler and Vancouver-area suburbs (Richmond, Burnaby, North Vancouber) and other neighborhood locations in addition to downtown Vancouver and the airport. On Friday and weekend morning departures, riders have the option of hot breakfasts; free movies are offered during the journey. Also available from the website is a C$20 (US$20/£10) SnowCard, which offers discounts on Snowbus transportation and lift-ticket packages, and at Vancouver and Whistler area restaurants, recreational clothing stores, and ski and board shops. One-way fares between Vancouver and Whistler are C$21 (US$21/£11). Snowbus operates daily, though only during ski season.

By Train The **Whistler Mountaineer,** a new route from Rocky Mountaineer Vacations (*©* **877/460-3200** or 604/606-7245; www.whistlermountaineer.com), offers stops in Vancouver and Whistler along the highly scenic Sea to Sky corridor. There's one train in each direction daily, departing 8:30am from North Vancouver Station, arriving at Whistler Station at 11:30am. The trains returns in the afternoon, departing Whistler Station at 2:30pm and arriving at North Vancouver Station at 6pm. Currently the train operates mid-April to mid-October only. The least expensive fair is C$110 (US$110/£55) adult, C$60 (US$60/£30) children 2 to 11 one-way, or C$199 (US$199/£100) adult, C$109 (US$109/£55) children round-trip.

GETTING AROUND The complex of villages and communities at Whistler can be initially confusing. Be sure to pick up a map when you get to Whistler and study it—the curving streets are made for pedestrians and defy easy negotiation by drivers, particularly in the winter darkness. **Whistler Village** is at the base of the ski runs at Whistler Peak. **Upper Village,** at the base of Blackcomb ski runs is just across Fitzsimmons Creek from Whistler Village. As development continues, the distinction between these two "villages" is disappearing, though Whistler Village is the center for most independent restaurants, shopping, and the youthful night-life scene. Upper Village, centered on the Four Seasons and Fairmont Chateau Whistler hotels, is quieter and more upscale. However, both villages are compact and pedestrian oriented, and signed trails and paths link together shops, lodgings, and restaurants in the central resort area. If you're staying in Whistler Village or Upper Village, you should plan to park your car and leave it for the duration of your stay. The walk between the two village resort areas takes about 10 minutes.

Many smaller inns, B&Bs, restaurants, and services are located outside the nucleus of Whistler Village and Upper Village. Creekside is a large development east (downhill) from Whistler Village, while the shores of Alta Lake are ringed with residential areas and golf courses.

By Bus The year-round Whistler and Valley Express (WAVE) **public bus system** (*©* **604/932-4020**) offers 14 routes in the Whistler area. Buses have both bike and ski racks. Most routes cross paths at the Gondola Transit Exchange off Blackcomb Way, near the base of the Whistler Mountain lifts. One-way fares are C$1.50 (US$1.50/75p) for adults and C$1.25 (US$1.25/65p) for seniors and students. For a route map, go to www.busonline.ca.

Whistler & the 2010 Winter Olympic & Paralympic Games

The 2010 Olympic Winter Games will be staged in Vancouver and Whistler from February 12 to 28, 2010. These cities will host the Paralympic Winter Games from March 12 to 21, 2010. For information on the games, contact **Vancouver 2010 Organizing Committee**, 202–1002 Lynham Rd., Whistler, BC V0N 1B1 (© **866/932-2010** or 604/932-2010; www.vancouver2010.com).

Events to be held in Whistler include:

- Alpine skiing (downhill, super G, giant slalom, slalom, combined)
- Nordic skiing (biathlon, cross-country skiing, ski jumping, Nordic combined)
- Sliding (bobsleigh, luge, skeleton)
- Alpine skiing (Paralympic)
- Biathlon (Paralympic)
- Cross-country skiing

Events will take place in three major competition venues: Alpine skiing events on Whistler Mountain's Creekside runs; bobsled, luge, and skeleton events at the new Sliding Centre on Blackcomb Mountain; and Nordic, biathlon, and ski-jumping competition events at newly developed facilities in Callahan Valley, about 10km (6 miles) southwest of Whistler.

All men's and women's downhill ski events will be held at the Whistler Creekside, including downhill, Super G, giant slalom, slalom, and combined. The men's events will all take place on the Dave Murray Downhill run, widely considered as one of the top three courses in the world. The women's and Paralympic alpine course will begin on Wild Card run, swing over to Lower Jimmie's Joker, and wind its way down a portion of Franz's Run to finally join up with the men's course on the Lower Dave Murray Downhill.

By Taxi   The village's taxis operate around the clock. Taxi tours, golf-course transfers, and airport transport are also offered by **Airport Limousine Service** (© **604/273-1331**), **Whistler Taxi** (© **604/938-3333**), and **Sea to Sky Taxi** (© **604/932-3333**).

By Car   Rental cars are available from **Avis** in the Cascade Lodge, 4315 Northlands Blvd. (© **800/TRY-AVIS** or 604/932-1236).

SPECIAL EVENTS   Downhill ski competitions are held December through May, including the **TELUS Winter Classic** (Jan), **Nokia Snowboard FIS World Cup** (Feb), and the **TELUS World Ski & Snowboard Festival** (Apr). In August, mountain bikers compete in **Crankworx.**

During the third week in July, the villages host **Whistler's Roots Weekend** (© **604/932-2394**). Down in the villages and up on the mountains, you'll hear the sounds of Celtic, zydeco, bluegrass, folk, and world-beat music at free and ticketed events. The **Whistler Summit Concert Series** (© **604/932-3434**) is held during August weekends. The mountains provide a stunning backdrop for the on-mountain concerts.

The second weekend in September ushers in the **Whistler Jazz & Blues Festival** (© **604/932-2394**), featuring live performances in the village squares and the surrounding clubs. **Cornucopia** (© **604/932-3434**) is Whistler's premier wine-and-food

A brand-new competition center is being built for the cross-country, ski-jumping, biathlon, and Nordic combined events at Callahan Valley. The construction project involves the competition facilities (including two ski jumps and three separate stadiums), 14km (8.7 miles) of competition trails, and 8km (5 miles) of training trails, as well as utility installation, access roads, parking lots, technical sport buildings, a day lodge, and other related infrastructure. The stadiums, each of which will house 12,000 fans, will be removed after the Olympics. An additional 20km to 25km (12–16 miles) of recreational trails will cover cross-country ski terrain next to the Winter Games Callahan Valley core area.

The Whistler Sliding Centre is located on Blackcomb Mountain. The project features construction of a new 1,700m (5,577-ft.) concrete sliding track, refrigeration facilities, and access road. Bobsleigh, luge, and skeleton events will take place here. The sliding track will remain after the Olympics, becoming part of the permanent recreational facilities at Whistler-Blackcomb.

The Whistler Olympic and Paralympic Village site is located within the Cheakamus Valley, near the so-called "Function Junction" at the western entrance to Whistler. Designed for 2,400 athletes and officials, the Whistler Olympic and Paralympic Village is about 10 minutes from all Whistler competition venues. A short shuttle ride will take athletes to the heart of Whistler Village and the nightly outdoor medal ceremonies at the Whistler Celebration Plaza, with the capacity for 8,000. The Paralympic Closing Ceremony will also be presented at this site.

festival. Held in November, the opening gala showcases top wineries from the Pacific region, plus lots of food events and tastings from local chefs.

SKIING & SNOWBOARDING

CROSS-COUNTRY SKIING   The 32km (20 miles) of easy to very difficult marked trails at **Lost Lake** start at the Lorimer Rd. bridge over Fitzsimmons Creek, just west of Upper Village. Passes are C$16 (US$16/£8) per day. A 1-hour cross-country lesson runs about C$35 (US$35/£18) and is available from **Cross Country Connection** (© 604/905-0071; www.crosscountryconnection.bc.ca), also at the trail head. They also offer Nordic ski rentals, though customers having lessons have dibs on rentals. The website also has a downloadable map of the trail system.

Lessons are also available from **Whistler Nordic Centre** at the Nicklaus North Golf Course Clubhouse (© 888/771-2382 or 604/932-7711; www.whistlerski-hike.com), with cross-country ski trails leading through the undulating golf course grounds along the shores of Green Lake. The Nordic Centre is a great place to learn or master cross-country skiing, with 5km (3 miles) of well-groomed novice trails; the trails also connect to the Lost Lake trail system for those who want more of a challenge. The **Valley Trail System** in the village becomes a well-marked cross-country ski trail during winter.

Peak to Peak

More superlatives for Whistler: Intrawest, the corporation behind Whistler Blackcomb Resort, is building a record-defying gondola that will link together the peaks of Whistler (elev. 2,182m/7,160 ft.) and Blackcomb (elev. 2,284m/7,494 ft.) mountains. Set to open in December 2008, the **Peak to Peak Gondola** will have the longest free-span lift in the world, at 3.024km (1¾ miles) and a total length of 4.4km (2¾ miles). The Peak to Peak Gondola will also be the highest detachable lift in the world, at 415m (1,362 ft.) above the valley floor. The gondola will include 28 cars carrying up to 28 passengers each, with cars leaving approximately every 54 seconds; it will be capable of carrying 2,050 people per hour each way. The lift will take 11 minutes to travel from peak to peak. Clearly, the new gondola will offer skiers greater flexibility for skiing the highest runs of both mountains, and will offer summer visitors one of the most attention-grabbing gondola rides in the world.

DOWNHILL SKIING   The **Whistler/Blackcomb Mountains,** 4545 Blackcomb Way, Whistler, BC V0N 1B4 (*(C)* **866/218-9690** or 604/932-3434; snow report 604/687-1032; www.whistlerblackcomb.com), are jointly operated by Intrawest, so your pass gives access to both ski areas. You can book nearly all accommodations and activities in Whistler from their website.

From its base in Whistler Village, **Whistler Mountain** has 1,530m (5,020 ft.) of vertical and over 100 marked runs that are serviced by a total of 20 lifts. From its base in Upper Village, **Blackcomb Mountain** has 1,610m (5,282 ft.) of vertical and over 100 marked runs that are served by a total of 17 lifts. Both mountains also have bowls and glade skiing, with Blackcomb offering glacier skiing well into August. Together, the two mountains comprise the largest ski resort in North America, offering over 8,100 skiable acres—3,000 more than the largest U.S resort.

During winter, lift tickets for 2 days of skiing (out of 3) on both mountains range from C$120 to C$164 (US$120–US$164/£60–£82) for adults, C$102 to C$139 (US$102–US$139/£51–£70) for seniors, and C$62 to $85 (US$62–US$85/£31–£43) for children 7 to 12. Lifts are open 8:30am to 3:30pm (to 4:30pm mid-Mar to closing, depending on weather and conditions). Whistler/Blackcomb offers ski lessons and guides for all levels and interests. (For skiers looking to try snowboarding, a rental package and a half-day lesson is a particularly attractive option.) Phone **Guest Relations** at *(C)* **604/932-3434** for details. Ski, snowboard, and boot rentals are available from the resort, and can be booked online. In addition, dozens of independent shops provide equipment rentals. **Affinity Sports** (www.affinityrentals.com) has six locations in the Whistler area, with online reservations available. **Summit Ski** (*(C)* **604/938-6225** or 604/932-6225; www.summitsport.com) has three locations in Whistler and rents high-performance and regular skis, snowboards, cross-country skis, and snowshoes.

HELI-SKIING & HELI-BOARDING   Forget lift lines and crowds. Ride a helicopter to the crest of a Coast Range peak and experience the ultimate in powder skiing. You'll need to be a confident intermediate to advanced skier in good shape to join a heli-ski trip. **Whistler Heli-Skiing** (*(C)* **888/HELISKI** or 604/932-4105; www.whistlerheliskiing.com), offers a three-run day, with 1,400m to 2,300m (4,593 ft.–7,546 ft.) of vertical helicopter lift, costing C$730 (US$730/£365) per person. **Coast**

Range Heli-Skiing (© **800/701-8744** or 604/894-1144; www.coastrangeheliskiing. com) offers a 4-run day, with 1,800m to 4,000m (5,906 ft.–13,123 ft.) of vertical helicopter lift, for C$845 (US$845/£423) per person. Both trips include a guide and lunch.

SNO-CAT SKIING & BOARDING   Lifts and choppers aren't the only way up a mountain. **Powder Mountain Catskiing** (© **877/PWDR-FIX** or 604/932-0169; www.powdermountaincatskiing.com) uses Sno-Cats to climb up into a private skiing area south of Whistler where skiers and boarders will find 1,600 skiable hectares (3,954 acres) on two mountains. The price—C$479 (US$479/£240) per person— pays for a full day of skiing, usually six to eight runs down 2,100 to 3,000 vertical meters (6,890–9,843 ft.) of untracked powder, plus transport to/from Whistler, breakfast, lunch, and guides.

OTHER WINTER ACTIVITIES

DOG SLEDDING   Explore the old-growth forests of the Soo Valley Wildlife Preserve while mushing a team of eager Huskies. **Cougar Mountain** (© **888/297-2222** or 604/932-4086; www.cougarmountain.ca) offers a choice of dog-sledding trips, and if the weather and terrain permits, you may even get to drive the dogs yourself. A 4-hour Woof Pack tour costs C$280 (US$280/£140) for two people sharing a sled.

ICE CLIMBING   Climb a frozen waterfall with Coast Mountain Guides (© **604/ 932-7711;** www.coastmountainguides.com). Guides provide all equipment; beginners are welcome. Climbs start at C$347 (US$347/£174) per person.

SLEIGH RIDING   For an old-fashioned horse-drawn sleigh ride, contact **Blackcomb Horsedrawn Sleigh Rides,** 103–4338 Main St., Whistler, BC V0N 1B4 (© **604/932-7631;** www.blackcombsleighrides.com). Giant Percheron horses lead the way and comfortable sleighs with padded seats and cozy blankets keep you warm. A number of tours are available, starting with basic half-hour rides for C$45 (US$45/ £23) for adults, and C$25 (US$25/£13) for children 3 to 12. Longer rides and dinner sleigh ride combos are also available.

SNOWMOBILING   The year-round ATV/snowmobile tours offered by **Canadian Snowmobile Adventures Ltd.,** Carleton Lodge (© **604/938-1616;** www.canadian snowmobile.com), are a unique way to take to the Whistler Mountain trails. Exploring the Fitzsimmons Creek watershed, a 2-hour tour costs C$119 (US$119/£60) for a driver and C$89 (US$89/£45) for a passenger. If you're up for more adventure, consider a night-time snowmobile tour to a remote mountain cabin, where a fondue dinner awaits, for C$169 (US$169/£85). For experienced snowmobilers, there's an 8-hour tour to a real mining ghost town, with lunch in a still-operational miner's pub; it costs C$600 (US$600/£300) per person.

SNOWSHOEING   Snowshoeing makes a great family outing; kids really enjoy the experience of walking on snow. Most ski-rental outfits also offer showshoe rentals, so you won't have to look far to find a pair. If you want to just rent the snowshoes and find your own way around, rentals are typically C$15 (US$15/£7.50) per day. **Outdoor Adventures@Whistler,** P.O. Box 1054, Whistler, BC V0N 1B0 (© **604/932-0647;** www.adventureswhistler.com), has guided tours for novices at C$69 (US$69/£35) for 1½ hours.

SUMMER ACTIVITIES

BIKING   Whistler is world famous for its mountain biking. While many gonzo riders come from around the world to test themselves on the many technical trails, others come to enjoy the gentler pleasures of simply biking through the forest.

Some of the best mountain-bike trails in the village are in Whistler and Blackcomb mountains' **Bike Park,** which offers 200km (124 miles) of lift-serviced trails and mountain pathways with more than 1,200m (3,937 ft.) of vertical drop. The park has three access lifts and two jump areas; the trail system is labeled from green circle, blue square, to black diamond. There's also the **Air Dome,** a 929 sq. m (10,000-sq.-ft.) covered indoor mountain bike–training facility with a huge foam pit, ramps, and a quarter pipe and half pipe. Per-day lift tickets and park admission are C$47 (US$47/ £24) adults, C$25 (US$25/£13) youths ages 10 to 12.

If you're not ready for daredevil riding on the mountain, the 30km (19-mile) paved **Valley Trail** is a pedestrian/bicycle route linking parks, neighborhoods, and playgrounds around Whistler Village. For other biking trails, check out the comprehensive Whistler biking website at **www.whistlermountainbike.com**.

In summer, nearly every ski shop switches gears and offers bike rentals. You'll have absolutely no problem finding a bike to rent in Whistler Village. If you want to call ahead and reserve a bike, try **Whistler Bike Company,** Hilton Whistler Resort, 4050 Whistler Way, Whistler Village (© **604/938-9511**). Prices range from C$30 (US$30/ £15) per half-day for a commuting-style bike to C$60 to C$85 (US$60–US$85/ £30–£43) per half-day for a high-end mountain bike.

CANOEING & KAYAKING   The 2-hour River of Golden Dreams Kayak & Canoe Tour offered by **Whistler Outdoor Experience,** P.O. Box 151, Whistler, BC V0N 1B0 (© **604/932-3389;** www.whistleroutdoor.com), is a great way to get acquainted with an exhilarating stretch of slow-moving glacial water that runs between Green Lake and Alta Lake behind the village of Whistler. Packages range from C$55 (US$55/£28) per person unguided to C$85 (US$85/£43) per person with a guide. **Outdoor Adventures Whistler** (© **604/932-0647;** www.adventureswhistler.com) offers canoe trips down the Lillooet River. A guided, 3-hour sunset cruise in six-person, voyagery-style canoes is C$109 (US$109/£55) adult, C$59 (US$59/£30) children 6 to 12.

FISHING   Spring runs of steelhead, rainbow trout, and Dolly Varden char; summer runs of cutthroat and salmon; and fall runs of coho salmon attract anglers from around the world to the many glacier-fed lakes and rivers in the area and to **Birkenhead Lake Provincial Park,** 67km (42 miles) north of Pemberton. Bring your favorite fly rod and don't forget to buy a fishing license when you arrive. **Whistler Flyfishing,** 117–4368 Main St. (© **888/822-3474** or 604/932-7221; www.whistlerfly fishing.com), offers half-day and full-day catch-and-release fishing trips in the surrounding glacier rivers. Half-day rates are C$175 (US$175/£88) per person, based on two people, which includes all fishing gear, round-trip transport to and from the Whistler Village Bus Loop, and a snack or lunch (but not a B.C. fishing license, which is required).

GOLF   Robert Trent Jones's Fairmont **Chateau Whistler Golf Club,** at the base of Blackcomb Mountain (© **604/938-2092,** or pro shop 604/938-2095), is an 18-hole, par-72 course. Greens fees are C$69 to C$195 (US$69–US$195/£35–£98). A multiple-award-winning golf course, **Nicklaus North at Whistler** (© **604/938-9898**) is a 5-minute drive north of the village on the shores of Green Lake. The 6,908-yard, par-71 course's mountain views are spectacular. Greens fees are C$125 to C$189

(US\$125–US\$189/£63–£95). The 6,676-yard **Whistler Golf Club** (© **800/376-1777** or 604/932-4544), designed by Arnold Palmer, features nine lakes, two creeks, and magnificent vistas. In addition to the 18-hole, par-72 course, the club offers a driving range, putting green, sand bunker, and pitching area. Greens fees are C\$99 to C\$159 (US\$99–US\$159/£50–£80).

HIKING   There are numerous easy hiking trails in and around Whistler. (Just remember—never hike alone, and bring plenty of water with you.) You can take ski lifts up to Whistler and Blackcomb mountains' trails during summer, but you have a number of other choices as well. The **Lost Lake Trail** starts at the northern end of the Day Skier Parking Lot at Blackcomb. The 30km (19 miles) of marked trails that wind around creeks, beaver dams, blueberry patches, and lush cedar groves are ideal for biking, cross-country skiing, or just strolling and picnicking.

The **Valley Trail System** is a well-marked paved trail connecting parts of Whistler. The trail starts on the west side of Highway 99 adjacent to the Whistler Golf Course and winds through quiet residential areas, as well as golf courses and parks. Garibaldi Provincial Park's **Singing Pass Trail** is a 4-hour hike of moderate difficulty. The fun way to experience this trail is to take the Whistler Mountain gondola to the top and walk down the well-marked path that ends in the village.

Whistler Mountain's premier chairlift—the Peak Chair—remains open in summer for transport to the mountain's 2,182m (7,159-ft.) summit for alpine sightseeing and hiking. Called the **Peak Adventure** (© **866/218-9690** or 604/932-3434; www.whistlerblackcomb.com), tickets are C\$30 (US\$30/£15) adult, C\$24 (US\$24/£12) seniors and youths 13 to 18, and C\$12 (US\$12/£6) children 7 to 12. In addition to the exhilarating open-air chairlift ride, you see ancient glaciers, snowcapped peaks, dormant volcanoes, and the beautiful Coast Mountain Range. At the top, there are more than 48km (30 miles) of alpine hiking trails including the Peak Interpretive Walk; guided hikes are available.

Nairn Falls Provincial Park is about 33km (21 miles) north of Whistler on Highway 99. It features a 1.5km-long (1-mile) trail leading you to a stupendous view of the icy-cold Green River as it plunges 60m (197 ft.) over a rocky cliff into a narrow gorge on its way downstream. On Highway 99 north of Mount Currie, **Joffre Lakes Provincial Park** is an intermediate-level hike leading past several brilliant-blue glacial lakes up to the very foot of a glacier. The **Ancient Cedars** area of Cougar Mountain is an awe-inspiring grove of towering cedars and Douglas firs. Some of the trees are over 1,000 years old and measure 2.5m (8 ft.) in diameter.

HORSEBACK RIDING   **Adventure Ranch** near Pemberton (© **604/894 5200;** www.adventureranch.net) offers 2-hour horseback tours (C\$65/US\$65/£33) from its Lillooet River–side ranch, 30 minutes from Whistler.

JET BOATING   **Whistler River Adventures** (© **604/932-3532;** www.whistlerriver.com) takes guests up the Lillooet River from near Pemberton. The tour surges past large rapids, spectacular glacier peaks, and traditional Native fishing camps. Deer, bear, osprey, and spawning salmon are frequently seen. This 3-hour-long trip is C\$99 (US\$99/£50); kids 10 to 16 get a C\$10 (US\$10/£5) discount.

RAFTING   **Whistler River Adventures** (see "Jet Boating," above) offers five different day trips on local rivers, ranging from a placid all-generation paddle to a roaring whitewater adventure. Four-hour paddle trips on the Cheakamus River are gentle enough for families (C\$89/US\$89/£45 adults, C\$69/US\$69/£35 youths 10–16, and

C$44/US$44/£22 children 5–9), while the 8-hour round-trip Squamish River white-water trip is for those seeking an adrenaline high (C$154/US$154/£77 adults, C$144/US$144/£72 youths 10–16). All trips include equipment and ground transport. The 8-hour trip includes a salmon barbecue lunch.

TENNIS The **Whistler Racquet & Golf Resort,** 4500 Northland Blvd. (© **604/ 932-1991;** www.whistlertennis.com), features three covered courts, seven outdoor courts, and a practice cage, all open to drop-in visitors. Indoor courts are C$32 (US$32/£16) per hour and outdoor courts are C$16 (US$16/£8) per hour. Adult and junior tennis camps are offered during summer. Camp prices range from C$300 to C$370 (US$300–US$370/£150–£185) for a 3-day camp; kids camps cost C$48 (US$48/£24) per day drop-in or C$195 (US$195/£98) for a 5-day camp.

There are **free public courts** at Myrtle Public School, Alpha Lake Park, Meadow Park, Millar's Pond, Brio, Blackcomb Benchlands, White Gold, and Emerald Park. Call © **604/938-PARK** for details.

ZIP LINING One of Whistler's newest thrills are the year-round steel zip-line rides offered by **Ziptrek Ecotours** (© **866/935-0001** or 604/935-0001; www.ziptrek. com). Zip lining involves gliding along a suspended steel cable using a pulley and climbing harness at speeds up to 89kmph (55mph). Guided tours include zip-line rides that range in height and length from 24m to 610m (79–2,000 ft.), spanning 11 hectares (27 acres) in the valley between Whistler and Blackcomb Mountains, an area of untouched coastal temperate rainforest. The new adrenaline-pumping Eagle tour drops 20 stories and ends in Whistler Village itself. Tickets are C$98 (US$98/£49) adults, C$78 (US$78/£39) seniors and youths 14 and under. For those not up to zip lining, Ziptrek also offers **TreeTrek,** a network of suspended boardwalks, aerial stairways, and bridges at heights of over 24m (80 ft.) in the tree canopy. Tickets are C$39 (US$39/£20) adults and C$29 (US$29/£15) seniors and youth 14 and under.

EXPLORING THE TOWN

SEEING THE SIGHTS Opening to the public in 2008, the **Squamish Lil'wat Cultural Centre** is an architecturally stunning showcase of soaring glass and stone, designed to celebrate the joint history and living cultures of the Squamish and Lil'wat Nations. The facility comprises 2,824 sq. m (30,400 sq. ft.) in total, including both indoor and outdoor space, anchored by the monumental Great Hall with traditional artifacts and 67m (220-ft.) glass plank walls revealing spectacular mountain and forest views. The center also features a gallery of Squamish and Lil'wat sacred cultural treasures and icons, plus a shop for First Nations art. Outdoors is a Squamish longhouse, which was the traditional dwelling of the Squamish people, and a replica Lil'wat *ístken* or pit house, which was the traditional dwelling of the Lil'wat people. The cultural center is located at the entrance to the Upper Village, along Lorimer Road, on a wedge of land between the Four Seasons Resort and The Fairmont Chateau Whistler. For information on hours and admissions, go to www.slcc.ca.

To learn more about Whistler's heritage, flora, and fauna, visit the **Whistler Museum & Archives Society,** 4329 Main St., off Northlands Boulevard (© **604/932-2019**). June through Labour Day, the museum is open daily 10am to 4pm; call ahead for winter opening hours. Admission is C$5 (US$5/£2.50) for adults, C$4 (US$4/£2) seniors and students, and C$3 (US$3/£1.50) youths 7 to 18.

The **Path Gallery,** 4338 Main St. © **604/932-7570**), is devoted to Northwest Coast Native art, including totem poles, carved masks, and prints. **Gallery Row** in the

Hilton Whistler Resort consists of three galleries: the **Whistler Village Art Gallery** (© 604/938-3001), the **Black Tusk Gallery** (© 604/905-5540), and the **Adele Campbell Gallery** (© 604/938-0887). Their collections include fine art, sculpture, and glass.

At the base of Blackcomb Mountain, the **Adventure Zone** offers a kid-centric collection of activities in a circuslike atmosphere. Activities including horseback riding, minigolf, bungee trampolines, flying trapeze, wall climbing, gondola rides, spinning human gyroscopes, zip lining, and luge rides. A five-adventure pass costs C$39 (US$39/£20); see www.whistlerblackcomb.com for more information.

Based at Blackcomb Mountain, the **Dave Murray Summer Ski Camp,** P.O. Box 98, Whistler, BC V0N 1B0 (© **604/932-5765;** www.skiandsnowboard.com), is North America's longest-running summer ski camp. Eight-day junior programs cost about C$1,750 (US$1,750/£875) mid-June to mid-July (lodging not included; day camp lessons cost C$185/US$185/£93).

SHOPPING   **Whistler Village** and the area surrounding the **Blackcomb Mountain lift** brim with clothing, jewelry, craft, specialty, gift, and equipment shops open daily 10am to 6pm. You'll have absolutely no problem finding interesting places to shop in Whistler—both quality and prices are high.

SPAS   Spas are definitely a growth industry in Whistler. Nearly all the large hotels now feature spas, and a number of independent spas line the streets of Whistler Village. The **Vida Wellness Spa** at Chateau Whistler Resort (© **604/938-2086**) is considered one of the best in Whistler. Open daily 8am to 9pm, it offers massage therapy, aromatherapy, skincare, body wraps, and steam baths. Another noteworthy hotel spa is the Westin Resort's **Avello Spa,** 400–4090 Whistler Way (© **877/935-7111** or 604/935-3444; www.whistlerspa.com), which offers a host of spa services as well as holistic and hydrotherapy treatments. The newest and swankiest is **The Spa at Four Seasons Resort** (© **604/966-2620**), with 15 treatment rooms, a Vichy shower, yoga and fitness classes, and a vast assortment of luxurious treatments from mineral scrubs to wildflower baths.

Solarice Wellness Centre and Spa, with locations at 4308 Main St. (© **866/ 368-0888** or 604/966-0888) and 4230 Gateway Dr. (© **888/935-1222** or 604/935-2222; www.sachaspa.com), is a highly atmospheric day spa with exotic-themed treatment rooms and a wide selection of beauty and relaxation treatments. The therapists at **Whistler Physiotherapy** (© **604/932-4001** or 604/938-9001; www.whistlerphysio.com) have a lot of experience with the typical ski, board, and hiking injuries. There are three locations: 339–4370 Lorimer Rd., at Marketplace; 202–2011 Innsbruck Dr., next to Boston Pizza in Creekside; and 4433 Sundial Place in Whistler Village.

WHERE TO STAY

South of Whistler on the Sea to Sky corridor is the very popular **Alice Lake Provincial Park.** About 27km (17 miles) north of Whistler, the well-maintained campground at **Nairn Falls,** Highway 99 (© **604/898-3678**), is more adult oriented, with pit toilets, pumped well water, fire pits, and firewood, but no showers. The 85 campsites at **Birkenhead Lake Provincial Park,** off Portage Road, Birken (© **604/ 898-3678**), fill up very quickly during summer. To reserve at any of these provincial parks, call **Discover Camping** at © **800/689-9025.** Campsites are C$14 (US$14/£7).

Tickets & Lodging for the 2010 Winter Olympics

If you hope to attend the 2010 Winter Games, a bit of preplanning will be necessary.

Tickets: In October 2008, 1.6 million tickets for the 2010 Olympic Winter Games go on sale; 250,000 Paralympic Winter Games tickets will be available in 2009. However, the process for buying these tickets is anything but straightforward. The Vancouver 2010 Organizing Committee website at www.vancouver2010.com is the best source of general information regarding tickets. However, only Canadian citizens can buy tickets through the official website. Non-Canadian residents must purchase tickets through the authorized sales agent for their respective National Olympic Committee. For example, U.S. citizens will purchase tickets to the 2010 Winter Games though **Jet Set Sports** (P.O. Box 366, Far Hills, NJ 07931; © **908/766-1001**; fax 908/766-4646; www.jetsetsports.com), the authorized ticket sales agent of the U.S. Olympic Committee.

The ticket-buying process will be staged in phases. In some cases, lotteries will be held to distribute tickets fairly to Olympic Games events where demand for tickets exceeds supply. You want to see figure skating? How about settling for a ticket for curling? The starting price for events tickets is C$25 (US$25/£13), and half of all tickets are priced at C$100 (US$100/£50) or less.

Beware! As early as 2007, the Vancouver news media was filled with stories of sports fans buying Winter Olympic tickets online. In all cases, these tickets were fraudulent. Until the official ticketing program has been launched in October 2008, any individual or group claiming to have access to 2010 Olympic Winter Games tickets is making that claim falsely. Once tickets have been made available, buyers should be aware that tickets bought from any unauthorized source may not be valid and may not be accepted for entry to 2010 Winter Games venues. If you are interested in attending the 2010 Winter Games, it is imperative to sign up at **www.vancouver2010.com** to receive ticket updates and announcements as they are made available. Caveat emptor.

Accommodations: If you plan to reserve a Whistler hotel room years in advance of the Olympics, you'll have to cool your heels until late 2008. Nearly all the hotels, condos, inns and other lodging options in Whistler have been asked to hold their rooms until all the groups that fall under the responsibility of the 2010 Organization Committee have secured lodging.

For a first-time visitor, figuring out lodging at Whistler can be rather intimidating. One of the easiest ways to book rooms, buy ski passes, and plan activities is to visit the official Whistler Blackcomb Resort website at **www.whistlerblackcomb.com**. Most hotels and condo developments are represented at this one-stop shopping and information site.

For the most part, lodgings in Whistler are of very high quality. The price of rooms is also quite high. The hotels listed below offer superlative rooms, many with fireplaces, balconies, kitchens, and beautiful furnishings, and the properties offer lots of

These include members of the International Olympic Committee, the National Olympic Committees of participating nations, International Sport Federations, international and domestic corporate sponsors, international and domestic news media, athletes' families, team coaches, support personnel, and security. At press time, it's impossible to know how many rooms in Whistler will remain for spectators after the bigwigs, officials, media, and family take their cut (it's estimated that this group will require about 5,000 beds), but most of the hoteliers I spoke to expect that few rooms will remain for the average consumer. In fact, there are rumors that cruise ships may be docked at Squamish in Howe Sound (60km/37 miles from Whistler), acting as hotels for stragglers. If you are hoping to stay in Whistler during the Olympics, you'll need to bird-dog the various hotel websites in October 2008 and to monitor the official Olympics website at www.vancouver2010.com. Best of luck.

To make it more challenging, the Olympic Committee hasn't announced yet whether the remaining rooms in Whistler will be released before the event tickets go on sale. You might end up with tickets to a Whistler event, but have no option of getting a room at the resort (or the other way around).

Clearly, once the unreserved rooms in Whistler are released, there will be a huge surge of demand, which will drive up prices. Accommodation pricing is the responsibility of the individual hotels and inns, and the organizing committee is not directly involved with setting prices for spectator accommodation, but is working with tourism organizations to encourage best practices and ensure a fair market value. Again, be very wary of reservations from nonauthorized sources or using your credit card to purchase room reservations from unfamiliar sources—there is already a lot of fraud surrounding Internet ticket and reservation sales for Olympic events and services.

Transportation: Even if you secure a ticket and have a room reservation, don't expect to squire the family SUV around Whistler during the Olympics. While the games are on, nearly all transportation to, from and within Whistler will be on public transport buses. Of course, the official line is that use of buses reduces impact on the environment, but the real reason has more to do with reducing traffic gridlock and enhancing security.

extras, including hot tubs, pools, ski storage, shopping arcades, and spas. However, the smaller inns recommended below offer great value and excellent accommodations, often with services and options that can, for many travelers, make them a more attractive option than the larger hotels. At these smaller, owner-operated inns, rates usually include breakfast, afternoon snacks, free Internet access, and parking, features that are usually available for an extra fee at hotels. These smaller inns are also located outside of the central villages and usually offer a quieter lodging experience than the hotels in Whistler Village.

In addition to the hotels and inns below, Whistler is absolutely loaded with condo developments. To reserve one of these units, which can range from studios, one- to five-bedroom fully furnished condos, town houses, and chalets with prices from around C$125 to C$1,500 (US$125–US$1,500/£63–£750) a night, for many travelers the easiest thing to do is simply decide on your price point and call one of the central booking agencies, such as **Resort Quest Whistler** (🕾 **800/892-2431** or 604/932-6699; www.resortquest.com/whistler) and **Whistler Superior Properties** (🕾 **877/535-8282** or 604/932-3510; www.whistlersuperior.com). **Whistler Accommodations** (🕾 **866/905-4607** or 604/905-4607; www.whistleraccommodation.com) focuses on condos and hotels in the Upper Village.

One other excellent booking service is **Allura Direct** (🕾 **866/4-ALLURA** or 604/707-6700; www.alluradirect.com), through which owners of rental properties in Whistler rent directly to the public (and you escape the 10% local hotel tax). The website has an excellent search engine, and offers lots of information and photos of numerous properties located throughout Whistler. Though owners are screened—we encountered no problems and got a fabulous deal on a one-bedroom condo—quality can vary, so we recommend you do your homework and book only with those owners who accept credit cards.

Reservations for peak winter periods should be made by September at the latest.

IN THE VILLAGE & UPPER VILLAGE

The Fairmont Chateau Whistler 🌟🌟🌟   Perennially rated the top ski resort hotel in North America by reader surveys in such magazines as *Condé Nast Traveler,* the Fairmont re-creates the look of a feudal castle at the foot of Blackcomb Mountain, but with every modern comfort added. Massive wooden beams support an airy peaked roof in the lobby, while in the hillside Mallard Bar, double-sided stone fireplaces cast a cozy glow on the couches and leather armchairs. Rooms and suites are very comfortable and beautifully furnished, and feature duvets, bathrobes, and soaker tubs (some offer stunning views of the slopes). Fairmont Gold service guests can have breakfast or relax après-ski in a private lounge with the feel of a Victorian library. All guests can use the heated outdoor pool and Jacuzzis, which look out over the base of the ski hill. The hotel's **Vida Wellness Spa** is generally cited as the best in town. The Fairmont pays attention to the needs of skiers, with a recreation concierge, ski storage next to the slopes, and ski valets to help make pre- and après-ski as expeditious and pleasant as possible.

4599 Chateau Blvd., Whistler, BC V0N 1B4. 🕾 **800/606-8244** or 604/938-8000. Fax 604/938-2058. www.fairmont. com/whistler. 550 units. Winter C$429–C$549 (US$429–US$549/£215–£275) double, C$570–C$1,399 (US$570–US$1,399/£285–£700) suite; summer C$159–C$335 (US$159–US$335/£80–£168) double, C$425–C$1,000 (US$425–US$1,000/£213–£500) suite. AE, MC, V. Underground valet parking C$25 (US$25/£13). Pets welcome. **Amenities:** 4 restaurants; bar; heated indoor/outdoor pool; 18-hole golf course; 2 tennis courts; health club; outstanding spa facility; Jacuzzi; children's programs; concierge; business center; shopping arcade; 24-hr. room service; in-room massage; babysitting; coin laundry; laundry service; same-day dry cleaning; nonsmoking rooms; concierge-level rooms; secure ski and bike storage; rooms for those w/limited mobility. *In room:* A/C, TV w/movie channels, dataport, minibar, coffeemaker, hair dryer, iron, safe.

Four Seasons Resort Whistler 🌟🌟🌟   Whistler has its share of grand hotels, but even in this exalted company the Four Seasons Resort stands alone. Easily the most refined and elegant of Whistler's hotels, the Four Seasons is monumental in scale while maintaining the atmosphere of a very intimate and sophisticated boutique hotel—a rare achievement. The expansive stone, glass, and timber lobby is like a modern-day hunting lodge—but with the addition of extraordinary contemporary art—while Fifty Two 80 Bistro & Bar, the hotel's fine-dining restaurant (p. 772), has a pleasing, slightly playful decor of stone, candy-colored tile and back-lit onyx.

The Four Season's urbane good taste extends to the large guest rooms, decorated in wood and cool earth tones and beautifully furnished with rich fabrics and leather furniture. All rooms have a balcony, fireplace, and very large, amenity-filled bathrooms with soaker tubs. The standard room is a very spacious 46 sq. m (500 sq. ft.), and superior and deluxe level rooms are truly large. A separate wing of the hotel contains private residences—139 sq. m to 344 sq. m (1,500–3,700 sq. ft.) apartments with two to four bedrooms. With 15 treatment rooms, the exquisite Spa at the Four Seasons Resort is Whistler's largest, and a heated outdoor pool and three whirlpool baths fill half the hotel courtyard. The Four Seasons Resort Whistler is a très chic, très elegant monument to refinement.

4591 Blackcomb Way, Whistler, BC V0N 1B4. ⓒ 888/935-2460 or 604/935-3400. Fax 604/935-3455. www.four seasons.com/whistler. 273 units. June 15–Sept 13 and Nov 27–Dec 19 C$295–C$650 (US$295–US$650/£148–£325) double; Sept 14–Nov 26 and April 13–June 14 C$245–C$550 (US$245–US$550/£123–£275) double; Dec 20–Dec 31 C$875–C$1,475 (US$875–US$1,475/£438–£738) double; Jan 1–Feb 7 C$395–C$895 (US$395–US$895/£198–£448) double; Feb 8–April 12 C$435–C$950 (US$435–US$950/£218–£475) double. AE, DC, DISC, MC, V. Underground valet parking C$28 (US$28/£14); self-parking C$23 (US$23/£12). **Amenities:** Restaurant; lounge; heated outdoor pool; fitness studio; superlative spa; hot tubs; concierge; business center; 24-hr. room service; laundry and dry-cleaning service; ski and bike storage; rooms for those w/limited mobility. In room: A/C, TV/DVD, CD player, dataport, high-speed Internet access, minibar, coffeemaker, hair dryer, iron, safe.

Pan Pacific Whistler Mountainside ⓡⓡ   The Pan Pacific's slightly older and more family-oriented Mountainside all-suite property has a lot going for it, with top-notch furnishings, kitchenettes, and loads of amenities. Comfortable as the rooms are, however, the true advantage to the Pan Pacific Mountainside is its location at the foot of the Whistler Mountain gondola. Not only can you ski right to your hotel, but thanks to a large heated outdoor pool and Jacuzzi deck, you can sit at the end of the day sipping a glass of wine, gazing up at the snowy slopes, and marvel at the ameliorative effects of warm water on aching muscles. With sofa beds and fold-down Murphy beds, the studio suites are fine for couples, while the one- and two-bedroom suites allow more space for larger groups or families with kids.

4320 Sundial Crescent, Whistler, BC V0N 1B4. ⓒ 888/905-9995 or 604/905-2999. Fax 604/905-2995. www.pan pacific.com. 121 units. Jan 1–April 26 C$199–C$849 (US$199–US$849/£200–£425) studio, C$299–C$1,049 (US$299–US$1,049/£150–£525) 1 bedroom, C$599–C$1,499 (US$599–US$1,499/£300–£750) 2 bedroom; April 27–Nov 19 C$129–C$329 (US$129–US$329/£65–£165) studio, C$169–C$429 (US$169–US$429/£85–£215) 1 bedroom, C$229–C$529 (US$229–US$529/£115–£265) 2 bedroom; Nov 20–Dec 31 C$199–C$849 (US$199–US$849/£100–£425) studio, C$299–C$1,049 (US$299–US$1,049/£150–£525) 1 bedroom, C$399–C$1,499 (US$399–US$1,499/£200–£750) 2 bedroom. Wheelchair-accessible units available. AE, DC, MC, V. Underground valet parking C$20 (US$20/£10). **Amenities:** Restaurant; pub; heated outdoor pool; fitness center; whirlpool; steam room; concierge; room service; self-serve laundry; ski, bike, and golf bag storage. In room: A/C, TV, pay movie channels, pay Nintendo, dataport w/high-speed Internet, wireless connectivity, fridge, coffeemaker, stove w/oven, microwave, dishwasher, hair dryer, iron.

Pan Pacific Whistler Village Centre ⓡⓡⓡ   The Pan Pacific chain now has two handsome properties in Whistler, both just steps off Blackcomb Way in Whistler Village. The newest is the Pan Pacific Village Centre, opened in 2005. An all-suite boutique property, the Village Centre is an imposing structure with curious gables and a dormered roofline, underscoring the fact that this is anything but an anonymous corporate hotel. All in all, suites in the Village Centre are more like apartments than hotel

rooms; it's also more couples-oriented than its family-friendly sister property. All one-, two- and three-bedroom suites have a balcony, fireplace, flatscreen TV, full kitchen with granite counters, soaker tub, bathrobes, handsome furniture, built-in cabinetry, and floor-to-ceiling windows to let in the amazing mountain vistas. The rooms come in two equally elegant color schemes, either "dawn," in shades of tan and light fir, or "dusk," with darker wood tones and rich upholstery. The penthouse suites are truly magnificent, with cathedral ceilings, massive stone fireplaces, multiple balconies, European appliances, dining rooms, and loads of room—the Blackcomb Suite has 156 sq. m (1,680 sq. ft.)!

The Village Centre has a fitness center with sauna, massage therapy and spa treatment rooms, a lap pool, and two hot tubs. Rates include a full breakfast buffet and afternoon/evening hors d'oeuvres in the Pacific Lounge, a guest-only facility with an outdoor patio.

4299 Blackcomb Way, Whistler, BC V0N 1B4. ⓒ 888/966-5575 or 604/966-5500. Fax 604/966-5501. www. panpacific.com. 83 units. Jan 1–Apr 26 C$249–C$999 (US$249–US$999/£125–£500) 1 bedroom, C$499–C$1,399 (US$499–US$1,399/£250–£700) 2 bedroom, C$1,299–C$2,799 (US$1,299–US$2,799/£650–£1,400) 3-bedroom penthouse; April 27–Nov 19 C$179–C$429 (US$179–US$429/£90–£215) 1 bedroom, C$249–C$529 (US$249–US$529/£125–£265) 2 bedroom, C$699–C$999 (US$699–US$999/£350–£500) 3-bedroom penthouse; Nov 20–Dec 31 C$249–C$999 (US$249–US$999/£125–£500) 1 bedroom, C$349–C$1,399 (US$349–US$1,399/£175–£700) 2 bedroom, C$799–C$2,799 (US$799–US$2,799/£400–£1,400) 3-bedroom penthouse. Wheelchair-accessible units available. AE, DC, DISC, MC, V. Underground valet parking C$20 (US$20/£10). **Amenities:** Restaurant; pub; heated outdoor pool; fitness center; whirlpool; sauna; concierge; room service; self-serve laundry; ski, bike, and golf bag storage. In room: A/C, TV, pay movie channels, pay Nintendo, Web TV, dataport w/high-speed Internet, wireless connectivity, fridge, microwave convection oven, coffeemaker, hair dryer, iron.

The Westin Resort and Spa Whistler 🕉🕉🕉
Talk about location: The all-suite Westin Resort snapped up the best piece of property in town and squeezed itself onto the mountainside at the bottom of the Whistler gondola. It's both central to all the restaurants and night spots in Whistler Village, yet slightly apart from the crowds. The two-towered hotel is built in the style of an enormous mountain chalet with cedar timbers and lots of local granite and basalt finishings. All 419 suites received an update in 2007 and offer full kitchens, soaker tubs, slate-lined showers, and an elegant and restful decor; there are even "workout" suites with an array of fitness equipment. The beds, Westin's signature Heavenly Beds, are indeed divine. If you're here to ski, expect little luxuries including a ski valet service and (no more cold toes!) a boot-warming service. That is certainly one of the reasons why the Westin has already grabbed several top awards; the hotel's **Avello Spa** is extremely well appointed for après-ski pampering and the indoor/outdoor pool, hot tubs, steam baths, and sauna will warm up ski-weary limbs.

4090 Whistler Way, Whistler, BC V0N 1B4. ⓒ 888/634-5577 or 604/905-5000. Fax 604/905-5589. www.westin whistler.com. 419 units. Apr 16–Nov 23 C$179–C$489 (US$179–US$489/£90–£245) junior suite, C$269–C$599 (US$269–US$599/£135–£300) 1-bedroom suite, C$429–C$1,049 (US$429–US$1,049/£215–£525) 2-bedroom suite; Nov 24–Apr 15 C$209–C$589 (US$209–US$589/£105–£295) junior suite, C$319–C$689 (US$319–US$689/£160–£345) 1-bedroom suite, C$539–C$1,519 (US$539–US$1,519/£270–£760) 2-bedroom suite. Children 17 and under stay free in parent's room. AE, DC, DISC, MC, V. Parking C$23 (US$23/£12). **Amenities:** Restaurant; bar; indoor and outdoor pool; nearby golf course; nearby tennis courts; health club; spa; indoor and outdoor Jacuzzi; sauna; bike rental; children's program; concierge; business center; Wi-Fi access; shopping arcade; salon; 24-hr. room service; massage; babysitting; laundry; dry cleaning; nonsmoking facility. In room: A/C, TV w/pay movies, dataport, fully appointed kitchen, coffeemaker, hair dryer, iron, safe.

OUTSIDE THE VILLAGE

Alpine Chalet Whistler ⋒⋒   This cozy alpine-style lodge sits in a quiet location near Alta Lake and the Whistler Golf Club. The entire inn, built in 2001, is designed to provide luxurious lodgings, privacy, and a welcoming sense of camaraderie in the comfortable, fireplace-dominated guest lounge. There are three room types: alpine rooms, comfortable lodge rooms that will suit the needs of most skiers and travelers; chalets, which are larger and feature fireplaces and other extras; and the master suite, the largest and most opulent room, with a fireplace, cathedral ceiling, Jacuzzi, and large private balcony. All rooms have balconies or terraces, fine linens, bathrobes, and other upscale amenities you'd expect at a classy hotel. Evening meals available by reservation.

3012 Alpine Crescent, Whistler, BC V0N 1B3. © 800/736-9967 or 604/935-3003. Fax 604/935-3008. www.whistler inn.com. 8 units. Jan 6–Apr 30 C$189–C$269 (US$189–US$269/£95–£135); Dec 19–Jan 5 C$259–C$399 (US$259–US$399/£130–£200); May 1–Dec 18 C$149–C$229 (US$149–US$229/£75–£115). Rates include full breakfast. MC, V. Free parking. **Amenities:** 8-person hot tub; steam room; guest lounge, heated ski lockers. *In room:* A/C, TV/DVD, high-speed Internet, hair dryer.

Cedar Springs Bed & Breakfast Lodge ⋒ *(Kids)*   The no-children policy at many Whistler inns can be a real challenge for families, but the Cedar Springs provides an excellent solution. Guests at this large and charming modern lodge a mile north of Whistler Village have a choice of king-, queen-, or twin-size beds in comfortably modern yet understated surroundings. Two family suites, with two queen and two twin beds, are just the ticket for families. What's more, the lodge is just next door to a park, biking paths, and a sports center with swimming pool. Cedar Springs also offers excellent accommodations for couples and solo travelers. The large honeymoon suite boasts a fireplace and balcony. Most rooms feature handmade pine furniture; all have bathrooms with heated tile floors. The guest sitting room has a TV, VCR, fireplace, and video library.

A sauna and hot tub on the sun deck overlooking the gardens add to the pampering after a day of play. A gourmet breakfast is served by the fireplace in the dining room, and guests are welcome to enjoy afternoon tea. Lodge owners Jackie and Jeorn offer lots of extras such as complimentary shuttle service to ski lifts, heated ski gear storage, bike rentals, and free Wi-Fi access.

8106 Cedar Springs Rd., Whistler, BC V0N 1B8. © 800/727-7547 or 604/938-8007. Fax 604/938-8023. www. whistlerbb.com. 8 units, 6 with bathroom. C$175–C$249 (US$175–US$249/£88–£125) double winter high season; C$89–C$165 (US$89–US$165/£45–£83) double spring, summer, fall. Rates include full breakfast and afternoon tea. MC, V. Free parking; 2-minute walk to public transport. Take Hwy. 99 north toward Pemberton 4km (2½ miles) past Whistler Village. Turn left onto Alpine Way, go a block to Rainbow Dr., and turn left; go a block to Camino St. and turn left. The lodge is a block down at the corner of Camino and Cedar Springs Rd. **Amenities:** Jacuzzi; sauna; guest lounge w/TV/VCR/DVD; courtesy car to ski slopes; nonsmoking rooms; secure ski and heated gear storage. *In room:* Free Wi-Fi, hair dryer, no phone.

Durlacher Hof Pension Inn ⋒⋒ *(Finds)*   This lovely inn boasts both an authentic Austrian feel and a sociable atmosphere. Both are the result of the exceptional care and service shown by owners Peter and Erika Durlacher. Guests are greeted by name at the entranceway, provided with slippers, and then given a tour of the three-story chalet-style property. The rooms vary in size from comfortable to quite spacious and come with goose-down duvets and fine linens, private bathrooms (some with jetted tubs) with deluxe toiletries, and incredible mountain views from private balconies. Better still is the downstairs lounge, with a welcoming fireplace and complimentary après-ski appetizers baked by Erika (these are delectable enough that guests are drawn from all over the inn to snack, share stories, and strategize on ways to obtain Erika's recipes). For much the same reason, many guests seem to linger over the complimentary (and substantial) hot breakfast. Peter and Erica are a font of knowledge about local restaurants and recreation; they will happily arrange tours and outings.

7055 Nesters Rd., Whistler, BC V0N 1B7. ⓒ 877/932-1924 or 604/932-1924. Fax 604/938-1980. www.durlacherhof. com. 8 units. Mid-Dec to Mar 31 C$129–C$499 (US$129–US$499/£65–£250) double; mid-June to Sept 30 C$99–C$299 (US$99–US$299/£50–£150) double. Discounted rates for spring and fall. Extra person C$35 (US$35/£18). Rates include full breakfast and afternoon tea. MC, V. Free parking. Take Hwy. 99 about 1km (½ mile) north of Whistler Village to Nester's Rd. Turn left and the inn is immediately on the right. **Amenities:** Jacuzzi; sauna; laundry service; dry cleaning; nonsmoking rooms; 1 room for those w/limited mobility. *In room:* TV, hair dryer, no phone.

Hostelling International Whistler *(Value)* One of the few inexpensive spots in Whistler, the hostel also happens to have one of the nicest locations: on the south edge of Alta Lake, with a dining room, deck, and lawn looking over the lake to Whistler Mountain. Inside, the hostel is extremely pleasant; there's a lounge with a wood-burning stove, a common kitchen, a piano, Ping-Pong tables, and a sauna, as well as a drying room for ski gear and storage for bikes, boards, and skis. In the summer, guests have use of a barbecue, canoe, and rowboat. As with all hostels, most rooms and facilities are shared. Beds at the hostel book up very early. Book by September at the latest for the winter ski season.

5678 Alta Lake Rd., Whistler, BC V0N 1B5. ⓒ 604/932-5492. Fax 604/932-4687. www.hihostels.ca. 33 beds in 4- to 8-bed dorms. C$20–C$26 (US$20–US$26/£10–£13) IYHA members; C$24–C$30 (US$24–US$30/£12–£15) nonmembers. Family and group memberships available. MC, V. Free parking. **Amenities:** Sauna; canoe and bike rental; nonsmoking facility.

Inn at Clifftop Lane *(★★)* This large home, built as a B&B, sits above the Whistler Village on a quiet side street just south of Whistler Creekside, and offers large and beautifully furnished rooms. The inn strikes that perfect balance between the hominess of a B&B and the formality of a small boutique hotel. Each of the guest rooms is spacious, with an easy chair and living area, plus a bathroom with a jetted tub and bathrobes. The home is filled with books and decorated with antiques and folk art collected during the owners' travels, lending a cheerful élan to the breakfast rooms and guest lounge. Outdoors, steps lead through the forest to a hot tub and a private deck. This is a great choice for travelers seeking understated comfort and elegance with friendly, professional service.

2828 Clifftop Lane, Whistler, BC V0N 1B2. ⓒ 888/281-2929 or 604/938-1229. Fax 604/938-9880. www.innat clifftop.com. 5 units. Summer low season from C$119–C$139 (US$119–US$139/£60–£70); winter high season from C$145–C$259 (US$145–US$259/£73–£130). Ski packages available. Rates include full breakfast. AE, MC, V. Free parking. **Amenities:** Hot tub; lounge; library, nonsmoking rooms. *In room:* TV, Wi-Fi access, hair dryer.

WHERE TO DINE

Whistler overflows with dining spots—you'll have no trouble finding excellent food. Note that many restaurants close for seasonal holidays or have shorter hours in late April and early November, the "mud" season. Call to confirm hours if you visit then. **Ingrid's Village Café,** just off the Village Square at 4305 Skiers Approach (ⓒ **604/932-7000**), is a locals' favorite for simple homelike food, for both quality and price. A large bowl of Ingrid's clam chowder costs just C$5 (US$5/£2.50), while a veggie burger comes in at C$6 (US$6/£3). It's open daily 8am to 6pm.

The **Citta Bistro,** in the Whistler Village Square (ⓒ **604/932-4177**), serves thin-crust pizzas such as the Californian Herb, topped with spiced chicken breast, sun-dried tomatoes, fresh pesto, and mozzarella, as well as gourmet burgers such as the Citta Extraordinaire, topped with bacon, cheddar, and garlic mushrooms. Main

courses are C$7 to C$14 (US$7–US$14/£3.50–£7); it's open daily noon to midnight.
Thai One On, 4557 Blackcomb Way, in the Le Chamois Hotel (© **604/932-4822**),
is Whistler's top Thai restaurant, with entrees from C$11 to C$21 (US$11–US$21/
£5.50–£11); it's open daily from 5 to 10pm.

The **Whistler Brewhouse,** 4355 Blackcomb Way (© **604/905-2739**), is a great
spot for a microbrew ale, a plate of wood-fired pizza or rotisserie chicken (C$15–
C$23/US$15–US$23/£7.50–£12), and a seat on the patio; the brewhouse is open
daily 11:30am to midnight, till 1am on weekends. **Sachi Sushi,** 4359 Main St. (© **604/
935-5649**), is the best of Whistler's many sushi restaurants—the udon noodles and
hot pots are excellent as well. Sushi rolls cost from C$8 to C$17 (US$8–US$17/
£4–£8.50); hours are Tuesday through Friday noon to 2:30pm and 5:30 to 10pm.

Après FRENCH   This intimate and very stylish restaurant is Whistler's sole bastion
of contemporary French cooking. French-born chef Eric Vernice has worked in London, New York, at a clutch of Michelon-starred restaurants in France, and in Whistler
as Bearfoot Bistro's first executive chef. Now in his own restaurant, Vernice creates
innovative cuisine that's rooted in the traditions of classic French cooking. Appetizers
are especially tempting, and grazing tapas-style through an evening's worth of small
plates is an excellent introduction to Vernice's cooking. Escargots are sautéed with garlic, prosciutto, and forest mushrooms; scallops and king crab are topped with crustacean foam and white truffle shavings. For main courses, the West Coast
Bouillabaisse is a tasty choice, or perhaps pan-seared duck breast with wild berry and
Sarawak pepper sauce. A six-course tasting menu is available for C$85 (US$85/£43).

103-4338 Main St. © 604/935-0200. www.apresrestaurant.com. Reservations recommended. Main courses C$22–
C$36 (US$22–US$36/£11–£18). MC, V. Tues–Sat 5:30pm–midnight. Call for spring and fall hours.

Araxi Restaurant & Bar ♠♠♠ WEST COAST   Frequently awarded for its wine
list, as well as voted best restaurant in Whistler, this is one of the resort's top places to
dine. And thanks to a major renovation, Araxi now has storage enough for its famous
12,000-bottle inventory of fine B.C. and foreign wines. Outside, the heated patio
seats 80 people amid barrels of flowers, while inside, the artwork, antiques, and terra-
cotta tiles provide a subtle Mediterranean ambience that serves as a theater for the
presentation of extraordinary food.

Diners have a choice of a la carte items or a monthly changing five-course tasting
menu for C$89 (US$89/£45). The kitchen makes the most of local ingredients (and in
fact has a "100-mile menu" featuring the best of local farmers and fishers) such as house-
smoked trout, Pemberton cheese and lamb, and Howe Sound oysters. Chef James Walt
has a deft hand, producing dishes that are inventive yet tradition-based and full of flavor: Boudin blanc sausage is fashioned from squab and fois gras, and presented with
Jerusalem artichoke purée; delicate lamb meat rillettes come with a single, perfect pumpkin ravioli. Don't hesitate to ask for a suggestion when contemplating the nearly ency-
clopedic wine list—the wine staff here is exceedingly friendly and knowledgeable.

4222 Village Sq. © 604/932-4540. www.araxi.com. Main courses C$25–C$45 (US$25–US$45/£13–£23). AE, MC,
V. Mid-May to Oct daily 11am–3pm and 5–11pm.

Bearfoot Bistro ♠♠♠ PACIFIC NORTHWEST   One of the very best in Whistler,
Barefoot Bistro has created an enormous following for its regional, seasonal cuisine. The
emphasis is on innovation, new flavors, and unusual preparations—in short, this is a
cutting-edge restaurant for serious gastronomes. In the dining room, choose either three
or five courses from the admirably broad menu, with selections such as lobster with

Meyer lemon, fava bean risotto, popcorn-crusted lingcod with littleneck clam–corn chowder, or braised pork belly with Dungeness crab grapefruit salad. There's nothing ordinary about the food, or the wine list, which has earned awards from *Wine Spectator* magazine. A number of specialty tasting menus are also available. Appetizers and more casual meals are available in the fireside room and the cozy Champagne Bar.

4121 Village Green. ⓒ 604/932-3433. www.bearfootbistro.com. Reservations recommended. 3-course menu C$45 (US$45/£23), 5-course menu C$98 (US$98/£49). AE, MC, V. Daily 5–10pm.

Fifty Two 80 Bistro & Bar SEAFOOD/CANADIAN ⓡ   The suave dining room at the upscale Four Seasons Resort Whistler celebrates "fire and ice"—fire from the stone fireplace and dramatic backlit onyx panels and ice from the display of fresh fish and shellfish that greets diners. The design may be high concept but the food is more easy-going and hearty. For appetizers, fresh shucked oysters or seared scallops with cauliflower purée are outstanding, and old-fashioned chicken supreme is made new again with local corn and wild mushrooms. Fresh lobster, prime Canadian steaks, spit-roasted meats, and fresh fish entrees round out the menu. Combine the a la carte selections into three- or four-course dinners for a great value on sublimely prepared food.

4591 Blackcomb Way (in the Four Seasons Whistler Resort). ⓒ 604/935-3400. Reservations required. Main courses C$18–C$46 (US$18–US$46/£9–£23); 3-course dinner C$39 (US$39/£20). AE, DC, DISC, MC, V. Daily 7am–10pm.

Rimrock Cafe and Oyster Bar ⓡⓡ SEAFOOD   Upstairs in a long narrow room with a high ceiling and a great stone fireplace at one end, Rimrock is very much like a Viking mead hall of old. It's not the atmosphere, however, that causes people to hop in a cab and make the C$5 (US$5/£2.50) journey out from Whistler Village. What draws folks in is the food. The first order of business should be a plate of oysters. Chef Rolf Gunther serves them up half a dozen ways, from raw with champagne to cooked in hell (broiled with fresh chiles). For my money, though, the signature Rimrock oyster is still the best: broiled with béchamel sauce and smoked salmon. Other appetizers are lightly seared ahi tuna or Québec foie gras with apple-raspberry salad. Main dishes are focused on seafood and game. Look for lobster and scallops with toasted almond butter and crispy leeks or grilled arctic Caribou with porcini cream and orange-cranberry relish. The accompanying wine list has a number of fine vintages from B.C., California, New Zealand, and Australia.

2117 Whistler Rd. ⓒ 877/932-5589 or 604/932-5565. www.rimrockwhistler.com. Main courses C$24–C$40 (US$24–US$40/£12–£20). AE, MC, V. Daily 11:30am–11:30pm.

WHISTLER AFTER DARK

For a town of just 10,000, Whistler has a more-than-respectable nightlife scene. You'll find concert listings in the *Pique*, a free local paper available at cafes and food stores. **Tommy Africa's,** 4216 Gateway Dr. (ⓒ 604/932-6090), and the dark and cavernous **Maxx Fish,** in Whistler Village Square below the Amsterdam Cafe (ⓒ 604/932-1904), cater to the 18- to 22-year-old crowd; you'll find lots of beat and not much light. The crowd at **Garfinkel's,** at the entrance to Village North (ⓒ 604/932-2323), is similar, though the cutoff age can reach as high as 26 or 27. **Buffalo Bills,** across from the Whistler Gondola (ⓒ 604/932-6613), and the **Savage Beagle,** opposite Starbucks in the Village (ⓒ 604/938-3337), cater to the 30-something crowd. Bills is bigger, with a pool table, a video ski machine, and a smallish dance floor. The Beagle has a fabulous selection of beer and bar drinks, with a pleasant little pub upstairs and a house-oriented dance floor below.

7 The Okanagan Valley: A Taste of the Grape ⟨★⟨★

The arid **Okanagan Valley** with its long chain of lakes is the ideal destination for fresh-watersports enthusiasts, golfers, skiers, and wine lovers. Ranches and small towns have flourished here for more than a century; the region's **fruit orchards and vineyards** will make you feel as if you've been transported to the Spanish countryside. Summer visitors get the pick of the fruit crop at insider prices from the many fruit stands that line Highway 97. Be sure to stop for a pint of cherries, a basket of apples, homemade jams, and other goodies.

An Okanagan region chardonnay won gold medals in 1994 at international competitions held in London and Paris. In 2000, several other Okanagan vintages picked up quite a number of medals at international competitions. And more than 70 other wineries produce vintages that are following right on their heels. Despite these coveted honors, the valley has received little international publicity. It's far less crowded and expensive than California's wine country, but no less extraordinary . Most visitors are Canadian, and the valley isn't yet a major tour-bus destination. Get here before they do.

Remember to bring your camera when you head out on the lake. If you spot its legendary underwater resident, **Ogopogo,** take a picture. The shy monster (depicted in ancient petroglyphs found in the valley as a snakelike beast with a horselike head) is said to be a distant cousin of Scotland's Loch Ness monster.

ESSENTIALS

VISITOR INFORMATION   The **Penticton Visitor Info Centre** is at 888 Westminster Ave. W., Penticton, BC V2A 8R2 (© **800/663-5052** or 250/493-4055; www. penticton.org). The **Kelowna Visitor Info Centre** is at 544 Harvey Ave., Kelowna, BC V1Y 6C9 (© **800/663-4345** or 250/861-1515; www.kelownachamber.org). For information about the Okanagan wineries, contact **Okanagan Wine Festivals** (© **250/ 861-6654**), which has a helpful website at www.owfs.com.

GETTING THERE   By Plane   Air Canada Jazz (© **800/247-2262;** www.flyjazz. ca) has frequent daily commuter flights from Calgary and Vancouver to Penticton and Kelowna. **Horizon Air** (© **800/547-9308;** www.horizonair.com) offers service from Seattle. **WestJet** (© **800/538-5696;** www.westjet.com) operates flights from Vancouver, Victoria, Calgary, and Edmonton.

By Car   The 395km (245-mile) drive from Vancouver to Penticton via the Trans-Canada Highway (Hwy. 1) and Highway 3 rambles through rich delta farmlands and the forested mountains of Manning Provincial Park and the Similkameen River region before descending into the Okanagan Valley's antelope-brush and sagebrush desert. For a more direct route to the valley, take the Trans-Canada Highway to the Coquihalla Toll Highway (C$10/US$10/£5) via Merritt and Hope. Using this expressway allows drivers to make the journey from Kelowna to Vancouver in 4 hours.

SPECIAL EVENTS   Be the first to taste the valley's best chardonnay, pinot noir, merlot, and ice wines at the **Okanagan Wine Festival** (© **250/861-6654;** www.owfs. com), during the first and second weeks in October at wineries and restaurants throughout the Okanagan Valley.

TASTING THE FRUITS OF THE VINEYARDS

British Columbia has a long history of producing wines, ranging from mediocre to really, truly bad. A missionary, Father Pandosy, planted apple trees and vineyards in 1859 and produced sacramental wines for the valley's mission. Over the years, more wineries cropped up, but few of them worried about the quality of their bottling, because they were subsidized by the B.C. government.

In the 1980s, the government threatened to pull its support of the industry unless it could produce an internationally competitive product. The vintners listened. Root stock was imported from France and Germany. European-trained master vintners were hired to oversee the development of the vines and the winemaking process. The climate and soil conditions turned out to be some of the best in the world for wine making, and today British Columbian wines are winning international gold medals. Competitively priced, at about C$15 to C$50 (US$15–US$50/£7.50–£25) per bottle, they represent some great bargains in well-balanced chardonnays, pinot blancs, and Gewürztraminers; full-bodied merlots, pinot noirs, and cabernets; and dessert ice wines that surpass the best muscat d'or.

Because U.S. visitors are allowed to bring back 1 liter (33.8 oz.) of wine per person without paying extra duty, Americans can bring a bottle of their favorite selection back home if they've visited Canada for more than 24 hours. Travelers from the United Kingdom can take back up to 2 liters of still wine without paying duty.

Most Okanagan wineries are found between the U.S. border and Kelowna along Highway 97, 130km (81 miles) of stunning lake and mountain scenery. Just across the U.S. border from Washington State, **Osoyoos** is a small agricultural town on Osoyoos Lake that's making a rapid transition to wine-country-resort destination. Just to the north, the unfussy town of **Oliver** was once mostly known for apricots and peaches, but now it's generally considered the top terrior for growing grapes in the Okanagan Valley.

Many Canadian retirees have chosen **Penticton** as their home because it has relatively mild winters and dry, desert-like summers. It's also a favorite destination for younger visitors, drawn by boating, water-skiing, sportfishing, and windsurfing on 128km-long (80-mile) Lake Okanagan. On the east shores of the lake, just past Penticton, is the Naramata Bench, another highly favored location for vineyards.

The town of **Kelowna** in the central valley is the hub of the B.C. winemaking industry and the valley's largest city, with a population of 105,000.

The valley's more than 100 vineyards and wineries conduct free tours and wine tastings throughout the year. Here are a few favorite stops; each of the following wineries is open daily for tastings from spring through late fall. Call ahead for winter hours.

Just north of Osoyoos, **Burrowing Owl Winery** ✿, halfway between Osoyoos and Oliver at 100 Burrowing Owl Pl. (© **877/498-0620** or 250/498-6202; www.bovwine. ca), makes exceptional wines; its award-winning merlot is one of B.C.'s top wines. Their **Sonora Room** dining room is an equally excellent vineyard restaurant (closed in winter), and the 10-bedroom **Guest House at Burrowing Owl** (p. 776) is a top boutique lodging.

The town of **Okanagan Falls** is 20km (12 miles) south of Penticton along Highway 97. Adjacent to a wilderness area and bird sanctuary overlooking Vaseaux Lake, **Blue Mountain Vineyards & Cellars**, Allendale Road (© **250/497-8244;** www. bluemountainwinery.com), offers tours by appointment and operates a wine shop and tasting room. Blasted Church Vineyards ✿, 378 Parsons Rd. (© **250/497-1125;** www. blastedchurch.com), has impossible-to-miss wine labels, and delicious and affordable wines. One of my favorites.

Near Oliver, **Tinhorn Creek Vineyards,** Road 7 (© **888/846-4676;** www.tinhorn. com), is one of the top Okanagan wineries. Specialties include Gewürztraminer, pinot gris, chardonnay, pinot noir, cabernet franc, merlot, and ice wine. Tinhorn Creek plans to open a vineyard restaurant in 2008. Also near Oliver, the **Hester Creek**

Estate Winery, Road 8 (© **250/498-4435;** www.hestercreek.com), has a wine boutique open daily 10am to 5pm, and tours of the wine-making area are available by appointment; especially nice here is the grapevine-shaded patio that invites picnickers.

Penticton is at the lower shores of Okanagan Lake, and rising immediately to the east is the Naramata Bench, home to some of the best Okanagan wineries. **La Frenz Winery,** 740 Naramata Rd. (© **250/492-6690;** www.lafrenzwinery.com), makes excellent small-lots bottlings of semillion, viognier, and merlot. **Poplar Grove Winery** ⚘, 1060 Poplar Gove Rd. (© **250/493-9463;** www.poplargrove.ca), produces a top-notch claret-style wine; try the cabernet franc if it's available—it's a wonderful wine that sells out every year.

Traveling north from Penticton on Highway 97 (the west side of the lake), you'll find other notable wineries. **Sumac Ridge Estate Winery,** 17403 Hwy. 97 (© **250/494-0451;** www.sumacridge.com), operates a wine shop and tasting room, plus the winery features a fine dining room, the **Cellar Door Bistro.**

Across Okanagan Lake from Kelown is **Westbank,** home to a number of well-established wineries. **Mission Hill Wines,** 1730 Mission Hill Rd. (© **250/768-7611;** www.missionhillwinery.com), was established in 1981 and has one of the most opulent wineries in B.C. The cabernet sauvignon and syrah is excellent. The **Hainle Vineyards Estate Winery,** 5355 Trepanier Bench Rd. (© **250/767-2525;** www.hainle.com), was the first Okanagan winery to produce ice wine. The winery's **Amphora Bistro** is open daily for lunch and dinner. **Quails' Gate Estate** ⚘, 3303 Boucherie Rd., Kelowna (© **250/769-4451;** www.quailsgate.com), has a beautiful new tasting room overlooking vineyards and the lake. If ice wines (made with grapes that have been allowed to stay on the vine through several frosts, dehydrating them and intensifying the sugars) are your favorite dessert potable, you'll want to taste the vintages here. An excellent restaurant, **Old Vines Patio and Restaurant,** is open year-round for lunch and dinner.

In and around **Kelowna** are some of the biggest names in British Columbia's wine-making industry. **Calona Vineyards,** 1125 Richter St., Kelowna (© **250/762-3332;** www.calonavineyards.ca), conducts tours and tastings through western Canada's oldest (since 1932) and largest winery. South of Kelowna on the east side of the lake is **Cedar Creek Estate Winery,** 5445 Lakeshore Rd. (© **250/764-8866;** www.cedar creek.bc.ca), which produces notable pinot noir, chardonnay, and meritage blends. The Terrace Restaurant is open for lunch daily.

SPORTS & OUTDOOR ACTIVITIES

BOATING & WATERSPORTS The Okanagan Valley's numerous local marinas offer full-service boat rentals. The **Marina on Okanagan Lake,** 291 Front St., Penticton (© **250/492-2628**), rents ski boats, Tigersharks (similar to jet skis or Sea-Doos), fishing boats, and tackle. In Kelowna, the marinas at the Grand Okanagan Resort and the Hotel Eldorado offer boat and watercraft rentals.

GOLF The Okanagan's warm climate is good for more than just growing grapes and apricots. The valley also boasts 50 golf courses; for complete information, contact www. totabc.com/trellis/golf. Here are two of the best. Les Furber's **Gallagher's Canyon Golf and Country Club,** 4320 McCulloch Rd., Kelowna (© **250/861-4240**), has an 18-hole course that features a hole overlooking the precipice of a gaping canyon and another that's perched on the brink of a ravine. It also has a 9-hole course, a midlength course, and a new double-ended learning center. Resting high on a wooded ridge between two lakes, Les Furber's **Predator Ridge,** 360 Commonage Rd., Vernon (© **250/542-3436**), has hosted the B.C. Open Championship in recent years. The par-5 4th hole can be played only over a huge midfairway lake; it's a challenge even for seasoned pros. The greens fees throughout the Okanagan Valley range from C$65 to C$175 (US$65–US$175/£33–£88) and are a good value not only because of the beautiful locations but also for the quality of service you'll find at each club.

SKIING   Cross-country and powder skiing are the Okanagan Valley's main winter attractions. Intermediate and expert downhill skiers frequent the **Apex Resort,** Green Mountain Road, Penticton (© 877/777-2739 or 250/292-8222; www.apexresort. com), with 56 runs and 52km (32 miles) of cross-country ski trails. Day passes are C$55 (US$55/£28) adult, C$45 (US$45/£23) senior and teens, and C$34 (US$34/£17) kids 12 and under. Facilities include an ice rink, snow golf, sleigh rides, casino nights, and racing competitions.

   Silver Star Mountain Ski Resort & Cross-Country Centre offers cross-country skiers 93km (58 miles) of trails (including 6.5km/4 miles lit for night skiing), plus 50km (31 miles) of trails in the adjacent Silver Star Provincial Park. The ski-in/ski-out resort resembles a 19th-century mining town. For off-piste fanatics, some of Canada's most extreme verticals are here among the resort's 72 downhill runs.

   Only a 15-minute drive from Westbank, **Crystal Mountain Resorts Ltd.** (© 250/768-5189, or 250/768-3753 for snow report; www.crystalresort.com) has a range of ski programs for all types of skiers, specializing in clinics for children, women, and seniors. The resort's 20 runs are 80% intermediate-to-novice grade and are serviced by one double chair and two T-bars. The runs are equipped for day and night skiing. There's also a half pipe for snowboarders. Lift tickets start at C$43 (US$43/£22) adults and C$35 (US$35/£18) youths.

   If you yearn for hip-deep dry powder, then head to **Big White Ski Resort,** Parkinson Way, Kelowna (© 250/765-3101, 250/765-SNOW for snow report, or 250/765-8888 for lodge reservations; www.bigwhite.com). The resort—B.C.'s second largest—spreads over a broad mountain featuring long, wide runs. Skiers cruise open bowls and tree-lined glades. There's an annual average of 5.5m (18 ft.) of fluffy powder, so it's no wonder the resort's 118 runs are so popular. Day passes are C$68 (US$68/£34) adult, C$56 (US$56/£28) senior and youths 13 to 18, C$33 (US$33/£17) kids 6 to 12. The resort also offers more than 40km (25 miles) of groomed cross-country ski trails, a recreational racing program, night skiing 5 nights a week—and 17,000 slopeside beds in a range of hotels, condos, and private home rentals.

WHERE TO STAY

The **B.C. Provincial Parks Service/Okanagan District** (© 250/494-6500; www.discovercamping.ca) maintains a number of provincial campgrounds in this area. They're open April to October, and fees are C$14 to C$21 (US$14–US$21/£7–£11) per night. There are 41 campsites at **Haynes Point Provincial Park** in Osoyoos, which has flush toilets, a boat launch, and visitor programs. This campground is popular with naturalists interested in hiking the "pocket desert." **Vaseaux Lake Provincial Park,** near Okanagan Falls, offers 12 campsites and great wildlife-viewing opportunities; deer, antelope, and even a number of California bighorn sheep live in the surrounding hills. And **Okanagan Lake Provincial Park** has 168 campsites nestled amid 10,000 imported trees. Facilities include free hot showers, flush toilets, a sani-station, and a boat launch.

IN & AROUND OSOYOOS

Guest House at Burrowing Owl ⊛   The top-echilon Burrowing Owl Winery offers 10 spectacular guest rooms in the midst of a vineyard. This newly constructed boutique inn offers large and airy rooms, filled with light, fine art, Native stone, and gracious good taste. Most rooms have king beds (two have two doubles), and all have balconies overlooking the grape vines and the nearby desert hills. Relax by the 25m (82-ft.) outdoor pool and patio, and contemplate dinner at the **Sonora Room** ⊛, the winery's excellent New Canadian restaurant.

100 Burrowing Owl Place (R.R. 1, Comp 20 Site 52) Oliver, BC V0N 1T0. ℂ **877/498-0620** or 250/498-0620. www.bovwine.ca. 10 units. C$350 (US$350/£175) double May 1–Oct 15. 2-night minimum stay in high season. Lower off-season rates. AE, MC, V. Free parking. **Amenities:** Restaurant; wine bar; outdoor pool; hot tub. *In room:* A/C, flat-screen TV, high-speed Internet access, fridge.

Spirit Ridge Vineyard Resort & Spa ⊛⊛
This luxury level lodging overlooks Lake Osoyoos, the steep-sloped Okangan Valley, and miles of vineyards. Opened in 2007, Spirit Ridge brings a Santa Fe look to the Sonoran desert landscape. Lodgings are in one-bedroom suites, or one- or two-bedroom villas, each with full kitchen, dining and living room (with fireplace), and balcony. The resort offers a full service spa plus the **Passate-mop Restaurant,** with "wine country comfort food." Guests have private access to beaches on Osoyoos Lake; 9-hole **Sonora Dunes Golf Course** (250/495-4653; www.sonoradunes.com) and **Nk'Mip Cellars Winery** (ℂ 250/495-2985; www.nkmip cellars.com) are adjacent.

1200 Rancher Creek Rd., Osoyoos, BC V0H 1V0. ℂ **877/313-9463** or 250/495-5445. Fax 250/495-5447. www.spirit ridge.ca. 94 units. C$289–C$349 (US$289–US$349/£145–£175) suite; C$349 (US$349/£175) 1-bedroom villa; C$429 (US$429/£215) 2-bedroom villa. AE, MC, V. Free parking. Pets welcome for C$20 (US$20/£10) daily fee. **Amenities:** Restaurant; lounge; outdoor pool; waterslide; golf course nearby; fitness center; spa; hot tub; room service. *In room:* AC, TV/DVD, Wi-Fi, full kitchen, coffeemaker, hair dryer, iron, fireplace.

IN PENTICTON

Naramata Heritage Inn & Spa ⊛
Built in 1908, the Naramata Inn served as a hotel, private residence, and girls' school before undergoing extensive and loving reno-vation as a classic wine country inn. If you're coming to the Okanagan for a romantic getaway, or simply have an aversion to the mom-and-pop motels and corporate hotels that dominate wine-country lodging, then look no further. This inn is a half-hour north-west of Penticton on the quiet side of Lake Okanagan in the tiny community of Nara-mata. It offers very charming rooms (note that some are authentically small), restored to glow with period finery but modern luxury: The linens are top-notch and the bath-room's heated tile floors are a nice touch on a cool morning. In addition to en-suite bath-rooms with showers, rooms also have a claw-foot tub in the bedroom for soaking and relaxing. The inn also offers a spa for upscale pampering, plus the best dining in the area. There are few places in the otherwise utilitarian Okanagan as unique as this.

3625 First St., Naramata, BC V0H 1N0 (19km/12 miles north of Penticton on the east side of Okanagan Lake). ℂ **866/617-1188** or 250/496-6808. www.naramatainn.com. 12 units. High season C$182–C$510 (US$182–US$510/£91–£255) double. Continental breakfast included in rates. Lower off-season rates. AE, MC, V. **Amenities:** Restaurant (p. 779); wine bar; spa; Wi-Fi access; limited room service. *In room:* A/C, hair dryer, iron, no phone.

Penticton Lakeside Resort Convention Centre & Casino
Set on the water's edge, the Penticton Lakeside Resort has its own stretch of sandy Lake Okanagan beach-front, where guests can sunbathe or stroll along the adjacent pier. The deluxe suites fea-ture Jacuzzis, and the lakeside rooms are highly recommended for their view. All rooms and suites are smartly furnished with quality furniture; all rooms have balconies (some suites have two-person Jacuzzi tubs). The menus at the Hooded Merganser Restaurant and the Barking Parrot Bar & Patio feature locally grown ingredients. Other facilities include an extensive pool and health club facility, and a casino.

21 W. Lakeshore Dr., Penticton, BC V2A 7M5. © **800/663-9400** or 250/493-8221. Fax 250/493-0607. www.rpbhotels. com. 204 units. C$197–C$222 (US$197–US$222/£99–£111) double; from C$255 (US$255/£128) suite. Lower off-season rates. AE, DC, DISC, MC, V. Free parking. When you arrive in town, follow the signs to Main St. Lakeshore Dr. is at the north end of Main St. Pets accepted with C$20 (US$20/£10) fee. **Amenities:** Restaurant; lounge; indoor pool; tennis courts; health club; Jacuzzi; sauna; watersports-equipment rental; children's center; concierge; tour desk; business center; 24-hr. room service; babysitting; same-day dry cleaning; volleyball court. *In room:* A/C, TV/VCR w/pay movies, dataport, coffeemaker, hair dryer, iron.

IN KELOWNA

Grand Okanagan Lakefront Resort & Conference Centre ★★★ (Kids)   This elegant lakeshore resort sits on 10 hectares (25 acres) of beach and parkland; its atmosphere is reminiscent of Miami Beach in the 1920s. The atrium lobby of the modern hotel has a fountain with a sculpted dolphin as its centerpiece. The newly updated rooms (2007) are spacious and regally outfitted with opulent furniture and upholstery, with views from every window. Suites offer Jacuzzi tubs and separate showers, and deluxe condos offer full kitchens—good for families. Grand Club rooms occupy the top two floors of the resort, and offer secured access, a private lounge (with complimentary breakfast), and extraordinary views. Two-bedroom units come with full kitchen, fireplace, three TVs, and washer and dryer. Even more fabulous are the Royal Private Villas, sumptuous guest units in their own building that are essentially luxury apartments, with access to a private infinity pool.

This is an ideal location for visitors who want to feel pampered in sophisticated surroundings while maintaining easy access to the waterfront. The restaurant and lounge overlook the resort's private marina, where guests can moor their small boats. Motorized swans and boats sized for kids offer fun for children in a protected waterway. The state-of-the-art fitness room and spa offers a variety of wellness and aesthetic treatments.

1310 Water St., Kelowna, BC V1Y 9P3. © **800/465-4651** or 250/763-4500. Fax 250/763-4565. www.grandokanagan. com. 390 units. C$159–C$339 (US$159–US$339/£80–£170) double; C$369–C$1,499 (US$369–US$1,499/£185–£750) suites, condos, or luxury villas. Extra person C$15 (US$15/£7.50). Off-season discounts available. AE, DC, MC, V. **Amenities:** 3 restaurants; pub; lounge; indoor and outdoor pools; health club w/spa; watersports-equipment rentals; concierge; business center; shopping arcade; salon; room service; laundry service; same-day dry cleaning; casino. *In room:* A/C, TV, high-speed Internet access, minibar (on request), coffeemaker, hair dryer, iron/ironing board.

Hotel Eldorado ★★   This is one of the most charming places to stay in Kelowna if you like historic inns. With a history dating back to 1926, the Eldorado has been fully restored and is now decorated with a unique mix of antiques; a wing with 30 new guest rooms and six luxury suites were added in 2005. All rooms are individually decorated, and there's a wide mix of floor plans and layouts, some with CD players and fridges. The third-floor guest rooms with views of the lake are the largest and quietest. Some rooms also feature lakeside balconies. On the premises are a boardwalk cafe, lounge, spa, and dining room. The staff can arrange boat moorage, boat rentals, and water-skiing lessons.

500 Cook Rd. (at Lakeshore Rd.), Kelowna, BC V1W 3G9. © **866/608 7500** or 250/763-7500. Fax 250/861-4779. www.eldoradokelowna.com. 55 units. C$189–C$449 (US$189–US$449/£95–£225). Lower off-season rates available. AE, DC, MC, V. From downtown follow Pandosy Rd. south 1.5km (1 mile). Turn right on Cook Rd. **Amenities:** Fine-dining restaurant; bar; boardwalk cafe; indoor pool; fitness center; spa services; Jacuzzi; steam room; marina. *In room:* A/C, TV, Wi-Fi access, coffeemaker, hair dryer, iron.

WHERE TO DINE

A number of vineyards in the Okanagan Valley now have restaurants; in fact, in good weather, these winery dining rooms are extremely charming places to eat, as most dining is alfresco (there are no bad views in the valley) and there's an explosion of local boutique and organic market produce available to young chefs. Of the wineries noted above, Sumac Ridge's **Cellar Door Bistro** (© **250/494-0451**) is open daily year-round for lunch and dinner; Quails' Gate's **Old Vines Patio and Restaurant** (© **800/420-9463** or 250/769-4451) is open year-round for lunch and dinner; Hainle's **Amphora Bistro** (© **250/767-2525**) is open Tuesday through Friday for lunch, and nightly for dinner; and Burrowing Owl's very impressive **Sonora Room** (© **877/498-0620** or 250/498-0620) is open daily for lunch, and Wednesday through Sunday for dinner (closed in winter).

IN & AROUND PENTICTON

Naramata Inn ⊕ PACIFIC NORTHWEST   Built in 1908, the Naramata Inn is resplendent in early-20th-century character. The Cobblestone Wine Bar serves some of the most sophisticated food in the Okanagan Valley, and with a very impressive wine list. Using only the freshest ingredients—many from its own garden—the Cobblestone offers a selection of tasting menus that focus on regional ingredients; wine pairings are available for each of the menus. Expect such refined dishes as seared deep sea scallop and kurabuta pork belly confit with parsnip ravioli, and double-smoked bacon-wrapped quail breast with matsutake mushrooms.

3625 First St., Naramata (19km/12 miles north of Penticton on the east side of Okanagan Lake). (© **250/496-5001.** www.naramatainn.com. Reservations required. 5-course menu C$70 (US$70/£35. MC, V. Rock Oven Dining Room May–Oct Thurs–Sun 6–9pm; Cobblestone Wine Bar and Restaurant Apr–Oct daily 11:30am–10pm, Nov–Mar Thurs–Sun 11:30am–10pm.

IN KELOWNA

Bouchons Bistro ⊕ FRENCH   This Gallic transplant offers classic French bistro fare just a few blocks from the Okanagan lakefront. The dining room, with ochre walls, stained-glass panels, and handwritten menus, actually feels Parisian. The menu doesn't stray far from classic French cuisine, though it's prepared with the freshest and best of local products; the level of cooking at Bouchons will make you appreciate French cuisine once again. Cassoulet is a house specialty, and you can't go wrong with duck confit glazed with honey and spices. The C$37 (US$37/£19) three-course prix-fixe menu is a very good value. The wine list is half French, half local Okanagan vintages. In summer, there's alfresco dining in the gardenlike patio.

1180 Sunset Dr. © **250/763-6595.** Reservations recommended. Main courses C$19–C$37 (US$19–US$37/£10–£19). MC, V. Daily 5:30–10pm.

Fresco ⊕⊕⊕ NEW CANADIAN   This coolly sophisticated restaurant is Kelowna's dining hot spot. The cooking focuses on fresh regional cuisine, while keeping the preparations relatively unfussy—as these things go with this class of cutting-edge cooking. The open kitchen overlooks a studied casual dining room; service is top-notch and the wine list celebrates the vintages of the Okanagan Valley. Start a meal with a Dungeness crab cake with apple slaw and black-mustard-seed mayonnaise, and move on to a main dish of grilled venison rib chop with cherry and tarragon bread pudding, or forest mushroom–crusted rack of lamb with Parmesan cheese gnocchi. Fresco's chef/owner Rod Butters has cooked at some of western Canada's top restaurants; this is his first solo venture. Stop by and see what's cooking.

1560 Water St. © **250/868-8805.** Reservations required. Main courses C$22–C$37 (US$22–US$37/£11–£19). AE, MC, V. Tues–Sat 5:30–10pm.

17

The Yukon, Northwest Territories & Nunavut

by Bill McRae

The Far North of Canada is one of North America's last great wilderness areas. The Yukon, the Northwest Territories, Nunavut, and the northernmost of British Columbia are home to the Inuit, Inuvialuit, and northern First Nations peoples like the Dene, vast herds of wildlife, and thousands of square miles of tundra and stunted subarctic forest. For centuries, names such as the Klondike, Hudson's Bay, and the Northwest Passage have conjured up powerful images of rugged determination in an untamed and harsh wilderness. For an area so little visited and so distant, the North has long played an integral role in the history and imagination of the Western world.

Yet the North has been changing rapidly, creating a whole pattern of paradoxes. The Arctic is a hotbed of mineral, oil, gas, and diamond exploration. Jobs and schools have brought Native people from their hunting camps to town, where they live in prefabs instead of igloos and drive trucks and snowmobiles out to their trap lines. Still, much of the money they spend in supermarkets they earn using ancestral hunting and artisan skills, and for many, life remains based on the pursuit of migrating game animals and marine creatures.

Native Canadians—including First Nations peoples (Indians), the Inuit, Inuvialuit, and the Métis, offspring of white and First Nations couples—make up the majority of the North's population. All of Canada's Native peoples were originally nomadic, traveling enormous distances in pursuit of migrating game animals. Today nearly all First Nations people have permanent homes in settlements, but many of them spend part of the year in remote tent camps hunting, fishing, and trapping. And though the Inuit no longer live in igloos, these snow houses are still built as temporary shelters when the occasion arises.

Survival is the key word for Native Canadians. They learned to survive in conditions that seem unimaginably harsh to more southerly peoples, relying on skills and technologies that become more wondrous the better you know them. Early white explorers quickly learned that in order to stay alive they had to adopt those skills and technologies as best they could. Those who refused to "go native" rarely survived in the great Canadian north.

Norse merchants and explorers traveling from Greenland may have been the first non-Native visitors to the Canadian North, as long as 800 years ago, but the first non-Native known to have penetrated the region was Martin Frobisher. His written account of meeting the Inuit, over 400 years old, is the earliest on record. At about the same time, European whalers, hunting whales for their oil, were occasionally forced ashore by storms or shipwrecks and depended on Inuit hospitality for survival. This almost-legendary hospitality, extended to any stranger who came to them, remains an outstanding characteristic of the Inuit. Whites began to move into the Canadian Arctic in greater number during the "fur rush" of the late 18th century. In the wake of the fur hunters and traders came Roman Catholic and Anglican missionaries, who built churches and opened schools.

For most of its recorded history, the Far North was governed from afar, first by Great Britain, then by the Hudson's Bay Company, and from 1867 by the new Canadian government in Ottawa. At that time the Northwest Territories included all of the Yukon, Saskatchewan, Alberta, and huge parts of other provinces. Then, in 1896, gold was discovered on Bonanza Creek in the midwestern Yukon region of Klondike. Tens of thousands of people flocked to the Yukon in a matter of months, giving birth to **Dawson City** in Klondike, **Whitehorse** (later the capital) in southcentral Yukon, and a dozen other tent communities, many of which eventually went bust along with the gold veins. The Yukon gold rush was the greatest in history; prospectors washed more than C$500,000 (US$500,000/£250,000) in gold out of the

gravel banks along the Klondike before industrial mining moved in, to reap in the millions. With its new wealth and population, the Yukon split off from the rest of the Northwest Territories in 1898.

The Northwest Territories didn't receive its own elected government until 1967, when the center of government was moved from Ottawa to the new territorial capital of **Yellowknife** and a representative assembly was elected. In 1999, the eastern section of the Northwest Territories, almost 2 million sq. km (about 772,000 sq. miles), became a separate and autonomous territory known as **Nunavut** (meaning "our land" in the Inuit language of Inuktitut), with its capital of **Iqaluit** (formerly Frobisher Bay) on Baffin Island. The rest of the pre-Nunavut Northwest Territories—1,172,000 sq. km (452,500 sq. miles) of land that contains the drainage of the Mackenzie River, a sizeable portion of arctic coast, the Great Slave and Great Bear lakes, and a few arctic island territories—has retained the Northwest Territories name.

1 Exploring the North

The Arctic isn't like any other place. That observation may seem elementary, but even a well-prepared first-timer will experience many things here to startle—and perhaps offend—the senses.

No matter where you start from, the Arctic is a long way away. By far the easiest way to get there is by plane. Whitehorse, Yellowknife, and Iqaluit all have airports with daily service from major Canadian cities. Each of these towns is a center for a network of smaller airlines with regularly scheduled flights to yet smaller communities; here you'll also find charter services to take you to incredibly out-of-the-way destinations.

Tucked inland just east of Alaska, the Yukon is home to one of the most notable fortune hunts of all times: the Klondike Gold Rush. From 1898 to 1920, Dawson City was the destination of tens of thousands of prospectors—and other types of gold diggers—who were lured north by the dream of easy wealth. Today, Dawson City and territorial capital Whitehorse are still very lively and filled with history, though many of today's travelers are drawn as much to recreation on the Yukon's rivers, lakes, and mountains as to the trail of bonanza gold.

Until 1999, the Northwest Territories designated the entire northern tier of Canada (except the Yukon). Then Nunavut, comprising the eastern mainland and many of the arctic islands, split away to form a separate territory and a de facto homeland for the Inuit peoples. Centered on Baffin Island and the capital Iqualuit, Nunavut is an extremely far-flung territory made of up remote Native villages, expanses of tundra, and craggy, glacier-crowned islands.

The remaining Northwest Territories is sometimes referred to as the western Arctic. Mining is the prime economic driver, with everything from gold to silver to diamonds extracted from the tundra. The capital of Yellowknife is a hells-a-poppin' kind of city, born of a gold rush and sustained by high-paying government and mining industry jobs. Vast glacial-dug lakes provide lakefront for rustic to ritzy fishing lodges.

VISITOR INFORMATION

For information, write **Tourism Yukon**, P.O. Box 2703, Whitehorse, YT Y1A 2C6 (© **800/661-0494;** www.touryukon.com). Be sure to ask for a copy of the official vacation guide *Yukon: Canada's True North.*

For the Northwest Territories, contact **NWT Arctic Tourism**, P.O. Box 610, Yellowknife, NT X1A 2N5 (© **800/661-0788** or 867/873-7200; www.explorenwt.com). Ask for the free map of the province (it's almost impossible to find a map of the Territories elsewhere) and *The Explorers' Guide,* with full listings of accommodations and outfitters.

Information on Nunavut is at **www.nunavuttourism.com,** where you can download a copy of the *Nunavut Travel Planner.* You can also call © **866/686-2888** or e-mail info@nunavuttourism.com to make inquiries or request the travel planner.

CLIMATE & SEASONS

During summer, the farther north you travel, the more daylight you get. Yellowknife and Whitehorse, in the south, bask under 20 hours of sunshine a day, followed by 4 hours of milky twilight bright enough to read a newspaper by. In northern Inuvik, Northwest Territories, the summer sun shines around the clock. In midwinter, however, these towns don't see the northern sun rise at all.

The North is divided into two climatic zones: **subarctic** and **arctic,** but the division doesn't follow the Arctic Circle. And while there are permanent ice caps in the far-northern islands, summer in the rest of the land gets considerably hotter than you might think. The average high temperatures in July and August for many subarctic regions can be in the 70s and 80s (20s Celsius), and the mercury has been known to climb into the 90s (30s Celsius). However, even in summer you should bring a warm sweater or ski jacket—and don't forget a pair of really sturdy shoes or boots.

In winter, weather conditions are truly arctic. The mercury may dip as low as –60°F (–51°C) for short periods. You'll need heavily insulated clothing and footwear to travel during this time of year. Spring is an increasingly popular time to visit, with clear sunny skies, highs around 20°F (–7°C), and days already longer than seems reasonable.

DRIVING THE NORTH

Setting out to drive the back roads of the Far North has a strange fascination for many people, most of whom own RVs. The most famous route through the North is the **Alaska Highway,** which was built during World War II to link the continental United States with Alaska via northern British Columbia and the Yukon. Today the route is mostly paved and isn't the adventure it once was. Off-road enthusiasts may prefer the **Mackenzie Highway,** linking **Edmonton** to **Yellowknife.** But even this road is mostly paved nowadays, which leaves the **Dempster Highway** ⚡ (© **867/979-2040** highway information), between **Dawson City** and **Inuvik,** as one of the few real back roads left.

Much of the North is served by good roads, though driving up here demands different preparations than you might be used to. It's a good idea to travel with a full 20-liter

The Yukon, the Northwest Territories & Nunavut

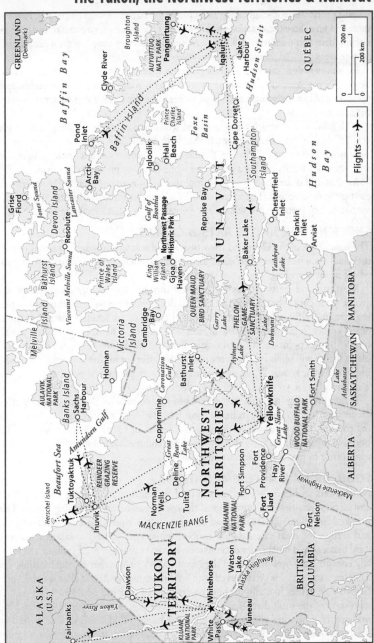

(5-gal.) gas can, even though along most routes gas stations appear frequently. However, there's no guarantee these stations will be open in the evenings, on Sunday, or at the precise moment you need to fill up. By all means, fill up every time you see a gas station in remote areas.

In summer, dust can be a serious nuisance, particularly on gravel roads. When it becomes a problem, close all windows and turn on your heater fan. This builds up air pressure inside your vehicle and helps to keep the dust out. Keep cameras in plastic bags for protection.

It's a good idea to attach a bug or gravel screen and plastic headlight guards to your vehicle. And it's absolutely essential that your windshield wipers are operative and your washer reservoir full. In the Yukon, the law requires that all automobiles drive with their headlights on; it's a good idea while traveling on any gravel road.

April and May are the spring slush months, when mud and water may render some road sections hazardous. The winter months, December through March, require a lot of special driving preparations; winter isn't a good time to plan a road trip to the North.

SHOPPING FOR NATIVE ARTS & CRAFTS

The handiwork of the Dene and Inuit people is absolutely unique. Some of it has utility value—you won't get finer, more painstakingly stitched cold-weather clothing anywhere in the world.

Most arts-and-crafts articles are handled through community cooperatives, thus avoiding the cut of the middleman. Official documentation will guarantee that a piece is a genuine Native Canadian object. Don't hesitate to ask retailers where a particular object comes from, what it's made of, and who made it. They'll be glad to tell you and frequently will point out where the artist lives and works. In the eastern Arctic particularly, artists will often approach tourists in the streets or in bars and restaurants, seeking to sell their goods. While these articles may lack the official paperwork, the price is often right; use your judgment when deciding to buy.

Before investing in Native art, make sure you know what the **import restrictions** are in your home country. In many countries, it's illegal to bring in articles containing parts of marine mammals (this includes walrus or narwhal ivory, as well as whale bones or polar-bear fur). Sealskin products are commonly prohibited. Consult a Customs office to find out what restrictions are in place.

FOOD, DRINK & ACCOMMODATIONS

Northerners traditionally lived off the land by hunting and fishing (many still do), and arctic specialties have now worked their way onto many fine-dining menus. **Caribou** and **musk ox** appear on almost all menus in the North and offer a different taste and texture for meat eaters. Good caribou, sometimes dressed in sauces made from local berries (wild blueberries or Saskatoon berries) tastes like mild venison and is usually cheaper than beef or lamb in the North. Musk ox is rather stronger tasting, with a chewy texture, and is often served with wild mushrooms. **Arctic char** is a mild pink-fleshed fish, rather like salmon but coarser grained and less oily. You won't find the mainstays of the Inuit diet—seal and whale meat—on most restaurant menus, but in outlying communities you won't have to look hard to find someone able to feed you some *maktaaq* (whale blubber and skin) or *igunaq* (aged, fermented meat, of walrus or seal). **Bannocks,** a type of baking-powder biscuit, and so-called **Eskimo doughnuts,** a cousin of Indian fry bread, are popular snacks to feed tourists. You'll have to decide how appetizing you find the delicacy known as **Eskimo ice cream** *(akutuq)*,

---

⌐Tips **Warning: Get Thee to an Outfitter**

Outdoor enthusiasts who want to get out onto the land, the water, or the gla-cier will need to have the assistance of an outfitter or a local tour provider. There are no roads to speak of here, so you'll need help simply to get wherever you're going. This usually involves a boat or an airplane trip. Sports-equipment rental is all but unheard of, and it's very foolish to head out into the wilds (which start at the edge of the village) without the advice and guidance of someone who knows the terrain, weather, and other general conditions. For all these reasons—and for the entree you'll get into the community—you should hire an outfitter. You'll end up saving money, time, and frustration.

---

a mousselike concoction made of whipped animal fats (caribou fat and seal oil, for instance) and berries.

Vegetarians aren't going to find much to eat in the North. The traditional arctic diet doesn't include much in the way of fruits or vegetables, and green stuff that's been air-freighted in is pretty sad looking by the time it reaches the table. Bring your own dietary supplements if you have a restricted diet.

No matter what you eat in the North, it's going to be expensive. In towns like Yel-lowknife or Inuvik, a normal entree at a decent hotel restaurant will cost at least C$35 (US$35/£18); at outlying villages, where hotels offer full board, a sandwich with fries will run C$25 (US$25/£13). Chances are excellent that, for the money, your food will be very pedestrian in quality. In most towns, the grocery-store chain The Northern shelters a few fast-food outlets, usually the only other dining option.

Alcohol is banned or highly restricted in most Native communities. Some towns are completely dry: No one, not even visitors in the privacy of their hotel rooms, is allowed to possess or consume alcohol. In some locales, RCMP officers will check the baggage of incoming travelers and confiscate alcohol. In other communities, alcohol is legal but regulated to such a degree the casual visitor will find it impossible to get hold of a drink. In other communities, alcohol is available in hotel bars or restaurants but not in stores (or even by room service). Alcohol is a major social problem in the North, so by all means respect the local laws regulating alcohol consumption.

Accommodations are the most expensive day-to-day outlay in the North. Almost every community, no matter how small, will have a hotel, but prices are very high. You can save some money with B&Bs or home stays, which also have the advantage of introducing you to the locals.

THE GREAT OUTDOORS

SEASONAL TRAVEL   Hiking and naturalist trips are popular in late July, August, and early September. The ice is off the ocean, allowing access by boat to otherwise-remote areas. Naturalist-led hikes out onto the tundra make great day trips.

While it may seem natural to plan a trip to the Arctic in summer, the Far North is a year-round destination. Late-winter dog-sledding trips out into the frozen wilder-ness are popular with adventurous souls. In May and June, dog-sled or snow-machine trips visit the edge of the ice floe, where wildlife viewing is superb. And in the dead of winter, there is the 24-hour darkness and the northern lights that lure people north.

MOSQUITOES, DEERFLIES & OTHER CRITTERS   During summer especially, two of the most commonly heard sounds in the North are the rhythmic buzzing of winged biting insects and the cursing of their human victims. **Insect repellent** is a necessity, as is having a place you can get away from the mosquitoes for a while. Some hikers wear expedition hats or head nets to ward off the worst attacks. Mosquitoes can go through light fabric, which is why it's better to wear sturdy clothes even on the hottest days. Wasps, hornets, and other stinging insects are common. If you're allergic, be ready with your serum.

CANOEING & DOG SLEDDING   If you want to see the land as early explorers and Natives did, try exploring the North via these two traditional methods. The following outfitters usually offer recreation in more than one part of the North or different recreational pursuits depending on the season.

Canoeing   The early French-Canadian trappers, or *voyageurs,* explored the North—particularly the Yukon—by canoe, and outfitters now offer multiday expeditions down the region's wide powerful rivers. A good place to go for some advice on guided tours on Yukon and Northwest Territories rivers is **Paddle Canada**, P.O. Box 398, 446 Main St. W., Merrickville, ON K0G 1N0 (© 888/252-6292 or 613/269-2910; www.paddling canada.com). **Kanoe People,** P.O. Box 31149, Whitehorse, YT Y1A 5P7 (© 867/668-4899; www.kanoepeople.com), offers both custom and guided canoe trips on Yukon rivers and lakes. River trips pass historic mining ghost towns and First Nation villages. A guided trip on the Yukon goes for 8 days and costs C$1,596 (US$1,596/£798), and one on the Telsin lasts 10 days at C$1,649 (US$1,649/£825). Bring your own sleeping bag, pad, and small personal gear (including fishing tackle) of choice; everything else—including camping equipment, food, and transportation from Whitehorse—is included.

Dog Sledding   An even more indigenous mode of transport in the North is travel by dog sled. While few people run dogs as their sole means of getting around any longer, the sport of dog sledding is hugely popular, and dog-sledding trips to otherwise-snowbound backcountry destinations make a great early-spring adventure.

In the Yukon, **Uncommon Journeys,** P.O. Box 20621, Whitehorse, YT Y1A 7A2 (© 867/668-2255; www.uncommonyukon.com), offers 7- and 10-day guided backcountry dog-sledding trips out into the northern wilderness. Seven-day trips start at C$3,290 (US$3,290/£1,645).

WILDLIFE   It's easy to confuse **caribou** with European reindeer, as the two look very much alike and, in fact, are generally classified as the same species. But while reindeer are mostly domesticated animals, caribou are wild, and still travel in huge migrating herds that stretch to the horizon, sometimes numbering 100,000 or more. Caribou form the major food and clothing supply for many Native Canadians, whose lives cycle around the movements of the herds.

The mighty **musk ox** is indigenous to the Arctic. About 12,000 of them live on the northern islands. Immense and prehistoric looking, the bulls weigh up to 590 kilograms (1,300 lb.). They appear even larger because they carry a mountain of shaggy hair. Underneath the coarse outer coat, musk oxen have a silky-soft layer of underwool, called *qiviut* in Inuit. One pound of qiviut can be spun into a 40-strand thread 40km (25 miles) long! As light as it is soft, a sweater made from the stuff will keep its wearer warm in subzero weather. And it doesn't shrink when wet. Qiviut is extremely expensive. Once spun, it can sell for as much as C$90 (US$90/£45) an ounce.

The monarch of the Arctic, the **polar bear** roams the coast and the shores of Hudson Bay; you'll have to travel quite a way over mighty tough country to see one in its habitat.

Weighing up to 658 kilograms (1,450 lb.), they're the largest land predators in North America. **Grizzly bears** are found in the boreal forests and river basins. Both animals are very dangerous; if you encounter them, give them a wide berth. The North is full of other animals much easier to observe than the bears. In the wooded regions, you'll come across **wolves** and **wolverines** (harmless to humans, despite the legends about them), **mink, lynx, otter, ptarmigan,** and **beaver.** The sleek and beautiful white or brown **arctic foxes** live in ice regions as well as beneath the tree line and near settlements.

Mid-July to late August, **seals, walruses, narwhals,** and **bowhead** and **beluga whales** are in their breeding grounds off the coast of Baffin Island and in Hudson Bay. And in the endless skies above there are **eagles, hawks, owls, razor-billed auks,** and **ivory gulls.**

2 The Alaska Highway: On to the Last Frontier ⟨★

Constructed as a military freight road during World War II to link Alaska to the Lower 48, the Alaska Highway—also known as the Alcan Highway, and Highway 97 in British Columbia—has become something of a pilgrimage route. The vast majority of people who make the trip are recent retirees, who take their newly purchased RVs and head up north; it's a rite of passage.

Strictly speaking, the Alaska Highway starts at the Mile 1 marker in **Dawson Creek,** on the eastern edge of British Columbia, and travels north and west for 2,242km (1,393 miles) to **Delta Junction,** in Alaska, passing through the Yukon along the way. The **Richardson Highway** (Alaska Rte. 4) covers the additional 158km (98 miles) from Delta Junction to **Fairbanks.** As recently as 25 years ago, much of the talk of the Alaska Highway had to do with conditions of the road itself, the freak rain and snowstorms, and the far-flung gas pumps. However, for the road's 50th anniversary in 1992, the final stretches of the road were paved.

While the days of tire-eating gravel roads and extra gas cans are largely past, there are several things to consider before setting out. First, this is a very *long* road. Popular wisdom states that if you drive straight out, it takes 3 days between Dawson Creek and Fairbanks. But much of the road is very winding, slow-moving RV traffic is heavy, and considerable portions are under reconstruction every summer. If you try to keep yourself to a 3-day schedule, you'll have a miserable time.

WHAT TO EXPECT

Summer is the only opportunity to repair the road, so construction crews really go to it; depend on lengthy delays and some very rugged detours. Visitor centers along the way get faxes of daily construction schedules and conditions, so stop for updates, or follow the links to "Road Conditions" from the website **www.themilepost.com.** You can also call ⟨ **867/456-7623** for 24-hour highway information.

While availability of gasoline isn't the problem that it once was, there are a couple of things to remember. Gas prices can be substantially higher than in, say, Edmonton or Calgary. Although there's gas at most of the communities that appear on the road map, most close up early in the evening. You'll find 24-hour gas stations and plenty of motel rooms in the towns of Dawson City, Fort St. John, Fort Nelson, Watson Lake, and Whitehorse.

Try to be patient when driving the Alaska Highway. In high season, the entire route, from Edmonton to Fairbanks, is one long caravan of RVs. Many people have their car in tow, a boat on the roof, and several bicycles chained to the spare tire. Thus encumbered, they lumber up the highway; loath (or unable) to pass one another. These convoys of RVs stretch on forever, the slowest of the party setting the pace for all.

DRIVING THE ALASKA HIGHWAY

This overview of the Alaska Highway is not meant to serve as a detailed guide for drivers. For that, you should purchase the annual *Alaska Milepost* (www.themilepost.com), which offers exhaustive, mile-by-mile coverage of the trip (and of other road trips into the Arctic of Alaska and Canada).

The route begins (or ends) at Dawson Creek, in British Columbia. Depending on where you start from, Dawson Creek is a long 590km (367-mile) drive from Edmonton or a comparatively short 406km (252 miles) from Prince George on Highway 97. Dawson Creek is a natural place to break up the journey, with ample tourist facilities. If you want to call ahead to ensure a room, try the **Ramada Limted Dawson Creek,** 1748 Alaska Ave. (© **800/663-2749** or 250/782-8595).

From Dawson Creek, the Alaska Highway soon crosses the Peace River and passes through **Fort St. John,** in the heart of British Columbia's far-north ranch country. The highway continues north, parallel to the Rockies. First the ranches thin, and then the forests thin. Moose are often seen from the road.

From Fort St. John to **Fort Nelson,** you'll find gas stations and cafes every 65 to 81km (40–50 miles), though lodging options are pretty dubious. Fort Nelson is thick with motels and gas stations; because it's hours from any other major service center, this is a good place to spend the night. Try the **Travelodge Fort Nelson,** 4711 50th Ave. S. (© **888/515-6375** or 250/774-3911; www.travelodgefortnelson.com).

At Fort Nelson, the Alaska Highway turns west and heads into the Rockies; from here, too, graveled **Liard Highway** (B.C. Hwy. 77; Northern Territories Hwy. 7) continues north to Fort Liard and Fort Simpson, the gateway to **Nahanni National Park,** a very worthy side trip.

A breathtaking, unspoiled wilderness of 4,766 sq. km (1,840 sq. miles) in the southwest corner of the Northwest Territory, Nahanni National Park is accessible only by foot, motorboat, canoe, or charter aircraft. Within the park, the South Nahanni River claws its path through the rugged Mackenzie Mountains, at one point charging over incredible Virginia Falls, at 105m (344 ft.), twice as high as Niagara and carrying more water. Below the falls, the river surges through one of the continent's deepest gorges, with canyon walls up to 1,333m (4,373 ft.) high. For most travelers, a flight-seeing day trip to the falls is adventure enough, though white-water raft trips from the base of the falls through the canyon (requiring 6 days or more) may be tempting to enthusiasts. **Wolverine Air** (© **888/695-2263;** www.wolverineair.com), in Fort Simpson, offers charter drop-offs to various park destinations or sightseeing day trips to the falls; a 3-hour flying-only tour costs C$1,095 (US$1,095/£548) for up to five people, while a 5½-hour flying tour with a stopover at the falls costs C$1,295 (US$1,295/£648) for up to three people. For a full listing of licensed rafting outfitters and for details about the park, contact **Nahanni National Park,** Box 348, Fort Simpson, NT X0E 0N0 (© **867/695-3151;** www.pc.gc.ca/pn-np/nt/nahanni).

From Fort Nelson, the Alaska Highway through the Rockies is mostly narrow and winding; you can depend on finding a construction crew working along this stretch. The Rockies are relatively modest mountains in this area, not as rugged or scenic as they are farther south in Jasper National Park. Once over the Continental Divide, the Alaska Highway follows tributaries of the Liard River through **Stone Mountain** and **Muncho Lake** provincial parks. Rustic lodges are scattered along the road. The lovely log **Northern Rockies Lodge** ⚓, at Muncho Lake (© **800/663-5269** or 250/776-3481; www.northern-rockies-lodge.com), offers lodge rooms and log cabins for C$105 to C$125 (US$105–US$125/£53–£63) and campsites for C$35 (US$35/£18).

At the town of **Liard River,** stop and stretch your legs or go for a soak at **Liard Hot Springs.** The provincial parks department maintains two nice soaking pools in the deep forest; the boardwalk out into the mineral-water marsh is pleasant even if you don't have time for a dip.

As you get closer to **Watson Lake** in the Yukon, you'll notice that mom-and-pop gas stations along the road will advertise that they have cheaper gas than at Watson Lake. Believe them, and fill up: Watson Lake is an unappealing town whose extortionately priced gas is probably its only memorable feature. **The Belvedere Motor Hotel,** 609 Frank Trail (© 867/536-7714), is the best spot to spend the night, with a restaurant and coffee shop on-site and rooms starting at C$89 (US$89/£45).

The long road between Watson Lake and **Whitehorse** travels through rolling hills and forest to Teslin and Atlin lakes, where the landscape becomes more mountainous and the gray clouds of the Gulf of Alaska's weather systems hang menacingly on the horizon. Whitehorse is the largest town along the route of the Alaska Highway, and unless you're in a great hurry, plan to spend at least a day here. See the Whitehorse section (following) for lodging suggestions.

Hope for good weather as you leave Whitehorse; the trip past **Kluane National Park** is one the most beautiful parts of the entire route. Tucked into the southwestern corner of the Yukon, a 2-hour drive from Whitehorse, these 22,015 sq. km (8,500 sq. miles) of glaciers, marshes, mountains, and sand dunes are unsettled and virtually untouched—and designated as a **UNESCO World Heritage Site.** Bordering on Alaska in the west, Kluane contains **Mount Logan** and **Mount St. Elias,** respectively the second- and third-highest peaks in North America.

Because Kluane is largely undeveloped and is preserved as a wilderness, casual exploration of Kluane is limited to a few day-hiking trails and to aerial sightseeing trips on small aircraft and helicopters. The vast expanse of ice and rock in the wilderness heart of Kluane is well beyond the striking range of the average outdoor enthusiast. The area's white-water rafting is world-class but likewise not for the uninitiated (for information on white-water expeditions in Kluane, see "Sports & Outdoor Activities," in the following section on Whitehorse).

Purists may object, but the only way the average person is going to have a chance to see the backcountry of Kluane Park is by airplane or helicopter. Located at the Haines Junction airport, **Trans North Helicopters** (© 867/668-2177; www.tntaheli.com) offers a 1-hour flight into Kluane Park and over Lowell Glacier and Lowell Lake. The fare is C$319 (US$319/£160) per person, based on a minimum group of four (for a minimum total cost of C$1,276 (US$1,276/£638).

The park's one easy day hike is at lovely **Kathleen Lake,** where there's an interpreted hike or else a longer trail along the lake's south bank. Rangers at the **visitor center** (at Haines Junction, open year-round; © 867/634-7250) can offer advice on other hikes; they also show an award-winning audiovisual presentation on the park. For more information on recreation in Kluane, see the website at **www.pc.gc.ca/pn-np/yt/kluane.**

After Kluane, the Alaska Highway edges by Kluane Lake before passing Beaver Creek and crossing over into Alaska. From the border crossing to Fairbanks, it's another 481km (298 miles).

3 Whitehorse: Capital of the Yukon ⚐

Born of the Klondike Gold Rush, Whitehorse was the head of riverboat navigation on the Yukon River for the thousands of prospectors who came north seeking fortunes.

Just south of the city (upriver), the Yukon River's treacherous Miles and White Horse Rapids (so called for whitecapped waves that resembled horses' manes) blocked riverboat transport. When the White Pass and Yukon Route railway arrived in Whitehorse from Skagway in 1902, the city's role as the transportation hub of the Yukon was cemented. Whitehorse boomed again during the 1940s when thousands of U.S. Army personnel arrived to complete the Alaska Highway, and by 1953, Whitehorse became the capital of the Yukon after Dawson City fizzled out along with its gold.

With a population of about 23,000, Whitehorse is home to almost three-quarters of the Yukon's population. It's no longer a frontier settlement, and food, lodging and hospitality are all of a high standard.

ESSENTIALS

GETTING THERE   **Whitehorse Airport** (© 867/667-8440), just off the Alaska Highway on a rise above the city, is served by **Air Canada Jazz** (© 888/247-2262; www.flyjazz.ca) from Vancouver. **Air North** (© 800/661-0407 in Canada, or 800/ 764-0407 from the U.S.; www.flyairnorth.com) flies into Whitehorse from Juneau and Fairbanks, Alaska, plus Edmonton, Calgary, and Vancouver. **First Air** (© 800/267-1247 or 613/688-2635; www.firstair.ca) links Whitehorse to Yellowknife, while **Condor Air** (© 800/524-6975; www7.condor.com) in summer offers twice-weekly nonstop flights between Whitehorse and Frankfurt, Germany (the Yukon is a very popular destination for German outdoor adventurers). Cab fare to downtown Whitehorse from the airport is around C$12 (US$12/£6). Whitehorse is 458km (285 miles) southeast of Beaver Creek (the Alaskan border).

VISITOR INFORMATION   Your first stop should be the **Yukon Visitor Information Centre,** Second and Hanson streets (© 867/667-3084). The third week in May to the third week in September, the center is open daily 8am to 8pm; winter hours are Monday to Friday 9am to 4:30pm. A bounty of information can be found at **www. visitwhitehorse.com, www.yukoninfo.com**, and **www.touryukon.com**.

GETTING AROUND   Public transit is handled by **Whitehorse Transit** (© 867/ 668-7433); fare is C$2 (US$2/£1). Car rental is available from **Budget** (© 800/858-5377 or 867/667-6200), **Hertz** (© 800/654-3131), and **National** (© 867/456-2277 in Canada, or 800/764-2277 in the U.S.). If you need a taxi, try **Yukon Taxi** (© 867/ 667-6677).

SPECIAL EVENTS   February is a happening month in Whitehorse. One of the top dog-sled races in North America, the **Yukon Quest** (www.yukonquest.org), runs 1,610km (1,000 miles) between Whitehorse and Fairbanks, Alaska. The town is filled with hundreds of yapping dogs and avid mushers, eager to vie for the C$125,000 (US$125,000/£63,000) top prize. Making even more noise is the **Frostbite Music Festival** (www.frostbitefest.ca), which attracts musicians and entertainers from across Canada. Immediately afterward is the **Yukon Sourdough Rendezvous** (www.yukon rendezvous.com), a midwinter festival commemorating the days of the gold rush with various old-fashioned competitions, like dog pulls, fiddling and costume contests, and a "mad trapper" competition.

In early summer, Whitehorse hosts the **Yukon International Storytelling Festival** (www.storytelling.yk.net), the third-largest event of its kind in the world. The festival highlights ancient stories of First Nations and Native circumpolar peoples, but features traditional stories from all over the world. Many stories are performed theatrically, with song, music, and dance.

EXPLORING WHITEHORSE

Whitehorse has a large collection of historic gold-rush buildings and landmarks scattered throughout the city, though without context they may just seem like old buildings. The **Yukon Historical and Museums Association,** Donnenworth House, 3126 Third Ave., next to Le Page Park and behind the T.C. Richard's Building (© 867/667-4704; http://heritageyukon.ca), offers Whitehorse Heritage Buildings walking tours in June, July, and August. Monday through Saturday, the hour-long tours are at 9am, 11am, 1pm, and 3pm and cost C$2 (US$2/£1). They pass many of the gold rush–era structures and historic sites, such the unusual log cabin skyscrapers, and are a good introduction to the town.

Be sure to stop by city hall, on Second Avenue, between Steele and Wood streets, for a free 3-day parking permit.

MacBride Museum 🍴 Covering half a city block, this log-cabin museum is crammed with relics from the gold-rush era and has a large display of Yukon wildlife and minerals, all lovingly arranged by a nonprofit society. Within the museum compound you'll find Sam McGee's Cabin (read Robert Service's poem on the cremation of same) and the old Whitehorse Telegraph Office. The MacBride has four galleries, open-air exhibits, and a gift shop.

1124 First Ave. (at Wood St.). © 867/667-2709. www.macbridemuseum.com. Admission C$7 (US$7/£3.50) adults, C$6 (US$6/£3) seniors, C$3.50 (US$3.50/£1.75) youths 6–16, free for children under 6. Mid-May to Aug daily 10am–5pm; Sept daily noon–5pm; winter Thurs–Sat noon–5pm.

Old Log Church Museum The first resident priest of Whitehorse arrived in 1900, and the town immediately proceeded to build a log church and rectory to house him and his services. They're now some of the oldest buildings in the city. The Old Log Church was once the Anglican cathedral for the diocese—the only wooden cathedral in the world—and today it is a museum of the Yukon's early missionaries, whalers, and explorers, and their contact with indigenous First Nations people. The collection of Inuvialuit artifacts from Herschel Island (off the Yukon's Arctic Ocean shore) is especially interesting. (On the next block over are two "log skyscrapers"—old two- and three-story log cabins used as apartments and offices.)

Elliott St. at Third Ave. © 867/668-2555. Admission C$3 (US$3/£1.50) adults, C$2.50 (US$2.50/£1.25) seniors and students, children under 12 free. Mid-May to mid-Sept daily 10am–6pm.

SS *Klondike* Take a tour of the largest of the 250 riverboats that chugged up and down the Yukon River between 1929 and 1955, primarily as a cargo transport. Actually, the one on view was built in 1936 to replace the first *Klondike,* which ran aground. The *Klondike* is now permanently dry-docked beside the river, and is a designated National Historic Site. The boat has been restored to its late 1930s glory.

Anchored at the Robert Campbell Bridge. © 867/667-4511 (summer and gift shop number) or 867/667-3910 in the off season. Admission C$6.15 (US$6.15/£3.10) adults, C$1.95 (US$1.95/£1) students. Tours on the hour: May 15–June 11 daily 9am–6pm; June 12–Aug 21 daily 9am–7:30pm; Aug 22–Sept 15 daily 10am–4pm.

Takhini Hot Springs A swimming pool fed by natural hot springs and surrounded by rolling hills and hiking trails, the developed Takhini Hot Springs might be just what you need after days on the Alaska Highway. After swimming, you can refresh yourself at the restaurant. Depending on the season, wall climbing, zip lining, camping, horseback riding, hiking, cross-country skiing, and wagon or sleigh rides are also available.

Off of the N. Klondike Hwy. (10 Hotsprings Rd.), 27km (17 miles) north of Whitehorse. © 867/633-2706. www.takhinihotsprings.yk.ca. Pool admission C$9.50 (US$9.50/£4.75) adults, C$7 (US$7/£3.50) youth and seniors, C$6 (US$6/£3) children 3–12. Late-May to mid-June daily noon–10pm; mid-June to mid-Sept daily 8am–10pm.

Whitehorse Fishway   Narrowly bounded by high basalt walls and once one of the roughest sections of the Yukon River, Miles Canyon is now the site of a hydroelectric dam and the world's longest wooden fish ladder. The native Chinook salmon that migrate past Whitehorse use the fishway to bypass the dam, on their way to completing one of the longest fish migrations in the world. Mid-July to mid-August you can view these magnificent fish through windows looking in on the ladder. Interpretive displays and an upper viewing deck show you the entire process by which the dam has ceased to be an obstruction to the salmon migration.

At the end of Nisutlin Dr., in suburban Riverdale. Free admission. Fish ladder open late June to early Sept daily 8:30am–8:30pm.

Yukon Arts Centre   This is the hub of visual and performance arts in Whitehorse and the Yukon. The gallery hosts 10 to 17 rotating exhibits yearly, featuring both regional and international artists, photographers, and themes. It also offers workshops, lectures, and children's programs. You can see world-class, local and touring theatrical, musical, and dance performances year-round in the center's 424-seat theater.

Yukon Place at Yukon College, off Range Rd. N; northwest of downtown. © 867/667-8575. www.yukonartscentre.com. Admission by donation. Gallery: Tues–Fri noon–6pm; Sat–Sun noon–5pm. Call or visit website for performance calendar.

Yukon Beringia Interpretive Centre 🕊 *Kids*   During the last ice age, a land bridge joined Asia to Alaska and the Yukon, forming a subcontinent known as Beringia. Bordered on all sides by glaciers, Beringia was once home to woolly mammoths and other fascinating Pleistocene-era animals, as well as to cave-dwelling humans. This museum presents the archaeological and paleontological past of Beringia, with life-size exhibits of ice-age animals, multimedia displays, films, and dioramas on its prehistoric people, animals, plants, and ecosystems. Try your hand at hurling an atlatl, which is a sling and spear weapon that early hunters used in these parts 10,000 years ago.

Adjacent to the Yukon Transportation Museum, on Electra Crescent; Mile 917 on the Alaska Hwy. © 867/667-8855. www.beringia.com. C$6 (US$6/£3) adults, C$5 (US$5/£2.50) seniors, C$4 (US$4/£2), students, children 5 and under free. Combo ticket with Yukon Transportation Museum C$9 (US$9/£4.50) single, C$25 (US$25/£13) family. Mid-May to Labour Day daily 9am–6pm; winter Sun 1–5pm.

Yukon Transportation Museum 🕊 *Kids*   This fascinating museum presents the development of travel, from dog sled to railway to bush plane, through to the building of the Alaska Highway. You'll come away with a new appreciation of how adventurous and arduous it once was to travel to the Yukon. The exhibits and vintage photos on travel by dog sled are especially interesting. There's also a replica of the historic aircraft *Queen of the Yukon,* the sister aircraft of *The Spirit of St. Louis.* A film details the building of the White Pass Railroad from Skagway to Whitehorse, and a model recreation of that railway features a replica of downtown Whitehorse in the 1920s and 1930s. Step outside the museum and you'll see its DC-3 weathervane, the world's largest, at the entrance of the Whitehorse airport.

30 Electra Crescent; Mile 917 on the Alaska Hwy., adjacent to Whitehorse Airport and the Beringia Centre (see above) © 867/668-4792. www.yukontransportationmuseum.ca. Admission C$6 (US$6/£3) adults, C$5 (US$5/£2.50) seniors, C$4 (US$4/£2) students, children 5 and under free. Combo ticket with Yukon Berengia Interpretive Centre C$9 (US$9/£4.50) single, C$25 (US$25/£13) family. Mid-May to Labour Day daily 10am–6pm.

TOURS & EXCURSIONS

CITY TOURS   In addition to the historical walking tours offered by Yukon Historical and Museums Association (see above), **Gray Line** offers a 7½-hour city bus tour with a river cruise on the Yukon River through Miles Canyon. Available June through September, the cost is C$57 (US$57/£29) adults, C$29 (US$29/£15) children. The Gray Line headquarters are in the Westmark Hotel, 201 Wood St., Whitehorse (© **800/478-6388** or 867/668-3225).

WILDLIFE TOURS   North of Whitehorse 26km (16 miles), the **Yukon Wildlife Preserve,** Box 20411, Mile 5, Takhini Hot Springs Rd., Whitehorse, YK Y1A 7A2, 1.5km (1 mile) east of the Takhini Hot Springs (© **867/456-7400;** www.yukon wildlife.ca), manages populations of many different indigenous animal species for breeding and conservation purposes, and is open for public viewing. The preserve covers hundreds of acres of forests, marshes, and meadows, and features such animals as bison, moose, musk ox, elk, mountain goats, and rare peregrine falcons. Local wildlife also frequents the preserve. From mid-June to September 1, the preserve offers five guided 90-minute driving tours; cost is C$22 (US$22/£11) adults, C$12 (US$12/£6) students, C$55 (US$55/£28) family.

RIVER CRUISES   The MV *Schwatka* (© **867/668-4716** for reservations) is a river craft that cruises the Yukon River through the famous Miles Canyon. This stretch—once the most hazardous section of water in the territory—is now dammed and tamed, though it still offers fascinating wilderness scenery. The cruise takes 2 hours, accompanied by narration telling the story of the old "wild river" times. Adults pay C$25 (US$25/£13), children pay half price. Trips are offered late May through September 15. The boat leaves 5km (3 miles) south of Whitehorse; follow the signs for Miles Canyon.

SHOPPING   The **Yukon Gallery,** 201B Main St. (© 867/667-2391; www.yukon gallery.ca), is Whitehorse's best commercial visual-arts gallery, featuring a large show space devoted to Yukon and regional artists. There's an extensive display of paintings and prints, as well as some ceramics and Northern crafts, like moose-hair tufting. **Mac's Fireweed Books,** 203 Main St. (© **800/661-0508** or 867/668-6104 or 800/ 661-0508; www.yukonbooks.com), is the best bookstore in town, specializing in Yukon-related books and "Arcticana," as well as a vast selection of magazines.

SPORTS & OUTDOOR ACTIVITIES

CANOEING   The rivers of the Yukon were once navigated only by Native canoeists, and the Yukon's swift-flowing wide rivers still make for great canoe trips. In addition to their multiday expeditions (see "The Great Outdoors," earlier in this chapter), **Kanoe People** (© **867/668-4899;** www.kanoepeople.com) offers a variety of planned, self-guided day trips on the Yukon River for C$65 to C$95 (US$65–US$95/£33–£48) per person. It also rents canoes, sea kayaks, and other equipment by the day or week. For day rentals costing C$40 (US$40/£20) for canoes or C$50 (US$50/£25) for kayaks, as well as a selection of easy day canoe trips, contact **Up North,** (© **867/667-7905;** www.upnorth.yk.ca), on the Yukon River across from the MacBride Museum (86 Wickstrom Rd.). You can also rent a canoe for a day and shoot the once-harrowing 40km (25-mile) Miles Canyon—C$55 (US$55/£28) pays for two shuttles and the canoe rental. Other day trips on the Yukon and multiday trips on the Teslin and Pelly rivers are also offered. In winter, Up North offers ice fishing, snowshoeing, and snowmobile tours, including multiday trips that trace a circuit of backcountry cabins and wall tents.

HIKING If you're looking for a short loop hike from downtown, the **Millennium Trail** is an excellent choice. Begin on either side of the Robert Campbell Bridge (the extension of Second Ave., south of Whitehorse) and follow the paved accessible foot path to a new footbridge directly below the Whitehorse Dam. The entire loop is 5km (3 miles). A longer loop is the Yukon River Loop Trail, which continues from the Millennium Trail on either side, passing the dam and the fish ladder and following Schwatka Lake to Miles Canyon. Here the Yukon River cuts a narrow passage through the underlying basalt. Though not very deep, the canyon greatly constricts the river, forming rapids that were once the object of dread to the greenhorn 98ers in their homemade boats. A footbridge crosses the river above Miles Canyon, making a 15km (9-mile) loop.

During July and August, the **Yukon Conservation Society,** 302 Hawkins St. (© 867/667-5678), offers free guided nature walks in the Whitehorse area. Contact them weekdays between 10am and 2pm for details. Hikes are given Monday to Friday, and on most days several destinations are offered, including the **Whitehorse Rapids Dam** and **Miles Canyon.** Most walks are only a couple of hours long. You must get yourself to the departure point for any hike, and be sure to bring comfortable shoes and insect repellent.

HORSEBACK RIDING At Fish Lake, just 20 minutes from Whitehorse, **Sky High Wilderness Ranches** (© 867/667-4321) offers a variety of guided horseback rides starting at C$30 (US$30/£15) an hour. The 3-hour Midnight Sun ride is a top choice, costing C$72 (US$72/£36). Sky High Wilderness Ranches also offers hostel lodging and tent camping, plus fishing in aptly named Fish Lake. The operation is 24km (15 miles) northwest of Whitehorse on the Fish Lake Road.

RAFTING Whitehorse-based white-water outfitter **Tatshenshini Expediting,** 1602 Alder St. (© 867/633-2742; www.tatshenshiniyukon.com), offers a fantastically exciting day trip down Kluane National Park's Tatshenshini River for C$125 (US$125/£63), not including transportation to/from Whitehorse. Participants must be 14 years of age or older. Longer trips from this outfitter include an 11-day trip down the Tatshenshini from Dalton Post and down the Alsek River to the Pacific for C$3,600 (US$3,600/ £1,800). Four- and six-day trips down the Alsek are also available. Call ahead because trip offerings vary from year to year and fill up fast.

WHERE TO STAY

There are a great number of campgrounds in and around Whitehorse; they represent the best alternative for travelers watching their money.

Tenters will like the **Robert Service Campground,** South Access Road (© 867/ 668-6678 or 867/668-3721), close to downtown and free of RVs. There are 48 unserviced tent sites, plus fire pits, washrooms, showers, and a picnic area. The rate is C$14 (US$14/£7) per tent. Just north of Whitehorse on the Dawson City road are a number of lakeside territorial parks with campgrounds. At Lake Laberge Park, you can camp "on the marge of Lake Lebarge" with the creatively spelled verses of Robert Service filling your thoughts. There's also camping at Takhini Hot Springs (see "Exploring Whitehorse," above).

Whitehorse has more than 25 hotels, motels, B&Bs, and chalets in and around the downtown area, including a couple opposite the airport. This is far more than you'd expect in a place its size, and the standards are mostly high. If you're on a budget, check out the new **Beez Kneez Bakpakers Hostel,** 408 Hoge St. (© 867/456-2333; www.bzkneez.com), near the south entrance to Whitehorse, with a large deck, full kitchen, and lots of friendly travelers to befriend; bunk accommodations cost C$25 (US$25/£13).

Best Western Gold Rush Inn   Modern, but with a Wild West motif, the Gold Rush Inn is one of the largest and most central lodgings in Whitehorse, within easy walking distance of attractions and shopping. All of the guest rooms are recently remodeled; a few come with bunk beds for kids. Some rooms have Jacuzzis and all have microwaves.

411 Main St., Whitehorse, YT Y1A 2B6. ℭ 800/661-0539 in the Yukon or northern B.C., 800/764-7604 in Alaska, or 867/668-4500. Fax 867/668-7432. www.goldrushinn.com. 101 units. C$129–C$189 (US$129–US$189/£65–£95) double. Weekend specials. Senior discounts. Children under 12 stay free in parent's room. AE, DC, DISC, MC, V. Free parking. Pets may be allowed. **Amenities:** Restaurant; tavern w/entertainment; salon; laundry services. *In room:* A/C, TV w/free and pay movies, fridge, microwave, coffeemaker, hair dryer.

Edgewater Hotel 𝕬𝕬   This small vintage boutique hotel has been operated by the same family for three generations. It's also in a location central to historic Whitehorse; overlooking the Yukon River across from the handsome (now defunct) rail station. A favorite of traveling businesspeople and government officials, the Edgewater has more polish than the other downtown hotels that focus on summer coach tours. Guest rooms are comfortably furnished: Standard rooms have one bed but no air-conditioning (rarely an issue at this latitude), while Deluxe rooms have two beds, double sinks, and A/C. The two suites are essentially one-bedroom apartments with full kitchens and two beds in the bedroom. All rooms have high-speed Internet, a flatscreen TV, fridge, and large work table. The Edgewater's two restaurants, including the Cellar Steakhouse & Wine Bar (p. 797), are among Whitehorse's finest.

101 Main St., Whitehorse, YT Y1A 2A7. ℭ 877/484-3334 or 867/667-2572. Fax 867/668-3014. www.edgewaterhotel. yk.ca. 30 units. C$159–C$179 (US$159–US$179/£80–£90) double; C$279 (US$279/£140) suite. Discounts for seniors and AAA/CAA members. AE, DC, MC, V. Free parking. **Amenities:** 2 restaurants. *In room:* A/C (in some rooms), TV, dataport, coffeemaker, hair dryer, iron.

Hawkins House 𝕬   All guest rooms have balconies in this modern but stylishly retro Victorian home. Rooms are decorated according to theme, but tastefully so: The Fireweed Room has rustic pine furniture a la Klondike, while the Fleur de Lys Room recalls Belle Epoque France. All the rooms have a queen-size bed and private phone lines. Breakfast is available for C$7 (US$7/£3.50). The proprietors also offer weekly vacation apartment rentals in an adjacent building.

303 Hawkins St., Whitehorse, YT Y1A 1X5. ℭ/fax 867/668-7638. 4 units. Winter C$124 (US$124/£62) double; spring and fall C$133 (US$133/£67) double; summer C$163 (US$163/£82) double. AE, DC, MC, V. Free on-site parking. **Amenities:** Jacuzzi; laundry service. *In room:* TV/VCR, fridge, coffeemaker.

High Country Inn 𝕬   One of the newest hotels in Whitehorse, the High Country Inn is attached to a small convention center just south of downtown. After staying in historic gold rush–era rooms across the North, the High Country Inn's very comfortable, corporate hotel rooms may be enticing. There's variation in room size; if you want extra space, ask for a room on the third or fourth floors, which have executive, Jacuzzi, and kitchenette suites. In summer, the deck at the Yukon Mining Company, the hotel's restaurant, is one of the city's most popular outdoor dining and drinking venues.

4051 Fourth Ave., Whitehorse, YT 1A 1W2. ℭ 800/554-4471 or 867/667-4519. Fax 867/667-6457. www.highcountry inn.ca. 84 units. C$169–C$259 (US$169–US$259/£85–£130) double. Off-season reduced rates. AE, MC, V. Free parking. Pets allowed. **Amenities:** Restaurant; lounge; complimentary airport shuttle; coin-op laundry; nonsmoking rooms. *In room:* TV, coffeemaker, hair dryer, iron/ironing board.

Midnight Sun Bed & Breakfast   This new B&B is within walking distance of downtown and offers four large guest rooms, all with private bathrooms, phones, high-speed Internet, and TVs. There's a guest lounge, plus a do-it-yourself barbecue area. Absolutely everything is shipshape and comfortable, and the welcome is hearty—you'll feel right at home.

6118 Sixth Ave, Whitehorse, YT Y1A 1N8. (✆ 866/284-4448 or 867/667-2255. Fax 867/668-4376. www.midnight sunbb.com. 4 units. C$119–C$140 (US$119–US$140/£60–£70) double. Off-season reduced rates and senior discount available. AE, MC, V. Free parking. **Amenities:** Guest laundry; nonsmoking facility. *In room:* TV.

River View Hotel *Value*   Don't let looks deceive. One of the oldest establishments in the Yukon, completely rebuilt in 1970, the River View breathes territorial tradition. The nondescript exterior belies comfortable, large, and fully modern guest rooms that represent a good deal in an otherwise expensive town. The lobby is crowded with Old Yukon memorabilia, from hand-cranked phones to moose antlers, and the Talisman Café has one of the best ethnic and vegetarian menus in town. You can't beat the location either: It's on the Yukon River, across from the MacBride Museum, and only 1 block from Main Street.

102 Wood St., Whitehorse, YT Y1A 2E3. (✆ 867/667-7801. Fax 867/668-6075. www.riverviewhotel.ca. 53 units. Fall–winter C$99 (US$99/£50); spring–summer C$129 (US$129/£65) double. Extra person C$10 (US$10/£5). DC, DISC, MC, V. Heated underground parking C$6 (US$6/£3). Pets allowed. **Amenities:** Restaurant; lounge w/entertainment; room service; coin-op laundry; nonsmoking rooms; pet rooms. *In room:* TV, coffeemaker, hair dryer.

Westmark Whitehorse Hotel *✿*   Centrally located in downtown Whitehorse, this regional chain has one of the busiest lobbies in town—the Gray Line/Holland America/Westours tour-booking office is located here. In addition, the hotel hosts one of Whitehorse's popular musical revues, the *Frantic Follies*. This is ground zero for bus-tour travelers, though there's plenty of reason to call for reservations if you're just traveling through. The guest rooms are spacious and well maintained and many accommodate travelers with disabilities. There's a small arcade alongside the hotel, housing a gift shop, barber, hairdresser, and a travel agency.

201 Wood St., Whitehorse, YT Y1A 2E4 (✆ 800/544-0970 or 867/393-9700. Fax 867/668-2789. www.westmark hotels.com. 180 units. C$149 (US$149/£75) double. Children under 12 stay free in parent's room. AE, DC, MC, V. Free parking. **Amenities:** Restaurant; lounge; guest laundry; rooms for those w/limited mobility. *In room:* TV, hair dryer, iron, voice mail.

WHERE TO DINE

Food is generally more expensive in Whitehorse than in the provinces, and this goes for wine as well. Be happy you didn't come during the gold rush, when a meal of beans, stewed apples, bread, and coffee could cost $5—the equivalent of as much as C$125 (US$125/£63) today!

Whitehorse is going through a coffeehouse craze, which is great for travelers wanting lattes, pastries, and inexpensive lunches. **Zola's Café Doré,** Haugen Center, on Main Street between Third and Fourth (✆ 867/668-5780), is a large and popular gathering spot in the center of town, with good coffee, pastries, and sandwiches. **Backerei,** 100 Main St. (✆ 867/633-6299), has more of an alternative feel, with home-baked breads and soups and salads for lunch. For straight-up Yukon java, go to **Midnight Sun Coffee Roastery,** 4168-C Fourth Ave. (✆ 867/633-4563), a Bohemian hangout specializing in fresh-roasted coffees—made in an antique roaster on the premises—as well as freshly baked muffins, croissants, cookies, pastries, and breakfast and lunch sandwiches.

Whitehorse is lucky to have an excellent local brewery, the **Yukon Brewing Company,** which makes "beer worth freezing for." It's available on draft at most bars and restaurants. Unfortunately, there's no brewpub, but if you enjoy the ales, consider a tour of the brewery at 102 Copper Rd. (© **867/668-4183**).

EXPENSIVE

Cellar Steakhouse & Wine Bar ⚜ CANADIAN   This plush lower-level dining room at the Edgewater Hotel (p. 795) has a big local reputation. Steaks, prime rib, and other hearty dishes are the specialty, though fresh local fish plays a big role on the menu too. In addition, there is a selection of tapas and appetizers (C$12–C$16/US$12–US$16/£6–£8)—oysters casino, seared ahi tuna, chicken wraps, and so on—to accompany a glass of wine or make a light meal. The dining room is refined and elegant, with a casual sophistication largely lacking at other Whitehorse restaurants that play at fine dining. The wine list is the city's finest. Upstairs, the Edge Bar & Grill offers more casual dining for three meals a day.

In the Edgewater Hotel, 101 Main St. © 867/667-2572. www.edgewaterhotel.yk.ca. Reservations recommended. Main courses C$24–C$45 (US$24–US$45/£12–£23). AE, DC, MC, V. Mon–Fri 11:30am–1:30pm; daily 5–10pm.

MODERATE

Klondike Rib & Salmon BBQ ⚜ BARBECUE/STEAK/SEAFOOD   One of the most popular places to eat in Whitehorse, this fast-paced restaurant looks a bit worn from the outside—no wonder, as it's in one of the city's oldest remaining buildings (a bakery from 1900)—but there's nothing old-fashioned about the quality or execution of the food served. Both ribs and chicken are smoked in house and are outstanding, and even standards like beef tenderloin get updated with apricot-mustard glaze and fresh pineapple salsa. Fresh wild local salmon is also excellent, as is arctic char and halibut. It wouldn't be northern food without game, and diners should consider wild stroganoff, with bison, caribou, and other wild meats in mushroom and brandy sauce. Even the burgers go Northern—would you like fries with your caribou or musk ox burgers? The dining room is delightfully atmospheric, but the real action is on the two small outdoor heated decks that flank the dining room.

Corner of Second Ave. and Steele St. © 867/667-7554. Reservations recommended. Main courses C$22–C$32 (US$22–US$32/£11–£16). MC, V. Daily 11am–2pm and 4–9pm. Closed mid-Sept to mid-May.

La Gourmandise ⚜ FRENCH CANADIAN   Cozy and romantic, La Gourmandise doesn't pretend to have a gold-rush past, and that's a good thing if you're weary of the huge servings of meat and potatoes typical of the North. Low key but sophisticated, La Gourmandise is like a venerable country inn in Québec, with low-ceilings, dark-wood beams, and two fireplaces. The food is likewise stylish and welcoming. Crepes (both savory and sweet) are the house specialty, though there's plenty else to choose from. Lunch-time soup, salad, and sandwiches give way at dinner to hearty dishes such as Québec salmon pie, stuffed chicken breast with wine and red-currant sauce, and filet mignon with wild mushrooms and goat cheese. Fresh local fish and seafood is also a specialty—there's a choice of four preparations for mussels.

4121 Fourth Ave. © 867/456-4127. Reservations recommended. Main courses C$8–C$10 (US$8–US$10/£4–£5) lunch, C$18–C$34 (US$18–US$34/£9–£17) dinner. MC, V. Mon–Fri 11am–2pm; Tues–Sat 5–10pm; Sun 10am–2pm.

INEXPENSIVE

Cranberry Bistro *Value* ETHNIC   This unassuming little restaurant is a favorite of locals at lunchtime, as it serves a changing menu of ethnic foods from around the world. The bistro supports its claim of being "passionate about food" by providing a selection of grilled panini sandwiches, salads, gourmet pizzas, and a changing selection of "ethnic street foods," which can range from spring rolls and ginger beef wontons to falafel and spanakopita. The bistro is right across from LePage Park, where musicians perform weekdays at noon during the summer—if you like, order lunch and head to the park. Just remember to return your plates and utensils when you're finished.

302 Wood St. (℃ 867/456-4898. Reservations not accepted. Main courses C$7–C$10 (US$7–US10/£3.50–£5). MC, V. Mon–Fri 9am–4pm.

Pasta Palace *Value* ITALIAN/EUROPEAN/TAPAS This is one of the few inexpensive restaurants in Whitehorse where you won't feel as if you're eating on a budget. The best thing about the menu is the extensive selection of tapas and appetizers available throughout the day. The selection includes inexpensive bruschettas, salads, and sandwiches under C$10 (US$10/£5). Full entrees are also good bargains, including full-flavored pasta dishes; steaks, chops, and kabobs; and a full seafood platter. The dining room isn't fancy, but service is prompt and friendly.

209 Main St. (near Second Ave.). (℃ 867/667-6888. Main courses C$8–C$25 (US$8–US$25/£4–£13). MC, V. Mon–Fri 8am–10pm; Sat 11am–10pm.

WHITEHORSE AFTER DARK

The top-of-the-bill attraction in Whitehorse is the *Frantic Follies* (℃ 867/668-2042; www.franticfollies.com), a singing, dancing, clowning, and declaiming gold-rush revue that has become famous throughout the North. The show is an entertaining mélange of skits; music-hall drollery; whooping, high-kicking, garter-flashing cancan dancers; sentimental ballads; and deadpan corn, interspersed with rolling recitations of Robert Service's poetry. Shows take place nightly May through September at the **Westmark Whitehorse Hotel** (p. 796). Tickets are C$24 (US$24/£12) for adults and C$10 (US$10/£5) for children.

Whitehorse has quite the local music scene. The bar at the **Capital Hotel,** 103 Main St. (℃ 867/667-2565), has live music nightly, while **Lizards Lounge** at the Town and Mountain Hotel, 401 Main St. (℃ 867/668-7644), also has live bands frequently. Also check out what's happening at the **Boiler Room** at the Yukon Inn, 4220 Fourth Ave. (℃ 867/667-2527), with live music and DJs.

4 The Chilkoot Trail & White Pass

South of Whitehorse, massive ranges of glacier-chewed peaks rise up to ring the Gulf of Alaska; stormy waters reach far inland as fjords and enormous glaciers spill into the sea (the famed Glacier Bay is here). This spectacularly scenic region is also the site of the **Chilkoot Trail,** which in 1898 saw 100,000 gold-rush stampeders struggle up its steep slopes. Another high mountain pass was transcribed in 1900 by the White Pass and Yukon Railroad on its way to the goldfields; excursion trains now run on these rails, considered a marvel of engineering.

To see these sites, most people embark on long-distance hiking trails, rail excursions, or cruise boats. Happily, two highways edge through this spectacular landscape; if you use the **Alaska Marine Highway ferries** (℃ 800/642-0066; www.dot.state.ak.us/amhs), this trip can be made as a loop from either Whitehorse or Haines Junction. Because the ferries keep an irregular schedule, you'll need to call or check the website to find out what the sailing times are on the day you plan to make the trip.

THE CHILKOOT TRAIL

In 1896, word of the great gold strikes on the Klondike reached the outside world, and nearly 100,000 people set out for the Yukon to seek their fortunes. There was no organized transportation into the Yukon, so the stampeders resorted to the most expedient methods. The **Chilkoot Trail,** long an Indian trail through one of the few glacier-free passes in the Gulf of Alaska, became the primary overland route to the Yukon River, Whitehorse, and the gold fields near Dawson City.

The ascent of the Chilkoot became the stuff of legend, and pictures of men and women clambering up the steep snowfields to Chilkoot Summit are one of the enduring images of the stampeder spirit. The Northwest Mounted Police demanded that anyone entering the Yukon carry a ton of provisions (literally); there were no supplies in the newly born gold camps on the Klondike, and malnutrition and lack of proper shelter were major problems. People were forced to make up to 30 trips up the trail in order to transport all their goods into Canada. Once past the RCMP station at Chilkoot Summit, the stampeders then had to build some sort of boat or barge to ferry their belongings across Bennett Lake and down the Yukon River.

Today, the Chilkoot Trail is a national historic park jointly administered by the Canadian and U.S. parks departments. The original trail is open year-round to hikers who wish to experience the route of the stampeders. The route also passes through marvelous glacier-carved valleys, coastal rainforest, boreal forest, and alpine tundra.

However, the Chilkoot Trail is as challenging today as it was 100 years ago. Though the trail is only a total of 53km (33 miles) in length, the vertical elevation gain is nearly 1,128m (3,700 ft.) and much of the path is very rocky. Weather, even in high summer, can be extremely changeable, making this always-formidable trail sometimes a dangerous one.

Most people make the trip from **Dyea,** 15km (9 miles) north of Skagway in Alaska over the Chilkoot Summit (the U.S.-Canadian border) to **Bennett** in northwest British Columbia, in 4 days. Many shuttles and taxis run from Skagway to the trail head at Dyea. The third day of the hike is the hardest, with a steep ascent to the pass and a 12km (7.5-mile) distance between campsites. At Bennett, there's no road or boat access; from the end of the trail, you'll need to make another 6km (4-mile) hike out along the rail tracks to Highway 2 near Fraser, British Columbia (the least expensive option), or you can ride the **White Pass and Yukon Railway** (✆ **800/343-7373;** www.whitepassrailroad.com) from Bennett out to Fraser for C$50 (US$50/£25) or down to Skagway for C$90 (US$90/£45). There's a C$18 (US$18/£9) surcharge for tickets purchased in Bennett, so plan ahead. Remember to take a passport with you on this hike—you're crossing an international border.

The Chilkoot Trail isn't a casual hike; you'll need to plan and provision for your trip carefully. And it isn't a wilderness hike, because between 75 and 100 people start the trail daily. Remember that the trail is preserved as a historic park; leave artifacts of the gold-rush days—the trail is strewn with boots, stoves, and other effluvia of the stampeders—as you found them.

Permits are also required to make the hike. The U.S. and Canadian parks authorities cooperate to administer these permits, and they can be obtained on either side of the border. Only 50 hikers are allowed per day from each side of the pass, and 42 of the permits may be reserved for $12 (£6) each—the other eight are held for last-minute hikers. The permits cost $53 (£27) for adults and $26 (£13) for children ages 6 to 17; the fees are the same in U.S. and Canadian dollars.

For details on the Chilkoot Trail, contact the **Klondike Gold Rush National Historic Park,** P.O. Box 517, Skagway, AK 99840 (✆ **907/983-2921;** www.nps.gov/klgo), or the **Canadian Parks Service,** Suite 200–300 Main St., Whitehorse, YT Y1A 2B5 (✆ **800/661-0486;** www.pc.gc.ca/lhn-nhs/yt/chilkoot).

WHITE PASS & THE YUKON ROUTE

In 1898, engineers began the task of excavating a railway line up to **White Pass.** Considered a marvel of engineering, the track edged around sheer cliffs on long trestles and tunneled through banks of granite. The train effectively ended traffic on the Chilkoot Trail, just to the north.

The White Pass and Yukon Route railroad now operates between Skagway, Alaska, and Bennett, British Columbia. Several trips are available on the historic line. Trains travel twice daily from Skagway to the summit of White Pass; the 3-hour return journey costs US$98 (C$98/£49) for adults. As this trip does not cross the U.S./Canadian border, U.S. citizens do not require a passport for passage. Late May through early September from Sunday to Friday, trains make a 6-hour one-way trip from Skagway to Lake Bennett, the end of the Chilkoot Trail, costing US$165 (C$165/£88) adults for diesel-powered engines; it's US$125 (C$125/£63) for a 4-hour round-trip journey on a steam-powered engine from Skagway to Fraser Meadows (Sat–Sun). As these trips cross an international border, passports are required. Connections between Fraser and Whitehorse via motor coach are available daily. Prices for children ages 3 to 12 on all rides are half the adult fare, and infants ride free.

The White Pass and Yukon excursion trains operate mid-May to the last weekend of September. Advance reservations are required; for details, contact the **White Pass and Yukon Route,** P.O. Box 435, Skagway, AK 99840 (© **800/343-7373;** www.whitepass railroad.com).

5 Dawson City: An Authentic Gold-Rush Town

Dawson City is as much of a paradox as it is a community today. Once the biggest Canadian city west of Winnipeg, with a population of 30,000, it withered to practically a ghost town after the stampeders stopped stampeding. In 1953 the seat of territorial government was shifted to Whitehorse, which might've spelled the end of Dawson—but didn't. For now, every summer the influx of tourists more than matches the stream of gold rushers in its heyday. The reason for this is the remarkable preservation and restoration work done by Parks Canada. Dawson today is the nearest thing to an authentic gold-rush town the world has to offer.

However, Dawson City is more than just a gold-rush theme park; it's a real town with 1,800 year-round residents (though population triples in summer with seasonal workers), many still working as miners (and many as sourdough wannabes). The citizens still like to party, stay up late, and tell tall tales to strangers, much as they did a century ago.

ESSENTIALS

GETTING THERE From Whitehorse you can catch an **Air North** plane for the 1-hour hop (© **800/764-0407** in the U.S., or 800/661-0407 in Canada). You can also fly round-trip from Fairbanks, Alaska. Call the Visitor Information Centre (see below) to inquire about bus service between Whitehorse and Dawson City—the service formerly operated by the **Dawson City Courier** is not running at press time, but a replacement has been promised.

The scenic 537km (334-mile) drive on the North Klondike Highway from Whitehorse to Dawson City takes 6 to 8 hours. If you're driving from the upper part of Alaska, from Chicken take the chip-sealed **Taylor Highway** across the border, where it becomes the paved **Top of the World Highway,** completing the trip to Dawson.

VISITOR INFORMATION The **Visitor Information Centre,** Front and King streets (© **867/993-5566**), provides details on all historic sights and attractions; the national park service also maintains an information desk here. It's open mid-May to mid-September daily 8am to 8pm. Walking tours of Dawson City, led by highly knowledgeable guides, depart from the center daily in summer, costing C$6 (US$6/£3). Visit **www.dawsoncity.ca** for current information.

SPECIAL EVENTS **Discovery Days** in mid-August commemorates the finding of the Klondike gold a century ago with dancing, music, parades, and canoe races. In mid-July the city hosts the **Dawson City Music Festival** (www.dcmf.com), featuring rock, folk, jazz, blues, world-beat, and traditional music from across Canada and beyond. Dawson also hosts a variety of winter events. In late February and early March, the **Trek over the Top** (www.trekoverthetop.com) features snowmobile races from Tok, Alaska, to Dawson City, and vice versa, via the Top of the World Highway. In mid-March, the **Percy De Wolfe Memorial Race and Mail Run,** a 336km (209-mile) dog-sled race from Dawson City to Eagle, Alaska, commemorates the route of historic Dawson mail carrier Percy De Wolfe.

EXPLORING DAWSON CITY & ENVIRONS

All of Dawson City and much of the surrounding area is preserved as a National Historic Site, and it's easy to spend a day wandering the boardwalks, looking at the old buildings, shopping the boutiques, and exploring vintage watering holes. About half of the buildings in the town are historic; the rest are artful contemporary reconstructions. **Dawson Historical National Historic Site Complex** (© **867/993-7200** or 867/993-7237; www.pc.gc.ca/lhn-nhs/yt/dawson) preserves 8 blocks and sites in and around Dawson City. The Parks Service fees are usually C$6 (US$6/£3) for each guided tour. A variety of tours are available, and combination tickets are available; tours are available June through mid-September. For current Parks Canada program information and tickets, head over to the Visitor Information Centre at Front and King streets.

Between the town and the mighty Yukon River is a dike channeling the once-devastating floodwaters. A path follows the dike and makes for a nice stroll. The **SS *Keno,*** a Yukon riverboat, is berthed along the dike (near Front and Queen Sts.). Built in Whitehorse in 1922, it was one of the last riverboats to travel on the Yukon—there were once more than 200 of them.

Dänojà Zho Cultural Centre The name of this new First Nations center translates as "Long Time Ago House." Built to celebrate and share the traditional lifestyle and history of the Tr'ondëk Hwëch'in people (more commonly referred to as the Hän), the center offers archeological artifacts, costumes, tools, photos, and presentations that tell the story of the Native inhabitants of the Klondike area. Especially interesting is the Hammerstone Gallery, which relates the events of the last century from a First Nation perspective. Ticket price includes a guided tour; the gift shop carries handmade clothing, books, music, and gifts.

On Front St., across from the Visitor Information Centre. © 867/993-6768. www.trondek.com. Admission C$5 (US$5/£2.50) adult, C$2.50 (US$2.50/£1.25) children 12 to 18, free for children under 12. June–Sept daily 10am–6pm.

Dawson City Museum 𝆏 In the grand old Territorial Administration building, this excellent museum should be your first stop on a tour of Dawson City. Well-curated displays explain the geology and paleontology of the area (this region was on the main migratory path between Asia and North America during the last ice age), as well as the history of the Native Hän peoples. The focus, of course, is the gold rush, and the museum explains various mining techniques; one of the galleries is dedicated to demonstrating the day-to-day life of early-1900s Dawson City. Various tours and programs are offered on the hour, including the excellent Oscar-nominated short documentary from 1957, *City of Gold.* Costumed docents are on hand to answer questions and recount episodes of history. On the grounds are early rail steam engines that served in the mines.

Fifth Ave. at Minto Park. © 867/993-5291. http://users.yknet.yk.ca/dcpages/Museum.html. Admission C$7 (US$7/£3.50) adults, C$5 (US$5/£2.50) students and seniors, C$16 (US$16/£8) families, free for small children. Mid-May to Mid-Sept daily 10am–6pm.

Robert Service Cabin   Poet Robert Service lived in this two-room log cabin from 1909 to 1912. Backed up against the steep cliffs edging Dawson City, Service's modest cabin today plays host to a string of pilgrims who come to hear an actor twice daily recite some of the most famous verses in the authentic milieu. Oddly enough, the bard of the gold rush neither took part in nor even saw the actual stampede. Born in England, he didn't arrive in Dawson until 1907—as a bank teller—when the rush was well and truly over. He got most of his plots by listening to old prospectors in the saloons, but the atmosphere he soaked in at the same time was genuine enough—and his imagination did the rest.

Note: In addition to the above performances, the Robert Service show, featuring long-time Service interpreter Tom Byrne, now takes place at the Westmark Inn Dawson City, Fifth and Harper streets (© **867/993-5542**). Tickets (C$10/US$10/£5 adult, half price for children under 12) are available at the hotel gift shop; performances are daily June through Labour Day at 3pm.

Eighth Ave. © 867/993-7200. Admission C$6 (US$6/£3). June to mid-Sept daily 9am–5pm; recitals daily at 10am and 3pm.

Jack London's Cabin and Interpretive Centre   American adventure writer Jack London lived in the Yukon less than a year—he left in June 1898 after a bout with scurvy—but his writings immortalized the North, particularly the animal stories like *The Call of the Wild, White Fang,* and *The Son of Wolf.* The cabin contains more than 60 photos, documents, newspaper articles, and other London memorabilia.

Eighth Ave. © 867/993-5575. Admission C$2 (US$2/£1). Mid-May to mid-Sept daily 11am–3pm; recitations daily at 12:30pm.

Bonanza Creek   The original Yukon gold strike and some of the richest pay dirt in the world were found on **Bonanza Creek,** an otherwise-insignificant tributary flowing north into the Klondike River. A century's worth of mining has left the stream bed piled into an orderly chaos of gravel heaps, the result of massive dredges. The national park service has preserved and interpreted a number of old prospecting sites; however, most of the land along Bonanza Creek is owned privately, so don't trespass, and by no means should you casually pan gold.

The **Discovery Claim,** about 16km (10 miles) up Bonanza Creek Road, is the spot, now marked by a National Historic Sites cairn, where George Carmack, Skookum Jim, and Tagish Charlie found the gold that unleashed the Klondike stampede in 1896. They staked out the first four claims (the fourth partner, Bob Henderson, wasn't present). Within a week, Bonanza and Eldorado creeks had been staked out from end to end, but none of the later claims matched the wealth of the first. Just over 12km (7½ miles) up Bonanza Creek, Parks Canada has preserved **Dredge no. 4** (© **867/993-7200**), the largest wooden-hulled gold dredges ever used in North America; it's open June through early to mid-September daily 9am to 5pm, with tours offered hourly to 4pm at C$6 (US$6/£3). Dredges—which augured up the permafrost, washed out the fine gravel, and sifted out the residual gold—were used after placer miners had panned out the easily accessible gold along the creek. Dredge no. 4 began operation in 1913 and could dig and sift 13,800 cubic m (18,000 cubic yd.) in 24 hours, thus doing the work of an army of prospectors. You can do some free panning yourself at Claim 6, 15km (9 miles) up Bonanza Road. Bring your own pan (BYOP)!

Head west on Bonanza Creek Rd., about 2km (1¼ miles) south of Dawson City.

THE KLONDIKE GOLD RUSH

The Klondike Gold Rush began with a wild war whoop from the throats of three men—two First Nations Canadians and one white—that broke the silence of Bonanza Creek on the morning of August 17, 1896: "Gold!" they screamed, "Gold, gold, gold!" That cry rang through the Yukon, crossed to Alaska, and rippled down into the United States. Soon the whole world echoed with it, and people as far away as China and Australia began selling their household goods and homes to scrape together the fare to a place few of them had ever heard of before.

Some 100,000 men and women from every corner of the globe set out on the Klondike stampede, descending on a territory populated by a few hundred souls. Tens of thousands came by the Chilkoot Pass from Alaska—the shortest route but also the toughest. Canadian law required each stampeder to carry a ton—literally 909 kilograms (2,000 lb.) of provisions up over the 914m (3,000-ft.) summit. Sometimes it took 30 or more trips up a 45-degree slope to get all the baggage over, and the entire trail—with only one pack—takes about 3½ days to hike. Many collapsed on the way, but the rest slogged on—on to the Klondike and the untold riches to be found there.

For some, the riches were real enough. The Klondike fields proved to be the richest ever found anywhere. Klondike stampeders were netting $300 to $400 in a single pan (and gold was then valued at around C$15/US$15/£7.50 an ounce)! What's more, unlike some gold that lies embedded in veins of hard rock, the Klondike gold came in dust or nugget forms buried in creek beds. This placer gold, as it's called, didn't have to be milled—it was already in an almost-pure state!

The trouble was that most of the clerks who dropped their pens and butchers who shed their aprons to join the rush came too late. By the time they had completed the backbreaking trip, all the profitable claims along the Klondike creeks had been staked out and were defended by grim men with guns in their fists.

Almost overnight, Dawson boomed into a roaring, bustling, gambling, whoring metropolis of 30,000 people, thousands of them living in tents. And here gathered those who made fortunes from the rush without ever handling a pan: the supply merchants, saloonkeepers, dance-hall girls, and cardsharps. There were also some oddly peripheral characters: a bank teller named Robert Service who listened to the tall tales of prospectors and set them to verse (he never panned gold himself). And a stocky 21-year-old former sailor from San Francisco who adopted a big mongrel dog in Dawson, then went home and wrote a book about his canine companion that sold half a million copies. The book was *The Call of the Wild;* the sailor, Jack London.

By 1903, more than C$500 million (US$500 million/£250 million) in gold had been shipped south from the Klondike, and the rush petered out. A handful of millionaires bought mansions in Seattle, tens of thousands went home with empty pockets, and thousands more lay dead in unmarked graves along the Yukon River. Within a decade, Dawson became a dreaming backwater haunted by 30,000 ghosts.

TOURS & EXCURSIONS

From June to mid-September the national park service offers C$6 (US$6/£3) **daily walking tours** ✦ of Dawson City; check for hours and sign up for the tours at the **Visitor Information Centre,** at Front and King streets (𝄢 **867/993-5566**). Up to eight different tours are offered in high season.

The **Yukon Queen II** is a "fast cat" catamaran that can carry 104 passengers over the 173km (108-mile) stretch of river from Dawson City to Eagle, Alaska. Tickets include meals; mid-May to mid-September, the 1-day round-trip journeys run daily. Adults pay C$90 (US$90/£45) each way. (Travelers can also fly back.) Book the boat trip and return flights through **Gray Line Yukon/Yukon Queen River Cruises** on Front Street (First Ave.) near the Visitor Information Centre (𝄢 **867/993-5599**); tickets go quickly, so reserve well in advance in high season; at all times, you'll need to reserve 1 day in advance for U.S. immigrations preapproval. If paying in cash, only U.S. dollars are accepted, even in Dawson City. If you want to stay overnight in Eagle, you'll have to make arrangements separately.

If you just want to get out on the Yukon River without the trip to Alaska, **Fishwheel Charters** (𝄢 **867-993-6237**) offers a fascinating 2-hour river journey into the traditional Hän culture that existed here long before the Klondike Gold Rush. The tour operator, himself a member of the Hän First Nation, provides background on traditional lifestyles and takes visitors past the Hän village of Moosehead, historic Fort Reliance, and a traditional fish camp. On the way back, the tour stops at Dog Island for tea and bannock. During high season, three trips daily are offered; cost is C$32 (US$32/£16) adults, C$10 (US$10/£5) children 10 and under. Inquire at the Visitor Information Centre for the location of ticket office.

WHERE TO STAY

The **Dawson City River Hostel** (𝄢 **867/993-6823** summer only; www.yukonhostels. com) is just across from the Dawson Ferry. Beds are available in a variety of shared and private rooms in riverfront cabins. There's no electricity (though there is the midnight sun for a nightlight), and wood fire heats the sauna and the prospector's bath house. The rate for Hostelling International members is C$18 (US$18/£9); for nonmembers, C$22 (US$22/£11). The **Gold Rush Campground** (𝄢 **867/993-5247;** www.goldrush campground.com), at the corner of Fourth Avenue and York Street, is right in Dawson and operated by very friendly folks; rates range from C$19 to C$39 (US$19–US$39/ £9.50–£20).

Each of the following, except the Dawson City Bunkhouse and the Westmark Inn, are open year-round.

Aurora Inn ✦ If the gold-rush theme prevalent in much of Dawson isn't your thing, then try the bright, airy rooms at the new Aurora Inn, a cosmopolitan country inn in the Swiss tradition. The large guest rooms are furnished with locally made pine furniture, and come in a variety of configurations, including top-of-the-line king suites with Jacuzzi tubs. Everything is notably well maintained and shipshape—you'll need to remove your shoes before going to your room. All rooms have private bathrooms and TVs, and there's also a common area with a large screen TV and VCR. The dining room here is one of Dawson's best (p. 806).

Fifth Ave. and Harper St. (Box 1748), Dawson City, YK Y0B 1G0. 𝄢 **867/993-6860.** Fax 867/993-5689. www.aurora inn.ca. 20 units. C$159–C$199 (US$159–US$199/£80–£100) double. Lower off-season rates. Children under 12 stay free in parent's room. MC, V. Free parking. **Amenities:** Restaurant; free airport shuttle. *In room:* TV, wireless Internet.

Bombay Peggy's Inn & Pub ⊹ Surprise your friends and family—and maybe yourself—by spending a few nights in a brothel. The structure that houses Bombay Peggy's was built in 1900 and served multiple purposes before becoming one of Dawson City's most notorious houses of ill repute. In its current incarnation, Bombay Peggy's takes the name of one of the brothel's leading madams and celebrates the building's long association with the hospitality industry. Rebuilt and modernized, Bombay Peggy's is now a small inn with large and stylish guest rooms, plus a pub and martini lounge on the main floor. The rooms are decorated with antiques, Oriental carpets, and tongue-in-cheek Victorian boudoir élan (you might choose to spend the night in the Lipstick Room, for instance); all rooms but the three "Snugs" have private bathrooms.

Corner of Second Ave. and Princess St., P.O. Box 411, Dawson City, YK Y0B 1G0. ⓒ 867/993-6969. Fax 867/ 993-6199. www.bombaypeggys.com. 9 units. C$99–C$195 (US$99–US$195/£50–£98) double. Lower off-season rates. AE, MC, V. **Amenities:** Pub. *In room:* A/C, wireless Internet.

Dawson City B&B This nicely decorated, large home fronted by two stories of decks is on the outskirts of Dawson City, beside Gateway Park and overlooking the Klondike and Yukon rivers, with excellent views. The grounds are very attractively gardened. Rooms are ample size, very clean, and simply but attractively furnished. Breakfasts are bounteous. Smoking is not permitted inside the house.

451 Craig St., Dawson City, YT Y0B 1G0. ⓒ **867/993-5649.** Fax 867/993-5648. www.dawsonbb.com. 7 units, 3 with bathroom. C$115–C$145 (US$115–US$145/£58–£73) double. Senior and AAA/CAA discounts. DC, MC, V. Free parking. Children under 12 not accepted. **Amenities:** Courtesy pickup; free bicycles and fishing rods. *In room:* TV.

Dawson City Bunkhouse *(Value)* One of the good lodging values in town, this handsome hotel looks Old West but is just a decade old. Guest rooms are small but bright and clean; the beds come with Hudson's Bay Company blankets. The cheapest rooms don't have private bathrooms, but toilets and showers are down the landing. Only the queen (sleeps three) and king (sleeps four) suites have private bathrooms. There's no heat in the rooms, so check Dawson temperatures before making a reservation—though it's rarely a problem under the summer's midnight sun.

Front and Princess sts., Dawson City, YT Y0B 1G0. ⓒ **867/993-6164.** Fax 867/993-6051. info@dawsoncitybunk house.com. 32 units, 20 with bathroom. C$59–C$89 (US$59–US$89/£30–£45) double. Senior discounts available. MC, V. Free parking. Closed mid-Sept to mid-May.

Downtown Hotel One of Dawson City's originals, the Downtown has been completely rebuilt, refurbished, and updated with all modern facilities, yet it preserves a real western-style atmosphere. The Jack London Grill and Sourdough Saloon (with its Sourtoe Cocktail) look right out of the gold-rush era; they're definitely worth a visit.

Second Ave. and Queen St., Dawson City, YT Y0B 1G0. ⓒ 867/993-5346. Fax 867/993-5076. www.downtownhotel. ca. 59 units. From C$108 (US$108/£54) double. Senior discount offered. Children under 6 stay free in parent's room. AE, DC, DISC, MC, V. Transportation available for travelers with disabilities. **Amenities:** Restaurant; lounge; Jacuzzi; courtesy limo; winter plug-ins available for car head-bolt heaters; Internet access in saloon. *In room:* TV w/pay movies, coffeemaker.

Eldorado Hotel ⊹ *(Value)* Another vintage hotel made over and modernized, the Eldorado offers clean and nicely appointed guest rooms in its original building or in an adjacent modern motel unit. Some rooms feature kitchenettes. The Eldorado also manages a true antique, the Yukon Hotel on Front Street. Built in 1897, the old two-story hotel is completely modern inside, and all rooms have kitchens. The Eldorado represents a good lodging value for the independent travelers—and if you wish, you can still pay for your room in gold dust.

Third Ave. and Princess St., Dawson City, YT Y0B 1G0. ℭ 800/764-3536 or 867/993-5451. Fax 867/993-5256. www. eldoradohotel.ca. 52 units. From C$138 (US$138/£69) double. Senior discounts available. Children under 12 stay free in parent's room. AE, DC, DISC, MC, V. **Amenities:** Restaurant; lounge; courtesy airport pickup; coin-op washers and dryers; executive-level suites; winter plug-ins available. *In room:* TV, kitchenette (in some rooms), coffeemaker.

Klondike Kate's Cabins   Near the well-loved restaurant with the same name (see below), these recently built modern log cabins are clean and full of character, all with private bathrooms and cable TV. Some cabins have fridges and microwaves, and some can sleep up to four. In summer, the cabins are cheerful with pots of flowers and chairs on porches; nonsmoking cabins are available.

1102 Third Ave. (Box 417), Dawson City, YT Y0B 1G0. ℭ 867/993-6527. Fax 867/993-6044. www.klondikekates.ca. 15 cabins. C$100–C$130 (US$100–US$130/£50–£115) double. MC, V. Free parking. Airport pickup available. Closed Oct–May. **Amenities:** Restaurant; nonsmoking cabins. *In rooms:* TV, Internet access.

Westmark Inn Dawson City 🕏🕏   The Westmark is Dawson City's largest and most comfortable hotel, with an entire street of newly constructed guest rooms added to their existing units in 2005. The Westmark is owned by the Holland America cruise line, so the hotel serves a lot of bus tour passengers, but if Dawson's antique hotels don't appeal, then call ahead and reserve brand-new rooms at this top-notch accommodation. Most rooms have two queen beds, though kings and triples are also available. Belinda's, the dining room, extends out onto a very large heated and covered deck, which overlooks a charming courtyard garden. A second-story lounge has a patio with views over Dawson.

Fifth Ave. and Harper St. (Box 420), Dawson City, YT Y0B 1G0. ℭ 800/544-0970 or 867/993-5542 (summer only). www.westmarkhotels.com. 179 units. C$125–C$159 (US$125–US$159/£63–£80) double. AE, MC, V. Free parking. Closed mid-Sept to mid-May. **Amenities:** Restaurant; lounge; laundry; nonsmoking rooms; rooms for those w/limited mobility. *In room:* TV, coffeemaker.

WHERE TO DINE

Food is generally good in Dawson City and, considering the isolation and transport costs, not too expensive. The Downtown and Eldorado hotels both have good dining rooms and are open for three meals a day. Many restaurants close in winter or keep shorter hours. The **River West Bistro,** Front and Queen streets (ℭ 867/993-6339), is the hub of the town, with excellent baked goods and espresso drinks in the morning, and burgers and sandwiches available the rest of the day. It's open 7am to 8pm Monday through Friday, and 8am to 8pm on Saturday and Sunday.

Aurora Inn 🕏 CONTINENTAL/GERMAN   The sunny, cheerful dining room at the Aurora Inn serves expertly prepared German- and Swiss-style food—the only cooking that approaches Euro-style cuisine in Dawson. The menu ranges from schnitzels to lamb chops and cheese fondue for two. Local salmon is pan-fried and served with homemade tartar sauce. All breads and desserts are homemade.

Fifth Ave. and Harper St. ℭ 867/993-6860. Main courses C$17–C$24 (US$17–US$24/£8.50–£12). MC, V. Daily 4–9pm.

Klondike Kate's Restaurant 🕏 CANADIAN   This friendly and informal cafe is in one of Dawson's oldest buildings, with a covered and heated deck off the side. The menu offers well-prepared standard Yukon fare—steak, salmon, ribs—plus more inventive specials that take advantage of seasonal and regional ingredients, including fresh morel mushroom soup, and a tomato-and–goat cheese salad with port and beet-juice vinaigrette. Reservations are a good idea because this is a very popular place—and with good reason.

At the corner of Third Ave. and King St. ℭ 867/993-6527. Main courses C$11–C$34 (US$11–US$34/£5.50–£17). MC, V. Apr–Sept daily 6:30am–11pm.

DAWSON CITY AFTER DARK

"After dark" is oxymoronic in summertime Dawson—the midnight sun brings out the partier in the residents, and you'll find plenty of late-night action. We overheard in one bar, "In summer, Dawson doesn't sleep. We have all winter for that." Dawson City is still full of honky-tonks and saloons, and most have some form of nightly live music. On warm summer evenings all the doors are thrown open and you can sample the music by strolling through town on the boardwalks; the music is far better than you'd expect for a town with fewer than 2,000 people. Some favorites: Both the lounge bar and the pub at the **Midnight Sun** (© 867/993-5495), at Third Avenue and Queen Street, have live bands nightly. The tavern at the **Westminster Hotel,** between Queen and Princess on Third, often features traditional Yukon fiddlers, as well as other local and touring musical acts. The pub at **Bombay Peggy's,** Second Avenue and Princess Street (© 867/993-6969), has occasional live music and a very lively and youthful cocktail crowd—don't be surprised when this spot gets raucous.

   Diamond Tooth Gertie's, Fourth and Queen streets (© 867/993-5575), is Dawson City's one remaining gambling hall, and it has an authentic gold-rush decor, from the shirt-sleeved honky-tonk pianist to the wooden floorboards. The games include black-jack, roulette, and poker, as well as slot machines; the minimum stakes are low, and the ambience is friendly rather than tense. The three nightly floor shows combine **cancan** dancing, throaty siren songs, and ragtime piano. May through September, Gertie's is open daily 2pm to 2am, and admission is C$6 (US$6/£3). An interesting side note: Gambling revenues from Gertie's support historic preservation in the Klondike.

   It's said that "strange things are done under the Midnight sun," but there's nothing much odder than the **Sourtoe Cocktail** at the Sourdough Saloon in the Downtown Hotel (Second Ave. and Queen St.). You can join 65,000 members of the Sourtoe Cocktail Club by tossing down a drink into which the bartender places a preserved human toe. Yes, a real human toe. Apparently, in the 1970s a habitué of the saloon, Dick Stevenson, discovered a severed human toe preserved in alcohol while cleaning out an old cabin (the story of this original severed toe involves a tale of frostbite and amputation during the 1920s). Remembering the poem *Ballad of the Ice-Worm Cocktail* by Robert Service, Stevenson came up with the idea for a very unique specialty cocktail. The toe makes the ultimate garnish for the cocktail of your choice; pick your liquor, and the bartender will slip in the digit. The toe, which is about as disturbing looking as you are currently imagining, must touch the drinker's lips during the consumption of the alcohol before he or she can claim to be a true Sourtoer. A Sourtoe Cocktail costs C$5 (US$5/£2.50), and after you finish the drink, you'll receive a certificate plus the right to disgust listeners for the rest of your life. For more on the Sourtoe Cocktail, see the website at **www.sourtoecocktailclub.com**.

6 The Top of the World Highway

The scenic **Top of the World Highway** links Dawson City to Tetlin Junction in Alaska. After the free Yukon River ferry crossing at Dawson City (depending on weather conditions, open mid-May to mid-Oct), this 282km (175-mile) paved or chip-sealed road rapidly climbs above the tree line where it follows meandering ridge tops—hence the name. The views are wondrous: Bare green mountains undulate for hundreds of miles into the distance; looking down, you can see clouds floating in deep valley clefts.

   After 106km (66 miles), the road crosses the U.S.-Canadian border; the border crossing is open mid-May through the first weekend in October, 8am to 8pm Pacific

Standard Time (note that the time in Alaska is an hour earlier). There are no restrooms, services, or currency exchange at the border.

The free ferry at Dawson City can get very backed up in high season; delays up to 3 hours are possible. Peak traffic in mid-summer is from 7 to 11am and 4 to 7pm. Commercial and local traffic has priority and doesn't have to wait in line. The Top of the World Highway isn't maintained during winter; it's generally free of snow April through mid-October.

7 North on the Dempster Highway to Inuvik

Forty kilometers (25 miles) east of Dawson City, the famed **Dempster Highway** *&* heads north 735km (456 miles) to **Inuvik,** Northwest Territories, on the Mackenzie River near the Arctic Ocean. The most northerly public road in Canada, the Dempster is another of those highways that exudes a strange appeal to RV travelers; locals in Inuvik refer to these tourists as "end of the roaders." It's a beautiful drive, especially early in the fall, when frost brings out the color in tiny tundra plants and migrating wildlife is more easily seen. The Dempster passes through a wide variety of landscapes, from tundra plains to rugged volcanic mountains; in fact, between Highway 2 and Inuvik the Dempster crosses the Continental Divide three times. **North Fork Pass** in the Ogilvie Mountains, with the knife-edged gray peaks of Tombstone Mountain incising the horizon to the west, is especially stirring. The Dempster crosses the Arctic Circle—one of only two roads in Canada to do so—at Mile 252.

The Dempster is a gravel road open year-round. It's in good shape in most sections, though very dusty; allow 12 hours to make the drive between Inuvik and Dawson City. There are services at three points only: Eagle Plains, Fort McPherson, and Arctic Red River. Don't depend on gas or food outside of standard daytime business hours. At the Peel and the Mackenzie rivers are free ferry crossings in summer; in winter, vehicles simply cross on the ice. For 2 weeks, during the spring thaw and the fall freeze-up, through traffic on the Dempster ceases. For details on ferries and road conditions, call *©* **877/ 456-7623** in the Yukon or 800/661-0752 in the Yukon or Northwest Territories.

Inuvik, 771km (478 miles) from Dawson City, is the town at the end of the long Dempster Highway—the most northerly road in Canada—and the most-visited center in the western Arctic. Because of its year-round road access from the Yukon and frequent flights from Yellowknife, Inuvik is becoming a tourist destination in itself and is the departure point for tours out to more far-flung destinations. Inuvik is on the Mackenzie River, one of the largest rivers in the world. Here, about 129km (80 miles) from its debouchment into the Arctic Ocean, the Mackenzie flows into its vast delta. Inuvik is also right at the northern edge of the taiga, near the beginning of the tundra, making this region a transition zone for a number of the larger Northern animals.

The town is home to a population of 3,500, composed of **Inuvialuit,** the Inuit people of the western Arctic; of **Gwich'in,** a Dene tribe from south of the Mackenzie River delta; and of more recent white settlers, many of whom work at public-sector jobs.

For more information about Inuvik and the surrounding area, go to the town's website at **www.inuvik.ca** or call *©* **867/777-8600.** Inuvik's best lodging choice is the **Finto Motor Inn,** 288 Mackenzie Rd. (P.O. Box 1925), Inuvik, NT X0E 0T0 (*©* **867/ 777-2647;** www.inuvikhotels.com), with nicely furnished modern rooms and the popular **Peppermill Restaurant,** which offers gourmet renditions of local game and fish in addition to traditional steaks and other meats.

The most famous landmark in Inuvik is **Our Lady of Victory Church,** a large round structure with a glistening dome, usually referred to as the Igloo Church. You should definitely stop at the **Western Arctic Visitor Centre** (© 867/777-4727) on the south end of town. Exhibits provide a good overview of the human and natural history of the area and of recreation and sightseeing options. June 15 through Labour Day, it's open daily from 10am to 5pm. Several art and gift shops offer local Inuit and Indian carvings and crafts; probably the best is **Northern Images,** 15 Mackenzie Rd. (© 867/777-2786).

EXPLORING OUTSIDE INUVIK

Inuvik may be the end of the road, but tour operators continue out from here to truly remote destinations. One of the best is **Arctic Nature Tours,** P.O. Box 1530, Inuvik, NT X0E 0T0 (© 867/777-3300; www.arcticnaturetours.com), which offers air and boat tours to the following destinations plus an imposing list of more specialized eco-tours. However, because minimum numbers are necessary for all tours, don't count on specific trips to run while you're visiting.

TUKTOYAKTUK   On the shores on the Arctic Ocean's Beaufort Sea, the little Native town known as "Tuk" is reached by a short flight from Inuvik. Tour operators in Inuvik offer half-day tours of Tuk (including the flight) for around C$280 (US$280/£140), focusing on the curious "pingos" (volcanolike formations made of buckled ice that occur only here and in one location in Siberia) and the Inuvialuit culture. Stops are made at the workshops of stone carvers and other artisans, and you'll get the chance to stick your toe in the Arctic Ocean.

MACKENZIE DELTA TRIPS   When the Mackenzie River meets the Arctic Ocean, it forms an enormous basin filled with a multitude of lakes, river channels, and marshlands. Two-hour wildlife-viewing trips on the mazelike delta are C$65 (US$65/£33).

HERSCHEL ISLAND   This island, 241km (150 miles) northwest of Inuvik, sits just off the northern shores of the Yukon in the Beaufort Sea. Long a base for Native hunters and fishers, in the late 1800s Herschel Island became a camp for American and then Hudson's Bay Company whalers. Today, it's a territorial park, preserving both the historic whaling camp and abundant tundra plant and wildlife (including arctic fox, caribou, grizzly bear, and many shorebirds).

Tours of the island are generally offered only in July and August, when the arctic ice floes move away from the island sufficiently to allow floatplanes to land in **Pauline Cove,** near the old whaling settlement. A day trip to the island, costing C$420 (US$420/£210), includes a brief tour of the whaling station and a chance to explore the tundra landscape and arctic shoreline. On the flight to the island, there's a good chance of seeing musk ox, nesting arctic swans, caribou, and grizzly bear in the Mackenzie River delta.

8 Yellowknife: Capital of the Northwest Territories ★

The capital of the Northwest Territories and the most northerly city in Canada, **Yellowknife** lies on the north shore of Great Slave Lake. The site was originally occupied by the Dogrib and Yellowknives (Chipewyan) Dene peoples, and whites didn't settle there until 1934, following the discovery of gold on the lakeshores.

Mirimar Con and Giant Yellowknife gold mines defined the community for 40 years, but today Yellowknife styles itself as Canada's diamond capital. Gold played out just as geologists traced a trail of micro diamonds to kimberlite pipes out on the tundra. As the seat of government, the city is at the center of a transportation network that connects communities across the Arctic.

Most of the old gold-boom vestiges are gone—the bordellos, gambling dens, log-cabin banks, and never-closing bars are merely memories now. But the original **Old Town** is there, a crazy tangle of wooden shacks hugging the lakeshore rocks, surrounded by small commercial airlines that supply mining camps and transport hunters and fishermen to wilderness lodges—on floats in summer, on skis in winter.

Yellowknife is a vibrant, youthful place, made expensive by isolation and high salaries paid to transient young professionals and local entrepreneurs who pay big-city prices for homes. A significant portion of Yellowknife consists of people in their late 20s and 30s. Yellowknife attracts young people just out of college looking for high-paying public-sector jobs, wilderness recreation, and the adventure of living in the Arctic. After a few years, however, many of them head back south to warmer climes. Yellowknife is also the center for a number of outlying Dene communities, which roots the city in a more long-standing traditional culture.

People are very friendly and outgoing and seem genuinely glad to see you. The party scene here is just about what you'd expect in a town surrounded by Dene villages and filled with geologists and young bureaucrats. There's a more dynamic nightlife here than the size of the population could possibly justify.

ESSENTIALS

GETTING THERE   **Yellowknife Airport** is 5km (3 miles) northeast of the town. **First Air** (🕐 800/267-1247 or 613/688-2635; www.firstair.ca), flies direct to Yellowknife from Edmonton and Whitehorse. **Canadian North** (🕐 800/661-1505; www.canadiannorth.com) provides daily flights from Ottawa, Edmonton, and Calgary.

If you're driving from Edmonton, take Highway 16 to Grimshaw. From there the **Mackenzie Highway** leads to the Northwest Territories border, 475km (295 miles) north, and on to Yellowknife via Fort Providence. The total distance from Edmonton is 1,524km (947 miles). Most of the road is now paved.

VISITOR INFORMATION   For information about the territory in general or Yellowknife in particular, contact one of the following: the **Northern Frontier Regional Visitors Centre**, No. 4, 4807 49th St., Yellowknife, NT X1A 3T5 (🕐 877/881-4262 or 867/873-4262; www.northernfrontier.com); or **NWT Arctic Tourism**, P.O. Box 610, Yellowknife, NT X1A 2N5 (🕐 800/661-0788 or 867/873-7200; www.explorenwt.com)

A useful phone number for motorists is the **ferry information line** at 🕐 800/661-0750 (NT only), which lets you know the status of the various car ferries along the Dempster and Mackenzie highways. At breakup and freeze-up time, there's usually a month's time when the ferries can't operate and the ice isn't yet thick enough to drive on.

CITY LAYOUT   The city's expanding urban center, **New Town**—a busy hub of modern hotels, shopping centers, office blocks, and government buildings—spreads above the town's historic birthplace, called **Old Town.** Together the two towns count about 18,000 inhabitants, by far the largest community in the Territories.

Most of New Town lies between rock-lined Frame Lake and Yellowknife Bay on Great Slave Lake. The main street in this part of town is **Franklin Avenue,** also called **50th Avenue.** Oddly, early town planners decided to start the young town's numbering system at the junction of 50th Avenue and 50th Street; even though the downtown area is only 10 blocks square, the street addresses give the illusion of a much larger city.

The junction of 48th Street and Franklin (50th) Avenue is pretty much the center of town. A block south are the post office and a number of enclosed shopping arcades (very practical up here, where winter temperatures would otherwise discourage shopping). Turn north and travel half a mile to Old Town and **Latham Island,** which stick out into Yellowknife Bay. This is still a bustling center for boats, floatplanes, B&Bs, and food and drink.

South of Frame Lake is the modern residential area, and just west is the airport. If you follow 48th Street out of town without turning onto the Mackenzie Highway, the street turns into the **Ingraham Trail,** a bush road heading out toward a series of lakes with fishing and boating access, hiking trails, and a couple of campgrounds. This is the main recreational playground for Yellowknifers, who love to canoe or kayak from lake to lake or all the way back to town.

GETTING AROUND   Monday through Saturday, **Yellowknife City Transit** (contact Cardinal Coach Lines at ℂ 867/873-4693, or city hall at ℂ 867/920-5653) loops through Yellowknife once an hour—sometimes with a bus available every half-hour—with stops at the airport and throughout downtown. The fares are C$2.50 (US$2.50/£1.25) for adults, C$1.50 (US$1.50/75p) for youth ages 6 to 17, and free for children 5 and under; tickets are available at City Hall and at various local shops.

For car rentals, **Budget** (ℂ 800/527-0700 in the U.S., 800/472-3325 in Canada, or 867/920-9209) and **National** (ℂ 888/878-5557 or 867/920-2970) have offices at the airport. **Rent-A-Relic,** 356 Old Airport Rd. (ℂ 867/873-3400), offers older models at substantial savings—and they'll pick you up and drop you off at the airport. At all these operations, the number of cars available during summer is rather limited and the demand very high. Try to book ahead as far as possible.

Taxis are pretty cheap in Yellowknife; call **City Cabs** (ℂ 867/873-4444) or **YK Cabs** (ℂ 867/873-8888) for a lift. A ride to the airport costs about C$15 (US$15/£7.50).

SPECIAL EVENTS   The **Caribou Carnival,** in late March, is a burst of spring fever that morphs into a month-long celebration of all things Northern: aurora viewing, erecting the Snow King's ice palace on Yellowknife Bay, igloo-building contests, and Inuit wrestling. The highlight is the Canadian Championship Dog Derby, a 3-day, 240km (149-mile) dog-sled race. The brief summer starts with late June's **Raven Mad Daze** and the **Solstice Celebration** (ℂ 867/766-3865; www.solsticefestival.ca), which draws throngs to Franklin Avenue for music, dancing, and street food. The **Festival of the Midnight Sun** is an arts festival in mid-July. There are a one-act play competition, various arts workshops (including lessons in Native beading and carving), and fine art on display all over town. Also in mid-July, the **Folk on the Rocks Music Festival** (www.folkontherocks.com) features a mix of northern (arctic) and southern Canadian folk, rock, blues, and other genres, plus Native musical performances.

EXPLORING YELLOWKNIFE

Stop by the **Northern Frontier Regional Visitor Centre** (ℂ 877/881-4262 or 867/873-4262; www.northernfrontier.com), on 49th Street (just north of 49th Ave.) on the west edge of town, to see a number of exhibits explaining the major points of local history, ecology, and Native culture. You'll want to put the kids on the "bush flight" elevator, which simulates a flight over Great Slave Lake while slowly rising to the second floor. The center also has a video library and information on walking trails, parks, and outdoor activities. Also pick up a free parking pass, enabling you to escape the parking meters. It's open May through August daily 8:30am to 6pm, and the rest of the year Monday through Friday 8:30am to 5:30pm and weekends noon to 4pm.

The **Prince of Wales Northern Heritage Centre** ⚔, on the shore of Frame Lake (© **867/873-7551;** www.pwnhc.ca), is a museum in a class all its own. You'll learn the history, background, and characteristics of the Dene and Inuit peoples, the Métis, and pioneer whites through dioramas; artifacts; and talking, reciting, and singing slide presentations. It depicts the human struggle with an environment so incredibly harsh that survival alone seems an accomplishment. Admission is free. June to August, it's open daily 10:30am to 5:30pm; September to May, it's open Tuesday to Friday 10:30am to 5pm and on weekends noon to 5pm.

Rising above Old Town, the **Bush Pilot's Monument** is a stone pillar paying tribute to the little band of airmen who opened up the Far North. The surrounding cluster of shacks and cottages is the original Yellowknife, built on the shores of a narrow peninsula jutting into Great Slave Lake. It's not exactly a pretty place, but definitely intriguing. Sprinkled along the inlets are half a dozen bush-pilot operations, minuscule airlines flying charter planes as well as scheduled routes to outlying areas. The little floatplanes shunt around like taxis, and you can watch a landing or takeoff every hour of the day. Off the tip of the Old Town peninsula lies **Latham Island,** which you can reach by a causeway. The island has a small Native Canadian community, a few luxury homes, and a number of B&Bs.

TOURS & EXCURSIONS

Aurora World Corp. (© **867/873-4776;** www.raventours.yk.com) offers a 2½-hour city tour, exploring the sights, culture, history, and ecology of Yellowknife. Aurora also offers a number of more specialized trips, particularly during the winter, including dog-sledding, snowmobiling, and wildlife tours, plus excursions just outside the city to view the Aurora Borealis. Yellowknife is on the 60th parallel which, at its longitude, places it directly within an oval-shaped range at which the aurora appears most often and vividly. Tours generally run 4 hours in length and include a meal of local foods, photography tips, and an astronomy lesson.

DogPaddle Adventures (© **867/444-2242;** www.dogpaddleadventures.com) offers, by season, canoe fishing trips or winter excursions involving dog-sled rides, snowmobiling, ice-fishing, and snow-shoeing, plus a primer on dog handling for mushers. Rates range between C$50 (US$50/£25) for an hour's dog-sled ride to C$250 (US$250/£125) per person for a day of ice-fishing and dog-sledding at a remote day camp.

SHOPPING

Yellowknife is a principal retail outlet for Northern artwork and craft items, as well as for the specialized clothing the climate demands. Some of it is so handsome that sheer vanity will make you wear it in more southerly temperatures.

Northern Images, 4801 Franklin Ave. (© **867/873-5944**), features authentic Native Canadian (Inuit and Dene) articles: apparel and carvings, graphic prints, silver jewelry, ornamental moose-hair tuftings, and porcupine quill work. Proceeds from sales go directly to Native artisans.

Gallery of the Midnight Sun, 5005 Bryson Dr. (© **867/873-8064;** www.gallery midnightsun.com), has a great selection of Northern sculptures (mainly Inuit stone carvings), and also sells a variety of apparel, paintings, and arctic crafts. To browse an excellent selection of paintings and other artworks by northern artists of all cultural backgrounds, visit **Birchwood Gallery,** 26-4910 50th Ave. (© **867/873-4050;** www. birchwoodgallery.com).

SPORTS & OUTDOOR ACTIVITIES

The town is ringed by hiking trails: some gentle, some pretty rugged. Most convenient for a short hike or a jog is the 9km (5.6-mile) trail around **Frame Lake,** accessible from the Northern Heritage Centre, the Prince of Wales Heritage Centre, and other points. Don't forget insect repellent and watch for black bears that wander close to the city and parks.

The other major focus of recreation in the Yellowknife area is the **Ingraham Trail,** a paved and then gravel road starting just northwest of town and winding east over 73km (45 miles) to Tibbet Lake. En route lay a string of lakes, mostly linked by the Cameron River, making this prime canoe and kayak country. Ingraham Trail also crosses by several territorial parks, two waterfalls, the Giant Mine, and waterfowl habitat, plus lots of picnic sites, camping spots, boat rentals, and fishing spots.

One of the largest lakes along the trail is **Prelude Lake,** 32km (20 miles) east of town; it's a wonderful setting for scenic boating. For boat rentals, you might check out **Overlander Sports** (© **867/873-2474;** www.overlandersports.com). For other rental providers, contact the visitor center (© **877/881-4262** or 867/873-4262; www.northern frontier.com).

CANOEING & KAYAKING   When you fly into Yellowknife, you'll notice that about half the land surface is composed of lakes, so it's no wonder that canoeing and kayaking are really popular here. **Narwal Adventure Training and Tours,** 101-5103 51st Ave. (© **867/873-6443;** www.ssimicro.com/~narwal), offers canoe and kayak rentals and instruction, and can provide guided tours of Great Slave and Prelude lakes. A daylong rental from Narwal is around C$45 (US$45/£23). The Northern Frontier Regional Visitor Centre offers maps of seven canoe paths through the maze of lakes, islands, and streams along the Ingraham Trail; with a few short portages, it's possible to float just about all the way from Prelude Lake to Yellowknife, about a 5-day journey.

FISHING TRIPS   Traditionally, fishing has been the main reason to visit the Yellowknife and the Great Slave Lake area. Lake trout, arctic grayling, northern pike, and whitefish grow to storied size in these Northern lakes; the pristine water conditions and general lack of anglers mean fishing isn't just good, it's great. Both **Bluefish Services** (© **867/873-4818**) and **Barbara Ann Charters** (© **867/873-9913**) offer fishing trips on Great Slave Lake directly from town, but most serious anglers fly in floatplanes to fishing lodges, either on Great Slave or on more remote lakes, for a wilderness fishing trip.

One of the best of the lodge outfitters on Great Slave Lake is the **Frontier Fishing Lodge** (© **780/465-6843;** www.frontierfishinglodge.com), 185km (115 miles) southeast of Yellowknife and accessible only by floatplane or boat. With comfortable lodge rooms or freestanding log cabins, a 3-day all-inclusive guided fishing trip costs around C$1,795 (US$1,795/£898). Nearly two dozen fishing-lodge outfitters operate in the Yellowknife area; contact the visitor center for a complete listing.

HIKING   The most popular hike along the **Ingraham Trail** is to **Cameron River Falls.** The well-signed trail head is 48km (30 miles) east of Yellowknife. Although not a long hike—allow 1½ hours for the round-trip—the trail to the falls is hilly. An easier trail is the **Prelude Lake Nature Trail,** winding along Prelude Lake through wildlife habitat. The 90-minute hike begins and ends at the lakeside campground. Closer to

Yellowknife, the **Prospectors Trail** at Fred Henne Park is an interpreted trail through gold-bearing rock outcroppings; signs tell the story of Yellowknife's rich geology.

WHERE TO STAY

The campground most convenient to Yellowknife is **Fred Henne Park** (© 867/ 920-2472 for information on all territorial parks), just east of the airport on Long Lake. Both RVs and tents are welcome; there are showers, kitchen shelters, potable water, camp stoves, and electrical outlets, but no RV hookups. At **Prelude Lake Territorial Park,** 29km (18 miles) east of Yellowknife, there are 28 rustic campsites, with no facilities beyond running water and firewood. **Reid Lake Territorial Park,** 61km (38 miles) east of Yellowknife, is near the opposite end of the Ingraham Trail, and is the starting point for popular canoe trips on the Cameron River. Reid Lake also has 28 campsites with running water and firewood. All three territorial park campsites are open mid-May to mid-September and charge the same fees: C$10, C$15, or C$20 (US$10, US$15, or US$20/£5, £7.50, or £10). All these provincial parks accept online reservations at www.campingnwt.ca.

EXPENSIVE

Chateau Nova ☆   Archival photos of Yellowknife's days of yore grace the walls of one of the town's newest hotels, which offers excellent amenities in a pleasant location right downtown. Guest rooms are large and comfortable, and have such amenities as bathrobes. Suites include a kitchenette, queen sleeper sofa in addition to a queen bed, and a Jacuzzi tub.

4401 50th Ave. Box 250, Yellowknife, NT X1A 2N2. © **877/839-1236** or 867/873-9700. Fax 867/873-9702. www. novahotels.ca. 60 units. C$194–$214 (US$194–$214/£97–£107) double. Additional person add C$15 (US$15/£7.50). Children under 12 stay free in parent's room (maximum of 2 children). AE, DC, DISC, MC, V. **Amenities:** Restaurant; lounge; exercise room; Jacuzzi; sauna; courtesy airport shuttle; business center; limited room service; laundry service; same-day dry cleaning; nonsmoking rooms; executive-level rooms. *In room:* A/C, TV/VCR, dataport, coffeemaker, hair dryer, iron.

Explorer Hotel ☆☆   The Explorer is a commanding snow-white structure overlooking both the city and a profusion of rock-lined lakes. It has long been Yellowknife's premier hotel—Queen Elizabeth herself has stayed here—and after a complete top-to-bottom renovation in 2005, the Explorer sparkles with renewed style and comfort. Guest rooms are spacious, many with kitchenettes. If you've arrived with business to do, you'll like the large desks, voice mail, and other business services. A wheelchair-accessible room is also available. The Trader's Grill and Trapline Lounge are among the Territories' finest restaurants.

4825 49th Ave., Yellowknife, NT X1A 2R3. © **800/661-0892** in Canada, or 867/873-3531. Fax 867/873-2789. www.explorerhotel.ca. 128 units. C$198–C$210 (US$198–US$210/£99–£105) double; from C$220 (US$220/£110) suite. AE, DC, MC, V. Free parking with winter plug-ins available for car head-bolt heaters. **Amenities:** 2 restaurants; exercise room; concierge; tour and activities desk; free airport shuttle; limited room service; same-day laundry and dry cleaning; nonsmoking rooms; executive-level rooms; 1 room for those w/limited mobility. *In room:* TV, dataport, coffeemaker, hair dryer.

Yellowknife Inn ☆   This inn is right in the center of Yellowknife and has recently been completely refurbished and updated. The new lobby is joined to a large shopping-and-dining complex, the Centre Square Mall, making this the place to stay in winter. Guest rooms are fair size, some with minibars, and offer amenities that have won an International Hospitality award. The walls are decorated with Inuit art. Guests receive a pass to local fitness facilities. The hotel will also store extra luggage or equipment if you're off to a secondary destination for a while.

5010 49th St., Yellowknife, NT X1A 2N4. © 800/661-0580 or 867/873-2601. Fax 867/873-2602. www.yellow knifeinn.com. 130 units. C$160–C$175 (US$160–US$175/£80–£88) double. Rates include breakfast. AE, DC, MC, V. Free parking. **Amenities:** Restaurant; lounge; courtesy limo; laundry services; nonsmoking rooms; executive suites; rooms for those w/ limited mobility. *In room:* TV, dataport, coffeemaker.

MODERATE

Captain Ron's   Located on Latham Island on the shores of Great Slave Lake, Captain Ron's is reached by causeway. It's a cozy and picturesque place with four guest rooms (which share two bathrooms) and a reading lounge with a fireplace and TV. Each room has a double bed, radio, and picture windows to take in the lake view.

8 Lessard Dr., Yellowknife, NT X1A 2G5. © 867/873-3746. 4 units. C$98 (US$98/£49) double. Rates include break-fast. V. *In room:* No phone.

Red Coach Inn *(Value)*   An attractive two-story wood structure, the Red Coach has undergone a complete renovation. Within walking distance to both New Town and Old Town, the Red Coach is also just around the corner from Great Slave Lake. Many units have pleasantly spacious kitchenettes stocked with electric ranges and all the necessary utensils. All rooms have two double beds, flatscreen TVs, and private full bathrooms. There are smoking and nonsmoking rooms available. Kerrin's Café, on-site, serves all three meals and can provide room service. Altogether, it's a great value for your money.

4115 Franklin Ave. (Box 596), Yellowknife, NT X1A 2N4. © 867/873-8511. Fax 867/873-5547. redcoach inn@theedge.ca. 42 units. C$129 (US$129/£65) double. Senior and corporate rates available. MC, V. Free parking with plug-ins. **Amenities:** Restaurant. *In room:* TV.

WHERE TO DINE
EXPENSIVE

L'Heritage Restaurant Francais FRENCH   This small, exquisite French restaurant is not exactly what you expect in rowdy Yellowknife, but it's quickly become one of the city's fine dining favorites. The French-born chef/owner brings European finesse to fish and meats of the North. In addition to classics like pork loin in mustard sauce and chicken braised in red wine, you'll find an arctic char burger and fondue with local game meats. The atmosphere is homey in a French Country sort of way.

5019 49th St. (upstairs). © 867/873-9561. Reservations recommended. Main courses C$20–C$37 (US$20–US$37/£10–£19). AE, MC. V. Mon–Sat 5–10pm.

Trader's Grill and Trapline Lounge *✦* INTERNATIONAL/NORTHERN   These two interlinked restaurants in the Explorer Hotel offer some of the best Northern cooking in the Northwest Territories. The menu lists a number of game dishes peculiar to the region (caribou and musk ox) but prepared with French sauces and finesse. Other dishes—steaks, pasta, and seafood—have a more international provenance.

In the Explorer Hotel, 4825 49th Ave. © 867/873-3531, ext. 7121. Reservations recommended. Main courses C$18–C$40 (US$18–US$40/£9–£20). AE, DC, MC, V. Mon–Sat 6am–2pm and 5–10pm (lunch buffet 11:30am–2pm); Sun 7am–10pm (brunch 10am–2pm). Lounge Mon–Sat 11am–11:30pm.

MODERATE

Bullock's Bistro NORTHERN   This bustling little restaurant doesn't have a lengthy menu, but it's doing something right: the dining room is usually filled to capacity for lunch and dinner. The secret is that Bullock's serves fish taken from Great Slave Lake—trout, cod, pike, and whitefish—in simple but delicious preparations. Go for the fish and chips, stay for the various fish chowders. The fish is always fresh and the ambience vibrant but informal.

3534 Weaver Rd., Old Town. © **867/873-3474**. Reservations recommended. Main courses C$10–C$20 (US$10–US$20/£5–£10). MC, V. Daily 11am–10pm.

Le Frolic Bistro & Bar ☆ BISTRO/PUB FARE   Bustling and convivial, this popular watering hole is a great spot to have an informal meal or to enjoy a drink and appetizer—there's a menu of dishes meant for sharing in addition to burgers and French bistro favorites. The atmosphere is friendly, with stained glass and dark paneling lending a pleasant air of formality.

5019 49th St. © **867/669-9852**. www.lefrolic.com. Main courses C$18–C$25 (US$18–US$25/£9–£13). AE, DISC, MC, V. Mon–Sat 11am–1am.

INEXPENSIVE

The **Heritage Café** at the **Northern Heritage Centre**, on Frame Lake (© **867/ 873-7551**), has a good selection of inexpensive lunch items; this is a fine place to go for soups, salads, sandwiches, and pasta dishes, whether or not you plan on visiting the museum. It's open Tuesday through Friday 11am to 4pm and Sunday noon to 4pm. The **Gold Range Bistro**, 5010 50th St. (© **867/873-4567**), offers home-style breakfast, lunch, and dinner. Pan-fried white fish on Friday is memorable.

Brand-name fast food is present in Yellowknife, and for people on a tight budget, this is probably the way to avoid the otherwise rather high cost of dining. All the downtown shopping arcades have inexpensive food outlets as well.

YELLOWKNIFE AFTER DARK

By and large, people in Yellowknife aren't scared of a drink, and nightlife revolves around bars and pubs. Increasingly, there's a music scene in Yellowknife; a number of local bands have developed national followings.

Officially called Bad Sam's, the **Gold Range Tavern**, in the Gold Range Hotel, 5010 50th St. (© **867/873-4441**), is better known by its local nickname—"Strange Range." The Range is an occasionally rip-roaring tavern that attracts the whole gamut of local and visiting characters in search of some after-dinner whoopee. You don't come here for a quiet evening, but you can't say you've seen Yellowknife if you haven't seen the Strange Range.

The pleasant **Black Knight Pub**, 4910 49th St. (© **867/920-4041**), has a selection of about 15 beers on tap, with an emphasis on English and Irish brews, as well as the largest selection of scotches in town (somewhere around 120!). It's open 11am until 2am, every day but Sunday. The **Top Knight**, a nightclub upstairs from the pub, offers dancing and informal dining.

9 Nunavut: The Inuit Homeland

Nunavut is one of the world's most remote and uninhabited areas, but one that holds many rewards for the traveler willing to get off the beaten path. Arctic landscapes can be breathtaking, traditional Inuit villages retain age-old hunting and fishing ways, and the **artwork** of the North is famous worldwide. In almost every community, artists engage in weaving; print making; or stone, ivory, and bone carving. Locally produced artwork is available from community co-ops, galleries, or from the artists themselves.

WHAT TO EXPECT

Traveling the wilds of Nunavut is a great adventure, but frankly it isn't for everyone. The Arctic is a very expensive place to travel. Airfare is very high—for example, flights between Ottawa and Iqaluit are usually over C$2,500 (US$2,500/£1,250), and it will cost even more again to fly from Iqaluit to Pond Inlet. While almost every little community has a serviceable hotel/restaurant, room prices are shockingly high; a hostel-style rustic room with full board costs as much as a decent room in Paris. Food costs are equally high (remember that food must be air-freighted in) and the quality is poor.

To reach anywhere in Nunavut, you'll need to fly on floatplanes, tiny commuter planes, and aircraft that years ago passed out of use in the rest of the world. Of course, all aircraft in the Arctic are regularly inspected and regulated for safety, but if you have phobias about flying, you may find the combination of rattling aircraft and changeable flying conditions unpleasant.

Nunavut is the homeland of the Inuit. Travelers are made welcome in nearly all Native villages, but it must be stressed that these communities aren't set up as holiday camps for southern visitors. Most people aren't English speakers; except for the local hotel, there may not be public areas open for non-Natives. You're definitely a guest here; while people are friendly and will greet you, you'll probably feel very much an outsider.

BAFFIN ISLAND: ADVENTURE & INUIT ART

One of the most remote and uninhabited areas in North America, rugged and beautiful **Baffin Island** is an excellent destination for the traveler willing to spend some time and money for an adventure vacation; it's also a great place if your mission is to find high-quality Inuit arts and crafts.

It's easy to spend a day or two exploring the galleries and museums of **Iqaluit,** the capital, but if you've come this far, you definitely should continue on to yet more remote and traditional communities. Iqaluit is the population and governmental center of Baffin, but far more scenic and culturally significant destinations are just a short plane ride away.

For information about Baffin Island communities, contact **Nunavut Tourism,** P.O. Box 1450, Iqaluit, NU X0A 0H0 (© **866/686-2888** or 867/979-6551; www.nunavut tourism.com). Any serious traveler should get hold of *The Nunavut Handbook,* an excellent government-sponsored guide loaded with information on Nunavut's land, wildlife, history, people, culture, and practical tips for travelers. The handbook is available from local bookstores and from **www.nunavuthandbook.com**.

GETTING THERE Iqaluit, 2,266km (1,408 miles) from Yellowknife, is the major transport hub on Baffin and is linked to the rest of Canada by flights from Montréal, Ottawa, Winnipeg, and Yellowknife on **First Air** (© **800/267-1247** or 613/688-2635; www.firstair.ca) and **Canadian North** (© **800/661-1505;** www.canadiannorth.com).

Because there are no roads linking communities here, travel between small villages is also by plane. First Air is the major local carrier, centering out of Iqaluit; a bevy of smaller providers fill in the gaps.

IQALUIT: GATEWAY TO BAFFIN ISLAND

On the southern end of the island, **Iqaluit** (pronounced Ee-ka-*loo*-eet) is the new capital of Nunavut and like most Inuit settlements is quite young; it grew up alongside a U.S. Air Force airstrip built here in 1942. The rambling village overlooking Frobisher Bay now boasts a rapidly growing population of more than 4,400 and is a hodgepodge of weather-proofed government and civic buildings.

Exploring Iqaluit

Begin at the **Unikkaarvik Visitor/Information Centre** (© **867/979-4636**), overlooking the bay, with a friendly staff to answer questions and a series of displays on local Native culture, natural history, and local art. There's even an igloo to explore.

June 1 to Labour Day, the center is open daily 10am to 5pm; the rest of the year, it's open Monday through Friday the same hours.

Next door is the **Nunatta Sunakkutaangit Museum** (© 867/979-5537), housed in an old Hudson's Bay Company building. The collection of arctic arts and crafts here is excellent; this is a good place to observe the stylized beauty of Native carvings. It's open Tuesday through Sunday 1 to 5pm. The **Government of Nunavut Building,** at Iqaluit's "four corners," also has a good display of Northern art in the lobby.

Iqaluit is the primary center for **Baffin Island art.** Local galleries carry works from communities around the island; ask at the visitor center for a map of arts-and-crafts locations if you're interested in buying; prices here can be at least half of what they are down south.

Where to Stay

Discovery Lodge Hotel, 1056 Apex Rd. (P.O. Box 387), Iqaluit, NU X0A 0H0 (© 867/979-4433; www.discoverylodge.com), is a newer hotel with nicely furnished, good-size guest rooms and an inviting public sitting area. The restaurant is one of Iqaluit's best. Double rooms begin at C$220 (US$220/£110). **Frobisher Inn,** on a hill above Iqaluit (P.O. Box 610, Iqaluit, NU X0A 0H0; © 867/979-2222; www. frobisherinn.com), or the "Frobe," as it's known by regulars, is in a complex that houses a cinema, a small shopping arcade, and the municipal pool. Recently updated guest rooms are pleasantly furnished and decorated, and the views on the bay side are quite panoramic. There's a very lively bar as well as an excellent restaurant, with a mix of French and Northern choices. Double rooms begin at C$220 (US$220/£110).

OTHER BAFFIN ISLAND DESTINATIONS

If you've come as far as Iqaluit, don't stop now. Smaller communities on Baffin Island are far more scenic and compelling than Iqaluit, and with excellent recreational opportunities. Each of the following Inuit communities is served by scheduled air service and will have a small hotel, store and guide services. For current information on these communities, consult the Nunavut tourism website at. www.nunavuttourism.com.

PANGNIRTUNG AND AUYUITTUQ NATIONAL PARK   Called "Pang" by Territorians, **Pangnirtung** is at the heart of one of the most scenic areas in Nunavut. Located on a deep, mountain-flanked fjord, Pang is the jumping-off point for 21,500 sq. km (8,300-sq.-mile) Auyuittuq National Park, often referred to as "the Switzerland of the Arctic."

Pang itself is a lovely little village of 1,200 people, with a postcard view up the narrow fjord to the glaciered peaks of Auyuittuq. The local population is very friendly and outgoing, which isn't the case in some other Inuit villages. The **Angmarlik Interpretive Centre** (© 867/473-8737) is definitely worth a stop, with well-presented displays on local Inuit history and culture.

Most people go to Pang to reach **Auyuittuq National Park,** 31km (19 miles) farther up Pangnirtung Fjord. *Auyuittuq* (pronounced Ow-you-*ee*-tuk) means "the land that never melts" and refers to the 5,698-sq.-km (2,200-sq.-mile) Penny Ice Cap, which covers the high plateaus of the park, and the glaciers that edge down into the lower valleys and cling to the towering granite peaks. The landscapes are extremely dramatic: Cliffs rise from the milky-green sea, terminating in hornlike glacier-draped peaks 2,333m (7,654 ft.) high; in fact, the world's longest uninterrupted cliff face (over 1km/½ mile of sheer rock) is in the park. Auyuittuq is largely the province of long-distance hikers and rock climbers; if you're looking for an adventurous walking holiday in magnificent scenery, this might be it. The best time to visit is July to mid-August, when the days are long and afternoons bring short-sleeve weather. For details, contact the Auyuittuq Park superintendent, P.O. Box 353, Pangnirtung, NU X0A 0R0 (© **867/473-2500;** www.pc.gc.ca/pn-np/nu/auyuittuq).

POND INLET   In many ways, the best reason to make the trip to Pond Inlet on Baffin's northern shore is simply to see the landscape. On a clear day, the 4-hour flight from Iqaluit up to Pond is simply astounding: hundreds of miles of knife-edged mountains, massive ice caps (remnants of the icefields that once covered all North America), glacier-choked valleys, and deep fjords flooded by the sea. It's an epic land-scape—in all the country, perhaps only the Canadian Rockies can match the eastern coast of Baffin Island for sheer scenic drama.

Pond Inlet sits on **Eclipse Sound,** near the top of Baffin Island in the heart of this rugged beauty. Opposite the town is **Bylot Island,** a wildlife refuge and part of Sirmi-lik (North Baffin) National Park. Its craggy peaks rear 2,167m (7,109 ft.) straight up from the sea; from its central ice caps, two massive glaciers pour down into the sound directly across from town.

Considering the amazing scenery in the area, Pond Inlet is relatively untouristy. The peak tourist season is May and June, when local outfitters offer trips out to the edge of the ice floes, the point where the ice of the protected bays meets the open water of the Arctic Ocean. In spring this is where you find much of the Arctic's **wildlife** 🐾: seals, walruses, bird life, polar bears, narwhals, and other species converge here to feed, often on one another. A wildlife-viewing trip out to the floe edge (by snowmobile or dogsled) requires at least 3 days, with 5-day trips advised for maximum viewing opportunities. Other recreation opportunities open up in August, when the ice clears out of Eclipse Sound. Bird-watching boat trips out to Bylot Island are offered (the rare ivory gull nests here), as well as narwhal-watching trips in the fjords. It's best to allow several days in Pond Inlet if you're coming for summer trips; the weather is very changeable this far north.

KIMMIRUT & KATANNILIK TERRITORIAL PARK   The center for Baffin Island's famed stone-carving industry, **Kimmirut,** formerly **Lake Harbour,** is located along a rocky harbor, directly south of Iqaluit on the southern shore of Baffin Island. While many people make the trip to this dynamic, picturesque community to visit the workshops of world-renowned carvers, there are other reasons to make the trip. **Katannilik Territorial Park** is a preserve of arctic wildlife and lush tundra vegetation and offers access to Soper River. The Soper, a Canadian Heritage River, is famed for its many waterfalls in side valleys and for its long-distance float and canoe trips.

Many people visit Katannilik Territorial Park for a less demanding version of rugged Auyuittuq National Park farther north. Wildlife viewing is good, and hiking trails wind through the park. Canoeing or kayaking the Soper River is a popular 3-day trip that's full of adventure but still suitable for a family. For more information on the park, con-tact the Katannilik Park manager, Lake Harbour, NU X0A 0N0 (© **867/939-2084;** www.nunavutparks.com).

OTHER NUNAVUT DESTINATIONS
BATHURST INLET   One of the most notable arctic lodges, **Bathurst Inlet Lodge** was founded in 1969 for naturalists and those interested in the Arctic's natural history and ecology. The lodge is at the mouth of the Burnside River on an arm of the Arctic Ocean in a rugged landscape of tundra and rocky cliffs. The lodge is housed in the

historic buildings of a former Oblate mission and the old Hudson's Bay Company trading post.

The lodge is open for a brief mid-summer season only. Rates will depend on the activities available during your visit, but are typically C$4,995 (US$4,995/£2,498) a week, which includes charter air transportation to/from Yellowknife, all meals, and programs. The lodge can make arrangements to suit your individual interests, including fishing, hiking, flight seeing, wildlife photography, and river floating.

For more details, contact **Bathurst Inlet Lodge,** P.O. Box 820, Yellowknife, NT X1A 2N6 (© **867/873-2595;** www.bathurstinletlodge.com).

QUTTINIRPAAQ (Ellesmere Island) National Park Reserve   A good part of the intrigue of **Ellesmere Island** is its absolute remoteness. A preserve of rugged glacier-choked mountains, icefields, mountain lakes and fjords, and arctic wildlife, Ellesmere Island National Park is the most northerly point in Canada. During the short summer, experienced hikers and mountaineers make their way to this wilderness area to explore some of the most isolated and inaccessible land in the world.

Getting to Ellesmere is neither easy nor cheap. From Resolute Bay (served by regularly scheduled flights on First Air), park visitors must charter a private airplane for the 960km (597-mile) flight farther north. There are no facilities or improvements in the park itself, so you must be prepared for extremes of weather and physical endurance. The most common activity is hiking from Lake Hazen at the center of the park to Tanquary Fjord in the southwest corner. This 129km (80-mile) trek crosses rugged tundra moorland, as well as several glaciers, and demands fords of major rivers. Needless to say, Ellesmere Island Park isn't for the uninitiated.

For more information and an up-to-date listing of outfitters who run trips into the park, contact **Quttinirpaaq National Park,** P.O. Box 278, Iqaluit, NU, X0A 0H0 (© **867/975-4673;** www.pc.gc.ca/pn-np/nu/quttinirpaaq).

Appendix:
Canada in Depth

by Bill McRae

Canada's sheer amount of elbow space can make you dizzy. At 6.1 million sq. km (3.8 million sq. miles), 322,000 sq. km (200,000 sq. miles) more than the United States, this colossal expanse contains only 33 million people—fewer than the state of California alone. Most of the population is clustered in a relatively narrow southern belt that boasts all the nation's large cities and nearly all its industries. The silent Yukon, Northwest Territories, and Nunavut—where 100,000 people dot 2.4 million sq. km (1.5 million sq. miles)—remain a frontier, stretching to the arctic shores and embracing thousands of lakes no one has ever charted, counted, or named.

It's impossible to easily categorize this land or its people—just when you think you know Canada, you discover another place, another temperament, a hidden side.

1 History 101

THE FOUNDING OF NEW FRANCE

The Vikings landed in Canada more than 1,000 years ago, but the French were the first Europeans to get a toehold in the country. In 1608, Samuel de Champlain established a settlement on the cliffs overlooking the St. Lawrence River—today's Québec City. This was exactly a year after the Virginia Company founded Jamestown. Hundreds of miles of unexplored wilderness lay between the embryo colonies, but they were inexorably set on a collision course.

The early stages of the struggle for the new continent were explorations—and the French outdid the English. Their fur traders, navigators, soldiers, and missionaries opened up not only Canada but also most of the United States. Relying on canoes for transport, these *voyageurs* discovered, mapped and settled at least 35 of the 50 United States. Gradually, they staked out an immense colonial empire that, in patches and minus recognized borders, stretched from Hudson Bay in the Arctic to the Gulf of Mexico. Christened

New France, it was run on an ancient seigniorial system, whereby settlers were granted land by the Crown in return for military service.

The military obligation was essential, for the colony knew hardly a moment of peace during its existence. New France blocked the path of western expansion by England's seaboard colonies with a string of forts that lined the Ohio-Mississippi Valley. The Anglo-Americans were determined to break through, and so the frontier clashes crackled and flared, with the native tribes participating ferociously. These miniature wars were nightmares of savagery, waged with knives and tomahawks as much as with muskets and cannons, characterized by raids and counterraids, burning villages, and massacred women and children.

The French retaliated in kind. They converted the Abenaki tribe to Christianity and encouraged them to raid deep into New England territory, where, in 1704, they totally destroyed the town of Deerfield, Massachusetts. The Americans answered with a punitive blitz expedition by the famous green-clad Roger's Rangers, who wiped out the main Abenaki village and slaughtered half its population.

By far the most dreaded of the tribes was the Iroquois, who played the same role in the Canadian east as the Sioux (another French label) played in the American West. Astute politicians, the Iroquois played the English against the French and vice versa, lending their scalping knives first to one side, then to the other. It took more than a century before they finally succumbed to the whites' smallpox, firewater, and gunpowder—in that order.

THE FALL OF QUÉBEC

There were only about 65,000 French settlers in the colony, but they more than held their own against the million Anglo-Americans, first and foremost because they were natural forest fighters—one French trapper could stalemate six redcoats in the woods. Mainly, however, it was because they made friends with the local tribes whenever possible. The majority of tribes sided with the French and made the English pay a terrible price for their blindness.

Even before French and English interests in the New World came to the point of armed struggle in the Seven Years' War, the British had largely taken control of Acadia (as the area of coastal Nova Scotia and New Brunswick was then known), though its lush forests and farmlands were dotted with French settlements. The governors knew there would be war, so, suspicious of Acadia's French-speaking inhabitants, they decided on a bold and ruthless plan: All Acadians who wouldn't openly pledge allegiance to the British sovereign would be deported. The order came in 1755, and French-speaking families throughout the province were forcibly moved from their homes, many resettling in the French territory of Louisiana, where their Cajun language and culture are still alive today. To replace the Acadians, shiploads of Scottish and Irish settlers arrived from the British Isles, and the province soon acquired the name Nova Scotia—New Scotland.

When the final round of fighting began in 1754, it opened with a series of shattering English debacles. The French had a brilliant commander, the Marquis de Montcalm, exactly the kind of unorthodox tactician needed for the fluid semi-guerrilla warfare of the American wilderness. Britain's proud General Braddock rode into a French-Indian ambush that killed him and scattered his army. Montcalm led an expedition against Fort Oswego that wiped out the stronghold and turned Lake Ontario into a French waterway. The following summer he repeated the feat

Dateline

- **1608** Samuel de Champlain founds the settlement of Kebec—today's Québec City.
- **1642** The French colony of Ville-Marie established, later renamed Montréal.
- **1759** The British defeat the French at the Plains of Abraham. Québec City falls.
- **1763** All "New France" (Canada) ceded to the British.
- **1775** American Revolutionary forces capture Montréal but are repulsed at Québec City.
- **1813** Americans blow up Fort York (Toronto) in the War of 1812.
- **1841** The Act of Union creates the United Provinces of Canada.
- **1855** Ottawa becomes Canada's capital.
- **1869** The Hudson's Bay Company sells Rupert's Land
to Canada. It becomes the Province of Alberta.
- **1873** The Northwest Mounted Police (the Mounties) are created.
- **1875** The west coast community of Gastown is incorporated as the city of Vancouver. The Northwest Mounted Police build the log fort that will develop into the city of Calgary.

with Fort William Henry, at the head of Lake George, which fell amid ghastly scenes of massacre, later immortalized by James Fenimore Cooper in *The Last of the Mohicans*. Middle New York now lay wide open to raids, and England's hold on America seemed to be slipping.

Then, like a cornered boxer bouncing from the ropes, the British came back with a devastating right-left-right that not only saved their colonies but also won them the entire continent. The first punches were against Fort Duquesne, in Pennsylvania, and against the Fortress of Louisbourg, on Cape Breton, both of which they took after bloody sieges. Then, where least expected, came the ultimate haymaker, aimed straight at the enemy's solar plexus—Québec.

In June 1759, a British fleet nosed its way from the Atlantic down the St. Lawrence River. In charge of the troops on board was the youngest general in the army, 32-year-old James Wolfe, whose military record was remarkable and whose behavior was so eccentric he had the reputation of being "mad as a March hare." The struggle for Québec dragged on until September, when Wolfe, near desperation, played his final card. He couldn't storm those gallantly defended fortress walls, though the British guns had shelled the town to rubble. Wolfe

therefore loaded 5,000 men into boats and rowed upriver to a cove behind the city. Then they silently climbed the towering cliff face in the darkness, and when morning came Wolfe had his army squarely astride Montcalm's supply lines. Now the French had to come out of their stronghold and fight in the open.

The British formed their famous "thin red line" across the bush-studded Plains of Abraham, just west of the city. Montcalm advanced on them with five regiments, all in step, and in the next quarter of an hour the fate of Canada was decided. The redcoats stood like statues as the French drew closer—100 yards, 60 yards, 40 yards. Then a command rang out, and (in such perfect unison it sounded like a single thunderclap) the English muskets crashed. The redcoats advanced four measured paces, halted, fired, advanced another four paces with robot precision—halted, fired again. Then it was all over.

The plain was covered with the fallen French. Montcalm lay mortally wounded, and the rest of his troops fled helter-skelter. Among the British casualties was Wolfe himself. With two bullets through his body, he lived just long enough to hear that he'd won. Montcalm died a few hours after him. Today, overlooking the boardwalk of Québec, you'll find a unique memorial to these men—a

---

- **1885** Under Louis Riel, the Métis rebel in western Saskatchewan.
- **1887** The transcontinental railroad reaches Vancouver, connecting Canada from ocean to ocean.
- **1896** The Klondike gold rush brings 100,000 people swarming into the Yukon.
- **1914** Canada enters World War I alongside Britain. Some 60,000 Canadians die in combat.

- **1920** The Northwest Territories separate from the Yukon.
- **1930** Depression and mass unemployment hit Canada.
- **1939** Canada enters World War II with Britain.
- **1947** Huge oil deposits are discovered at Leduc, southwest of Edmonton. The Alberta oil boom begins.
- **1959** The opening of the St. Lawrence Seaway turns Toronto into a major seaport.

- **1967** Montréal hosts the World Expo.
- **1968** The Parti Québécois is founded by René Lévesque. The separatist movement begins.
- **1970** Cabinet Minister Pierre Laporte is kidnapped and murdered. The War Measures Act is imposed on Québec.
- **1976** Montréal becomes the site of the Olympic Games.

continues

statue commemorating both the victor and vanquished of the same battle.

A CONFEDERATION OF PROVINCES

Canada has always been a loosely linked country, a confederation of provinces, not a union of states. Canadians are quick to tell you theirs is a "cultural mosaic" of people, not a "melting pot." These factors account in great part for two of Canada's most striking characteristics: its cultural vitality and its habits of mistrust and contention.

THE U.S. INVASION

The capture of Québec determined the war and left Britain ruler of all North America down to the Mexican border. Yet, oddly enough, this victory generated Britain's worst defeat. For if the French had held Canada, the British government would certainly have been more careful in its treatment of the American colonists. As it was, the British felt cocksure and decided to make the colonists themselves pay for the outrageous costs of the French and Indian Wars. The taxes slapped on all imports—especially tea—infuriated the colonists to the point of open rebellion against the Crown. The rest of this story—the America Revolution of 1775–1783—is, as they say, history.

But if the British misjudged the temper of the colonists, the Americans were equally wrong about the mood of the Canadians. General George Washington felt sure the French in the north would join the American Revolution, or at least not resist an invasion of American soldiers. He was terribly mistaken on both counts. The French had little love for either of the English-speaking antagonists. But they were staunch Royalists and devout Catholics, with no sympathy for the "godless" republicans from the south. Only a handful changed sides, and most French Canadians fought grimly shoulder to shoulder with their erstwhile enemies.

Thirty-eight years later, in the War of 1812, another U.S. army marched up the banks of the Richelieu River where it flows from Lake Champlain to the St. Lawrence. And once again the French Canadians stuck by the British and flung back the invaders. The war ended in a draw, but with surprisingly happy results. Britain and the young United States agreed to demilitarize the Great Lakes and to extend their mutual border along the 49th parallel to the Rockies.

LOYALISTS & IMMIGRANTS

One of the side effects of the American Revolution was an influx of English-speaking newcomers for Canada. About

- **1988** Calgary hosts the Winter Olympics.
- **1989** The Canada-U.S. Free Trade Agreement eliminates all tariffs on goods of national origin moving between the two countries.
- **1995** Québec votes narrowly to remain in Canada.
- **1999** Nunavut severs itself from the rump Northwest Territories to become a self-governed territory and Inuit homeland.
- **2003** Vancouver is awarded 2010 Olympic Winter Games as tourism starts to rebound following major drop due to SARS outbreak in Toronto and discovery of mad cow disease in some Alberta cattle.
- **2005** Canada's Civil Marriage Act, legalizing same-sex marriage, receives royal assent. Michaëlle Jean, born in Haiti, becomes the 27th governor general of Canada, the first black person to hold that position.
- **2007** The Canadian dollar reaches, then exceeds the value of U.S. dollar for the first time since 1957.

50,000 Americans who had remained faithful to George III, the United Empire Loyalists, migrated to Canada because they were given rough treatment in the States. They settled mostly in Nova Scotia and began to populate the almost-empty shores of what's now New Brunswick.

After the Napoleonic Wars, a regular tide of immigrants came from England, which was going through the early and cruelest stages of the Industrial Revolution. They were fleeing from the hideously bleak factory towns, from workhouses, starvation wages, and impoverished Scottish farms. Even the unknown perils of the New World seemed preferable to these blessings of the Dickens era. By 1850, more than half a million immigrants had arrived, pushing Canada's population above two million. The population centers began to shift westward, away from the old seaboard colonies in the east, opening up the territories eventually called Ontario, Manitoba, and Saskatchewan.

With increased population came the demand for confederation, largely because the various colony borders hampered trade. Britain complied rather promptly. In 1867, Parliament passed an act creating a federal union out of the colonies of Upper and Lower Canada, Nova Scotia, and New Brunswick. British Columbia hesitated over whether to remain separate, join the United States, or merge with Canada, but finally voted itself in. Remote Newfoundland hesitated longest of all, a distinct colony until 1949, when it became Canada's 10th province.

THE METIS REBELLION

Geographically, Canada stretched from the Atlantic to the Pacific, but in reality most of the immense region in between lay beyond the rule of Ottawa, the nation's capital. The endless prairies and forest lands of the west and northwest were inhabited by about 40,000 people, more than half of them nomadic tribes

pushed there by the waves of white settlers. They lived by hunting, fishing, and trapping, depending largely on buffalo for food, clothing, and shelter. As the once-enormous herds began to dwindle, life grew increasingly hard for the nomads. Adding to their troubles were whiskey traders peddling poisonous rotgut for furs and packs of outlaws who took what they wanted at gunpoint.

Ordinary law officers were nearly useless. In 1873, the federal government created a quite extraordinary force: the Northwest Mounted Police, now called the Royal Canadian Mounted Police (and now rarely mounted). The scarlet-coated Mounties earned a legendary reputation for toughness, fairness, and the ability to hunt down wrongdoers. And unlike their American counterparts, they usually brought in prisoners alive.

But even the Mounties couldn't handle the desperate uprising that shook western Saskatchewan in 1885. As the railroad relentlessly pushed across the prairies and the buffalo vanished, the people known as the Métis felt they had to fight for their existence. The Métis, offspring of French trappers and Native women, were superb hunters and trackers. The westward expansion had driven them from Manitoba to the banks of the Saskatchewan River, where some 6,000 of them now made their last stand against iron rails and wooden farmhouses. They had a charismatic leader in Louis Riel, a man educated enough to teach school and mad enough to think God wanted him to found a new religion.

With Riel's rebels rose their natural allies, the Plains tribes, under chiefs Pound-maker and Big Bear. Together, they were a formidable force. The Métis attacked the Mounted Police at Duck Lake, cut the telegraph wires, and proclaimed an independent republic. Their allies stormed the town of Battleford, then captured and burned Fort Pitt. The alarmed administration in Ottawa sent an army marching westward under General Middleton, equipped with artillery and Gatling machine guns. The Métis checked them briefly at Fish Creek but had to fall back on their main village of Batoche. There the last battle of the west took place—long lines of redcoats charging with fixed bayonets, the Métis fighting from house to house, from rifle pits and crude trenches, so short of ammunition they had to shoot lead buttons instead of bullets.

Batoche fell (you can still see the bullet marks on the houses there), and the rebellion was completely crushed shortly afterward. Louis Riel was tried for treason and murder. Though any court today probably would've found him insane, the Canadian authorities hanged him.

RAILROADS, WHEAT & WAR

The reason the army crushed Riel's rebellion so quickly was also the reason for its outbreak: the Canadian Pacific Railway. The railroad was more than a marvel of engineering—it formed a steel band holding the country together, enabling Canada to live up to its motto, *A Mari Usque ad Mare* ("From Sea to Sea").

Though the free-roaming prairie people hated the iron horse, railroads were vital to Canada's survival as a nation. They had to be pushed through, against all opposition, because the isolated provinces threatened to drift into the orbit of the United States. Without the western provinces, the Dominion would cease to exist. As one journalist of the time put it: "The whistle of a locomotive is the true cradle song and anthem of our country." As Canada's transportation system developed, the central provinces emerged as one of the world's biggest

breadbaskets. In just a decade, wheat production zoomed from 56 million bushels to more than 200 million, putting Canada on a par with the United States and Russia as a granary.

And despite the bitterness engendered by Riel's execution, in the following year Canada elected its first prime minister of French heritage. Sir Wilfrid Laurier had one foot in each ethnic camp and proved to be a superlative leader—according to some, the best his country ever produced. His term of office (1896–1911) was a period in which Canada flexed its muscles like a young giant and looked forward to unlimited growth and a century of peaceful prosperity—just like an equally optimistic American neighbor to the south.

With the onset of World War I, the Dominion went to war allied with Britain and likewise tried to fight it on a volunteer basis. It didn't work. The tall, healthy Canadians, together with the Australians, formed the shock troops of the British Empire and earned that honor with torrents of blood. The entire western front in France was littered with Canadian bones. The flow of volunteers became a trickle, and in 1917 the Dominion was forced to introduce conscription. The measure ran into violent opposition from the French-speaking minority, who saw conscription as a device to thin out their numbers.

The draft law went through, but it strained the nation's unity almost to the breaking point. The results were ghastly. More than 60,000 Canadians fell in battle, a terrible bloodletting for a country of 250,000. (In World War II, by contrast, Canada lost 40,000 from a population of 11.5 million.)

2 Toward World Power

Between the world wars, the fortunes of Canada more or less reflected those of the United States, except that Canada was

never foolish enough to join the "noble experiment" of Prohibition. Some of its citizens, in fact, waxed rich on the lucrative bootlegging trade across the border.

But the Great Depression, coupled with disastrous droughts in the western provinces, hit all the harder in Canada. There was no equivalent of Roosevelt's New Deal in the Dominion. The country staggered along from one financial crisis to the next until the outbreak of World War II totally transformed the situation. The war provided the boost Canada needed to join the ranks of the major industrial nations. And the surge of postwar immigration provided the numbers required to work the new industries. From 1941 to 1974, Canada doubled in population and increased its gross national product nearly tenfold.

With the discovery of huge uranium deposits in Ontario and Saskatchewan, Canada was in the position to add nuclear energy to its power resources. And the opening of the St. Lawrence Seaway turned Toronto—more than 1,600km (1,000 miles) from the nearest ocean—into a major seaport. All these achievements propelled Canada into its present position: a powerhouse of manufacturing and trade, with a standard of living to exceed that of the United States. But, simultaneously, old ghosts were raising their heads again.

TROUBLE IN QUEBEC

As an ethnic enclave, the French Canadians had more than won their battle for survival. From their original 65,000 settlers, they had grown to more than six million, without receiving reinforcements from overseas. They had preserved and increased their presence by means of large families, rigid cultural cohesion, and the unifying influence of their Catholic faith. But they had fallen far behind the English-speaking majority economically and politically. Few held top positions in industry or finance, and they enjoyed relatively little say in national matters.

What rankled them most was that Canada never recognized French as a second national language; the French were expected to be bilingual if they wanted good careers, but the English-speakers got along nicely with just their own tongue. On a general cultural basis, as well, the country overwhelmingly reflected Anglo-Saxon attitudes rather than an Anglo-French mixture.

By the early 1960s, this discontent led to a dramatic radicalization of Québécois politics. A new separatist movement arose that regarded Québec not as simply 1 of 10 provinces but as *l'état du Québec,* a distinct state that might, if it chose, break away from the country. The most extreme faction, the Front de Liberation du Québec (FLQ), was frankly revolutionary and terrorist. It backed its demands with bombs, arson, and murder, culminating in the kidnap-killing of Cabinet Minister Pierre Laporte in October 1970.

The Ottawa government, under Prime Minister Pierre Trudeau, imposed the War Measures Act and moved 10,000 troops into the province. The police used their exceptional powers under the act to break up civil disorders, arrest hundreds of suspects, and catch the murderers of Laporte. In the 1973 provincial elections, the separatists were badly defeated, winning only 6 seats from a total of 110.

The crisis eventually calmed down. In some ways, its effects were beneficial. The federal government redoubled its efforts to remove the worst grievances of the French Canadians. Federal funds flowed to French schools outside Québec (nearly half the schoolchildren of New Brunswick, for example, are French-speaking). French Canadians were appointed to senior positions. Most important, all provinces were asked to make French an official language, which entailed making signs, government forms, transportation schedules, and other printed matter bilingual. Civil servants had to bone up on French to pass their

Canada's Cultural Mosaic

Canada has sought "unity through diversity" as a national ideal, and its people are even more diverse than its scenery. In the eastern province of Québec live six million French Canadians, whose motto, *Je me souviens* ("I remember"), has kept them "more French than France" through 2 centuries of Anglo domination. They've transformed Canada into a bilingual country where everything official—including parking tickets and airline passes—comes in two tongues.

The English-speaking majority of the populace is a mosaic rather than a block. Two massive waves of immigration—one before 1914, the other between 1945 and 1972—poured 6.5 million assorted Europeans and Americans into the country, providing muscles and skills, as well as a kaleidoscope of cultures. The 1990s saw another wave of immigration—largely from Asia and particularly from Hong Kong—that has transformed the economics and politics of British Columbia. Thus, Nova Scotia is as Scottish as haggis and kilts, Vancouver has the largest Chinese population outside Asia, the plains of Manitoba are sprinkled with the onion-shaped domes of Ukrainian churches, and Ontario offers Italian street markets and a theater festival featuring the works of Shakespeare at, yes, Stratford.

You can attend a Native Canadian tribal assembly, a Chinese New Year dragon parade, an Inuit spring celebration, a German Bierfest, a Highland gathering, or a Slavic folk dance. There are group settlements on the prairies where the working parlance is Danish, Czech, or Hungarian, and entire villages speak Icelandic.

exams, and the business world began to stipulate bilingualism for men and women aiming at executive positions. All these measures were already afoot before the turmoil began, but there's no doubt that bloodshed helped to accelerate them.

UNION OR SEPARATION?

Ever since the violent crisis, Canadian politicians of all hues have been trying to patch up some sort of compromise that would enable their country to remain united. They appeared close to success when they formulated the so-called Meech Lake Accord in the 1980s. Québec's premier set up a commission to study ways to change the province's constitutional relationship with Ottawa's federal government. This aroused the ire of other provinces, which failed to see why Québec should be granted a "special" position in Canada. During this time, the separatist Parti Québécois rallied its forces and staged a political comeback. The Meech Lake agreement became too unwieldy to pass muster, and an alliance of French Canadians, Native Canadian groups, western Canadian libertarians—and the province of New Brunswick—drove a stake through the heart of the accord. So the proposals, memorandums, and referendums go on and on; each one vetoed by the other camp and none coming closer to a solution.

The rift between Québec's French and English speakers—and between Québec and the other provinces—is still wide, though an improving Québec economy has generally muted resentments in the past few years. To make the situation even more complex, the only population segment in Québec that's growing is that of non-English- and non-French-speaking immigrants. Winning over the immigrant vote is suddenly big political business in Québec.

In October 1995, Québec again faced a referendum asking whether the French-speaking province should separate from the rest of Canada, and suddenly Canada teetered on the brink of splitting apart. The vote went in favor of the pro-unity camp by a razor-thin margin, but the issue was hardly resolved: In all likelihood, it lives to be reborn as another referendum. Meanwhile, as public officials debate separatism, Québec's younger generation is voting with its feet. Many of its brightest and best are heading west, particularly to more prosperous B.C. and Alberta. However, these western provinces—no lovers of Ottawa—themselves dream of loosening the federal laws binding them to eastern Canada.

By now, most Canadians are heartily tired of the Québec debate, though nobody seems to have a clear idea how to end it. Some say secession is the only way out; others favor the Swiss formula of biculturalism and bilingualism. For Québec, the breakaway advocated by Francophone hotheads could spell economic disaster. Most of Canada's industrial and financial power is in the English-speaking provinces. An independent Québec would be a poor country. But all Canada would be poorer by losing the special flavor and rich cultural heritage imparted by the presence of La Belle Province.

3 Onward Into the 21st Century: The Creation of Nunavut & More

Elements of the Canadian economy are still adapting to the landmark North American Free Trade Agreement concluded with the States in 1989. While free trade hasn't done much to revive the smokestack industries that once were the engines of eastern Canada, the agreement, combined with a weak Canadian dollar in the 1990s, was actually good for much of Canada's huge agricultural heartland. However, the globalization of trade is transforming the Canadian economy in ways that produce confusion and hostility in some citizens. Many Canadians are deeply ambivalent about being so closely linked to their powerful southern neighbor, and the trade agreement (and U.S. culture in general) often gets the blame for everything that's going wrong with Canada. Yet 85% of Canada's trade is with its southern neighbor—so it's a relationship that will need to be worked out in some form or other.

Public interest in protecting the environment runs high, as reflected in public policy. Recycling is commonplace, and communities across the country have made great strides in balancing economic interests with environmental goals. On Vancouver Island, for example, environmentalists and timber companies agreed in 1995 on forestry standards that satisfy both parties. When salmon fishing boats blockaded an Alaska ferry in Prince Rupert in 1997, the issue for the Canadians was perceived overfishing by Americans. Salmon have been reduced to an endangered species in much of the Pacific Northwest, and the Canadians consequently don't think much of U.S. fisheries policies.

In 1999, the huge Northern Territories divided in two. The eastern half, which takes in Baffin Island, the land around Hudson's Bay, and most of the arctic islands, is now called Nunavut and essentially functions as an Inuit homeland. The rump Northwest Territories officially retains the territory's old name, though many refer to the region as the Western Arctic.

The success of the Nunavut negotiations has emboldened other Native groups to settle their own land claims with the Canadian government. While many of the claims in northern Canada can be settled by transferring government land and money to Native groups, those in southern Canada are more complex. Some tribes assert a prior claim to land currently owned by non-Indians; in other areas, Native groups refuse to abide by environmental laws that seek to protect endangered runs of salmon. The situation in a number of communities has moved beyond protests and threats to armed encounters and road barricades. The path seems set for more and increasingly hostile confrontations between official Canada and its Native peoples.

The early years of the 21st century have been generally positive for Canada. The Canadian economy has strengthened markedly, and the Canadian dollar is stronger against the U.S. dollar than it has been in decades. In 2007, the loonie pulled ahead of the U.S. in value for the first time since 1957. At the same time, Canada has begun to distance itself from the dictates of Washington and is charting its own path on international issues. Canada did not join the U.S.-led "Alliance of the Willing" in its war against Iraq, and its determination to hold the U.S. accountable to pro-Canadian World Trade Organization decisions in the long-running softwood lumber disputes further marks a newfound Canadian policy independence.

Indeed, as the U.S. follows an increasingly unilateralist international program and as Canada embraces progressive policies in issues such as the legalization of marijuana and sanctioning of same-sex unions, Canada finds itself at odds with its powerful neighbor. With social and political values more in line with the nations of "Old Europe," one can foresee Canada increasingly charting its own way on the international stage. In fact, in 2003 the English newsmagazine *The Economist,* in a series of articles titled "Canada's New Spirit," stated, "Canada has been going through quite a renaissance, in public policy as well as its economy. Indeed, a cautious case can be made that Canada is now rather cool."

Index

FROMMER'S® COMPLETE TRAVEL GUIDES

FROMMER'S® DAY BY DAY GUIDES

PAULINE FROMMER'S GUIDES: SEE MORE. SPEND LESS.

FROMMER'S® PORTABLE GUIDES

Acapulco, Ixtapa & Zihuatanejo
Amsterdam
Aruba, Bonaire & Curacao
Australia's Great Barrier Reef
Bahamas
Big Island of Hawaii
Boston
California Wine Country
Cancún
Cayman Islands
Charleston
Chicago
Dominican Republic

Florence
Las Vegas
Las Vegas for Non-Gamblers
London
Maui
Nantucket & Martha's Vineyard
New Orleans
New York City
Paris
Portland
Puerto Rico
Puerto Vallarta, Manzanillo &
    Guadalajara

Rio de Janeiro
San Diego
San Francisco
Savannah
St. Martin, Sint Maarten, Anguila &
    St. Bart's
Turks & Caicos
Vancouver
Venice
Virgin Islands
Washington, D.C.
Whistler

FROMMER'S® CRUISE GUIDES

Alaska Cruises & Ports of Call

Cruises & Ports of Call

European Cruises & Ports of Call

FROMMER'S® NATIONAL PARK GUIDES

Algonquin Provincial Park
Banff & Jasper
Grand Canyon

National Parks of the American West
Rocky Mountain
Yellowstone & Grand Teton

Yosemite and Sequoia & Kings
    Canyon
Zion & Bryce Canyon

FROMMER'S® WITH KIDS GUIDES

Chicago
Hawaii
Las Vegas
London

National Parks
New York City
San Francisco

Toronto
Walt Disney World® & Orlando
Washington, D.C.

FROMMER'S® PHRASEFINDER DICTIONARY GUIDES

Chinese
French

German
Italian

Japanese
Spanish

SUZY GERSHMAN'S BORN TO SHOP GUIDES

France
Hong Kong, Shanghai & Beijing
Italy

London
New York
Paris

San Francisco
Where to Buy the Best of Everything

FROMMER'S® BEST-LOVED DRIVING TOURS

Britain
California
France
Germany

Ireland
Italy
New England
Northern Italy

Scotland
Spain
Tuscany & Umbria

THE UNOFFICIAL GUIDES®

Adventure Travel in Alaska
Beyond Disney
California with Kids
Central Italy
Chicago
Cruises
Disneyland®
England
Hawaii

Ireland
Las Vegas
London
Maui
Mexico's Best Beach Resorts
Mini Mickey
New Orleans
New York City
Paris

San Francisco
South Florida including Miami &
    the Keys
Walt Disney World®
Walt Disney World® for
    Grown-ups
Walt Disney World® with Kids
Washington, D.C.

SPECIAL-INTEREST TITLES

Athens Past & Present
Best Places to Raise Your Family
Cities Ranked & Rated
500 Places to Take Your Kids Before They Grow Up
Frommer's Best Day Trips from London
Frommer's Best RV & Tent Campgrounds in the U.S.A.

Frommer's Exploring America by RV
Frommer's NYC Free & Dirt Cheap
Frommer's Road Atlas Europe
Frommer's Road Atlas Ireland
Retirement Places Rated

There's a parking lot where my ocean view should be.

 À la place de la vue sur l'océan, me voilà avec une vue sur un parking.

 Anstatt Meerblick habe ich Sicht auf einen Parkplatz.

 Al posto della vista sull'oceano c'è un parcheggio.

 No tengo vista al mar porque hay un parque de estacionamiento.

 Há um parque de estacionamento onde deveria estar a minha vista do ocea.

 Ett parkeringsområde har byggts på den plats där min utsikt över oceanen borde vara.

Er ligt een parkeerterrein waar mijn zee-uitzicht zou moeten zijn.

نالك موقف للسيارات مكان ما وجب ان يكون المنظر الخلاب المطل على المحيط .

眼前に広がる紺碧の海・・・じゃない。窓の外は駐車場

停车场的位置应该是我的海景所在。

I'm fluent in pig latin.

Hotel mishaps aren't bound by geography.
Neither is our Guarantee. It covers your entire travel experience, including the price. So if you don't get the ocean view you booked, we'll work with our travel partners to make it right, right away. See www.travelocity.com/guarantee for details.

 travelocity
You'll never roam alone.